PCI Express System Architecture

The PC System Architecture Series

MindShare, Inc.

Please see our web site at www.awprofessional.com/series/mindshare for more information on these titles.

AGP System Architecture: Second Edition
0-201-70069-7

CardBus System Architecture
0-201-40997-6

FireWire® System Architecture: Second Edition
0-201-48535-4

InfiniBand System Architecture
0-321-11765-4

ISA System Architecture: Third Edition
0-201-40996-8

PCI Express System Architecture
0-321-15630-7

PCI System Architecture: Fourth Edition
0-201-30974-2

PCI-X System Architecture
0-201-72682-3

PCMCIA System Architecture: Second Edition
0-201-40991-7

Pentium® Pro and Pentium® II System Architecture: Second Edition
0-201-30973-4

Pentium® Processor System Architecture: Second Edition
0-201-40992-5

Plug and Play System Architecture
0-201-41013-3

Protected Mode Software Architecture
0-201-55447-X

Universal Serial Bus System Architecture: Second Edition
0-201-30975-0

HyperTransport™ System Architecture
0-321-16845-3

PCI Express System Architecture

MINDSHARE, INC.
Ravi Budruk
Don Anderson
Tom Shanley

Addison-Wesley

Boston • San Francisco • New York • Toronto • Montreal
London • Munich • Paris • Madrid
Capetown • Sydney • Tokyo • Singapore • Mexico City

The publisher offers discounts on this book when ordered in quantity for bulk purchases and special sales. For more information, please contact:

U.S. Corporate and Government Sales
(800) 382-3419
corpsales@pearsontechgroup.com

For sales outside of the U.S., please contact:

International Sales
(317) 581-3793
international@pearsontechgroup.com

Visit Addison-Wesley on the Web: www.awprofessional.com

Library of Congress Cataloging-in-Publication Data

Budruk, Ravi.
PCI express system architecture / Mindshare, Inc., Ravi Buduk ... [et al.].
p. cm.
Includes index.
ISBN 0-321-15630-7 (alk. paper)
1. Computer architecture. 2. Microcomputers—buses. 3. Computer architecture. I. Budruk, Ravi II. Mindshare, Inc. III. Title.

QA76.9.A73P43 2003
004.2 '2—dc22 2003015461

Set in 10 point Palatino by MindShare, Inc.

Text printed on recycled and acid-free paper.

ISBN 0321156307

2 3 4 5 6 7 CRS 06 05 04 03

2nd Printing December 2003

To my parents Aruna and Shripal Budruk
who started me on the path to Knowledge

Contents

About This Book

Part One: The Big Picture

Chapter 1: Architectural Perspective

Contents

Contents

Chapter 2: Architecture Overview

Part Two: Transaction Protocol

Chapter 3: Address Spaces & Transaction Routing

Chapter 5: ACK/NAK Protocol

Chapter 6: QoS/TCs/VCs and Arbitration

Chapter 7: Flow Control

Chapter 8: Transaction Ordering

Chapter 9: Interrupts

Chapter 10: Error Detection and Handling

Part Three: The Physical Layer

Chapter 11: Physical Layer Logic

Chapter 12: Electrical Physical Layer

Chapter 13: System Reset

Chapter 14: Link Initialization & Training

Contents

Part Four: Power-Related Topics

Chapter 15: Power Budgeting

Chapter 16: Power Management

Contents

Part Five: Optional Topics

Chapter 17: Hot Plug

Contents

Part Six: PCI Express Configuration

Chapter 19: Configuration Overview

Chapter 20: Configuration Mechanisms

Chapter 21: PCI Express Enumeration

Chapter 22: PCI Compatible Configuration Registers

Chapter 23: Expansion ROMs

Chapter 24: Express-Specific Configuration Registers

Appendices

Figures

Figures

Figures

Figures

Figures

Figures

Tables

Tables

Tables

Tables

Acknowledgments

Thanks to those who made significant contributions to this book:

Joe Winkles — for this superb job of technical editing.

Jay Trodden — for his contribution in developing the chapter on *Transaction Routing* and *Packet-Based Transactions*.

Mike Jackson — for his contribution in preparing the *Card Electromechanical* chapter.

Dave Dzatko — for research and editing.

Special thanks to Catalyst Enterprises, Inc. for supplying:
Appendix A: *Test, Debug and Verification*

Special thanks to PLX Technology for contributing two appendices:
Appendix B: *Markets & Applications for the PCI Express™ Architecture*
Appendix C: *Implementing Intelligent Adapters and Multi-Host Systems With PCI Express™ Technology*

Thanks also to the PCI SIG for giving permission to use some of the mechanical drawings from the specification.

The MindShare Architecture Series

The MindShare Architecture book series currently includes the books listed in Table 1 below. The entire book series is published by Addison-Wesley.

Table 1: PC Architecture Book Series

Category	Title	Edition	ISBN
Processor Architecture	80486 System Architecture	3rd	0-201-40994-1
	Pentium Processor System Architecture	2nd	0-201-40992-5
	Pentium Pro and Pentium II System Architecture	2nd	0-201-30973-4
	PowerPC System Architecture	1st	0-201-40990-9
Bus Architecture	PCI System Architecture	4th	0-201-30974-2
	PCI-X System Architecture	1st	0-201-72682-3
	EISA System Architecture	Out-of-print	0-201-40995-X
	Firewire System Architecture: IEEE 1394a	2nd	0-201-48535-4
	ISA System Architecture	3rd	0-201-40996-8
	Universal Serial Bus System Architecture 2.0	2nd	0-201-46137-4
	HyperTransport System Architecture	1st	0-321-16845-3
	PCI Express System Architecture	***1st***	***0-321-15630-7***
Network Architecture	Infiniband Network Architecture	1st	0-321-11765-4

Table 1: PC Architecture Book Series (Continued)

Category	Title	Edition	ISBN
Other Architectures	PCMCIA System Architecture: 16-Bit PC Cards	2nd	0-201-40991-7
	CardBus System Architecture	1st	0-201-40997-6
	Plug and Play System Architecture	1st	0-201-41013-3
	Protected Mode Software Architecture	1st	0-201-55447-X
	AGP System Architecture	1st	0-201-37964-3

Cautionary Note

The reader should keep in mind that MindShare's book series often details rapidly evolving technologies, as is the case with PCI Express. This being the case, it should be recognized that the book is a "snapshot" of the state of the technology at the time the book was completed. We make every attempt to produce our books on a timely basis, but the next revision of the specification is not introduced in time to make necessary changes. This PCI Express book complies with revision 1.0a of the *PCI Express™ Base Specification* released and trademarked by the PCI Special Interest Group. Several expansion card form-factor specifications are planned for PCI Express, but only the Electromechanical specification, revision 1.0 was released when this book was completed. However, the chapter covering the Card Electromechanical topic reviews several form-factors that were under development at the time of writing.

Intended Audience

This book is intended for use by hardware and software design and support personnel. The tutorial approach taken may also make it useful to technical personnel not directly involved design, verification, and other support functions.

Prerequisite Knowledge

It is recommended that the reader has a reasonable background in PC architecture, including experience or knowledge of an I/O bus and related protocol. Because PCI Express maintains several levels of compatibility with the original PCI design, critical background information regarding PCI has been incorporated into this book. However, the reader may find it beneficial to read the MindShare publication entitled *PCI System Architecture*, which focusses on and details the PCI architecture.

Topics and Organization

Topics covered in this book and the flow of the book are as follows:

Part 1: Background and Comprehensive Overview. Provides an architectural perspective of the PCI Express technology by comparing and contrasting it with the PCI and PCI-X buses. It also introduces the major features of the PCI Express architecture.
Part 2: PCI Express Transaction Protocol. Includes packet format and field definition and use, along with transaction and link layer functions.
Part 3: Physical Layer Description. Describes the physical layer functions, link training and initialization, reset, and electrical signaling.
Part 4: Power-Related Topics. Discusses Power Budgeting and Power Management.
Part 5: Optional Topics. Discusses the major features of PCI Express that are optional, including Hot Plug and Expansion Card implementation details.
Part 6: PCI Express Configuration. Discusses the configuration process, accessing configuration space, and details the content and use of all configuration registers.
Appendix:

- **Test, Debug, and Verification**
- **Markets & Applications for the PCI Express™ Architecture**
- **Implementing Intelligent Adapters and Multi-Host Systems With PCI Express™ Technology**
- **PCI Express Class Codes**
- **Legacy Support for Locking**

Documentation Conventions

This section defines the typographical convention used throughout this book.

PCI Express™

PCI Express™ is a trademark of the PCI SIG. This book takes the liberty of abbreviating PCI Express as "PCI-XP" primarily in illustration where limited space is an issue.

Hexadecimal Notation

All hex numbers are followed by a lower case "h." For example:

89F2BD02h
0111h

Binary Notation

All binary numbers are followed by a lower case "b." For example:

1000 1001 1111 0010b
01b

Decimal Notation

Number without any suffix are decimal. When required for clarity, decimal numbers are followed by a lower case "d." Examples:

9
15
512d

Bits Versus Bytes Notation

This book represents bit with lower case "b" and bytes with an upper case "B." For example:

Megabits/second = Mb/s
Megabytes/second = MB/s

Bit Fields

Groups bits are represented with the high-order bits first followed by the low-order bits and enclosed by brackets. For example:

[7:0] = bits 0 through 7

Active Signal States

Signals that are active low are followed by #, as in PERST# and WAKE#. Active high signals have no suffix, such as POWERGOOD.

Visit Our Web Site

Our web site lists all of our courses and the delivery options available for each course:

- Information on MindShare courses:
    - Self-paced DVDs and CDs
    - Live web-delivered classes
    - Live on-site classes.
- Free short courses on selected topics
- Technical papers
- Errata for a number of our books

All of our books are listed and can be ordered in bound or e-book versions.

www.mindshare.com

We Want Your Feedback

MindShare values you comments and suggestions. Contact us at:

Phone: (719) 487-1417 or within the U.S. (800) 633-1440
Fax: (719) 487-1434 (Fax)
Technical seminars: E-mail nancy@mindshare.com
Technical questions: E-mail don@mindshare.com or tom@mindshare.com
General information: E-mail info@mindshare.com

Mailing Address:

MindShare, Inc.
4285 Slash Pine Drive
Colorado Springs, CO 80908

Part One

The Big Picture

1 Architectural Perspective

This Chapter

This chapter describes performance advantages and key features of the PCI Express (PCI-XP) Link. To highlight these advantages, this chapter describes performance characteristics and features of predecessor buses such as PCI and PCI-X buses with the goal of discussing the evolution of PCI Express from these predecessor buses. The reader will be able to compare and contrast features and performance points of PCI, PCI-X and PCI Express buses. The key features of a PCI Express system are described. In addition, the chapter describes some examples of PCI Express system topologies.

The Next Chapter

The next chapter describes in further detail the features of the PCI Express bus. It describes the layered architecture of a device design while providing a brief functional description of each layer. The chapter provides an overview of packet formation at a transmitter device, the transmission and reception of the packet over the PCI Express Link and packet decode at a receiver device.

Introduction To PCI Express

PCI Express is the third generation high performance I/O bus used to interconnect peripheral devices in applications such as computing and communication platforms. The first generation buses include the ISA, EISA, VESA, and Micro Channel buses, while the second generation buses include PCI, AGP, and PCI-X. PCI Express is an all encompassing I/O device interconnect bus that has applications in the mobile, desktop, workstation, server, embedded computing and communication platforms.

The Role of the Original PCI Solution

Don't Throw Away What is Good! Keep It

The PCI Express architects have carried forward the most beneficial features from previous generation bus architectures and have also taken advantages of new developments in computer architecture.

For example, PCI Express employs the same usage model and load-store communication model as PCI and PCI-X. PCI Express supports familiar transactions such as memory read/write, IO read/write and configuration read/write transactions. The memory, IO and configuration address space model is the same as PCI and PCI-X address spaces. By maintaining the address space model, existing OSs and driver software will run in a PCI Express system without any modifications. In other words, PCI Express is software backwards compatible with PCI and PCI-X systems. In fact, a PCI Express system will boot an existing OS with no changes to current drivers and application programs. Even PCI/ACPI power management software will still run.

Like predecessor buses, PCI Express supports chip-to-chip interconnect and board-to-board interconnect via cards and connectors. The connector and card structure are similar to PCI and PCI-X connectors and cards. A PCI Express motherboard will have a similar form factor to existing FR4 ATX motherboards which is encased in the familiar PC package.

Make Improvements for the Future

To improve bus performance, reduce overall system cost and take advantage of new developments in computer design, the PCI Express architecture had to be significantly re-designed from its predecessor buses. PCI and PCI-X buses are multi-drop parallel interconnect buses in which many devices share one bus.

PCI Express on the other hand implements a serial, point-to-point type interconnect for communication between two devices. Multiple PCI Express devices are interconnected via the use of switches which means one can practically connect a large number of devices together in a system. A point-to-point interconnect implies limited electrical load on the link allowing transmission and reception frequencies to scale to much higher numbers. Currently PCI Express transmission and reception data rate is 2.5 Gbits/sec. A serial interconnect between two devices results in fewer pins per device package which reduces PCI Express chip and board design cost and reduces board design complexity. PCI Express performance is also highly scalable. This is achieved by implementing scalable numbers for pins and signal Lanes per interconnect based on communication performance requirements for that interconnect.

PCI Express implements switch-based technology to interconnect a large number of devices. Communication over the serial interconnect is accomplished using a packet-based communication protocol. Quality Of Service (QoS) features provide differentiated transmission performance for different applications. Hot Plug/Hot Swap support enables "always-on" systems. Advanced power management features allow one to design for low power mobile applications. RAS (Reliable, Available, Serviceable) error handling features make PCI Express suitable for robust high-end server applications. Hot plug, power management, error handling and interrupt signaling are accomplished in-band using packet based messaging rather than side-band signals. This keeps the device pin count low and reduces system cost.

The configuration address space available per function is extended to 4KB, allowing designers to define additional registers. However, new software is required to access this extended configuration register space.

Looking into the Future

In the future, PCI Express communication frequencies are expected to double and quadruple to 5 Gbits/sec and 10 Gbits/sec. Taking advantage of these frequencies will require Physical Layer re-design of a device with no changes necessary to the higher layers of the device design.

Additional mechanical form factors are expected. Support for a Server IO Module, Newcard (PC Card style), and Cable form factors are expected.

Predecessor Buses Compared

In an effort to compare and contrast features of predecessor buses, the next section of this chapter describes some of the key features of IO bus architectures defined by the PCI Special Interest Group (PCISIG). These buses, shown in Table 1-1 on page 12, include the PCI 33 MHz bus, PCI- 66 MHz bus, PCI-X 66 MHz/133 MHz buses, PCI-X 266/533 MHz buses and finally PCI Express.

Table 1-1: Bus Specifications and Release Dates

Bus Type	Specification Release	Date of Release
PCI 33 MHz	2.0	1993
PCI 66 MHz	2.1	1995
PCI-X 66 MHz and 133 MHz	1.0	1999
PCI-X 266 MHz and 533 MHz	2.0	Q1, 2002
PCI Express	1.0	Q2, 2002

Author's Disclaimer

In comparing these buses, it is not the authors' intention to suggest that any one bus is better than any other bus. Each bus architecture has its advantages and disadvantages. After evaluating the features of each bus architecture, a particular bus architecture may turn out to be more suitable for a specific application than another bus architecture. For example, it is the system designers responsibility to determine whether to implement a PCI-X bus or PCI Express for the I/O interconnect in a high-end server design. Our goal in this chapter is to document the features of each bus architecture so that the designer can evaluate the various bus architectures.

Bus Performances and Number of Slots Compared

Table 1-2 on page 13 shows the various bus architectures defined by the PCISIG. The table shows the evolution of bus frequencies and bandwidths. As is obvious, increasing bus frequency results in increased bandwidth. However, increasing bus frequency compromises the number of electrical loads or number of connectors allowable on a bus at that frequency. At some point, for a given bus architecture, there is an upper limit beyond which one cannot further increase the bus frequency, hence requiring the definition of a new bus architecture.

Table 1-2: Comparison of Bus Frequency, Bandwidth and Number of Slots

Bus Type	Clock Frequency	Peak Bandwidth *	Number of Card Slots per Bus
PCI 32-bit	33 MHz	133 MBytes/sec	4-5
PCI 32-bit	66 MHz	266 MBytes/sec	1-2
PCI-X 32-bit	66 MHz	266 MBytes/sec	4
PCI-X 32-bit	133 MHz	533 MBytes/sec	1-2
PCI-X 32-bit	266 MHz effective	1066 MBytes/sec	1
PCI-X 32-bit	533 MHz effective	2131 MByte/sec	1
*** Double all these bandwidth numbers for 64-bit bus implementations**			

PCI Express Aggregate Throughput

A PCI Express interconnect that connects two devices together is referred to as a Link. A Link consists of either x1, x2, x4, x8, x12, x16 or x32 signal pairs in each direction. These signals are referred to as Lanes. A designer determines how many Lanes to implement based on the targeted performance benchmark required on a given Link.

Table 1-3 shows aggregate bandwidth numbers for various Link width implementations. As is apparent from this table, the peak bandwidth achievable with PCI Express is significantly higher than any existing bus today.

Let us consider how these bandwidth numbers are calculated. The transmission/reception rate is 2.5 Gbits/sec per Lane per direction. To support a greater degree of robustness during data transmission and reception, each byte of data transmitted is converted into a 10-bit code (via an 8b/10b encoder in the transmitter device). In other words, for every Byte of data to be transmitted, 10-bits of encoded data are actually transmitted. The result is 25% additional overhead to transmit a byte of data. Table 1-3 accounts for this 25% loss in transmission performance.

PCI Express implements a dual-simplex Link which implies that data is transmitted and received simultaneously on a transmit and receive Lane. The aggregate bandwidth assumes simultaneous traffic in both directions.

To obtain the aggregate bandwith numbers in Table 1-3 multiply 2.5 Gbits/sec by 2 (for each direction), then multiply by number of Lanes, and finally divide by 10-bits per Byte (to account for the 8-to-10 bit encoding).

Table 1-3: PCI Express Aggregate Throughput for Various Link Widths

PCI Express Link Width	x1	x2	x4	x8	x12	x16	x32
Aggregate Bandwidth (GBytes/sec)	0.5	1	2	4	6	8	16

Performance Per Pin Compared

As is apparent from Figure 1-1, PCI Express achieves the highest bandwidth per pin. This results in a device package with fewer pins and a motherboard implementation with few wires and hence overall reduced system cost per unit bandwidth.

In Figure 1-1, the first 7 bars are associated with PCI and PCI-X buses where we assume 84 pins per device. This includes 46 signal pins, interrupt and power management pins, error pins and the remainder are power and ground pins. The last bar associated with a x8 PCI Express Link assumes 40 pins per device which include 32 signal lines (8 differential pairs per direction) and the rest are power and ground pins.

Figure 1-1: Comparison of Performance Per Pin for Various Buses

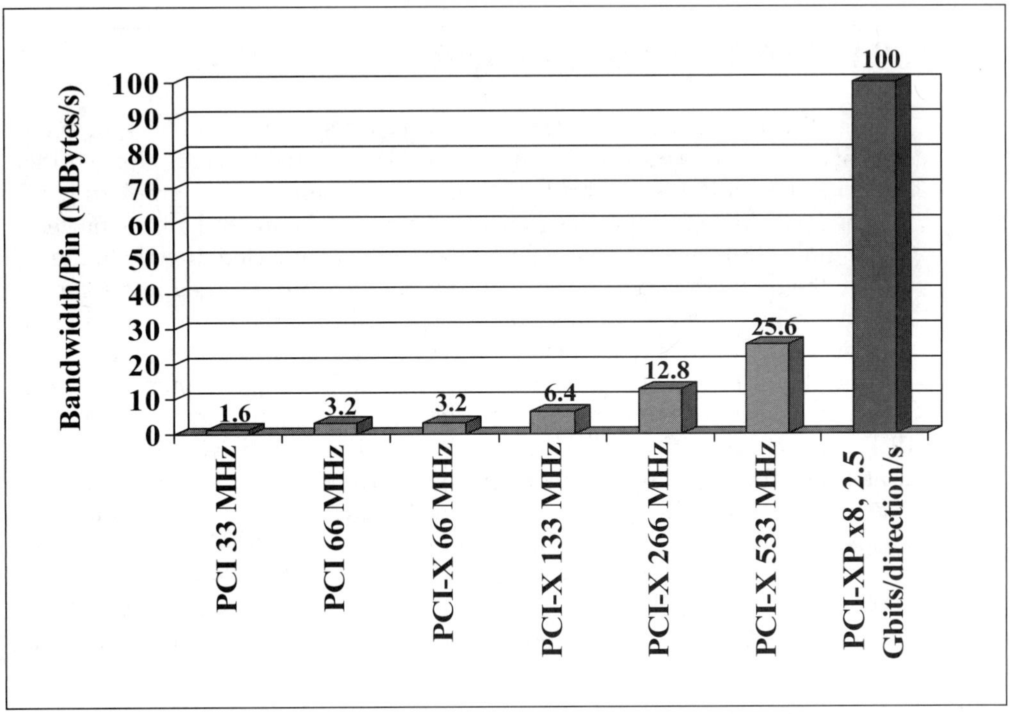

I/O Bus Architecture Perspective

33 MHz PCI Bus Based System

Figure 1-2 on page 17 is a 33 MHz PCI bus based system. The PCI system consists of a Host (CPU) bus-to-PCI bus bridge, also referred to as the North bridge. Associated with the North bridge is the system memory bus, graphics (AGP) bus, and a 33 MHz PCI bus. I/O devices share the PCI bus and are connected to it in a multi-drop fashion. These devices are either connected directly to the PCI bus on the motherboard or by way of a peripheral card plugged into a connector on the bus. Devices connected directly to the motherboard consume one electrical load while connectors are accounted for as 2 loads. A South bridge bridges the PCI bus to the ISA bus where slower, lower performance peripherals exist. Associated with the south bridge is a USB and IDE bus. A CD or hard disk is associated with the IDE bus. The South bridge contains an interrupt controller (not shown) to which interrupt signals from PCI devices are connected. The interrupt controller is connected to the CPU via an INTR signal or an APIC bus. The South bridge is the central resource that provides the source of reset, reference clock, and error reporting signals. Boot ROM exists on the ISA bus along with a Super IO chip, which includes keyboard, mouse, floppy disk controller and serial/parallel bus controllers. The PCI bus arbiter logic is included in the North bridge.

Figure 1-3 on page 18 represents a typical PCI bus cycle. The PCI bus clock is 33 MHz. The address bus width is 32-bits (4GB memory address space), although PCI optionally supports 64-bit address bus. The data bus width is implemented as either 32-bits or 64-bits depending on bus performance requirement. The address and data bus signals are multiplexed on the same pins (AD bus) to reduce pin count. Command signals (C/BE#) encode the transaction type of the bus cycle that master devices initiate. PCI supports 12 transaction types that include memory, IO, and configuration read/write bus cycles. Control signals such as FRAME#, DEVSEL#, TRDY#, IRDY#, STOP# are handshake signals used during bus cycles. Finally, the PCI bus consists of a few optional error related signals, interrupt signals and power management signals. A PCI master device implements a minimum of 49 signals.

Any PCI master device that wishes to initiate a bus cycle first arbitrates for use of the PCI bus by asserting a request (REQ#) to the arbiter in the North bridge. After receiving a grant (GNT#) from the arbiter and checking that the bus is idle, the master device can start a bus cycle.

Figure 1-2: 33 MHz PCI Bus Based Platform

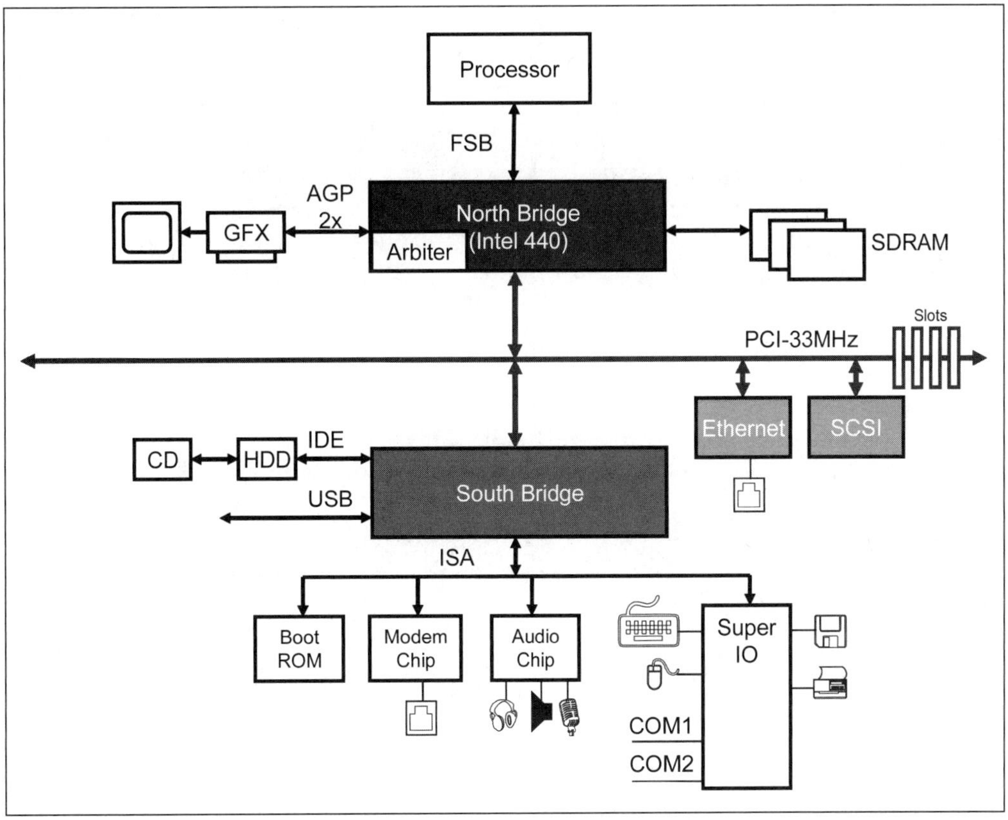

Electrical Load Limit of a 33 MHz PCI Bus

The PCI specification theoretically supports 32 devices per PCI bus. This means that PCI enumeration software will detect and recognize up to 32 devices per bus. However, as a rule of thumb, a PCI bus can support a maximum of 10-12 electrical loads (devices) at 33 MHz. PCI implements a static clocking protocol with a clock period of 30 ns at 33 MHz.

PCI implements reflected-wave switching signal drivers. The driver drives a half signal swing signal on the rising edge of PCI clock. The signal propagates down the PCI bus transmission line and is reflected at the end of the transmission line where there is no termination. The reflection causes the half swing signal to double. The doubled (full signal swing) signal must settle to a steady state value with sufficient setup time prior to the next rising edge of PCI clock where receiving devices sample the signal. The total time from when a driver drives a signal until the receiver detects a valid signal (including propagation time and reflection delay plus setup time) must be less than the clock period of 30 ns.

Figure 1-3: Typical PCI Burst Memory Read Bus Cycle

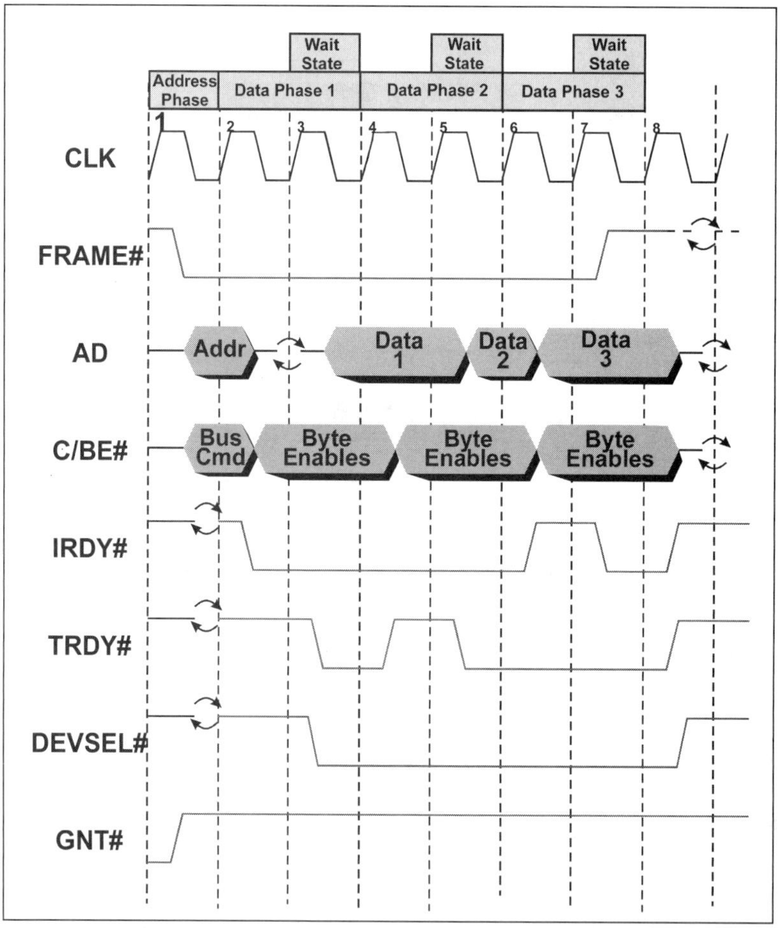

The more electrical loads on a bus, the longer it takes for the signal to propagate and double with sufficient setup to the next rising edge of clock. As mentioned earlier, a 33 MHz PCI bus meets signal timing with no more than 10-12 loads. Connectors on the PCI bus are counted as 2 loads because the connector is accounted for as one load and the peripheral card with a PCI device is the second load. As indicated in Table 1-2 on page 13 a 33 MHz PCI bus can be designed with a maximum of 4-5 connectors.

To connect any more than 10-12 loads in a system requires the implementation of a PCI-to-PCI bridge as shown in Figure 1-4. This permits an additional 10-12 loads to be connected on the secondary PCI bus 1. The PCI specification theoretically supports up to 256 buses in a system. This means that PCI enumeration software will detect and recognize up to 256 PCI bridges per system.

Figure 1-4: 33 MHz PCI Based System Showing Implementation of a PCI-to-PCI Bridge

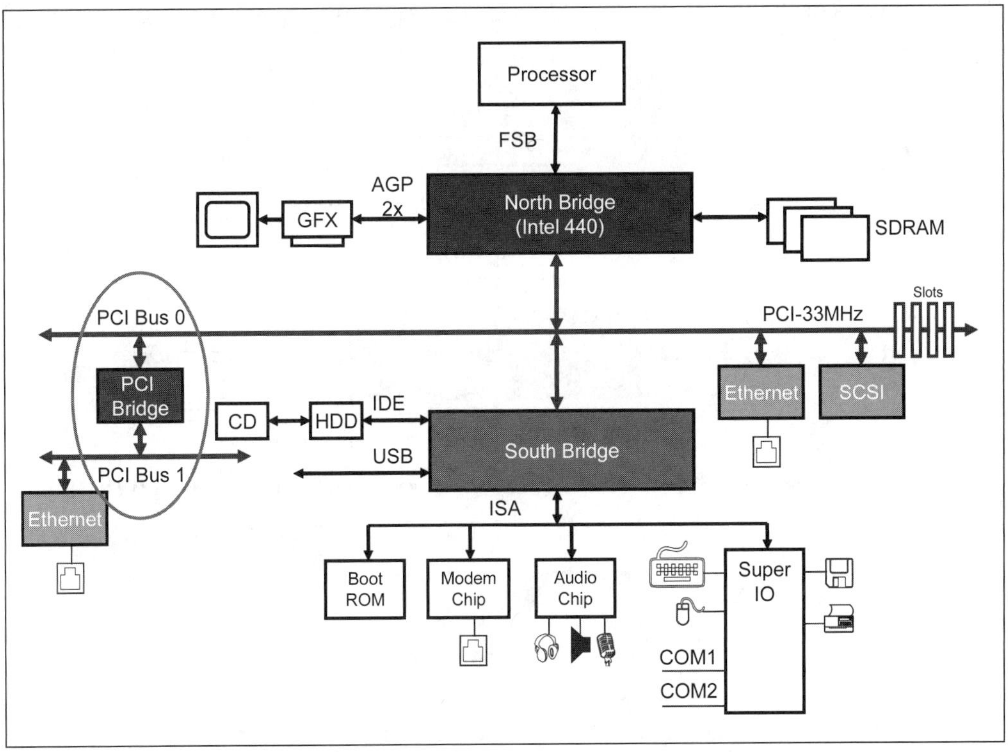

PCI Transaction Model - Programmed IO

Consider an example in which the CPU communicates with a PCI peripheral such as an Ethernet device shown in Figure 1-5. Transaction 1 shown in the figure, which is initiated by the CPU and targets a peripheral device, is referred to as a programmed IO transaction. Software commands the CPU to initiate a memory or IO read/write bus cycle on the host bus targeting an address mapped in a PCI device's address space. The North bridge arbitrates for use of the PCI bus and when it wins ownership of the bus generates a PCI memory or IO read/write bus cycle represented in Figure 1-3 on page 18. During the first clock of this bus cycle (known as the address phase), all target devices decode the address. One target (the Ethernet device in this example) decodes the address and claims the transaction. The master (North bridge in this case) communicates with the claiming target (Ethernet controller). Data is transferred between master and target in subsequent clocks after the address phase of the bus cycle. Either 4 bytes or 8 bytes of data are transferred per clock tick depending on the PCI bus width. The bus cycle is referred to as a burst bus cycle if data is transferred back-to-back between master and target during multiple data phases of that bus cycle. Burst bus cycles result in the most efficient use of PCI bus bandwidth.

Figure 1-5: PCI Transaction Model

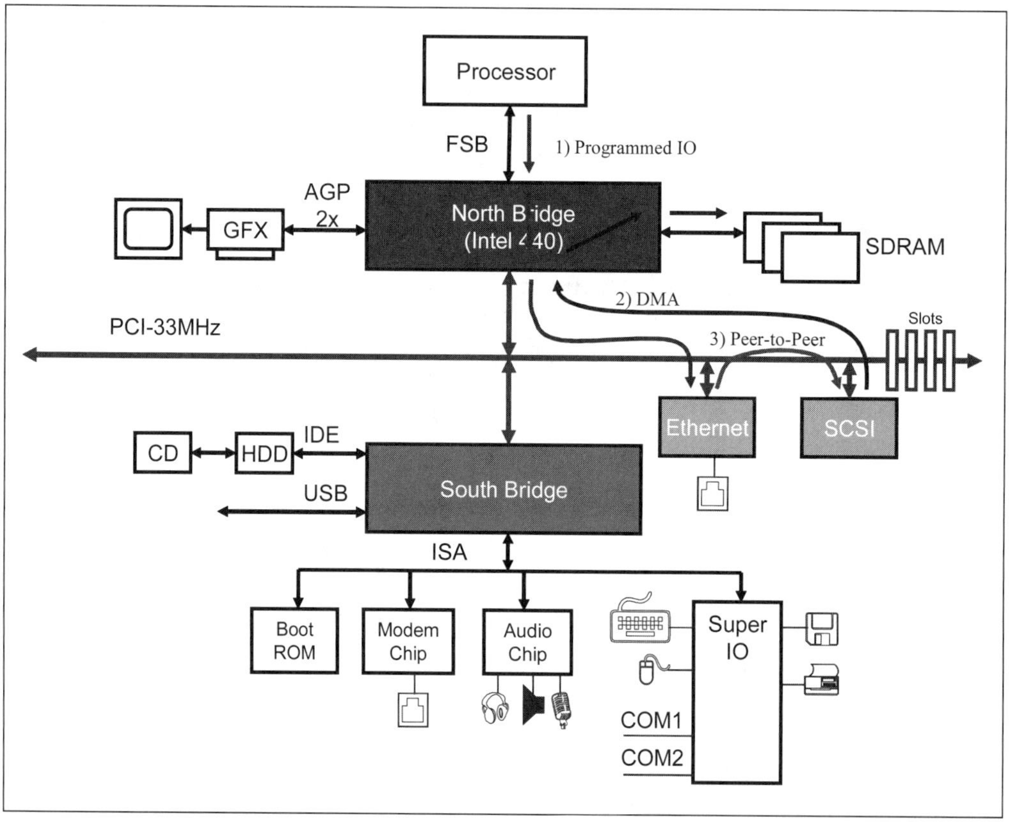

At 33 MHz and the bus width of 32-bits (4 Bytes), peak bandwidth achievable is 4 Bytes x 33 MHz = 133 MBytes/sec. Peak bandwidth on a 64-bit bus is 266 Mbytes/sec. See Table 1-2 on page 13.

Efficiency of the PCI bus for data payload transport is in the order of 50%. Efficiency is defined as number of clocks during which data is transferred divided by the number of total clocks, times 100. The lost performance is due to bus idle time between bus cycles, arbitration time, time lost in the address phase of a bus cycle, wait states during data phases, delays during transaction retries (not discussed yet), as well as latencies through PCI bridges.

PCI Transaction Model - Direct Memory Access (DMA)

Data transfer between a PCI device and system memory is accomplished in two ways:

The first less efficient method uses programmed IO transfers as discussed in the previous section. The PCI device generates an interrupt to inform the CPU that it needs data transferred. The device interrupt service routine (ISR) causes the CPU to read from the PCI device into one of its own registers. The ISR then tells the CPU to write from its register to memory. Similarly, if data is to be moved from memory to the PCI device, the ISR tells the CPU to read from memory into its own register. The ISR then tells the CPU to write from its register to the PCI device. It is apparent that the process is very inefficient for two reasons. First, there are two bus cycles generated by the CPU for every data transfer, one to memory and one to the PCI device. Second, the CPU is busy transferring data rather than performing its primary function of executing application code.

The second more efficient method to transfer data is the DMA (direct memory access) method illustrated by Transaction 2 in Figure 1-5 on page 20, where the PCI device becomes a bus master. Upon command by a local application (software) which runs on a PCI peripheral or the PCI peripheral hardware itself, the PCI device may initiate a bus cycle to talk to memory. The PCI bus master device (SCSI device in this example) arbitrates for the PCI bus, wins ownership of the bus and initiates a PCI memory bus cycle. The North bridge which decodes the address acts as the target for the transaction. In the data phase of the bus cycle, data is transferred between the SCSI master and the North bridge target. The bridge in turn generates a DRAM bus cycle to communicate with system memory. The PCI peripheral generates an interrupt to inform the system software that the data transfer has completed. This bus master or DMA method of data transport is more efficient because the CPU is not involved in the data move and further only one burst bus cycle is generated to move a block of data.

PCI Transaction Model - Peer-to-Peer

A Peer-to-peer transaction shown as Transaction 3 in Figure 1-5 on page 20 is the direct transfer of data between two PCI devices. A master that wishes to initiate a transaction, arbitrates, wins ownership of the bus and starts a transaction. A target PCI device that recognizes the address claims the bus cycle. For a write bus cycle, data is moved from master to target. For a read bus cycle, data is moved from target to master.

PCI Bus Arbitration

A PCI device that wishes to initiate a bus cycle arbitrates for use of the bus first. The arbiter implements an arbitration algorithm with which it decides who to grant the bus to next. The arbiter is able to grant the bus to the next requesting device while a bus cycle is in progress. This arbitration protocol is referred to as hidden bus arbitration. Hidden bus arbitration allows for more efficient hand over of the bus from one bus master device to another with only one idle clock between two bus cycles (referred to as back-to-back bus cycles). PCI protocol does not provide a standard mechanism by which system software or device drivers can configure the arbitration algorithm in order to provide for differentiated class of service for various applications.

Figure 1-6: PCI Bus Arbitration

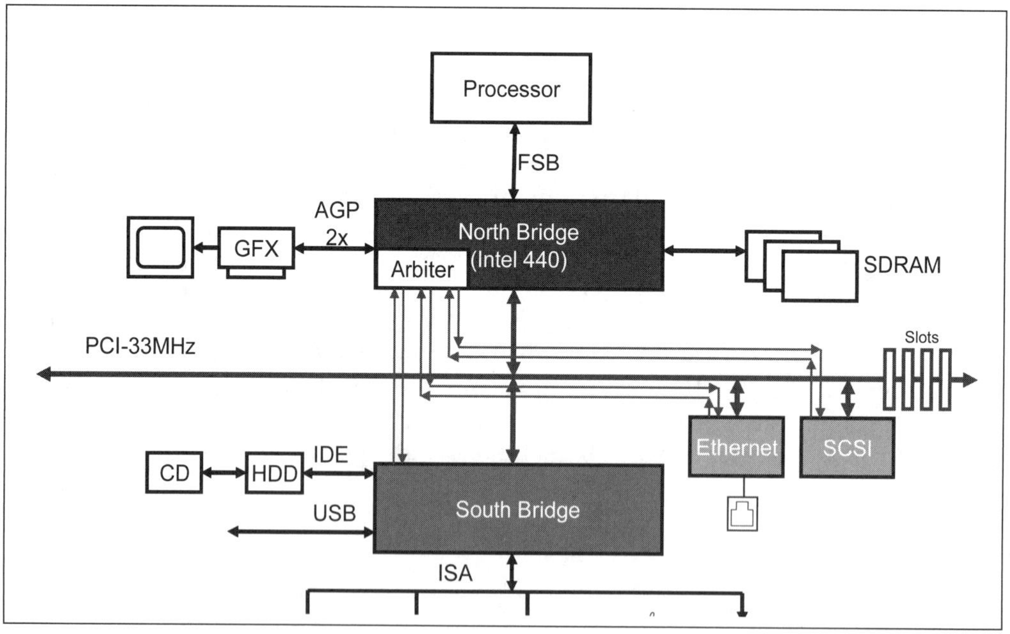

PCI Delayed Transaction Protocol

PCI Retry Protocol: When a PCI master initiates a transaction to access a target device and the target device is not ready, the target signals a transaction retry. This scenario is illustrated in Figure 1-7.

Figure 1-7: PCI Transaction Retry Mechanism

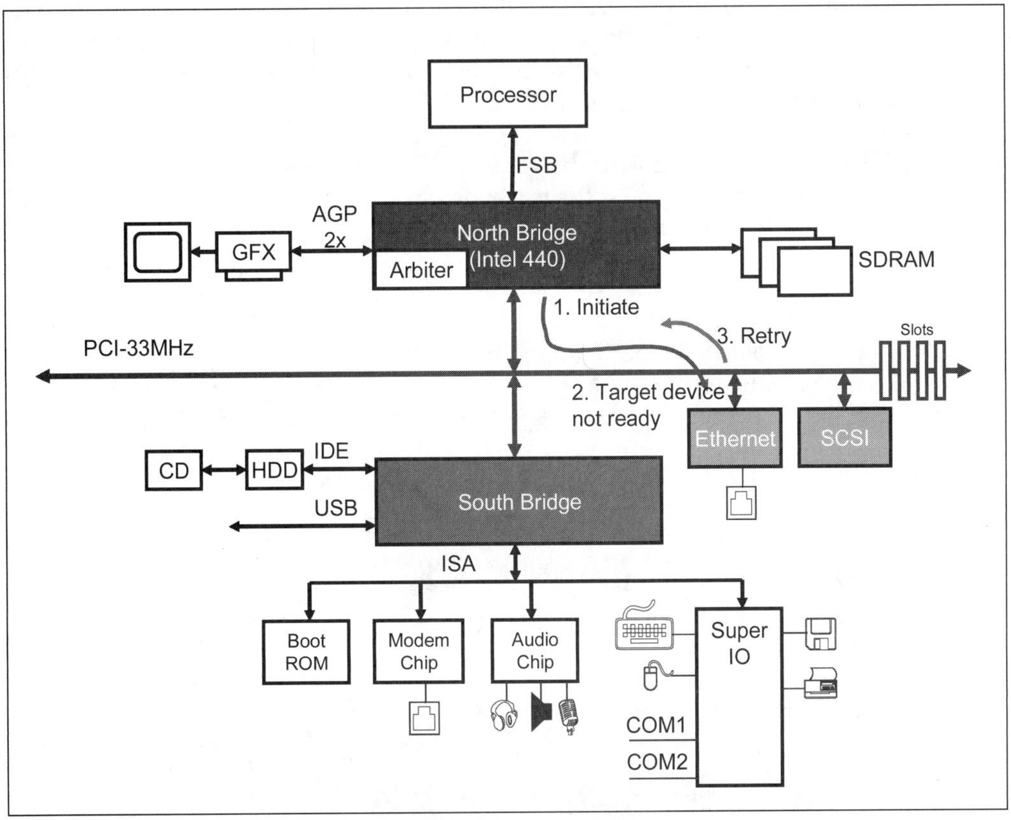

Consider the following example in which the North bridge initiates a memory read transaction to read data from the Ethernet device. The Ethernet target claims the bus cycle. However, the Ethernet target does not immediately have the data to return to the North bridge master. The Ethernet device has two choices by which to delay the data transfer. The first is to insert wait-states in the data phase. If only a few wait-states are needed, then the data is still transferred efficiently. If however the target device requires more time (more than 16 clocks from the beginning of the transaction), then the second option the target has is to signal a retry with a signal called STOP#. A retry tells the master to end the bus cycle prematurely without transferring data. Doing so prevents the bus from being held for a long time in wait-states, which compromises the bus efficiency. The bus master that is retried by the target waits a minimum of 2 clocks and must once again arbitrate for use of the bus to re-initiate the identical bus cycle. During the time that the bus master is retried, the arbiter can grant the bus to other requesting masters so that the PCI bus is more efficiently utilized. By the time the retried master is granted the bus and it re-initiates the bus cycle, hopefully the target will claim the cycle and will be ready to transfer data. The bus cycle goes to completion with data transfer. Otherwise, if the target is still not ready, it retries the master's bus cycle again and the process is repeated until the master successfully transfers data.

PCI Disconnect Protocol: When a PCI master initiates a transaction to access a target device and if the target device is able to transfer at least one doubleword of data but cannot complete the entire data transfer, it disconnects the bus cycle at the point at which it cannot continue the data transfer. This scenario is illustrated in Figure 1-8.

Figure 1-8: PCI Transaction Disconnect Mechanism

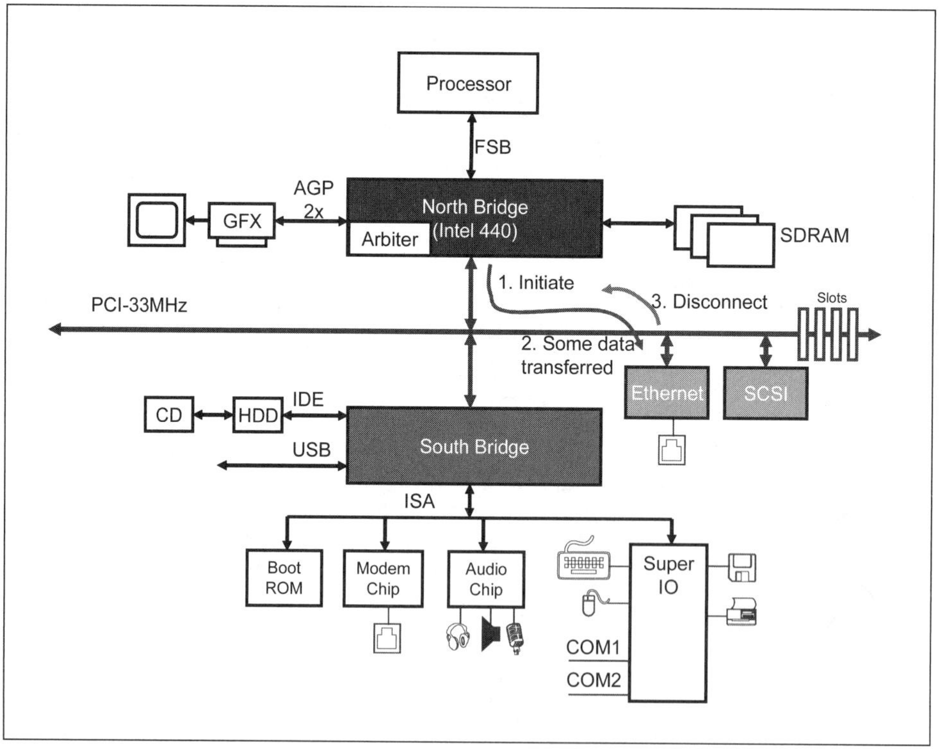

Consider the following example in which the North bridge initiates a burst memory read transaction to read data from the Ethernet device. The Ethernet target device claims the bus cycle and transfers some data, but then runs out of data to transfer. The Ethernet device has two choices to delay the data transfer. The first option is to insert wait-states during the current data phase while waiting for additional data to arrive. If the target needs to insert only a few wait-states, then the data is still transferred efficiently. If however the target device requires more time (the PCI specification allows maximum of 8 clocks in the data phase), then the target device must signal a disconnect. To do this the target asserts STOP# in the middle of the bus cycle to tell the master to end the bus cycle prematurely. A disconnect results in some data is transferred, while a retry does not. Disconnect frees the bus from long periods of wait states. The disconnected master waits a minimum of 2 clocks before once again arbitrating for use of the bus and continuing the bus cycle at the disconnected address. During the time that the bus master is disconnected, the arbiter may grant the bus to other requesting masters so that the PCI bus is utilized more efficiently. By the time the disconnected master is granted the bus and continues the bus cycle, hopefully the target is ready to continue the data transfer until it is completed. Otherwise, the target once again retries or disconnects the master's bus cycle and the process is repeated until the master successfully transfers all its data.

PCI Interrupt Handling

Central to the PCI interrupt handling protocol is the interrupt controller shown in Figure 1-9. PCI devices use one-of-four interrupt signals (INTA#, INTB#, INTC#, INTD#) to trigger an interrupt request to the interrupt controller. In turn, the interrupt controller asserts INTR to the CPU. If the architecture supports an APIC (Advanced Programmable Interrupt Controller) then it sends an APIC message to the CPU as opposed to asserting the INTR signal. The interrupted CPU determines the source of the interrupt, saves its state and services the device that generated the interrupt. Interrupts on PCI INTx# signals are sharable. This allows multiple devices to generate their interrupts on the same interrupt signal. OS software has the overhead to determine which one of the devices sharing the interrupt signal generated the interrupt. This is accomplished by polling the Interrupt Pending bit mapped in a device's memory space. Doing so incurs additional latency in servicing the interrupting device.

Figure 1-9: PCI Interrupt Handling

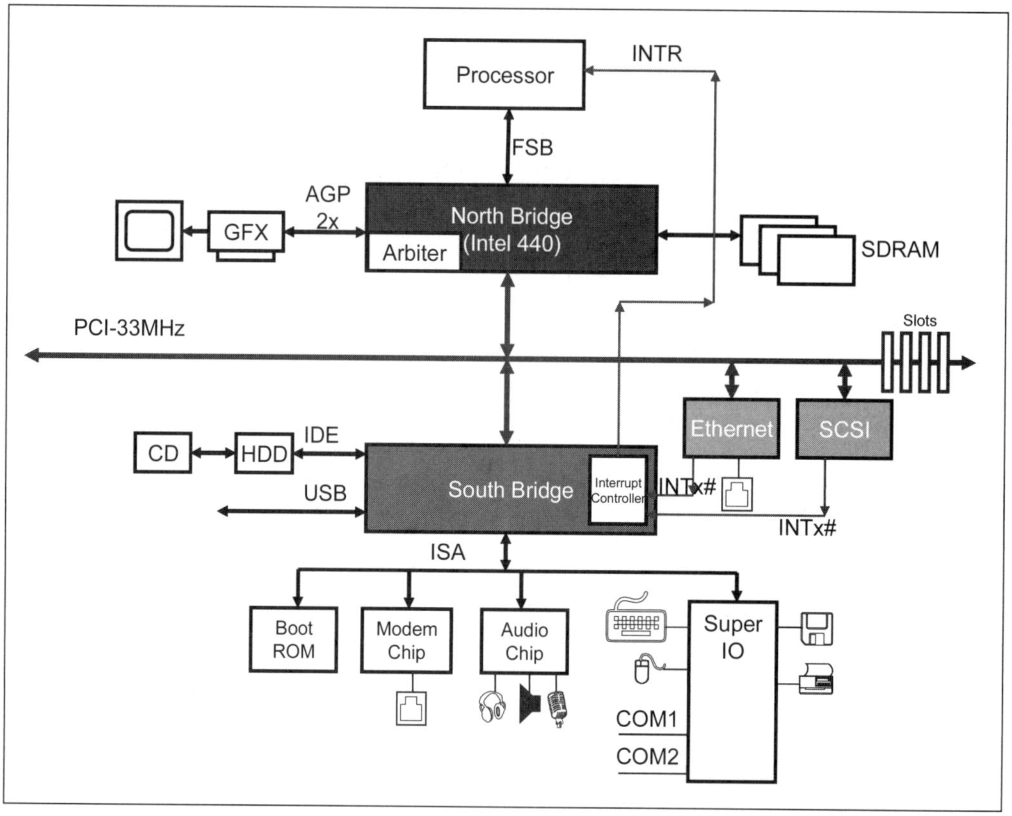

PCI Error Handling

PCI devices are optionally designed to detect address and data phase parity errors during transactions. Even parity is generated on the PAR signal during each bus cycle's address and data phases. The device that receives the address or data during a bus cycle uses the parity signal to determine if a parity error has occurred due to noise on the PCI bus. If a device detects an address phase parity error, it asserts SERR#. If a device detects a data phase parity error, it asserts PERR#. The PERR# and SERR# signals are connected to the error logic (in the South bridge) as shown in Figure 1-10 on page 27. In many systems, the error logic asserts the NMI signal (non-maskable interrupt signal) to the CPU upon detecting PERR# or SERR#. This interrupt results in notification of a parity error and the system shuts down (We all know the blue screen of death). Kind of draconian don't you agree?

Figure 1-10: PCI Error Handling Protocol

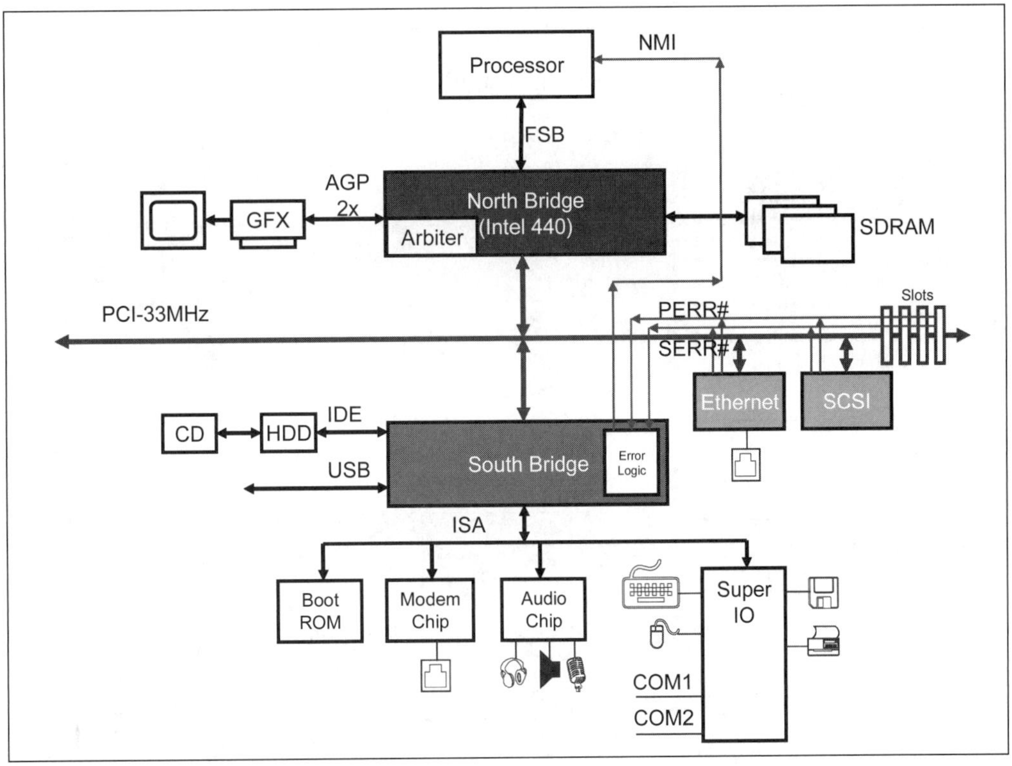

Unfortunately, PCI error detection and reporting is not robust. PCI errors are fatal uncorrectable errors that many times result in system shutdown. Further, errors are detectable as long as an odd number of signals are affected by noise. Given the poor PCI error detection protocol and error handling policies, many system designs either disable or do not support error checking and reporting.

PCI Address Space Map

PCI architecture supports 3 address spaces shown in Figure 1-11. These are the memory, IO and configuration address spaces. The memory address space goes up to 4 GB for systems that support 32-bit memory addressing and optionally up to 16 EB (exabytes) for systems that support 64-bit memory addressing. PCI supports up to 4GB of IO address space, however, many platforms limit IO space to 64 KB due to X86 CPUs only supporting 64 KB of IO address space. PCI devices are configured to map to a configurable region within either the memory or IO address space.

Figure 1-11: Address Space Mapping

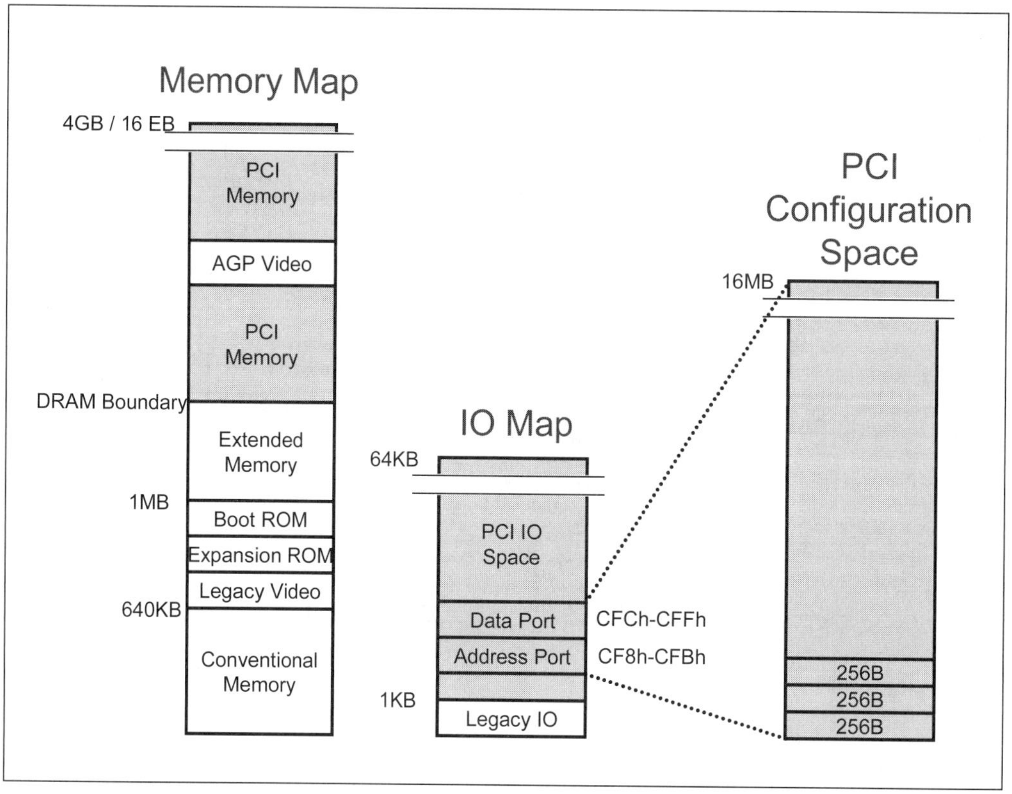

PCI device configuration registers map to a third space called configuration address space. Each PCI function may have up to 256 Bytes of configuration address space. The configuration address space is 16 MBytes. This is calculated by multiplying 256 Bytes, by 8 functions per device, by 32 devices per bus, by 256 buses per system. An x86 CPU can access memory or IO address space but does not support configuration address space directly. Instead, CPUs access PCI configuration space indirectly by indexing through an IO mapped Address Port and Data Port in the host bridge (North bridge or MCH). The Address Port is located at IO address CF8h-CFBh and the Data Port is mapped to location CFCh-CFFh.

PCI Configuration Cycle Generation

PCI configuration cycle generation involves two steps.

Step 1: The CPU generates an IO write to the Address Port at IO address CF8h in the North bridge. The data written to the Address Port is the configuration register address to be accessed.

Figure 1-12: PCI Configuration Cycle Generation

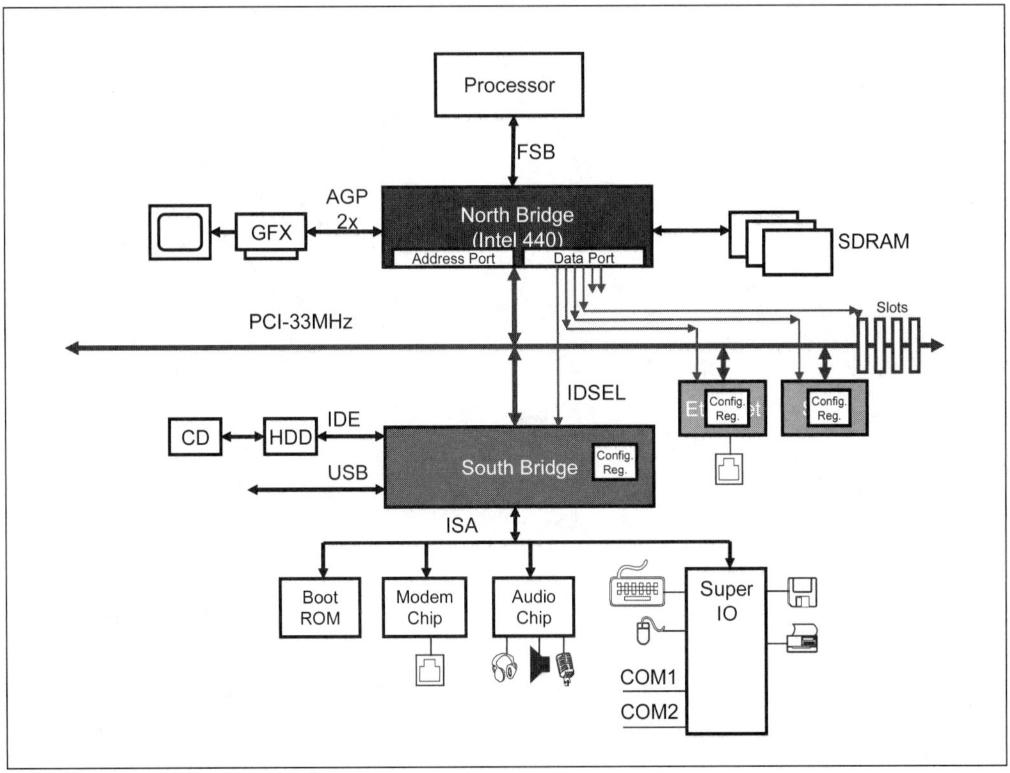

Step 2: The CPU either generates an IO read or IO write to the Data Port at location CFCh in the North bridge. The North bridge in turn then generates either a configuration read or configuration write transaction on the PCI bus.

The address for the configuration transaction address phase is obtained from the contents of the Address register. During the configuration bus cycle, one of the point-to-point IDSEL signals shown in Figure 1-12 on page 29 is asserted to select the device whose register is being accessed. That PCI target device claims the configuration cycle and fulfills the request.

PCI Function Configuration Register Space

Each PCI device contains up to 256 Bytes of configuration register space. The first 64 bytes are configuration header registers and the remaining 192 Bytes are device specific registers. The header registers are configured at boot time by the Boot ROM configuration firmware and by the OS. The device specific registers are configured by the device's device driver that is loaded and executed by the OS at boot time.

Figure 1-13: 256 Byte PCI Function Configuration Register Space

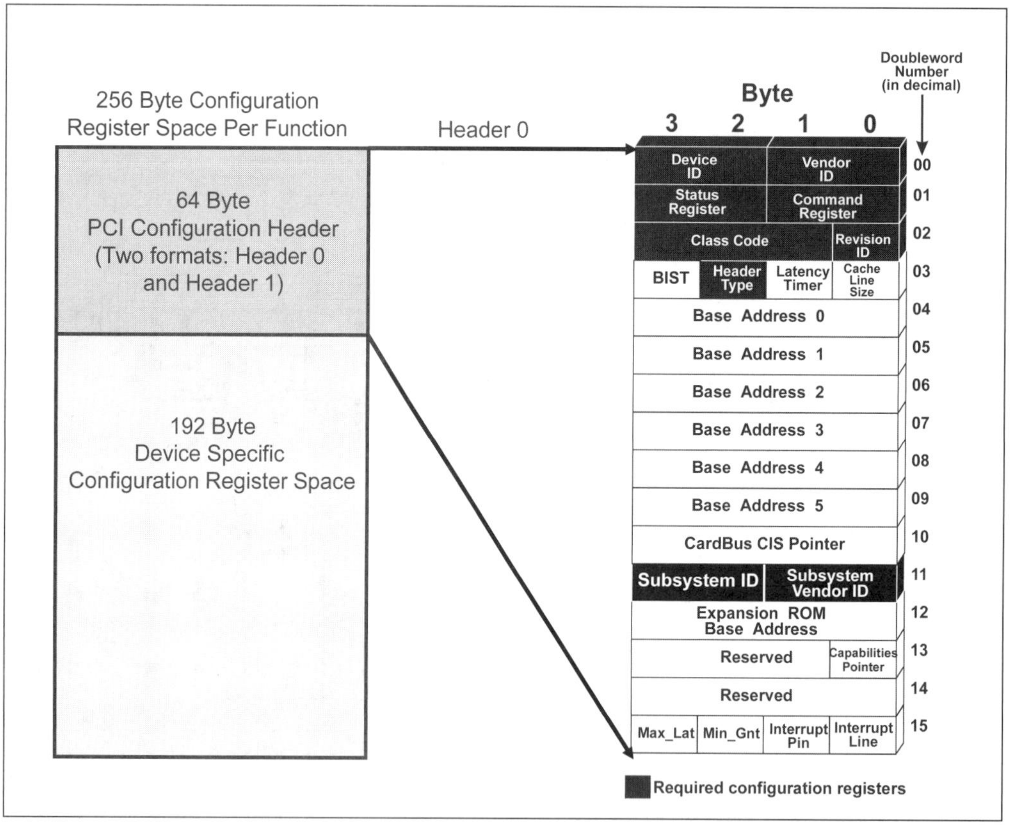

Within the header space, the Base Address registers are one of the most important registers configured by the 'Plug and Play' configuration software. It is via these registers that software assigns a device its memory and/or IO address space within the system's memory and IO address space. No two devices are assigned the same address range, thus ensuring the 'plug and play' nature of the PCI system.

PCI Programming Model

Software instructions may cause the CPU to generate memory or IO read/write bus cycles. The North bridge decodes the address of the resulting CPU bus cycles, and if the address maps to PCI address space, the bridge in turn generates a PCI memory or IO read/write bus cycle. A target device on the PCI bus claims the cycle and completes the transfer. In summary, the CPU communicates with any PCI device via the North bridge, which generates PCI memory or IO bus cycles on the behalf of the CPU.

An intelligent PCI device that includes a local processor or bus master state machine (typically intelligent IO cards) can also initiate PCI memory or IO transactions on the PCI bus. These masters can communicate directly with any other devices, including system memory associated with the North bridge.

A device driver executing on the CPU configures the device-specific configuration register space of an associated PCI device. A configured PCI device that is bus master capable can initiate its own transactions, which allows it to communicate with any other PCI target device including system memory associated with the North bridge.

The CPU can access configuration space as described in the previous section.

PCI Express architecture assumes the identical programming model as the PCI programming model described above. In fact, current OSs written for PCI systems can boot a PCI Express system. Current PCI device drivers will initialize PCI Express devices without any driver changes. PCI configuration and enumeration firmware will function unmodified on a PCI Express system.

Limitations of a 33 MHz PCI System

As indicated in Table 1-2 on page 13, peak bandwidth achievable on a 64-bit 33 MHz PCI bus is 266 Mbytes/sec. Current high-end workstation and server applications require greater bandwidth.

Applications such as gigabit Ethernet and high performance disc transfers in RAID and SCSI configurations require greater bandwidth capability than the 33 MHz PCI bus offers.

Latest Generation of Intel PCI Chipsets

Figure 1-14 shows an example of a later generation Intel PCI chipset. The two shaded devices are NOT the North bridge and South bridge shown in earlier diagrams. Instead, one device is the Memory Controller Hub (MCH) and the other is the IO Controller Hub (ICH). The two chips are connected by a proprietary Intel high throughput, low pin count bus called the Hub Link.

Figure 1-14: Latest Generation of PCI Chipsets

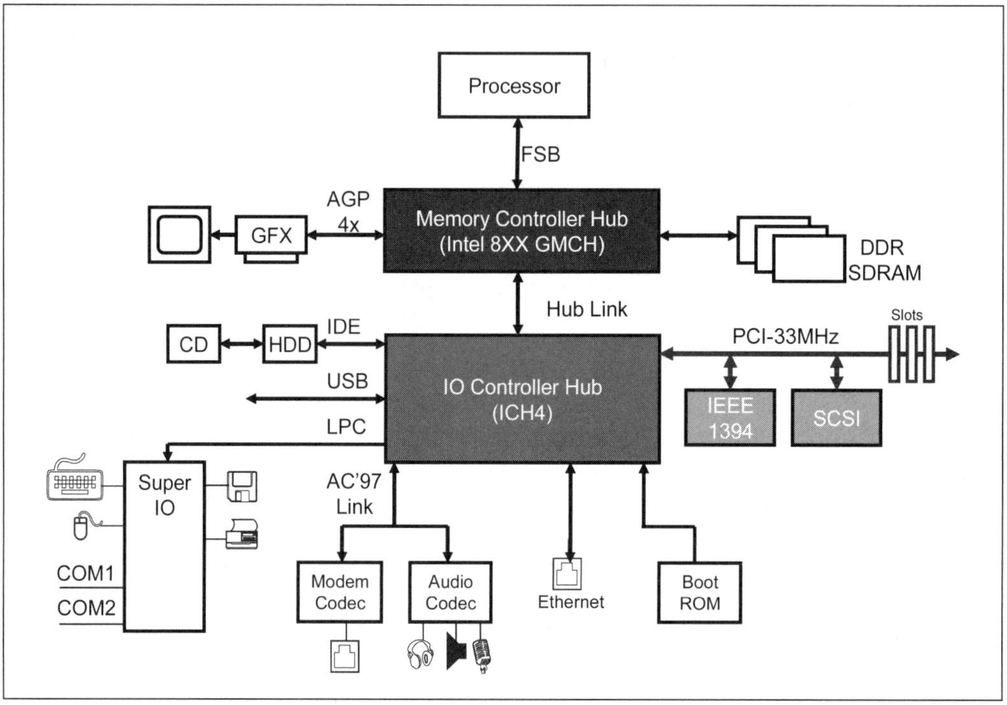

The ICH includes the South bridge functionality but does not support the ISA bus. Other buses associated with ICH include LPC (low pin count) bus, AC'97, Ethernet, Boot ROM, IDE, USB, SMbus and finally the PCI bus. The advantage of this architecture over previous architectures is that the IDE, USB, Ethernet and audio devices do not transfer their data through the PCI bus to memory as is the case with earlier chipsets. Instead they do so through the Hub Link. Hub Link is a higher performance bus compared to PCI. In other words, these devices bypass the PCI bus when communicating with memory. The result is improved performance.

66 MHz PCI Bus Based System

High end systems that require better IO bandwidth implement a 66 MHz 64-bit PCI buses. This PCI bus supports peak data transfer rate of 533 MBytes/sec.

The PCI 2.1 specification released in 1995 added 66MHz PCI support.

Figure 1-15 shows an example of a 66 MHz PCI bus based system. This system has similar features to that described in Figure 1-14 on page 32. However, the MCH chip in this example supports two additional Hub Link buses that connect to P64H (PCI 64-bit Hub) bridge chips, providing access to the 64-bit, 66 MHz buses. These buses each support 1 connector in which a high-end peripheral card may be installed.

Figure 1-15: 66 MHz PCI Bus Based Platform

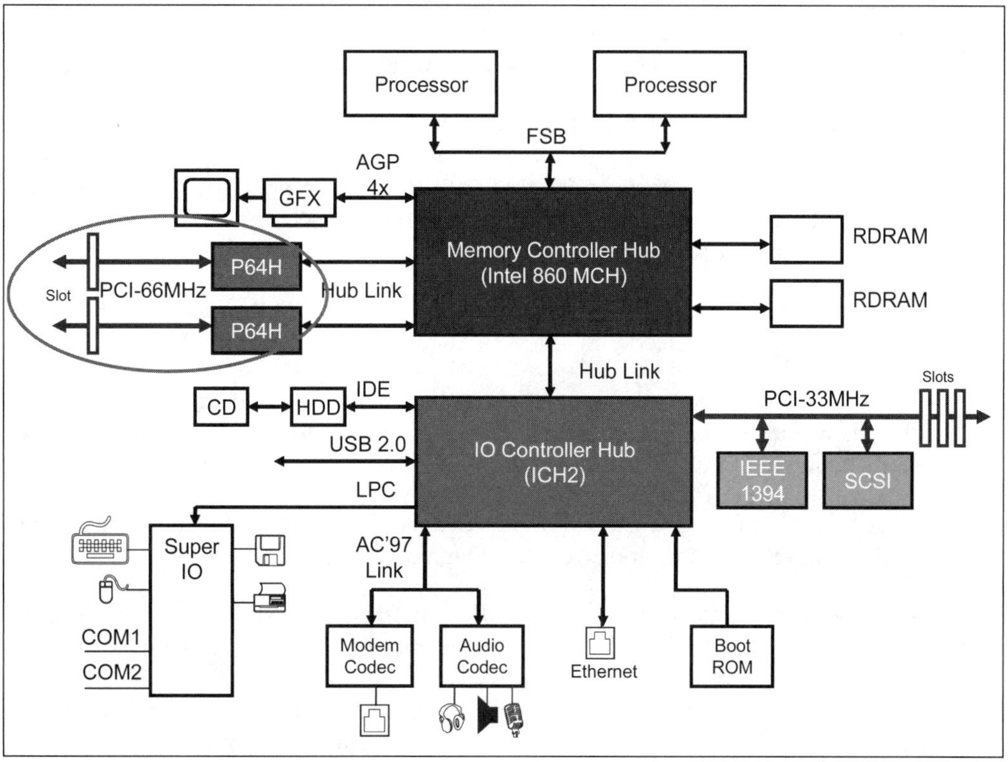

Limitations of 66 MHz PCI bus

The PCI clock period at 66 MHz is 15 ns. Recall that PCI supports reflected-wave signaling drivers that are weaker drivers, which have slower rise and fall times as compared to incident-wave signaling drivers. It is a challenge to design a 66 MHz device or system that satisfies the signal timing requirements.

A 66 MHz PCI based motherboard is routed with shorter signal traces to ensure shorter signal propagation delays. In addition, the bus is loaded with fewer loads in order to ensure faster signal rise and fall times. Taking into account typical board impedances and minimum signal trace lengths, it is possible to interconnect a maximum of four to five 66 MHz PCI devices. Only one or two connectors may be connected on a 66 MHz PCI bus. This is a significant limitation for a system which requires multiple devices interconnected.

The solution requires the addition of PCI bridges and hence multiple buses to interconnect devices. This solution is expensive and consumes additional board real estate. In addition, transactions between devices on opposite sides of a bridge complete with greater latency because bridges implement delayed transactions. This requires bridges to retry all transactions that must cross to the other side (with the exception of memory writes which are posted).

Limitations of PCI Architecture

The maximum frequency achievable with the PCI architecture is 66 MHz. This is a result of the static clock method of driving and latching signals and because reflected-wave signaling is used.

PCI bus efficiency is in the order of 50% or 60%. Some of the factors that contribute towards this reduced efficiency are listed below.

The PCI specification allows master and target devices to insert wait-states during data phases of a bus cycle. Slow devices will add wait-states which reduces the efficiency of bus cycles.

PCI bus cycles do not indicate transfer size. This makes buffer management within master and target devices inefficient.

Delayed transactions on PCI are handled inefficiently. When a master is retried, it guesses when to try again. If the master tries too soon, the target may retry the transaction again. If the master waits too long to retry, the latency to complete a data transfer is increased. Similarly, if a target disconnects a transaction the master must guess when to resume the bus cycle at a later time.

All PCI bus master accesses to system memory result in a snoop access to the CPU cache. Doing so results in additional wait states during PCI bus master accesses of system memory. The North bridge or MCH must assume all system memory address space is cachable even though this may not be the case. PCI bus cycles provide no mechanism by which to indicate an access to non-cachable memory address space.

PCI architecture observes strict ordering rules as defined by the specification. Even if a PCI application does not require observation of these strict ordering rules, PCI bus cycles do not provide a mechanism to allow relaxed ordering rule. Observing relaxed ordering rules allows bus cycles (especially those that cross a bridge) to complete with reduced latency.

PCI interrupt handling architecture is inefficient especially because multiple devices share a PCI interrupt signal. Additional software latency is incurred while software discovers which device or devices that share an interrupt signal actually generated the interrupt.

The processor's NMI interrupt input is asserted when a PCI parity or system error is detected. Ultimately the system shuts down when an error is detected. This is a severe response. A more appropriate response might be to detect the error and attempt error recovery. PCI does not require error recovery features, nor does it support an extensive register set for documenting a variety of detectable errors.

These limitations above have been resolved in the next generation bus architectures, namely PCI-X and PCI Express.

66 MHz and 133 MHz PCI-X 1.0 Bus Based Platforms

Figure 1-16 on page 36 is an example of an Intel 7500 server chipset based system. This chipset has similarities to the 8XX chipset described earlier. MCH and ICH chips are connected via a Hub Link 1.0 bus. Associated with ICH is a 32-bit 33 MHz PCI bus. The 7500 MCH chip includes 3 additional high performance Hub Link 2.0 ports. These Hub Link ports are connected to 3 Hub Link-to-PCI-X Hub 2 bridges (P64H2). Each P64H2 bridge supports 2 PCI-X buses that can run at frequencies up to 133MHz. Hub Link 2.0 Links can sustain the higher bandwidth requirements for PCI-X traffic that targets system memory.

Figure 1-16: 66 MHz/133 MHz PCI-X Bus Based Platform

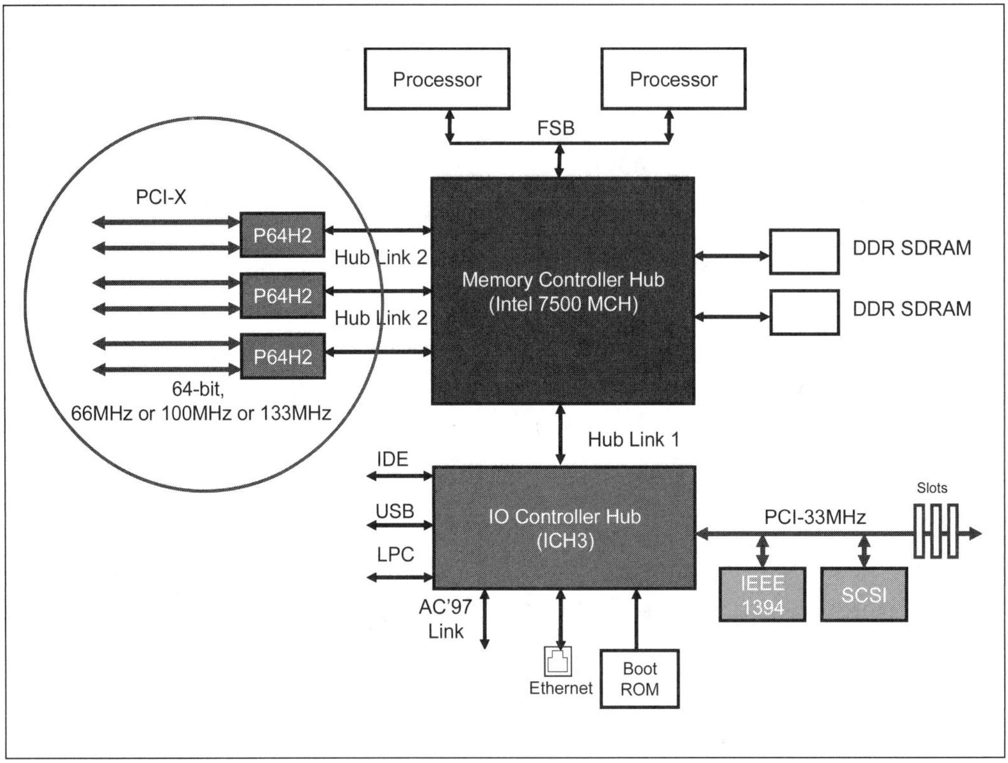

PCI-X Features

The PCI-X bus is a higher frequency, higher performance, higher efficiency bus compared to the PCI bus.

PCI-X devices can be plugged into PCI slots and vice-versa. PCI-X and PCI slots employ the same connector format. Thus, PCI-X is 100% backwards compatible to PCI from both a hardware and software standpoint. The device drivers, OS, and applications that run on a PCI system also run on a PCI-X system.

PCI-X signals are registered. A registered signal requires smaller setup time to sample the signal as compared with a non-registered signal employed in PCI. Also, PCI-X devices employ PLLs that are used to pre-drive signals with smaller clock-to-out time. The time gained from reduced setup time and clock-to-out time is used towards increased clock frequency capability and the ability to support more devices on the bus at a given frequency compared to PCI. PCI-X supports 8-10 loads or 4 connectors at 66 MHz and 3-4 loads or 1-2 connectors at 133 MHz.

The peak bandwidth achievable with 64-bit 133 MHz PCI-X is 1064 MBytes/sec.

Following the first data phase, the PCI-X bus does not allow wait states during subsequent data phases.

Most PCI-X bus cycles are burst cycles and data is generally transferred in blocks of no less than 128 Bytes. This results in higher bus utilization. Further, the transfer size is specified in the attribute phase of PCI-X transactions. This allows for more efficient device buffer management. Figure 1-17 is an example of a PCI-X burst memory read transaction.

Figure 1-17: Example PCI-X Burst Memory Read Bus Cycle

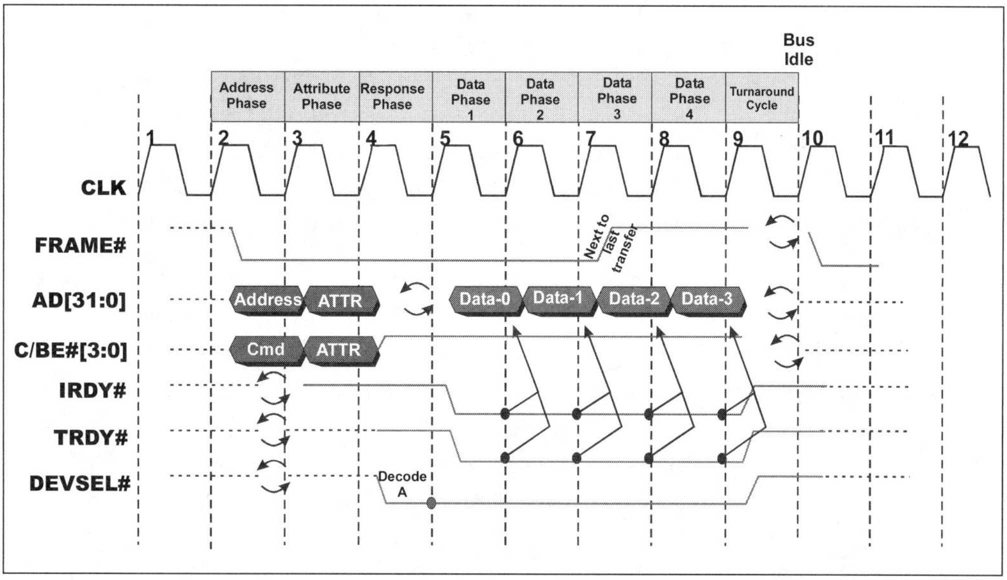

PCI-X Requester/Completer Split Transaction Model. Consider an example of the split transaction protocol supported by PCI-X for delaying transactions. This protocol is illustrated in Figure 1-18. A requester initiates a read transaction. The completer that claims the bus cycles may be unable to return the requested data immediately. Rather than signaling a retry as would be the case in PCI protocol, the completer memorizes the transaction (address, transaction type, byte count, requester ID are memorized) and signals a split response. This prompts the requester to end the bus cycle, and the bus goes idle. The PCI-X bus is now available for other transactions, resulting in more efficient bus utilization. Meanwhile, the requester simply waits for the completer to supply it the requested data at a later time. Once the completer has gathered the requested data, it then arbitrates and obtains bus ownership and initiates a split completion bus cycle during which it returns the requested data. The requester claims the split completion bus cycle and accepts the data from the completer.

The split completion bus cycle is very much like a write bus cycle. Exactly two bus transactions are needed to complete the entire data transfer. In between these two bus transactions (the read request and the split completion transaction) the bus is utilized for other transactions. The requester also receives the requested data in a very efficient manner.

PCI Express architecture employs a similar transaction protocol.

Figure 1-18: PCI-X Split Transaction Protocol

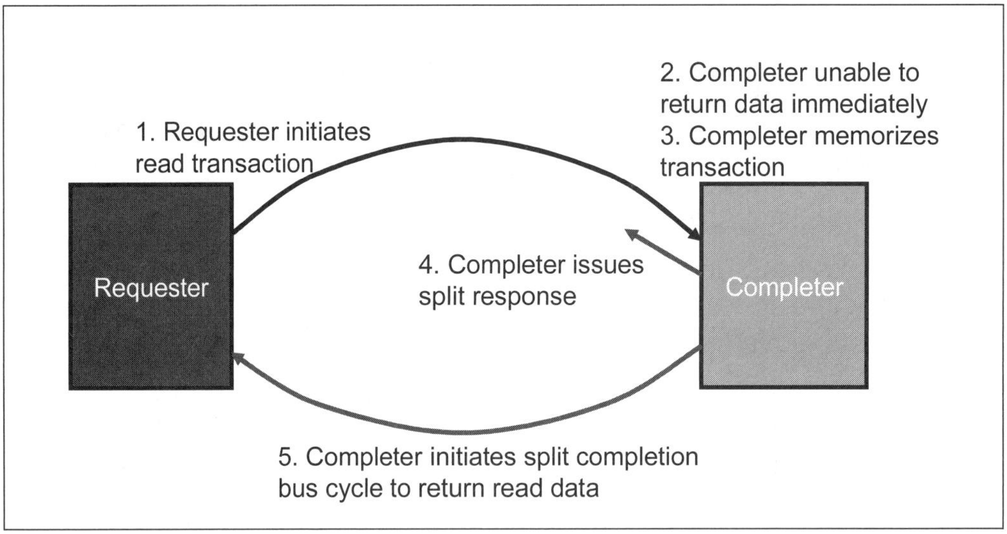

These performance enhancement features described so far contribute towards an increased transfer efficiency of 85% for PCI-X as compared to 50%-60% with PCI protocol.

PCI-X devices must support Message Signaled Interrupt (MSI) architecture, which is a more efficient architecture than the legacy interrupt architecture described in the PCI architecture section. To generate an interrupt request, a

PCI-X devices initiates a memory write transaction targeting the Host (North) bridge. The data written is a unique interrupt vector associated with the device generating the interrupt. The Host bridge interrupts the CPU and the vector is delivered to the CPU in a platform specific manner. With this vector, the CPU is immediately able to run an interrupt service routine to service the interrupting device. There is no software overhead in determining which device generated the interrupt. Also, unlike in the PCI architecture, no interrupt pins are required.

PCI Express architecture implements the MSI protocol, resulting in reduced interrupt servicing latency and elimination of interrupt signals.

PCI Express architecture also supports the RO bit and NS bit feature with the result that those transactions with either NS=1 or RO=1 complete with better performance than transactions with NS=0 or RO=0. PCI transactions by definition assume NS=0 and RO=0.

- **NS** — No Snoop (NS) may be used when accessing system memory. PCI-X bus masters can use the NS bit to indicate whether the region of memory being accessed is cachable (NS=0) or not (NS=1). For those transactions with NS=1, the Host bridge does not snoop the processor cache. The result is improved performance during accesses to non-cachable memory.
- **RO** — Relaxed Ordering (RO) allows transactions that do not have any order of completion requirements to complete more efficiently. We will not get into the details here. Suffice it to say that transactions with the RO bit set can complete on the bus in any order with respect to other transactions that are pending completion.

The PCI-X 2.0 specification released in Q1 2002 was designed to further increase the bandwidth capability of PCI-X bus. This bus is described next.

DDR and QDR PCI-X 2.0 Bus Based Platforms

Figure 1-19 shows a hypothetical PCI-X 2.0 system. This diagram is the author's best guess as to what a PCI-X 2.0 system will look like. PCI-X 2.0 devices and connectors are 100% hardware and software backwards compatible with PCI-X 1.0 as well as PCI devices and connectors. A PCI-X 2.0 bus supports either Dual Data Rate (DDR) or Quad Data Rate (QDR) data transport using a PCI-X 133 MHz clock and strobes that are phase shifted to provide the necessary clock edges.

Figure 1-19: Hypothetical PCI-X 2.0 Bus Based Platform

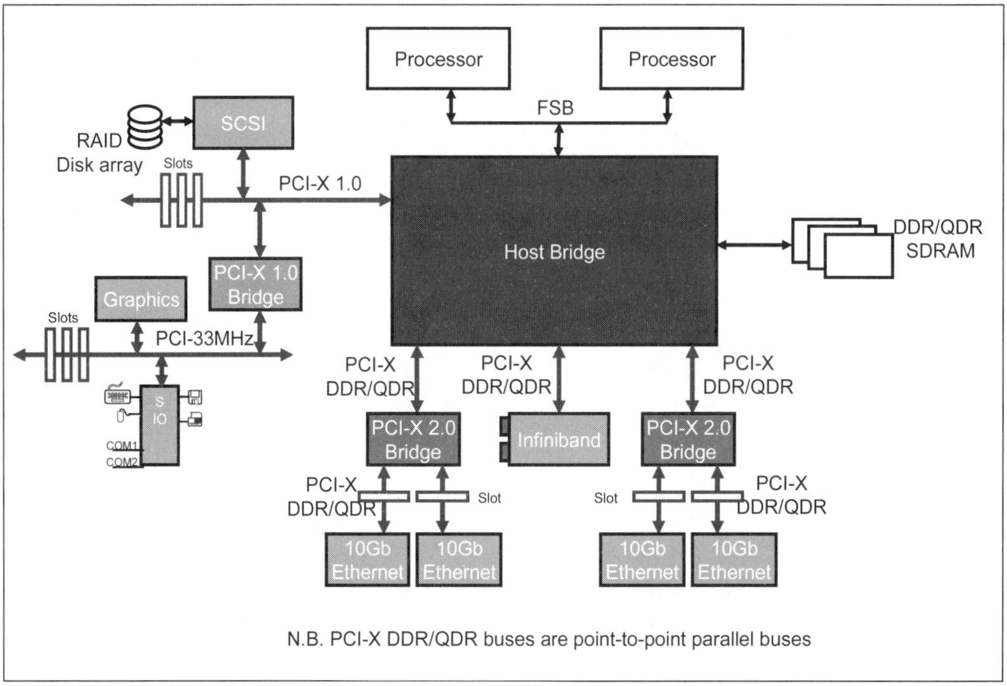

A design requiring greater than 1 GByte/sec bus bandwidth can implement the DDR or QDR protocol. As indicated in Table 1-2 on page 13, PCI-X 2.0 peak bandwidth capability is 4256 MBytes/sec for a 64-bit 533 MHz effective PCI-X bus. With the aid of a strobe clock, data is transferred two times or four times per 133 MHz clock.

PCI-X 2.0 devices also support ECC generation and checking. This allows auto-correction of single bit errors and detection and reporting of multi-bit errors. Error handling is more robust than PCI and PCI-X 1.0 systems making this bus more suited for high-performance, robust, non-stop server applications.

Some noteworthy points to remember are that with very fast signal timing, it is only possible to support one connector on the PCI-X 2.0 bus. This implies that a PCI-X 2.0 bus essentially becomes a point-to-point connection with no multi-drop capability as with its predecessor buses.

PCI-X 2.0 bridges are essentially switches with one primary bus and one or more downstream secondary buses as shown in Figure 1-19 on page 40.

The PCI Express Way

PCI Express provides a high-speed, high-performance, point-to-point, dual simplex, differential signaling Link for interconnecting devices. Data is transmitted from a device on one set of signals, and received on another set of signals.

The Link - A Point-to-Point Interconnect

As shown in Figure 1-20, a PCI Express interconnect consists of either a x1, x2, x4, x8, x12, x16 or x32 point-to-point Link. A PCI Express Link is the physical connection between two devices. A Lane consists of signal pairs in each direction. A x1 Link consists of 1 Lane or 1 differential signal pair in each direction for a total of 4 signals. A x32 Link consists of 32 Lanes or 32 signal pairs for each direction for a total of 128 signals. The Link supports a symmetric number of Lanes in each direction. During hardware initialization, the Link is initialized for Link width and frequency of operation automatically by the devices on opposite ends of the Link. No OS or firmware is involved during Link level initialization.

Figure 1-20: PCI Express Link

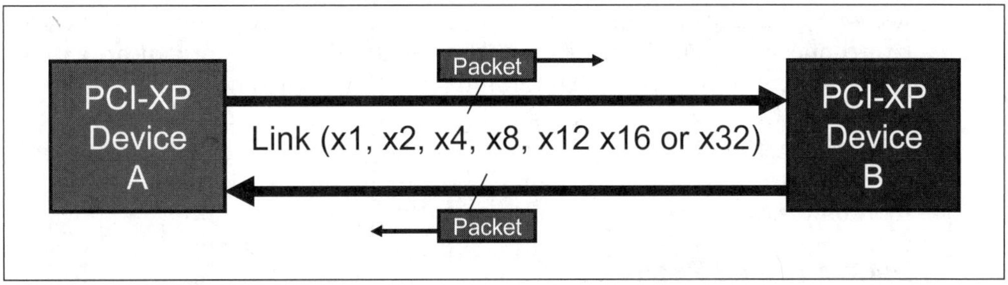

Differential Signaling

PCI Express devices employ differential drivers and receivers at each port. Figure 1-21 shows the electrical characteristics of a PCI Express signal. A positive voltage difference between the D+ and D- terminals implies Logical 1. A negative voltage difference between D+ and D- implies a Logical 0. No voltage difference between D+ and D- means that the driver is in the high-impedance tristate condition, which is referred to as the electrical-idle and low-power state of the Link.

The PCI Express Differential Peak-to-Peak signal voltage at the transmitter ranges from 800 mV - 1200 mV, while the differential peak voltage is one-half these values. The common mode voltage can be any voltage between 0 V and 3.6 V. The differential driver is DC isolated from the differential receiver at the opposite end of the Link by placing a capacitor at the driver side of the Link. Two devices at opposite ends of a Link may support different DC common mode voltages. The differential impedance at the receiver is matched with the board impedance to prevent reflections from occurring.

Figure 1-21: PCI Express Differential Signal

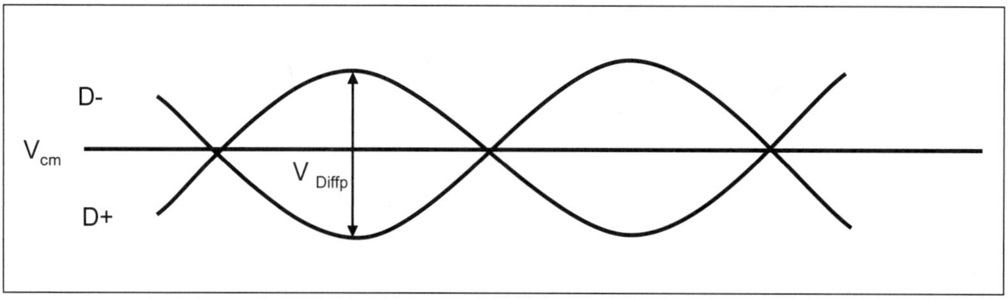

Switches Used to Interconnect Multiple Devices

Switches are implemented in systems requiring multiple devices to be interconnected. Switches can range from a 2-port device to an n-port device, where each port connects to a PCI Express Link. The specification does not indicate a maximum number of ports a switch can implement. A switch may be incorporated into a Root Complex device (Host bridge or North bridge equivalent), resulting in a multi-port root complex. Figure 1-23 on page 52 and Figure 1-25 on page 54 are examples of PCI Express systems showing multi-ported devices such as the root complex or switches.

Packet Based Protocol

Rather than bus cycles we are familiar with from PCI and PCI-X architectures, PCI Express encodes transactions using a packet based protocol. Packets are transmitted and received serially and byte striped across the available Lanes of the Link. The more Lanes implemented on a Link the faster a packet is transmitted and the greater the bandwidth of the Link. The packets are used to support the split transaction protocol for non-posted transactions. Various types of packets such as memory read and write requests, IO read and write requests, configuration read and write requests, message requests and completions are defined.

Bandwidth and Clocking

As is apparent from Table 1-3 on page 14, the aggregate bandwidth achievable with PCI Express is significantly higher than any bus available today. The PCI Express 1.0 specification supports 2.5 Gbits/sec/lane/direction transfer rate.

No clock signal exists on the Link. Each packet to be transmitted over the Link consists of bytes of information. Each byte is encoded into a 10-bit symbol. All symbols are guaranteed to have one-zero transitions. The receiver uses a PLL to recover a clock from the 0-to-1 and 1-to-0 transitions of the incoming bit stream.

Address Space

PCI Express supports the same address spaces as PCI: memory, IO and configuration address spaces. In addition, the maximum configuration address space per device function is extended from 256 Bytes to 4 KBytes. New OS, drivers and applications are required to take advantage of this additional configuration address space. Also, a new messaging transaction and address space provides messaging capability between devices. Some messages are PCI Express standard messages used for error reporting, interrupt and power management messaging. Other messages are vendor defined messages.

PCI Express Transactions

PCI Express supports the same transaction types supported by PCI and PCI-X. These include memory read and memory write, I/O read and I/O write, configuration read and configuration write. In addition, PCI Express supports a new transaction type called Message transactions. These transactions are encoded using the packet-based PCI Express protocol described later.

PCI Express Transaction Model

PCI Express transactions can be divided into two categories. Those transactions that are non-posted and those that are posted. Non-posted transactions, such as memory reads, implement a split transaction communication model similar to the PCI-X split transaction protocol. For example, a requester device transmits a non-posted type memory read request packet to a completer. The completer returns a completion packet with the read data to the requester. Posted transactions, such as memory writes, consist of a memory write packet transmitted uni-directionally from requester to completer with no completion packet returned from completer to requester.

Error Handling and Robustness of Data Transfer

CRC fields are embedded within each packet transmitted. One of the CRC fields supports a Link-level error checking protocol whereby each receiver of a packet checks for Link-level CRC errors. Packets transmitted over the Link in error are recognized with a CRC error at the receiver. The transmitter of the packet is notified of the error by the receiver. The transmitter automatically retries sending the packet (with no software involvement), hopefully resulting in auto-correction of the error.

In addition, an optional CRC field within a packet allows for end-to-end data integrity checking required for high availability applications.

Error handling on PCI Express can be as rudimentary as PCI level error handling described earlier or can be robust enough for server-level requirements. A rich set of error logging registers and error reporting mechanisms provide for improved fault isolation and recovery solutions required by RAS (Reliable, Available, Serviceable) applications.

Quality of Service (QoS), Traffic Classes (TCs) and Virtual Channels (VCs)

The Quality of Service feature of PCI Express refers to the capability of routing packets from different applications through the fabric with differentiated priorities and deterministic latencies and bandwidth. For example, it may be desirable to ensure that Isochronous applications, such as video data packets, move through the fabric with higher priority and guaranteed bandwidth, while control data packets may not have specific bandwidth or latency requirements.

PCI Express packets contain a Traffic Class (TC) number between 0 and 7 that is assigned by the device's application or device driver. Packets with different TCs can move through the fabric with different priority, resulting in varying performances. These packets are routed through the fabric by utilizing virtual channel (VC) buffers implemented in switches, endpoints and root complex devices.

Each Traffic Class is individually mapped to a Virtual Channel (a VC can have several TCs mapped to it, but a TC cannot be mapped to multiple VCs). The TC in each packet is used by the transmitting and receiving ports to determine which VC buffer to drop the packet into. Switches and devices are configured to arbitrate and prioritize between packets from different VCs before forwarding. This arbitration is referred to as VC arbitration. In addition, packets arriving at different ingress ports are forwarded to their own VC buffers at the egress port. These transactions are prioritized based on the ingress port number when being merged into a common VC output buffer for delivery across the egress link. This arbitration is referred to as Port arbitration.

The result is that packets with different TC numbers could observe different performance when routed through the PCI Express fabric.

Flow Control

A packet transmitted by a device is received into a VC buffer in the receiver at the opposite end of the Link. The receiver periodically updates the transmitter with information regarding the amount of buffer space it has available. The transmitter device will only transmit a packet to the receiver if it knows that the receiving device has sufficient buffer space to hold the next transaction. The protocol by which the transmitter ensures that the receiving buffer has sufficient space available is referred to as flow control. The flow control mechanism guarantees that a transmitted packet will be accepted by the receiver, baring error conditions. As such, the PCI Express transaction protocol does not require support of packet retry (unless an error condition is detected in the receiver), thereby improving the efficiency with which packets are forwarded to a receiver via the Link.

MSI Style Interrupt Handling Similar to PCI-X

Interrupt handling is accomplished in-band via PCI-X-like MSI protocol. PCI Express device use a memory write packet to transmit an interrupt vector to the root complex host bridge device, which in-turn interrupts the CPU. PCI Express devices are required to implement the MSI capability register block. PCI Express also supports legacy interrupt handling in-band by encoding interrupt signal transitions (for INTA#, INTB#, INTC# and INTD#) using Message transactions. Only endpoint devices that must support legacy functions and PCI Express-to-PCI bridges are allowed to support legacy interrupt generation.

Power Management

The PCI Express fabric consumes less power because the interconnect consists of fewer signals that have smaller signal swings. Each device's power state is individually managed. PCI/PCI Express power management software determines the power management capability of each device and manages it individually in a manner similar to PCI. Devices can notify software of their current power state, as well as power management software can propagate a wake-up event through the fabric to power-up a device or group of devices. Devices can also signal a wake-up event using an in-band mechanism or a side-band signal.

With no software involvement, devices place a Link into a power savings state after a time-out when they recognize that there are no packets to transmit over the Link. This capability is referred to as Active State power management.

PCI Express supports device power states: D0, D1, D2, D3-Hot and D3-Cold, where D0 is the full-on power state and D3-Cold is the lowest power state.

PCI Express also supports the following Link power states: L0, L0s, L1, L2 and L3, where L0 is the full-on Link state and L3 is the Link-Off power state.

Hot Plug Support

PCI Express supports hot plug and surprise hot unplug without usage of side-band signals. Hot plug interrupt messages, communicated in-band to the root complex, trigger hot plug software to detect a hot plug or removal event. Rather than implementing a centralized hot plug controller as exists in PCI platforms, the hot plug controller function is distributed to the port logic associated with a hot plug capable port of a switch or root complex. 2 colored LEDs, a Manually-operated Retention Latch (MRL), MRL sensor, attention button, power control signal and PRSNT2# signal are some of the elements of a hot plug capable port.

PCI Compatible Software Model

PCI Express employs the same programming model as PCI and PCI-X systems described earlier in this chapter. The memory and IO address space remains the same as PCI/PCI-X. The first 256 Bytes of configuration space per PCI Express function is the same as PCI/PCI-X device configuration address space, thus ensuring that current OSs and device drivers will run on a PCI Express system. PCI Express architecture extends the configuration address space to 4 KB per functional device. Updated OSs and device drivers are required to take advantage and access this additional configuration address space.

PCI Express configuration model supports two mechanisms:

1. PCI compatible configuration model which is 100% compatible with existing OSs and bus enumeration and configuration software for PCI/PCI-X systems.
2. PCI Express enhanced configuration mechanism which provides access to additional configuration space beyond the first 256 Bytes and up to 4 KBytes per function.

Mechanical Form Factors

PCI Express architecture supports multiple platform interconnects such as chip-to-chip, board-to-peripheral card via PCI-like connectors and Mini PCI Express form factors for the mobile market. Specifications for these are fully defined. See "Add-in Cards and Connectors" on page 685 for details on PCI Express peripheral card and connector definition.

PCI-like Peripheral Card and Connector. Currently, x1, x4, x8 and x16 PCI-like connectors are defined along with associated peripheral cards. Desktop computers implementing PCI Express can have the same look and feel as current computers with no changes required to existing system form factors. PCI Express motherboards can have an ATX-like motherboard form factor.

Mini PCI Express Form Factor. Mini PCI Express connector and add-in card implements a subset of signals that exist on a standard PCI Express connector and add-in card. The form factor, as the name implies, is much smaller. This form factor targets the mobile computing market. The Mini PCI Express slot supports x1 PCI Express signals including power management signals. In addition, the slot supports LED control signals, a USB interface and an SMBus interface. The Mini PCI Express module is similar but smaller than a PC Card.

Mechanical Form Factors Pending Release

As of May 2003, specifications for two new form factors have not been released. Below is a summary of publicly available information about these form factors.

NEWCARD Form Factor. Another new module form factor that will service both mobile and desktop markets is the NEWCARD form factor. This is a PCMCIA PC card type form factor, but of nearly half the size that will support x1 PCI Express signals including power management signals. In addition, the slot supports USB and SMBus interfaces. There are two size form factors defined, a narrower version and a wider version though the thickness and depth remain the same. Although similar in appearance to Mini PCI Express Module, this is a different form factor.

Server IO Module (SIOM) Form Factor. These are a family of modules that target the workstation and server market. They are designed with future support of larger PCI Express Lane widths and higher frequency bit rates beyond 2.5 Gbits/s Generation 1 transmission rates. Four form factors are under consideration. The base module with single- and double-width modules. Also, the full height with single- and double-width modules.

PCI Express Topology

Major components in the PCI Express system shown in Figure 1-22 include a root complex, switches, and endpoint devices.

Figure 1-22: PCI Express Topology

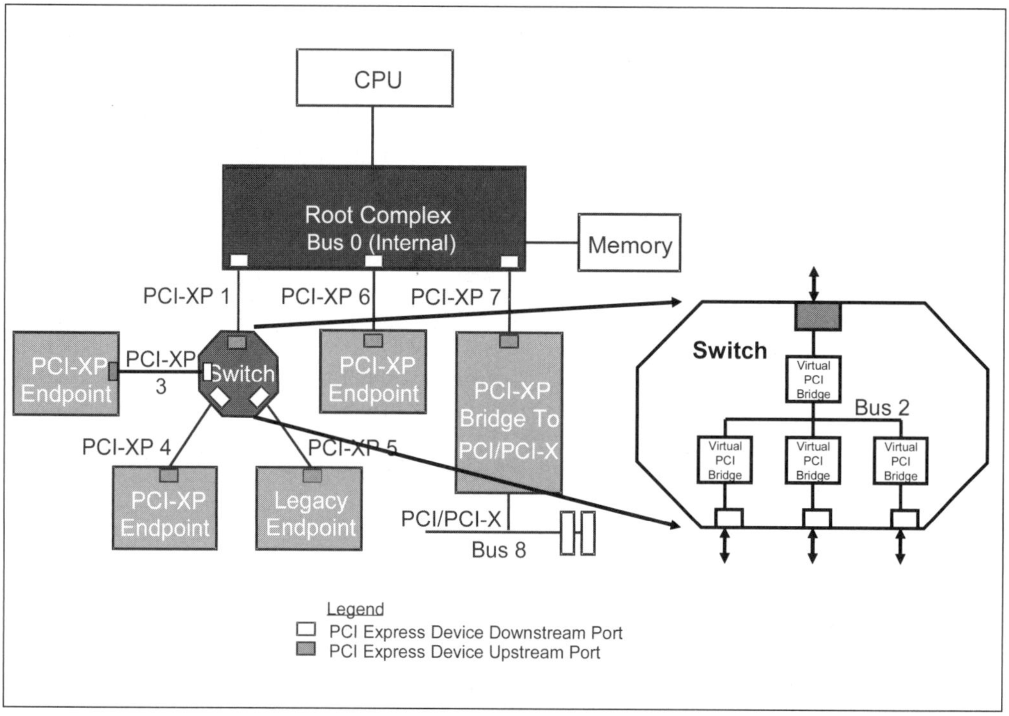

The **Root Complex** denotes the device that connects the CPU and memory subsystem to the PCI Express fabric. It may support one or more PCI Express ports. The root complex in this example supports 3 ports. Each port is connected to an endpoint device or a switch which forms a sub-hierarchy. The root complex generates transaction requests on the behalf of the CPU. It is capable of initiating configuration transaction requests on the behalf of the CPU. It generates both memory and IO requests as well as generates locked transaction requests on the behalf of the CPU. The root complex as a completer does not respond to locked requests. Root complex transmits packets out of its ports and receives packets on its ports which it forwards to memory. A multi-port root complex may also route packets from one port to another port but is NOT required by the specification to do so.

Root complex implements central resources such as: hot plug controller, power management controller, interrupt controller, error detection and reporting logic. The root complex initializes with a bus number, device number and function number which are used to form a requester ID or completer ID. The root complex bus, device and function numbers initialize to all 0s.

A **Hierarchy** is a fabric of all the devices and Links associated with a root complex that are either directly connected to the root complex via its port(s) or indirectly connected via switches and bridges. In Figure 1-22 on page 48, the entire PCI Express fabric associated with the root is one hierarchy.

A **Hierarchy Domain** is a fabric of devices and Links that are associated with one port of the root complex. For example in Figure 1-22 on page 48, there are 3 hierarchy domains.

Endpoints are devices other than root complex and switches that are requesters or completers of PCI Express transactions. They are peripheral devices such as Ethernet, USB or graphics devices. Endpoints initiate transactions as a requester or respond to transactions as a completer. Two types of endpoints exist, PCI Express endpoints and legacy endpoints. **Legacy Endpoints** may support IO transactions. They may support locked transaction semantics as a completer but not as a requester. Interrupt capable legacy devices may support legacy style interrupt generation using message requests but must in addition support MSI generation using memory write transactions. Legacy devices are not required to support 64-bit memory addressing capability. **PCI Express Endpoints** must not support IO or locked transaction semantics and must support MSI style interrupt generation. PCI Express endpoints must support 64-bit memory addressing capability in prefetchable memory address space, though their non-prefetchable memory address space is permitted to map the below 4GByte boundary. Both types of endpoints implement Type 0 PCI configuration headers and respond to configuration transactions as completers. Each endpoint is initialized with a device ID (**requester ID** or **completer ID)** which consists of a bus number, device number, and function number. Endpoints are always device 0 on a bus.

Multi-Function Endpoints. Like PCI devices, PCI Express devices may support up to 8 functions per endpoint with at least one function number 0. However, a PCI Express Link supports only one endpoint numbered device 0.

PCI Express-to-PCI(-X) Bridge is a bridge between PCI Express fabric and a PCI or PCI-X hierarchy.

A **Requester** is a device that originates a transaction in the PCI Express fabric. Root complex and endpoints are requester type devices.

A **Completer** is a device addressed or targeted by a requester. A requester reads data from a completer or writes data to a completer. Root complex and endpoints are completer type devices.

A **Port** is the interface between a PCI Express component and the Link. It consists of differential transmitters and receivers. An **Upstream Port** is a port that points in the direction of the root complex. A **Downstream Port** is a port that points away from the root complex. An endpoint port is an upstream port. A root complex port(s) is a downstream port. An **Ingress Port** is a port that receives a packet. An **Egress Port** is a port that transmits a packet.

A **Switch** can be thought of as consisting of two or more logical PCI-to-PCI bridges, each bridge associated with a switch port. Each bridge implements configuration header 1 registers. Configuration and enumeration software will detect and initialize each of the header 1 registers at boot time. A 4 port switch shown in Figure 1-22 on page 48 consists of 4 virtual bridges. These bridges are internally connected via a non-defined bus. One port of a switch pointing in the direction of the root complex is an upstream port. All other ports pointing away from the root complex are downstream ports.

A switch forwards packets in a manner similar to PCI bridges using memory, IO or configuration address based routing. Switches must forward all types of transactions from any ingress port to any egress port. Switches forward these packets based on one of three routing mechanisms: address routing, ID routing, or implicit routing. The logical bridges within the switch implement PCI configuration header 1. The configuration header contains memory and IO base and limit address registers as well as primary bus number, secondary bus number and subordinate bus number registers. These registers are used by the switch to aid in packet routing and forwarding.

Switches implement two arbitration mechanisms, port arbitration and VC arbitration, by which they determine the priority with which to forward packets from ingress ports to egress ports. Switches support locked requests.

Enumerating the System

Standard PCI Plug and Play enumeration software can enumerate a PCI Express system. The Links are numbered in a manner similar to the PCI depth first search enumeration algorithm. An example of the bus numbering is shown in Figure 1-22 on page 48. Each PCI Express Link is equivalent to a logical PCI bus. In other words, each Link is assigned a bus number by the bus enumerating software. A PCI Express endpoint is device 0 on a PCI Express Link of a given bus number. Only one device (device 0) exists per PCI Express Link. The internal bus within a switch that connects all the virtual bridges together is also numbered. The first Link associated with the root complex is number bus 1. Bus 0 is an internal virtual bus within the root complex. Buses downstream of a PCI Express-to-PCI(-X) bridge are enumerated the same way as in a PCI(-X) system.

Endpoints and PCI(-X) devices may implement up to 8 functions per device. Only 1 device is supported per PCI Express Link though PCI(-X) buses may theoretically support up to 32 devices per bus. A system could theoretically include up to 256 PCI Express Link and PCI(-X) buses.

PCI Express System Block Diagram

Low Cost PCI Express Chipset

Figure 1-23 on page 52 is a block diagram of a low cost PCI Express based system. As of the writing of this book (April 2003) no real life PCI Express chipset architecture designs were publicly disclosed. The author describes here a practical low cost PCI Express chipset whose architecture is based on existing non-PCI Express chipset architectures. In this solution, AGP which connects MCH to a graphics controller in earlier MCH designs (see Figure 1-14 on page 32) is replaced with a PCI Express Link. The Hub Link that connects MCH to ICH is replaced with a PCI Express Link. And in addition to a PCI bus associated with ICH, the ICH chip supports 4 PCI Express Links. Some of these Links can connect directly to devices on the motherboard and some can be routed to connectors where peripheral cards are installed.

The CPU can communicate with PCI Express devices associated with ICH as well as the PCI Express graphics controller. PCI Express devices can communicate with system memory or the graphics controller associated with MCH. PCI devices may also communicate with PCI Express devices and vice versa. In other words, the chipset supports peer-to-peer packet routing between PCI Express endpoints and PCI devices, memory and graphics. It is yet to be determined if the first generation PCI Express chipsets, will support peer-to-peer packet routing between PCI Express endpoints. Remember that the specification does not require the root complex to support peer-to-peer packet routing between the multiple Links associated with the root complex.

This design does not require the use of switches if the number of PCI Express devices to be connected does not exceed the number of Links available in this design.

Figure 1-23: Low Cost PCI Express System

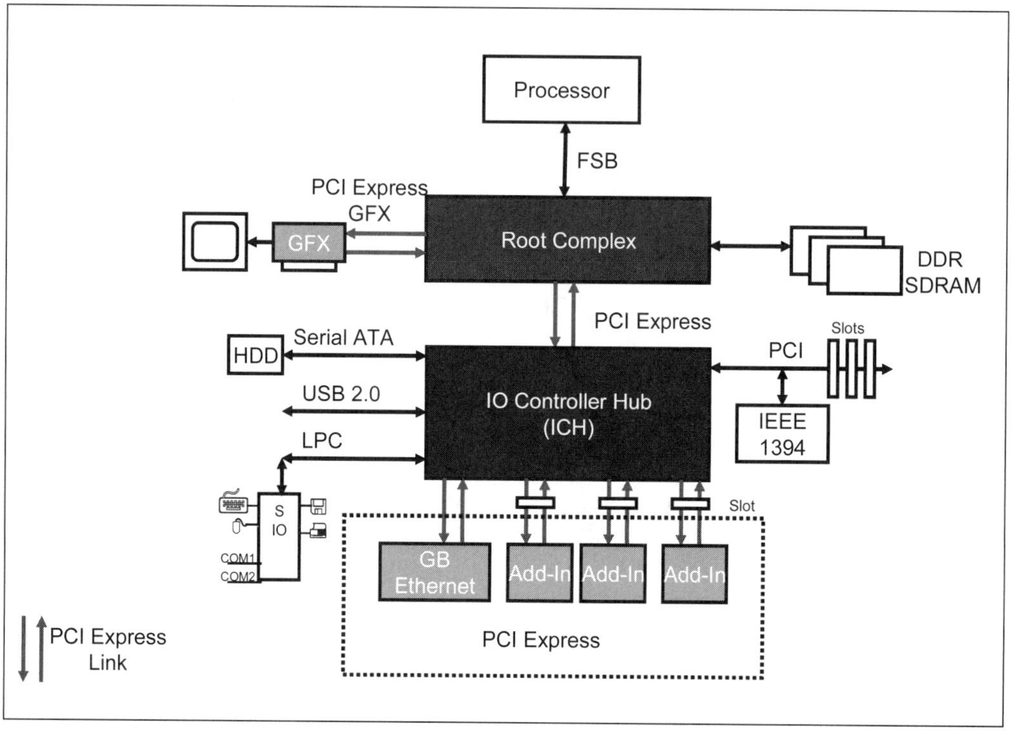

Another Low Cost PCI Express Chipset

Figure 1-24 on page 53 is a block diagram of another low cost PCI Express system. In this design, the Hub Link connects the root complex to an ICH device. The ICH device may be an existing design which has no PCI Express Link associated with it. Instead, all PCI Express Links are associated with the root complex. One of these Links connects to a graphics controller. The other Links directly connect to PCI Express endpoints on the motherboard or connect to PCI Express endpoints on peripheral cards inserted in slots.

Figure 1-24: Another Low Cost PCI Express System

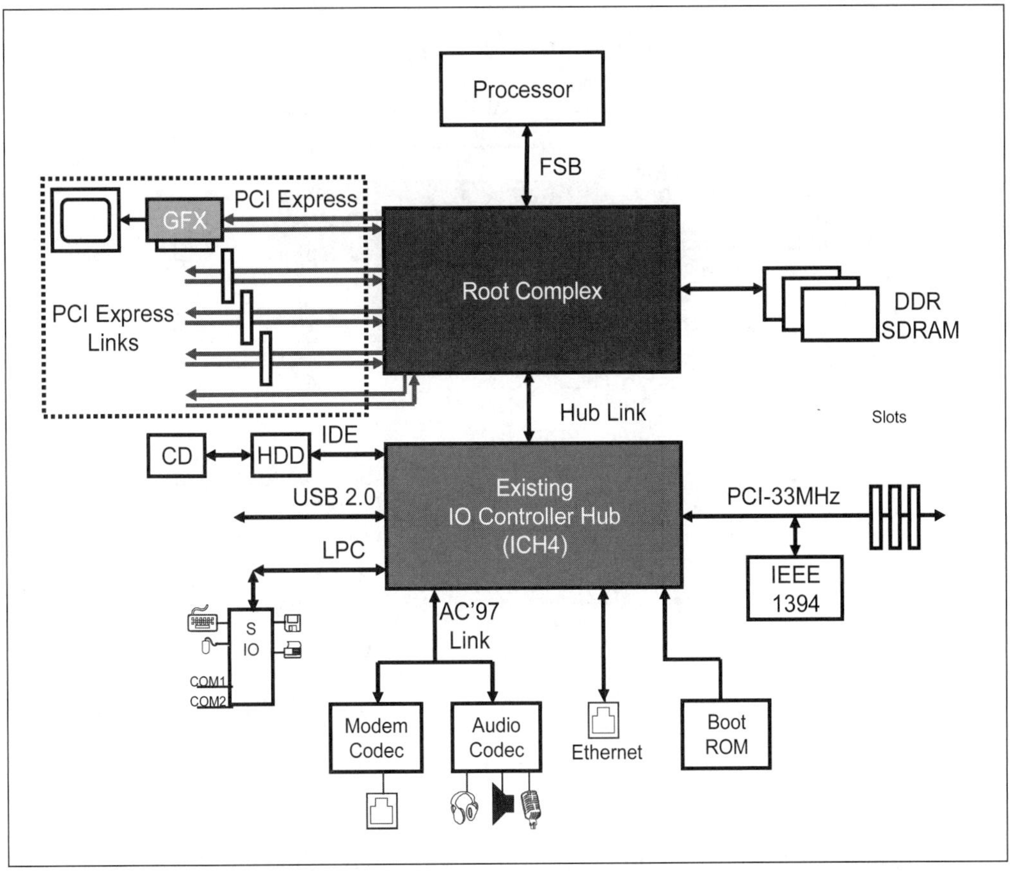

High-End Server System

Figure 1-25 shows a more complex system requiring a large number of devices connected together. Multi-port switches are a necessary design feature to accomplish this. To support PCI or PCI-X buses, a PCI Express-to-PCI(-X) bridge is connected to one switch port. PCI Express packets can be routed from any device to any other device because switch support peer-to-peer packet routing (Only multi-port root complex devices are not required to support peer-to-peer functionality).

Figure 1-25: PCI Express High-End Server System

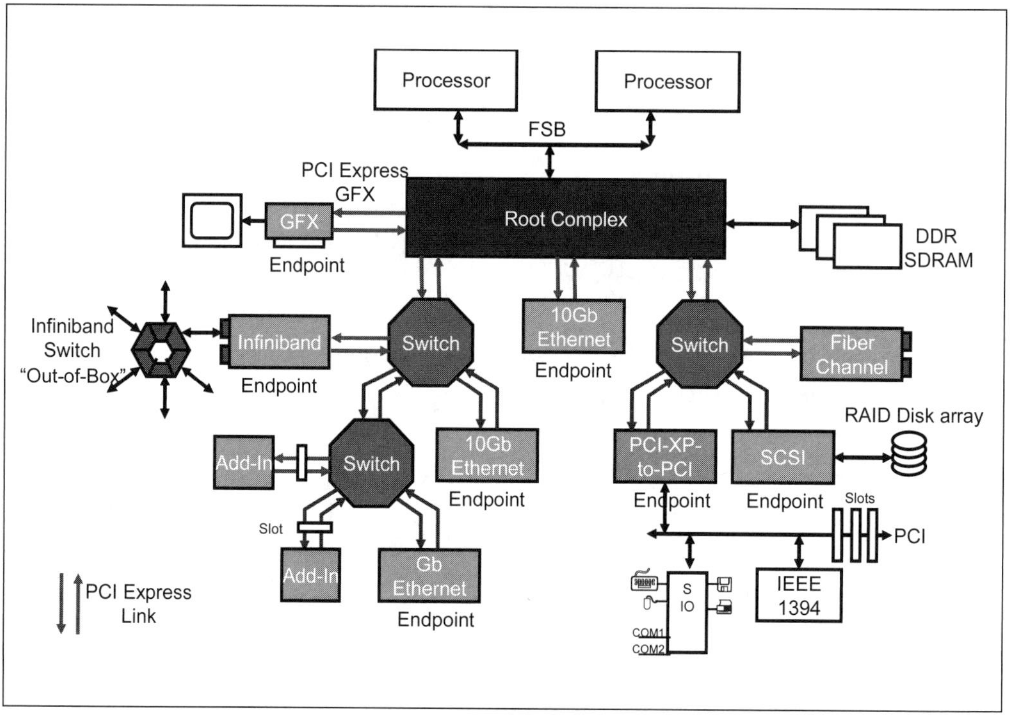

PCI Express Specifications

As of the writing of this book (May 2003) the following are specifications released by the PCISIG.

- PCI Express 1.0a Base Specification released Q2, 2003
- PCI Express 1.0a Card Electomechanical Specification released Q2, 2002
- PCI Express 1.0 Base Specification released Q2, 2002
- PCI Express 1.0 Card Electomechanical Specification released Q2, 2002
- Mini PCI Express 1.0 Specification released Q2, 2003

As of May 2003, the specifications pending release are: the PCI Express-to-PCI Bridge specification, Server IO Module specification, Cable specification, Backplane specification, updated Mini PCI Express specification, and NEWCARD specification.

2 Architecture Overview

Previous Chapter

The previous chapter described performance advantages and key features of the PCI Express (PCI-XP) Link. To highlight these advantages, the chapter described performance characteristics and features of predecessor buses such as PCI and PCI-X buses with the goal of discussing the evolution of PCI Express from these predecessor buses. It compared and contrasted features and performance points of PCI, PCI-X and PCI Express buses. The key features of a PCI Express system were described. The chapter in addition described some examples of PCI Express system topologies.

This Chapter

This chapter is an introduction to the PCI Express data transfer protocol. It describes the layered approach to PCI Express device design while describing the function of each device layer. Packet types employed in accomplishing data transfers are described without getting into packet content details. Finally, this chapter outlines the process of a requester initiating a transaction such as a memory read to read data from a completer across a Link.

The Next Chapter

The next chapter describes how packets are routed through a PCI Express fabric consisting of switches. Packets are routed based on a memory address, IO address, device ID or implicitly.

Introduction to PCI Express Transactions

PCI Express employs packets to accomplish data transfers between devices. A root complex can communicate with an endpoint. An endpoint can communicate with a root complex. An endpoint can communicate with another endpoint. Communication involves the transmission and reception of packets called Transaction Layer packets (TLPs).

PCI Express transactions can be grouped into four categories:

1) memory, 2) IO, 3) configuration, and 4) message transactions. Memory, IO and configuration transactions are supported in PCI and PCI-X architectures, but the message transaction is new to PCI Express. **Transactions** are defined as a series of one or more packet transmissions required to complete an information transfer between a requester and a completer. Table 2-1 is a more detailed list of transactions. These transactions can be categorized into non-posted transactions and posted transactions.

Table 2-1: PCI Express Non-Posted and Posted Transactions

Transaction Type	Non-Posted or Posted
Memory Read	Non-Posted
Memory Write	Posted
Memory Read Lock	Non-Posted
IO Read	Non-Posted
IO Write	Non-Posted
Configuration Read (Type 0 and Type 1)	Non-Posted
Configuration Write (Type 0 and Type 1)	Non-Posted
Message	Posted

For Non-posted transactions, a requester transmits a TLP request packet to a completer. At a later time, the completer returns a TLP completion packet back to the requester. Non-posted transactions are handled as split transactions similar to the PCI-X split transaction model described on page 37 in Chapter 1. The purpose of the completion TLP is to confirm to the requester that the completer has received the request TLP. In addition, non-posted read transactions contain data in the completion TLP. Non-Posted write transactions contain data in the write request TLP.

For Posted transactions, a requester transmits a TLP request packet to a completer. The completer however does NOT return a completion TLP back to the requester. Posted transactions are optimized for best performance in completing the transaction at the expense of the requester not having knowledge of successful reception of the request by the completer. Posted transactions may or may not contain data in the request TLP.

PCI Express Transaction Protocol

Table 2-2 lists all of the TLP request and TLP completion packets. These packets are used in the transactions referenced in Table 2-1. Our goal in this section is to describe how these packets are used to complete transactions at a system level and not to describe the packet routing through the PCI Express fabric nor to describe packet contents in any detail.

Table 2-2: PCI Express TLP Packet Types

TLP Packet Types	Abbreviated Name
Memory Read Request	MRd
Memory Read Request - Locked access	MRdLk
Memory Write Request	MWr
IO Read	IORd
IO Write	IOWr
Configuration Read (Type 0 and Type 1)	CfgRd0, CfgRd1
Configuration Write (Type 0 and Type 1)	CfgWr0, CfgWr1
Message Request without Data	Msg
Message Request with Data	MsgD
Completion without Data	Cpl
Completion with Data	CplD
Completion without Data - associated with Locked Memory Read Requests	CplLk
Completion with Data - associated with Locked Memory Read Requests	CplDLk

Non-Posted Read Transactions

Figure 2-1 shows the packets transmitted by a requester and completer to complete a non-posted read transaction. To complete this transfer, a requester transmits a non-posted read request TLP to a completer it intends to read data from. Non-posted read request TLPs include memory read request (MRd), IO read request (IORd), and configuration read request type 0 or type 1 (CfgRd0, CfgRd1) TLPs. Requesters may be root complex or endpoint devices (endpoints do not initiate configuration read/write requests however).

The request TLP is routed through the fabric of switches using information in the header portion of the TLP. The packet makes its way to a targeted completer. The completer can be a root complex, switches, bridges or endpoints.

When the completer receives the packet and decodes its contents, it gathers the amount of data specified in the request from the targeted address. The completer creates a single completion TLP or multiple completion TLPs with data (CplD) and sends it back to the requester. The completer can return up to 4 KBytes of data per CplD packet.

The completion packet contains routing information necessary to route the packet back to the requester. This completion packet travels through the same path and hierarchy of switches as the request packet.

Requesters uses a tag field in the completion to associate it with a request TLP of the same tag value it transmitted earlier. Use of a tag in the request and completion TLPs allows a requester to manage multiple outstanding transactions.

If a completer is unable to obtain requested data as a result of an error, it returns a completion packet without data (Cpl) and an error status indication. The requester determines how to handle the error at the software layer.

Figure 2-1: Non-Posted Read Transaction Protocol

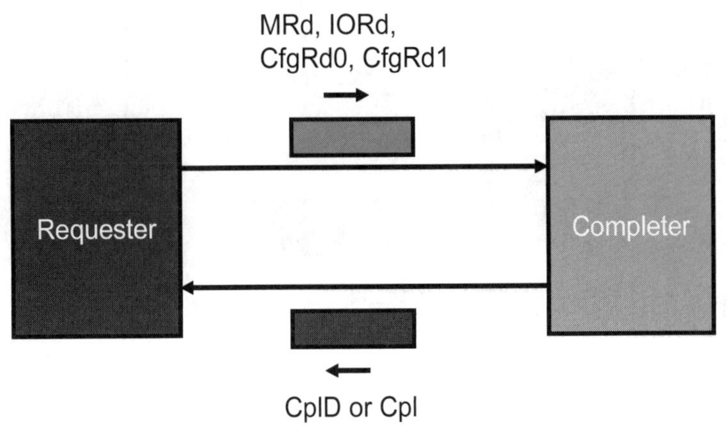

Legend:
MRd = Memory Read Request
IORd = IO Read Request
CfgRd0 = Type 0 Configuration Read Request
CfgRd1 = Type 1 Configuration Read Request
CplD = Completion with data for normal completion of MRd, IORd, CfgRd0, CfgRd1
Cpl = Completion without data for error completion of MRd, IORd, CfgRd0, CfgRd1

Non-Posted Read Transaction for Locked Requests

Figure 2-2 on page 60 shows packets transmitted by a requester and completer to complete a non-posted locked read transaction. To complete this transfer, a requester transmits a memory read locked request (MRdLk) TLP. The requester can only be a root complex which initiates a locked request on the behalf of the CPU. Endpoints are not allowed to initiate locked requests.

The locked memory read request TLP is routed downstream through the fabric of switches using information in the header portion of the TLP. The packet makes its way to a targeted completer. The completer can only be a legacy endpoint. The entire path from root complex to the endpoint (for TCs that map to VC0) is locked including the ingress and egress port of switches in the pathway.

Figure 2-2: Non-Posted Locked Read Transaction Protocol

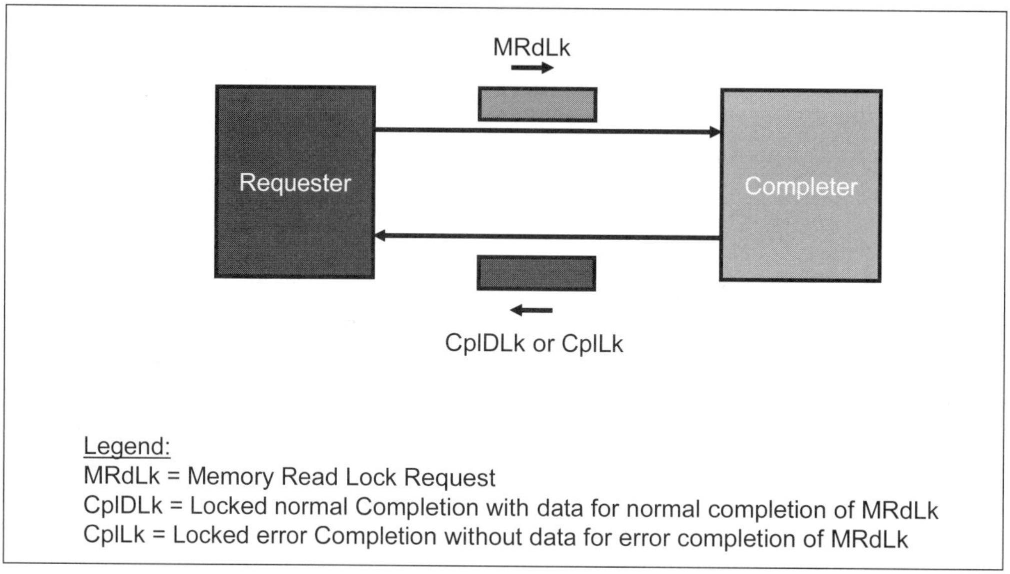

When the completer receives the packet and decodes its contents, it gathers the amount of data specified in the request from the targeted address. The completer creates one or more locked completion TLP with data (CplDLk) along with a completion status. The completion is sent back to the root complex requester via the path and hierarchy of switches as the original request.

The CplDLk packet contains routing information necessary to route the packet back to the requester. Requesters uses a tag field in the completion to associate it with a request TLP of the same tag value it transmitted earlier. Use of a tag in the request and completion TLPs allows a requester to manage multiple outstanding transactions.

If the completer is unable to obtain the requested data as a result of an error, it returns a completion packet without data (CplLk) and an error status indication within the packet. The requester who receives the error notification via the CplLk TLP must assume that atomicity of the lock is no longer guaranteed and thus determine how to handle the error at the software layer.

The path from requester to completer remains locked until the requester at a later time transmits an unlock message to the completer. The path and ingress/egress ports of a switch that the unlock message passes through are unlocked.

Non Posted Write Transactions

Figure 2-3 on page 61 shows the packets transmitted by a requester and completer to complete a non-posted write transaction. To complete this transfer, a requester transmits a non-posted write request TLP to a completer it intends to write data to. Non-posted write request TLPs include IO write request (IOWr), configuration write request type 0 or type 1 (CfgWr0, CfgWr1) TLPs. Memory write request and message requests are posted requests. Requesters may be a root complex or endpoint device (though not for configuration write requests).

Figure 2-3: Non-Posted Write Transaction Protocol

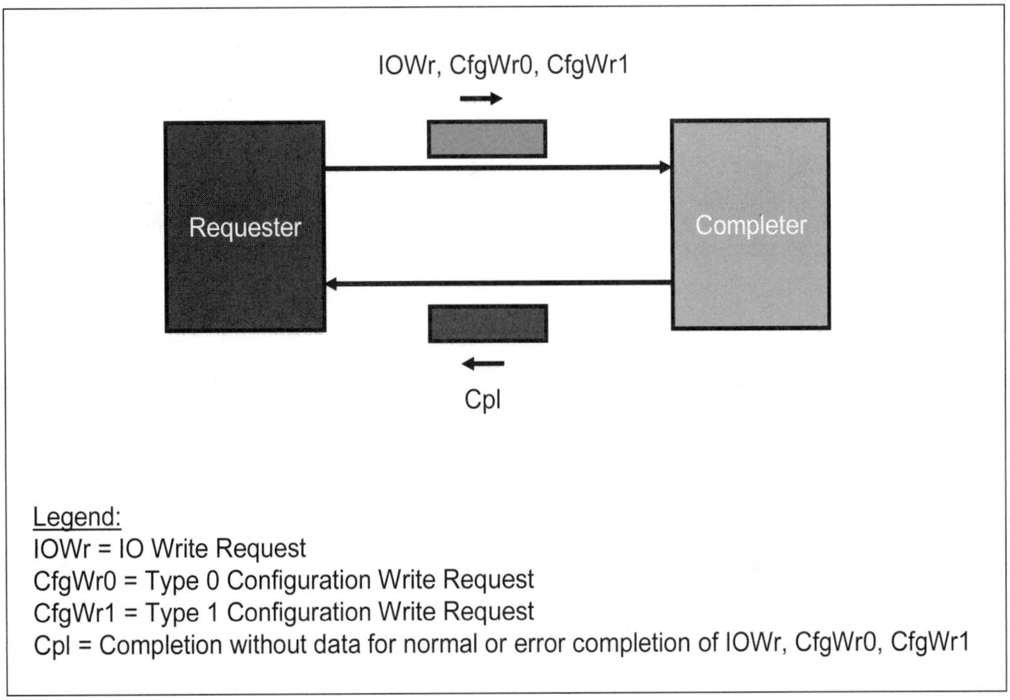

A request packet with data is routed through the fabric of switches using information in the header of the packet. The packet makes its way to a completer.

When the completer receives the packet and decodes its contents, it accepts the data. The completer creates a single completion packet without data (Cpl) to confirm reception of the write request. This is the purpose of the completion.

The completion packet contains routing information necessary to route the packet back to the requester. This completion packet will propagate through the same hierarchy of switches that the request packet went through before making its way back to the requester. The requester gets confirmation notification that the write request did make its way successfully to the completer.

If the completer is unable to successfully write the data in the request to the final destination or if the write request packet reaches the completer in error, then it returns a completion packet without data (Cpl) but with an error status indication. The requester who receives the error notification via the Cpl TLP determines how to handle the error at the software layer.

Posted Memory Write Transactions

Memory write requests shown in Figure 2-4 are posted transactions. This implies that the completer returns no completion notification to inform the requester that the memory write request packet has reached its destination successfully. No time is wasted in returning a completion, thus back-to-back posted writes complete with higher performance relative to non-posted transactions.

The write request packet which contains data is routed through the fabric of switches using information in the header portion of the packet. The packet makes its way to a completer. The completer accepts the specified amount of data within the packet. Transaction over.

If the write request is received by the completer in error, or is unable to write the posted write data to the final destination due to an internal error, the requester is not informed via the hardware protocol. The completer could log an error and generate an error message notification to the root complex. Error handling software manages the error.

Figure 2-4: Posted Memory Write Transaction Protocol

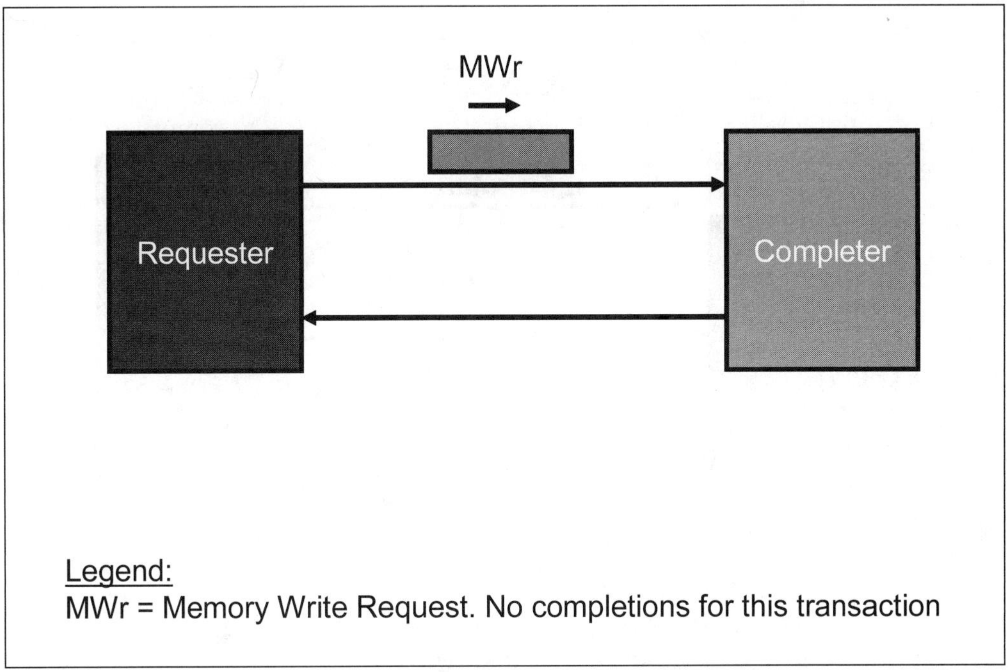

Posted Message Transactions

Message requests are also posted transactions as pictured in Figure 2-5 on page 64. There are two categories of message request TLPs, Msg and MsgD. Some message requests propagate from requester to completer, some are broadcast requests from the root complex to all endpoints, some are transmitted by an endpoint to the root complex. Message packets may be routed to completer(s) based on the message's address, device ID or routed implicitly. Message request routing is covered in Chapter 3.

The completer accepts any data that may be contained in the packet (if the packet is MsgD) and/or performs the task specified by the message.

Message request support eliminates the need for side-band signals in a PCI Express system. They are used for PCI style legacy interrupt signaling, power management protocol, error signaling, unlocking a path in the PCI Express fabric, slot power support, hot plug protocol, and vender defined purposes.

Figure 2-5: Posted Message Transaction Protocol

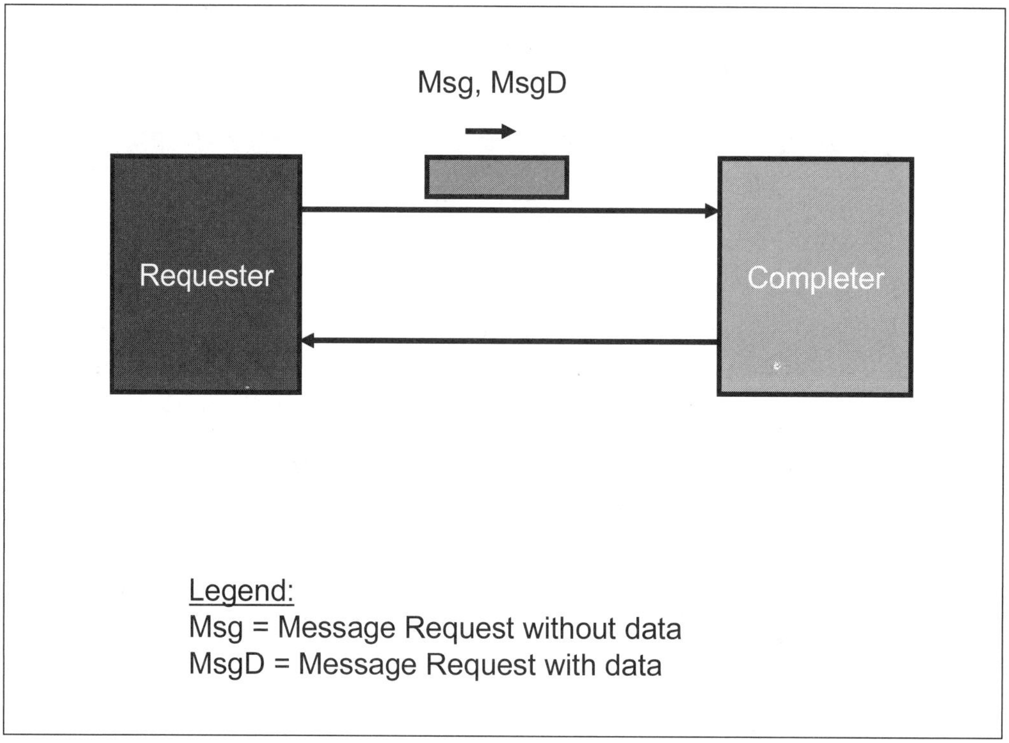

Some Examples of Transactions

This section describes a few transaction examples showing packets transmitted between requester and completer to accomplish a transaction. The examples consist of a memory read, IO write, and Memory write.

Memory Read Originated by CPU, Targeting an Endpoint

Figure 2-6 shows an example of packet routing associated with completing a memory read transaction. The root complex on the behalf of the CPU initiates a non-posted memory read from the completer endpoint shown. The root complex transmits an MRd packet which contains amongst other fields, an address, TLP type, requester ID (of the root complex) and length of transfer (in doublewords) field. Switch A which is a 3 port switch receives the packet on its upstream port. The switch logically appears like a 3 virtual bridge device connected by an internal bus. The logical bridges within the switch contain memory and IO base and limit address registers within their configuration space similar to PCI bridges. The MRd packet address is decoded by the switch and compared with the base/limit address range registers of the two downstream logical bridges. The switch internally forwards the MRd packet from the upstream ingress port to the correct downstream port (the left port in this example). The MRd packet is forwarded to switch B. Switch B decodes the address in a similar manner. Assume the MRd packets is forwarded to the right-hand port so that the completer endpoint receives the MRd packet.

Figure 2-6: Non-Posted Memory Read Originated by CPU and Targeting an Endpoint

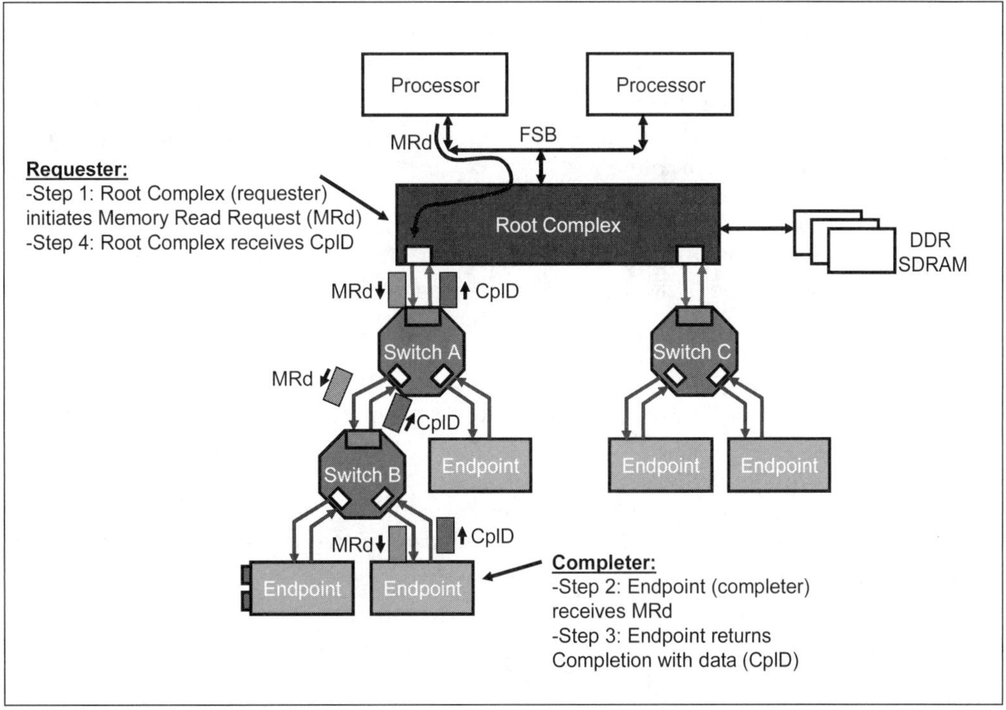

The completer decodes the contents of the header within the MRd packet, gathers the requested data and returns a completion packet with data (CplD). The header portion of the completion TLP contains the requester ID copied from the original request TLP. The requester ID is used to route the completion packet back to the root complex.

The logical bridges within Switch B compares the bus number field of the requester ID in the CplD packet with the secondary and subordinate bus number configuration registers. The CplD packet is forwarded to the appropriate port (in this case the upstream port). The CplD packet moves to Switch A which forwards the packet to the root complex. The requester ID field of the completion TLP matches the root complex's ID. The root complex checks the completion status (hopefully "successful completion") and accepts the data. This data is returned to the CPU in response to its pending memory read transaction.

Memory Read Originated by Endpoint, Targeting System Memory

In a similar manner, the endpoint device shown in Figure 2-7 on page 67 initiates a memory read request (MRd). This packet contains amongst other fields in the header, the endpoint's requester ID, targeted address and amount of data requested. It forwards the packet to Switch B which decodes the memory address in the packet and compares it with the memory base/limit address range registers within the virtual bridges of the switch. The packet is forwarded to Switch A which decodes the address in the packet and forwards the packet to the root complex completer.

The root complex obtains the requested data from system memory and creates a completion TLP with data (CplD). The bus number portion of the requester ID in the completion TLP is used to route the packet through the switches to the endpoint.

A requester endpoint can also communicate with another peer completer endpoint. For example an endpoint attached to switch B can talk to an endpoint connected to switch C. The request TLP is routed using an address. The completion is routed using bus number. Multi-port root complex devices are not required to support port-to-port packet routing. In which case, peer-to-peer transactions between endpoints associated with two different ports of the root complex is not supported.

Figure 2-7: Non-Posted Memory Read Originated by Endpoint and Targeting Memory

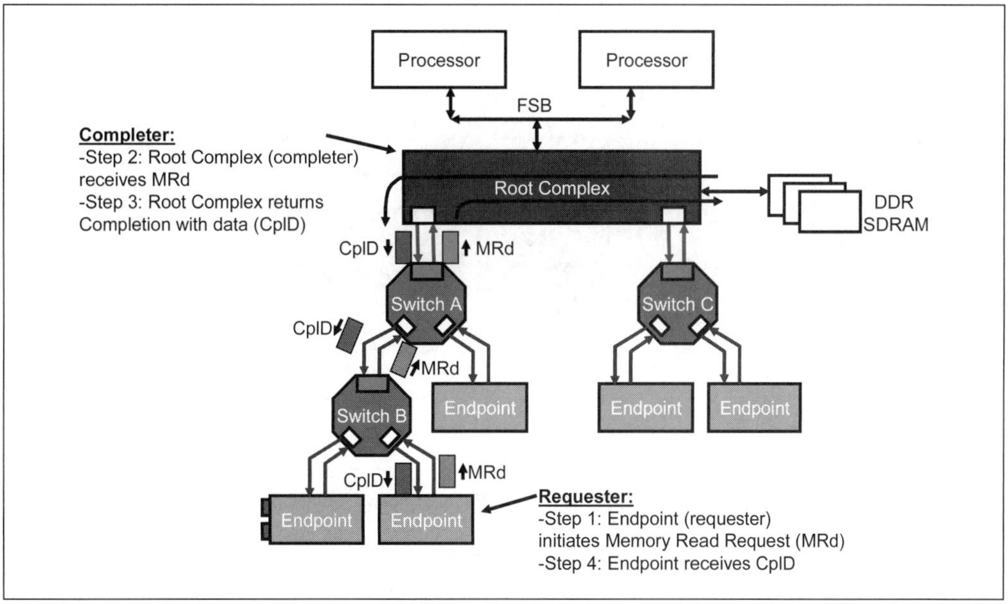

IO Write Initiated by CPU, Targeting an Endpoint

IO requests can only be initiated by a root complex or a legacy endpoint. PCI Express endpoints do not initiate IO transactions. IO transactions are intended for legacy support. Native PCI Express devices are not prohibited from implementing IO space, but the specification states that a PCI Express Endpoint must not depend on the operating system allocating I/O resources that are requested.

IO requests are routed by switches in a similar manner to memory requests. Switches route IO request packets by comparing the IO address in the packet with the IO base and limit address range registers in the virtual bridge configuration space associated with a switch

Figure 2-8 on page 68 shows routing of packets associated with an IO write transaction. The CPU initiates an IO write on the Front Side Bus (FSB). The write contains a target IO address and up to 4 Bytes of data. The root complex creates an IO Write request TLP (IOWr) using address and data from the CPU transaction. It uses its own requester ID in the packet header. This packet is routed through switch A and B. The completer endpoint returns a completion without data (Cpl) and completion status of 'successful completion' to confirm the reception of good data from the requester.

Figure 2-8: IO Write Transaction Originated by CPU, Targeting Legacy Endpoint

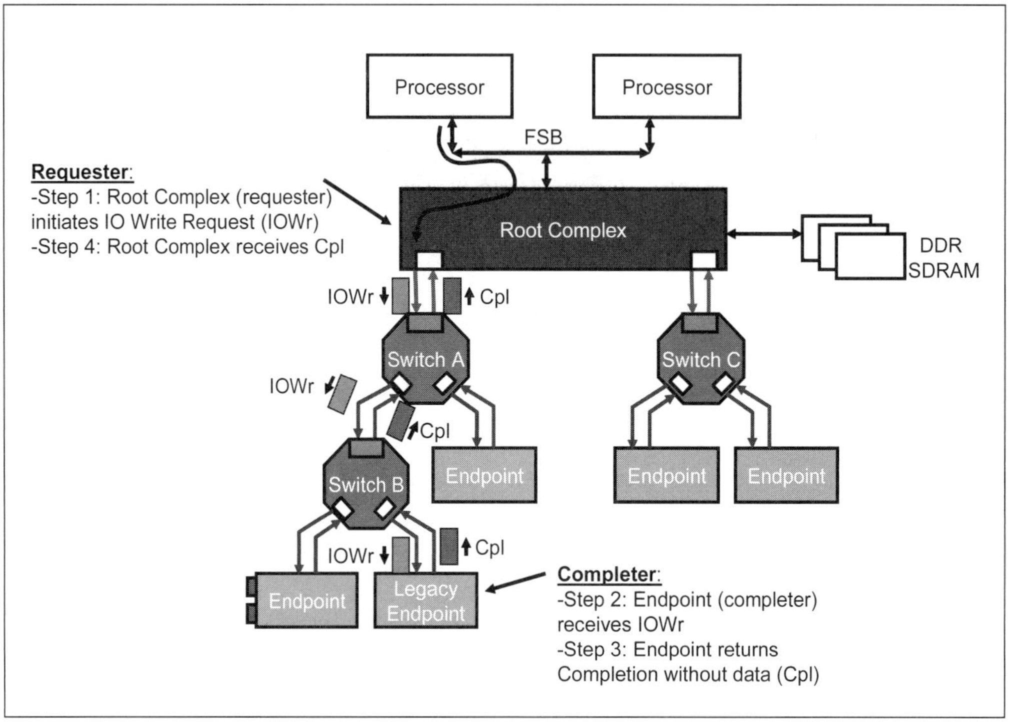

Memory Write Transaction Originated by CPU and Targeting an Endpoint

Memory write (MWr) requests (and message requests Msg or MsgD) are posted transactions. This implies that the completer does not return a completion. The MWr packet is routed through the PCI Express fabric of switches in the same manner as described for memory read requests. The requester root complex can write up to 4 KBytes of data with one MWr packet.

Figure 2-9 on page 69 shows a memory write transaction originated by the CPU. The root complex creates a MWr TLP on behalf of the CPU using target address and data from the CPU FSB transaction. This packet is routed through switch A and B. The packet reaches the endpoint and the transaction is complete.

Figure 2-9: Memory Write Transaction Originated by CPU, Targeting Endpoint

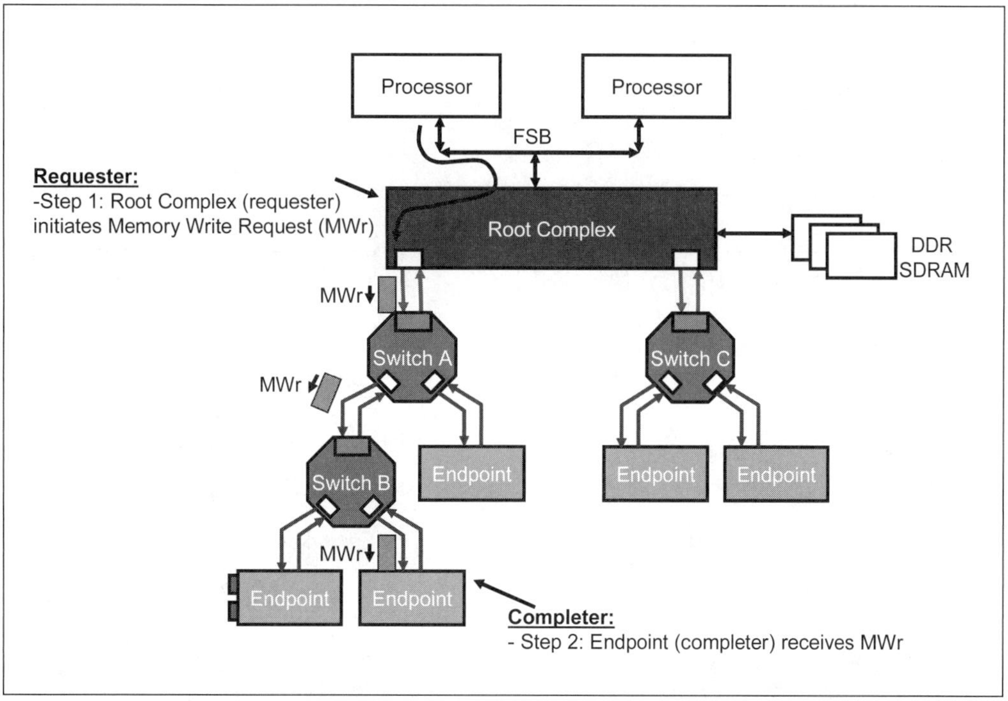

PCI Express Device Layers

Overview

The PCI Express specification defines a layered architecture for device design as shown in Figure 2-10 on page 70. The layers consist of a Transaction Layer, a Data Link Layer and a Physical layer. The layers can be further divided vertically into two, a transmit portion that processes outbound traffic and a receive portion that processes inbound traffic. However, a device design does not have to implement a layered architecture as long as the functionality required by the specification is supported.

Figure 2-10: PCI Express Device Layers

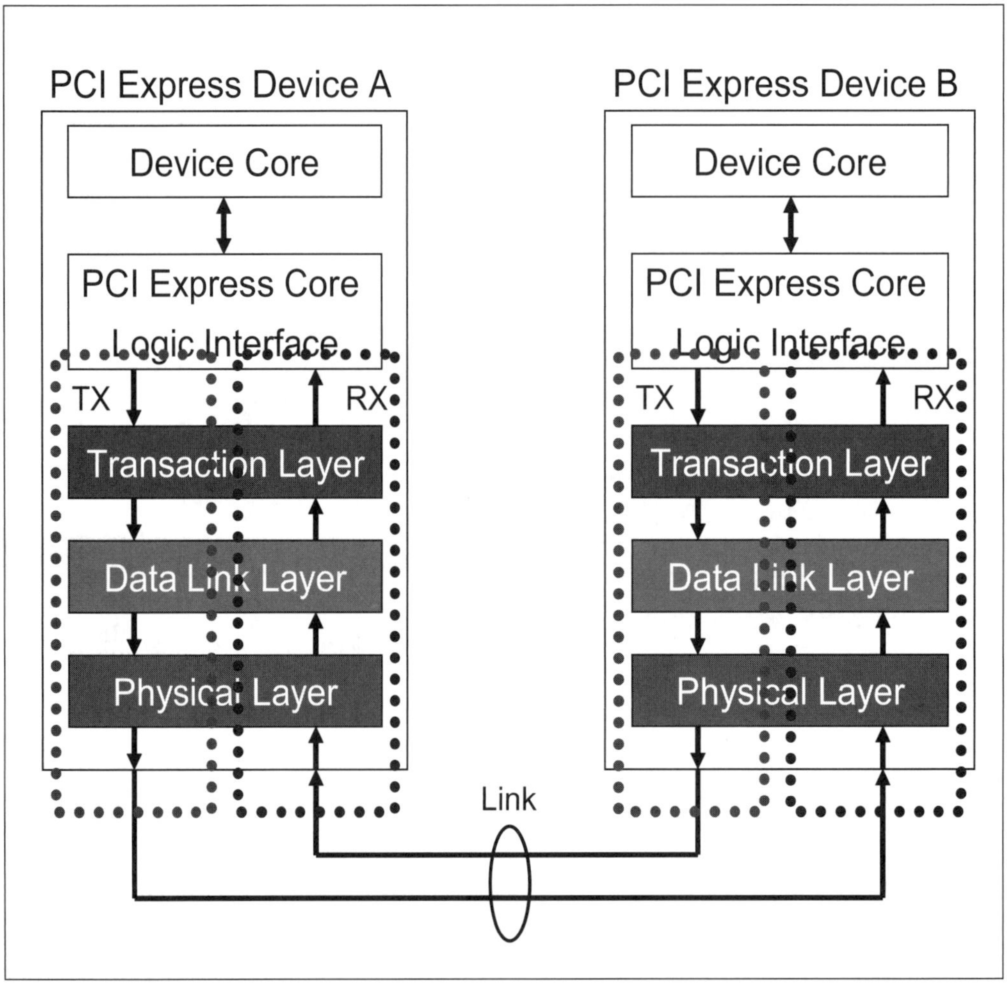

The goal of this section is to describe the function of each layer and to describe the flow of events to accomplish a data transfer. Packet creation at a transmitting device and packet reception and decoding at a receiving device are also explained.

Transmit Portion of Device Layers

Consider the transmit portion of a device. Packet contents are formed in the Transaction Layer with information obtained from the device core and application. The packet is stored in buffers ready for transmission to the lower layers. This packet is referred to as a Transaction Layer Packet (TLP) described in the earlier section of this chapter. The Data Link Layer concatenates to the packet additional information required for error checking at a receiver device. The packet is then encoded in the Physical layer and transmitted differentially on the Link by the analog portion of this Layer. The packet is transmitted using the available Lanes of the Link to the receiving device which is its neighbor.

Receive Portion of Device Layers

The receiver device decodes the incoming packet contents in the Physical Layer and forwards the resulting contents to the upper layers. The Data Link Layer checks for errors in the incoming packet and if there are no errors forwards the packet up to the Transaction Layer. The Transaction Layer buffers the incoming TLPs and converts the information in the packet to a representation that can be processed by the device core and application.

Device Layers and their Associated Packets

Three categories of packets are defined, each one is associated with one of the three device layers. Associated with the Transaction Layer is the Transaction Layer Packet (TLP). Associated with the Data Link Layer is the Data Link Layer Packet (DLLP). Associated with the Physical Layer is the Physical Layer Packet (PLP). These packets are introduced next.

Transaction Layer Packets (TLPs)

PCI Express transactions employ TLPs which originate at the Transaction Layer of a transmitter device and terminate at the Transaction Layer of a receiver device. This process is represented in Figure 2-11 on page 72. The Data Link Layer and Physical Layer also contribute to TLP assembly as the TLP moves through the layers of the transmitting device. At the other end of the Link where a neighbor receives the TLP, the Physical Layer, Data Link Layer and Transaction Layer disassemble the TLP.

Figure 2-11: TLP Origin and Destination

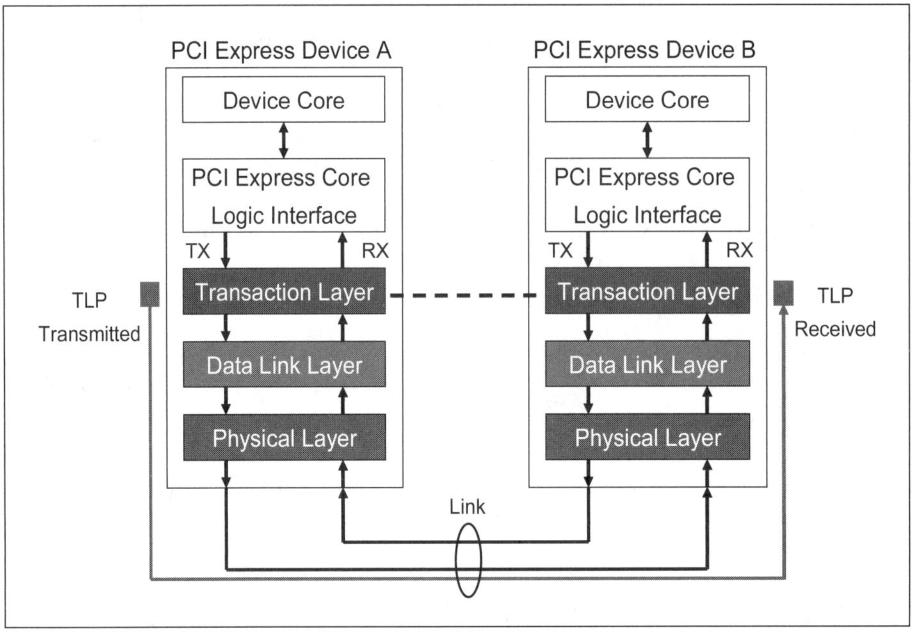

TLP Packet Assembly. A TLP that is transmitted on the Link appears as shown in Figure 2-12 on page 73.

The software layer/device core sends to the Transaction Layer the information required to assemble the core section of the TLP which is the header and data portion of the packet. Some TLPs do not contain a data section. An optional End-to-End CRC (ECRC) field is calculated and appended to the packet. The ECRC field is used by the ultimate targeted device of this packet to check for CRC errors in the header and data portion of the TLP.

The core section of the TLP is forwarded to the Data Link Layer which then appends a sequence ID and another LCRC field. The LCRC field is used by the neighboring receiver device at the other end of the Link to check for CRC errors in the core section of the TLP plus the sequence ID. The resultant TLP is forwarded to the Physical Layer which concatenates a Start and End framing character of 1 byte each to the packet. The packet is encoded and differentially transmitted on the Link using the available number of Lanes.

Figure 2-12: TLP Assembly

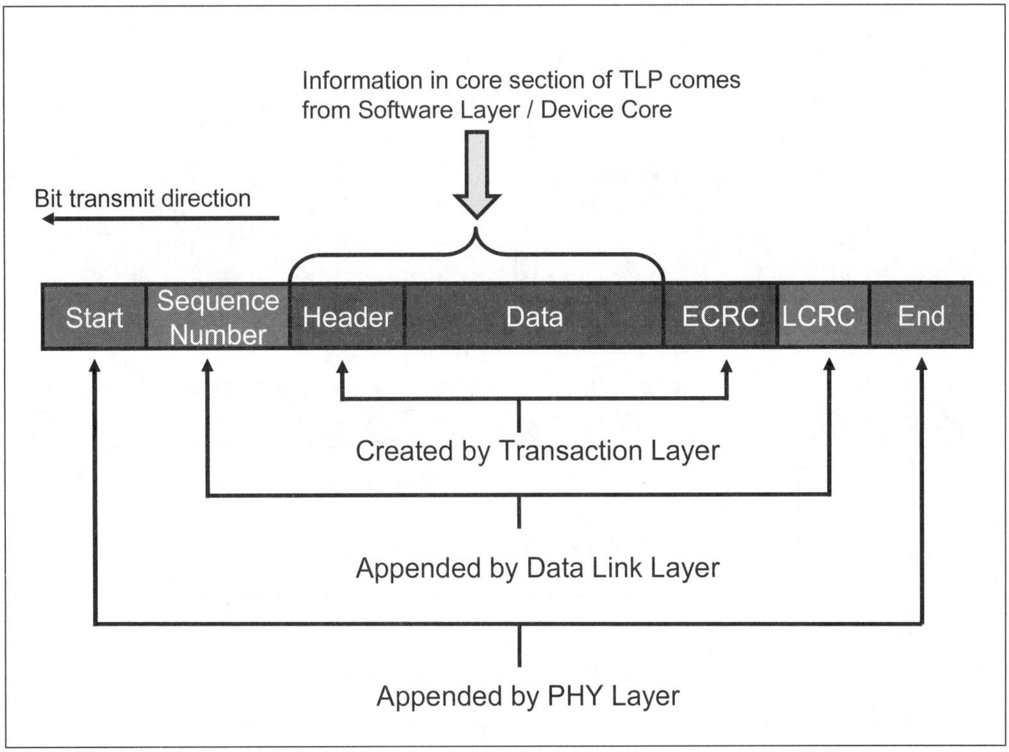

TLP Packet Disassembly. A neighboring receiver device receives the incoming TLP bit stream. As shown in Figure 2-13 on page 74 the received TLP is decoded by the Physical Layer and the Start and End frame fields are stripped. The resultant TLP is sent to the Data Link Layer. This layer checks for any errors in the TLP and strips the sequence ID and LCRC field. Assume there are no LCRC errors, then the TLP is forwarded up to the Transaction Layer. If the receiving device is a switch, then the packet is routed from one port of the switch to an egress port based on address information contained in the header portion of the TLP. Switches are allowed to check for ECRC errors and even report the errors it finds and error. However, a switch is not allowed to modify the ECRC that way the targeted device of this TLP will detect an ECRC error if there is such an error.

The ultimate targeted device of this TLP checks for ECRC errors in the header and data portion of the TLP. The ECRC field is stripped, leaving the header and data portion of the packet. It is this information that is finally forwarded to the Device Core/Software Layer.

Figure 2-13: TLP Disassembly

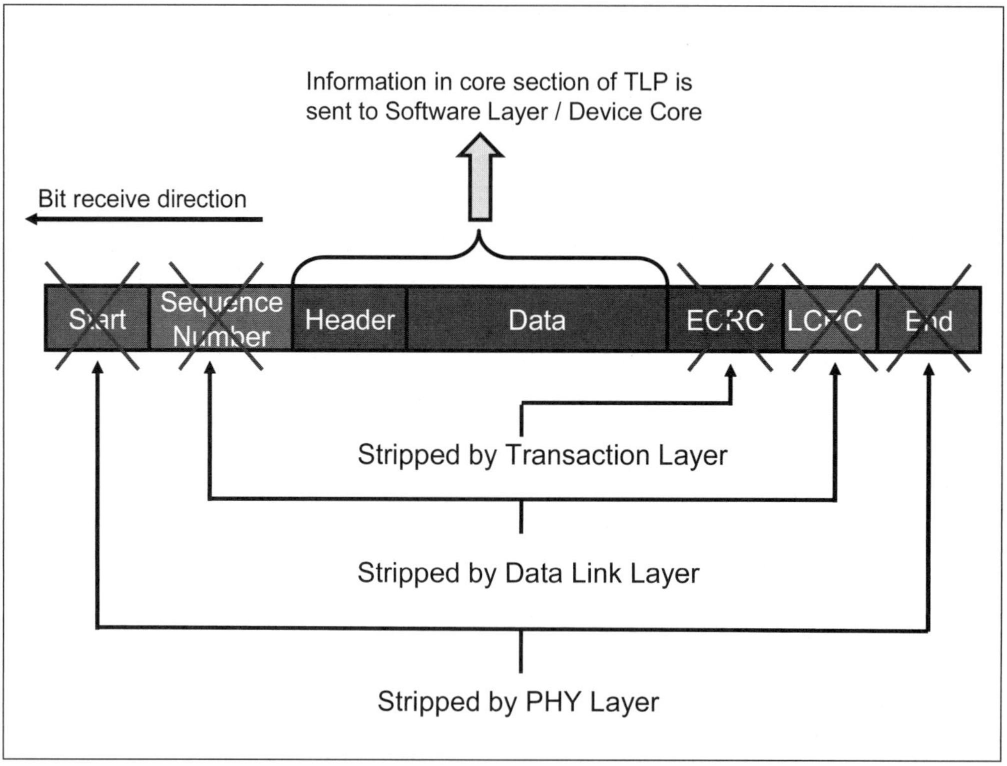

Data Link Layer Packets (DLLPs)

Another PCI Express packet called DLLP originates at the Data Link Layer of a transmitter device and terminates at the Data Link Layer of a receiver device. This process is represented in Figure 2-14 on page 75. The Physical Layer also contributes to DLLP assembly and disassembly as the DLLP moves from one device to another via the PCI Express Link.

DLLPs are used for Link Management functions including TLP acknowledgement associated with the ACK/NAK protocol, power management, and exchange of Flow Control information.

DLLPs are transferred between Data Link Layers of the two directly connected components on a Link. DLLPs do not pass through switches unlike TLPs which do travel through the PCI Express fabric. DLLPs do not contain routing information. These packets are smaller in size compared to TLPs, 8 bytes to be precise.

Figure 2-14: DLLP Origin and Destination

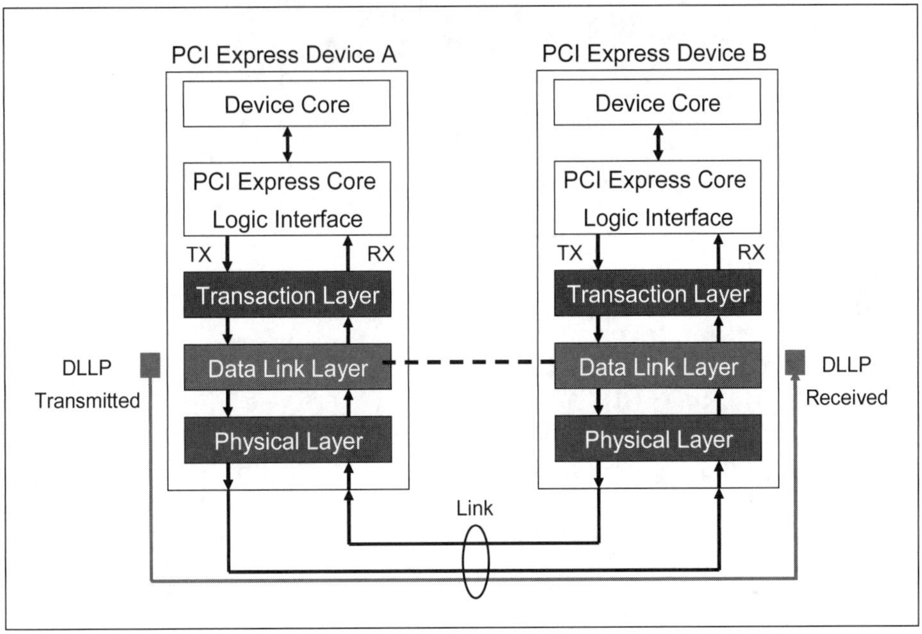

DLLP Assembly. The DLLP shown in Figure 2-15 on page 76 originates at the Data Link Layer. There are various types of DLLPs some of which include Flow Control DLLPs (FCx), acknowledge/ no acknowledge DLLPs which confirm reception of TLPs (ACK and NAK), and power management DLLPs (PMx). A DLLP type field identifies various types of DLLPs. The Data Link Layer appends a 16-bit CRC used by the receiver of the DLLP to check for CRC errors in the DLLP.

The DLLP content along with a 16-bit CRC is forwarded to the Physical Layer which appends a Start and End frame character of 1 byte each to the packet. The packet is encoded and differentially transmitted on the Link using the available number of Lanes.

Figure 2-15: DLLP Assembly

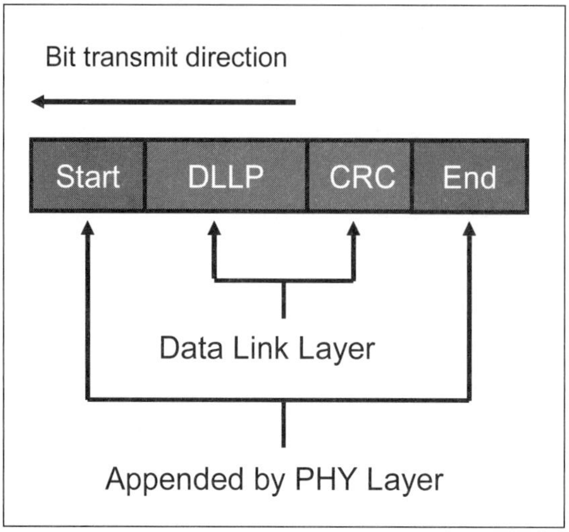

DLLP Disassembly. The DLLP is received by Physical Layer of a receiving device. The received bit stream is decoded and the Start and End frame fields are stripped as depicted in Figure 2-16. The resultant packet is sent to the Data Link Layer. This layer checks for CRC errors and strips the CRC field. The Data Link Layer is the destination layer for DLLPs and it is not forwarded up to the Transaction Layer.

Figure 2-16: DLLP Disassembly

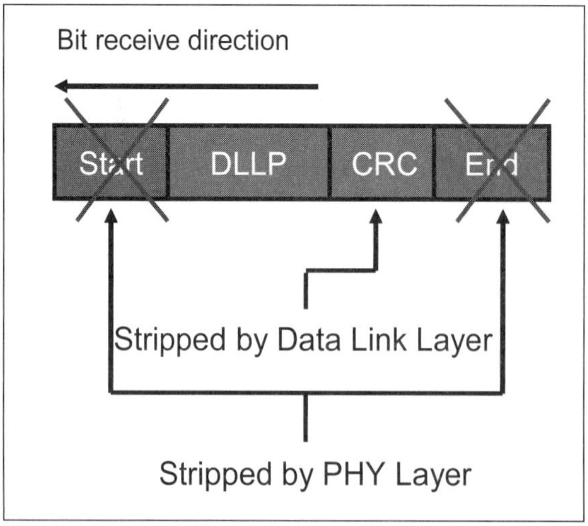

Physical Layer Packets (PLPs)

Another PCI Express packet called PLP originates at the Physical Layer of a transmitter device and terminates at the Physical Layer of a receiver device. This process is represented in Figure 2-17 on page 77. The PLP is a very simple packet that starts with a 1 byte COM character followed by 3 or more other characters that define the PLP type as well as contain other information. The PLP is a multiple of 4 bytes in size, an example of which is shown in Figure 2-18 on page 78. The specification refers to this packet as the Ordered-Set. PLPs do not contain any routing information. They are not routed through the fabric and do not propagate through a switch.

Some PLPs are used during the Link Training process described in "Ordered-Sets Used During Link Training and Initialization" on page 504. Another PLP is used for clock tolerance compensation. PLPs are used to place a Link into the electrical idle low power state or to wake up a link from this low power state.

Figure 2-17: PLP Origin and Destination

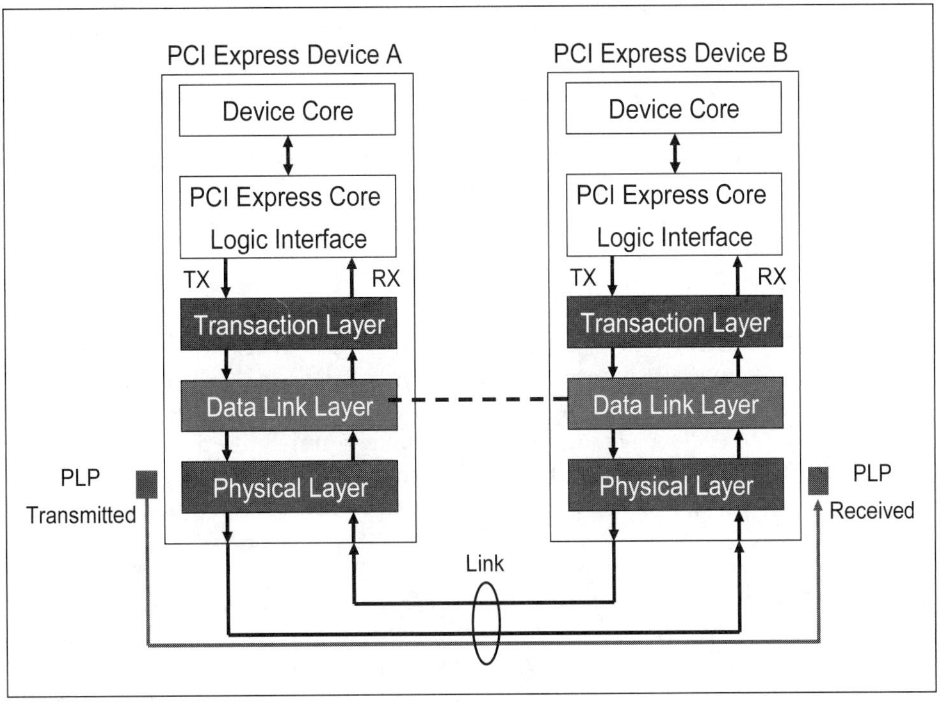

Figure 2-18: PLP or Ordered-Set Structure

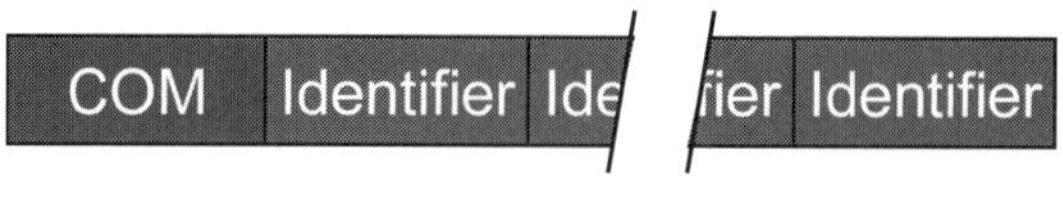

Function of Each PCI Express Device Layer

Figure 2-19 on page 79 is a more detailed block diagram of a PCI Express Device's layers. This block diagram is used to explain key functions of each layer and explain the function of each layer as it relates to generation of outbound traffic and response to inbound traffic. The layers consist of Device Core/Software Layer, Transaction Layer, Data Link Layer and Physical Layer.

Device Core / Software Layer

The Device Core consists of, for example, the root complex core logic or an endpoint core logic such as that of an Ethernet controller, SCSI controller, USB controller, etc. To design a PCI Express endpoint, a designer may reuse the Device Core logic from a PCI or PCI-X core logic design and wrap around it the PCI Express layered design described in this section.

Transmit Side. The Device Core logic in conjunction with local software provides the necessary information required by the PCI Express device to generate TLPs. This information is sent via the Transmit interface to the Transaction Layer of the device. Example of information transmitted to the Transaction Layer includes: transaction type to inform the Transaction Layer what type of TLP to generate, address, amount of data to transfer, data, traffic class, message index etc.

Receive Side. The Device Core logic is also responsible to receive information sent by the Transaction Layer via the Receive interface. This information includes: type of TLP received by the Transaction Layer, address, amount of data received, data, traffic class of received TLP, message index, error conditions etc.

Transaction Layer

The transaction Layer shown in Figure 2-19 is responsible for generation of outbound TLP traffic and reception of inbound TLP traffic. The Transaction Layer supports the split transaction protocol for non-posted transactions. In other words, the Transaction Layer associates an inbound completion TLP of a given tag value with an outbound non-posted request TLP of the same tag value transmitted earlier.

Figure 2-19: Detailed Block Diagram of PCI Express Device's Layers

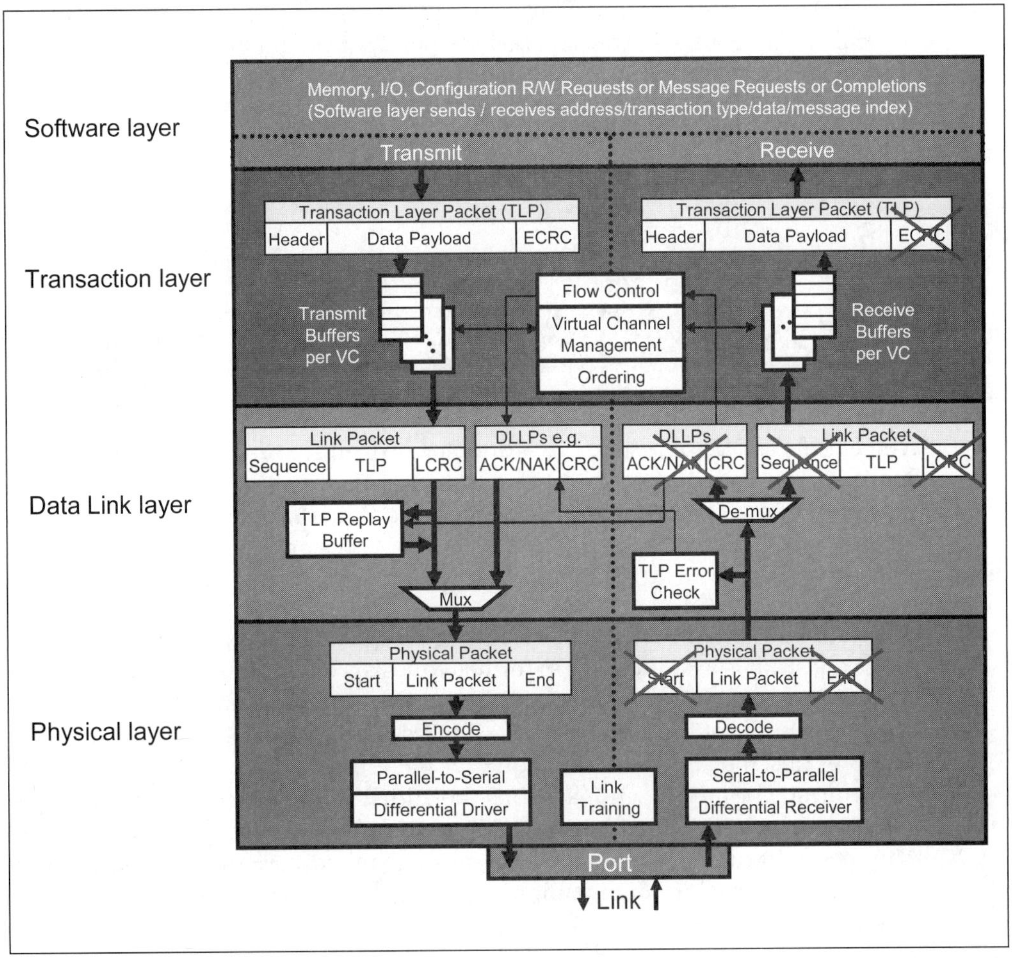

The transaction layer contains virtual channel buffers (VC Buffers) to store outbound TLPs that await transmission and also to store inbound TLPs received from the Link. The flow control protocol associated with these virtual channel buffers ensures that a remote transmitter does not transmit too many TLPs and cause the receiver virtual channel buffers to overflow. The Transaction Layer also orders TLPs according to ordering rules before transmission. It is this layer that supports the Quality of Service (QoS) protocol.

The Transaction Layer supports 4 address spaces: memory address, IO address, configuration address and message space. Message packets contain a message.

Transmit Side. The Transaction Layer receives information from the Device Core and generates outbound request and completion TLPs which it stores in virtual channel buffers. This layer assembles Transaction Layer Packets (TLPs). The major components of a TLP are: Header, Data Payload and an optional ECRC (specification also uses the term Digest) field as shown in Figure 2-20.

Figure 2-20: TLP Structure at the Transaction Layer

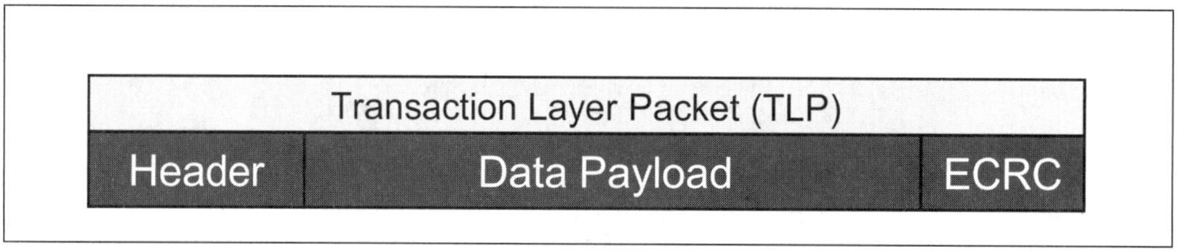

The Header is 3 doublewords or 4 doublewords in size and may include information such as; Address, TLP type, transfer size, requester ID/completer ID, tag, traffic class, byte enables, completion codes, and attributes (including "no snoop" and "relaxed ordering" bits). The TLP types are defined in Table 2-2 on page 57.

The address is a 32-bit memory address or an extended 64-bit address for memory requests. It is a 32-bit address for IO requests. For configuration transactions the address is an ID consisting of Bus Number, Device Number and Function Number plus a configuration register address of the targeted register. For completion TLPs, the address is the requester ID of the device that originally made the request. For message transactions the address used for routing is the destination device's ID consisting of Bus Number, Device Number and Function Number of the device targeted by the message request. Message requests could also be broadcast or routed implicitly by targeting the root complex or an upstream port.

The transfer size or length field indicates the amount of data to transfer calculated in doublewords (DWs). The data transfer length can be between 1 to 1024 DWs. Write request TLPs include data payload in the amount indicated by the length field of the header. For a read request TLP, the length field indicates the amount of data requested from a completer. This data is returned in one or more completion packets. Read request TLPs do not include a data payload field. Byte enables specify byte level address resolution.

Request packets contain a requester ID (bus#, device#, function #) of the device transmitting the request. The tag field in the request is memorized by the completer and the same tag is used in the completion.

A bit in the Header (TD = TLP Digest) indicates whether this packet contains an ECRC field also referred to as Digest. This field is 32-bits wide and contains an End-to-End CRC (ECRC). The ECRC field is generated by the Transaction Layer at time of creation of the outbound TLP. It is generated based on the entire TLP from first byte of header to last byte of data payload (with the exception of the EP bit, and bit 0 of the Type field. These two bits are always considered to be a 1 for the ECRC calculation). The TLP never changes as it traverses the fabric (with the exception of perhaps the two bits mentioned in the earlier sentence). The receiver device checks for an ECRC error that may occur as the packet moves through the fabric.

Receiver Side. The receiver side of the Transaction Layer stores inbound TLPs in receiver virtual channel buffers. The receiver checks for CRC errors based on the ECRC field in the TLP. If there are no errors, the ECRC field is stripped and the resultant information in the TLP header as well as the data payload is sent to the Device Core.

Flow Control. The Transaction Layer ensures that it does not transmit a TLP over the Link to a remote receiver device unless the receiver device has virtual channel buffer space to accept TLPs (of a given traffic class). The protocol for guaranteeing this mechanism is referred to as the "flow control" protocol. If the transmitter device does not observe this protocol, a transmitted TLP will cause the receiver virtual channel buffer to overflow. Flow control is automatically managed at the hardware level and is transparent to software. Software is only involved to enable additional buffers beyond the default set of virtual channel buffers (referred to as VC 0 buffers). The default buffers are enabled automatically after Link training, thus allowing TLP traffic to flow through the fabric immediately after Link training. Configuration transactions use the default virtual channel buffers and can begin immediately after the Link training process. Link training process is described in Chapter 14, entitled "Link Initialization & Training," on page 499.

Refer to Figure 2-21 on page 82 for an overview of the flow control process. A receiver device transmits DLLPs called Flow Control Packets (FCx DLLPs) to the transmitter device on a periodic basis. The FCx DLLPs contain flow control credit information that updates the transmitter regarding how much buffer space is available in the receiver virtual channel buffer. The transmitter keeps track of this information and will only transmit TLPs out of its Transaction Layer if it knows that the remote receiver has buffer space to accept the transmitted TLP.

Figure 2-21: Flow Control Process

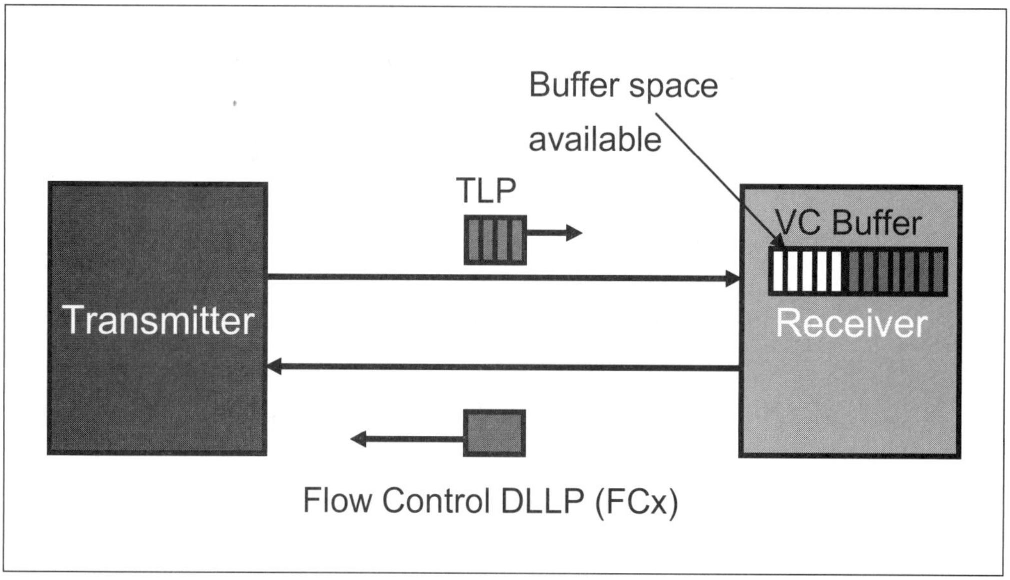

Quality of Service (QoS). Consider Figure 2-22 on page 83 in which the video camera and SCSI device shown need to transmit write request TLPs to system DRAM. The camera data is time critical isochronous data which must reach memory with guaranteed bandwidth otherwise the displayed image will appear choppy or unclear. The SCSI data is not as time sensitive and only needs to get to system memory correctly without errors. It is clear that the video data packet should have higher priority when routed through the PCI Express fabric, especially through switches. QoS refers to the capability of routing packets from different applications through the fabric with differentiated priorities and deterministic latencies and bandwidth. PCI and PCI-X systems do not support QoS capability.

Consider this example. Application driver software in conjunction with the OS assigns the video data packets a traffic class of 7 (TC7) and the SCSI data packet a traffic class of 0 (TC0). These TC numbers are embedded in the TLP header. Configuration software uses TC/VC mapping device configuration registers to map TC0 related TLPs to virtual channel 0 buffers (VC0) and TC7 related TLPs to virtual channel 7 buffers (VC7).

Figure 2-22: Example Showing QoS Capability of PCI Express

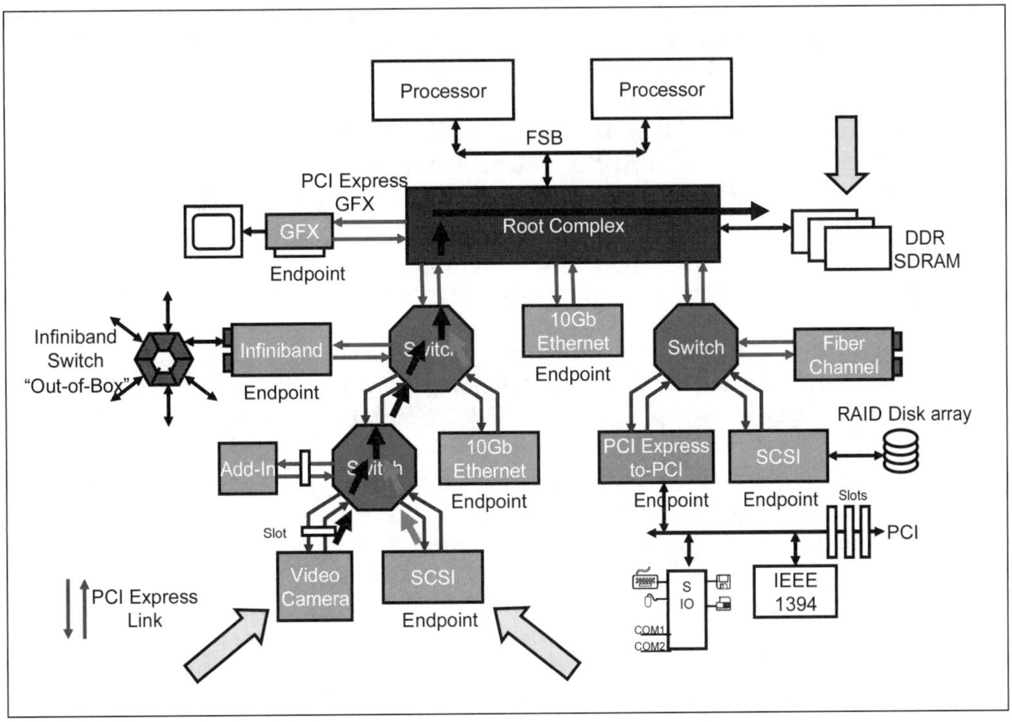

As TLPs from these two applications (video and SCSI applications) move through the fabric, the switches post incoming packets moving upstream into their respective VC buffers (VC0 and VC7). The switch uses a priority based arbitration mechanism to determine which of the two incoming packets to forward with greater priority to a common egress port. Assume VC7 buffer contents are configured with higher priority than VC0. Whenever two incoming packets are to be forwarded to one upstream port, the switch will always pick the VC7 packet, the video data, over the VC0 packet, the SCSI data. This guarantees greater bandwidth and reduced latency for video data compared to SCSI data.

A PCI Express device that implements more than one set of virtual channel buffers has the ability to arbitrate between TLPs from different VC buffers. VC buffers have configurable priorities. Thus traffic flowing through the system in different VC buffers will observe differentiated performances. The arbitration mechanism between TLP traffic flowing through different VC buffers is referred to as VC arbitration.

Also, multi-port switches have the ability to arbitrate between traffic coming in on two ingress ports but using the same VC buffer resource on a common egress port. This configurable arbitration mechanism between ports supported by switches is referred to as Port arbitration.

Traffic Classes (TCs) and Virtual Channels (VCs). TC is a TLP header field transmitted within the packet unmodified end-to-end through the fabric. Local application software and system software based on performance requirements decides what TC label a TLP uses. VCs are physical buffers that provide a means to support multiple independent logical data flows over the physical Link via the use of transmit and receiver virtual channel buffers.

PCI Express devices may implement up to 8 VC buffers (VC0-VC7). The TC field is a 3-bit field that allows differentiation of traffic into 8 traffic classes (TC0-TC7). Devices must implement VC0. Similarly, a device is required to support TC0 (best effort general purpose service class). The other optional TCs may be used to provide differentiated service through the fabric. Associated with each implemented VC ID, a transmit device implements a transmit buffer and a receive device implements a receive buffer.

Devices or switches implement TC-to-VC mapping logic by which a TLP of a given TC number is forwarded through the Link using a particular VC numbered buffer. PCI Express provides the capability of mapping multiple TCs onto a single VC, thus reducing device cost by means of providing limited number of VC buffer support. TC/VC mapping is configured by system software through configuration registers. It is up to the device application software to determine TC label for TLPs and TC/VC mapping that meets performance requirements. In its simplest form TC/VC mapping registers can be configured with a one-to-one mapping of TC to VC.

Consider the example illustrated in Figure 2-23 on page 85. The TC/VC mapping registers in Device A are configured to map, TLPs with TC[2:0] to VC0 and TLPs with TC[7:3] to VC1. The TC/VC mapping registers in receiver Device B must also be configured identically as Device A. The same numbered VC buffers are enabled both in transmitter Device A and receiver Device B.

If Device A needs to transmit a TLP with TC label of 7 and another packet with TC label of 0, the two packets will be placed in VC1 and VC0 buffers, respectively. The arbitration logic arbitrates between the two VC buffers. Assume VC1 buffer is configured with higher priority than VC0 buffer. Thus, Device A will forward the TC7 TLPs in VC1 to the Link ahead of the TC0 TLPs in VC0.

When the TLPs arrive in Device B, the TC/VC mapping logic decodes the TC label in each TLP and places the TLPs in their associated VC buffers.

In this example, TLP traffic with TC[7:3] label will flow through the fabric with higher priority than TC[2:0] traffic. Within each TC group however, TLPs will flow with equal priority.

Figure 2-23: TC Numbers and VC Buffers

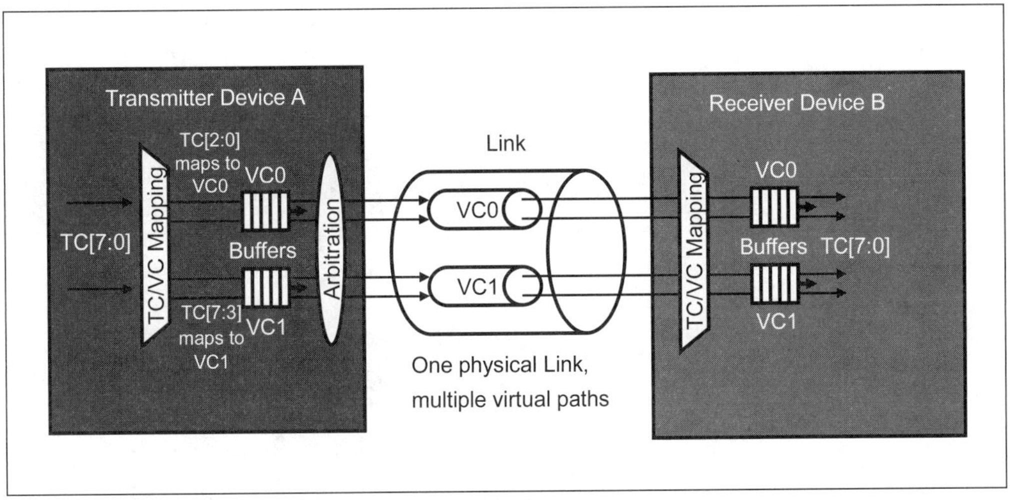

Port Arbitration and VC Arbitration. The goals of arbitration support in the Transaction Layer are:

- To provide differentiated services between data flows within the fabric.
- To provide guaranteed bandwidth with deterministic and smallest end-to-end transaction latency.

Packets of different TCs are routed through the fabric of switches with different priority based on arbitration policy implemented in switches. Packets coming in from ingress ports heading towards a particular egress port compete for use of that egress port.

Switches implement two types of arbitration for each egress port: Port Arbitration and VC Arbitration. Consider Figure 2-24 on page 86.

Port arbitration is arbitration between two packets arriving on different ingress ports but that map to the same virtual channel (after going through TC-to-VC mapping) of the common egress port. The port arbiter implements round-robin, weighted round-robin or programmable time-based round-robin arbitration schemes selectable through configuration registers.

VC arbitration takes place after port arbitration. For a given egress port, packets from all VCs compete to transmit on the same egress port. VC arbitration resolves the order in which TLPs in different VC buffers are forwarded on to the Link. VC arbitration policies supported include, strict priority, round-robin and weighted round-robin arbitration schemes selectable through configuration registers.

Independent of arbitration, each VC must observe transaction ordering and flow control rules before it can make pending TLP traffic visible to the arbitration mechanism.

Figure 2-24: Switch Implements Port Arbitration and VC Arbitration Logic

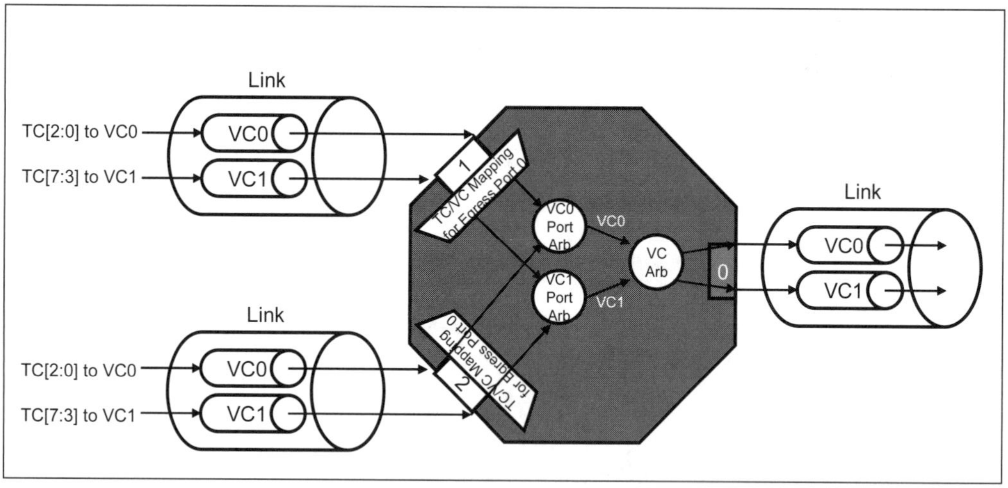

Endpoint devices and a root complex with only one port do not support port arbitration. They only support VC arbitration in the Transaction Layer.

Transaction Ordering. PCI Express protocol implements PCI/PCI-X compliant producer-consumer ordering model for transaction ordering with provision to support relaxed ordering similar to PCI-X architecture. Transaction ordering rules guarantee that TLP traffic associated with a given traffic class is routed through the fabric in the correct order to prevent potential deadlock or live-lock conditions from occurring. Traffic associated with different TC labels have no ordering relationship. Chapter 8, entitled "Transaction Ordering," on page 315 describes these ordering rules.

The Transaction Layer ensures that TLPs for a given TC are ordered correctly with respect to other TLPs of the same TC label before forwarding to the Data Link Layer and Physical Layer for transmission.

Power Management. The Transaction Layer supports ACPI/PCI power management, as dictated by system software. Hardware within the Transaction Layer autonomously power manages a device to minimize power during full-on power states. This automatic power management is referred to as Active State Power Management and does not involve software. Power management software associated with the OS power manages a device's power states though power management configuration registers. Power management is described in Chapter 16.

Configuration Registers. A device's configuration registers are associated with the Transaction Layer. The registers are configured during initialization and bus enumeration. They are also configured by device drivers and accessed by runtime software/OS. Additionally, the registers store negotiated Link capabilities, such as Link width and frequency. Configuration registers are described in Part 6 of the book.

Data Link Layer

Refer to Figure 2-19 on page 79 for a block diagram of a device's Data Link Layer. The primary function of the Data Link Layer is to ensure data integrity during packet transmission and reception on each Link. If a transmitter device sends a TLP to a remote receiver device at the other end of a Link and a CRC error is detected, the transmitter device is notified with a NAK DLLP. The transmitter device automatically replays the TLP. This time hopefully no error occurs. With error checking and automatic replay of packets received in error, PCI Express ensures very high probability that a TLP transmitted by one device will make its way to the final destination with no errors. This makes PCI Express ideal for low error rate, high-availability systems such as servers.

Transmit Side. The Transaction Layer must observe the flow control mechanism before forwarding outbound TLPs to the Data Link Layer. If sufficient credits exist, a TLP stored within the virtual channel buffer is passed from the Transaction Layer to the Data Link Layer for transmission.

Consider Figure 2-25 on page 88 which shows the logic associated with the ACK-NAK mechanism of the Data Link Layer. The Data Link Layer is responsible for TLP CRC generation and TLP error checking. For outbound TLPs from transmit Device A, a Link CRC (LCRC) is generated and appended to the TLP. In addition, a sequence ID is appended to the TLP. Device A's Data Link Layer preserves a copy of the TLP in a replay buffer and transmits the TLP to Device B. The Data Link Layer of the remote Device B receives the TLP and checks for CRC errors.

Figure 2-25: Data Link Layer Replay Mechanism

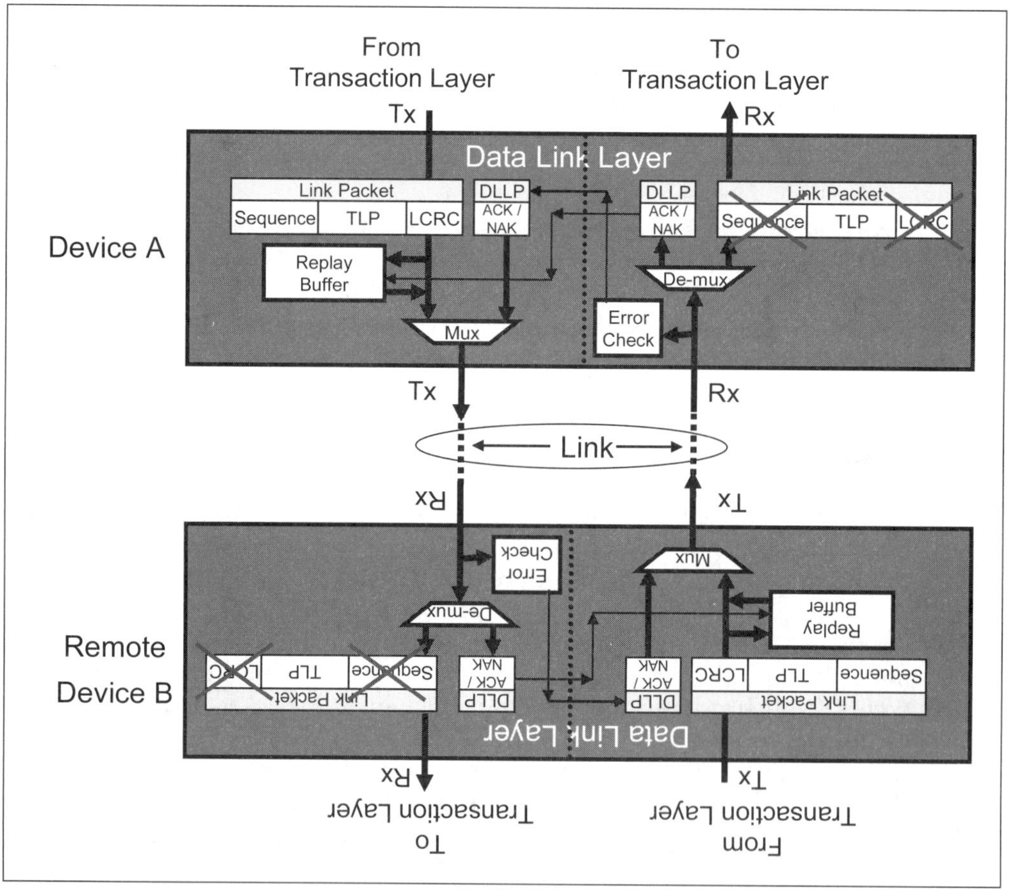

If there is no error, the Data Link Layer of Device B returns an ACK DLLP with a sequence ID to Device A. Device A has confirmation that the TLP has reached Device B (not necessarily the final destination) successfully. Device A clears its replay buffer of the TLP associated with that sequence ID.

If on the other hand a CRC error is detected in the TLP received at the remote Device B, then a NAK DLLP with a sequence ID is returned to Device A. An error has occurred during TLP transmission. Device A's Data Link Layer replays associated TLPs from the replay buffer. The Data Link Layer generates error indications for error reporting and logging mechanisms.

In summary, the replay mechanism uses the sequence ID field within received ACK/NAK DLLPs to associate it with outbound TLPs stored in the replay buffer. Reception of ACK DLLPs cause the replay buffer to clear TLPs from the buffer. Receiving NAK DLLPs cause the replay buffer to replay associated TLPs.

For a given TLP in the replay buffer, if the transmitter device receives a NAK 4 times and the TLP is replayed 3 additional times as a result, then the Data Link Layer logs the error, reports a correctable error, and re-trains the Link.

Receive Side. The receive side of the Data Link Layer is responsible for LCRC error checking on inbound TLPs. If no error is detected, the device schedules an ACK DLLP for transmission back to the remote transmitter device. The receiver strips the TLP of the LCRC field and sequence ID.

If a CRC error is detected, it schedules a NAK to return back to the remote transmitter. The TLP is eliminated.

The receive side of the Data Link Layer also receives ACKs and NAKs from a remote device. If an ACK is received the receive side of the Data Link layer informs the transmit side to clear an associated TLP from the replay buffer. If a NAK is received, the receive side causes the replay buffer of the transmit side to replay associated TLPs.

The receive side is also responsible for checking the sequence ID of received TLPs to check for dropped or out-of-order TLPs.

Data Link Layer Contribution to TLPs and DLLPs. The Data Link Layer concatenates a 12-bit sequence ID and 32-bit LCRC field to an outbound TLP that arrives from the Transaction Layer. The resultant TLP is shown in Figure 2-26 on page 90. The sequence ID is used to associate a copy of the outbound TLP stored in the replay buffer with a received ACK/NAK DLLP inbound from a neighboring remote device. The ACK/NAK DLLP confirms arrival of the outbound TLP in the remote device.

The 32-bit LCRC is calculated based on all bytes in the TLP including the sequence ID.

A DLLP shown in Figure 2-26 on page 90 is a 4 byte packet with a 16-bit CRC field. The 8-bit DLLP Type field indicates various categories of DLLPs. These include: ACK, NAK, Power Management related DLLPs (PM_Enter_L1, PM_Enter_L23, PM_Active_State_Request_L1, PM_Request_Ack) and Flow Control related DLLPs (InitFC1-P, InitFC1-NP, InitFC1-Cpl, InitFC2-P, InitFC2-NP, InitFC2-Cpl, UpdateFC-P, UpdateFC-NP, UpdateFC-Cpl). The 16-bit CRC is calculated using all 4 bytes of the DLLP. Received DLLPs which fail the CRC check are discarded. The loss of information from discarding a DLLP is self repairing such that a successive DLLP will supersede any information lost. ACK and NAK DLLPs contain a sequence ID field (shown as Misc. field in Figure 2-26) used by the device to associate an inbound ACK/NAK DLLP with a stored copy of a TLP in the replay buffer.

Figure 2-26: TLP and DLLP Structure at the Data Link Layer

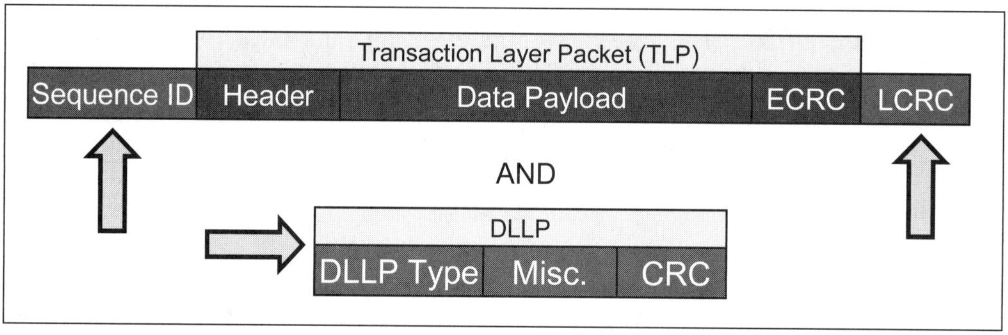

Non-Posted Transaction Showing ACK-NAK Protocol. Next the steps required to complete a memory read request between a requester and a completer on the far end of a switch are described. Figure 2-27 on page 91 shows the activity on the Link to complete this transaction:

Step 1a: Requester transmits a memory read request TLP (MRd). Switch receives the MRd TLP and checks for CRC error using the LCRC field in the MRd TLP.

Step 1b: If no error then switch returns ACK DLLP to requester. Requester discards copy of the TLP from its replay buffer.

Step 2a: Switch forwards the MRd TLP to the correct egress port using memory address for routing. Completer receives MRd TLP. Completer checks for CRC errors in received MRd TLP using LCRC.

Step 2b: If no error then completer returns ACK DLLP to switch. Switch discards copy of the MRd TLP from its replay buffer.

Step 3a: Completer checks for CRC error using optional ECRC field in MRd TLP. Assume no End-to-End error. Completer returns Completion (CplD) with Data TLP whenever it has the requested data. Switch receives CplD TLP and checks for CRC error using LCRC.

Step 3b: If no error then switch returns ACK DLLP to completer. Completer discards copy of the CplD TLP from its replay buffer.

Step 4a: Switch decodes Requester ID field in CplD TLP and routes the packet to the correct egress port. Requester receives CplD TLP. Requester checks for CRC errors in received CplD TLP using LCRC.

Step 4b: If no error then requester returns ACK DLLP to switch. Switch discards copy of the CplD TLP from its replay buffer. Requester determines if there is error in CplD TLP using CRC field in optional ECRC field. Assume no End-to-End error. Requester checks completion error code in CplD. Assume completion code of 'Successful Completion'. To associate the completion with the original request, requester matches tag in CplD with original tag of MRd request. Requester accepts data.

Figure 2-27: Non-Posted Transaction on Link

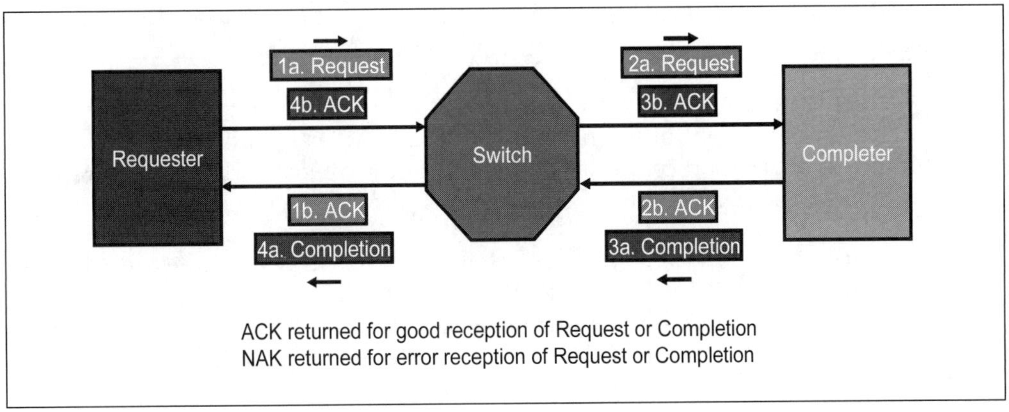

Posted Transaction Showing ACK-NAK Protocol. Below are the steps involved in completing a memory write request between a requester and a completer on the far end of a switch. Figure 2-28 on page 92 shows the activity on the Link to complete this transaction:

Step 1a: Requester transmits a memory write request TLP (MWr) with data. Switch receives MWr TLP and checks for CRC error with LCRC field in the TLP.

Step 1b: If no error then switch returns ACK DLLP to requester. Requester discards copy of the TLP from its replay buffer.

Step 2a: Switch forwards the MWr TLP to the correct egress port using memory address for routing. Completer receives MWr TLP. Completer checks for CRC errors in received MRd TLP using LCRC.

Step 2b: If no error then completer returns ACK DLLP to switch. Switch discards copy of the MWr TLP from its replay buffer. Completer checks for CRC error using optional digest field in MWr TLP. Assume no End-to-End error. Completer accepts data. There is no completion associated with this transaction.

Figure 2-28: Posted Transaction on Link

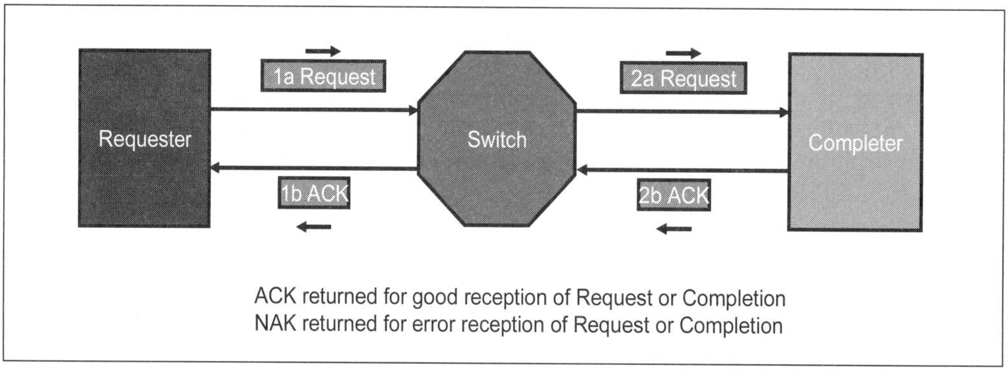

Other Functions of the Data Link Layer. Following power-up or Reset, the flow control mechanism described earlier is initialized by the Data Link Layer. This process is accomplished automatically at the hardware level and has no software involvement.

Flow control for the default virtual channel VC0 is initialized first. In addition, when additional VCs are enabled by software, the flow control initialization process is repeated for each newly enabled VC. Since VC0 is enabled before all other VCs, no TLP traffic will be active prior to initialization of VC0.

Physical Layer

Refer to Figure 2-19 on page 79 for a block diagram of a device's Physical Layer. Both TLP and DLLP type packets are sent from the Data Link Layer to the Physical Layer for transmission over the Link. Also, packets are received by the Physical Layer from the Link and sent to the Data Link Layer.

The Physical Layer is divided in two portions, the Logical Physical Layer and the Electrical Physical Layer. The Logical Physical Layer contains digital logic associated with processing packets before transmission on the Link, or processing packets inbound from the Link before sending to the Data Link Layer. The Electrical Physical Layer is the analog interface of the Physical Layer that connects to the Link. It consists of differential drivers and receivers for each Lane.

Transmit Side. TLPs and DLLPs from the Data Link Layer are clocked into a buffer in the Logical Physical Layer. The Physical Layer frames the TLP or DLLP with a Start and End character. The symbol is a framing code byte which a receiver device uses to detect the start and end of a packet. The Start and End characters are shown appended to a TLP and DLLP in Figure 2-29 on page 94. The diagram shows the size of each field in a TLP or DLLP.

The transmit logical sub-block conditions the received packet from the Data Link Layer into the correct format for transmission. Packets are byte striped across the available Lanes on the Link.

Each byte of a packet is then scrambled with the aid of Linear Feedback Shift Register type scrambler. By scrambling the bytes, repeated bit patterns on the Link are eliminated, thus reducing the average EMI noise generated.

The resultant bytes are encoded into a 10b code by the 8b/10b encoding logic. The primary purpose of encoding 8b characters to 10b symbols is to create sufficient 1-to-0 and 0-to-1 transition density in the bit stream to facilitate recreation of a receive clock with the aid of a PLL at the remote receiver device. Note that data is not transmitted along with a clock. Instead, the bit stream contains sufficient transitions to allow the receiver device to recreate a receive clock.

The parallel-to-serial converter generates a serial bit stream of the packet on each Lane and transmits it differentially at 2.5 Gbits/s.

Receive Side. The receive Electrical Physical Layer clocks in a packet arriving differentially on all Lanes. The serial bit stream of the packet is converted into a 10b parallel stream using the serial-to-parallel converter. The receiver logic also includes an elastic buffer which accommodates for clock frequency variation between a transmit clock with which the packet bit stream is clocked into a receiver and the receiver clock. The 10b symbol stream is decoded back to the 8b representation of each symbol with the 8b/10b decoder. The 8b characters are de-scrambled. The Byte unstriping logic, re-creates the original packet stream transmitted by the remote device.

Figure 2-29: TLP and DLLP Structure at the Physical Layer

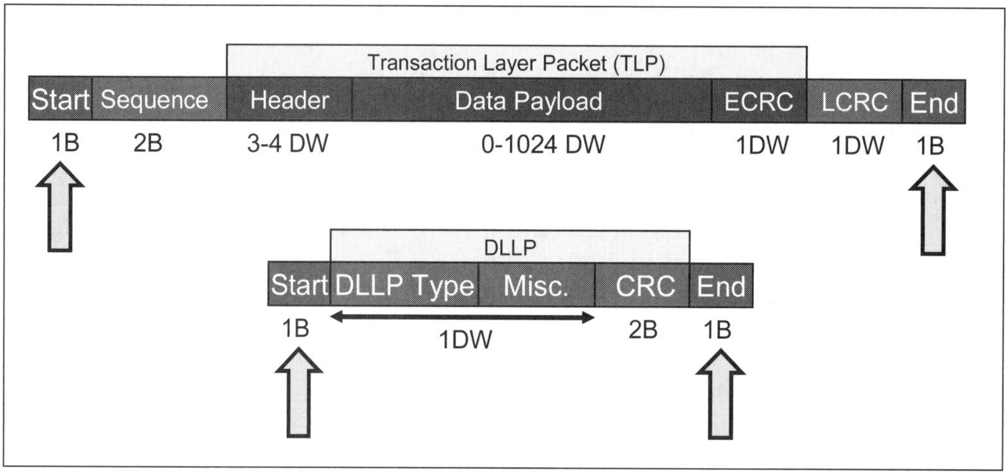

Link Training and Initialization. An additional function of the Physical Layer is Link initialization and training. Link initialization and training is a Physical Layer controlled process that configures and initializes each Link for normal operation. This process is automatic and does not involve software. The following are determined during the Link initialization and training process:

- Link width
- Link data rate
- Lane reversal
- Polarity inversion.
- Bit lock per Lane
- Symbol lock per Lane
- Lane-to-Lane de-skew within a multi-Lane Link.

Link width. Two devices with a different number of Lanes per Link may be connected. E.g. one device has x2 port and it is connected to a device with x4 port. After initialization the Physical Layer of both devices determines and sets the Link width to the minimum Lane width of x2. Other Link negotiated behaviors include Lane reversal and splitting of ports into multiple Links.

Lane reversal if necessary is an optional feature. Lanes are numbered. A designer may not wire the correct Lanes of two ports correctly. In which case training allows for the Lane numbers to be reversed so that the Lane numbers of adjacent ports on each end of the Link match up. Part of the same process may allow for a multi-Lane Link to be split into multiple Links.

Polarity inversion. The D+ and D- differential pair terminals for two devices may not be connected correctly. In which case the training sequence receiver reverses the polarity on the differential receiver.

Link data rate. Training is completed at data rate of 2.5 Gbit/s. In the future, higher data rates of 5 Gbit/s and 10 Gbit/s will be supported. During training, each node advertises its highest data rate capability. The Link is initialized with the highest common frequency that devices at opposite ends of a Link support.

Lane-to-Lane De-skew. Due to Link wire length variations and different driver/receiver characteristics on a multi-Lane Link, bit streams on each Lane will arrive at a receiver skewed with respect to other Lanes. The receiver circuit must compensate for this skew by adding/removing delays on each Lane. Relaxed routing rules allow Link wire lengths in the order of 20"-30".

Link Power Management. The normal power-on operation of a Link is called the L0 state. Lower power states of the Link in which no packets are transmitted or received are L0s, L1, L2 and L3 power states. The L0s power state is automatically entered when a time-out occurs after a period of inactivity on the Link. Entering and exiting this state does not involve software and the exit latency is the shortest. L1 and L2 are lower power states than L0s, but exit latencies are greater. The L3 power state is the full off power state from which a device cannot generate a wake up event.

Reset. Two types of reset are supported:

- Cold/warm reset also called a Fundamental Reset which occurs following a device being powered-on (cold reset) or due to a reset without circulating power (warm reset).
- Hot reset sometimes referred to as protocol reset is an in-band method of propagating reset. Transmission of an ordered-set is used to signal a hot reset. Software initiates hot reset generation.

On exit from reset (cold, warm, or hot), all state machines and configuration registers (hot reset does not reset sticky configuration registers) are initialized.

Electrical Physical Layer. The transmitter of one device is AC coupled to the receiver of another device at the opposite end of the Link as shown in Figure 2-30. The AC coupling capacitor is between 75-200 nF. The transmitter DC common mode voltage is established during Link training and initialization. The DC common mode impedance is typically 50 ohms while the differential impedance is 100 ohms typical. This impedance is matched with a standard FR4 board.

Figure 2-30: Electrical Physical Layer Showing Differential Transmitter and Receiver

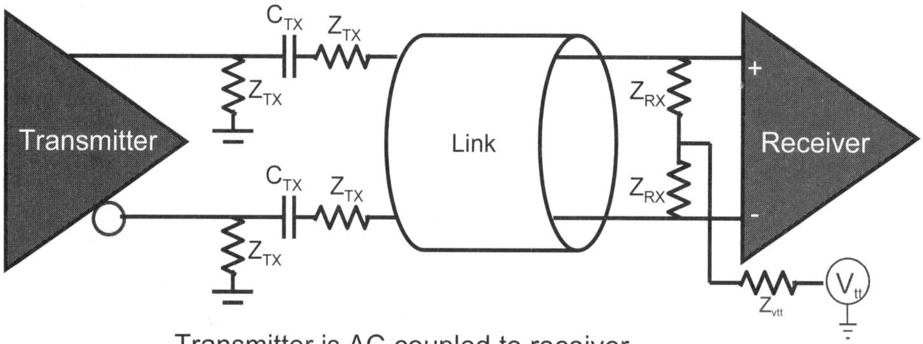

Transmitter is AC coupled to receiver

DC common mode impedance is 50 Ohms

Differential impedance is 100 Ohms

Coupling capacitor is between 75-200 nF

Example of a Non-Posted Memory Read Transaction

Let us put our knowledge so far to describe the set of events that take place from the time a requester device initiates a memory read request, until it obtains the requested data from a completer device. Given that such a transaction is a non-posted transaction, there are two phases to the read process. The first phase is the transmission of a memory read request TLP from requester to completer. The second phase is the reception of a completion with data from the completer.

Memory Read Request Phase

Refer to Figure 2-31. The requester Device Core or Software Layer sends the following information to the Transaction Layer:

32-bit or 64-bit memory address, transaction type of memory read request, amount of data to read calculated in doublewords, traffic class if other than TC0, byte enables, attributes to indicate if 'relaxed ordering' and 'no snoop' attribute bits should be set or clear.

Figure 2-31: Memory Read Request Phase

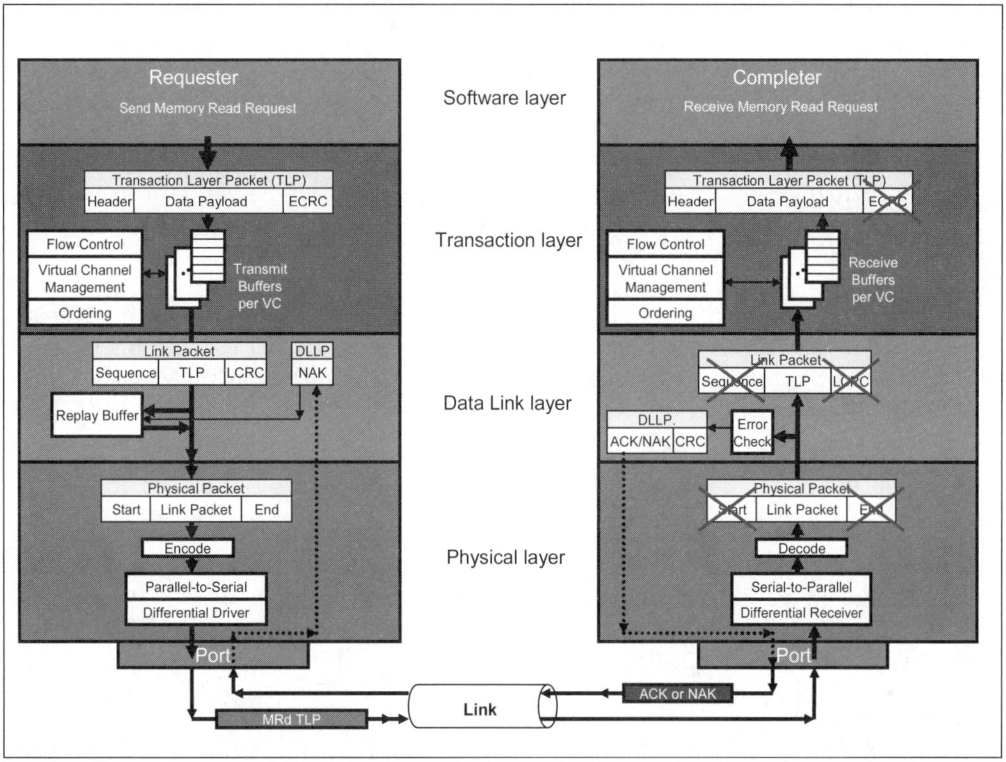

The Transaction layer uses this information to build a MRd TLP. The exact TLP packet format is described in a later chapter. A 3 DW or 4 DW header is created depending on address size (32-bit or 64-bit). In addition, the Transaction Layer adds its requester ID (bus#, device#, function#) and an 8-bit tag to the header. It sets the TD (transaction digest present) bit in the TLP header if a 32-bit

End-to-End CRC is added to the tail portion of the TLP. The TLP does not have a data payload. The TLP is placed in the appropriate virtual channel buffer ready for transmission. The flow control logic confirms there are sufficient "credits" available (obtained from the completer device) for the virtual channel associated with the traffic class used.

Only then the memory read request TLP is sent to the Data Link Layer. The Data Link Layer adds a 12-bit sequence ID and a 32-bit LCRC which is calculated based on the entire packet. A copy of the TLP with sequence ID and LCRC is stored in the replay buffer.

This packet is forwarded to the Physical Layer which tags on a Start symbol and an End symbol to the packet. The packet is byte striped across the available Lanes, scrambled and 10 bit encoded. Finally the packet is converted to a serial bit stream on all Lanes and transmitted differentially across the Link to the neighbor completer device.

The completer converts the incoming serial bit stream back to 10b symbols while assembling the packet in an elastic buffer. The 10b symbols are converted back to bytes and the bytes from all Lanes are de-scrambled and un-striped. The Start and End symbols are detected and removed. The resultant TLP is sent to the Data Link Layer.

The completer Data Link Layer checks for LCRC errors in the received TLP and checks the Sequence ID for missing or out-of-sequence TLPs. Assume no error. The Data Link Layer creates an ACK DLLP which contains the same sequence ID as contained in the memory read request TLP received. A 16-bit CRC is added to the ACK DLLP. The DLLP is sent back to the Physical Layer which transmits the ACK DLLP to the requester.

The requester Physical Layer reformulates the ACK DLLP and sends it up to the Data Link Layer which evaluates the sequence ID and compares it with TLPs stored in the replay buffer. The stored memory read request TLP associated with the ACK received is discarded from the replay buffer. If a NAK DLLP was received by the requester instead, it would re-send a copy of the stored memory read request TLP.

In the mean time the Data Link Layer of the completer strips the sequence ID and LCRC field from the memory read request TLP and forwards it to the Transaction Layer.

The Transaction Layer receives the memory read request TLP in the appropriate virtual channel buffer associated with the TC of the TLP. The Transaction layer checks for ECRC error. It forwards the contents of the header (address, requester ID, memory read transaction type, amount of data requested, traffic class etc.) to the completer Device Core/Software Layer.

Completion with Data Phase

Refer to Figure 2-32 on page 99 during the following discussion. To service the memory read request, the completer Device Core/Software Layer sends the following information to the Transaction Layer:

Requester ID and Tag copied from the original memory read request, transaction type of completion with data (CplD), requested amount of data with data length field, traffic class if other than TC0, attributes to indicate if 'relaxed ordering' and 'no snoop' bits should be set or clear (these bits are copied from the original memory read request). Finally, a completion status of successful completion (SC) is sent.

Figure 2-32: Completion with Data Phase

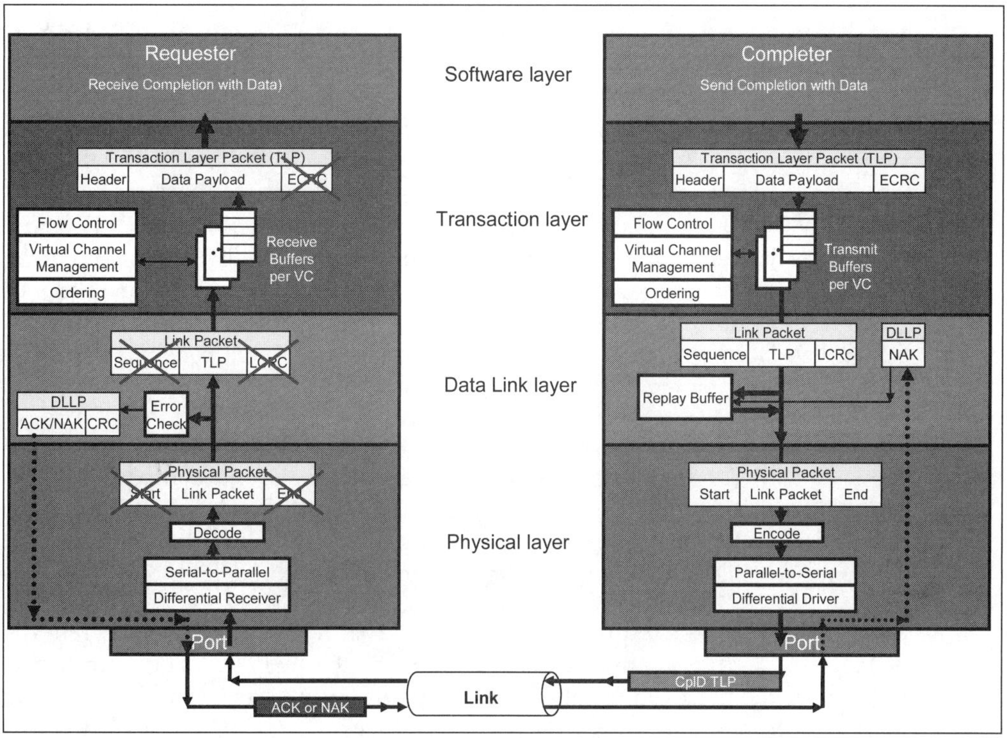

The Transaction layer uses this information to build a CplD TLP. The exact TLP packet format is described in a later chapter. A 3 DW header is created. In addition, the Transaction Layer adds its own completer ID to the header. The TD (transaction digest present) bit in the TLP header is set if a 32-bit End-to-End CRC is added to the tail portion of the TLP. The TLP includes the data payload. The flow control logic confirms sufficient "credits" are available (obtained from the requester device) for the virtual channel associated with the traffic class used.

Only then the CplD TLP is sent to the Data Link Layer. The Data Link Layer adds a 12-bit sequence ID and a 32-bit LCRC which is calculated based on the entire packet. A copy of the TLP with sequence ID and LCRC is stored in the replay buffer.

This packet is forwarded to the Physical Layer which tags on a Start symbol and an End symbol to the packet. The packet is byte striped across the available Lanes, scrambled and 10 bit encoded. Finally the CplD packet is converted to a serial bit stream on all Lanes and transmitted differentially across the Link to the neighbor requester device.

The requester converts the incoming serial bit stream back to 10b symbols while assembling the packet in an elastic buffer. The 10b symbols are converted back to bytes and the bytes from all Lanes are de-scrambled and un-striped. The Start and End symbols are detected and removed. The resultant TLP is sent to the Data Link Layer.

The Data Link Layer checks for LCRC errors in the received CplD TLP and checks the Sequence ID for missing or out-of-sequence TLPs. Assume no error. The Data Link Layer creates an ACK DLLP which contains the same sequence ID as contained in the CplD TLP received. A 16-bit CRC is added to the ACK DLLP. The DLLP is sent back to the Physical Layer which transmits the ACK DLLP to the completer.

The completer Physical Layer reformulates the ACK DLLP and sends it up to the Data Link Layer which evaluates the sequence ID and compares it with TLPs stored in the replay buffer. The stored CplD TLP associated with the ACK received is discarded from the replay buffer. If a NAK DLLP was received by the completer instead, it would re-send a copy of the stored CplD TLP.

In the mean time, the requester Transaction Layer receives the CplD TLP in the appropriate virtual channel buffer mapped to the TLP TC. The Transaction Layer uses the tag in the header of the CplD TLP to associate the completion with the original request. Transaction layer checks for ECRC error. It forwards the header contents and data payload including the Completion Status to the requester Device Core/Software Layer. Memory read transaction DONE.

Hot Plug

PCI Express supports native hot-plug though hot-plug support in a device is not mandatory. Some of the elements found in a PCI Express hot plug system are:

- Indicators which show the power and attention state of the slot.
- Manually-operated Retention Latch (MRL) that holds add-in cards in place.
- MRL Sensor that allow the port and system software to detect the MRL being opened.
- Electromechanical Interlock which prevents removal of add-in cards while slot is powered.
- Attention Button that allows user to request hot-plug operations.
- Software User Interface that allows user to request hot-plug operations.
- Slot Numbering for visual identification of slots.

When a port has no connection or a removal event occurs, the port transmitter moves to the electrical high impedance detect state. The receiver remains in the electrical low impedance state.

PCI Express Performance and Data Transfer Efficiency

As of May 2003, no realistic performance and efficiency numbers were available. However, Table 2-3 shows aggregate bandwidth numbers for various Link widths after factoring the overhead of 8b/10b encoding.

Table 2-3: PCI Express Aggregate Throughput for Various Link Widths

PCI Express Link Width	x1	x2	x4	x8	x12	x16	x32
Aggregate Bandwidth (GBytes/sec)	0.5	1	2	4	6	8	16

DLLPs are 2 doublewords in size. The ACK/NAK and flow control protocol utilize DLLPs, but it is not expected that these DLLPs will use up a significant portion of the bandwidth.

The remainder of the bandwidth is available for TLPs. Between 6-7 doublewords of the TLP is overhead associated with Start and End framing symbols, sequence ID, TLP header, ECRC and LCRC fields. The remainder of the TLP contains between 0-1024 doublewords of data payload. It is apparent that the bus efficiency is significantly low if small size packets are transmitted. The efficiency numbers are very high if TLPs contain significant amounts of data payload.

Packets can be transmitted back-to-back without the Link going idle. Thus the Link can be 100% utilized.

The switch does not introduce any arbitration overhead when forwarding incoming packets from multiple ingress ports to one egress port. However, it is yet to be seen what the effect is of the Quality of Service protocol on actual bandwidth numbers for given applications.

There is overhead associated with the split transaction protocol, especially for read transactions. For a read request TLP, the data payload is contained in the completion. This factor has to be accounted for when determining the effective performance of the bus. Posted write transactions improve the efficiency of the fabric.

Switches support cut-through mode. That is to say that an incoming packet can be immediately forwarded to an egress port for transmission without the switch having to buffer up the packet. The latency for packet forwarding through a switch can be very small allowing packets to travel from one end of the PCI Express fabric to another end with very small latency.

Part Two

Transaction Protocol

3 Address Spaces & Transaction Routing

The Previous Chapter

The previous chapter introduced the PCI Express data transfer protocol. It described the layered approach to PCI Express device design while describing the function of each device layer. Packet types employed in accomplishing data transfers were described without getting into packet content details. Finally, this chapter outlined the process of a requester initiating a transaction such as a memory read to read data from a completer across a Link.

This Chapter

This chapter describes the general concepts of PCI Express transaction routing and the mechanisms used by a device in deciding whether to accept, forward, or reject a packet arriving at an ingress port. Because Data Link Layer Packets (DLLPs) and Physical Layer *ordered set* link traffic are never forwarded, the emphasis here is on Transaction Layer Packet (TLP) types and the three routing methods associated with them: address routing, ID routing, and implicit routing. Included is a summary of configuration methods used in PCI Express to set up PCI-compatible plug-and-play addressing within system IO and memory maps, as well as key elements in the PCI Express packet protocol used in making routing decisions.

The Next Chapter

The next chapter details the two major classes of packets are *Transaction Layer Packets* (TLPs), and *Data Link Layer Packets* (DLLPs). The use and format of each TLP and DLLP packet type is covered, along with definitions of the field within the packets.

Introduction

Unlike shared-bus architectures such as PCI and PCI-X, where traffic is visible to each device and routing is mainly a concern of bridges, PCI Express devices are dependent on each other to accept traffic or forward it in the direction of the ultimate recipient.

Figure 3-1: Multi-Port PCI Express Devices Have Routing Responsibilities

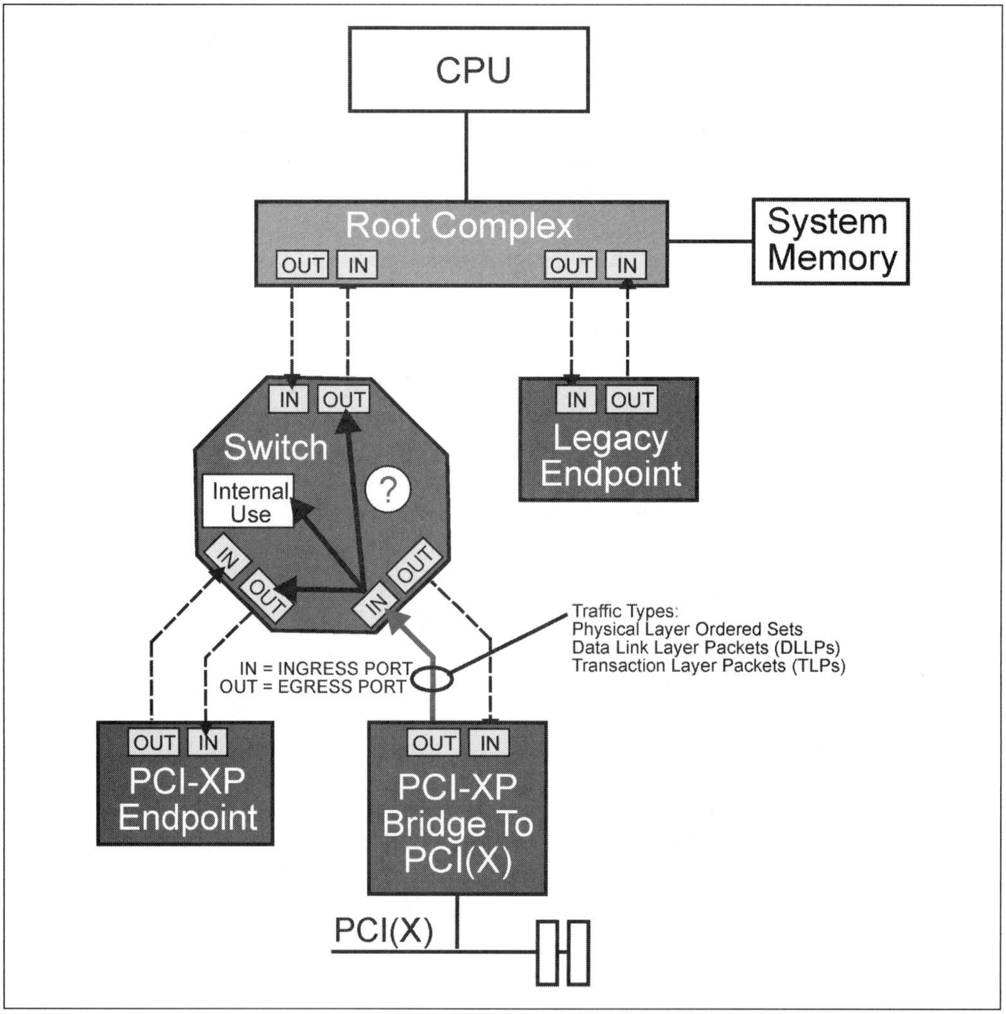

As illustrated in Figure 3-1 on page 106, a PCI Express topology consists of independent, point-to-point links connecting each device with one or more neighbors. As traffic arrives at the inbound side of a link interface (called the *ingress port*), the device checks for errors, then makes one of three decisions:

1. Accept the traffic and use it internally.
2. Forward the traffic to the appropriate outbound *(egress)* port.
3. Reject the traffic because it is neither the intended target nor an interface to it (note that there are also other reasons why traffic may be rejected)

Receivers Check For Three Types of Link Traffic

Assuming a link is fully operational, the physical layer receiver interface of each device is prepared to monitor the logical idle condition and detect the arrival of the three types of link traffic: Ordered Sets, DLLPs, and TLPs. Using control (K) symbols which accompany the traffic to determine framing boundaries and traffic type, PCI Express devices then make a distinction between traffic which is local to the link vs. traffic which may require routing to other links (e.g. TLPs). Local link traffic, which includes Ordered Sets and Data Link Layer Packets (DLLPs), isn't forwarded and carries no routing information. Transaction Layer Packets (TLPs) can and do move from link to link, using routing information contained in the packet headers.

Multi-port Devices Assume the Routing Burden

It should be apparent in Figure 3-1 on page 106 that devices with multiple PCI Express ports are responsible for handling their own traffic as well as forwarding other traffic between ingress ports and any enabled egress ports. Also note that while peer-peer transaction support is required of switches, it is optional for a multi-port Root Complex. It is up to the system designer to account for peer-to-peer traffic when selecting devices and laying out a motherboard.

Endpoints Have Limited Routing Responsibilities

It should also be apparent in Figure 3-1 on page 106 that endpoint devices have a single link interface and lack the ability to route inbound traffic to other links. For this reason, and because they don't reside on shared busses, endpoints never expect to see ingress port traffic which is not intended for them (this is different than shared-bus PCI(X), where devices commonly decode addresses and commands not targeting them). Endpoint routing is limited to accepting or rejecting transactions presented to them.

System Routing Strategy Is Programmed

Before transactions can be generated by a requester, accepted by the completer, and forwarded by any devices in the path between the two, all devices must be configured to enforce the system transaction routing scheme. Routing is based on traffic type, system memory and IO address assignments, etc. In keeping with PCI plug-and-play configuration methods, each PCI express device is discovered, memory and IO address resources are assigned to them, and switch/bridge devices are programmed to forward transactions on their behalf. Once routing is programmed, bus mastering and target address decoding are enabled. Thereafter, devices are prepared to generate, accept, forward, or reject transactions as necessary.

Two Types of Local Link Traffic

Local traffic occurs between the transmit interface of one device and the receive interface of its neighbor for the purpose of managing the link itself. This traffic is never forwarded or flow controlled; when sent, it must be accepted. Local traffic is further classified as *Ordered Sets* exchanged between the Physical Layers of two devices on a link or Data Link Layer packets (DLLPs) exchanged between the Data Link Layers of the two devices.

Ordered Sets

These are sent by each physical layer transmitter to the physical layer of the corresponding receiver to initiate link training, compensate for clock tolerance, or transition a link to and from the Electrical Idle state. As indicated in Table 3-1 on page 109, there are five types of Ordered Sets.

Each ordered set is constructed of 10-bit control (K) symbols that are created within the physical layer. These symbols have a common name as well as a alph-numeric code that defines the 10 bits pattern of 1s and 0s, of which they are comprised. For example, the SKP (Skip) symbol has a 10-bit value represented as K28.0.

Figure 3-2 on page 110 illustrates the transmission of Ordered Sets. Note that each ordered set is fixed in size, consisting of 4 or 16 characters. Again, the receiver is required to consume them as they are sent. Note that the COM control symbol (K28.5) is used to indicate the start of any ordered set.

Refer to the "8b/10b Encoding" on page 419 for a thorough discussion of Ordered Sets.

Table 3-1: Ordered Set Types

Ordered Set Type	Symbols	Purpose
Fast Training Sequence (FTS)	COM, 3 FTS	Quick synchronization of bit stream when leaving L0s power state.
Training Sequence One (TS1)	COM, Lane ID, 14 more	Used in link training, to align and synchronize the incoming bit stream at startup, convey reset, other functions.
Training Sequence Two (TS2)	COM, Lane ID, 14 more	See TS1.
Electrical Idle (IDLE)	COM, 3 IDL	Indicates that link should be brought to a lower power state (L0s, L1, L2).
Skip	COM, 3 SKP	Inserted periodically to compensate for clock tolerances.

Figure 3-2: PCI Express Link Local Traffic: Ordered Sets

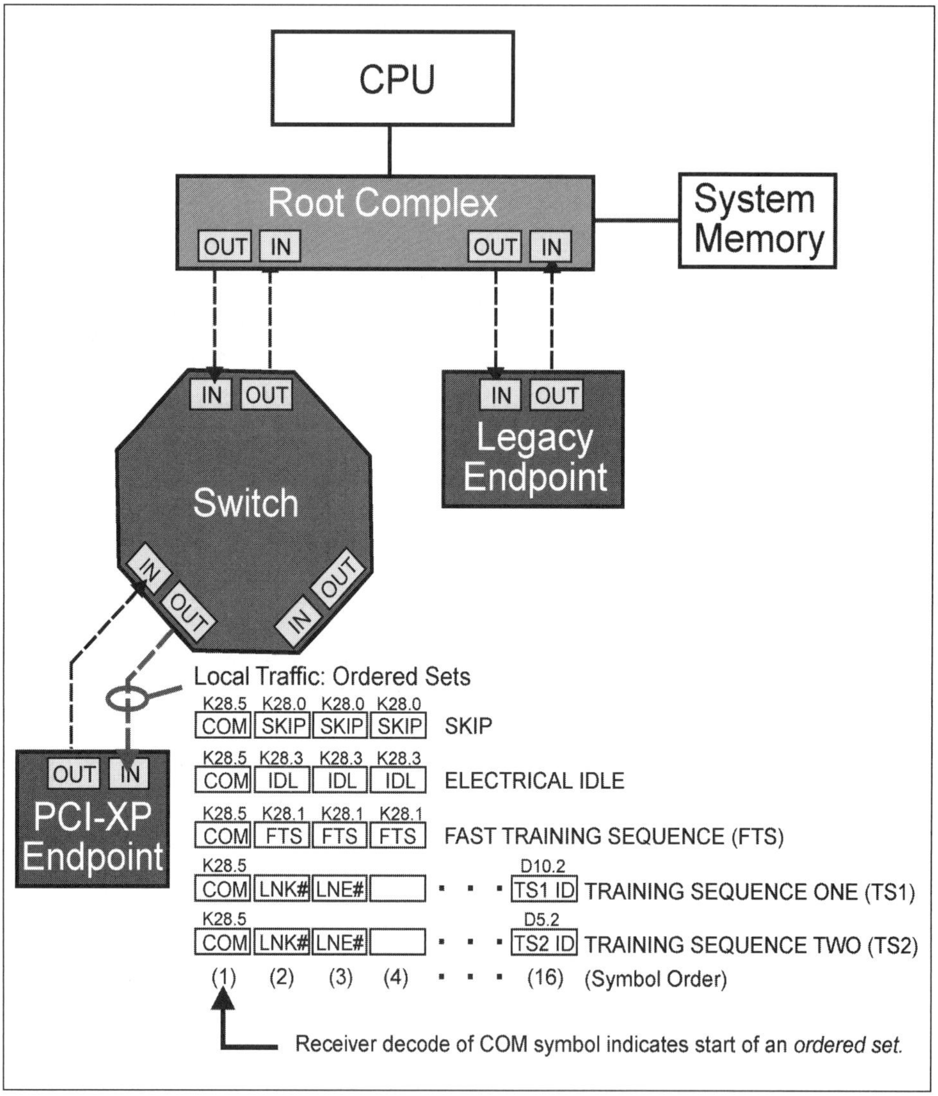

Data Link Layer Packets (DLLPs)

The other type of local traffic sent by a device transmit interface to the corresponding receiver of the device attached to it are Data Link Layer Packets (DLLPs). These are also used in link management, although they are sourced at the device Data Link Layer rather that the Physical Layer. The main functions of DLLPs are to facilitate Link Power Management, TLP Flow Control, and the acknowledgement of successful TLP delivery across the link.

Table 3-2: Data Link Layer Packet (DLLP) Types

DLLP	Purpose
Acknowledge (Ack)	Receiver Data Link Layer sends Ack to indicate that no CRC or other errors have been encountered in received TLP(s). Transmitter retains copy of TLPs until Ack'd
No Acknowledge (Nak)	Receiver Data Link Layer sends Nak to indicate that a TLP was received with a CRC or other error. All TLPs remaining in the transmitter's Retry Buffer must be resent, in the original order.
PM_Enter_L1; PM_Enter_L23	Following a software configuration space access to cause a device power management event, a downstream device requests entry to link L1 or Level 2-3 state
PM_Active_State_Req_L1	Downstream device autonomously requests L1 Active State
PM_Request_Ack	Upstream device acknowledges transition to L1 State
Vendor-Specific DLLP	Reserved for vendor-specific purposes
InitFC1-P InitFC1-NP InitFC1-Cpl	Flow Control Initialization Type One DLLP awarding posted (P), nonposted (NP), or completion (Cpl) flow control credits.
InitFC2-P InitFC2-NP InitFC2-Cpl	Flow Control Initialization Type Two DLLP confirming award of InitFC1 posted (P), nonposted (NP), or completion (Cpl) flow control credits.
UpdateFC-P UpdateFC-NP UpdateFC-Cpl	Flow Control Credit Update DLLP awarding posted (P), nonposted (NP), or completion (Cpl) flow control credits.

As described in Table 3-2 on page 111 and shown in Figure 3-3 on page 112, there are three major types of DLLPs: Ack/Nak, Power Management (several variants), and Flow Control. In addition, a vendor-specific DLLP is permitted in the specification. Each DLLP is 8 bytes, including a Start Of DLLP (SDP) byte, 2-byte CRC, and an End Of Packet (END) byte in addition to the 4 byte DLLP core (which includes the *type* field and any required attributes).

Figure 3-3: PCI Express Link Local Traffic: DLLPs

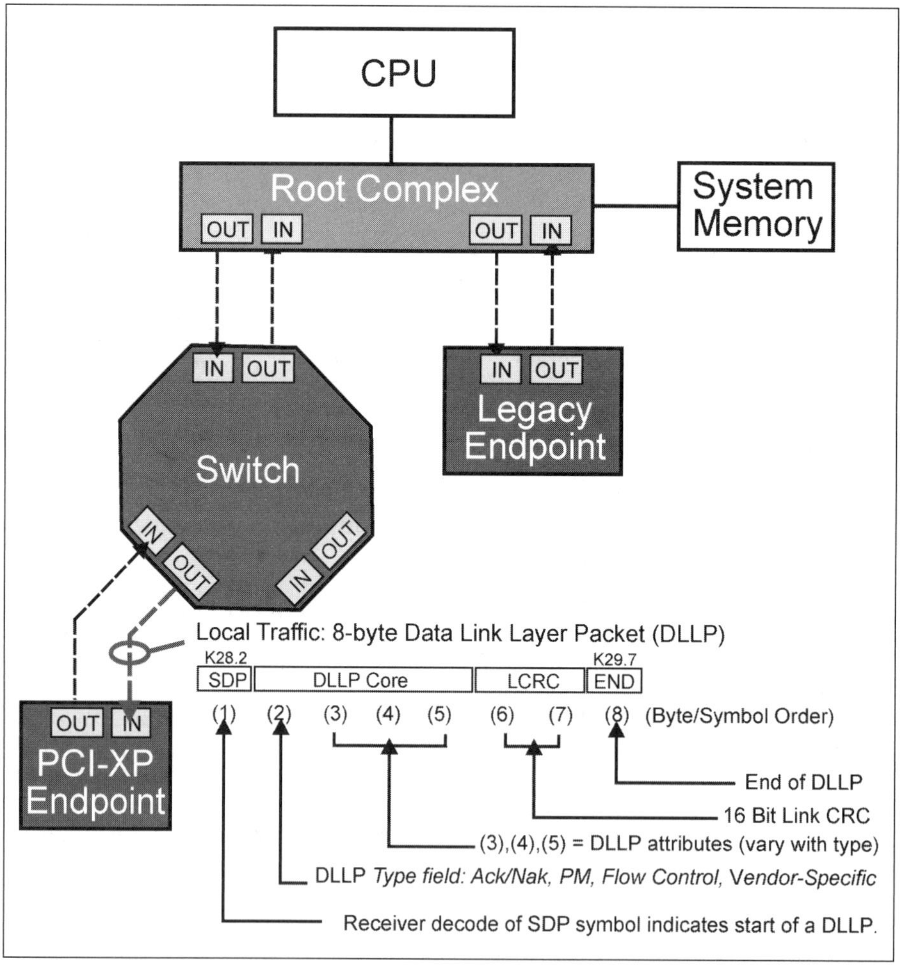

Note that unlike Ordered Sets, DLLPs always carry a 16-bit CRC which is verified by the receiver before carrying out the required operation. If an error is detected by the receiver of a DLLP, it is dropped. Even though DLLPs are not acknowledged, time-out mechanisms built into the specification permit recovery from dropped DLLPs due to CRC errors.

Refer to "Data Link Layer Packets" on page 198 for a thorough discussion of Data Link Layer packets.

Transaction Layer Packet Routing Basics

The third class of link traffic originates in the Transaction Layer of one device and targets the Transaction Layer of another device. These Transaction Layer Packets (TLPs) are forwarded from one link to another as necessary, subject to the routing mechanisms and rules described in the following sections. Note that other chapters in this book describe additional aspects of Transaction Layer Packet handling, including Flow Control, Quality Of Service, Error Handling, Ordering rules, etc. The term transaction is used here to describe the exchange of information using Transaction Layer Packets. Because Ordered Sets and DLLPs carry no routing information and are not forwarded, the routing rules described in the following sections apply only to TLPs.

TLPs Used to Access Four Address Spaces

As transactions are carried out between PCI Express requesters and completers, four separate address spaces are used: Memory, IO, Configuration, and Message. The basic use of each address space is described in Table 3-3 on page 113.

Table 3-3: PCI Express Address Space And Transaction Types

Address Space	Transaction Types	Purpose
Memory	Read, Write	Transfer data to or from a location in the system memory map
IO	Read, Write	Transfer data to or from a location in the system IO map
Configuration	Read, Write	Transfer data to or from a location in the configuration space of a PCI-compatible device.

Table 3-3: PCI Express Address Space And Transaction Types (Continued)

Address Space	Transaction Types	Purpose
Message	Baseline, Vendor-specific	General in-band messaging and event reporting (without consuming memory or IO address resources)

Split Transaction Protocol Is Used

Accesses to the four address spaces in PCI Express are accomplished using split-transaction requests and completions.

Split Transactions: Better Performance, More Overhead

The split transaction protocol is an improvement over earlier bus protocols (e.g. PCI) which made extensive use of bus wait-states or delayed transactions (retries) to deal with latencies in accessing targets. In PCI Express, the completion following a request is initiated by the completer only when it has data and/or status ready for delivery. The fact that the completion is separated in time from the request which caused it also means that two separate TLPs are generated, with independent routing for the request TLP and the Completion TLP. Note that while a link is free for other activity in the time between a request and its subsequent completion, a split-transaction protocol involves some additional overhead as two complete TLPs must be generated to carry out a single transaction.

Figure 3-4 on page 115 illustrates the request-completion phases of a PCI Express split transaction. This example represents an endpoint read from system memory.

Figure 3-4: PCI Express Transaction Request And Completion TLPs

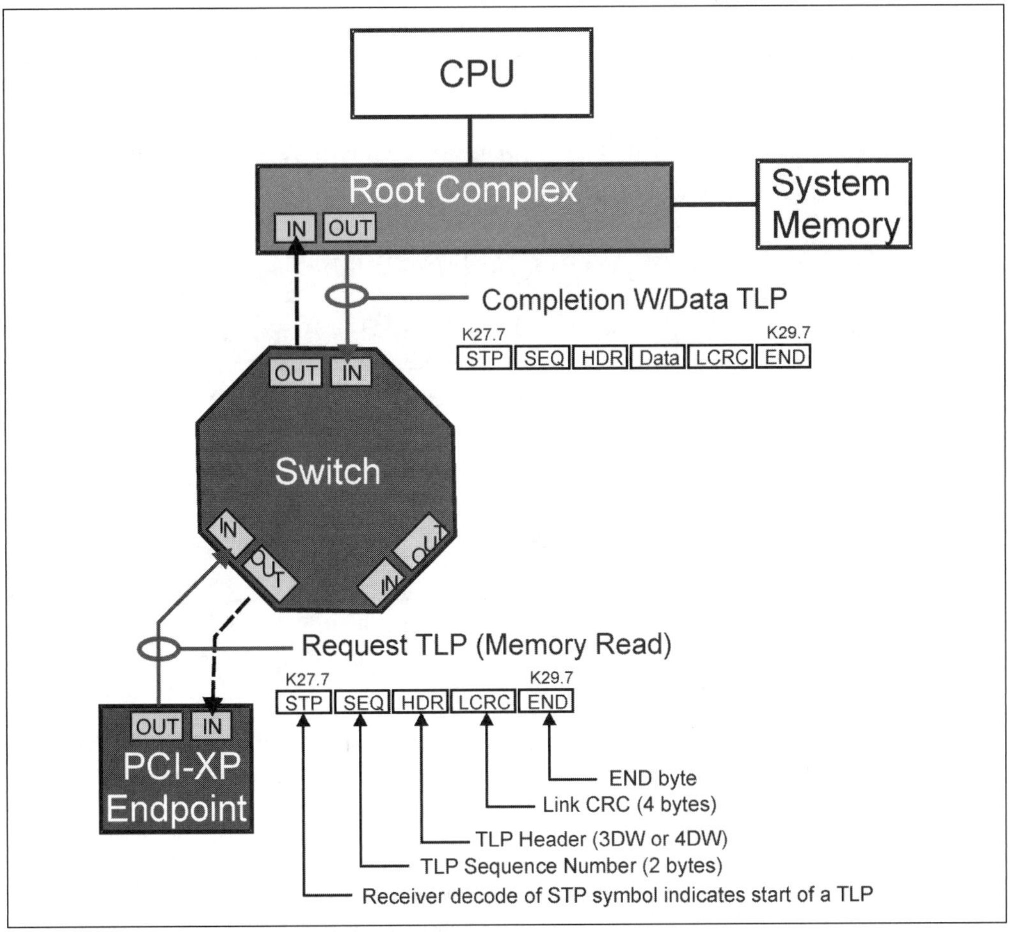

Write Posting: Sometimes a Completion Isn't Needed

To mitigate the penalty of the request-completion latency, messages and some write transactions in PCI Express are posted, meaning the write request (including data) is sent, and the transaction is over from the requester's perspective as soon as the request is sent out of the egress port; responsibility for delivery is now the problem of the next device. In a multi-level topology, this has the advantage of being much faster than waiting for the entire request-completion transit, but — as in all posting schemes — uncertainty exists concerning when (and if) the transaction completed successfully at the ultimate recipient.

In PCI Express, write posting to memory is considered acceptable in exchange for the higher performance. On the other hand, writes to IO and configuration space may change device behavior, and write posting is not permitted. A completion will always be sent to report status of the IO or configuration write operation.

Table 3-4 on page 116 lists PCI Express posted and non-posted transactions.

Table 3-4: PCI Express Posted and Non-Posted Transactions

Request	How Request Is Handled
Memory Write	All Memory Write requests are posted. No completion is expected or sent.
Memory Read Memory Read Lock	All memory read requests are non-posted. A completion with data (CplD or CplDLK) will be returned by the completer with requested data and to report status of the memory read
IO Write	All IO Write requests are non-posted. A completion without data (Cpl) will be returned by the completer to report status of the IO write operation.
IO Read	All IO read requests are non-posted. A completion with data (CplD) will be returned by the completer with requested data and to report status of the IO read operation.
Configuration Write Type 0 and Type 1	All Configuration Write requests are non-posted. A completion without data (Cpl) will be returned by the completer to report status of the configuration space write operation.
Configuration Read Type 0 and Type 1	All configuration read requests are non-posted. A completion with data (CplD) will be returned by the completer with requested data and to report status of the read operation.
Message Message With Data	While the routing method varies, all message transactions are handled in the same manner as memory writes in that they are considered posted requests

Three Methods of TLP Routing

All of the TLP variants, targeting any of the four address spaces, are routed using one of the three possible schemes: Address Routing, ID Routing, and Implicit Routing. Table 3-5 on page 117 summarizes the PCI Express TLP header type variants and the routing method used for each. Each of these is described in the following sections.

Table 3-5: PCI Express TLP Variants And Routing Options

TLP Type	Routing Method Used
Memory Read (MRd), Memory Read Lock (MRdLk), Memory Write (MWr)	Address Routing
IO Read (IORd), IO Write (IOWr)	Address Routing
Configuration Read Type 0 (CfgRd0), Configuration Read Type 1 (CfgRd1) Configuration Write Type 0 (CfgWr0), Configuration Write Type 1(CfgWr1)	ID Routing
Message (Msg), Message With Data (MsgD)	Address Routing, ID Routing, or Implicit routing
Completion (Cpl), Completion With Data (CplD)	ID Routing

PCI Express Routing Is Compatible with PCI

As indicated in Table 3-5 on page 117, memory and IO transactions are routed through the PCI Express topology using address routing to reference system memory and IO maps, while configuration cycles use ID routing to reference the completer's (target's) logical position within the PCI-compatible bus topology (using Bus Number, Device Number, Function Number in place of a linear address). Both address routing and ID routing are completely compatible with routing methods used in the PCI and PCIX protocols when performing memory, IO, or configuration transactions. PCI Express completions also use the ID routing scheme.

PCI Express Adds Implicit Routing for Messages

PCI Express adds the third routing method, implicit routing, which is an option when sending messages. In implicit routing, neither address or ID routing information applies; the packet is routed based on a code in the packet header indicating it is destined for device(s) with known, fixed locations (the Root Complex, the next receiver, etc.).

While limited in the cases it can support, implicit routing simplifies routing of messages. Note that messages may optionally use address or ID routing instead.

Why Were Messages Added to PCI Express Protocol? PCI and PCI-X protocols support *load and store* memory and IO read-write transactions, which have the following features:

1. The transaction initiator drives out a memory or IO start address selecting a location within the desired target.
2. The target claims the transaction based on decoding and comparing the transaction start address with ranges it has been programmed to respond to in its configuration space Base Address Registers.
3. If the transaction involves bursting, then addresses are indexed after each data transfer.

While PCI Express also supports load and store transactions with its memory and IO transactions, it adds in-band messages. The main reason for this is that the PCI Express protocol seeks to (and does) eliminate many of the sideband signals related to interrupts, error handling, and power management which are found in PCI(X)-based systems. Elimination of signals is very important in an architecture with the scalability possible with PCI Express. It would not be efficient to design a PCI Express device with a two lane link and then saddle it with numerous additional signals to handle auxiliary functions.

The PCI Express protocol replaces most sideband signals with a variety of in-band packet types; some of these are conveyed as Data Link Layer packets (DLLPs) and some as Transaction Layer packets (TLPs).

How Implicit Routing Helps with Messages. One side effect of using in-band messages in place of hard-wired sideband signals is the problem of delivering the message to the proper recipient in a topology consisting of numerous point-to-point links. The PCI Express protocol provides maximum flexibility in routing message TLPs; they may use address routing, ID routing, or the third method, implicit routing. Implicit routing takes advantage of the fact that, due to their architecture, switches and other multi-port devices have a fundamental sense of upstream and downstream, and where the Root Complex is to be found. Because of this, a message header can be routed implicitly with a simple code indicating that it is intended for the Root Complex, a broadcast downstream message, should terminate at the next receiver, etc.

The advantage of implicit routing is that it eliminates the need to assign a set of memory mapped addresses for all of the possible message variants and program all of the devices to use them.

Header Fields Define Packet Format and Routing

As depicted in Figure 3-5 on page 119, each Transaction Layer Packet contains a three or four double word (12 or 16 byte) header. Included in the 3DW or 4DW header are two fields, *Type* and *Format* (Fmt), which define the format of the remainder of the header and the routing method to be used on the entire TLP as it moves between devices in the PCI Express topology.

Figure 3-5: Transaction Layer Packet Generic 3DW And 4DW Headers

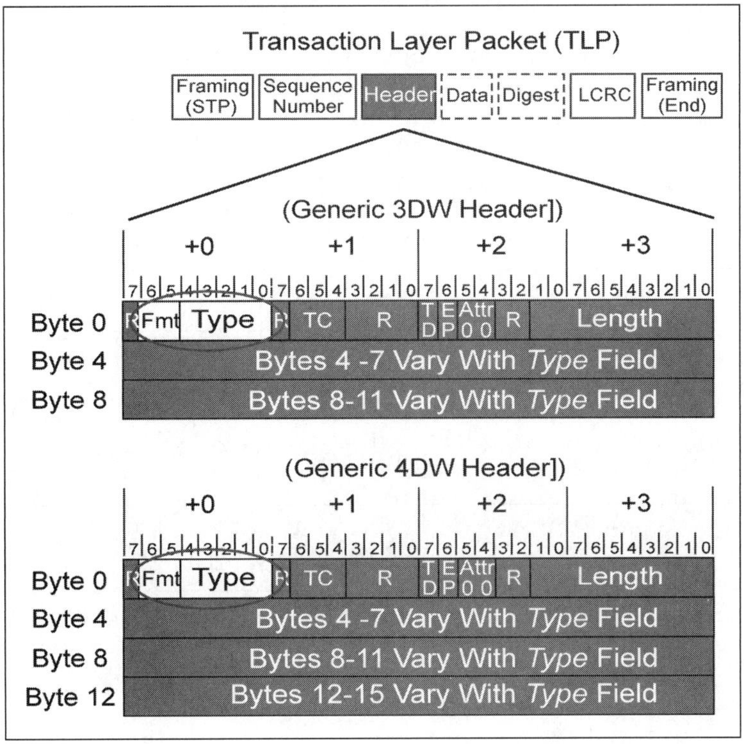

Using TLP Header Information: Overview

General

As TLPs arrive at an ingress port, they are first checked for errors at both the physical and data link layers of the receiver. Assuming there are no errors, TLP routing is performed; basic steps include:

1. The TLP header *Type* and *Format* fields in the first DWord are examined to determine the size and format of the remainder of the packet.
2. Depending on the routing method associated with the packet, the device will determine if it is the intended recipient; if so, it will accept (consume) the TLP. If it is not the recipient, and it is a multi-port device, it will forward the TLP to the appropriate egress port--subject to the rules for ordering and flow control for that egress port.
3. If it is neither the intended recipient nor a device in the path to it, it will generally reject the packet as an Unsupported Request (UR).

Header Type/Format Field Encodings

Table 3-6 on page 120 below summarizes the encodings used in TLP header Type and Format fields. These two fields, used together, indicate TLP format and routing to the receiver.

Table 3-6: TLP Header Type and Format Field Encodings

TLP	FMT[1:0]	TYPE [4:0]
Memory Read Request (MRd)	00 = 3DW, no data 01 = 4DW, no data	0 0000
Memory Read Lock Request (MRdLk)	00 = 3DW, no data 01 = 4DW, no data	0 0001
Memory Write Request (MWr)	10 = 3DW, w/ data 11 = 4DW, w/ data	0 0000
IO Read Request (IORd)	00 = 3DW, no data	00010
IO Write Request (IOWr)	10 = 3DW, w/ data	0 0010

Table 3-6: TLP Header Type and Format Field Encodings (Continued)

TLP	FMT[1:0]	TYPE [4:0]
Config Type 0 Read Request (CfgRd0)	00 = 3DW, no data	0 0100
Config Type 0 Write Request (CfgWr0)	10 = 3DW, w/ data	0 0100
Config Type 1 Read Request (CfgRd1)	00 = 3DW, no data	0 0101
Config Type 1 Write Request (CfgWr1)	10 = 3DW, w/ data	0 0101
Message Request (Msg)	01 = 4DW, no data	1 0 RRR* (for RRR, see routing subfield)
Message Request W/Data (MsgD)	11 = 4DW, w/ data	1 0 RRR* (for RRR, see routing subfield)
Completion (Cpl)	00 = 3DW, no data	0 1010
Completion W/Data (CplD)	10 = 3DW, w/ data	0 1010
Completion-Locked (CplLk)	00 = 3DW, no data	0 1011
Completion W/Data (CplDLk)	10 = 3DW, w/ data	0 1011

Applying Routing Mechanisms

Once configuration of the system routing strategy is complete and transactions are enabled, PCI Express devices decode inbound TLP headers and use corresponding fields in configuration space Base Address Registers, Base/Limit registers, and Bus Number registers to apply address, ID, and implicit routing to the packet. Note that there are actually two levels of decision: the device first determines if the packet targets an internal location; if not, and the device is a switch, it will evaluate the packet to see if it should be forwarded out of an egress port. A third possibility is that the packet has been received in error or is malformed; in this case, it will be handled as a receive error. There are a number of cases when this may happen, and a number of ways it may be handled. Refer to "PCI Express Error Checking Mechanisms" on page 356 for a description of error checking and handling. The following sections describe the basic features of each routing mechanism; we will assume no errors are encountered.

Address Routing

PCI Express transactions using address routing reference the same system memory and IO maps that PCI and PCIX transactions do. Address routing is used to transfer data to or from memory, memory mapped IO, or IO locations. Memory transaction requests may carry either 32 bit addresses using the 3DW TLP header format, or 64 bit addresses using the 4DW TLP header format. IO transaction requests are restricted to 32 bits of address using the 3DW TLP header format, and should only target legacy devices.

Memory and IO Address Maps

Figure 3-6 on page 122 depicts generic system memory and IO maps. Note that the size of the system memory map is a function of the range of addresses that devices are capable of generating (often dictated by the CPU address bus). As in PCI and PCI-X, PCI Express permits either 32 bit or 64 bit memory addressing. The size of the system IO map is limited to 32 bits (4GB), although in many systems only the lower 16 bits (64KB) are used.

Figure 3-6: Generic System Memory And IO Address Maps

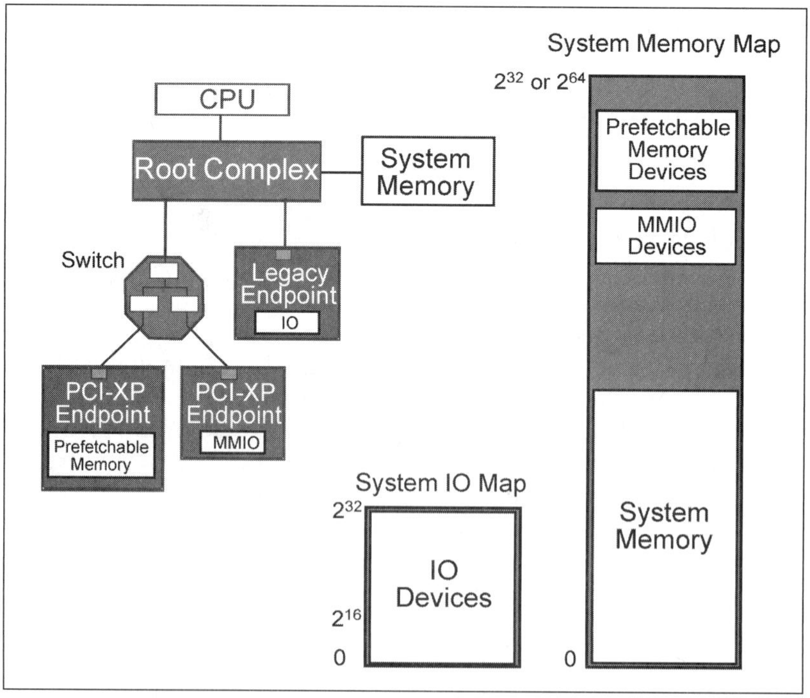

Key TLP Header Fields in Address Routing

If the Type field in a received TLP indicates address routing is to be used, then the Address Fields in the header are used to performing the routing check. There are two cases: 32-bit addresses and 64-bit addresses.

TLPs with 3DW, 32-Bit Address. For IO or a 32-bit memory requests, only 32 bits of address are contained in the header. Devices targeted with these TLPs will reside below the 4GB memory or IO address boundary. Figure 3-7 on page 123 depicts this case.

Figure 3-7: 3DW TLP Header Address Routing Fields

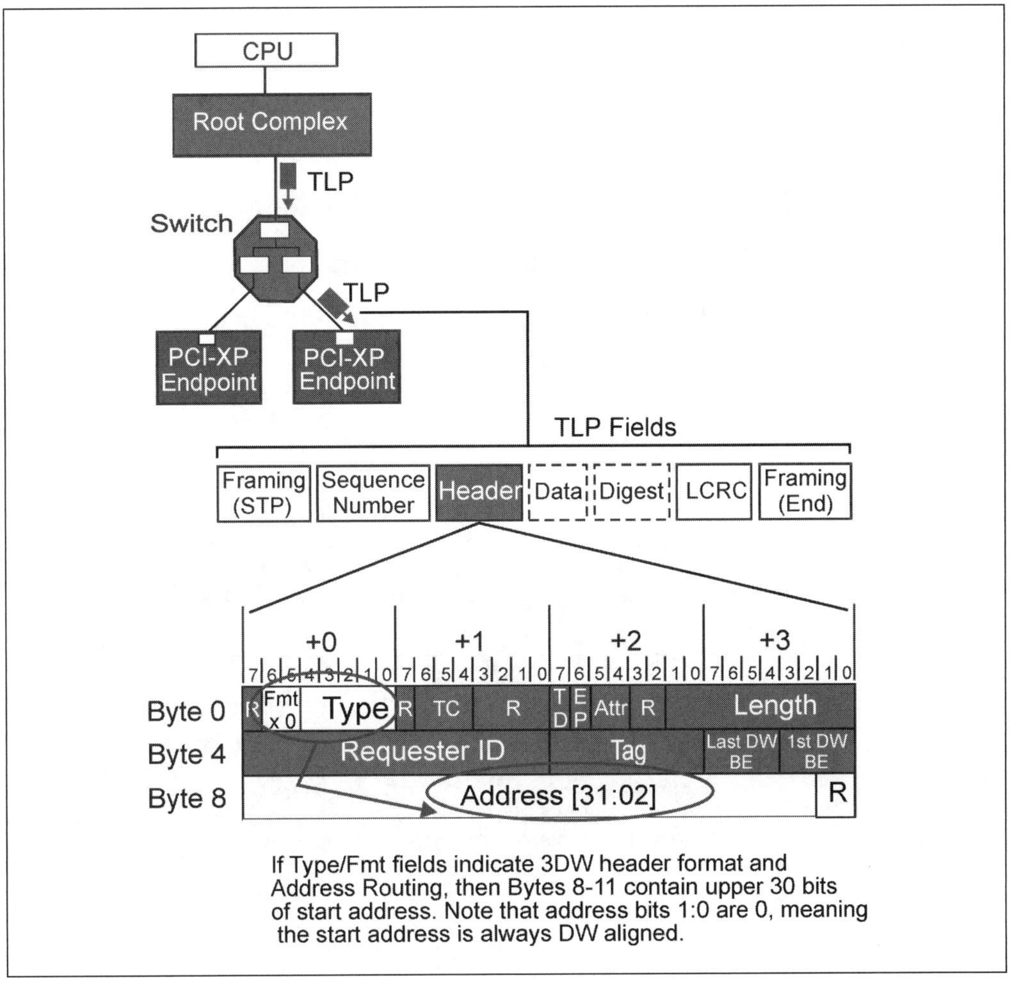

TLPs With 4DW, 64-Bit Address. For 64-bit memory requests, 64 bits of address are contained in the header. Devices targeted with these TLPs will reside above the 4GB memory boundary. Figure 3-8 on page 124 shows this case.

Figure 3-8: 4DW TLP Header Address Routing Fields

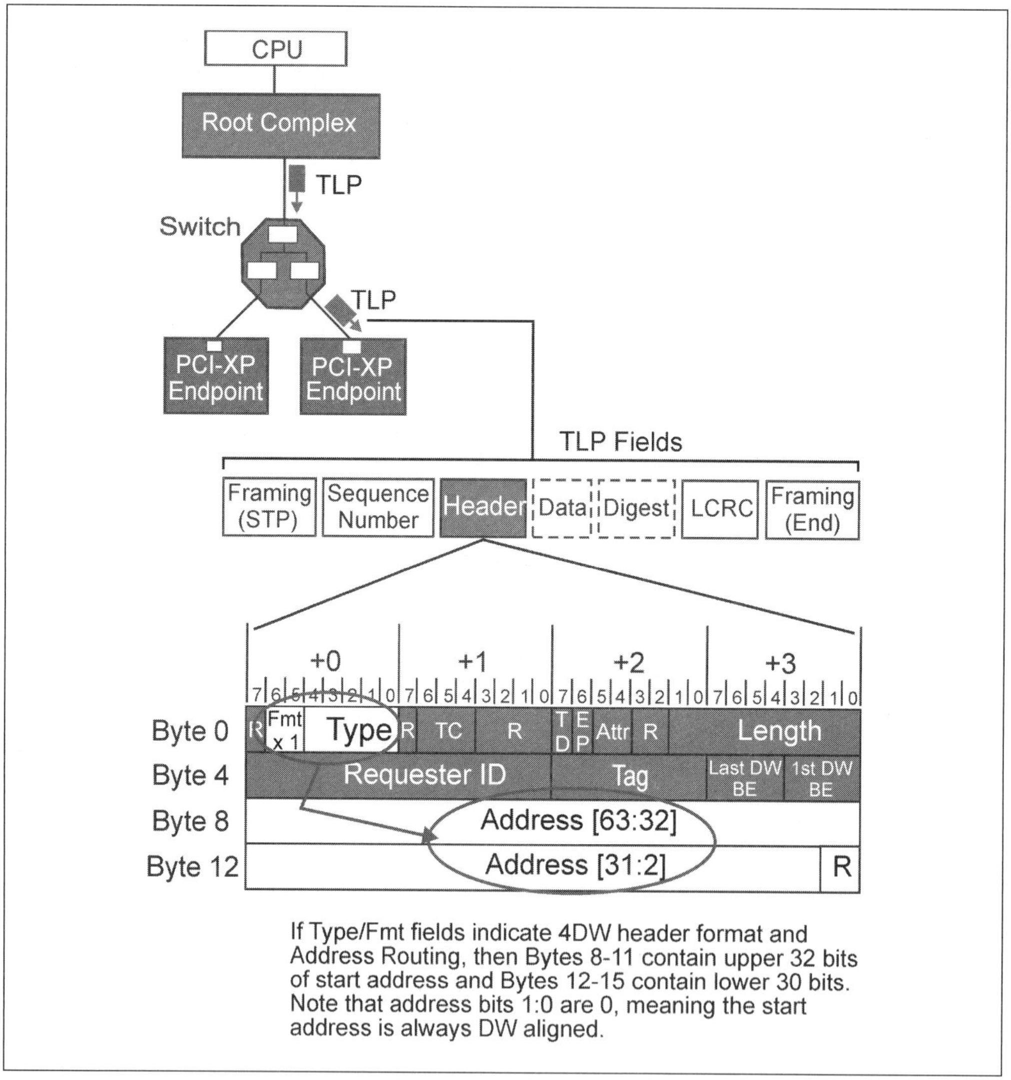

An Endpoint Checks an Address-Routed TLP

If the Type field in a received TLP indicates address routing is to be used, then an endpoint device simply checks the address in the packet header against each of its implemented BARs in its Type 0 configuration space header. As it has only one link interface, it will either claim the packet or reject it. Figure 3-9 on page 125 illustrates this case.

Figure 3-9: Endpoint Checks Routing Of An Inbound TLP Using Address Routing

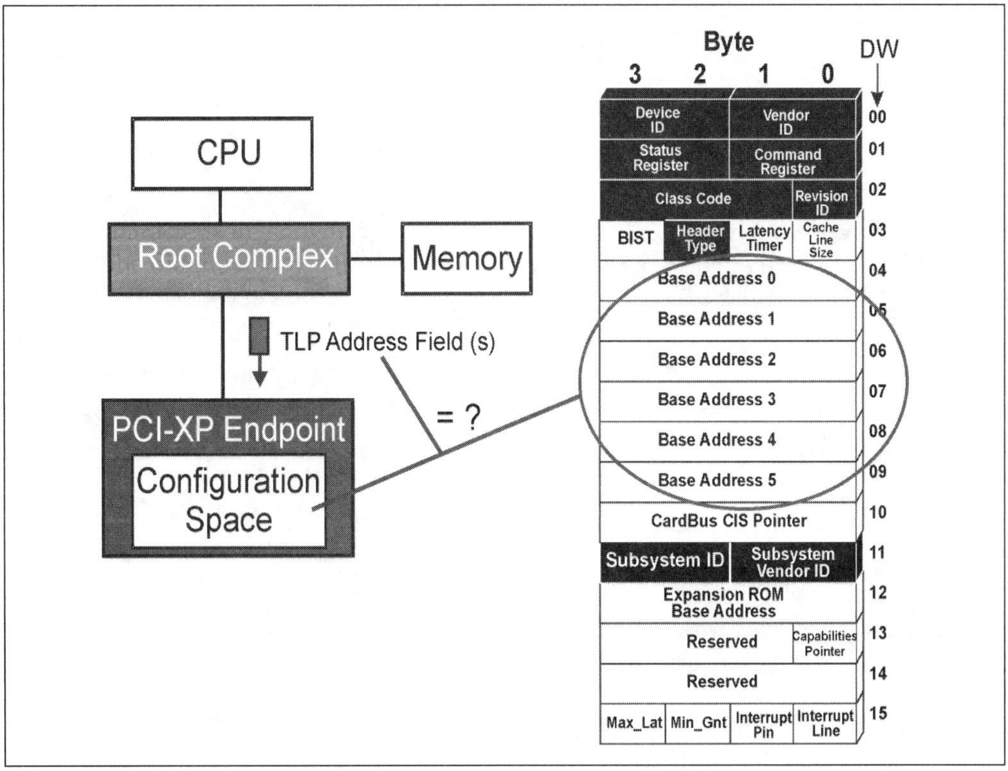

A Switch Receives an Address Routed TLP: Two Checks

General. If the Type field in a received TLP indicates address routing is to be used, then a switch first checks to see if it is the intended completer. It compares the header address against target addresses programmed in its two BARs. If the address falls within the range, it consumes the packet. This case is indicated by (1) in Figure 3-10 on page 126. If the header address field does not match a range programmed in a BAR, it then checks the Type 1 configuration space header for each downstream link. It checks the non-prefetchable memory (MMIO) and prefetchable Base/Limit registers if the transaction targets memory, or the I/O Base and Limt registers if the transaction targets I/O address space. This check is indicated by (2) in Figure 3-10 on page 126.

Figure 3-10: Switch Checks Routing Of An Inbound TLP Using Address Routing

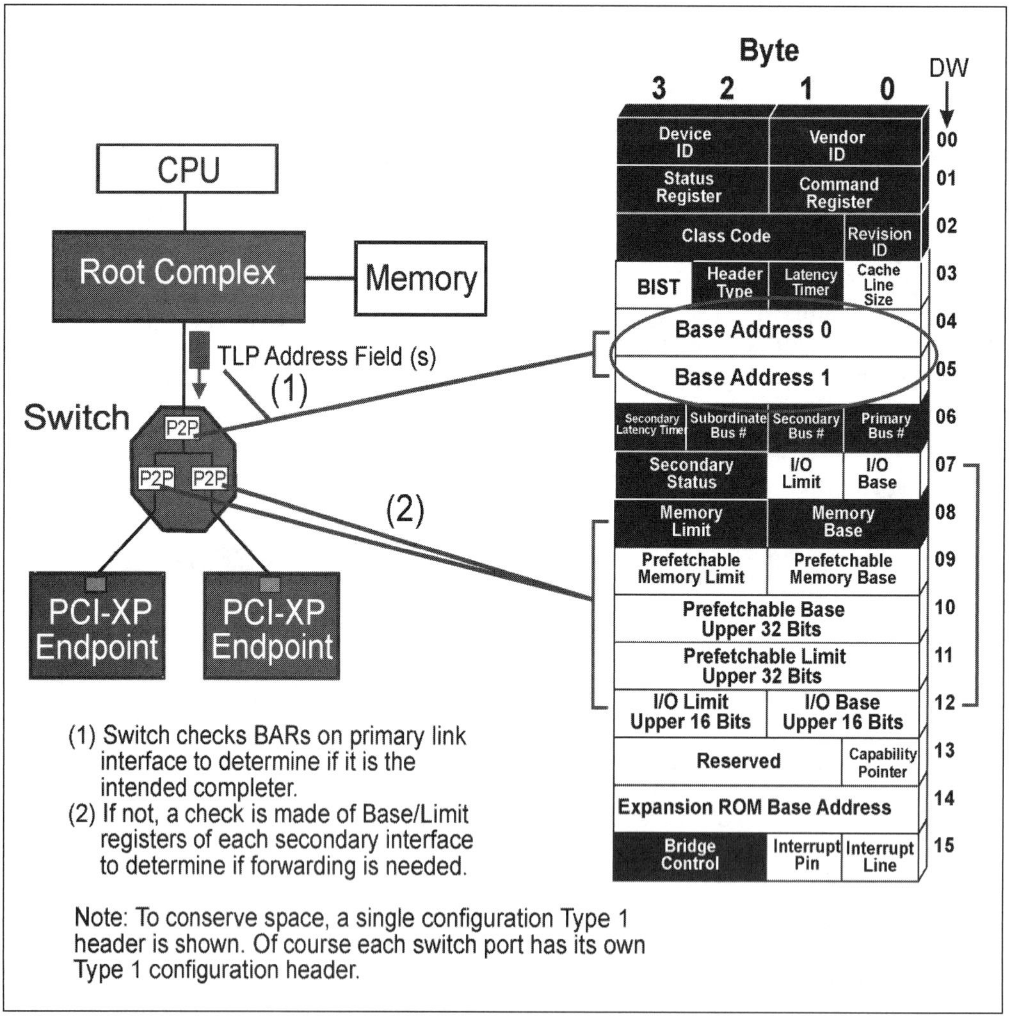

Other Notes About Switch Address-Routing. The following notes also apply to switch address routing:

1. If the address-routed packet address falls in the range of one of its secondary bridge interface Base/Limit register sets, it will forward the packet downstream.
2. If the address-routed packet was moving downstream (was received on the primary interface) and it does not map to any BAR or downstream link Base/Limit registers, it will be handled as an unsupported request on the primary link.
3. Upstream address-routed packets are always forwarded to the upstream link if they do not target an internal location or another downstream link.

ID Routing

ID routing is based on the logical position (Bus Number, Device Number, Function Number) of a device function within the PCI bus topology. ID routing is compatible with routing methods used in the PCI and PCIX protocols when performing Type 0 or Type 1 configuration transactions. In PCI Express, it is also used for routing completions and may be used in message routing as well.

ID Bus Number, Device Number, Function Number Limits

PCI Express supports the same basic topology limits as PCI and PCI-X:

1. A maximum of 256 busses/links in a system. This includes busses created by bridges to other PCI-compatible protocols such as PCI, PCI-X, AGP, etc.
2. A maximum of 32 devices per bus/link. Of course, While a PCI(X) bus or the internal bus of a switch may host more than one downstream bridge interface, external PCI Express links are always point-to-point with only two devices per link. The downstream device on an external link is device 0.

- A maximum of 8 internal functions per device.

A significant difference in PCI Express over PCI is the provision for extending the amount of configuration space per function from 256 bytes to 4KB. Refer to the "Configuration Overview" on page 711 for a detailed description of the compatible and extended areas of PCI Express configuration space.

Key TLP Header Fields in ID Routing

If the Type field in a received TLP indicates ID routing is to be used, then the ID fields in the header are used to perform the routing check. There are two cases: ID routing with a 3DW header and ID routing with a 4DW header.

3DW TLP, ID Routing. Figure 3-11 on page 128 illustrates a TLP using ID routing and the 3DW header.

Figure 3-11: 3DW TLP Header ID Routing Fields

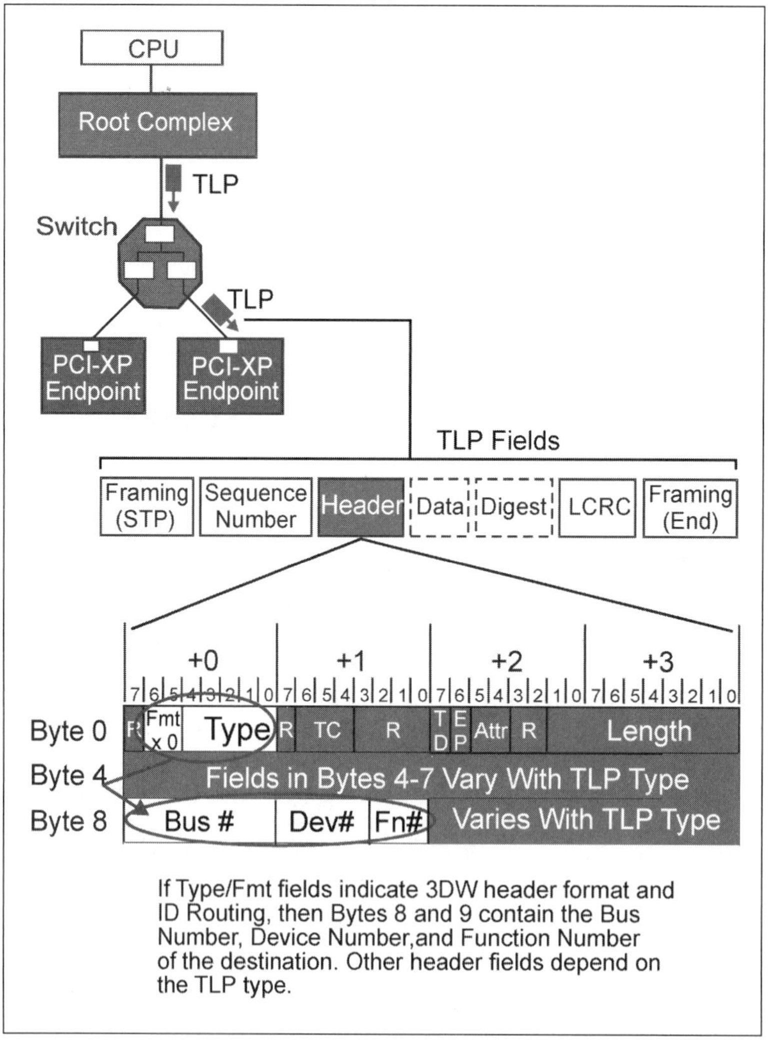

4DW TLP, ID Routing. Figure 3-12 on page 129 illustrates a TLP using ID routing and the 4DW header.

Figure 3-12: 4DW TLP Header ID Routing Fields

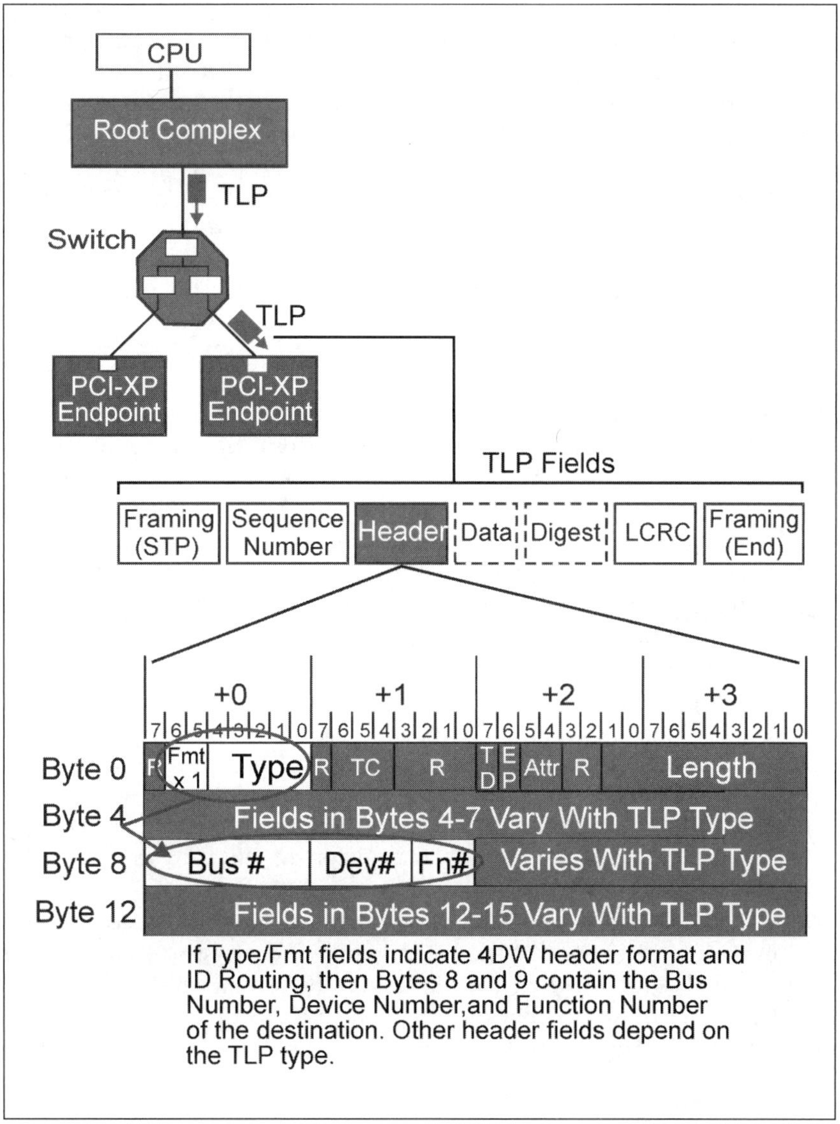

An Endpoint Checks an ID-Routed TLP

If the Type field in a received TLP indicates ID routing is to be used, then an endpoint device simply checks the ID field in the packet header against its own Bus Number, Device Number, and Function Number(s). In PCI Express, each device "captures" (and remembers) its own Bus Number and Device Number contained in TLP header bytes 8-9 each time a configuration write (Type 0) is detected on its primary link. At reset, all bus and device numbers in the system revert to 0, so a device will not respond to transactions other than configuration cycles until at least one configuration write cycle (Type 0) has been performed. Note that the PCI Express protocol does not define a configuration space location where the device function is required to store the captured Bus Number and Device Number information, only that it must do it.

Once again, as it has only one link interface, an endpoint will either claim an ID-routed packet or reject it. Figure 3-11 on page 128 illustrates this case.

A Switch Receives an ID-Routed TLP: Two Checks

If the Type field in a received TLP indicates ID routing is to be used, then a switch first checks to see if it is the intended completer. It compares the header ID field against its own Bus Number, Device Number, and Function Number(s). This is indicated by (1) in Figure 3-13 on page 131. As in the case of an endpoint, a switch captures its own Bus Number and Device number each time a configuration write (Type 0) is detected on i's primary link interface. If the header ID agrees with the ID of the switch, it consumes the packet. If the ID field does not match i's own, it then checks the Secondary-Subordinate Bus Number registers in the configuration space for each downstream link. This check is indicated by (2) in Figure 3-13 on page 131.

Other Notes About Switch ID Routing

1. If the ID-routed packet matches the range of one of its secondary bridge interface Secondary-Subordinate registers, it will forward the packet downstream.
2. If the ID-routed packet was moving downstream (was received on the primary interface) and it does not map to any downstream interface, it will be handled as an unsupported request on the primary link.
3. Upstream ID-routed packets are always forwarded to the upstream link if they do not target an internal location or another downstream link.

Figure 3-13: Switch Checks Routing Of An Inbound TLP Using ID Routing

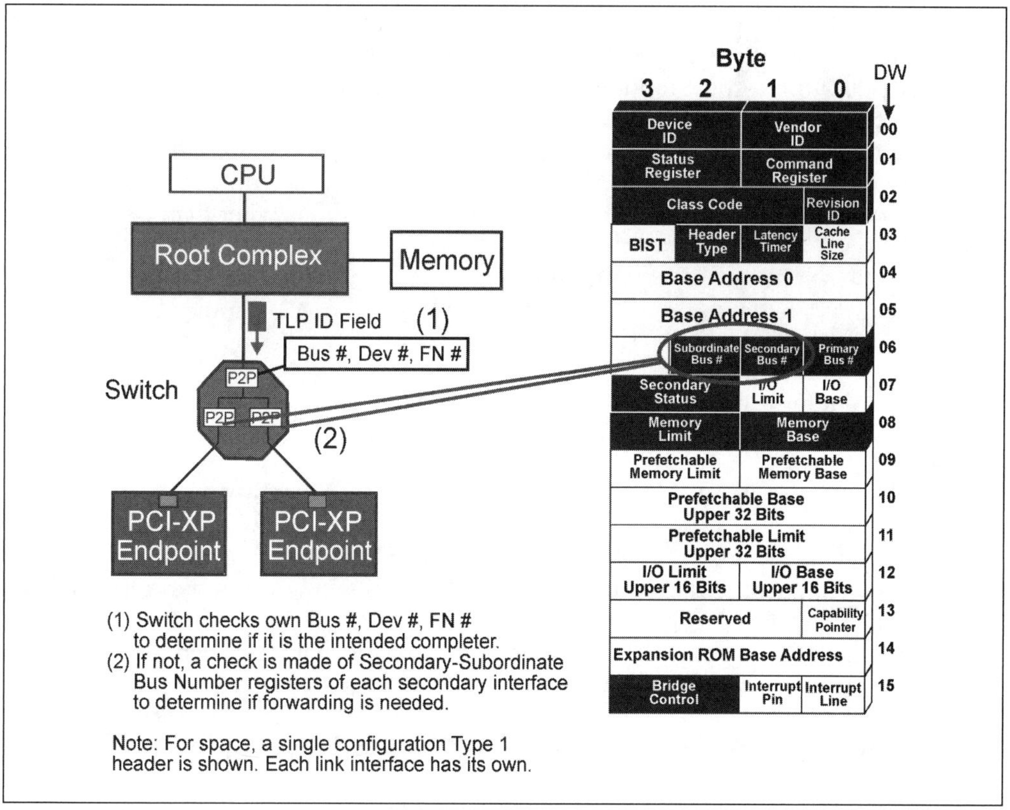

Implicit Routing

Implicit routing is based on the intrinsic knowledge PCI Express devices are required to have concerning upstream and downstream traffic and the existence of a single PCI Express Root Complex at the top of the PCI Express topology. This awareness allows limited routing of packets without the need to assign and include addresses with certain message packets. Because the Root Complex generally implements power management and interrupt controllers, as well as system error handling, it is either the source or recipient of most PCI Express messages.

Only Messages May Use Implicit Routing

With the elimination of many sideband signals in the PCI Express protocol, alternate methods are required to inform the host system when devices need service with respect to interrupts, errors, power management, etc. PCI Express addresses this by defining a number of special TLPs which may be used as virtual wires in conveying sideband events. Message groups currently defined include:

- Power Management
- INTx legacy interrupt signaling
- Error signaling
- Locked Transaction support
- Hot Plug signaling
- Vendor-specific messages
- Slot Power Limit messages

Messages May Also Use Address or ID Routing

In systems where all or some of this event traffic should target the system memory map or a logical location in the PCI bus topology, address routing and ID routing may be used in place of implicit routing. If address or ID routing is chosen for a message, then the routing mechanisms just described are applied in the same way as they would for other posted write packets.

Routing Sub-Field in Header Indicates Routing Method

As a message TLP moves between PCI Express devices, packet header fields indicate both that it is a message, and whether it should be routed using address, ID, or implicitly.

Key TLP Header Fields in Implicit Routing

If the Type field in a received message TLP indicates implicit routing is to be used, then the routing sub-field in the header is also used to determine the message destination when the routing check is performed. Figure 3-14 on page 133 illustrates a message TLP using implicit routing.

Figure 3-14: 4DW Message TLP Header Implicit Routing Fields

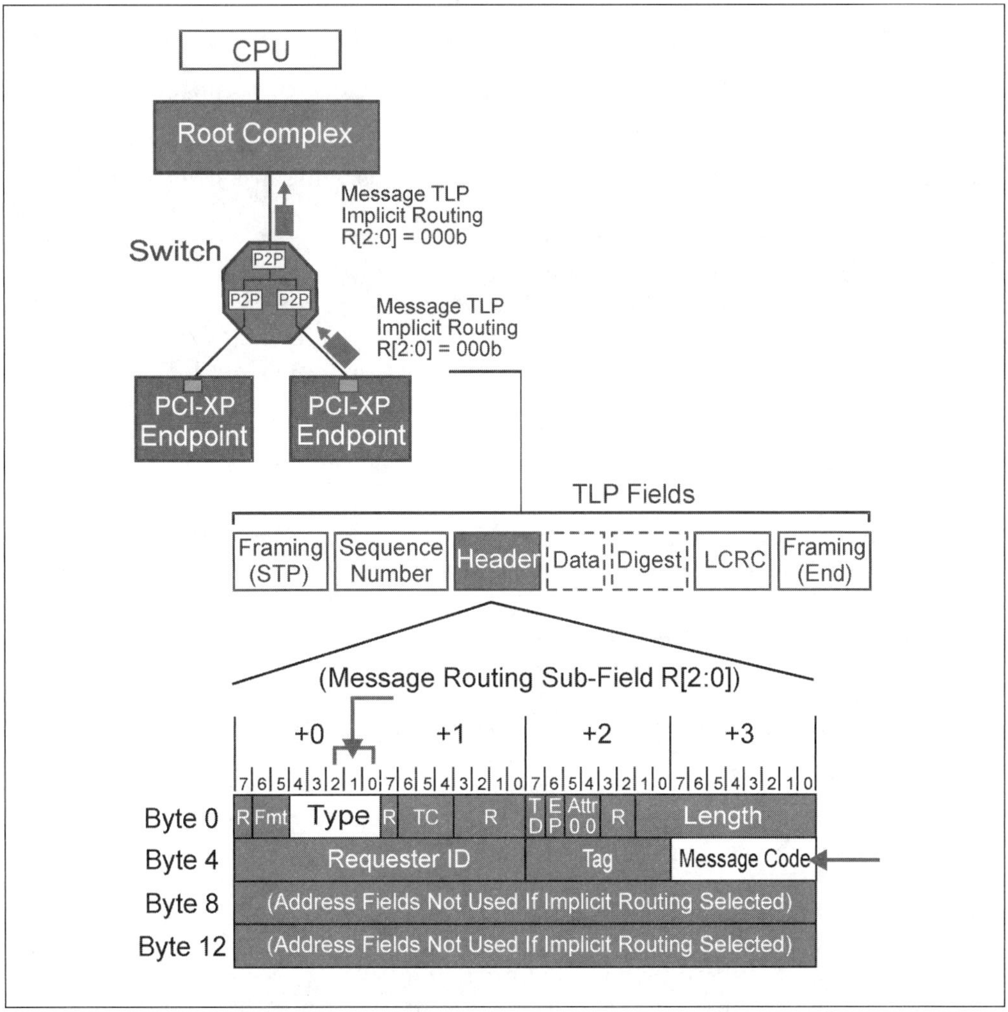

Message Type Field Summary

Table 3-7 on page 134 summarizes the use of the TLP header Type field when a message is being sent. As shown, the upper two bits of the 5 bit Type field indicate the packet is a message, and the lower three bits are the routing sub-field which specify the routing method to apply. Note that the 4DW header is always used with message TLPs, regardless of the routing option selected.

Table 3-7: Message Request Header Type Field Usage

Type Field Bits	Description
Bit 4:3	Defines the type of transaction: 10b = Message Transaction
Bit 2:0	Message Routing Subfield R[2:0], used to select message routing: • 000b = Route to Root Complex • 001b = Use Address Routing • 010b = Use ID Routing • 011b = Route as a Broadcast Message from Root Complex • 100b = Local message; terminate at receiver (INTx messages) • 101b = Gather & route to Root Complex (PME_TO_Ack message)

An Endpoint Checks a TLP Routed Implicitly

If the Type field in a received message TLP indicates implicit routing is to be used, then an endpoint device simply checks that the routing sub-field is appropriate for it. For example, an endpoint may accept a broadcast message or a message which terminates at the receiver; it won't accept messages which implicitly target the Root Complex.

A Switch Receives a TLP Routed Implicitly

If the Type field in a received message TLP indicates implicit routing is to be used, then a switch device simply considers the ingress port it arrived on and whether the routing sub-field code is appropriate for it. Some examples:

1. The upstream link interface of a switch may legitimately receive a broadcast message routed implicitly from the Root Complex. If it does, it will forward it intact onto all downstream links. It should not see an implicitly routed broadcast message arrive on a downstream ingress port, and will handle this as a malformed TLP.
2. The switch may accept messages indicating implicit routing to the root complex on secondary links; it will forward all of these upstream because it "knows" the location of the Root Complex is on its primary side. It would not accept messages routed implicitly to the Root Complex if they arrived on the primary link receive interface.

3. If the implicitly routed message arrives on either upstream or downstream ingress ports, the switch may consume the packet if routing indicates it should terminate at receiver.
4. If messages are routed using address or ID methods, a switch will simply perform normal address checks in deciding whether to accept or forward it.

Plug-And-Play Configuration of Routing Options

PCI-compatible configuration space and PCI Express extended configuration space are covered in detail in the Part 6. For reference, the programming of three sets of configuration space registers related to routing is summarized here.

Routing Configuration Is PCI-Compatible

PCI Express supports the basic 256 byte PCI configuration space common to all compatible devices, including the Type 0 and Type 1 PCI configuration space header formats used by non-bridge and switch/bridge devices, respectively. Devices may implement basic PCI-equivalent functionality with no change to drivers or Operating System software.

Two Configuration Space Header Formats: Type 0, Type 1

PCI Express endpoint devices support a single PCI Express link and use the Type 0 (non-bridge) format header. Switch/bridge devices support multiple links, and implement a Type 1 format header for each link interface. Figure 3-15 on page 136 illustrates a PCI Express topology and the use of configuration space Type 0 and Type 1 header formats.

Routing Registers Are Located in Configuration Header

As with PCI, registers associated with transaction routing are located in the first 64 bytes (16 DW) of configuration space (referred to in PCI Express as the PCI 2.3 compatible header area). The three sets of registers of principal interest are:

1. *Base Address Registers (BARs)* found in Type 0 and Type 1 headers.
2. Three sets of *Base/Limit Register* pairs supported in the Type 1 header of switch/bridge devices.
3. Three *Bus Number Registers,* also found in Type 1 headers of bridge/devices.

Figure 3-16 on page 137 illustrates the Type 0 and Type 1 PCI Express Configuration Space header formats. Key routing registers are indicated.

Figure 3-15: PCI Express Devices And Type 0 And Type 1 Header Use

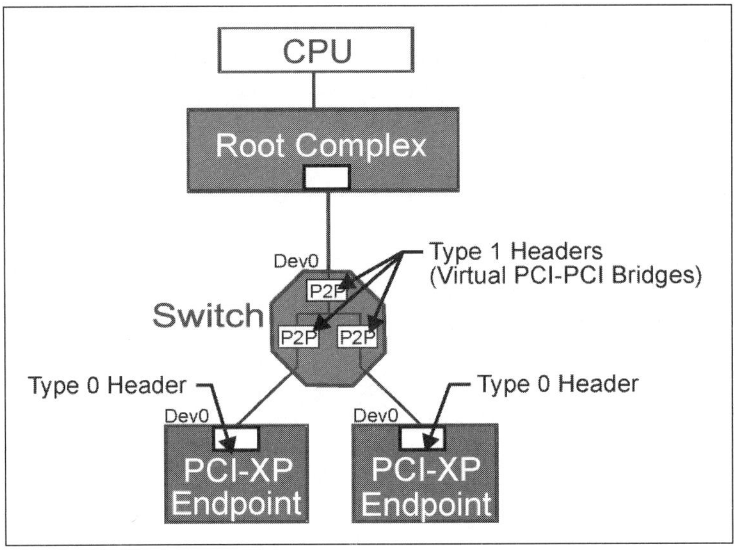

Base Address Registers (BARs): Type 0, 1 Headers

General

The first of the configuration space registers related to routing are the Base Address Registers (BARs) These are marked "<1" in Figure 3-16 on page 137, and are implemented by all devices which require system memory, IO, or memory mapped IO (MMIO) addresses allocated to them as targets. The location and use of BARs is compatible with PCI and PCI-X. As shown in Figure 3-16 on page 137, a Type 0 configuration space header has 6 BARs available for the device designer (at DW 4-9), while a Type 1 header has only two BARs (at DW 4-5).

After discovering device resource requirements, system software programs each BAR with start address for a range of addresses the device may respond to as a completer (target). Set up of BARs involves several things:

1. The device designer uses a BAR to hard-code a request for an allocation of one block of prefetchable or non-prefetchable memory, or of IO addresses in the system memory or IO map. A pair of adjacent BARs are concatenated if a 64-bit memory request is being made.

2. Hard-coded bits in the BAR include an indication of the request type, the size of the request, and whether the target device may be considered prefetchable (memory requests only).

Figure 3-16: PCI Express Configuration Space Type 0 and Type 1 Headers

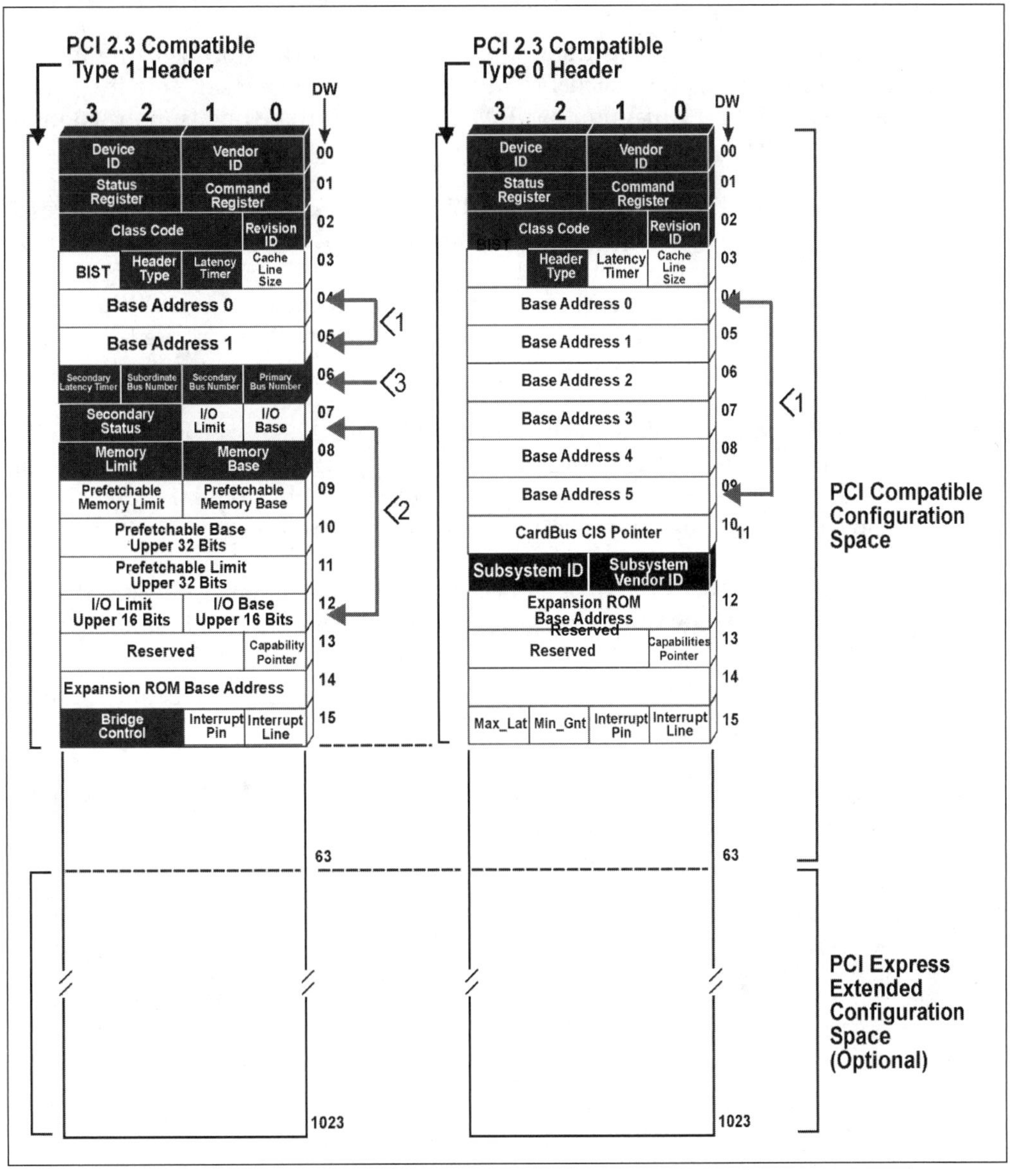

During enumeration, all PCI-compatible devices are discovered and the BARs are examined by system software to decode the request. Once the system memory and IO maps are established, software programs upper bits in implemented BARs with the start address for the block allocated to the target.

BAR Setup Example One: 1MB, Prefetchable Memory Request

Figure 3-17 depicts the basic steps in setting up a BAR which is being used to track a 1 MB block of prefetchable addresses for a device residing in the system memory map. In the diagram, the BAR is shown at three points in the configuration process:

1. The uninitialized BAR in Figure 3-17 is as it looks after power-up or a reset. While the designer has tied lower bits to indicate the request type and size, there is no requirement about how the upper bits (which are read-write) must come up in a BAR, so these bits are indicated with XXXXX. System software will first write all 1's to the BAR to set all read-write bits = 1. Of course, the hard-coded lower bits are not affected by the configuration write.
2. The second view of the BAR shown in Figure 3-17 is as it looks after configuration software has performed the write of all 1's to it. The next step in configuration is a read of the BAR to check the request. Table 3-8 on page 140 summarizes the results of this configuration read.

3. The third view of the BAR shown in Figure 3-17 on page 139 is as it looks after configuration software has performed another configuration write (Type 0) to program the start address for the block. In this example, the device start address is 2GB, so bit 31 is written = 1 (2^{31} = 2GB) and all other upper bits are written = 0's.

At this point the configuration of the BAR is complete. Once software enables memory address decoding in the PCI command register, the device will claim memory transactions in the range 2GB to 2GB+1MB.

Figure 3-17: 32-Bit Prefetchable Memory BAR Set Up

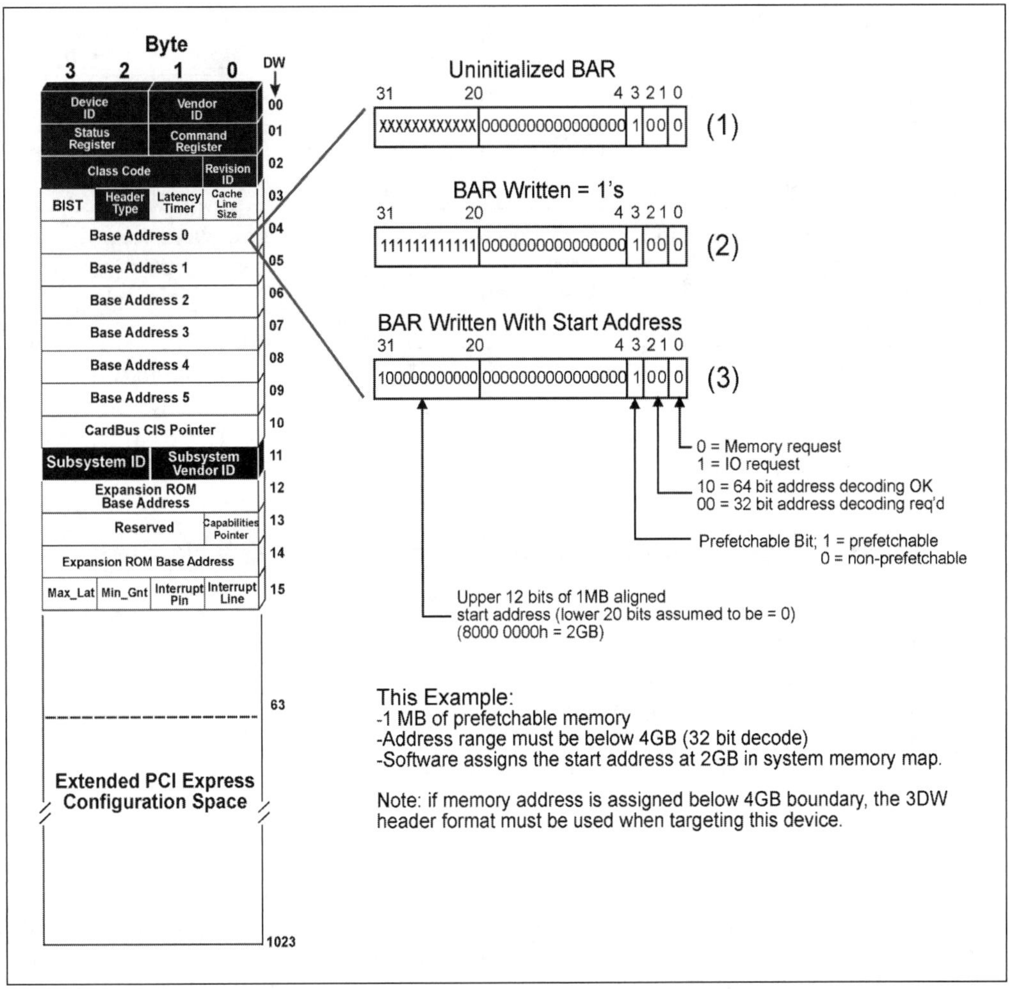

Table 3-8: Results Of Reading The BAR after Writing All "1s" To It

BAR Bits	Meaning
0	Read back as a "0", indicating a memory request
2:1	Read back as 00b indicating the target only supports a 32 bit address decoder
3	Read back as a "1", indicating request is for prefetchable memory
19:4	All read back as "0", used to help indicate the size of the request (also see bit 20)
31:20	All read back as "1" because software has not yet programmed the upper bits with a start address for the block. Note that because bit 20 was the first bit (above bit 3) to read back as written (=1); this indicates the memory request size is 1MB (2^{20} = 1MB).

BAR Setup Example Two: 64-Bit, 64MB Memory Request

Figure 3-18 on page 141 depicts the basic steps in setting up a pair of BARs being used to track a 64 MB block of prefetchable addresses for a device residing in the system memory map. In the diagram, the BARs are shown at three points in the configuration process:

1. The uninitialized BARs are as they look after power-up or a reset. The designer has hard-coded lower bits of the lower BAR to indicate the request type and size; the upper BAR bits are all read-write. System software will first write all 1's to both BARs to set all read-write bits = 1. Of course, the hard-coded bits in the lower BAR are unaffected by the configuration write.
2. The second view of the BARs in Figure 3-18 on page 141 shows them as they look after configuration software has performed the write of all 1's to both. The next step in configuration is a read of the BARs to check the request. Table 3-9 on page 142 summarizes the results of this configuration read.
3. The third view of the BAR pair Figure 3-18 on page 141 indicates conditions after configuration software has performed two configuration writes (Type 0) to program the two halves of the 64 bit start address for the block. In this example, the device start address is 16GB, so bit 1 of the Upper BAR (address bit 33 in the BAR pair) is written = 1 (2^{33} = 16GB); all other read-write bits in both BARs are written = 0's.

At this point the configuration of the BAR pair is complete. Once software enables memory address decoding in the PCI command register, the device will claim memory transactions in the range 16GB to 16GB+64MB.

Figure 3-18: 64-Bit Prefetchable Memory BAR Set Up

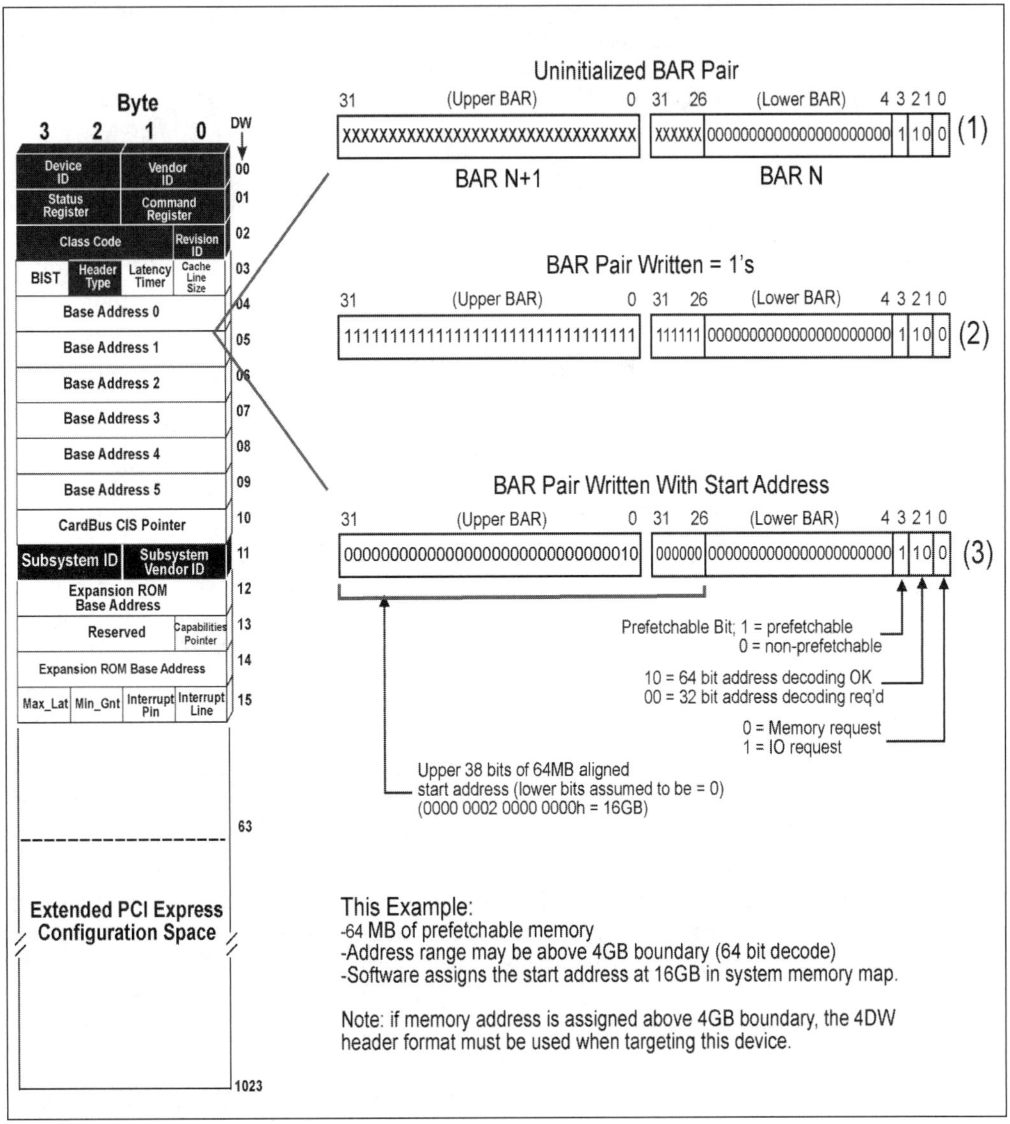

Table 3-9: Results Of Reading The BAR Pair after Writing All "1s" To Both

BAR	BAR Bits	Meaning
Lower	0	Read back as a "0", indicating a memory request
Lower	2:1	Read back as 10 b indicating the target supports a 64 bit address decoder, and that the first BAR is concatenated with the next
Lower	3	Read back as a "1", indicating request is for prefetchable memory
Lower	25:4	All read back as "0", used to help indicate the size of the request (also see bit 26)
Lower	31:26	All read back as "1" because software has not yet programmed the upper bits with a start address for the block. Note that because bit 26 was the first bit (above bit 3) to read back as written (=1); this indicates the memory request size is 64MB (2^{26} = 64MB).
Upper	31:0	All read back as "1". These bits will be used as the upper 32 bits of the 64-bit start address programmed by system software.

BAR Setup Example Three: 256-Byte IO Request

Figure 3-19 on page 143 depicts the basic steps in setting up a BAR which is being used to track a 256 byte block of IO addresses for a legacy PCI Express device residing in the system IO map. In the diagram, the BAR is shown at three points in the configuration process:

1. The uninitialized BAR in Figure 3-19 is as it looks after power-up or a reset. System software first writes all 1's to the BAR to set all read-write bits = 1. Of course, the hard-coded bits are unaffected by the configuration write.
2. The second view of the BAR shown in Figure 3-19 on page 143 is as it looks after configuration software has performed the write of all 1's to it. The next step in configuration is a read of the BAR to check the request. Table 3-10 on page 144 summarizes the results of this configuration read.
3. The third view of the BAR shown Figure 3-19 on page 143 is as it looks after configuration software has performed another configuration write (Type 0) to program the start address for the IO block. In this example, the device start address is 16KB, so bit 14 is written = 1 (2^{14} = 16KB); all other upper bits are written = 0's.

At this point the configuration of the IO BAR is complete. Once software enables IO address decoding in the PCI command register, the device will claim IO transactions in the range 16KB to 16KB+256.

Figure 3-19: IO BAR Set Up

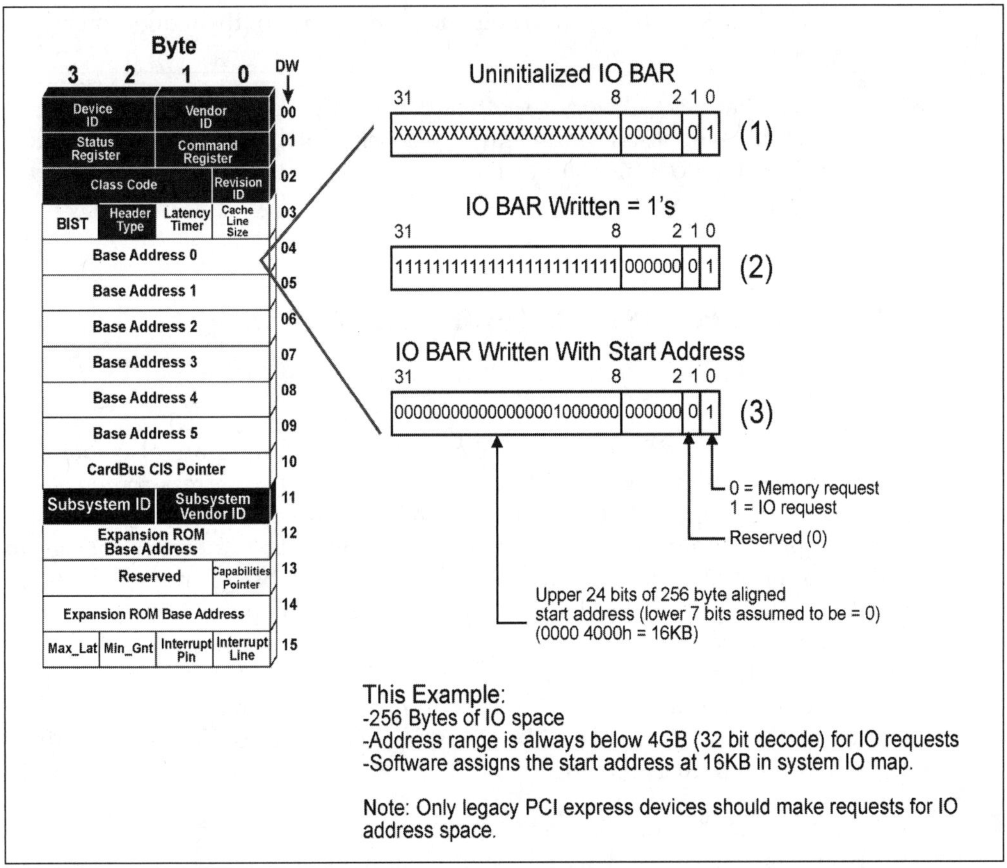

Table 3-10: Results Of Reading The IO BAR after Writing All "1s" To It

BAR Bits	Meaning
0	Read back as a "1", indicating an IO request
1	Reserved. Tied low and read back as "0".
7:2	All read back as "0", used to help indicate the size of the request (also see bit 8)
31:8	All read back as "1" because software has not yet programmed the upper bits with a start address for the block. Note that because bit 8 was the first bit (above bit 1) to read back as written (=1); this indicates the IO request size is 256 bytes ($2^8 = 256$).

Base/Limit Registers, Type 1 Header Only

General

The second set of configuration registers related to routing are also found in Type 1 configuration headers and used when forwarding address-routed TLPs. Marked "<2" in Figure 3-16 on page 137, these are the three sets of Base/Limit registers programmed in each bridge interface to enable a switch/bridge to claim and forward address-routed TLPs to a secondary bus. Three sets of Base/Limit Registers are needed because transactions are handled differently (e.g. prefetching, write-posting, etc.) in the prefetchable memory, non-prefetchable memory (MMIO), and IO address domains. The Base Register in each pair establishes the start address for the community of downstream devices and the Limit Register defines the upper address for that group of devices. The three sets of Base/Limit Registers include:

- Prefetchable Memory Base and Limit Registers
- Non-Prefetchable Memory Base and Limit Register
- I/O Base and Limit Registers

Prefetchable Memory Base/Limit Registers

The Prefetchable Memory Base/Limit registers are located at DW 9 and Prefetchable Memory Base/Limit Upper registers at DW 10-11 within the header 1. These registers track all downstream prefetchable memory devices. Either 32 bit or 64 bit addressing can be supported by these registers. If the

Upper Registers are not implemented, only 32 bits of memory addressing is available, and the TLP headers mapping to this space will be the 3DW format. If the Upper registers and system software maps the device above the 4GB boundary, TLPs accessing the device will carry the 4DW header format. In the example shown in Figure 3-20 on page 145, a 6GB prefetchable address range is being set up for the secondary link of a switch.

Register programming in the example shown in Figure 3-20 on page 145 is summarized in Table 3-11.

Figure 3-20: 6GB, 64-Bit Prefetchable Memory Base/Limit Register Set Up

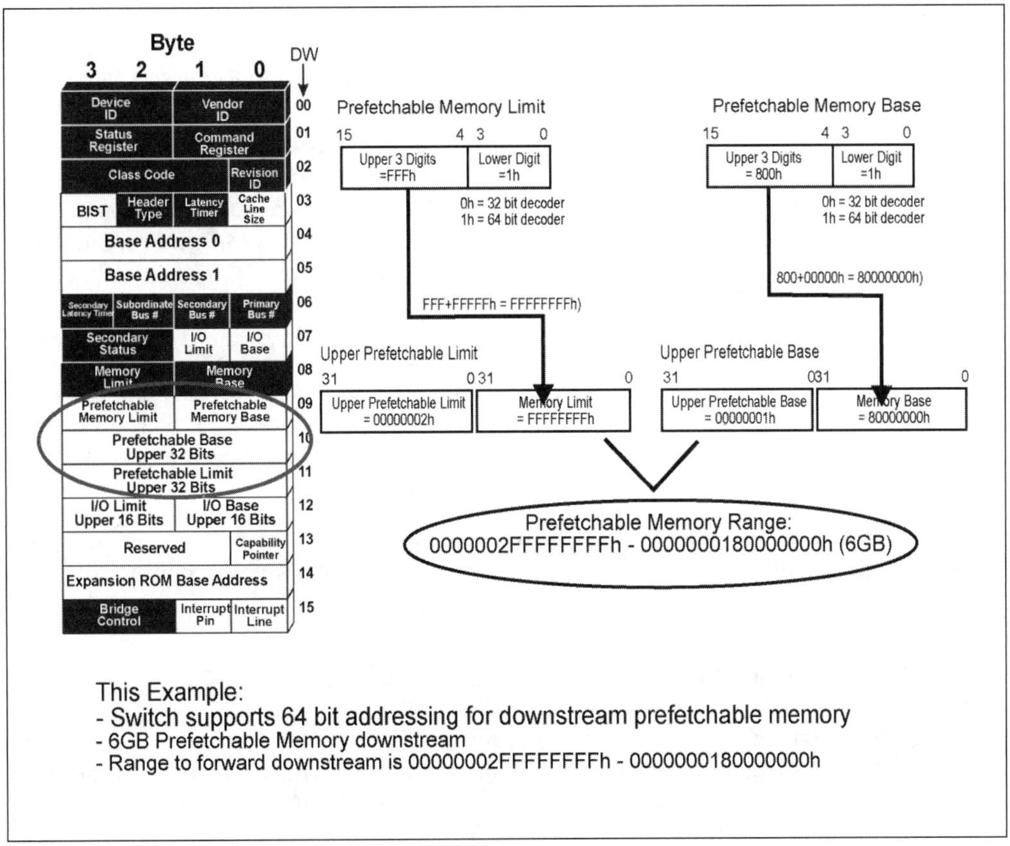

Table 3-11: 6 GB, 64-Bit Prefetchable Base/Limit Register Setup

Register	Value	Use
Prefetchable Memory Base	8001h	Upper 3 nibbles (800h) are used to provide most significant 3 digits of the 32-bit Base Address for Prefetchable Memory behind this switch. The lower 5 digits of the address are assumed to be 00000h. The least significant nibble of this register value (1h) indicates that a 64 bit address decoder is supported and that the Upper Base/Limit Registers are also used.
Prefetchable Memory Limit	FFF1h	Upper 3 nibbles (FFFh) are used to provide most significant 3 digits of the 32-bit Limit Address for Prefetchable Memory behind this switch. The lower 5 digits of the address are assumed to be FFFFFh. The least significant nibble of this register value (1h) indicates that a 64 bit address decoder is supported and that the Upper Base/Limit Registers are also used.
Prefetchable Memory Base Upper 32 Bits	00000001h	Upper 32 bits of the 64-bit Base address for Prefetchable Memory behind this switch.
Prefetchable Memory Limit Upper 32 Bits	00000002h	Upper 32 bits of the 64-bit Limit address for Prefetchable Memory behind this switch.

Non-Prefetchable Memory Base/Limit Registers

Non-Prefetchable Memory Base/Limit (at DW 8). These registers are used to track all downstream non-prefetchable memory (memory mapped IO) devices. Non-prefetchable memory devices are limited to 32 bit addressing; TLPs targeting them always use the 3DW header format.

Register programming in the example shown in Figure 3-21 on page 147 is summarized in Table 3-12.

Figure 3-21: 2MB, 32-Bit Non-Prefetchable Base/Limit Register Set Up

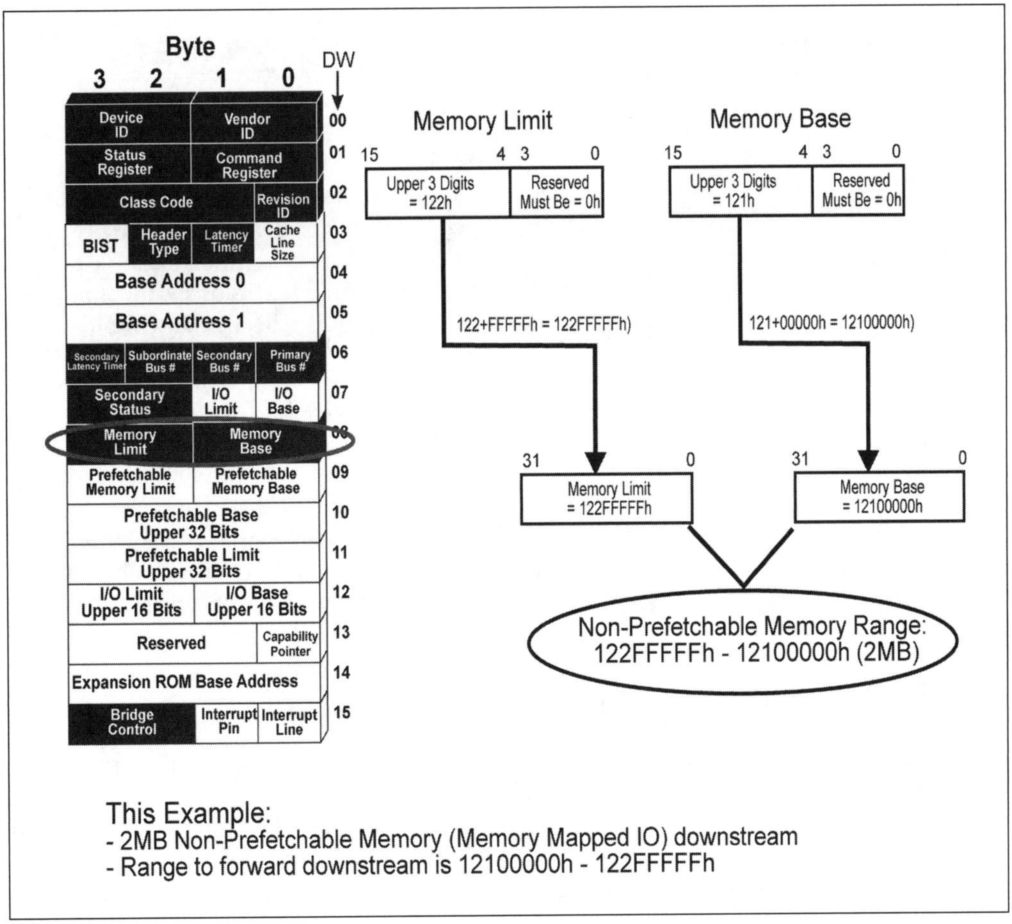

Table 3-12: 2MB, 32-Bit Non-Prefetchable Base/Limit Register Setup

Register	Value	Use
Memory Base (Non-Prefetchable)	1210h	Upper 3 nibbles (121h) are used to provide most significant 3 digits of the 32-bit Base Address for Non-Prefetchable Memory behind this switch. The lower 5 digits of the address are assumed to be 00000h. The least significant nibble of this register value (0h) is reserved and should be set = 0.
Memory Limit (Non-Prefetchable)	1220h	Upper 3 nibbles (122h) are used to provide most significant 3 digits of the 32-bit Limit Address for Prefetchable Memory behind this switch. The lower 5 digits of the address are assumed to be FFFFFh. The least significant nibble of this register value (0h) is reserved and should be set = 0.

IO Base/Limit Registers

IO Base/Limit (at DW 7) and IO Base/Limit Upper registers (at DW 12). These registers are used to track all downstream IO target devices. If the Upper Registers are used, then IO address space may be extended to a full 32 bits (4GB). If they are not implemented, then IO address space is limited to 16 bits (64KB). In either case, TLPs targeting these IO devices always carry the 3DW header format.

Register programming in the example shown in Figure 3-22 on page 149 is summarized in Table 3-13 on page 150.

Figure 3-22: IO Base/Limit Register Set Up

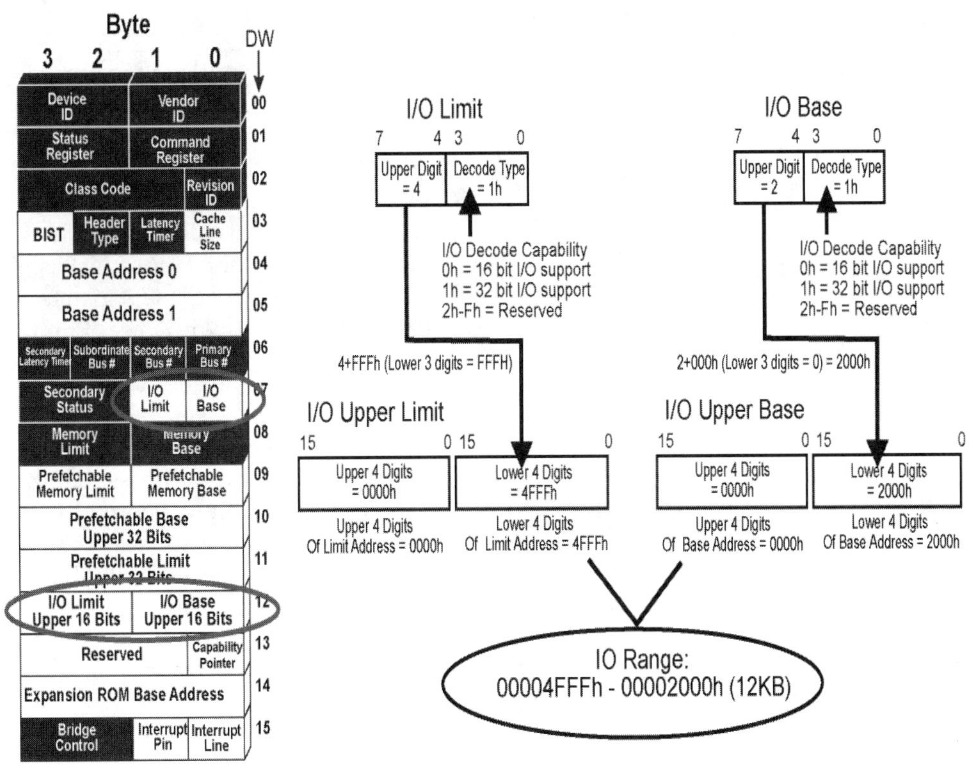

This Example:
- 12KB IO Behind Bridge
- Range to forward downstream is 4FFFh - 2000h.
- Because bridge supports Upper I/O Base/Limit registers, these will be programmed = 0.

Table 3-13: 256 Byte IO Base/Limit Register Setup

Register	Value	Use
IO Base	21h	Upper nibble (2h) specifies the most significant hex digit of the 32 bit IO Base address (the lower digits are 000h) The lower nibble (1h) indicates that the device supports 32 bit IO behind the bridge interface. This also means the device implements the Upper IO Base/ Limit register set, and those registers will be concatenated with Base/Limit.
IO Limit	41h	Upper nibble (4h) specifies the most significant hex digit of the 32 bit IO Limit address (the lower digits are FFFh). The lower nibble (1h) indicates that the device supports 32 bit IO behind the bridge interface. This also means the device implements the Upper IO Base/ Limit register set, and those registers will be concatenated with Base/Limit.
IO Base Upper 16 Bits	0000h	Upper 16 bits of the 32-bit Base address for IO behind this switch.
IO Limit Upper 16 Bits	0000h	Upper 16 bits of the 32-bit Limit address for IO behind this switch.

Bus Number Registers, Type 1 Header Only

The third set of configuration registers related to routing are used when forwarding ID-routed TLPs, including configuration cycles and completions and optionally messages. These are marked "<3" in Figure 3-16 on page 137. As in PCI, a switch/bridge interface requires three registers: Primary Bus Number, Secondary Bus Number, and Subordinate bus number. The function of these registers is summarized here.

Primary Bus Number

The Primary Bus Number register contains the bus (link) number to which the upstream side of a bridge (switch) is connected. In PCI Express, the primary bus is the one in the direction of the Root Complex and host processor.

Secondary Bus Number

The Secondary Bus Number register contains the bus (link) number to which the downstream side of a bridge (switch) is connected.

Subordinate Bus Number

The Subordinate Bus Number register contains the highest bus (link) number on the downstream side of a bridge (switch). The Subordinate and Secondary Bus Number registers will contain the same value unless there is another bridge (switch) on the secondary side.

A Switch Is a Two-Level Bridge Structure

Because PCI does not natively support bridges with multiple downstream ports, PCI Express switch devices appear logically as two-level PCI bridge structures, consisting of a single bridge to the primary link and an internal PCI bus which hosts one or more virtual bridges to secondary interfaces. Each bridge interface has an independent Type 1 format configuration header with its own sets of Base/Limit Registers and Bus Number Registers. Figure 3-23 on page 152 illustrates the bus numbering associated with the external links and internal bus of a switch. Note that the secondary bus on the primary link interface is the internal virtual bus, and that the primary interface of all downstream link interfaces connect to the internal bus logically.

Figure 3-23: Bus Number Registers In A Switch

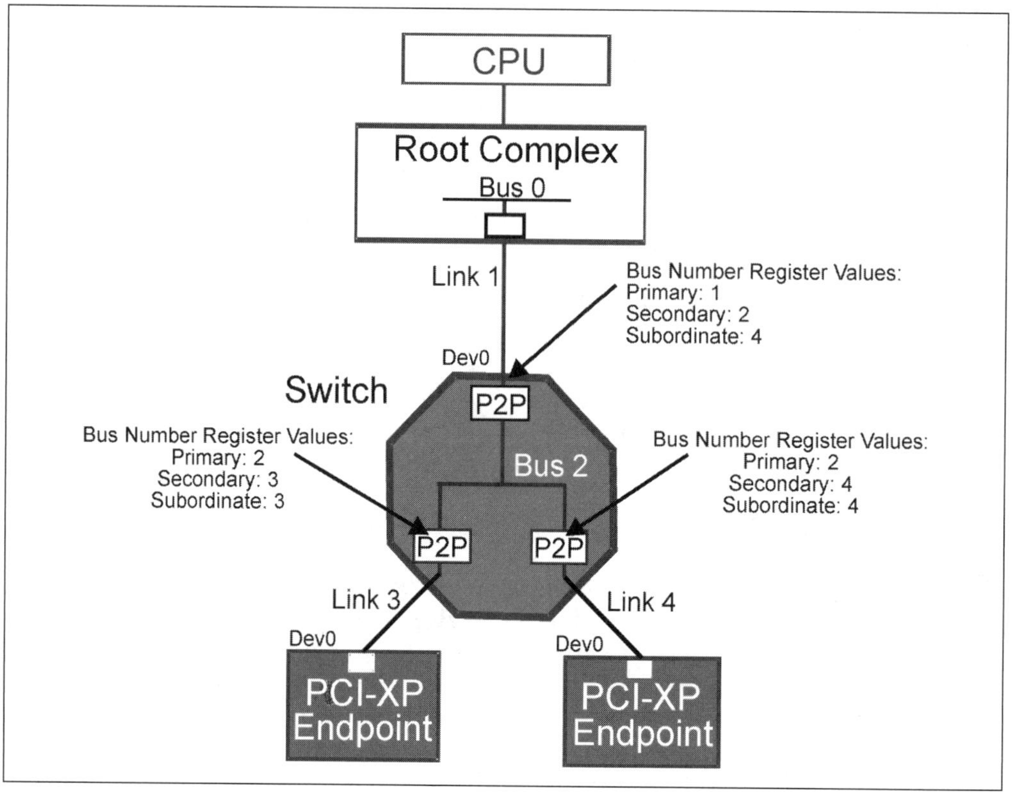

4 Packet-Based Transactions

The Previous Chapter

The previous chapter described the general concepts of PCI Express transaction routing and the mechanisms used by a device in deciding whether to accept, forward, or reject a packet arriving at an ingress port. Because Data Link Layer Packets (DLLPs) and Physical Layer *ordered set* link traffic are never forwarded, the emphasis here is on Transaction Layer Packet (TLP) types and the three routing methods associated with them: address routing, ID routing, and implicit routing. Included is a summary of configuration methods used in PCI Express to set up PCI-compatible plug-and-play addressing within system IO and memory maps, as well as key elements in the PCI Express packet protocol used in making routing decisions.

This Chapter

Information moves between PCI Express devices in packets, and the two major classes of packets are *Transaction Layer Packets* (TLPs), and *Data Link Layer Packets* (DLLPs). The use, format, and definition of all TLP and DLLP packet types and their related fields are detailed in this chapter.

The Next Chapter

The next chapter discusses the Ack/Nak Protocol that verifies the delivery of TLPs between each port as they travel between the requester and completer devices. This chapter details the hardware retry mechanism that is automatically triggered when a TLP transmission error is detected on a given link.

Introduction to the Packet-Based Protocol

The PCI Express protocol improves upon methods used by earlier busses (e.g. PCI) to exchange data and to signal system events. In addition to supporting basic memory, IO, and configuration read/write transactions, the links eliminate many sideband signals and replaces them with in-band messages.

With the exception of the logical idle indication and physical layer *Ordered Sets*, all information moves across an active PCI Express link in fundamental chunks called packets which are comprised of 10 bit control (K) and data (D) symbols. The two major classes of packets exchanged between two PCI Express devices are high level *Transaction Layer Packets* (TLPs), and low-level link maintenance packets called *Data Link Layer Packets* (DLLPs). Collectively, the various TLPs and DLLPs allow two devices to perform memory, IO, and Configuration Space transactions reliably and use messages to initiate power management events, generate interrupts, report errors, etc. Figure 4-1 on page 155 depicts TLPs and DLLPs on a PCI Express link.

Why Use A Packet-Based Transaction Protocol

There are some distinct advantages in using a packet-based protocol, especially when it comes to data integrity. Three important aspects of PCI Express packet protocol help promote data integrity during link transmission:

Packet Formats Are Well Defined

Some early bus protocols (e.g. PCI) allow transfers of indeterminate (and unlimited) size, making identification of payload boundaries impossible until the end of the transfer. In addition, an early transaction end might be signaled by either agent (e.g. target disconnect on a write or pre-emption of the initiator during a read), resulting in a partial transfer. In these cases, it is difficult for the sender of data to calculate and send a checksum or CRC covering an entire payload, when it may terminate unexpectedly. Instead, PCI uses a simple parity scheme which is applied and checked for each bus phase completed.

In contrast, each PCI Express packet has a known size and format, and the packet *header*--positioned at the beginning of each DLLP and TLP packet-- indicates the packet type and presence of any optional fields. The size of each packet field is either fixed or defined by the packet type. The size of any data payload is conveyed in the TLP header *Length* field. Once a transfer commences, there are no early transaction terminations by the recipient. This structured packet format makes it possible to insert additional information into the packet into prescribed locations, including framing symbols, CRC, and a packet sequence number (TLPs only).

Figure 4-1: TLP And DLLP Packets

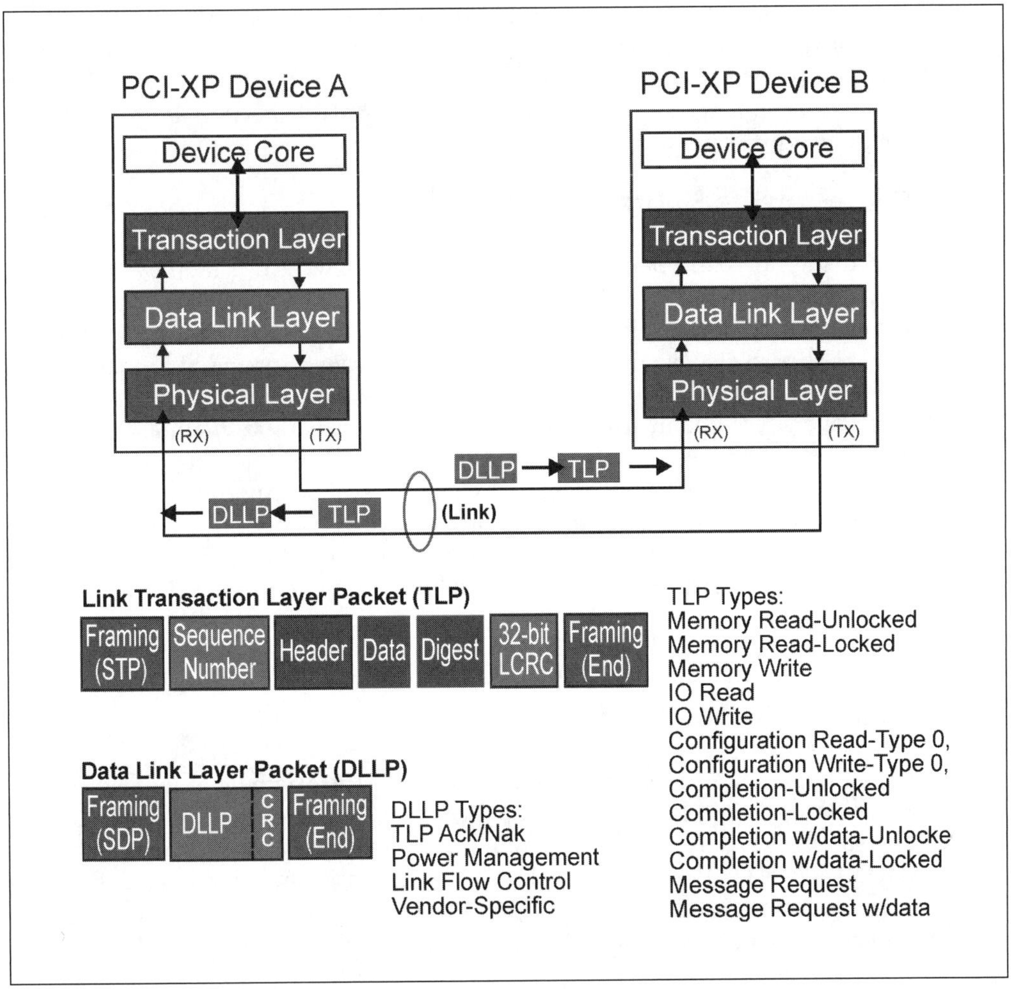

Framing Symbols Indicate Packet Boundaries

Each TLP and DLLP packet sent is framed with a Start and End control symbol, clearly defining the packet boundaries to the receiver. Note that the Start and End control (K) symbols appended to packets by the transmitting device are 10 bits each. This is a big improvement over PCI and PCI-X which use the assertion and de-assertion of a single FRAME# signal to indicate the beginning and end of a transaction. A glitch on the FRAME# signal (or any of the other PCI/PCIX control signals) could cause a target to misconstrue bus events. In contrast, a PCI Express receiver must properly decode a complete 10 bit symbol before concluding link activity is beginning or ending. Unexpected or unrecognized control symbols are handled as errors.

CRC Protects Entire Packet

Unlike the side-band parity signals used by PCI devices during the address and each data phase of a transaction, the in-band 16-bit or 32-bit PCI Express CRC value "protects" the entire packet (other than framing symbols). In addition to CRC, TLP packets also have a packet *sequence number* appended to them by the transmitter so that if an error is detected at the receiver, the specific packet(s) which were received in error may be resent. The transmitter maintains a copy of each TLP sent in a *Retry Buffer* until it is checked and acknowledged by the receiver. This TLP acknowledgement mechanism (sometimes referred to as the *Ack/Nak* protocol) forms the basis of link-level TLP error correction and is very important in deep topologies where devices may be many links away from the host in the event an error occurs and CPU intervention would otherwise be needed.

Transaction Layer Packets

In PCI Express terminology, high-level transactions originate at the device core of the transmitting device and terminate at the core of the receiving device. The Transaction Layer is the starting point in the assembly of outbound Transaction Layer Packets (TLPs), and the end point for disassembly of inbound TLPs at the receiver. Along the way, the Data Link Layer and Physical Layer of each device contribute to the packet assembly and disassembly as described below.

TLPs Are Assembled And Disassembled

Figure 4-2 on page 158 depicts the general flow of TLP assembly at the transmit side of a link and disassembly at the receiver. The key stages in Transaction Layer Packet protocol are listed below. The numbers correspond to those in Figure 4-2.

1. Device B's core passes a request for service to the PCI Express hardware interface. How this done is not covered by the PCI Express Specification, and is device-specific. General information contained in the request would include:
   — The PCI Express command to be performed
   — Start address or ID of target (if address routing or ID routing are used)
   — Transaction type (memory read or write, configuration cycle, etc.)
   — Data payload size (and the data to send, if any)
   — Virtual Channel/Traffic class information
   — Attributes of the transfer: No Snoop bit set?, Relaxed Ordering set?, etc.
2. The Transaction Layer builds the TLP header, data payload, and digest based on the request from the core. Before sending a TLP to the Data Link Layer, flow control credits and ordering rules must be applied.
3. When the TLP is received at the Data Link Layer, a Sequence Number is assigned and a Link CRC is calculated for the TLP (includes Sequence Number). The TLP is then passed on to the Physical Layer.
4. At the Physical Layer, byte striping, scrambling, encoding, and serialization are performed. STP and END control (K) characters are appended to the packet. The packet is sent out on the transmit side of the link.
5. At the Physical Layer receiver of Device A, de-serialization, framing symbol check, decoding, and byte un-striping are performed. Note that at the Physical Layer, the first level or error checking is performed (on the control codes).
6. The Data Link Layer of the receiver calculates CRC and checks it against the received value. It also checks the Sequence Number of the TLP for violations. If there are no errors, it passes the TLP up to the Transaction Layer of the receiver. The information is decoded and passed to the core of Device A. The Data Link Layer of the receiver will also notify the transmitter of the success or failure in processing the TLP by sending an Ack or Nak DLLP to the transmitter. In the event of a Nak (No Acknowledge), the transmitter will re-send all TLPs in its Retry Buffer.

Figure 4-2: PCI Express Layered Protocol And TLP Assembly/Disassembly

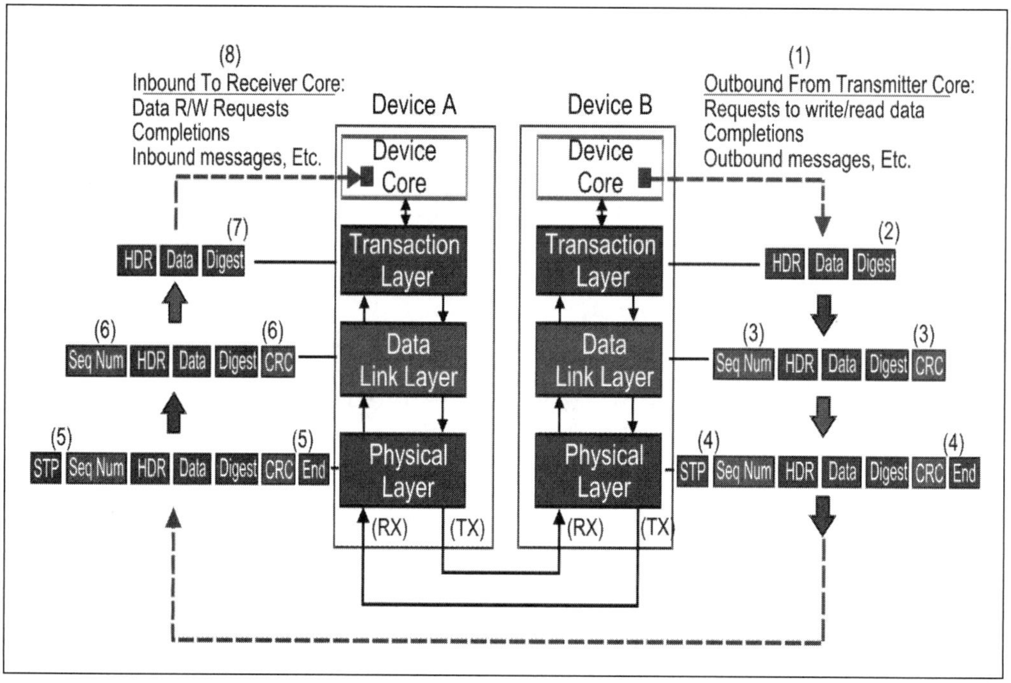

Device Core Requests Access to Four Spaces

Transactions are carried out between PCI Express requesters and completers, using four separate address spaces: Memory, IO, Configuration, and Message. (See Table 4-1.)

Table 4-1: PCI Express Address Space And Transaction Types

Address Space	Transaction Types	Purpose
Memory	Read, Write	Transfer data to or from a location in the system memory map. The protocol also supports a *locked memory* read transaction.
IO	Read, Write	Transfer data to or from a location in the system IO map. PCI Express IO address assignment to legacy devices. IO addressing is not permitted for Native PCI Express devices.
Configuration	Read, Write	Transfer data to or from a location in the configuration space of a PCI Express device. As in PCI, configuration is used to discover device capabilities, program plug-and-play features, and check status using the 4KB PCI Express configuration space.
Message	Baseline, Vendor-specific	Provides in-band messaging and event reporting (without consuming memory or IO address resources). These are handled the same as posted write transactions.

TLP Transaction Variants Defined

In accessing the four address spaces, PCI Express Transaction Layer Packets (TLPs) carry a header field, called the *Type* field, which encodes the specific command variant to be used. Table 4-2 on page 160 summarizes the allowed transactions:

Table 4-2: TLP Header Type Field Defines Transaction Variant

TLP *Type*	Acronym
Memory Read Request	(MRd)
Memory Read Lock Request	(MRdLk)
Memory Write Request	(MWr)
IO Read Request	(IORd)
IO Write Request	(IOWr)
Config Type 0 Read Request	(CfgRd0)
Config Type 0 Write Request	(CfgWr0)
Config Type 1 Read Request	(CfgRd1)
Config Type 1 Write Request	(CfgWr1)
Message Request	(Msg)
Message Request W/Data	(MsgD)
Completion	(Cpl)
Completion W/Data	(CplD)
Completion-Locked	(CplLk)
Completion W/Data	(CplDLk)

TLP Structure

The basic usage of each component of a Transaction Layer Packet is defined in Table 4-3 on page 161.

Table 4-3: TLP Header Type Field Defines Transaction Variant

TLP Component	Protocol Layer	Component Use
Header	Transaction Layer	3DW or 4DW (12 or 16 bytes) in size. Format varies with type, but Header defines transaction parameters: • Transaction type • Intended recipient address, ID, etc. • Transfer size (if any), Byte Enables • Ordering attribute • Cache coherency attribute • Traffic Class
Data	Transaction Layer	Optional field. 0-1024 DW Payload, which may be further qualified with Byte Enables to get byte address and byte transfer size resolution.
Digest	Transaction Layer	Optional field. If present, always 1 DW in size. Used for end-to-end CRC (ECRC) and data poisoning.

Generic TLP Header Format

Figure 4-3 on page 162 illustrates the format and contents of a generic TLP 3DW header. In this section, fields common to nearly all transactions are summarized. In later sections, header format differences associated with the specific transaction types are covered.

Figure 4-3: Generic TLP Header Fields

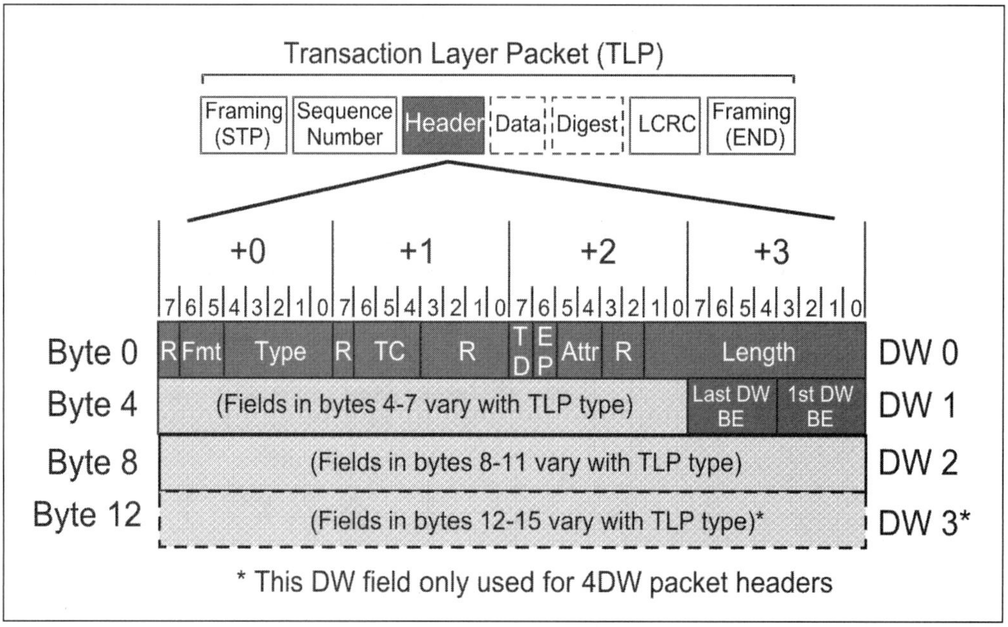

Generic Header Field Summary

Table 4-4 on page 163 summarizes the size and use of each of the generic TLP header fields. Note that fields marked "R" in Figure 4-3 on page 162 are reserved and should be set = 0.

·

Table 4-4: Generic Header Field Summary

Header Field	Header Location	Field Use
Length [9:0]	Byte 3 Bit 7:0 Byte 2 Bit 1:0	TLP data payload transfer size, in DW. Maximum transfer size is 10 bits, 2^{10} = 1024 DW (4KB). Encoding: 00 0000 0001b = 1DW 00 0000 0010b = 2DW . . 11 1111 1111b = 1023 DW 00 0000 0000b = 1024 DW
Attr (Attributes)	Byte 2 Bit 5:4	Bit 5 = Relaxed ordering. When set = 1, PCI-X relaxed ordering is enabled for this TLP. If set = 0, then strict PCI ordering is used. Bit 4 = No Snoop. When set = 1, requester is indicating that no host cache coherency issues exist with respect to this TLP. System hardware is not required to cause processor cache snoop for coherency. When set = 0, PCI -type cache snoop protection is required.
EP (Poisoned Data)	Byte 2 Bit 6	If set = 1, the data accompanying this data should be considered invalid although the transaction is being allowed to complete normally.
TD (TLP Digest Field Present)	Byte 2 Bit 7	If set = 1, the optional 1 DW TLP Digest field is included with this TLP that contains an ECRC value. Some rules: Presence of the Digest field must be checked by all receivers (using this bit). • A TLP with TD = 1, but no Digest field is handled as a Malformed TLP. • If a device supports checking ECRC and TD=1, it must perform the ECRC check. • If a device does not support checking ECRC (optional) at the ultimate destination, the device must ignore the digest.

Table 4-4: Generic Header Field Summary

Header Field	Header Location	Field Use
TC (Traffic Class)	Byte 1 Bit 6:4	These three bits are used to encode the traffic class to be applied to this TLP and to the completion associated with it (if any). 000b = Traffic Class 0 (Default) . . 111b = Traffic Class 7 TC 0 is the default class, and TC 1-7 are used in providing differentiated services. See "Traffic Classes and Virtual Channels" on page 256 for additional information.
Type[4:0]	Byte 0 Bit 4:0	These 5 bits encode the transaction variant used with this TLP. The Type field is used with Fmt [1:0] field to specify transaction type, header size, and whether data payload is present. See below for additional information of Type/Fmt encoding for each transaction type.
Fmt[1:0] Format	Byte 0 Bit 6:5	These two bits encode information about header size and whether a data payload will be part of the TLP: 00b 3DW header, no data 01b 4DW header, no data 10b 3DW header, with data 11b 4DW header, with data See below for additional information of Type/Fmt encoding for each transaction type.
First DW Byte Enables	Byte 7 Bit 3:0	These four high-true bits map one-to-one to the bytes within the first double word of payload. Bit 3 = 1: Byte 3 in first DW is valid; otherwise not Bit 2 = 1: Byte 2 in first DW is valid; otherwise not Bit 1 = 1: Byte 1 in first DW is valid; otherwise not Bit 9 = 1: Byte 0 in first DW is valid; otherwise not See below for details on Byte Enable use.

Table 4-4: Generic Header Field Summary

Header Field	Header Location	Field Use
Last DW Byte Enables	Byte 7 Bit 7:4	These four high-true bits map one-to-one to the bytes within the first double word of payload. Bit 3 = 1: Byte 3 in last DW is valid; otherwise not Bit 2 = 1: Byte 2 in last DW is valid; otherwise not Bit 1 = 1: Byte 1 in last DW is valid; otherwise not Bit 9 = 1: Byte 0 in last DW is valid; otherwise not See below for details on Byte Enable use.

Header *Type/Format* Field Encodings

Table 4-5 on page 165 summarizes the encodings used in TLP header Type and Format (Fmt) fields.

Table 4-5: TLP Header Type and Format Field Encodings

TLP	FMT[1:0]	TYPE [4:0]
Memory Read Request (MRd)	00 = 3DW, no data 01 = 4DW, no data	0 0000
Memory Read Lock Request (MRdLk)	00 = 3DW, no data 01 = 4DW, no data	0 0001
Memory Write Request (MWr)	10 = 3DW, w/ data 11 = 4DW, w/ data	0 0000
IO Read Request (IORd)	00 = 3DW, no data	00010
IO Write Request (IOWr)	10 = 3DW, w/ data	0 0010
Config Type 0 Read Request (CfgRd0)	00 = 3DW, no data	0 0100
Config Type 0 Write Request (CfgWr0)	10 = 3DW, w/ data	0 0100
Config Type 1 Read Request (CfgRd1)	00 = 3DW, no data	0 0101
Config Type 1 Write Request (CfgWr1)	10 = 3DW, w/ data	0 0101

Table 4-5: TLP Header Type and Format Field Encodings

TLP	FMT[1:0]	TYPE [4:0]
Message Request (Msg)	01 = 4DW, no data	1 0 rrr* (for rrr, see routing subfield)
Message Request W/Data (MsgD)	11 = 4DW, w/ data	1 0rrr* (for rrr, see routing subfield)
Completion (Cpl)	00 = 3DW, no data	0 1010
Completion W/Data (CplD)	10 = 3DW, w/ data	0 1010
Completion-Locked (CplLk)	00 = 3DW, no data	0 1011
Completion W/Data (CplDLk)	10 = 3DW, w/ data	0 1011

The Digest and ECRC Field

The digest field and End-to-End CRC (ECRC) is optional as is a device's ability to generate and check ECRC. If supported and enabled by software, devices must calculate and apply ECRC for all TLPs that the device originates. Also, devices that support ECRC checking must also support Advanced Error Reporting.

ECRC Generation and Checking. This book does not detail the algorithm and process of calculating ECRC, but is defined within the specification. ECRC covers all fields that do not change as the TLP is forwarded across the fabric. The ECRC includes all invariant fields of the TLP header and the data payload, if present. All variant fields are set to 1 for calculating the ECRC, include:

- **Bit 0 of the Type field is variant** — this bit changes when the transaction type is altered for a packet. For example, a configuration transaction being forwarded to a remote link (across one or more switches) begins as a type 1 configuration transaction. When the transaction reaches the destination link, it is converted to a type 0 configuration transaction by changing bit 0 of the type field.
- Error/Poisoned (EP) bit — this bit can be set as a TLP traverses the fabric in the event that the data field associated with the packet has been corrupted. This is also referred to as error forwarding.

Who Can Check ECRC? The ECRC check is intended for the device that is the ultimate receipient of the TLP. Link CRC checking verifies that a TLP traverses a given link before being forwarded to the next link, but ECRC is intended to verify that the packet send has not been altered in its journey between the Requester and Completer. Switches in the path must maintain the integrity of the TD bit because corruption of TD will cause an error at the ultimate target device.

The specification makes two statements regarding a Switch's role in ECRC checking:

- A switch that supports ECRC checking performs this check on TLPs destined to a location within the Switch itself. "On all other TLPs a Switch must preserve the ECRC (forward it untouched) as an integral part of the TLP."
- "Note that a Switch may perform ECRC checking on TLPs passing through the Switch. ECRC Errors detected by the Switch are reported in the same way any other device would report them, but do not alter the TLPs passage through the Switch."

These statements may appear to contradict each other. However, the first statement does not explicitly state that an ECRC check cannot be made in the process of forwarding the TLP untouched. The second statement clarifies that it is possible for switches, as well as the ultimate target device, to check and report ECRC.

Using Byte Enables

As in the PCI protocol, PCI Express requires a mechanism for reconciling its DW addressing and data transfers with the need, at times, for byte resolution in transfer sizes and transaction start/end addresses. To achieve byte resolution, PCI Express makes use of the two Byte Enable fields introduced earlier in Figure 4-3 on page 162 and in Table 4-4 on page 163.

The First DW Byte Enable field and the Last DW Byte Enable fields allow the requester to qualify the bytes of interest within the first and last double words transferred; this has the effect of allowing smaller transfers than a full double word and offsetting the start and end addresses from DW boundaries.

Byte Enable Rules.

1. Byte enable bits are high true. A value of "0" indicates the corresponding byte in the data payload should not be written by the completer. A value of "1", indicates it should.
2. If the valid data transferred is all within a single aligned double word, the

Last DW Byte enable field must be = 0000b.
3. If the header Length field indicates a transfer is more than 1DW, the First DW Byte Enable must have at least one bit enabled.
4. If the Length field indicates a transfer of 3DW or more, then neither the First DW Byte Enable field or the Last DW Byte Enable field may have discontinuous byte enable bits set. In these cases, the Byte Enable fields are only being used to offset the effective start address of a burst transaction.
5. Discontinuous byte enable bit patterns in the First DW Byte enable field are allowed if the transfer is 1DW.
6. Discontinuous byte enable bit patterns in both the First and Second DW Byte enable fields are allowed only if the transfer is Quadword aligned (2DWs).
7. A write request with a transfer length of 1DW and no byte enables set is legal, but has no effect on the completer.
8. If a read request of 1 DW is done with no byte enable bits set, the completer returns a 1DW data payload of undefined data. This may be used as a Flush mechanism. Because of ordering rules, a flush may be used to force all previously posted writes to memory before the completion is returned.

An example of byte enable use in this case is illustrated in Figure 4-4 on page 168. Note that the transfer length must extend from the first DW with any valid byte enabled to the last DW with any valid bytes enabled. Because the transfer is more than 2DW, the byte enables may only be used to specify the start address location (2d) and end address location (34d) of the transfer.

Figure 4-4: Using First DW and Last DW Byte Enable Fields

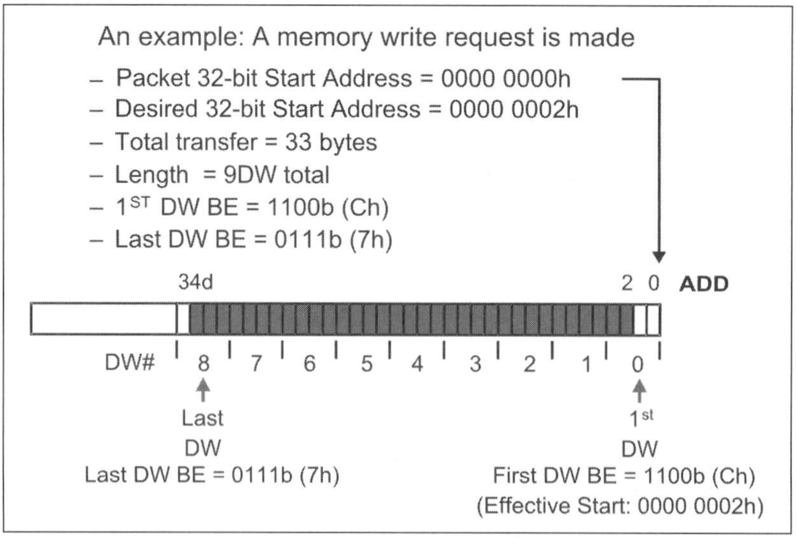

Transaction Descriptor Fields

As transactions move between requester and completer, it is important to uniquely identify a transaction, since many split transactions may be pending at any instant. To this end, the specification defines several important header fields that when used together form a unique Transaction Descriptor as illustrated in Figure 4-5.

Figure 4-5: Transaction Descriptor Fields

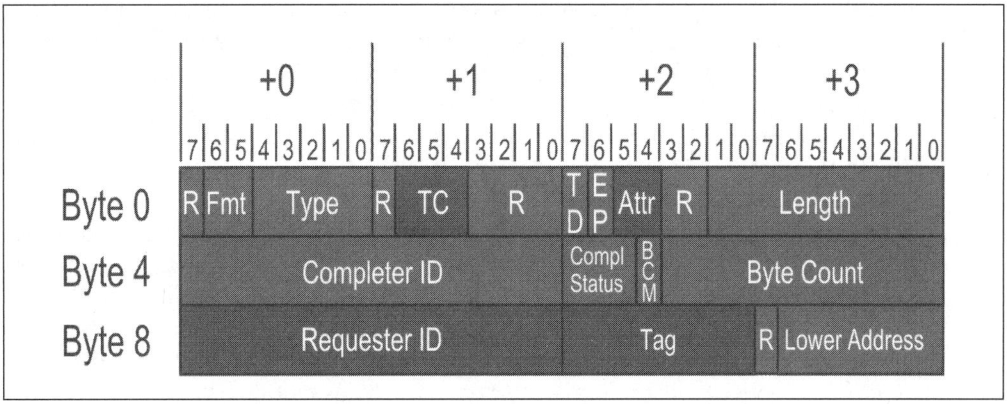

While the Transaction Descriptor fields are not in adjacent header locations, collectively they describe key transaction attributes, including:

Transaction ID. This is comprised of the Bus, Device, and Function Number of the TLP requester AND the Tag field of the TLP.

Traffic Class. Traffic Class (TC 0 -7) is inserted in the TLP by the requester, and travels unmodified through the topology to the completer. At every link, Traffic Class is mapped to one of the available virtual channels.

Transaction Attributes. These consist of the Relaxed Ordering and No Snoop bits. These are also set by the requester and travel with the packet to the completer.

Additional Rules For TLPs With Data Payloads

The following rules apply when a TLP includes a data payload.

1. The Length field refers to data payload only; the Digest field (if present) is not included in the Length.
2. The first byte of data in the payload (immediately after the header) is always associated with the lowest (start) address.
3. The Length field always represents an integral number of doublewords (DW) transferred. Partial doublewords are qualified using First and Last Byte Enable fields.
4. The PCI Express specification states that when multiple transactions are returned by a completer in response to a single memory request, that each intermediate transaction must end on naturally-aligned 64 and 128 byte address boundaries for a root complex (this is termed the Read Completion Boundary, or RCB). All other devices must break such transactions at naturally-aligned 128 byte boundaries. This behavior promotes system performance related to cache lines.
5. The Length field is reserved when sending message TLPs using the transaction *Msg*. The Length field is valid when sending the message with data variant *MsgD*.
6. PCI Express supports load tuning of links. This means that the data payload of a TLP must not exceed the current value in the Max_Payload_Size field of the Device Control Register. Only write transactions have data payloads, so this restriction does not apply to reads. A receiver is required to check for violations of the Max_Payload_Size limit during writes; violations are handled as Malformed TLPs.
7. Receivers also must check for discrepancies between the value in the Length field and the actual amount of data transferred in a TLP with data. Violations are also handled as Malformed TLPs.
8. Requests must not mix combinations of start address and transfer length which will cause a memory space access to cross a 4KB boundary. While checking is optional in this case, receivers checking for violations of this rule will report it as a Malformed TLP.

Building Transactions: TLP Requests & Completions

In this section, the format of 3DW and 4DW headers used to accomplish specific transaction types are described. Many of the generic fields described previously apply, but an emphasis is placed on the fields which are handled differently between transaction types.

IO Requests

While the PCI Express specification discourages the use of IO transactions, an allowance is made for legacy devices and software which may rely on a compatible device residing in the system IO map rather than the memory map. While the IO transactions can technically access a 32-bit IO range, in reality many systems (and CPUs) restrict IO access to the lower 16 bits (64KB) of this range. Figure 4-6 on page 171 depicts the system IO map and the 16/32 bit address boundaries. PCI Express non-legacy devices are memory-mapped, and not permitted to make requests for IO address allocation in their configuration Base Address Registers.

Figure 4-6: System IO Map

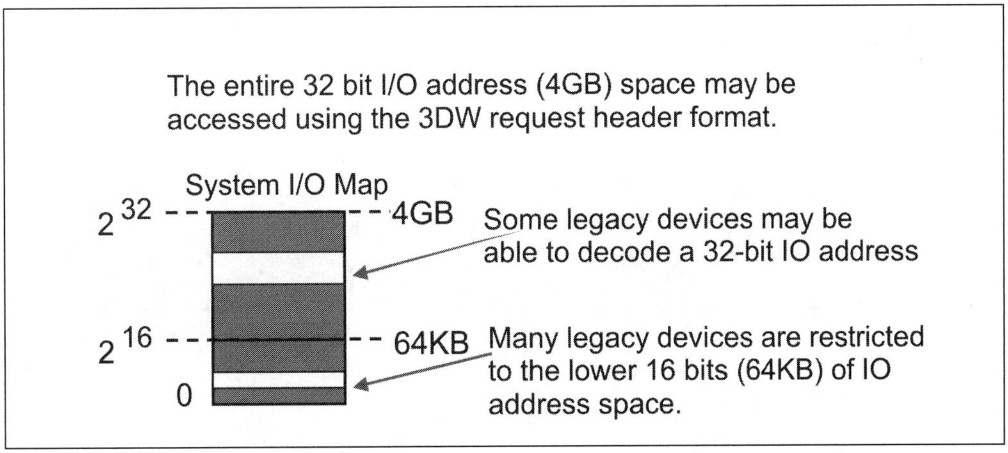

IO Request Header Format. Figure 4-7 on page 172 depicts the format of the 3DW IO request header. Each field in the header is described in the section that follows.

Figure 4-7: 3DW IO Request Header Format

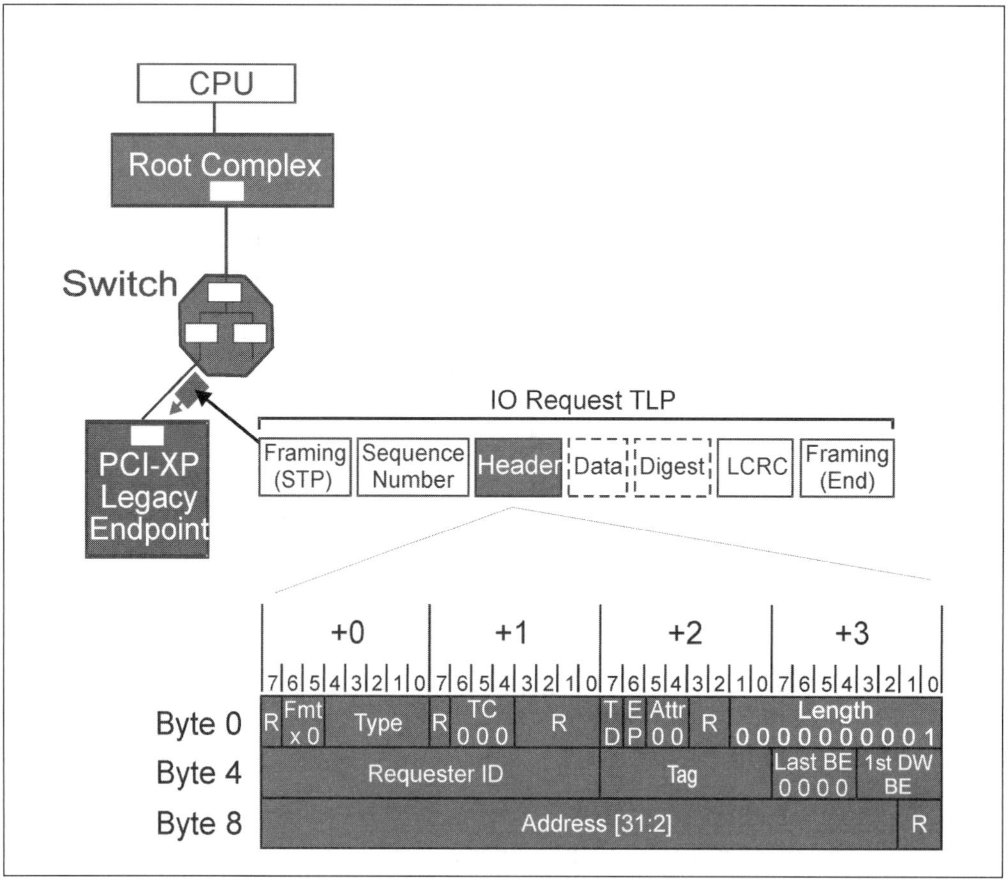

Definitions Of IO Request Header Fields. Table 4-6 on page 173 describes the location and use of each field in an IO request header.

Table 4-6: IO Request Header Fields

Field Name	Header Byte/Bit	Function
Length 9:0	Byte 3 Bit 7:0 Byte 2 Bit 1:0	Indicates data payload size in DW. For IO requests, this field is always = 1. Byte Enables are used to qualify bytes within DW.
Attr 1:0 (Attributes)	Byte 2 Bit 5:4	Attribute 1: Relaxed Ordering Bit Attribute 0: No Snoop Bit Both of these bits are always = 0 in IO requests.
EP	Byte 2 Bit 6	If = 1, indicates the data payload (if present) is poisoned.
TD	Byte 2 Bit 7	If = 1, indicates the presence of a digest field (1 DW) at the end of the TLP (preceding LCRC and END)
TC 2:0 (Transfer Class)	Byte 2 Bit 6:4	Indicates transfer class for the packet. TC is = 0 for all IO requests.
Type 4:0	Byte 0 Bit 4:0	TLP packet type field. Always set to 00010b for IO requests
Fmt 1:0 (Format)	Byte 0 Bit 6:5	Packet Format. IO requests are: 00b = IO Read (3DW without data) 10b = IO Write (3DW with data)
1st DW BE 3:0 (First DW Byte Enables)	Byte 7 Bit 3:0	These high true bits map one-to-one to qualify bytes within the DW payload. For IO requests, any bit combination is valid (including none)
Last BE 3:0 (Last DW Byte Enables)	Byte 7 Bit 7:4	These high true bits map one-to-one to qualify bytes within the last DW transferred. For IO requests, these bits must be 0000b. (Single DW)

Table 4-6: IO Request Header Fields

Field Name	Header Byte/Bit	Function
Tag 7:0	Byte 6 Bit 7:0	These bits are used to identify each outstanding request issued by the requester. As non-posted requests are sent, the next sequential tag is assigned. Default: only bits 4:0 are used (32 outstanding transactions at a time) If Extended Tag bit in PCI Express Control Register is set = 1, then all 8 bits may be used (256 tags).
Requester ID 15:0	Byte 5 Bit 7:0 Byte 4 Bit 7:0	Identifies the requester so a completion may be returned, etc. Byte 4, 7:0 = Bus Number Byte 5, 7:3 = Device Number Byte 5, 2:0 = Function Number
Address 31:2	Byte 8 Bit 7:2 Byte 7 Bit 7:0 Byte 6 Bit 7:0 Byte 5 Bit 7:0	The upper 30 bits of the 32-bit start address for the IO transfer. Note that the lower two bits of the 32 bit address are reserved (00b), forcing the start address to be DW aligned.

Memory Requests

PCI Express memory transactions include two classes: Read Request/Completion and Write Request. Figure 4-8 on page 175 depicts the system memory map and the 3DW and 4DW memory request packet formats. When request memory data transfer it is important to remember that memory transactions are never permitted to cross 4KB boundaries.

Figure 4-8: 3DW And 4DW Memory Request Header Formats

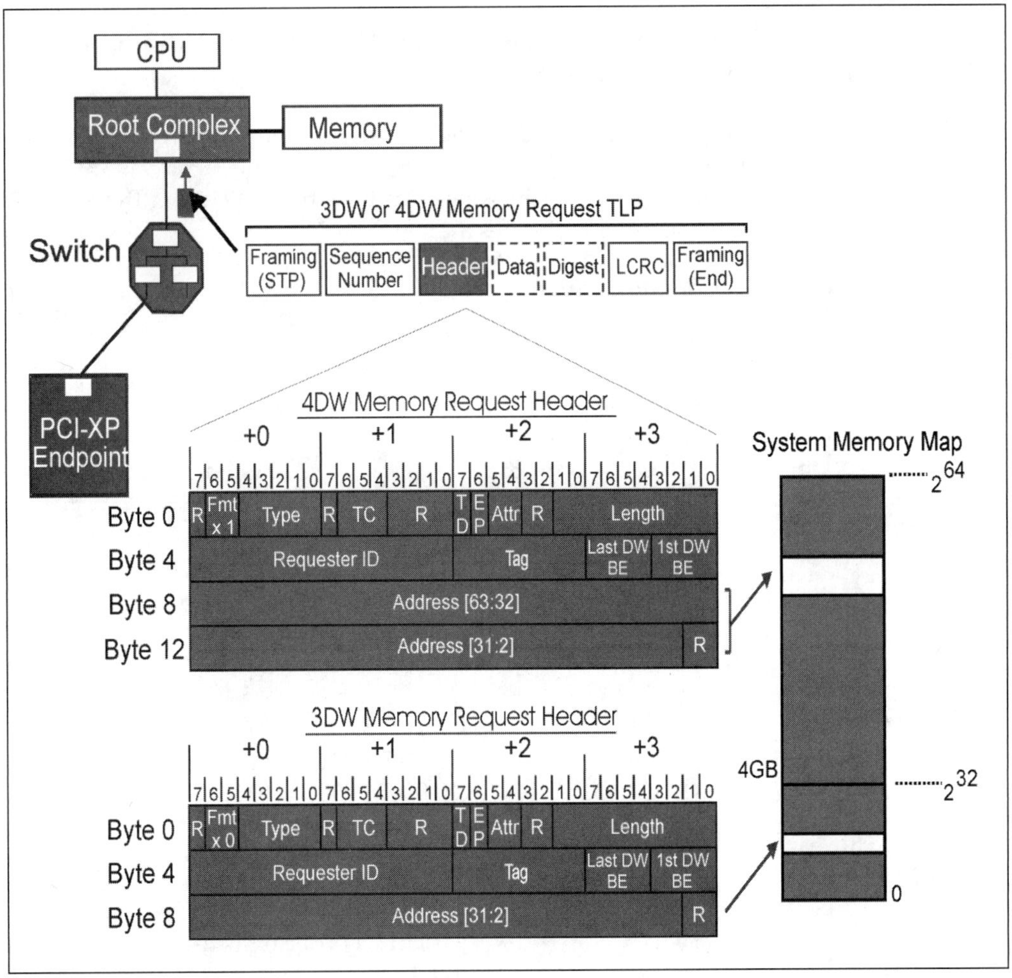

Description of 3DW And 4DW Memory Request Header Fields.

The location and use of each field in a 4DW memory request header is listed in Table 4-7 on page 176.

Note: The difference between a 3DW header and a 4DW header is the location and size of the starting Address field:

- For a 3DW header (32 bit addressing): Address bits 31:2 are in Bytes 8-11, and 12-15 are not used.
- For a 4DW header (64 bit addressing): Address bits 31:2 are in Bytes 12-15, and address bits 63:32 are in Bytes 8-11.

Otherwise the header fields are the same.

Table 4-7: 4DW Memory Request Header Fields

Field Name	Header Byte/Bit	Function
Length [9:0]	Byte 3 Bit 7:0 Byte 2 Bit 1:0	TLP data payload transfer size, in DW. Maximum transfer size is 10 bits, 2^{10} = 1024 DW (4KB). Encoding: 00 0000 0001b = 1DW 00 0000 0010b = 2DW . . 11 1111 1111b = 1023 DW 00 0000 0000b = 1024 DW
Attr (Attributes)	Byte 2 Bit 5:4	Bit 5 = Relaxed ordering. When set = 1, PCI-X relaxed ordering is enabled for this TLP. If set = 0, then strict PCI ordering is used. Bit 4 = No Snoop. When set = 1, requester is indicating that no host cache coherency issues exist with respect to this TLP. System hardware is not required to cause processor cache snoop for coherency. When set = 0, PCI -type cache snoop protection is required.

Table 4-7: 4DW Memory Request Header Fields

Field Name	Header Byte/Bit	Function
EP (Poisoned Data)	Byte 2 Bit 6	If set = 1, the data accompanying this data should be considered invalid although the transaction is being allowed to complete normally.
TD (TLP Digest Field Present)	Byte 2 Bit 7	If set = 1, the optional 1 DW TLP Digest field is included with this TLP. Some rules: Presence of the Digest field must be checked by all receivers (using this bit) • A TLP with TD = 1, but no Digest field is handled as a Malformed TLP. • If a device supports checking ECRC and TD=1, it must perform the ECRC check. • If a device does not support checking ECRC (optional) at the ultimate destination, the device must ignore the digest field.
TC (Traffic Class)	Byte 1 Bit 6:4	These three bits are used to encode the traffic class to be applied to this TLP and to the completion associated with it (if any). 000b = Traffic Class 0 (Default) . . 111b = Traffic Class 7 TC 0 is the default class, and TC 1-7 are used in providing differentiated services. See "Traffic Classes and Virtual Channels" on page 256 for additional information.

Table 4-7: 4DW Memory Request Header Fields

Field Name	Header Byte/Bit	Function
Type[4:0]	Byte 0 Bit 4:0	TLP packet Type field: 00000b = Memory Read or Write 00001b = Memory Read Locked Type field is used with Fmt [1:0] field to specify transaction type, header size, and whether data payload is present.
Fmt 1:0 (Format)	Byte 0 Bit 6:5	Packet Format: 00b = Memory Read (3DW w/o data) 10b = Memory Write (3DW w/ data) 01b = Memory Read (4DW w/o data) 11b = Memory Write (4DW w/ data)
1st DW BE 3:0 (First DW Byte Enables)	Byte 7 Bit 3:0	These high true bits map one-to-one to qualify bytes within the DW payload.
Last BE 3:0 (Last DW Byte Enables)	Byte 7 Bit 7:4	These high true bits map one-to-one to qualify bytes within the last DW transferred.
Tag 7:0	Byte 6 Bit 7:0	These bits are used to identify each outstanding request issued by the requester. As non-posted requests are sent, the next sequential tag is assigned. Default: only bits 4:0 are used (32 outstanding transactions at a time) If Extended Tag bit in PCI Express Control Register is set = 1, then all 8 bits may be used (256 tags).
Requester ID 15:0	Byte 5 Bit 7:0 Byte 4 Bit 7:0	Identifies the requester so a completion may be returned, etc. Byte 4, 7:0 = Bus Number Byte 5, 7:3 = Device Number Byte 5, 2:0 = Function Number

Table 4-7: 4DW Memory Request Header Fields

Field Name	Header Byte/Bit	Function
Address 31:2	Byte 15 Bit 7:2 Byte 14 Bit 7:0 Byte 13 Bit 7:0 Byte 12 Bit 7:0	The lower 32 bits of the 64 bit start address for the memory transfer. Note that the lower two bits of the 32 bit address are reserved (00b), forcing the start address to be DW aligned.
Address 63:32	Byte 11 Bit 7:2 Byte 10 Bit 7:0 Byte 9 Bit 7:0 Byte 8 Bit 7:0	The upper 32 bits of the 64-bit start address for the memory transfer.

Memory Request Notes. Features of memory requests include:

1. Memory transfers are never permitted to cross a 4KB boundary.
2. All memory mapped writes are posted, resulting in much higher performance.
3. Either 32 bit or 64 bit addressing may be used. The 3DW header format supports 32 bit addresses and the 4DW header supports 64 bits.
4. The full capability of burst transfers is available with a transfer length of 0-1024 DW (0-4KB).
5. Advanced PCI Express Quality of Service features, including up to 8 transfer classes and virtual channels may be implemented.
6. The No Snoop attribute bit in the header may be set = 1, relieving the system hardware from the burden of snooping processor caches when PCI Express transactions target main memory. Optionally, the bit may be deasserted in the packet, providing PCI-like cache coherency protection.
7. The Relaxed Ordering bit may also be set = 1, permitting devices in the path between the packet and its destination to apply the relaxed ordering rules available in PCI-X. If deasserted, strong PCI producer-consumer ordering is enforced.

Configuration Requests

To maintain compatibility with PCI, PCI Express supports both Type 0 and Type 1 configuration cycles. A Type 1 cycle propagates downstream until it reaches the bridge interface hosting the bus (link) that the target device resides on. The configuration transaction is converted on the destination link from Type 1 to Type 0 by the bridge. The bridge forwards and converts configuration cycles using previously programmed Bus Number registers that specify its primary, secondary, and subordinate buses. Refer to the "PCI-Compatible Configuration Mechanism" on page 723 for a discussion of routing these transactions.

Figure 4-9 on page 180 illustrates a Type 1 configuration cycle making its way downstream. At the destination link, it is converted to Type 0 and claimed by the endpoint device. Note that unlike PCI, only one device (other than the bridge) resides on a link. For this reason, no IDSEL or other hardware indication is required to instruct the device to claim the Type 0 cycle; any Type 0 configuration cycle a device sees on its primary link will be claimed.

Figure 4-9: 3DW Configuration Request And Header Format

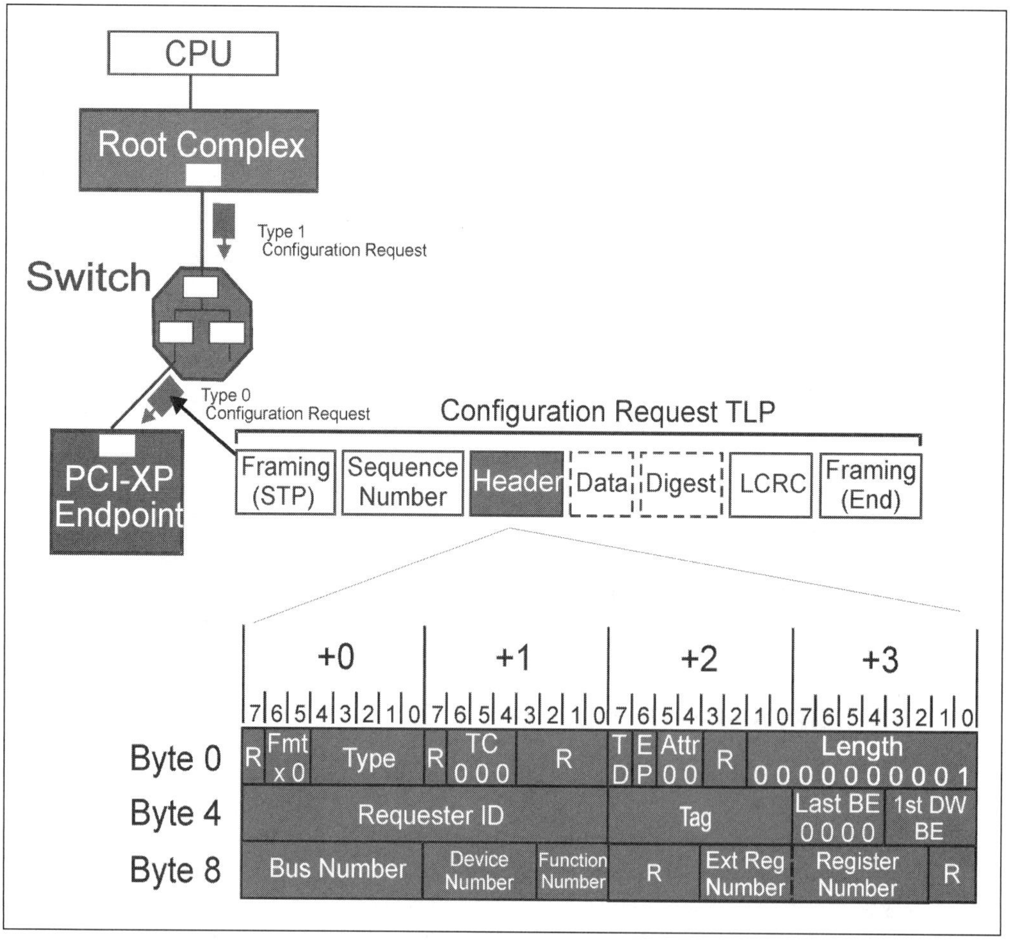

Definitions Of Configuration Request Header Fields. Table 4-8 on page 181 describes the location and use of each field in the configuration request header illustrated in Figure 4-9 on page 180.

Table 4-8: Configuration Request Header Fields

Field Name	Header Byte/Bit	Function
Length 9:0	Byte 3 Bit 7:0 Byte 2 Bit 1:0	Indicates data payload size in DW. For configuration requests, this field is always = 1. Byte Enables are used to qualify bytes within DW (any combination is legal)
Attr 1:0 (Attributes)	Byte 2 Bit 5:4	Attribute 1: Relaxed Ordering Bit Attribute 0: No Snoop Bit Both of these bits are always = 0 in configuration requests.
EP	Byte 2 Bit 6	If = 1, indicates the data payload (if present) is poisoned.
TD	Byte 2 Bit 7	If = 1, indicates the presence of a digest field (1 DW) at the end of the TLP (preceding LCRC and END)
TC 2:0 (Transfer Class)	Byte 2 Bit 6:4	Indicates transfer class for the packet. TC is = 0 for all Configuration requests.
Type 4:0	Byte 0 Bit 4:0	TLP packet type field. Set to: 00100b = Type 0 config request 00101b = Type 1 config request
Fmt 1:0 (Format)	Byte 0 Bit 6:5	Packet Format. Always a 3DW header 00b = configuration read (no data) 10b = configuration write (with data)
1st DW BE 3:0 (First DW Byte Enables)	Byte 7 Bit 3:0	These high true bits map one-to-one to qualify bytes within the DW payload. For config requests, any bit combination is valid (including none)

Table 4-8: Configuration Request Header Fields

Field Name	Header Byte/Bit	Function
Last BE 3:0 (Last DW Byte Enables)	Byte 7 Bit 7:4	These high true bits map one-to-one to qualify bytes within the last DW transferred. For config requests, these bits must be 0000b. (Single DW)
Tag 7:0	Byte 6 Bit 7:0	These bits are used to identify each outstanding request issued by the requester. As non-posted requests are sent, the next sequential tag is assigned. Default: only bits 4:0 are used (32 outstanding transactions at a time) If Extended Tag bit in PCI Express Control Register is set = 1, then all 8 bits may be used (256 tags).
Requester ID 15:0	Byte 5 Bit 7:0 Byte 4 Bit 7:0	Identifies the requester so a completion may be returned, etc. Byte 4, 7:0 = Bus Number Byte 5, 7:3 = Device Number Byte 5, 2:0 = Function Number
Register Number	Byte 11 Bit 7:2	These bits provide the lower 6 bits of DW configuration space offset. The Register Number is used in conjunction with Ext Register Number to provide the full 10 bits of offset needed for the 1024 DW (4096 byte) PCI Express configuration space.
Ext Register Number (Extended Register Number)	Byte 10 Bit 3:0	These bits provide the upper 4 bits of DW configuration space offset. The Ext Register Number is used in conjunction with Register Number to provide the full 10 bits of offset needed for the 1024 DW (4096 byte) PCI Express configuration space. For compatibility, this field can be set = 0, and only the lower 64DW (256 bytes will be seen) when indexing the Register Number.

Table 4-8: Configuration Request Header Fields

Field Name	Header Byte/Bit	Function
Completer ID 15:0	Byte 9 Bit 7:0 Byte 8 Bit 7:0	Identifies the completer being accessed with this configuration cycle. The Bus and Device numbers in this field are "captured" by the device on each configuration Type 0 write. Byte 8, 7:0 = Bus Number Byte 9, 7:3 = Device Number Byte 9, 2:0 = Function Number

Configuration Request Notes. Configuration requests always use the 3DW header format and are routed by the contents of the ID field.

All devices "capture" the Bus Number and Device Number information provided by the upstream device during each Type 0 configuration write cycle. Information is contained in Byte 8-9 (Completer ID) of configuration request.

Completions

Completions are returned following each non-posted request:

- Memory Read request may result in completion with data (CplD)
- IO Read request may result in a completion with or without data (CplD)
- IO Write request may result in a completion without data (Cpl)
- Configuration Read request may result in a completion with data (CplD)
- Configuration Write request may result in a completion without data (Cpl)

Many of the fields in the completion must have the same values as the associated request, including Traffic Class, Attribute bits, and the original Requester ID which is used to route the completion back to the original requester. Figure 4-10 on page 184 depicts a completion returning after a non-posted request, as well as the 3DW completion header format.

Figure 4-10: 3DW Completion Header Format

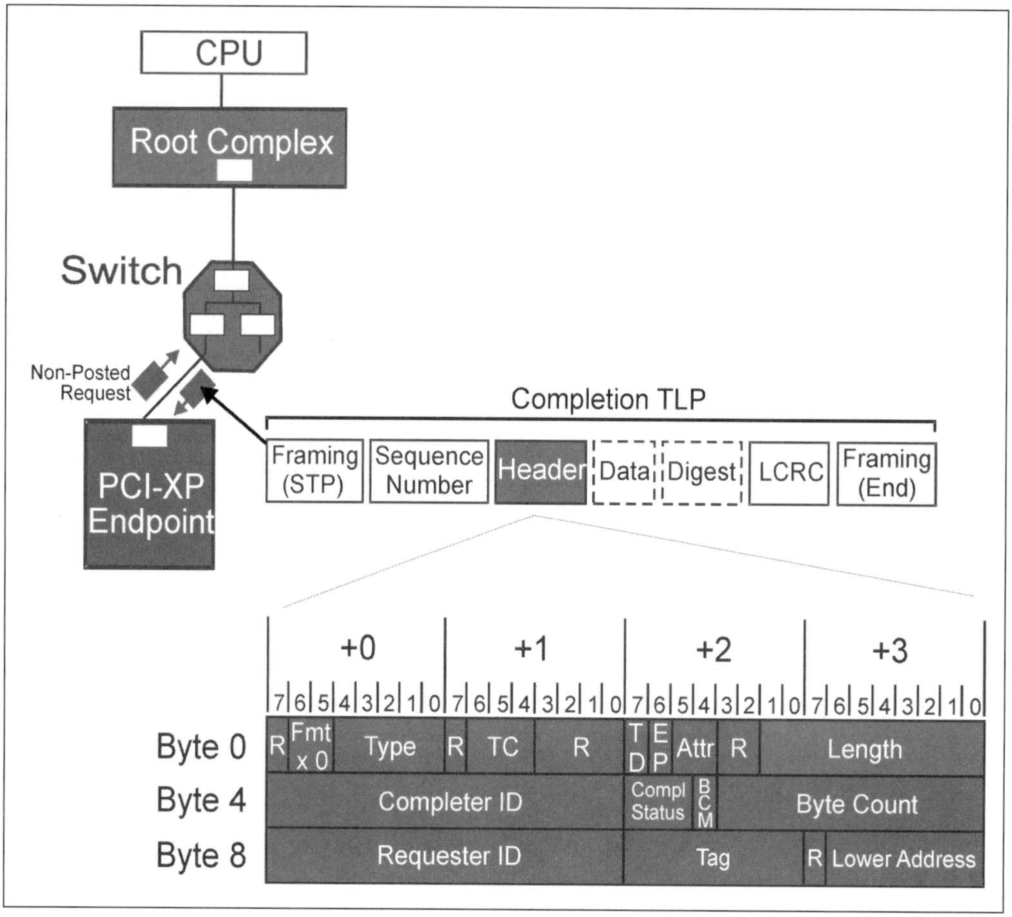

Definitions Of Completion Header Fields. Table 4-9 on page 185 describes the location and use of each field in a completion header.

Table 4-9: Completion Header Fields

Field Name	Header Byte/Bit	Function
Length 9:0	Byte 3 Bit 7:0 Byte 2 Bit 1:0	Indicates data payload size in DW. For completions, this field reflects the size of the data payload associated with this completion.
Attr 1:0 (Attributes)	Byte 2 Bit 5:4	Attribute 1: Relaxed Ordering Bit Attribute 0: No Snoop Bit For a completion, both of these bits are set to same state as in the request.
EP	Byte 2 Bit 6	If = 1, indicates the data payload is poisoned.
TD	Byte 2 Bit 7	If = 1, indicates the presence of a digest field (1 DW) at the end of the TLP (preceding LCRC and END)
TC 2:0 (Transfer Class)	Byte 2 Bit 6:4	Indicates transfer class for the packet. For a completion, TC is set to same value as in the request.
Type 4:0	Byte 0 Bit 4:0	TLP packet type field. Always set to 01010b for a completion.
Fmt 1:0 (Format)	Byte 0 Bit 6:5	Packet Format. Always a 3DW header 00b = Completion without data (Cpl) 10b = Completion with data (CplD)
Byte Count	Byte 7 Bit 7:0 Byte 6 Bit 3:0	This is the remaining byte count until a read request is satisfied. Generally, it is derived from the original request Length field. See "Data Returned For Read Requests:" on page 188 for special cases caused by multiple completions.

Table 4-9: Completion Header Fields

Field Name	Header Byte/Bit	Function
BCM (Byte Count Modified)	Byte 6 Bit 4	Set = 1 only by PCI-X completers. Indicates that the byte count field (see previous field) reflects the first transfer payload rather than total payload remaining. See "Using The Byte Count Modified Bit" on page 188.
CS 2:0 (Completion Status Code)	Byte 6 Bit 7:5	These bits encoded by the completer to indicate success in fulfilling the request. 000b = Successful Completion (SC) 001b = Unsupported Request (UR) 010b = Config Req Retry Status (CR S) 100b = Completer abort. (CA) others: reserved. See "Summary of Completion Status Codes:" on page 187.
Completer ID 15:0	Byte 5 Bit 7:0 Byte 4 Bit 7:0	Identifies the completer. While not needed for routing a completion, this information may be useful if debugging bus traffic. Byte 4 7:0 = Completer Bus # Byte 5 7:3 = Completer Dev # Byte 5 2:0 = Completer Function #
Lower Address 6:0	Byte 11 Bit 6:0	The lower 7 bits of address for the first enabled byte of data returned with a read. Calculated from request Length and Byte enables, it is used to determine next legal Read Completion Boundary. See "Calculating Lower Address Field" on page 187.
Tag 7:0	Byte 10 Bit 7:0	These bits are set to reflect the Tag received with the request. The requester uses them to associate inbound completion with an outstanding request.

Table 4-9: Completion Header Fields

Field Name	Header Byte/Bit	Function
Requester ID 15:0	Byte 9 Bit 7:0 Byte 8 Bit 7:0	Copied from the request into this field to be used in routing the completion back to the original requester. Byte 4, 7:0 = Requester Bus # Byte 5, 7:3 = Requester Device # Byte 5, 2:0 = Requester Function #

Summary of Completion Status Codes: (Refer to Completion Status field in table Table 4-9 on page 185).

- 000b (SC) Successful Completion code indicates the original request completed properly at the target.
- 001b (UR) Unsupported Request code indicates original request failed at the target because it targeted an unsupported address, carried an unsupported address or request, etc. This is handled as an uncorrectable error. See the "Unsupported Request" on page 365 for details.
- 010b (CRS) Configuration Request Retry Status indicates target was temporarily off-line and the attempt should be retried. (e.g. initialization delay after reset, etc.).
- 100b (CA) Completer Abort code indicates that completer is off-line due to an error (much like target abort in PCI). The error will be logged and handled as an uncorrectable error.

Calculating The Lower Address Field (Byte 11, bits 7:0): Refer to the Lower Address field in Table 4-9 on page 185. The Lower Address field is set up by the completer during completions with data (CplD) to reflect the address of the first enabled byte of data being returned in the completion payload. This must be calculated in hardware by considering both the DW start address and the byte enable pattern in the First DW Byte Enable field provided in the original request. Basically, the address is an offset from the DW start address:

- If the First DW Byte Enable field is 1111b, all bytes are enabled in the first DW and the offset is 0. The byte start address is = DW start address.
- If the First DW Byte Enable field is 1110b, the upper three bytes are enabled in the first DW and the offset is 1. The byte start address is = DW start address + 1.

- If the First DW Byte Enable field is 1100b, the upper two bytes are enabled in the first DW and the offset is 2. The byte start address is = DW start address + 2.
- If the First DW Byte Enable field is 1000b, only the upper byte is enabled in the first DW and the offset is 3. The byte start address is = DW start address + 3.

Once calculated, the lower 7 bits are placed in the Lower Address field of the completion header in the event the start address was not aligned on a Read Completion Boundary (RCB) and the read completion must break off at the first RCB. Knowledge of the RCB is necessary because breaking a transaction must be done on RCBs which are based on start address--not transfer size.

Using The Byte Count Modified Bit. Refer to the Byte Count Modified Bit in Table 4-9 on page 185. This bit is only set by a PCI-X completer (e.g. a bridge from PCI Express to PCI-X) in a particular circumstance. Rules for its assertion include:

1. It is only set = 1 by a PCI-X completer if a read request is going to be broken into multiple completions
2. The BCM bit is only set for the first completion of the series. It is set to indicate that the first completion contains a Byte Count field that reflects the first completion payload rather than the total remaining (as it would in normal PCI Express protocol). The receiver then recognizes that the completion will be followed by others to satisfy the original request as required.
3. For the second and any other completions in the series, the BCM bit must be deasserted and the Byte Count field will reflect the total remaining count--just as in normal PCI Express protocol.
4. PCI Express devices receiving completions with the BCM bit set must interpret this case properly.
5. The Lower Address field is set up by the completer during completions with data (CplD) to reflect the address of the first enabled byte of data being returned

Data Returned For Read Requests:

1. Completions for read requests may be broken into multiple completions, but total data transfer must equal size of original request
2. Completions for multiple requests may not be combined
3. IO and Configuration reads are always 1 DW, so will always be satisfied with a single completion
4. A completion with a Status Code other than SC (successful completion) terminates a transaction.

5. The Read Completion Boundary (RCB) must be observed when handling a read request with multiple completions. The RCB is 64 bytes or 128 bytes for the root complex; the value used should be visible in a configuration register.
6. Bridges and endpoints may implement a bit for selecting the RCB size (64 or 128 bytes) under software control.
7. Completions that do not cross an aligned RCB boundary must complete in one transfer.
8. Multiple completions for a single read request must return data in increasing address order.

Receiver Completion Handling Rules:

1. A completion received without a match to an outstanding request is an Unexpected Completion. It will be handled as an error.
2. Completions with a completion status other than Successful Completion (SC) or Configuration Request Retry Status (CRS) will be handled as an error and buffer space associated with them will be released.
3. When the Root Complex receivers a CRS status during a configuration cycle, its handling of the event is not defined except after reset (when a period is defined when it must allow it).
4. If CRS is received for a request other than configuration, it is handled as a Malformed TLP.
5. Completions received with status = a reserved code alias to Unsupported Requests.
6. If a read completion is received with a status other than Successful Completion (SC), no data is received with the completion and a CPl (or CplLk) is returned in place of a CplD (or CplDLk).
7. In the event multiple completions are being returned for a read request, a completion status other than Successful Completion (SC) immediately ends the transaction. Device handling of data received prior to the error is implementation-specific.
8. In maintaining compatibility with PCI, a Root Complex may be required to synthesize a read value of a "1's" when a configuration cycle ends with a completion indicating an Unsupported Request. (This is analogous to master aborts which occur when PCI enumeration probes devices which are not in the system).

Message Requests

Message requests replace many of the interrupt, error, and power management sideband signals used on earlier bus protocols. All message requests use the 4DW header format, and are handled much the same as posted memory write transactions. Messages may be routed using address, ID, or implicit routing. The *routing subfield* in the packet header indicates the routing method to apply, and which additional header registers are in use (address registers, etc.). Figure 4-11 on page 190 depicts the message request header format.

Figure 4-11: 4DW Message Request Header Format

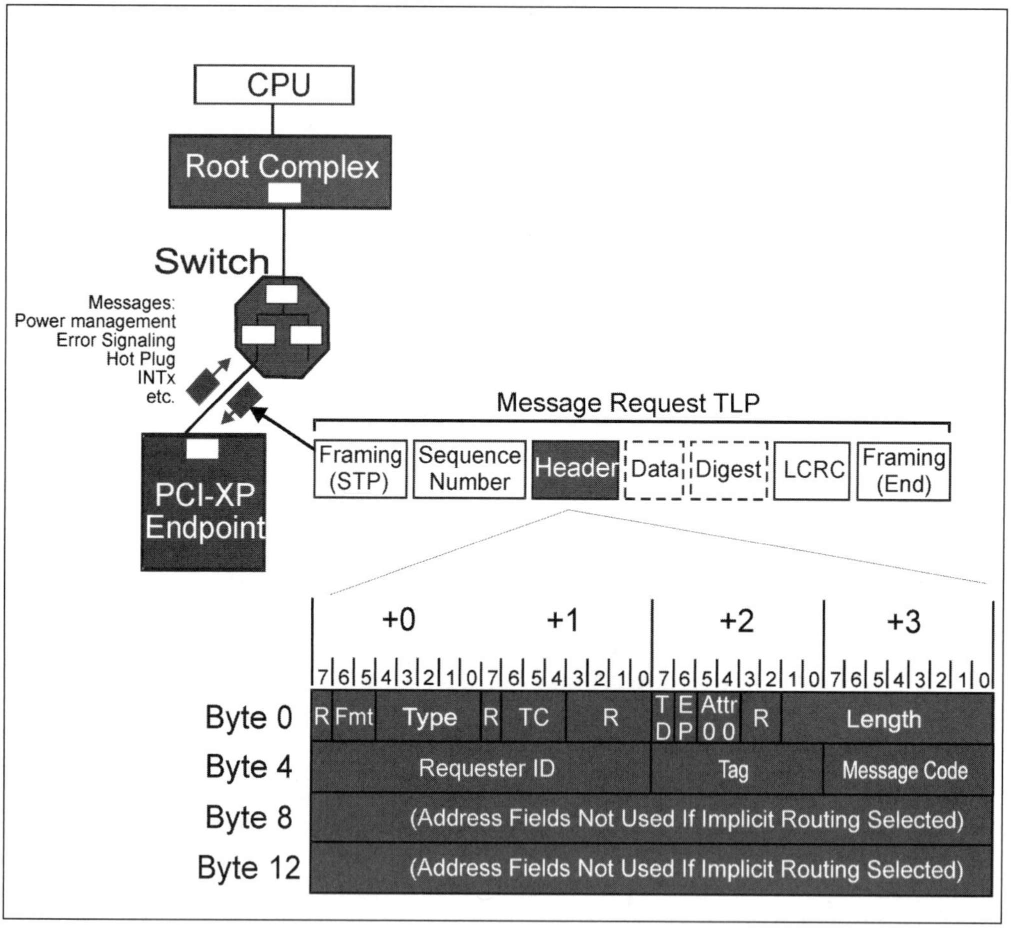

Definitions Of Message Request Header Fields. Table 4-10 on page 191 describes the location and use of each field in a message request header.

Table 4-10: Message Request Header Fields

Field Name	Header Byte/Bit	Function
Length 9:0	Byte 3 Bit 7:0 Byte 2 Bit 1:0	Indicates data payload size in DW. For message requests, this field is always 0 (no data) or 1 (one DW of data)
Attr 1:0 (Attributes)	Byte 2 Bit 5:4	Attribute 1: Relaxed Ordering Bit Attribute 0: No Snoop Bit Both of these bits are always = 0 in message requests.
EP	Byte 2 Bit 6	If = 1, indicates the data payload (if present) is poisoned.
TD	Byte 2 Bit 7	If = 1, indicates the presence of a digest field (1 DW) at the end of the TLP (preceding LCRC and END)
TC 2:0 (Transfer Class)	Byte 2 Bit 6:4	Indicates transfer class for the packet. TC is = 0 for all message requests.
Type 4:0	Byte 0 Bit 4:0	TLP packet type field. Set to: Bit 4:3: 10b = Msg Bit 2:0 (Message Routing Subfield) 000b = Routed to Root Complex 001b = Routed by address 010b = Routed by ID 011b = Root Complex Broadcast Msg 100b = Local; terminate at receiver 101b = Gather/route to Root Complex 0thers = reserved
Fmt 1:0 (Format)	Byte 0 Bit 6:5	Packet Format. Always a 4DW header 01b = message request without data 11b = message request with data

Table 4-10: Message Request Header Fields

Field Name	Header Byte/Bit	Function
Message Code 7:0	Byte 7 Bit 7:0	This field contains the code indicating the type of message being sent. 0000 0000b = Unlock Message 0001 xxxxb = Power Mgmt Message 0010 0xxxb = INTx Message 0011 00xxb = Error Message 0100 xxxxb = Hot Plug Message 0101 0000b = Slot Power Message 0111 111xb = Vendor Type 0 Message 0111 1111b = Vendor Type 1 Message
Tag 7:0	Byte 6 Bit 7:0	As all message requests are posted, no tag is assigned to them. These bits should be = 0.
Requester ID 15:0	Byte 5 Bit 7:0 Byte 4 Bit 7:0	Identifies the requester sending the message. Byte 4, 7:0 = Requester Bus # Byte 5, 7:3 = Requester Device # Byte 5, 2:0 = Requester Function #
Address 31:2	Byte 11 Bit 7:2 Byte 10 Bit 7:0 Byte 9 Bit 7:0 Byte 8 Bit 7:0	If address routing was selected for the message (see Type 4:0 field above), then this field contains the lower part of the 64-bit starting address. Otherwise, this field is not used.
Address 63:32	Byte 15 Bit 7:2 Byte 14 Bit 7:0 Byte 13 Bit 7:0 Byte 12 Bit 7:0	If address routing was selected for the message (see Type 4:0 field above), then this field contains the upper 32 bits of the 64 bit starting address. Otherwise, this field is not used.

Message Notes: The following tables specify the message coding used for each of the seven message groups, and is based on the message code field listed in Table 4-10 on page 191. The defined groups include:

1. INTx Interrupt Signaling
2. Power Management
3. Error Signaling
4. Lock Transaction Support
5. Slot Power Limit Support
6. Vendor Defined Messages
7. Hot Plug Signaling

INTx Interrupt Signaling. While many devices are capable of using the PCI 2.3 Message Signaled Interrupt (MSI) method of delivering interrupts, some devices may not support it. PCI Express defines a virtual wire alternative in which devices simulate the assertion and deassertion of the INTx (INTA-INTD) interrupt signals seen in PCI-based systems. Basically, a message is sent to inform the upstream device an interrupt has been asserted. After servicing, the device which sent the interrupt sends a second message indicating the virtual interrupt signal is being released. Refer to the "Message Signaled Interrupts" on page 331 for details. Table 4-11 summarizes the INTx message coding at the packet level.

Table 4-11: INTx Interrupt Signaling Message Coding

INTx Message	Message Code 7:0	Routing 2:0
Assert_INTA	0010 0000b	100b
Assert_INTB	0010 0001b	100b
Assert_INTC	0010 0010b	100b
Assert_INTD	0010 0011b	100b
Deassert_INTA	0010 0100b	100b
Deassert_INTB	0010 0101b	100b
Deassert_INTC	0010 0110b	100b
Deassert_INTD	0010 0111b	100b

Other INTx Rules:

1. The INTx Message type does not include a data payload. The Length field is reserved.
2. Assert_INTx and Deassert_INTx are only issued by upstream ports. Checking violations of this rule is optional. If checked, a TLP violation is handled as a Malformed TLP.
3. These messages are required to use the default traffic class, TC0. Receivers must check for violation of this rule (handled as Malformed TLPs).
4. Components at both ends of the link must track the current state of the four virtual interrupts. If the logical state of one of the interrupts changes at the upstream port, the port must send the appropriate INTx message to the downstream port on the same link.
5. INTx signaling is disabled when the Interrupt Disable bit of the Command Register is set = 1 (just as it would be if physical interrupt lines are used).
6. If any virtual INTx signals are active when the Interrupt Disable bit is set in the device, the device must transmit a corresponding Deassert_INTx message onto the link.
7. Switches must track the state of the four INTx signals independently for each downstream port and combine the states for the upstream link.
8. The Root Complex must track the state of the four INTx lines independently and convert them into system interrupts in a system-specific way.
9. Because of switches in the path, the Requester ID in an INTx message may be the last transmitter, not the original requester.

Power Management Messages. PCI Express is compatible with PCI power management, and adds the PCI Express active link management mechanism. Refer to Chapter 16, entitled "Power Management," on page 567 for a description of power management. Table 4-12 on page 194 summarizes the four power management message types.

Table 4-12: Power Management Message Coding

Power Management Message	Message Code 7:0	Routing 2:0
PM_Active_State_Nak	0001 0100b	100b
PM_PME	0001 1000b	000b
PM_Turn_Off	0001 1001b	011b
PME_TO_Ack	0001 1011b	101b

Other Power Management Message Rules:

1. Power Management Message type does not include a data payload. The Length field is reserved.
2. These messages are required to use the default traffic class, TC0. Receivers must check for violation of this rule (handled as Malformed TLPs).
3. PM_PME is sent upstream by component requesting event.
4. PM_Turn_Off is broadcast downstream
5. PME_TO_Ack is sent upstream by endpoint. For switch with devices attached to multiple downstream ports, this message won't be sent upstream until all it is first received from all downstream ports.

Error Messages. Error messages are sent upstream by enabled devices that detect correctable, non-fatal uncorrectable, and fatal non-correctable errors. The device detecting the error is defined by the Requester ID field in the message header. Table 4-13 on page 195 describes the three error message types.

Table 4-13: Error Message Coding

Error Message	Message Code 7:0	Routing 2:0
ERR_COR	0011 0000b	000b
ERR_NONFATAL	0011 0001b	000b
ERR_FATAL	0011 0011b	000b

Other Error Signaling Message Rules:

1. These messages are required to use the default traffic class, TC0. Receivers must check for violation of this rule (handled as Malformed TLPs).
2. This message type does not include a data payload. The Length field is reserved.
3. The Root Complex converts error messages into system-specific events.

Unlock Message. The Unlock message is sent to a completer to release it from lock as part of the PCI Express Locked Transaction sequence. Table 4-14 on page 196 summarizes the coding for this message.

Table 4-14: Unlock Message Coding

Unlock Message	Message Code 7:0	Routing 2:0
Unlock	0000 0000b	011b

Other Unlock Message Rules:

1. These messages are required to use the default traffic class, TC0. Receivers must check for violation of this rule (handled as Malformed TLPs).
2. This message type does not include a data payload. The Length field is reserved.

Slot Power Limit Message. This message is sent from a downstream switch or Root Complex port to the upstream port of the device attached to it. It conveys a slot power limit which the downstream device then copies into the Device Capabilities Register for its upstream port. Table 4-15 summarizes the coding for this message.

Table 4-15: Slot Power Limit Message Coding

Unlock Message	Message Code 7:0	Routing 2:0
Set_Slot_Power_Limit	0101 0000b	100b

Other Set_Slot_Power_Limit Message Rules:

1. These messages are required to use the default traffic class, TC0. Receivers must check for violation of this rule (handled as Malformed TLPs).
2. This message type carries a data payload of 1 DW. The Length field is set = 1. Only the lower 10 bits of the 32-bit data payload is used for slot power scaling; the upper bits in the data payload must be set = 0.
3. This message is sent automatically anytime the link transitions to DL_Up status or if a configuration write to the Slot Capabilities Register occurs when the Data Link Layer reports DL_Up status.
4. If a card in a slot consumes less power than the power limit specified for the card/form factor, it may ignore the message.

Hot Plug Signaling Message. These messages are passed between downstream ports of switches and Root Ports that support Hot Plug Event signaling. Table 4-16 summarizes the Hot Plug message types.

Table 4-16: Hot Plug Message Coding

Error Message	Message Code 7:0	Routing 2:0
Attention_Indicator_On	0100 0001b	100b
Attention_Indicator_Blink	0100 0011b	100b
Attention_Indicator_Off	0100 0000b	100b
Power_Indicator_On	0100 0101b	100b
Power_Indicator_Blink	0100 0111b	100b
Power_Indicator_Off	0100 0100b	100b
Attention_Button_Pressed	0100 1000b	100b

Other Hot Plug Message Rules:

- The Attention and Power indicator messages are all driven by the switch/ root complex port to the card.
- The Attention Button message is driven upstream by a slot device that implements a switch.

Data Link Layer Packets

The primary responsibility of the PCI Express Data Link Layer is to assure that integrity is maintained when TLPs move between two devices. It also has link initialization and power management responsibilities, including tracking of the link state and passing messages and status between the Transaction Layer above and the Physical Layer below.

In performing its role, the Data Link Layer exchanges traffic with its neighbor using Data Link Layer Packets (DLLPs). DLLPs originate and terminate at the Data Link Layer of each device, without involvement of the Transaction Layer. DLLPs and TLPs are interleaved on the link. Figure 4-12 on page 198 depicts the transmission of a DLLP from one device to another.

Figure 4-12: Data Link Layer Sends A DLLP

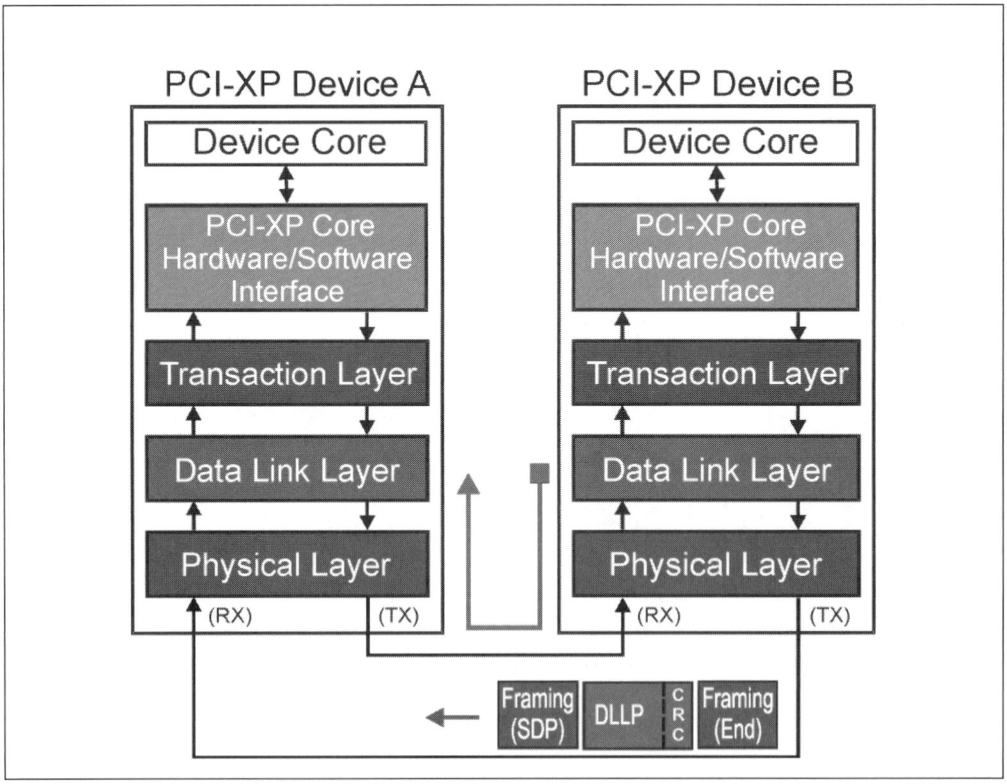

Types Of DLLPs

There are three important groups of DLLPs used in managing a link:

1. TLP Acknowledgement Ack/Nak DLLPs
2. Power Management DLLPs
3. Flow Control Packet DLLPs

In addition, the specification defines a vendor-specific DLLP.

DLLPs Are Local Traffic

DLLPs have a simple packet format. Unlike TLPs, they carry no target information because they are used for nearest-neighbor communications only.

Receiver handling of DLLPs

The following rules apply when a DLLP is sent from transmitter to receiver:

1. As DLLPs arrive at the receiver, they are immediately processed. They cannot be flow controlled.
2. All received DLLPs are checked for errors. This includes a control symbol check at the Physical Layer after deserialization, followed by a CRC check at the receiver Data Link Layer. A 16 bit CRC is calculated and sent with the packet by the transmitter; the receiver calculates its own DLLP checksum and compares it to the received value.
3. Any DLLPs that fail the CRC check are discarded. There are several reportable errors associated with DLLPs.
4. Unlike TLPs, the is no acknowledgement protocol for DLLPs. The PCI Express specification has time-out mechanisms which are intended to allow recovery from lost or discarded DLLPs.
5. Assuming no errors occur, the DLLP type is determined and it is passed to the appropriate internal logic:
   — Power Management DLLPs are passed to the device power management logic
   — Flow Control DLLPs are passed to the Transaction Layer so credits may be updated.
   — Ack/Nak DLLPs are routed to the Data Link Layer transmit interface so TLPs in the retry buffer may be discarded or resent.

Sending A Data Link Layer Packet

DLLPs are assembled on the transmit side and disassembled on the receiver side of a link. These packets originate at the Data Link Layer and are passed to the Physical Layer. There, framing symbols are added before the packet is sent. Figure 4-13 on page 200 depicts a generic DLLP in transit from Device B to Device A.

Figure 4-13: Generic Data Link Layer Packet Format

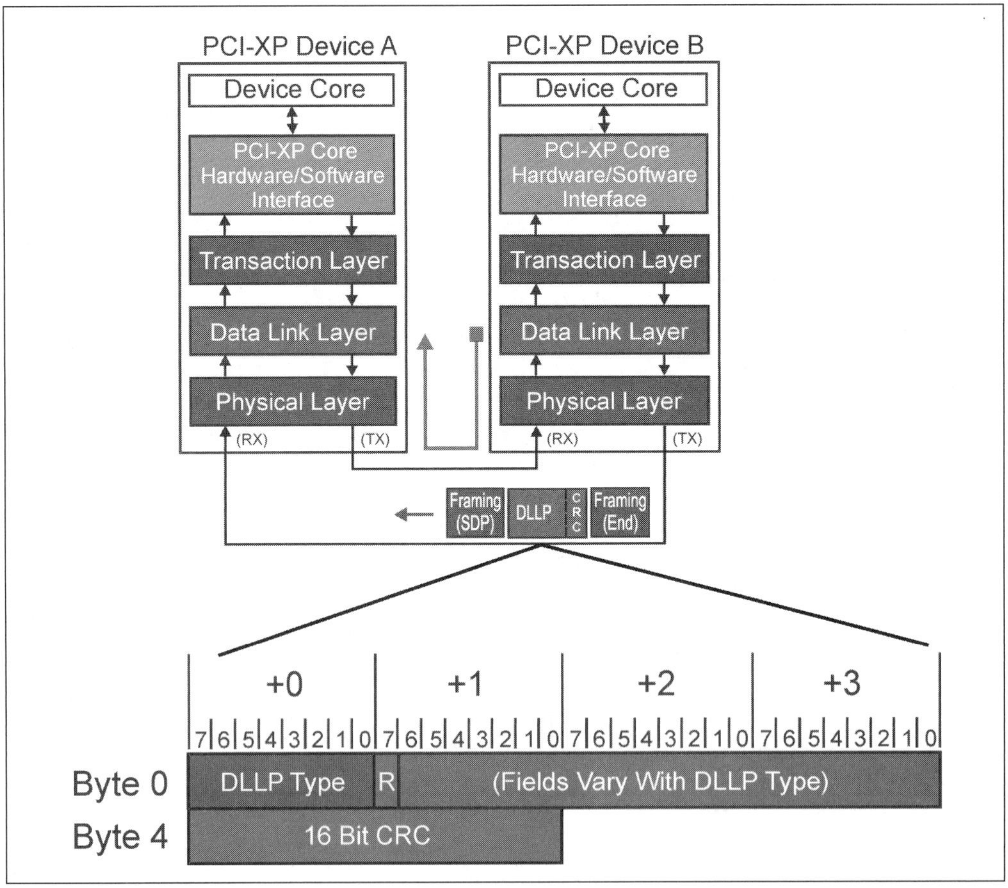

Fixed DLLP Packet Size: 8 Bytes

All Data Link Layer Packets consist of the following components:

1. A 1 DW core (4 bytes) consisting of the one byte Type field and three additional bytes of attributes. The attributes vary with the DLLP type.
2. A 16 bit CRC value which is calculated based on the DW core contents, then appended to it.
3. These 6 bytes are then passed to the Physical Layer where a Start Of DLLP (SDP) control symbol and an End Of Packet (END) control symbol are added to it. Before transmission, the Physical Layer encodes the 8 bytes of information into eight 10-bit symbols for transmission to the receiver.

Note that there is never a data payload with a DLLP; all information of interest is carried in the Type and Attribute fields.

DLLP Packet Types

The three groups of DLLPs are defined with a number of variants. Table 4-17 summarizes each variant as well as their *DLLP Type* field coding.

Table 4-17: DLLP Packet Types

DLLP Type	Type Field Encoding	Purpose
Ack (TLP Acknowledge)	0000 0000b	TLP transmission integrity
Nak (TLP No Acknowledge)	0001 0000b	TLP transmission integrity
PM_Enter_L1	0010 0000b	Power Management
PM_Enter_L23	0010 0001b	Power Management
PM_Active_State_Request_L1	0010 0011b	Power Management
PM_Request_Ack	0010 0100b	Power Management
Vendor Specific	0011 0000b	Vendor
InitFC1-P xxx=VC #	0100 0xxxb	TLP Flow Control

Table 4-17: DLLP Packet Types

DLLP Type		Type Field Encoding	Purpose
InitFC1-NP	xxx=VC #	0101 0xxxb	TLP Flow Control
InitFC1-Cpl	xxx=VC #	0110 0xxxb	TLP Flow Control
InitFC2-P	xxx=VC #	1100 0xxxb	TLP Flow Control
InitFC2-NP	xxx=VC #	1101 0xxxb	TLP Flow Control
InitFC2-Cpl	xxx=VC #	1110 0xxxb	TLP Flow Control
UpdateFC-P	xxx=VC #	1000 0xxxb	TLP Flow Control
UpdateFC-NP	xxx=VC #	1001 0xxxb	TLP Flow Control
UpdateFC-Cpl	xxx=VC #	1010 0xxxb	TLP Flow Control
Reserved		Others	Reserved

Ack Or Nak DLLP Packet Format

The format of the DLLP used by a receiver to Ack or Nak the delivery of a TLP is illustrated in Figure 4-14.

Figure 4-14: Ack Or Nak DLLP Packet Format

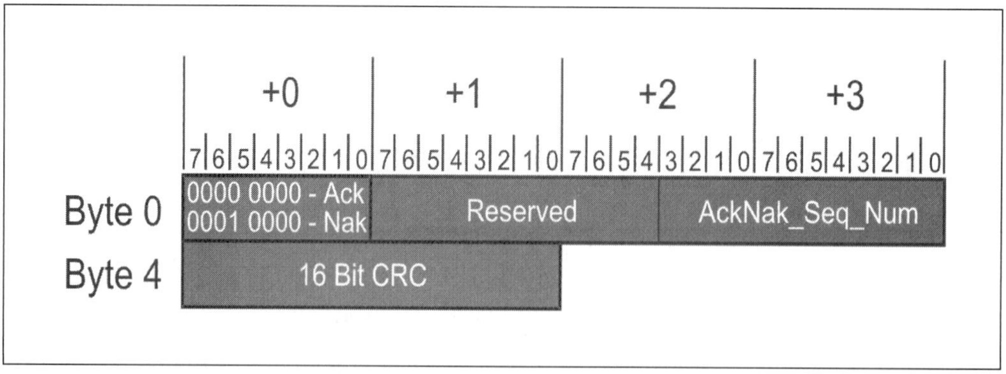

Definitions Of Ack Or Nak DLLP Fields. Table 4-18 describes the fields contained in an Ack or Nak DLLP.

Table 4-18: Ack or Nak DLLP Fields

Field Name	Header Byte/Bit	DLLP Function
AckNak_Seq_Num [11:0]	Byte 3 Bit 7:0 Byte 2 Bit 3:0	**For an ACK DLLP:** • For good TLPs received with Sequence Number = NEXT_RCV_SEQ count (count before incrementing), use NEXT_RCV_SEQ count - 1 (count after incrementing minus 1). • For TLP received with Sequence Number earlier than NEXT_RCV_SEQ count (duplicate TLP), use NEXT_RCV_SEQ count - 1. **For a NAK DLLP:** • Associated with a TLP that failed the CRC check, use NEXT_RCV_SEQ count - 1. • For a TLP received with Sequence Number later than NEXT_RCV_SEQ count, use NEXT_RCV_SEQ count - 1. Upon receipt, the transmitter will purge TLPs with equal to and earlier Sequence Numbers and replay the remainder TLPs.
Type 7:0	Byte 0 Bit 7:0	Indicates the type of DLLP. For the Ack/Nak DLLPs: • 0000 0000b = ACK DLLP. • 0001 0000b = NAK DLLP.
16-bit CRC	Byte 5 Bit 7:0 Byte 4 Bit 7:0	16-bit CRC used to protect the contents of this DLLP. Calculation is made on Bytes 0-3 of the ACK/NAK.

Power Management DLLP Packet Format

PCI Express power management DLLPs and TLPs replace most signals associated with power management state changes. The format of the DLLP used for power management is illustrated in Figure 4-15.

Figure 4-15: Power Management DLLP Packet Format

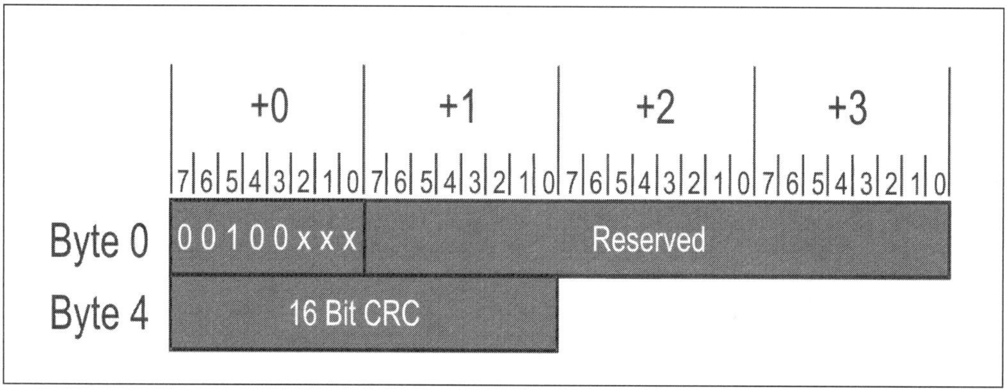

Definitions Of Power Management DLLP Fields. Table 4-19 describes the fields contained in a Power Management DLLP.

Table 4-19: Power Management DLLP Fields

Field Name	Header Byte/Bit	DLLP Function
Type 7:0	Byte 0 Bit 7:0	This field indicates type of DLLP. For the Power Management DLLPs: 0010 0000b = PM_Enter_L1 0010 0001b = PM_Enter_L2 0010 0011b = PM_Active_State_Request 0010 0100b = PM_Request_Ack
Link CRC	Byte 5 Bit 7:0 Byte 4 Bit 7:0	16 Bit CRC sent to protect the contents of this DLLP. Calculation is made on Bytes 0-3, regardless of whether fields are used.

Flow Control Packet Format

PCI Express eliminates many of the inefficiencies of earlier bus protocols through the use of a credit-based flow control scheme. This topic is covered in detail in Chapter 7, entitled "Flow Control," on page 285. Three slightly different DLLPs are used to initialize the credits and to update them as receiver buffer space becomes available. The two flow control initialization packets are referred to as InitFC1 and InitFC2. The Update DLLP is referred to as UpdateFC.

The generic DLLP format for all three flow control DLLP variants is illustrated in Figure 4-16 on page 205.

Figure 4-16: Flow Control DLLP Packet Format

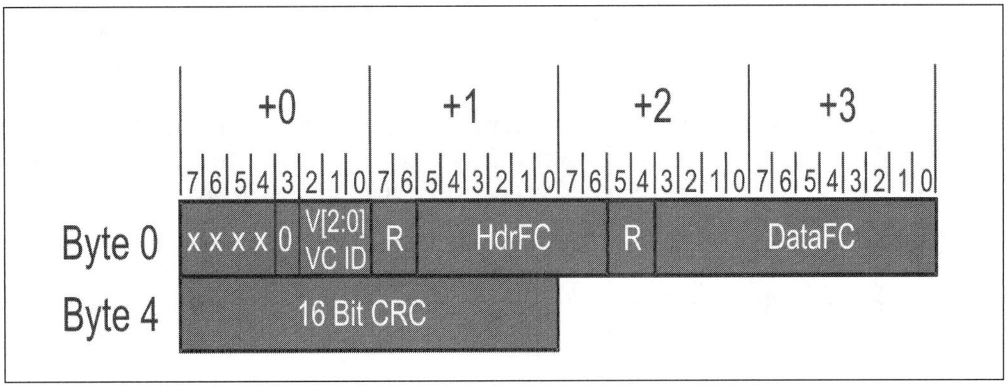

Definitions Of Flow Control DLLP Fields. Table 4-20 on page 206 describes the fields contained in a flow control DLLP.

Table 4-20: Flow Control DLLP Fields

Field Name	Header Byte/Bit	DLLP Function
DataFC 11:0	Byte 3 Bit 7:0 Byte 2 Bit 3:0	This field contains the credits associated with data storage. Data credits are in units of 16 bytes per credit, and are applied to the flow control counter for the virtual channel indicated in V[2:0], and for the traffic type indicated by the code in Byte 0, Bits 7:4.
HdrFC 11:0	Byte 2 Bit 7:6 Byte 1 Bit 5:0	This field contains the credits associated with header storage. Data credits are in units of 1 header (including digest) per credit, and are applied to the flow control counter for the virtual channel indicated in V[2:0], and for the traffic type indicated by the code in Byte 0, Bits 7:4.
VC [2:0]	Byte 0 Bit 2:0	This field indicates the virtual channel (VC 0-7) receiving the credits.
Type 3:0	Byte 0 Bit 7:4	This field contains a code indicating the type of FC DLLP: 0100b = InitFC1-P (Posted Requests) 0101b = InitFC1-NP (Non-Posted Requests) 0110b = InitFC1-Cpl (Completions) 0101b = InitFC2-P (Posted Requests) 1101b = InitFC2-NP (Non-Posted Requests) 1110b = InitFC2-Cpl (Completions) 1000b = UpdateFC-P (Posted Requests) 1001b = UpdateFC-NP (Non-Posted Requests) 1010b = UpdateFC-Cpl (Completions)
Link CRC	Byte 5 Bit 7:0 Byte 4 Bit 7:0	16 Bit CRC sent to protect the contents of this DLLP. Calculation is made on Bytes 0-3, regardless of whether fields are used.

Vendor Specific DLLP Format

PCI Express reserves a DLLP type for vendor specific use. Only the Type code is defined. The Vendor DLLP is illustrated in Figure 4-17.

Figure 4-17: Vendor Specific DLLP Packet Format

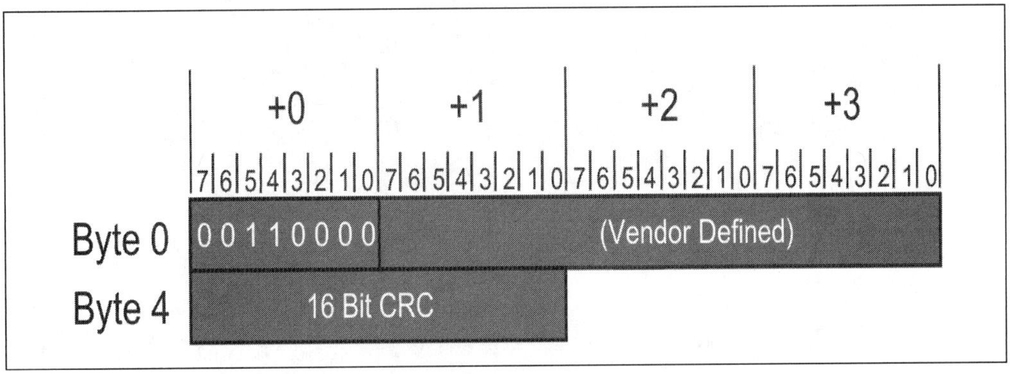

Definitions Of Vendor Specific DLLP Fields. Table 4-21 on page 207 describes the fields contained in a Vendor-Specific DLLP

Table 4-21: Vendor-Specific DLLP Fields

Field Name	Header Byte/Bit	DLLP Function
Type 3:0	Byte 0 Bit 7:4	This field contains a code indicating the Vendor-specific DLLP: 0011 0000b = Vendor specific DLLP
Link CRC	Byte 5 Bit 7:0 Byte 4 Bit 7:0	16 Bit CRC sent to protect the contents of this DLLP. Calculation is made on Bytes 0-3, regardless of whether fields are used.

5 ACK/NAK Protocol

The Previous Chapter

Information moves between PCI Express devices in packets. The two major classes of packets are Transaction Layer Packets (TLPs), and Data Link Layer Packets (DLLPs). The use, format, and definition of all TLP and DLLP packet types and their related fields were detailed in that chapter.

This Chapter

This chapter describes a key feature of the Data Link Layer: 'reliable' transport of TLPs from one device to another device across the Link. The use of ACK DLLPs to confirm reception of TLPs and the use of NAK DLLPs to indicate error reception of TLPs is explained. The chapter describes the rules for replaying TLPs in the event that a NAK DLLP is received.

The Next Chapter

The next chapter discusses Traffic Classes, Virtual Channels, and Arbitration that support Quality of Service concepts in PCI Express implementations. The concept of Quality of Service in the context of PCI Express is an attempt to predict the bandwidth and latency associated with the flow of different transaction streams traversing the PCI Express fabric. The use of QoS is based on application-specific software assigning Traffic Class (TC) values to transactions, which define the priority of each transaction as it travels between the Requester and Completer devices. Each TC is mapped to a Virtual Channel (VC) that is used to manage transaction priority via two arbitration schemes called port and VC arbitration.

Reliable Transport of TLPs Across Each Link

The function of the Data Link Layer (shown in Figure 5-1 on page 210) is two fold:

- 'Reliable' transport of TLPs from one device to another device across the Link.
- The receiver's Transaction Layer should receive TLPs in the same order that the transmitter sent them. The Data Link Layer must preserve this order despite any occurrence of errors that require TLPs to be replayed (retried).

Figure 5-1: Data Link Layer

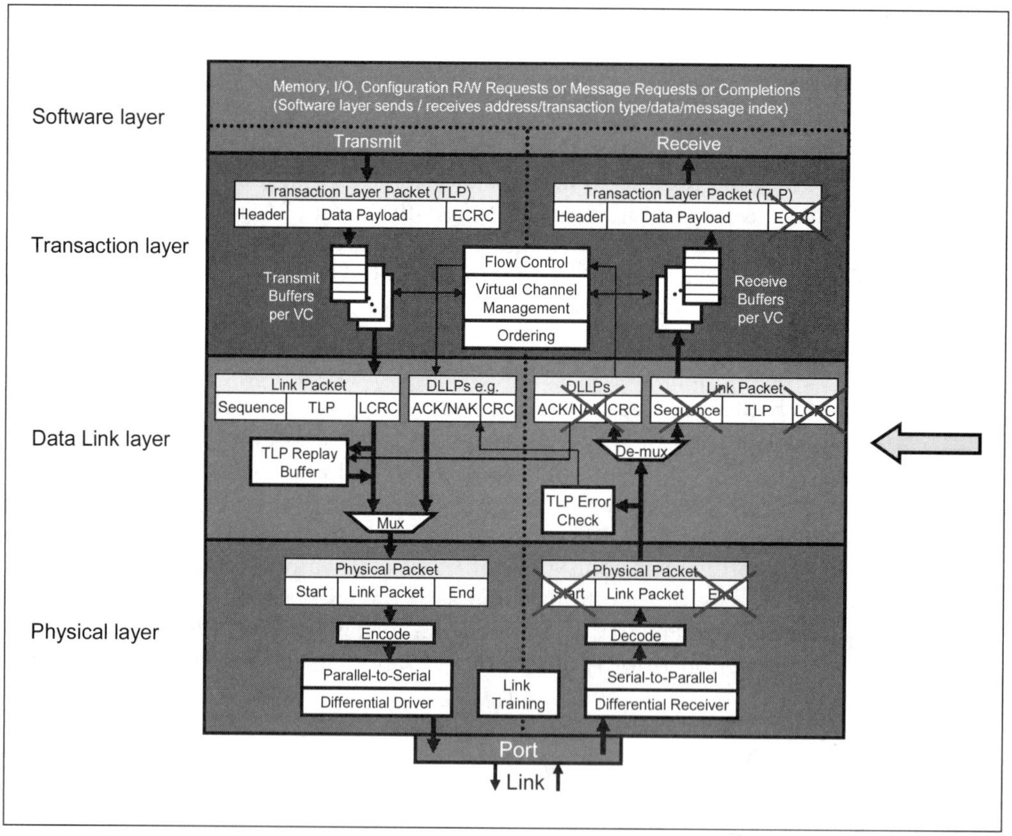

The ACK/NAK protocol associated with the Data Link Layer is described with the aid of Figure 5-2 on page 211 which shows sub-blocks with greater detail. For every TLP that is sent from one device (Device A) to another (Device B) across one Link, the receiver checks for errors in the TLP (using the TLP's LCRC field). The receiver Device B notifies transmitter Device A on good or bad reception of TLPs by returning an ACK or a NAK DLLP. Reception of an ACK DLLP by the transmitter indicates that the receiver has received one or more TLP(s) successfully. Reception of a NAK DLLP by the transmitter indicates that the receiver has received one or more TLP(s) in error. Device A which receives a NAK DLLP then re-sends associated TLP(s) which will hopefully, arrive at the receiver successfully without error.

The error checking capability in the receiver and the transmitter's ability to re-send TLPs if a TLP is not received correctly is the core of the ACK/NAK protocol described in this chapter.

Definition: As used in this chapter, the term Transmitter refers to the device that sends TLPs.

Definition: As used in this chapter, the term Receiver refers to the device that receives TLPs.

Figure 5-2: Overview of the ACK/NAK Protocol

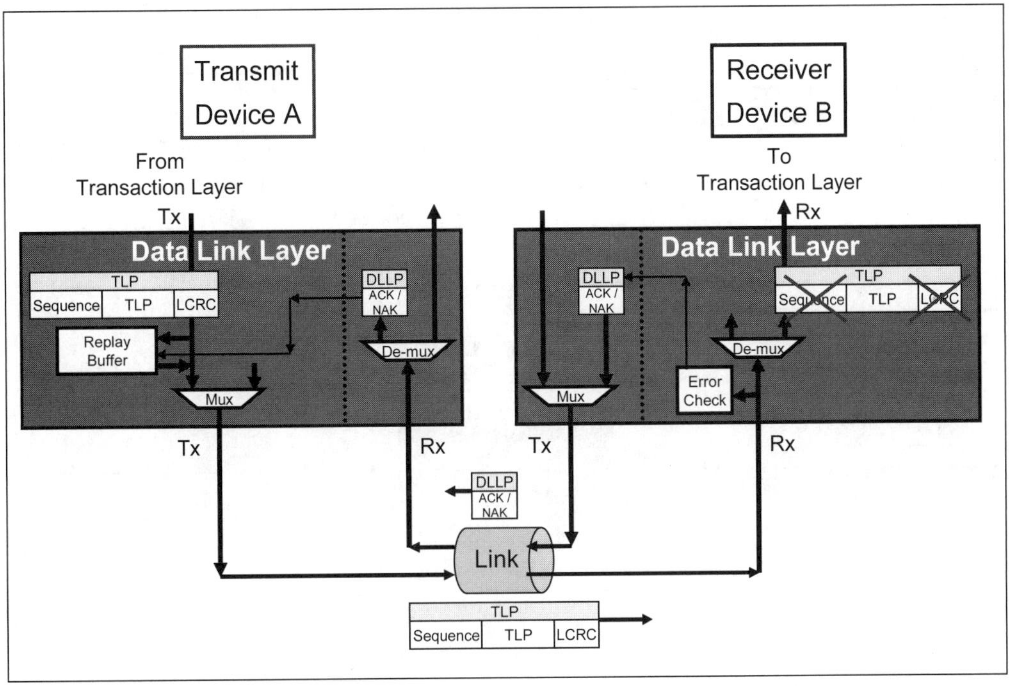

Elements of the ACK/NAK Protocol

Figure 5-3 is a block diagram of a transmitter and a remote receiver connected via a Link. The diagram shows all of the major Data Link Layer elements associated with reliable TLP transfer from the transmitter's Transaction Layer to the receiver's Transaction Layer. Packet order is maintained by the transmitter's and receiver's Transaction Layer.

Figure 5-3: Elements of the ACK/NAK Protocol

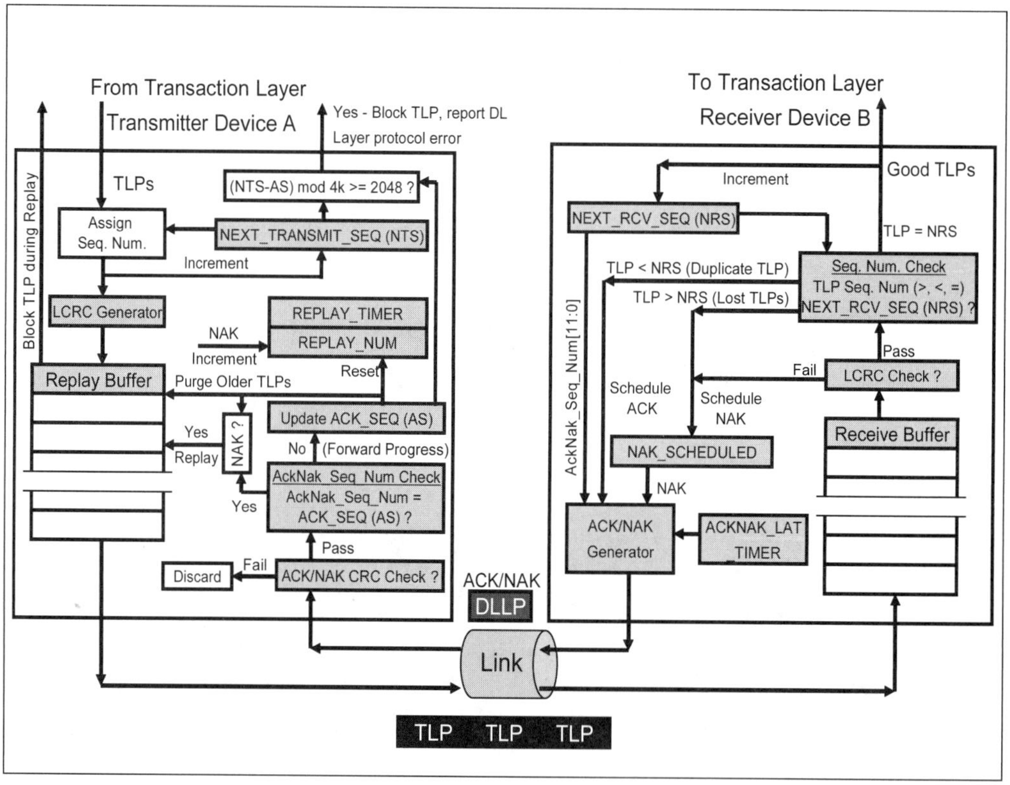

Transmitter Elements of the ACK/NAK Protocol

Figure 5-4 on page 215 illustrates the transmitter Data Link Layer elements associated with processing of outbound TLPs and inbound ACK/NAK DLLPs.

Replay Buffer

The replay buffer stores TLPs with all fields including the Data Link Layer-related Sequence Number and LCRC fields. The TLPs are saved in the order of arrival from the Transaction Layer before transmission. Each TLP in the Replay Buffer contains a Sequence Number which is incrementally greater than the sequence number of the previous TLP in the buffer.

When the transmitter receives acknowledgement via an ACK DLLP that TLPs have reached the receiver successfully, it purges the associated TLPs from the Replay Buffer. If, on the other hand, the transmitter receives a NAK DLLP, it replays (i.e., re-transmits) the contents of the buffer.

NEXT_TRANSMIT_SEQ Counter

This counter generates the Sequence Number assigned to each new transmitted TLP. The counter is a 12-bit counter that is initialized to 0 at reset, or when the Data Link Layer is in the inactive state. It increments until it reaches 4095 and then rolls over to 0 (i.e., it is a modulo 4096 counter).

LCRC Generator

The LCRC Generator provides a 32-bit LCRC for the TLP. The LCRC is calculated using all fields of the TLP including the Header, Data Payload, ECRC and Sequence Number. The receiver uses the TLP's LCRC field to check for a CRC error in the received TLP.

REPLAY_NUM Count

This 2-bit counter stores the number of replay attempts following either reception of a NAK DLLP, or a REPLAY_TIMER time-out. When the REPLAY_NUM count rolls over from 11b to 00b, the Data Link Layer triggers a Physical Layer Link-retrain (see the description of the LTSSM recovery state on page 532). It waits for completion of re-training before attempting to transmit TLPs once again. The REPLAY_NUM counter is initialized to 00b at reset, or when the Data Link Layer is inactive. It is also reset whenever an ACK is received, indicating that forward progress is being made in transmitting TLPs.

REPLAY_TIMER Count

The REPLAY_TIMER is used to measure the time from when a TLP is transmitted until an associated ACK or NAK DLLP is received. The REPLAY_TIMER is started (or restarted, if already running) when the last Symbol of any TLP is sent. It restarts from 0 each time that there are outstanding TLPs in the Replay Buffer and an ACK DLLP is received that references a TLP still in the Replay Buffer. It resets to 0 and holds when there are no outstanding TLPs in the Replay Buffer, or until restart conditions are met for each NAK received (except during a replay), or when the REPLAY_TIMER expires. It is not advanced (i.e., its value remains fixed) during Link re-training.

ACKD_SEQ Count

This 12-bit register tracks or stores the Sequence Number of the most recently received ACK or NAK DLLP. It is initialized to all 1s at reset, or when the Data Link Layer is inactive. This register is updated with the AckNak_Seq_Num [11:0] field of a received ACK or NAK DLLP. The ACKD_SEQ count is compared with the NEXT_TRANSMIT_SEQ count.

IF (NEXT_TRANSMIT_SEQ - ACKD_SEQ) mod 4096 ≥ 2048 THEN
New TLPs from Transaction Layer are not accepted by Data Link Layer until this equation is no longer true. In addition, a Data Link Layer protocol error which is a fatal uncorrectable error is reported. This error condition occurs if there is a separation greater than 2047 between NEXT_TRANSMIT_SEQ and ACKD_SEQ. i.e, a separation greater than 2047 between the sequence number of a TLP being transmitted and that of a TLP in the replay buffer that receives an ACK or NAK DLLP.

Also, the ACKD_SEQ count is used to check for forward progress made in transmitting TLPs. If no forward progress is made after 3 additional replay attempts, the Link in re-trained.

DLLP CRC Check

This block checks for CRC errors in DLLPs returned from the receiver. Good DLLPs are further processed. If a DLLP CRC error is detected, the DLLP is discarded and an error reported. No further action is taken.

Definition: The Data Link Layer is in the inactive state when the Physical Layer reports that the Link is non-operational or nothing is connected to the Port. The Physical Layer is in the non-operational state when the Link Training and Status State Machine (LTSSM) is in the Detect, Polling, Configuration, Disabled, Reset or Loopback states during which LinkUp = 0 (see Chapter 14 on 'Link Initialization and Training'). While in the inactive state, the Data Link Layer state machines are initialized to their default values and the Replay Buffer is cleared. The Data Link Layer exits the inactive state when the Physical Layer reports LinkUp = 1 and the Link Disable bit of the Link Control register = 0.

Figure 5-4: Transmitter Elements Associated with the ACK/NAK Protocol

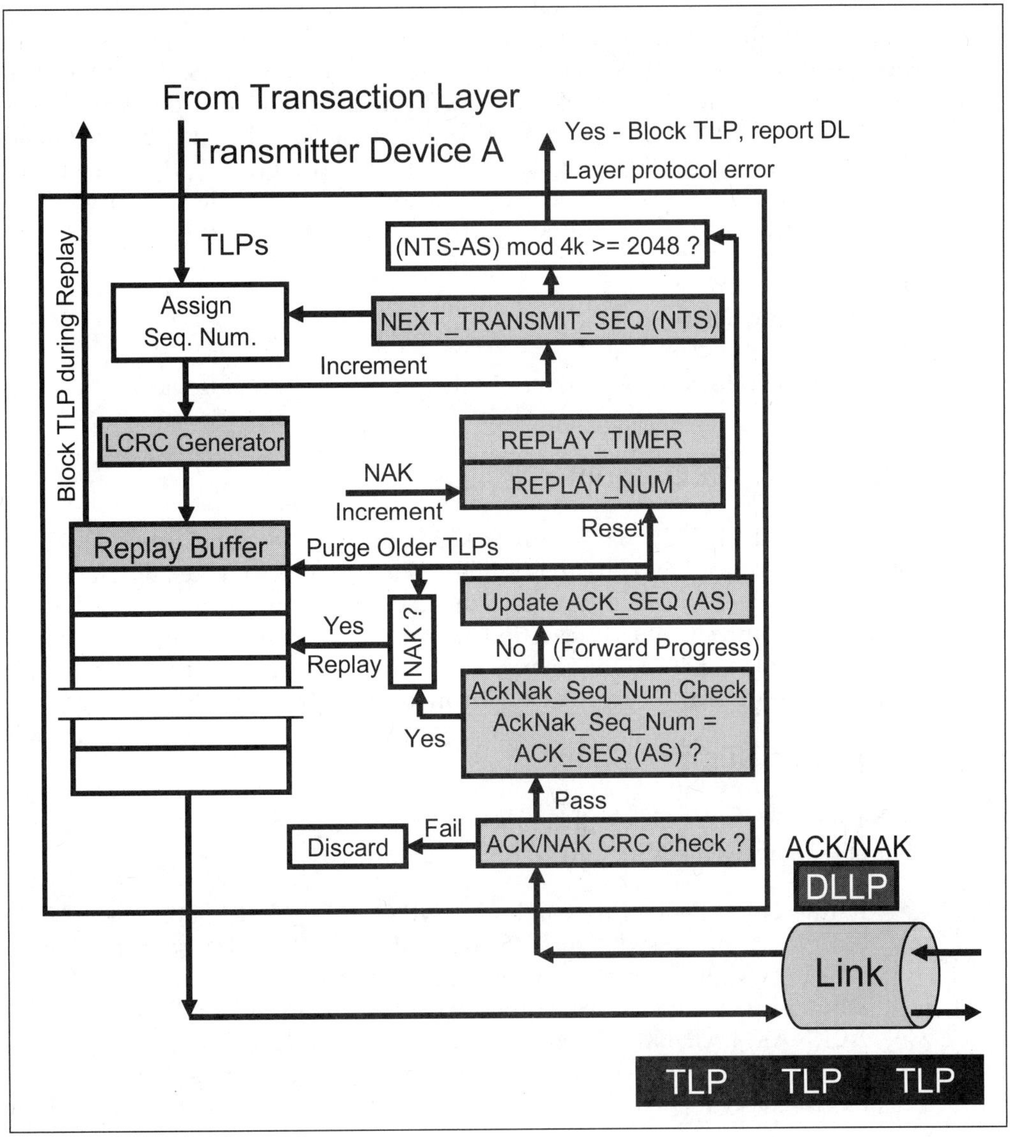

Receiver Elements of the ACK/NAK Protocol

Figure 5-5 on page 218 illustrates the receiver Data Link Layer elements associated with processing of inbound TLPs and outbound ACK/NAK DLLPs.

Receive Buffer

The receive buffer temporarily stores received TLPs while TLP CRC and Sequence Number checks are performed. If there are no errors, the TLP is processed and transferred to the receiver's Transaction Layer. If there are errors associated with the TLP, it is discarded and a NAK DLLP may be scheduled (more on this later in this chapter). If the TLP is a duplicate TLP (more on this later in this chapter), it is discarded and an ACK DLLP is scheduled. If the TLP is a 'nullified' TLP, it is discarded and no further action is taken (see "Switch Cut-Through Mode" on page 248).

LCRC Error Check

This block checks for LCRC errors in the received TLP using the TLP's 32-bit LCRC field.

NEXT_RCV_SEQ Count

The 12-bit NEXT_RCV_SEQ counter keeps track of the next expected TLP's Sequence Number. This counter is initialized to 0 at reset, or when the Data Link Layer is inactive. This counter is incremented once for each good TLP received that is forwarded to the Transaction Layer. The counter rolls over to 0 after reaching a value of 4095. The counter is not incremented for TLPs received with CRC error, nullified TLPs, or TLPs with an incorrect Sequence Number.

Sequence Number Check

After the CRC error check, this block verifies that a received TLP's Sequence Number matches the NEXT_RCV_SEQ count.

- If the TLP's Sequence Number = NEXT_RCV_SEQ count, the TLP is accepted, processed and forwarded to the Transaction Layer. NEXT_RCV_SEQ count is incremented. The receiver continues to process inbound TLPs and does not have to return an ACK DLLP until the ACKNAK_LATENCY_TIMER expires or exceeds its set value.
- If the TLP's Sequence Number is an earlier Sequence Number than NEXT_RCV_SEQ count and with a separation of no more than 2048 from

NEXT_RCV_SEQ count, the TLP is a duplicate TLP. It is discarded and an ACK DLLP is scheduled for return to the transmitter.

- If the TLP's Sequence Number is a later Sequence Number than NEXT_RCV_SEQ count, or for any other case other than the above two conditions, the TLP is discarded and a NAK DLLP may be scheduled (more on this later) for return to the transmitter.

NAK_SCHEDULED Flag

The NAK_SCHEDULED flag is set when the receiver schedules a NAK DLLP to return to the remote transmitter. It is cleared when the receiver sees the first TLP associated with the replay of a previously-Nak'd TLP. The specification is unclear about whether the receiver should schedule additional NAK DLLP for bad TLPs received while the NAK_SCHEDULED flag is set. It is the authors' interpretation that the receiver must not schedule the return of additional NAK DLLPs for subsequently received TLPs while the NAK_SCHEDULED flag remains set.

ACKNAK_LATENCY_TIMER

The ACKNAK_LATENCY_TIMER monitors the elapsed time since the last ACK or NAK DLLP was scheduled to be returned to the remote transmitter. The receiver uses this timer to ensure that it processes TLPs promptly and returns an ACK or a NAK DLLP when the timer expires or exceeds its set value. The timer value is set based on a formula described in "Receivers ACKNAK_LATENCY_TIMER" on page 237.

ACK/NAK DLLP Generator

This block generates the ACK or NAK DLLP upon command from the LCRC or Sequence Number check block. The ACK or NAK DLLP contains an AckNak_Seq_Num[11:0] field obtained from the NEXT_RCV_SEQ counter. ACK or NAK DLLPs contain a AckNak_Seq_Num[11:0] value equal to NEXT_RCV_SEQ count - 1.

Figure 5-5: Receiver Elements Associated with the ACK/NAK Protocol

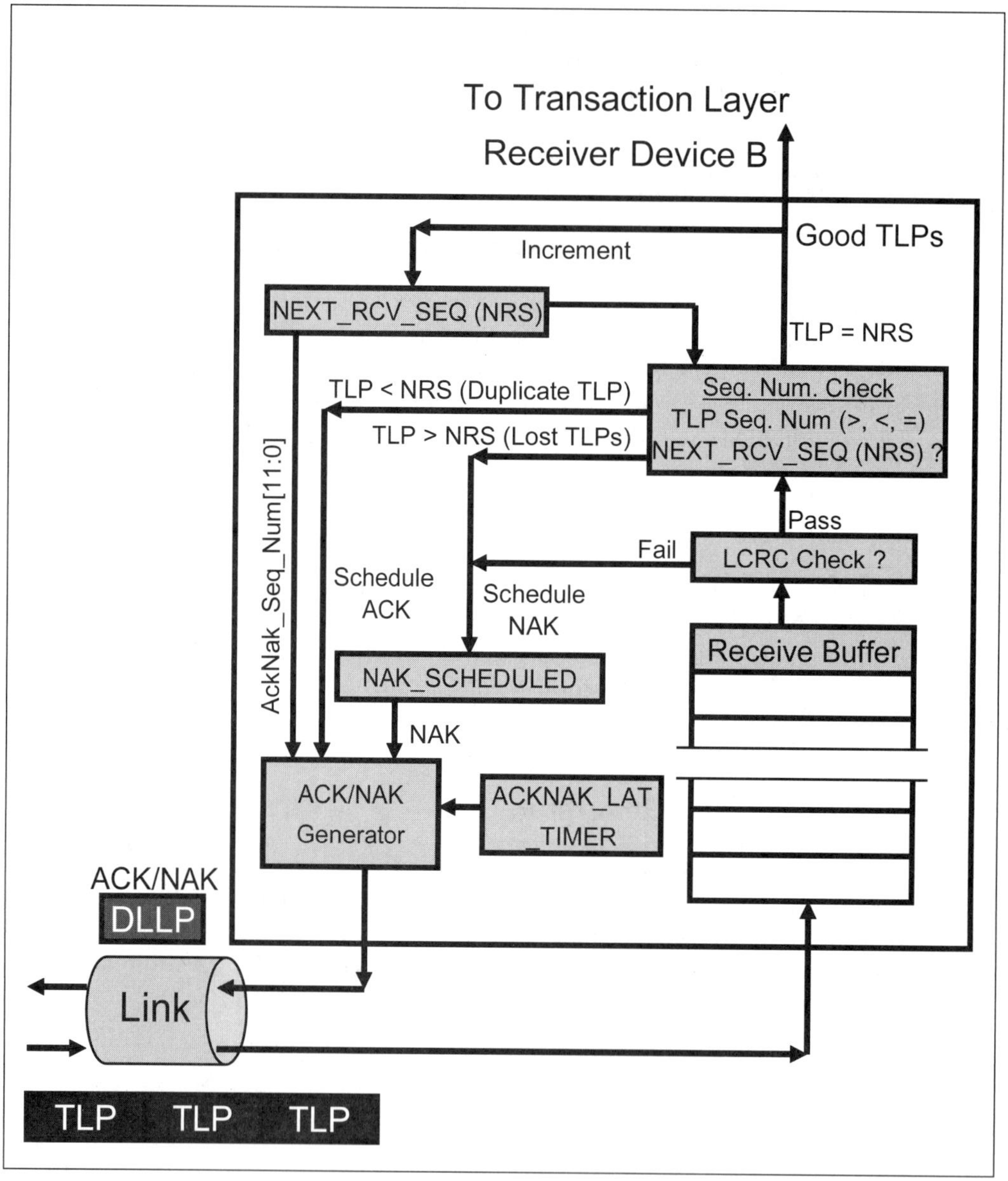

ACK/NAK DLLP Format

The format of an ACK or NAK DLLP is illustrated in Figure 5-6 on page 219. Table 5-6 describes the ACK or NAK DLLP Fields.

Figure 5-6: Ack Or Nak DLLP Packet Format

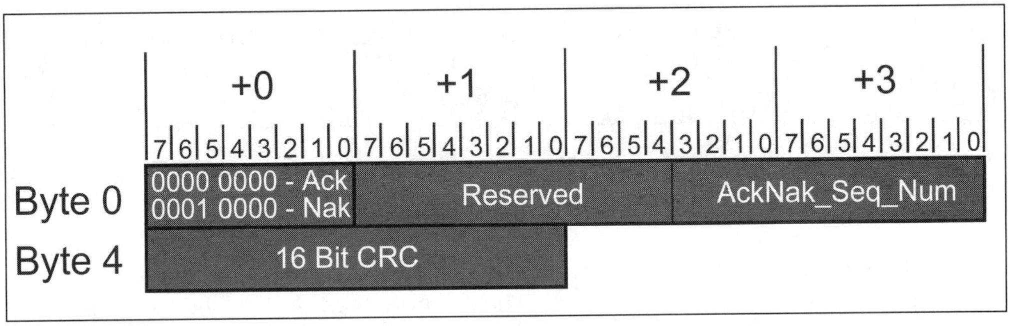

Table 5-1: Ack or Nak DLLP Fields

Field Name	Header Byte/Bit	DLLP Function
AckNak_Seq_Num [11:0]	Byte 3 Bit 7:0 Byte 2 Bit 3:0	**For an ACK DLLP:** • For good TLPs received with Sequence Number = NEXT_RCV_SEQ count (count before incrementing), use NEXT_RCV_SEQ count - 1 (count after incrementing minus 1). • For TLP received with Sequence Number earlier than NEXT_RCV_SEQ count (duplicate TLP), use NEXT_RCV_SEQ count - 1. **For a NAK DLLP:** • Associated with a TLP that fails the CRC check, use NEXT_RCV_SEQ count - 1. • For a TLP received with Sequence Number later than NEXT_RCV_SEQ count, use NEXT_RCV_SEQ count - 1. Upon receipt, the transmitter will purge TLPs with equal to and earlier Sequence Numbers and replay the remainder TLPs.

Table 5-1: Ack or Nak DLLP Fields (Continued)

Field Name	Header Byte/Bit	DLLP Function
Type 7:0	Byte 0 Bit 7:0	Indicates the type of DLLP. For the Ack/ Nak DLLPs: • 0000 0000b = ACK DLLP. • 0001 0000b = NAK DLLP.
16-bit CRC	Byte 5 Bit 7:0 Byte 4 Bit 7:0	16-bit CRC used to protect the contents of this DLLP. Calculation is made on Bytes 0-3 of the ACK/NAK.

ACK/NAK Protocol Details

This section describes the detailed transmitter and receiver behavior in processing TLPs and ACK/NAK DLLPs. The examples demonstrate flow of TLPs from transmitter to the remote receiver in both the normal non-error case, as well as the error cases.

Transmitter Protocol Details

This section delves deeper into the ACK/NAK protocol. Consider the transmit side of a device's Data Link Layer shown in Figure 5-4 on page 215.

Sequence Number

Before a transmitter sends TLPs delivered by the Transaction Layer, the Data Link Layer appends a 12-bit Sequence Numbers to each TLP. The Sequence Number is generated by the 12-bit NEXT_TRANSMIT_SEQ counter. The counter is initialized to 0 at reset, or when the Data Link Layer is in the inactive state. It increments after each new TLP is transmitted until it reaches its maximum value of 4095, and then rolls over to 0. For each new TLP sent, the transmitter appends the Sequence Number from the NEXT_TRANSMIT_SEQ counter.

Keep in mind that an incremented Sequence Number does not necessarily mean a greater Sequence Number (since the counter rolls over when after it reaches a maximum value of 4095).

32-Bit LCRC

The transmitter also appends a 32-bit LCRC (Link CRC) calculated based on TLP contents which include the Header, Data Payload, ECRC and Sequence Number.

Replay (Retry) Buffer

General. Before a device transmits a TLP, it stores a copy of the TLP in a buffer associated with the Data Link Layer referred to as the Replay Buffer (the specification uses the term Retry Buffer). Each buffer entry stores a complete TLP with all of its fields including the Header (up to 16 bytes), an optional Data Payload (up to 4KB), an optional ECRC (up to four bytes), the Sequence Number (12-bits wide, but occupies two bytes) and the LCRC field (four bytes). The buffer size is unspecified. The buffer should be big enough to store transmitted TLPs that have not yet been acknowledged via ACK DLLPs.

When the transmitter receives an ACK DLLP, it purges from the Replay Buffer TLPs with equal to or earlier Sequence Numbers than the Sequence Number received with the ACK DLLPs.

When the transmitter receives NAK DLLPs, it purges the Replay Buffer of TLPs with Sequence Numbers that are equal to or earlier than the Sequence Number that arrives with the NAK and replays (re-transmits) TLPs of later Sequence Numbers (the remainder TLPs in the Replay Buffer). This implies that a NAK DLLP inherently acknowledges TLPs with equal to or earlier Sequence Numbers than the AckNak_Seq_Num[11:0] of the NAK DLLP and replays the remainder TLPs in the Replay Buffer. Efficient replay strategies are discussed later.

Replay Buffer Sizing. The Replay Buffer should be large enough so that, under normal operating conditions, TLP transmissions are not throttled due to a Replay Buffer full condition. To determine what buffer size to implement, one must consider the following:

- ACK DLLP delivery Latency from the receiver.
- Delays cause by the physical Link interconnect and the Physical Layer implementations.
- Receiver L0s exit latency to L0. i.e., the buffer should ideally be big enough to hold TLPs while the Link which is in L0s is returned to L0.

Transmitter's Response to an ACK DLLP

General. If the transmitter receives an ACK DLLP, it has positive confirmation that its transmitted TLP(s) have reached the receiver successfully. The transmitter associates the Sequence Number contained in the ACK DLLP with TLP entries contained in the Replay Buffer.

A single ACK DLLP returned by the receiver Device B may be used to acknowledge multiple TLPs. It is not necessary that every TLP transmitted must have a corresponding ACK DLLP returned by the remote receiver. This is done to conserve bandwidth by reducing the ACK DLLP traffic on the bus. The receiver gathers multiple TLPs and then collectively acknowledges them with one ACK DLLP that corresponds to the last received good TLP. In InfiniBand, this is referred to as ACK coalescing.

The transmitter's response to reception of an ACK DLLP include:

- Load ACKD_SEQ register with AckNak_Seq_Num[11:0] of the ACK DLLP.
- Reset the REPLAY_NUM counter and REPLAY_TIMER to 0.
- Purge the Replay Buffer as described below.

Purging the Replay Buffer. An ACK DLLP of a given Sequence Number (contained in the AckNak_Seq_Num[11:0] field) acknowledges the receipt of a TLP with that Sequence Number in the transmitter Replay Buffer, PLUS all TLPs with earlier Sequence Numbers. In other words, an ACK DLLP with a given Sequence Number not only acknowledges a specific TLP in the Replay Buffer (the one with that Sequence Number), but it also acknowledges TLPs of earlier (logically lower) Sequence Numbers. The transmitter purges the Replay Buffer of all TLPs acknowledged by the ACK DLLP.

Examples of Transmitter ACK DLLP Processing

Example 1. Consider Figure 5-7 on page 223, with the emphasis on the transmitter Device A.

1. Device A transmits TLPs with Sequence Numbers 3, 4, 5, 6, 7 where TLP 3 is the first TLP sent and TLP 7 is the last TLP sent.
2. Device B receives TLPs with Sequence Numbers 3, 4, 5 in that order. TLP 6, 7 are still en route.
3. Device B performs the error checks and collectively acknowledges good receipt of TLPs 3, 4, 5 with the return of an ACK DLLP with a Sequence Number of 5.
4. Device A receives ACK 5.

5. Device A purges TLP 3, 4, 5 from the Replay Buffer.
6. When Device B receives TLP 6, 7, steps 3 through 5 may be repeated for those packets as well.

Figure 5-7: Example 1 that Shows Transmitter Behavior with Receipt of an ACK DLLP

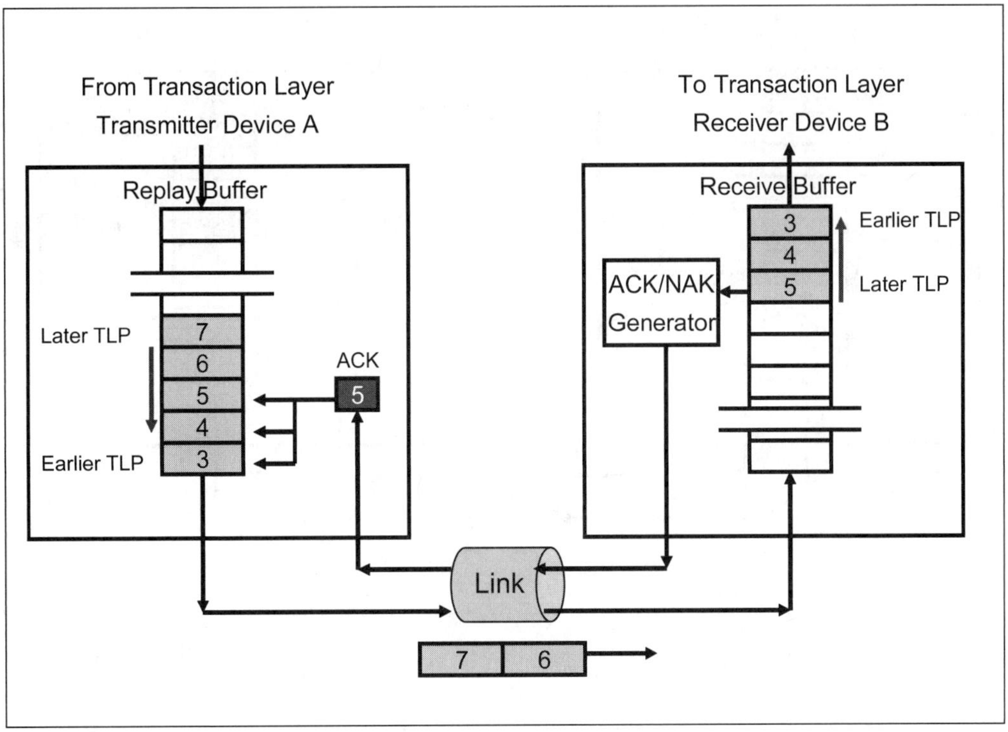

Example 2. Consider Figure 5-8, with the emphasis on the transmitter Device A.

1. Device A transmits TLPs with Sequence Numbers 4094, 4095, 0, 1, 2 where TLP 4094 is the first TLP sent and TLP 2 is the last TLP sent.
2. Device B receives TLPs with Sequence Numbers 4094, 4095, 0, 1 in that order. TLP 2 is still en route.
3. Device B performs the error checks and collectively acknowledges good receipt of TLPs 4094, 4095, 0, 1 with the return of an ACK DLLP with a Sequence Number of 1.
4. Device A receives ACK 1.
5. Device A purges TLP 4094, 4095, 0, 1 from the Replay Buffer.
6. When Device B ultimately receives TLP 2, steps 3 through 5 may be repeated for TLP 2.

Figure 5-8: Example 2 that Shows Transmitter Behavior with Receipt of an ACK DLLP

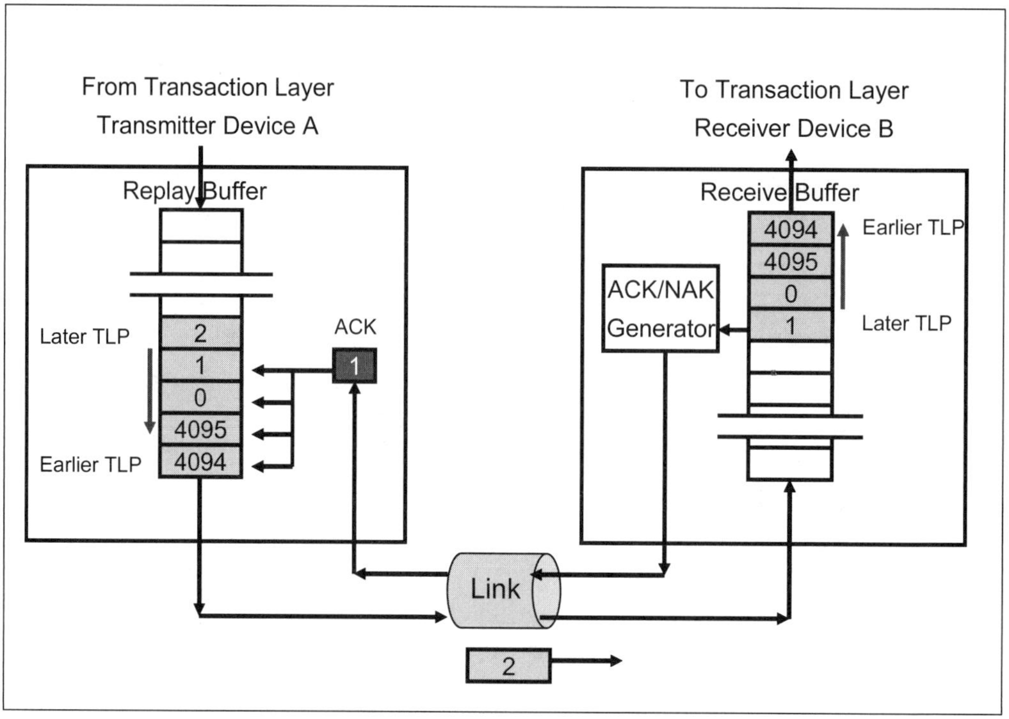

Transmitter's Response to a NAK DLLP

A NAK DLLP received by the transmitter implies that a TLP transmitted at an earlier time was received by the receiver in error. The transmitter first purges from the Replay Buffer any TLP with Sequence Numbers equal to or earlier than the NAK DLLP's AckNak_Seq_Num[11:0]. It then replays (retries) the remainder TLPs starting with the TLP with Sequence Number immediately after the AckNak_Seq_Num[11:0] of the NAK DLLP until the newest TLP. In addition, the transmitter's response to reception of a NAK DLLP include:

- Reset REPLAY_NUM and REPLAY_TIMER to 0 only if the NAK DLLP's AckNak_Seq_Num[11:0] is later than the current ACKD_SEQ value (forward progress is made in transmitting TLPs).
- Load ACKD_SEQ register with AckNak_Seq_Num[11:0] of the NAK DLLP.

TLP Replay

When a Replay becomes necessary, the transmitter blocks the delivery of new TLPs by the Transaction Layer. It then replays (re-sends or retries) the contents of the Replay Buffer starting with the earliest TLP first (of Sequence Number = AckNak_Seq_Num[11:0] + 1) until the remainder of the Replay Buffer is replayed. After the replay event, the Data Link Layer unblocks acceptance of new TLPs from the Transaction Layer. The transmitter continues to save the TLPs just replayed until they are finally acknowledged at a later time.

Efficient TLP Replay

ACK DLLPs or NAK DLLPs received during replay must be processed. This means that the transmitter must process the DLLPs and, at the very least, store them until the replay is finished. After replay is complete, the transmitter evaluates the ACK or NAK DLLPs and performs the appropriate processing.

A more efficient design might begin processing the ACK/NAK DLLPs while the transmitter is still in the act of replaying. By doing so, newly received ACK DLLPs are used to purge the Replay Buffer even while replay is in progress. If another NAK DLLP is received in the meantime, at the very least, the TLPs that were acknowledged have been purged and would not be replayed.

During replay, if multiple ACK DLLPs are received, the ACK DLLP received last with the latest Sequence Number can collapse earlier ACK DLLPs of earlier Sequence Numbers. During the replay, the transmitter can concurrently purge TLPs of Sequence Number equal to and earlier than the AckNak_Seq_Num[11:0] of the last received ACK DLLP.

Example of Transmitter NAK DLLP Processing

Consider Figure 5-9 on page 226, with focus on transmitter Device A.

1. Device A transmits TLPs with Sequence Number 4094, 4095, 0, 1, and 2, where TLP 4094 is the first TLP sent and TLP 2 is the last TLP sent.
2. Device B receives TLPs 4094, 4095, and 0 in that order. TLP 1, 2 are still en route.
3. Device B receives TLP 4094 with no error and hence NEXT_RCV_SEQ count increments to 4095
4. Device B receives TLP 4095 with a CRC error.
5. Device B schedules the return of a NAK DLLP with Sequence Number 4094 (NEXT_RCV_SEQ count - 1).

6. Device A receives NAK 4094 and blocks acceptance of new TLPs from its Transaction Layer until replay completes.
7. Device A first purges TLP 4094 (and earlier TLPs; none in this example).
8. Device A then replays TLPs 4095, 0, 1, and 2, but does not purge them.

Figure 5-9: Example that Shows Transmitter Behavior on Receipt of a NAK DLLP

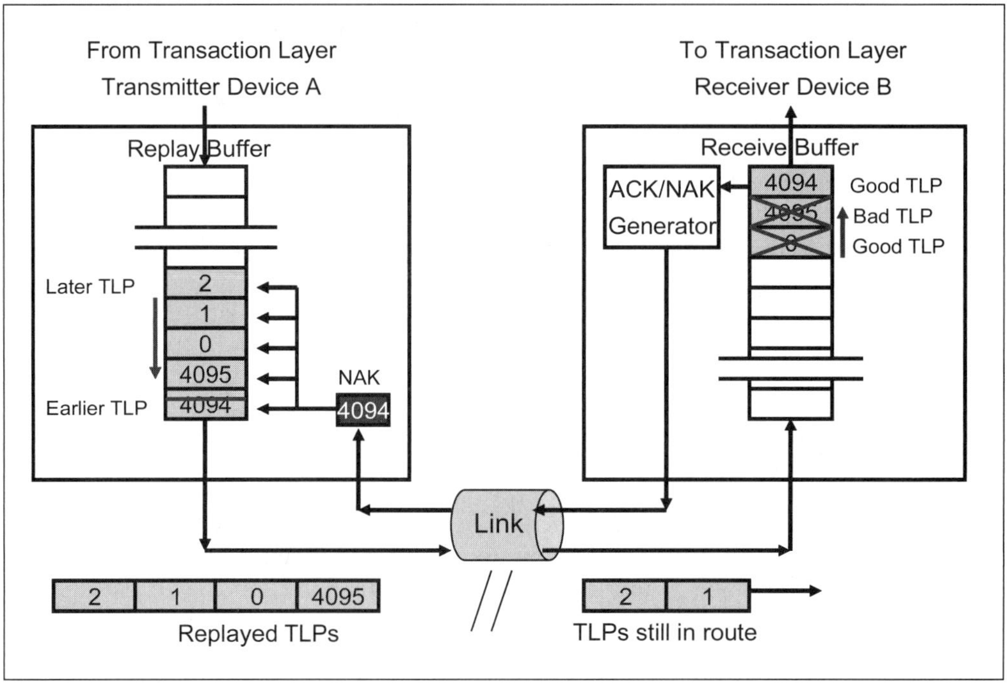

Repeated Replay of TLPs. Each time the transmitter receives a NAK DLLP, it replays the Replay Buffer contents. The transmitter uses a 2-bit Replay Number counter, referred to as the REPLAY_NUM counter, to keep track of the number of replay events. Reception of a NAK DLLP increments REPLAY_NUM. This counter is initialized to 0 at reset, or when the Data Link Layer is inactive. It is also reset if an ACK or NAK DLLP is received with a later Sequence Number than that contained in the ACKD_SEQ register. As long as forward progress is made in transmitting TLPs the REPLAY_NUM counter resets. When a fourth NAK is received, indicating no forward progress has been made after several tries, the counter rolls over to zero. The transmitter will not replay the TLPs a fourth time but instead it signals a replay number rollover error. The device assumes that the Link is non-functional or that there is a Physical Layer problem at either the transmitter or receiver end.

What Happens After the Replay Number Rollover? A transmitter's Data Link Layer triggers the Physical Layer to re-train the Link. The Physical Layer Link Training and Status State Machine (LTSSM) enters the Recovery State (see "Recovery State" on page 532). The Replay Number Rollover error bit is set ("Advanced Correctable Error Handling" on page 384) in the Advanced Error Reporting registers (if implemented). The Replay Buffer contents are preserved and the Data Link Layer is not initialized by the re-training process. Upon Physical Layer re-training exit, assuming that the problem has been cleared, the transmitter resumes the same replay process again. Hopefully, the TLPs can be re-sent successfully on this attempt.

The specification does not address a device's handling of repeated re-train attempts. The author recommends that a device track the number of re-train attempts. After a re-train rollover the device could signal a Data Link Layer protocol error indicating the severity as an Uncorrectable Fatal Error.

Transmitter's Replay Timer

The transmitter implements a REPLAY_TIMER to measure the time from when a TLP is transmitted until the transmitter receives an associated ACK or NAK DLLP from the remote receiver. A formula (described below) determines the timer's expiration period. Timer expiration triggers a replay event and the REPLAY_NUM count increments. A time-out may arise if an ACK or NAK DLLP is lost en route, or because of an error in the receiver that prevents it from returning an ACK or NAK DLLP. Timer-related rules are:

- The Timer starts (if not already started) when the last symbol of any TLP is transmitted.
- The Timer is reset to 0 and restarted when:
  - — A Replay event occurs and the last symbol of the first TLP is replayed.
  - — For each ACK DLLP received, as long as there are unacknowledged TLPs in the Replay Buffer,
- The Timer is reset and held when:
  - — There are no TLPs to transmit, or when the Replay Buffer is empty.
  - — A NAK DLLP is received. The timer restarts when replay begins.
  - — When the timer expires.
  - — The Data Link Layer is inactive.
- Timer is Held during Link training or re-training.

REPLAY_TIMER Equation. The timer is loaded with a value that reflects the worst-case latency for the return of an ACK or NAK DLLP. This time depends on the maximum data payload allowed for a TLP and the width of the Link.

The equation to calculate the REPLAY_TIMER value required is:

$$\left(\frac{(Max\_Payload\_Size + TLPOverhead) * AckFactor}{LinkWidth} + InternalDelay\right) * 3 + Rx\_L0s\_Adjustment$$

The value in the timer represents a symbol time (4ns).

The equation fields are defined as follows:

- **Max_Payload_Size** is the value in the Max_Payload_Size field of the Device Control Register ("Device Capabilities Register" on page 900).
- **TLP Overhead** includes the additional TLP fields beyond the data payload (header, digest, LCRC, and Start/End framing symbols). In the specification, the overhead value is treated as a constant of 28 symbols.
- The **Ack Factor** is a fudge factor that represents the number of maximum-sized TLPs (based on Max_Payload) that can be received before an ACK DLLP must be sent. The AF value ranges from 1.0 to 3.0 and is used to balance Link bandwidth efficiency and Replay Buffer size. Figure 5-10 on page 229 summarizes the Ack Factor values for various Link widths and payloads. These Ack Factor values are chosen to allow implementations to achieve good performance without requiring a large uneconomical buffer.
- **Link Width** ranges from 1-bit wide to 32-bits wide.
- **Internal Delay** is the receiver's internal delay between receiving a TLP, processing it at the Data Link Layer, and returning an ACK or NAK DLLP. It is treated as a constant of 19 symbol times in these calculations.
- **Rx_L0s_Adjustment** is the time required by the receive circuits to exit from L0s to L0, expressed in symbol times.

REPLAY_TIMER Summary Table. Figure 5-10 on page 229 is a summary table that shows possible timer load values with various variables plugged into the REPLAY_TIMER equation.

Figure 5-10: Table and Equation to Calculate REPLAY_TIMER Load Value

Max_Payload Size	X1 Link	X2 Link	X4 Link	X8 Link	X12 Link	x16 Link	X32 Link
128 Bytes	711	384	219	201	174	144	99
256 Bytes	1248	651	354	321	270	216	135
512 Bytes	1677	867	462	258	327	258	156
1024 Bytes	3213	1635	846	450	582	450	252
2048 Bytes	6285	3171	1614	834	1095	834	444
4096 Bytes	12,429	6243	3150	1602	2118	1602	828

The table summarizes values calculated using the equation, minus the Rx_L0s_Adjustment term

Example: Assume a 2-lane link with a Max_Payload of 2048 bytes.

$$\left[\frac{(\text{Max\_Payload\_Size} + \text{TLP Overhead}) * \text{AckFactor}}{\text{LinkWidth}} + \text{Internal Delay}\right] * 3$$

$$\left[\frac{(2048 + 28) * 1.0}{2} + 19\right] * 3 = \underline{3171} \text{ (about a 12.7uS timeout period)}$$

Transmitter DLLP Handling

The DLLP CRC Error Checking block determines whether there is a CRC error in the received DLLP. The DLLP includes a 16-bit CRC for this purpose (see Table 5-1 on page 219). If there are no DLLP CRC errors, then the DLLPs are further processed. If a DLLP CRC error is detected, the DLLP is discarded, and the error is reported as a DLLP CRC error to the error handling logic which logs the error in the optional Advanced Error Reporting registers (see Bad DLLP in "Advanced Correctable Error Handling" on page 384). No further action is taken.

Discarding an ACK or NAK DLLP received in error is not a severe response because a subsequently received DLLP will accomplish the same goal as the discarded DLLP. The side effect of this action is that associated TLPs are purged a little later than they would have been or that a replay happens at a later time. If a subsequent DLLP is not received in time, the transmitter REPLAY_TIMER expires anyway, and the TLPs are replayed.

Receiver Protocol Details

Consider the receive side of a device's Data Link Layer shown in Figure 5-5 on page 218.

TLP Received at Physical Layer

TLPs received at the Physical Layer are checked for STP and END framing errors as well as other receiver errors such as disparity errors. If there are no errors, the TLPs are passed to the Data Link Layer. If there are any errors, the TLP is discarded and the allocated storage is freed up. The Data Link Layer is informed of this error so that it can schedule a NAK DLLP. (see "Receiver Schedules a NAK" on page 233).

Received TLP Error Check

The receiver accepts TLPs from the Link into a receiver buffer and checks for CRC errors. The receiver calculates an expected LCRC value based on the received TLP (excluding the LCRC field) and compares this value with the TLP's 32-bit LCRC. If the two match, the TLP is good. If the two LCRC values do not match, the received TLP is bad and the receiver schedules a NAK DLLP to be returned to the remote transmitter. The receiver also checks for other types of non-CRC related errors (such as that described in the next section).

Next Received TLP's Sequence Number

The receiver keeps track of the next expected TLP's Sequence Number via a 12-bit counter referred to as the NEXT_RCV_SEQ counter. This counter is initialized to 0 at reset, or when the Data Link Layer is inactive. This counter is incremented once for each good TLP that is received and forwarded to the Transaction Layer. The counter rolls over to 0 after reaching a value of 4095.

The receiver uses the NEXT_RCV_SEQ counter to identify the Sequence Number that should be in the next received TLP. If a received TLP has no LCRC error, the device compares its Sequence Number with the NEXT_RCV_SEQ count. Under normal operational conditions, these two numbers should match. If this is the case, the receiver accepts the TLP, forwards the TLP to the Transaction Layer, increments the NEXT_RCV_SEQ counter and is ready for the next TLP. An ACK DLLP may be scheduled for return if the ACKNAK_LATENCY_TIMER expires or exceeds its set value. The receiver is ready to perform a comparison on the next received TLP's Sequence Number.

In some cases, a received TLP's Sequence Number may not match the NEXT_RCV_SEQ count. The received TLP's Sequence Number may be either logically greater than or logically less than NEXT_RCV_SEQ count (a logical number in this case accounts for the count rollover, so in fact a logically greater number may actually be a lower number if the count rolls over). See "Receiver Sequence Number Check" on page 234 for details on these two abnormal conditions.

For a TLP received with a CRC error, or a nullified TLP or a TLP for which the Sequence Number check described above fails, the NEXT_RCV_SEQ counter is not incremented.

Receiver Schedules An ACK DLLP

If the receiver does not detect an LCRC error (see "Received TLP Error Check" on page 230) or a Sequence Number related error (see "Next Received TLP's Sequence Number" on page 230) associated with a received TLP, it accepts the TLP and sends it to the Transaction Layer. The NEXT_RCV_SEQ counter is incremented and the receiver is ready for the next TLP. At this point, the receiver can schedule an ACK DLLP with the Sequence Number of the received TLP (see the AckNak_Seq_Num[11:0] field described in Table 5-1 on page 219). Alternatively, the receiver could also wait for additional TLPs and schedule an ACK DLLP with the Sequence Number of the last good TLP received.

The receiver is allowed to accumulate a number of good TLPs and then sends one aggregate ACK DLLP with a Sequence Number of the latest good TLP received. The coalesced ACK DLLP acknowledges the good receipt of a collection of TLPs starting with the oldest TLP in the transmitter's Replay Buffer and ending with the TLP being acknowledged by the current ACK DLLP. By doing so, the receiver optimizes the use of Link bandwidth due to reduced ACK DLLP traffic. The frequency with which ACK DLLPs are scheduled for return is described in "Receivers ACKNAK_LATENCY_TIMER" on page 237. When the ACKNAK_LATENCY_ TIMER expires or exceeds its set value and TLPs are received, an ACK DLLP with a Sequence Number of the last good TLP is returned to the transmitter.

When the receiver schedules an ACK DLLP to be returned to the remote transmitter, the receiver might have other packets (TLPs, DLLPs or PLPs) enqueued that also have to be transmitted on the Link in the same direction as the ACK DLLP. This implies that the receiver may not immediately return the ACK DLLP to the transmitter, especially if a large TLP (with up to a 4KB data payload) is already being transmitted (see "Recommended Priority To Schedule Packets" on page 244).

The receiver continues to receive TLPs and as long as there are no detected errors (LCRC or Sequence Number errors), it forwards the TLPs to the Transaction Layer. When the receiver has the opportunity to return the ACK DLLP to the remote transmitter, it appends the Sequence Number of the latest good TLP received and returns the ACK DLLP. Upon receipt of the ACK DLLP, the remote transmitter purges its Replay Buffer of the TLPs with matching Sequence Numbers and all TLPs transmitted earlier than the acknowledged TLP.

Example of Receiver ACK Scheduling

Example: Consider Figure 5-11 on page 233, with focus on the receiver Device B.

1. Device A transmits TLPs with Sequence Numbers 4094, 4095, 0, 1, and 2, where TLP 4094 is the first TLP sent and TLP 2 is the last TLP sent.
2. Device B receives TLPs with Sequence Numbers 4094, 4095, 0, and 1, in that order. NEXT_RCV_SEQ count increments to 2. TLP 2 is still en route.
3. Device B performs error checks and issues a coalesced ACK to collectively acknowledge receipt of TLPs 4094, 4095, 0, and 1, with the return of an ACK DLLP with Sequence Number of 1.
4. Device B forwards TLPs 4094, 4095, 0, and 1 to its Transaction Layer.
5. When Device B ultimately receives TLP 2, steps 3 and 4 may be repeated for TLP 2.

Figure 5-11: Example that Shows Receiver Behavior with Receipt of Good TLP

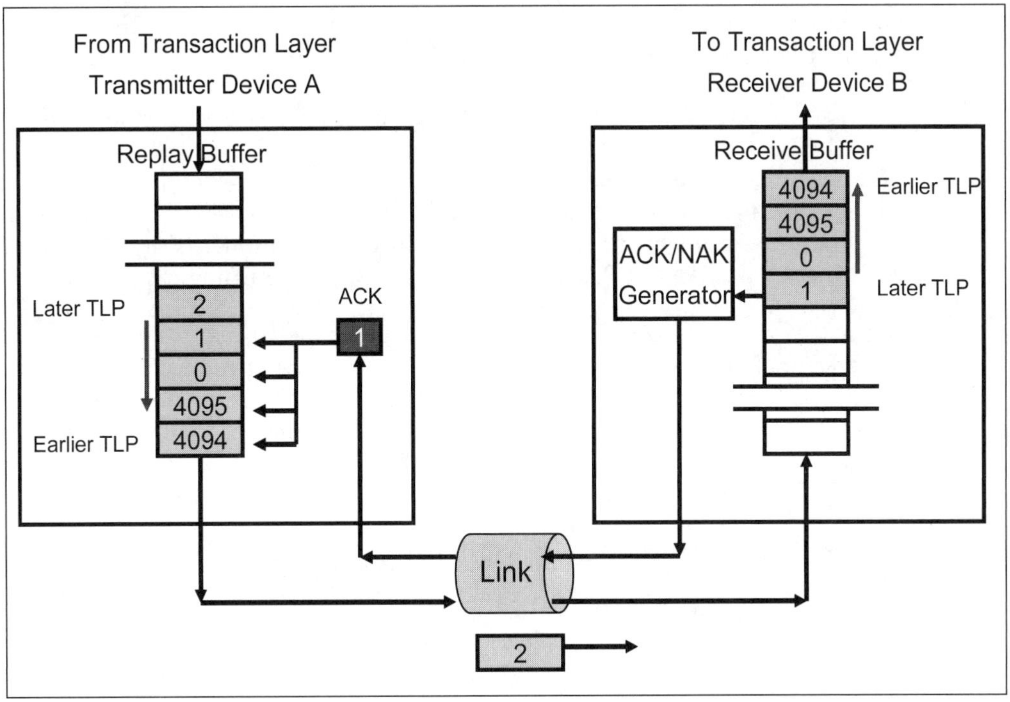

NAK Scheduled Flag

The receiver implements a Flag bit referred to as the NAK_SCHEDULED flag. When a receiver detects a TLP CRC error, or any other non-CRC related error that requires it to schedule a NAK DLLP to be returned, the receiver sets the NAK_SCHEDULED flag and clears it when the receiver detects replayed TLPs from the transmitter for which there are no CRC errors.

Receiver Schedules a NAK

Upon receipt of a TLP, the first type of error condition the receiver may detect is a TLP LCRC error (see "Received TLP Error Check" on page 230). The receiver discards the bad TLP. If the NAK_SCHEDULED flag is clear, it schedules a NAK DLLP to return to the transmitter. The NAK_SCHEDULED flag is then set. The receiver uses the NEXT_RCV_SEQ count - 1 count value as the AckNak_Seq_Num [11:0] field in the NAK DLLP (Table 5-1 on page 219). At the time the receiver schedules a NAK DLLP to return to the transmitter, the Link may be in use to transmit other queued TLPs, DLLPs or PLPs. In that case, the receiver delays the transmission of the NAK DLLP (see "Recommended Priority To Schedule Packets" on page 244). When the Link becomes available, however, it sends the NAK DLLP to the remote transmitter. The transmitter replays the TLPs from the Replay Buffer (see "TLP Replay" on page 225).

In the meantime, TLPs currently en route continue to arrive at the receiver. These TLPs have later Sequence Numbers than the NEXT_RCV_SEQ count. The receiver discards them. The specification is unclear about whether the receiver should schedule a NAK DLLP for these TLPs. It is the authors' interpretation that the receiver must not schedule the return of additional NAK DLLPs for subsequently received TLPs while the NAK_SCHEDULED flag remains set.

The receiver detects a replayed TLP when it receives a TLP with Sequence Numbers that matches NEXT_RCV_SEQ count. If the replayed TLPs arrive with no errors, the receiver increments NEXT_RCV_SEQ count and clears the NAK_SCHEDULED flag. The receiver may schedule an ACK DLLP for return to the transmitter if the ACKNAK_LATENCY_TIMER expires. The good replayed TLPs are forwarded to the Transaction Layer.

There is a second scenario under which the receiver schedules NAK DLLPs to return to the transmitter. If the receiver detects a TLP with a later Sequence Number than the next expected Sequence Number indicated by NEXT_RCV_SEQ count or for which the TLP has a Sequence Number that is separated from NEXT_RCV_SEQ count by more than 2048, the above described procedure is repeated. See "Receiver Sequence Number Check" below for the reasons why this could happen.

The two error conditions just described wherein a NAK DLLP is scheduled for return are reported as errors associated with the Data Link Layer. The error reported is a bad TLP error with a severity of correctable.

Receiver Sequence Number Check

Every received TLP that passes the CRC check goes through a Sequence Number check. The received TLPs Sequence Number is compared with the NEXT_RCV_SEQ count. Below are three possibilities:

- **TLP Sequence Number equal NEXT_RCV_SEQ count**. This situation results when a good TLP is received. It also occurs when a replayed TLP is received. The TLP is accepted and forwarded to the Transaction Layer. NEXT_RCV_SEQ count is incremented and an ACK DLLP may be scheduled (according to the ACK DLLP scheduling rules described in "Receiver Schedules An ACK DLLP" on page 231).

- **TLP Sequence Number is logically less than NEXT_RCV_SEQ count (earlier Sequence Number).** This situation results when a duplicate TLP is received as the result of a replay event. The duplicate TLP is discarded. NEXT_RCV_SEQ count is not incremented. An ACK DLLP is scheduled so that the transmitter can purge its Replay Buffer of the duplicate TLP(s). The receiver uses the NEXT_RCV_SEQ count - 1 in the ACK DLLP's AckNak_Seq_Num[11:0] field. What scenario results in a duplicate TLP being received? Consider this example. A receiver accepts a TLP and returns an associated ACK DLLP and increments the NEXT_RCV_SEQ count. The ACK DLLP is lost en route to the transmitter. As a result, this TLP remains in the remote transmitter's Replay Buffer. The transmitter's REPLAY_TIMER expires when no further ACK DLLPs are received. This causes the transmitter to replay the entire contents of the Replay Buffer. The receiver sees these TLPs with earlier Sequence Numbers than the NEXT_RCV_SEQ count and discards them because they are duplicate TLPs. More precisely, a TLP is a duplicate TLP if:
  `(NEXT_RCV_SEQ - TLP Sequence Number) mod 4096 <= 2048.`
  An ACK DLLP is returned for every duplicate TLP received.
- **TLP Sequence Number is logically greater than NEXT_RCV_SEQ count (later Sequence Number)**. This situation results when one or more TLPs are lost en route. The receiver schedules a NAK DLLP for return to the transmitter if NAK_SCHEDULED flag is clear (see NAK DLLP scheduling rules described in "Receiver Schedules a NAK" on page 233). NEXT_RCV_SEQ count does not increment when the receiver receives such TLPs of later Sequence Number.

Receiver Preserves TLP Ordering

In addition to guaranteeing reliable TLP transport, the ACK/NAK protocol preserves packet ordering. The receiver's Transaction Layer receives TLPs in the same order that the transmitter sent them.

A transmitter correctly orders TLPs according to the ordering rules before transmission in order to maintain correct program flow and to eliminate the occurrence of potential deadlock and livelock conditions (see Chapter 8, entitled "Transaction Ordering," on page 315). The Receiver is required to preserve TLP order (otherwise, application program flow is altered). To preserved this order, the receiver applies three rules:

- When the receiver detects a bad TLP, it discards the TLP and all new TLPs that follow in the pipeline until the replayed TLPs are detected.
- Also, duplicate TLPs are discarded.
- TLPs received after one or more lost TLPs are received are discarded.

For TLPs that arrive after the first bad TLP, the motivation to discard these TLPs, not forward them to the Transaction Layer and schedule a NAK DLLP is as follows. When the receiver detects a bad TLP, it discards it and any new TLPs in the pipeline. The receiver then waits for TLP replay. After verifying that there are no errors in the replayed TLP(s), the receiver forwards them to the Transaction Layer and resumes acceptance of new TLPs in the pipeline. Doing so preserves TLP receive and acceptance order at the receivers Transaction Layer.

Example of Receiver NAK Scheduling

Example: Consider Figure 5-12 on page 237 with emphasis on the receiver Device B.

1. Device A transmits TLPs with Sequence Numbers 4094, 4095, 0, 1, and 2, where TLP 4094 is the first TLP sent and TLP 2 is the last TLP sent.
2. Device B receives TLPs 4094, 4095, and 0, in that order. TLPs 1 and 2 are still in flight.
3. Device B receives TLP 4094 with no errors and forwards it to the Transaction Layer. NEXT_RCV_SEQ count increments to 4095.
4. Device B detects an LCRC error in TLP 4095 and hence returns a NAK DLLP with a Sequence Number of 4094 (NEXT_RCV_SEQ count - 1). The NAK_SCHEDULED flag is set. NEXT_RCV_SEQ count does not increment.
5. Device B discards TLP 4095.
6. Device B also discards TLP 0, even though it is a good TLP. Also TLP 1 and 2 are discarded when they arrive.
7. Device B does not schedule a NAK DLLP for TLP 0, 1 and 2 because the NAK_SCHEDULED flag is set.
8. Device A receives NAK 4094.
9. Device A does not accept any new TLPs from its Transaction Layer.
10. Device A first purges TLP 4094.
11. Device A then replays TLPs 4095, 0, 1, and 2, but continues to save these TLPs in the Replay Buffer. It then accepts TLPs from the Transaction Layer.
12. Replayed TLPs 4095, 0, 1, and 2 arrive at Device B in that order.
13. After verifying that there are no CRC errors in the received TLPs, device B detects TLP 4095 as a replayed TLP because it has a Sequence Number equal to NEXT_RCV_SEQ count. NAK_SCHEDULED flag is cleared.
14. Device B forwards these TLPs to the Transaction Layer in this order: 4095, 0, 1, and 2.

Figure 5-12. Example that Shows Receiver Behavior When It Receives Bad TLPs

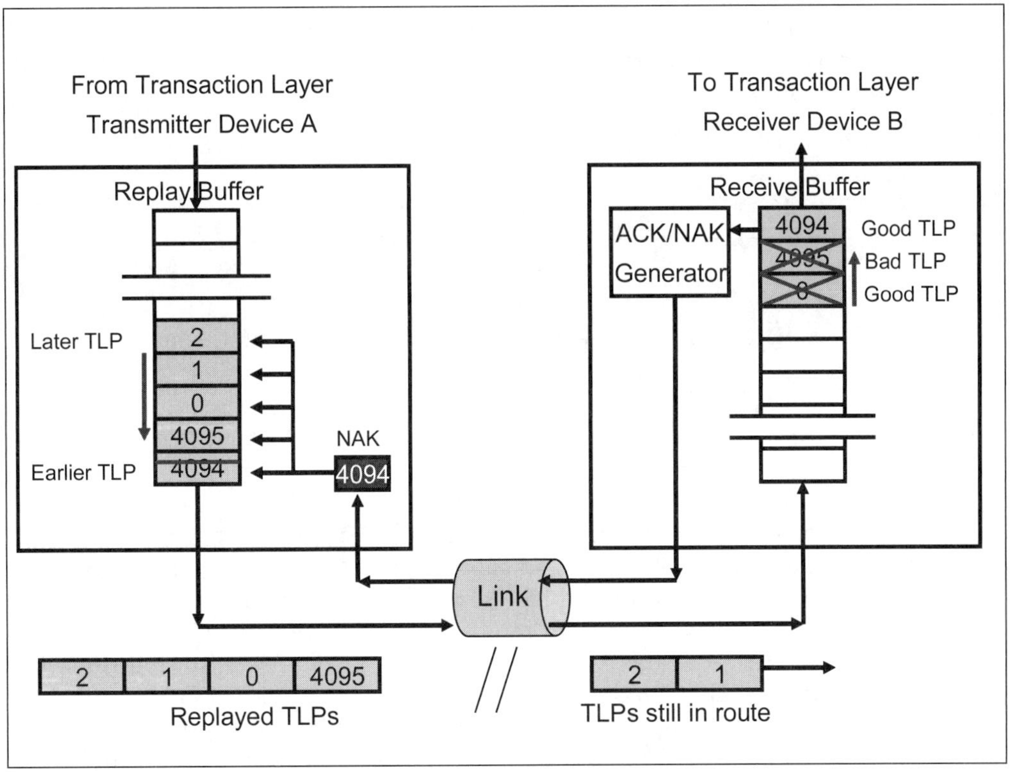

Receivers ACKNAK_LATENCY_TIMER

The ACKNAK_LATENCY_TIMER measures the duration since an ACK or NAK DLLP was scheduled for return to the remote transmitter. This timer has a value that is approximately 1/3 that of the transmitter REPLAY_TIMER. When the timer expires, the receiver schedules an ACK DLLP with a Sequence Number of the last good unacknowledged TLP received. The timer guarantees that the receiver schedules an ACK or NAK DLLP for a received TLP before the transmitter's REPLAY_TIMER expires causing it to replay.

The timer resets to 0 and restarts when an ACK or NAK DLLP is scheduled.

The timer resets to 0 and holds when:

- All received TLPs have been acknowledged.
- The Data Link Layer is in the inactive state.

ACKNAK_LATENCY_TIMER Equation. The receiver's ACKNAK_LATENCY_TIMER is loaded with a value that reflects the worst-case transmission latency in sending an ACK or NAK in response to a received TLP. This time depends on the anticipated maximum payload size and the width of the Link.

The equation to calculate the ACKNAK_LATENCY_TIMER value required is:

$$\frac{(Max\_Payload\_Size + TLPOverhead) * AckFactor}{LinkWidth} + InternalDelay + Tx\_L0s\_Adjustment$$

The value in the timer represents symbol times (a symbol time = 4 ns).

The fields above are defined as follows:

- **Max_Payload_Size** is the value in the Max_Payload_Size field of the Device Control Register (see page 900).
- **TLP Overhead** includes the additional TLP fields beyond the data payload (header, digest, LCRC, and Start/End framing symbols). In the specification, the overhead value is treated as a constant of 28 symbols.
- The **Ack Factor** is the biggest number of maximum-sized TLPs (based on Max_Payload) which can be received before an ACK DLLP is sent. The AF value (it's a fudge factor) ranges from 1.0 to 3.0, and is used to balance Link bandwidth efficiency and Replay Buffer size. Figure 5-10 on page 229 summarizes the Ack Factor values for various Link widths and payloads. These Ack Factor values are chosen to allow implementations to achieve good performance without requiring a large, uneconomical buffer.
- **Link Width** ranges from 1-bit wide to 32-bits wide.
- **Internal Delay** is the receiver's internal delay between receiving a TLP, processing it at the Data Link Layer, and returning an ACK or NAK DLLP. It is treated as a constant of 19 symbol times in these calculations.
- **Tx_L0s_Adjustment**: If L0s is enabled, the time required for the transmitter to exit L0s, expressed in symbol times. Note that setting the Extended Sync bit of the Link Control register affects the exit time from L0s and must be taken into account in this adjustment.

It turns out that the entries in this table are approximately a third in value of the REPLAY_TIMER latency values in Figure 5-10 on page 229.

ACKNAK_LATENCY_TIMER Summary Table. Figure 5-13 on page 239 is a summary table that shows possible timer load values with various variables plugged into the ACKNAK_LATENCY_TIMER equation.

Figure 5-13: Table to Calculate ACKNAK_LATENCY_TIMER Load Value

Max_Payload Size	X1 Link	X2 Link	X4 Link	X8 Link	X12 Link	x16 Link	X32 Link
128 Bytes	237 (AF=1.4)	128 (AF=1.4)	73 (AF=1.4)	67 (AF=2.5)	58 (AF=3.0)	48 (AF=3.0)	33 (AF=3.0)
256 Bytes	416 (AF=1.4)	217 (AF=1.4)	118 (AF=1.4)	107 (AF=2.5)	90 (AF=3.0)	72 (AF=3.0)	45 (AF=3.0)
512 Bytes	559 (AF=1.0)	289 (AF=1.0)	154 (AF=1.0)	86 (AF=1.0)	109 (AF=2.0)	86 (AF=2.0)	52 (AF=2.0)
1024 Bytes	1071 (AF=1.0)	545 (AF=1.0)	282 (AF=1.0)	150 (AF=1.0)	194 (AF=2.0)	150 (AF=2.0)	84 (AF=2.0)
2048 Bytes	2095 (AF=1.0)	1057 (AF=1.0)	538 (AF=1.0)	278 (AF=1.0)	365 (AF=2.0)	278 (AF=2.0)	148 (AF=2.0)
4096 Bytes	4143 (AF=1.0)	2081 (AF=1.0)	1050 (AF=1.0)	534 (AF=1.0)	706 (AF=2.0)	534 (AF=2.0)	276 (AF=2.0)

Error Situations Reliably Handled by ACK/NAK Protocol

This section describes the possible sources of errors that may occur in delivery of TLPs from a transmitter to a receiver across a Link. The ACK/NAK protocol guarantees reliable delivery of TLPs despite the unlikely event that these errors occur. Below is a bullet list of errors and the related error correction mechanism the protocol uses to resolve the error:

- **Problem**: CRC error occurs in transmission of a TLP (see "Transmitter's Response to a NAK DLLP" on page 224 and "Receiver Schedules a NAK" on page 233.)
  Solution: Receiver detects LCRC error and schedules a NAK DLLP with Sequence Number = NEXT_RCV_SEQ count - 1. Transmitter replays TLPs.

- **Problem**: One or more TLPs are lost en route to the receiver.
  Solution: The receiver performs a sequence number check on all received TLPs. The receiver expects TLPs to arrive with each TLP that has an incremented 12-bit Sequence Number from that in the previous TLP. If one or more TLPs are lost en route, a TLP will have a Sequence Number issued later than expected Sequence Number reflected in the NEXT_RCV_SEQ count. The receiver schedules a NAK DLLP with a Sequence Number = NEXT_RCV_SEQ count - 1. Transmitter replays the Replay Buffer contents.

- **Problem**: Receiver returns an ACK DLLP, but it is corrupted en route to the transmitter. The remote Transmitter detects a CRC error in the DLLP (DLLP is covered by 16-bit CRC, see "ACK/NAK DLLP Format" on page 219). In fact, the transmitter does not know that the malformed DLLP just received is supposed to be an ACK DLLP. All it knows is that the packet is a DLLP.
  Solution:
  — **Case 1:** The Transmitter discards the DLLP. A subsequent ACK DLLP received with a later Sequence Number causes the transmitter Replay Buffer to purge all TLPs with equal and earlier generated Sequence Numbers. The transmitter never knew that anything went wrong.
  — **Case 2:** The Transmitter discards the DLLP. A subsequent NAK DLLP received with a later generated Sequence Number causes the transmitter Replay Buffer to purge TLPs with equal to an earlier Sequence Numbers. The transmitter then replay all TLPs with later Sequence Numbers till the last TLP in the Replay Buffer. The transmitter never knew that anything went wrong.
- **Problem**: ACK or NAK DLLP for received TLPs are not returned by the receiver by the proper ACKNAK_LATENCY_TIMER time-out. The associated TLPs remain in the transmitter Replay Buffer.
  Solution: The REPLAY_TIMER times-out and the transmitter replays its Replay Buffer.
- **Problem**: The Receiver returns a NAK DLLP but it is corrupted en route to the transmitter. The remote Transmitter detects a CRC error in the DLLP. In fact, the transmitter does not know that the DLLP received is supposed to be an NAK DLLP. All it knows is that the packet is a DLLP.
  Solution: The Transmitter discards the DLLP. The receiver discards all subsequently received TLPs and awaits the replay. Given that the NAK was rejected by the transmitter, it's REPLAY_TIMER expires and triggers the replay.
- **Problem**: Due to an error in the receiver, it is unable to schedule an ACK or NAK DLLP for a received TLP.
  Solution: The transmitter REPLAY_TIMER will expire and result in TLP replay.

ACK/NAK Protocol Summary

Refer to Figure 5-3 on page 212 and the following subsections for a summary of the elements of the Data Link Layer.

Transmitter Side

Non-Error Case (ACK DLLP Management)

- Unless blocked by the Data Link Layer, the Transaction Layer passes down the Header, Data, and Digest information for each TLP to be sent.
- Each TLP is assigned a 12-bit Sequence Number using current NEXT_TRANSMIT_SEQ count.
- A check is made to see if the acceptance of new TLPs from the Transaction Layer should be blocked. The transmitter performs a modulo 4096 subtraction of the ACKD_SEQ count from the NEXT_TRANSMIT_SEQ count to see if the result is >= 2048d. If it is, further TLPs are blocked until incoming ACK/NAK DLLPs render the equation untrue.
- The NEXT_TRANSMIT_SEQ counter increments by one for each TLP processed. Note: if the transmitter wants to nullify a TLP being sent, it sends an inverted CRC to the physical layer and indicates an EDB end (End Bad Packet) symbol should be used (NEXT_TRANSMIT_SEQ is not incremented). See the "Switch Cut-Through Mode" on page 248 for details.
- A 32-bit LCRC value is calculated for the TLP (the LCRC calculation includes the Sequence Number).
- A copy of the TLP is placed in the Replay Buffer and the TLP is forwarded to the Physical Layer for transmission.
- The Physical Layer adds STP and END framing symbols, then transmits the packet.
- At a later time, assume the transmitter receives an ACK DLLP from the receiver. It performs a CRC error check and, if the check fails, discards the ACK DLLP (the same holds true if a bad NAK DLLP is received). If the check is OK, it purges the Replay buffer of TLPs from the oldest TLP up to and including the TLP with Sequence Number that matches the Sequence Number in the ACK DLLP.

Error Case (NAK DLLP Management)

Repeat the process described in the previous section, but this time, assume that the transmitter receives a NAK DLLP:

- Upon receipt of the NAK DLLP with no CRC error, the transmitter follows the following sequence of steps in performing the Replay. NOTE: this is the same sequence of events which would occur if the REPLAY_TIMER expires instead.
  - The REPLAY_NUM is incremented. The maximum number of attempts to clear (ACK) all unacknowledged TLPs in the Replay Buffer is four.
  - If the REPLAY_NUM count rolls over from 11b to 00b, the transmitter instructs the Physical Layer to re-train the Link.
  - If REPLAY_NUM does not roll over, proceed.
  - Block acceptance of new TLPs from the Transaction Layer.
  - Complete transmission of any TLPs in progress.
  - Purge any TLPs of equal or earlier Sequence Numbers than NAK DLLP's AckNak_Seq_Num[11:0].
  - Re-transmit TLPs with later Sequence Numbers than the NAK DLLP's AckNak_Seq_Num[11:0].
  - ACK DLLPs or NAK DLLPs received during replay must be processed. The transmitter may disregard them until replay is complete or use them during replay to skip transmission of newly acknowledged TLPs. Earlier Sequence Numbers can be collapsed when an ACK DLLP is received with a later Sequence Number. Also, ACK DLLPs with later Sequence Numbers than a NAK DLLP received earlier supersede the earlier NAK DLLP.
  - When the replay is complete, unblock TLPs and return to normal operation.

Receiver Side

Non-Error Case

TLPs are received at the Physical Layer where they are checked for framing errors and other receiver-related errors. Assume that there are no errors. If the Physical Layer reports the end symbol was EDB and the CRC value was inverted, this is not an error condition; discard the packet and free any allocated space (see "Switch Cut-Through Mode" on page 248). There will be no ACK or NAK DLLP returned for this case.

The sequence of steps performed are as follows:

- Calculate the CRC for the incoming TLP and check it against the LCRC provided with the packet. If the CRC passes, go to the next step.
- Compare the Sequence Number for the inbound packet against the current value in the NEXT_RCV_SEQ count.
- If they are the same, this is the next expected TLP. Forward the TLP to the Transaction Layer. Also increment the NEXT_RCV_SEQ count.
- Clear the NAK_SCHEDULED flag if set.
- If the ACKNAK_LATENCY_TIMER expires, schedule and ACK DLLP with AckNak_Seq_Num[11:0] = NEXT_RCV_SEQ count - 1.

Error Case

TLPs are received at the Physical Layer where they are checked for framing errors and other receiver-related errors. In the event of an error, the Physical Layer discards the packet, reports the error, and frees any storage allocated for the TLP. If the EDB is set and the CRC is not inverted, this is a bad packet: discard the TLP and set the error flag. If the NAK_SCHEDULED flag is clear, set it, and schedule a NAK DLLP with the NEXT_RCV_SEQ count - 1 value used as the Sequence Number.

- If there are no Physical Layer errors detected, forward the TLP to the Data Link Layer.
- Calculate the CRC for the incoming TLP and check it against the LCRC provided with the packet. If the CRC fails, set the NAK_SCHEDULED flag. Schedule a NAK DLLP with NEXT_RCV_SEQ count - 1 used as the Sequence Number. If LCRC error check passes, go to the next bullet.
- If the LCRC check passes, then compare the Sequence Number for the inbound packet against the current value in the NEXT_RCV_SEQ count. If the TLP Sequence Number is not equal to NEXT_RCV_SEQ count and if (NEXT_RCV_SEQ - TLP Sequence Number) mod 4096 <= 2048, the TLP is a duplicate TLP. Discard the TLP, and schedule an ACK with NEXT_RCV_SEQ count - 1 value used as AckNak_Seq_Num[11:0].
- Discard TLPs received with Sequence Number other than the Sequence Number described by the above bullet. If the NAK_SCHEDULED flag is clear, set it, and schedule a NAK DLLP with NEXT_RCV_SEQ count - 1 used as AckNak_Seq_Num[11:0]. If the NAK _SCHEDULED flag bit is already set, keep it set and do not schedule a NAK DLLP.

Recommended Priority To Schedule Packets

A device may have many types of TLPs, DLLPs and PLPs to transmit on a given Link. The following is a recommended but not required set of priorities for scheduling packets:

1. Completion of any TLP or DLLP currently in progress (highest priority).
2. PLP transmissions.
3. NAK DLLP.
4. ACK DLLP.
5. FC (Flow Control) DLLP.
6. Replay Buffer re-transmissions.
7. TLPs that are waiting in the Transaction Layer.
8. All other DLLP transmissions (lowest priority)

Some More Examples

To demonstrate the reliable TLP delivery capability provided by the ACK/NAK Protocol, the following examples are provided.

Lost TLP

Consider Figure 5-14 on page 245 which shows the ACK/NAK protocol for handling lost TLPs.

1. Device A transmits TLPs 4094, 4095, 0, 1, and 2.
2. Device B receives TLPs 4094, 4095, and 0, for which it returns ACK 0. These TLPs are forwarded to the Transaction Layer. NEXT_RCV_SEQ is incremented and the next value of NEXT_RCV_SEQ count is 1. Device B is ready to receive TLP 1.
3. Seeing ACK 0, Device A purges TLPs 4094, 4095, and 0 from its replay buffer.
4. TLP 1 is lost en route.
5. TLP 2 arrives instead. Upon performing a Sequence Number check, Device B realizes that TLP 2's Sequence Number is greater than NEXT_RCV_SEQ count.
6. Device B discards TLP 2 and schedules NAK 0 (NEXT_RCV_SEQ count - 1).
7. Upon receipt of NAK 0, Device A replays TLPs 1 and 2.
8. TLPs 1 and 2 arrive without error at Device B and are forwarded to the Transaction Layer.

Figure 5-14: Lost TLP Handling

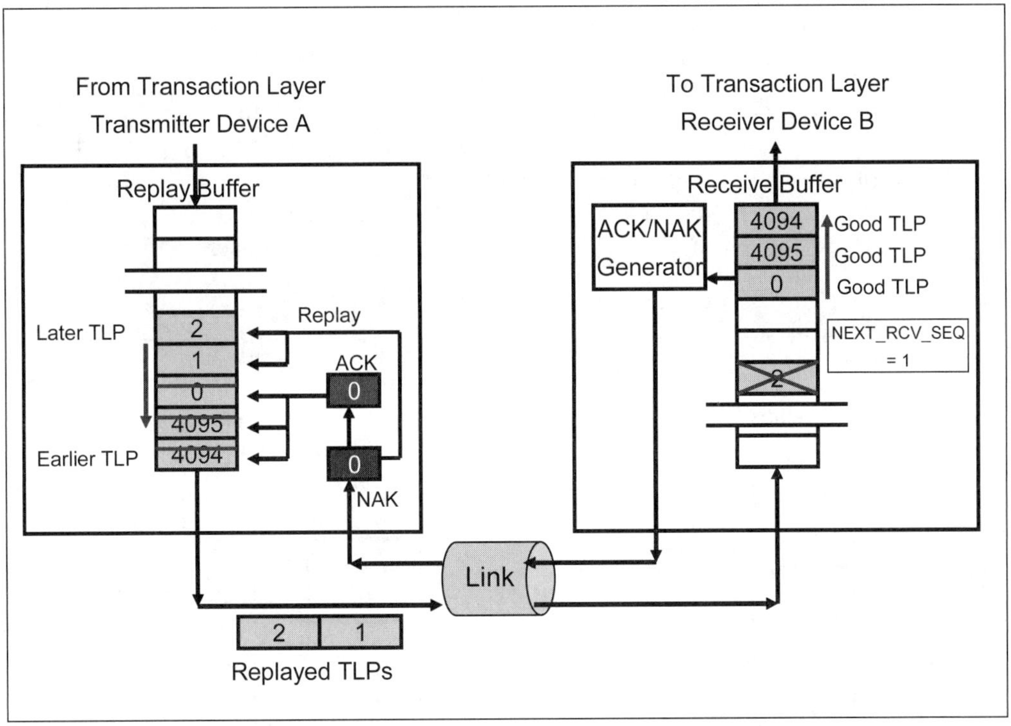

Lost ACK DLLP or ACK DLLP with CRC Error

Consider Figure 5-15 on page 246 which shows the ACK/NAK protocol for handling a lost ACK DLLP.

1. Device A transmits TLPs 4094, 4095, 0, 1, and 2.
2. Device B receives TLPs 4094, 4095, and 0, for which it returns ACK 0. These TLPs are forwarded to the Transaction Layer. NEXT_RCV_SEQ is incremented and the next value of NEXT_RCV_SEQ count is set to 1.
3. ACK 0 is lost en route. TLPs 4094, 4095, and 0 remain in Device A's Replay Buffer.
4. TLPs 1 and 2 arrive at Device B shortly thereafter. NEXT_RCV_SEQ count increments to 3.
5. Device B returns ACK 2 and sends TLPs 1 and 2 to the Transaction Layer.
6. ACK 2 arrives at Device A.
7. Device A purges its Replay Buffer of TLPs 4094, 4095, 0, 1, and 2.

The example would be the same if a CRC error existed in ACK packet 0. Device A would detect the CRC error in ACK 0 and discard it. When received later, ACK 2 would cause the Replay Buffer to purge all TLPs (4094 through 2).

If ACK 2 is also lost or corrupted, and no further ACK or NAK DLLPs are returned to Device A, its REPLAY_TIMER will expire. This results in replay of its entire buffer. Device B receives TLP 4094, 4095, 0, 1 and 2 and detects them as duplicate TLPs because their Sequence Numbers are earlier than NEXT_RCV_SEQ count of 3. These TLPs are discarded and ACK DLLPs with AckNak_Seq_Num[11:0] = 2 are returned to Device A for each duplicate TLP.

Figure 5-15: Lost ACK DLLP Handling

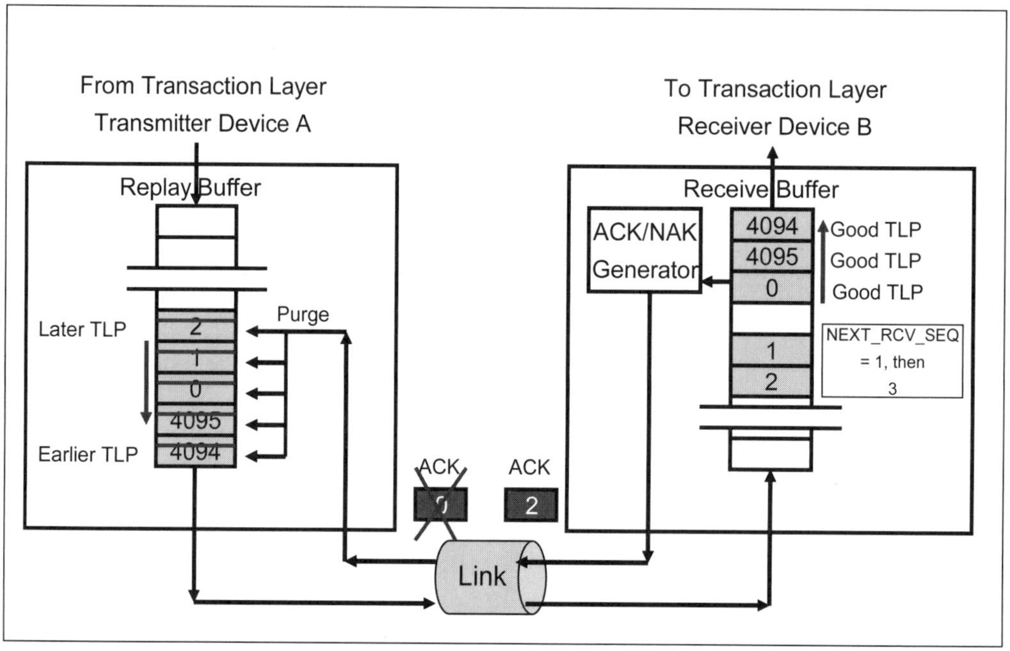

Lost ACK DLLP followed by NAK DLLP

Consider Figure 5-16 on page 247 which shows the ACK/NAK protocol for handling a lost ACK DLLP followed by a valid NAK DLLP.

1. Device A transmits TLPs 4094, 4095, 0, 1, and 2.
2. Device B receives TLPs 4094, 4095, and 0, for which it returns ACK 0. These TLPs are forwarded to the Transaction Layer. NEXT_RCV_SEQ is incre-

mented and the next value of NEXT_RCV_SEQ count is 1.

3. ACK 0 is lost en route. TLPs 4094, 4095, and 0 remain in Device A's Replay Buffer.
4. TLPs 1 and 2 arrive at Device B shortly thereafter. TLP 1 is good and NEXT_RCV_SEQ count increments to 2. TLP 1 is forwarded to the Transaction Layer.
5. TLP 2 is corrupt. NEXT_RCV_SEQ count remains at 2.
6. Device B returns a NAK with a Sequence Number of 1 and discards TLP 2.
7. NAK 1 arrives at Device A.
8. Device A first purges TLP 4094, 4095, 0 and 1
9. Device A replays TLP 2.
10. TLP 2 arrive at Device B. The NEXT_RCV_SEQ count is 2.
11. Device B accepts good TLP 2 and forwards it to the Transaction Layer. NEXT_RCV_SEQ increments to 3.
12. Device B may return an ACK with a Sequence Number of 2 if the ACKNAK_LATENCY_TIMER expires.
13. Upon receipt of ACK 2, Device A purges TLP 2.

Figure 5-16: Lost ACK DLLP Handling

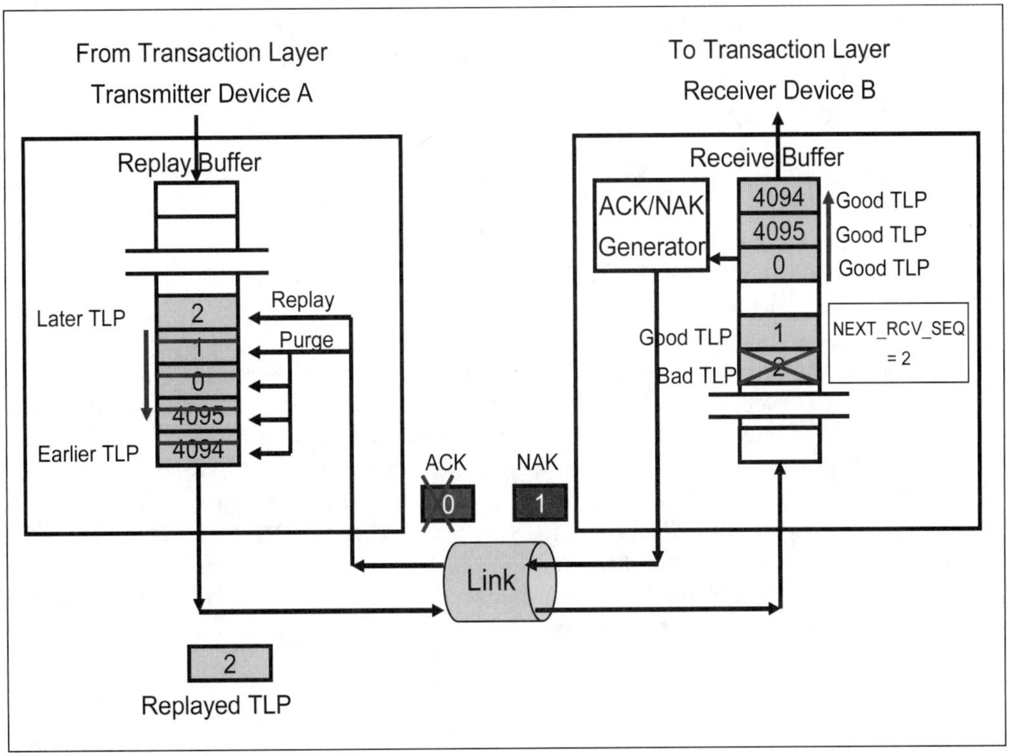

Switch Cut-Through Mode

PCI Express supports a switch-related feature that allows TLP transfer latency through a switch to be significantly reduced. This feature is referred to as the 'cut-through' mode. Without this feature, the propagation time through a switch could be significant.

Without Cut-Through Mode

Background

Consider an example where a large TLP needs to pass through a switch from one port to another. Until the tail end of the TLP is received by the switch's ingress port, the switch is unable to determine if there is a CRC error. Typically, the switch will not forward the packet through the egress port until it determines that there is no CRC error. This implies that the latency through the switch is at least the time to clock the packet into the switch. If the packet needs to pass through many switches to get to the final destination, the latencies would add up, increasing the time to get from source to destination.

Possible Solution

One option to reduce latency would be to start forwarding the TLP through the switch's egress port before the tail end of the TLP has been received by the switch ingress port. This is fine as long as the packet is not corrupted. Consider what would happen if the TLP were corrupt. The packet would begin transmitting through the egress port before the switch realized that there is an error. After the switch detects the CRC error, it would return a NAK to the TLP source and discard the packet, *but part of the packet has already been transmitted and its transmission cannot be cleanly aborted in mid-transmit*. There is no point keeping a copy of the bad TLP in the egress port Replay Buffer because it is bad. The TLP source port would at a later time replay after receiving the NAK DLLP. The TLP is already outbound and en route to the Endpoint destination. The Endpoint receives the packet, detects a CRC error, and returns a NAK to the switch. The switch is expected to replay the TLP, but the switch has already discarded the TLP due to the detected error on the inbound TLP. The switch is stuck between a rock and a hard place!

Switch Cut-Through Mode

Background

The PCI Express protocol permits the implementation of an optional feature referred to as cut-through mode. Cut-though is the ability to start streaming a packet through a switch without waiting for the receipt of the tail end of the packet. If, ultimately, a CRC error is detected when the CRC is received at the tail end of the packet, the packet that has already begun transmission from the switch egress port can be 'nullified'.

A **nullified** packet is a packet that terminates with an EDB symbol as opposed to an END. It also has an inverted 32-bit LCRC.

Example That Demonstrates Switch Cut-Through Feature

Consider the example in Figure 5-17 that illustrates the cut-though mode of a switch.

A TLP with large data payload passes from the left, through the switch, to the Endpoint on the right. The steps as the packet is routed through the switch are as follows:

1. A TLP is inbound to a switch. While en route, the packet's contents is corrupted.
2. The TLP header at the head of the TLP is decoded by the switch and the packet is forwarded to the egress port before the switch becomes aware of a CRC error. Finally, the tail end of the packet arrives in the switch ingress port and it is able to complete a CRC check.
3. The switch detects a CRC error for which the switch returns a NAK DLLP to the TLP source.
4. On the egress port, the switch replaces the END framing symbol at the tail end of the bad TLP with the EDB (End Bad) symbol. The CRC is also inverted from what it would normally be. The TLP is now 'nullified'. Once the TLP has exited the switch, the switch discards its copy from the Replay Buffer.
5. The nullified packet arrives at the Endpoint. The Endpoint detects the EDB symbol and the inverted CRC and discards the packet.
6. The Endpoint does not return a NAK DLLP (otherwise the switch would be obliged to replay).

When the TLP source device receives the NAK DLLP, it replays the packet. This time no error occurs on the switch's ingress port. As the packet arrives in the switch, the header is decoded and the TLP is forwarded to the egress port with very short latency. When the tail end of the TLP arrives at the switch, a CRC check is performed. There is no error, so an ACK is returned to the TLP source which then purges its replay buffer. The switch stores a copy of the TLP in its egress port Replay Buffer. When the TLP reaches the destination Endpoint, the Endpoint device performs a CRC check. The packet is a good packet terminated with the END framing symbol. There are no CRC errors and so the Endpoint returns an ACK DLLP to the switch. The switch purges the copy of the TLP from its Replay Buffer. The packet has been routed from source to destination with minimal latency.

Figure 5-17: Switch Cut-Through Mode Showing Error Handling

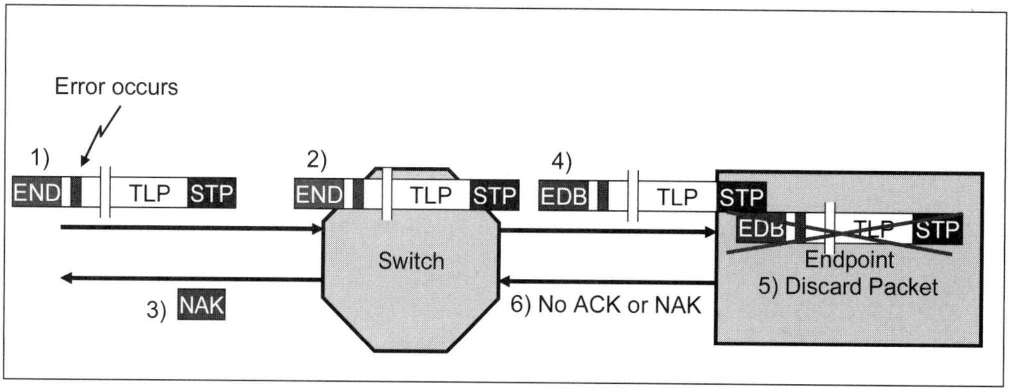

6 QoS/TCs/VCs and Arbitration

The Previous Chapter

The previous chapter detailed the Ack/Nak Protocol that verifies the delivery of TLPs between each port as they travel between the requester and completer devices. This chapter details the hardware retry mechanism that is automatically triggered when a TLP transmission error is detected on a given link.

This Chapter

This chapter discusses Traffic Classes, Virtual Channels, and Arbitration that support Quality of Service concepts in PCI Express implementations. The concept of Quality of Service in the context of PCI Express is an attempt to predict the bandwidth and latency associated with the flow of different transaction streams traversing the PCI Express fabric. The use of QoS is based on application-specific software assigning Traffic Class (TC) values to transactions, which define the priority of each transaction as it travels between the Requester and Completer devices. Each TC is mapped to a Virtual Channel (VC) that is used to manage transaction priority via two arbitration schemes called port and VC arbitration.

The Next Chapter

The next chapter discusses the purposes and detailed operation of the Flow Control Protocol. This protocol requires each device to implement credit-based link flow control for each virtual channel on each port. Flow control guarantees that transmitters will never send Transaction Layer Packets (TLPs) that the receiver can't accept. This prevents receive buffer over-runs and eliminates the need for inefficient disconnects, retries, and wait-states on the link. Flow Control also helps enable compliance with PCI Express ordering rules by maintaining separate virtual channel Flow Control buffers for three types of transactions: Posted (P), Non-Posted (NP) and Completions (Cpl).

Quality of Service

Quality of Service (QoS) is a generic term that normally refers to the ability of a network or other entity (in our case, PCI Express) to provide predictable latency and bandwidth. QoS is of particular interest when applications require guaranteed bus bandwidth at regular intervals, such as audio data. To help deal with this type of requirement PCI Express defines isochronous transactions that require a high degree of QoS. However, QoS can apply to any transaction or series of transactions that must traverse the PCI Express fabric. Note that QoS can only be supported when the system and device-specific software is PCI Express aware.

QoS can involve many elements of performance including:

- Transmission rate
- Effective Bandwidth
- Latency
- Error rate
- Other parameters that affect performance

Several features of PCI Express architecture provide the mechanisms that make QoS achievable. The PCI Express features that support QoS include:

- Traffic Classes (TCs)
- Virtual Channels (VCs)
- Port Arbitration
- Virtual Channel Arbitration
- Link Flow Control

PCI Express uses these features to support two general classes of transactions that can benefit from the PCI Express implementation of QoS.

Isochronous Transactions — from Iso (same) + chronous (time), these transactions require a constant bus bandwidth at regular intervals along with guaranteed latency. Isochronous transactions are most often used when a synchronous connection is required between two devices. For example, a CD-ROM drive containing a music CD may be sourcing data to speakers. A synchronous connection exists when a headset is plugged directly into the drive. However, when the audio card is used to deliver the audio information to a set of external speakers, isochronous transactions may be used to simplify the delivery of the data.

Asynchronous Transactions This class of transactions involves a wide variety of applications that have widely varying requirements for bandwidth and latency. QoS can provide the more demanding applications (those requiring higher bandwidth and shorter latencies) with higher priority than the less demanding applications. In this way, software can establish a hierarchy of traffic classes for transactions that permits differentiation of transaction priority based on their requirements. The specification refers to this capability as differentiated services.

Isochronous Transaction Support

PCI Express supports QoS and the associated TC, VC, and arbitration mechanisms so that isochronous transactions can be performed. A classic example of a device that benefits from isochronous transaction support is a video camera attached to a tape deck. This real-time application requires that image and audio data be transferred at a constant rate (e.g., 64 frames/second). This type of application is typically supported via a direct synchronous attachment between the two devices.

Synchronous Versus Isochronous Transactions

Two devices connected directly perform synchronous transfers. A synchronous source delivers data directly to the synchronous sink through use of a common reference clock. In our example, the video camera (synchronous source) sends audio and video data to the tape deck (synchronous sink), which immediately stores the data in real time with little or no data buffering, and with only a slight delay due to signal propagation.

When these devices are connected via PCI Express a synchronous connection is not possible. Instead, PCI Express emulates synchronous connections through the use of isochronous transactions and data buffering. In this scenario, isochronous transactions can be used to ensure that a constant amount of data is delivered at specified intervals (100µs in this example), thus achieving the required transmission characteristics. Consider the following sequence (Refer to Figure 6-1 on page 254):

1. The synchronous source (video camera and PCI Express interface) accumulates data in Buffer A during service interval 1 (SI 1).
2. The camera delivers the accumulated data to the synchronous sink (tape deck) sometime during the next service interval (SI 2). The camera also accumulates the next block of data in Buffer B as the contents of Buffer A is delivered.

3. The tape deck buffers the incoming data (in its Buffer A), which can then be delivered synchronously for recording on tape during service interval 3. During SI 3 the camera once again accumulates data into Buffer A, and the cycle repeats.

Figure 6-1: Example Application of Isochronous Transaction

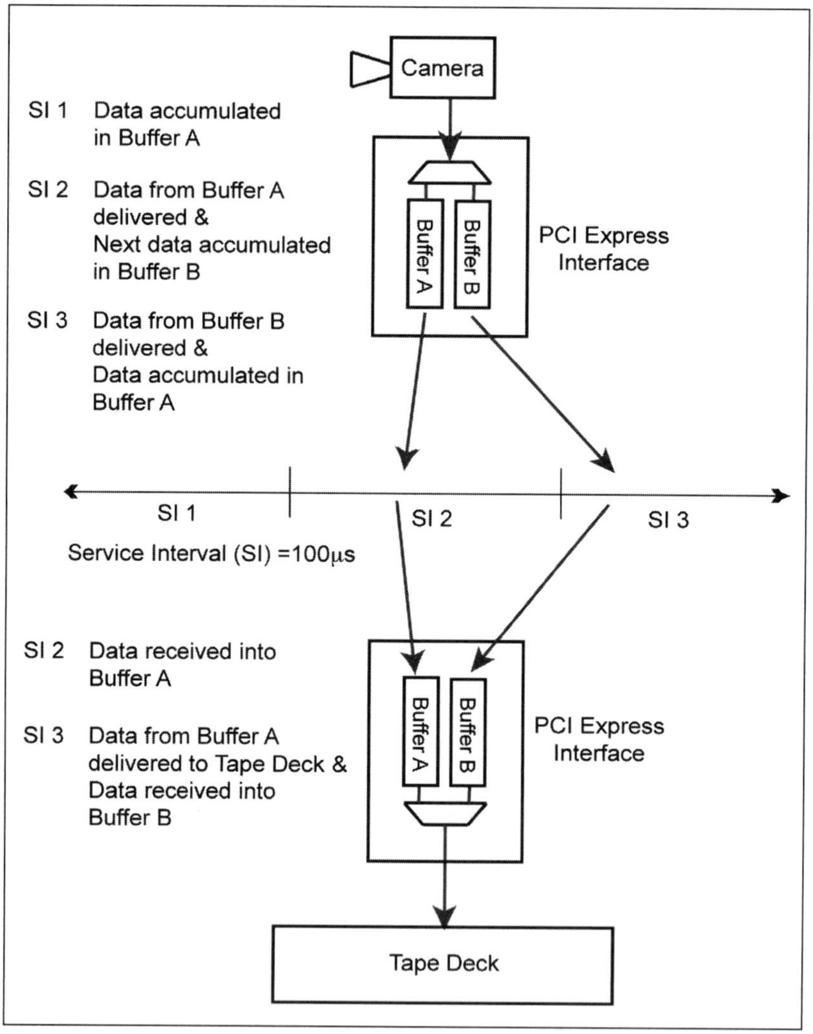

Isochronous Transaction Management

Management of an isochronous communications channel is based on a Traffic Class (TC) value and an associated Virtual Channel (VC) number that software assigns during initialization. Hardware components including the Requester of a transaction and all devices in the path between the requester and completer are configured to transport the isochronous transactions from link to link via a hi-priority virtual channel.

The requester initiates isochronous transactions that include a TC value representing the desired QoS. The Requester injects isochronous packets into the fabric at the required rate (service interval), and all devices in the path between the Requester and Completer must be configured to support the transport of the isochronous transactions at the specified interval. Any intermediate device along the path must convert the TC to the associated VC used to control transaction arbitration. This arbitration results in the desired bandwidth and latency for transactions with the assigned TC. Note that the TC value remains constant for a given transaction while the VC number may change from link to link.

Differentiated Services

Various types of asynchronous traffic (all traffic other than isochronous) have different priority from the system perspective. For example, ethernet traffic requires higher priority (smaller latencies) than mass storage transactions. PCI Express software can establish different TC values and associated virtual channels and can set up the communications paths to ensure different delivery policies are established as required. Note that the specification does not define specific methods for identifying delivery requirements or the policies to be used when setting up differentiated services.

Perspective on QOS/TC/VC and Arbitration

PCI does not include any QoS-related features similar to those defined by PCI Express. Many questions arise regarding the need for such an elaborate scheme for managing traffic flow based on QoS and differentiated services. Without implementing these new features, the bandwidth available with a PCI Express system is far greater and latencies much shorter than PCI-based implementations, due primarily to the topology and higher delivery rates. Consequently, aside from the possible advantage of isochronous transactions, there appears to be little advantage to implementing systems that support multiple Traffic

Classes and Virtual Channels.

While this may be true for most desktop PCs, other high-end applications may benefit significantly from these new features. The PCI Express specification also opens the door to applications that demand the ability to differentiate and manage system traffic based on Traffic Class prioritization.

Traffic Classes and Virtual Channels

During initialization a PCI Express device-driver communicates the levels of QoS that it desires for its transactions, and the operating system returns TC values that correspond to the QoS requested. The TC value ultimately determines the relative priority of a given transaction as it traverses the PCI Express fabric. Two hardware mechanisms provide guaranteed isochronous bandwidth and differentiated services:

- Virtual Channel Arbitration
- Port Arbitration

These arbitration mechanisms use VC numbers to manage transaction priority. System configuration software must assign VC IDs and set up the association between the traffic class assigned to a transaction and the virtual channel to be used when traversing each link. This is done via VC configuration registers mapped within the extended configuration address space. The list of these registers and their location within configuration space is illustrated in Figure 6-2.

Figure 6-2: VC Configuration Registers Mapped in Extended Configuration Address Space

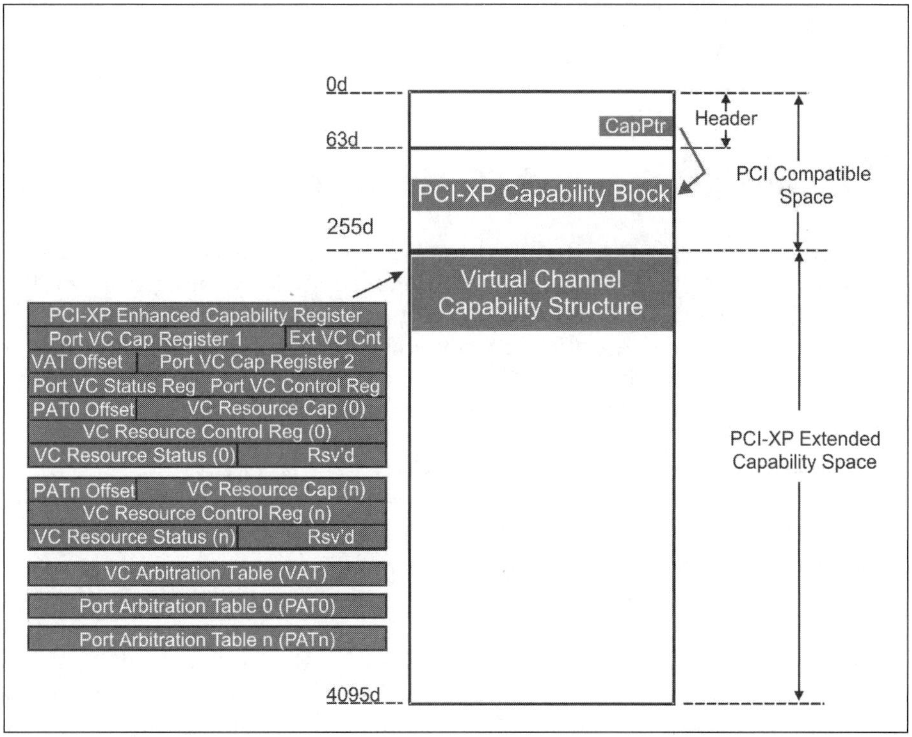

The TC value is carried in the transaction packet header and can contain one of eight values (TC0-TC7). TC0 must be implemented by all PCI Express devices and the system makes a "best effort" when delivering transactions with the TC0 label. TC values of TC1-TC7 are optional and provide seven levels of arbitration for differentiating between packet streams that require varying amounts of bandwidth. Similarly, eight VC numbers (VC0-VC7) are specified, with VC0 required and VC1-VC7 optional. ("VC Assignment and TC Mapping" on page 258 discusses VC initialization).

Note that TC0 is hardwired to VC0 in all devices. If configuration software is not PCI Express aware all transactions will use the default TC0 and VC0; thereby eliminating the possibility of supporting differentiated services and isochronous transactions. Furthermore, the specification requires some transaction types to use TC0/VC0 exclusively:

- Configuration
- I/O

- INTx Message
- Power Management Message
- Error Signaling Message
- Unlock Message
- Set_Slot_Power_Limit Message

VC Assignment and TC Mapping

Configuration software designed for PCI Express sets up virtual channels for each link in the fabric. Recall that the default TC and VC assignments following Cold Reset will be TC0 and VC0, which is used when the configuration software is not PCI Express aware. The number of virtual channels used depends on the greatest capability shared by the two devices attached to a given link. Software assigns an ID for each VC and maps one or more TCs to each.

Determining the Number of VCs to be Used

Software checks the number of VCs supported by the devices attached to a common link and assigns the greatest number of VCs that both devices have in common. For example, consider the three devices attached to the switch in Figure 6-3 on page 259. In this example, the switch supports all 8 VCs on each of its ports; while Device A supports only the default VC, Device B supports 4 VC s, and Device C support 8 VCs. When configuring VCs for each link, software determines the maximum number of VCs supported by both devices at each end of the link and assigns that number to both devices. The VC assignment applies to transactions flowing across a link in both directions.

Figure 6-3: The Number of VCs Supported by Device Can Vary

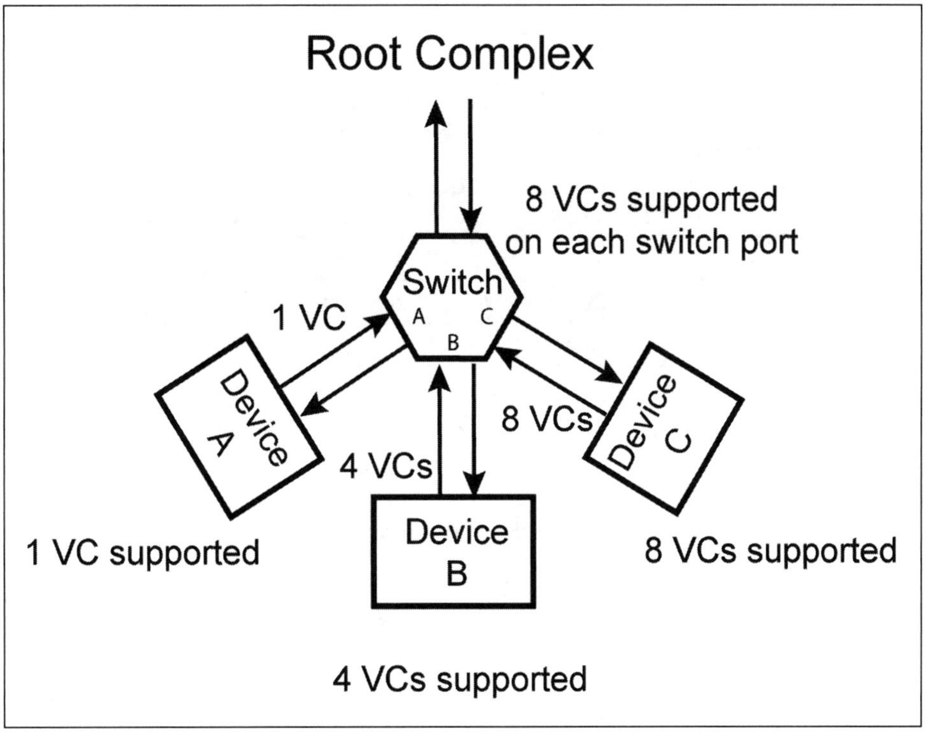

Note that even though switch port A supports all 8 VCs Device A supports a single VC, leaving 7 VCs unused within switch port A. Similarly, 4 VCs are used by switch port B. Software of course configures and enables all 8 VCs within switch port C.

Configuration software determines the maximum number of VCs supported by each port interface by reading its *Extended VC Count* field contained within the "Virtual Channel Capability" registers. The smaller of the two values governs the maximum number of VCs supported by this link for both transmission and reception of transactions. Figure 6-4 on page 260 illustrates the location and format of the Extended VC Count field. Software may restrict the number of VCs configured and enabled to fewer than actually allowed. This may be done to achieve the QoS desired for a given platform or application.

Figure 6-4: Extended VCs Supported Field

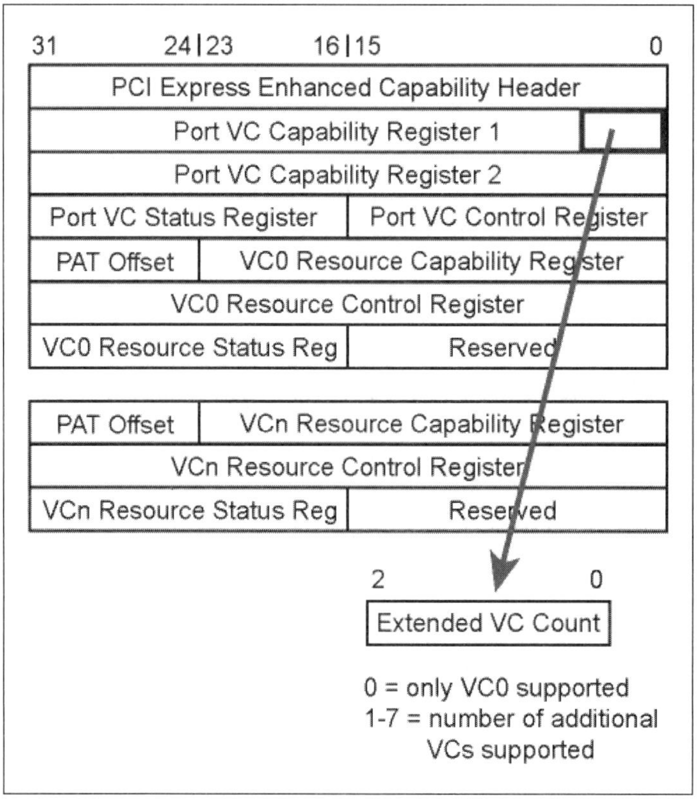

Assigning VC Numbers (IDs)

Configuration software must assign VC numbers or IDs to each of the virtual channels, except VC0 which is always hardwired. As illustrated in Figure 6-5 on page 261, the VC Capabilities registers include 3 DWs used for configuring each VC. The first set of registers (starting at offset 10h) always applies to VC0. The *Extended VCs Count* field (described above) defines the number of additional VC register sets implemented by this port, each of which permits configuration of an additional VC. Note that these register sets are mapped in configuration space directly following the VC0 registers. The mapping is expressed as an offset from each of the three VC0 DW registers:

- 10h + (n*0Ch)
- 14h + (n*0Ch)
- 18h + (n*0Ch)

The value "n" represents the number of additional VCs implemented. For example, if the *Extended VCs Count* contains a value of 3, then n=1, 2, and 3 for the three additional register sets. Note that these numbers simply identify the register sets for each VC supported and is not the VC ID.

Software assigns a VC ID for each of the additional VCs being used via the *VC ID* field within the VCn Resource Control Register. (See Figure 6-5) These IDs are not required to be assigned contiguous values, but the same VC value can be used only once.

Figure 6-5: VC Resource Control Register

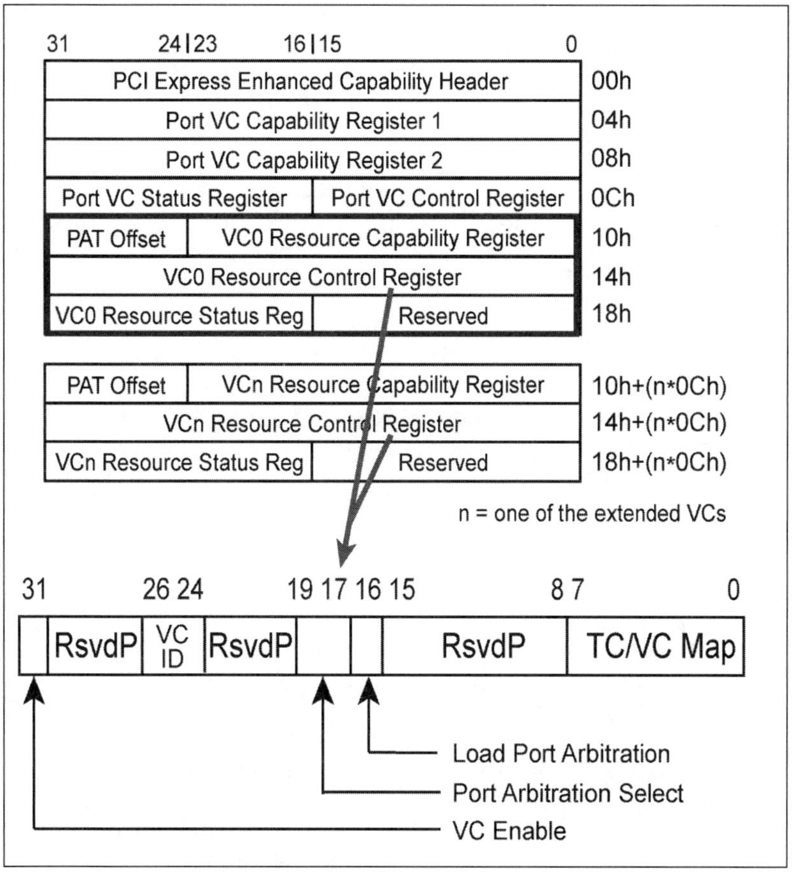

Assigning TCs to each VC — TC/VC Mapping

The Traffic Class value assigned by a requester to each transaction must be associated with a VC as it traverses each link on its journey to the recipient. Also, the VC ID associated with a given TC may change from link to link. Configuration software establishes this association during initialization via the *TC/VC Map* field of the VC Resource Control Register. This 8-bit field permits any TC value to be mapped to the selected VC, where each bit position represents the corresponding TC value (i.e., bit 0 = TC0:: bit 7 = TC7). Setting a bit assigns the corresponding TC value to the VC ID. Figure 6-6 shows a mapping example where TC0 and TC1 are mapped to VC0 and TC2::TC4 are mapped to VC3.

Figure 6-6: TC to VC Mapping Example

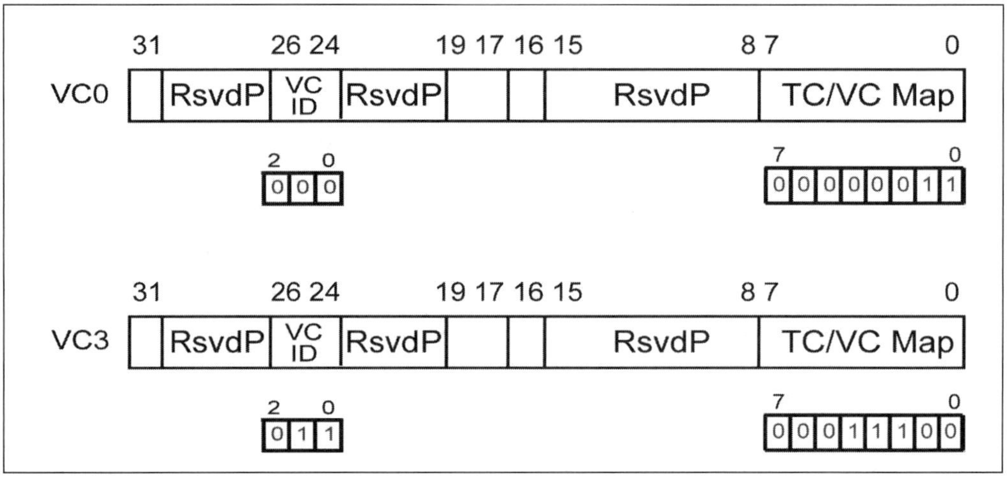

Software is permitted a great deal of flexibility in assigning VC IDs and mapping the associated TCs. However, the specification states several rules associated with the TC/VC mapping:

- TC/VC mapping must be identical for the two ports attached to the same link.
- One TC must not be mapped to multiple VCs in any PCI Express Port.
- One or multiple TCs can be mapped to a single VC.

Table 6-1 on page 263 lists a variety of combinations that may be implemented. This is intended only to illustrate a few combinations, and many more are possible.

Table 6-1: Example TC to VC Mappings

TC	VC Assignment	Comment
TC0	VC0	Default setting, used by all transactions.
TC0-TC1 TC2-TC7	VC0 VC7	VCs are not required to be assigned consecutively. Multiple TCs can be assigned to a single VC.
TC0 TC1 TC6 TC7	VC0 VC1 VC6 VC7	Several transaction types must use TC0/VC0. (1) TCs are not required to be assigned consecutively. Some TC/VC combinations can be used to support an isochronous connection.
TC0 TC1 TC2 TC3 TC4 TC5 TC6 TC7	VC0 VC1 VC2 VC3 VC4 VC5 VC6 VC7	All TCs can be assigned to the corresponding VC numbers.
TC0 TC1-TC4	VC0 VC6	The VC number that is assigned need not match one of the corresponding TC numbers.
TC0 TC1-TC2 TC2	VC0 VC1 VC2	**Illegal**. A TC number can be assigned to only one VC number. This example shows TC2 mapped to both VC1 and VC2, which is not allowed.

Arbitration

Two types of transaction arbitration provide the method for managing isochronous transactions and differentiated services:

- **Virtual Channel (VC) Arbitration** — determines the priority of transactions being transmitted from the same port, based on their VC ID.
- **Port Arbitration** — determines the priority of transactions with the same VC assignment at the egress port, based on the priority of the port at which the transactions arrived. Port arbitration applies to transactions that have the same VC ID at the egress port, therefore a port arbitration mechanism exists for each virtual channel supported by the egress port.

Arbitration is also affected by the requirements associated with transaction ordering and flow control. These additional requirements are discussed in subsequent chapters, but are mentioned in the context of arbitration as required in the following discussions.

Virtual Channel Arbitration

In addition to supporting QoS objectives, VC arbitration should also ensure that forward progress is made for all transactions. This prevents inadvertent split transaction time-outs. Any device that both initiates transactions and supports two or more VCs must implement VC arbitration. Furthermore, other device types that support more than one VC (e.g., switches) must also support VC arbitration.

VC arbitration allows a transmitting device to determine the priority of transactions based on their VC assignment. Key characteristics of VCs that are relevant to VC arbitration include:

- Each VC supported and enabled provides its own buffers and flow control.
- Transactions mapped to the same VC are issued in strict order (unless the "Relaxed Ordering" attribute bit is set).
- No ordering relationship exists between transactions assigned to different VCs.

Figure 6-7 on page 265 illustrates the concept of VC arbitration. In this example two VCs are implemented (VC0 and VC1) and transmission priority is based on a 3:1 ratio, where 3 VC1 transactions are sent to each VC0 transaction. The device core issues transactions (that include a TC value) to the TC/VC Mapping logic. Based on the associated VC value, the transaction is routed to the appropriate VC buffer where it awaits transmission. The VC arbiter determines the VC buffer priority when sending transactions.

This example illustrates the flow of transaction in only one direction. The same logic exists for transmitting transactions simultaneously in the opposite direction. That is, the root port also contains transmit buffers and an arbiter and the endpoint device contains receive buffers.

Figure 6-7: Conceptual VC Arbitration Example

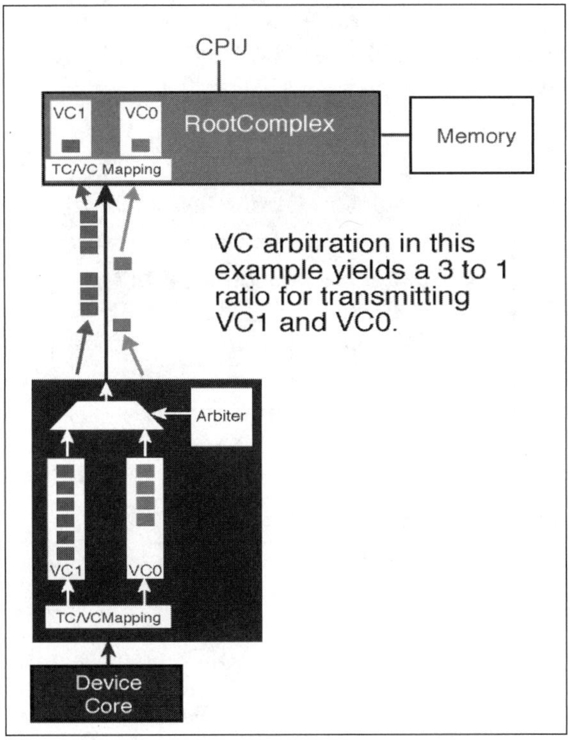

A variety of VC arbitration mechanisms may be employed by a given design. The method chosen by the designer is specified within the VC capability registers. In general, there are three approaches that can be taken:

- Strict Priority Arbitration for all VCs
- Split Priority Arbitration — VCs are segmented into low- and high-priority groups. The low-priority group uses some form of round robin arbitration and the high-priority group uses strict priority.
- Round robin priority (standard or weighted) arbitration for all VCs

Strict Priority VC Arbitration

The specification defines a default priority scheme based on the inherent priority of VC IDs (VC0=lowest priority and VC7=highest priority). The arbitration mechanism is hardware based, and requires no configuration. Figure 6-8 illustrates a strict priority arbitration example that includes all VCs. The VC ID governs the order in which transactions are sent. The maximum number of VCs that use strict priority arbitration cannot be greater than the value in the *Extended VC Count* field. (See Figure 6-4 on page 260.) Furthermore, if the designer has chosen strict priority arbitration for all VCs supported, the *Low Priority Extended VC Count* field of Port VC Capability Register 1 is hardwired to zero. (See Figure 6-9 on page 267.)

Figure 6-8: Strict Arbitration Priority

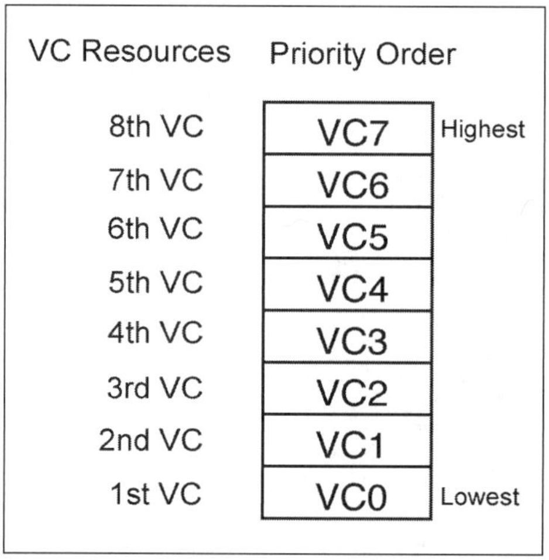

Strict priority requires that VCs of higher priority get precedence over lower priority VCs based on the VC ID. For example, if all eight VCs are governed by strict priority, transactions with a VC ID of VC0 can only be sent when no transactions are pending transmission in VC1-VC7. In some circumstances strict priority can result in lower priority transactions being starved for bandwidth and experiencing extremely long latencies. Conversely, the highest priority transactions receive very high bandwidth with minimal latencies. The specification requires that high priority traffic be regulated to avoid starvation, and further defines two methods of regulation:

- The originating port can manage the injection rate of high priority transactions, to permit greater bandwidth for lower priority transactions.
- Switches can regulate multiple data flows at the egress port that are vying for link bandwidth. This method may limit the throughput from high bandwidth applications and devices that attempt to exceed the limitations of the available bandwidth.

The designer of a device may also limit the number of VCs that participate in strict priority by specifying a split between the low- and high-priority VCs as discussed in the next section.

Low- and High-Priority VC Arbitration

Figure 6-9 on page 267 illustrates the *Low Priority Extended VC Count* field within VC Capability Register 1. This read-only field specifies a VC ID value that identifies the upper limit of the low-priority arbitration group for the design. For example, if this count contains a value of 4, then VC0-VC4 are members of the low-priority group and VC5-VC7 use strict priority. Note that a *Low Priority Extended VC Count* of 7 means that no strict priority is used.

Figure 6-9: Low Priority Extended VC Count

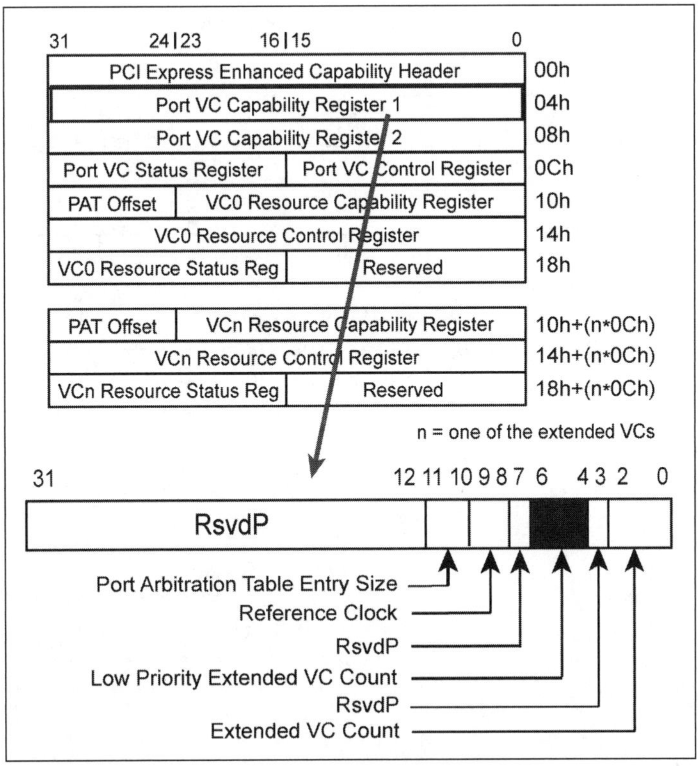

As depicted in Figure 6-11 on page 269, the high-priority VCs continue to use strict priority arbitration, while the low-priority arbitration group uses one of the other prioritization methods supported by the device. VC Capability Register 2 reports which alternate arbitration methods are supported for the low priority group, and the VC Control Register permits selection of the method to be used by this group. See Figure 6-10 on page 268. The low-priority arbitration schemes include:

- Hardware Based Fixed Arbitration Scheme — the specification permits the vendor to define a hardware-based fixed arbitration scheme that provides all VCs with the same priority. (e.g. round robin).
- Weighted Round Robin (WRR) — with WRR some VCs can be given higher priority than others because they have more positions within the round robin than others. The specification defines three WRR configurations, each with a different number of entries (or phases).

Figure 6-10: Determining VC Arbitration Capabilities and Selecting the Scheme

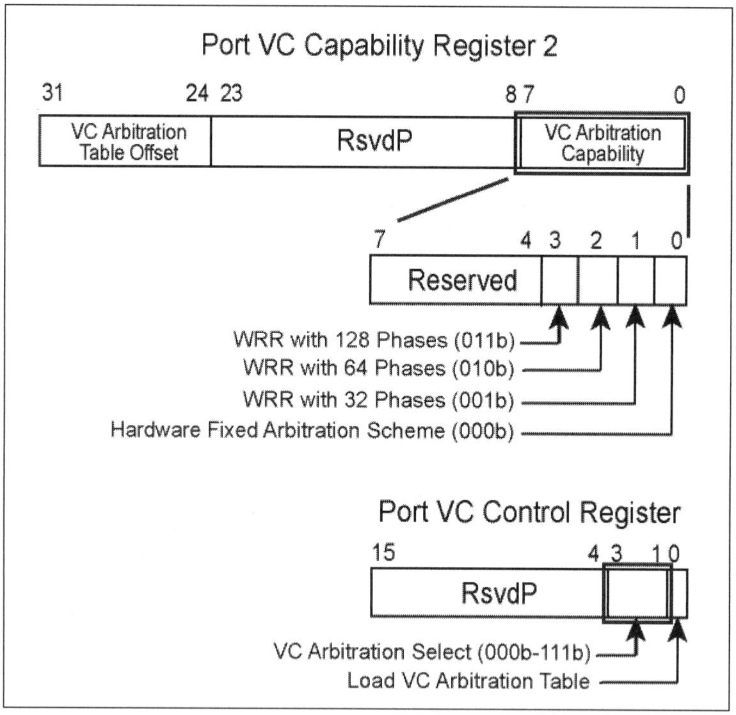

Figure 6-11: VC Arbitration with Low- and High-Priority Implementations

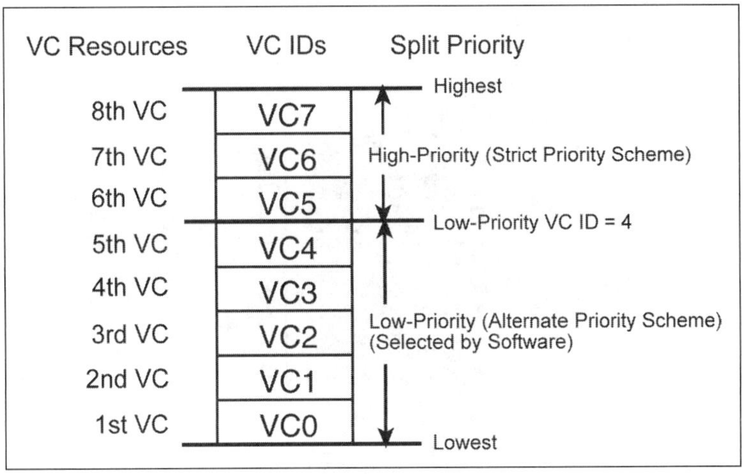

Hardware Fixed Arbitration Scheme. This selection defines a hardware-based VC arbitration scheme that requires no additional software setup. The specification mentions standard Round Robin arbitration as an example scheme that the designer may choose. In such a scheme, transactions pending transmission within each low-priority VC are sent during each pass through the round robin. The specification does not preclude other implementation-specific schemes.

Weighted Round Robin Arbitration Scheme. The weighted round robin (WRR) approach permits software to configure the VC Arbitration table. The number of arbitration table entries supported by the design is reported in the *VC Arbitration Capability* field of Port VC Capability Register 2. The table size is selected by writing the corresponding value in to the *VC Arbitration Select* field of the Port VC Control Register. See Figure 6-10 on page 268. Each entry in the table represents one phase that software loads with a low priority VC ID value. The VC arbiter repeatedly scans all table entries in a sequential fashion and sends transactions from the VC buffer specified in the table entries. Once a transaction has been sent, the arbiter immediately proceeds to the next phase.

Software can set up the VC arbitration table such that some VCs are listed in more entries than others; thereby, allowing differentiation of QoS between the VCs. This gives software considerable flexibility in establishing the desired priority. Figure 6-12 on page 270 depicts the weighted round robin VC arbitration concept.

Figure 6-12: Weighted Round Robin Low-Priority VC Arbitration Table Example

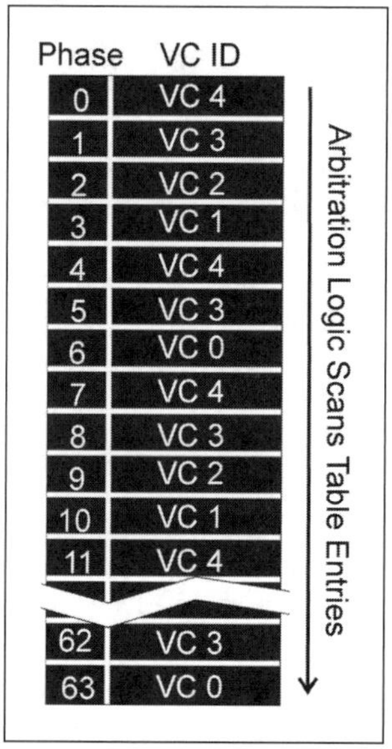

Round Robin Arbitration (Equal or Weighted) for All VCs

The hardware designer may choose to implement one of the round robin forms of VC arbitration for all VCs. This is accomplished by specifying the highest VC number supported by the device as a member of the low priority group (via the *Lowest Priority Extended Count* field. In this case, all VC priorities are managed via the VC arbitration table. Note that the VC arbitration table is not used when the Hardware Fixed Round Robin scheme is selected. See page 269.

Loading the Virtual Channel Arbitration Table

The VC Arbitration Table (VAT) is located at an offset from the beginning of the extended configuration space as indicated by the VC Arbitration Table Offset field. This offset is contained within Port VC Capability Register 2. (See Figure 6-13 on page 271.)

Figure 6-13: VC Arbitration Table Offset and Load VC Arbitration Table Fields

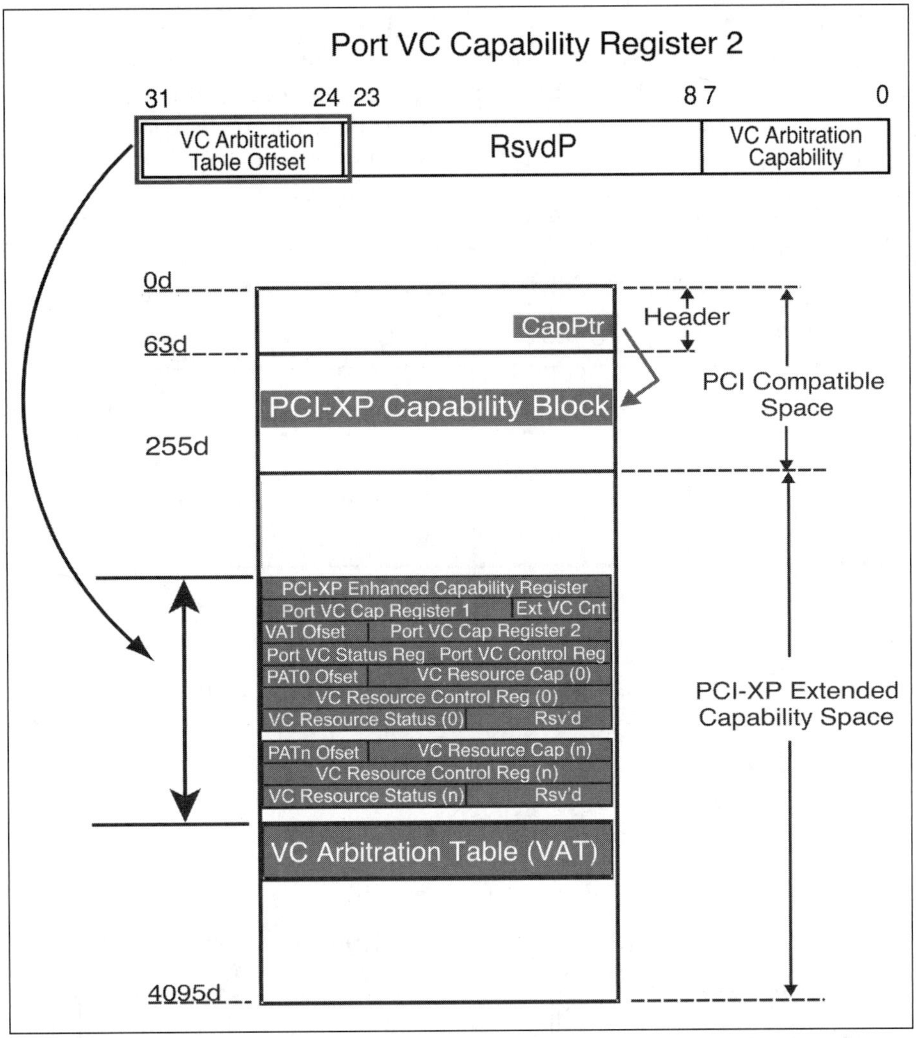

Refer to Figure 6-14 on page 272 during the following discussion. Each entry within the VAT is a 4-bit field that identifies the VC ID of the virtual channel buffer that is scheduled to deliver data during this corresponding phase. The table length is a function of the hardware design and the arbitration scheme selected if choices are supported by the design as illustrated in Figure 6-10 on page 268.

The table is loaded by configuration software to achieve the priority order desired for the virtual channels. Hardware sets the *VC Arbitration Table Status* bit when software updates any entry within the table. Once the table is loaded, software sets the *Load VC Arbitration Table* bit within the Port VC Control register. This bit causes hardware to load the new values into the VC Arbiter. Hardware clears the *VC Arbitration Table Status* bit when table loading is complete; thereby, permitting software to verify successful loading.

Figure 6-14: Loading the VC Arbitration Table Entries

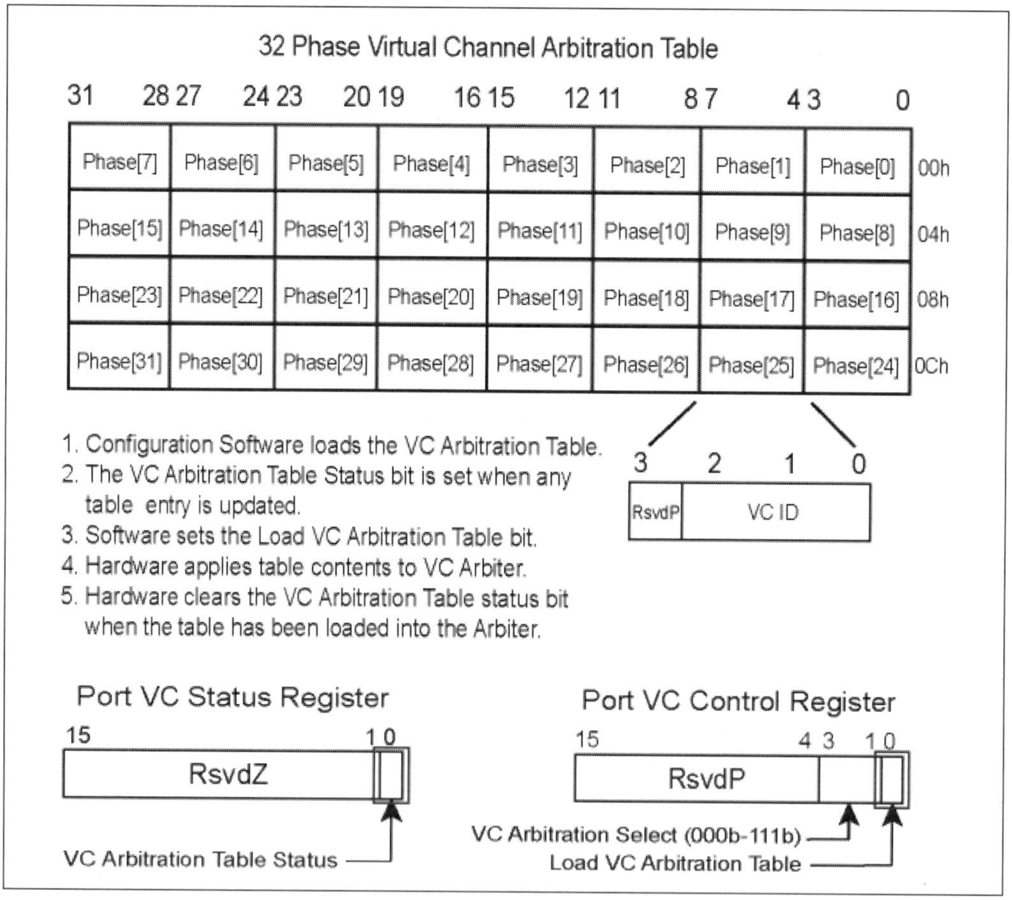

VC Arbitration within Multiple Function Endpoints

The specification does not state how an endpoint should manage the arbitration of data flows from different functions within an endpoint. However it does state that "Multi-function Endpoints... should support PCI Express VC-based arbitration control mechanisms if multiple VCs are implemented for the PCI Express Link." VC arbitration when there are multiple functions raises interesting questions about the approach to be taken. Of course when the device functions support only VC0, no VC arbitration is necessary. The specification leaves the approach open to the designer.

Figure 6-15 on page 274 shows a functional block diagram of an example implementation in which two functions are implemented within an endpoint device, each of which supports two VCs. The example approach is based upon the goal of using a standard PCI Express core to interface both functions to the link. The transaction layer within the link performs the TC/VC mapping and VC arbitration. The device-specific portion of the design is the function arbiter that determines the priority of data flows from the functions to the transaction layer of the core. Following are key considerations for such an approach:

- Rather than duplicating the TC/VC mapping within each function, the standard device core performs the task. An important consideration for this decision is that all functions must use the same TC/VC mapping. The specification requires that the TC/VC mapping be the same for devices at each end of a link. This means that each function within the endpoint must have the same mappings.
- The function arbiter used TC values to determine the priority of transactions being delivered from the two functions, and selects the highest priority transaction from the functions when forwarding transactions to the transaction layer of the PCI Express core. The arbitration algorithm is hardwired based on the applications associated with each function.

Figure 6-15: Example Multi-Function Endpoint Implementation with VC Arbitration

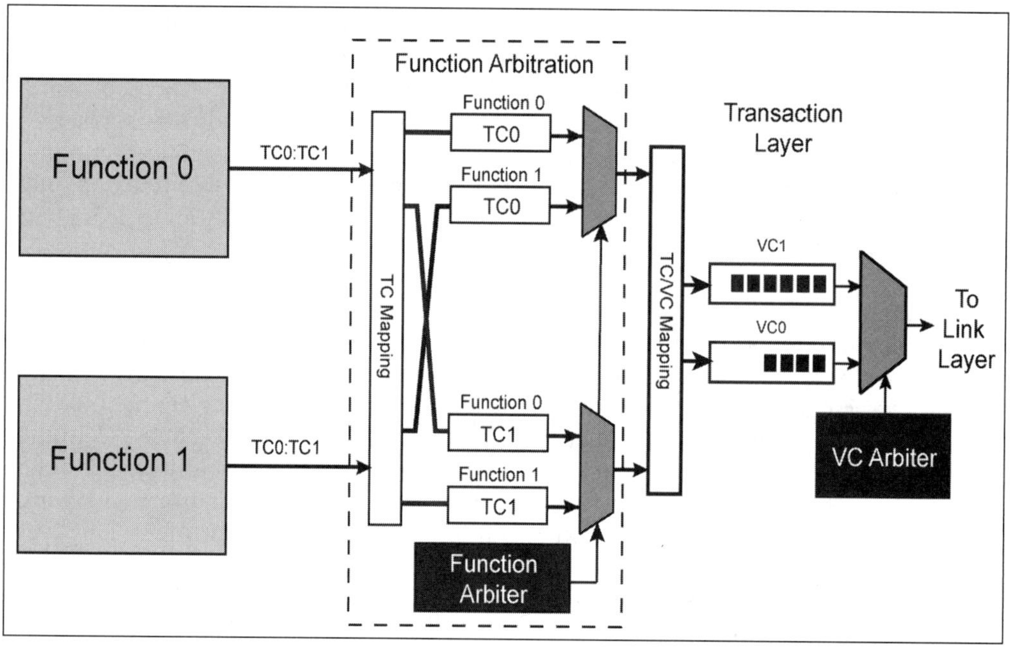

Port Arbitration

When traffic from multiple ports vie for limited bandwidth associated with a common egress port, arbitration is required. The concept of port arbitration is pictured in Figure 6-16 on page 275. Note that port arbitration exists in three locations within a system:

- Egress ports of switches
- Root Complex ports when peer-to-peer transactions are supported
- Root Complex egress ports to that lead to sources such as main memory

Port arbitration requires software configuration, which is handled via PCI-to-PCI bridge (PPB) configuration in both switches and peer-to-peer transfers within the Root Complex and by the Root Complex Register Block when accessing shared root complex resources such as main memory. Port arbitration occurs independently for each virtual channel supported by the egress port. In the example below, root port 2 supports peer-to-peer transfers from root ports 1 and 2; however, peer-to-peer transfer support between root complex ports is not required.

Because port arbitration is managed independently for each VC of the egress port or RCRB, a port arbitration table is required for each VC that supports programmable port arbitration as illustrated in Figure 6-17 on page 276. Port arbitration tables are supported only by switches and RCRBs and are not allowed for endpoints, root ports and PCI Express bridges.

Figure 6-16: Port Arbitration Concept

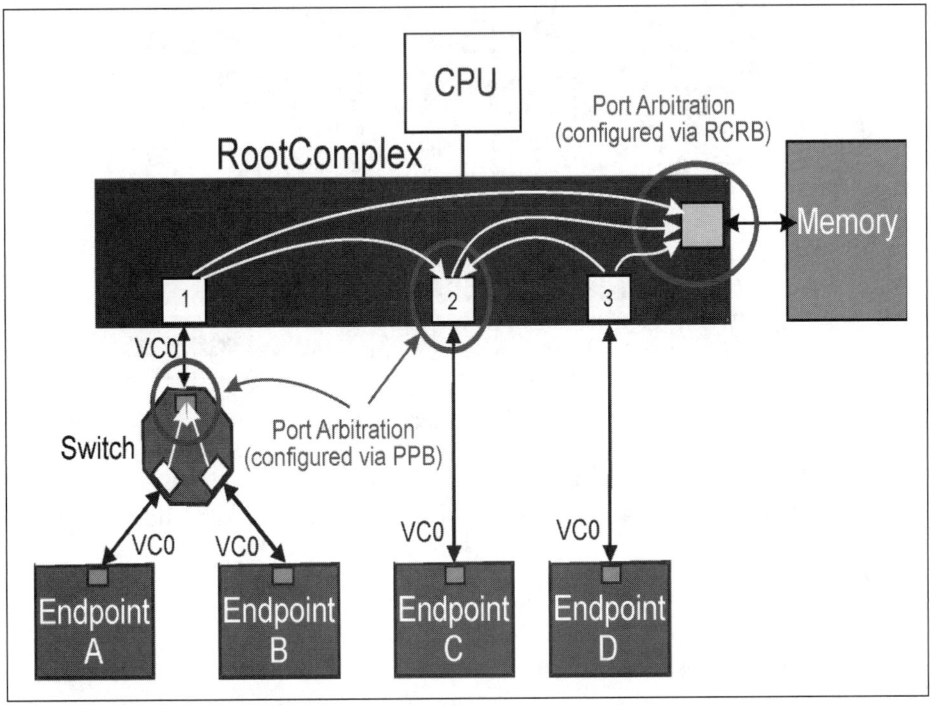

Figure 6-17: Port Arbitration Tables Needed for nEach VC

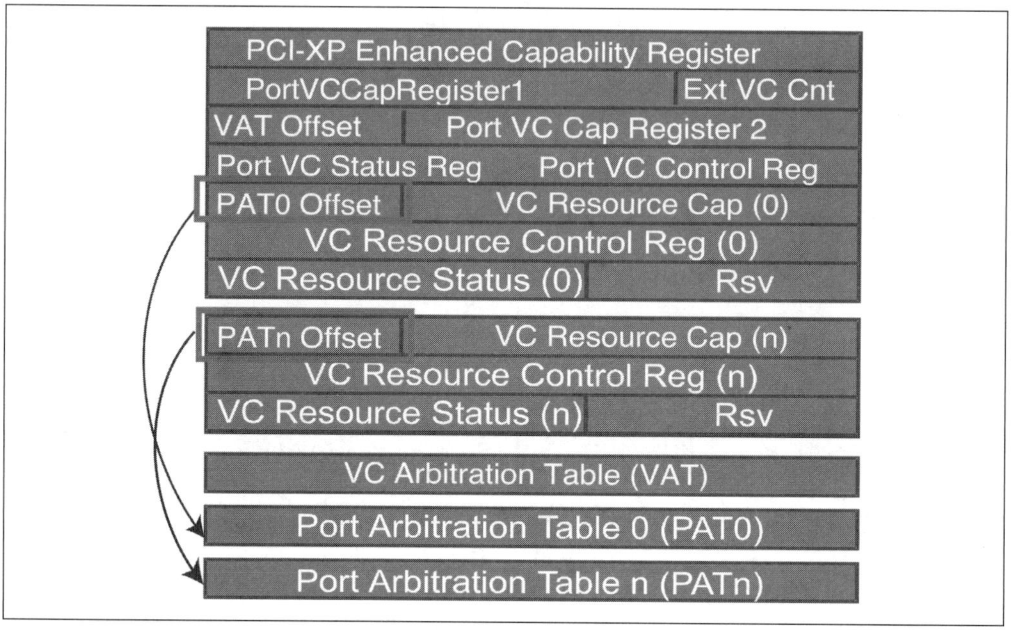

The process of arbitrating between different packet streams also implies the use of additional buffers to accumulate traffic from each port in the egress port as illustrated in Figure 6-18 on page 277. This example illustrates two ingress ports (1 and 2) whose transactions are routed to an egress port (3). The action taken by the switch include:

1. Transactions arriving at the ingress ports are directed to the appropriate flow control buffers based on the TC/VC mapping.
2. Transactions are forwarded from the flow control buffers to the routing logic is consulted to determine the egress port.
3. Transactions are routed to the egress port (3) where TC/VC mapping determines into which VC buffer the transactions should be placed.
4. A set of VC buffers is associated with each of the egress ports. Note that the ingress port number is tracked until transactions are placed in their VC buffer.
5. Port arbitration logic determines the order in which transactions are sent from each group of VC buffers.

Figure 6-18: Port Arbitration Buffering

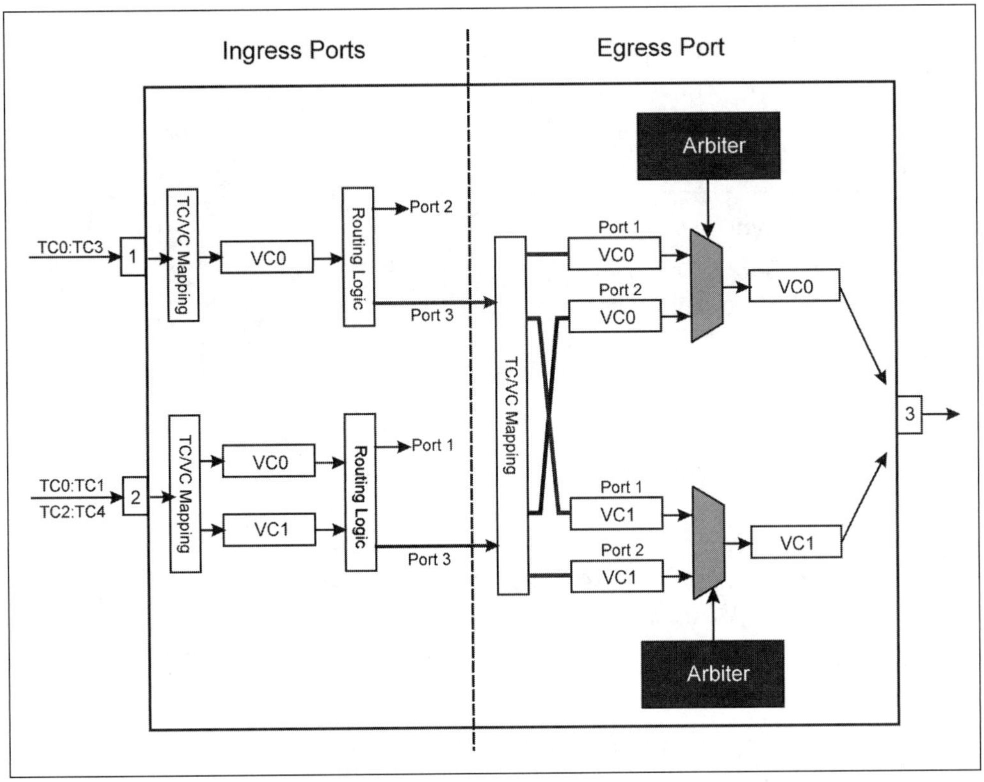

The Port Arbitration Mechanisms

The actual port arbitration mechanisms defined by the specification are similar to the models used for VC arbitration and include:

- Non-configurable hardware-fixed arbitration scheme
- Weighted Round Robin (WRR) arbitration with 32 phases
- WRR arbitration with 64 phases
- WRR arbitration with 128 phases
- Time-based WRR arbitration with 128 phases
- WRR arbitration with 256 phases

Configuration software must determine the port arbitration capability for a switch or RCRB and select the port arbitration scheme to be used for each enabled VC. Figure 6-19 on page 278 illustrates the registers and fields involved in determining port arbitration capabilities and selecting the port arbitration scheme to be used by each VC.

Figure 6-19: Software checks Port Arbitration Capabilities and Selects the Scheme to be Used.

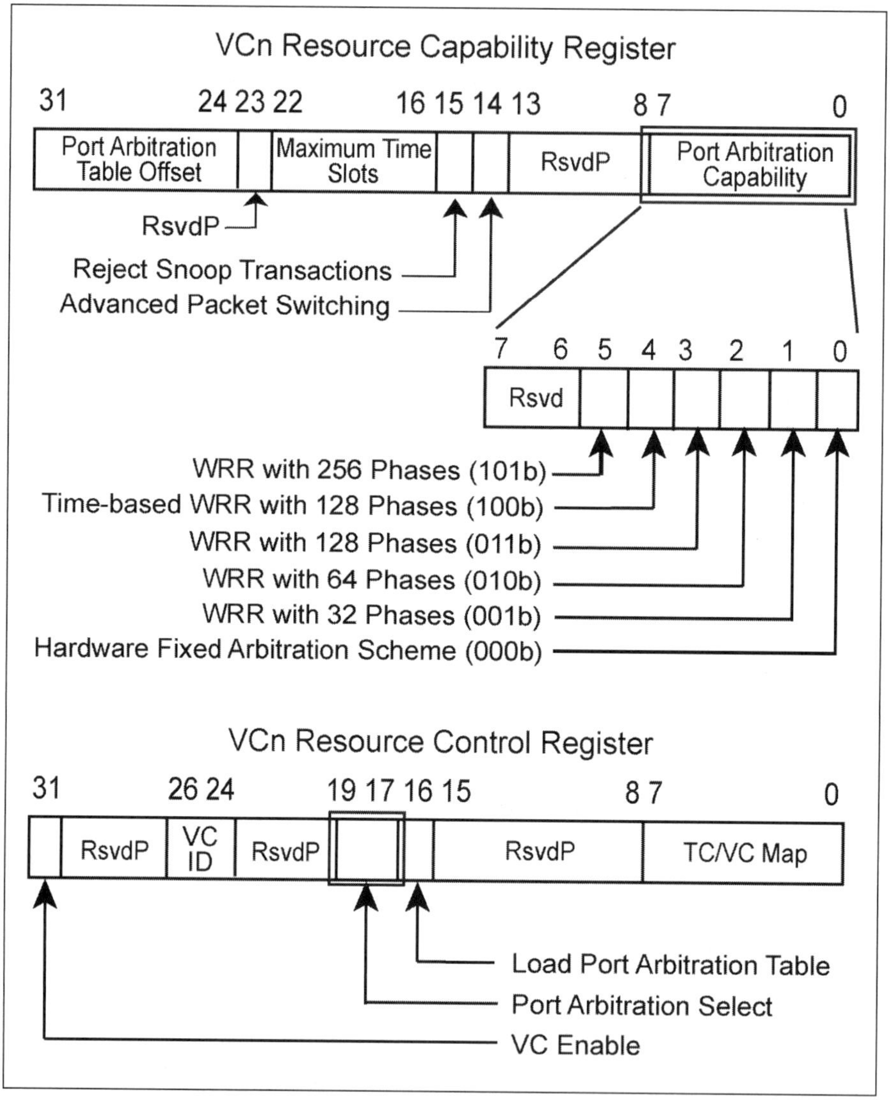

Non-Configurable Hardware-Fixed Arbitration. This port arbitration mechanism does not require configuration of the port arbitration table. Once selected by software, the mechanism is managed solely by hardware. The actual arbitration scheme is based on a round-robin or similar approach where each port has the same priority. This type of mechanism ensures a type of fairness and ensures that all transactions can make forward progress. However, it does not service the goals of differentiated services and does not support isochronous transactions.

Weighted Round Robin Arbitration. Like the weighted round robin mechanism used for VC arbitration, software loads the port arbitration table such that some ports can receive higher priority than others based on the number of phases in the round robin that are allocated for each port. This approach allows software to facilitate differentiated services by assigning different weights to traffic coming from different ports.

As the table is scanned each table phase specifies a port number that identifies the VC buffer from which the next transaction is sent. Once the transaction is delivered arbitration control logic immediately proceeds to the next phase. For a given port, if no transaction is pending transmission the arbiter advances immediately to the next phase.

The specification defines four table lengths for WRR port arbitration, determined by the number of phases used by the table. The table length selections include:

- 32 phases
- 64 phases
- 128 phases
- 256 phases

Time-Based, Weighted Round Robin Arbitration. The time-based WRR mechanism is required for supporting isochronous transactions. Consequently, each switch egress port and RCRB that supports isochronous transactions must implement time-based WRR port arbitration.

Time-based weighted round robin adds the element of a virtual timeslot for each arbitration phase. Just as in WRR the port arbiter delivers one transaction from the Ingress Port VC buffer indicated by the Port Number of the current phase. However, rather than immediately advancing to the next phase, the time-based arbiter waits until the current virtual timeslot elaspses before advancing. This ensures that transactions are accepted from the ingress port buffer at regular intervals. Note that the timeslot does not govern the duration of the transfer, but rather the interval between transfers. The maximum duration of a transaction is the time it takes to complete the round robin and return to the original timeslot. Each timeslot is defined as 100ns.

Also, it is possible that no transaction is delivered during a timeslot, resulting in an idle timeslot. This occurs when:

- no transaction is pending for the selected ingress port during the current phase, or
- the phase contains the port number of this egress port

Time-based WRR arbitration supports a maximum table length of 128 phases. The actual number of phases implemented is reported via the *Maximum Time Slot* field of each virtual channel that supports Timed WRR arbitration. See the Figure 6-20 on page 280 which illustrate the *Maximum Time Slots* Field within the VCn Resource Capability register. See MindShare's website for a white paper on example applications of Time-Based WRR.

Figure 6-20: Maximum Time Slots Register

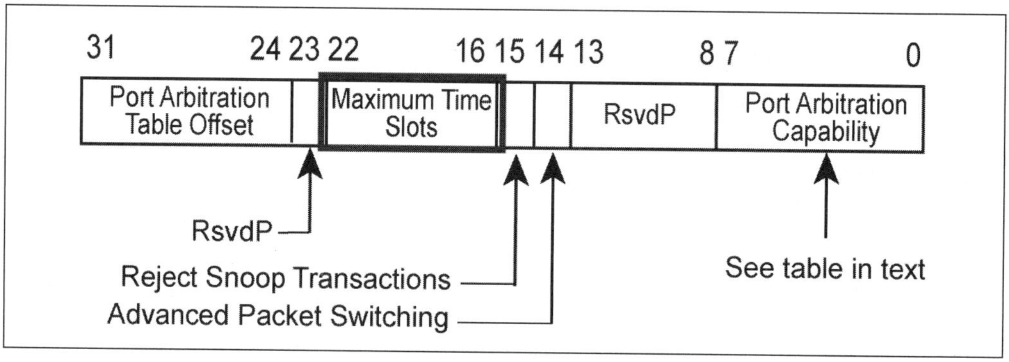

Loading the Port Arbitration Tables

A port arbitration table is required for each VC supported by the egress port.

The actual size and format of the Port Arbitration Tables are a function of the number of phases and the number of ingress ports supported by the Switch, RCRB, or Root Port that supports peer-to-peer transfers. The maximum number of ingress ports supported by the Port Arbitration Table is 256 ports. The actual number of bits within each table entry is design dependent and governed by the number of ingress ports whose transactions can be delivered to the egress port. The size of each table entry is reported in the 2-bit *Port Arbitration Table Entry Size* field of Port VC Capability Register 1. The permissible values are:

- 00b — 1 bit
- 01b — 2 bits
- 10b — 4 bits
- 11b — 8 bits

Configuration software loads each table with port numbers to accomplish the desired port priority for each VC supported. As illustrated in Figure 6-21 on page 281, the port arbitration table format depends on the size of each entry and the number of time slots supported by this design.

Figure 6-21: Format of Port Arbitration Table

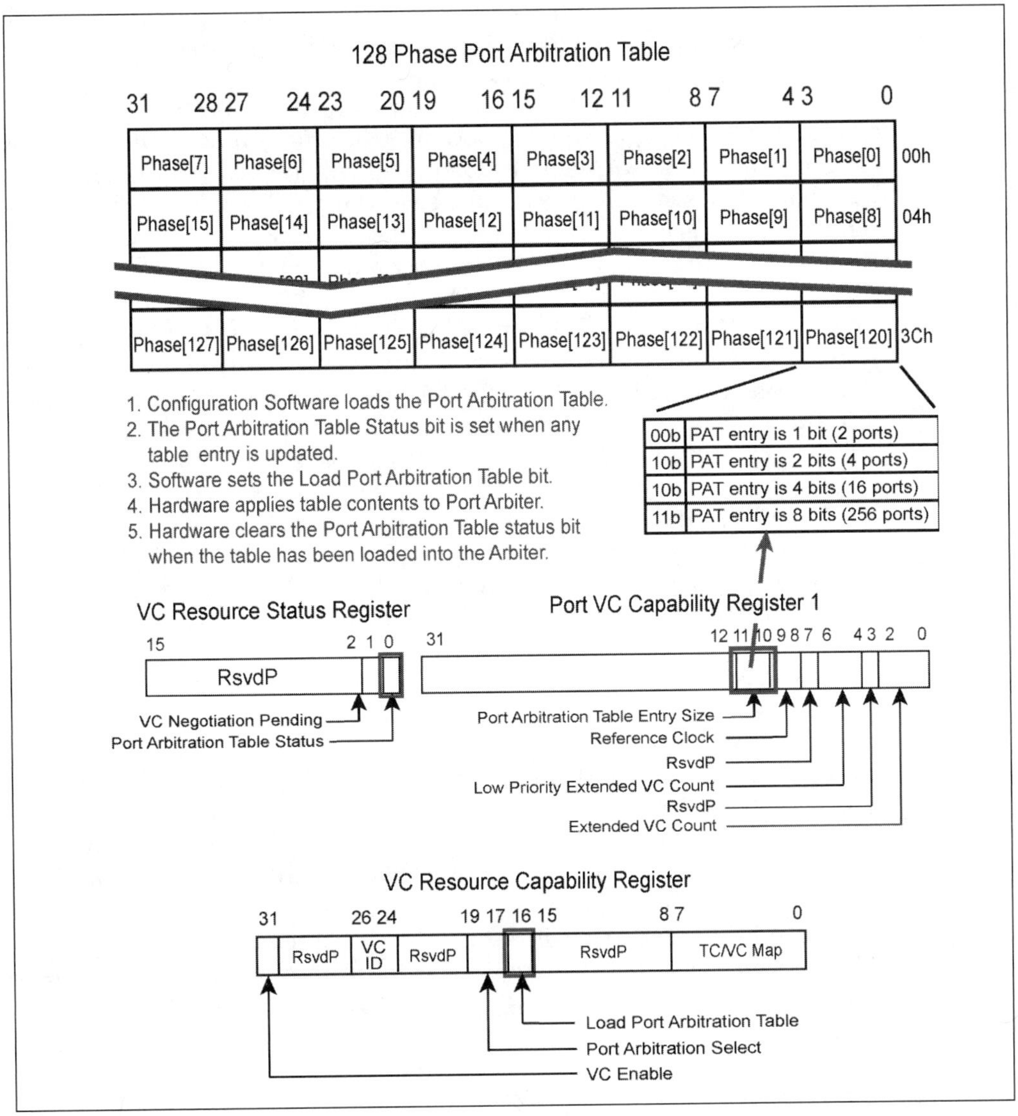

Switch Arbitration Example

This section provides an example of a three-port switch with both Port and VC arbitration illustrated. The example presumes that packets arriving on ingress ports 0 and 1 are moving in the upstream direction and port 2 is the egress port facing the Root Complex. This example serves to summarize port and VC arbitration and illustrate their use within a PCI Express switch. Refer to Figure 6-22 on page 283 during the following discussion.

1. Packets arrive at ingress port 0 and are placed in a receiver flow control buffer based on TC/VC mapping associated with port 0. As indicated, TLPs carrying traffic class TC0 or TC1 are sent to the VC0 receiver flow control buffers. TLPs carrying traffic class TC3 or TC5 are sent to the VC1 receiver flow control buffers. No other TCs are permitted on this link.
2. Packets arrive at ingress port 1 and are placed in a receiver flow control buffer based on port 1 TC/VC mapping. As indicated, TLPs carrying traffic class TC0 are sent to the VC0 receiver flow control buffers. TLPs carrying traffic class TC2-TC4 are sent to the VC3 receiver flow control buffers. NO OTHER TCs are permitted on this link.
3. The target egress port is determined from routing information in each packet. Address routing is applied to memory or IO request TLPs, ID routing is applied to configuration or completion TLPs, etc.
4. All packets destined for egress port 2 are subjected to the TC/VC mapping for that port. As shown, TLPs carrying traffic class TC0-TC2 are managed as virtual channel 0 (VC0) traffic, TLPs carrying traffic class TC3-TC7 are managed as VC1 traffic.
5. Independent Port Arbitration is applied to packets within each VC. This may be a fixed or weighted round robin arbitration used to select packets from all possible different ingress ports. Port arbitration ultimately results in all VCs of a given type being routed to the same VC buffer.
6. Following Port Arbitration, VC arbitration determines the order in which transactions pending transmission within the individual VC buffers will be transferred across the link. The arbitration algorithm may be fixed or weighted round robin. The arbiter selects transactions from the head of each VC buffer based on the priority scheme implemented.
7. Note that the VC arbiter selects packets for transmission only if sufficient flow control credits exist.

Figure 6-22: Example of Port and VC Arbitration within A Switch

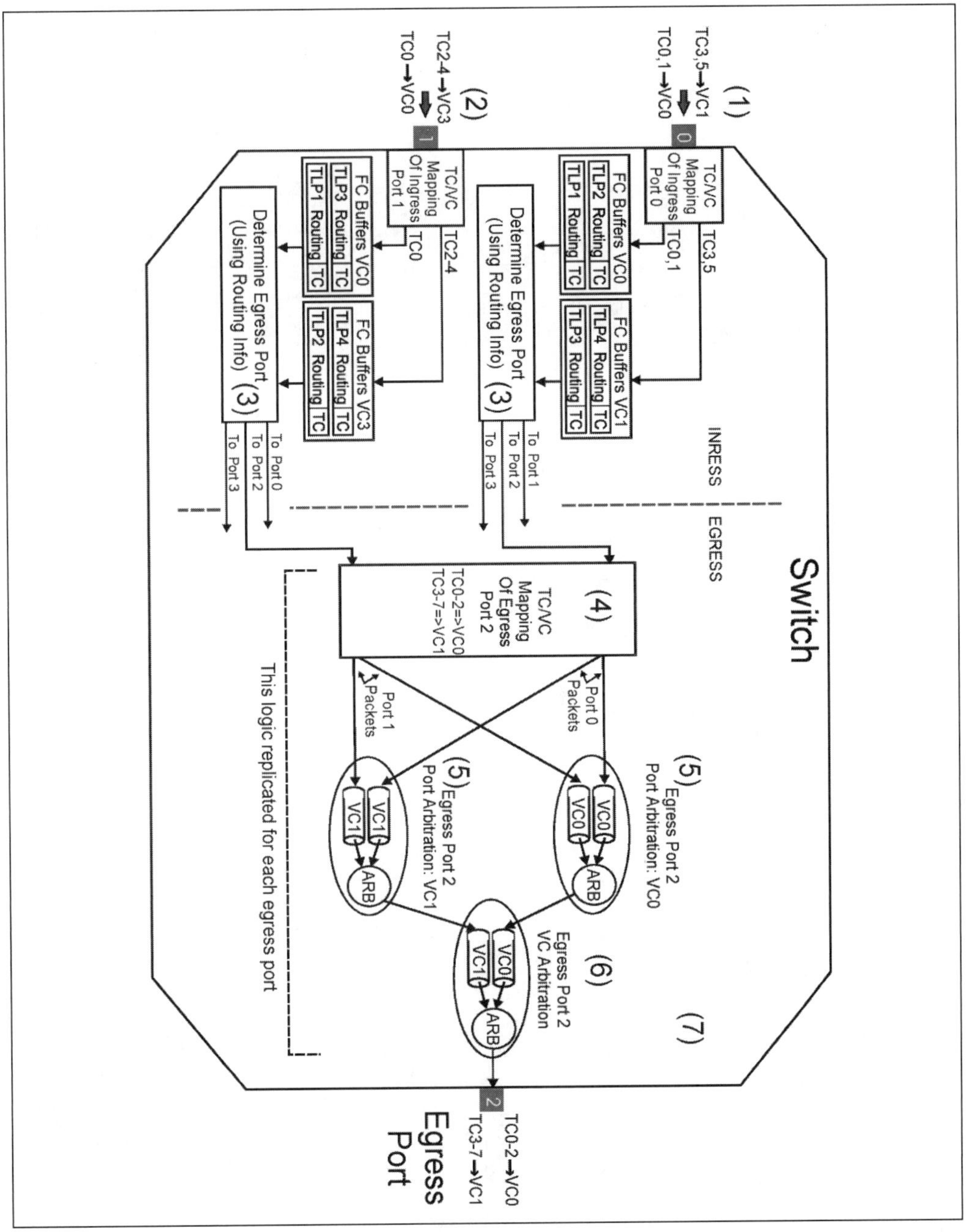

7 Flow Control

The Previous Chapter

This previous chapter discussed Traffic Classes, Virtual Channels, and Arbitration that supports Quality of Service concepts in PCI Express implementations. The concept of Quality of Service in the context of PCI Express is an attempt to predict the bandwidth and latency associated with the flow of different transaction streams traversing the PCI Express fabric. The use of QoS is based on application-specific software assigning Traffic Class (TC) values to transactions, which define the priority of each transaction as it travels between the Requester and Completer devices. Each TC is mapped to a Virtual Channel (VC) that is used to manage transaction priority via two arbitration schemes called port and VC arbitration.

This Chapter

This chapter discusses the purposes and detailed operation of the Flow Control Protocol. This protocol requires each device to implement credit-based link flow control for each virtual channel on each port. Flow control guarantees that transmitters will never send Transaction Layer Packets (TLPs) that the receiver can't accept. This prevents receive buffer over-runs and eliminates the need for inefficient disconnects, retries, and wait-states on the link. Flow Control also helps enable compliance with PCI Express ordering rules by maintaining separate virtual channel Flow Control buffers for three types of transactions: Posted (P), Non-Posted (NP) and Completions (Cpl).

The Next Chapter

The next chapter discusses the ordering requirements for PCI Express devices, as well as PCI and PCI-X devices that may be attached to a PCI Express fabric. The discussion describes the Producer/Consumer programming model upon which the fundamental ordering rules are based. It also describes the potential performance problems that can emerge when strong ordering is employed, describes the weak ordering solution, and specifies the rules defined for deadlock avoidance.

Flow Control Concept

The ports at each end of every PCI Express link must implement Flow Control. Before a transaction packet can be sent across a link to the receiving port, the transmitting port must verify that the receiving port has sufficient buffer space to accept the transaction to be sent. In many other architectures including PCI and PCI-X, transactions are delivered to a target device without knowing if it can accept the transaction. If the transaction is rejected due to insufficient buffer space, the transaction is resent (retried) until the transaction completes. This procedure can severely reduce the efficiency of a bus, by wasting bus bandwidth when other transactions are ready to be sent.

Because PCI Express is a point-to-point implementation, the Flow Control mechanism would be ineffective, if only one transaction stream was pending transmission across a link. That is, if the receive buffer was temporarily full, the transmitter would be prevented from sending a subsequent transaction due to transaction ordering requirements, thereby blocking any further transfers. PCI Express improves link efficiency by implementing multiple flow-control buffers for separate transaction streams (virtual channels). Because Flow Control is managed separately for each virtual channel implemented for a given link, if the Flow Control buffer for one VC is full, the transmitter can advance to another VC buffer and send transactions associated with it.

The link Flow Control mechanism uses a credit-based mechanism that allows the transmitting port to check buffer space availability at the receiving port. During initialization each receiver reports the size of its receive buffers (in Flow Control credits) to the port at the opposite end of the link. The receiving port continues to update the transmitting port regularly by transmitting the number of credits that have been freed up. This is accomplished via Flow Control DLLPs.

Flow control logic is located in the transaction layer of the transmitting and receiving devices. Both transmitter and receiver sides of each device are involved in flow control. Refer to Figure 7-1 on page 287 during the following descriptions.

- **Devices Report Buffer Space Available** — The receiver of each node contains the Flow Control buffers. Each device must report the amount of flow control buffer space they have available to the device on the opposite end of the link. Buffer space is reported in units called Flow Control Credits (FCCs). The number of Flow Control Credits within each buffer is forwarded from the transaction layer to the transmit side of the link layer as illustrated in Figure 7-1. The link creates a Flow Control DLLP that carries this credit information to the receiver at the opposite end of the link. This is done for each Flow Control Buffer.

- **Receiving Credits** — Notice that the receiver in Figure 7-1 also receives Flow Control DLLPs from the device at the opposite end of the link. This information is transferred to the transaction layer to update the Flow Control Counters that track the amount of Flow Control Buffer space in the other device.
- **Credit Checks Made** — Each transmitter check consults the Flow Control Counters to check available credits. If sufficient credits are available to receive the transaction pending delivery then the transaction is forwarded to the link layer and is ultimately sent to the opposite device. If enough credits are not available the transaction is temporarily blocked until additional Flow Control credits are reported by the receiving device.

Figure 7-1: Location of Flow Control Logic

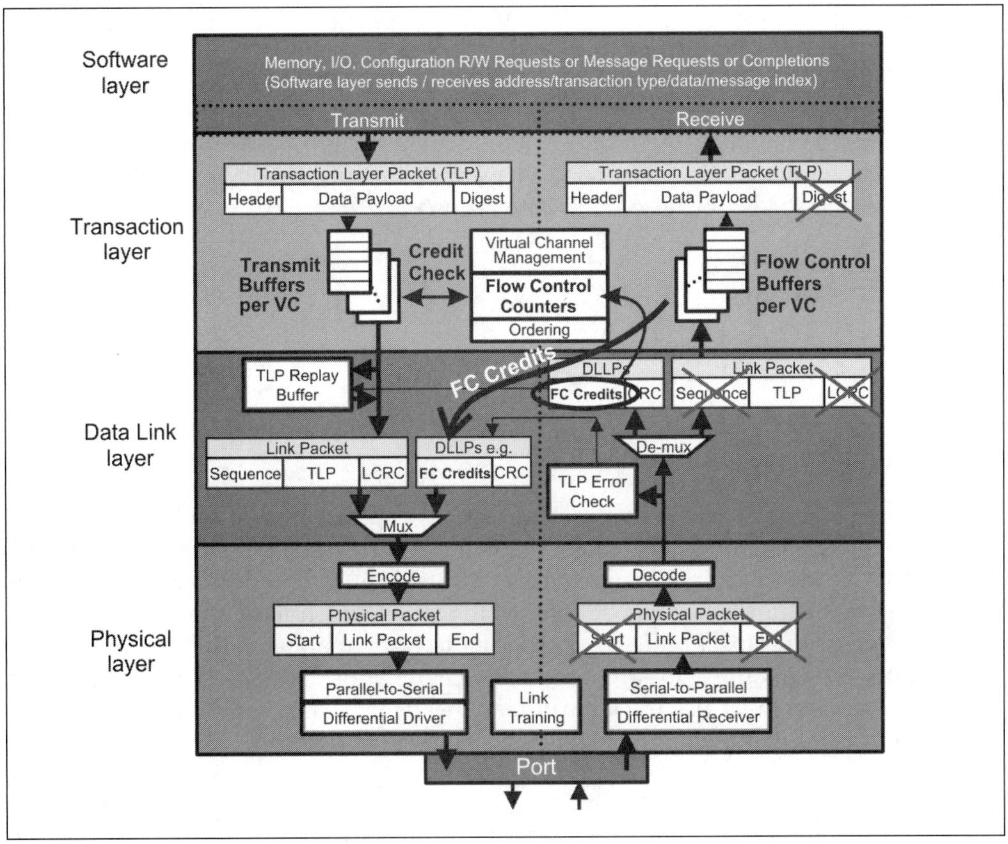

Flow Control Buffers

Flow control buffers are implemented for each VC resource supported by a PCI Express port. Recall that devices at each end of the link may not support the same number of VC resources, therefore the maximum number of VCs configured and enabled by software is the greatest number of VCs in common between the two ports.

VC Flow Control Buffer Organization

Each VC Flow Control buffer at the receiver is managed for each category of transaction flowing through the virtual channel. These categories are:

- Posted Transactions — Memory Writes and Messages
- Non-Posted Transactions — Memory Reads, Configuration Reads and Writes, and I/O Reads and Writes
- Completions — Read Completions and Write Completions

In addition, each of these categories is separated into header and data portions of each transaction. Flow control operates independently for each of the six buffers listed below (also see Figure 7-2 on page 289).

- Posted Header
- Posted Data

- Non-Posted Header
- Non-Posted Data

- Completion Header
- Completion Data

Some transactions consist of a header only (e.g., read requests) while others consist of a header and data (e.g., write requests). The transmitter must ensure that both header and data buffer space is available as required for each transaction before the transaction can be sent. Note that when a transaction is received into a VC Flow Control buffer that ordering must be maintained when the transactions are forwarded to software or to an egress port in the case of a switch. The the receiver must also track the order of header and data components within the Flow Control buffer.

Figure 7-2: Flow Control Buffer Organization

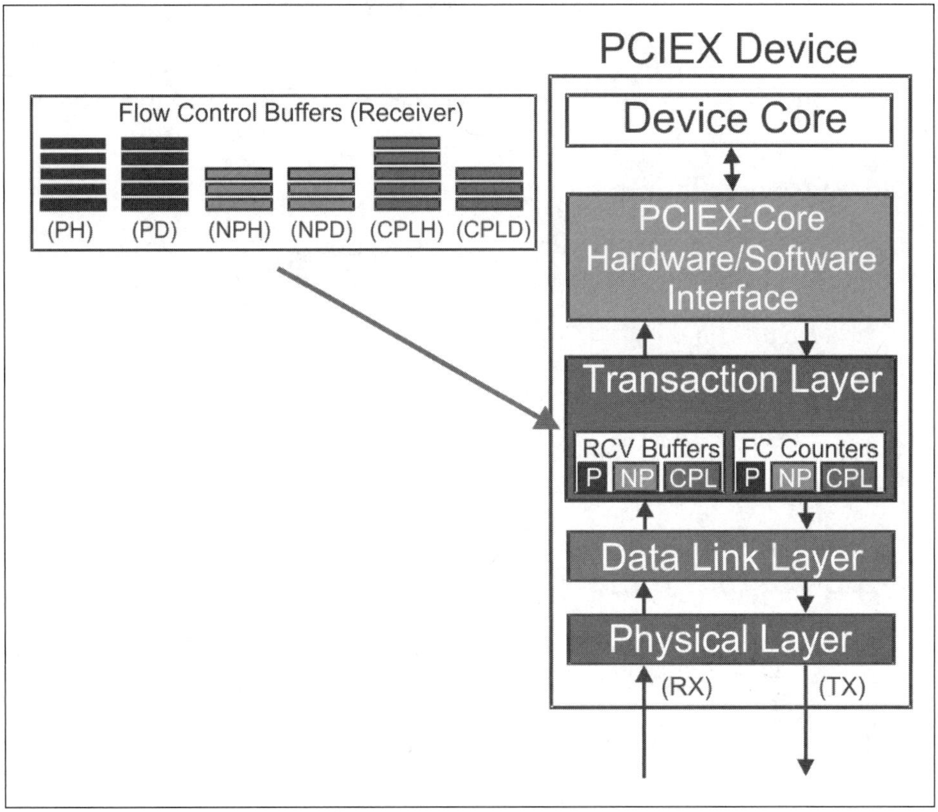

Flow Control Credits

Buffer space is reported by the receiver in units called Flow Control credits. The unit value of Flow Control credits (FCCs) may differ between header and data as listed below:

- Header FCCs — maximum header size + digest
  - o 4 DWs for completions
  - o 5 DWs for requests
- Data FCCs — 4 DWs (aligned 16 bytes)

Flow control credits are passed within the header of the link layer Flow Control Packets. Note that DLLPs do not require Flow Control credits because they originate and terminate at the link layer.

Maximum Flow Control Buffer Size

The maximum buffer size that can be reported via the Flow Control Initialization and Update packets for the header and data portions of a transaction are as follows:

128 Credits for headers

- 2,560 bytes Request Headers @ 20 bytes/credit
- 2048 bytes for completion headers @ 16 bytes/credit

2048 Credits for data

- 32KB @ 16 bytes/credit

The reason for these limits is discussed in the section entitled "Stage 1 — Flow Control Following Initialization" page 296, step 2.

Introduction to the Flow Control Mechanism

The specification defines the requirements of the Flow Control mechanism by describing conceptual registers and counters along with procedures and mechanisms for reporting, tracking, and calculating whether a transaction can be sent. These elements define the functional requirements; however, the actual implementation may vary from the conceptual model. This section introduces the specified model that serves to explain the concept and define the requirements. The approach taken focuses on a single flow control example for a non-posted header. The concepts discussed apply to all Flow Control buffer types.

The Flow Control Elements

Figure 7-3 identifies and illustrates the elements used by the transmitter and receiver when managing flow control. This diagram illustrates transactions flowing in a single direction across a link, but of course another set of these elements is used to support transfers in the opposite direction. The primary function of each element within the transmitting and receiving devices is listed below. Note that for a single direction these Flow Control elements are duplicated for each Flow Control receive buffer, yielding six sets of elements. This example deals with non-posted header flow control.

Transmitter Elements

- **Pending Transaction Buffer** — holds transactions that are pending transfer within the same virtual channel.
- **Credit Consumed Counter** — tracks the size of all transactions sent from the VC buffer (of the specified type, e.g., non-posted headers) in Flow Control credits. This count is abbreviated "CC."
- **Credit Limit Register** — this register is initialized by the receiving device when it sends Flow Control initialization packets to report the size of the corresponding Flow Control receive buffer. Following initialization, Flow Control update packets are sent periodically to add more Flow Control credits as they become available at the receiver. This value is abbreviated "CL."
- **Flow Control Gating Logic** — performs the calculations to determine if the receiver has sufficient Flow Control credits to receive the pending TLP (PTLP). In essence, this check ensures that the total CREDITS_CONSUMED (CC) plus the credit required for the next packet pending transmission (PTLP) does not exceed the CREDIT_LIMIT (CL). This specification defines the following equation for performing the check, with all values represented in credits:

$$CL - (CC + PTLP) mod 2^{[FieldSize]} \leq 2^{[FieldSize]}/2$$

For an example application of this equation, See "Stage 1 — Flow Control Following Initialization" on page 294.

Receiver Elements

- **Flow Control (Receive) Buffer** — stores incoming header or data information.
- **Credit Allocated** — This counter tracks the total Flow Control credits that have been allocated (made available) since initialization. It is initialized by hardware to reflect the size of the associated Flow Control buffer. As the buffer fills the amount of available buffer space decreases until transactions are removed from the buffer. The number of Flow Control credits associated with each transaction removed from the buffer is added to the CREDIT_ALLOCATED counter; thereby keeping a running count of new credits made available.
- **Credits Received Counter (optional)** — this counter keeps track of the total size of all data received from the transmitting device and placed into the Flow Control buffer (in Flow Control credits). When flow control is functioning properly, the CREDITS_RECEIVED count should be the same as

CREDITS_CONSUMED count at the transmitter and be equal to or less than the CREDIT_ALLOCATED count. If this is not true, then a flow control buffer overflow has occurred and error is detected. Although optional the specification recommends its use.

Flow control management is based on keeping track of Flow Control credits using modulo counters. Consequently, the counters are designed to role over when the count saturates. The width of the counters depend on whether flow control is tracking transaction headers or data:

- Header flow control uses modulo 256 counters (8-bits wide)
- Data flow control uses modulo 4096 counters (12-bits wide)

In addition, all calculations are made using unsigned arithmetic. The operation of the counters and the calculations are explained by example on page 290.

Figure 7-3: Flow Control Elements

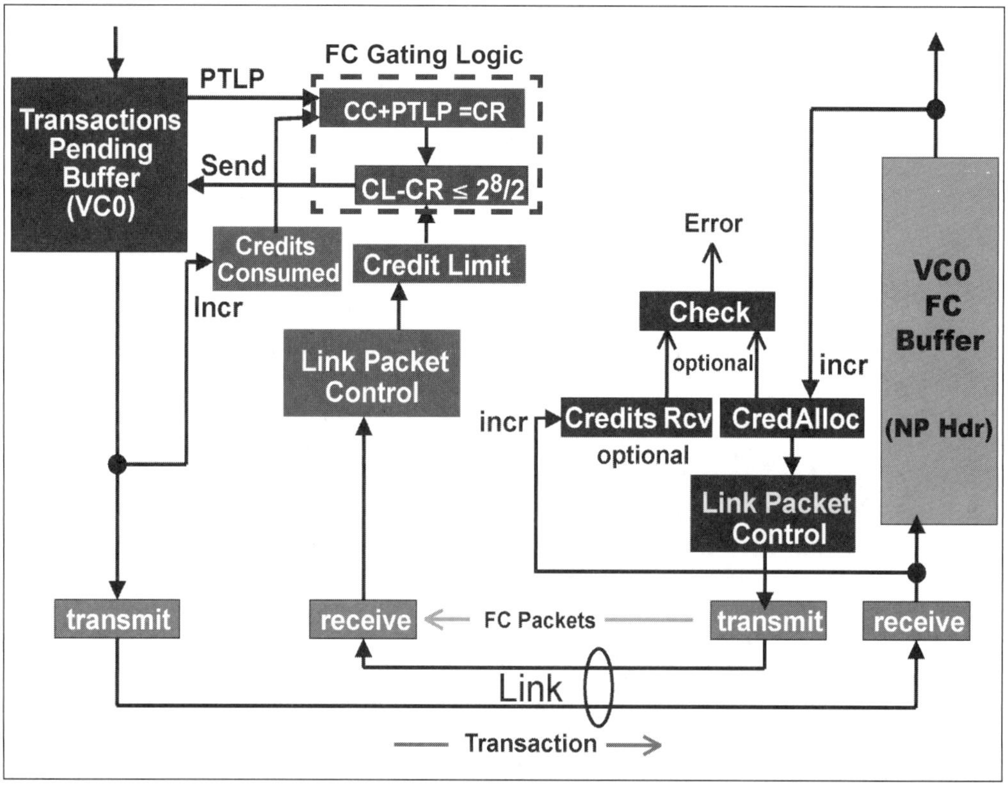

Flow Control Packets

The transmit side of a device reports flow control credit information from its receive buffers to the opposite device. The specification defines three types of Flow Control packets:

- Flow Control Init1 — used to report the size of the Flow Control buffers for a given virtual channel
- Flow Control Init2 — same as Flow Control Init1 except it is used to verify completion of flow control initialization at each end of the link (receiving device ignores flow control credit information)
- Flow Control Update — used to update Credit Limit periodically

Each Flow Control packet contains the header and data flow control credit information for each virtual channel and type of Flow Control packet. The packet fields that carry the header and data Flow Control credits reflect the counter width as discussed in the previous section. Figure 7-4 pictures the format and content of these packets.

Figure 7-4: Types and Format of Flow Control Packets

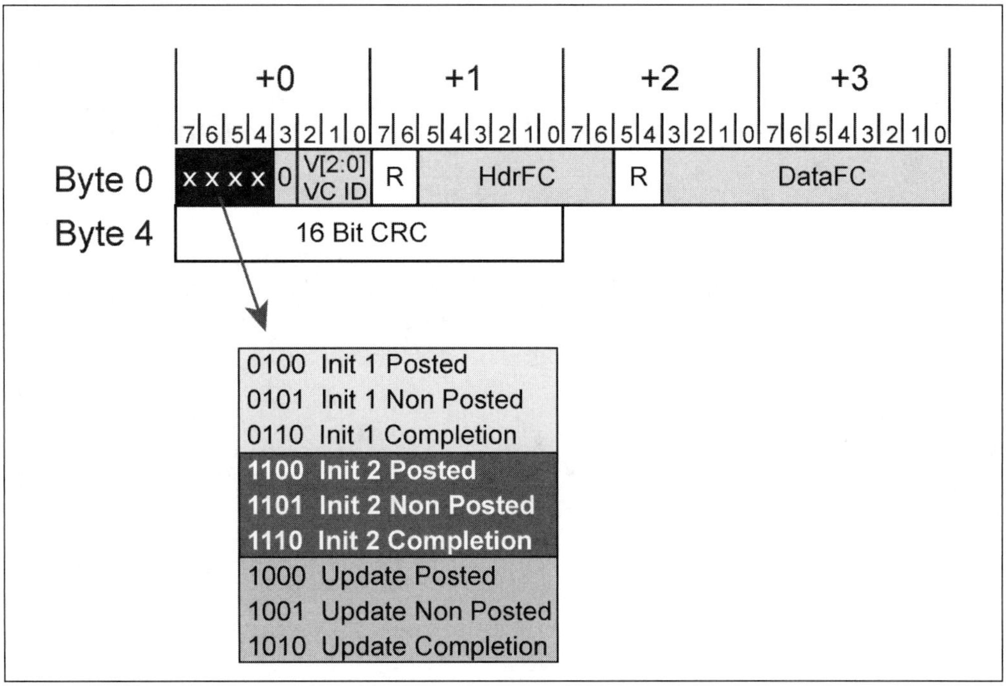

Operation of the Flow Control Model - An Example

The purpose of this example is to explain the operation of the Flow Control mechanism based on the conceptual model presented by the specification. The example uses the non-posted header Flow Control buffer type, and spans four stages to capture the nuances of the flow control implementation:

Stage One — Immediately following initialization, the several transactions are tracked to explain the basic operation of the counters and registers as they track transactions as they are sent across the link. In this stage, data is accumulating within the Flow Control buffer, but no transactions are being removed.

Stage Two — If the transmitter sends non-posted transactions at a rate such that the Flow Control buffer is filled faster than the receiver can forward transactions from the buffer, the buffer will fill. Stage two describes this circumstance.

Stage Three — The modulo counters are designed to roll over and continue counting from zero. This stage describes the flow control operation at the point of the CREDITS_ALLOCATED count rolling over to zero.

Stage Four — The specification describes the optional error check that can be made by the receiver in the event of a Flow Control buffer overflow. This error check is described in this section.

Stage 1 — Flow Control Following Initialization

The assumption made in this example is that flow control initialization has just completed and the devices are ready for normal operation. The Flow Control buffer is presumed to be 2KB in size, which represents 102d (66h) Flow Control units with 20 bytes/header. Figure 7-5 on page 295 illustrates the elements involved with the values that would be in each counter and register following flow control initialization.

Figure 7-5. Flow Control Elements Following Initialization

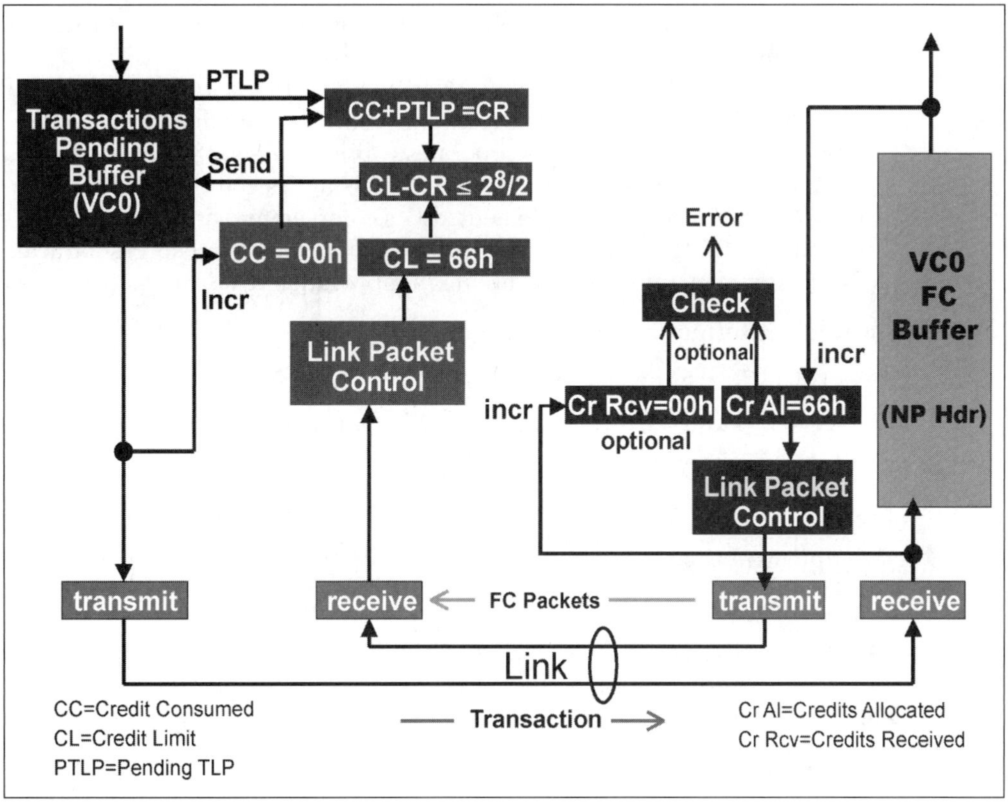

The transmitter must check Flow Control credit prior to sending a transaction. In the case of headers the number of Flow Control units required is always one. The transmitter takes the following steps to determine if the transaction can be sent. For simplicity, this example ignores the possibility of data being included in the transaction.

The credit check is made using unsigned arithmetic (2's complement) in order to satisfy the following formula:

$$CL - (CC + PTLP) mod 2^{[FieldSize]} \leq 2^{[FieldSize]}/2$$

Substituting values from Figure 7-5 yields:

$$66h - (00h + 01h) mod 2^8 \leq 2^8/2$$

$$66h - 01h \ mod 256 \leq 80h$$

1. The current CREDITS_CONSUMED count (CC) is added to the PTLP credits required, to determine the CUMULATIVE_CREDITS_REQUIRED (CR), or 00h + 01h =01h. Sufficient credits exist if this value is equal to or less than the credit limit.
2. The CUMULATIVE_CREDITS_REQUIRED count is subtracted from the CREDIT_LIMIT count (CL) to determine if sufficient credits are available. The following description incorporates a brief review of 2's complement subtraction. When performing subtraction using 2's complement the number to be subtracted is complemented (1's complement) and 1 is added (2's complement). This value is then added to the number being subtracted from. Any carry due to the addition is simply ignored.

The numbers to subtract are:

`CL 01100110b (66h) - CR 00000001b (01h) = n`

Number to be subtracted is converted to 2's complement:

`00000001b > 11111110b` (1's complement)

`11111110b +1 = 11111111b` (1's complement +1 = 2's complement)

2's complement is added.

```
01100110
11111111 (add)
01100101 = 01100101b = 65h
```

Is result <= 80h?

`Yes, 65h <= 80h` (send transaction)

The result of the subtraction must be equal to or less than 1/2 the maximum value that can be tracked with a modulo 256 counter (128). This approach is taken to ensure unique results from the unsigned arithmetic. For example, unsigned 2's-complement subtraction yields the same results for both 0-128 and 255-127, as shown below.

```
  00h(0)   -  80h(128)= -80h(128)
00000000b - 1000000b = n
00000000b + 01111111+1b (add 2's complement)
00000000b + 10000000b = 10000000b(10h)
```

```
 FFh(255)  -  7Fh(127) = +80h(128)
11111111b - 01111111b = n
11111111b + 10000000+1 (add 2's complement)
11111111b + 10000001b = 10000000b(10h)
```

To ensure that conflicts such as the one above do not occur, the maximum number of unused credits that can be reported is limited to $2^8/2$ (128) credits for headers and $2^{12}/2$ (2048) credits for data. This means that the CREDITS_ALLOCATED count must never exceed the CREDITS_CONSUMED count by more than 128 for headers and 2048 for data. This ensures that any result < 1/2 the maximum register count is a positive number and represents credits available, and results > 1/2 the maximum count are negative numbers that indicate credits not available.

3. The CREDITS_CONSUMED count increments by one when the transaction is forwarded to the link layer.
4. When the transaction arrives at the receiver, the transaction header is placed into the Flow Control buffer and the CREDITS_RECEIVED counter (optional) increments by one. Note that CREDIT_ALLOCATED does not change.

Figure 7-6 on page 297 illustrates the Flow Control elements following transfer of the first transaction.

Figure 7-6: Flow Control Elements Following Delivery of First Transaction

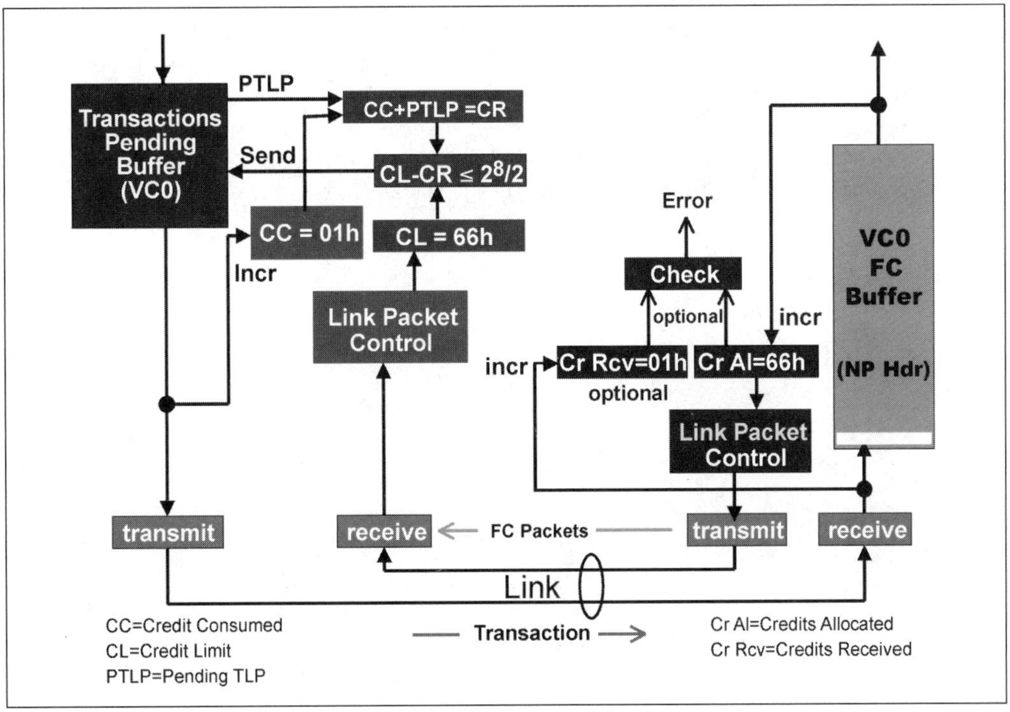

Stage 2 — Flow Control Buffer Fills Up

This example presumes that the receiving device has been unable to move transactions from the Flow Control buffer since initialization. This could be caused if the device core was temporarily busy and unable to process transactions. Consequently, the Flow Control buffer has completely filled. Figure 7-7 on page 299 illustrates this scenario.

Again the transmitter checks Flow Control credits to determine if the next pending TLP can be sent. The unsigned arithmetic is performed to subtract the Credits Required from the CREDIT_LIMIT:

66h(CL) - 67h (CR) <= 80h
01100110b - 01100111b <= 10000000b (if yes, send transaction)

CL 01100110(66)
CR 10011001 (add 2's complement of 67h)
11111111 = FFh<=80h (not true, don't send packet)

Not until the receiver moves one or more transactions from the Flow Control buffer can the pending transaction be sent. When the first transaction is moved from the Flow Control buffer, the CREDIT_ALLOCATED count is increased to 67h. When the Update Flow Control packet is delivered to the transmitter, the new CREDIT_LIMIT will be loaded into the CL register. The resulting check will pass the test, thereby permitting the packet to be sent.

CL 01100111 (67)
CR 10011001 add 2's complement of 67
00000000 = 00h<=80h (send transaction)

Figure 7-7. Flow Control Elements with Flow Control Buffer Filled

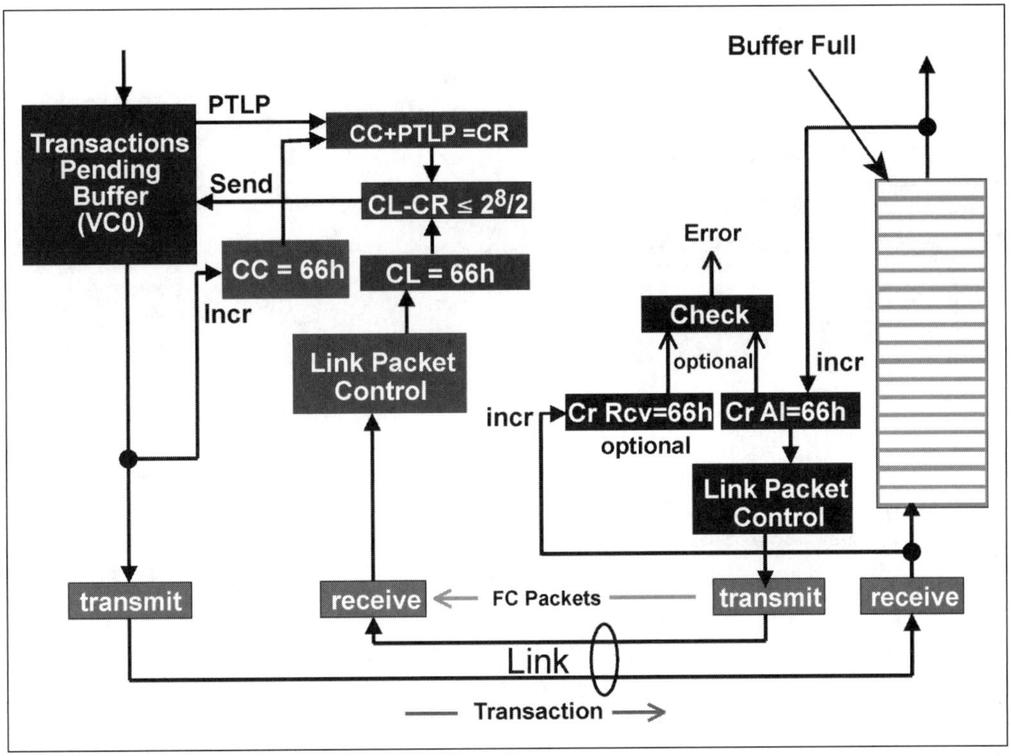

Stage 3 — The Credit Limit count Rolls Over

The receiver's CREDIT_LIMIT (CL) always runs ahead of (or is equal to) the CREDITS_CONSUMED (CC) count. Each time the transmitter performs a credit check, it adds the credits required (CR) for a TLP to the current CREDITS_CONSUMED count and subtracts the result from the current CREDIT_LIMIT to determine if enough credits are available to send the TLP.

Because both the CL count and the CC count only index up, they are allowed to roll over from maximum count back to 0. A problem appears to arise when the CL count (which, again, is running ahead) has rolled over and the CC has not. Figure 7-8 shows the CL and CR counts before and after CL rollover.

Figure 7-8: Flow Control Rollover Problem

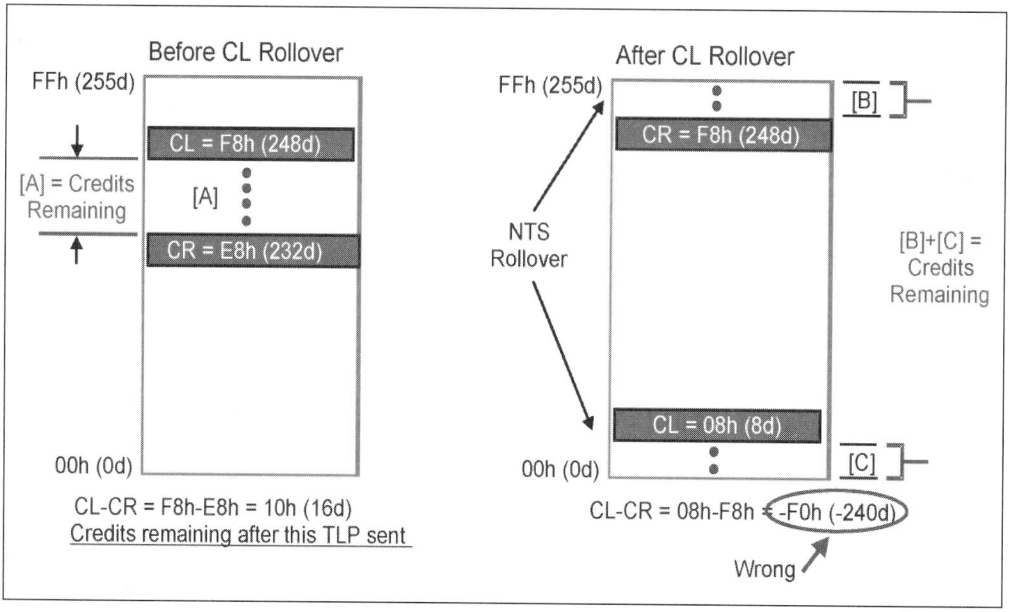

If a simple subtraction is performed in the rollover case, the result is negative. This indicates that credits are not available. However, because unsigned arithmetic is used the problem does not arise. See below:

`CL 00001000` (08h)
`CR 11111000` (F8h) > `00000111+1` = 2's complement

`CL 00001000` (08h)
`CR 00001000` (add 2's complement)
`   00010000 or 10h`

Stage 4 — FC Buffer Overflow Error Check

The specification recommends implementation of the optional FC buffer overflow error checking mechanism. These optional elements include:

- CREDITS_RECEIVED counter
- Error Check Logic

These elements permit the receiver to track Flow Control credits in the same manner as the transmitter. That is, the transmitter CREDIT_LIMIT count should be the same as the receiver's CREDITS_ALLOCATED count (after an Update DLLP is sent) and the receiver's CREDITS_RECEIVED count should be the same as the transmitter's CREDITS_CONSUMED count. If flow control is working correctly the following will be true:

- the transmitter's CREDITS_CONSUMED count should always be ≤ its CREDIT_LIMIT
- the receiver's CREDITS_RECEIVED count (CR) should always be ≤ its CREDITS_ALLOCATED count (CA)

An overflow condition is detected when the following formula is satisfied. Note that the field size is either 8 (headers) or 12 (data):

$$(CA - CR)mod2^{[FieldSize]} > 2^{[FieldSize]}/2$$

If the formula is true, then the result is negative; thus, more credits have been sent to the FC buffer than were available and an overflow has occurred. Note that the 1.0a version of the specification defines the equation as ≥ rather than > as shown above. This appears to be an error, because when CA=CR no overflow condition exists. For example, for the case right after initialization where the receiver advertises that it has 128 credits for the transmitter to use, CA = 128, and CR = 0 because it hasn't received anything yet, then this equation evaluates true. Which means it has overflowed, when actually all we have done is advertise our max allowed number of credits. If the equation evaluates for only > and not ≥, then everything seems to work.

Infinite Flow Control Advertisement

PCI Express defines an infinite Flow Control credit value. A device that advertises infinite Flow Control credits need not send Flow Control Update packets following initialization and the transmitter will never be blocked from sending transactions. During flow control initialization, a device advertises "infinite" credits by delivering a zero in the credit field of the FC_INIT1 DLLP.

Who Advertises Infinite Flow Control Credits?

It's interesting to note that the minimum Flow Control credits that must be advertised includes infinite credits for completion transactions in certain situations. See Table 7-1 on page 303. These requirements involve devices that originate requests for which completions are expected to be returned (i.e., Endpoints and root ports that do not support peer-to-peer transfers). It does not include devices that merely forward completions (switches and root ports that support peer-to-peer transfers). This implies a requirement that any device initiating a request must commit buffer space for the expected completion header and data (if applicable). This guarantees that no throttling would ever occur when completions cross the final link to the original requester. This type of rule is required of PCI-X devices that initiate split transactions. Multiple searches of the specification failed to reveal this requirement explicitly stated for PCI Express devices; however, it is implied by the requirement to advertise infinite Flow Control credits.

Note also that infinite flow control credits can only be advertised during initializtion. This must be true, because the CA counter in the receiver could rollover to 00h and send an Update FC packet with the credit field set to 00h. If the Link is in the DL_Init state, this means infinite credits, but if the Link is in the DL_Active state, this does not mean infinite credits.

Special Use for Infinite Credit Advertisements.

The specification points out a special consideration for devices that do not need to implement all the FC buffer types for all VCs. For example, the only Non-Posted writes are I/O Writes and Configuration Writes both of which are permitted only on VC0. Thus, Non-Posted data buffers are not needed for VC1 - VC7. Because no Flow Control tracking is needed, a device can simply advertise infinite Flow Control credits during initialization, thereby eliminating the need to send needless FC_Update packets.

Header and Data Advertisements May Conflict

An infinite Flow Control advertisement might be sent for either the Data or header buffers (with same FC type) but not both. In this case, Update DLLPs are required for one buffer but not the other. This simply means that the device requiring credits will send an Update DLLP with the corresponding field containing the CREDITS_ALLOCATED credit information, and the other field must be set to zero (consistent with its advertisement).

The Minimum Flow Control Advertisement

The minimum number of credits that can be reported for the different Flow Control buffer types is listed in Table 7-1 on page 303.

Table 7-1: Required Minimum Flow Control Advertisements

Credit Type	Minimum Advertisement
Posted Request Header (PH)	1 unit. Credit Value = one 4DW HDR + Digest = 5DW.
Posted Request Data (PD)	Largest possible setting of the Max_Payload_Size; for the component divided by FC Unit Size (4DW). Example: If the largest Max_Payload_Size value supported is 1024 bytes, the smallest permitted initial credit value would be 040h.
Non-Posted Request HDR (NPH)	1 unit. Credit Value = one 4 DW HDR + Digest = 5DW.
Non-Posted Request Data (NPD)	1 unit. Credit Value = 4DW.
Completion HDR (CPLH)	1 unit. Credit Value = one 3DW HDR + Digest = 4DW; for Root Complex with peer-to-peer support and Switches. Infinite units. Initial Credit Value = all 0's for Root Complex with no peer-to-peer support and Endpoints.
Completion Data (CPLD)	n units. Value of largest possible setting of Max_Payload_Size or size of largest Read Request (which ever is smaller) divided by FC Unit Size (4DW); for Root Complex with peer-to-peer support and Switches. Infinite units. Initial Credit Value = all 0's; for Root Complex with no peer-to-peer support and Endpoints.

Flow Control Initialization

Prior to sending any transactions, flow control initialization must be performed. Initialization occurs for each link in the system and involves a handshake between the devices attached to the same link. TLPs associated with the virtual channel being initialized cannot be forwarded across the link until Flow Control Initialization is performed successfully.

Once initiated, the flow control initialization procedure is fundamentally the same for all Virtual Channels. The small differences that exist are discussed later. Initialization of VC0 (default VC) must be done in hardware so that configuration transactions can traverse the PCI Express fabric. Other VCs initialize once configuration software has set up and enabled the VCs at both ends of the link. Enabling a VC triggers hardware to perform flow control initialization for this VC.

Figure 7-9 pictures the Flow Control counters within the devices at both ends of the link, along with the state of flag bits used during initialization.

Figure 7-9: Initial State of Example FC Elements

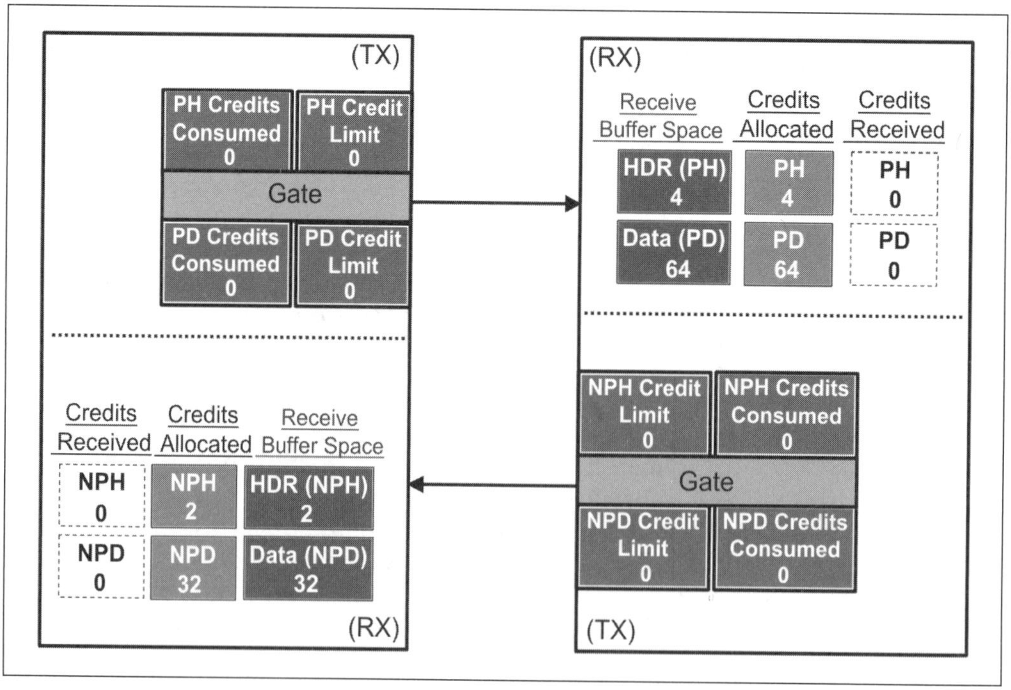

The FC Initialization Sequence

PCI Express defines two stages in flow control initialization: FC_INIT1 and FC_INIT2. Each stage of course involves the use of the Flow Control packets (FCPs).

- Flow Control Init1 — reports the size of the Flow Control buffers for a given virtual channel
- Flow Control Init2 — verifies that the device transmitting the Init2 packet has completed the flow control initialization for the specified VC and buffer type.

FC Init1 Packets Advertise Flow Control Credits Available

During the FC_INIT1 state, a device continuously outputs a sequence of 3 InitFC1 Flow Control packets advertising its posted, non-posted, and completion receiver buffer sizes. (See Figure 7-10.) Each device also waits to receive a similar sequence from its neighbor. Once a device has received the complete sequence and sent its own, it initializes transmit counters, sets an internal flag FI1, and exits FC_INIT1. This process is illustrated in Figure 7-11 on page 306 and described below. The example shows Device A reporting Non-Posted Buffer Credits and Device B reporting Posted Buffer Credits. This illustrates that the devices need not be in synchronization regarding what they are reporting. In fact, the two device will typically not start the flow control initialization process at the same time.

Figure 7-10: INIT1 Flow Control Packet Format and Contents

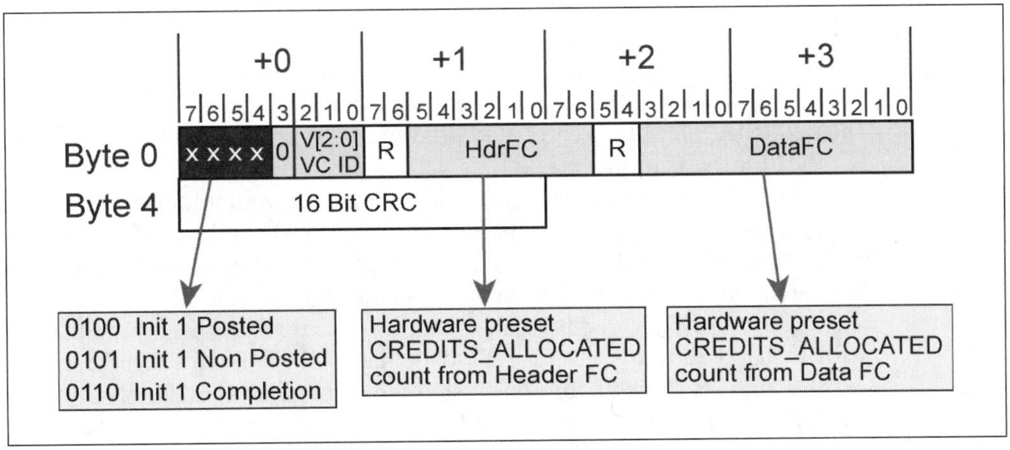

Figure 7-11: Devices Send and Initialize Flow Control Registers

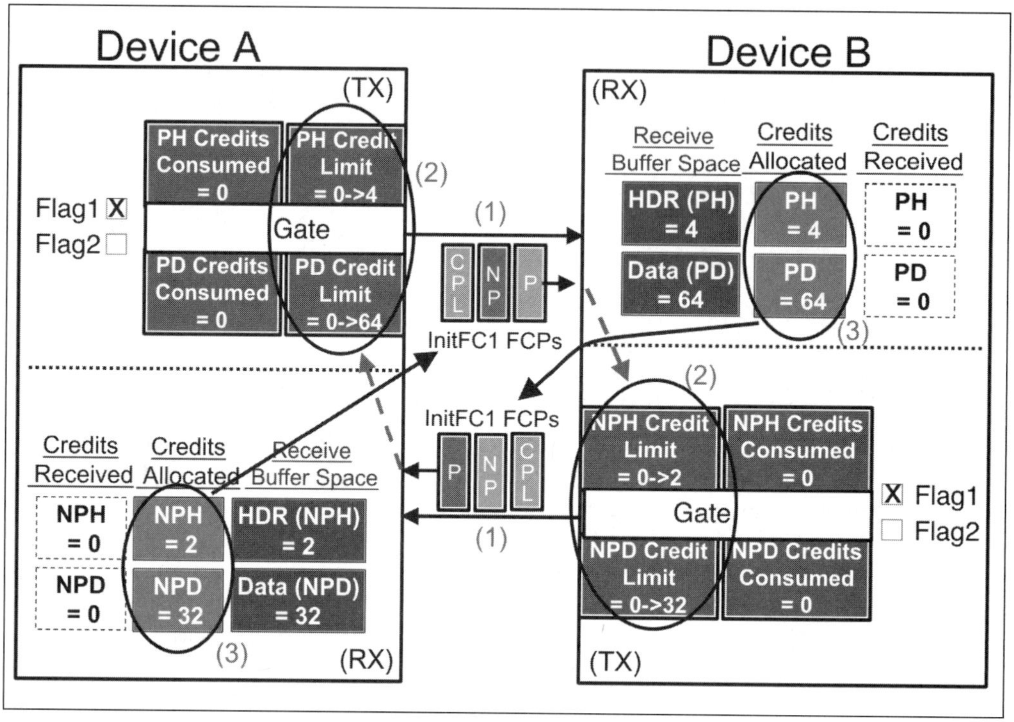

1. Each device sends InitFC1 type Flow Control packets (FCPs) to advertise the size of its respective receive buffers. A separate FCP for posted requests (P), non-posted requests (NP) and completion (CPL) packet types is required. The order in which this sequence of three FCPs is sent is:
   - Header and Data buffer credit units for Posted Requests (P).
   - Header and Data buffer credit units for Non-Posted Requests (NP)
   - Header and Data buffer credit units for Completions (CPL)

   The sequence of FCPs is repeated continuously until a device leaves the FC_INIT1 initialization state.
2. In the meantime, devices take the credit information and initialize the transmit credit limit registers. In this example, Device A loads its PH transmit Credit Limit register with a value of 4, which was reported by Device B for its posted request header FC buffer. It also loads its PD Credit Limit register with a value of 64d credits (1024 bytes worth of data) for accompanying posted data. Similarly, Device B loads its NPH transmit Credit Limit counter with a value of 2 for non-posted request headers and its NPD transmit counter with a value of 32d credits (512 bytes worth of data) for accompanying non-posted data.

3. Note that when this process is complete, the Credits Allocated counter in the receivers and the corresponding Credit Limit counters in the transmitters will be equal.
4. Once a device receives Init1 FC values for a given buffer type (e.g., Posted) and has recorded them, the FC_INIT1 state is complete for that Flow Control buffer. Once all FC buffers for a given VC have completed the FC_INIT1 state, Flag 1 (Fl1) is set and the device ceases to send FCInit1 DLLPs and advances to FC Init2 state. Note that receipt of an Init2 FC packets may also cause Fl1 to be set. This can occur if the neighboring device has already advanced to the FC Init2 state.

FC Init2 Packets Confirm Successful FC Initialization

PCI Express defines the InitFC2 state that is used for feedback to verify the Flow Control initialization has been successful for a given VC. During FC_INIT2, each device continuously outputs a sequence of 3 InitFC2 Flow Control packets; however, credit values are discarded during the FC_INIT2 state. Note that devices are permitted to send TLPs upon entering the FC_INIT2 state. Figure 7-12 illustrates InitFC2 behavior, which is described following the illustration.

Figure 7-12: Device Confirm that Flow Control Initialization is Completed for a Given Buffer

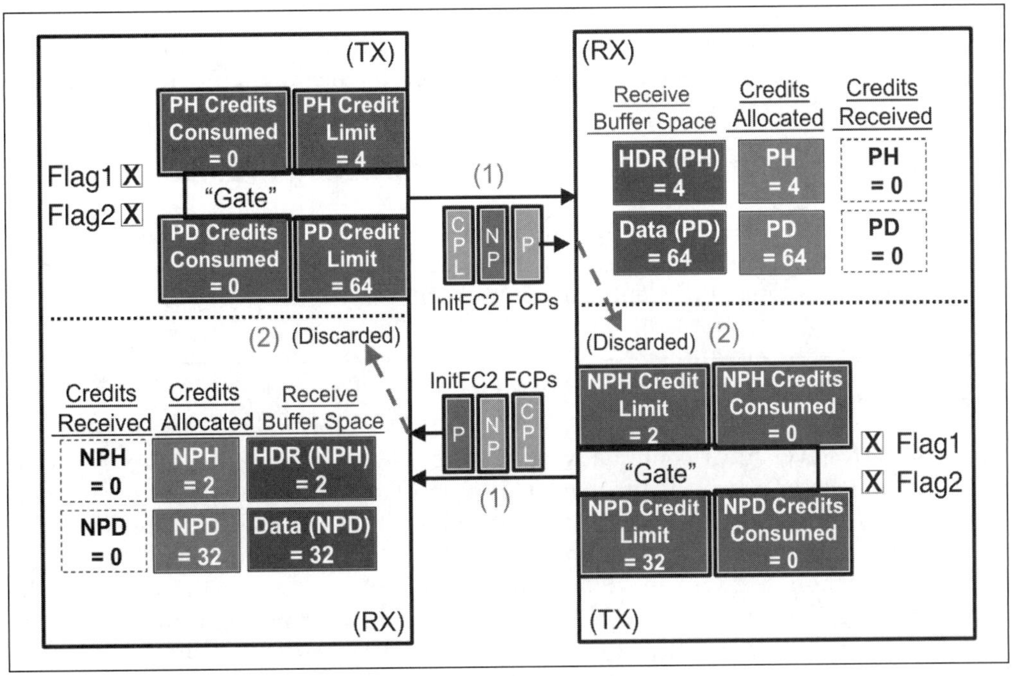

1. At the start of initialization state FC_INIT2, each device commences sending InitFC2 type Flow Control packets (FCPs) to indicate it has completed the FC_INIT1 state. Devices use the same repetitive sequence when sending FCPs in this state as before:
   - Header and Data buffer credit allocation for Posted Requests (P)
   - Header and Data buffer credit allocation for Non-Posted Requests (NP)
   - Header and Data buffer credit allocation for Completions (CPL)
2. All credits reported in InitFC2 FCPs may be discarded, as the transmitter Credit Limit counters were already set up in FC_INIT1.
3. Once a device receives an FC_INIT2 packet for any buffer type, it sets an internal flag (FI2). (It doesn't wait to receive an FC_Init2 for each type.) Note that FI2 is also set upon receipt of an UpdateFC packet or TLP.

Rate of FC_INIT1 and FC_INIT2 Transmission

The specification defines the latency between sending FC_INIT DLLPs as follows:

- **VC0**. Hardware initiated flow control of VC0 requires that FC_INIT1 and FC_INIT2 packets be transmitted "continuously at the maximum rate possible." That is, the resend timer is set to a value of zero.
- **VC1-VC7**. When software initiates flow control initialization, the FC_INIT sequence is repeated "when no other TLPs or DLLPs are available for transmission." However, the latency between the beginning of one sequence to the next can be no greater than 17µs.

Violations of the Flow Control Initialization Protocol

A violation of the flow control initialization protocol can be optionally checked by a device. An error detected can be reported as a Data Link Layer protocol error. See "Link Flow Control-Related Errors" on page 363.

Flow Control Updates Following FC_INIT

The receiver must continually update its neighboring device to report additional Flow Control credits that have accumulated as a result of moving transactions from the Flow Control buffer. Figure 7-13 on page 309 illustrates an example where the transmitter was previously blocked from sending header transactions because the Flow Control buffer was full. In the example, the receiver has just removed three headers from the Flow Control buffer. More space is now available, but the neighboring device has no knowledge of this. As each header is removed from the Flow Control buffer, the

CREDITS_ALLOCATED count increments. The new count is delivered to the CREDIT_LIMIT register of the neighboring device via an update Flow Control packet. The updated credit limit allows transmission of additional transactions.

Figure 7-13: Flow Control Update Example

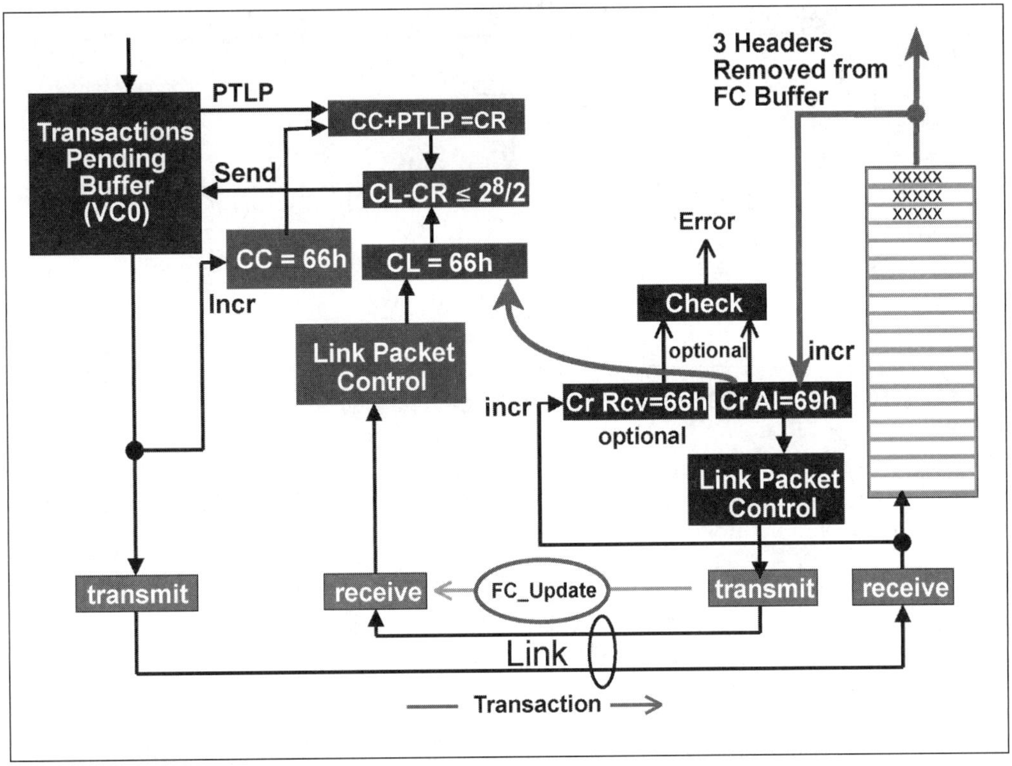

FC_Update DLLP Format and Content

Recall that update Flow Control packets, like the Flow Control initialization packets contain two update fields, one for header and one for data for the selected credit type (P, NP, and Cpl). Figure 7-14 on page 310 depicts the content of the update packet. The receiver's CREDITS_ALLOCATED counts that are reported in the HdrFC and DataFC fields may have been updated many times or not at all since the last update packet sent.

Figure 7-14: Update Flow Control Packet Format and Contents

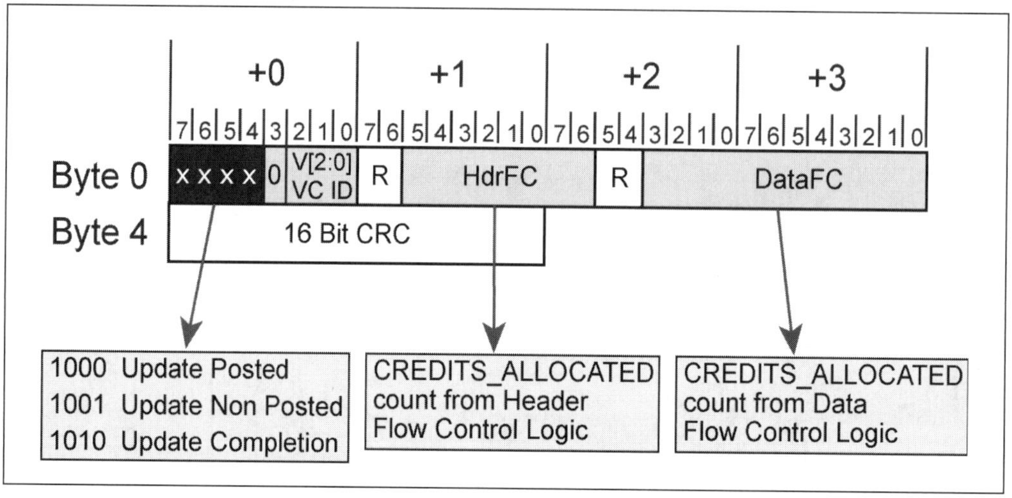

Flow Control Update Frequency

The specification defines a variety of rules and suggested implementations that govern when and how often Flow Control Update DLLPs should be sent. The motivation includes:

- Notifying the transmitting device as early as possible about new credits allocated, which allows previously blocked transactions to continue.
- Establishing worst-case latency between FC Packets.
- Balancing the requirements and variables associated with flow control operation. This involves:
  - o the need to report credits available often enough to prevent transaction blocking
  - o the desire to reduce the link bandwidth required to send FC_Update DLLPs
  - o selecting the optimum buffer size
  - o the maximum data payload size
- Detecting violation of the maximum latency between Flow Control packets.

The update frequency limits specified assume that the link is in the active state (L0 or LOs (s=standby). All other link states represent more aggressive power management with longer recovery latencies that require link recovery prior to sending packets.

Immediate Notification of Credits Allocated

When a Flow Control buffer has filled to the extent that maximum-sized packets cannot be sent, the specification requires immediate delivery of an FC_Update DLLP when the deficit is eliminated. Specifically, when additional credits are allocated by a receiver that guarantee sufficient space now exists to accepts another maximum-sized packet, an Update packet must be sent. Two cases exist:

- **Maximum Packet Size = 1 Credit.** When packet transmission is blocked due to a buffer full condition for non-infinite NPH, NPD, PH, and CPLH buffer types, an UpdateFC packet must be scheduled for Transmission when one or more credits are made available (allocated) for that buffer type.
- **Maximum Packet Size = Max_Payload_Size.** Flow Control buffer space may decrease to the extent that a maximum-sized packet cannot be sent for non-infinite PD and CPLD credit types. In this case, when one or more additional credits are allocated, an Update FCP must be scheduled for transmission.

Maximum Latency Between Update Flow Control DLLPs

The transmission frequency of Update FCPs for each FC credit type (non-infinite) must be scheduled for transmission at least once every 30 µs (-0%/+50%). If the Extended Sync bit within the Control Link register is set, Updates must be scheduled no later than every 120 µs (-0%/+50%). Note that Update FCPs may be scheduled for transmission more frequently than is required.

Calculating Update Frequency Based on Payload Size and Link Width

The specification offers a formula for calculating the frequency at which update packets need to be sent for maximum data payloads sizes and link widths. The formula, shown below, defines FC Update delivery intervals in symbol times (.4ns).

$$\frac{(MaxPayloadSize + TLPOverhead) \times UpdateFactor}{LinkWidth} + InternalDelay$$

where:

- **MaxPayloadSize** = The value in the Max_Payload_Size field of the Device Control register
- **TLPOverhead** = the constant value (28 symbols) representing the addi-

tional TLP components that consume Link bandwidth (header, LCRC, framing Symbols)

- **UpdateFactor** = the number of maximum size TLPs sent during the interval between UpdateFC Packets received. This number balances link bandwidth efficiency and receive buffer sizes – the value varies with Max_Payload_Size and Link width
- **LinkWidth** = The operating width of the Link negotiated during initialization
- **InternalDelay** = a constant value of 19 symbol times that represents the internal processing delays for received TLPs and transmitted DLLPs

The simple relationship defined by the formula show that for a given data payload and buffer size, the frequency of update packet delivery becomes higher as the link width increases. This relatively simple approach suggests a timer implementation that triggers scheduling of update packets. Note that this formula does not account for delays associated with the receiver or transmitter being in the L0s power management state.

The specification recognizes that the formula will be inadequate for many applications such as those that stream large blocks of data. These applications may require buffer sizes larger than the minimum specified, as well as a more sophisticated update policy in order to optimize performance and reduce power consumption. Because a given solution is dependent on the particular requirements of an application, no definition for such policies is provided.

Error Detection Timer — A Pseudo Requirement

The specification defines an optional time-out mechanism that is highly recommended. So much so, that the specification points out that it is expected to become a requirement in futures versions of the spec. This mechanism detects prolonged absences of Flow Control packets. The maximum latency between FC packets for a given Flow Control credit type is specified to be no greater than 120µs. This error detection timer has a maximum limit of 200µs, and it gets reset any time a Flow Control packet of any type is received. If a time-out occurs, this suggests a serious problem with a device's ability to report Flow Control credits. Consequently, a time-out triggers the Physical Layer to enter its Recovery state which retrains the link and hopefully clears the error condition. Characteristics of this timer include:

- operational only when the link is in its active state (L0 or L0s)
- maximum count limited to 200 µs (-0%/+50%)

- timer is reset when any Init or Update FCP is received, or optionally the timer may be reset by the receipt of any type of DLLP
- when timer expires Physical Layer enters the Link Training Sequence State Machine (LTSSM) Recovery state

8 Transaction Ordering

The Previous Chapter

The previous chapter discussed the purposes and detailed operation of the Flow Control Protocol. This protocol requires each device to implement credit-based link flow control for each virtual channel on each port. Flow control guarantees that transmitters will never send Transaction Layer Packets (TLPs) that the receiver can't accept. This prevents receive buffer over-runs and eliminates the need for inefficient disconnects, retries, and wait-states on the link. Flow Control also helps enable compliance with PCI Express ordering rules by maintaining separate Virtual Channel Flow Control buffers for three types of transactions: Posted (P), Non-Posted (NP) and Completions (Cpl).

This Chapter

This chapter discusses the ordering requirements for PCI Express devices as well as PCI and PCI-X devices that may be attached to a PCI Express fabric. The discussion describes the Producer/Consumer programming model upon which the fundamental ordering rules are based. It also describes the potential performance problems that can emerge when strong ordering is employed and specifies the rules defined for deadlock avoidance.

The Next Chapter

Native PCI Express devices that require interrupt support must use the Message Signaled Interrupt (MSI) mechanism defined originally in the PCI 2.2 specification. The next chapter details the MSI mechanism and also describes the legacy support that permits virtualization of the PCI INTx signals required by devices such as PCI Express-to-PCI Bridges.

Introduction

As with other protocols, PCI Express imposes ordering rules on transactions moving through the fabric at the same time. The reasons for the ordering rules include:

- Ensuring that the completion of transactions is deterministic and in the sequence intended by the programmer.
- Avoiding deadlocks conditions.
- Maintaining compatibility with ordering already used on legacy buses (e.g., PCI, PCI-X, and AGP).
- Maximize performance and throughput by minimizing read latencies and managing read/write ordering.

PCI Express ordering is based on the same Producer/Consumer model as PCI. The split transaction protocol and related ordering rules are fairly straight forward when restricting the discussion to transactions involving only native PCI Express devices. However, ordering becomes more complex when including support for the legacy buses mentioned in bullet three above.

Rather than presenting the ordering rules defined by the specification and attempting to explain the rationale for each rule, this chapter takes the building block approach. Each major ordering concern is introduced one at a time. The discussion begins with the most conservative (and safest) approach to ordering, progresses to a more aggressive approach (to improve performance), and culminates with the ordering rules presented in the specification. The discussion is segmented into the following sections:

1. The Producer/Consumer programming model upon which the fundamental ordering rules are based.
2. The fundamental PCI Express device ordering requirements that ensure the Producer/Consumer model functions correctly.
3. The Relaxed Ordering feature that permits violation of the Producer/Consumer ordering when the device issuing a request knows that the transaction is not part of a Producer/Consumer programming sequence.
4. Modification of the strong ordering rules to improve performance.
5. Avoiding deadlock conditions and support for PCI legacy implementations.

Producer/Consumer Model

Readers familiar with the Producer/Consumer programming model may choose to skip this section and proceed directly to "Native PCI Express Ordering Rules" on page 318.

The Producer/Consumer model is a common methodology that two requester-capable devices might use to communicate with each other. Consider the following example scenario:

1. A network adapter begins to receive a stream of compressed video data over the network and performs a series of memory write transactions to deliver the stream of compressed video data into a **Data buffer** in memory (in other words the network adapter is the **Producer** of the data).
2. After the **Producer** moves the data to memory, it performs a memory write transaction to set an indicator (or **Flag**) in a memory location (or a register) to indicate that the data is ready for processing.
3. Another requester (referred to as the **Consumer**) periodically performs a memory read from the **Flag** location to see if there's any data to be processed. In this example, this requester is a video decompressor that will decompress and display the data.
4. When it sees that the **Flag** has been set by the **Producer**, it performs a memory write to clear the **Flag,** followed by a burst memory read transaction to read the compressed data (it consumes the data; hence the name **Consumer**) from the **Data buffer** in memory.
5. When it is done consuming the **Data**, the **Consumer** writes the completion status into the **Status** location. It then resumes periodically reading the **Flag** location to determine when more data needs to be processed.
6. In the meantime, the **Producer** has been reading periodically from the **Status** location to see if data processing has been completed by the other requester (the **Consumer**). This location typically contains zero until the other requester completes the data processing and writes the completion status into it. When the **Producer** reads the **Status** and sees that the **Consumer** has completed processing the **Data**, the **Producer** then performs a memory write to clear the **Status** location.
7. The process then repeats whenever the **Producer** has more data to be processed.

Ordering rules are required to ensure that the Producer/Consumer model works correctly no matter where the **Producer**, the **Consumer**, the **Data** buffer, the **Flag** location, and the **Status** location are located in the system (in other words, no matter how they are distributed on various links in the system).

Native PCI Express Ordering Rules

PCI Express transaction ordering for native devices can be summarized with four simple rules:

1. PCI Express requires strong ordering of transactions (i.e., performing transactions in the order issued by software) flowing through the fabric that have the same TC assignment (see item 4 for the exception to this rule). Because all transactions that have the same TC value assigned to them are mapped to a given VC, the same rules apply to transactions within each VC.
2. No ordering relationship exists between transactions with different TC assignments.
3. The ordering rules apply in the same way to all types of transactions: memory, IO, configuration, and messages.
4. Under limited circumstances, transactions with the Relaxed Ordering attribute bit set can be ordered ahead of other transactions with the same TC.

These fundamental rules ensure that transactions always complete in the order intended by software. However, these rules are extremely conservative and do not necessarily result in optimum performance. For example, when transactions from many devices merge within switches, there may be no ordering relationship between transactions from these different devices. In such cases, more aggressive rules can be applied to improve performance as discussed in "Modified Ordering Rules Improve Performance" on page 322.

Producer/Consumer Model with Native Devices

Because the Producer/Consumer model depends on strong ordering, when the following conditions are met native PCI Express devices support this model without additional ordering rules:

1. All elements associated with the Producer/Consumer model reside within native PCI Express devices.
2. All transactions associated with the operation of the Producer/Consumer model transverse only PCI Express links within the same fabric.
3. All associated transactions have the same TC values. If different TC values are used, then the strong ordering relationship between the transactions is no longer guaranteed.
4. The Relaxed Ordering (RO) attribute bit of the transactions must be cleared to avoid reordering the transactions that are part of the Producer/Consumer transaction series.

When PCI legacy devices reside within a PCI Express system, the ordering rules become more involved. Consequently, additional ordering rules apply because of PCI's delayed transaction protocol. Without ordering rules, this protocol could permit Producer/Consumer transactions to complete out of order and cause the programming model to break.

Relaxed Ordering

PCI Express supports the Relaxed Ordering mechanism introduced by PCI-X; however, PCI Express introduces some changes (discussed later in this chapter). The concept of Relaxed Ordering in the PCI Express environment allows switches in the path between the Requester and Completer to reorder some transactions just received before others that were previously enqueued.

The ordering rules that exist to support the Producer/Consumer model may result in transactions being blocked, when in fact the blocked transactions are completely unrelated to any Producer/Consumer transaction sequence. Consequently, in certain circumstances, a transaction with its Relaxed Ordering (RO) attribute bit set can be re-ordered ahead of other transactions.

The Relaxed Ordering bit may be set by the device if its device driver has enabled it to do so (by setting the Enable Relaxed Ordering bit in the Device Control register—see Table 24 - 3 on page 906). Relaxed ordering gives switches and the Root Complex permission to move this transaction ahead of others, whereas the action is normally prohibited.

RO Effects on Memory Writes and Messages

PCI Express Switches and the Root Complex are affected by memory write and message transactions that have their RO bit set. Memory write and Message transactions are treated the same in most respects—both are handled as posted operations, both are received into the same Posted buffer, and both are subject to the same ordering requirements. When the RO bit is set, switches handle these transactions as follows:

- Switches are permitted to reorder memory write transactions just posted ahead of previously posted memory write transactions or message transactions. Similarly, message transactions just posted may be ordered ahead of previously posted memory write or message transactions. Switches must also forward the RO bit unmodified. The ability to reorder these transactions within switches is not supported by PCI-X bridges. In PCI-X, all posted writes must be forwarded in the exact order received. Another difference between the PCI-X and PCI Express implementations is that message transactions are not defined for PCI-X.

- The Root Complex is permitted to order a just-posted write transaction ahead of another write transaction that was received earlier in time. Also, when receiving write requests (with RO set), the Root Complex is required to write the data payload to the specified address location within system memory, but is permitted to write each byte to memory in any address order.

RO Effects on Memory Read Transactions

All read transactions in PCI Express are handled as split transactions. When a device issues a memory read request with the RO bit set, the request may traverse one or more switches on its journey to the Completer. The Completer returns the requested read data in a series of one or more split completion transactions, and uses the same RO setting as in the request. Switch behavior for the example stated above is as follow:

1. A switch that receives a memory read request with the RO bit set must forward the request in the order received, and must not reorder it ahead of memory write transactions that were previously posted. This action guarantees that all write transactions moving in the direction of the read request are pushed ahead of the read. Such actions are not necessarily part of the Producer/Consumer programming sequence, but software may depend on this flushing action taking place. Also, the RO bit must not be modified by the switch.
2. When the Completer receives the memory read request, it fetches the requested read data and delivers a series of one or more memory read Completion transactions with the RO bit set (because it was set in the request).
3. A switch receiving the memory read Completion(s) detects the RO bit set and knows that it is allowed to order the read Completion(s) ahead of previously posted memory writes moving in the direction of the Completion. If the memory write transaction were blocked (due to flow control), then the memory read Completion would also be blocked if the RO was not set. Relaxed ordering in this case improves read performance.

Table 8-1 summarizes the relaxed ordering behavior allowed by switches.

Table 8-1: Transactions That Can Be Reordered Due to Relaxed Ordering

These Transactions with RO=1 Can Pass	These Transactions
Memory Write Request	Memory Write Request
Message Request	Memory Write Request
Memory Write Request	Message Request
Message Request	Message Request
Read Completion	Memory Write Request
Read Completion	Message Request

Summary of Strong Ordering Rules

The PCI Express specification defines strong ordering rules associated with transactions that are assigned the same TC value, and further defines a Relaxed Ordering attribute that can be used when a device knows that a transaction has no ordering relationship to other transactions with the same TC value. Table 8-2 on page 322 summarizes the PCI Express ordering rules that satisfy the Producer/Consumer model and also provides for Relaxed Ordering. The table represents a draconian approach to ordering and does not consider issues of performance, preventing deadlocks, etc.

The table applies to transactions with the same TC assignment that are moving in the same direction. These rules ensure that transactions will complete in the intended program order and eliminates the possibility of deadlocks in a pure PCI Express implementation (i.e., systems with no PCI Bridges). Columns 2 - 6 represent transactions that have previously latched by a PCI Express device, while column 1 represents subsequently-latched transactions. The ordering relationship between the transaction in column 1 to other transactions previously enqueued is expressed in the table on a row-by-row basis. Note that these rules apply uniformly to all transaction types (Memory, Messages, IO, and Configuration). The table entries are defined as follows:

No — The transaction in column 1 must not be permitted to proceed ahead of the previously enqueued transaction in the corresponding columns (2-6).

Y/N (Yes/No) — The transaction in column 1 is allowed to proceed ahead of the previously enqueued transaction because its Relaxed Ordering bit is set (1), but it is not required to do so.

Table 8-2: Fundamental Ordering Rules Based on Strong Ordering and RO Attribute

	Row Pass Column?	Posted Request: Memory Write or Message Request (Col 2)	Non-Posted Request: Read Request (Col 3)	Non-Posted Request: I/O or Configuration Write Request (Col 4)	Completion: Read Completion (Col 5)	Completion: I/O or Configuration Write Completion (Col 6)
Posted Request	Memory Write or Message Request (Row A)	a) No b) Y/N	No	No	No	No
Non-Posted Request	Read Request (Row B)	No	No	No	No	No
Non-Posted Request	I/O or Configuration Write Request (Row C)	No	No	No	No	No
Completion	Read Completion (Row D)	a) No b) Y/N	No	No	No	No
Completion	I/O or Configuration Write Completion (Row E)	No	No	No	No	No

Note that the shaded area represents the ordering requirements that ensure the Producer/Consumer model functions correctly and is consistent with the basic rules associated with strong ordering. The transaction ordering associated with columns 3 - 6 play no role in the Producer/Consumer model.

Modified Ordering Rules Improve Performance

This section describes how temporary transaction blocking can occur when the strong ordering rules listed in Table 8-2 are rigorously enforced. Modification of strong ordering between transactions that do not violate the Produce/Consumer programming model can eliminate many blocking conditions and improve link efficiency.

Strong Ordering Can Result in Transaction Blocking

Maintaining the strong ordering relationship between transactions would likely result in instances where all transactions would be blocked due to a single receive buffer being full. The strong ordering requirements to support the Producer/Consumer model cannot be modified (except in the case of relaxed ordering described previously). However, transaction sequences that do not occur within the Producer/Consumer programming model can be modified to a weakly ordered scheme that can lead to improved performance.

The Problem

Consider the following example illustrated in Figure 8-1 on page 323 when strong ordering is maintained for all transaction sequences. This example depicts transmitter and receiver buffers associated with the delivery of transactions in a single direction (from left to right) for a single Virtual Channel (VC), and the transmit and receive buffers are organized in the same way. Also, recall that each of the transaction types (Posted, Non-Posted, and Completions) have independent flow control within the same VC. The numbers within the transmit buffers show the order in which these transactions were issued to the transmitter. In addition, the non-posted receive buffer is currently full. Consider the following sequence.

1. Transaction 1 (a memory read—non-posted operation) is the next transaction that must be sent (based on strong ordering). The flow control mechanism detects that insufficient credits are available, so Transaction 1 cannot be sent.
2. Transaction 2 (a posted memory write) is the next transaction pending. When consulting Table 8-2 (based on strong ordering), entry A3 specifies that a memory write must not pass a previously posted read transaction.
3. Because all entries in Table 8-2 are "No", all transactions are blocked due to the non-posted receive buffer being filled.

Figure 8-1: Example of Strongly Ordered Transactions that Results in Temporary Blocking

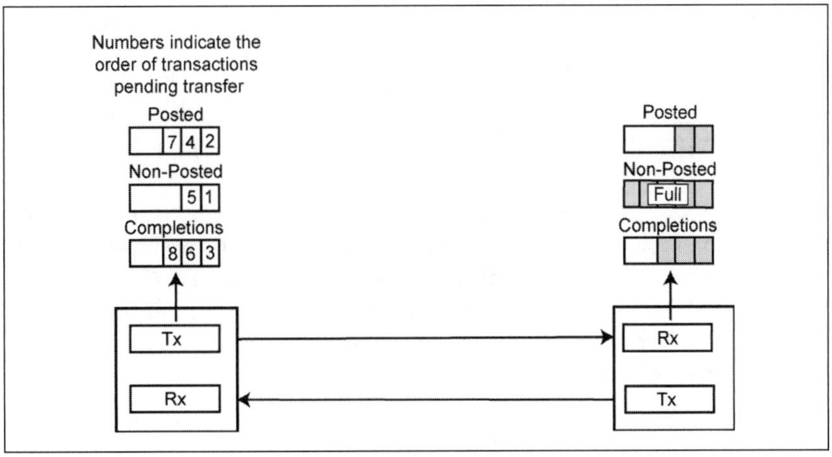

The Weakly Ordered Solution

As discussed previously, strong ordering is required to support the Producer/Consumer model. This requirement is satisfied entirely by the shaded area in Table 8-2. The non-shaded area deals with transaction sequences that do not occur in the Producer/Consumer programming model, and therefore can be modified. Table 8-3 on page 326 lists these entries as weakly ordered. The modified entries are defined as:

Y/N (Yes/No) — The transaction in column 1 is allowed to proceed ahead of the previously enqueued transaction because the entry is not related to the Producer/Consumer strong ordering requirements and can be weakly ordered to improve performance.

Consider the scenario in Figure 8-1 with weak ordering employed:

1. Transaction 1 (a memory read—non-posted operation) is the next transaction that must be sent. The flow control mechanism detects that insufficient credits are available, so Transaction 1 cannot be sent.
2. The next transaction pending (2) is a posted memory write operation. When consulting Table 8-3 on page 326, entry A3 (Y/N) allows the transmitter to reorder transaction 2 ahead of transaction 1. No blocking occurs!
3. The remaining transactions pending will also complete ahead of transaction 1 if the non-posted buffer remains full. When flow control credits are returned for the non-posted operations, transaction 1 will be the next transaction sent.

In summary, these examples illustrate how strong ordering can temporarily block all transactions pending delivery, and that weak ordering rules can be used to improve link efficiency without violating the Producer/Consumer model.

Order Management Accomplished with VC Buffers

As the previous example illustrated, transaction ordering is managed within the Virtual Channel buffers. These buffers are grouped into Posted, Non-Posted, and Completion transactions and flow control is managed independently for each group. This makes it much easier to implement the modified (weak) ordering described in the previous example. See Chapter 7, entitled "Flow Control," on page 285 for details.

Recall that transactions are mapped to Virtual Channels using the transaction's TC. If each TC is mapped to a separate VC, then each VC buffer will contain transactions with a single TC assignment. In this situation, VC flow control permits optimum flow of transactions.

Summary of Modified Ordering Rules

Table 8-3 on page 326 lists and highlights the modified ordering rules that allow switches to move some transactions ahead of others that may be stalled due to a receive buffer full condition. Definition of the entries are the same as the previous table:

No—The transaction in column 1 must not be permitted to proceed ahead of the previously enqueued transaction in the corresponding columns (2-6).

Y/N (Yes/No)—The transaction in column 1 is allowed to proceed ahead of the previously enqueued transaction because:

- its Relaxed Ordering bit is set (1), but it is not required to do so.
- the entry is not subject to the Producer/Consumer strong ordering requirements and is weakly ordered to improve performance.

Note: The "No" entry in Row D, Column 5 (D5) applies to cases where a Completer returns multiple Completions in response to a single read request. These Completions must return in order (i.e., Completions with the same transaction ID).

Upon examination of the table, some readers may question whether programs will operate correctly when weak ordering is employed. For example, note that a write transaction is permitted to be reordered ahead of a previously latched read request (entry A3). A programmer who reads from a location followed by a write to the same location must not expect these operations to complete in program order. Note that the ordering rules only guarantee proper operation of the Producer/Consumer programming model. If a programmer requires a read operation to complete ahead of a write transaction, then the write must not be issued until the read transaction completes.

Table 8-3: Weak Ordering Rules Enhance Performance

Row Pass Column?		Posted Request	Non-Posted Request		Completion	
		Memory Write or Message Request (Col 2)	Read Request (Col 3)	I/O or Configuration Write Request (Col 4)	Read Completion (Col 5)	I/O or Configuration Write Completion (Col 6)
Posted Request	Memory Write or Message Request (Row A)	a) No b) Y/N	Y/N	Y/N	Y/N	Y/N
Non-Posted Request	Read Request (Row B)	No	Y/N	Y/N	Y/N	Y/N
	I/O or Configuration Write Request (Row C)	No	Y/N	Y/N	Y/N	Y/N
Completion	Read Completion (Row D)	a) No b) Y/N	Y/N	Y/N	a) Y/N b) No	Y/N
	I/O or Configuration Write Completion (Row E)	No	Y/N	Y/N	Y/N	Y/N

Support for PCI Buses and Deadlock Avoidance

Because the PCI bus employs delayed transactions, several deadlock scenarios can develop. These deadlock avoidance rules are included in PCI Express ordering to ensure that no deadlocks occur regardless of topology. Adhering to the ordering rules prevent problems when boundary conditions develop due to unanticipated topologies (e.g., two PCI Express to PCI bridges connected across the PCI Express fabric). Refer to the MindShare book entitled *PCI System Architecture, Fourth Edition* (published by Addison-Wesley) for a detailed explanation of the scenarios that are the basis for the PCI ordering rules related to deadlock avoidance. Table 8-4 on page 327 lists and highlights the deadlock avoidance ordering rules. Note that avoiding the deadlocks involves "Yes" entries in each case. If blocking occurs, the transaction in column 1 must be moved ahead of the transaction specified in the column where the "Yes" entry exists. Note also that the "Yes" entries in A5b and A6b apply only to PCI Express to PCI Bridges and PCI Express to PCI-X Bridges.

Table 8-4: Ordering Rules with Deadlock Avoidance Rules

Row Pass Column?		Posted Request: Memory Write or Message Request (Col 2)	Non-Posted Request: Read Request (Col 3)	Non-Posted Request: I/O or Configuration Write Request (Col 4)	Completion: Read Completion (Col 5)	Completion: I/O or Configuration Write Completion (Col 6)
Posted Request	Memory Write or Message Request (Row A)	a) No b) Y/N	Yes	Yes	a) Y/N b) Yes	a) Y/N b) Yes
Non-Posted Request	Read Request (Row B)	No	Y/N	Y/N	Y/N	Y/N
Non-Posted Request	I/O or Configuration Write Request (Row C)	No	Y/N	Y/N	Y/N	Y/N
Completion	Read Completion (Row D)	a) No b) Y/N	Yes	Yes	a) Y/N b) No	Y/N
Completion	I/O or Configuration Write Completion (Row E)	Y/N	Yes	Yes	Y/N	Y/N

The specification provides the following explanation of the table entries:

- **A2a** — A Memory Write or Message Request with the Relaxed Ordering Attribute bit clear (0b) must not pass any other Memory Write or Message Request.
- **A2b** — A Memory Write or Message Request with the Relaxed Ordering Attribute bit set (1b) is permitted to pass any other Memory Write or Message Request.
- **A3, A4** — A Memory Write or Message Request must be allowed to pass Read Requests and I/O or Configuration Write Requests to avoid deadlocks.
- **A5a, A6a** — Endpoints, Switches, and Root Complexes may either allow Memory Write and Message Requests to pass Completions or to be blocked by Completions.
- **A5b, A6b** —PCI Express to PCI Bridges and PCI Express to PCI-X Bridges (when operating in PCI mode), must allow Memory Write and Message Requests to pass Completions traveling in the PCI Express to PCI direction (Primary side of Bridge to Secondary side of Bridge) to avoid deadlock.

- **B2, C2** — These Requests cannot pass a Memory Write or Message Request. This preserves strong write ordering required to support the Producer/ Consumer model.
- **B3, B4, C3, C4** — Read Requests and I/O or Configuration Write Requests are permitted to be blocked by or to pass other Read Requests and I/O or Configuration Write Requests.
- **B5, B6, C5, C6** — The Requests specified are permitted to be blocked by or to pass Completions.
- **D2a** — If the Relaxed Ordering attribute bit is not set, then a Read Completion cannot pass a previously enqueued Memory Write or Message Request.
- **D2b** —If the Relaxed Ordering attribute bit is set, then a Read Completion is permitted to pass a previously enqueued Memory Write or Message Request.
- **D3, D4, E3, E4** — Completions must be allowed to pass Read and I/O or Configuration Write Requests to avoid deadlocks.
- **D5a** — Read Completions associated with different Read Requests are allowed to be blocked by or to pass each other.
- **D5b** — When multiple completions are returned in response to a single Read Request, the completions must return the requested read data in the proper address order. Note that the data returned in each completion is delivered in ascending address order. Switches can recognize this condition because each completion will have the same Transaction ID. Completions with different transaction IDs can be reordered without concern.
- **D6 Read** — Completions are permitted to be blocked by or to pass I/O or Configuration Write Completions.
- **E2** — I/O or Configuration Write Completions are permitted to be blocked by or to pass Memory Write and Message Requests. Such transactions are actually moving in the opposite direction, and have no ordering relationship.
- **E5, E6** — I/O or Configuration Write Completions are permitted to be blocked by or to pass Read Completions and other I/O or Configuration Write Completions.

The specification also states the following additional rules:

- For Root Complex and Switch, Memory Write combining (as defined in the PCI Specification) is prohibited. Note: This is required so that devices can be permitted to optimize their receive buffer and control logic for Memory Write sizes matching their natural expected sizes, rather than being required to support the maximum possible Memory Write payload size.
- Combining of Memory Read Requests, and/or Completions for different Requests is prohibited.
- The No Snoop bit does not affect the required ordering behavior.

9 Interrupts

The Previous Chapter

This chapter discusses the ordering requirements for PCI Express devices as well as PCI and PCI-X devices that may be attached to a PCI Express fabric. The discussion describes the Producer/Consumer programming model upon which the fundamental ordering rules are based. It also describes the potential performance problems that can emerge when strong ordering is employed and specifies the rules defined for deadlock avoidance.

This Chapter

Native PCI Express devices that require interrupt support must use the Message Signaled Interrupt (MSI) mechanism defined originally in the PCI 2.2 version of the specification. This chapter details the MSI mechanism and also describes the legacy support that permits virtualization of the PCI INTx signals required by devices such as PCI Express-to-PCI Bridges.

The Next Chapter

To this point it has been presumed that transactions traversing the fabric have not encountered any errors that cannot be corrected by hardware. The next chapter discusses both correctable and non-correctable errors and discusses the mechanisms used to report them. The PCI Express architecture provides a rich set of error detection, reporting, and logging capabilities. PCI Express error reporting classifies errors into three classes: correctable, non-fatal, and fatal. Prior to discussing the PCI Express error reporting capabilities, including PCI-compatible mechanisms, a brief review of the PCI error handling is included as background information.

Two Methods of Interrupt Delivery

Interrupt delivery is conditionally optional for PCI Express devices. When a native PCI Express function does depend upon delivering interrupts to call its device driver, Message Signaled Interrupts (MSI) must be used. However, in the event that a device connecting to a PCI Express link cannot use MSIs (i.e., legacy devices), an alternate mechanism is defined. Both mechanisms are summarized below:

Native PCI Express Interrupt Delivery — PCI Express eliminates the need for sideband signals by using the Message Signaled Interrupt (MSI), first defined by the 2.2 version of the PCI Specification (as an optional mechanism) and later required by PCI-X devices. The term "Message Signaled Interrupt" can be misleading in the context of PCI Express because of possible confusion with PCI Express's "Message" transactions. A Message Signaled Interrupt is not a PCI Express Message, instead it is simply a Memory Write transaction. A memory write associated with an MSI can only be distinguished from other memory writes by the address locations they target, which are reserved by the system for Interrupt delivery.

Legacy PCI Interrupt Delivery — This mechanism supports devices that must use PCI-Compatible interrupt signaling (i.e., INTA#, INTB#, INTC#, and INTD#) defined for the PCI bus. Legacy functions use one of the interrupt lines to signal an interrupt. An INTx# signal is asserted to request interrupt service and deasserted when the interrupt service accesses a device-specific register, thereby indicating the interrupt is being serviced. PCI Express defines in-band messages that act as virtual INTx# wires, which target the interrupt controller located typically within the Root Complex.

Figure 9-1 illustrates the delivery of interrupts from three types of devices:

- Native PCI Express device — must use MSI delivery
- Legacy endpoint device — must support MSI and optionally support INTx messages. Such devices may be boot devices that must use legacy interrupts during boot, but once its driver loads MSIs are used.
- PCI Express-to-PCI (X) Bridge — must support INTx messages

Figure 9-1: Native PCI Express and Legacy PCI Interrupt Delivery

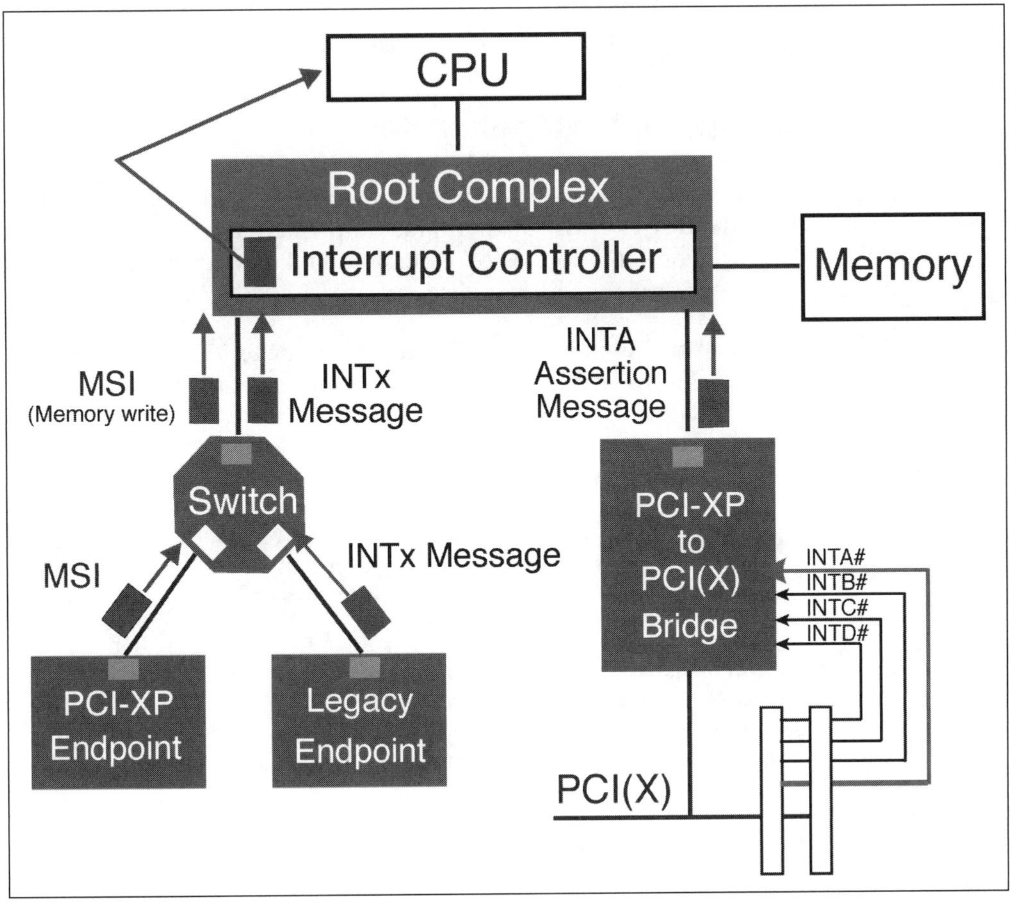

Message Signaled Interrupts

Message Signaled Interrupts (MSIs) are delivered to the Root Complex via memory write transactions. The MSI Capability register provides all the information that the device requires to signal MSIs. This register is set up by configuration software and includes the following information:

- Target memory address
- Data Value to be written to the specified address location
- The number of messages that can be encoded into the data

See "Description of 3DW And 4DW Memory Request Header Fields" on page 176 for a review of the Memory Write Transaction Header. Note that MSIs always have a data payload of 1DW.

The MSI Capability Register Set

A PCI Express function indicates its support for MSI via the MSI Capability registers. Each native PCI Express function must implement a single MSI register set within its own configuration space. Note that the PCI Express specification defines two register formats:

1. 64-bit memory addressing format (Figure 9-2 on page 332) — required by all native PCI Express devices and optionally implemented by Legacy endpoints.
2. 32-bit memory addressing format (Figure 9-3 on page 332) — optionally supported by Legacy endpoints.

Figure 9-2: 64-bit MSI Capability Register Format

31 … 16	15 … 8	7 … 0	
Message Control Register	Pointer to Next ID	Capability ID = 05h	Dword 0
Least-Significant 32-bits of Message Address Register		0 0	Dword 1
Most-Significant 32-bits of Message Address Register			Dword 2
	Message Data Register		Dword 3

Figure 9-3: 32-bit MSI Capability Register Set Format

31 … 16	15 … 8	7 … 0	
Message Control Register	Pointer to Next ID	Capability ID = 05h	Dword 0
Message Address Register		0 0	Dword 1
	Message Data Register		Dword 2

The following sections describe each field within the MSI registers.

Capability ID

The Capability ID that identifies the MSI register set is **05h**. This is a hardwired, read-only value.

Pointer To Next New Capability

The second byte of the register set either points to the next New Capability's register set or contains 00h if this is the end of the New Capabilities list. This is a hardwired, read-only value. If non-zero, it must be a dword-aligned value.

Message Control Register

Figure 9-4 on page 333 and Table 9-1 on page 333 illustrate the layout and usage of the Message Control register.

Figure 9-4: Message Control Register

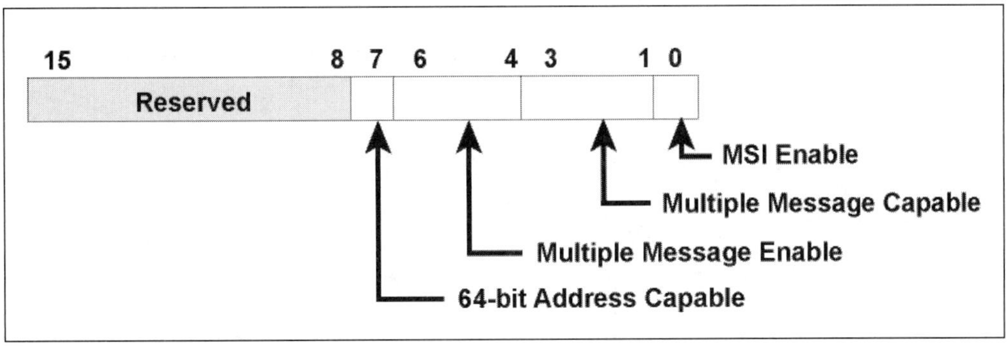

Table 9-1: Format and Usage of Message Control Register

Bit(s)	Field Name	Description
15:8	Reserved	Read-Only. Always zero.
7	64-bit Address Capable	Read-Only. • 0 = Function does not implement the upper 32-bits of the Message Address register and is incapable of generating a 64-bit memory address. • 1 = Function implements the upper 32-bits of the Message Address register and is capable of generating a 64-bit memory address.

Table 9-1: Format and Usage of Message Control Register (Continued)

Bit(s)	Field Name	Description
6:4	Multiple Message Enable	Read/Write. After system software reads the Multiple Message Capable field (see next row in this table) to determine how many messages are requested by the device, it programs a 3-bit value into this field indicating the actual number of messages allocated to the device. The number allocated can be equal to or less than the number actually requested. The state of this field after reset is 000b. The field is encoded as follows: **Value** — **Number of Messages Requested** 000b — 1 001b — 2 010b — 4 011b — 8 100b — 16 101b — 32 110b — Reserved 111b — Reserved
3:1	Multiple Message Capable	Read-Only. System software reads this field to determine how many messages the device would like allocated to it. The requested number of messages is a power of two, therefore a device that would like three messages must request that four messages be allocated to it. The field is encoded as follows: **Value** — **Number of Messages Requested** 000b — 1 001b — 2 010b — 4 011b — 8 100b — 16 101b — 32 110b — Reserved 111b — Reserved

Table 9-1: Format and Usage of Message Control Register (Continued)

Bit(s)	Field Name	Description
0	MSI Enable	Read/Write. State after reset is 0, indicating that the device's MSI capability is disabled. • **0** = Function is **disabled** from using **MSI**. It must use INTX Messages to deliver interrupts (legacy endpoint or bridge). • **1** = Function is **enabled** to use **MSI** to request service and is forbidden to use its interrupt pin.

Message Address Register

The lower two bits of the 32-bit Message Address register are hardwired to zero and cannot be changed. In other words, the address assigned by system software is always aligned on a dword address boundary.

The upper 32-bits of the Message Address register are required for native PCI Express devices and optional for legacy endpoints. This register is present if Bit 7 of the Message Control register is set. If present, it is a read/write register and it is used in conjunction with the Message Address register to assign a 32-bit or a 64-bit memory address to the device:

- If the upper 32-bits of the Message Address register are set to a non-zero value by the system software, then a 64-bit message address has been assigned to the device using both the upper and lower halves of the register.
- If the upper 32-bits of the Message Address register are set to zero by the system software, then a 32-bit message address has been assigned to the device using both the upper and lower halves of the register.

Message Data Register

The system software assigns the device a base message data pattern by writing it into this 16-bit, read/write register. When the device must generate an interrupt request, it writes a 32-bit value to the memory address specified in the Message Address register. The data written has the following format:

- The upper 16 bits are always set to zero.
- The lower 16 bits are supplied from the Message Data register. If more than one message has been assigned to the device, the device modifies the lower bits (the number of modifiable bits depends on how many messages have been assigned to the device by the configuration software) of the data from

the Message Data register to form the appropriate message for the event it wishes to report to its driver. For an example, refer to the example cited in "Basics of Generating an MSI Interrupt Request" on page 338.

Basics of MSI Configuration

The following list specifies the steps taken by software to configure MSI interrupts for a PCI Express device. Refer to Figure 9-5 on page 337.

1. At startup time, the configuration software scans the PCI bus(es) (referred to as bus enumeration) and discovers devices (i.e., it performs configuration reads for valid Vendor IDs).When a PCI Express function is discovered, the configuration software reads the Capabilities List Pointer to obtain the location of the first Capability register within the chain of registers.
2. The software then searches the capability register sets until it discovers the MSI Capability register set (Capability ID of 05h).
3. Software assigns a dword-aligned memory address to the device's Message Address register. This is the destination address of the memory write used when delivering an interrupt request.
4. Software checks the Multiple Message Capable field in the device's Message Control register to determine how many event-specific messages the device would like assigned to it.
5. The software then allocates a number of messages equal to or less than what the device requested. At a minimum, one message will be allocated to the device.
6. The software writes the base message data pattern into the device's Message Data register.
7. Finally, the software sets the MSI Enable bit in the device's Message Control register, thereby enabling it to generate interrupts using MSI memory writes.

Figure 9-5: Device MSI Configuration Process

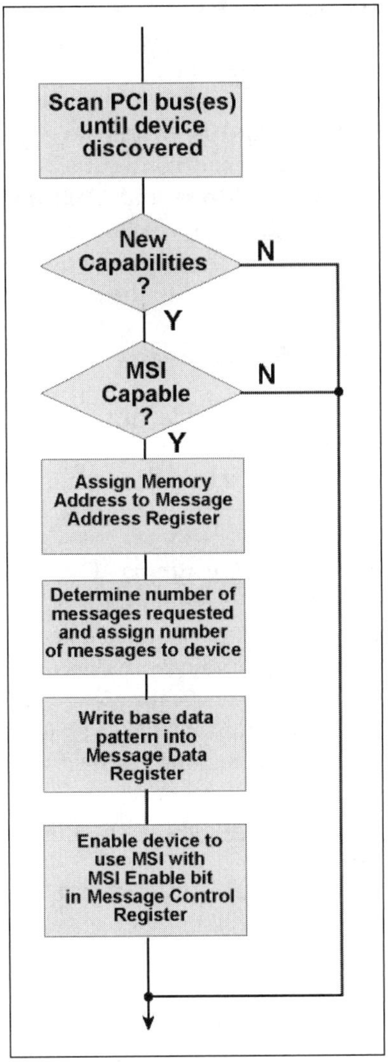

Basics of Generating an MSI Interrupt Request

When a PCI Express function generates an interrupt request to the processor it performs a memory write transaction. The associated data is platform specific and is always 1DW in size, and is written to a pre-defined memory address location. As described earlier, the configuration software is responsible for priming the function's MSI Address and Data registers with the appropriate memory address and the data to be written to that address when generating a request. It also primes a field in the Message Control register with the number of messages that have been allocated to the device.

Memory Write Transaction (MSI)

When the device must generate an interrupt request, it writes the Message Data register contents to the memory address specified in its Message Address register. Figure 9-6 on page 339 illustrates the contents of the Memory Write Transaction Header and Data field. Key points include:

- Format field must be 11b, indicating a 4DW header with Data (native functions) and may be 10b for Legacy Endpoints.
- Header Attribute bits (No Snoop and Relaxed Ordering) must be zero.
- Length field must be 01h to indicate maximum data payload of 1DW.
- First BE field must be 0011b, indicating valid data in lower 16 bits.
- Last BE field must be 0000b, indicating a single DW transaction.
- Address fields within the header come directly from the address fields within the MSI Capability registers.
- Lower 16 bits of the Data payload come directly from the data field within the MSI Capability registers.

Figure 9-6: Format of Memory Write Transaction for Native-Deive MSI Delivery

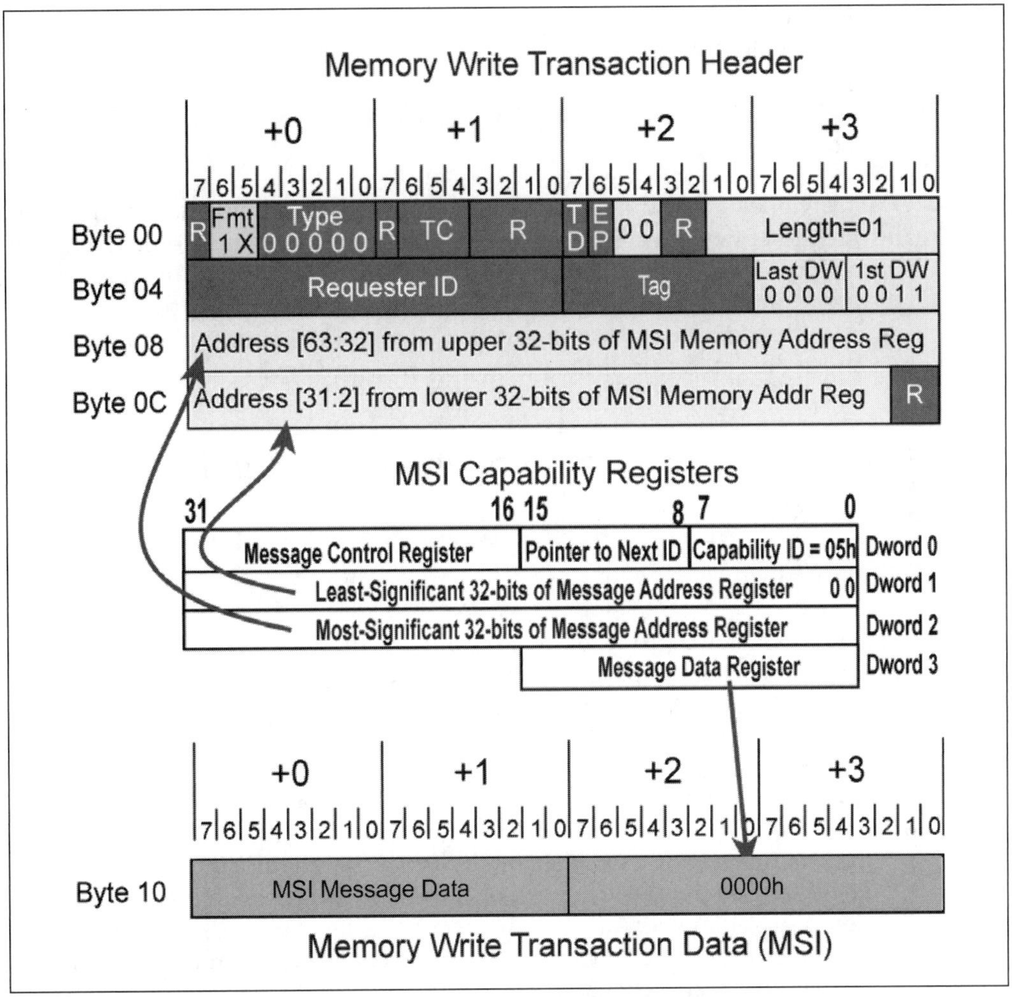

Multiple Messages

If the system software allocated more than one message to the device, it is permitted to modify the lower bits of the assigned Message Data value to send a different message for each device-specific event type that requires servicing by the device driver.

As an example, assume the following:

- Four messages have been allocated to a device.
- A data value of 0500h has been assigned to the device's Message Data register.
- Memory address 0A000000h has been written into the device's Message Address register.

When any one of four different device-specific events occurs, the device generates a request by performing a dword write to memory address 0A000000h with a data value of 00000500h, 00000501h, 00000502h, or 00000503h. In other words, the device automatically appends the value 0000h to the upper part of its assigned message data value (to make a 32-bit value) and modifies the lower two bits of the value to indicate the specific message type.

Memory Synchronization When Interrupt Handler Entered

The Problem

Assume that a PCI Express device performs one or more memory write transactions to deliver data (application data) into main memory, followed by an MSI (which notifies software that new application data has been moved to memory). Also assume the following:

- application data transactions have a Traffic Class of Zero (TC0) and will always flow through VC0 buffers.
- the MSI transaction uses TC1, and it flows through the VC1 buffers.
- These transactions traverse one or more switches on their way to the Root Complex and memory.
- VC arbitration is set up so that VC1 transactions have a much higher priority than VC0 transactions.

Flow Control and VC arbitration associated with the delivery of the data and the MSI may result in the MSI transaction being moved ahead of the application data transactions based on the goals of differentiated services. This is possible because there is no ordering relationship maintained between transactions that have different TC values and VC assignments. Consequently, the MSI may arrive at the Root Complex well ahead of the corresponding application data.

When the CPU is interrupted by the MSI, the currently-executing program is suspended and the processor executes the interrupt handler within the

Requester's device driver. The driver may immediately read data from the target memory buffer in main memory. If some of the application data transactions that are still making their way upstream, the driver will fetch and process old data.

Solving the Problem

The problem can be solved in two ways:

1. Ensure that the TC numbers of the Memory Write data and the MSI are the same. The MSI must also have its relaxed ordering bit cleared.
2. The driver can solve this problem by performing a dummy read (Memory Read Dword with all Byte Enables deasserted) from a location within its device before processing the data. The read must also have the same TC number as the Memory Write data. The read completion returned to the Root Complex will travel in the same VC as the Memory Write data, thereby ensuring that the write data will be pushed ahead of the read completion and into memory prior to the completion being received by the driver. Recall that the ordering rules require that all transactions with the same TC must be performed in order. The only exception is a transaction with the relaxed ordering bit set.

Interrupt Latency

The time from signaling an interrupt request until software services the device is referred to as its interrupt latency. As with the other interrupt request delivery mechanisms the MSI capability does not provide interrupt latency guarantees.

MSI Results In ECRC Error

Because MSIs are delivered as Memory Write transactions, and error associated with delivery of an MSI is treated the same as any other Memory Write error condition. See "ECRC Generation and Checking" on page 361 for treatment of ECRC errors.

Some Rules, Recommendations, etc.

1. It is the specification's intention that mutually-exclusive messages will be assigned to devices by the system software and that each message will be converted to an exclusive interrupt level upon delivery to the processor.

2. More than one MSI capability register set per function is prohibited.
3. A read from the Message Address register produces undefined results.
4. Reserved registers and bits are read-only and always return zero when read.
5. System software can modify Message Control register bits, but the device is prohibited from doing so. In other words, it's not permitted to modify the bits via the "back door."
6. At a minimum, a single message will be assigned to each device.
7. System software must not write to the upper half of the dword that contains the Message Data register.
8. If the device writes the same message multiple times, only one of those messages is guaranteed to be serviced. If all of them must be serviced, the device must not generate the same message again until the driver services the earlier one.
9. If a device has more than one message assigned, and it writes a series of different messages, it is guaranteed that all of them will be serviced.

Legacy PCI Interrupt Delivery

This section provides background information regarding the standard PCI interrupt delivery using INTx signals. This is followed by a detailed discussion of how PCI Express supports virtual INTx signaling. Readers familiar with PCI interrupt handling may wish to proceed to "Virtual INTx Signaling" on page 347.

Background — PCI Interrupt Signaling

PCI devices that use interrupts have two options:

1. INTx# active low-level signals that can be shared. These signals were defined in the original specification.
2. Message Signaled Interrupts introduced with the 2.2 version of the specification are optional for PCI devices. These MSIs are compatible with PCI Express and require no modification by devices or by PCI Express-to-PCI Bridges.

Device INTx# Pins

Each physical PCI component can implement up to 4 INTx# signals (INTA#, INTB#, INTC#, and INTD#). Because PCI devices (like PCI Express devices) can support up to 8 functions, four interrupt pins are supported. However, if a maximum of eight functions are implemented and all required interrupts then the

INTx# signals would have to be shared. Also, no single function is permitted to use more than one INTx# signal.

Determining if a Function Uses INTx# Pins

Each PCI function indicates support for an INTx# signal via the standard configuration header. The read-only Interrupt Pin register illustrated in Figure 9-7 on page 343, contains the information needed by configuration software to determine if INTx signals are supported and, if so, which INTx# signal is used by this function.

Figure 9-7: Interrupt Pin Register within PCI Configuration Header

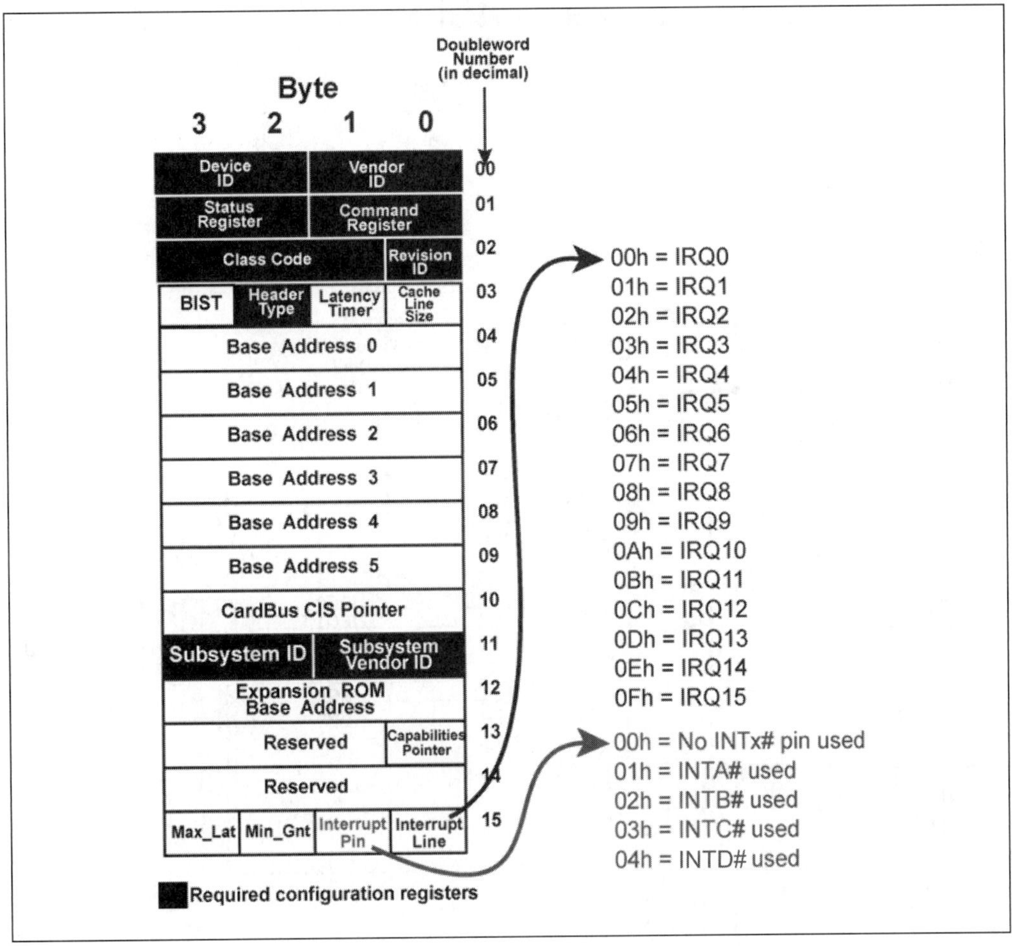

Interrupt Routing

The system designer determines the routing of INTx pins from devices. The INTx signals used by each device can be routed in a variety of ways so that ultimately the each INTx pin will go to an input of the interrupt controller. Figure 9-8 on page 344 illustrates a variety of PCI devices using INTx pins to signal interrupts. As is typical, all PCI INTx signals are routed to one of four inputs. All INTx signals routed to a given input will be directed to a specific input to the interrupt controller, thus each of the INTx routed to the common interrupt input will also have the same interrupt Line number assigned to it by platform software. For example, IRQ15 has three PCI INTx inputs from different devices — INTB#, INTA#, and INTA#. Consequently, the functions using these INTx lines will share IRQ15 and its associated interrupt vector.

Figure 9-8: INTx Signal Routing is Platform Specific

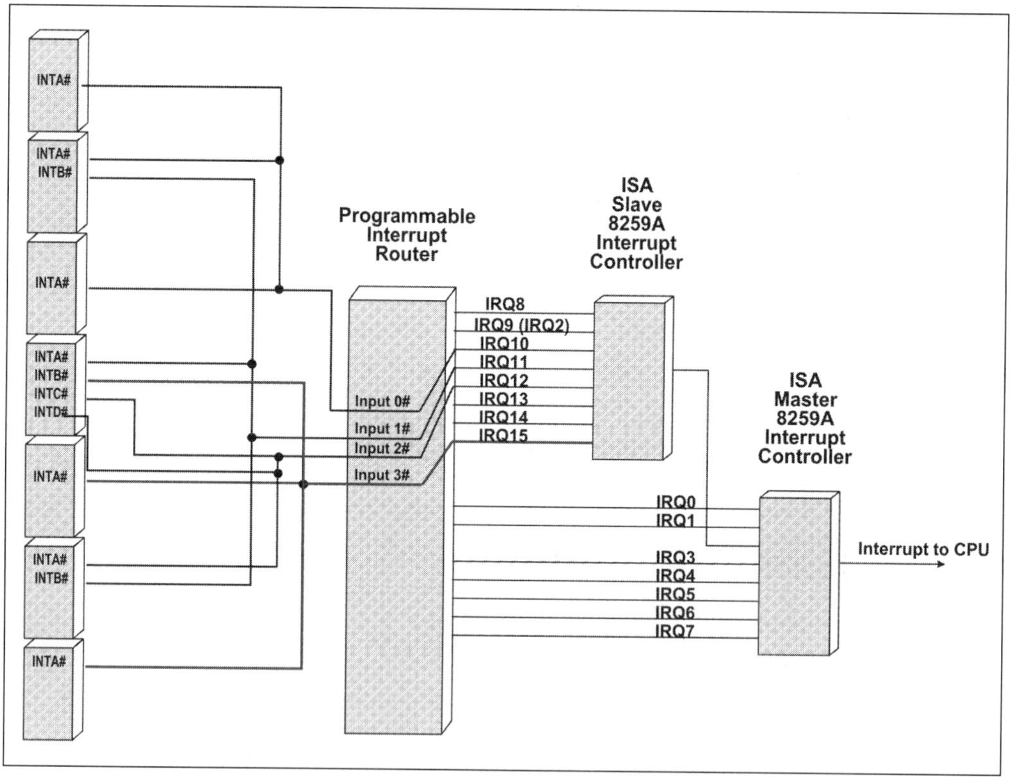

Associating the INTx# Line to an IRQ Number

Based on the routing of the INTx pin associated with each function, the Interrupt Line number is reported by configuration software (also pictured in Figure 9-7 on page 343). The value ultimately tells the function's device driver which interrupt vector will be reported when an interrupt occurs from this function. Therefore, when this function generates an interrupt the CPU will receive the vector number that corresponds to the IRQ specified in the Interrupt Line register. The CPU uses this vector to index into the interrupt service table to fetch the entry point of the interrupt service routine associated with the function's device driver. The method used to communicate this information is operating environment specific (e.g., the Windows XP or Linux).

Note that because the INTx# lines can be wire ORed from different devices, the interrupt line number assignment will be the same for those devices whose INTx# lines are wired together. In these cases, an interrupt signaled by any of the devices sharing the same IRQ will cause the same vector to be sent to the CPU. Software must ensure that all service routines that share the same IRQ input chain the service routines together so that all devices can be checked to determine which one(s) caused the interrupt request. Once again the mechanism used for chaining the service routines is operating environment specific.

INTx# Signaling

The INTx# lines are active low signals implemented as open-drain with a pullup resistor provided on each line by the system. Multiple devices connected to the same PCI interrupt request signal line can assert it simultaneously without damage.

When a device signals an interrupt it also sets a bit within a device-specific register to indicate that an interrupt is pending. This register can be mapped into memory or I/O address space and is read by device-specific software to verify that an interrupt is pending completion. When this bit is cleared, the INTx signal is deasserted.

The device must also set the Interrupt Status bit located in the Configuration Status register. This bit can be read by system software to see if an interrupt is currently pending completion. (See Figure 9-10 on page 347.)

Interrupt Disable. The 2.3 specification added an interrupt disable bit (Bit 10) to the configuration command register. See Figure 9-9 on page 346. The bit is cleared at reset permitting generation of INTx signal generation. Software may set this bit thereby inhibiting generation of INTx signaling. Note that the Interrupt Disable bit has no effect on Message Signalled Interrupts (MSI). MSIs are enabled via the MSI capability command register.

Figure 9-9: Configuration Command Register — Interrupt Disable Field

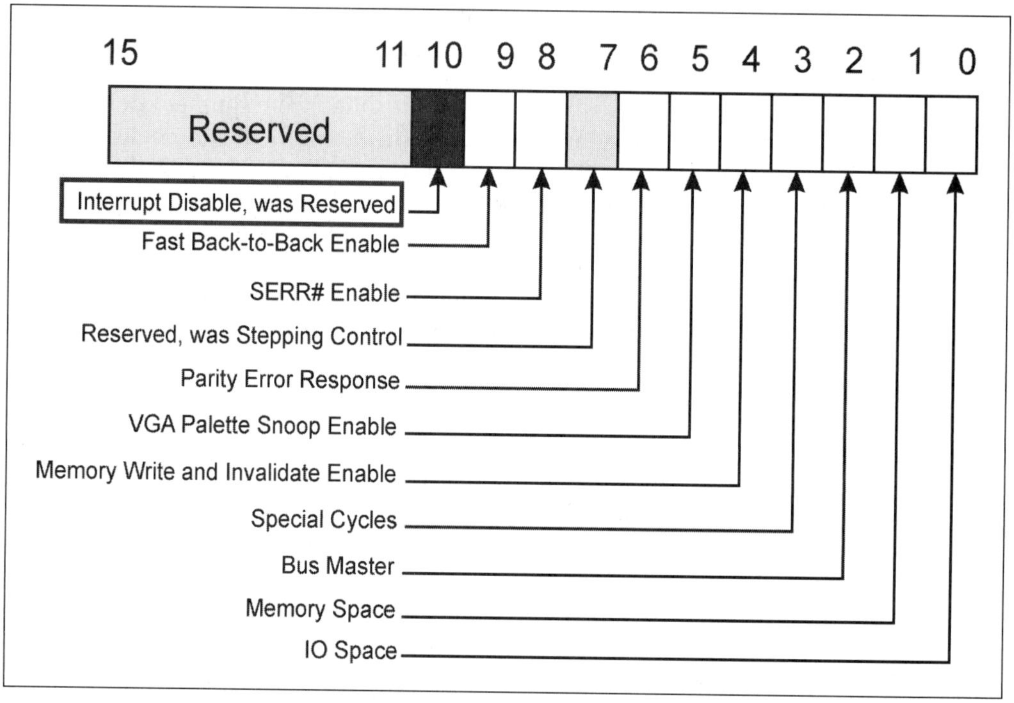

Interrupt Status. The PCI 2.3 specification added an interrupt status bit to the configuration status register (pictured in Figure 9-10 on page 347). A function must set this status bit when an interrupt is pending. In addition, if the Interrupt Disable bit in the configuration command register is cleared (i.e. interrupts enabled), then the function's INTx# signal is asserted, but only after the interrupt status bit is set. This bit is unaffected by the state of the interrupt disable bit, and it has no effect on the MSI mechanism. Note also that the bit is read only.

Figure 9-10: Configuration Status Register — Interrupt Status Field

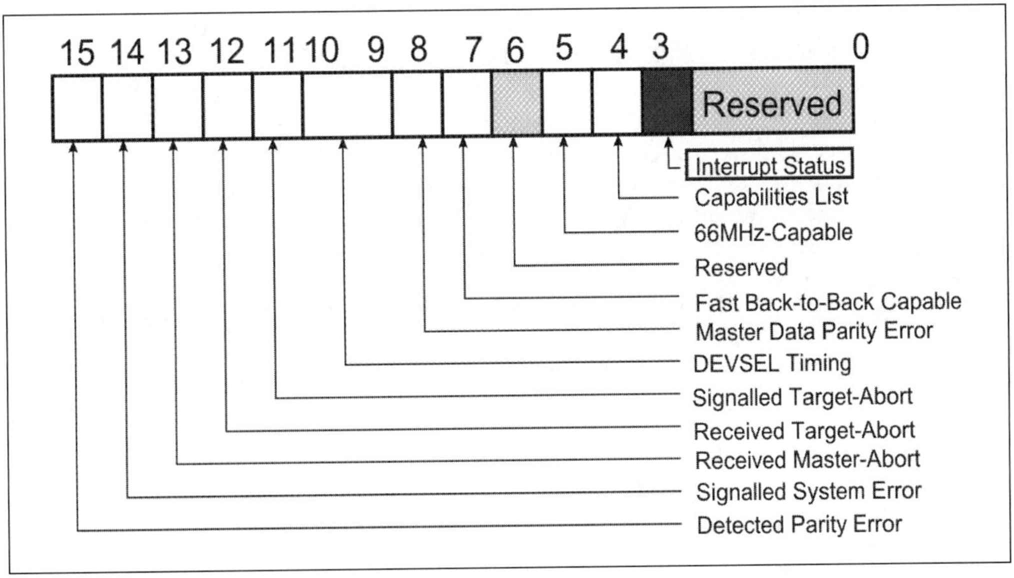

Virtual INTx Signaling

When circumstances make it impossible to use MSIs standard compatible INTx signaling may be used. Following are two examples of devices that cannot use MSI:

PCI Express-to-PCI(X) bridges — PCI devices will likely use the INTx signals to deliver an interrupt request (MSI is optional). Because PCI Express does not support sideband interrupt signaling, an INTx virtual wire message is used to signal the interrupt controller (located in the Root Complex). The interrupt controller in turn delivers an interrupt request to the CPU, including the vector number that identifies the entry point of the interrupt service routine.

Boot Devices — Standard PC systems typically use the legacy interrupt subsystem (8259 interrupt controller and related signals) during the boot sequence. Furthermore, the MSI subsystem cannot be used because it typically initializes after the Operating System (OS) loads and device drivers initialize. PCI Express devices involved in initializing the system and loading the OS (e.g., video, hard drive, and keyboard) are called "boot devices." Boot devices must use legacy interrupt support until the OS and device drivers for their devices install, after which they use MSI.

Virtual INTx Wire Delivery

Figure 9-11 on page 348 illustrates an example PCI Express system that implements a legacy boot device and a PCI Express-to-PCI Bridge. The bridge can never issue MSIs because it does not know the source of the INTx# signals; whereas, the boot device can signal interrupt via MSI following the boot sequence. Figure 9-11 depicts the bridge using an INTB messages to signal the assertion and deassertion of INTB# from the PCI bus. The legacy device is shown signaling an INTA from its function. Note that INTx signaling involves two messages:

- The **Assert_INTx** messages that indicates a high to low transition of the virtual INTx# signal.
- The **Deassert_INTx** messages that indicates a low to high transition of the virtual INTx# signal.

When a Legacy device delivers an Assert_INTx message, it also sets its Interrupt Pending bit located in memory or I/O space and also sets the Interrupt Pending bit located within the Configuration Status register (Figure 9-10).

Figure 9-11: Legacy Devices use INTx Messages to Virtualize INTA#-INTD# Signal Transitions

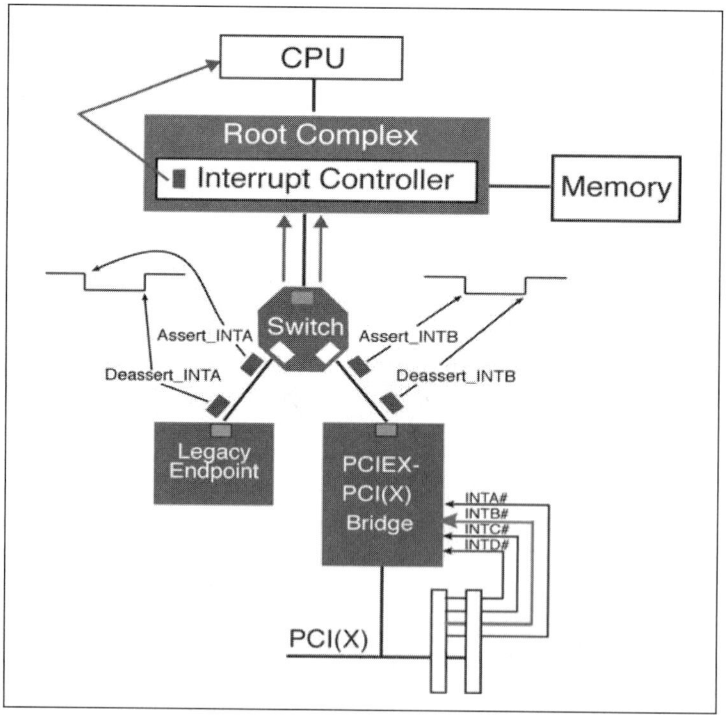

Collapsing INTx Signals within a Bridge

Switches that have multiple downstream ports to which legacy devices attach must ensure that INTx transactions are delivered upstream in the correct fashion. The specific requirement is to ensure that the interrupt controller receives INTx messages that represent the wire-ORed behavior of legacy PCI implementations. As illustrated in Figure 9-8 on page 344, INTx lines may be shared when one or more INTx lines are tied together (wire-ORed). Consequently, when more than one devices signals an interrupt at roughly the same time only the first assertion is seen by the interrupt controller. Similarly, when one of these devices deasserts its INTx line, the line remains asserted and only the last deassertion will be seen by the interrupt controller.

Two or more legacy PCI Express devices sending the same INTx message on different ports of the same switch, must be treated as wire-ORed messages. This ensures that the interrupt controller observes the correct transitions. Figure 9-12 on page 350 illustrates two legacy devices issuing INTA messages to the Switch. Note that because the INTA messages overlap, the second Assert_INTA is blocked because an Assert_INTA message has been registered and no deassertion has yet occurred. Similarly the first Deassert_INTA message is blocked because two Assert_INTAs are outstanding and this is the first deassert message, so another will follow. This ensures that the interrupt controller will never receive two Assert_INTx messages of the same type nor two Deassert_INTX messages of the same type.

As described above, switches must track the state of each of the INTx messages at each port and transfer only those that represent a valid change in the virtual signaling.

Figure 9-12: Switch Collapses INTx Message to Achieve Wired-OR Characteristics

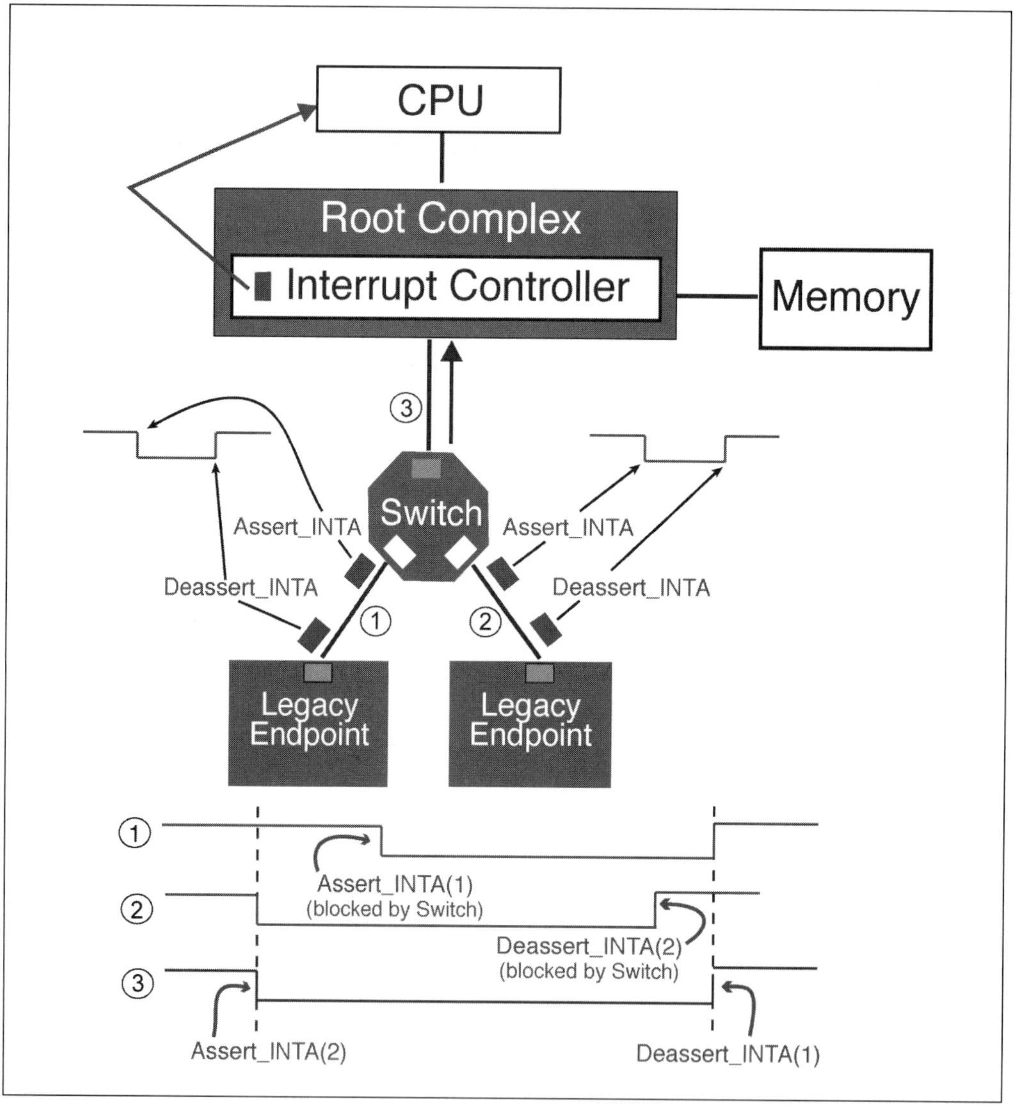

INTx Message Format

Figure 9-13 on page 351 depicts the format of the INTx message header and defines the message types supported. INTx messages are always delivered from upstream ports of Endpoints, Bridges, and Switches. The routing employed is "Local-Terminate at Receiver," with the interrupt controller as the ultimate destination. The message code field identifies the message type and eight codes are used by the INTx messages as listed in Table 9-2.

Figure 9-13: INTx Message Format and Types

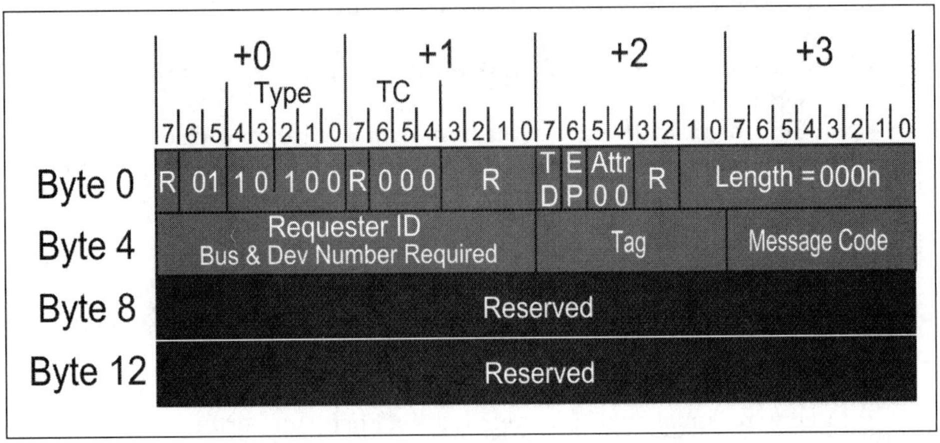

Table 9-2: INTx Message Codes

INTx Messages	Message Code
Assert_INTA	0010 0000
Assert_INTB	0010 0001
Assert_INTC	0010 0010
Assert_INTD	0010 0011
Deassert_INTA	0010 0100
Deassert_INTB	0010 0101
Deassert_INTC	0010 0110
Deassert_INTD	0010 0111

The rules associated with the delivery of INTx messages are consistent with other message types, but have some unique characteristics. The INTx message rules are summarized below:

- Assert_INTx and Deassert_INTx are only issued in the upstream direction by Legacy Endpoint or Bridge devices. Note that an otherwise native PCI Express endpoint is allowed to send INTx messages prior to its device drivers being loaded, because it is a boot device.
- Switches must issue INTx messages upstream when there is a change of the "collapsed" interrupt due to one of the downstream ports receiving an assert or deassert message. (See "Collapsing INTx Signals within a Bridge" on page 349.)
- Devices on either side of a link must track the current state of INTA-INTD assertion.
- A Switch tracks the state of the four virtual wires for each of its downstream ports, and presents a collapsed set of virtual wires on its upstream port.
- The Root Complex must track the state of the four virtual wires (A-D) for each downstream port.
- INTx signaling may be disabled with the Interrupt Disable bit in the Command Register.
- If any INTx virtual wires are active and device interrupts are then disabled, a corresponding Deassert_INTx message must be sent.
- If a switch downstream port goes to DL_Down status, any active INTx virtual wires must be deasserted, and the upstream port updated accordingly (Deassert_INTx message required if that INTx was in active state).

Devices May Support Both MSI and Legacy Interrupts

When a PCI Express device supports both INTx messages and MSI, only one of the mechanism will be enabled at any given time. The most likely type of device that would support both capabilities is a boot device. A system in which a boot device resides may not support MSI during the boot sequence. Consequently configuration software will initialize interrupts by loading a Line register value and enabling the device for legacy operation just as is done for PCI devices. Once the OS loads, the device's MSI register set is loaded and the MSI enable bit is set. Setting this bit disables the devices ability to use INTx messages and enables the delivery of MSIs.

Note also that setting the Interrupt Disable bit in the Configuration Command register also inhibits the generation of INTx messages.

Special Consideration for Base System Peripherals

Interrupts may also originate in embedded legacy hardware, such as an I/O Controller Hub or Super I/O device. Some of the typical legacy devices required in such systems include:

- Serial ports
- Parallel ports
- Keyboard and Mouse Controller
- System Timer
- IDE controllers

These devices typically require a very specific IRQ line, which allows legacy software to interact with them correctly.

Using the INTx messages does not guarantee that the devices will receive the IRQ assignment that they require. Many different approaches and strategies may be employed to ensure they get the IRQs required. Following is an example system that supports legacy interrupt assignment.

Example System

Figure 9-14 on page 354 illustrates a PCI Express system that includes an existing I/O Controller Hub (ICH) that attaches to the Root Complex via a proprietary link. The interrupt controller that is embedded within the ICH is an IOAPIC that can generate an MSI when it receives an interrupt request at its inputs. In such an implementation, software can assign the legacy vector number to each input, to ensure the correct legacy software is called.

The advantage to this approach is that existing hardware can be used to support the legacy requirements within a PCI Express platform. This system also requires that the MSI subsystem be configured for use during the boot sequence. The example illustrated eliminates the need for INTx messages, unless a PCI Express expansion device incorporates a PCI Express-to-PCI Bridge.

Figure 9-14: PCI Express System with PCI-Based IO Controller Hub

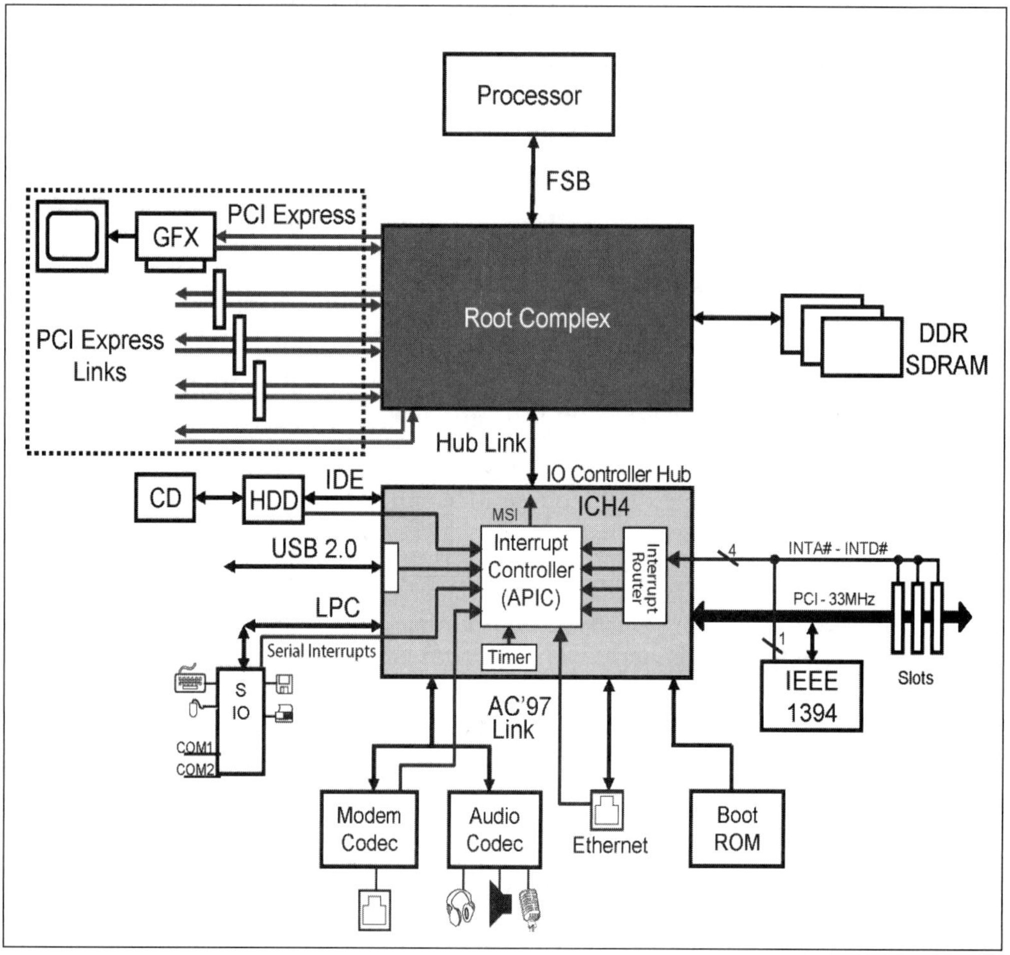

10 Error Detection and Handling

The Previous Chapter

Native PCI Express devices that require interrupt support must use the Message Signaled Interrupt (MSI) mechanism defined originally in the PCI 2.2 version of the specification. The previous chapter detailed the MSI mechanism and also described the legacy support that permits virtualization of the PCI INTx signals required by devices such as PCI Express-to-PCI Bridges.

This Chapter

To this point it has been presumed that transactions traversing the fabric have not encountered any errors that cannot be corrected by hardware. This chapter discusses both correctable and non-correctable errors and discusses the mechanisms used to report them. The PCI Express architecture provides a rich set of error detection, reporting, and logging capabilities. PCI Express error reporting classifies errors into three classes: correctable, non-fatal, and fatal. PCI Express error reporting capabilities include PCI-compatible mechanisms, thus a brief review of the PCI error handling is included as background information.

The Next Chapter

The next chapter describes the Logical Physical Layer core logic. It describes how an outbound packet is processed before clocking the packet out differentially. The chapter also describes how an inbound packet arriving from the Link is processed and sent to the Data Link Layer. Sub-block functions of the Physical Layer such as Byte Striping and Un-Striping logic, Scrambler and De-Scrambler, 8b/10b Encoder and Decoder, Elastic Buffers are discussed, and more.

Background

The original PCI bus implementation provides for basic parity checks on each transaction as it passes between two devices residing on the same bus. When a transaction crosses a bridge, the bridge is involved in the parity checks at both the originating and destination busses. Any error detected is registered by the device that has detected the error and optionally reported. The PCI architecture provides a method for reporting the following types of errors:

- data parity errors — reported via the PERR# (Parity Error) signal
- data parity errors during multicast transactions (special cycles) — reported via the SERR# (System Error) signal
- address and command parity errors — reported via the SERR# signal
- other types of errors (e.g. device specific) — reported via SERR#

Errors reported via PERR# are considered potentially recoverable, whereas, errors reported via SERR# are considered unrecoverable. How the errors reported via PERR# are handled is left up to the implementer. Error handling may involve only hardware, device-specific software, or system software. Errors signaled via SERR# are reported to the system and handled by system software. (See MindShare's PCI System Architecture book for details.)

PCI-X uses the same error reporting signals as PCI, but defines specific error handling requirements depending on whether device-specific error handling software is present. If a device-specific error handler is not present, then all parity errors are reported via SERR#.

PCI-X 2.0 adds limited support for Error Correction Codes (ECC) designed to automatically detect and correct single-bit errors within the address or data. (See MindShare's PCI-X System Architecture book for details.)

Introduction to PCI Express Error Management

PCI Express defines a variety of mechanisms used for checking errors, reporting those errors and identifying the appropriate hardware and software elements for handling these errors.

PCI Express Error Checking Mechanisms

PCI Express error checking focuses on errors associated with the PCI Express interface and the delivery of transactions between the requester and completer functions. Figure 10-1 on page 357 illustrates the scope of the error checking that is the focus of this chapter. Errors within a function that do not pertain to a given transaction are not reported through the error handling procedures defined by the PCI Express specification, and it is recommended that such errors be handled using proprietary methods that are reported via device-specific interrupts. Each layer of the PCI Express interface includes error checking capability as described in the following sections.

Figure 10-1: The Scope of PCI Express Error Checking and Reporting

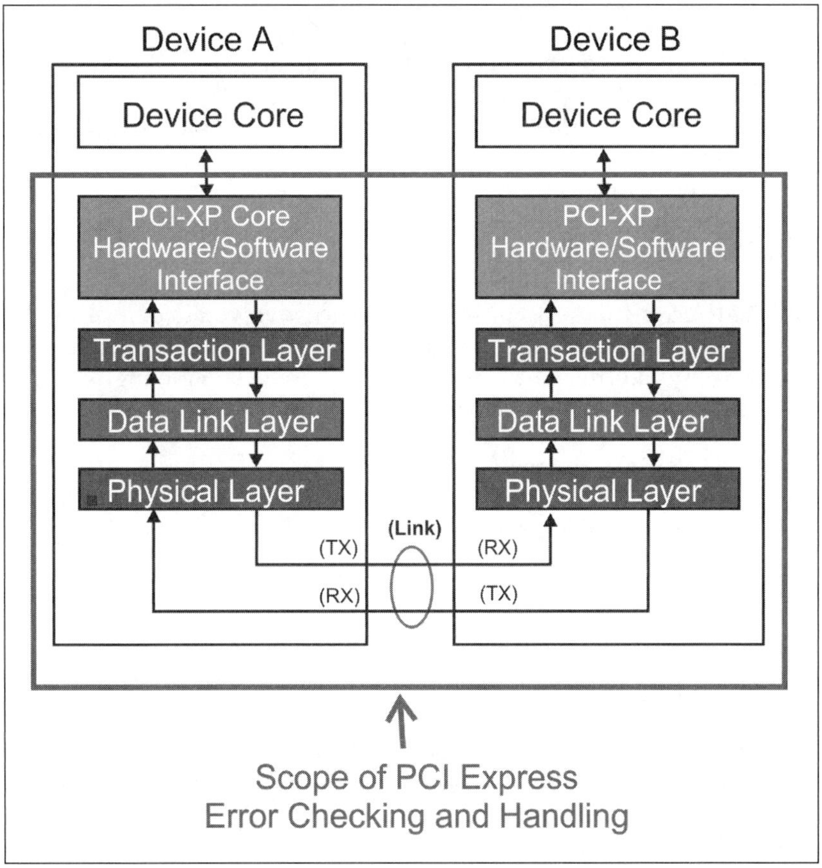

Transaction Layer Errors

The transaction layer checks are performed only by the Requestor and Completer. Packets traversing switches do not perform any transaction layer checks. Checks performed at the transaction layer include:

- ECRC check failure (optional check based on end-to-end CRC)
- Malformed TLP (error in packet format)
- Completion Time-outs during split transactions
- Flow Control Protocol errors (optional)
- Unsupported Requests
- Data Corruption (reported as a poisoned packet)
- Completer Abort (optional)
- Unexpected Completion (completion does not match any Request pending completion)
- Receiver Overflow (optional check)

Data Link Layer Errors

Link layer error checks occur within a device involved in delivering the transaction between the requester and completer functions. This includes the requesting device, intermediate switches, and the completing device. Checks performed at the link layer include:

- LCRC check failure for TLPs
- Sequence Number check for TLP s
- LCRC check failure for DLLPs
- Replay Time-out
- Replay Number Rollover
- Data Link Layer Protocol errors

Physical Layer Errors

Physical layer error checks are also performed by all devices involved in delivering the transaction, including the requesting device, intermediate switches, and the completing device. Checks performed at the physical layer include:

- Receiver errors (optional)
- Training errors (optional)

Error Reporting Mechanisms

PCI Express provides three mechanisms for establishing the error reporting policy. These mechanisms are controlled and reported through configuration registers mapped into three distinct regions of configuration space. (See Figure 10-2 on page 360.) The various error reporting features are enabled as follows:

- PCI-compatible Registers (required) — this error reporting mechanism provides backward compatibility with existing PCI compatible software and is enabled via the PCI configuration *Command Register.* This approach requires that PCI Express errors be mapped to PCI compatible error registers.
- PCI Express Capability Registers (required) — this mechanism is available only to software that has knowledge of PCI Express. This required error reporting is enabled via the PCI Express *Device Control Register* mapped within PCI-compatible configuration space.
- PCI Express Advanced Error Reporting Registers (optional) — this mechanism involves registers mapped into the extended configuration address space. PCI Express compatible software enables error reporting for individual errors via the *Error Mask Register.*

The specification refers to baseline (required) error reporting capabilities and advanced (optional) error reporting capabilities. The baseline error reporting mechanisms require access to the PCI-compatible registers and PCI Express Capability registers (bullets 1 and 2 above), while advanced error reporting (bullet 3) requires access to the Advanced Error Reporting registers that are mapped into extended configuration address space as illustrated in Figure 10-2. This chapter details all error reporting mechanisms.

Figure 10-2: Location of PCI Express Error-Related Configuration Registers

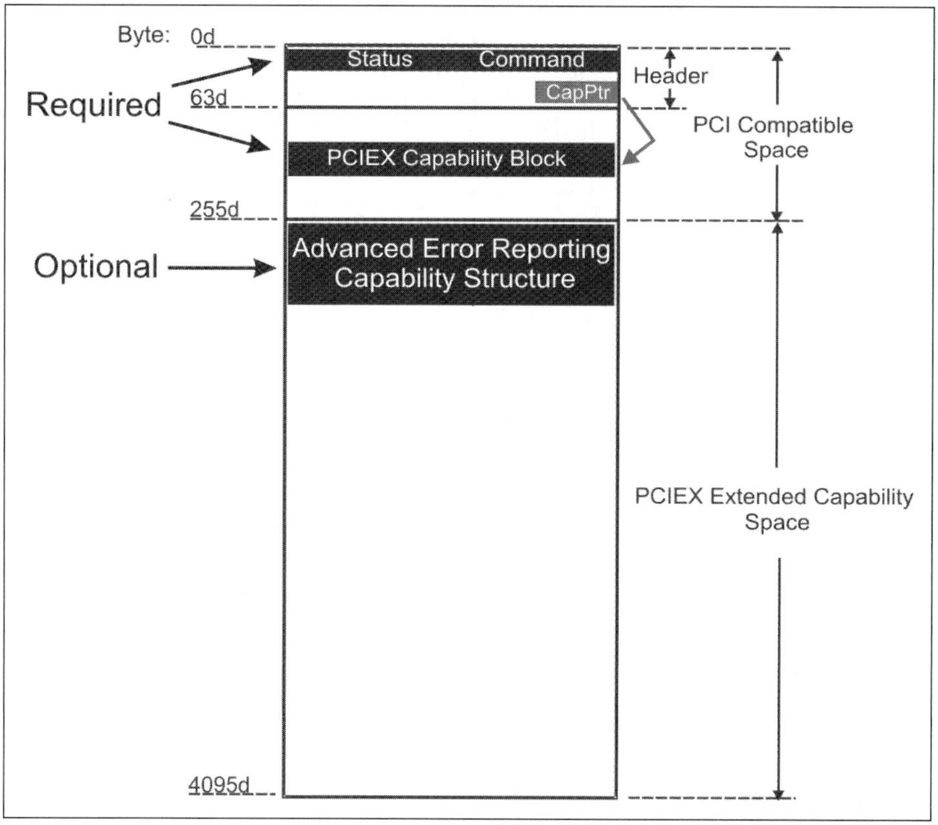

Error Handling Mechanisms

Errors are categorized into three classes that specify the severity of an error as listed below. Note also the specification defines the entity that should handle the error based on its severity:

- Correctable errors — handled by hardware
- Uncorrectable errors-nonfatal — handled by device-specific software
- Uncorrectable errors-fatal — handled by system software

By defining errors into these classes, error handling software can be partitioned into separate handlers to perform the actions required for a given platform. The actions taken based on severity of an error might range from monitoring the effects of correctable errors on system performance to simply resetting the system or PCI Express sub-system in the event of a fatal error.

Note that regardless of the severity of a given error, software can establish a policy whereby any error can be reported to the system (via the Root Complex) for the purpose of tracking and logging. (See page 390 for details.)

Sources of PCI Express Errors

This section provides a more detailed description of the error checks made by PCI Express interfaces when handling transactions.

ECRC Generation and Checking

ECRC generation and checking is optional and only supported by devices and systems that implement Advanced Error Reporting. Devices that support ECRC must implement the Advanced Error Capabilities and Control Register. Configuration software checks this register to determine if ECRC is supported, and to enable ECRC support.

A PCI Express device that originates a transaction (Request or Completion) can create and append a 32-bit CRC (within the digest field) that covers the header and data portions of the transaction. This CRC is termed end-to-end (ECRC) and is typically checked and reported by the ultimate recipient of the transaction. Switches in the path between the originating and receiving devices may optionally check and report ECRC errors, or merely forward the packet without checking the ECRC. If a Switch detects an ECRC error it must still forward the packet unaltered as it would any other packet. Switches may also be the originator or recipient of a transaction in which case they can participate in ECRC generation and checking in this role.

The actions taken when an ECRC error is detected is considered beyond the scope of the specification. However, the possible actions taken will likely depend on whether the ECRC error occurs in a Request or Completion:

- **ECRC in Request** — completers that detect an ECRC error may simply drop the transaction without forwarding it to the receiving function and as a result not return a completion. This ultimately will result in a completion time-out within the requesting device. The requester could then reschedule the transaction under software control.

- **ECRC in Completion** — requesters that detect an ECRC error may drop the packet and report the error to the function's device driver via a function-specific interrupt. The driver would check the status bits in the *Uncorrectable Error Status Register* to detect the nature of the error and potentially reschedule the transaction in the event that a prefetchable address location was being accessed.

Note that ECRC errors may also result in error messages being sent to the host for handling or logging.

Data Poisoning (Optional)

Data poisoning provides a way of indicating that data associated with a transaction is corrupted. When a TLP is received that contains a data field, the recipient will know that data is corrupted if the poisoned bit is set. Figure 10-3 illustrates the Error/Poisoned bit (EP) located within the first Dword of a packet.

Figure 10-3: The Error/Poisoned Bit within Packet Headers

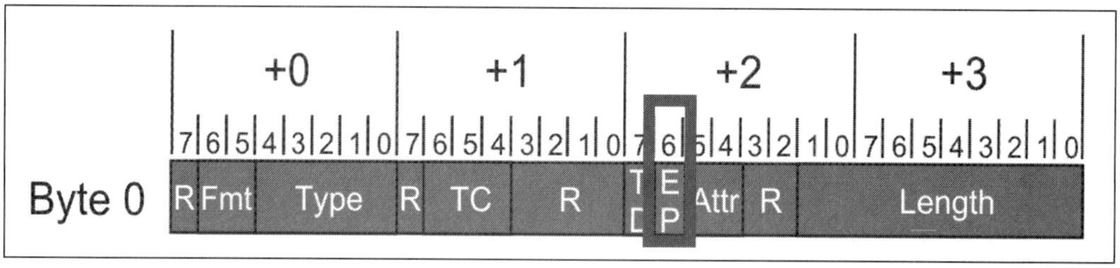

The specification includes three examples of data corruption that could result in data poisoning being used. In each of these cases, the error can be forwarded to the recipient via the data poisoning bit in the transaction header.

- When a Requester wishes to perform a Memory Write transaction it must first fetch the data it wishes to send to the completer from local memory. In the event of a parity error when reading the data, the data can be marked as poisoned.
- When a Completer must return data in response to a Memory Read request, the data it fetches from memory may incur a parity error.
- Data that is stored in a cache or buffer that has error checking may also result in data corruption being detected. The specification does not indicate where these caches or buffers may be located, but it is conceivable that any device that originates a transaction or forwards it may indicate that the data has been poisoned.

The specification states that data poisoning applies to data associated with both posted and non-posted writes and read completions. Therefore data poisoning can be used in conjunction with Memory, I/O, and Configuration transactions that have a data payload.

Data poisoning can only be done at the transaction layer of a device. The link layer does not process or in any way affect the contents of the TLP header. The transaction layer indicates that data is corrupted by setting the Data Error/Poisoned bit (E/P) in the Write request or Read Completion transaction header.

Data poisoning errors are enabled and reported via the Uncorrectable Error Registers.

TC to VC Mapping Errors

All PCI Express ports that implement the extended VC capability (endpoints, switches, and root ports) must check to verify that the TC of each inbound packet is mapped to an active VC. Packets with TC's that fail this check are treated as malformed TLPs. Similarly, when switches forward packets, they must also verify that the target outbound port of the switch also supports the packet's TC. If not, the packet is treated as a malformed TLP.

A requester or completer may implement more than one Virtual Channel (VC) and enable more than one Traffic Class (TC). If the device core issues a request to send a transaction with a TC number that is not enabled (pointing to an active VC) within the TC to VC mapping tables, the transaction is rejected and a malformed TLP is indicated. If the device has implemented the PCI Express Virtual Channel Capability structure (supports multiple VCs and/or TC filtering), then the malformed TLP error is detected at the transmitting device. However, if the device only supports the default TC0/VC0 configuration, then this error would be detected at the first receiving device along the packet's path that implements the extended VC capability and applies TC filtering.

Note also that the TC to VC mapping is a transaction layer function. (See "Assigning TCs to each VC — TC/VC Mapping" on page 262 for details).

Link Flow Control-Related Errors

Prior to forwarding the packet to the link layer for transmission across the link, the transaction layer must check flow control credits to ensure that the receive buffers in the adjacent node (switch or completer) have sufficient room to hold the transaction. Flow control protocol errors may occur that will likely prevent transactions from being sent. These errors can be reported to the Root Complex and are considered uncorrectable. The uncorrectable error registers are used to enable and check status for Flow Control (FC) errors. *The specification does not require that these errors be checked and reported.*

All five conditions that cause flow control related errors (flow control protocol errors and receiver overflow errors) are detected by and associated with the port receiving the flow control information. These error conditions are:

- The specification defines the minimum credit size that can be initially reported for each Flow Control type. During FC initialization for any Virtual Channel, if a receiver fails to advertise VC credit value equal to or greater than those permitted, it is considered an FC protocol error.
- The maximum number of data payload credits that can be reported is restricted to 2048 unused credits and 128 unused credits for headers. Exceeding these limits is considered an FC protocol error.
- During FC initialization receivers are allowed to report infinite FC credits. FC updates are required following initialization. FC updates are allowed providing that the credit value field is set to zero, which is ignored by the recipient. If the data field contains any value other than zero, it is considered an FC protocol error.
- During FC initialization either the Data or header FC advertisement (but not both) for a given FC type may be infinite. FC update packets are required to report credits for the buffer that advertised limited FC credits. However the update credit value for the buffer advertised as infinite must be set to zero and ignored by the receiver. A non-zero credit value could cause an FC protocol error.
- A specific check can be made at the receiving port to determine if a flow control receive buffer has overflowed, resulting in lost data. This check is optional and considered an FC protocol error.

Flow Control Protocol errors are reported as uncorrectable errors, if supported and enabled.

Malformed Transaction Layer Packet (TLP)

When the ultimate recipient of a transaction receives a request or completion packet into the transaction layer, the packet format is checked for violations of the TLP formatting rules. The specification defines the following items that cause a malformed packet:

- Data payload exceeds Max payload size.
- The actual data length does not match data length specified in the header.
- Start Memory DW address and length field results in the transaction crossing a 4KB boundary.
- TD field =1 (indicating Digest included) but no digest field is present.
- Byte Enable violation detected.
- Packets which use an undefined Type field values.
- Multiple completion packets are used to send read data back to the requester and the data size returned in any of the completion packets violates the Read Completion Boundary (RCB) value.
- Completions with a Configuration Request Retry Status in response to a Request other than a Configuration Request.
- Traffic Class field (TC) contains a value not assigned to an enabled Virtual Channel (VC) within the TC - VC mapping for the receiving device.
- Transaction type requiring use of TC0 has TC value other than zero:
  - I/O Read or Write requests and completions
  - Configuration Read or Write requests and completions
  - Error messages
  - INTx messages
  - Power Management messages
  - Unlock messages
  - Slot Power messages
- Routing is incorrect for transaction type (e.g., transactions requiring routing to Root Complex detected moving away from Root Complex).

Split Transaction Errors

A variety of failures can occur during a split transaction. When a transaction request is sent to a destination device a completion transaction is expected in response (except for Memory Write and Message transactions which are posted transactions). The various failure modes that can occur are discussed in the following sections.

Unsupported Request

When a recipient of a transaction request detects that it does not support this transaction, it returns a completion transaction with unsupported request (UR) specified in the completion status field. The specification defines a number of specific conditions that cause UR to be returned in the completion status field:

- Request type not supported.
- Message request received with unsupported or undefined message code.

- Request does not reference address space mapped within device.
- Request contains an address that cannot be routed to any egress port of a bridge or a switch (i.e., address is not mapped to any port's base and limit registers).
- Poisoned Write Request addresses an I/O or Memory mapped control space in the Completer. Such transactions must be discarded by the Completer and reported as a UR.
- PCI Express endpoint device receives a MRdLk (lock) transaction. (Recall that lock is not supported by endpoint devices.)
- The downstream port of the Root Complex or Switch receives a configuration request with a Device number of 1-31. The port must terminate the transaction and not initiate a configuration transaction on the downstream link. Instead a completion transaction is returned with UR status.
- A configuration access that targets an un-implemented Bus, Dev, or Function results in termination of the transaction, and a completion transaction is returned with UR status.
- Type 1 configuration request received at endpoint.
- A completion is received at the requester with a reserved completion code. This must be interpreted as a UR.
- A function is in the D1 or D2 power management states and a request other than a configuration request is received.
- A configuration access that targets a bus that is not in the range of buses downstream of that port according to the secondary and subordinate register values.
- A configuration request passing through a PCI Express - PCI Bridge for which the Extended Register Address field is non-zero that is directed toward a PCI bus that does not support Extended Configuration Space.
- A transaction headed for a port with the Reject Snoop Transactions field set in the VC Resource Capability register that does not have the No Snoop bit set in the TLP header.
- A transaction is targeting a device on a PCI bus but is Master Aborted after the request was accepted by the bridge.

Completer Abort

These type of error checks are optional. Three circumstances can occur that could result in a Completer returning an abort to the Requester:

1. A Completer receives a request that it cannot complete because the request violates the programming rules for the device. As an example, some devices may be designed to permit access to a single location within a specific DWord, while any attempt to access the other locations within the same DWord would fail. Such restrictions are not violations of the specification,

but rather legal restrictions associated with an implementation-specific programming interface for this function. Accesses to such devices are based upon the expectation that only the device-driver for this device understands how to access its function.

2. A completer receives a request that it cannot process because of some permanent error condition associated with the device. For example, a PCI Express wireless LAN card that is not accepting PCI Express transactions because it will not transmit or receive data over its radio unless there is an approved antenna attached.
3. A PCI Express to PCI Bridge may receive a request that targets a PCI or PCI-X bus. These buses support a signaling convention that allows the target device to indicate that it has aborted the request (target abort) because it cannot complete the request due to some permanent condition or violation of the function's programming rules. The bridge in turn would return a PCI Express completion transaction indicating CA status.

A Completer that aborts a request may report the error to the Root Complex as a Non-Fatal Error message. Further, if the aborted request requires a completion, the completion status would be reported as CA.

Unexpected Completion

A completion transaction that arrives at a Requester uses the transaction descriptor (Requester ID and Tag) to match the request to which this completion applies. In rare circumstances the transaction descriptor may not match a request that is pending completion. The typical reason for this unexpected completion is that the completion was mis-routed on its journey back to the intended requester. Consequently, two requesters will be surprised:

1. the requester that has received the unexpected completion, and
2. the requester that fails to receive the completion (thereby causing a completion time-out)

A Non-Fatal Error message can be sent by the device that receives the unexpected completion.

Completion Time-out

The previous discussion points out that a completion transaction can be routed to the wrong device. Consequently, the pending request will never receive its completion. The specification defines the completion time-out mechanism to identify this situation and report the error to requester software for possible recovery. The specification clearly defines that the intent of the completion time-out is to detect when a completion has no reasonable chance of returning and not related to expected latencies associated with split transactions.

The completion time-out mechanism must be implemented by any device that initiates requests that require completions to be returned. An exception is allowed for devices that only initiate configuration transactions. The specification defines the permissible range of the time-out value as follows:

- It is strongly recommended that a device not time-out earlier than 10ms after sending a request; however, if the device requires greater granularity a time-out can occur as early as 50μs.
- Devices must time-out no later than 50ms.

Note that for Memory Read requests a request may require two or more completions to return all of the requested data. All of the data must be returned prior to the time-out. If some but not all of the data has been returned when the time-out occurs, the requester may either discarded or keep the data.

Error Classifications

Errors are categorized into three classes that specify the severity of an error as listed below. Note also the specification defines the entity that should handle the error based on its severity:

- Correctable errors — handled by hardware
- Uncorrectable errors-nonfatal — handled by device-specific software
- Uncorrectable errors-fatal — handled by system software

By defining errors into these classes, error handling software can be partitioned into separate handlers to perform the actions required of a given platform. The actions taken based on severity of an error might range from monitoring the effects of correctable errors on system performance to simply resetting the system in the event of a fatal error.

Note that regardless of the severity of a given error, software can establish a policy whereby the system is notified of all errors for the purpose of tracking and logging each category.

Correctable Errors

The specification defines correctable errors as those errors that are corrected solely by hardware. Such errors may have an impact on performance (i.e., latency and bandwidth), but no information is lost as a result of the error. These types of error can be reported to software, which can take a variety of actions, Including:

- log the error
- update calculations of PCI Express performance
- track errors to project possible weaknesses within the fabric. This can suggest areas where greater potential exists for fatal errors in the future.

Uncorrectable Non-Fatal Errors

Non-fatal errors mean that the integrity of the PCI Express fabric is not affected, but that information has been lost. Non-fatal errors typically mean that a transaction has been corrupted, and the PCI Express hardware cannot correct the error. However, the PCI Express fabric continues to function correctly and other transactions are unaffected. Recovery from a non-fatal error may or may not be possible. The possibility of recovery rests in the hands of the device-specific software associated with the requester that initiated the transaction.

Uncorrectable Fatal Errors

Fatal errors indicate that a link in the PCI Express fabric is no longer reliable. Data has been lost and every attempt to recover data under software control will likely fail also. Such conditions affect all transactions that traverse a given link. In some cases, the error condition leading to the fatal errors may be resolved by resetting the link. Alternatively, the specification invites implementation-specific approaches, in which software may attempt to limit the effects of the failure. The specification does not define any particular actions that should or could be taken by software.

How Errors are Reported

PCI Express includes two methods of reporting errors:

- error message transactions — used to report errors to the host
- completion status — used by the completer to report errors to the requester

Each reporting mechanism is described below.

Error Messages

As discussed previously, PCI reports errors via the PERR# and SERR# signals. Because PCI Express eliminates theses error-related signals, error messages have been defined to replace these signals by acting as virtual wires. Furthermore, these messages provide additional information that could not be conveyed directly via the PERR# and SERR# signals. This includes identification of the device that detected the error and an indication of the severity of each error.

Figure 10-4 illustrates the format of the error messages. Note that these packets are routed to the Root Complex for handling by system software. The message code defines the type of message being signaled. As one might guess, the specification defines three basic types of error messages shown in Table 10-1.

Figure 10-4: Basic Format of the Error Messages

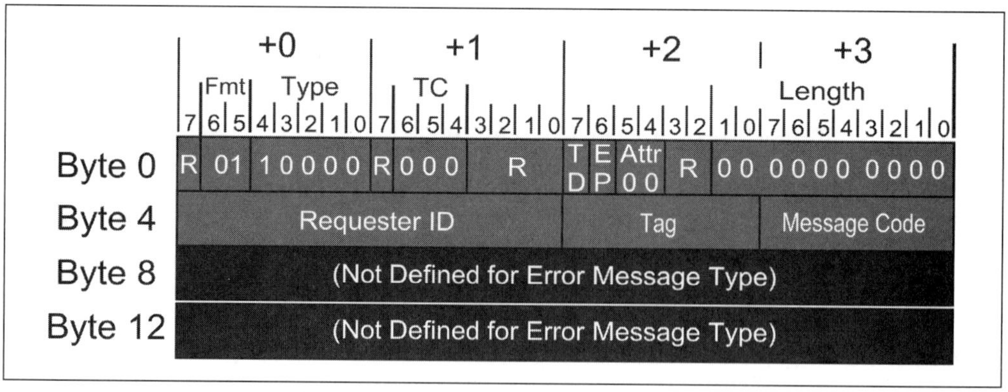

Table 10-1: Error Message Codes and Description

Message Code	Name	Description
30h	ERR_COR	used when a PCI Express device detects a correctable error
31h	ERR_NONFATAL	used when a device detects a non-fatal, uncorrectable error
33h	ERR_FATAL	used when a device detects a fatal, uncorrectable error

Completion Status

PCI Express defines a *completion status* field within the completion header that enables the transaction completer to report errors back to the requester. Figure 10-5 illustrates the location of the completion field and Table 10-2 defines the completion values. Note that the shaded status entries represent error conditions that can be reported via error messages.

Figure 10-5: Completion Status Field within the Completion Header

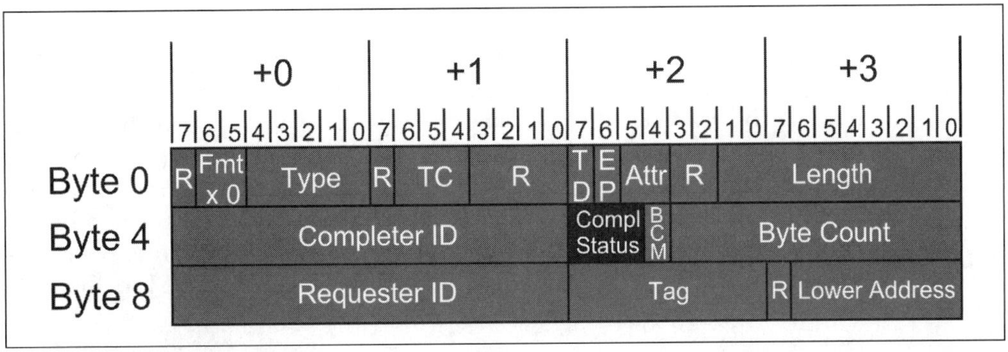

Table 10-2: Completion Code and Description

Status Code	Completion Status Definition
000b	Successful Completion (SC)
001b	Unsupported Request (UR)
010b	Configuration Request Retry Status (CRS)
011b	Completer Abort (CA)
100b - 111b	Reserved

Baseline Error Detection and Handling

This section defines the required support for detecting and reporting PCI Express errors. Each PCI Express compliant devices must include:

- PCI-Compatible support — required to support operating environments that have no knowledge of PCI Express.
- PCI Express Error reporting — available to operating environments that do have knowledge of PCI Express.

PCI-Compatible Error Reporting Mechanisms

Each PCI Express must map required PCI Express error support to the PCI-related error registers. This involves enabling error reporting and setting status bits that can be read by PCI-compliant software. To understand the features available from the PCI-compatible point of view consider the error-related bits of the Command and Status registers located within the Configuration header. While the command and status register bits have the PCI name, some of the field definitions have been modified to reflect the related PCI Express error conditions and reporting mechanisms. The PCI Express errors tracked by the PCI-compatible registers are:

- Transaction Poisoning/Error Forwarding (optional)
- Completer Abort (CA) detected by a completer
- Unrecognizable Request (UR) detected by a completer

The PCI mechanism for reporting errors is the assertion of PERR# (data parity errors) and SERR# (unrecoverable errors). The PCI Express mechanisms for reporting these events are via the split transaction mechanism (transaction completions) and virtual SERR# signaling via error messages.

Configuration Command and Status Registers

Figure 10-6 illustrates the command register and the location of the error-related fields. These bits are set to enable baseline error reporting under control of PCI-compatible software. Table 10-3 defines the specific effects of each bit.

Figure 10-6: PCI-Compatible Configuration Command Register

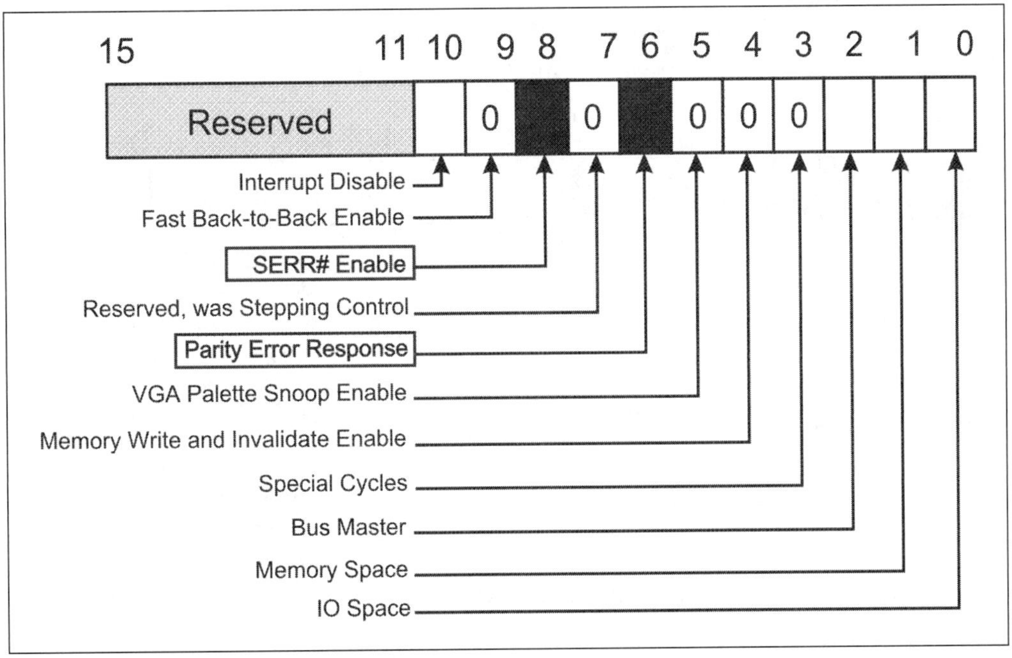

Table 10-3: Error-Related Command Register Bits

Name	Description
SERR# Enable	Setting this bit (1) enables the generation of the appropriate PCI Express error messages to the Root Complex. Error messages are sent by the device that has detected either a fatal or non-fatal error.

Table 10-3: Error-Related Command Register Bits (Continued)

Name	Description
Parity Error Response	This bit enables poisoned TLP reporting. This error is typically reported as an Unsupported Request (UR) and may also result in a non-fatal error message if SERR# enable=1b. Note that reporting in some cases is device-specific.

Figure 10-7 illustrates the configuration status register and the location of the error-related bit fields. Table 10-4 on page 374 defines the circumstances under which each bit is set and the actions taken by the device when error reporting is enabled.

Figure 10-7: PCI-Compatible Status Register (Error-Related Bits)

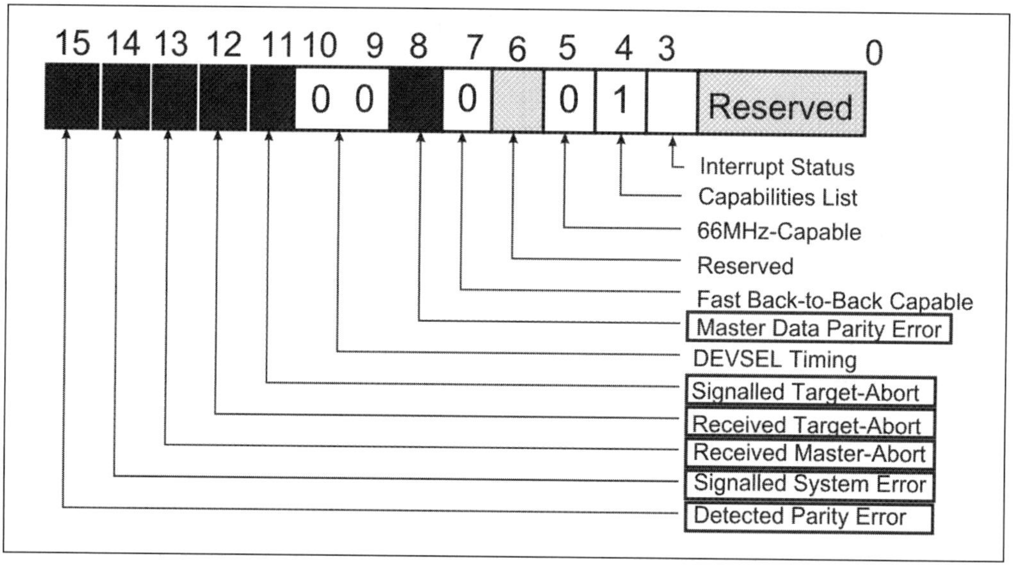

Table 10-4: Description of PCI-Compatible Status Register Bits for Reporting Errors

Error-Related Bit	Description
Detected Parity Error	Set by the interface that receives a Write Request or Read Completion transaction with the poisoned bit set. This action pertains to the requestors, completers, and switches. (This bit is updated regardless of the state of the Parity Error enable bit.)

Table 10-4. Description of PCI Compatible Status Register Bits for Reporting Errors

Error-Related Bit	Description
Signalled System Error	This bit is set by a device that has detected an uncorrectable error and reported it via an error message (requires SERR# enable bit to be set in the Command register to send error message).
Received Master Abort	Set by a requester that receives a completion transaction with Unsupported Request (UR) in the completion status field.
Received Target Abort	Set by a requester that receives a completion transaction with Completer Abort (CA) in the completion status field.
Signalled Target Abort	Set by a completer when aborting a request that violates the device's programming rules.
Master Data Parity Error	Set by a transmitter that initiates or forwards a transaction with the poisoned bit set and to a receiver device that received a completion with the poisoned bit set. This bit is set by a device that either: • receives a completion packet that has been poisoned • transmits a write packet that has been poisoned

PCI Express Baseline Error Handling

The Baseline capability also requires use of the PCI Express capability registers. These registers include error detection and handling bit fields that provide finer granularity regarding the nature of an error that is supplied with standard PCI error handling.

Figure 10-8 on page 376 illustrates the PCI Express capability register set. These registers provide support for:

- Enabling/disabling error reporting (Error Message Generation)
- Providing error status
- Providing status for link training errors
- Initiating link re-training

Figure 10-8: PCI Express Capability Register Set

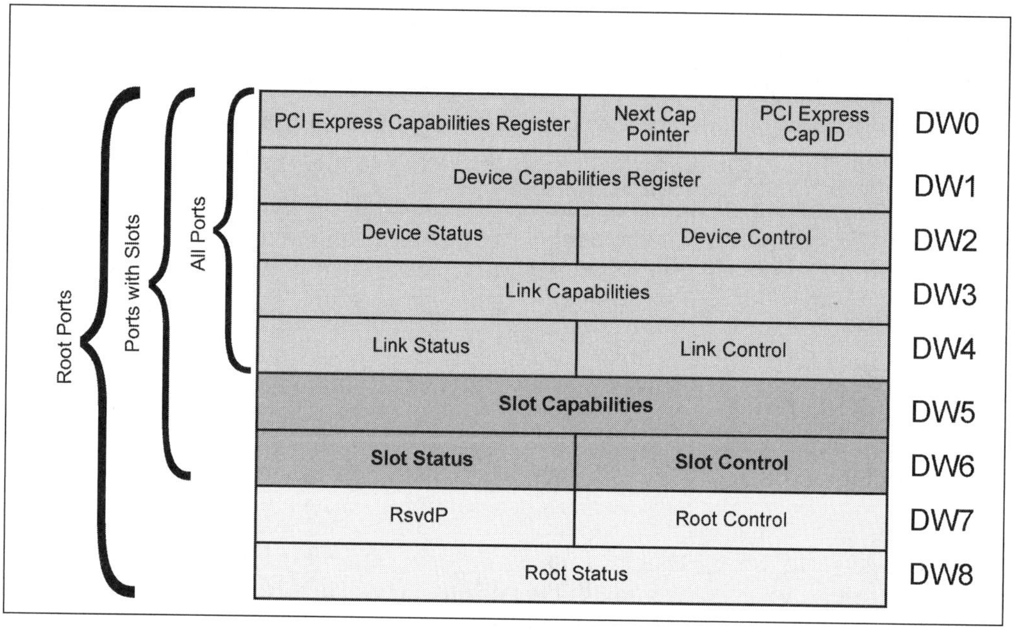

Enabling/Disabling Error Reporting

The Device Control and Device Status registers permit software to enable generation of Error Messages for four error-related events and to check status information to determine which type of error has been detected:

- Correctable Errors
- Non-Fatal Errors
- Fatal Errors
- Unsupported Request Errors

Note that the only specific type of error condition identified is the unsupported request (UR). No granularity is provided for determining other types of error conditions that occur. Only the classification of the error is reported within the device status register. Table 10-5 on page 377 lists each error type and its associated error classification.

Table 10-5: Default Classification of Errors

Classification	Name of Error	Layer Detected
Correctable	Receiver Error	Physical
Correctable	Bad TLP	Link
Correctable	Bad DLLP	Link
Correctable	Replay Time-out	Link
Correctable	Replay Number Rollover	Link
Uncorrectable - Non Fatal	Poisoned TLP Received	Transaction
Uncorrectable - Non Fatal	ECRC Check Failed	Transaction
Uncorrectable - Non Fatal	Unsupported Request	Transaction
Uncorrectable - Non Fatal	Completion Time-out	Transaction
Uncorrectable - Non Fatal	Completion Abort	Transaction
Uncorrectable - Non Fatal	Unexpected Completion	Transaction
Uncorrectable - Fatal	Training Error	Physical
Uncorrectable - Fatal	DLL Protocol Error	Link
Uncorrectable - Fatal	Receiver Overflow	Transaction
Uncorrectable - Fatal	Flow Control Protocol Error	Transaction
Uncorrectable - Fatal	Malformed TLP	Transaction

Enabling Error Reporting — Device Control Register. Setting the corresponding bit in the Device Control Register enables the generation of the corresponding Error Message which reports errors associated with each classification. (Refer to Figure 10-9 on page 378.) Unsupported Request errors are specified as Non-Fatal errors and are reported via a Non-Fatal Error Message, but only when the *UR Reporting Enable* bit is set.

Figure 10-9: Device Control Register Bit Fields Related to Error Handling

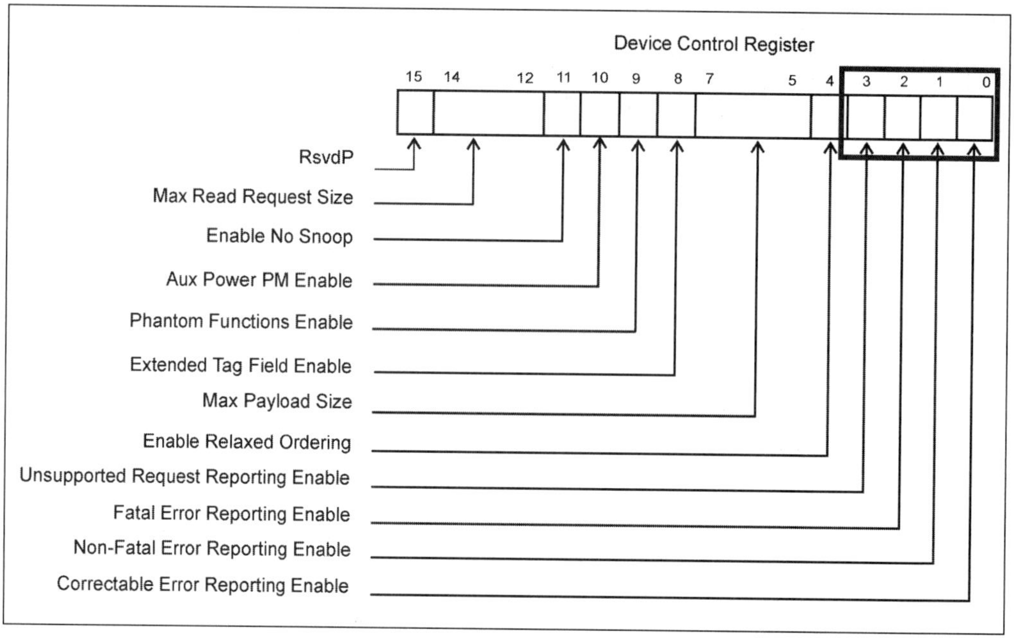

Error Status — Device Status Register. See Figure 10-10 on page 379. An error status bit is set any time an error associated with its classification is detected. These bits are set irrespective of the setting of the Error Reporting Enable bits within the Device Control Register. Because Unsupported Request errors are by default considered Non-Fatal Errors, when these errors occur both the *Non-Fatal Error status* bit and the *Unsupported Request* status bit will be set. Note that these bits are cleared by software when writing a one (1) to the bit field.

Figure 10-10. Device Status Register Bit Fields Related to Error Handling

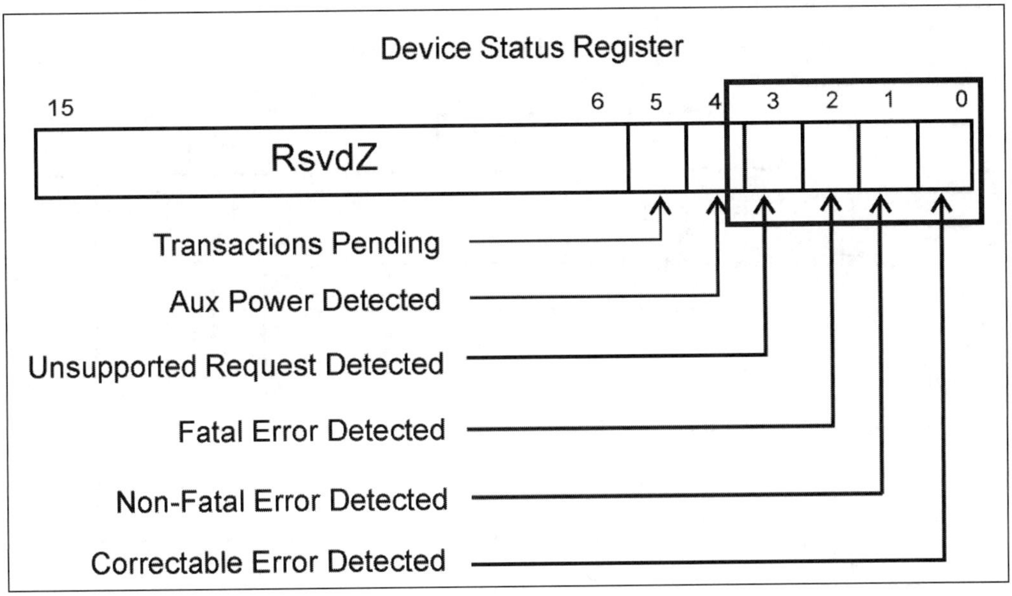

Link Errors

The physical link connecting two devices may fail causing a variety of errors. Link failures are typically detected within the physical layer and communicated to the Data Link Layer. Because the link has incurred errors, the error cannot be reported to the host via the failed link. Therefore, link errors must be reported via the upstream port of switches or by the Root Port itself. Also the related fields in the PCI Express Link Control and Status registers are only valid in Switch and Root downstream ports (never within endpoint devices or switch upsteam ports). This permits system software to access link-related error registers on the port that is closest to the host.

If software can isolate one or more errors to a given link, one method of attempting to clear a non-correctable error is to retrain the link. The Link Control Register includes a bit that when set forces the Root or Switch port to retrain the link. If transaction (upon completion of the retraining) can once again traverse the link without errors, the problem will have been solved. Figure 10-11 illustrates the Link Control Register and highlights the *Retrain Link* field that software sets to initiate retaining.

Figure 10-11: Link Control Register Allows Retraining of Link

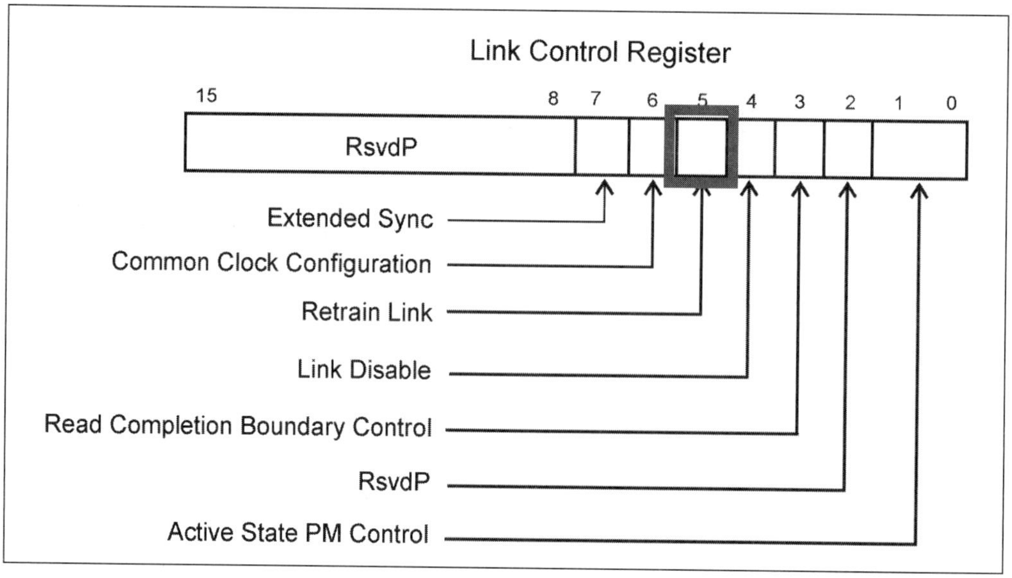

Software can monitor the *Link Training* bit in the Link Status Register to determine when retraining has completed. Software can also check the *Link Training Error* bit to verify that link training was successful. Link Training errors are reported via the Fatal Error Message. Figure 10-12 highlights these status bits.

Figure 10-12: Link Retraining Status Bits within the Link Status Register

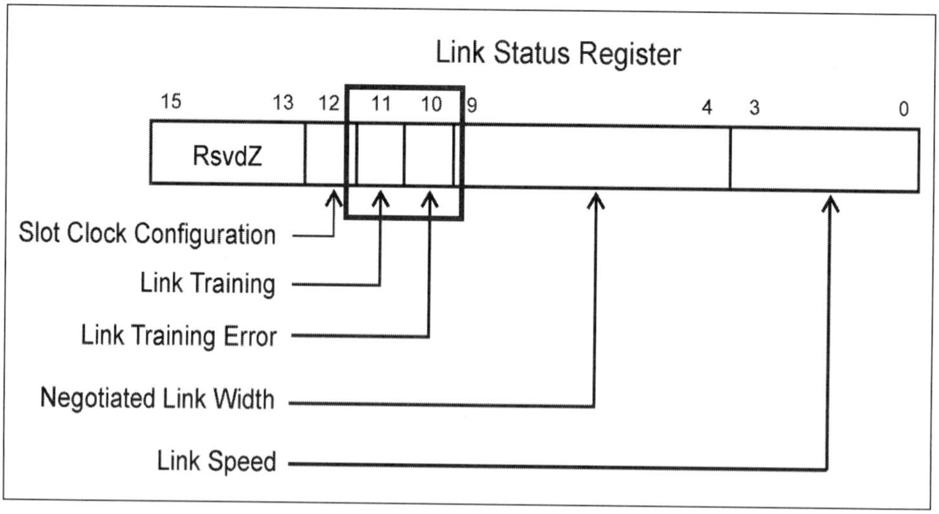

Root'o Rooponoo to Error Mooongo

When a message is received by the Root Complex the action that it takes when reporting the error message to the host system is determined in part by the Root Control Register settings. Figure 10-13 depicts this register and highlights the three bit fields that specify whether an error should be reported as a fatal System Error (SERR set enables generation of a system error). In x86 systems it is likely that a Non-Maskable Interrupt (NMI) will be signaled if the error is to be reported as a SERR.

The PME Interrupt Enable bit (3) allows software to enable and disable interrupt generation upon the Root Complex detecting a PME Message transaction.

Other options for reporting error messages are not configurable via standard registers. The most likely scenario is that a system interrupt will be signaled to the processor that will call an Error Handler, which may attempt to clear the error condition and/or simply log the error.

Figure 10-13: Root Control Register

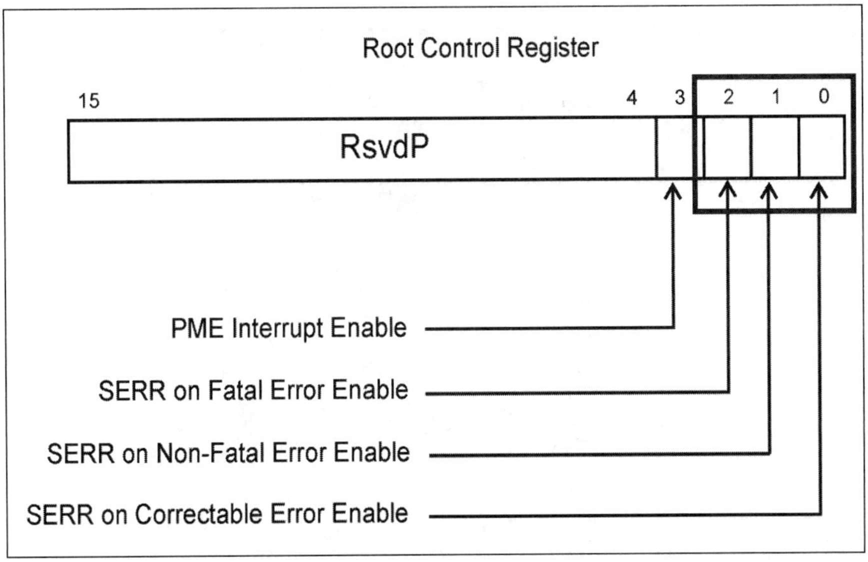

Advanced Error Reporting Mechanisms

Advanced Error Reporting requires implementation of the Advanced Error Reporting registers illustrated in Figure 10-14 on page 382. (Note that the lighter fields at the bottom of the Capability register diagram are used only for root ports, discussed later.) These registers provide several additional error reporting features:

- finer granularity in defining the actual type of error that has occurred within each classification.
- ability to specify the severity of each uncorrectable error type to determine whether it should be reported as a fatal or non-fatal error.
- support for logging errors.
- enable/disable Root Complex to report errors to the system.
- identify source of the error.
- ability to mask reporting individual types of errors.

Figure 10-14: Advanced Error Capability Registers

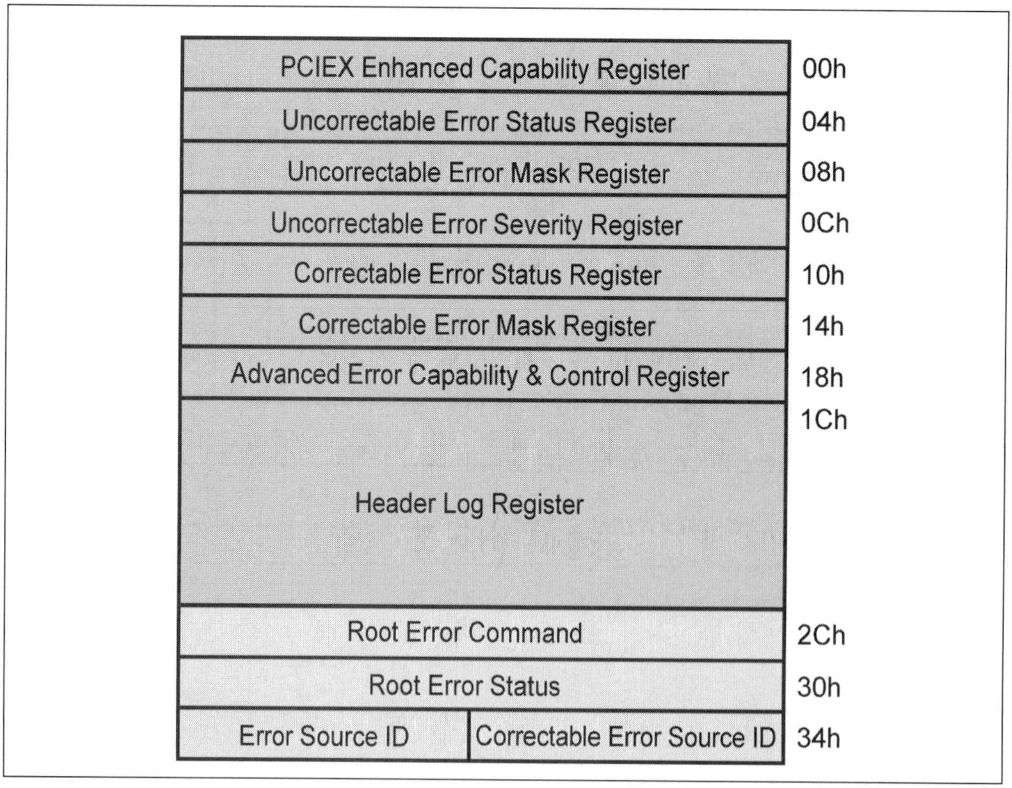

ECRC Generation and Checking

End-to-End CRC (ECRC) generation and checking can be enabled only if the Advanced Error Reporting Capability registers are implemented. Specifically, the Advanced Error Capability and Control register provides control over ECRC generation and checking as illustrated in Figure 10-15 on page 383.

Figure 10-15: The Advanced Error Capability & Control Register

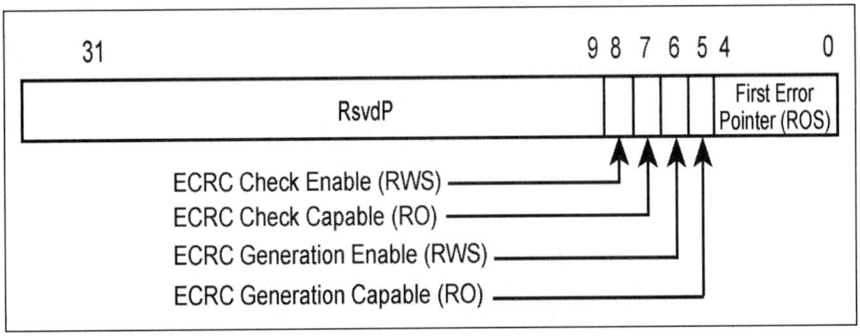

This register reports whether this device supports ECRC generation and checking. If so, configuration software can enable one or both features.

In some cases, multiple uncorrectable errors may be detected prior to software reading and clearing the register. The First Error Pointer field identifies the bit position within the Advanced Uncorrectable Status register corresponding to the error that occurred first. (See Figure 10-18 on page 387.)

The First Error Pointer and the ECRC Check and Generation Enable bits must be implemented as sticky bits.

Handling Sticky Bits

Several of the Advanced Configuration Error Registers employ sticky fields. Many of these fields are single bits. The designations of sticky fields are as follows:

- ROS — Read Only/Sticky
- RWS — Read/Write/Sticky
- RW1CS — Read/Write 1 to Clear/Sticky

Sticky error register fields behave differently in that a Hot Reset has no affect on the contents of these fields. For all other register fields, Hot Reset forces default values into the fields. Sticky bits are important in error handling to ensure that Error-related control and status information is not lost due to a Hot Reset. Software may initiate a Hot Reset in an attempt to clear errors.

Advanced Correctable Error Handling

Advanced error reporting provides the ability to pinpoint specific correctable errors. These errors can selectively cause the generation of a Correctable Error Message being sent to the host system:

- Receiver Errors (optional) — caused when the Physical Layer detects an error in the incoming packet (TLP or DLLP). The Physical Layer discards the packet, frees buffer space allocated to the packet, and signals the Link Layer that a receive error has occurred. This error is reported by setting a status bit and must not result in the Link Layer also reporting an error for this packet (e.g., the Link Layer must not report a Bad TLP or Bad DLLP).
- Bad TLPs — caused when the Link Layer detects a packet with a bad CRC check, an incorrectly nullified packet, or an incorrect Packet Sequence Number (not a duplicate). In each case, the Link Layer discards the packet and reports a NAK DLLP to the transmitter, which triggers a transaction retry.
- Bad DLLPs — caused by a CRC check failure. This type of error may be corrected by a subsequent DLLP or a time-out that results ultimately in DLLP retry. The exact corrective action depends on the type of DLLP that has failed and the circumstances associated with packet transmission.
- REPLAY_NUM Rollover — the REPLAY_NUM is a count maintained within the transmitting side of the link layer that keeps track of the number of times that a transaction had been retransmitted without successful delivery. When the count rolls over, hardware automatically retrains the link in an attempt to clear the fault condition.
- Replay Timer Time-out — this timer is maintained within the transmitting side of the Link Layer and is intended to trigger a retry when forward progress in sending TLPs has stopped. A time-out occurs when unacknowledged TLPs have not received an acknowledgement within the time-out period. A time-out results in a retry of all unacknowledged TLPs.

Knowledge of which error has occurred can help system software to make better predictions of components that are likely to fail completely in the future. Software may also choose to mask recognition of some correctable errors while reporting others.

Advanced Correctable Error Status

When a correctable error occurs the corresponding bit within the Advanced Correctable Error Status register is set. (See Figure 10-16.) These bits are automatically set by hardware and are cleared by software when writing a "1" to the bit position. These bits are set whether or not the error is reported via an Error Message. Each status bit in this register is designated RW1CS.

Figure 10-16: Advanced Correctable Error Status Register

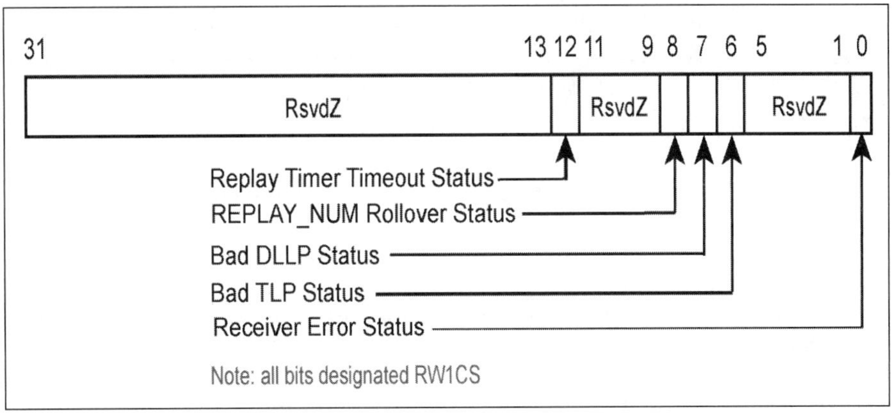

Advanced Correctable Error Reporting

Whether a particular correctable error is reported to the host is specified by the Correctable Mask register illustrated in Figure 10-17. The default state of the mask bits are cleared (0), thereby causing a Correctable Error message to be delivered when any of the correctable errors are detected. Software may choose to set one or more bits to prevent a Correctable Error Message from being sent when the selected error is detected. Each bit in this register is designated RWS.

Figure 10-17: Advanced Correctable Error Mask Register

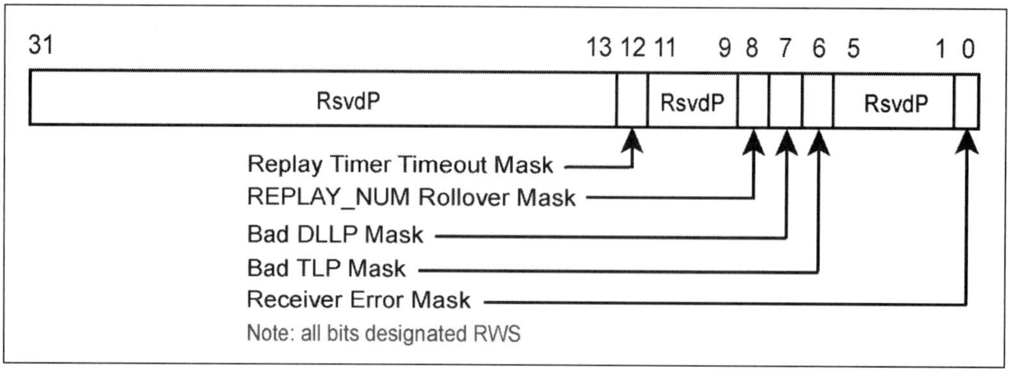

Advanced Uncorrectable Error Handling

Advanced error reporting provides the ability to pinpoint which uncorrectable error has occurred. Furthermore software can specify the severity of each error and select which errors will result in an Error Message being sent to the host system (Root Complex).

- Training Errors (optional) — caused by failure in the link training sequence at the Physical Layer.
- Data Link Protocol Errors — caused by Link Layer protocol errors including the ACK/NAK retry mechanism. *[Note: The specification states that "Violations of Flow Control initialization protocol are Data Link Layer Protocol Errors" and that checking these errors is optional. It seems likely that these error should be treated as Flow Control Protocol errors (which are optional) and not Data Link Layer Protocol errors (which are required)].*
- Poisoned TLP Errors — caused by data corruption storage error within memory or data buffers.
- Flow Control Protocol Errors (optional) — errors associated with failures of the flow control mechanism within the transaction layer.
- Completion Time-out Errors — caused by excessive delays in the return of the expected completion. This error is detected by the Requester.
- Completer Abort Errors (optional) — occurs when the Completer cannot fulfill the transaction request due to a variety of possible problems with the request or failure of the completer device.
- Unexpected Completion Errors — occurs when a requester receives a completion transaction that does not match an request pending completion.
- Receiver Overflow Errors (optional) — caused by a flow-control buffer overflow condition.

- Malformed TLPs — caused by processing errors associated with the transaction header. This error is detected within the Transaction Layer of the device receiving the TLP.
- ECRC Errors (optional) — caused by an End-to-End CRC (ECRC) check failure within the transaction layer of the receiving device.
- Unsupported Request Errors — occurs when the Completer does not support the request. The request is correctly formed and has not incurred any detected error during transport, however the transaction cannot be fulfilled by the completer due to a variety of reasons including illegal access and invalid command for this device.

The errors noted as optional in the list above may not be implemented in the Advanced Uncorrectable register set.

Advanced Uncorrectable Error Status

When an uncorrectable error occurs the corresponding bit within the Advanced Uncorrectable Error Status register is set. (See Figure 10-18 on page 387.) These bits are automatically set by hardware and are cleared by software when writing a "1" to the bit position. These bits are set whether or not the error is reported via an Error Message. Each status bit in this register is designated RW1CS.

Figure 10-18: Advanced Uncorrectable Error Status Register

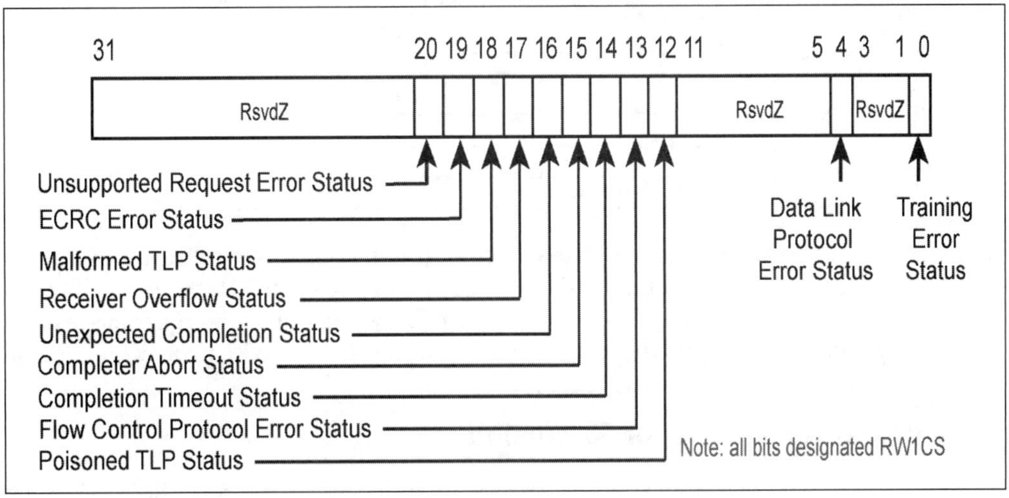

Selecting the Severity of Each Uncorrectable Error

Advanced error handling permits software to select the severity of each error within the Advanced Uncorrectable Error Severity register. This gives software the opportunity to treat errors according to the severity associated with a given application. For example, Poisoned TLP data associated with audio data being sent to a speaker, while not correctable has no serious side effects relative to the integrity of the system. However, if real-time status information is being retrieved that will help make critical decisions, any errors in this data can be very serious. Figure 10-19 illustrates the Error Severity register. The default values are illustrated in the individual bit fields. These represent the default severity levels for each type of error (1 = Fatal, 0 = Non-Fatal).

Figure 10-19: Advanced Uncorrectable Error Severity Register

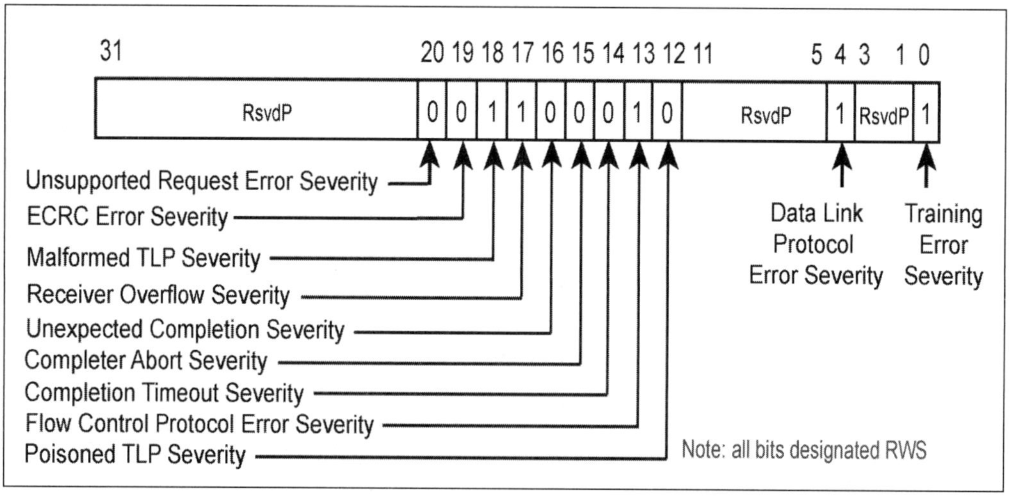

Those uncorrectable errors that are selected to be non fatal will result in a Non-Fatal Error Message being delivered and those selected as Fatal errors will result in a Fatal Error Message delivered. However, whether or not an Error Message is generated for a given error is specified in the Advanced Uncorrectable Mask register.

Uncorrectable Error Reporting

Software can mask out specific errors so that they never cause an Error Message to be generated. The default condition is to generate Error Messages for each type of error (all bits are cleared). Figure 10-20 on page 389 depicts the Advanced Uncorrectable Error Mask register.

Figure 10-20: Advanced Uncorrectable Error Mask Register

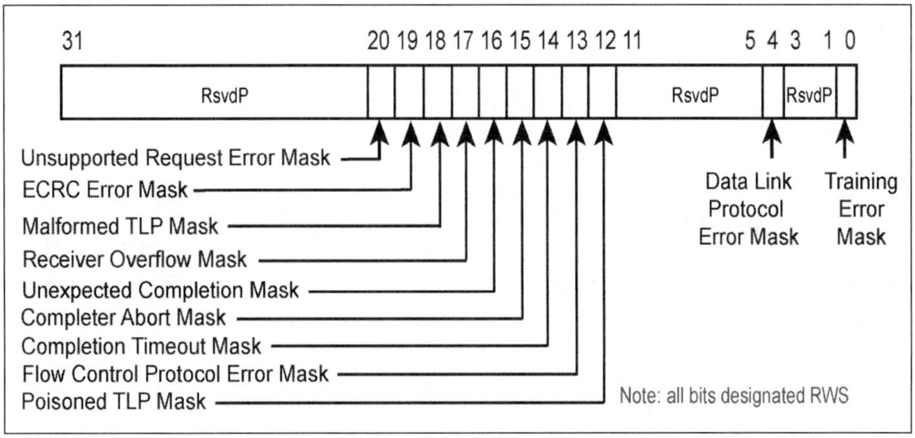

Error Logging

A four DWord portion of the Advanced Error Registers block is reserved for storing the header of the transaction that has incurred a failure. Only a select group of Transaction Layer errors result in the transaction header being logged. Table 10-6 lists the transactions that are logged.

Table 10-6: Transaction Layer Errors That are Logged

Name of Error	Default Classification
Poisoned TLP Received	Uncorrectable - Non Fatal
ECRC Check Failed	Uncorrectable - Non Fatal
Unsupported Request	Uncorrectable - Non Fatal
Completion Abort	Uncorrectable - Non Fatal
Unexpected Completion	Uncorrectable - Non Fatal
Malformed TLP	Uncorrectable - Fatal

The format of the header is preserved when captured and placed into the register. That is, the illustration of header format in this book is exactly how the headers will appear within the Error Logging register. Note also that the contents of this register are designated ROS.

Root Complex Error Tracking and Reporting

The Root Complex is the target of all Error Messages issued by devices within the PCI Express fabric. Errors received by the Root Complex result in status registers being updated and the error being conditionally reported to the appropriate software handler or handlers.

Root Complex Error Status Registers

When the Root Complex receives an Error Message, it sets status bits within the Root Error Status register (Figure 10-21 on page 391). This register indicates the types of errors received and also indicates when multiple errors of the same type have been received. Note that an error detected at the root port is treated as if the port sent itself an Error Message.

The Advanced Root Error Status register tracks the occurrence of errors as follows:

Correctable Errors

- Sets the "Received Correctable Error" bit upon receipt of the first ERR_COR Message, or detection of a root port correctable error.
- Sets the "Multiple Correctable Error Message Received" bit upon receipt of an ERR_COR Message, or detection of a root port correctable error when the "Received Correctable Error" bit is already set.

Uncorrectable Errors

- Sets the "Received Uncorrectable Error" bit upon receipt of the first ERR_FATAL or ERR_NONFATAL Error Message, or detection of a root port uncorrectable error.
- Set the "Multiple Uncorrectable Error Message Received" bit upon receipt of an ERR_FATAL or ERR_NONFATAL Message, or detection of a root port correctable error when the "Received Uncorrectable Error" bit is already set.

Detecting and Reporting First Uncorrectable Fatal versus Non-Fatal Errors

If the system wishes to implement separate software error handlers for Correctable, Non-Fatal, and Fatal errors. The Root Error Status register includes bits to differentiate Correctable from Uncorrectable Errors but needs additional bits to also determine whether Uncorrectable errors are fatal or non-fatal:

- If the first Uncorrectable Error Message received is FATAL the "First Uncorrectable Fatal" bit is also set along with the "Fatal Error Message Received" bit.
- If the first Uncorrectable Error Message received is NONFATAL the "Non-Fatal Error Message Received" bit is set. (If a subsequent Uncorrectable Error is Fatal, the "Fatal Error Message Received" bit will be set, but because the "First Uncorrectable Fatal" remains cleared, software knows that the first Uncorrectable Error received was Non-Fatal.)

Figure 10-21: Root Error Status Register

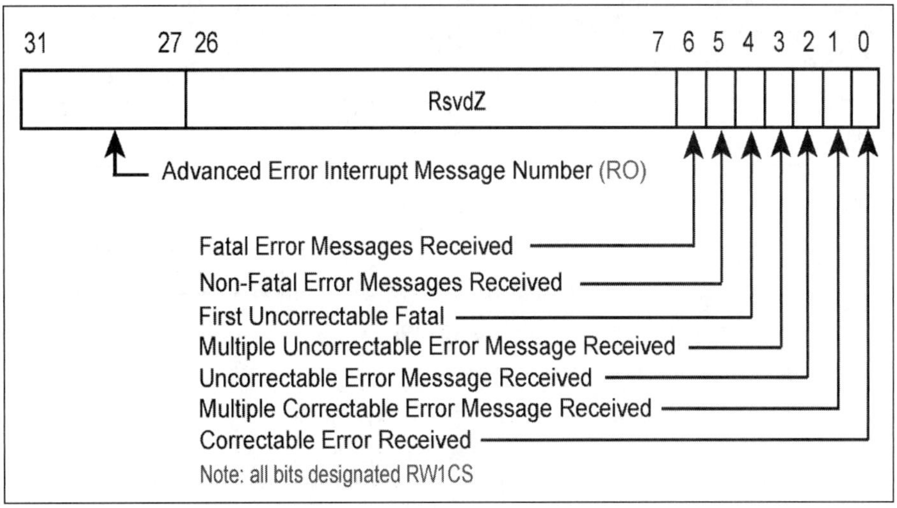

Advanced Source ID Register

Software error handlers may need to read and clear error status registers within the device that detected and reported the error. The Error Messages contain the ID of the device reporting the error. The Source ID register captures the Error Message ID associated with the first Fatal and first Non-Fatal Error message received by the Root Complex. The format of this register is shown in Figure 10-22 on page 391.

Figure 10-22: Advanced Source ID Register

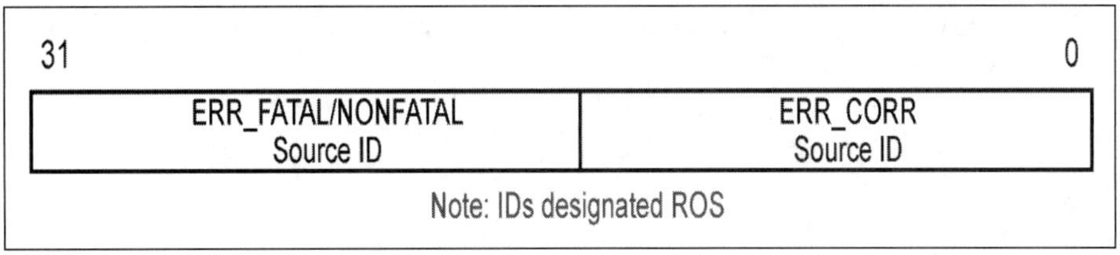

Root Error Command Register

The Root Error Status register sets status bits that determines whether a Correctable, Fatal, or Non-Fatal error has occurred. In conjunction with these status bits the Root Complex can also generate separate interrupts that call handlers for each of the error categories. The Root Error Command register enables interrupt generation for all three categories as pictured in Figure 10-23 on page 392.

Figure 10-23: Advanced Root Error Command Register

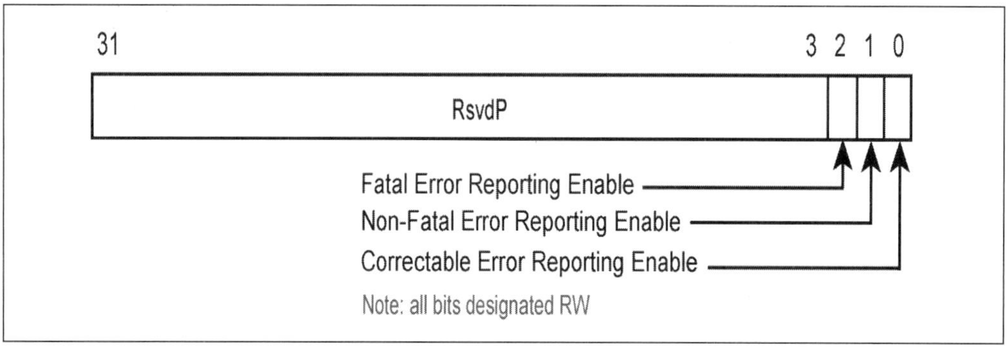

Reporting Errors to the Host System

Software error handlers will initially read Root Complex status registers to determine the nature of the error, and may also need to read device-specific error registers of the device that reported the error.

Summary of Error Logging and Reporting

The actions taken by a function when an error is detected is governed by the type of error and the settings of the error-related configuration registers. The specification includes the flow chart in Figure 10-24 on page 393 that specifies the actions taken by a device upon detecting an error. This flow chart presumes that PCI Express compatible software is being used and does not cover the case of error handling when only legacy PCI software is used.

Figure 10-24: Error Handling Flow Chart

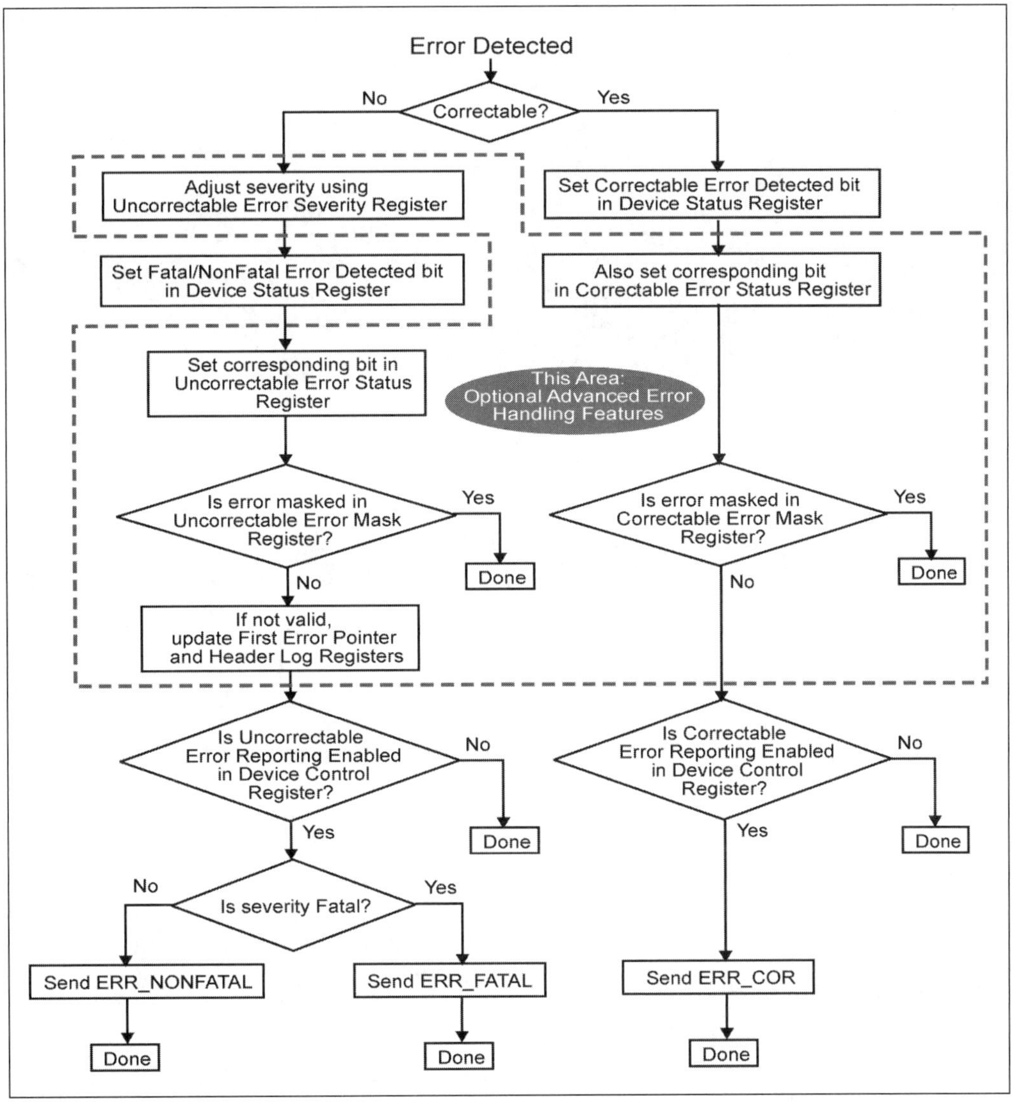

Part Three

The Physical Layer

11 Physical Layer Logic

The Previous Chapter

The previous chapter discussed both correctable and non-correctable errors and the mechanisms used to log and report them. Prior to discussing the PCI Express error reporting capabilities, a brief review of the PCI error handling was included as background information.

This Chapter

This chapter describes the Logical characteristics of the Physical Layer core logic. It describes how an outbound packet is processed before clocking the packet out differentially. The chapter also describes how an inbound packet arriving from the Link is processed and sent to the Data Link Layer. The chapter describes sub-block functions of the Physical Layer such as Byte Striping and Un-Striping logic, Scrambler and De-Scrambler, 8b/10b Encoder and Decoder, Elastic Buffers and more.

The Next Chapter

The next chapter describes the electrical characteristics of the Physical Layer. It describes the analog characteristics of the differential drivers and receivers that connect a PCI Express device to the Link.

Physical Layer Overview

The Physical Layer shown in Figure 11-1 on page 398 connects to the Link on one side and interfaces to the Data Link Layer on the other side. The Physical Layer processes outbound packets before transmission to the Link and processes inbound packets received from the Link. The two sections of the Physical Layer associated with transmission and reception of packets are referred to as the transmit logic and the receive logic throughout this chapter.

The transmit logic of the Physical Layer essentially processes packets arriving from the Data Link Layer, then converts them into a serial bit stream. The bit stream is clocked out at 2.5 Gbits/s/Lane onto the Link.

The receive logic clocks in a serial bit stream arriving on the Lanes of the Link with a clock that is recovered from the incoming bit stream. The receive logic converts the serial bit steam into a parallel symbol stream, processes the incoming symbols, assembles packets and sends them to the Data Link Layer.

Figure 11-1: Physical Layer

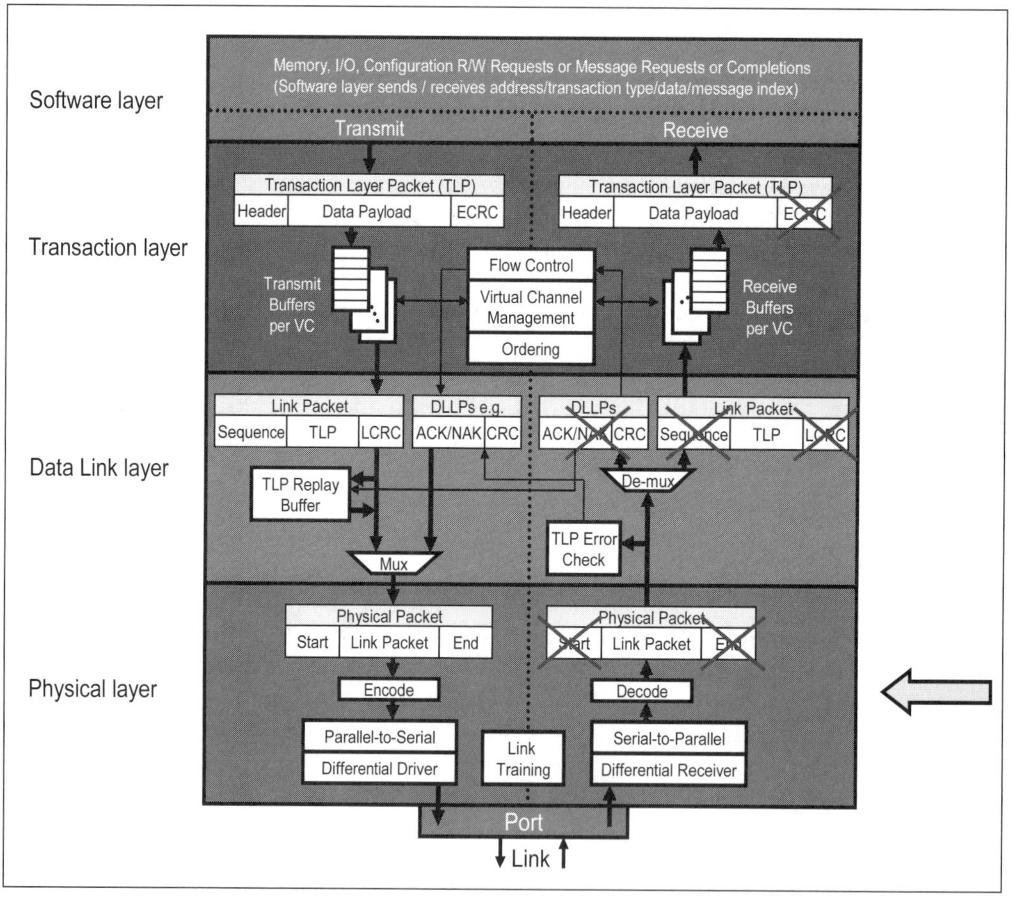

In the future, data rates per Lane are expected to go to 5 Gbits/s, 10 Gbits/s and beyond. When this happens, an existing design can be adapted to the higher data rates by redesigning the Physical Layer while maximizing reuse of the Data Link Layer, Transaction Layer and Device Core/Software Layer. The Physical Layer may be designed as a standalone entity separate from the Data Link Layer and Transaction Layer. This allows a design to be migrated to higher data rates or even to an optical implementation if such a Physical Layer is supported in the future.

Two sub-blocks make up the Physical Layer. These are the logical Physical Layer and the electrical Physical Layer as shown in Figure 11-2. This chapter describes the logical sub-block, and the next chapter describes the electrical sub-block. Both sub-blocks are split into transmit logic and receive logic (independent of each other) which allow dual simplex communication.

Figure 11-2: Logical and Electrical Sub-Blocks of the Physical Layer

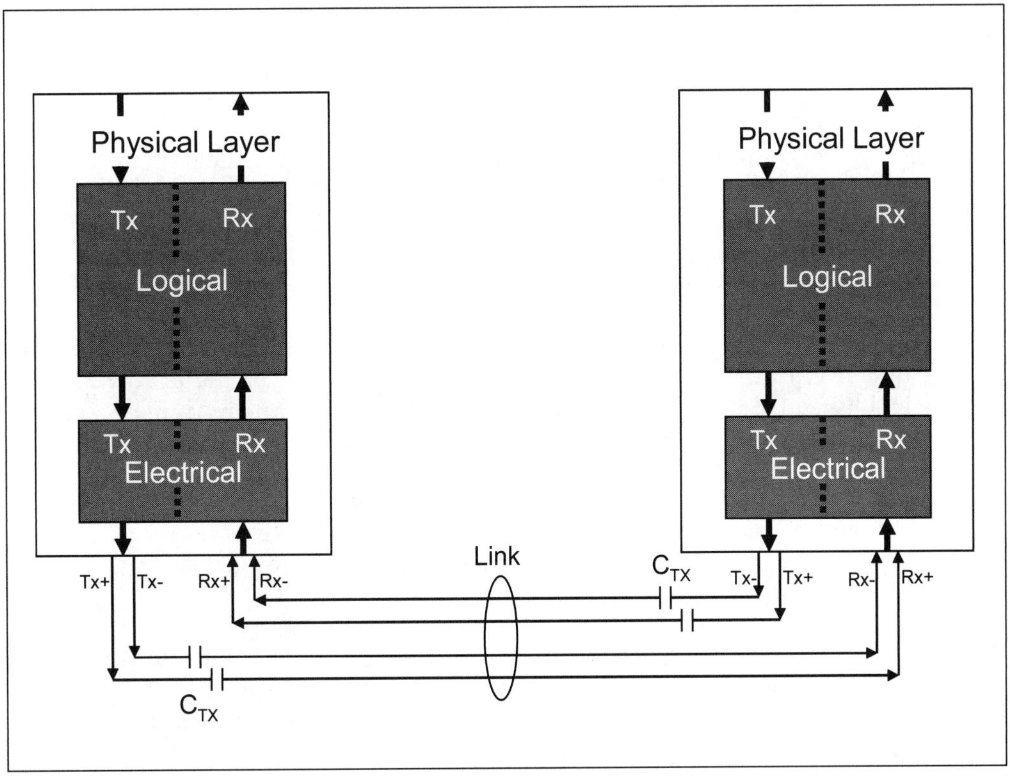

Disclaimer

To facilitate description of the Physical Layer functionality, an example implementation is described that is not necessarily the implementation assumed by the specification nor is a designer compelled to implement a Physical Layer in such a manner. A designer may implement the Physical Layer in any manner that is compliant with the functionality expected by the PCI Express specification.

Transmit Logic Overview

Figure 11-3 on page 401 shows the elements that make up the transmit logic:

- a multiplexer (mux),
- byte striping logic (only necessary if the link implements more than one data lane),
- scramblers,
- 8b/10b encoders,
- and parallel-to-serial converters.

TLPs and DLLPs from the Data Link layer are clocked into a Tx (transmit) Buffer. With the aid of a multiplexer, the Physical Layer frames the TLPs or DLLPs with Start and End characters. These characters are framing symbols which the receiver device uses to detect start and end of packet.

The framed packet is sent to the **Byte Striping logic** which multiplexes the bytes of the packet onto the Lanes. One byte of the packet is transferred on one Lane, the next byte on the next Lane and so on for the available Lanes.

The **Scrambler** uses an algorithm to pseudo-randomly scramble each byte of the packet. The Start and End framing bytes are not scrambled. Scrambling eliminates repetitive patterns in the bit stream. Repetitive patterns result in large amounts of energy concentrated in discrete frequencies which leads to significant EMI noise generation. Scrambling spreads energy over a frequency range, hence minimizing average EMI noise generated.

The scrambled 8-bit characters (8b characters) are encoded into 10-bit symbols (10b symbols) by the **8b/10b Encoder** logic. And yes, there is a 25% loss in transmission performance due to the expansion of each byte into a 10-bit character. A **Character** is defined as the 8-bit un-encoded byte of a packet. A **Symbol** is defined as the 10-bit encoded equivalent of the 8-bit character. The purpose of

8b/10b Encoding the packet characters is primarily to create sufficient 1 to 0 and 0-to-1 transition density in the bit stream so that the receiver can re-create a receive clock with the aid of a **receiver Phase Lock Loop (PLL)**. Note that the clock used to clock the serial data bit stream out of the transmitter is not itself transmitted onto the wire. Rather, the receive clock is used to clock in an inbound packet.

The 10b symbols are converted to a serial bit stream by the **Parallel-to-Serial converter**. This logic uses a 2.5 GHz clock to serially clock the packets out on each Lane. The serial bit stream is sent to the electrical sub-block which **differentially transmits** the packet onto each Lane of the Link.

Figure 11-3: Physical Layer Details

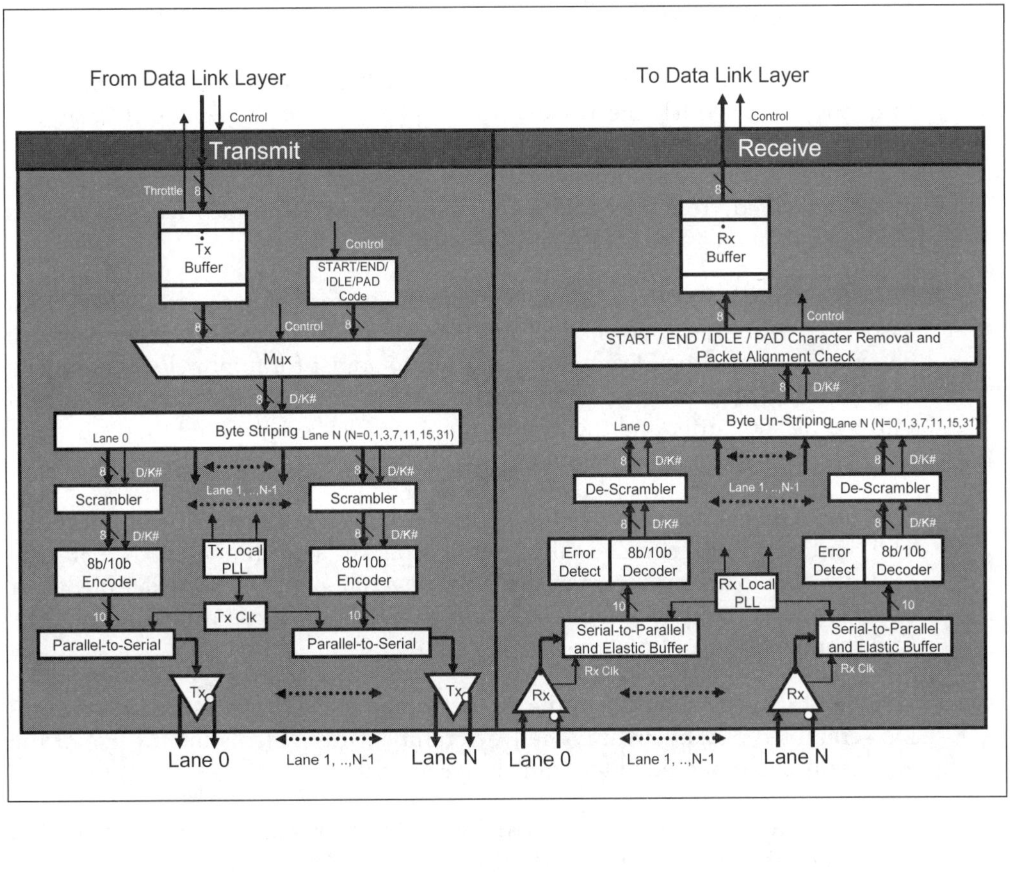

Receive Logic Overview

Figure 11-3 shows the elements that make up the receiver logic:

- receive PLL,
- serial-to-parallel converter,
- elastic buffer,
- 8b/10b decoder,
- de-scrambler,
- byte un-striping logic (only necessary if the link implements more than one data lane),
- control character removal circuit,
- and a packet receive buffer.

As the data bit stream is received, the **receiver PLL** is synchronized to the clock frequency with which the packet was clocked out of the remote transmitter device. The transitions in the incoming serial bit stream are used to re-synchronize the PPL circuitry and maintain bit and symbol lock while generating a clock recovered from the data bit stream. The serial-to-parallel converter is clocked by the recovered clock and outputs 10b symbols.

The 10b symbols are clocked into the **Elastic Buffer** using the recovered clock associated with the receiver PLL. The Elastic Buffer is used for clock tolerance compensation; i.e. the Elastic Buffer is used to adjust for minor clock frequency variation between the recovered clock used to clock the incoming bit stream into the Elastic Buffer and the locally-generated clock associated that is used to clock data out of the Elastic Buffer.

The 10b symbols are converted back to 8b characters by the **8b/10b Decoder**. The Start and End characters that frame a packet are eliminated. The 8b/10b Decoder also looks for errors in the incoming 10b symbols. For example, error detection logic can check for invalid 10b symbols or detect a missing Start or End character.

The **De-Scrambler** reproduces the de-scrambled packet stream from the incoming scrambled packet stream. The De-Scrambler implements the inverse of the algorithm implemented in the transmitter Scrambler.

The bytes from each Lane are **un-striped** to form a serial byte stream that is loaded into the **receive buffer** to feed to the Data Link layer.

Physical Layer Link Active State Power Management

The full-on power state of the Physical Layer and Link is called the L0 state. Devices support two lower power states, L0s (L0 suspend) and L1 Active that are actively and automatically managed by the Physical Layer. L1 Active power state is a lower power state than L0s and is optionally supported. The L0s power state is managed by the Physical Layer. The L1 Active power state is managed by a combination of Data Link Layer and Physical Layer.

A Link can be placed in the L0s power state in one direction independent of the other direction while a Link in the L1 Active power state is in this state in both directions.

Software enables support of the L0s and L1 Active power states via configuration registers. After reset, these registers are in a state that disables lower power state functionality. The Physical Layer automatically manages entering these lower power states upon detection of a period of inactivity on the Link. Once a device is in L0s or L1 Active and it intends to transmit packets, it can transition its Link power state back to L0. The exit latency from L1 Active is greater than the exit latency from L0s.

Additional details on Link Active State Power Management are covered in "Link Training and Status State Machine (LTSSM)" on page 508 on Link Training and "Link Active State Power Management" on page 608.

Link Training and Initialization

The Physical Layer is responsible for the Link Initialization and Training. The process is described in "Link Initialization and Training Overview" on page 500.

Transmit Logic Details

Figure 11-4 on page 406 shows the transmit logic of the Logical Physical Layer. This section describes packet processing from the time packets are received from the Data Link Layer until the packet is clocked out of the Physical Layer onto the Link.

Tx Buffer

The Tx Buffer receives TLPs and DLLPs from the Data Link Layer. Along with the packets, the Data Link Layer indicates the start and end of the packet using a 'Control' signal so that the Physical Layer can append Start and End framing characters to the packet. The Tx Buffer uses a 'throttle' signal to throttle the flow of packets from the Data Link Layer in case the Tx Buffer fills up.

Multiplexer (Mux) and Mux Control Logic

General

The Mux shown in Figure 11-5 on page 407 primarily gates packet characters from the Tx Buffer to the Byte Striping logic (only necessary if the link implements more than one data lane). However, under certain circumstances, the Mux may gate other inputs to the Byte Striping logic. Here is a summary of the four Mux inputs and when they are gated:

- **Transmit Data Buffer**. When the Data Link Layer supplies a packet to be transmitted, the Mux gates the packet's character stream through to the Byte Striping logic. Characters within the Tx Buffer are Data or 'D' characters. Hence the D/K# signal is driven High when Tx Buffer contents are gated. See "Definition of Characters and Symbols" on page 405.
- **Start and End characters.** These Control characters are appended to the start and end of every TLP and DLLP as shown in Figure 11-6 on page 408. These framing characters allow a receiver to easily detect the start and end of a packet. There are two types of Start characters, one is the start TLP character (STP) and the other is the start DLLP character (SDP). There are two types of end characters, the End Good TLP or DLLP character (END), and the End Bad TLP character (EDB). See Table 11-5 on page 432 for a list of Control characters. A control signal from the Data Link Layer in combination with the packet type determine what type of framing character to gate. Start and End characters are Control or 'K' characters, hence the D/K# signal is driven low when the Start and End characters are gated out at the start and end of a packet, respectively.

- **Ordered-Sets.** Ordered-Sets are multiples of 4 character sequences that starts with a comma (COM) control character followed by other characters. They are transmitted during special events as described below:
  - During Link training, **Training Sequence 1 and 2 (TS1 and TS2) Ordered-Sets** are transmitted over the Link. Link training occurs after fundamental reset, hot reset, or after certain error conditions occur. Refer to "Ordered-Sets Used During Link Training and Initialization" on page 504 for detailed usage of TS1 and TS2 Ordered-Sets.
  - At periodic intervals, the Mux gates the **SKIP Ordered-Set** pattern through to the Byte Striping logic to facilitate clock tolerance compensation in the receiver circuit of the port at the other end of the Link. For a detailed description, refer to "Inserting Clock Compensation Zones" on page 436 and "Receiver Clock Compensation Logic" on page 442.
  - When a device wants to place its transmitter in the electrical Idle state, it must inform the remote receiver at the other end of the Link. The device gates an **electrical Idle Ordered-Set** to do so.
  - When a device wants to change the Link power state from L0s low power state to the L0 full-on power state, it transmits **Fast Training Sequence (FTS) Ordered-Sets** to the receiver. The receiver uses this Ordered-Set to re-synchronize its PLL to the transmitter clock.
- Ordered-Sets begin with a K character and, depending on the type of set, may contain D or K characters. Hence, during transmission of an Ordered-Set, the D/K# signal is driven Low for a clock and then may be driven High or Low there after.
- **Logical Idle Sequence.** When there are no packets to transmit on the Link (referred to as Logical Idle Link), rather than leave the Link in a floating state or drive nothing, logical Idle characters are gated. Doing so guarantees signal transitions on the Link thus allowing the receiver's PLL to maintain clock synchronization with the transmit clock. In addition, the receiver is able to maintain bit and symbol lock. The logical Idle sequence consists of transmitting 00h characters. It therefore consists of D type characters, hence, the D/K# signal is high while the Mux is gating logical Idle sequences.

Definition of Characters and Symbols

Each character is 8-bits in size. They can be grouped into two categories, Control or 'K' characters, and Data or 'D' characters. From the standpoint of 8b/10b Encoding, D characters are encoded into a different 10-bit symbol than K characters of the same 8-bit value. Each 10-bit encoded character is referred to as a symbol.

Figure 11-4: Physical Layer Transmit Logic Details

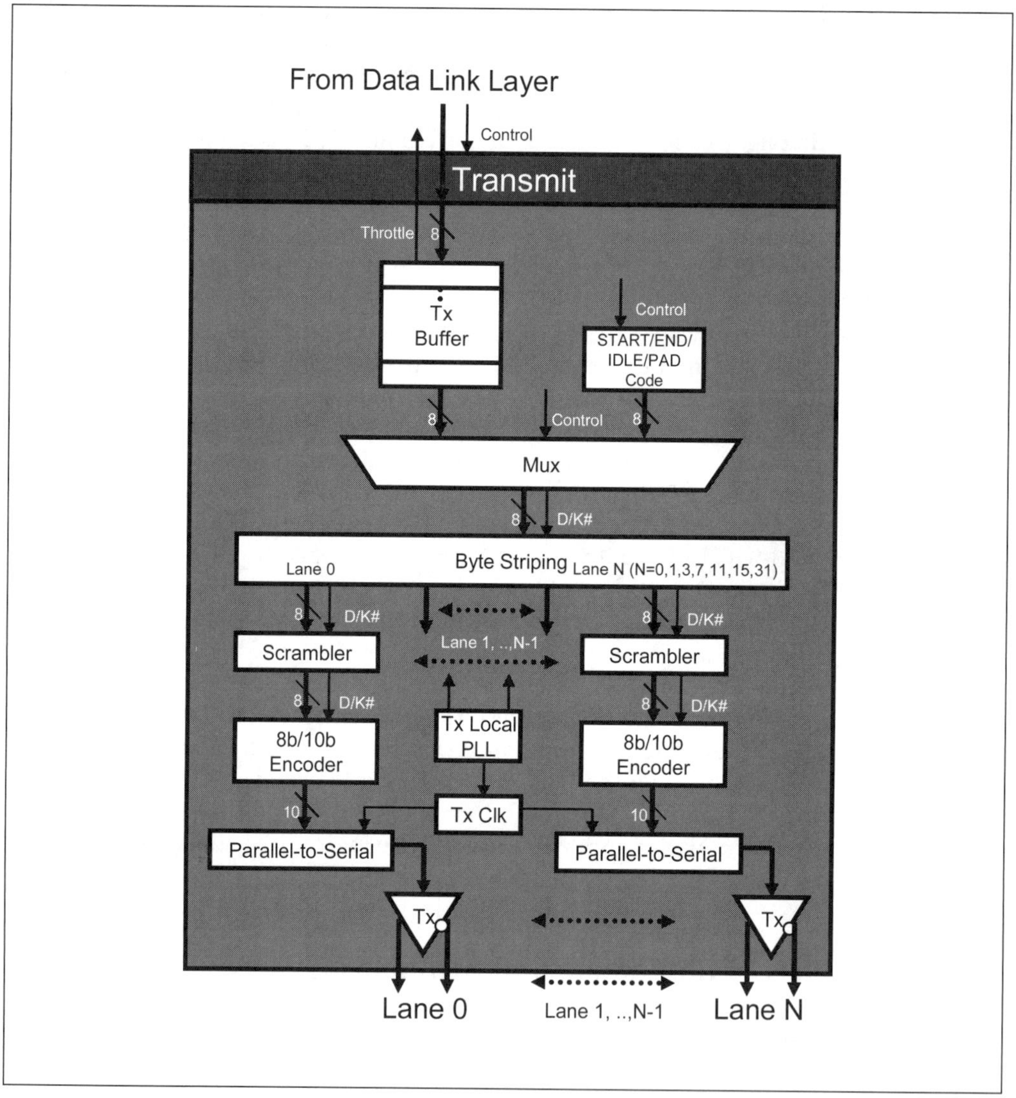

Figure 11-5: Transmit Logic Multiplexer

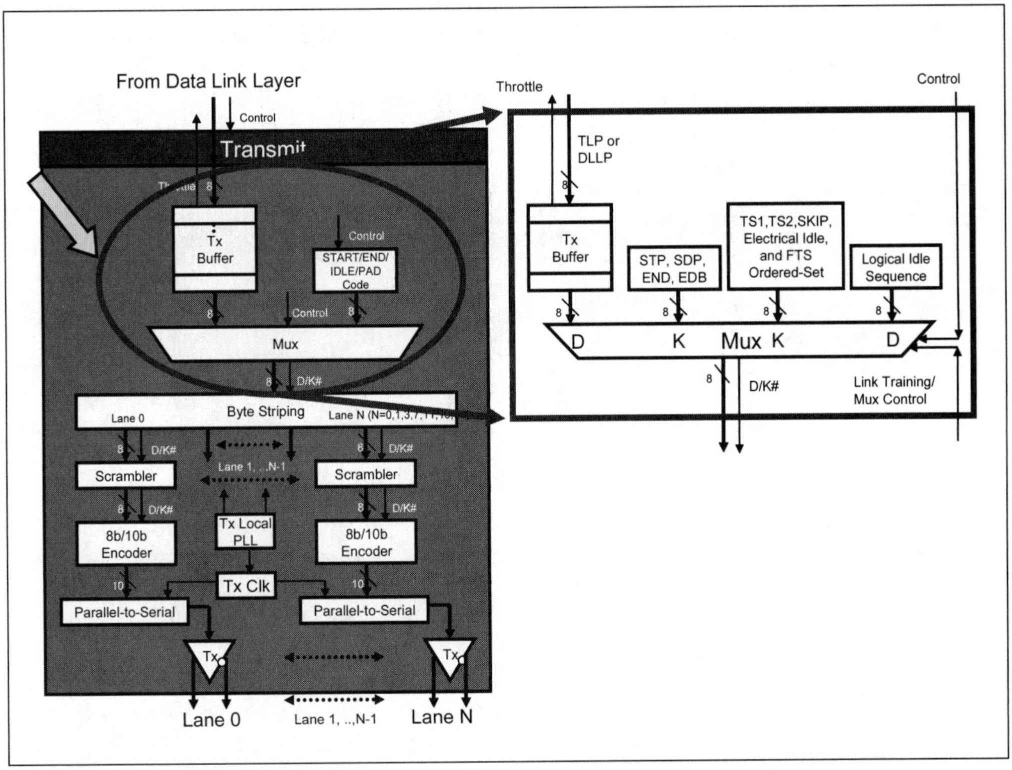

Figure 11-6: TLP and DLLP Packet Framing with Start and End Control Characters

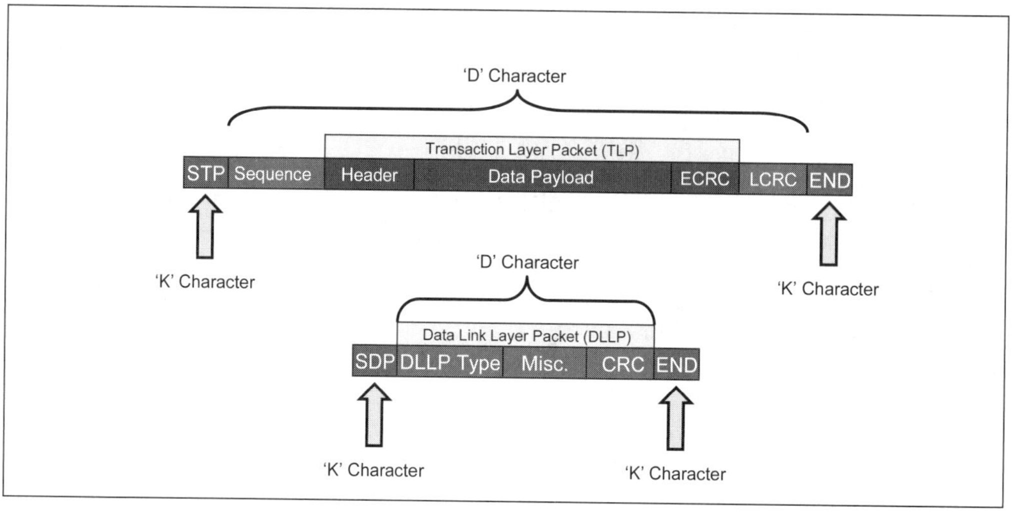

Byte Striping (Optional)

When a port implements more than one data Lane (i.e., more than one serial data path on the external Link), the packet data is striped across the 2, 4, 8, 12, 16, or 32 Lanes by the Byte Striping logic. Striping means that each consecutive outbound character in a character stream is multiplexed onto the consecutive Lanes. Examples of Byte Striping are illustrated in Figure 11-7 on page 409, Figure 11-8 on page 410, Figure 11-9 on page 411. The number of Lanes used is configured during the Link training process.

Disclaimer: This example assumes that the Byte Striping logic is implemented before the Scrambler and 8b/10b Encoder. Every Lane implements a Scrambler and an 8b/10b Encoder. This permits a receiver Physical Layer to detect errors on any Lane independent of the other Lanes. For example, an error that may have occurred in the transmitter Scrambler or 8b/10b Encoder is detectable if a receiver detects an invalid 10b character on a given Lane. When an error is detected on a Lane and cannot be cleared, the Lane could be disabled and the Link re-trained and re-initialized with fewer Lanes. This error recovery feature is suggested and not required by specification.

On the other hand, to simplify and reduce the size of the Physical Layer logic, a designer may choose to place the Byte Striping logic after the Scrambler and 8b/10b Encoder but before the Parallel-to-Serial converter. This reduces the number of Scramblers and 8b/10b Encoders to one. If the receiver detects an error in the incoming bit stream however, it cannot isolate the error to a particular Lane.

Figure 11-7: x1 Byte Striping

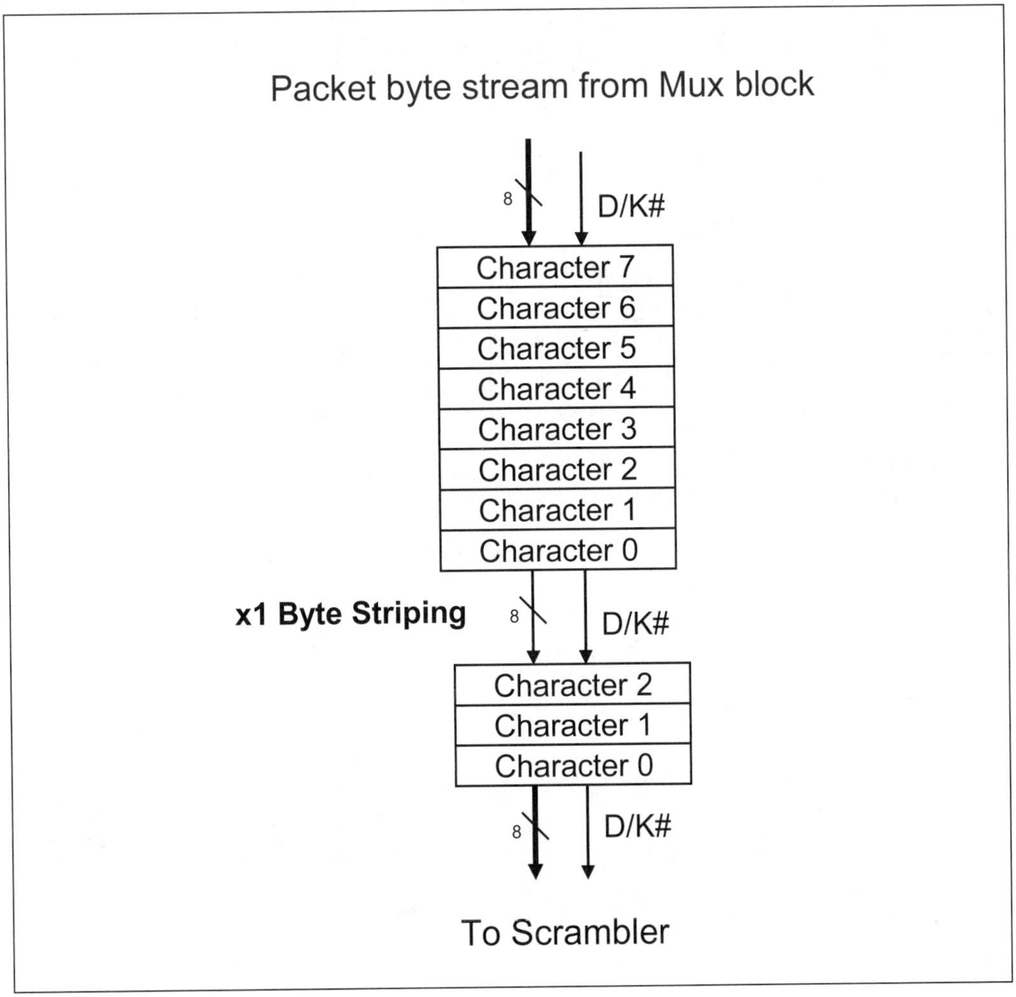

Figure 11-8: x4 Byte Striping

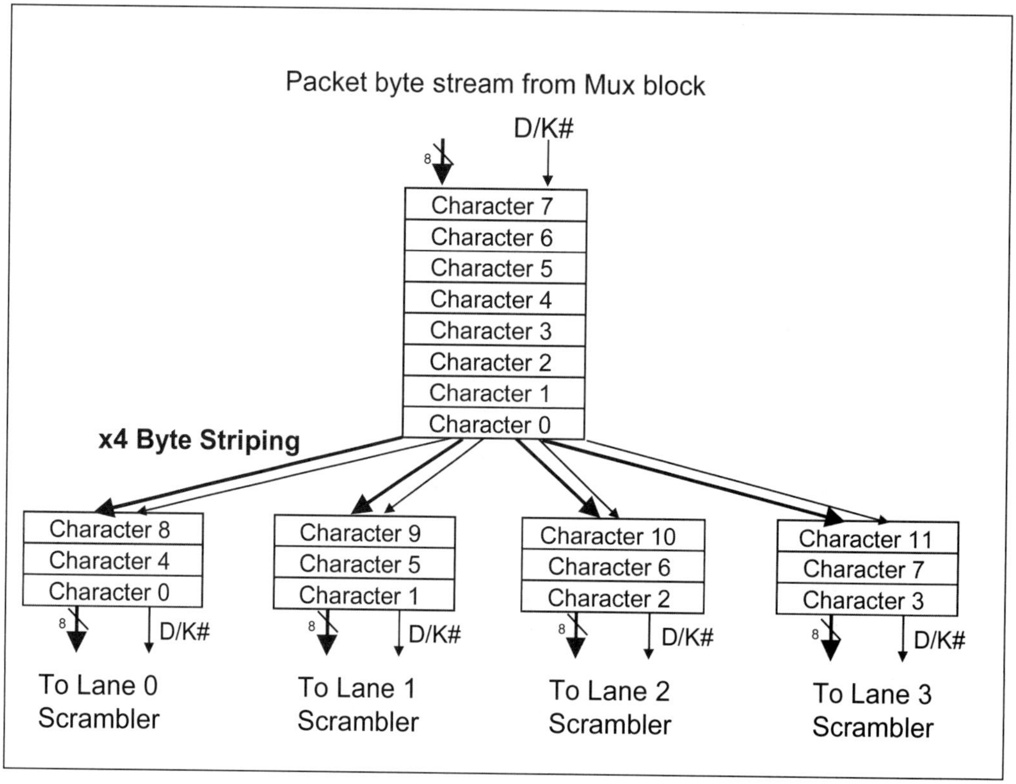

Figure 11-9: x8, x12, x16, x32 Byte Striping

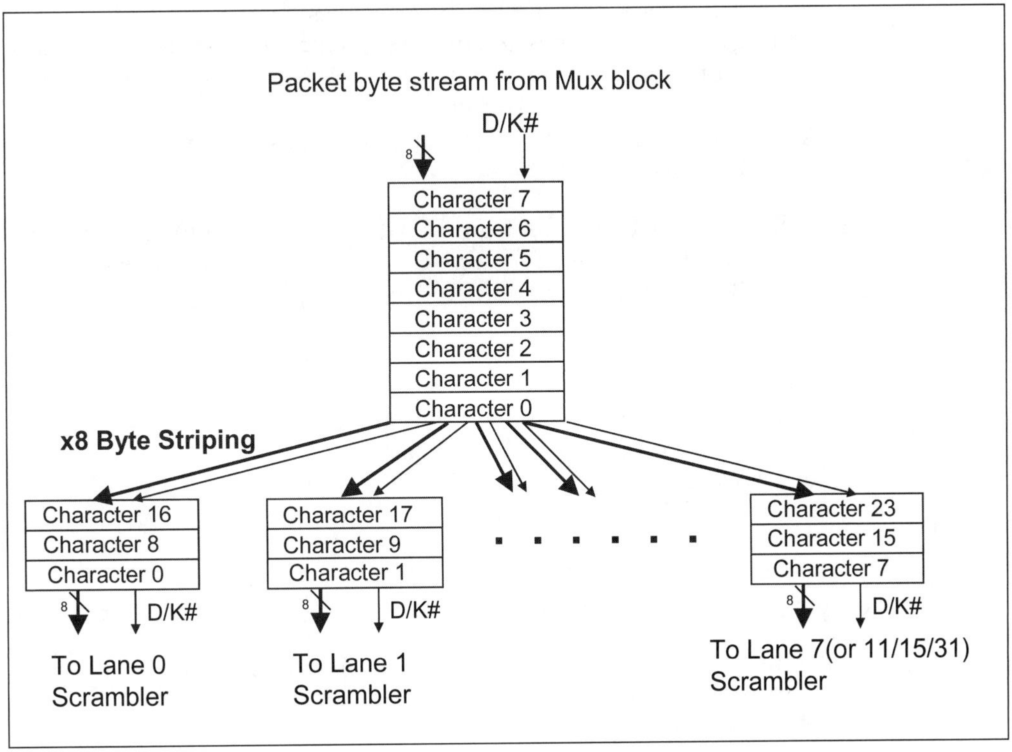

Packet Format Rules

After passing through the Byte Striping logic, a TLP or DLLP character stream is striped across the Lanes. This section describes the rules used to byte stripe packets so that the packets are correctly striped across the Lanes of the Link.

General Packet Format Rules. The following are the general packet format rules:

- The total packet length (including Start and End characters) of each packet must be a multiple of four characters.
- TLPs always start with the STP character.
- DLLPs always start with SDP and are 8 characters long (6 characters + SDP + END)

- All TLPs terminate with either an END or EDB character.
- DLLPs terminate with the END character.
- STP and SDP characters must be placed on Lane 0 when starting the transmission of a packet after the transmission of Logical Idles. If not starting a packet transmission from Logical Idle (i.e. back-to-back transmission of packets), then STP and SDP must start on a Lane number divisible by 4.
- Any violation of these rules may be reported as a Receiver Error to the Data Link Layer.

x1 Packet Format Example. Figure 11-10 on page 413 illustrates the format of packets transmitted over a x1 Link (i.e., a Link with only one Lane operational). The illustration shows the following sequence of packets:

1. One TLP.
2. One 8-byte DLLP.
3. One clock compensation packet consisting of a SKIP Ordered-Set (i.e., a COM followed by three SKP characters).
4. Two TLPs.
5. One 8-byte DLLP.
6. One TLP.
7. A Flow Control Packet.
8. Logical Idles transmitted because there are no more packets to transmit.

x4 Packet Format Rules. The following rules apply when a packet is transmitted over a x4 Link (i.e., a Link with four Lanes):

- STP and SDP characters are always transmitted on Lane 0.
- END and EDB characters are always transmitted on Lane 3.
- When an Ordered-Set such as the SKIP Ordered-Set is transmitted (for clock compensation in the receiver), it must be sent on all four Lanes simultaneously.
- When Logical Idle sequences are transmitted, they must be transmitted on all Lanes.
- Any violation of these rules may be reported as a Receiver Error to the Data Link Layer.

x4 Packet Format Example. Figure 11-11 on page 414 illustrates the format of packets transmitted over a x4 Link (i.e., a Link with four data Lanes operational). The illustration shows the following sequence of packets:

1. One TLP.
2. A SKIP Ordered-Set transmitted on all Lanes for periodic receiver clock compensation.

3. A DLLP.
4. Logical Idles on all Lanes because there are no more packets to transmit.

Figure 11-10: x1 Packet Format

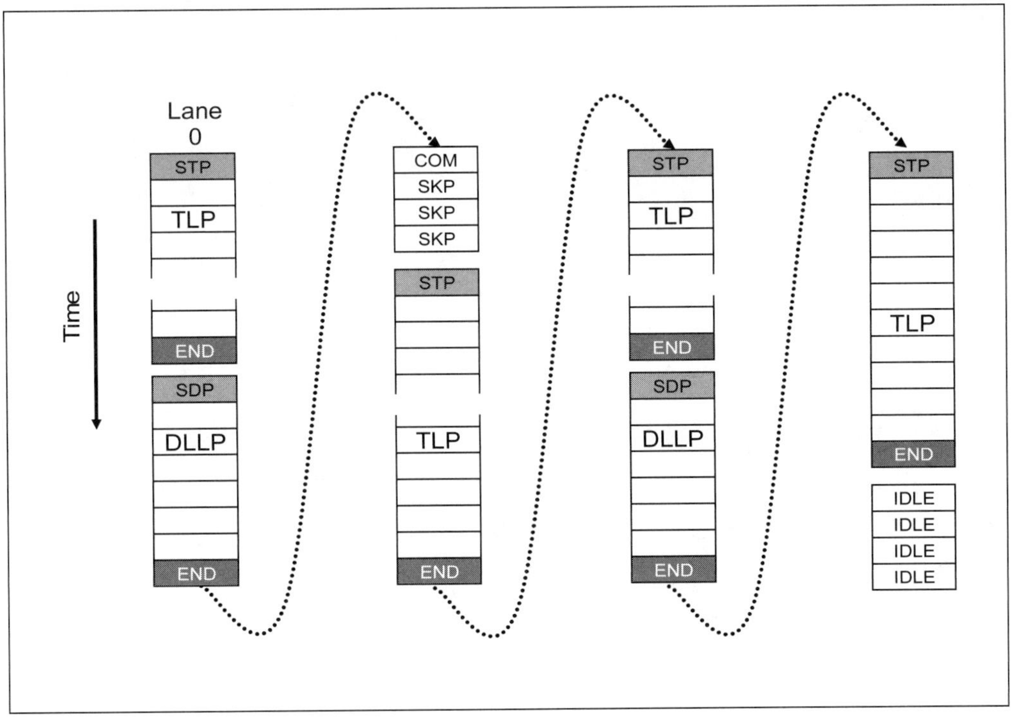

x8, x12, x16 or x32 Packet Format Rules. The following rules apply when a packet is transmitted over a x8, x12, x16, or x32 Link:

- STP/SDP characters are always transmitted on Lane 0 when transmission starts after a period during which Logical Idles are transmitted.
- STP/SDP characters may only be transmitted on Lane numbers divisible by 4 when transmitting back-to-back packets.
- END/EDB characters are transmitted on Lane numbers divisible by 4 less 1.
- If a packet doesn't end on the last Lane and there are no more packet transmissions, PAD symbols are transmitted on the Lanes above the Lane on which the END/EDB character is transmitted. This keeps the Link aligned so that transmission of the Logical Idle sequence can start on all Lanes at the same time.

- When an Ordered-Set such as the SKIP Ordered-Set is transmitted (for clock compensation in the receiver), it must be sent on all four Lanes simultaneously.
- When Logical Idle sequences are transmitted, they must be transmitted on all Lanes.
- Any violation of these rules may be reported as a Receiver Error to the Data Link Layer.

Figure 11-11: x4 Packet Format

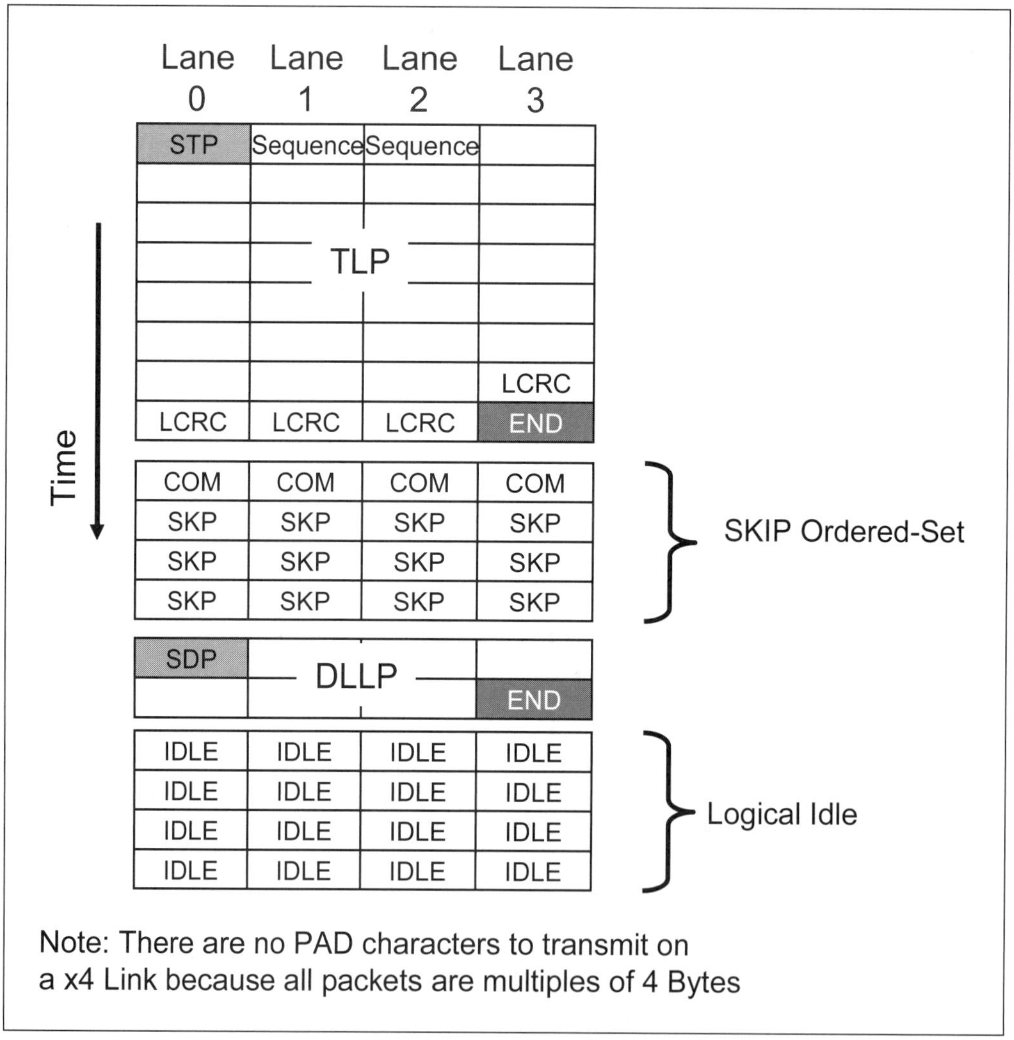

x8 Packet Format Example. Figure 11-12 on page 415 illustrates the format of packets transmitted over a x8 Link (i.e., a Link with 8 Lanes operational). The illustration shows the following sequence of packets:

1. A TLP.
2. A SKIP Ordered-Set transmitted on all Lanes for periodic receiver clock compensation.
3. A DLLP.
4. A TLP that ends on Lane 3. The remaining Lanes are filled with PADs so that the Link is aligned for the next transmission.
5. Logical Idles on all Lanes because there are no more packets to transmit.

Figure 11-12: x8 Packet Format

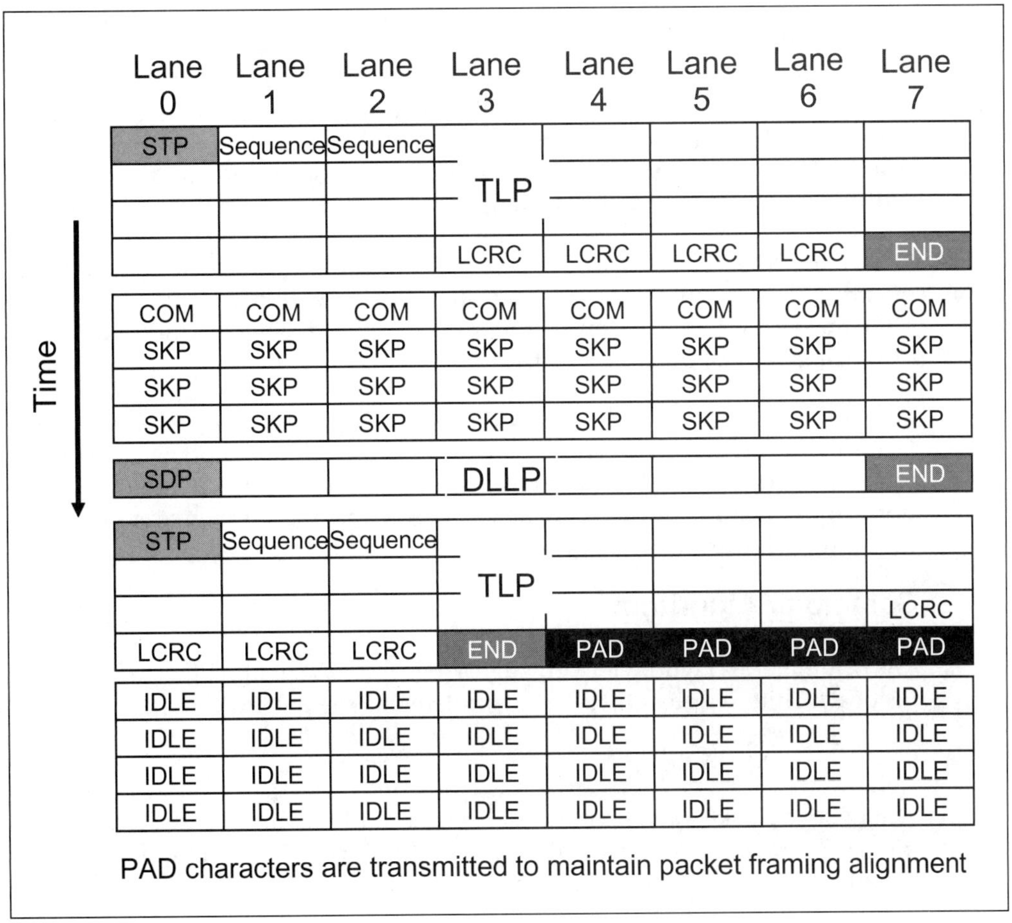

Scrambler

After byte striping, the outbound packets are transmitted across the Lanes. As shown in Figure 11-4 on page 406, each Lane in the Physical Layer design incorporates a Scrambler.

Purpose of Scrambling Outbound Transmission

The Scrambler eliminates generation of repetitive patterns on a transmitted data stream. As an example, when scrambled, a stream of 0s will result in a pseudo-random bit pattern.

Repetitive patterns result in large amount of energy concentrated in discrete frequencies which results in significant EMI noise generated. By scrambling the transmitted data, repetitive patterns—such as 10101010—are eliminated. As a result, no single frequency component of the signal is transmitted for significant periods of time. Thus the radiated EMI energy of a transmission is spread over a range in the frequency spectrum. This technique referred to as 'spread spectrum' effectively 'whitens' the frequency content of a signal and reduces the radiated power at any particular frequency.

On a bare systemboard with the wires of the Link un-shielded and high frequency transmission of 2.5 Gbits/s, EMI noise generation is significant. Scrambling makes the radiated power from the Link effectively look like white noise. This helps meet FCC requirements.

Also, on a multi-Lane Link with wires routed in close proximity, a scrambled transmission on one Lane generates white noise which does not interfere or correlate with another Lane's data transmission. This 'spatial frequency de-correlation' or reduction of crosstalk noise assists the receiver on each Lane to distinguish the desired signal from the background white noise.

Scrambler Algorithm

The Scrambler in Figure 11-13 on page 418 is implemented with a 16-bit Linear Feedback Shift Registers (LFSR) that implements the polynomial:

$$G(x) = X^{16} + X^5 + X^4 + X^3 + 1$$

The LFSR is clocked at the bit transfer rate. The LFSR output is serially clocked into an 8-bit register that is XORed with the 8-bit characters to form the scrambled data.

Implementation Note: The LFSR bit rate clock is 8 times the frequency (2GHz) of the byte clock (250MHz) that feeds the Scrambler output.

Some Scrambler implementation rules:

- On a multi-Lane Link implementation, Scramblers associated with each Lane must operate in concert, maintaining the same simultaneous value in each LFSR.
- Scrambling is applied to 'D' characters associated with TLP and DLLPs, including the Logical Idle (00h) sequence. 'D' characters within the TS1 and TS2 Ordered-Set are not scrambled.
- 'K' characters and characters within Ordered-Sets—such as TS1, TS2, SKIP, FTS and Electrical Idle Ordered-Sets—are not scrambled. These characters bypass the scrambler logic.
- Compliance Pattern related characters are not scrambled.
- When a COM character exits the Scrambler, (COM does not get scrambled) it initializes the LFSR. The initialized value of the 16-bit LFSR is FFFFh. Similarly on the receiver side, when a COM character enters the De-Scrambler, it is initialized.
- With one exception, the LFSR serially advances eight times for every character (D or K character) transmission. The LFSR does NOT advance on SKP characters associated with the SKIP Ordered-Set. The reason the LFSR is not advanced for SKPs is because a receiver of inbound packets may add or delete SKP symbols to perform clock tolerance compensation. Changing the number of characters in the receiver from the number of characters transmitted will cause the value in the receiver LFSR to lose synchronization with the transmitter LFSR value. For a detailed description, refer to "Inserting Clock Compensation Zones" on page 436 and "Receiver Clock Compensation Logic" on page 442.
- By default, Scrambling is always enabled. Although the specification does allow the Scrambler to be disabled for test and debug purposes, it does not provide a standard software or configuration register-related method to disable the Scrambler.

Figure 11-13: Scrambler

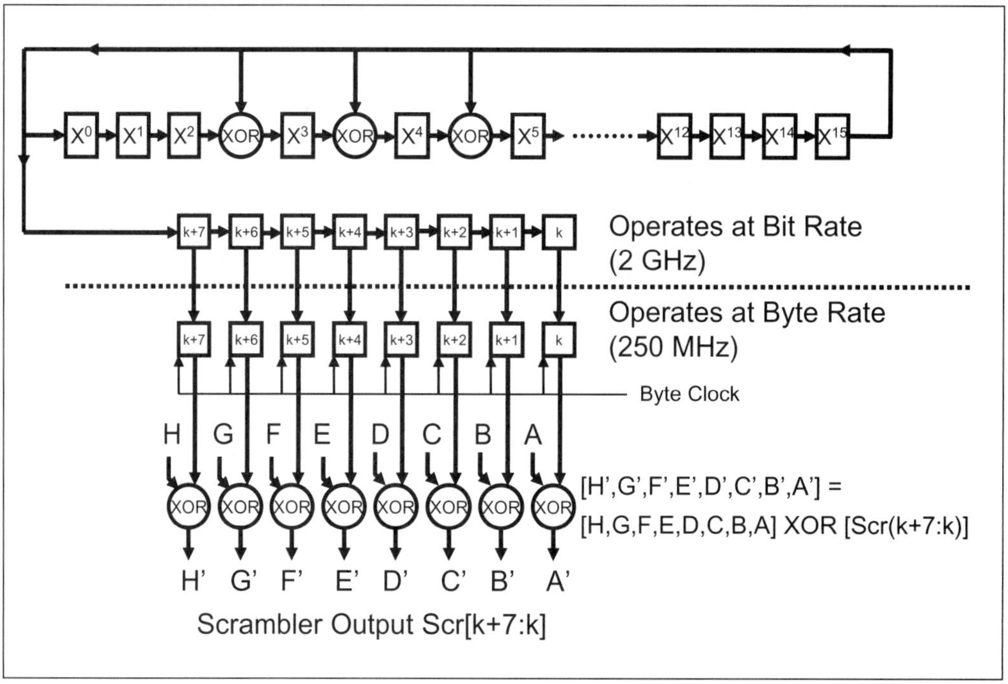

Disabling Scrambling

As stated in the previous section, the Scrambler can be disabled to help facilitate test and debug. Software or test equipment may tell a device to disable scrambling. However, the specification does not indicate the mechanism by which a device's Physical Layer is instructed to disable scrambling.

Scrambling is disabled in the Configuration State of Link Training described on the page 519. The device receiving the software request to disable scrambling will do so during the Link Training Configuration State, and transmits at least two TS1/TS2 Ordered-Sets with the disable scrambling bit set on all its configured Lanes to the remote device it is connected to. The remote receiver device disables its Scrambler/De-Scrambler. It is required that the Port that is sending the Disable Scrambling request will also disable scrambling.

8b/10b Encoding

General

Each Lane of a device's transmitter implements an 8-bit to 10-bit Encoder that encodes 8-bit data or control characters into 10-bit symbols. The coding scheme was invented by IBM in 1982 and is documented in the ANSI X3.230-1994 document, clause 11 (and also IEEE 802.3z, 36.2.4) and US Patent Number 4,486,739 entitled "Byte Oriented DC Balanced 8b/10b Partitioned Block Transmission Code". 8b/10b coding is now widely used in architectures such as Gigabit Ethernet, Fibre Channel, ServerNet, FICON, IEEE1394b, InfiniBand, etc.

Purpose of Encoding a Character Stream

The primary purpose of this scheme is to embed a clock into the serial bit stream transmitted on all Lanes. No clock is therefore transmitted along with the serial data bit stream. This eliminates the need for a high frequency 2.5GHz clock signal on the Link which would generate significant EMI noise and would be a challenge to route on a standard FR4 board. Link wire routing between two ports is much easier given that there is no clock to route, removing the need to match clock length to Lane signal trace lengths. Two devices are connected by simply wiring their Lanes together.

Below is a summary of the **advantages** of 8b/10b encoding scheme:

- **Embedded Clock.** Creates sufficient 0-to-1 and 1-to-0 transition density (i.e., signal changes) to facilitate re-creation of the receive clock on the receiver end using a PLL (by guaranteeing a limited run length of consecutive ones or zeros). The recovered receive clock is used to clock inbound 10-bit symbols into an elastic buffer. Figure 11-14 on page 420 illustrates the example case wherein 00h is converted to 1101000110b, where an 8-bit character with no transitions has 5 transitions when converted to a 10b symbol. These transitions keep the receiver PLL synchronized to the transmit circuit clock:
  - — Limited 'run length' means that the encoding scheme ensures the signal line will not remain in a high or low state for an extended period of time. The run length does not exceed five consecutive 1s or 0s.
  - — 1s and 0s are clocked out on the rising-edge of the transmit clock. At the receiver, a PLL can recreate the clock by sync'ing to the leading edges of 1s and 0s.
  - — Limited run length ensures minimum frequency drift in the receiver's PLL relative to the local clock in the transmit circuit.

Figure 11-14: Example of 8-bit Character of 00h Encoded to 10-bit Symbol

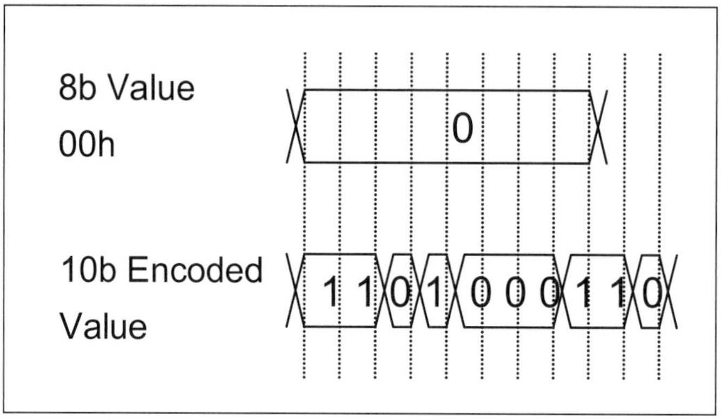

- **DC Balance.** Keeps the number of 1s and 0s transmitted as close to equal as possible, thus maintaining DC balance on the transmitted bit stream to an average of half the signal threshold voltage. This is very important in capacitive- and transformer-coupled circuits.
  — Maintains a balance between the number of 1s and 0s on the signal line, thereby ensuring that the received signal is free of any DC component. This reduces the possibility of inter-bit interference. Inter-bit interference results from the inability of a signal to switch properly from one logic level to the other because the Lane coupling capacitor or intrinsic wire capacitance is over-charged.
- **Encoding of Special Control Characters.** Permits the encoding of special control ('K') characters such as the Start and End framing characters at the start and end of TLPs and DLLPs.
- **Error Detection.** A secondary benefit of the encoding scheme is that it facilitates the detection of most transmission errors. A receiver can check for 'running disparity' errors, or the reception of invalid symbols. Via the running disparity mechanism (see "Disparity" on page 423), the data bit stream transmitted maintains a balance of 1s and 0s. The receiver checks the difference between the total number of 1s and 0s transmitted since link initialization and ensures that it is as close to zero as possible. If it isn't, a disparity error is detected and reported, implying that a transmission error occurred.

The **disadvantage** of 8b/10b encoding scheme is that, due to the expansion of each 8-bit character into a 10-bit symbol prior to transmission, the actual transmission performance is degraded by 20% or said another way, the transmission overhead is increased by 25% (everything good has a price tag).

Properties of 10-bit (10b) Symbols

- For 10-bit symbol transmissions, the average number of 1s transmitted over time is equal to the number of 0s transmitted, no matter what the 8-bit character to be transmitted is; i.e., the symbol transmission is DC balanced.
- The bit stream never contains more than five continuous 1s or 0s (limited-run length).
- Each 10-bit symbol contains:
  - Four 0s and six 1s (not necessarily contiguous), or
  - Six 0s and four 1s (not necessarily contiguous), or
  - Five 0s and five 1s (not necessarily contiguous).
- Each 10-bit symbol is subdivided into two sub-blocks: the first is six bits wide and the second is four bits wide.
  - The 6-bit sub-block contains no more than four 1s or four 0s.
  - The 4-bit sub-block contains no more than three 1s or three 0s.
- Any symbol with other than the above properties is considered invalid and a receiver consider this an error.
- An 8-bit character is submitted to the 8b/10b encoder along with a signal indicating whether the character is a Data (D) or Control (K) character. The encoder outputs the equivalent 10-bit symbol along with a current running disparity (CRD) that represents the sum of 1s and 0s for this transmission link since link initialization. See "Disparity" on page 423 for more information.
- The PCI Express specification defines Control characters that encode into the following Control symbols: STP, SDP, END, EDB, COM, PAD, SKP, FTS, and IDL (see "Control Character Encoding" on page 430).

Preparing 8-bit Character Notation

8b/10b conversion lookup tables refer to all 8-bit characters using a special notation (represented by Dxx.y for Data characters and Kxx.y. for Control characters). Figure 11-15 on page 422 illustrates the notation equivalent for any 8-bit D or K character. Below are the steps to covert the 8-bit number to its notation equivalent.

In Figure 11-15 on page 422, the example character is the Data character, 6Ah.

1. The bits in the character are identified by the capitalized alpha designators A through H.
2. The character is partitioned into two sub-blocks: one 3-bits wide and the other 5-bits wide.
3. The two sub-blocks are flipped.
4. The character takes the written form Zxx.y, where:
5. Z = D or K for Data or Control,
6. xx = the decimal value of the 5-bit field,
7. y = the decimal value of the 3-bit field.
8. The example character is represented as D10.3 in the 8b/10b lookup tables.

Figure 11-15: Preparing 8-bit Character for Encode

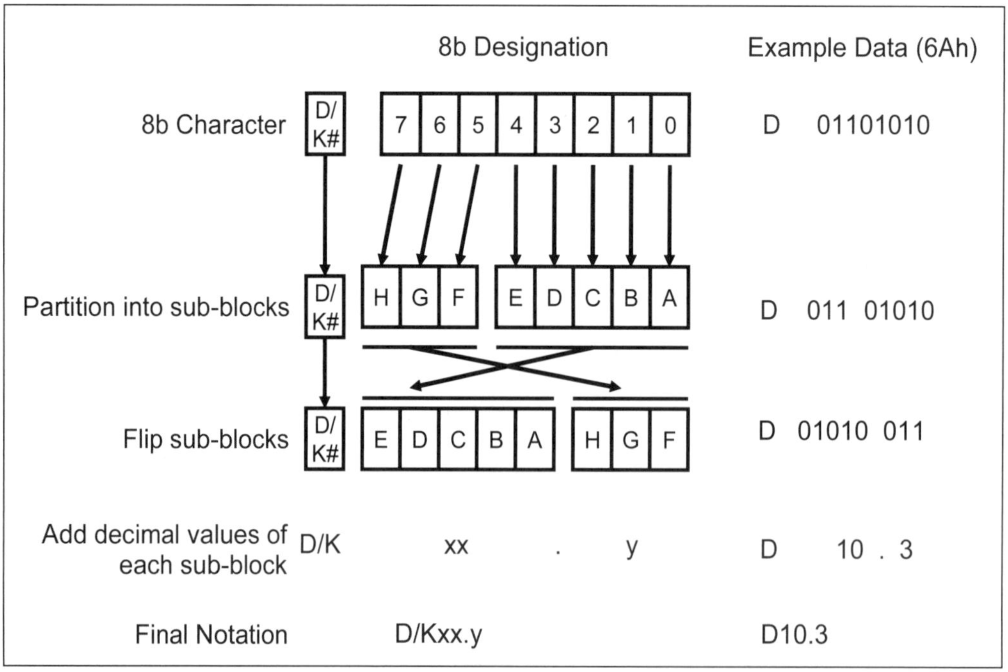

Disparity

Definition. Character disparity refers to the difference between the number of 1s and 0s in a 10-bit symbol:

- When a symbol has more 0s than 1s, the symbol has negative (–) disparity (e.g., 0101000101b).
- When a symbol has more 1s than 0s, the symbol has positive (+) disparity (e.g., 1001101110b).
- When a symbol has an equal number of 1s and 0s, the symbol has neutral disparity (e.g., 0110100101b).
- Each 10-bit symbol contains one of the following numbers of ones and zeros (not necessarily contiguous):
  - Four 0s and six 1s (+ disparity).
  - Six 0s and four 1s (– disparity).
  - Five 0s and five 1s (neutral disparity).

Two Categories of 8-bit Characters. There are two categories of 8-bit characters:

- Those that encode into 10-bit symbols with + or – disparity.
- Those that encode into 10-bit symbols with neutral disparity.

CRD (Current Running Disparity). The CRD reflects the total number of 1s and 0s transmitted over the link since link initialization and has the following characteristics:

- Its current state indicates the balance of 1s and 0s transmitted since link initialization.
- The CRD's initial state (before any characters are transmitted) can be + or –.
- The CRD's current state can be either positive (if more 1s than 0s have been transmitted) or negative (if more 0s than 1s).
- Each character is converted via a table lookup with the current state of the CRD factored in.
- As each new character is encoded, the CRD either remains the same (if the newly generated 10-bit character has neutral disparity) or it flips to the opposite polarity (if the newly generated character has + or – disparity).

8b/10b Encoding Procedure

Refer to Figure 11-16 on page 425. The encode is accomplished by performing two table lookups in parallel (not shown separately in the illustration):

- First Table Lookup: Three elements are submitted to a 5-bit to 6-bit table for a lookup (see Table 11-1 on page 427 and Table 11-2 on page 429):
  - The 5-bit portion of the 8-bit character (bits A through E).
  - The Data/Control (D/K#) indicator.
  - The current state of the CRD (positive or negative).
  - The table lookup yields the upper 6-bits of the 10-bit symbol (bits *abcdei*).
- Second Table Lookup: Three elements are submitted to a 3-bit to 4-bit table for a lookup (see Table 11-3 on page 429 and Table 11-4 on page 430):
  - The 3-bit portion of the 8-bit character (bits F through H).
  - The same Data/Control (D/K#) indicator.
  - The current state of the CRD (positive or negative).
  - The table lookup yields the lower 4-bits of the 10-bit symbol (bits *fghj*).

The 8b/10b encoder computes a new CRD based on the resultant 10-bit symbol and supplies this CRD for the 8b/10b encode of the next character. If the resultant 10-bit symbol is neutral (i.e., it has an equal number of 1s and 0s), the polarity of the CRD remains unchanged. If the resultant 10-bit symbol is + or –, the CRD flips to its opposite state. It is an error if the CRD is currently + or – and the next 10-bit symbol produced has the same polarity as the CRD (unless the next symbol has neutral disparity, in which case the CRD remains the same).

The 8b/10b encoder feeds a Parallel-to-Serial converter which clocks 10-bit symbols out in the bit order 'abcdeifghj' (shown in Figure 11-16 on page 425).

Example Encodings. Figure 11-17 on page 426 illustrates some example 8-bit to 10-bit encodings. The following is an explanation of the conversion of the 8-bit Data character 6Ah:

- The 8-bit character is broken down into its two sub-blocks: 011b and 01010b.
- The two sub-blocks are flipped and represented as the D10.3 character. The binary-weighted value of the 5-bit block is 10d and the value of the 3-bit field is 3d.
- The two blocks are submitted to the data character lookup tables (Table 11-1 on page 427 and Table 11-3 on page 429 are for D lookups) along with the current state of the CRD).

- The last two columns show the 10-bit symbol produced by the two parallel table lookups (Table 11-1 on page 427 and Table 11-3 on page 429) when the CRD is negative or positive.

Figure 11-16: 8-bit to 10-bit (8b/10b) Encoder

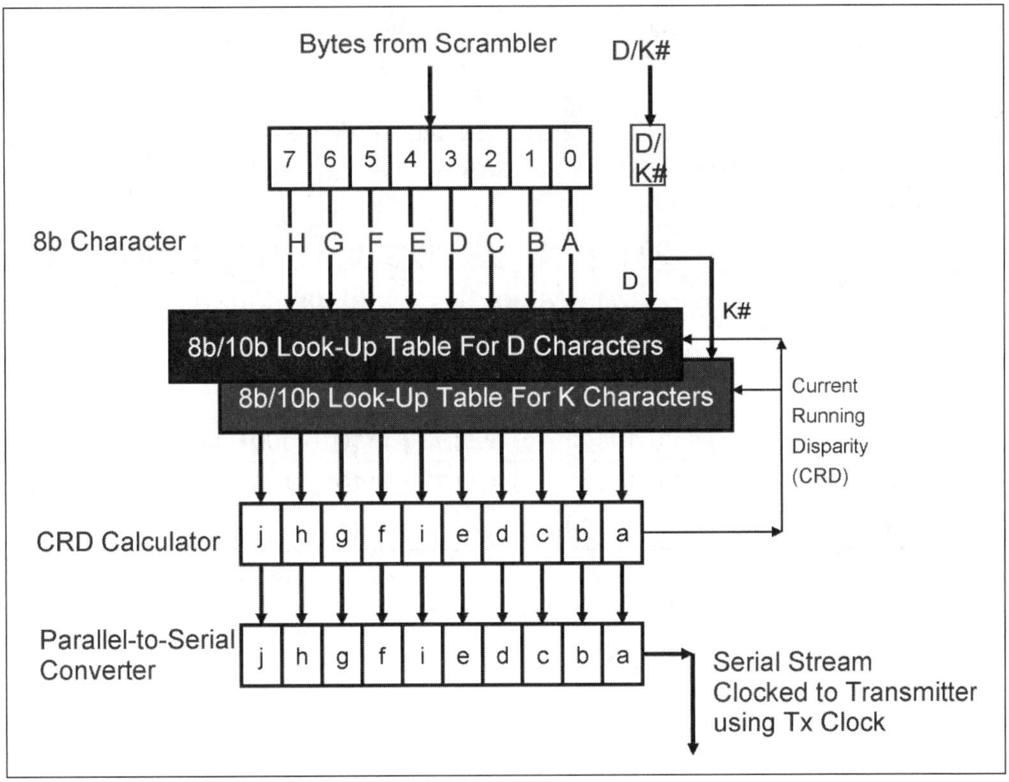

Example Transmission. Figure 11-18 on page 427 illustrates the encode and transmission of three characters: the first one is the control character BCh (K28.5), the second character is also BCh (K28.5) and the third character is the data character 6Ah (D10.3):

- If the initial CRD is negative at the time of the encode, the K28.5 is encoded into 001111 1010b (positive disparity), flipping the CRD from negative to positive.
- If the CRD is positive at the time of the encode, the K28.5 is encoded into 110000 0101b (negative disparity), flipping the CRD from positive to negative.

- The D10.3 is encoded into 010101 1100b (neutral disparity). The CRD therefore remains unchanged (negative) for the next encoding (not shown).
- Notice that the resultant symbol stream is DC balanced.

Figure 11-17: Example 8-bit/10-bit Encodings

Encode to this if CRD is positive
Encode to this if CRD is negative
This is 8-bit character

D or K Character	Hex Byte	Binary Bits HGF EDCBA	Byte Name	CRD – abcdei fghj	CRD + abcdei fghj
Data (D)	6A	011 01010	D10.3	010101 1100	010101 0011
Data (D)	1B	000 11011	D27.0	110110 0100	001001 1011
Data (D)	F7	111 10111	D23.7	111010 0001	000101 1110
Control (K)	F7	111 10111	K23.7	111010 1000	000101 0111
Control (K)	BC	101 11100	K28.5	001111 1010	110000 0101

If character encode yields neutral disparity, then CRD remains unchanged, else it flips

Figure 11-18: Example 8-bit/10-bit Transmission

Use these two characters in the example below:

D/K#	Hex Byte	Binary Bits HGF EDCBA	Byte Name	CRD – abcdei fghj	CRD + abcdei fghj
Control (K)	BC	101 11100	K28.5	001111 1010	110000 0101
Data (D)	6A	011 01010	D10.3	010101 1100	010101 0011

Example Transmission

	CRD	Character	CRD	Character	CRD	Character	CRD
Character to be transmitted		K28.5 (BCh)		K28.5 (BCh)		D10.3 (6Ah)	
Bit stream transmitted	-	Yields 001111 1010 CRD is +	+	Yields 110000 0101 CRD is -	-	Yields 010101 1100 CRD is neutral	-

Initialized value of CRD is don't care. Receiver can determine from incoming bit stream

The Lookup Tables

The following four tables define the table lookup for the two sub-blocks of 8-bit Data and Control characters.

Table 11-1: 5-bit to 6-bit Encode Table for Data Characters

Data Byte Name	Unencoded Bits EDCBA	Current RD – abcdei	Current RD + abcdei
D0	00000	100111	011000
D1	00001	011101	100010
D2	00010	101101	010010
D3	00011	110001	110001
D4	00100	110101	001010
D5	00101	101001	101001

Table 11-1: 5-bit to 6-bit Encode Table for Data Characters (Continued)

Data Byte Name	Unencoded Bits EDCBA	Current RD – abcdei	Current RD + abcdei
D6	00110	011001	011001
D7	00111	111000	000111
D8	01000	111001	000110
D9	01001	100101	100101
D10	01010	010101	010101
D11	01011	110100	110100
D12	01100	001101	001101
D13	01101	101100	101100
D14	01110	011100	011100
D15	01111	010111	101000
D16	10000	011011	100100
D17	10001	100011	100011
D18	10010	010011	010011
D19	10011	110010	110010
D20	10100	001011	001011
D21	10101	101010	101010
D22	10110	011010	011010
D23	10111	111010	000101
D24	11000	110011	001100
D25	11001	100110	100110
D26	11010	010110	010110
D27	11011	110110	001001
D28	11100	001110	001110

Table 11-1: 5-bit to 6-bit Encode Table for Data Characters (Continued)

Data Byte Name	Unencoded Bits EDCBA	Current RD – abcdei	Current RD + abcdei
D29	11101	101110	010001
D30	11110	011110	100001
D31	11111	101011	010100

Table 11-2: 5-bit to 6-bit Encode Table for Control Characters

Data Byte Name	Unencoded Bits EDCBA	Current RD – abcdei	Current RD + abcdei
K28	11100	001111	110000
K23	10111	111010	000101
K27	11011	110110	001001
K29	11101	101110	010001
K30	11110	011110	100001

Table 11-3: 3-bit to 4-bit Encode Table for Data Characters

Data Byte Name	Unencoded Bits HGF	Current RD - fghj	Current RD + fghj
--.0	000	1011	0100
--.1	001	1001	1001
--.2	010	0101	0101
--.3	011	1100	0011
--.4	100	1101	0010
--.5	101	1010	1010

Table 11-3: 3-bit to 4-bit Encode Table for Data Characters

Data Byte Name	Unencoded Bits HGF	Current RD - fghj	Current RD + fghj
--.6	110	0110	0110
--.7	111	1110/0111	0001/1000

Table 11-4: 3-bit to 4-bit Encode Table for Control Characters

Data Byte Name	Unencoded Bits HGF	Current RD – fghj	Current RD + fghj
--.0	000	1011	0100
--.1	001	0110	1001
--.2	010	1010	0101
--.3	011	1100	0011
--.4	100	1101	0010
--.5	101	0101	1010
--.6	110	1001	0110
--.7	111	0111	1000

Control Character Encoding

Table 11-5 on page 432 shows the encoding of the PCI Express-defined Control characters. These characters are not scrambled by the transmitter logic, but are encoded into 10-bit symbols. Because these Control characters are not scrambled, the receiver logic can easily detect these symbols in an incoming symbol stream.

These Control characters have the following properties

- **COM** (comma) character. The COM character is used as the first character of any Ordered-Set. Ordered-Sets are a collection of multiples of 4 characters that are used for specialized purposes (see "Ordered-Sets" on page 433). The 10-bit encoding of the COM (K28.5) character contains two bits of one polarity followed by five bits of the opposite polarity (001111 1010 or 110000 0101). The COM (and FTS) symbols are the only two symbols that have this property, thereby making it easy to detect at the receiver's Physical Layer. A receiver detects the COM pattern to detect the start of an Ordered-Set. In particular, the COM character associated with TS1, TS2, or FTS Ordered-Sets are used by a receiver to achieve bit and symbol lock on the incoming symbol stream. See "Link Training and Initialization" on page 403 for more details.
- **PAD** character. On a multi-Lane Link, assume the transmitter transmits the END character associated with a packet end on an intermediate Lane such as Lane 3 of a x8 Link. If the Link goes to the Logical Idle state after the transmission of the packet's END character, then the PAD character is used to fill in the remaining Lanes. This is done so packets as well as Logical Idle sequences always begin on Lane 0. For more information, see "x8, x12, x16 or x32 Packet Format Rules" on page 413 and "x8 Packet Format Example" on page 415.
- **SKP** (skip) character. The SKP character is used as part of the SKIP Ordered-Set. The SKIP Ordered-Set is transmitted for clock tolerance compensation. For a detailed description, refer to "Inserting Clock Compensation Zones" on page 436 and "Receiver Clock Compensation Logic" on page 442.
- **STP** (Start TLP) character. This character is inserted to identify the start of a TLP.
- **SDP** (Start DLLP) character. This character is inserted to identify the start of a DLLP.
- **END** character. This character is inserted to identify the end of a TLP or DLLP that has not experienced any CRC errors on previously-traversed links.
- **EDB** (EnD Bad packet) character. This character is inserted to identify the end of a TLP that a forwarding device (such as a switch) wishes to 'nullify'. Cut-through mode is a mode in which the switch forwards a packet from its ingress port to an egress port with minimal latency without having to buffer the incoming packet first. A switch may have started forwarding a packet in cut-through mode and then discovered that the packet is corrupted. It therefore must instruct the receiver of this packet to discard it. To nullify a TLP, the switch ends the packet with the EDB character and inverts the LCRC from its calculated value. A receiver that receives such a nullified

packet discards it and does not return an ACK or NAK. Also see the chapter on Ack/Nak for a detailed description of the switch cut-through mode.

- **FTS** (Fast Training Sequence) character. This character is used as part of the FTS Ordered-Set. FTS Ordered-Sets are transmitted by a device in order to transition a Link from the low power L0s low power state back to the full-on L0 state.
- **IDL** (Idle) character. This character is used as part of the Electrical Idle Ordered-Set. The Ordered-Set is transmitted to inform the receiver that the Link is about to transition to the L0s low power state (also referred to as the Electrical Idle state of the Link).

Table 11-5: Control Character Encoding and Definition

Character Name	8b Name	10b (CRD-)	10b (CRD+)	Description
COM	K28.5 (BCh)	001111 1010	110000 0101	First character in any Ordered-Set. Detected by receiver and used to achieve symbol lock during TS1/TS2 Ordered-Set reception at receiver
PAD	K23.7 (F7h)	111010 1000	000101 0111	Packet Padding character
SKP	K28.0 (1Ch)	001111 0100	110000 1011	Used in SKIP Ordered-Set. This Ordered-Set is used for Clock Tolerance Compensation
STP	K27.7 (FBh)	110110 1000	001001 0111	Start of TLP character
SDP	K28.2 (5Ch)	001111 0101	110000 1010	Start of DLLP character
END	K29.7 (FDh)	101110 1000	010001 0111	End of Good Packet character
EDB	K30.7 (FEh)	011110 1000	100001 0111	Character used to mark the end of a 'nullified' TLP.

Table 11-5: Control Character Encoding and Definition

Character Name	8b Name	10b (CRD-)	10b (CRD+)	Description
FTS	K28.1 (3Ch)	001111 1001	110000 0110	Used in FTS Ordered-Set. This Ordered-Set used to exit from L0s low power state to L0
IDL	K28.3 (7Ch)	001111 0011	110000 1100	Used in Electrical Idle Ordered-Set. This Ordered-Set used to place Link in Electrical Idle state

Ordered-Sets

General. Ordered-Sets are Physical Layer Packets (PLPs) consisting of a series of characters starting with the COM character and consisting a total of four characters. When transmitted, they are transmitted on all Lanes. Ordered-Sets are used for special functions such as:

- Link Training. See "Link Training and Initialization" on page 403 for a detailed description.
- Clock Tolerance Compensation. See "Inserting Clock Compensation Zones" on page 436 and "Receiver Clock Compensation Logic" on page 442.
- Placing the Link into the low power L0s state (also referred to as the Electrical Idle Link state).
- Changing the Link state from the low power L0s state (also referred to as Electrical Idle state) to the full-on L0 state.

The PCI Express specification defines five Ordered-Sets:

- Training Sequence 1 (TS1),
- Training Sequence 2 (TS2),
- SKIP,
- Fast Training Sequence (FTS)
- and Electrical IDLE Ordered-Sets.

A brief description of each Ordered-Set follows.

TS1 and TS2 Ordered-Sets. These two Ordered-Sets are used during Link training. They are transmitted by a port's transmitter to the other port's receiver, where they are used to achieve bit and symbol lock. They are also used by the ports at opposite ends of a Link to number their Links and Lanes. These Ordered-Sets are used during Link speed and width negotiation.

SKIP Ordered-Set. In a multi-lane implementation, the SKIP Ordered-Set is periodically transmitted on all Lanes to allow the receiver clock tolerance compensation logic to compensate for clock frequency variations between the clock used by the transmitting device to clock out the serial bit stream and the receiver device's local clock. The receiver adds a SKP symbol to a SKIP Ordered-Set in the receiver elastic buffer to prevent a potential buffer underflow condition from occurring due to the transmitter clock being slower than the local receiver clock. Alternately, the receiver deletes a SKP symbol from the SKIP Ordered-Set in the receiver elastic buffer to prevent a potential buffer overflow condition from occurring due to the transmitter clock being faster than the local receiver clock. For a detailed description, refer to "Inserting Clock Compensation Zones" on page 436 and "Receiver Clock Compensation Logic" on page 442.

Electrical Idle Ordered-Set. A transmitter device that wishes to place the Link in the Electrical Idle state (aka the L0s low power state) transmits this Ordered-Set to a receiver. Upon receipt, the differential receivers prepare for this low power state during which the transmitter driver can be in the low- or high-impedance state and packet transmission stops. The differential receiver remains in the low-impedance state while in this state.

FTS Ordered-Set. FTS Ordered-Sets are transmitted by a device to transition a Link from the low power L0s state back to the full-on L0 state. The receiver detects the FTS Ordered-Set and uses it to achieve bit and symbol lock as well as to re-synchronize its receiver PLL to the transmitter clock used to transmit the serial bit stream. See the Link Training and Power Management chapters for more details on FTS Ordered-Set usage.

Parallel-to-Serial Converter (Serializer)

The 8b/10b Encoder on each Lane feeds the Parallel-to-Serial converter associated with that Lane. The Parallel-to-Serial converter clocks 10-bit symbols out in the bit order 'abcdeifghj', with the least significant bit (a) shifted out first and the most significant bit (j) shifted out last (as shown in Figure 11-16 on page 425). The symbols supplied by the 8b/10b Encoder are clocked into the converter at 250MHz. The serial bit stream is clocked out of the Parallel-to-Serial converter at 2.5GHz.

Differential Transmit Driver

The differential driver that actually drives the serialized bit stream onto the wire (or fiber) uses NRZ encoding and drives the serial bit stream at the 2.5Gbit/s transfer rate. The differential driver output per Lane consists of two signals (D+ and D-). A logical one is signaled by driving the D+ signal high and the D- signal low, thus creating a positive voltage difference between the D+ and D- signals. A logical zero is signaled by driving the D+ signal low and the D- signal high, thus creating a negative voltage difference between the D+ and D- signals.

Differential peak-to-peak voltage driven by the transmitter is between 800mV (min.) and 1200mV (max).

- Logical 1 is signalled with a positive differential voltage.
- Logical 0 is signalled with a negative differential voltage.

During the Link's electrical Idle state, the transmitter drives a differential peak voltage between 0mV and 20mV (the transmitter may be in the low- or high-impedance state).

Details regarding the electrical characteristics of the driver are discussed in "Transmitter Driver Characteristics" on page 477

Transmit (Tx) Clock

The serial output of the Parallel-to-Serial converter on each Lane is clocked out to the differential driver by the Tx Clock signal (see Figure 11-16 on page 425). Tx clock frequency is 2.5GHz and it must be accurate to +/–300ppm from a center frequency of 2.5GHz (or 600ppm total). The clock can skew by one clock every 1666 clock cycles. Note that this Tx Clock is different from the local clock of the Physical Layer which is a much slower clock. The Physical Layer receives a clock from an external source. PCI Express devices on peripheral cards as well as system boards may use a 100MHz clock supplied by the system board. This clock is multiplied by a factor with the aid of a PLL internal to the Physical Layer. The resultant local clock, which runs at a much slower frequency than 2.5GHz, clocks Physical Layer logic such as the Byte Striping logic, the Scrambler, the 8b/10b Encoder, the buffers, etc. The PLL also produces the 2.5GHz Tx clock used to feed the Parallel-to-Serial converters.

Other Miscellaneous Transmit Logic Topics

Logical Idle Sequence

In order to keep the receiver's PLL sync'd up (i.e., to keep it from drifting), something must be transmitted during periods when there are no TLPs, DLLPs or PLPs to transmit. The logical Idle sequence is transmitted during these times. The Idle sequence is gated to the Mux as described in the section "Multiplexer (Mux) and Mux Control Logic" on page 404. Some properties of the Logical Idle sequence are:

- The logical Idle sequence consists of the 8-bit Data character with a value of 00h.
- When transmitted, it is simultaneously transmitted on all Lanes. The Link is said to be in the logical Idle state (not to be confused with electrical Idle—the state when the Link is not driven and there are no packet transmissions and the receiver PLL loses synchronization).
- The logical Idle sequence is scrambled. This implies that, on the Link, the logical Idle sequence has a pseudo-random value. A receiver can distinguish the logical Idle sequence from other packet transmissions because it occurs outside the packet framing context (i.e., the logical Idle sequence occurs after an END or EDB Control symbol, but before an STP or SDP Control symbol).
- The logical Idle Sequence is 8b/10b encoded.
- During Logical Idle sequence transmission, SKIP Ordered-Sets are also transmitted periodically.

Inserting Clock Compensation Zones

Background. When the receiver logic receives a symbol stream, it sometimes needs to add or remove a symbol from the received symbol stream to compensate for transmitter verses receiver clock frequency variations (for background, refer to "Receiver Clock Compensation Logic" on page 442).

It should be obvious that the receiver logic can't arbitrarily pick a symbol to add or delete. This means that, on a periodic basis, the transmit logic must transmit a special Control character sequence that can be used for this purpose. This sequence is referred to as the SKIP Ordered-Set (see Figure 11-19) which consists of a COM character followed by three SKP characters.

SKIP Ordered-Set Insertion Rules. A transmitter is required to transmit SKIP Ordered-Sets on a periodic basis. The following rules apply:

- The set must be scheduled for insertion at most once every 1180 symbol clocks (i.e., symbol times) and at least once every 1538 symbol clocks.
- When it's time to insert a SKIP Ordered-Set, it is inserted at the next packet boundary (not in the middle of a packet). SKIP Ordered-Sets are inserted between packets simultaneously on all Lanes. If a long packet transmission is already in progress, the SKIP Ordered-Sets are accumulated and then inserted consecutively at the next packet boundary.
- In a multi-Lane environment, the SKIP Ordered-Set must be transmitted on all Lanes simultaneously (see Figure 11-11 on page 414 and Figure 11-12 on page 415). When necessary, the Link is padded so as to allow all the transmission of the SKIP Ordered-Sets to start on the same clock (see Figure 11-12 on page 415).
- During all lower power Link states, any counter(s) used to schedule SKIP Ordered-Sets must be reset.
- SKIP Ordered-Sets must not be transmitted while the Compliance Pattern is in progress.

Figure 11-19: SKIP Ordered-Set

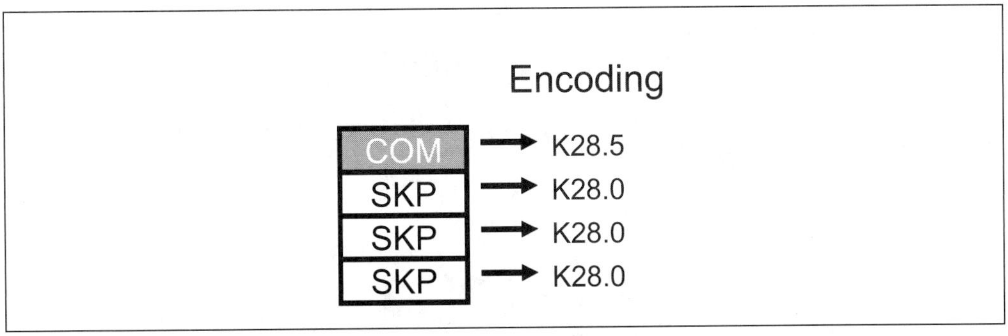

Receive Logic Details

Figure 11-20 shows the receiver logic of the Logical Physical Layer. This section describes packet processing from the time the data is received serially on each Lane until the packet byte stream is clocked to the Data Link Layer.

Figure 11-20: Physical Layer Receive Logic Details

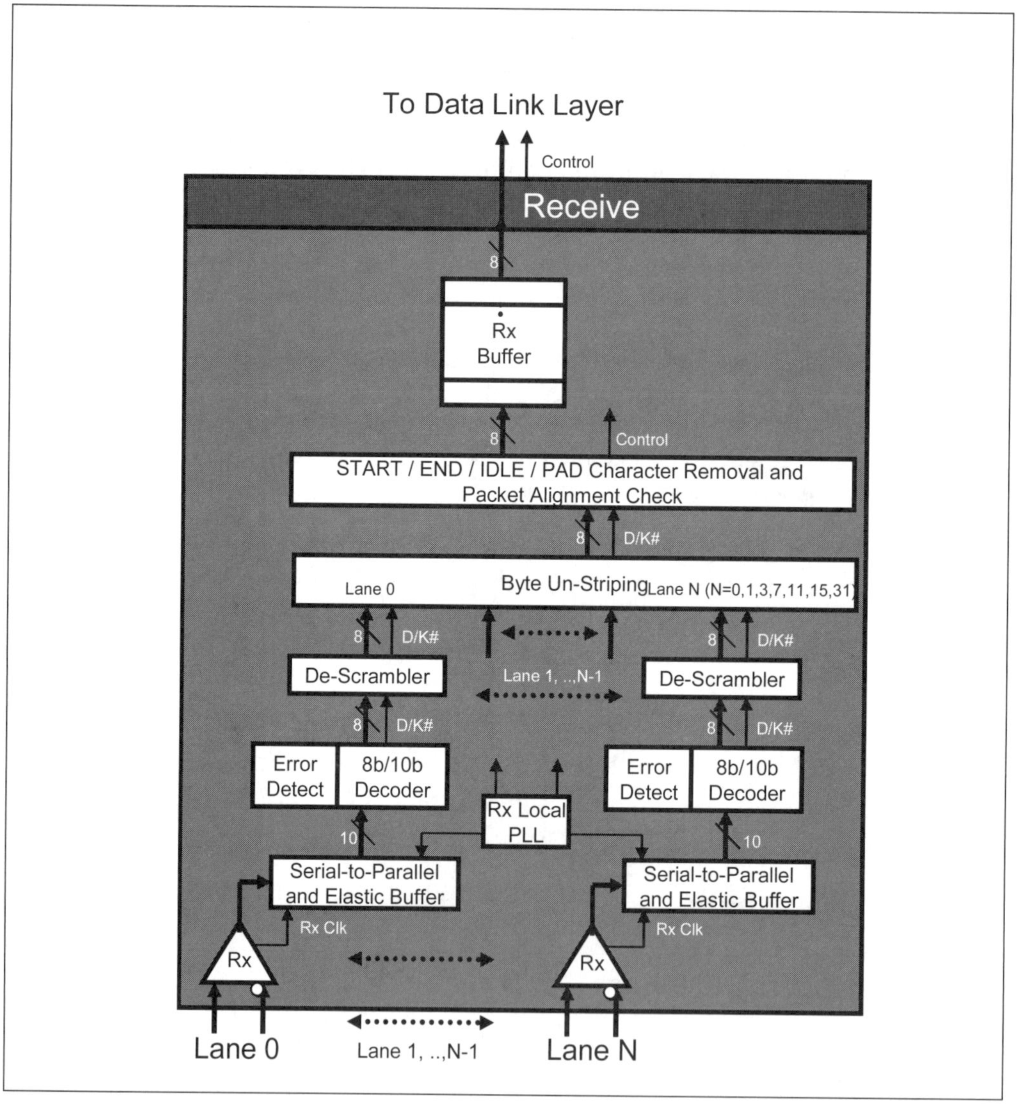

Figure 11-21 illustrates the receiver logic's front end on each Lane. This is comprised of:

- The differential receiver.
- The Rx Clock recovery logic.
- The COM symbol and Ordered-Set detector.
- The Serial-to-Parallel converter (Deserializer).
- The Lane-to-Lane De-Skew logic (delay circuit).
- The Elastic Buffer and Clock Tolerance Compensation logic.

Figure 11-21: Receiver Logic's Front End Per Lane

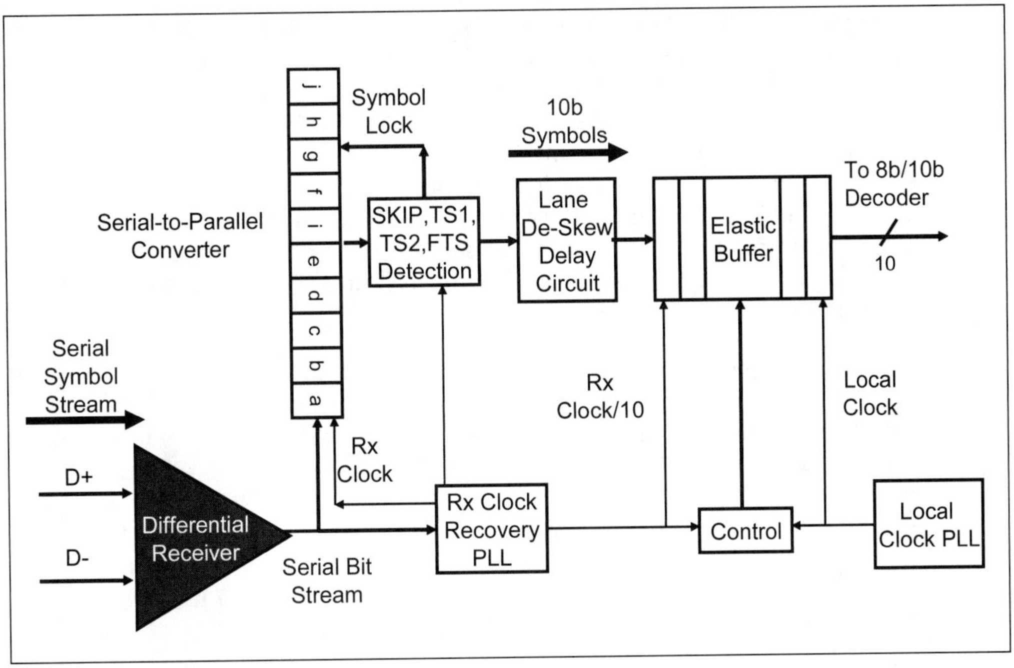

Differential Receiver

Refer to Figure 11-21. The differential receiver on each Lane senses differential peak-to-peak voltage differences > 175 mV but < 1200 mV:

- + difference = Logical 1.
- – difference = Logical 0.

A signal peak-to-peak difference < 65 mV is considered a signal absent condition and the Link is in the electrical Idle state. During this time, the receiver degates its input to prevent the error circuit from detecting an error. A signal peak-to-peak differential voltage between 65mV and 175mV serves as noise guard band.

Rx Clock Recovery

General

Using a PLL (Phase-Locked Loop), the receiver circuit generates the Rx Clock from the data bit transitions in the input data stream. This recovered clock has the same frequency (2.5GHz) as that of the Tx Clock used by the transmitting device to clock the data bit stream onto the wire (or fiber). The Rx Clock is used to clock the inbound serial symbol stream into the Serial-to-Parallel converter (Deserializer). The 10-bit symbol stream produced by the Deserializer is clocked into the elastic buffer with a divide by 10 version of the Rx Clock. The Rx Clock is different from the Local Clock that is used to clock symbols out of the Elastic Buffer to the 10b/8b decoder. The Local Clock must be accurate to within +/– 300ppm from center frequency.

Achieving Bit Lock

Recollect that the inbound serial symbol stream is guaranteed to have frequent 1-to-0 and 0-to-1 transitions due to the 8b/10b encoding scheme. A transition is guaranteed at least every 5 bit-times. The receiver PLL uses the transitions in the received bit-stream to synchronize the Rx Clock with the Tx Clock that was used at the transmitter to clock out the serialized bit stream. When the receiver PLL locks on to the Tx Clock frequency, the receiver is said to have achieved **"Bit Lock"**.

During Link training, the transmitter device sends a long series of back-to-back TS1 and TS2 Ordered-Sets to the receiver and the receiver uses the bit transitions in these Ordered-Sets to achieve Bit Lock. Once the Link is in the full-on L0 state, transitions on the Link occur on a regular basis and the receiver PLL is able to maintain Bit Lock.

Losing Bit Lock

If the Link is put in a low power state (such as L0s) where packet transmission ceases, the receiver's PLL gradually loses synchronization. The transmitter sends an electrical Idle Ordered-Set to tell the receiver to de-gate its input to prevent the error circuit from detecting an error.

Regaining Bit Lock

When the Link is in the L0s state, the transmitter sends a few FTS Ordered-sets (on the order of four FTSs) to the receiver and the receiver uses these to regain Bit Lock. Only a few FTSs are needed by the receiver in order to achieve Bit Lock (thus the wake up latency is of short duration). Because the Link is in the L0s state for a short time, the receiver PLL does not completely lose synchronization with the Tx Clock before it receives the FTSs.

Serial-to-Parallel converter (Deserializer)

The incoming serial data on each Lane is clocked into that Lane's Deserializer (the serial-to-parallel converter) by the Rx clock (see Figure 11-21 on page 439). The 10-bit symbols produced are clocked into an Elastic Buffer using a divide-by-10 version of the Rx Clock.

Symbol Boundary Sensing (Symbol Lock)

When the receive logic starts receiving a bit stream, it is JABOB (just a bunch of bits) with no markers to differentiate one symbol from another. The receive logic must have some way to determine the start and end of a 10-bit symbol. The Comma (COM) symbol serves this purpose.

The 10-bit encoding of the COM (K28.5) symbol contains two bits of one polarity followed by five bits of the opposite polarity (0011111010b or 1100000101b). Unless an error occurs, no other character has this property, thereby making it easily detectable. Recollect that the COM Control character, like all other Control characters, is not scrambled by the transmitter. This makes the COM easily detectable by the COM detector which looks for two consecutive 0s or two consecutive 1s followed by a string of five 1s or five 0s, respectively. Upon detection of the COM symbol, the COM Detector knows that the next bit received after the COM symbol is the first bit of a valid 10-bit symbol. The Deserializer is then initialized so that it can henceforth generate valid 10-bit symbols. The Deserializer is said to achieve **'Symbol Lock'**.

The COM symbol is utilized to achieve Symbol Lock under the following circumstances:

- During Link training when the Link is first established, TS1 and TS2 Ordered-Sets are transmitted (and each set begins with a COM symbol).
- During Link retraining initiated due to a problem on the Link, TS1 and TS2 Ordered-Sets are transmitted (and each set begins with a COM symbol).
- FTS Ordered-Sets are sent by a transmitter to inform the receiver to regain Bit Lock and Symbol Lock and change the state of the Link from L0s to L0.

Receiver Clock Compensation Logic

Background

Consider a transmitter at one end of a Link and the receiver at the opposite end. The transmit clock accuracy must be 2.5GHz +/– 300 ppm (parts per million). Once the Link is trained, the receive clock (Rx Clock) in the receiver is the same as the transmit clock (Tx Clock) at the other end of the Link (because the receive clock is derived from the bit stream that was transmitted at the remote end's transmit clock frequency). If the transmitter's Tx Clock at one end of the Link operates at +300 ppm and the Local Clock (shown in Figure 11-21 on page 439—not the Rx Clock) at the receiver at the other end operates at –300 ppm, this results in a worst-case 600 ppm difference between the two clocks.

In this scenario, the transmitter at one end of the Link is operating at 2.5GHz +300 ppm, while the receiver's local clock is operating at a frequency of 2.5GHz – 300ppm. The Tx Clock of the transmitter and Local Clock of the receiver can therefore shift one clock every 1666 clocks.

The Elastic Buffer's Role in the Receiver

It is a common design practice to clock most of the receive path logic using the Physical Layer's local clock. To compensate for the frequency difference between the Rx Clock (which is derived from the remote port's transmit frequency) and the Local Clock (which is derived from the local port's transmit frequency), an elastic buffer (see Figure 11-21 on page 439) is incorporated in the very early stages of the receive path.

Symbols arrive at the differential receiver as a bit stream and are presented to the Deserializer. The receive PLL recovers the clock (Rx Clock) embedded in the bit stream and the Deserializer converts the incoming bit stream into a series of 10-bit symbols. The symbols are clocked into the input side of the Elastic Buffer using the Rx Clock recovered from the incoming bit stream and are clocked out of the buffer using the receiver's local clock. As previously cited, these two clocks can be as much as 600ppm out of sync with each other.

The Elastic Buffer compensates for the difference between the two clocks by either deleting a SKP symbol from or inserting a SKP symbol into the symbols contained in the Elastic Buffer:

- If the transmit clock frequency is greater than the receive clock frequency by up to 600ppm, a SKP symbol is deleted from the buffer.
- If the transmit clock frequency is less than the receive clock frequency by up to 600ppm, a SKP symbol is added to the buffer.

The transmitter on the other end periodically transmits a special symbol sequence called the SKIP Ordered-Set (see Figure 11-19 on page 437 and "Inserting Clock Compensation Zones" on page 436) from which the "don't care" SKP symbol can be deleted or to which a "don't care" SKP symbol can be added. The SKIP Ordered-Set consists of four control symbols (a COM and three SKPs; the Skips are the "don't care" characters, hence the name "Skip"). Deleting or adding a SKP symbol to the SKIP Ordered-Set in the Elastic Buffer prevents a buffer overflow or underflow condition, respectively.

Loss of symbol(s) caused by Elastic Buffer overflow or underflow triggers a Receiver Error indication to the Data Link Layer and results in the automatic initiation of Link error recovery.

The transmitter schedules a SKIP Ordered-Set transmission once every 1180 to 1538 symbol times. However, if the transmitter starts a maximum sized TLP transmission right at the 1538 symbol time boundary when a SKIP Ordered-Set is scheduled to be transmitted, the SKIP Ordered-Set transmission is deferred. Receivers must be tolerant to receive and process SKIP Ordered-Sets that have a maximum separation dependent on the maximum packet payload size a device supports. The formula for the maximum number of Symbols (n) between SKIP Ordered-Sets is:

$n = 1538 + (\text{maximum packet payload size} + 28)$

28 is the number of symbols associated with the header (16 bytes), the optional ECRC (4 bytes), the LCRC (4 bytes), the sequence number (2 bytes) and framing symbols STP and END (2 bytes).

Lane-to-Lane De-Skew

Not a Problem on a Single-Lane Link

The problem of Lane-to-Lane skew is obviously only an issue on multi-Lane Links.

Flight Time Varies from Lane-to-Lane

Symbols are transmitted simultaneously on all Lanes using the same transmit clock, but they cannot be expected to arrive at the receiver at the same time (i.e., without Lane-to-Lane skew). A multi-Lane Link may have many sources of Lane-to-Lane skew. These sources include but are not limited to:

- Chip differential drivers and receivers.
- Printed wiring board impedance variations.
- Lane wire length miss-matches.
- Delays injected by the serialization and de-serialization logic.

When the byte-striped serial bit streams associated with a packet arrive on all Lanes at the receiver, it must remove this Lane-to-Lane skew in order to receive and process the data correctly. This process is referred to as Link deskew. Receivers use TS1 or TS2 Ordered-Sets during Link training or FTS Ordered-Sets during L0s exit to perform Link de-skew functions.

If Lane Data Is Not Aligned, Byte Unstriping Wouldn't Work

Havoc would ensue if the symbols transmitted on each Lane simultaneously were to arrive at each Lane receiver at different times and were then de-serialized and fed to the Byte Unstriping Logic. Gibberish would be fed to the Link Layer as packet data.

TS1/TS2 or FTS Ordered-Sets Used to De-Skew Link

The unique structure and length of the TS1/TS2 and FTS sets, and the fact that they are transmitted simultaneously on all Lanes, are used by the receiver's De-Skew logic to determine the amount of misalignment between Lanes. The specification doesn't define the method used to achieve multi-Lane alignment. As an example, the receiver logic could compensate for the misalignment by tuning an automatic delay circuit in each Lane's receiver (see Figure 11-21 on page 439 and Figure 11-22 on page 445).

The receiver must be capable of de-skewing up to 20ns of Lane-to-Lane skew as defined by the $L_{RX\text{-}SKEW}$ parameter shown in Table 12-2 on page 480.

De-Skew During Link Training, Retraining and L0s Exit

TS1 and TS2 Ordered-Sets are only transmitted during initial Link training or during Link retraining (i.e., recovery). FTS Ordered-Sets are transmitted during L0s exit. De-skew is therefore only performed by the receiver at those times and is not done on a periodic basis.

Lane-to-Lane De-Skew Capability of Receiver

The Lane-to-Lane de-skew parameter $L_{RX\text{-}SKEW}$ shown in Table 12-2 on page 480 requires that the receiver be capable of de-skewing Lane delays of up to 20ns. The transmitter is allowed to introduce a minimal Lane-to-Lane skew at the output pad defined by the $L_{TX\text{-}SKEW}$ parameter (see Table 12-1 on page 477) of 1.3ns.

Figure 11-22: Receiver's Link De-Skew Logic

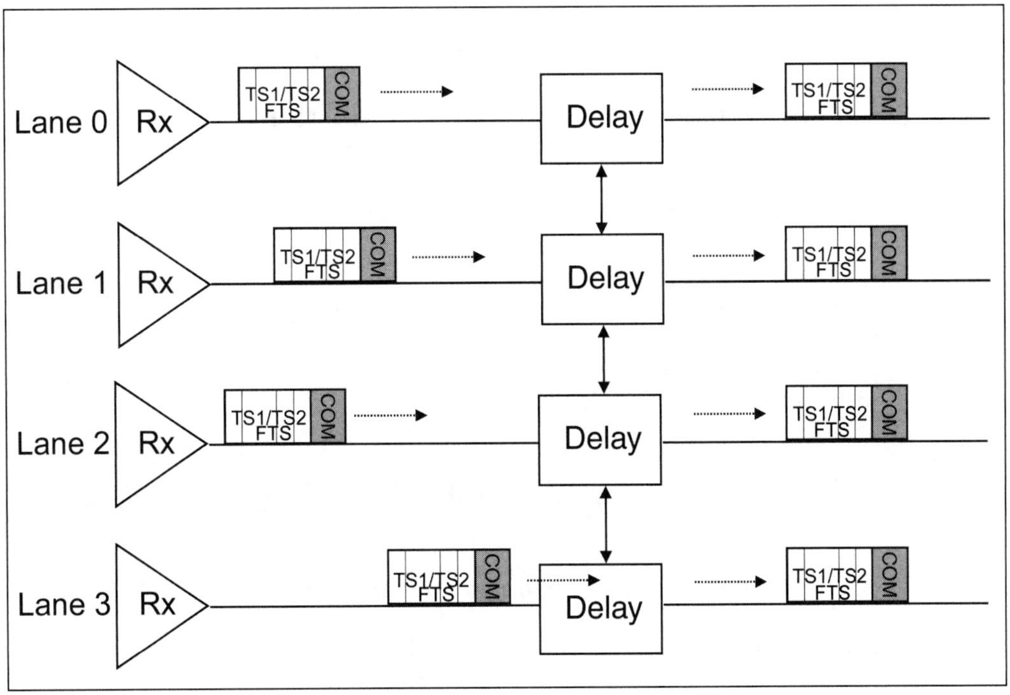

8b/10b Decoder

General

Refer to Figure 11-23 on page 447. Each receiver Lane incorporates a 10b/8b Decoder which is fed from the Elastic Buffer. The 8b/10b Decoder uses two lookup tables (the D and K tables) to decode the 10-bit symbol stream into 8-bit Data (D) or Control (K) characters plus the D/K# signal. The state of the D/K# signal indicates that the received symbol is:

- A Data (D) character if a match for the received symbol is discovered in the D table. D/K# is driven High.
- A Control (K) character if a match for the received symbol is discovered in the K table. D/K# is driven Low.

Disparity Calculator

The decoder determines the initial disparity value based on the disparity of the first symbol received. After the first symbol, once the disparity is initialized in the decoder, it expects the calculated disparity for each subsequent symbol received to toggle between + and - unless the symbol received has neutral disparity in which case the disparity remains the same value.

Code Violation and Disparity Error Detection

General. The error detection logic of the 8b/10b Decoder detects errors in the received symbol stream. It should be noted that it doesn't catch all possible transmission errors. The specification requires that these errors be detected and reported as a Receiver Error indication to the Data Link Layer. The two types of errors detected are:

- Code violation errors (i.e., a 10-bit symbol could not be decoded into a valid 8-bit Data or Control character).
- Disparity errors.

There is no automatic hardware error correction for these errors at the Physical Layer.

Code Violations. The following conditions represent code violations:

- Any 6-bit sub-block containing more than four 1s or four 0s is in error.
- Any 4-bit sub-block containing more than three 1s or three 0s is in error.

- Any 10-bit symbol containing more than six 1s or six 0s is in error.
- Any 10-bit symbol containing more than five consecutive 1s or five consecutive 0s is in error.
- Any 10-bit symbol that doesn't decode into an 8-bit character is in error.

Disparity Errors

A character that encodes into a 10-bit symbol with disparity other than neutral is encoded into a 10-bit symbol with polarity opposite to that of the CRD.

If the next symbol does not have neutral disparity and its disparity is the same as the CRD, a disparity error is detected.

- Some disparity errors may not be detectable until the subsequent symbol is processed (see Figure 11-24 on page 448).
- If two bits in a symbol flip in error, the error may not be detected (and the symbol may decode into a valid 8-bit character). The error goes undetected at the Physical Layer.

Figure 11-23: 8b/10b Decoder per Lane

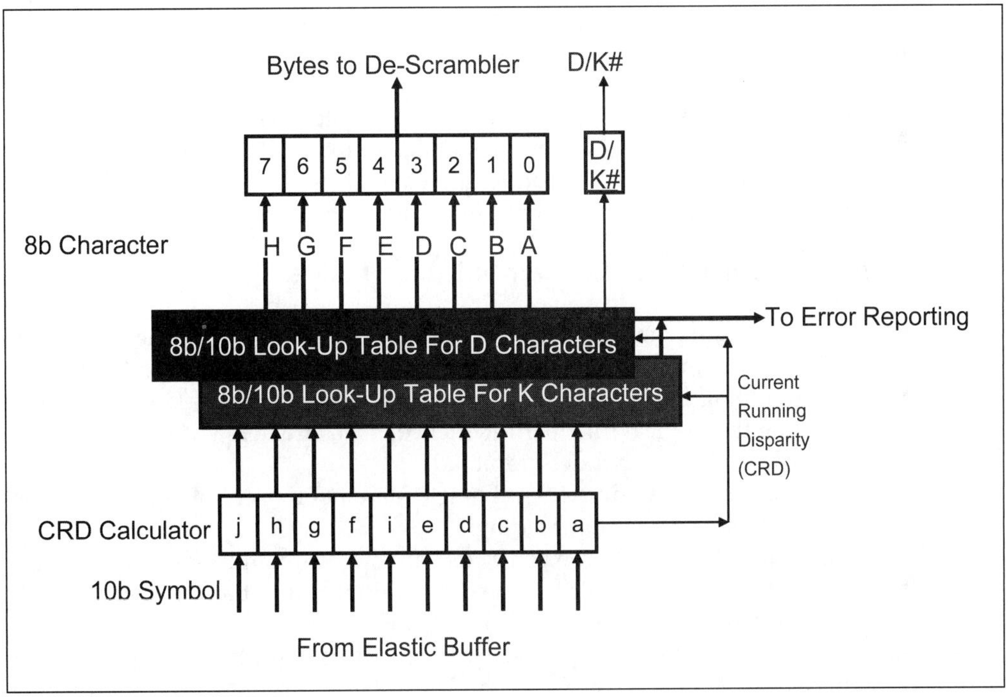

Figure 11-24: Example of Delayed Disparity Error Detection

	CRD	Character	CRD	Character	CRD	Character	CRD
Transmitted Character Stream	-	D21.1	-	D10.2	-	D23.5	+
Transmitted Bit Stream	-	101010 1001	-	010101 0101	-	111010 1010	+
Bit Stream After Error	-	101010 1011	+	010101 0101	+	111010 1010	+
Decoded Character Stream	-	D21.0	+	D10.2	+	Invalid	+

Error occurs here

Error detected here

De-Scrambler

The De-Scrambler is fed by the 8b/10b Decoder block. The De-Scrambler only de-scrambles Data (D) characters associated with a TLP or DLLP (D/K# is high). It does not de-scramble Control (K) characters or Ordered-Sets. K characters and Ordered-Sets sourced from the 8b/10b decoder are valid as is.

Some De-Scrambler Implementation Rules:

- On a multi-Lane Link, De-Scramblers associated with each Lane must operate in concert, maintaining the same simultaneous value in each LFSR.
- De-scrambling is applied to 'D' characters associated with TLP and DLLPs including the Logical Idle (00h) sequence. 'D' characters within the TS1 and TS2 Ordered-Set are not de-scrambled.
- 'K' characters and Ordered-Set characters are not de-scrambled. These characters bypass the de-scrambler logic.
- Compliance Pattern related characters are not de-scrambled.
- When a COM character enters the De- Scrambler, it initializes the LFSR. The initialized value of the 16-bit LFSR is FFFFh.
- With one exception, the LFSR serially advances eight times for every character (D or K character) received. The LFSR does NOT advance on SKP characters associated with the SKIP Ordered-Sets received. The reason the

LFSR is not advanced on detecting SKPs is because there may be a difference between the number of SKP characters transmitted and the SKP characters exiting the Elastic Buffer (as discussed in "Receiver Clock Compensation Logic" on page 442).

- By default, the De-Scrambler is always enabled. The specification does allow the De-Scrambler to be disabled for test and debug purposes. However the specification does not provide a standard software method or configuration register-related method for disabling the De-Scrambler.

Disabling De-Scrambling

If the receiver De-Scrambler receives at least two TS1/TS2 Ordered-Sets with the disable scrambling bit set from the remote device on all of its configured Lanes, it disables its De-Scrambler.

Byte Un-Striping

Figure 11-25 on page 449 illustrates an example of eight decoded 8-bit character streams from the eight De-Scramblers of a x8 Link being un-striped into a single byte stream which is fed to the Filter logic (see the next section).

Figure 11-25: Example of x8 Byte Un-Striping

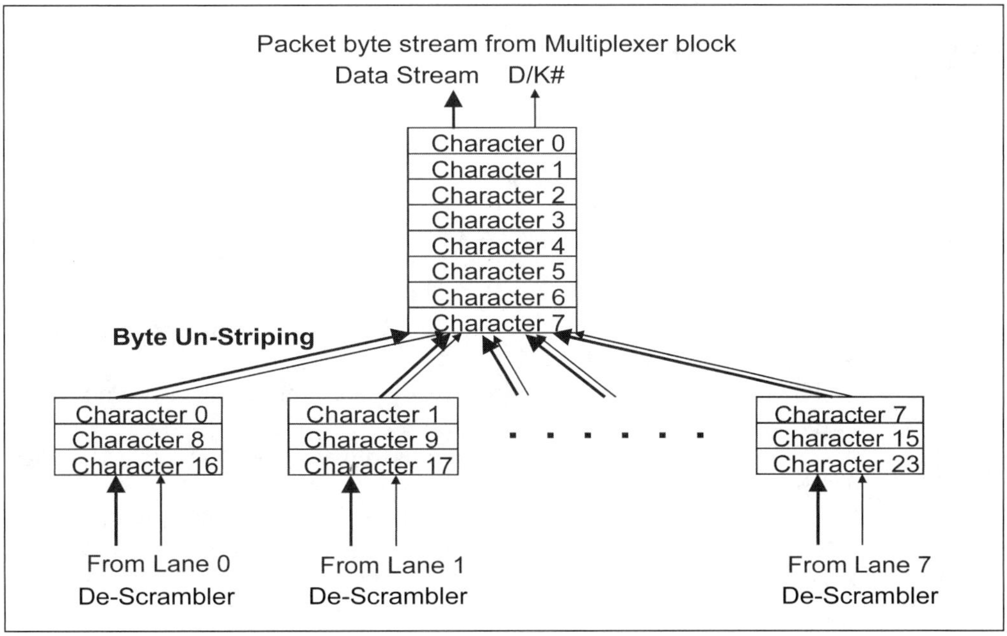

Filter and Packet Alignment Check

The serial byte stream supplied by the byte un-striping logic contains TLPs, DLLPs, Logical Idle sequences, Control characters such as STP, SDP, END, EDB, and PADs, as well as the types of Ordered-Sets. Of these characters, the Logical Idle sequence, the control characters and Ordered-Sets are detected and eliminated. What remains are TLPs and DLLPs which are sent to the Rx Buffer along with boundary characters indicating the start and end of each TLP and DLLP.

Receive Buffer (Rx Buffer)

The Rx Buffer holds received TLPs and DLLPs after the start and end characters have been eliminated. The received packets are ready to send to the Data Link Layer.

The interface between the Physical Layer and Data Link Layer is unspecified. Hence, the designer is free to decide what data bus width interface to implement. As an example, we can assume the interface clock to be 250MHz. In that case, the width of the data bus connecting the Data Link Layer to the Physical Layer interface can = the number of Lanes supported by the device x eight bits.

Physical Layer Error Handling

When the Physical Layer logic detects an error, it sends a Receiver Error indication to the Data Link Layer. The specification lists a few of these errors, but it is far from being an exhaustive error list. It is up to the designer to determine what Physical Layer errors to detect and report.

Some of these errors include:

- 8b/10b Decoder-related disparity errors (described in "Disparity Errors" on page 447). This check is required.
- 8b/10b Decoder-related code violation errors (described in "Code Violations" on page 446). This check is required.
- Elastic Buffer overflow or underflow caused by loss of symbol(s) (described in "The Elastic Buffer's Role in the Receiver" on page 442).
- The packet received is not consistent with the packet format rules described in "General Packet Format Rules" on page 411. This condition is optionally checked.

- Loss of Symbol Lock (see "Symbol Boundary Sensing (Symbol Lock)" on page 441).
- Loss of Lane-to-Lane de-skew (see "Lane-to-Lane De-Skew" on page 444).

Response of Data Link Layer to 'Receiver Error' Indication

If the Physical Layer indicates a Receiver Error to the Data Link Layer, the Data Link Layer discards the TLP currently being received and frees any storage allocated for the TLP. The Data Link Layer schedules a NAK DLLP for transmission back to the transmitter of the TLP. Doing so automatically causes the transmitter device to replay TLPs from the Replay Buffer, resulting in possible auto-correction of the error. The Data Link Layer may also direct the Physical Layer to initiate Link re-training (i.e., link recovery).

Detected Link errors may also result in the Physical Layer initiating the Link retraining (recovery) process.

In addition, the device that detects a Receiver Error sets the Receiver Error Status bit in the Correctable Error Status register (see Figure 24-20 on page 936) of the PCI Express Extended Advanced Error Capabilities register set. If enabled to do so, the device sends an ERR_COR (correctable error) message to the Root Complex (See "Advanced Uncorrectable Error Handling" on page 386 for details on error logging and reporting).

12 Electrical Physical Layer

The Previous Chapter

The previous chapter described:

- The logical Physical Layer core logic and how an outbound packet is processed before clocking the packet out differentially.
- How an inbound packet arriving from the Link is processed and sent to the Data Link Layer.
- Sub-block functions of the Physical Layer such as Byte Striping and unstriping logic, Scrambler and De-Scrambler, 8b/10b Encoder and decoder, Elastic Buffers and more.

This Chapter

This chapter describes the Physical Layer's electrical interface to the link. It describes the analog characteristics of the differential drivers and receivers that connect a PCI Express device to the Link. Timing and driver/receiver parameters are documented here.

The Next Chapter

The next chapter describes the three types of reset, namely: cold reset, warm reset and hot reset. It also describes the usage of a side-band reset signal called PERST#. The effect of reset on devices and the system is described.

Electrical Physical Layer Overview

The electrical sub-block associated with each lane (see Figure 12-1 on page 454) provides the physical interface to the Link. This sub-block contains differential drivers (transmitters) and differential receivers (receivers). The transmitter serializes outbound symbols on each Lane and converts the bit stream to electrical signals that have an embedded clock. The receiver detects electrical signaling on each Lane and generates a serial bit stream that it de-serializes into symbols, and supplies the symbol stream to the logical Physical Layer along with the clock recovered from the inbound serial bit stream.

In the future, this sub-block could be redesigned to support a cable interface or an optical (i.e., fiber) interface.

In addition, the electrical Physical Layer contains a Phase Lock Loop (PLL) that drives the Serializer in the transmitter and a receiver PLL that is sync'd to the transitions in the incoming serial symbol stream.

Figure 12-1: Electrical Sub-Block of the Physical Layer

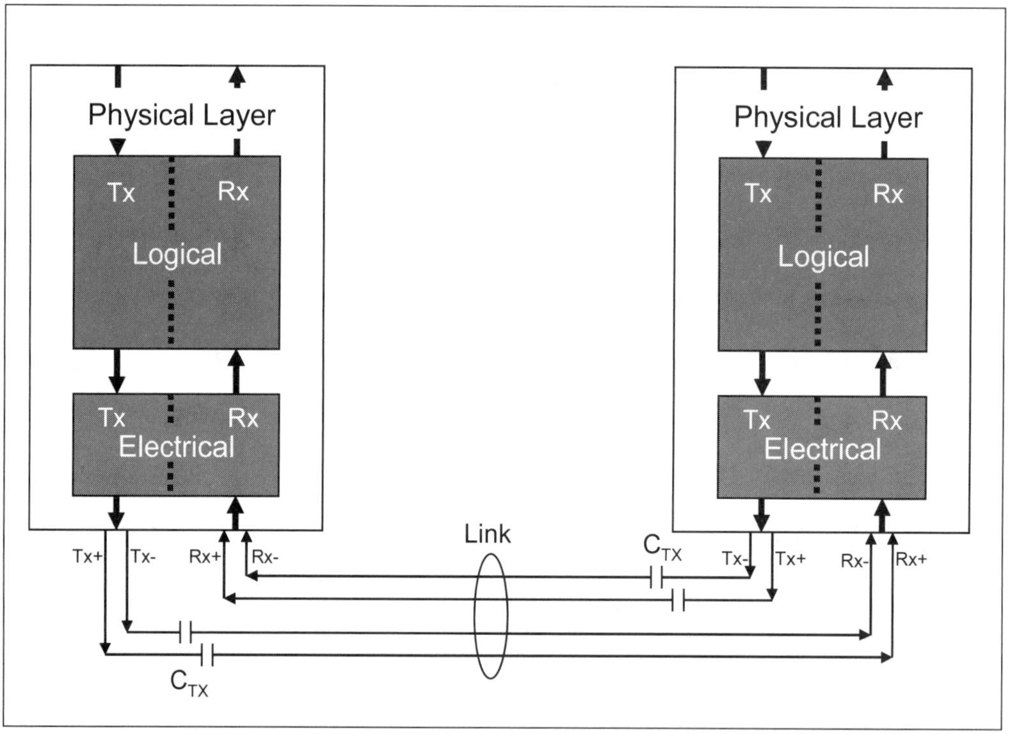

When the Link is in the L0 full-on state, the differential drivers drive the differential voltage associated with a logical 1 and logical 0 while driving the correct DC common mode voltage. The receivers sense differential voltages that indicate a logical 1 or 0 and, inaddition, can sense the electrical idle state of the Link. An eye diagram clearly illustrates the electrical characteristics of a driver and receiver and addresses signaling voltage levels, skew and jitter issues.

The electrical Physical Layer is responsible for placing the differential drivers, differential receivers, and the Link in the correct state when the Link is placed in a low power state such as L0s, L1, or L2. While in the L2 low power state, a device can signal a wake-up event upstream via a Beacon signaling mechanism.

The differential drivers support signal de-emphasis (or pre-emphasis; see "De-Emphasis (or Pre-Emphasis)" on page 466) to help reduce the bit error rate (BER)—especially on a lossy Link.

The drivers and receivers are short-circuit tolerant, making them ideally suited for hot insertion and removal events. The Link connecting two devices is AC coupled. A capacitor at the transmitter side of the Link DC de-couples it from the receiver. As a result, two devices at opposite ends of a Link can have their own ground and power planes. See Figure 12-1 on page 454 for the capacitor (C_{TX}) placement on the Link.

High Speed Electrical Signaling

Refer to Figure 12-2. High-speed LVDS (Low-Voltage Differential Signaling) electrical signaling is used in driver and receiver implementations. Drivers and receivers from different manufacturers must be inter-operable and may be designed to be hot-pluggable. A standard FR4 board can be used to route the Link wires. The following sections describe the electrical characteristics of the driver, receiver, and the Link represented in the Figure.

Figure 12-2: Differential Transmitter/Receiver

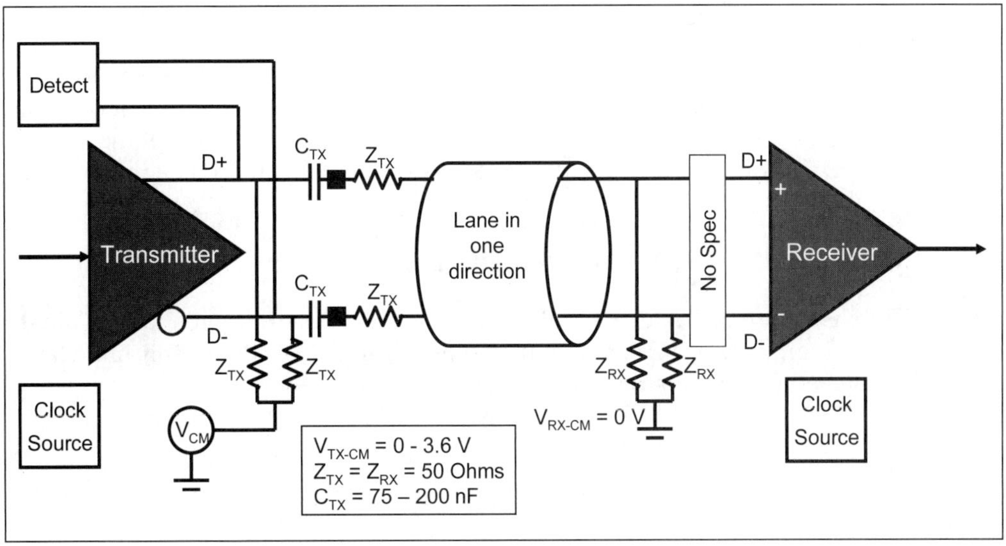

Clock Requirements

General

The transmitter clocks data out at 2.5Gbits/s. The clock used to do so must be accurate to +/- 300 ppm of the center frequency. It is allowed to skew a maximum of 1 clock every 1666 clocks. The two devices at the opposite ends of a Link could have their transmit clocks out of phase by as much as 600 ppm.

A device may derive its clock from an external clock source. The system board supplies a 100 MHz clock that is made available to devices on the system board as well as to add-in cards via the connector. With the aid of PLLs, a device may generate its required clocks from this 100 MHz clock.

Spread Spectrum Clocking (SSC)

Spread spectrum clocking is a technique used to modulate the clock frequency slowly so as to reduce EMI radiated noise at the center frequency of the clock. With SSC, the radiated energy does not produce a noise spike at 2.5GHz because the radiated energy is spread over a small frequency range around 2.5GHz.

SCC is not required by the specification. However, if supported, the following rules apply:

- The clock can be modulated by +0% to -0.5% from nominal a frequency of 2.5GHz.
- The modulation rate must be between 30KHz and 33KHz.
- The +/- 300 ppm requirement for clock frequency accuracy still holds. Further, the maximum of 600 ppm frequency variation between the two devices at opposite ends of a Link also remains true. This almost certainly imposes a requirement that the two devices at opposite ends of the Link be driven from the same clock source when the clock is modulated with SSC.

Impedance and Termination

The characteristic impedance of the Link is 100 Ohms differential (nominal), while single-ended DC common mode impedance is 50 Ohms. This impedance is matched to the transmitter and receiver impedances.

Transmitter Impedance Requirements

Transmitters must meet the $Z_{TX-DIFF-DC}$ (see Table 12-1 on page 477) parameters anytime differential signals are transmitted during the full-on L0 power state.

When a differential signal is not driven (e.g., in the lower power states), the transmitter may keep its output impedance at a minimum Z_{TX-DC} (see Table 12-1 on page 477) of 40 Ohms, but may also place the driver in a high impedance state. Placing a driver in the high impedance state may be helpful while in L0s or L1 low power states to help reduce power drain in these states.

Receiver Impedance Requirements

The receiver is required to meet the $Z_{RX-DIFF-DC}$ (see Table 12-2 on page 480) parameter of 100 Ohms anytime differential signals are transmitted during the full-on L0 power state, as well as in all other lower power states wherein adequate power is provided to the device. A receiver is excluded from this impedance requirement when the device is powered down (e.g., in the L2 and L3 power states and during Fundamental Reset).

When a receiver is powered down to the L2 or L3 state, or during Fundamental Reset, its receiver goes to the high impedance state and must meet the $Z_{RX-HIGH-IMP-DC}$ parameter of 200 KOhms minimum (see Table 12-2 on page 480).

DC Common Mode Voltages

Transmitter DC Common Mode Voltage

Once driven after power-on and during the Detect state of Link training, the transmitter DC common mode voltage $V_{TX-DC-CM}$ (see Table 12-1 on page 477) must remain at the same voltage. The common mode voltage is turned off only when the transmitter is placed in the L2 or L3 low power state, during which main power to the device is removed. A designer can choose any common mode voltage in the range of 0V to 3.6V.

Receiver DC Common Mode Voltage

The receiver is DC de-coupled from the transmitter by a capacitor. This allows the receiver to have its own DC common mode voltage. This voltage is specified at 0V. The specification is unclear about the meaning of this 0V receiver DC common mode voltage requirement and does not require the common mode voltage to be 0V at the input to the receiver differential amplifier. Rather, a simple bias voltage network allows the receiver to operate at optimal common mode. See Figure 12-3 on page 458.

Figure 12-3: Receiver DC Common Mode Voltage Requirement

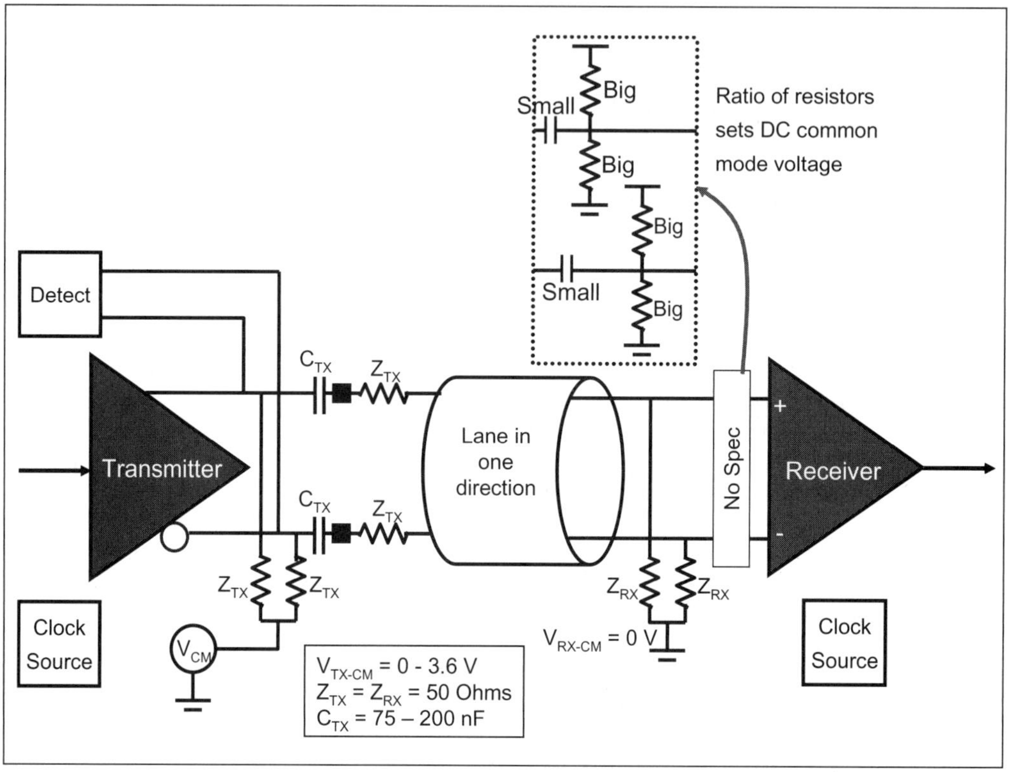

ESD and Short Circuit Requirements

All signals and power pins must withstand (without damage) a 2000V Electro-Static Discharge (ESD) using the human body model and 500V using the charged device model. For more details on this topic, see the JEDEC JESE22-A114-A specification.

The ESD requirement not only protects against electro-static damage, but facilitates support of surprise hot insertion and removal events. Transmitters and receivers are also required to be short-circuit tolerant. They must be able to withstand sustained short-circuit currents (on D+ or D- to ground) of $I_{TX\text{-}SHORT}$ (see Table 12-2 on page 480) in the order of 90mA (the maximum current a transmitter is required to provide).

Receiver Detection

General

The Detect block in the transmitter shown in Figure 12-2 on page 455 is required to detect the presence or absence of a receiver at the other end of the Link after coming out of reset or power-on. The Detect state of the Link Training state machine is responsible for making this determination.

Detection is accomplished when the transmitter changes the DC common mode voltage from one value to another. By design, the transmitter detect logic has knowledge of the rate at which the lines charge with or without a receiver.

With a Receiver Attached

With a receiver attached at the other end of the Link, the charge time (RC time constant) is relatively long due to the large coupling capacitor (C_{TX}). See the lower half of Figure 12-4 on page 460.

Time Constant to Charge ~= Z_{TX} * (C_{TX} + $C_{interconnect}$ + C_{pad}) => Large value

Without a Receiver Attached

Without a receiver attached at the other end of the Link, the charge time (RC time constant) is relatively short because the large coupling capacitor (C_{TX}) does NOT come into play. See the upper half of Figure 12-4 on page 460.

Time Constant to Charge ~= Z_{TX} * ($C_{interconnect}$ + C_{pad}) => Small value

Procedure To Detect Presence or Absence of Receiver

1. After reset or power-up, the transmitter drives a stable voltage on the D+ and D- terminals. This can be V_{DD} (3.6 V), Ground or any common mode voltage in-between V_{DD} and Ground.
2. Transmitter changes the common mode voltage:
   - If the initial common mode voltage is V_{DD}, then it drives the voltage towards Ground.
   - If the initial common mode voltage is Ground, then it drives the voltage towards V_{DD}.
   - If the initial common mode voltage is between V_{DD} and Ground, the transmitter drives the voltage in the opposite direction (the direction it must be driven to attain to the initial common mode voltage).

3. The transmitter detects the presence of a receiver by determining the charge time:
   — A Receiver is present if the charge time is long.
   — A Receiver is absent if the charge time is short.

Figure 12-4: Receiver Detection Mechanism

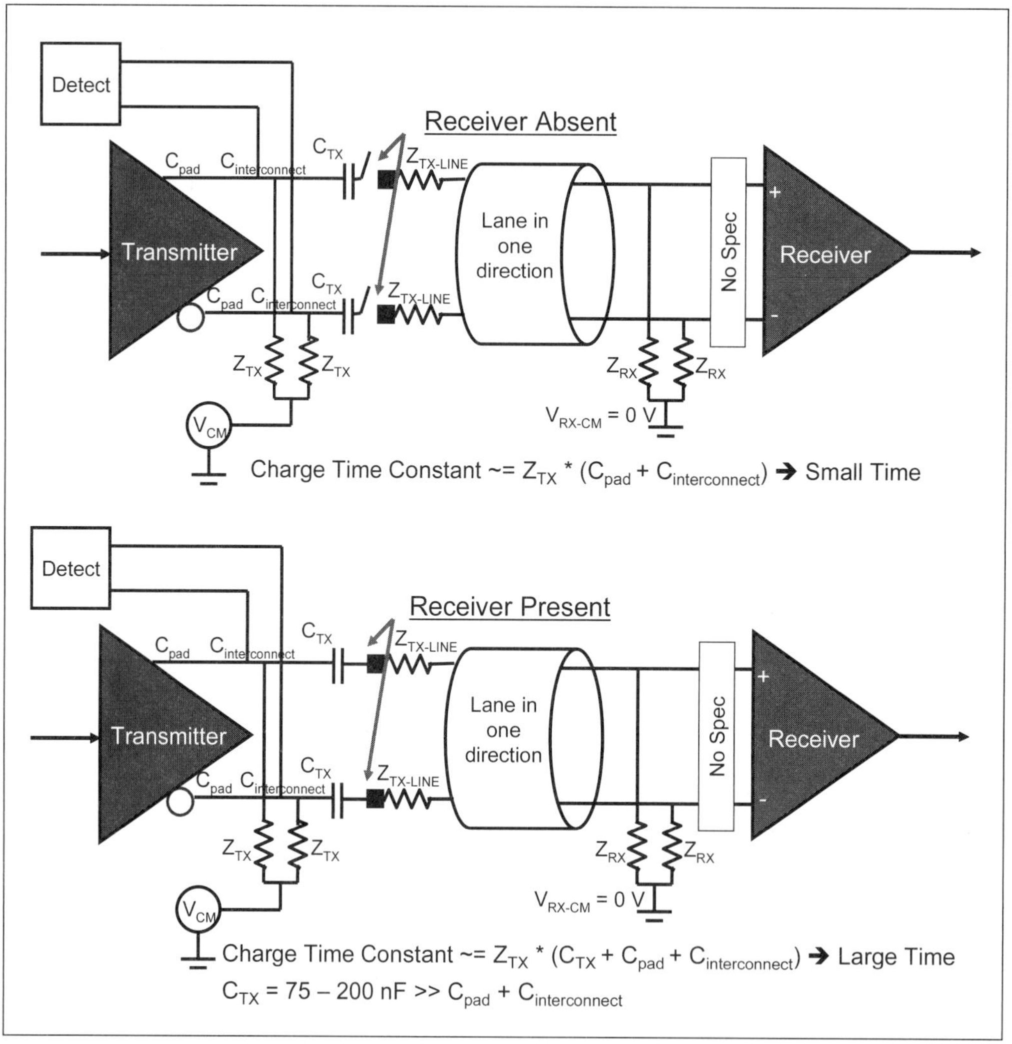

Differential Drivers and Receivers

Differential signaling (as opposed to the single-ended signaling employed in PCI and PCI-X) is ideal for high frequency signaling.

Advantages of Differential Signaling

Some of the advantages of differential signaling (versus single-ended signaling) are:

- Can achieve higher frequency transmission rate because the signal swing is smaller.
- Less EMI noise emitted due to noise cancellation of D+ signal emission with D- signal emission.
- Noise immunity, because any noise that couples into one signal will also couple into the other signal.
- Can signal three signal states: logical 1, logical 0 and electrical Idle.
- Smaller signal swing means less power consumption on the Link.

Differential Voltages

The differential driver uses NRZ encoding to drive the serial bit stream. The differential driver output consists of two signals, D+ and D-. A logical one is signaled by driving the D+ signal high and the D- signal low, creating a positive voltage difference between the D+ and D- signals. A logical Zero is signaled by driving the D+ signal low and the D- signal high, creating a negative voltage difference between the D+ and D- signals.

The differential peak-to-peak voltage driven by the transmitter $V_{TX\text{-}DIFFp\text{-}p}$ (see Table 12-1 on page 477) is between 800 mV (minimum) and 1200 mV (max).

- Logical 1 is signaled with a positive differential voltage.
- Logical 0 is signaled with a negative differential voltage.

During the Link electrical Idle state, the transmitter drives a differential peak voltage $V_{TX\text{-}IDLE\text{-}DIFFp}$ (see Table 12-1 on page 477) of between 0 mV and 20 mV. In this state, the transmitter may be in the low- or high-impedance state.

The receiver is able to sense a logical 1, a logical 0, as well as the electrical idle state of the Link by detecting the voltage on the Link via a differential receiver amplifier. Due to signal loss along the Link at high frequency, the receiver must be designed to sense an attenuated version of the differential signal driven by the transmitter. The receiver sensitivity is defined by the differential peak-to-peak voltage $V_{RX\text{-}DIFFp\text{-}p}$ (see Table 12-2 on page 480) of between 175 mV and 1200 mV.

Differential Voltage Notation

General. A differential signal voltage is defined by taking the difference in the voltage on the two conductors, D+ and D-. The voltage with respect to ground on each conductor is V_{D+} and V_{D-}. The differential voltage is $V_{DIFF} = V_{D+} - V_{D-}$. The Common Mode voltage, V_{CM}, is defined as the mean voltage of D+ and D-. $V_{CM} = (V_{D+} + V_{D-}) / 2$.

In defining differential voltages, the specification uses two parameters: 1) The differential peak-to-peak voltage, and 2) the Differential peak voltage. These voltages are defined by the following equations and are illustrated in Figure 12-5 on page 463.

- Differential Peak Voltage => $V_{DIFFp} = (\max |V_{D+} - V_{D-}|)$. Assume symmetric signal swing.
- Differential Peak-to-Peak Voltage => $V_{DIFFp\text{-}p} = (2 * \max |V_{D+} - V_{D-}|)$. Assume symmetric signal swing.
- Peak Common Mode Voltage => $V_{CMp} = (\max |V_{D+} + V_{D-}| / 2)$.

Differential Peak Voltage. The differential peak voltage is easily represented in a diagram as the differential voltage associated with signaling a logical 1 or logical 0.

Differential Peak-to-Peak Voltage. The differential peak-to-peak voltage is not easily represented in a diagram. One can think of the differential peak-to-peak voltage as the sum total of the differential voltage for signaling a logical 1 and for signaling a logical 0. One can think of this voltage as the total voltage swing a receiver experiences between receiving a logical 1 and receiving a logical 0.

Common Mode Voltage. The common mode voltage is the center voltage with respect to ground when the D+ and D- signals cross-over one another, assuming these two signals are symmetric. When a differential driver does not drive a differential voltage, it drives a common mode voltage with both D+ and D- signals at the same voltage (the signals do not swing).

Figure 12-5: Pictorial Representation of Differential Peak-to-Peak and Differential Peak Voltages

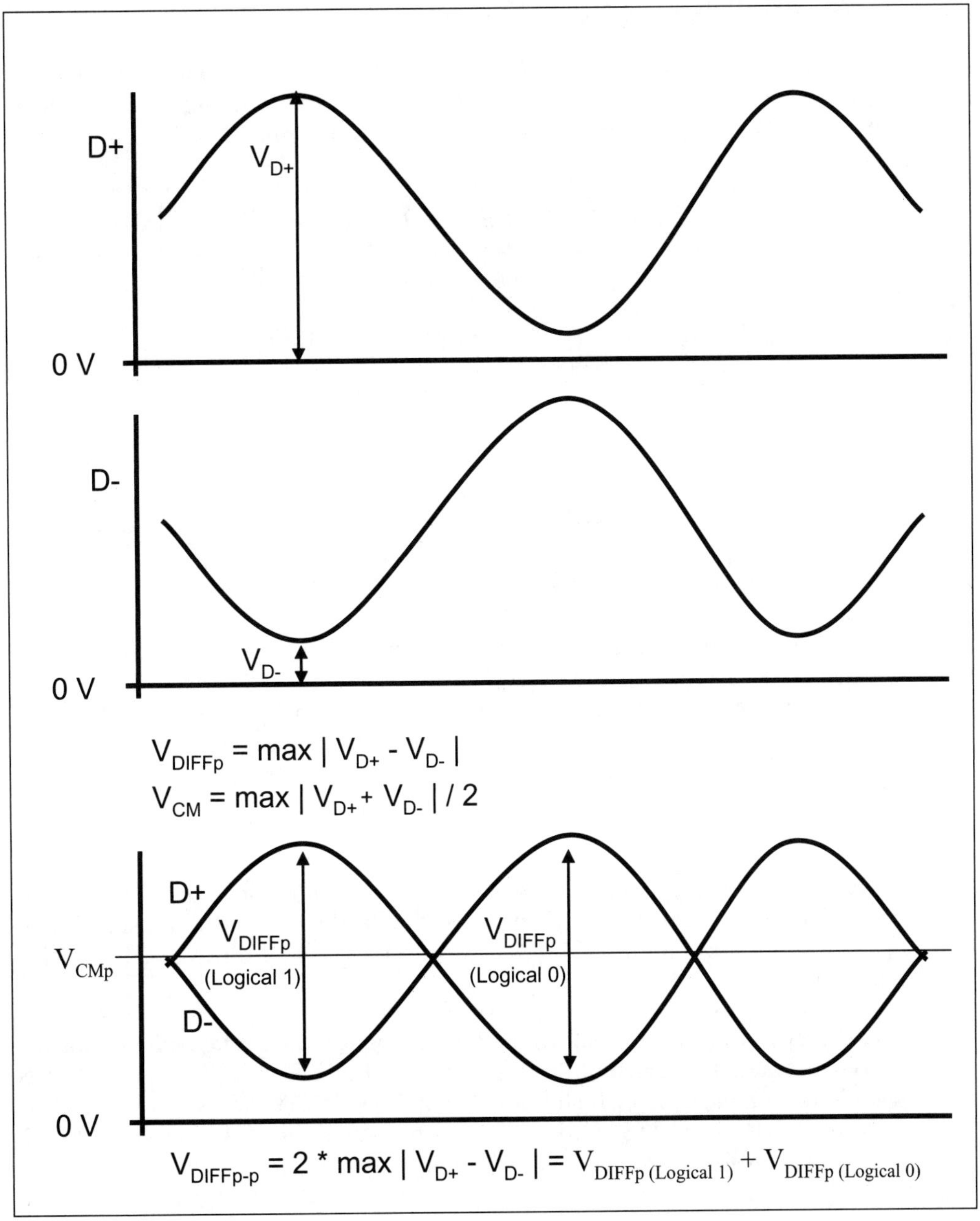

Electrical Idle

The electrical idle state of the Link is the state wherein the transmitter D+ and D- voltages are held at a steady, constant voltage (the common mode voltage). This state is used in power savings states such as L0s and L1, as well as the Link Inactive or Link Disable states.

Figure 12-6: Electrical Idle Ordered-Set

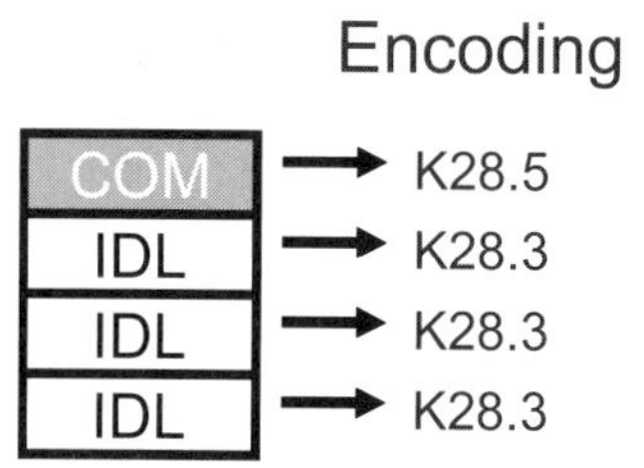

Transmitter Responsibility

A transmitter that wishes to place a Link in the electrical Idle state must first transmit the electrical Idle Ordered-Set shown in Figure 12-6. After doing so, the transmitter must go to the electrical Idle state within $T_{TX\text{-}IDLE\text{-}SET\text{-}TO\text{-}IDLE}$ time (see Table 12-1 on page 477) which is less that 20 UI (Unit Intervals = 400ps, 20 UI = 8 ns). The differential peak voltage driven by the transmitter in the electrical Idle state is $V_{TX\text{-}IDLE\text{-}DIFFp}$ (see Table 12-1 on page 477) which is less than a 20mV peak.

The transmitter can then remain in the low impedance state or go to the high impedance state. Once in the electrical Idle state, the transmitter must remain in this state for a minimum of $T_{TX\text{-}IDLE\text{-}MIN}$ (see Table 12-1 on page 477) which is 50 UI (20ns).

To exit electrical Idle and return the Link to the full-on L0 state when transmission resumes, the transmitter must do so within $T_{TX\text{-}IDLE\text{-}TO\text{-}DIFF\text{-}DATA}$ (see Table 12-1 on page 477) which is less that 20 UI (8ns). The transmitter sends FTS Ordered-Sets or TS1/TS2 Ordered sets to transition the Link state from the L0s or L1 state, respectively, back to L0 full-on state.

Receiver Responsibility

A receiver determines that the Link is going to enter electrical Idle state when it sees two out of the three IDLs of the Ordered-Set. The receiver de-gates the error reporting logic to prevent reporting errors due to unreliable activity on the Link and also immediately arms its electrical Idle Exit detector.

A receiver is able to detect an exit from the electrical Idle state when it detects a differential peak-to-peak voltage on the Link of greater than $V_{RX\text{-}IDLE\text{-}DET\text{-}DIFFpp}$ (see Table 12-2 on page 480) of 65mV. In the electrical Idle state, the receiver PLL will over time, lose clock synchronization because the receiver input is at a steady state voltage. To exit the electrical Idle state, a transmitter sends FTS or TS1/TS2 Ordered-Sets that the receiver uses to achieve Bit Lock and Symbol Lock and to resync the receiver PLL with the transmitter.

Power Consumed When Link Is in Electrical Idle State

In the electrical Idle state, the Link consumes less power because there are no Link voltage transitions that occur and the transmitter can de-gate its output stage. The Link is in either the L0s, L1, or the Disabled state while it remains in the electrical Idle state. The recommended power consumed in L0s is less than 20mW/Lane, while it is less than 5mW/Lane in the L1 state. The recommended power consumed per Lane in L0 is on the order of 80mW.

Electrical Idle Exit

A receiver detects electrical Idle exit when it receives a valid differential voltage within the $V_{RX\text{-}DIFFp\text{-}p}$ of 175 mV - 1200 mV. A transmitter typically sends TS1 Ordered-Sets to signal electrical Idle exit to a receiver.

Transmission Line Loss on Link

The transmitter drives a minimum differential peak-to-peak voltage $V_{TX\text{-}DIFFp\text{-}p}$ of 800mV. The receiver sensitivity is designed for a minimum differential peak-to-peak voltage ($V_{RX\text{-}DIFFp\text{-}p}$) of 175 mV. This translates to a 13.2dB loss budget that a Link is designed for. Although a board designer can determine the attenuation loss budget of a Link plotted against various frequencies, the transmitter and receiver eye diagram measurement are the ultimate determinant of loss budget for a Link. Eye diagrams are described in "LVDS Eye Diagram" on page 470. A transmitter that drives up to the maximum allowed differential peak-to-peak voltage of 1200mV can compensate for a lossy Link that has worst-case attenuation characteristics.

AC Coupling

PCI Express requires AC coupling capacitors be placed in close proximity to the transmitter on each Lane's differential signal pair. The AC coupling capacitor, C_{TX} (see Table 12-2 on page 480), is of a value between 75nF and 200nF. The capacitors can be integrated onto the system board, or integrated into the device itself. An add-in card with a PCI Express device on it must either place the capacitors on the card in close proximity to the transmitter, or integrate the capacitors into the PCI Express silicon.

The AC coupling capacitors eliminate DC common mode voltage sharing between two devices at opposite ends of the Link. This simplifies the device design by allowing each device to operate with its own transmitter DC common voltage. Each device can operate with its own power and ground plane, independent of the remote device at the opposite end of the Link.

De-Emphasis (or Pre-Emphasis)

PCI Express employs the concept of **de-emphasis** to help reduce the effect of the inter-symbol interference that may occur, especially on more lossy Link transmission lines. Supporting this mandatory feature reduces the Bit Error Rate (BER).

What is De-Emphasis?

A transmitted differential signal is de-emphasized when multiple bits of the same polarity are transmitted back-to-back as shown in Figure 12-7 on page 467. The Figure show a transmission of '1000010000'. Some rules related to signal de-emphasis are:

- An individual bit (that has the opposite polarity of the preceding bit) is not de-emphasized. It transmitted at the peak-to-peak differential voltage as specified by $V_{TX\text{-}DIFFp\text{-}p}$ (see Table 12-1 on page 477).
- The first bit of a series of same polarity bits is also not de-emphasized.
- Only subsequent bits of the same polarity after the first bit (of the same polarity) are de-emphasized.
- The de-emphasized voltage is 3.5dB nominal (actually, the 3dB - 4dB range is fine) less than the pre-emphasized voltage $V_{TX\text{-}DIFFp\text{-}p\text{-}MIN}$ (see Table 12-1 on page 477). The de-emphasized voltage translates to about 300mV differential peak-to-peak less than 800mV.
  566mV (3dB) >= $V_{TX\text{-}DEEMPH\text{-}DIFFp\text{-}p\text{-}MIN}$ >= 505 mV (4 dB) (see Table 12-1 on page 477).

- The Beacon signal is de-emphasized according to a slightly different rule. See "Beacon Signaling" on page 469.

Figure 12-7: Transmission with De-emphasis

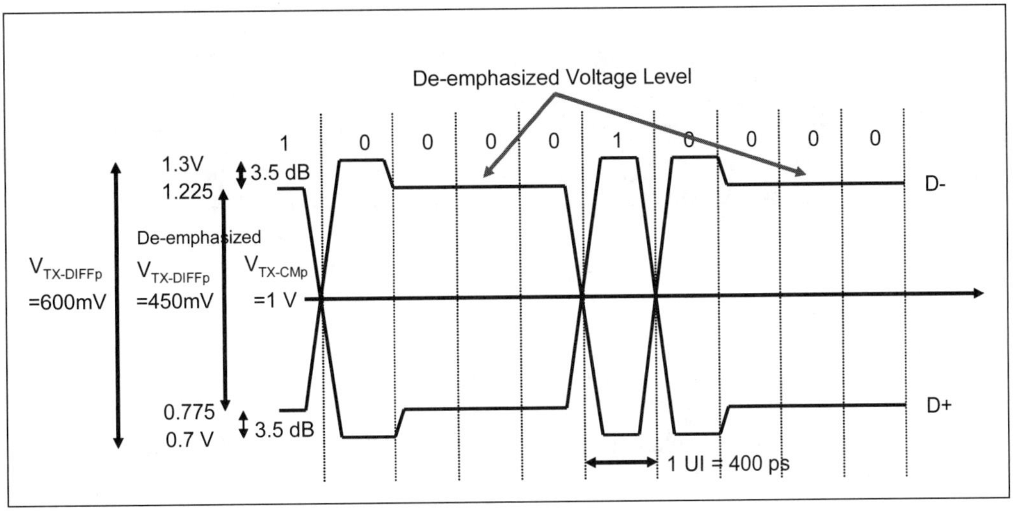

What is the Problem Addressed By De-emphasis?

As bit transmission frequencies increase, the bit-time or Unit Interval (UI) decreases. At the 2.5GBit/s transmission rate, the Unit Interval is a very small (400ps). The capacitive effects on the Link transmission line become more apparent. The line capacitors (C_{pad} + $C_{interconnect}$ + C_{TX}) store charge. When a signal has been held at a constant differential voltage (as in transmission of successive bits of the same polarity), the line capacitors charge up. The line does not easily change voltage when the signal polarity has to flip immediately to the opposite value. This results in what is referred to as **inter-symbol interference**.

Consider the example in Figure 12-8 on page 468 wherein a transmitter sends the bit pattern '111101111'. The string of the first four logical 1s charges the line capacitors. When the transmitter follows this string with a logical 0, the capacitors cannot discharge fast enough and then charge to the opposite polarity, so that the receiver will register the logical 0. The result is inter-symbol interference at the receiver. A receiver eye diagram would show the 'lonely' logical 0 with a narrower eye.

Figure 12-8: Problem of Inter-Symbol Interference

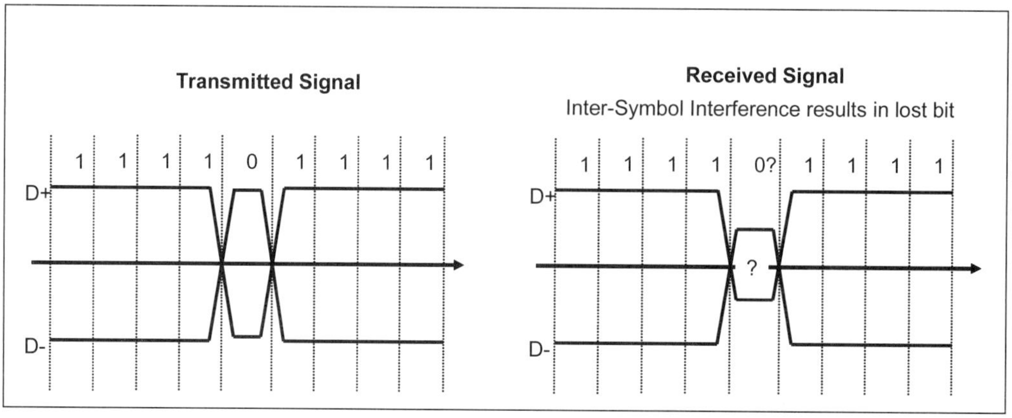

Solution

Rather than thinking that each subsequent bit transmitted after the first bit of the same polarity must be de-emphasized by 3.5dB (the PCI Express specification prefers to use the term de-emphasis), think of the first bit of a string of same polarity bits as being pre-emphasized by 3.5dB.

Figure 12-9: Solution is Pre-emphasis

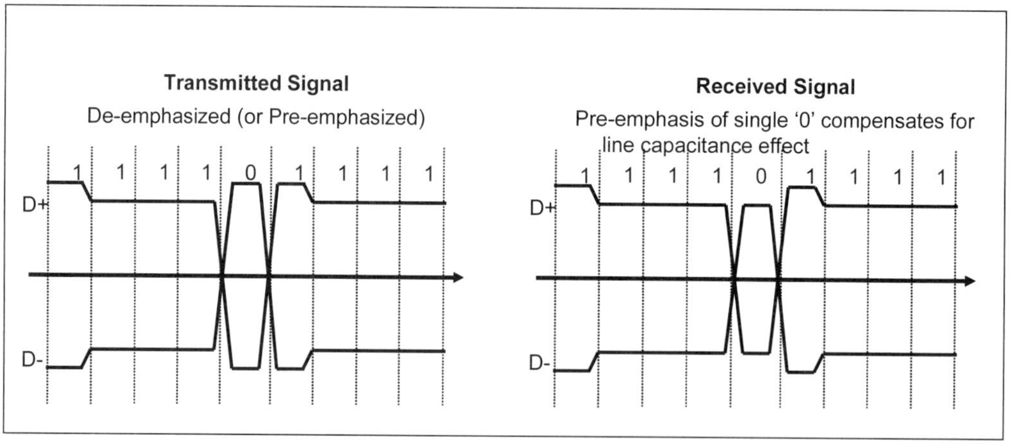

Consider the solution in Figure 12-9. By pre-emphasizing the 'lonely' logical 0 bit, the transmitter is given sufficient additional drive strength to overcome the capacitive effect of the previous string of logical 1s.

PCI Express device receivers are designed to detect differential signals that are attenuated by the Link transmission line by as much as 11-13.2dB from the transmitted value. The de-emphasis requirement for the transmitted signal is designed to accommodate systems with Link transmission lines that have this worst-case loss budget. Of course, for lower loss systems, there is more voltage margin at a receiver that receives a de-emphasized signal.

Beacon Signaling

General

A PCI Express device that is in the L2 low power state can generate a wake up event to inform the system that it wishes to move to the full-on L0 state. The Beacon signaling mechanism is one of two methods a device may employ to accomplish this. The other method (see "WAKE#" on page 696) is via the assertion of the WAKE# signal (if it is supported by the device).

While a device is in the L2 power state, its main power source and clock are turned off (as described in "" on page 484). However, an auxiliary power source (V_{aux}) keeps a limited portion of the device powered, including the wake up signaling logic.

When in the L2 low power state, a downstream device signals a **Beacon** wake up signal upstream to start the L2 exit sequence. If a switch or bridge receives the Beacon signal on its downstream port, it must forward the wake up event to its upstream port. This can be done by either forwarding the Beacon signal to the upstream port or by using WAKE# assertion to the power management logic. See "WAKE# (AUX Power)" on page 643.

When a device's Link power state is L2, even though the main power to the device is powered off, a limited portion of the device is powered by V_{aux}. The powered portion of the device allows the device to signal the wake up event via the Beacon. An upstream device such as a switch, bridge or Root Complex that is also in L2 power state is able to sense the Beacon because the receiver Beacon signal detection logic is also powered by V_{aux}.

Properties of the Beacon Signal

- It is a relatively low frequency, DC balanced differential signal consisting of periodic arbitrary data wherein the pulse width of the signal is at least 2ns but no greater than 16µs. A low frequency differential sine wave may suffice.
- The maximum time between pulses can be no larger than 16µs.

- The transmitted Beacon signal must meet the electrical voltage specifications documented in Table 12-1 on page 477.
- The signal must be DC balanced within a maximum time of 32µs.
- Beacon signaling, like normal differential signaling, must be done with the transmitter in the low impedance mode (50 Ohm single-ended, 100 Ohms differential impedance).
- When signaled, the Beacon signal must be transmitted on Lane 0, but does not have to be transmitted on other Lanes.
- With one exception, the transmitted Beacon signal must be de-emphasized according to the rules defined in the previous section. For Beacon pulses greater than 500ns, the Beacon signal voltage must be 6db de-emphasized from the $V_{TX\text{-}DIFFp\text{-}p}$ specification. The Beacon signal voltage may be de-emphasized by up to 3.5dB for Beacon pulses smaller than 500ns.

LVDS Eye Diagram

Jitter, Noise, and Signal Attenuation

As the bit stream travels from the transmitter on one end of a link to the receiver on the other end, it is subject to the following disruptive influences:

- Deterministic (i.e., predictable) jitter induced by the Link transmission line.
- Data-dependent jitter induced by the dynamic data patterns on the Link.
- Noise induced into the signal pair.
- Signal attentuation due to the impedance effect of the transmission line.

The Eye Test

Refer to Figure 12-10 on page 472. In order to ensure that the differential receiver receives an in-specification signal, an eye test is performed. The following description of the eye diagram was provided by James Edwards from an article he authored for *OE Magazine*. The author of this book has added some additional comments [in brackets].

> "The most common time domain measurement for a transmission system is the eye diagram. The eye diagram is a plot of data points repetitively sampled from a pseudo-random bit sequence and displayed by an oscilloscope. The time window of observation is two data periods wide. For a [PCI Express link running at 2.5Gbits/s], the period is 400ps, and the time win-

dow is set to 800ps. The oscilloscope sweep is triggered by every data clock pulse. An eye diagram allows the user to observe system performance on a single plot.

To observe every possible data combination, the oscilloscope must operate like a multiple-exposure camera. The digital oscilloscope's display persistence is set to infinite. With each clock trigger, a new waveform is measured and overlaid upon all previous measured waveforms. To enhance the interpretation of the composite image, digital oscilloscopes can assign different colors to convey information on the number of occurrences of the waveforms that occupy the same pixel on the display, a process known as color-grading. Modern digital sampling oscilloscopes include the ability to make a large number of automated measurements to fully characterize the various eye parameters."

The oscilloscope is set for infinite-persistence and a pattern generator is set up to generate a pseudo-random data pattern.

Optimal Eye

The most ideal reading would paint an eye pattern such as that shown in the center of Figure 12-10 on page 472 (labelled "Optimal Eye Opening"). It should be noted, however, that as long as the pattern painted resides totally within the region noted as "Normal," the transmitter and Link are within tolerance. Note that in these eye diagrams, the differential voltage parameters and values shown are peak differential voltages as opposed to peak-to-peak voltages documented in the specification. This is done because peak differential voltages can be represented in an eye diagram whereas peak-to-peak differential voltages cannot be represented in an eye diagram. See Figure 12-13 on page 475 for an example oscilloscope screen capture of an optimal eye.

Jitter Widens or Narrows the Eye Sideways

Refer to Figure 12-11 on page 473. Jitter will cause a clock pulse to occur either before or after the "Optimal Eye Opening" resulting in an eye opening wider or narrower horizontally than the optimal width. Once again, as long as the amount of jitter doesn't cause the window to widen beyond the normal zone, it is still within tolerance. The jitter specification J_T (see Table 12-1 on page 477) is a maximum of 3 UIs. See Figure 12-14 on page 476 for an example oscilloscope screen capture of an Eye Diagram showing how out-of-spec jitter causes horizontal widening or narrowing of the eye.

Noise and Signal Attenuation Heighten the Eye

Refer to Figure 12-12 on page 474. Noise or signal attenuation will cause the signal's voltage level to overshoot or undershoot the "Optimal Eye Opening" zone. As long as the amount of undershoot or overshoot doesn't cause the window height to dip below or extend above the normal zone, it is still within tolerance. See Figure 12-14 on page 476 for an example oscilloscope screen capture of an eye diagram showing how significant noise or signal attenuation causes the vertical widening or narrowing of the eye.

Figure 12-10: LVDS (Low-Voltage Differential Signal) Transmitter Eye Diagram

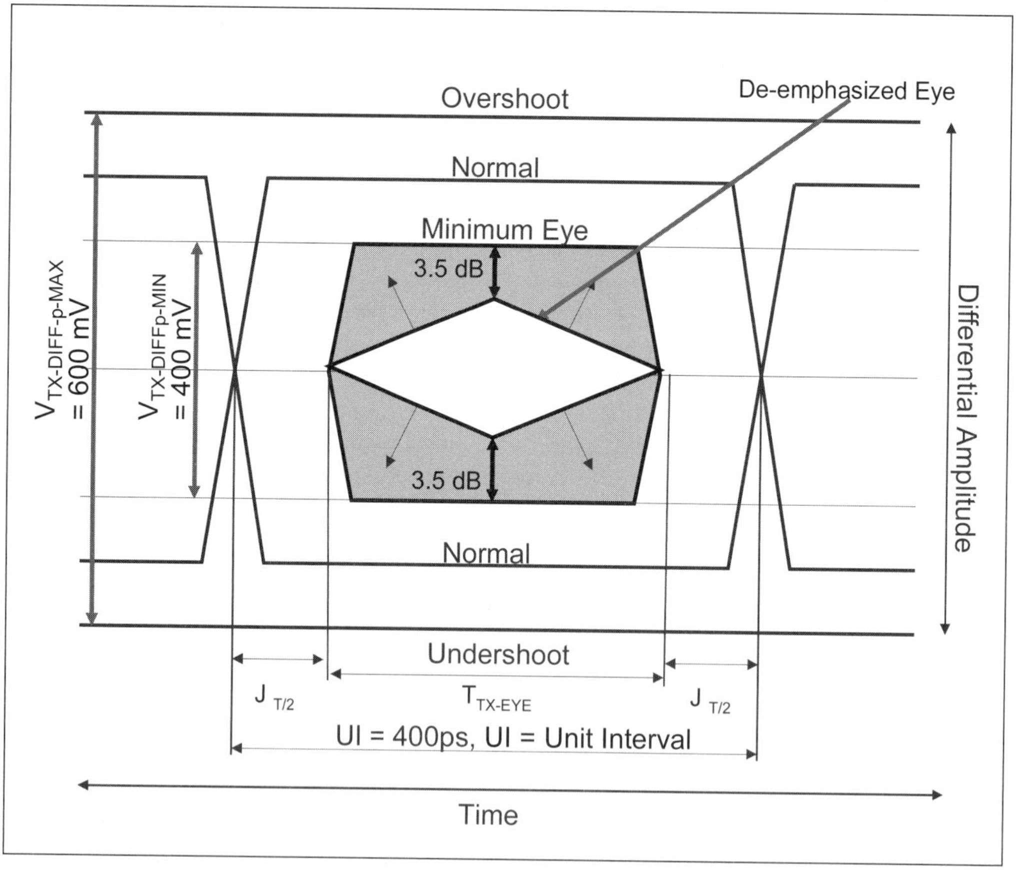

Figure 12-11: Transmitter Eye Diagram Jitter Indication

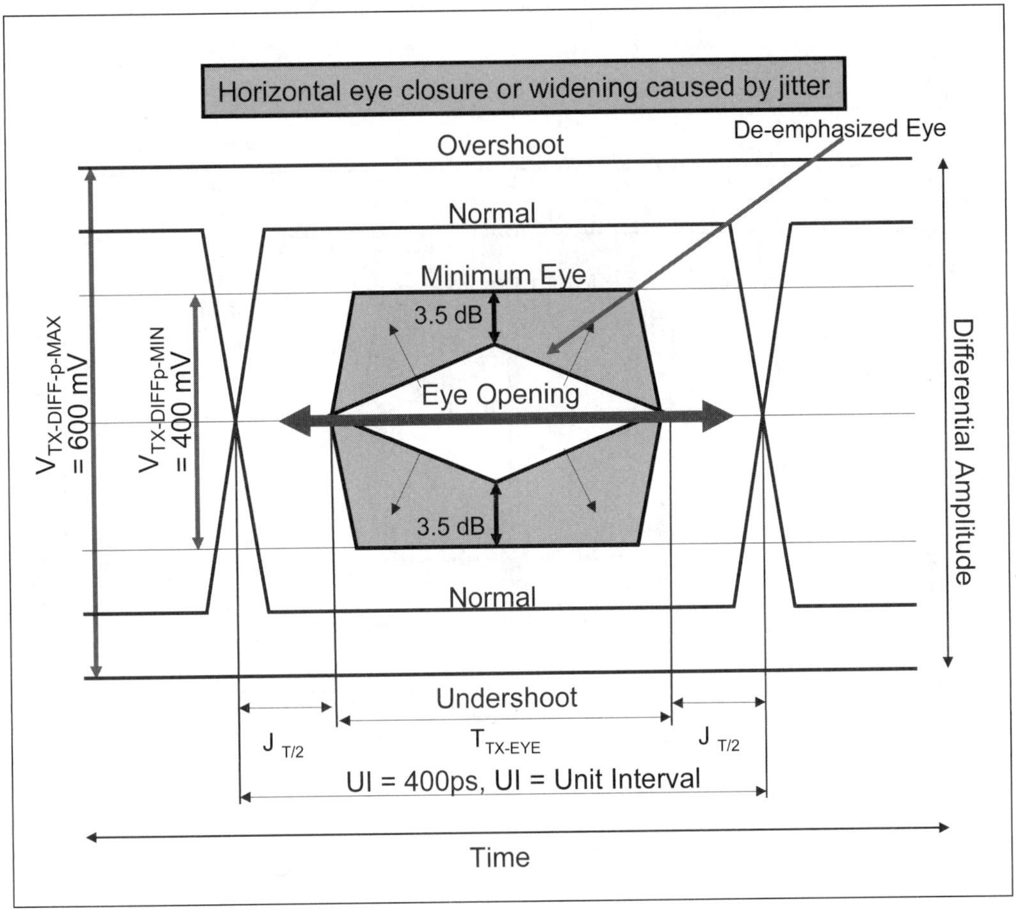

Figure 12-12: Transmitter Eye Diagram Noise/Attenuation Indication

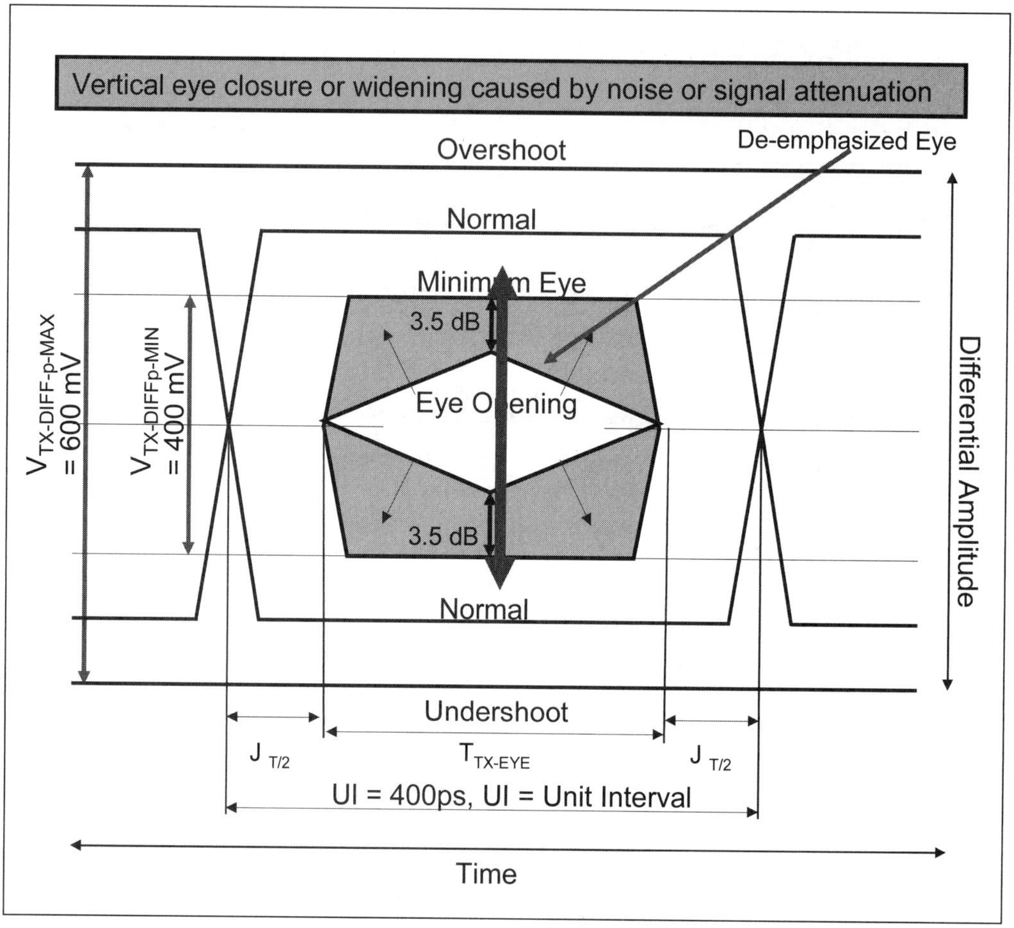

Figure 12-13: Screen Capture of a Normal Eye (With no De-emphasis Shown)

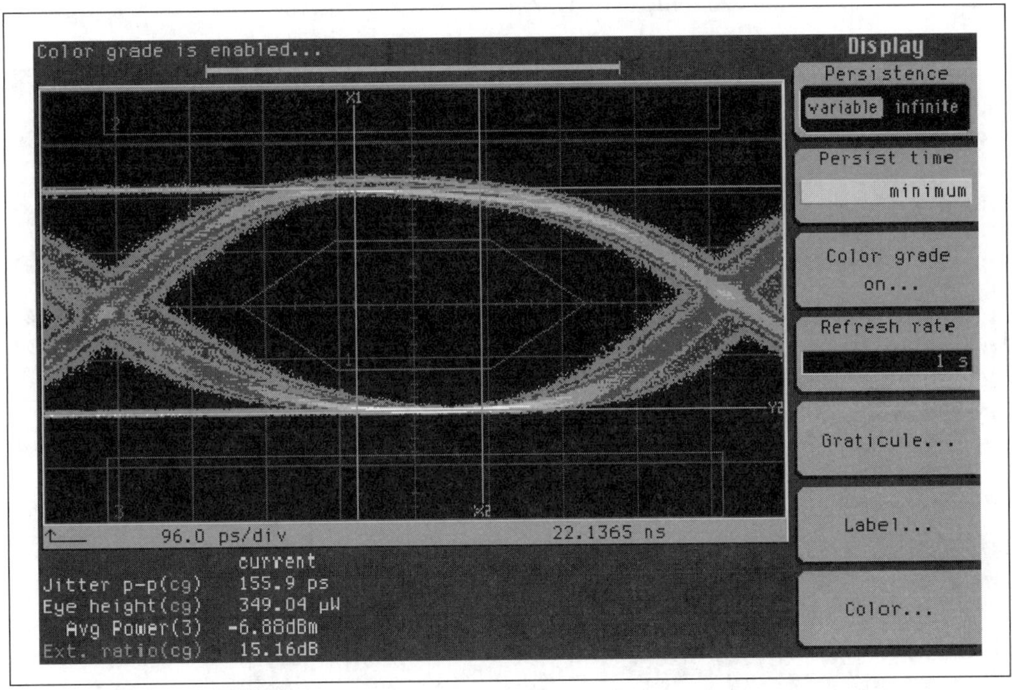

Figure 12-14: Screen Capture of a Bad Eye Showing Effect of Jitter, Noise and Signal Attenuation (With no De-emphasis Shown)

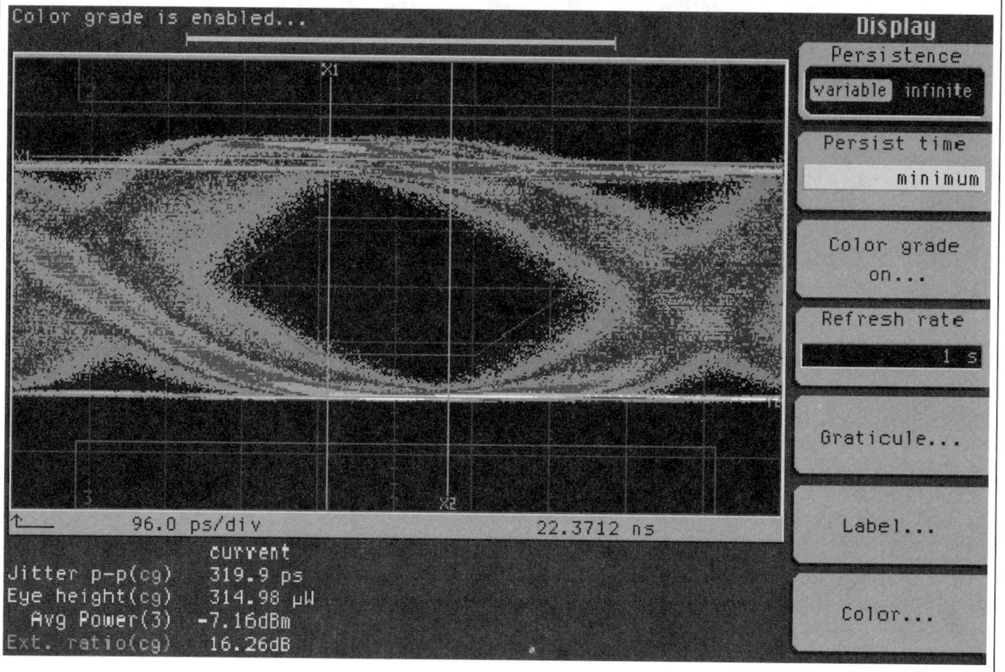

Transmitter Driver Characteristics

General

Table 12-1 on this page lists the transmitter driver characteristics.

Table 12-1: Output Driver Characteristics

Item	Max.	Min.	Units	Notes
UI	400.12	399.88	ps	Unit Interval = the bit time. 400 ps nominal.
$T_{TX\text{-}EYE}$		0.7	UI	Minimum eye width from which maximum jitter can be derived. $J_T = 1 - T_{TX\text{-}EYE}$
J_T	0.3		UI	Maximum jitter spec shown in Figure 12-11 on page 473.
$T_{TX\text{-}RISE}$ $T_{TX\text{-}FALL}$		0.125	UI	Rise and Fall time for differential signal measured at the 20%/80% voltage point.
$V_{TX\text{-}DIFFp\text{-}p}$	1200	800	mV	Peak-to-peak differential voltage.
$V_{TX\text{-}DIFFp}$	600	400	mV	Half of $V_{TX\text{-}DIFFp\text{-}p}$.
$V_{TX\text{-}DC\text{-}CM}$	3.6	0	V	DC common mode voltage.
$V_{TX\text{-}DEEMPH\text{-}DIFFp\text{-}p\text{-}MIN}$	566	505	mV	Range of minimum differential peak-to-peak voltages for de-emphasized bits. This is a 3dB - 4dB de-emphasis from pre-emphasized $V_{TX\text{-}DIFFp\text{-}p\text{-}MIN}$ of 800mV.
$I_{TX\text{-}SHORT}$	90		mA	Total current transmitter can provide when shorted to ground.

Table 12-1: Output Driver Characteristics (Continued)

Item	Max.	Min.	Units	Notes
$V_{TX\text{-}IDLE\text{-}DIFFp}$	20	0	mV	Peak differential voltage under electrical Idle state of Link.
$T_{TX\text{-}IDLE\text{-}MIN}$		50	UI	Minimum time a transmitter must be in electrical Idle.
$T_{TX\text{-}IDLE\text{-}SET\text{-}TO\text{-}IDLE}$	20		UI	Time allowed for transmitter to meet electrical Idle transmitter specification after sending electrical Idle Ordered-Set.
$T_{TX\text{-}IDLE\text{-}TO\text{-}DIFF\text{-}DATA}$	20		UI	Maximum time allowed for transmitter to meet differential transmission specification after electrical Idle exit.
$Z_{TX\text{-}DIFF\text{-}DC}$	120	80	Ohms	Transmitter differential mode low impedance. Typical value is 100 Ohms.
$Z_{TX\text{-}DC}$		40	Ohms	Requires minimum D+ and D- line impedance during all power states.
C_{TX}	200	75	nF	AC coupling capacitor on each Lane placed in close proximity to transmitter.
$L_{TX\text{-}SKEW}$	1.3		ns	Maximum Lane-to-Lane skew at transmitter between any two Lanes.

Transmit Driver Compliance Test and Measurement Load

The AC timing and voltage parameters shown in Table 12-1 on page 477 is measured within 0.2 inches from the package pins into the test load shown in Figure 12-15.

A 50 Ohm probe, or a resistor attached to ground, when attached to the transmit signal pair causes the device to go into the Compliance state of the Link Training and Status State Machine (LTSSM) (see "Polling.Configuration SubState" on page 517). During this state, the device outputs the compliance pattern which can be used for interoperability testing, EMI noise testing, Lane-to-Lane interference testing, Bit Error Rate determination, Transmit and Receive Eye measurements, etc.

Figure 12-15: Compliance Test/Measurement Load

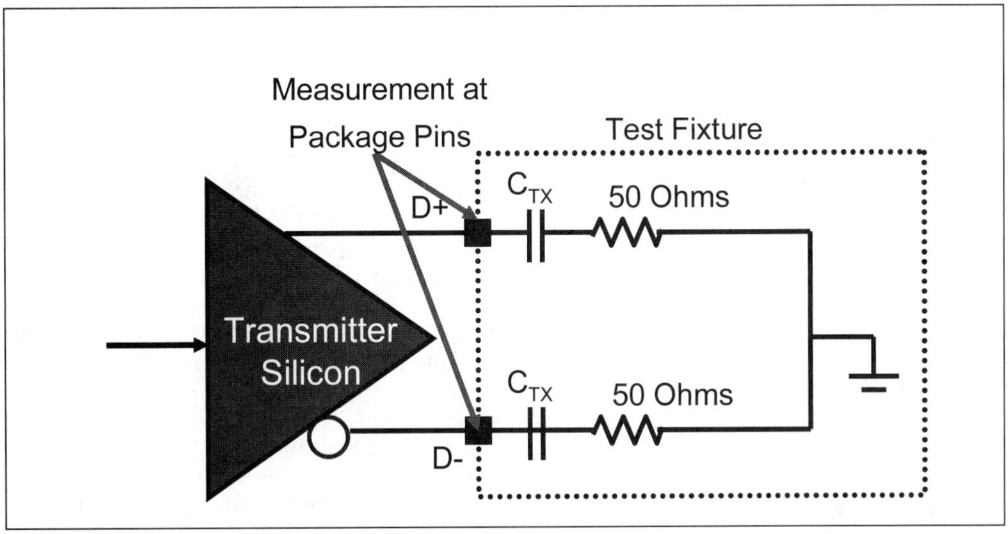

Input Receiver Characteristics

Table 12-2 on this page lists the input receiver characteristics. The receiver Eye Diagram in Figure 12-16 on page 481 illustrates some of the parameters listed in Table 12-2.

Table 12-2: Input Receiver Characteristics

Item	Max.	Min.	Units	Notes
UI	400.12	399.88	ps	Unit Interval =the bit time. 400ps nominal.
$T_{RX\text{-}EYE}$		0.4	UI	Minimum eye width from which maximum jitter is derived. $J_T = 1 - T_{RX\text{-}EYE}$
J_T	0.3		UI	Maximum jitter spec.
$V_{RX\text{-}DIFFp\text{-}p}$	1200	175	mV	Peak-to-peak differential voltage sensitivity of receiver.
$V_{RX\text{-}DIFFp}$	600	88	mV	Half of $V_{RX\text{-}DIFFp\text{-}p}$.
$V_{RX\text{-}IDLE\text{-}DET\text{-}DIFFp\text{-}p}$	175	65	mV	This is the electrical Idle detect threshold voltage. Any voltage less than 65mV peak-to-peak implies that the Link is in electrical Idle.
$Z_{RX\text{-}DIFF\text{-}DC}$	120	80	Ohms	Receiver DC differential mode impedance. 100 Ohms nominal.
$Z_{RX\text{-}\text{-}DC}$	60	40	Ohms	Requires minimum D+ and D- line impedance during all power states.
$Z_{RX\text{-}\text{-}HIGH\text{-}IMP\text{-}DC}$		200k	Ohms	Requires minimum D+ and D- line impedance when the receiver terminations do not have power (e.g., in the L2 low power state, or during Fundamental Reset).
$L_{RX\text{-}SKEW}$	20		ns	Lane-to-Lane skew that a receiver must be able to compensate for.

Figure 12-16: Receiver Eye Diagram

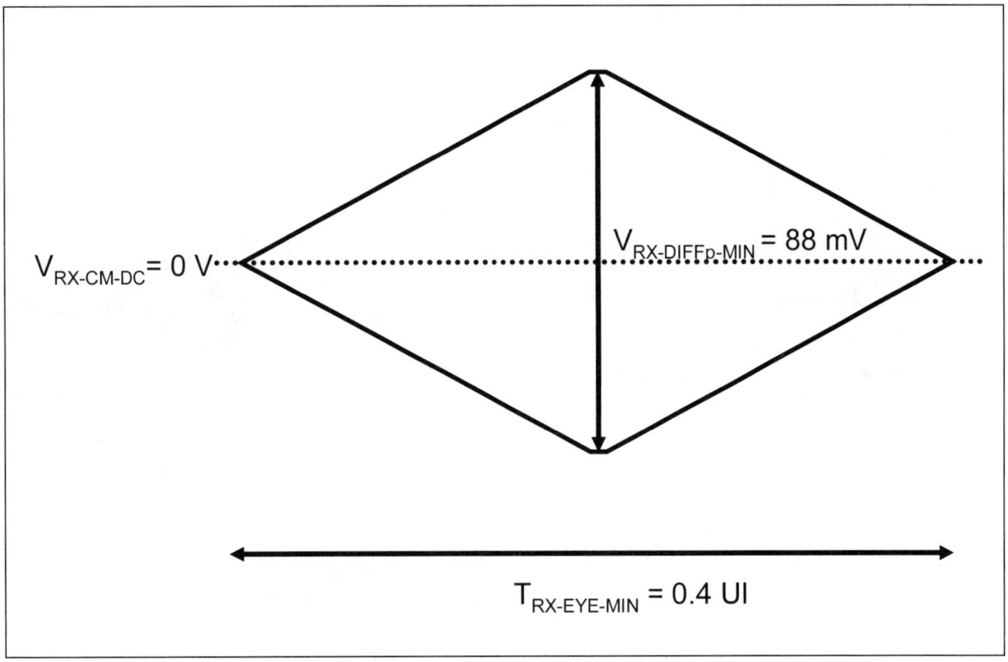

Electrical Physical Layer State in Power States

Figure 12-17 on page 482 through Figure 12-21 on page 486 illustrate the electrical state of the Physical Layer while the link is in various power management states.

Figure 12-17: L0 Full-On Link State

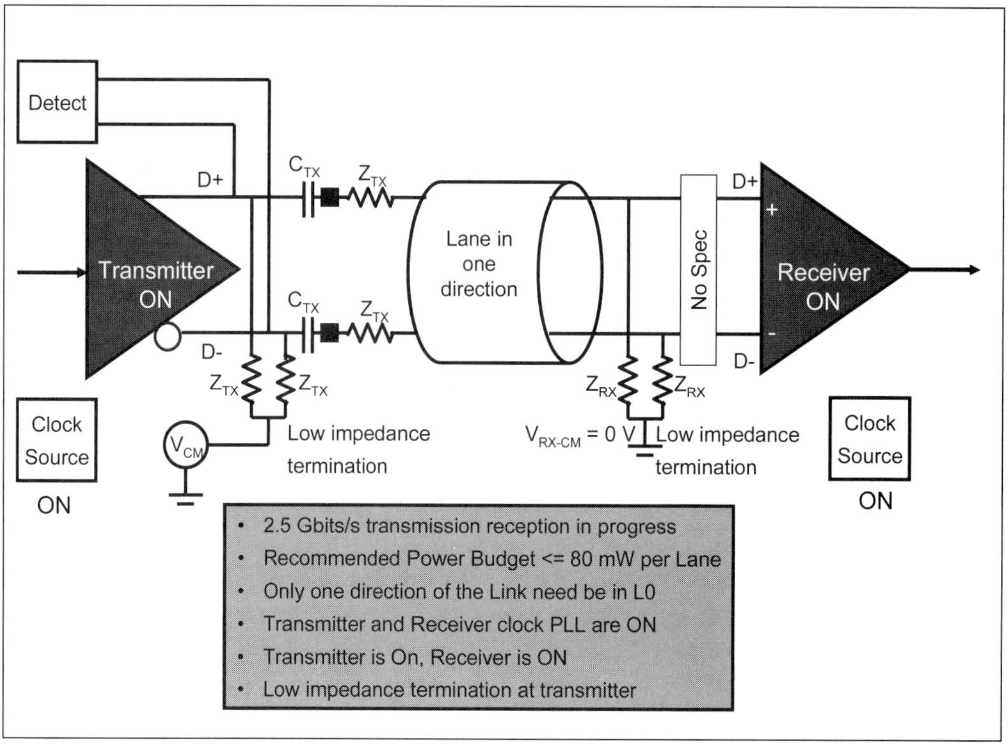

Figure 12-18: L0s Low Power Link State

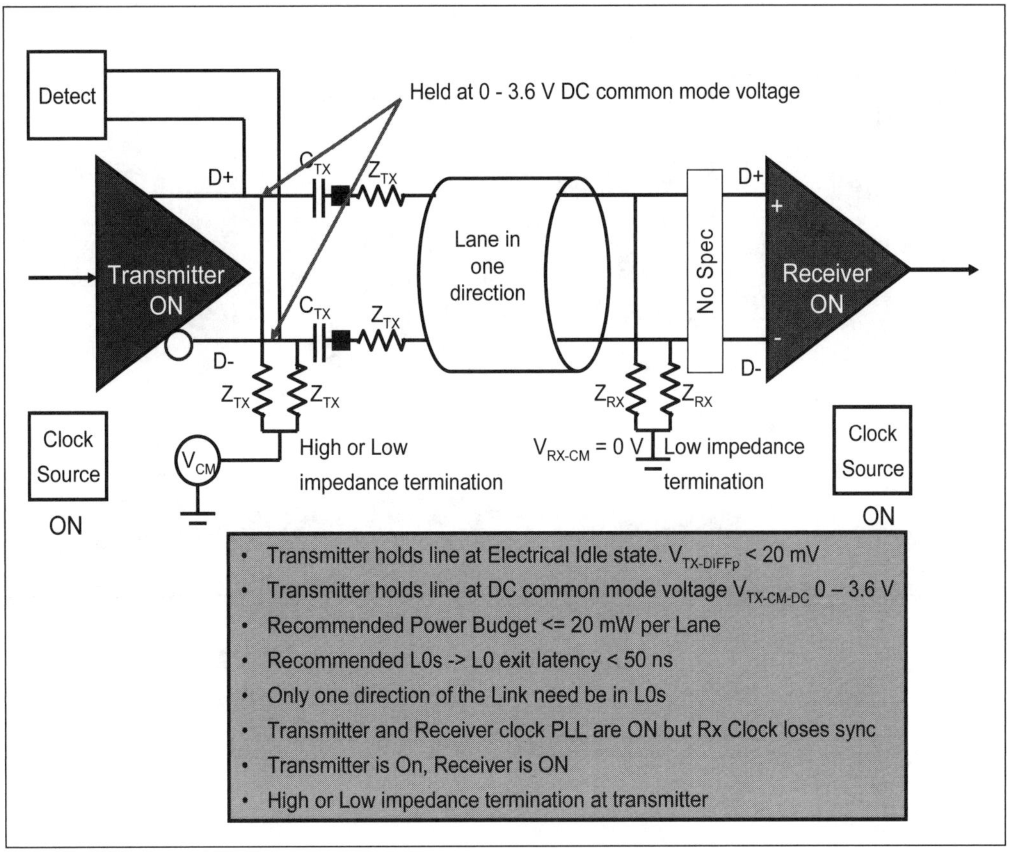

Figure 12-19: L1 Low Power Link State

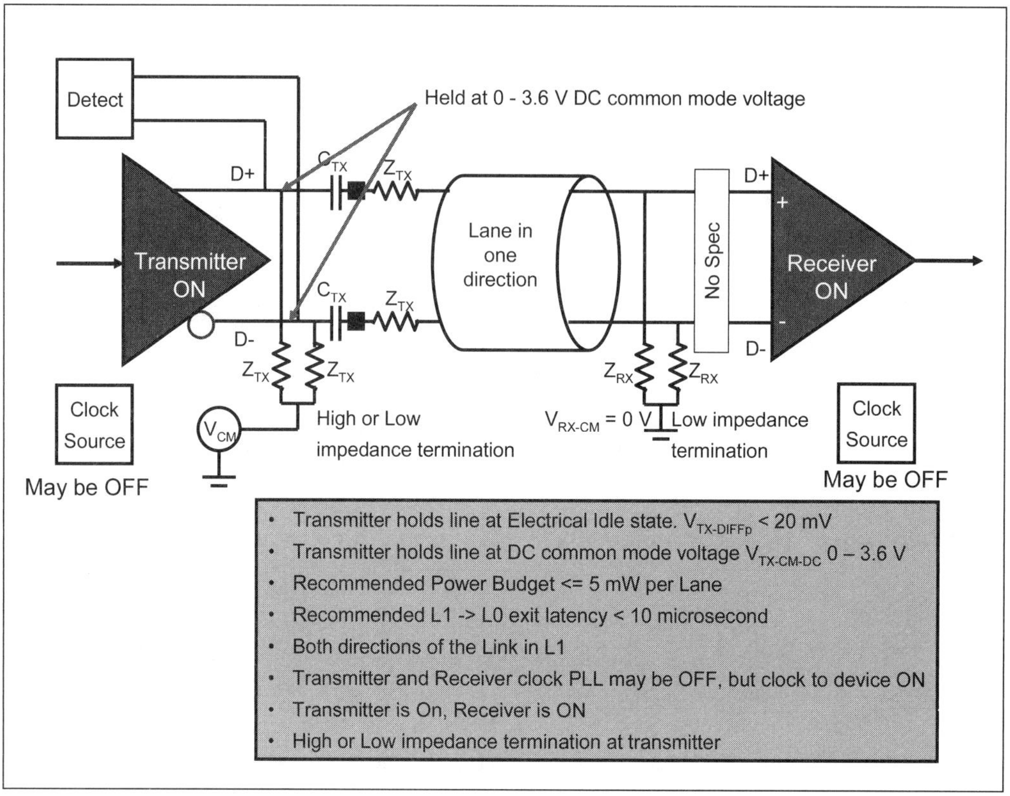

Figure 12-20. L2 Low Power Link State

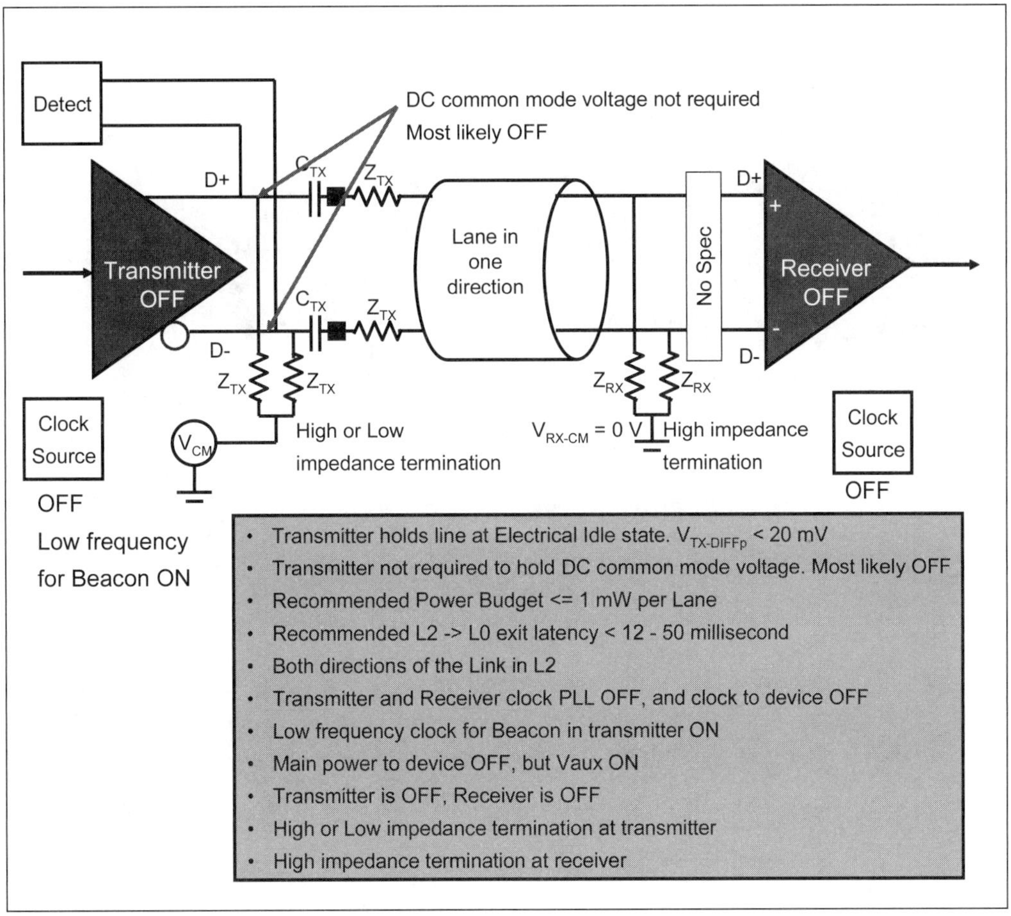

Figure 12-21: L3 Link Off State

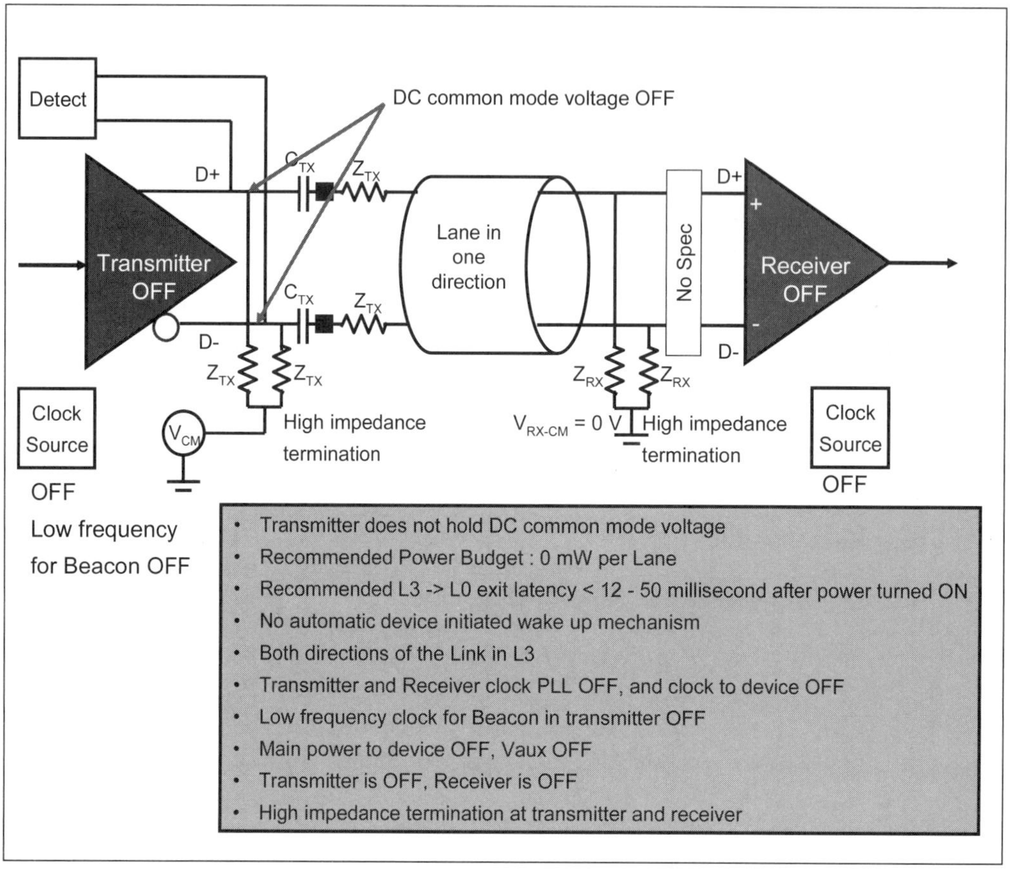

13 System Reset

The Previous Chapter

The previous chapter describes the Electrical Physical Layer. It describes the analog characteristics of the differential drivers and receivers that connect a PCI Express device to the Link. Timing and driver/receiver parameters are documented in that chapter.

This Chapter

This chapter describes 3 types of system reset generation capabilities: cold reset, warm reset and hot reset. The chapter also describes the usage of a side-band reset signal called PERST#. It describes the usage of the TS1 Ordered-Set to generate an in-band Hot Reset. The effect of reset on a device and system is described.

The Next Chapter

The next chapter describes the function of the Link Training and Status State Machine (LTSSM) of the Physical Layer. The chapter describes the initialization process of the Link from Power-On or Reset, until the full-on L0 state, where traffic on the Link can begin. In addition, the chapter describes the lower power management states L0s, L1, L2, L3 and briefly describes entry and exit procedure to/from these states.

Two Categories of System Reset

The PCI Express specification describes two reset generation mechanisms. The first mechanism is a system generated reset referred to as **Fundamental Reset**. The second mechanism is an In-band Reset (communicated downstream via the Link from one device to another) referred to as the **Hot Reset**.

Fundamental Reset

Fundamental Reset causes a device's state machines, hardware logic, port states and configuration registers (except sticky registers of a device that can draw valid V_{aux}) to initialize to their default conditions.

There are two types of Fundamental Reset:

- **Cold Reset**. This is a reset generated as a result of application of main power to the system.
- **Warm Reset.** Triggered by hardware without the removal and re-application of main power. A Warm Reset could be triggered due to toggling of the system 'POWERGOOD' signal with the system power stable. The mechanism for generating a Warm Reset is not defined by specification. It is up to the system designer to optionally provide a mechanism to generate a Warm Reset.

When Fundamental Reset is asserted:

- The receiver terminations are required to meet the $Z_{RX\text{-}HIGH\text{-}IMP\text{-}DC}$ parameter of 200 kOhms minimum (see Table 12-2 on page 480).
- The transmitter terminations are required to meet the output impedance at minimum $Z_{TX\text{-}DC}$ (see Table 12-1 on page 477) of 40 Ohms, but may place the driver in a high impedance state.
- The transmitter holds a constant DC common mode voltage between 0 V and 3.6 V.

After Fundamental Reset Exit:

- The receiver must re-enable its receiver terminations $Z_{RX\text{-}DIFF\text{-}DC}$ (see Table 12-2 on page 480) of 100 Ohms within 5 ms of Fundamental Reset exit. The receiver is now ready to detect electrical signaling on the Link.
- After Fundamental Reset exit, the Link Training state machine enters the 'Detect' state and the transmitter is ready to detect the presence of a receiver at the other end of the Link.
- The transmitter holds a constant DC common mode voltage between 0 V and 3.6 V.

Methods of Signaling Fundamental Reset

Fundamental Reset may be signaled via an auxiliary side-band signal called PERST# (PCI Express Reset, asserted low). When PERST# is not provided to an add-in card or component, Fundamental Reset is generated autonomously by the component or add-in card.

Below is a description of the two mechanisms of Fundamental Reset generation.

PERST# Type Fundamental Reset Generation. A central resource device, e.g. a chipset, in the PCI Express system provides this source of reset. For example, the IO Controller Hub (ICH) chip in Figure 13-1 on page 490 may generate PERST#. The system power supply (not shown in figure) generates a 'POWERGOOD' signal once main power is turned on and stable. The ICH Reset logic in-turn uses this signal to assert PERST# when POWERGOOD (asserted High) is deasserted. If power is cycled, POWERGOOD toggles and causes PERST# to assert and deassert. This is the Cold Reset. If the system provides a method of toggling POWERGOOD without cycling through power (as via a button on the chassis) then also PERST# asserts and deasserts. This is the Warm Reset.

The PERST# signal feeds all PCI Express devices on the motherboard including the connectors and graphics controller. Devices may choose to use PERST# but are not required to use it as the source of reset.

The PERST# signal also feeds the PCI Express-to-PCI-X bridge shown in the figure. The bridge forwards this reset to the PCI-X bus as PCI-X bus RST#. ICH also generates PRST# for the PCI bus.

Autonomous Method of Fundamental Reset Generation. A device can be designed to generate its own Fundamental Reset upon detection of application (or re-application) of main power. The specification does not describe the mechanism for doing so. The self reset generation mechanism can be built into the device or may be designed as external logic, for example, on a add-in card that detects Power-On and generates a local reset to the device.

The device must also generate an autonomous Fundamental Reset if it detects its power go outside of the limits specified.

A device should support the autonomous method of triggering a Fundamental Reset given that the specification is not clear about requirement of system PERST# support.

Figure 13-1: PERST# Generation

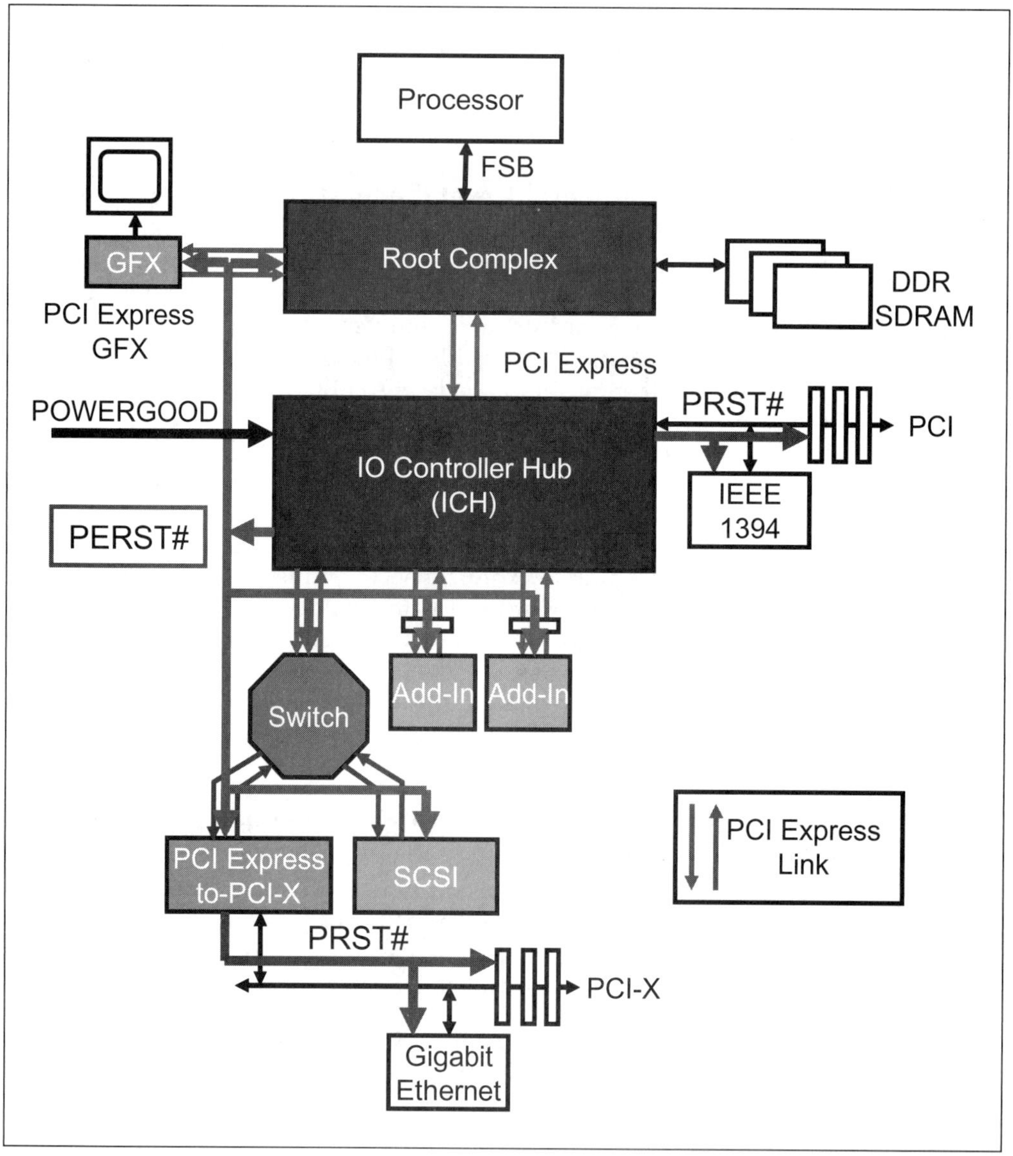

In-Band Reset or Hot Reset

Hot Reset is propagated in-band via the transmission of TS1 Ordered-Sets (shown in Figure 13-2) with bit 0 of symbol 5 in the TS1 Ordered-Set asserted. The TS1 Ordered-Set is transmitted on all Lanes with the correct Link # and Lane# symbols. These TS1 Ordered-Sets are continuously transmitted for 2 ms. Both transmitter and receiver of Hot Reset end up in the detect state (see "Hot Reset State" on page 544). Hot Reset, in general, is a software generated reset.

Figure 13-2: TS1 Ordered-Set Showing the Hot Reset Bit

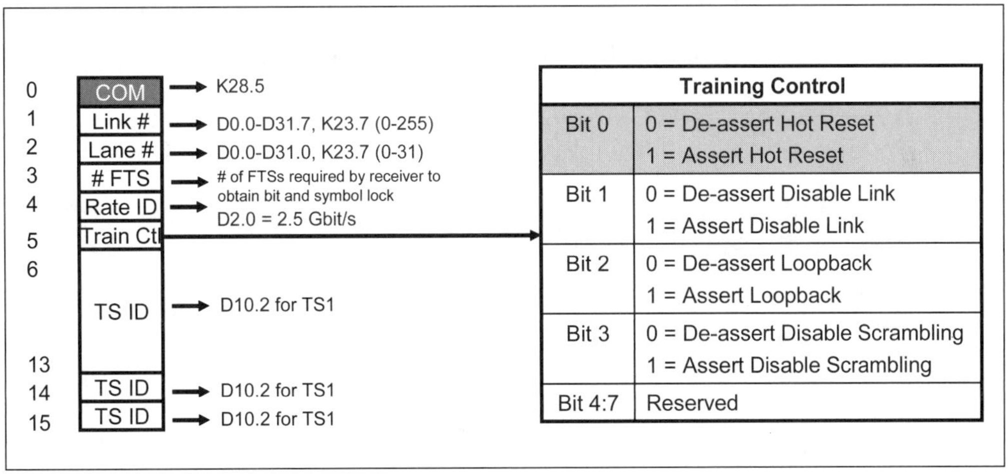

Hot Reset is propagated downstream. Hot Reset is not propagated upstream. This means that only the Root Complex and Switches are able to generate Hot Reset. Endpoints do not generate Hot Reset. A switch that receives a Hot Reset TS1 Ordered-Set on its upstream port must pass it to all its downstream ports. In addition, the switch resets itself. All devices downstream of a switch that receive the Hot Reset TS1 Ordered-Set will reset themselves.

Response to Receiving a Hot Reset Command

When a device receives a Hot Reset command:

- It goes to the 'Detect' Link State (via the Recovery and Hot Reset state) of the Link Training state machine and starts the Link training process, followed by initialization of VC0.
- Its state machines, hardware logic, port states and configuration registers (except sticky registers) initialize to their default conditions.

Switches Generate Hot Reset on Their Downstream Ports

The following are a list of bullets that indicate when a switch generates a Hot Reset on ALL its downstream ports:

- Switch receives a Hot Reset on its upstream port
- The Data Link Layer of the switch upstream port reports a DL_Down state. This state occurs when the upstream port has been disconnected or when the upstream port has lost connection with an upstream device due to an error that is not recoverable by the Physical Layer and Data Link Layer.
- Software sets the 'Secondary Bus Reset' bit of the Bridge Control configuration register associated with the upstream port.

Bridges Forward Hot Reset to the Secondary Bus

If a bridge such as a PCI Express-to-PCI(-X) bridge detects a Hot Reset on its upstream port, it must assert the PRST# signal on its secondary PCI(-X) bus.

How Does Software Tell a Device (e.g. Switch or Root Complex) to Generate Hot Reset?

Software tells a root complex or switch to generate a Hot Reset on a specific port by writing a 1 followed by 0 to the 'Secondary Bus Reset' bit in the Bridge Control register of that associated port's configuration header. See Figure 13-3 on page 493 for the location of this bit. Consider the example shown in Figure 13-4 on page 494. Software writes a 1 to the 'Secondary Bus Reset' register of Switch A's downstream left side port. Switch A generates a Hot Reset on that port by forwarding TS1 Ordered-Sets with the Hot Reset bit set. Switch A does not generate a Hot Reset on its right side port. Switch B receives this Hot Reset on its upstream port and forwards it on all downstream ports to the two endpoints.

If software writes to the 'Secondary Bus Reset' bit of the switch's upstream port, then the switch generates a Hot Reset on ALL its downstream ports. Consider the example shown in Figure 13-5 on page 495. Software writes a 1 to the 'Secondary Bus Reset' register of Switch C's upstream port. Switch C generates a Hot Reset on ALL downstream ports by forwarding TS1 Ordered-Sets with the Hot Reset bit set on both ports. The PCI Express-to-PCI bridge receives this Hot Reset and forwards it on to the PCI bus by asserting PRST#.

A device is in the L0 state when the 'Secondary Bus Reset' bit is set. The device (upstream device) then goes through the Recovery state of the LTSSM (see "Recovery State" on page 532) before it generates the TS1 Ordered-Sets with the Hot Reset bit set and then enters the Hot Reset state (see "Hot Reset State" on page 544). The Hot Reset TS1 Ordered-Sets are generated continuously for 2 ms and then the device exits to the Detect state where it is ready to start the Link training and initialization process.

The receiver (downstream device) of the Hot Reset TS1 Ordered-Sets will enter the Hot Reset state through the Recovery state. It exits to the Detect state if it receives at least two Hot Reset TS1 Ordered-Sets. Both upstream and downstream devices are initialized and end up in the Detect state from which they are ready to being Link training and initialization. If the downstream device is a switch or bridge, it passes on the Hot Reset to its downstream ports or bus.

Figure 13-3: Secondary Bus Reset Register to Generate Hot Reset

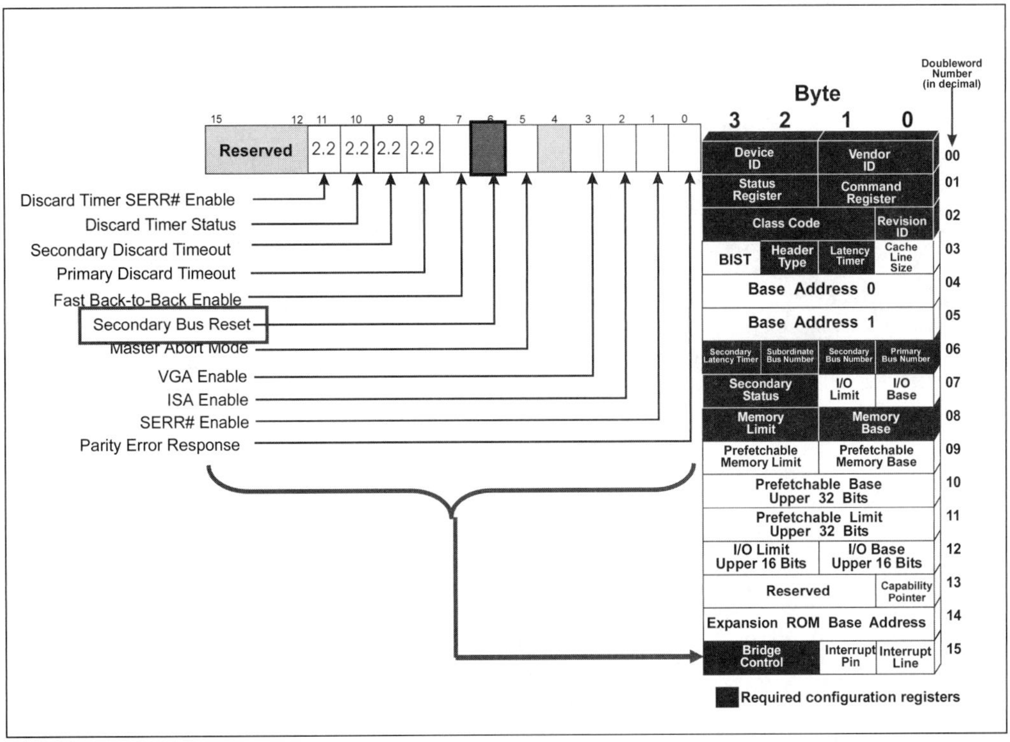

Figure 13-4: Switch Generates Hot Reset on One Downstream Port

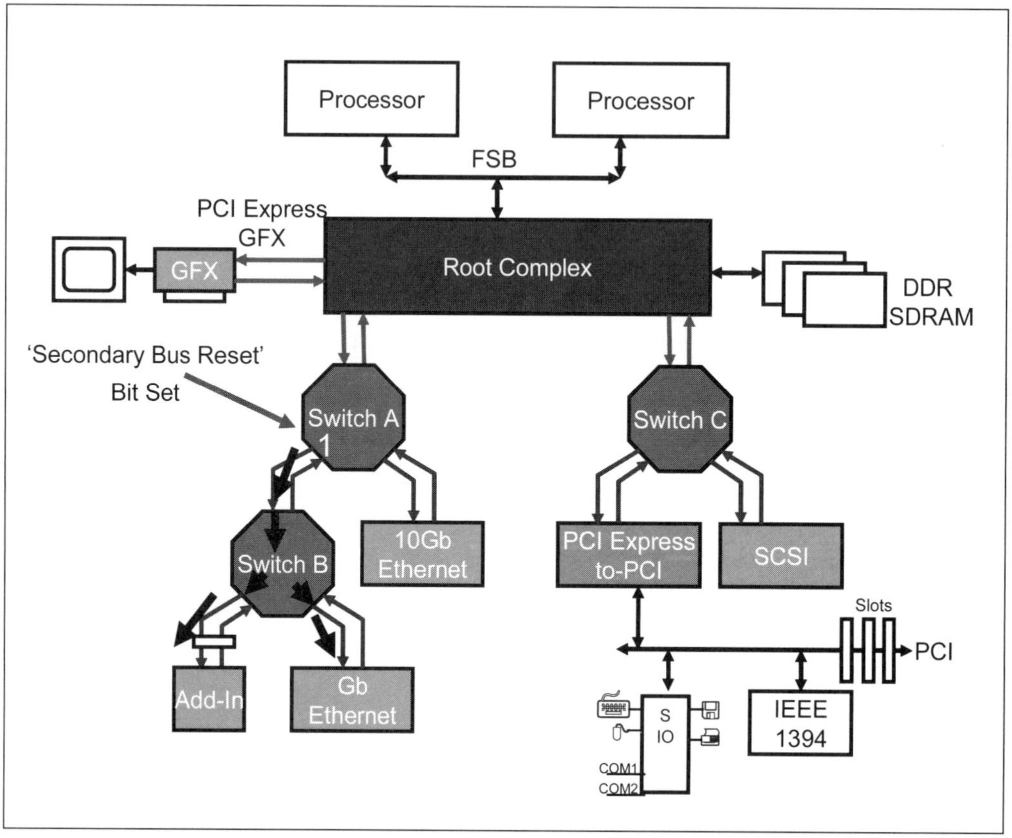

Figure 13-5: Switch Generates Hot Reset on All Downstream Ports

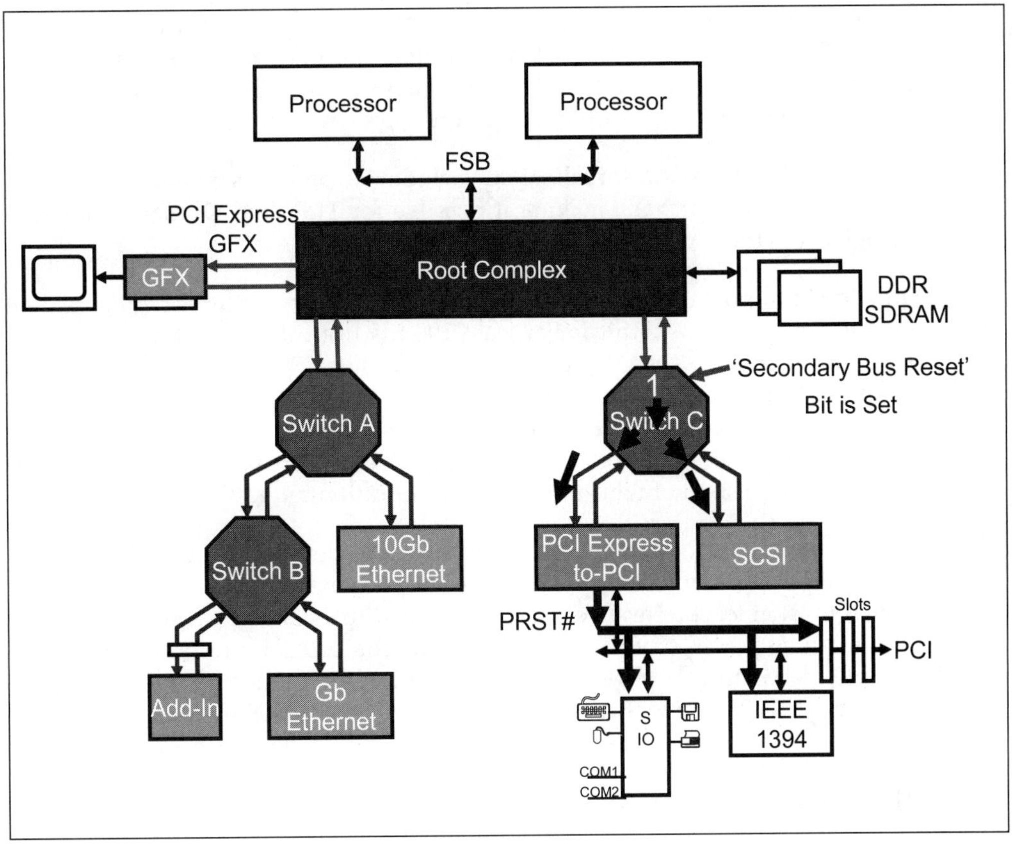

Reset Exit

After exiting the reset state, Link training and initialization must begin within 80 ms. Devices may exit the reset state at different times, since reset signaling is asynchronous. This means that in fact two devices on opposite ends of the Link who are reset may not start the Link training process at the same time.

After Link Training and Initialization each device proceeds through Flow Control initialization for VC0, making it possible for TLPs and DLLPs to be transferred across the Link.

To allow components who have been reset to perform internal initialization, system software must wait for at least 100 ms from the end of a reset (cold/warm/hot) before issuing Configuration Requests to PCI Express devices. To be software visible, devices must be ready to receive configuration request after 100 ms from the end of Reset. The specification does not address how software measures this wait time of 100 ms. It could be as simple as software starts a software loop at the end of which the first configuration request is initiated.

If software initiates a configuration request to a device after the 100 ms wait time from the end of Reset and the device is not done with its internal initialization, it must at least return a completion TLP, with a completion status of "Configuration Request Retry Status (CRRS)". The completion is returned to the root complex who initiated the configuration request on the behalf of the CPU. The completion TLP terminates the configuration request. Either the root complex may re-issue the configuration request or have the CPU retry the request again.

The Root Complex and/or system software must allow 1.0 second (+50%/-0%) after a reset before it may determine that a device which fails to return a successful Completion status for a valid Configuration Request is broken. This delay is analogous to the Trhfa parameter specified for PCI/PCI-X, and is intended to allow sufficient time for devices to complete self initialization.

Link Wakeup from L2 Low Power State

When a device's Link is in the L2 low power state, its main power is turned off though V_{aux} is still applied. A device returns to the full-on L0 power state by one of two methods. Either the device signals a wakeup event or Power Management software triggers the wakeup procedure "Waking Non-Communicating Links" on page 642.

Device Signals Wakeup

The powered down device (device(s) are in $D3_{Cold}$ with V_{aux} valid) whose Link is in L2 state, is able to signal a wakeup event either through signaling a Beacon (see "Beacon Signaling" on page 469) upstream towards the root complex or by asserting WAKE#. The wakeup event ultimately results in the power controller re-applying power and clock to the device (or group of devices) who signaled the wakeup. The power controller also causes (either autonomously or under software control) a PERST# Reset to the device or group of devices whose power and clock has been re-applied. If the device does not support PERST#, it must autonomously generate its own Fundamental Reset when it senses main power re-applied to it. Upon exit from Fundamental Reset, the device proceeds with Link training and initialization. The device, which is now in the $D0_{unintialized}$ state, can now send a PM_PME TLP message upstream to the root complex to inform Power Management software of the wakeup event.

Power Management Software Generates Wakeup Event

Power Management software can wake up a device or group of devices (device(s) are in $D3_{Cold}$) whose Link is in L2 state. Power Management software causes the power controller to re-apply power and clock to the device or group of devices. The power controller also causes (either autonomously or under software control) a PERST# Reset. If the device does not support PERST#, it must autonomously generate its own Fundamental Reset when it senses main power re-applied to it. Upon exit from Fundamental Reset, the device proceeds with Link training and initialization. The device is now in the $D0_{unintialized}$ state. It will have to be configured to bring it to the D0 state.

14 Link Initialization & Training

The Previous Chapter

The previous chapter described three types of system reset generation capabilities: cold reset, warm reset and hot reset. The chapter also described the usage of the side-band reset signal PERST#. The effect of reset on a device and system was described.

This Chapter

This chapter describes the function of the Link Training and Status State Machine (LTSSM) of the Physical Layer. The chapter describes the initialization process of the Link from Power-On or Reset, until the full-on L0 state, where traffic on the Link can begin. In addition, the chapter describes the lower power management states L0s, L1, L2, L3 and briefly describes entry and exit procedure to/from these states.

The Next Chapter

The next chapter describes the mechanical form factor for the PCI Express connector and add-in card. Different slot form factors are defined to support x1, x4, x8 and x16 Lane widths. In addition, the next chapter describes the Mini PCI Express form factor which targets the mobile market, Server IO Module (SIOM) form factor which targets the workstation and server market, and the NEWCARD form factor which targets both mobile and desktop markets.

Link Initialization and Training Overview

General

Link initialization and training is a Physical Layer control process that configures and initializes a device's Physical Layer, port, and associated Link so that normal packet traffic can proceed on the Link. This process is automatically initiated after reset without any software involvement. A sub-set of the Link training and initialization process, referred to as Link re-training, is initiated automatically as a result of a wakeup event from a low power mode, or due to an error condition that renders the Link inoperable. The Link Training and Status State Machine (LTSSM) is the Physical Layer sub-block responsible for the Link training and initialization process (see Figure 14-1).X

A receiver may optionally check for violations of the Link training and initialization protocol. If such an error occurs, it may be reported as a 'Link Training Error' to the error reporting logic (see "Link Errors" on page 379).

The following are configured during the Link training and initialization process:

- **Link Width** is established and set. Two devices with a different number of port Lanes may be connected. For example, one device with a x2 port may be connected to a device with a x4 port. During Link training and initialization, the Physical Layer of both devices determines and sets the Link width to the minimum Lane width of the two (i.e., x2). Other Link negotiated behaviors include Lane reversal, splitting of ports into multiple Links, and the configuration of a cross-Link.
- **Lane Reversal** on a multi-Lane device's port (if reversal is required). The Lanes on a device's port are numbered by design. When wiring up a Link to connect two devices, a board designer should match up the lane numbers of each device's port so that Lane 0 of one device's port connects to Lane 0 of the remote device's port, Lane *n* to Lane *n* of the remote device's port, and so on.

Figure 14-1: Link Training and Status State Machine Location

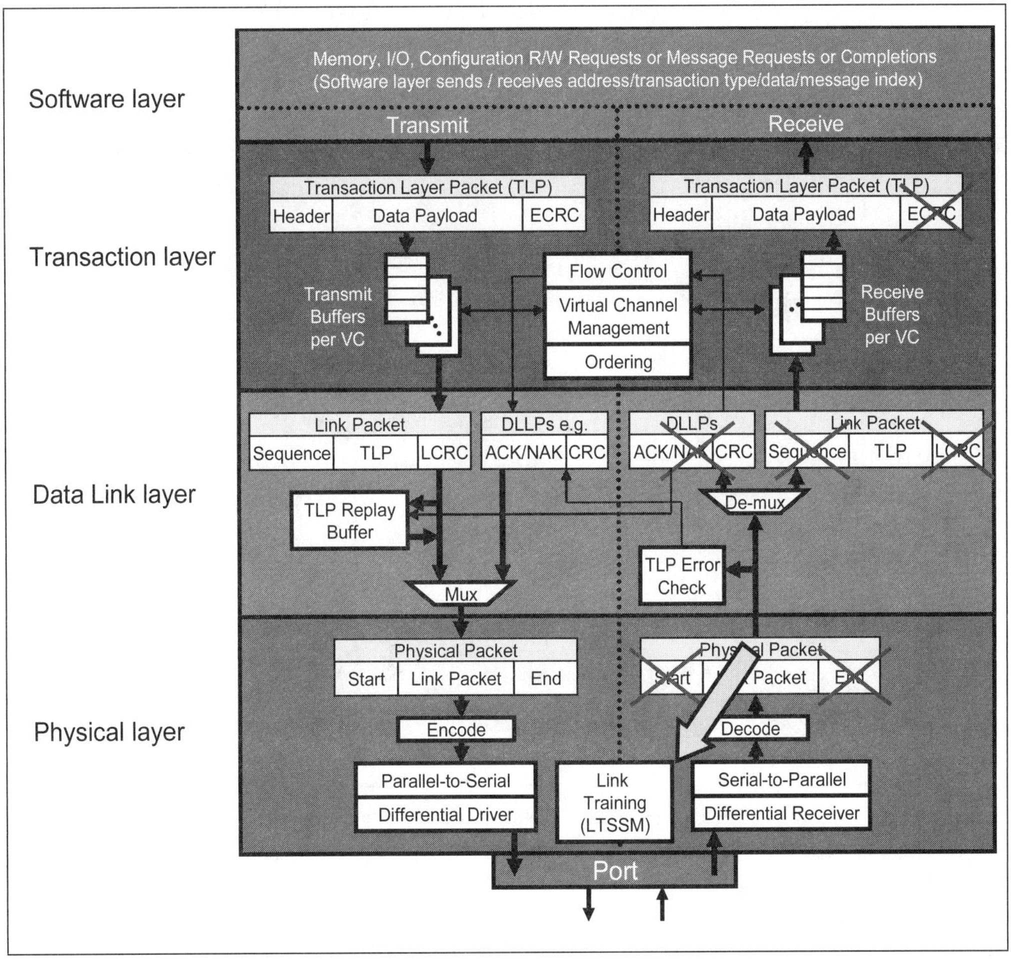

Due to the way the Lanes are organized on the pins of the device's package, it may not be possible to match up the Lanes of the two devices without crisscrossing the wires (see Figure 14-2 on page 502). Crisscrossed wires will introduce interference into the Link. If however, one or both of the devices support Lane Reversal, the designer could wire the Lanes in parallel fashion. During the Link training and initialization process, one device reverses the Lane numbering so the Lane numbers of the two ports would match up (Figure 14-2 on page 502). Unfortunately, the specification does not require devices to support the Lane Reversal feature. Hence, the designer must verify that at least one of the two devices connected via a Link supports this feature before wiring the Lanes of the two ports in reverse order. If the device supports this feature, the Lane Reversal process may permit a multi-Lane Link to be split into multiple Links that connect to multiple devices. More on this feature later.

Figure 14-2: Example Showing Lane Reversal

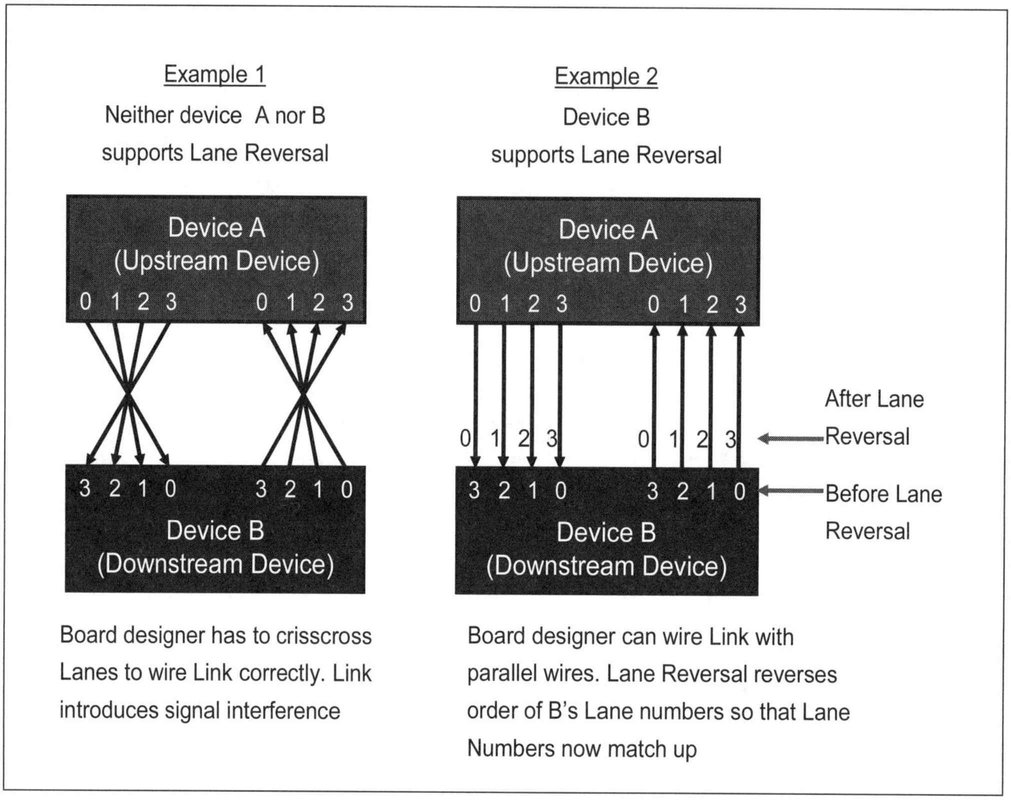

- **Polarity Inversion** may be necessary. The D+ and D- differential pair terminals for two devices may not be connected correctly, or may be intentionally reversed so that the signals do not crisscross when wiring the Link. If Lanes are wired with D+ and D- of one device wired to D- and D+ of the remote device, respectively, the Polarity Inversion feature reverses the D+ and D- signal polarities of the receiver differential terminal. Figure 14-3 illustrates the benefit of this feature on a x1 Link. Support for Polarity Inversion is mandatory.

Figure 14-3: Example Showing Polarity Inversion

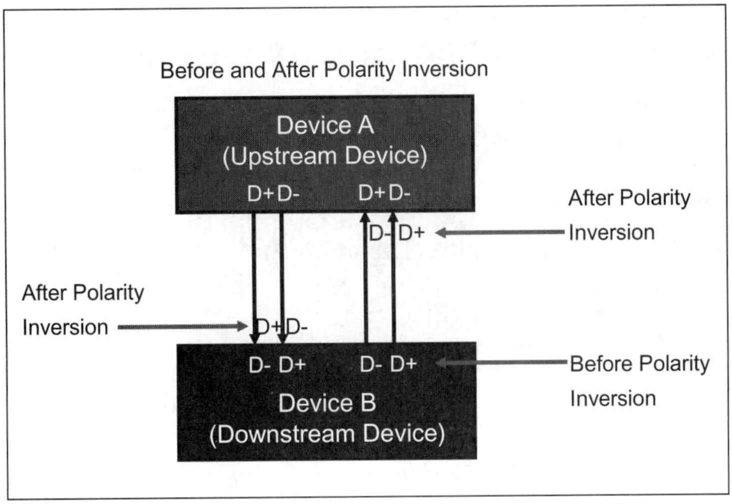

- **Link Data Rate.** Link initialization and training is completed at the default 2.5Gbit/s Generation 1 data rate. In the future, Generation 2 PCI Express will support higher data rates of 5Gbit/s and 10Gbit/s. During training, each node advertises its highest data rate capability. The Link is then initialized with the highest common frequency that both neighbors can support.
- **Bit Lock.** Before Link training begins, the receiver PLL is not yet sync'd with the remote transmitter's transmit clock, and the receiver is unable to differentiate between one received bit and another. During Link training, the receiver PLL is sync'd to the transmit clock and the receiver is then able to shift in the received serial bit stream. See "Achieving Bit Lock" on page 440.
- **Symbol Lock.** Before training, the receiver has no way of discerning the boundary between two, 10-bit sympols. During training, when TS1 and TS2 Ordered-Sets are exchanged, the receiver is able to locate the COM symbol (using its unique encoding) and uses it to initialize the deserializer. See "Symbol Boundary Sensing (Symbol Lock)" on page 441.
- **Lane-to-Lane De-skew.** Due to Link wire length variations and the different driver/receiver characteristics on a multi-Lane Link, each of the parallel bit streams that represent a packet are transmitted simultaneously, but they do not arrive at the receivers on each lane at the same time. The receiver circuit must compensate for this skew by adding or removing delays on each Lane so that the receiver can receive and align the serial bit streams of the packet (see "Lane-to-Lane De-Skew" on page 444). This deskew feature combined with the Polarity Inversion and Lane Reversal features, greatly simplifies

the designer's task of wiring up the high speed Link.

Ordered-Sets Used During Link Training and Initialization

Physical Layer Packets (PLPs), referred to as Ordered-Sets, are exchanged between neighboring devices during the Link training and initialization process. These packets were briefly described in the section on "Ordered-Sets" on page 433. The five Ordered-Sets are:

- Training Sequence 1 and 2 (TS1 and TS2),
- Electrical Idle,
- Fast Training Sequence (FTS), and
- Skip (SKIP) Ordered-Sets.

Their character structure is summarized in Figure 14-4 on page 504.

Figure 14-4: Five Ordered-Sets Used in the Link Training and Initialization Process

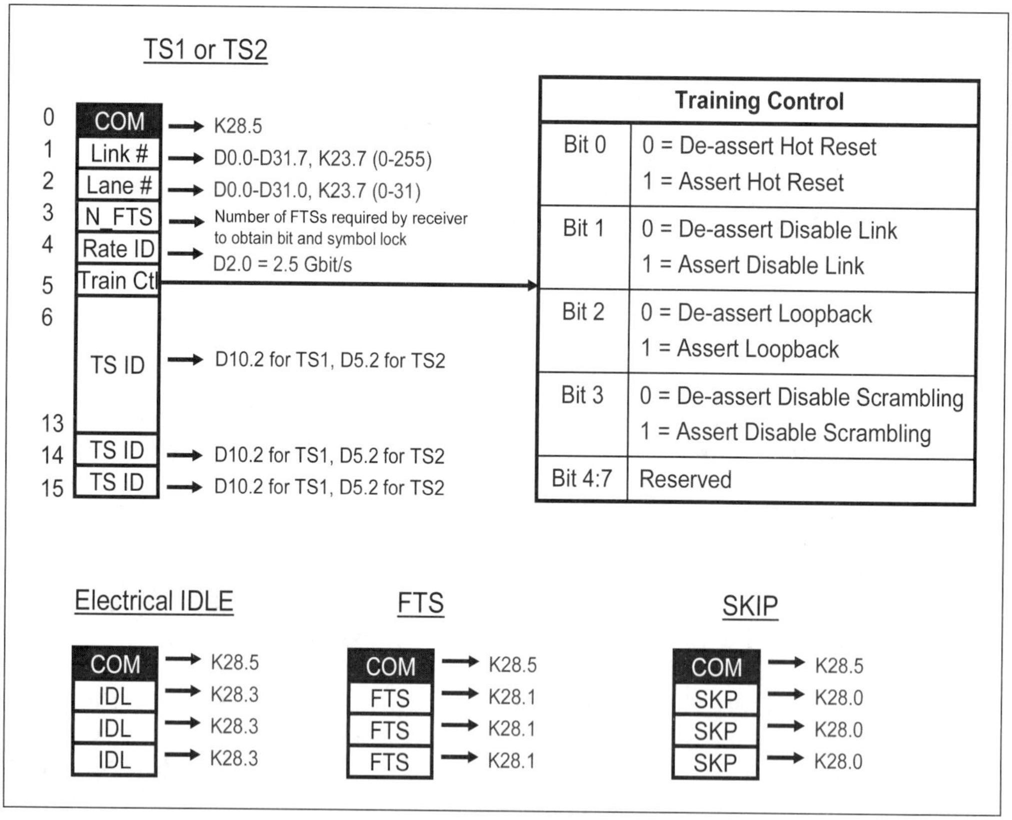

TS1 and TS2 Ordered-Sets

The TS1 and TS2 Ordered-Sets are each comprised up of 16 symbols. Structurally, there is not much difference between a TS1 and TS2 Ordered-Set, other than the TS Identifier (symbols 6-15) which contains a D10.2 for TS1 and D5.2 for the TS2 Ordered-Set. They are exchanged during the Polling, Configuration and Recovery states of the LTSSM described in "Link Training and Status State Machine (LTSSM)" on page 508. The TS1 and TS2 symbols consist of:

- **Symbol 0 (COM):** The K28.5 character identifies the start of an Ordered-Set. The receiver uses this character to achieve Bit Lock and Symbol Lock as described in "Achieving Bit Lock" on page 440 and "Symbol Boundary Sensing (Symbol Lock)" on page 441. By locating this character on a synchronized transmission of TS1 or TS2 Ordered-Sets on a multi-Lane Link, the receiver can de-skew the Lanes.
- **Symbol 1 (Link #):** In the early stages of Link training, when the TS1 and TS2 Ordered-Sets are exchanged, this field contains the PAD symbol (transmitted as a null symbol). During the configuration state of the LTSSM, this field contains an assumed Link Number. TS1 and TS2 Ordered-Sets driven from different ports of a switch contain different Link Numbers.
- **Symbol 2 (Lane #):** In the early stages of Link training when the TS1 and TS2 Ordered-Sets are exchanged, this field contains the PAD symbol (transmitted as a null symbol). During the configuration state of the LTSSM, this field contains an assumed Lane Number for each Lane of a Link. The TS1 and TS2 Ordered-Sets driven on each Lane of a given link contain different numbers.
- **Symbol 3 (N_FTS):** Contains the number of Fast Training Sequences. The exchange of FTS Ordered-Sets is used to achieve Bit Lock and Symbol Lock when exiting from the L0s to the L0 power state. During Link training at Link initialization, when TS1 or TS2 Ordered-Sets are exchanged, the receiver sends the remote transmitter the N_FTS field to indicate how many FTS Ordered-Sets it must receive to reliably obtain Bit and Symbol Lock. Armed with this information, the transmitter sends at least that many FTS Ordered-Sets during exit from the L0s state. A typical value is between two and four. This implies that the transmitter must send at least that many FTS Ordered-Sets during exit from the L0s state. For example, N_FTS = 4 translates to 4 FTS Ordered-Sets = 4 x 4 symbols = 16 x 4ns/symbol = 64ns, the period of time it takes the receiver's PLL to achieve Bit and Symbol Lock during exit from the L0s state. When the Extended Synch bit is set in the transmitter device, 4096 FTS Ordered-Sets must be sent in order to provide external Link monitoring tools with enough time to achieve Bit and Symbol

Lock synchronization. During the FTS Ordered set exchange, if the N_FTS period of time expires and the Receiver has not yet obtained Bit Lock, Symbol Lock, and Lane-to-Lane de-skew on all Lanes of the configured Link, the Receiver must transition to the Recovery state of the LTSSM.

- **Symbol 4 (Rate ID):** Each device informs its neighbor what data transfer rate it supports. A value of D2.0 indicates a 2.5Gbits/s transfer rate, while other values are currently reserved.
- **Symbol 5 (Training Control):** A device that sends TS1 and TS2 Ordered-Sets uses this symbol to communicate additional information such as:
  - — Bit 0, when set, indicates Hot Reset.
  - — Bit 1, when set, indicates Link Disable.
  - — Bit 2, when set, indicates Enable Loopback.
  - — Bit 3, when set, indicates disable scrambling.
  - — The remainder of the bits are reserved.

  Only one bit can be set in this field per Ordered-Set.
- **Symbol 6-15 (Training Sequence ID):** Driven with D10.2 for TS1 Ordered-Sets and D5.2 for TS2 Ordered-Sets.

See Table 14-1 for a summary of this information.

Table 14-1: Summary of TS1 and TS2 Ordered-Set Contents

Symbol Number	Allowed Value	Encoded Character Value	Description
0	Comma	K28.5	This is the COM (Comma) symbol.
1	0-255	D0.0 - D31.7, K23.7 (PAD)	Link Number. Uses the PAD symbol when there is no Link Number to communicate.
2	0-31	D0.0 - D31.0, K23.7 (PAD)	Lane Number. Use the PAD symbol when no there is no Lane Number to communicate.
3	0-255	D0.0 - D31.7	N_FTS. This is the number of FTS Ordered-Sets required by receiver to obtain Bit and Symbol Lock during exit from the L0s state.

Table 14-1: Summary of TS1 and TS2 Ordered-Set Contents (Continued)

Symbol Number	Allowed Value	Encoded Character Value	Description
4	2	D2.0	Data Rate Identifier: • Bit 0 = Reserved. • Bit 1 = 1, Generation1 (2.5Gbits/s). • Bits 7:2 = Reserved.
5	Bit 0 = 0,1 Bit 1 = 0,1 Bit 2 = 0,1 Bit 3 = 0,1 Bit 4:7 = 0	D0.0, D1.0, D2.0, D4.0, D8.0	Training Control. 0=De-assert, 1 = Assert: • Bit 0 - Hot Reset, • Bit 1 - Disable Link • Bit 2 - Enable Loopback • Bit 3 - Disable Scrambling • Bit 4:7 - Reserved, Set to 0
6-15		D10.2 for TS1 ID D5.2 for TS2 ID	TS1/TS2 Ordered-Set Identifier.

Electrical Idle Ordered-Set

The Electrical Idle Ordered-Set consists of four symbols, starting with the COM symbol and followed by three IDL symbols. This Ordered-Set is transmitted to a receiver prior to the transmitter placing its transmit half of the Link in the Electrical Idle state. The receiver detects this Ordered-Set, de-gates its error detection logic and prepares for the Link to go to the Electrical Idle state. Shortly after transmitting the Electrical Idle Ordered-Set, the transmitter drives a differential voltage of less than 20mV peak. For more details on Electrical Idle Ordered-Set usage and the Electrical Idle Link state, see "Electrical Idle" on page 464 .

FTS Ordered-Set

The FTS Ordered-Set consists of four symbols, starting with the COM symbol and followed by three FTS symbols. A transmitter that wishes to transition the state of its Link from the L0s low power state (Electrical Idle) to the L0 state sends a defined number of FTS Ordered-Sets to the receiver. The minimum number of FTS Ordered-Sets that the transmitter must send to the receiver is sent to the transmitter by the receiver during Link training and initialization. See "TS1 and TS2 Ordered-Sets" on page 505, Symbol 3.

SKIP Ordered-Set

The Skip Ordered-Set consists of four symbols, starting with the COM symbol and followed by three SKP symbols. It is transmitted at regular intervals from the transmitter to the receiver and is used for Clock Tolerance Compensation as described in "Inserting Clock Compensation Zones" on page 436 and "Receiver Clock Compensation Logic" on page 442.

Link Training and Status State Machine (LTSSM)

General

Figure 14-5 on page 510 illustrates the top-level states of the Link Training and Status State Machine (LTSSM). Each state consists of substates that, taken together, comprise that state. The first LTSSM state entered after exiting Fundamental Reset (Cold or Warm Reset) or Hot Reset is the Detect state.

The LTSSM consists of 11 top-level states: Detect, Polling, Configuration, Recovery, L0, L0s, L1, L2, Hot Reset, Loopback, and Disable. These states can be grouped into five categories:

1. The Link Training states.
2. A Link Re-Training State.
3. The Power Management states.
4. The Active Power Management states, and
5. Other states.

Upon any type of Reset exit, the flow of the LTSSM is through the following **Link Training states**:

Detect => Polling => Configuration => L0

If a Link error occurs while in the L0 state and it renders the Link inoperable, the LTSSM transitions to the **Link Re-Training state** (the Recovery state). In this state, the Link is retrained and returned to normal operation (i.e., the L0 state). A Link that is placed in a low power state (such as L1 or L2), returns to the L0 state via the Recovery state.

Without any high-level software involvement, if there are no packets transmitted on the Link (i.e., if the Logical Idle Sequence is transmitted) and a time-out occurs, the device may place its Link into a low power state such as L0s or L1. These are the **Active Power Management** states.

Power management software may place a device into one of the lower device power states such as D1, D2, $D3_{Hot}$ or $D3_{Cold}$. Doing so causes the Link to transition from L0 to one of the lower **Power Management states** such as L1 or L2.

While in the Configuration or the Recovery state, a Link can be directed to enter the Disable state or the Loopback state. While in the Recovery state, a device that receives the Electrical Idle Ordered-Set transits through the Hot Reset state before going to the Detect state. The three states—Disable, Loopback, and Hot Reset—are part of the **Other states** group.

Figure 14-5: Link Training and Status State Machine (LTSSM)

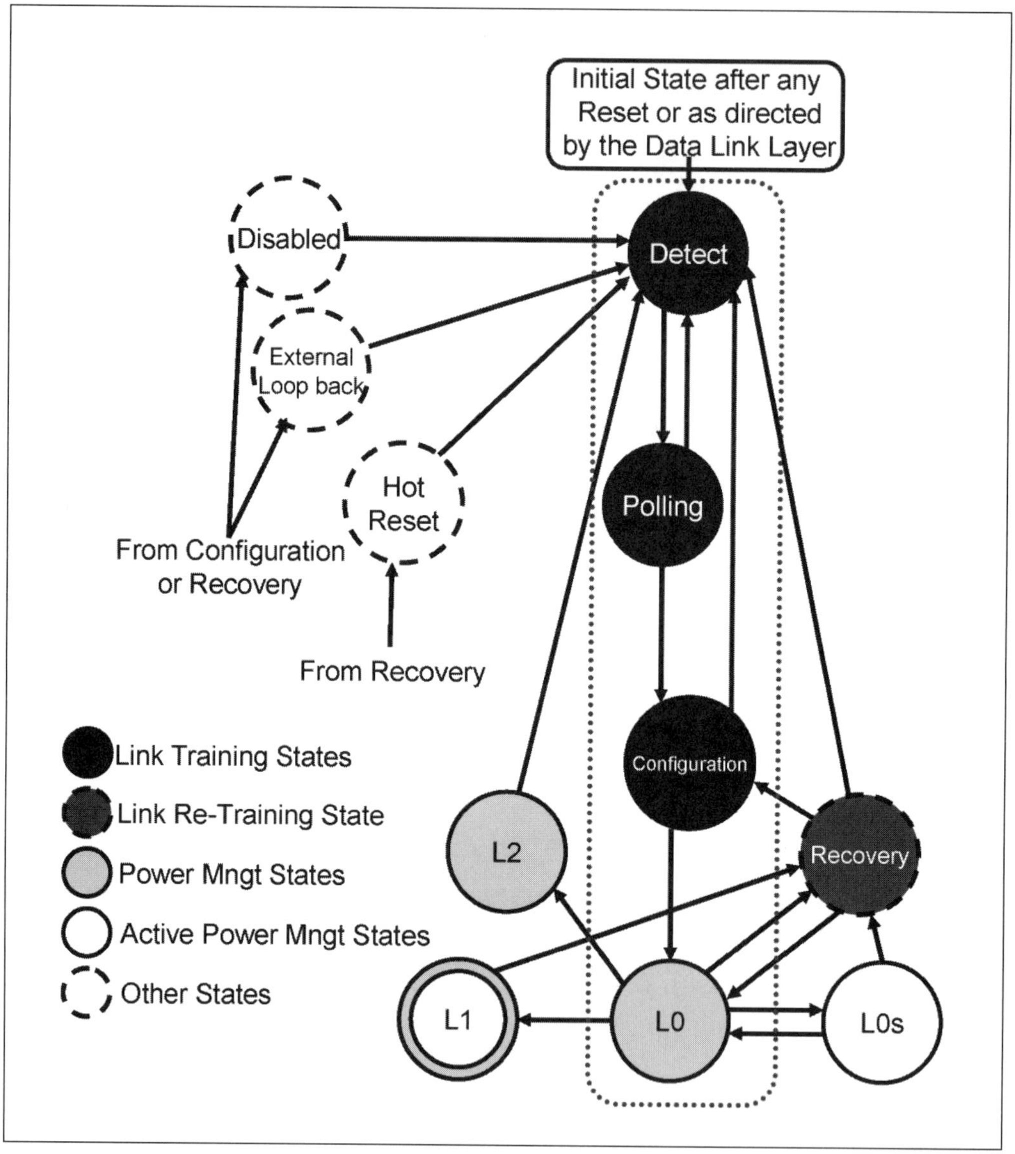

Overview of LTSSM States

Below is a brief description of the 11 LTSSM states:

- **Detect:** This is the initial state after reset. While the spec states that the LTSSM may also enter the Detect state as directed by the Data Link Layer, it does not indicate under what circumstances this would occur. In this state, a device detects the presence or absence of a device connected at the far end of the Link. The Detect state may also be entered from a number of other LTSSM states as described later in this chapter.
- **Polling:** The following conditions are established during the Polling state:
  - Bit Lock.
  - Symbol Lock.
  - Lane Polarity.
  - Lane Data Rate.
  - Compliance testing also occurs in this state.

    During compliance testing, the transmitter outputs a specified compliance pattern. This is intended to be used with test equipment to verify that all of the voltage, noise emission and timing specifications are within tolerance. During the Polling state, a device transmits TS1 and TS2 Ordered-Sets and responds to received TS1 and TS2 Ordered-Sets. Higher bit rate support is advertised via the exchange of TS1 and TS2 Ordered-Sets with the Rate ID field = the highest supported rate.
- **Configuration:** The following conditions are established during the Configuration state:
  - Link width.
  - Link Number.
  - Lane reversal.
  - Polarity inversion (if necessary).
  - Lane-to-Lane de-skew is performed.

    Both transmitter and receiver are communicating at the negotiated data rate (as of 6/16/03, the generation 1 data rate of 2.5Gb/s). During this state, scrambling can be disabled, the Disable and Loopback states can be entered, and the number of FTS Ordered-Sets required to transition from the L0s state to the L0 state is established.
- **L0:** This is the normal, fully active state of a Link during which TLPs, DLLPs and PLPs can be transmitted and received.
- **Recovery:** This state is entered from the L0 state due to an error that renders the Link inoperable. Recovery is also entered from the L1 state when the Link needs re-training before it transitions to the L0 state. In Recovery, Bit Lock and Symbol Lock are re-established in a manner similar to that used in

the Polling state. However, the time to transition through this state is much shorter than having to go through the Polling state and then transitioning to the L0 state. Lane-to-Lane de-skew is performed. The number of FTS Ordered-Sets required to transition from the L0s state to the L0 state is re-established.

- **L0s:** This is a low power, Active Power Management state. It takes a very short time (in the order of 50ns) to transit from the L0s state back to the L0 state (because the LTSSM does not have to go through the Recovery state). This state is entered after a transmitter sends and the remote receiver receives Electrical Idle Ordered-Sets while in the L0 state. Exit from the L0s state to the L0 state involves sending and receiving FTS Ordered-Sets. When transitioning from L0s exit to L0, Lane-to-Lane de-skew must be performed, and Bit and Symbol Lock must be re-established.
- **L1:** This is an even lower power state than L0s. L1 exit latency (via Recovery) is longer compared to L0s exit latency (see "Electrical Physical Layer State in Power States" on page 481). Entry into L1 can occur in one of two ways:
  — The first is automatic and does not involve higher-level software. A device with no scheduled TLPs or DLLPs to transmit can automatically place its Link in the L1 state after first being in the L0 state (while the device remains in the D0 power state).
  — The second is as a result of commands received from the power management software placing a device into a lower power device state (D1, D2, or $D3_{Hot}$). The device automatically places its Link in the L1 state.
- **L2:** This is the lowest power state. Most of the transmitter and receiver logic is powered down (with the exception of the receiver termination, which must be powered for the receiver to be in a low impedance state). Main power and the clock are not guaranteed, though V_{aux} power is available. When Beacon support is required by the associated system or form factor specification, an upstream port that supports this wakeup capability must be able to send the Beacon signal and a downstream port must be able to detect the Beacon signal (see "Beacon Signaling" on page 469). Beacon signaling or the WAKE# signal is used by a device in the $D3_{Cold}$ state to trigger a system wakeup event (i.e., a request for main power supply re-activation). Another power state defined by the specification is the L3 state, but this state does not relate to the LTSSM states. The L3 Link state is the full-off state where the V_{aux} power signal is not available. A device in L3 cannot trigger a wakeup event unless power is re-applied to the device through some other mechanism.
- **Loopback:** This state is used as a test and fault isolation state. Only entry and exit of this state is specified. The details of what occurs in this state are unspecified. Testing can occur on a per Lane basis or on the entire config-

ured Link. The Loopback Master device sends TS1 Ordered-Sets to the Loopback Slave with the Loopback bit set in the TS1 Training Control field. The Loopback Slave enters Loopback when it receives two consecutive TS1 Ordered-Sets with the Loopback bit set. How the Loopback Master enters into the Loopback state is device specific. Once in the Loopback state, the Master can send any pattern of symbols, as long as the 8b/10b encoding rules are followed.

- **Disable:** This state allows a configured Link to be disabled (e.g., due to a surprise removal of the remote device). In this state, the transmitter driver is in the electrical high impedance state and the receiver is enabled and in the low impedance state. Software commands a device to enter the Disable state by setting the Disable bit in the Link Control register. The device then transmits 16 TS1 Ordered-Sets with the Disable Link bit set in the TS1 Training Control field. A connected receiver is Disabled when it receives TS1 Ordered-Sets with the Disable Link bit set.
- **Hot Reset:** This state is entered when directed to do so by a device's higher layer, or when a device receives two, consecutive TS1 Ordered-Sets with the Hot Reset bit set in the TS1 Training Control field (see "In-Band Reset or Hot Reset" on page 491).

Detailed Description of LTSSM States

The subsections that follow provide a description of each of the LTSSM states. Most of the 11 LTSSM states are divided into two or more substates. SubState diagrams are used in the dicussions that follow to illustrate the substates.

Detect State

This state is the initial state at power-on time after a Fundamental Reset or after a Hot Reset command generated by the Software Layer. Entry into this state must occur within 80ms of Reset as described in "Reset Exit" on page 496. The Detect state can also be entered from the Disable, Loopback or L2 states. The Detect state is entered if the Configuration, Recovery or Polling states do not complete sucessfully. Figure 14-6 shows the Detect substate machine.

Detect.Quiet SubState

Entry—

From Fundamental Reset or Hot Reset. Also from L2, Loopback, Disable, Polling, Configuration and Recovery states.

During Detect Quiet—

- The transmitter is in the Electrical Idle state. The Electrical Idle Ordered-Set does not have to be transmitted before placing the Link in the Electrical Idle state.
- The transmitter drives a DC common mode voltage (it does not have to meet the 0 - 3.6 V specification).
- 2.5Gbit/s (Generation 1) transfer rate is initialized (but this is not the rate that will necessarily be advertised via the TS1 and TS2 Ordered-Sets).
- The Data Link Layer is sent LinkUp = 0.

Exit to Detect.Active—

After 12 ms timeout or when Link exits the Electrical Idle state.

Detect.Active SubState

Entry from Detect.Quiet—

This state is entered after 12ms or when the Link exits the Electrical Idle state.

During Detect.Active—

The transmitter device detects if receivers are connected on all Lanes of the Link. The transmitter starts at a stable DC common mode voltage on all Lanes. This voltage can be V_{DD}, GND, or some other stable voltage in-between. The transmitter then drives a DC common mode voltage other than the one currently presented. A receiver is detected based on the rate at which the D+ and D- lines charge to the new voltage. At design time, the device is designed with knowledge of the charge time to change the voltage (based on the assumed line impedance and transmitter impedance without receiver termination). With a receiver attached at the other end, the charge time will be longer than if there is no connected receiver. For more details on the receiver detection process, see "Receiver Detection" on page 459.

Exit to Detect.Quiet—

Occurs if a receiver is not detected. The loop from Detect.Quiet to Detect.Active is repeated every 12ms, as long as no receiver is attached. The next state is Polling if a Receiver is detected on all unconfigured Lanes.

Exit to Polling—

If the device detects a receiver attached. The Device must now drive a DC common voltage within the 0 - 3.6 V $V_{TX\text{-}CM\text{-}DC}$ specification.

Special Case—

If all Lanes of a device are not connected to a receiver. For example, a x4 device is connected to a x2 device. In that case, the device detects that some Lanes (two Lanes) are connected to a receiver, while others are not. Those Lanes connected to a receiver belong to one LTSSM.There are two choices at this point:

- Those Lanes not connected to a receiver belong to another LTSSM (if they can operate as a separate Link—see "Designing Devices with Links that can be Merged" on page 522). The other LTSSM continues to repeat the receiver detection sequence described above.
- Those Lanes that are not connected to a receiver and cannot become part of another Link and LTSSM must transition the unconnected Lanes to the Electrical Idle state.

Figure 14-6: Detect State Machine

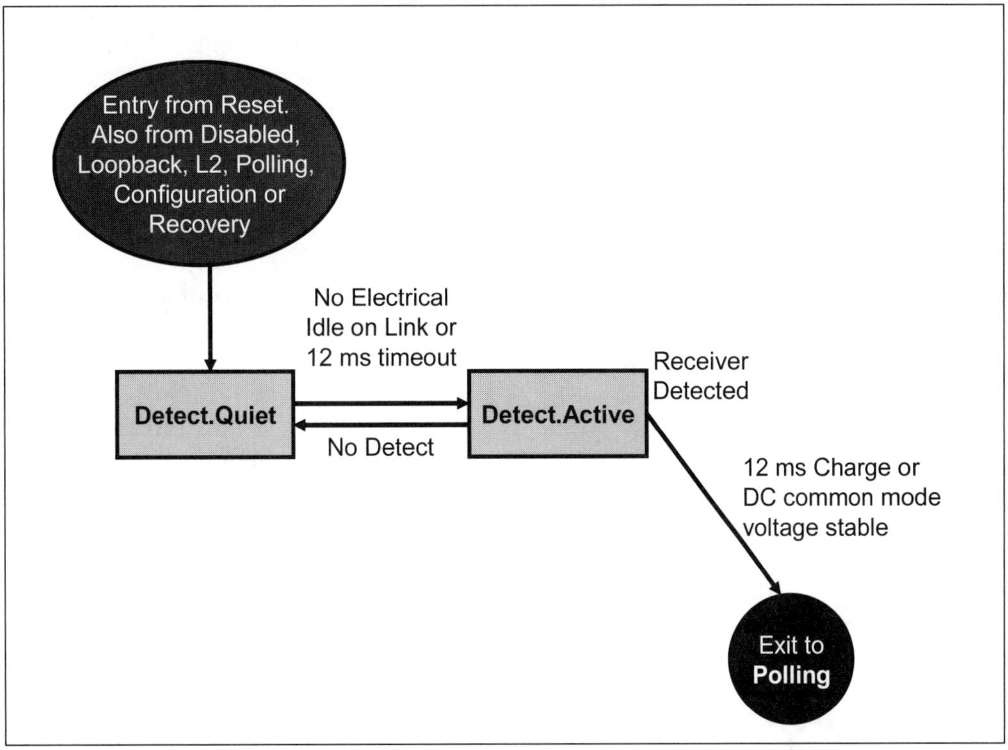

Polling State

Introduction

This state is the first time in the Link training and initialization process that PLPs (such as TS1 and TS2 Ordered-Sets) are exchanged between the two connected devices. Figure 14-7 shows the substates of the Polling state machine.

Polling.Active SubState

Entry from Detect—

Transmitters drive a DC common mode voltage within the spec limits on all Lanes on which it detected a receiver.

Entry from Polling.Compliance—

If Electrical Idle exit is detected at the receiver on ALL Lanes that detected a receiver during Detect, the Transmitter exits Polling.Compliance by transmitting 1024 TS1 Ordered-Sets.

Entry from Polling.Speed—

While in Polling.Speed, the Transmitter enters the Electrical Idle state for a minimum of $T_{TX\text{-}IDLE\text{-}MIN}$ and no longer than 2ms. An Electrical Idle ordered set is sent prior to entering the Electrical Idle state. The DC common mode voltage does not have to be within specification. The Data rate is changed on all Lanes to the highest common data rate supported on both sides of the Link indicated by the training sequence.

During Polling.Active—

- Bit/Symbol Lock are obtained as described in the next bullet (see "Symbol Boundary Sensing (Symbol Lock)" on page 441 and "Achieving Bit Lock" on page 440 for further details).
- The transmitters of the two connected devices transmit a minimum of 1024 consecutive TS1 Ordered-Sets on all connected Lanes. The two devices come out of the Detect state at different times, hence the TS1 Ordered-Set exchange of the two devices are not synchronized with one another. The PAD symbol is used in the Lane and Link Numbers fields of the TS1 Ordered-Sets. 1024 TS1 Ordered-Sets amounts to 64μs of time to achieve Bit and Symbol lock.

Exit to Polling.Configuration—

The next state will be Polling.Configuration if one of the following conditions is true:

- If a device receives eight consecutive TS1 or TS2 Ordered-Sets (or their complement due to polarity inversion) with Lane and Link set to the PAD symbol on ALL Lanes and at least 1024 TS1 Ordered Sets are transmitted, or
- After a 24ms timeout, if:
  - A device receives eight consecutive TS1 or TS2 Ordered-Sets (or their complement) with the Lane and Link numbers set to PAD symbol on ANY Lanes that detected a receiver during Detect, AND
  - at least 1024 TS1 Ordered-Sets were transmitted, AND
  - all Lanes that detected a receiver detected an exit from Electrical Idle at least once since entering Polling.Active (this prevents one or more bad transmitters or receivers from holding up Link configuration).

Exit to Polling.Compliance—

If at least one Lane that detected a receiver during Detect has never detected an exit from Electrical Idle since entering Polling.Active (a passive test load such as a resistor on at least one Lane forces all Lanes into Polling.Compliance).

Exit to Detect—

If no TS1 or TS2 Ordered-Sets are received with the Link and Lane number fields set to the PAD symbol on any Lane. Also, the highest advertised speed must be lowered to generation 1 (if not already advertised as such).

Polling.Configuration SubState

Entry from Polling.Active—

Enters Polling.Configuration if **either** of the following two conditions are true:

— If a device receives eight consecutive TS1 or TS2 Ordered-Sets (or their complement due to polarity inversion) with the Lane and Link numbers set to the PAD symbol on ALL Lanes and at least 1024 TS1 Ordered Sets are transmitted, **or**

— After a 24ms timeout, if a device receives eight consecutive TS1 or TS2 Ordered-Sets (or their complement) with the Lane and Link numbers set to the PAD symbol on ANY Lanes that detected a receiver while in the Detect state, and at least 1024 TS1 Ordered-Sets were transmitted, AND all Lanes that detected a receiver detected an exit from Electrical Idle at least once since entering Polling.Active (prevents one or more bad transmitters or receivers from holding up Link configuration).

During Polling.Configuration—

— If a receiver sees the complement of the TS1/TS2 Ordered-Sets, it has to invert the polarity of its differential input pair terminals. Basically, if D21.5 rather than D10.2 is received in the TS1 Ordered-Set, or if D26.5 rather than D5.2 is received for the TS2 Ordered-Set, then the receiver (not the transmitter) must invert its signal polarity. Polarity Inversion is a mandatory feature (see "Link Initialization and Training Overview" on page 500 for example of Polarity Inversion) and must be implemented on all Lanes independently.

— The Transmitter sends more than eight TS2 Ordered-Sets.

Exit to Configuration—

Assumes that no speed > 2.5Gbits/s is identified in the Data Rate Identifier field of the TS2 Ordered-Set. After receiving eight consecutive TS2 Ordered-Sets and transmitting 16 TS2 Ordered-Sets after receiving one TS2 Ordered-Set, exit to Configuration.

Exit to Polling.Speed—

The next state is Polling.Speed after eight consecutive TS2 Ordered Sets, with Link and Lane numbers set to the PAD symbol (K23.7), are received on any Lanes that detected a Receiver during Detect, 16 TS2 Ordered Sets are transmitted after receiving one TS2 ordered set, and at least one of those same Lanes is transmitting and receiving a Data Rate Identifier greater than 2.5Gb/s.

Exit to Detect—

If neither of the two exit conditions are met, exit to Detect after a 48ms time-out.

Polling.Compliance SubState

Entry from Polling.Active—

The next substate is Polling.Compliance if at least one Lane that detected a receiver during Detect has never detected an exit from the Electrical Idle state on its receiver since entering Polling.Active (a passive test load, such as a resistor, on at lease one Lane forces all Lanes into Polling.Compliance).

During Polling.Compliance—

A test probe (of 50 Ohms impedance) or a 50 Ohm impedance to ground hooked to the transmit pair on any Lane causes the device to enter Polling.Compliance (see "Transmit Driver Compliance Test and Measurement Load" on page 479"). In this state, the device (a pattern generator) is required to generate the compliance pattern on the Link. The compliance pattern selected produces the worst case interference between neighboring Lanes and results in the worst case EMI . Test equipment hooked to the Link is used to test for EMI noise, cross-talk, Bit Error Rate (BER), etc.

- The Transmitter outputs the compliance pattern on all Lanes that detected a receiver during Detect. The pattern consists of the 8b/10b symbols K28.5, D21.5, K28.5, and D10.2. Current running disparity (CRD) must be set to negative before sending the first symbol.
- No Skip Ordered-Sets are transmitted during Polling.Compliance.

Polling.Compliance Exit—

The compliance state is exited when an Electrical Idle exit is detected on all the Lanes that detected a receiver during Detect. The transmitter exits Polling.Compliance by transmitting 1024 TS1 Ordered-Sets.

Polling.Speed SubState

Entry from Polling.Configuration—

Polling.Speed is entered if:

- Eight consecutive TS2 Ordered-Sets are received, and
- 16 TS2 Ordered-Sets are transmitted after receiving one TS2, and
- at least one of the Lanes is transmitting and receiving with a Data Rate Identifier in the TS2 Ordered-Set that is higher than 2.5Gb/s.

During Polling.Speed—

- In this state, the transmitter enters the Electrical Idle state for at least 50 UI (20ns), but no longer than 2ms. An Electrical Idle Ordered-Set is sent prior to entering the Electrical Idle state and the DC common mode voltage ($V_{TX\text{-}CM\text{-}DC}$) does not have to be within the specified tolerance.
- During this state, the data rate is changed on all Lanes to the highest common data rate supported by both ends of the Link.

Exit to Polling.Active—

This is the default.

Figure 14-7: Polling State Machine

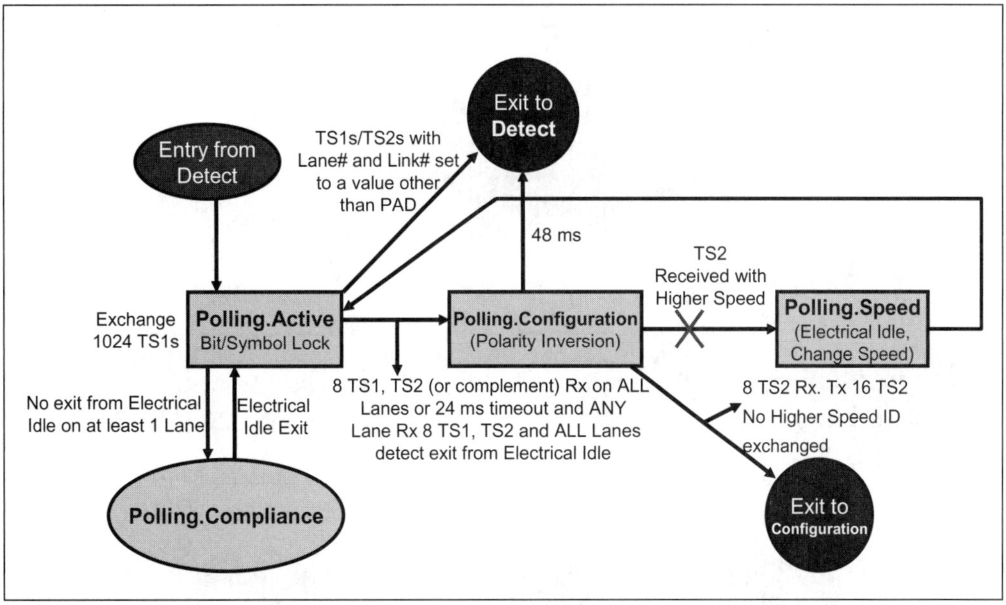

Configuration State

General

The main function of this state is the assignment of Link numbers and Lane numbers to each Link that is connected to a different device. The Link is also De-skewed in this state.

An upstream device sends TS1 Ordered-Sets on all downstream Lanes. This starts the Link numbering and Lane numbering process. If the width determination and Lane numbering is completed successfully, then TS2 Ordered-Sets are transmitted to the neighboring device to confirm the Link Width, Link Number and Lane Number for each Link connected to a different device.

While in the Configuration state, the Link Training bit in the Link Status register is set by hardware (see Figure 14-22 on page 552). This bit is set on Root Complex ports and on downstream Switch ports. It is not set in Endpoints or a Switch upstream ports.

Figure 14-8: Configuration State Machine

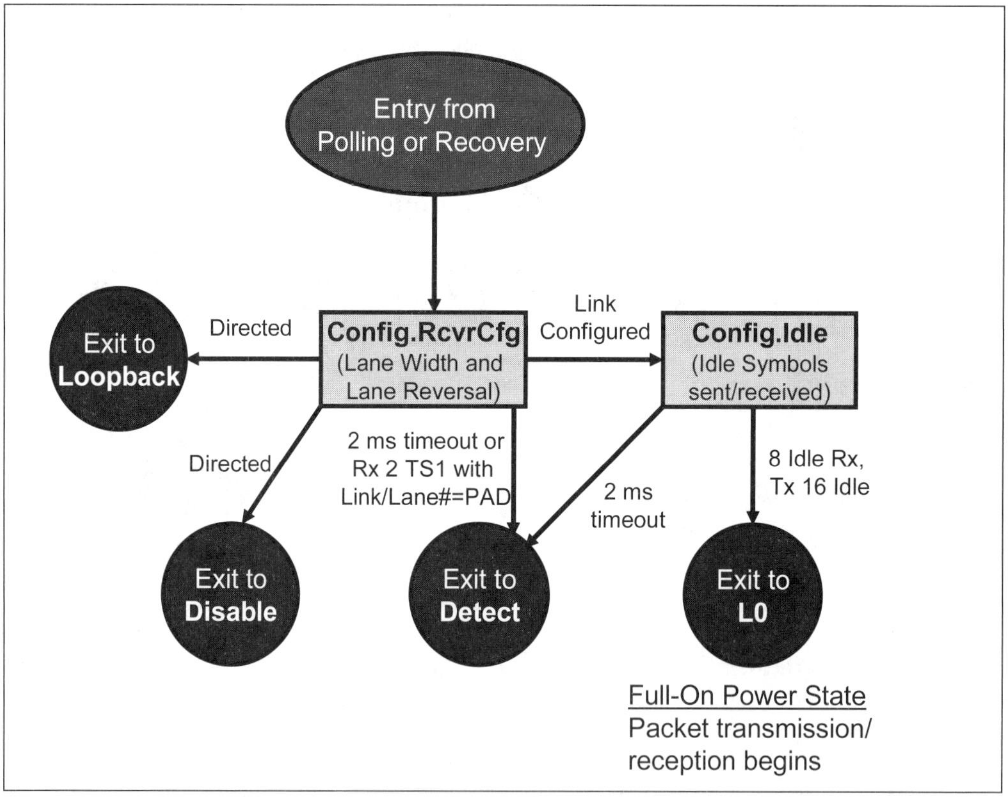

Configuration.RcvrCfg SubState

Entry from Polling or Recovery—

This state is entered after the normal completion of the Polling state (as described in "Polling.Configuration SubState" on page 517). It is also entered if the Recovery state fails to complete successfully (as described in"Recovery State" on page 532).

During Configuration.RcvrCfg—

- The Link Number of each Link connected to a unique device is negotiated.
- The Lanes of each unique Link are numbered starting with Lane 0. If necessary, the Lane Numbers are reversed.
- Those Lanes that are not part of a new Link are disabled and enter the Electrical Idle state. Disabled Lanes are re-enabled if the device enters the Detect state again.
- Each device advertises its N_FTS value in the TS1/TS2 Ordered-Sets it sends to the remote device.
- A receiver uses the COM symbol in the received TS1 and TS2 Ordered-Sets to de-skew the Lanes of the Link (see "Lane-to-Lane De-Skew" on page 444).

Rather than go through a tedious process to explain the Configuration.RcvrCfg function, three examples are presented in "Examples That Demonstrate Configuration.RcvrCfg Function" on page 524. That section describes the Link Numbering and Lane Numbering procedure.

Exit to Configuration.Idle—

When the Link Numbering and Lane Numbering process has completed successfully.

Exit to Detect—

The next state is Detect if, after a 2ms timeout, no Link or Lanes could be configured, or if all Lanes receive two consecutive TS1 Ordered-Sets with the Link and Lane Number fields set to the PAD symbol.

Exit to Disable or Loopback—

If directed to enter the Disable or Loopback state by higher layers:

- Software can inform a Loopback Master connected to the Link to enter the Loopback state in an implementation specific manner. The Loopback Master device continuously sends TS1 Ordered-Sets to the Loopback Slave with the Loopback bit set in the TS1 Training Control field until the Loopback slave returns TS1 Ordered-Sets with the Loopback bit set. The Loopback Slave enters Loopback when it receives two consecutive TS1 Ordered-Sets with the Loopback bit set.

— Similarly, software can command a device to enter the Disable state by setting the Disable bit in the Link Control register (see Figure 14-23 on page 553). This device (a downstream port) then transmits 16 TS1 Ordered-Sets with the Disable Link bit set in the TS1 Training Control field. A connected receiver (on an upstream port) is disabled when it receives TS1 Ordered-Sets with the Disable Link bit set.

Configuration.Idle SubState

Entry from Configuration.RcvrCfg—

When the Link Numbering and Lane Numbering process has completed successfully.

During Configuration.Idle—

The Link is fully configured. Bit Lock and Symbol Lock have been achieved. The Link data rate has been selected. The Link and Lane Numbers have been assigned.

— The Transmitter sends Logical Idle sequences (see "Logical Idle Sequence" on page 436) on all configured Lanes. At least 16 Logical Idle sequences are sent.

— The Receiver waits for the receipt of the Logical Idle data.

— The receivers Data Link Layer LinkUp status bit is set to 1.

Exit to L0—

Occurs when eight Logical Idle symbols are received on all configured Lanes and 16 Logical Idles are sent after receiving 1 Logical Idle. L0 is the full-on power state during which normal packet transmission and reception can occur. The differential transmitters and receivers are enabled in the low impedance state.

Exit to Detect—

Occurs when, after a 2ms timeout, no Logical Idle symbols have been exchanged.

Designing Devices with Links that can be Merged

General. A designer decides how many Lanes to implement on a given Link based on performance requirements for that Link. The specification requires that a device that implements a multi-Lane Link must be designed to operate as a one-x1 Link also. This allows such a multi-Lane Link device to operate when and if it connects to a x1 Link device (Link performance is lower, however).

An optional feature allows two or more downstream Links (associated with different ports) of a switch to be combined to form a wider Link that is connected to one device. Figure 14-9 on page 524 shows a Switch with one upstream port and four downstream ports. The Switch supports eight upstream Lanes and eight downstream Lanes. On the downstream side, the Switch supports four ports. It is therefore four-x2 capable. By combining two ports, it is also two-x4 capable. As required by the specification, each port must be x1 capable.

Four-x2 Configuration. The Switch is capable of supporting up to four downstream ports, with each port a x2 port (four-x2 capable on the downstream side) that connects to four devices (left side of Figure 14-9 on page 524). The bridge internally consists of one upstream logical bridge and four downstream logical bridges.

During Link Training, while in the Configuration.RcvrCfg substate, the LTSSM of each switch downstream port establishes that it is connected to four devices with x2 Links each. Essentially, the switch consists of four ports, four LTSSMs, four Physical Layers, four Data Link Layers and four Transaction Layers.

Two-x4 Configuration. This switch design also allows its downstream Lanes to be combined into two downstream x4 ports (right side of Figure 14-9). In other words, the eight downstream Lanes may be wired to two, independent x4 devices. In thise case, the switch consists of one upstream logical bridge and two downstream logical bridges.

During Link Training, while in the Configuration.RcvrCfg substate, the LTSSM of each switch downstream port establishes that it is connected to two downstream devices with x4 Links each. Essentially, the switch in this configuration has two downstream ports and the four switch LTSSMs are merged into two LTSSMs. The switch has two Physical Layers, two Data Link Layers and two Transaction Layers on the downstream side.

The switch is capable of four-x2 Links on the downstream side (left) or two-x4 Links (right), depending on how the designer chooses to wire up the downstream switch Lanes.

During the Configuration.RcvrCfg state, the LTSSM discovers how the downstream Lanes are wired. Each Link that connects to a unique device is numbered uniquely and each Lane of a Link is also numbered. Designing a switch with this capability is no trivial task, so the feature that permits the combining or splitting of Links to form a wider or narrower Link is optional.

It is a requirement that each multi-Lane port be able to operate as a x1 port when connected to a x1 device.

Figure 14-9: Combining Lanes to form Links

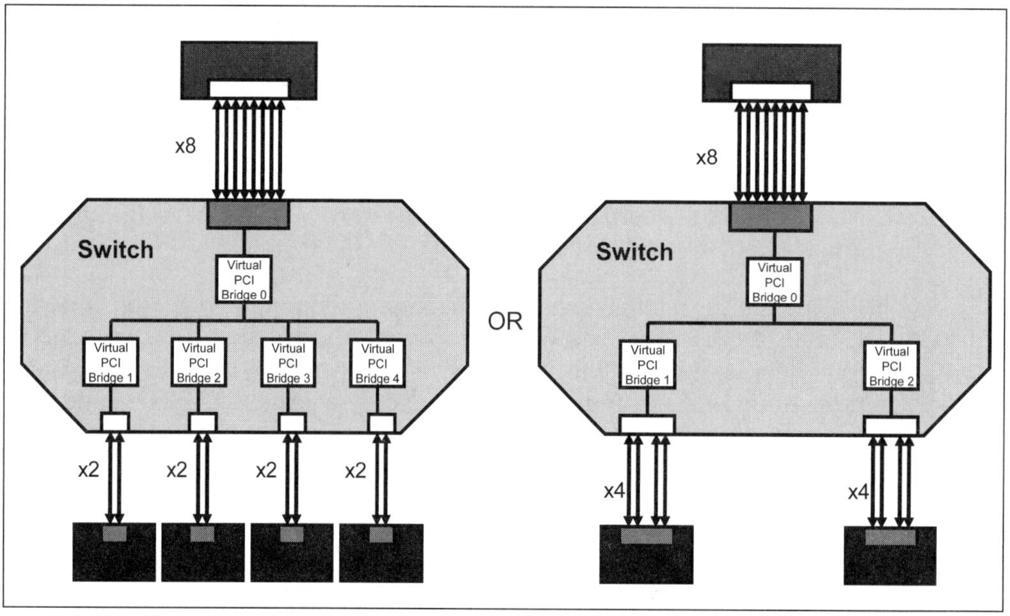

Examples That Demonstrate Configuration.RcvrCfg Function

The Link numbering and Lane numbering process is initiated by an upstream device during the Configuration.RcvrCfg substate. A Root Complex or a Switch downstream port would initiate the Configuration.RcvrCfg process. Endpoints and upstream ports are downstream devices and do not initiate this process.

TS1 and TS2 Ordered-Sets are transmitted and received during this substate. Upon exit from the Configuration.RcvrCfg substate, each Link has been initialized with a Link number (this indirectly establishes the number of ports a device supports). Each Lane has also been initialized with a Lane number (this indirectly establishes the Link width).

Three examples are covered in the next three sections.

RcvrCfg Example 1

Consider Figure 14-10 on page 527. Device A is one-x4 capable, one-x2 capable and one-x1 capable (One-x1 support is required by the spec). Device B is one-x4 capable, one-x2 capable and one-x1 capable (it is required to support this capability by the spec). The device pins associated with each Lane are physically numbered 0, 1, 2 and 3 (shown in the Figure 14-10), though the assigned Logical Lane numbers may have been changed while in Configuration.RcvrCfg sub-state (in this example, the Logical Lane Number remains the same as the physical Lane Number).

Link Number Negotiation.

1. **Mechanism**: Upstream Device A transmits TS1 Ordered-Sets with the Link Number for each group of connected Lanes set to a device-specific initial value. As an example, a switch with four downstream ports may initially set the Link numbers to 0, 1, 2, and 3. The Lane Number field is initially set to the PAD symbol (K23.7).
   Actions Taken: This implies that Device A sends four TS1 Ordered-Sets on the four Lanes. The four TS1 Ordered-Sets each contain a Link Number *n, n, n, n,* and the Lane Number fields are set to the PAD symbol. Even though Device A is also capable of One-x1 and One-x2 operation, Device A starts by assuming the capability that maximizes the use of all connected Lanes.
2. **Mechanism**: Downstream Device B returns TS1 Ordered-Sets on all connected Lanes that received TS1 Ordered-Sets with the assigned common Link Number for Lanes it can support as one Link. The Lane Numbers are initailly set to the PAD symbol (K23.7).
   Actions Taken: Device B returns a TS1 Ordered-Set on all four Lanes. The TS1 Ordered-Sets on each Lane contains Link Number *n*. The Lane Number field contains the PAD symbol. Device A sees the TS1 Ordered-Set with Link numbers of *n* on each Lane. Device A establishes that its four Lanes are connected to one downstream device and that the Link is numbered as *n*. Device A has received confirmation from Device B that its Link can be numbered *n,* where *n* is a number between 0 and 255. The Link is configured as a One-x4 Link.

The Link Number of *n* is a logical Link Number that is not stored in a defined configuration register. This number is hard-wired by design, and not related to the Port Number field of the Link Capability Register.

Also, the Negotiated Link Width field in the Link Status register of both the upstream and downstream devices are updated with "000100", indicating a x4 Link (see Figure 14-22 on page 552).

Lane Number Negotiation.

3. **Mechanism**: Upstream Device A sends TS1 Ordered-Sets on all connected Lanes with the configured Link Number and unique Lane Numbers starting with 0 for each Lane. PAD symbols are no longer sent in the Lane Number field.
   Actions Taken: Device A sends four TS1 Ordered-Sets with Link Number of *n* and Lane Numbers of 0, 1, 2 and 3, respectively, on each connected Lane.
4. **Mechanism**: Downstream Device B returns TS1 Ordered-Sets on all connected Lanes with the same Link Number as contained in the received TS1 Ordered-Sets and the same Lane Numbers for each Lane as indicated in the received TS1 Ordered-Sets.
   If the downstream device's Lanes are hooked in the reverse manner and it does not support the Lane Reversal feature, it returns the TS1 Ordered-Sets with the Lane Number field indicating the manner in which it wants the Lanes to be numbered. Hopefully, the upstream device supports Lane Reversal and accepts the reverse order in which the downstream device wants the Lanes numbered.
   Actions Taken: Device B returns four TS1 Ordered-Sets with a Link Number of *n* and Lane Numbers of 0, 1, 2 and 3, respectively, on each connected Lane.

Confirmation of Link Number and Lane Number Negotiated.

5. **Step 5 and 6. Mechanism**: Device A and B confirm the Link Number and Lane Numbers negotiated by exchanging TS2 Ordered-Sets.
   Actions Taken: Device A and B exchange TS2 Ordered-Sets with the Link Number set to *n* and the Lane Numbers set to 0, 1, 2 and 3, respectively, for each of the four Lanes. In this example, the Logical Lane Numbers of both devices remain the same as the physical Lane Numbers.

Figure 14-10. Example 1 Link Numbering and Lane Numbering

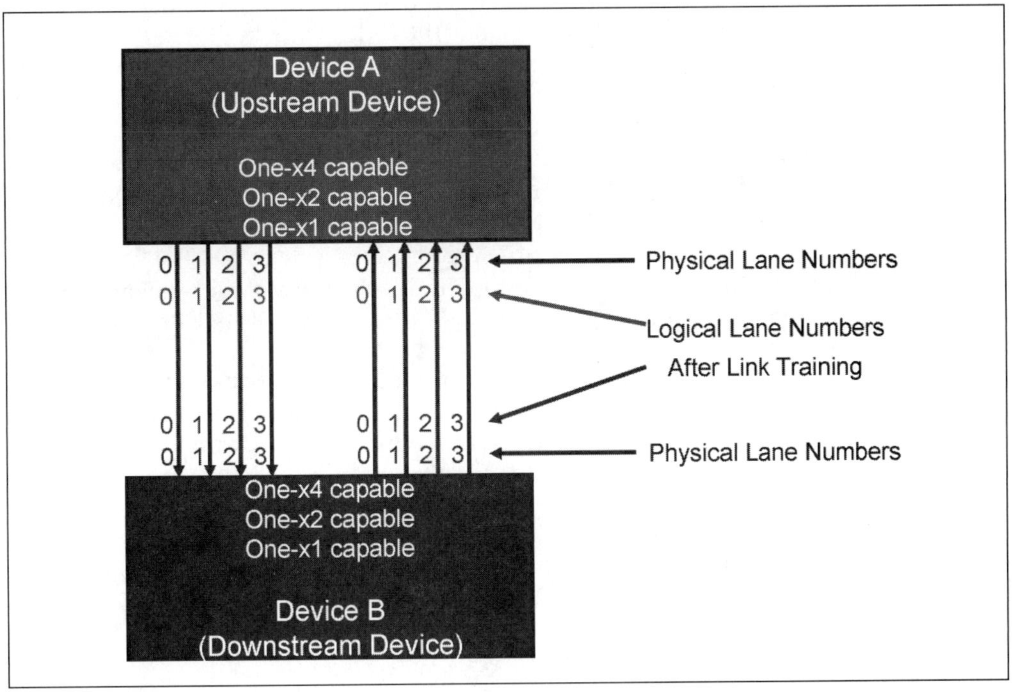

RcvrCfg Example 2

Consider Figure 14-11 on page 529. This is an example in which upstream device A is capable of one-x4, or two-x2, or two-x1. The narrowest Link capability that uses ALL Lanes is two-x2. The two ports of Device A are each x2 capable and the physical Pin Number (Lane number) of each port is 0 and 1. Device B and C each have one port that is x2 capable and the physical Pin Number (Lane number) of each port is 0 and 1.

Using a strapping option on Device A (or by default), it starts the Configuration.RcvrCfg substate by reporting its two-x2 capability when transmitting TS1 Ordered-Sets to the downstream devices.

Link Number Negotiation:

1. **Mechanism:** Upstream Device A transmits TS1 Ordered-Sets with an assumed Link Number value for each group of Lanes capable of acting as unique Links. For now, the Lane Number is set to the PAD symbol (K23.7)

Actions Taken: Device A sends TS1 Ordered-Sets on all four Lanes. The TS1 Ordered-Set on each Lane contains Link number *n*, *n*, *n*+1, and *n*+1. The Lane Number field contains the PAD symbol.

2. **Mechanism:** Downstream Devices B and C return TS1 Ordered-Sets containing the Link number for Lanes it can support as one Link. The Lane Number is initially set to the PAD symbol (K23.7).
   Actions Taken: Device B and C return TS1 Ordered-Sets on each Lane, each containing a Link Number of *n* for Device B and a Link Number of *n*+1 for Device C. The Lane Number field is initially set to the PAD symbol. Device A receives TS1 Ordered-Sets on two of the Lanes with a Link Number of *n* and TS1 Ordered-Sets on the other two Lanes with a Link Number of *n*+1.

The Link Number of *n* and n+1 is a logical Link Number that is not stored in a defined configuration register. This number is not related to the Port Number field of the Link Capability Register of upstream Device A's port or Device B's or Device C's port.

Also, the Negotiated Link Width field in the Link Status register of both upstream ports and downstream ports are updated with "000010," indicating a x2 Link (see Figure 14-22 on page 552).

Lane Number Negotiation.

3. **Mechanism:** Device A realizes that its Lanes are divided into two Links and sends TS1 Ordered-Sets on all connected Lanes with Link Number *n* on two Lanes and Link Number *n*+1 on the other two Lanes. PAD symbols are no longer sent in the Lane Number field.
   Actions Taken: Device A sends a TS1 Ordered-Set on two Lanes with a Link Number of *n* in both of the TS1s, a Lane Number of 0 in one of the TS1s, and a Lane Number of 1 in the other TS1. Device A also sends a TS1 on each of the other two Lanes with a Link Number of *n*+1 in both of the TS1s, a Lane Number of 0 in one TS1, and a Lane Number of 1 in the other TS1.
4. **Mechanism:** Downstream Device B and C returns TS1s on all connected Lanes with the same Link Number as contained in the received TS1 Ordered-Sets and the same Lane Numbers for each Lane as in the received TS1 Ordered-Sets.
   If the downstream devices' Lanes are hooked in the reverse manner and they do not support the Lane Reversal feature, they return the TS1 Ordered-Sets with the Lane Number fields reversed. Hopefully, the upstream device supports Lane Reversal and accepts the reverse order that the downstream devices want the Lanes numbered.

Actions Taken: Device B returns TS1s on each Lane with Link Number of *n* and a Lane Number of 0 in one TS1 Ordered-Set and a Lane Number of 1 in the other. Device C returns a TS1 on each Lane with a Link Number of *n*+1 and a Lane Number of 0 in one TS1 Ordered-Set and a Lane Number of 1 in the other.

Confirmation of Link Number and Lane Number Negotiated.

5. **Step 5 and 6 Mechanism:** Device A and B/C confirm the Link Numbers and Lane Numbers negotiated by exchanging TS2 Ordered-Sets.
   Actions Taken: Device A and B exchange a TS2 Ordered-Set on each Lane with the Link Number set to *n* and the Lane Numbers set to 0 and 1, respectively, for each of the two Lanes on the first Link. Device A and C exchange a TS2 Ordered-Set on each Lane with the Link Number set to *n*+1 and the Lane Numbers set to 0 and 1, respectively, for each of the two Lanes of the second Link. Each Lane of the two Links in this example are logically numbered 0 and 1, matching the physical Pin number (Lane number) of each Lane.

Figure 14-11: Example 2 Link Numbering and Lane Numbering

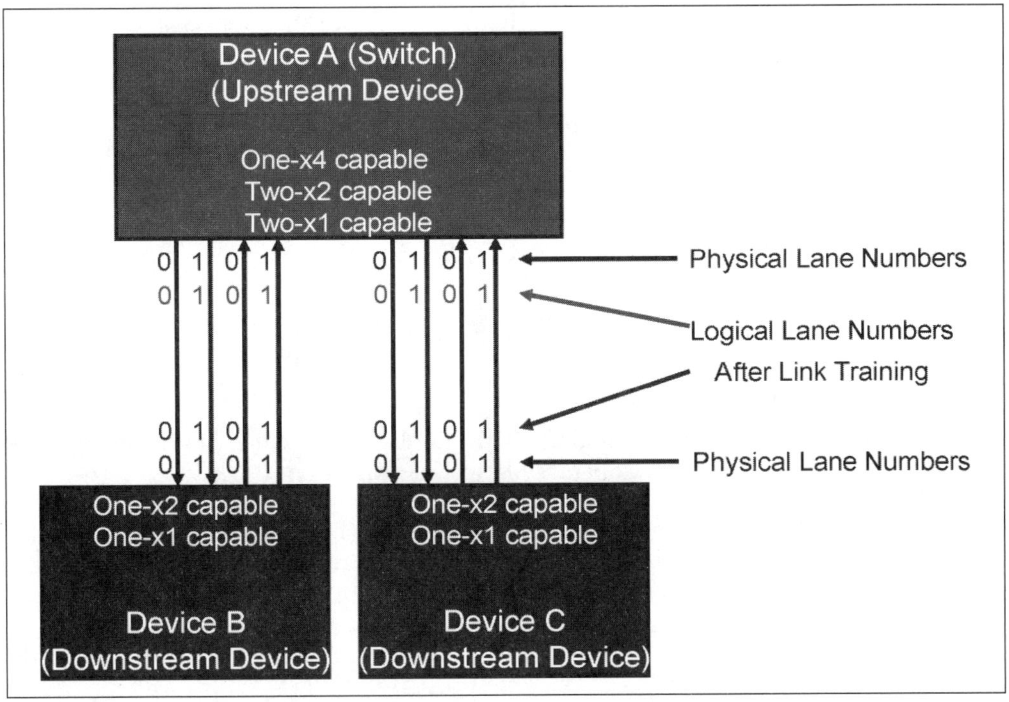

RcvrCfg Example 3

Consider Figure 14-12 on page 532. This is an example in which upstream device A is capable of one-x4, or two-x2, or two-x1 (the same as Device A in the previous example). The narrowest Link capability that uses ALL Lanes is two-x2. Each Lane of Device A's two ports are physically numbered 0 and 1.

Via a strapping option on Device A (or by default), it reports its two-x2 capability when transmitting TS1 Ordered-Sets to the downstream device. In this example, Device A initially assumes that it has two-x2 downstream Links. Also, both of Device A's Links are connected to downstream Device B. Device B is x4 capable. Its pins (or Lanes) are physically numbered 3, 2, 1, 0, respectively. In this example, assume that Device B does **not** support Lane Reversal, but Device A does support Lane Reversal.

Link Number Negotiation.

1. **Mechanism:** Upstream Device A transmits TS1 Ordered-Sets with an assumed Link Number field for each group of Lanes capable of being unique Links that use up all the Lanes. For now, the Lane Number is set to the PAD symbol (K23.7).
   Actions Taken: Device A sends four TS1 Ordered-Sets on the four Lanes. Each TS1 Ordered-Set contains the respective Link number (*n, n, n+1, n+1*). The Lane Number field is initially set to the PAD symbol.
2. **Mechanism:** Downstream Device B returns TS1 Ordered-Sets with an assigned common Link number for Lanes it can support as one Link. The Lane Number is initially set to the PAD symbol (K23.7).
   Actions Taken: Device B returns TS1 Ordered-Sets on each Lane, each containing a Link Number of *n*. The Lane Number field is initially set to the PAD symbol. Device A sees TS1 Ordered-Sets on four Lanes with a Link Number of *n*, telling Device A that its four Lanes are connected to one downstream device and that the Link should be numbered *n*.

The Link Number of *n* is a logical Link Number that is not stored in a defined configuration register. This number is not related to the Port Number field of the Link Capability Register.

Also, the Negotiated Link Width field in the Link Status register of both the upstream port and the downstream port are updated with "000100", indicating a x4 Link (see Figure 14-22 on page 552).

Lane Number Negotiation.

3. **Mechanism:** Device A realizes that its four Lanes are combined into one Link (One-x4) and sends TS1 Ordered-Sets on all connected Lanes with one assumed Link Number, *n*, and a unique Lane Number is assigned to each Lane of the Link. PAD symbols are no longer sent in the Lane Number field.
   Actions Taken: Device A sends TS1 Ordered-Sets on four Lanes with a Link Number of n and Lane Numbers 0, 1, 2, and 3, respectively, numbered left to right.
4. **Mechanism:** Downstream Device B returns a TS1 on all connected Lanes with the same Link Number *n* as contained in the received TS1 Ordered-Set. Assume that the Lanes are hooked up in reverse manner as shown in Figure 14-12 on page 532 and that Device B does not support the Lane Reversal feature.
   If the downstream device's Lanes are reversed and it does not support Lane Reversal, it returns the TS1 Ordered-Sets with the Lane Number fields reversed. Hopefully, the upstream device supports Lane Reversal and accepts the reverse ordering of the Lanes.
   Actions Taken: Device B returns a TS1 Ordered-Set on each Lane with a Link Number of *n* and Lane Numbers of 3, 2, 1 and 0, respectively, numbered from left to right.

Confirmation of Link Number and Lane Number Negotiated.

5. **Step 5 and 6 Mechanism:** Device A and B confirm the Link Number and the Lane Numbers negotiated by exchanging of TS2 Ordered-Sets.
   Actions Taken: Device A and B exchange a TS2 Ordered-Set on each Lane with the Link Number set to *n* and the Lane Numbers set to 3, 2, 1 and 0 (Lanes reversed), respectively, for each of the four Lanes.

Device A's physical Pin Numbers (Lane numbers) for the four Lanes from left to right are 0, 1, and 0, 1 (the same numbers repeated—because Device A is two-x2 port capable). However, Device A ends up with logical Lane Numbers of 3, 2, 1, 0, from left to right. Device B's physical Pin Numbers are 3, 2, 1 and 0, from left to right. The logical Lane Numbers remain the same as the physical Lane Numbers: 3, 2, 1 and 0.

Consider what would happen if Device A did not support Lane Reversal (Lane Reversal is an optional feature). In Step 4, Device B returns four TS1 Ordered-Sets with Lane Numbers of 3, 2, 1 and 0. Device A would not be able to reverse the physical Lane numbers of 0, 1, 2 and 3 that it proposed in Step 3. The Link training process freezes at this point. This is a Link training error and is reported by the upstream device (Device A) via the Link Training Error bit in the Link Status register (see Figure 14-22 on page 552). A system designer would be wrong to hook the Lanes of two devices that do not support Lane Reversal in a reversed manner.

Figure 14-12: Example 3 Link Numbering and Lane Numbering

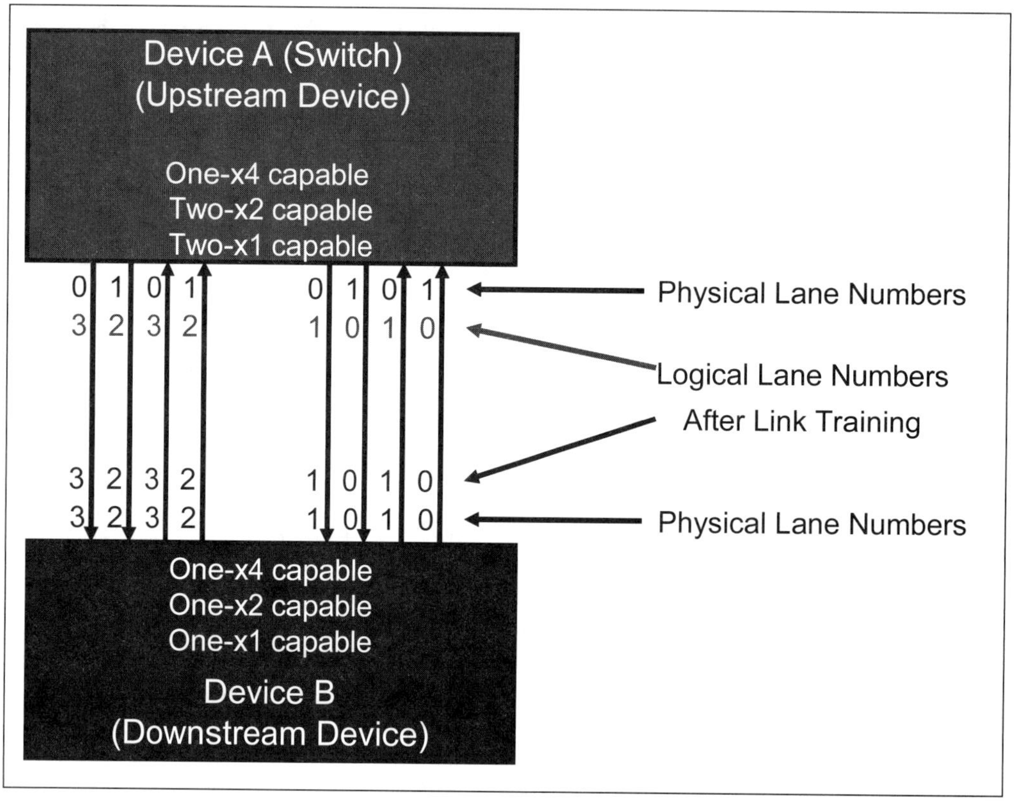

Recovery State

The Recovery state is also referred to as the Re-Training state. It is not entered during Link training (which occurs when a device comes out of reset). The Recovery state is entered when a receiver needs to regain Bit and Symbol Lock, or if an error occurs while in L0 that renders the Link inoperable. Rather than going through the Polling and Configuration states (which have longer latencies associated with them), the Recovery state has a much shorter latency (the PLLs are already operational and may only need to be sync'd). The number of

FTS Ordered-Sets (N_FTS) required for L0s exit is re-established in Recovery and the Link is de-skewed. The Link Number, Lane Numbers and bit transfer rate (2.5Gbits/s) remain unchanged. If any of these three variables have changed since the time the link was in the Configuration state, the LTSSM transitions from the Recovery state to the Configuration state.

Reasons that a Device Enters the Recovery State

- Exit from L1 (requires that the receiver be re-trained).
- Exit from L0s when the receiver is unable to achieve Bit/Symbol Lock due to the reception of an insufficient number of FTS Ordered-Sets.
- In case of an error that renders the Link unreliable, software sets the Retrain Link bit in the Link Control Register (see Figure 14-23 on page 553).
- An error condition that occurs in the L0 state that renders the Link unreliable may automatically cause the Data Link Layer or Physical Layer logic to initiate a re-train cycle.
- Reception of TS1 or TS2 Ordered-Sets on any configured Lane from a remote transmitter signals the receiver to retrain the link.
- A receiver detects that the Link has transitioned to the Electrical Idle state on all configured Lanes without first receiving the Electrical Idle Ordered-Sets from the transmitter.

Initiating the Recovery Process

Both devices on a Link go through Recovery together. One of the two devices initiates the Recovery process, transmitting TS1 Ordered-Sets to its neighbor. The neighbor goes through Recovery and returns the favor by returning TS1 Ordered-Sets that the initiator's receiver uses to go through Recovery. In transmitting and receiving TS1 Ordered-Sets, both the receiver and the transmitter of the Ordered-Sets regains Bit/Symbol Lock, and then returns to the L0 state.

Refer to Figure 14-13 on page 537 for the detailed steps involved in completing the Recovery process described below.

Recovery.RcvrLock SubState

Entry from L0—

A device enters Recovery for the reasons sited in "Reasons that a Device Enters the Recovery State" on page 533.

Entry from L1—

The Receiver detects Electrical Idle exit, or when directed by higher-level software. Electrical Idle exit means that the receiver detected a valid differential voltage and starts seeing TS1 Ordered-Sets.

Entry from L0s—

The Receiver enters into Recovery when it detects an N_FTS timeout (i.e., if the receiver is unable to re-obtain Bit/Symbol Lock after receiving N_FTS FTS Ordered-Sets, or if it receives an insufficient number of FTS Ordered-Sets, then instead of going to L0, it goes to Recovery).

During Recovery.RcvrLock—

— The transmitter sends TS1 Ordered-Sets on all configured Lanes (with the same Link and Lane Numbers as set during the Configuration state). The specification is unclear about how many TS1 Ordered-Sets the transmitter should send, but the author ventures to guess that it should send TS1 Ordered-Sets until this substate is exited.

— If the Extended Sync bit is set by software in the Link Control register (see Figure 14-23 on page 553), the transmitter must send a minimum of 1024 TS1 Ordered-Sets to allow an external monitoring device (i.e., a tool), if connected, to sync (obtain Bit/Symbol Lock).

— The receiver uses the received TS1 Ordered-Sets to obtain Bit/Symbol Lock.

— A device advertises its N_FTS value via the TS1 Ordered-Sets it sends to the remote device. This number can change from what it was during the Configuration state.

— A receiver uses the COM symbol in the received TS1 and TS2 Ordered-Sets to de-skew the Lanes of the Link (see "Lane-to-Lane De-Skew" on page 444).

Exit to Recovery.RcvrCfg—

A receiver moves to Recover.RcvrCfg if eight consecutive TS1 or TS2 Ordered-Sets are received without Link and Lane Number changes.

Exit to Configuration—

After 24ms, if the receiver detects at least one TS1 (but not eight consecutive TS1 Ordered-Sets) on ANY configured Lanes and the Link Number and Lane Number are the same as the numbers Transmitted in the TS1 Ordered-Sets, then it exits to Configuration.

Exit to Detect—

After a 24ms timeout, if the receiver does not detect TS1 or TS2 Ordered-Sets, or it detects TS1 or TS2 Ordered-Sets with the Link or Lane Number different from the numbers in the transmitted TS1 or TS2 Ordered-Sets, then it exits to Detect.

Recovery.RcvrCfg SubState

Entry from Recovery.RcvrLock—

A receiver moves to Recover.RcvrCfg if eight consecutive TS1 or TS2 Ordered-Sets are received without Link and Lane Number changes.

During Recovery.RcvrCfg—

— The Transmitter sends TS2s on all configured Lanes (with the same Link and Lane Numbers configured earlier). Again, the specification is unclear about how many TS2 Ordered-Sets the transmitter should send, but the author ventures to guess that it should send TS2 Ordered-Sets until this substate is exited.

— If the N_FTS value changes, the device must note the new value.

— If the Link was not de-skewed in the Recovery.RcvrLock substate, a receiver uses the COM symbol in the received TS1 and TS2 Ordered-Sets to de-skew the Lanes of the Link (see "Lane-to-Lane De-Skew" on page 444).

Exit to Recovery.Idle—

If eight consecutive TS2 Ordered-Sets are received with no Link/Lane Number changes and 16 TS2 Ordered-Sets are sent after receiving one TS1 or TS2 Ordered-Set, then exit to Recovery.Idle.

Exit to Configuration—

If eight consecutive TS1 Ordered-Sets are received on ANY Lane with Link or Lane Numbers that do not match what is being transmitted, then exit to Configuration state.

Exit to Detect—

Exit to Detect after a 48ms timeout and the state machine has not exited to Recovery.Idle or Configuration state.

Recovery.Idle SubState

Entry from Recovery.RcvrCfg—

Enter from Recovery.RcvrCfg if eight consecutive TS2 Ordered-Sets are received with no Link/Lane Number changes and 16 TS2 Ordered-Sets are sent after receiving one TS1 or TS2 Ordered-Set.

During Recovery.Idle—

— The Transmitter sends Logical Idle symbols on all configured Lanes unless exiting to Disable, Hot Reset, Configuration, or Loopback.

— The Receiver waits for the receipt of Logical Idle symbols on all Lanes.

Exit to Disable, Loopback or Hot Reset—

If directed by higher layers to enter the Disable, Loopback or Hot Reset state. The device transmits TS1 or TS2 (TS2 not valid for Hot Reset case) with the Disable, Loopback or Hot Reset bits set.

If a device receives two consecutive TS1s or TS2s (TS2 not valid for Hot Reset case) with the Disable, Loopback or Hot Reset bit set, it exits to the Disable, Loopback or Hot Reset state respectively.

Software can inform a Loopback Master connected to the Link to enter the Loopback state using an implementation specific mechanism. The Loopback Master device continuously sends TS1 Ordered-Sets to the Loopback

Slave with the Loopback bit set in the TS1 Training Control field until the Loopback slave returns TS1 Ordered-Sets with the Loopback bit set. The Loopback Slave enters Loopback when it receives two consecutive TS1s with the Loopback bit set.

Similarly, software can command a device to enter the Disable state by setting the Disable bit in the Link Control register (see Figure 14-23 on page 553). This device (a downstream port) then transmits 16 TS1 Ordered-Sets with the Disable Link bit set in the TS1 Training Control field. A connected receiver (on the upstream port) is disabled when it receives a TS1 with the Disable Link bit set.

Similarly, software can command a device to enter the Hot Reset state by setting the Secondary Bus Reset bit in the Bridge Control register (see "In-Band Reset or Hot Reset" on page 491). This device (a downstream port) then transmits TS1 Ordered-Sets continuously for 2ms with the Hot Reset bit set in the TS1 Training Control field. A receiver (in the upstream port) detects the Hot Reset when it receives at least two TS1 Ordered-Sets with the Hot Reset bit set.

Exit to Configuration—

Exits to the Configuration state if directed by a higher layer to re-configure the link, or if two consecutive TS1s are received with Lane numbers set to the PAD symbol.

Exit to L0—

If eight Logical Idle symbols are received on all configured Lanes.

Exit to Detect—

Exit to Detect after a 2ms timeout if the LTSSM does not exit to any of the other states above.

Figure 14-13: Recovery State Machine

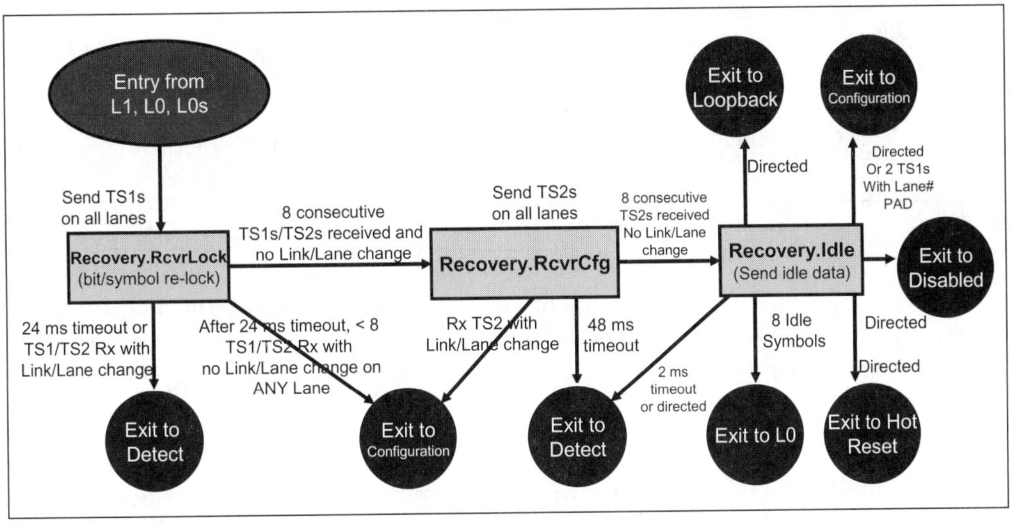

L0 State

Enter from Configuration—

This state is entered from Configuration.Idle substate if eight Logical Idle symbols are received on all configured Lanes and 16 Logical Idles are sent after receiving one Logical Idle.

Enter from Recovery—

This state is entered from the Recovery.Idle substate if eight Logical Idle symbols are received on all configured Lanes.

Enter from L0s—

This state is entered from L0s if a device receives the appropriate number of FTS Ordered-Sets and re-obtains Bit and Symbol Lock.

During L0—

- This is the fully-operational Link state during which TLP, DLLP and PLP transmission and reception can occur.
- The differential transmitters and receivers are enabled in the low impedance state.
- LinkUp=1

Exit to Recovery—

A device enters Recovery for any of the reasons sited in "Reasons that a Device Enters the Recovery State" on page 533.

Exit to L0s—

The Transmitter enters L0s when directed to do so by its higher layers. A Receiver enters L0s when it receives an Electrical Idle Ordered-Set and the Link transitions to the Electrical Idle state.

Exit to L1—

See "L1 State" on page 541 for a detailed description.

Exit to L2—

See "L2 State" on page 543 for a detailed description.

L0s State

This is a lower power state that has the shortest exit latency to L0. Devices manage entry and exit from this state automatically without any higher level software involvement.

L0s Transmitter State Machine

Figure 14-14 on page 539 shows the transmitter state machine associated with L0s state entry and exit.

Tx_L0s.Entry SubState.

Entry from L0—

The L0s state machine is entered when the device is directed to do so by an upper layer. This may occur via a timeout mechanism triggered due to periods of inactivity (no TLP, DLLP or PLP transmission activity) on the Link.

During Tx_L0s.Entry—

— The Transmitter sends an Electrical Idle Ordered-Set and the Link enters the Electrical Idle state.

— The Transmitter drives a DC common mode voltage between 0 - 3.6 V.

Exit to Tx_L0s.Idle—

Exit to Tx_L0s.Idle after 50 UI (20ns) while the transmitter drives a stable DC common mode voltage.

Tx_L0s.Idle SubState.

*Entry from Tx_L0s.Entry—*Enter Tx_L0s.Idle after 50 UI (20 ns) while the transmitter drives a stable DC common mode voltage.

During Tx_L0s.Idle—

— The Link is in the Electrical Idle state.

— The transmitter's output impedance could be low or high.

Exit to Tx_L0s.FTS—

Exit to Tx_L0s.FTS if directed to do so by a higher layer. For example, when it is time for a device to resume packet transmission, it will exit this state.

Tx_L0s.FTS SubState.

Entry from Tx_L0s.Idle—

Enter Tx_L0s.FTS if directed to do so by a higher layer.

During Tx_L0s.FTS—

— To exit the Electrical Idle substate, the transmitter sends the number of FTS Ordered-Sets specified by N_FTS. The N_FTS number is defined during Link Training (Configuration and Recovery states) during which each device advertises the number of FTS sets it requires to achieve lock.

— If the Extended Synch bit is set (see Figure 14-23 on page 553), the transmitter sends 4096 FTS Ordered-Sets instead of N_FTS number of FTS Ordered-Sets.

— Follow this by one Skip Ordered-Set. No SKIP Ordered-Sets are transmitted during the transmission of FTS Ordered-Sets.

Exit to L0—

Exit to L0 state after the Skip Ordered-Set transmission.

Figure 14-14: L0s Transmitter State Machine

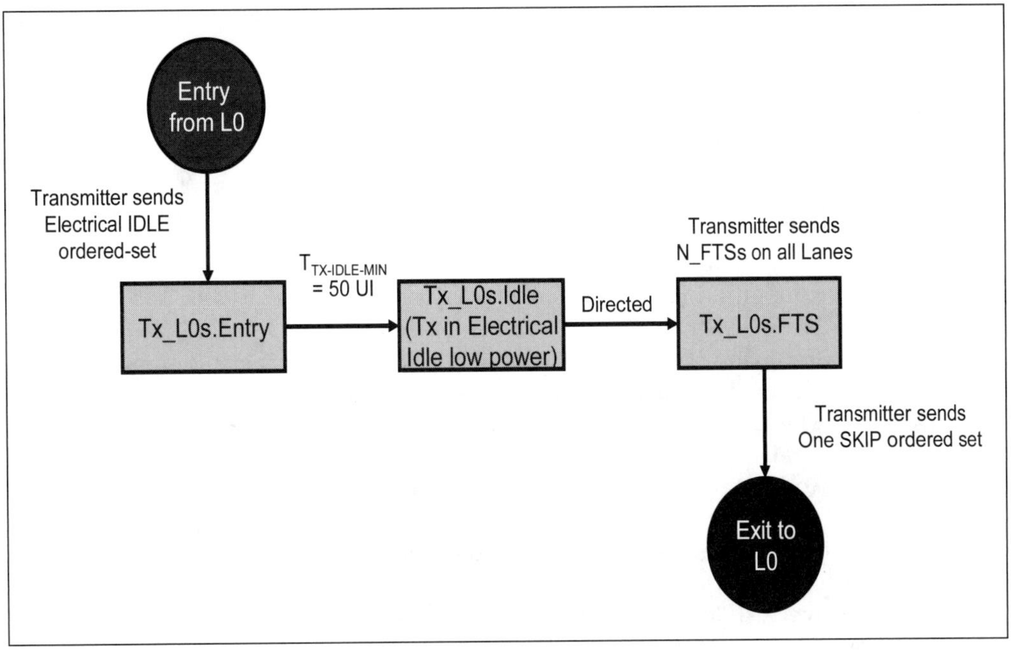

L0s Receiver State Machine

Figure 14-15 on page 541 shows the receiver state machine associated with L0s state entry and exit.

Rx_L0s.Entry SubState.
Entry from L0—
This lower power state is entered if a receiver receives an Electrical Idle Ordered-Set.
During Rx_L0s.Entry—
— Wait in the state for minimum of 50 UI (20ns).
— The receiver's input impedance remains low.
Exit to Rx_L0s.Idle—
Exit to Rx_L0s.Idle after 50 UI (20ns).

Rx_L0s.Idle SubState.
Entry from Rx_L0s.Entry—
Enter Rx_L0s.Idle after 50 UI (20ns).
During Rx_L0s.Idle—
Wait until the receiver detects an Electrical Idle exit (i.e., a valid differential voltage is seen on the receivers).
Exit to Rx_L0s.FTS—
The next state is Rx_L0s.FTS if the receiver detects Electrical Idle exit on any configured Lane.

Rx_L0s.FTS SubState.
Entry from Rx_L0s.Idle—
Enter this state from Rx_L0s.Idle if the receiver detects Electrical Idle exit on any configured Lane.
During Rx_L0s.FTS—
— Receiver obtains Bit/Symbol Lock if a sufficient number of FTS Ordered-Sets are received.
— The receiver must be able to receive packets after this state.
Exit to L0—
Exit to L0 state after Skip Ordered-Set reception and a sufficient number of FTS Ordered-Sets are received (as advertised during the Configuration or Recovery states via the N_FTS field of the TS1/TS2 Ordered-Set).
Exit to Recovery—
Recovery state is entered if an N_FTS timeout occurs (i.e., if the receiver receives an insufficient FTS Ordered-Sets to re-obtain Bit/Symbol Lock).

Figure 14-15: L0s Receiver State Machine

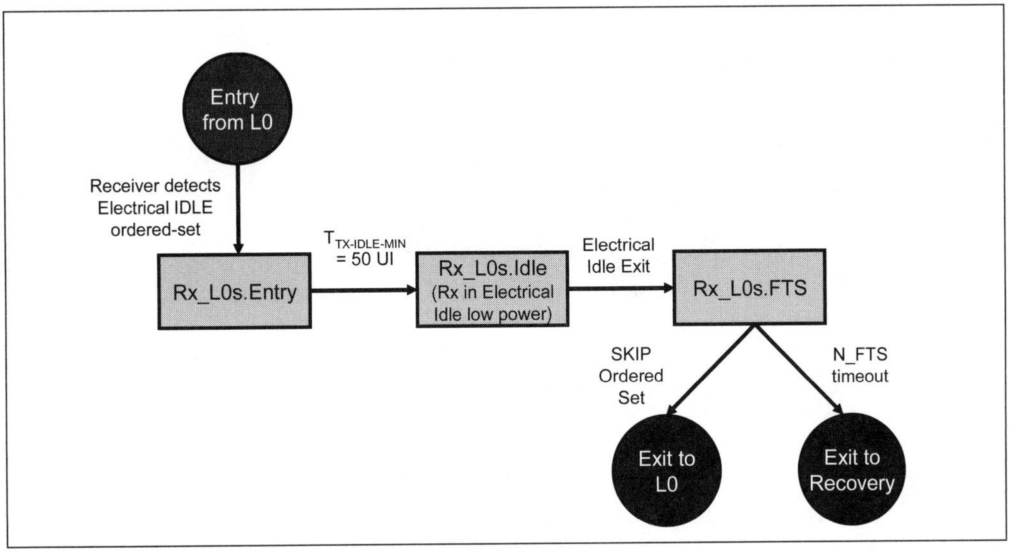

L1 State

This is a lower power state than L0s and has a longer exit latency than the L0s exit latency. Devices can manage entry and exit from this state automatically without any higher level software involvement. In addition, Power management software may direct a device to place its upstream Link into L1 (both directions of the Link go to L1) when the device is placed in a lower power device state such as D1, D2, or D3.

Figure 14-16 on page 542 shows the L1 entry and Exit state machine. This state machine is described in the subsections that follow.

L1.Entry SubState

Entry from L0—
The L0s state machine is entered when a device's higher layer directs the device to do so.
During L1.Entry—

- The Transmitter sends an Electrical Idle Ordered-Set and the Link enters the Electrical Idle state.

- The Transmitter drives a DC common mode voltage between 0 - 3.6 V.

Exit to L1.Idle—
Exit to L1.Idle after 50 UI (20ns), while the transmitter drives a stable DC common mode voltage.

L1.Idle SubState

Entry from L1.Entry—
Enter L1.Idle after 50 UI (20ns), while the transmitter drives a stable DC common mode voltage.

During L1.Idle—

- The Link is in the Electrical Idle state.
- The transmitter's output impedance could be low or high, while the receiver's remains in the low impedance state.
- Remain in this state until the receiver detects Electrical Idle exit (a valid differential voltage associated with the reception of a TS1 Ordered-Set used to signal L1 exit).

Exit to Recovery—
Exit to Recovery after the receiver detects the Electrical Idle exit condition, or if the device is directed to do so.

Figure 14-16: L1 State Machine

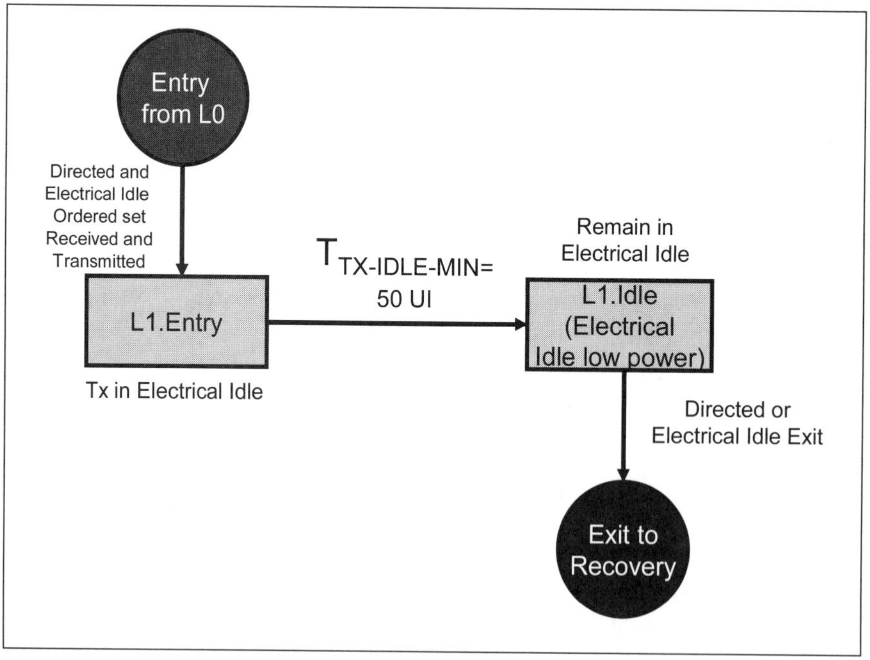

L2 State

This is even lower power state than L1 and has a longer exit latency than L1 exit latency. Power Management software directs a device to place its upstream Link into L2 (both directions of the Link go to L2) when the device is placed in a lower power device state such as $D3_{Cold}$.

Figure 14-17 on page 544 shows the L2 entry and Exit state machine. This state machine is described next.

L2.Idle SubState

Entry from L0—
This state is entered when directed to do so by higher layers and an Electrical Idle Ordered-Set is exchanged between neighbors across a Link.
During L2.Idle—

- The Receiver remains in the low impedance state.
- The Transmitter must remain in the Electrical Idle state for a minimum of 50 UI (20ns).
- The Receiver starts looking for the Electrical exit condition.
- DC common mode voltage doesn't have to be in spec. May be turned off.

Exit to L2.TransmitWake—
When an upstream port is directed to send the Beacon signal due to a wakeup event. Also, when a Beacon is received on at least Lane 0 of a switch downstream port.
Exit to Detect—
When a Beacon is received on at least Lane 0 of a Root Complex downstream port or if a Root Port is directed by a higher layer to go to the Detect state. Also, exit to Detect if an upstream Lane detects the Electrical Idle exit condition.

L1.TransmitWake SubState

Entry from L1.Idle—
Enter into L2.TransmitWake when an upstream port is directed to send the Beacon signal due to a wakeup event. Also, exit to L2.TransmitWake when a Beacon signal is received on at least Lane 0 of a switch downstream port.
During L1.TransmitWake—
Transmit the Beacon signal on at least Lane 0 of the upstream port in the direction of the Root Complex.
*Exit to Detect—*Go to Detect if an upstream port detects Electrical Idle exit condition.

Figure 14-17: L2 State Machine

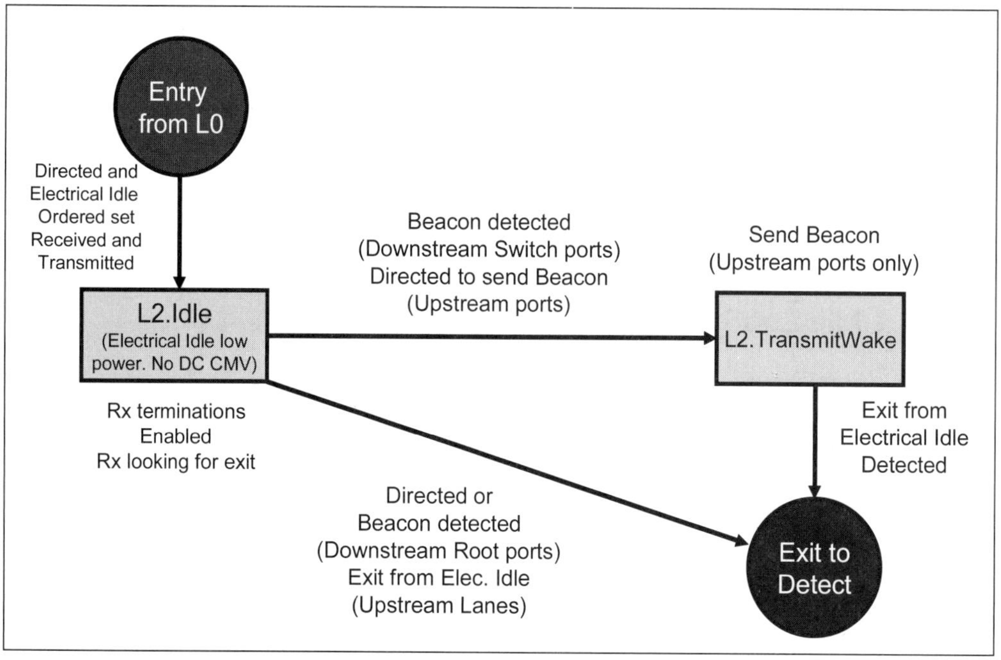

Hot Reset State

Hot Reset is an in-band signaled reset triggered by software as explained in "In-Band Reset or Hot Reset" on page 491. The state machine in Figure 14-18 on page 545 describes entry to and exit from the Hot Reset state.

Entry from Recovery—
Links that are directed to do so by higher layers enter Hot Reset through the Recovery state.
During Hot Reset—

- On all Lanes, the transmitter (on a downstream port) continuously transmits TS1s with the Hot Reset bit set and containing the configured Link and Lane Numbers. The Hot Reset initiator also resets itself.
- A receiver detects Hot Reset when it detects at least two TS1s with the Hot Reset bit set. It enters the Hot Reset state through recovery.
- LinkUp = 0.

Exit to Detect—
Exit to detect after a 2ms timeout.

Figure 14-18: Hot Reset State Machine

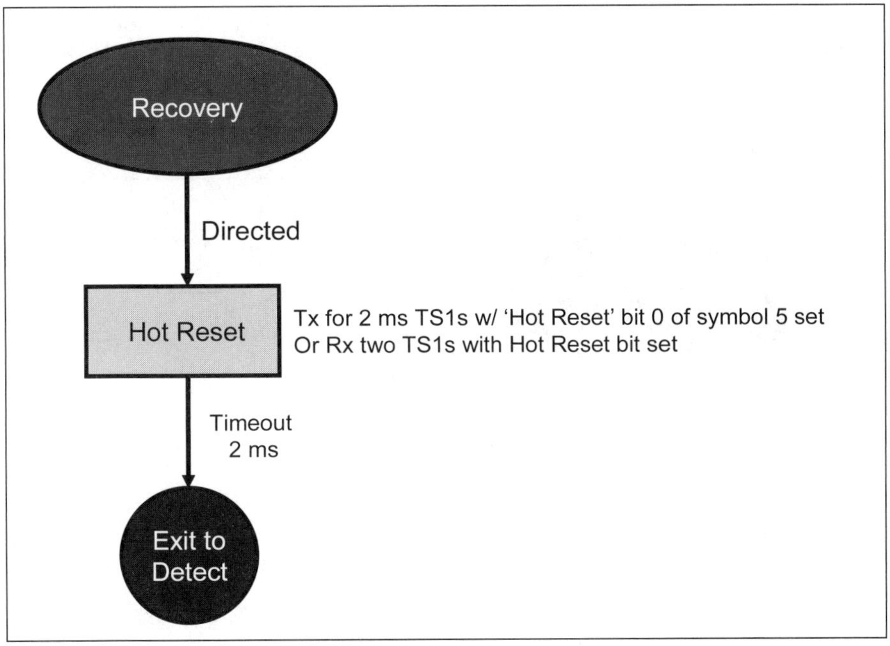

Disable State

A Disabled Link is a Link that is off and does not have to have the DC common mode voltage driven. If, for example, software wishes to turn off a faulty Link, it can do so by setting the Link Disable bit (see Figure 14-23 on page 553) in the Link Control register of a device. That device transmits TS1s with the Link Disable bit asserted. The state machine in Figure 14-19 on page 546 describes entry to and exit from the Disable state.

Entry from Configuration or Recovery—
All Lanes transmit 16 TS1 Ordered-Sets with the Link Disable bit asserted and then transition to Electrical Idle after transmitting the Electrical Idle Ordered-Set. If no Electrical Idle Ordered-Set is transmitted, then the receiver transitions to the Detect state after 2ms. The DC common mode voltage does not have to be within spec while in Detect.
During Disable—
- Remain in Disable state until the Disable exit condition is detected.
- The DC common mode voltage does not have to be within spec.
- LinkUp = 0.

Exit to Detect—
Exit to detect after a 2ms timeout wherein no Electrical Idle Ordered-set is received, or Disable entry, or an Electrical Idle exit is sensed, or as directed by higher layers.

Figure 14-19: Disable State Machine

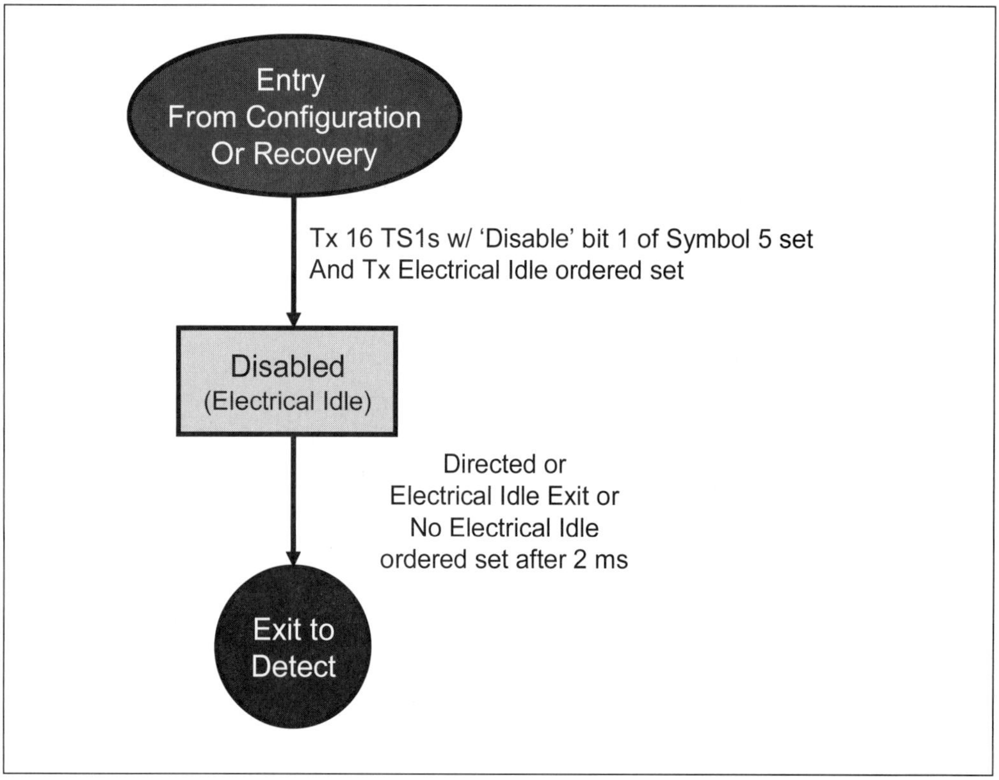

Loopback State

The Loopback feature is a test and debug feature and is not used in normal operation. A Loopback master device (such as a tester) when connected to a device's Link (the device under test is the Loopback slave when in the Loopback state) can place the Link and Loopback slave into the Loopback state by transmitting TS1 Ordered-Sets with the Loopback bit asserted. The Loopback master can serve as the BIST (Built In Self Test) engine.

Once in this state, the Loopback master sends valid 8b/10b encoded symbols to the Loopback slave. The Loopback slave turns around and feeds back the symbol stream. The Loopback slave continues to perform clock tolerance compensation, so the master must ensure that it inserts Skip Ordered-Sets at the correct intervals. To perform clock tolerance compensation, the Loopback slave may have to add or delete SKP symbols to the Skip Ordered-Set that it feeds back with the symbol stream to the Loopback master. If SKP symbols are added by the Loopback slave, they have to be of the same disparity as the received SKP symbols.

The Loopback state is exited when the Loopback master transmits the Electrical Idle Ordered-Set and the receiver detects that the Link has transitioned to the Electrical Idle state.

See Figure 14-20 on page 549 for a description of Loopback entry and exit procedure.

Loopback.Entry SubState

Entry—

As directed by higher layers, a Loopback master can transmit TS1 Ordered-Sets with the Loopback bit set.

During Loopback.Entry—

- The Loopback Master continuously transmits TS1 Ordered-Sets with the Loopback bit set.
- The Loopback Slave returns the identical TS1 Ordered-Sets.
- LinkUp = 0.

Exit to Loopback.Active—

When the master receives TS1 Ordered-Sets, the slave has entered the Loopback.Active substate.

Exit to Loopback.Exit—

If the master does not receive identical TS1 Ordered-Sets, or does not receive TS1 Ordered-Sets for 100ms, it transitions to the Loopback.Exit state.

Loopback.Active SubState

Entry from Loopback.Entry—

If the master receives TS1s identical to those it transmitted, the slave has entered the Loopback.Active substate.

During Loopback.Active—

- The Loopback master transmits valid 8b/10b symbols with valid disparity.
- The Loopback Slave returns the identical 8b/10b symbos with valid disparity while performing periodically performing clock tolerance compensation.

Exit to Loopback.Exit—

The Loopback master transmits at least 1ms of Electrical Idle Ordered-Sets. A receiver detects Loopback exit when it receives the Electrical Idle Ordered-Set, or senses the Electrical Idle state of the Link.

Loopback.Exit SubState

Entry from Loopback.Active—

The Loopback master transmits at least 1ms of Electrical Idle Ordered-Sets and then enters the Electrical Idle state. A receiver detects Loopback exit when it receives the Electrical Idle Ordered-Set, or senses the Electrical Idle state of the Link.

During Loopback.Exit—

- The Loopback master transmits Electrical Idle Ordered-Sets for at least 2ms.
- The Loopback Slave must enter Electrical Idle on all Lanes for 2ms. Before entering Loopback.Exit, the slave must echo back all symbols it received from the master.

The device then exits to the Detect state.

Figure 14-20: Loopback State Machine

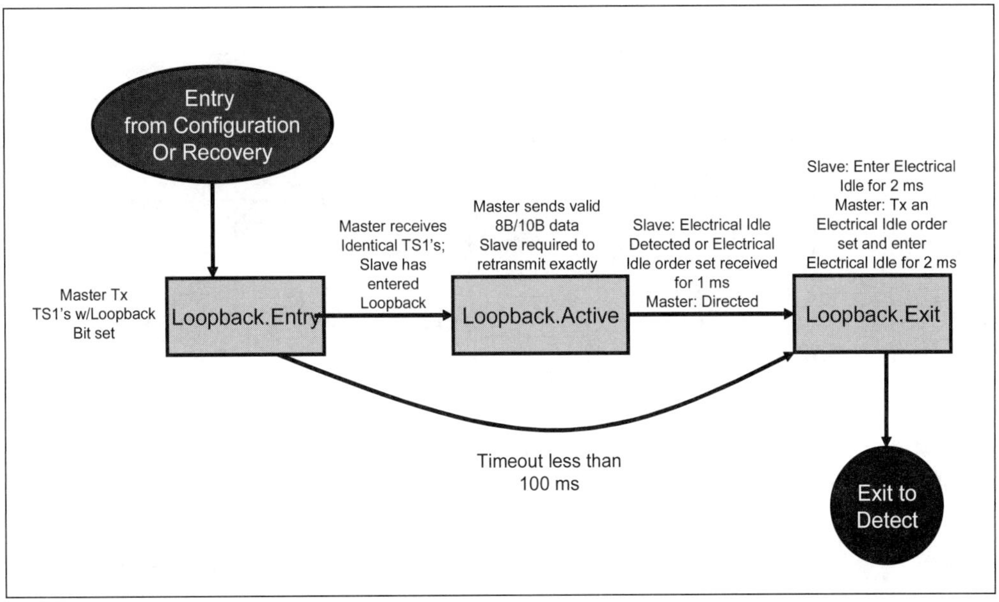

LTSSM Related Configuration Registers

Only those bits associated with the Link Training and Initialization state are described here.

Link Capability Register

The Link Capability Register is pictured in Figure 14-21 on page 550 and each bit field is described in the subsections that follow.

Maximum Link Speed[3:0]

This bit must currently be hard-wired to 0001b, indicating that its supported speed is the Generation 1 Link speed of 2.5Gbits/s. All other encodings are reserved.

Figure 14-21: Link Capabilities Register

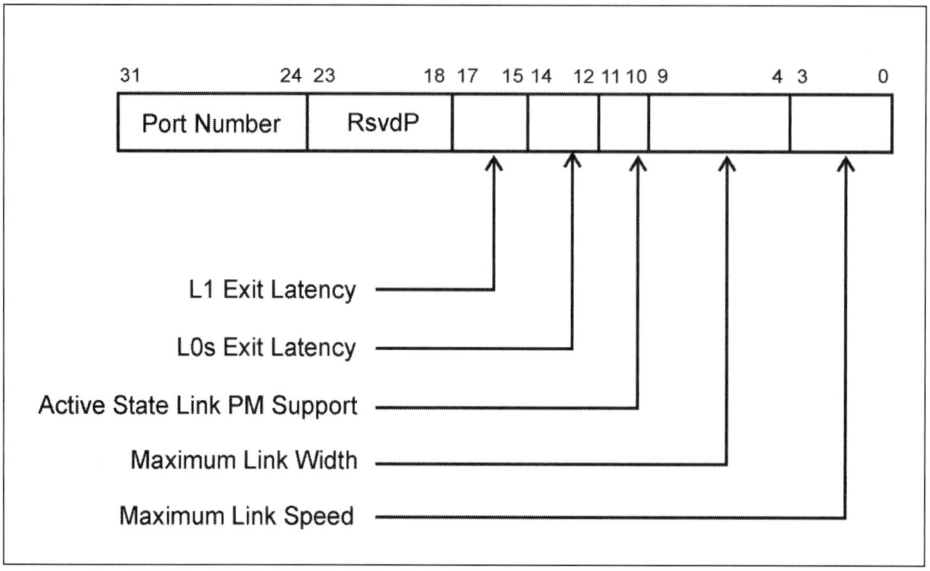

Maximum Link Width[9:4]

This field indicates the maximum width of the PCI Express Link. The values that are defined are:

- 000000b: Reserved.
- 000001b: x1.
- 000010b: x2.
- 000100b: x4.
- 001000b: x8.
- 001100b: x12.
- 010000b: x16.
- 100000b: x32.
- All others are reserved.

This register is either hard-wired or is automatically updated by hardware after passing through the Detect state of the LTSSM. This bit cannot be cleared or written by software.

Link Status Register

The Link Status Register is pictured in Figure 14-22 on page 552 and each bit field is described in the subsections that follow.

Link Speed[3:0]:

This field is read-only and indicates the negotiated Link speed of the PCI Express Link. It is updated during the Polling state of the LTSSM. Currently, the only defined encoding is 0001b, indicating a Link speed of 2.5Gbits/s.

Negotiate Link Width[9:4]

This field indicates the result of link width negotiation. There are seven possible widths, all other encodings are reserved. The defined encodings are:

- 000001b: for x1.
- 000010b for x2.
- 000100b for x4.
- 001000b for x8.
- 001100b for x12.
- 010000b for x16.
- 100000b for x32.

Training Error[10]

This bit is set by hardware when a Link Training error has occurred. It is cleared by the hardware upon successful training of the Link when the Link has entered the L0 (active) state. This bit is only supported in upstream devices such as a Root Complex or Switch down stream ports.

Link Training[11]

This bit is set by the hardware while Link Training is in progress and is cleared when Link Training completes. The LTSSM is either in the Configuration or Recovery state when this bit is set.

Figure 14-22: Link Status Register

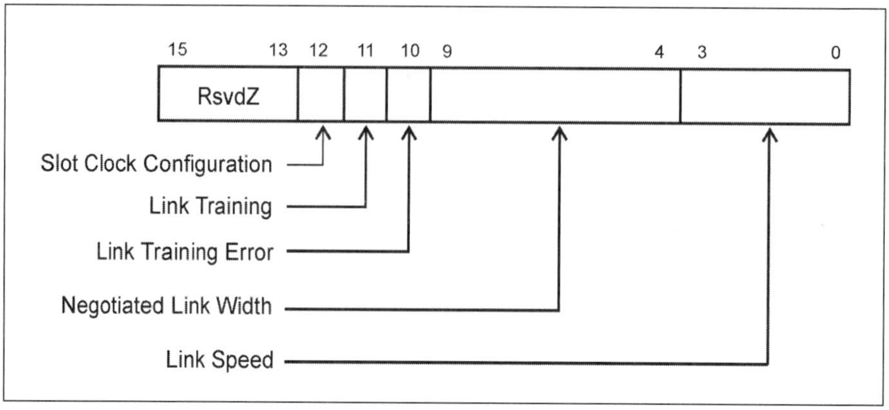

Link Control Register

The Link Control Register is pictured in Figure 14-23 on page 553 and each bit field is described in the subsections that follow.

Link Disable

When set to one, the link is disabled. It is not applicable to and is reserved for Endpoint devices and for an upstream port on a Switch. When this bit is written, any read immediately reflects the value written, regardless of the state of the Link. Writing this bit causes the device to transmit 16 TS Ordered-Sets with the Link Disable bit asserted.

Retrain Link

This bit allows software to initiate Link re-training. This could be used in error recovery. The bit is not applicable to and is reserved for Endpoint devices and the upstream ports of a Switch. When set to one, this directs the LTSSM to the Recovery state before the completion of the Configuration write request is returned.

Extended Synch

This bit is used to force the transmission of 4096 FTS (Fast Training Sequence) Ordered-Sets in L0s followed by a single Skip Ordered-Set prior to entering L0. It also forces the transmission of 1024 TS1 Ordered-Sets in L1 prior to entering the Recovery state. This extended sync permits external tools monitoring the link time to achieve Bit and Symbol Lock before the Link enters the L0 or Recovery states and resumes normal communication.

Figure 14-23: Link Control Register

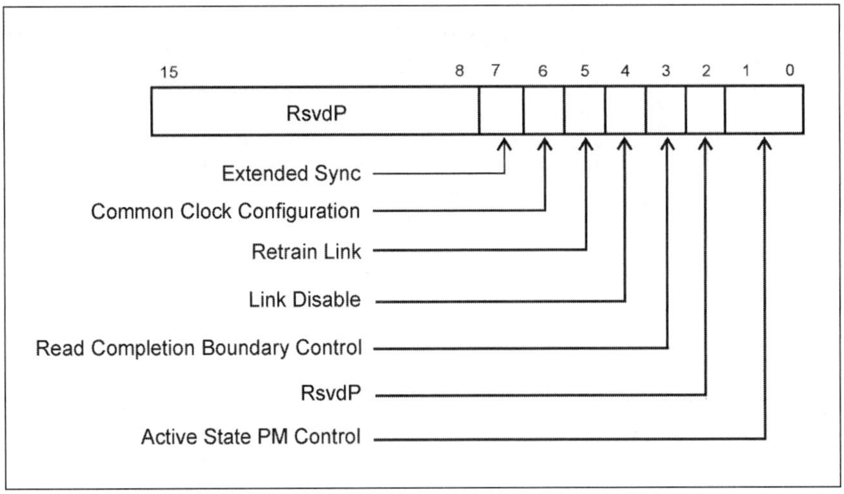

Part Four

Power-Related Topics

15 *Power Budgeting*

The Previous Chapter

The previous chapter described the function of the Link Training and Status State Machine (LTSSM) of the Physical Layer. It also described the initialization process of the Link from Power-On or Reset, until the full-on L0 state, where traffic on the Link can begin. In addition, the chapter described the lower power management states L0s, L1, L2, L3 and briefly discusses entry and exit procedure to/from these states.

This Chapter

This chapter describes the mechanisms that software can use to determine whether the system can support an add-in card based on the amount of power and cooling capacity it requires.

The Next Chapter

The next chapter provides a detailed description of PCI Express power management, which is compatible with revision 1.1 of the *PCI Bus PM Interface Specification* and the *Advanced Configuration and Power Interface,* revision 2.0 (ACPI). In addition PCI Express defines extensions that are orthogonal to the PCI-PM specification. These extensions focus primarily on Link Power and PM event management. This chapter also provides an overall context for the discussion of power management, by including a description of the OnNow Initiative, ACPI, and the involvement of the Windows OS is also provided.

Introduction to Power Budgeting

The primary goal of the PCI Express power budgeting capability is to allocate power for PCI Express hot plug devices, which can be added to the system during runtime. This capability ensures that the system can allocate the proper amount of power and cooling for these devices.

The specification states that "power budgeting capability is optional for PCI Express devices implemented in a form factor which does not require hot plug, or that are integrated on the system board." None of the form factor specifications released at the time of this writing required support for hot plug and did not require the power budgeting capability. However, form factor specifications under development will require hot plug support and may also require power budgeting capability.

System power budgeting is always required to support all system board devices and add-in cards. The new power budgeting capability provides mechanisms for managing the budgeting process. Each form factor specification defines the minimum and maximum power for a given expansion slot. For example, the Electromechanical specification limits the amount of power an expansion card can consume prior to and during configuration, but after a card is configured and enabled, it can consume the maximum amount of power specified for the slot. Chapter 18, entitled "Add-in Cards and Connectors," on page 685. Consequently, in the absence of the power budgeting capability registers, the system designer is responsible for guaranteeing that power has been budgeted correctly and that sufficient cooling is available to support any compliant card installed into the connector.

The specification defines the configuration registers that are designed to support the power budgeting process, but does not define the power budgeting methods and processes. The next section describes the hardware and software elements that would be involved in power budgeting, including the specified configuration registers.

The Power Budgeting Elements

Figure 15-2 illustrates the concept of Power Budgeting for hot plug cards. The role of each element involved in the power budgeting, allocation, and reporting process is listed and described below:

- System Firmware Power Management (used during boot time)
- Power Budget Manager (used during run time)
- Expansion Ports (ports to which card slots are attached)
- Add-in Devices (Power Budget Capable)

System Firmware — System firmware, having knowledge of the system design, is responsible for reporting system power information. The specification recommends the following power information be reported to the PCI Express power budget manager, which allocates and verifies power consumption and dissipation during runtime:

- Total system power available.
- Power allocated to system devices by firmware
- Number and type of slots in the system.

Firmware may also allocate power to PCI Express devices that support the power budgeting capability configuration register set (e.g., a hot-plug device used during boot time). The Power Budgeting Capability register (see Figure 15-1) contains a System Allocated bit that is intended to be set by firmware to notify the power budget manager that power for this device has been included in the system power allocation. Note that the power manager must read and save power information for hot-plug devices that are allocated by the system, in case they are removed during runtime.

Figure 15-1: System Allocated Bit

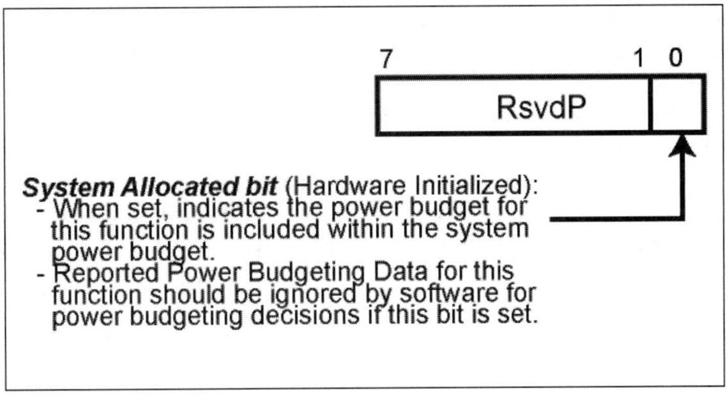

The Power Manager — The power manager initializes when the OS installs, at which time it receives power-budget information from system firmware. The specification does not define the method for communicating this information.

The power budget manager is responsible for allocating power for all PCI Express devices. This allocation includes:

- PCI Express devices that have not already been allocated by the system (includes embedded devices that support power budgeting).
- Hot-plugged devices installed at boot time.
- New devices added during runtime.

Expansion Ports — Figure 15-2 on page 561 illustrates a hot plug port that must have the Slot Power Limit and Slot Power Scale fields within the Slot Capabilities register implemented. The firmware or power budget manager must load these fields with a value that represents the maximum amount of power supported by this port. When software writes to these fields the port delivers the Set_Slot_Power_Limit message to the device. These fields are also written when software configures a card that has been added during a hot plug installation.

The PCI Express specification requires that:

- Any downstream port of a Switch or a Root Complex that has a slot attached (i.e., the Slot Implemented bit within its PCI Express Capabilities register is set) must implement the Slot Capabilities register.
- Software must initialize the Slot Power Limit Value and Scale fields of the Slot Capabilities register of the Switch or Root Complex Downstream Port that is connected to an add-in slot.
- The Upstream Port of an Endpoint, Switch, or a PCI Express-PCI Bridge must implement the Device Capabilities register.
- When a card is installed in a slot, and software updates the power limit and scale values in the Downstream port of the Switch or Root Complex, that port will automatically transmit the Set_Slot_Power_Limit message to the Upstream Port of the Endpoint, Switch, or a PCI Express-PCI Bridge on the installed card.
- The recipient of the Message must use the value in the Message data payload to limit usage of the power for the entire card/module, unless the card/module will never exceed the lowest value specified in the corresponding electromechanical specification.

Add-in Devices—Expansion cards that support the power budgeting capability must include the:

- Slot Power Limit Value and Slot Limit Scale fields within the Device Capabilities register.
- Power Budgeting Capability register set for reporting power-related information.

These devices must not consume more power than the lowest power specified by the form factor specification. Once power budgeting software allocates additional power via the Set_Slot_Power_Limit message, the device can consume the power specified, but not until it has been configured and enabled.

Device Driver The device's software driver is responsible for verifying that sufficient power is available for proper device operation prior to enabling it. If the power is lower than that required by the device, the device driver is responsible for reporting this to a higher software authority.

Figure 15-2: Elements Involved in Power Budget

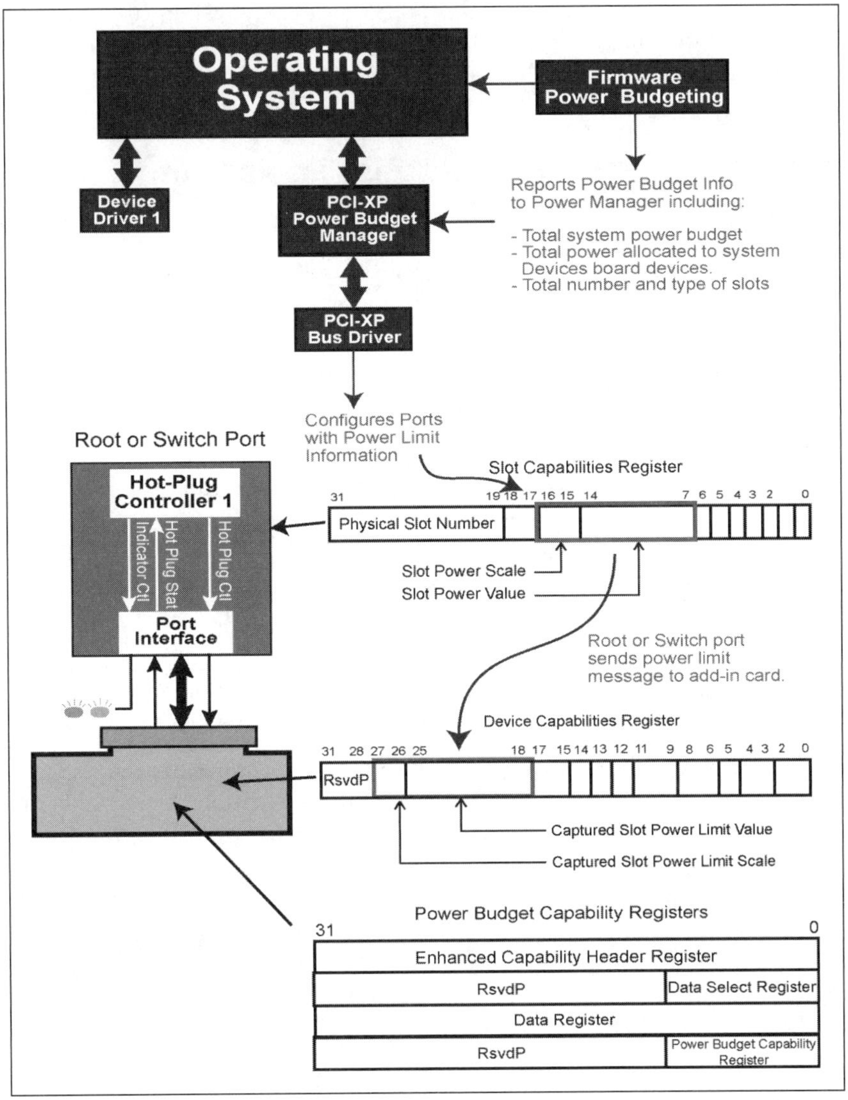

Slot Power Limit Control

Software is responsible for determining the maximum amount of power that an expansion device is allowed to consume. This power allocation is based on the power partitioning within the system, thermal capabilities, etc. Knowledge of the system's power and thermal limits comes from system firmware. The firmware or power manager (which receives power information from firmware) is responsible for reporting the power limits to each expansion port.

Expansion Port Delivers Slot Power Limit

Software writes to the *Slot Power Limit Value* and *Slot Power Limit Scale* fields of the Slot Capability register to specify the maximum power that can be consumed by the device. Software is required to specify a power value that reflects one of the maximum values defined by the specification. For example, the electromechanical specification defines maximum power listed in Table 15-1.

Table 15-1: Maximum Power Consumption for System Board Expansion Slots

	X1 Link		X4/X8 Link	X16 Link	
Standard Height	10W (max)	25W (max)	25W (max)	25W (max)	40W (max)
Low Profile Card	10W (max)		10W (max)	25W (max)	

When these registers are written by power budget software, the expansion port sends a Set_Slot_Power_Limit message to the expansion device. This procedure is illustrated in Figure 15-3 on page 563.

Figure 15-3: Slot Power Limit Sequence

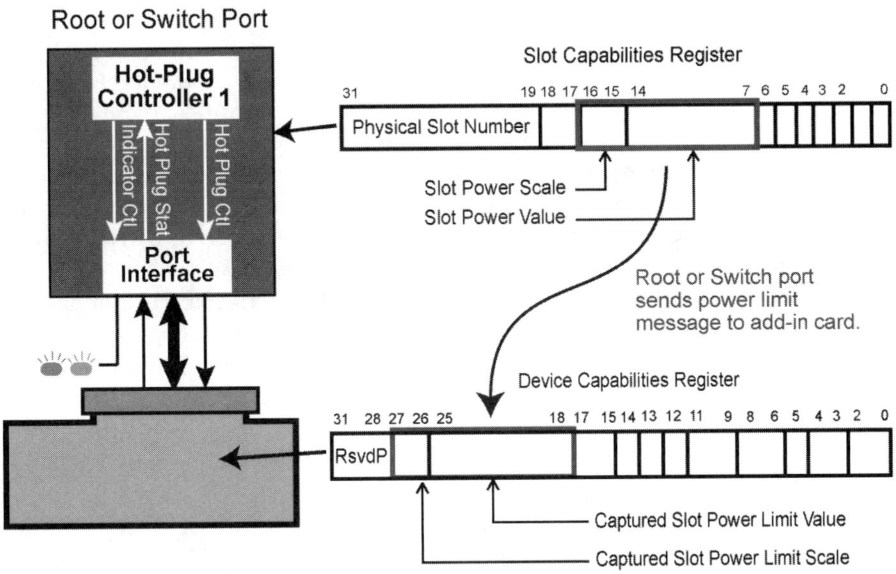

1. When Hot Plug software is notified of a card insertion request, Power and Clock are restored to the slot.
2. Hot Plug software calls configuration and power budgeting software to configure and allocate power to the device.
3. Power budget software may interrogate the card to determine its power requirements and characteristics.
4. Power is then allocated based on the device's requirements and the system's capabilities
5. Power software writes to the Slot Power Scale and Slot Power Value fields within the expansion port.
6. Writes to these fields command the port to send the Set_Slot_Power_Limit message to convey the contents of the Slot Power fields.
7. The slot receives the message and updates its Captured Slot Power Limit Value and Scale fields.
8. These values limit the power that the expansion device can consume once it is enabled by its device driver.

Expansion Device Limits Power Consumption

The device driver reads the values from the Slot Power Limit and Scale fields to verify that the power available is sufficient to operate the device. Several conditions may exist:

- The power available is ≥ the power required to operate the device at full capability. In this case, the driver enables the device by writing to the configuration Command register, permitting the device to consume up to the amount of power specified in the Power Limit fields.
- The power available is sufficient to operate the device but not at full capability. In this case, the driver is required to configure the device such that it consumes no more power than specified in the Power Limit fields.
- The power available is < the power required to operate the device. In this case, the driver must not enable the card and must report the inadequate power condition to the upper software layers, which ideally would inform the end user of the power-related problem.
- The power available exceeds the maximum power specified by the form factor specification. This condition should not occur. However, if it does, the device is not permitted to consume power beyond the maximum permitted by the form factor.
- The power available is < the lowest value specified by the form factor specification. This is a violation of the specification, which states that the expansion port "must not transmit a Set_Slot_Power_Limit Message which indicates a limit that is lower than the lowest value specified in the electromechanical specification for the slot's form factor." See Table 15-1 on page 562.

Some devices implemented on expansion devices may consume less power than the lowest limit specified for the form factor. Such devices are permitted to discard the information delivered in the Set_Slot_Power_Limit Messages. When the Slot Power Limit Value and Scale fields are read, these devices return zeros.

The Power Budget Capabilities Register Set

These registers permit power budgeting software to allocate power more effectively based on information provided by the device through its power budget data select and data register. This feature is similar to the data select and data fields within the power management capability registers. However, the power budget registers provide more detailed information that is useful to software when determining the effects of expansion cards that are added during runtime on the system power budget and cooling requirements. Through this capability, a device can report the power it consumes:

- from each power rail
- in various power management states
- in different operating conditions

These registers are not required for devices implemented on the system board or on expansion devices that do not support hot plug. Figure 15-4 on page 565 illustrates the power budget capabilities register set and shows the data select and data field that provide the method for accessing the power budget information.

The power budget information is maintained within a table that consists of one or more 32-bit entries. Each table entry contains power budget information for the different operating modes supported by the device. Each table entry is selected via the data select field, and the selected entry is then read from the data field. The index values start at zero and are implemented in sequential order. When a selected index returns all zeros in the data field, the end of the power budget table has been located. Figure 15-5 on page 566 illustrates the format and types of information available from the data field.

Figure 15-4: Power Budget Capability Registers

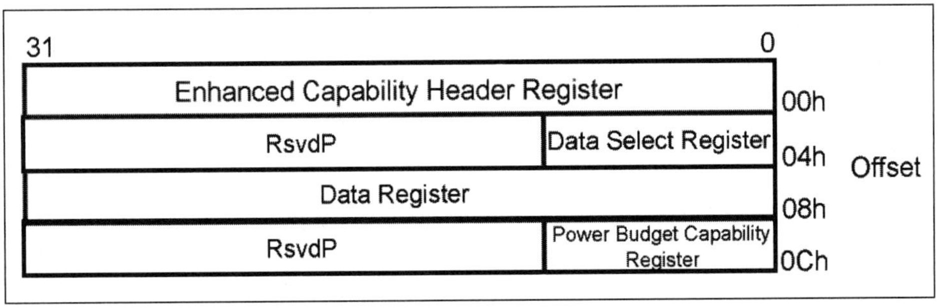

Figure 15-5: Power Budget Data Field Format and Definition

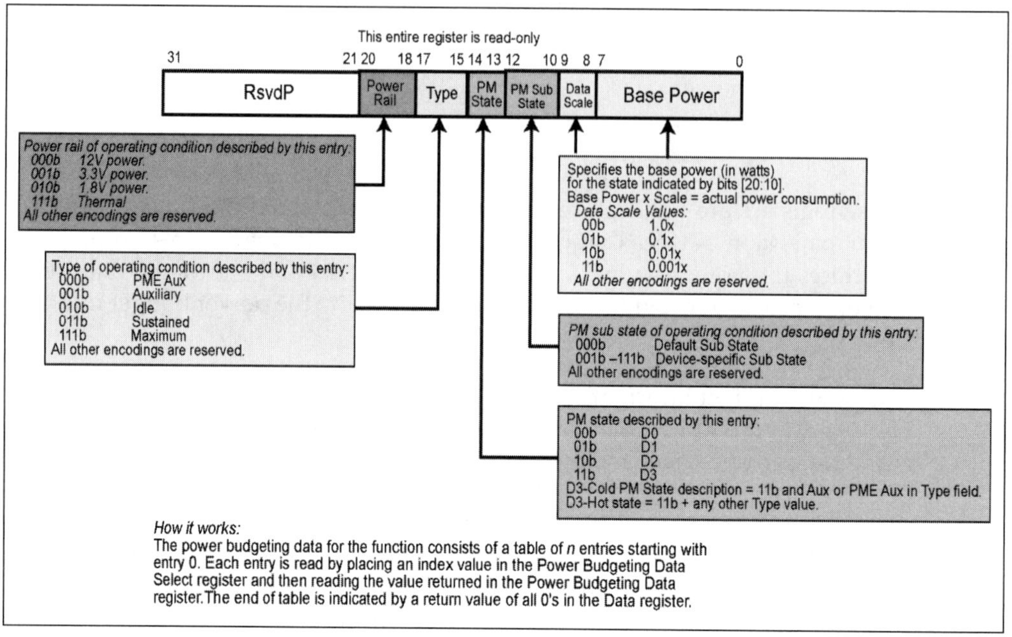

16 Power Management

The Previous Chapter

The previous chapter described the mechanisms that software can use to determine whether the system can support an add-in card based on the amount of power and cooling capacity it requires.

This Chapter

This chapter provides a detailed description of PCI Express power management, which is compatible with revision 1.1 of the *PCI Bus PM Interface Specification* and the *Advanced Configuration and Power Interface,* revision 2.0 (ACPI). In addition PCI Express defines extensions that are orthogonal to the PCI-PM specification. These extensions focus primarily on Link Power and PM event management. This chapter also provides an overall context for the discussion of power management, by including a description of the OnNow Initiative, ACPI, and the involvement of the Windows OS is also provided.

The Next Chapter

PCI Express includes native support for hot plug implementations. The next chapter discusses hot plug and hot removal of PCI Express devices. The specification defines a standard usage model for all device and platform form factors that support hot plug capability. The usage model defines, as an example, how push buttons and indicators (LED's) behave, if implemented on the chassis, add-in card or module. The definitions assigned to the indicators and push buttons, described in this chapter, apply to all models of hot plug implementations.

Introduction

PCI Express power management (PM) defines two major areas of support:

- **PCI-Compatible Power Management**. PCI Express power management is based upon hardware and software compatible with the *PCI Bus Power Management Interface Specification*, Revision 1.1 (also referred to as PCI-PM) and the *Advanced Configuration and Power Interface Specification*, Revision 2.0 (commonly known as ACPI). This support requires that all PCI Express functions include the PCI Power Management Capability registers, which permits transitions between function PM states.
- **Native PCI Express Extensions**. These extensions define autonomous hardware-based Link Power Management, mechanisms for waking the system, a Message transaction to report Power Management Events (PME), and low power to active state latency reporting and calculation.

This chapter is segmented into five major sections:

1. The first section is intended as a primer for the discussion of power management, by reviewing the role of system software in controlling power management features. This section restricts the discussion to the power-management software from the Windows Operating System perspective.
2. The second section "Function Power Management" on page 585 discusses PCI-PM required by PCI Express for placing functions into their low power states. This section also documents the PCI-PM capability registers used in PCI Express. Note that some of the register definitions are modified or not used by PCI Express functions.
3. Next, "Link Active State Power Management" on page 608 describes the autonomous Link power management that occurs when a device is in its active state (D0). Active State Power Management (ASPM) is a hardware-based link power conservation mechanism. Software enables ASPM and reads latency values to determine the level of ASPM appropriate, but does not initiate transitions into ASPM.
4. The third section "Software Initiated Link Power Management" on page 629 discusses the link power management, which is triggered by PCI-PM software when it changes the power state of a device. PCI Express devices are required to automatically conserve link power when software places a device into a low power state, including D3cold, (caused by the reference clock and main power being completely removed from a device).
5. Finally, "Link Wake Protocol and PME Generation" on page 638 covers Power Management Events (PME) and wakeup signaling. Devices may

request that software return them to the active state so they can handle an event that has occurred. This is done by sending PME messages. When power has been removed from a device, auxiliary power is required to monitor events and to signal Wakeup for reactivating the link. Once a device has been re-powered and the link has been re-trained the PME message can be sent.

Primer on Configuration Software

The *PCI Bus PM Interface Specification* describes how to implement the PCI PM registers that are required in PCI Express. These registers permit the OS to manage the power environment of both PCI and PCI Express functions.

Rather than immediately diving into a detailed nuts-and-bolts description of the *PCI Bus PM Interface Specification*, it's a good idea to begin by describing where it fits within the overall context of the OS and the system. Otherwise, this would just be a disconnected discussion of registers, bits, signals, etc. with no frame of reference.

Basics of PCI PM

The most popular OSs currently in use on PC-compatible machines are Windows 98/NT/2000/XP. This section provides an overview of how the OS interacts with other major software and hardware elements to manage the power usage of individual devices and the system as a whole. Table 16-1 on page 569 introduces the major elements involved in this process and provides a very basic description of how they relate to each other. It should be noted that neither the PCI Power Management spec nor the ACPI spec (Advanced Configuration and Power Interface) dictate the policies that the OS uses to manage power. It does, however, define the registers (and some data structures) that are used to control the power usage of PCI and PCI Express functions.

Table 16-1: Major Software/Hardware Elements Involved In PC PM

Element	Responsibility
OS	Directs the **overall system power management**.To accomplish this goal, the OS issues requests to the ACPI Driver, WDM (Windows Driver Model) device drivers, and to the PCI Express Bus Driver. Application programs that are power conservation-aware interact with the OS to accomplish device power management.

Table 16-1: Major Software/Hardware Elements Involved In PC PM (Continued)

Element	Responsibility
ACPI Driver	Manages configuration, power management, and thermal control of **devices embedded on the system board that do not adhere to any industry standard interface specification**. Examples could be chipset-specific registers, system board-specific registers that control power planes, etc. The PM registers within PCI Express functions (embedded or otherwise) are defined by the PCI PM spec and are therefore not managed by the ACPI driver, but rather by the PCI Express Bus Driver (see entry in this table).
WDM Device Driver	The WDM driver is a **Class driver** that can work with any device that falls within the Class of devices that it was written to control. The fact that it's not written for a specific device from a specific vendor means that it doesn't have register and bit-level knowledge of the device's interface. When it needs to issue a command to or check the status of the device, it issues a request to the **Miniport** driver supplied by the vendor of the specific device. The WDM also doesn't understand device characteristics that are peculiar to a specific bus implementation of that device type. As an example, the WDM doesn't understand a PCI Express device's configuration register set. It depends on the **PCI Express Bus Driver** to communicate with PCI Express configuration registers. When it receives requests from the OS to control the power state of its PCI Express device, it passes the request to the PCI Express Bus Driver: When a request to power down its device is received from the OS, the WDM saves the contents of its associated PCI Express function's device-specific registers (in other words, it performs a context save) and then passes the request to the PCI Express Bus Driver to change the power state of the device. Conversely, when a request to re-power the device is received from the OS, the WDM passes the request to the PCI Express Bus Driver to change the power state of the device. After the PCI Express Bus Driver has re-powered the device, the WDM then restores the context to the PCI Express function's device-specific registers.
Miniport Driver	**Supplied by the vendor of a device**, it receives requests from the WDM Class driver and converts them into the proper series of accesses to the device's register set.

Table 16-1: Major Software/Hardware Elements Involved In PC PM (Continued)

Element	Responsibility
PCI Express Bus Driver	This driver is **generic to all PCI Express-compliant devices**. It **manages their power states and configuration registers**, but does not have knowledge of a PCI Express function's device-specific register set (that knowledge is possessed by the Miniport Driver that the WDM driver uses to communicate with the device's register set). It receives requests from the device's WDM to change the state of the device's power management logic: When a request is received to power down the device, the PCI Express Bus Driver is responsible for saving the context of the function's PCI Express configuration Header registers and any New Capability registers that the device implements. Using the device's PCI Express configuration Command register, it then disables the ability of the device to act as a Requester or to respond as the target of transactions. Finally, it writes to the PCI Express function's PM registers to change its state. Conversely, when the device must be re-powered, the PCI Express Bus Driver writes to the PCI Express function's PM registers to change its state. It then restores the function's PCI Express configuration Header registers to their original state.
PCI Express PM registers within each PCI Express function's PCI Express configuration space.	**The location, format and usage of these registers is defined by the PCI Express PM spec**. The PCI Express Bus Driver understands this spec and therefore is the entity responsible for accessing a function's PM registers when requested to do so by the function's device driver (i.e., its WDM).
System Board power plane and bus clock control logic	The implementation and control of this logic is typically system board design-specific and is therefore **controlled by the ACPI Driver** (under the OS's direction).

OnNow Design Initiative Scheme Defines Overall PM

A whitepaper on Microsoft's website clearly defines the goals of the OnNow Design Initiative and the problems it addresses. The author has taken the liberty of reproducing the text verbatim from the *Goals* section of that paper.

Goals

The OnNow Design Initiative represents the overall guiding spirit behind the sought-after PC design. The following are the major goals as stated in an OnNow document:

- The PC is ready for use immediately when the user presses the On button.
- The PC is perceived to be off when not in use but is still capable of responding to wake-up events. Wake-up events might be triggered by a device receiving input such as a phone ringing, or by software that has requested the PC to wake up at some predetermined time.
- Software adjusts its behavior when the PC's power state changes. The operating system and applications work together intelligently to operate the PC to deliver effective power management in accordance with the user's current needs and expectations. For example, applications will not inadvertently keep the PC busy when it is not necessary, and instead will proactively participate in shutting down the PC to conserve energy and reduce noise.
- All devices participate in the device power management scheme, whether originally installed in the PC or added later by the user. Any new device can have its power state changed as system use dictates.

System PM States

Table 16-2 on page 572 defines the possible states of the overall system with reference to power consumption. The "Working", "Sleep", and "Soft Off" states are defined in the OnNow Design Initiative documents.

Table 16-2: System PM States as Defined by the OnNow Design Initiative

Power State	Description
Working	The system is completely usable and the OS is performing power management on a device-by-device basis. As an example, the modem may be powered down during periods when it isn't being used.

Table 16-2: System PM States as Defined by the OnNow Design Initiative (Continued)

Power State	Description
Sleeping	The system appears to be off and power consumption has been reduced. The sleep levels a system may implement is system design-specific. The amount of time it takes to return to the "Working" state is inversely proportional to the selected level of power conservation. Here are some examples: • The system may keep power applied to main memory, thereby preserving the OS and application programs in memory. The processor's register set contents may also be preserved. In this case, program execution can be resumed very quickly. • The system may copy the complete contents of main memory and the processor's register set contents to disk, and then remove power from the processor and main memory. In this case, the restart time will be longer because memory must restore both before resuming program execution.
Soft Off	The system appears to be off and power consumption has been greatly reduced. It requires a full reboot to return to the "Working" state (because the contents of memory have been lost).
No Power	This state isn't listed in the OnNow Design Initiative documents. The system has been disconnected from its power source.

Device PM States

The OnNow Design Initiative also defines the PM states at the device level. They are listed and defined in Table 16-4 on page 574. Table 16-3 on page 573 presents the same information in a slightly different form.

Table 16-3: OnNow Definition of Device-Level PM States

State	Description
D0	**Device support: Mandatory**. State in which device is on and running. It is receiving full power from the system and is delivering full functionality to the user. This is the initial state entered after a device completes reset.

Table 16-3: OnNow Definition of Device-Level PM States (Continued)

State	Description
D1	**Device support: Optional**. Class-specific low-power state (refer to "Device Class-Specific PM Specifications" on page 576) in which device context (see "Definition of Device Context" on page 574) may or may not be lost.
D2	**Device support: Optional**. Class-specific low-power state ("Device Class-Specific PM Specifications" on page 576) in which device context (see "Definition of Device Context" on page 574) may or may not be lost. Attains greater power savings than D1. A device in the D2 state can cause devices to lose some context.
D3	**Device support: Mandatory**. State in which device is off. Device context is lost. Power can be removed from the device.

Table 16-4: Concise Description of OnNow Device PM States

Device Power State	Power Consumption	Time to Return to D0 State
D0	Highest	NA
D1	< D0	Faster than D2
D2	< D1	Faster than D3
D3	For all intents and purposes, **none**, although there might be some negligible consumption.	Slowest

Definition of Device Context

General. During normal operation, the operational state of a device is constantly changing. Software external to the device (e.g., its device driver, the PCI Express Bus Driver, etc.) writes values into some of its registers, reads its status, etc. In addition, the device may contain a processor that executes device-specific code to control the device's interaction with the system as well as with an external element such as a network. The state of the device at a given instant in time is defined by (but not limited to) the following:

- The contents of the device's PCI Express configuration registers.
- The state of the device's IO registers that its device driver interacts with.
- If the device contains a processor, its current program pointer as well as the contents of some of the processor's other registers.

This is referred to as the current *device context*. Some or all of this information might be lost if the device's PM state is changed to a more aggressive power conservation level:

- If the device is placed in the D1 or D2 state, it may or may not lose some of this context information.
- If the device is placed in the D3 state, it will lose its context information.

Assume that a device is placed in a more aggressive power conservation state that causes it to lose some or all of its context information. If the device's context information is not restored when the device is placed back in the D0 state (i.e., fully-operational), it will no longer function correctly.

PM Event (PME) Context. Assume that the OS sets up a modem to wake up the system if the phone rings (in other words, on a Ring Detect) and that the system is then commanded to power down by the OS (e.g., in response to the user depressing the power switch). Remember that "power down" is a relative term within the context of power management. The chipset has power applied and monitors the PME# signal. To support this feature, the modem must implement:

- A PME (Power Management Event) Message capability.
- A PME enable/disable control bit.
- A PME status bit that indicates whether or not the device has send a PME message.
- One or more device-specific control bits that are used to selectively enable/disable the various device-specific events (such as Ring Detect) that can cause the device to send a PME message.
- Corresponding device-specific status bits that indicate why the device issued a PME message.

It should be obvious that the modem could not wake the system (by sending a PME message) if the logic described in the bullet list also lost power when the device is commanded to enter the D3 (off) state. It wouldn't "remember" that it was supposed to do so or why, would not be enabled to do so, etc. In other words, for the Ring Detect to successfully wake the system, the device's PME context information must not be lost when the device is placed in the D3 state.

Device Class-Specific PM Specifications

Default Device Class Specification. As mentioned earlier in this chapter, the OnNow Design Initiative provides a basic definition of the four possible power states (D0 - through - D3). It also defines the minimum PM states that all device types must implement. The document that provides this definition is the *Default Device Class Power Management spec*. This document mandates that all devices, irrespective of device category, must implement the PM states defined in Table 16-5 on page 576.

Table 16-5: Default Device Class PM States

State	Description
D0	Device is on and running. It is receiving full power from the system and is delivering full functionality to the user.
D1	This state is not defined and not used.
D2	This state is not defined and not used.
D3	Device is off and not running. Device context is assumed lost, and there is no need for any of it to be preserved in hardware. This state should consume the minimum power possible. Its only requirement is to recognize a bus-specific command to re-enter D0. Power can be removed from the device while in D3. If power is removed, the device will receive a bus-specific hardware reset upon reapplication of power, and should initialize itself as in a normal power on.

Device Class-Specific PM Specifications. Above and beyond the power states mandated by the *Default Device Class Specification*, certain categories (i.e., Classes) of devices may require:

- the implementation of the intermediate power states (D1 and/or D2)
- that devices within a class exhibit certain common characteristics when in a particular power state.

The rules associated with a particular device class are found in a set of documents referred to as *Device Class Power Management Specifications*. Currently, Device Class Power Management Specifications exist for the following device classes:

- Audio
- Communications

- Display
- Input
- Network
- PC Card
- Storage

They are available on Microsoft's Hardware Developers' web site.

Power Management Policy Owner

General. A device's PM policy owner is defined as the software module that makes decisions regarding the PM state of a device.

In Windows OS Environment. In a Windows environment, the policy owner is the class-specific driver (i.e., the WDM) associated with devices of that class.

PCI Express Power Management vs. ACPI

PCI Express Bus Driver Accesses PCI Express Configuration and PM Registers

As indicated in Table 16-1 on page 569 and Figure 16-1 on page 578, the PCI Express Bus Driver understands the location, format and usage of the PM registers defined in the PCI Power Management spec. It therefore is the software entity that is called whenever the OS needs to change the power state of a PCI Express device (or to determine its current power state and capabilities), or to access its configuration registers. Likewise,

- The IEEE 1394 Bus Driver understands the location, format and usage of the PM registers defined in the 1394 Power Management spec.
- The USB Bus Driver understands the location, format and usage of the PM registers defined in the USB Power Management spec.

Note that a discussion of the 1394 and USB Bus drivers is outside the scope of this book.

ACPI Driver Controls Non-Standard Embedded Devices

There are devices embedded on the system board whose register sets do not adhere to any particular industry standard spec. At boot time, the BIOS reports these devices to the OS via a set of tables (the **ACPI tables**; also referred to as the **namespace**; ACPI stands for Advanced Configuration and Power Interface).

When the OS needs to communicate with any of these devices, it calls the ACPI Driver. The ACPI Driver executes a handler (referred to as a **Control Method**) associated with the device. The handler is found in the ACPI tables that were passed to the OS by the BIOS at boot time. The handler is written by the system board designer in a special interpretive language referred to as ACPI Source Language, or **ASL**. The format of ASL is defined in the ACPI spec. The ASL source is then compiled into ACPI Machine Language, or **AML**. Note that AML is not a processor-specific machine language. It is a tokenized (i.e., compressed) version of the ASL source code. The ACPI Driver incorporates an AML token interpreter that enables it to "execute" a Control Method.

A discussion of ACPI is outside the scope of this book. It is only mentioned because the OS uses a combination of ACPI and Bus Driver services (such as the PCI Express (PCI-XP) Bus Driver) to manage the system's power and configuration.

Figure 16-1: Relationship of OS, Device Drivers, Bus Driver, PCI Express Registers, and ACPI

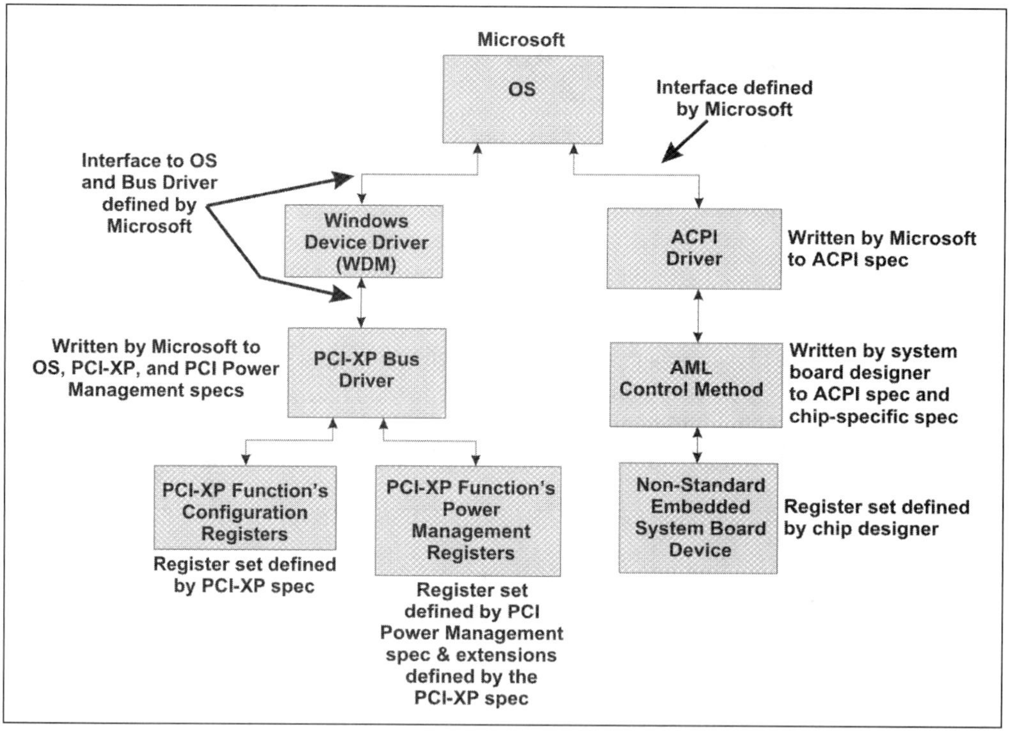

Some Example Scenarios

Figure 16-2 on page 581, Figure 16-3 on page 583, and Figure 16-4 on page 584 illustrate some example PM scenarios. *It should be noted that these illustrations are meant to be introductory in nature and do not cover all possible power state changes.* The examples focus on turning a PCI Express function Off (from a power perspective), or turning it On. This implies two possible states for a device (D0 and D3). While it's possible a function only has two states, a function may additionally implement other optional, intermediate power states (D1 and/or D2). The possible power states are discussed later in this chapter.

The following are some of the terms used in the illustrations:

- **IO Request Packet, or IRP**. The OS communicates a request to a Windows device driver by issuing an IRP to it. There are different categories of IRPs; for example, a Power IRP is used to request a change in the PM state of a device to or get its current PM state.
- **Windows Driver Model, or WDM**. A device driver written for the Windows environment that controls a device or a group of similar devices (e.g., network adapters).
- **General Purpose Event, or GPE**. ACPI-related events. The chipset implements a GPE register which is used to selectively enable or disable recognition of various GPEs. When recognition of a specific GPE is enabled (such as a PM event) and that event occurs, the chipset generates an SCI (System Control Interrupt) to the processor. This invokes the GPE handler within the ACPI Driver which then reads the GPE Status registers in the chipset to determine which GPE caused the interrupt.
- **System Control Interrupt, or SCI**. A system interrupt used by hardware to notify the OS of ACPI events. The SCI is an active low, shareable, level-sensitive interrupt.
- **Control Method**. A Control Method is a definition of how the OS can perform a simple hardware task. For example, the OS invokes a Control Method to read the temperature of a thermal zone. See the definition of ASL. An ACPI-compatible system must provide a minimal set of common Control Methods in the ACPI tables. The OS provides a set of well-defined Control Methods that ACPI table developers can reference in their Control Methods. OEMs can support different revisions of chipsets with one BIOS by either including Control Methods in the BIOS that test configurations and respond as needed or by including a different set of Control Methods for each chipset revision.

- **ACPI Source Language, or ASL**. Control Methods are written in a language called ASL which is then compiled into **AML (ACPI Machine Language)**. AML is comprised of a highly-compressed series of **tokens** that represent the ASL code. The AML code is interpreted and executed by an AML interpreter incorporated within the ACPI Driver.

Scenario—OS Wishes To Power Down PCI Express Devices. Figure 16-2 on page 581 illustrates the basic series of actions required when the OS wishes to power down all PCI Express devices and associated links in the fabric (i.e., remove the reference clock and Vcc) to conserve maximum power. Before doing this, it must first ensure that all functions within all PCI Express devices have been powered down.

1. If all of the PCI functions within all PCI Express devices are already powered down, skip to step 11.
2. The OS issues a Power IRP to the device driver (WDM) to transition all device functions to the lowest power state.
3. The WDM saves the current content of the functions device-specific registers.
4. The WDM disables the device's ability to generate interrupt requests by clearing its interrupt enable bit in its function-specific register set.
5. The WDM passes the Power IRP to the PCI Express Bus Driver.
6. The Bus Driver saves the current content of the function's configuration Header registers and any New Capability register sets that it may implement, along with extended configuration registers.
7. The PCI Express Bus Driver disables the function's ability to act as a Requester and Completer by clearing the appropriate bits in its configuration Command register.
8. The PCI Express Bus Driver writes to the function's PCI PM registers to set the lowest power state (off).
9. The PCI Express Bus Driver passes an IRP completion notice to the WDM.
10. The WDM passes the IRP completion notice to the OS. Steps 2-through-10 are repeated until all PCI functions within all devices have been placed in the powered down state.
11. The OS issues a Power IRP to the ACPI driver requesting that it turn off the reference clock and Vcc.
12. The ACPI driver runs the appropriate AML Control Method to turn off the clock and power.
13. The ACPI driver passes the IRP completion notice to the OS.

Figure 16-2: Example of OS Powering Down All Functions On PCI Express Links and then the Links Themselves

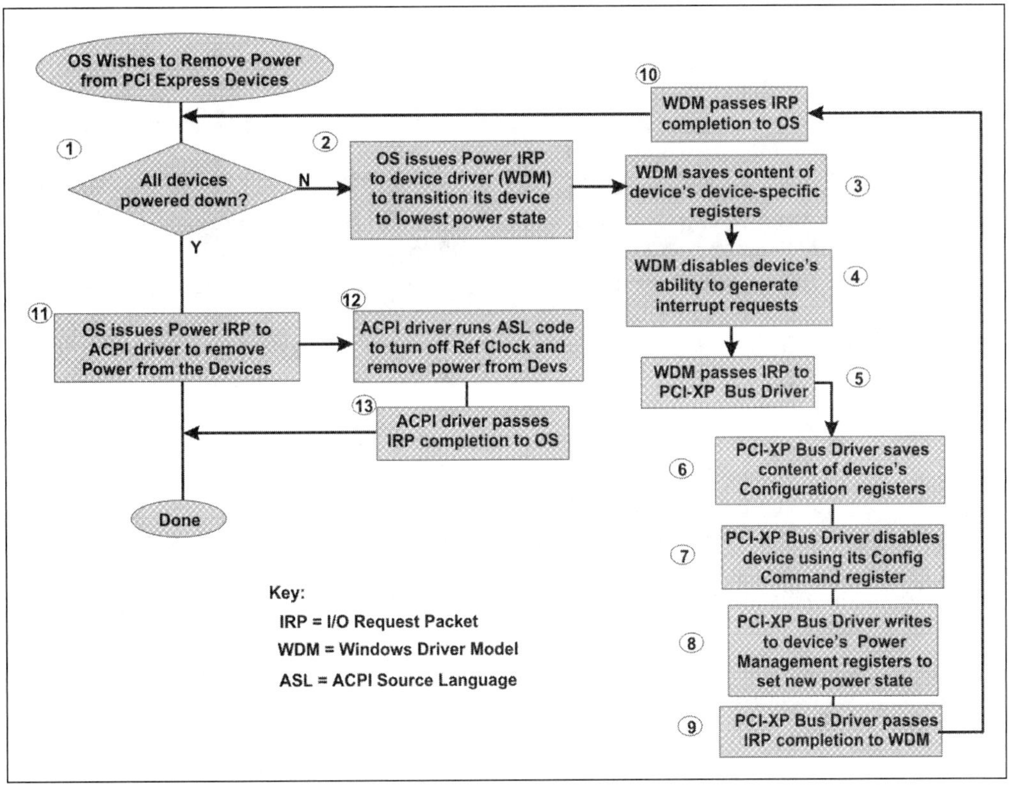

Scenario—Restore All Functions To Powered Up State. Figure 16-3 on page 583 illustrates the basic series of actions required when the OS wishes to power up a PCI Express function that was placed in the powered down state earlier.

1. It's possible that the OS had removed power to all PCI Express devices and turned off the PCI Express reference clock as in the previous example. To restore function back to their operating condition, the OS issues a Power (i.e., Power Management) IRP to the ACPI Driver requesting that the links be turned back on. In response, the ACPI Driver would execute the AML code necessary to turn on the PCI Express reference clock generator and re-apply power to the devices. It should be obvious that PCI-XP devices closest to the Host Bridge/Root Complex must be powered up first. When the ACPI Driver has completed this operation, it issues an IRP completion notice back to the OS. If the reference clock and power had not been turned off earlier, this step can be skipped.
2. The OS issues a Power IRP to the PCI Express device's WDM requesting that the device be restored to the full power state. The WDM passes the IRP to the PCI Express Bus Driver.
3. The PCI Express Bus Driver writes to the device's PCI Express PM registers to power up device.
4. The PCI Express Bus Driver restores the contents of the device's PCI Express configuration Header registers and any New Capability register sets that the device implements. This automatically restores the device's PCI Express configuration Command register enable bits to their original states.
5. The PCI Express Bus Driver passes an IRP completion notice back to the WDM.
6. The WDM restores the content of the device's device-specific IO or memory-mapped IO registers. This causes the device's interrupt enable bit to be restored, re-enabling the device's ability to generate interrupt requests. The device is now ready to resume normal operation.
7. The WDM returns an IRP completion notice to the OS.

Figure 16-3: Example of OS Restoring a PCI Express Function To Full Power

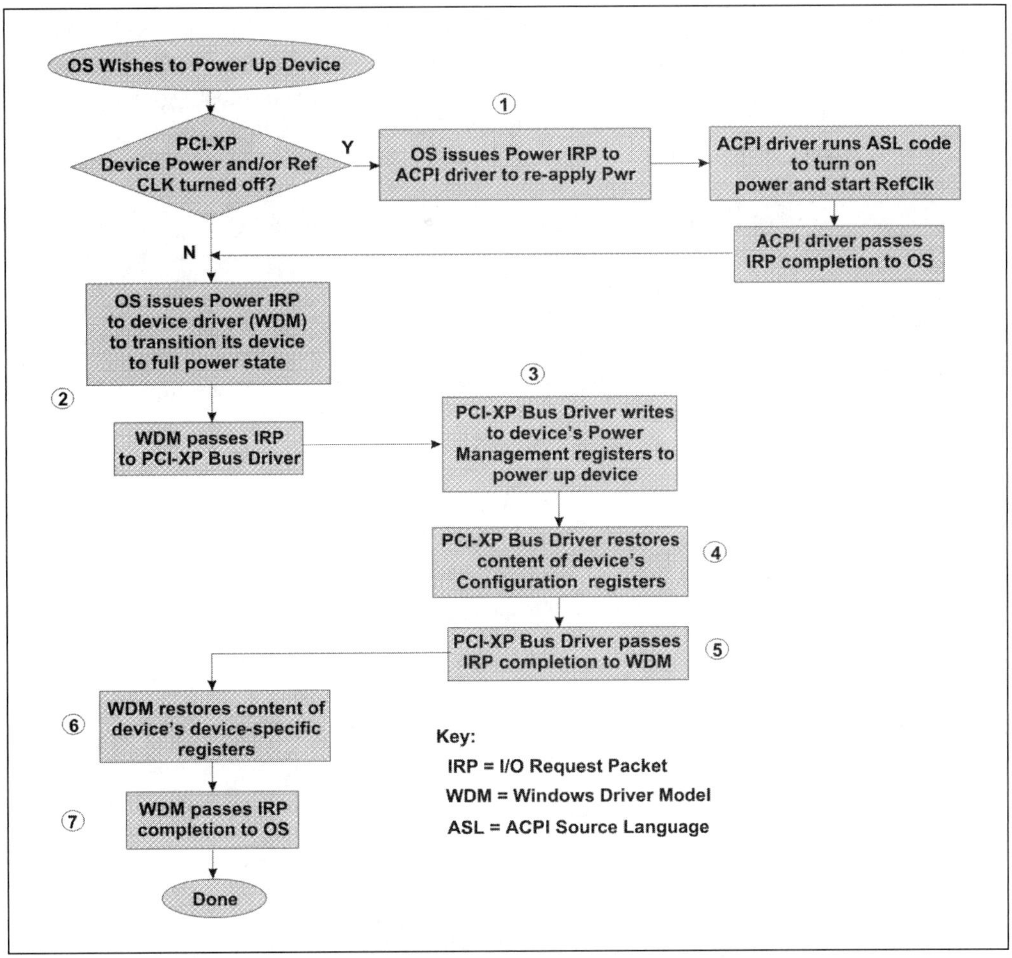

Scenario—Setup a Function-Specific System WakeUp Event. Figure 16-4 on page 584 illustrates the OS preparing a PCI Express device so that it will wake up the system (send a PME message) when a particular device-specific event occurs.

1. The OS issues a Power IRP to the device driver (WDM) to enable the device to wake up the system on a specified event.
2. The WDM writes to device-specific registers within the device to enable the event that will cause the system to wake up.
3. The WDM passes the IRP to the PCI Express Bus driver.

4. The PCI Express Bus Driver writes to the function's PM registers to enable its PME# logic.
5. The PCI Express Bus Driver returns the IRP completion notice to the WDM.
6. The WDM returns the IRP completion notice to the OS.
7. The OS issues a Power IRP to the ACPI driver requesting that the PCI Express Power Management Event (PME) monitoring logic be enabled to generate an ACPI interrupt (referred to as an SCI, or System Control Interrupt).
8. The ACPI driver enables the chipset's GPE logic to generate an SCI when PME# is detected asserted.
9. The ACPI driver returns the IRP completion notice to the OS.

Figure 16-4: OS Prepares a Function To Cause System WakeUp On Device-Specific Event

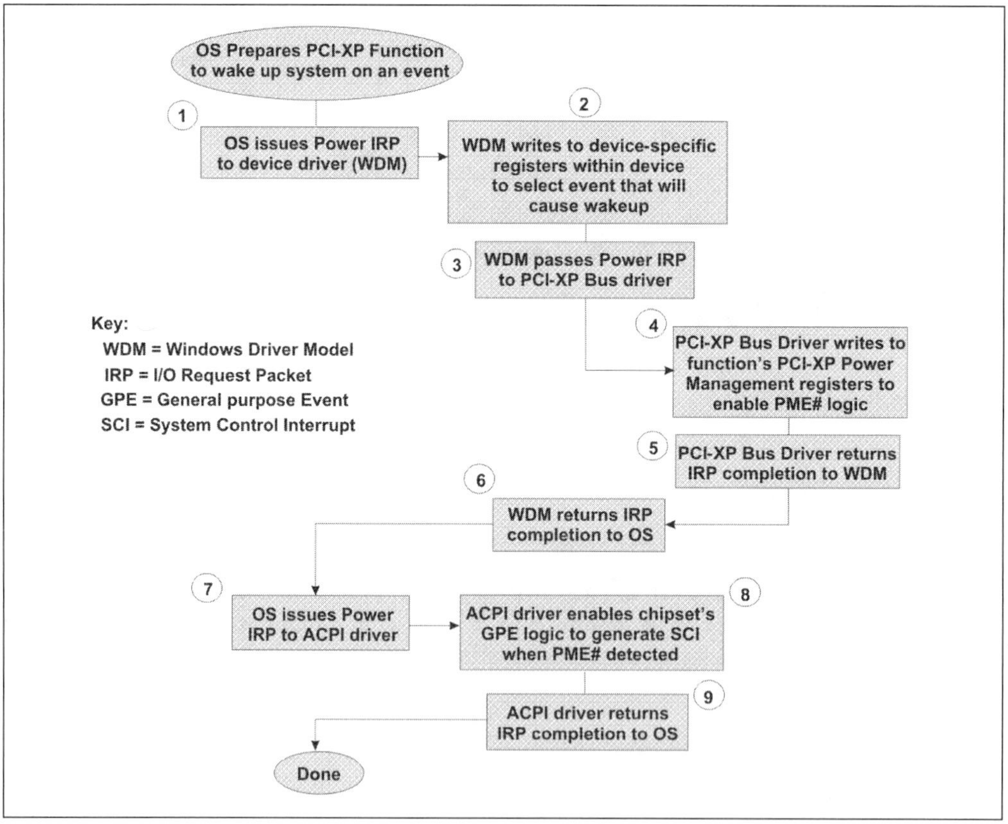

Function Power Management

PCI Express devices are required to support power management. Consequently, several registers and related bit fields must be implemented as discussed below.

The PM Capability Register Set

The PCI-PM specification defines the PM Capability register set that is located in PCI-compatible configuration space above the configuration header. The register is one in potentially many Capability registers that are linked together via pointers. The Capability ID of the PM register set is 01h. To determine the location of the PM registers software can perform the following checks. The registers described below must be implemented by PCI Express devices:

1. Software **checks** bit 4 (**Capabilities List bit**) of the function's **Configuration Status register**. A one indicates that the Capabilities Pointer register is implemented in the first byte of dword 13d of the function's configuration Header space.
2. The programmer then **reads** the dword-aligned pointer from the **Capabilities Pointer register** and uses it to read the indicated dword from the function's configuration space. This is the first dword of the first New Capability register set.
3. Refer to Figure 16-5 on page 586. If the first (i.e., least-significant) byte of the dword read contains **Capability ID 01h**, this identifies it as the PM register set used to control the function's power state. If the ID is something other than 01h, then this is the register set for a New Capability other than PM (e.g., PCI Express Capability registers). The byte immediately following the Capability ID byte is the *Pointer to Next Capability* field that specifies the start location (within the function's configuration space) of the register set for the next New Capability (if there are any additional New Capabilities). 00h indicates there isn't any, while a non-zero value is a valid pointer. As **software traverses the linked-list** of the function's New Capabilities, its PM register set will be located. A detailed description of the PM registers can be found in "Detailed Description of PCI-PM Registers" on page 596.

Figure 16-5: PCI Power Management Capability Register Set

31	16	15 8	7 0	
Power Management Capabilities (PMC)		Pointer to Next Capability	Capability ID 01h	1st Dword
Data Register	Bridge Support Extensions (PMCSR_BSE)	Control/Status Register (PMCSR)		2nd Dword

Device PM States

Each PCI Express function must support the full-on (D0) PM state and the full-off (D3) PM state. The D1 and D2 PM states are optional, as are the PM registers. The sections that follow provide a description of the possible PM states that may be supported by a PCI Express function.

D0 State—Full On

Mandatory. In this state, no power conservation is in effect and the device is fully-functional. All PCI Express functions must support the D0 state. There are two substates of the D0 PM state: D0 Uninitialized and D0 Active. No software-based power conservation is in effect in either of these two states. However, PCI Express defines Active State Power Management (ASPM) that is handled autonomously under hardware control to reduce link power consumption when the device is in this state. Table 16-6 on page 587 summarizes the PM policies while in the D0 state.

D0 Uninitialized. A function enters the D0 Uninitialized state in one of two ways:

- As a result of the Fundamental Reset being dectected, or
- When commanded to transition from the $D3_{hot}$ to the D0 PM state by software.

In either case, the function may exhibit characteristics that it has after detecting Fundamental Reset. In other words, its registers may be returned to their default state (before the function was configured and enabled by software) though this is not required. The function exhibits the following characteristics:

- It only responds to PCI Express configuration transactions.
- Its Command register enable bits are all returned to their default states.
- It cannot initiate transactions.
- It cannot act as the target of memory or IO transactions.

D0 Active. Once the function has been configured and enabled by software, it is in the D0 Active PM state and is fully functional.

Table 16-6: D0 Power Management Policies

Link PM State	Function PM State	Registers and/or State that must be valid	Power	Actions permitted to Function	Actions permitted by Function
L0	D0 uninitialized	PME context **	< 10W	PCI Express config transactions.	None
L0 L0s (required)* L1 (optional)*	D0 active	all	full	Any PCI Express transaction.	Any transaction, interrupt, or PME. **
L2/L3	D0 active	N/A***			

* Active State Power Management

** If PME supported in this state.

*** This combination of Bus/Function PM states not allowed.

D1 State—Light Sleep

Optional. This is a light sleep power conservation state. The function cannot:

- initiate TLPs (except PME Message TLP, if enabled)
- act as the target of transactions other than PCI Express configuration transactions. The function's PM registers are implemented in its configuration space and software must be able to access these registers while the device is in the D1 state.

Other characteristics of the D1 state are:

- Link automatically enters the L1 power conservation state when PM software places the function into the D1 state.
- The function may reactivate the link and send a PME message to notify PM software that the function has experienced an event that requires it be returned to full power (assuming that it supports the generation of PM events while in the D1 state and has been enabled to do so).
- The function may or may not lose its context in this state. If it does and the device supports PME, it must maintain its PME context (see "PM Event (PME) Context" on page 575) while in this state.
- The function must be returned to the D0 Active PM state in order to be fully-functional.

Table 16-7 lists the PM policies while in the D1 state.

Table 16-7: D1 Power Management Policies

Link PM State	Function PM State	Registers and/or State that must be valid	Power	Actions permitted to Function	Actions permitted by Function
L1	D1	Device class-specific registers and PME context. **	≤ D0 uninitialized	PCI Express config transactions and transactions permitted by device class PM spec (typically none). This requires the device to transition from L1 back to L0, which is triggered by the upstream port detecting a configuration transaction targeting the device.	PME Messages. ** Transactions are typically not permitted (but device class spec may permit). This requires the device to transition from L1 back to L0, which is triggered by the internal PME.
L2-L3		NA *			

* This combination of Bus/Function PM states not allowed.

** If PME supported in this state.

D2 State—Deep Sleep

Optional. This power state provides more power conservation than the D1 PM state and less than the $D3_{hot}$ PM state. The function cannot:

- initiate TLPs (except PME Message TLP).
- act as the target of transactions other than PCI Express configuration transactions. The function's PM registers are implemented in its configuration space and software must be able to access these registers while the device is in the D2 state.

Other characteristics of the D2 state are:

- The function transitions its link to the L1 state when PM software transitions function to the D2 state.
- The function may send a PME message to notify PM software that it needs to be returned to the active state to handle an event that has occurred (assuming that it supports the generation of PM events while in the D2 state and has been enabled to do so).
- The function may or may not lose its context in this state. If the function loses context and the device supports PME messages, it must maintain its PME context (see "PM Event (PME) Context" on page 575) while in this state.
- The function must be returned to the D0 Active PM state in order to be fully-functional.

Table 16-8 on page 590 illustrates the PM policies while in the D2 state.

Table 16-8: D2 Power Management Policies

Link PM State	Function PM State	Registers and/or State that must be valid	Power	Actions permitted to Function	Actions permitted by Function
L1	D2	Device class-specific registers and PME context. *	≤ next lower supported PM state or ≤ D0 uninitialized.	PCI Express config transactions and transactions permitted by device class PM spec (typically none). This requires the device to transition from L1 back to L0, which is triggered by the upstream port detecting a configuration transaction targeting the device.	PME Messages. ** Transactions are typically not permitted (but device class spec may permit). This requires the device to transition from L1 back to L0, which is triggered by the internal PME.
L2/L3		N/A**			

* If PME supported in this state.

** This combination of Bus/Function PM states not allowed.

D3—Full Off

Mandatory. All functions must support the D3 PM state. This is the PM state in which power conservation is maximized. There are two ways that a function can be placed into the D3 PM state:

- Removal of power (Vcc) from the device. This is referred to as the **D3$_{cold}$** PM state. The function could transition into the D3$_{cold}$ state for one of two reasons: if the link it resides on is placed in the L2 or L3 state; or the system is unplugged.
- Power is still applied to the function and software commands the function to enter the D3 state. This is referred to as the **D3$_{hot}$** PM state.

The following two sections describe the D3$_{hot}$ and D3$_{cold}$ PM states.

$D3_{Hot}$ State, Mandatory. As mentioned in the previous section, a function is placed into the $D3_{hot}$ PM state under program control (by writing the appropriate value into the PowerState field of its PMCSR register).

The function cannot:

- initiate TLPs (except PME Message TLP, if enabled and PME_TO_ACK Message TLP).
- act as the target of transactions other than PCI Express configuration transactions and PME_Turn_Off Message TLP. The function's PM registers are implemented in its configuration space and software must be able to access these registers while the device is in the $D3_{hot}$ state.

Other characteristics of the $D3_{hot}$ state are:

- The function transitions its link to the L1 state when PM software transitions function to the $D3_{hot}$ state.
- The function may send a PME message to notify PM software of its need to be returned to the full active state (assuming that it supports the generation of PM events while in the $D3_{hot}$ state and has been enabled to do so).
- The function almost certainly loses its context in this state. If it does and the device supports the generation of PME messages while in the $D3_{hot}$ state, it must maintain its PME context (see "PM Event (PME) Context" on page 575) while in this state.
- The function must be returned to the D0 Active PM state in order to be fully-functional.

The function exits the $D3_{hot}$ state under two circumstances:

- If Vcc is subsequently removed from the device, it transitions from $D3_{hot}$ to the $D3_{cold}$ PM state.
- Software can write to the PowerState field of the function's PMCSR register to change its PM state to $D0_{uninitialized}$.

When programmed to exit $D3_{hot}$ and return to the D0 PM state, the function returns to the D0 Uninitialized PM state (but Fundamental Reset is not required to be asserted). Table 16-9 on page 592 lists the PM policies while in the $D3_{hot}$ state.

Table 16-9: $D3_{hot}$ Power Management Policies

Bus PM State	Function PM State	Registers and/or State that must be valid	Power	Actions permitted to Function	Actions permitted by Function
L0	$D3_{hot}$	NA*			
L1		PME context. **	≤ next lower supported PM state or ≤ D0 uninitialized.	PCI Express config transactions & PME_Turn_Off broadcast message*** (These can only occur after the link transitions back to its L0 state.	PME message** PME_TO_ACK message*** PM_Enter_L23 DLLP*** (These can occur only after the link returns to L0)
L2/L3 Ready		L2/L3 Ready entered following the PME_Turn_Off handshake sequence, which prepares a device for power removal***			
L2/L3		NA *			

* This combination of Bus/Function PM states not allowed.

** If PME supported in this state.

*** See "L2/L3 Ready Handshake Sequence" on page 634 for details regarding the sequence.

$D3_{Cold}$ State. Mandatory. Every PCI Express function enters the $D3_{Cold}$ PM state upon removal of power (Vcc) from the function. When power is restored, a Fundamental Reset must also be asserted or the device must generate an internal reset. The function then transitions from the $D3_{Cold}$ state to the $D0_{Uninitialized}$ state. A function capable of generating a PME must maintain its PME context while in this state and when transitioning to the D0 state. Since power has been removed from the function, the function must utilize some auxiliary power source to maintain the PME context while in $D3_{Cold}$ state. When the device goes to $D0_{Uninitialized}$ state, if capable and enabled to do so, it generates a PME message to inform the system of the wake up event. For more information on the auxiliary power source, refer to "Auxiliary Power" on page 645.

Table 16-10 on page 593 illustrates the PM policies while in the $D3_{Cold}$ state.

Table 16-10. $D3_{cold}$ Power Management Policies

Bus PM State	Function PM State	Registers and/or State that must be valid	Power	Actions permitted to Function	Actions permitted by Function
L0	$D3_{cold}$				
L1					
L2		PME context *	AUX Power	Bus reset only	Signal Beacon** or WAKE#**
L3		None			None

* If PME supported in this state.

** The method used to signal a wake to restore clock and power depends on form factor.

Function PM State Transitions

Figure 16-6 on page 594 illustrates the permissible PM state transitions for a PCI Express function. Table 16-11 on page 594 provides a description of each transition.

Table 16-12 on page 596 illustrates the delays involved in transitioning from one state to another from both a hardware and a software perspective.

Figure 16-6: PCI Express Function Power Management State Transitions

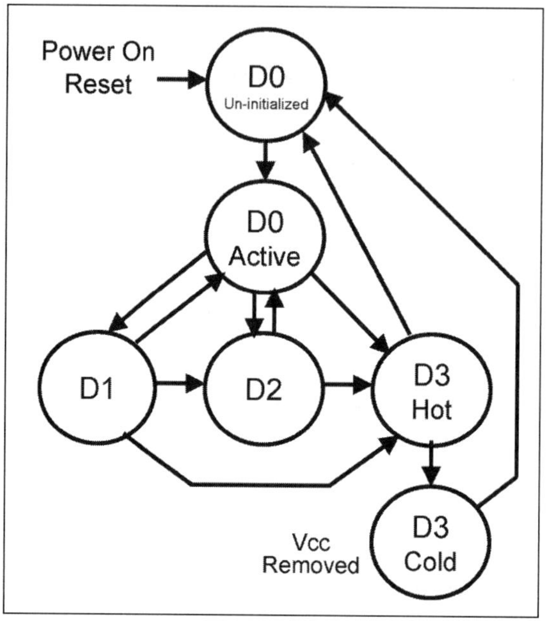

Table 16-11: Description of Function State Transitions

From State	To State	Description
D0 Uninitialized	D0 Active	Occurs under program control when function has been completely configured and enabled by its driver.
D0 Active	D1	Occurs when software writes to the PowerState field in the function's PMCSR register and sets the state to D1.
	D2	Occurs when software writes to the PowerState field in the function's PMCSR register and sets the state to D2.
	$D3_{hot}$	Occurs when software writes to the PowerState field in the function's PMCSR register and sets the state to $D3_{hot}$.

Table 16-11: Description of Function State Transitions (Continued)

From State	To State	Description
D1	D0 Active	Occurs when software writes to the PowerState field in the function's PMCSR register and sets the state to D0.
	D2	Occurs when software writes to the PowerState field in the function's PMCSR register and sets the state to D2.
	$D3_{hot}$	Occurs when software writes to the PowerState field in the function's PMCSR register and sets the state to $D3_{hot}$.
D2	D0 Active	Occurs when software writes to the PowerState field in the function's PMCSR register and sets the state to D0.
	$D3_{hot}$	Occurs when software writes to the PowerState field in the function's PMCSR register and sets the state to $D3_{hot}$.
$D3_{hot}$	$D3_{cold}$	Occurs when the Power Control logic removes Power from the function.
	D0 Uninitialized	Occurs when software writes to the PowerState field in the function's PMCSR register and sets the state to D0.
$D3_{cold}$	D0 Uninitialized	Wake event causes power (Vcc) to be restored, Fundamental Reset also becomes active. This causes the function to return to the D0 Uninitialized state. If wake not supported, Fundamental Reset causes the transition to the D0 Uninitialized state.

Table 16-12: Function State Transition Delays

Initial State	Next State	Minimum software-guaranteed delays
D0	D1	0
D0 or D1	D2	200µs from new state setting to first access to function (including config accesses).
D0, D1, or D2	$D3_{hot}$	10ms from new state setting to first access to function (including config accesses).
D1	D0	0
D2	D0	200µs from new state setting to first access to function (including config accesses).
$D3_{hot}$	D0	10ms from new state setting to first access to function (including config accesses).
$D3_{cold}$	D0	

Detailed Description of PCI-PM Registers

The *PCI Bus PM Interface spec* defines the PM registers (see Figure 16-7 on page 596) that are implemented in both PCI and PCI Express functions. These registers provide software with information regarding the function's PM capabilities and permit software to control the PM properties of the function. Since the PM registers are implemented in the PCI Express function's configuration space, software uses PCI configuration accesses to read and write the PM registers. The sections that follow provide a detailed description of these registers.

Figure 16-7: PCI Function's PM Registers

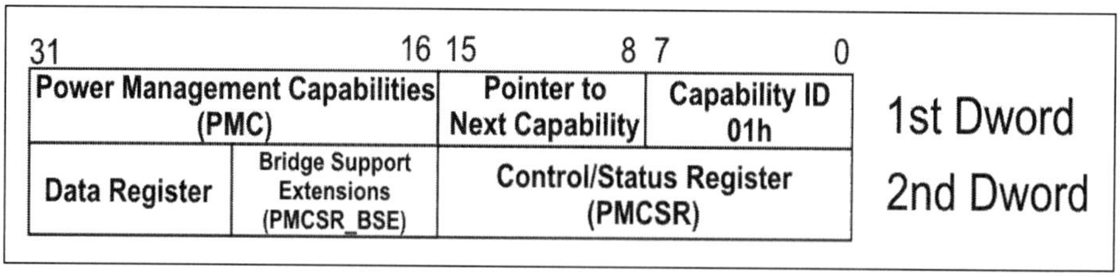

PM Capabilities (PMC) Register

Mandatory for function that implements PM. This 16-bit read-only register is interrogated by software to determine the PM capabilities of the function. Figure 16-8 on page 597 illustrates the register and Table 16-13 on page 597 describes each bit field.

Figure 16-8: Power Management Capabilities (PMC) Register - Read Only

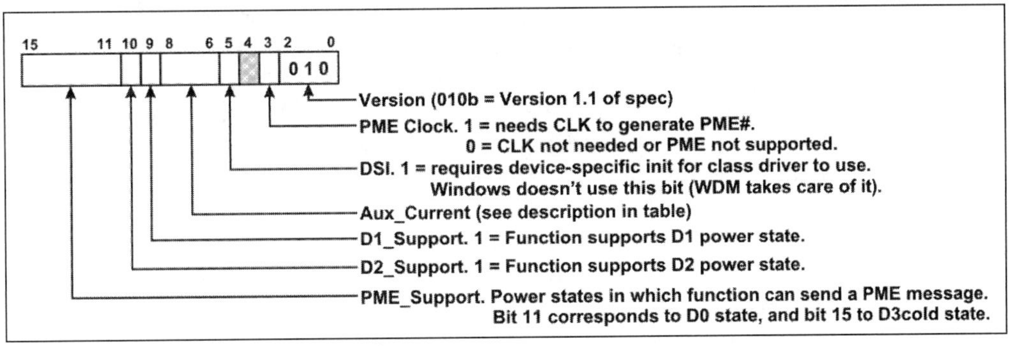

Table 16-13: The PMC Register Bit Assignments

Bit(s)	Description
15:11	**PME_Support** field. Indicates the PM states within which the function is capable of sending a PME message (Power Management Event). 0 in a bit indicates PME notification is not supported in the respective PM state. **<u>Bit</u>** **<u>Corresponds to PM State</u>** 11 D0 12 D1 13 D2 14 $D3_{hot}$ 15 $D3_{cold}$ (function requires aux power for PME logic and Wake signaling via beacon or WAKE# pin) Systems that support wake from $D3_{cold}$ must also support aux power. Similarly, components that support wake must use aux power to signal the wakeup. Bits 31, 30, and 27 must be set to 1b for virtual PCI-PCI Bridges implemented within Root and Switch Ports. This is required for ports that forward PME Messages.
10	**D2_Support** bit. 1 = Function supports the D2 PM state.

Table 16-13: The PMC Register Bit Assignments (Continued)

<table>
<tr><th>Bit(s)</th><th>Description</th></tr>
<tr><td>9</td><td>D1_Support bit. 1 = Function supports the D1 PM state.</td></tr>
<tr><td>8:6</td><td>Aux_Current field. For a function that supports generation of the PME message from the $D3_{cold}$ state, this field reports the current demand made upon the 3.3Vaux power source (see "Auxiliary Power" on page 645) by the function's logic that retains the PME context information. This information is used by software to determine how many functions can simultaneously be enabled for PME generation (based on the total amount of current each draws from the system 3.3Vaux power source and the power sourcing capability of the power source).
<ul>
<li>If the function does not support PME notification from within the $D3_{cold}$ PM state, this field is not implemented and always returns zero when read. Alternatively, a new feature defined by PCI Express permits devices that do not support PMEs to report the amount of Aux current they draw when enabled by the Aux Power PM Enable bit within the Device Control register.</li>
<li>If the function implements the Data register (see "Data Register" on page 603), this field is not implemented and always returns zero when read. The Data register then takes precedence over this field in reporting the 3.3Vaux current requirements for the function.</li>
<li>If the function supports PME notification from the $D3_{cold}$ state and does not implement the Data register, then the Aux_Current field reports the 3.3Vaux current requirements for the function. It is encoded as follows:</li>
</ul>
<table>
<tr><th>Bit
8 7 6</th><th>Max Current Required</th></tr>
<tr><td>1 1 1</td><td>375mA</td></tr>
<tr><td>1 1 0</td><td>320mA</td></tr>
<tr><td>1 0 1</td><td>270mA</td></tr>
<tr><td>1 0 0</td><td>220mA</td></tr>
<tr><td>0 1 1</td><td>160mA</td></tr>
<tr><td>0 1 0</td><td>100mA</td></tr>
<tr><td>0 0 1</td><td>55mA</td></tr>
<tr><td>0 0 0</td><td>0mA</td></tr>
</table>
</td></tr>
</table>

Table 16-13: The PMC Register Bit Assignments (Continued)

Bit(s)	Description
5	**Device-Specific Initialization (DSI)** bit. A one in this bit indicates that immediately after entry into the D0 Uninitialized state, the function requires additional configuration above and beyond setup of its PCI configuration Header registers before the Class driver can use the function. Microsoft OSs do not use this bit. Rather, the determination and initialization is made by the Class driver.
4	Reserved.
3	**PME Clock** bit. Does not apply to PCI Express. Must be hardwired to 0.
2:0	**Version** field. This field indicates the version of the PCI Bus PM Interface spec that the function complies with. **Bit** **2 1 0** — **Complies with Spec Version** 0 0 1 — 1.0 0 1 0 — 1.1 (required by PCI Express)

PM Control/Status (PMCSR) Register

Mandatory for all PCI Express Devices. This register is used for the following purposes:

- If the function implements PME capability, this register contains a PME Status bit that reflects whether or not a previously-enabled PME has occurred or not.
- If the function implements PME capability, this register contains a PME Enable bit that permits software to enable or disable the function's ability to assert the PME message or WAKE# signal.
- If the optional Data register is implemented (see "Data Register" on page 603), this register contains two fields that:
  - permit software to select the information that can be read through the Data register;
  - and provide the scaling factor that the Data register value must be multiplied by.
- The register's PowerState field can be used by software to determine the current PM state of the function and to place the function into a new PM state.

Figure 16-9 on page 600 and Table 16-14 on page 600 provide a description of the PMCSR bit fields. Note that PME is the abbreviation for Power Management Event.

Figure 16-9: Power Management Control/Status (PMCSR) Register - R/W

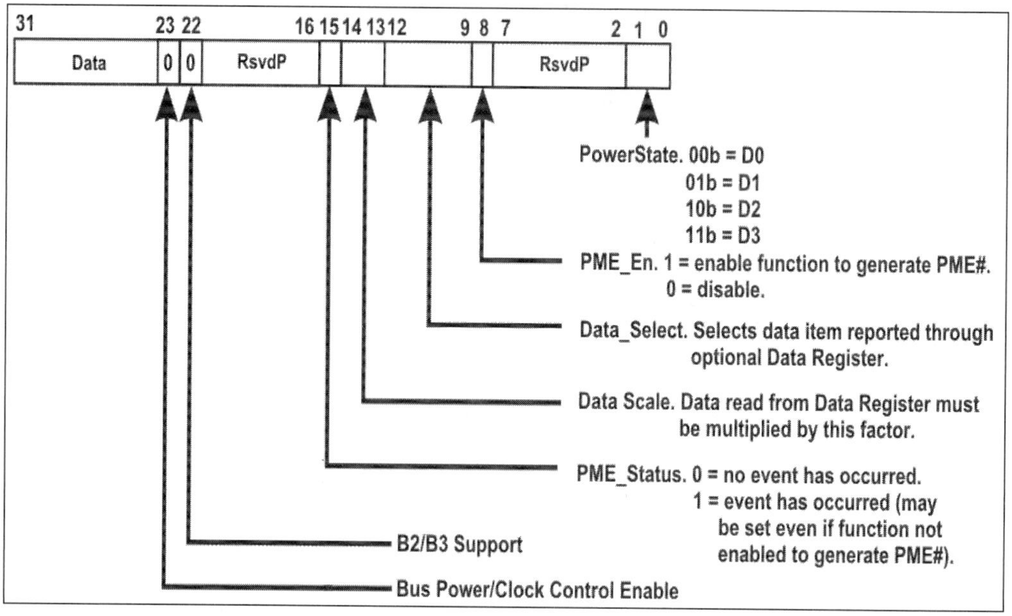

Table 16-14: PM Control/Status Register (PMCSR) Bit Assignments

Bit(s)	Value at Reset	Read/ Write	Description
31:24	all zeros	Read-only	See "Data Register" on page 603.
23	zero	Read-only	Not used in PCI Express
22	zero	Read-only	Not used in PCI Express
21:16	all zeros	Read-only	Reserved

Table 16 14: PM Control/Status Register (PMCSR) Bit Assignments (Continued)

Bit(s)	Value at Reset	Read/ Write	Description
15	See Description.	Read/Write. To Clear a one bit, write a one to it.	**PME_Status** bit. **Optional**. Only implemented if the function supports PME notification, otherwise this bit is always zero. If the function supports PME, this bit reflects whether the function has experienced a PME (even if the PME_En bit in this register has disabled the function's ability to send a PME message). If set to one, the function has experienced a PME. Software clears this bit by writing a one to it. After reset, this bit is zero if the function doesn't support PME from $D3_{cold}$. If the function supports PME from $D3_{cold}$: • this bit is indeterminate at initial OS boot time. • otherwise, it reflects whether the function has experienced a PME. If the function supports PME from $D3_{cold}$, the state of this bit must persist (is sticky) while the function remains in the $D3_{cold}$ state and during the transition from $D3_{cold}$ to the D0 Uninitialized state. This implies that the PME logic must use an aux power source to power this logic during these conditions (see "Auxiliary Power" on page 645).
14:13	Device-specific	Read-only	**Data_Scale** field. **Optional**. If the function does not implement the Data register (see "Data Register" on page 603), this field is hardwired to return zeros. If the Data register is implemented, the Data_Scale field is mandatory and must be implemented as a read-only field. The value read from this field represents the scaling factor that the value read from the Data register must be multiplied by. The value and interpretation of the Data_Scale field depends on the data item selected to be viewed through the Data register by the Data_Select field (see description in the next row of this table).

Table 16-14: PM Control/Status Register (PMCSR) Bit Assignments (Continued)

Bit(s)	Value at Reset	Read/ Write	Description
12:9	0000b	Read/Write	**Data_Select** field. **Optional**. If the function does not implement the Data register (see "Data Register" on page 603), this field is hardwired to return zeros. If the Data register is implemented, the Data_Select field is mandatory and is implemented as a read/write field. The value placed in this register selects the data value to be viewed through the Data register. That value must then be multiplied by the value read from the Data_Scale field (see previous row in this table).
8	See Description.	Read/Write	**PME_En** bit. **Optional**. 1 = enable function's ability to send PME messages when an event occurs. 0 = disable. If the function does not support the generation of PMEs from any power state, this bit is hardwired to always return zero when read. After reset, this bit is zero if the function doesn't support PME from $D3_{cold}$. If the function supports PME from $D3_{cold}$: • this bit is indeterminate at initial OS boot time. • otherwise, it enables or disables whether the function can send a PME message in case a PME occurs. If the function supports PME from $D3_{cold}$, the state of this bit must persist while the function remains in the $D3_{cold}$ state and during the transition from $D3_{cold}$ to the D0 Uninitialized state. This implies that the PME logic must use an aux power source to power this logic during these conditions.
7:2	all zeros	Read-only	Reserved

Table 16-14: PM Control/Status Register (PMCSR) Bit Assignments (Continued)

Bit(s)	Value at Reset	Read/ Write	Description
1:0	00b	R/W	**PowerState** field. **Mandatory**. Software uses this field to determine the current PM state of the function (by reading this field) or to place it into a new PM state (by writing to this field). If software selects a PM state that isn't supported by the function, the writes must complete normally, but the write data is discarded and no state change occurs. **1 0** — **PM State** 0 0 — D0 0 1 — D1 1 0 — D2 1 1 — $D3_{hot}$

Data Register

Optional, read-only. Refer to Figure 16-10 on page 605. The Data register is an optional, 8-bit, read-only register. If implemented, the Data register provides the programmer with the following information:

- Power consumed in the selected PM state. This information is useful in power budgeting.
- Power dissipated in the selected PM state.This information is useful in managing the thermal environment.
- Other, device-specific information regarding the function's operational characteristics. Currently, the spec only defines power consumption and power dissipation information to be reported through this register.

If the Data register is implemented,

- the Data_Select and Data_Scale fields of the PMCSR registers must also be implemented
- the Aux_Current field of the PMC register must not be implemented.

Determining Presence of the Data Register. Perform the following procedure to determine the presence of the Data register:

1. Write a value of 0000b into the Data_Select field of the PMCSR register.
2. Read from either the Data register or the Data_Scale field of the PMCSR register. A non-zero value indicates that the Data register as well as the Data_Scale and Data_Select fields of the PMCSR registers are implemented. If a value of zero is read, go to step 3.
3. If the current value of the Data_Select field is a value other than 1111b, go to step 4. If the current value of the Data_Select field is 1111b, all possible Data register values have been scanned and returned zero, indicating that neither the Data register nor the Data_Scale and Data_Select fields of the PMCSR registers are implemented.
4. Increment the content of the Data_Select field and go to step 2.

Operation of the Data Register. The information returned is typically a static copy of the function's worst-case power consumption and power dissipation characteristics (obtained from the device's data sheet) in the various PM states. To use the Data register, the programmer uses the following sequence:

1. Write a value into the Data_Select field (see Table 16-15 on page 605) of the PMCSR register to select the data item to be viewed through the Data register.
2. Read the data value from Data register.
3. Multiply the value by the scaling factor read from the Data_Scale field of the PMCSR register (see "PM Control/Status (PMCSR) Register" on page 599).

Multi-Function Devices. In a multi-function PCI Express device, each function must supply its own power-oriented information and the power information related to their common logic must be reported through function zero's Data register (see Data Select Value = 8 in Table 16-15 on page 605).

Virtual PCI-to-PCI Bridge Power Data. The specification does not overtly state a requirement for PCI-to-PCI bridge functions that are part of a port within the Root Complex or Switch regarding data field use. However, to maintain PCI-PM compatibility bridges must report the power information they consume. In this same fashion software could read the virtual PPB Data registers at each port of a switch to determine the power consumed by the switch in each power state. Based on PCI-PM each PCI Express function would be responsible for reporting its own power-related data.

Figure 16-10: PM Registers

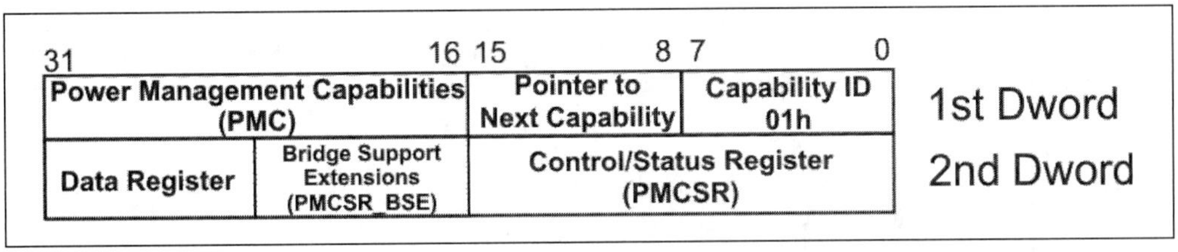

Table 16-15: Data Register Interpretation

Data Select Value	Data Reported in Data Register	Interpretation of Data Scale Field in PMCSR	Units/ Accuracy
00h	Power consumed in D0 state	00b = unknown 01b = multiply by 0.1 10b = multiply by 0.01 11b = multiply by 0.001	Watts
01h	Power consumed in D1 state		
02h	Power consumed in D2 state		
03h	Power consumed in D3 state		
04h	Power dissipated in D0 state		
05h	Power dissipated in D1 state		
06h	Power dissipated in D2 state		
07h	Power dissipated in D3 state		
08h	In a multi-function PCI device, function 0 indicates the power consumed by the logic that is common to all of the functions residing within this package.		

Table 16-15: Data Register Interpretation (Continued)

<table>
<tr><th>Data Select Value</th><th>Data Reported in Data Register</th><th>Interpretation of Data Scale Field in PMCSR</th><th>Units/ Accuracy</th></tr>
<tr><td>09h-0Fh. Spec actually shows this as decimal values 9-15. Author has chosen to represent in hex.</td><td>Reserved for future use of function 0 in a multi-function device.</td><td rowspan="2">Reserved</td><td rowspan="2">TBD</td></tr>
<tr><td>08h-0Fh. Spec actually shows this as decimal values 8-15. Author has chosen to represent in hex.</td><td>Reserved (single function devices and other functions (greater than function 0) within a multi-function device</td></tr>
</table>

Introduction to Link Power Management

PCI-PM compatible software places devices into one of four states as described in previous sections. PCI Express defines link power management that relates to each of the four device states. Table 16-16 on page 607 lists the Device states (D-States) and the associated Link states (L-states) permitted by the specification. Each relationship is described below:

D0 — When a device is in the D0 state is it fully powered and fully functional and the link is typically active (e.g. in the L0 state). PCI Express devices are required to support Active State Power Management (ASPM) that permits link power conservation even when the device is in the D0 state. Two low-power states are defined:

- L0 standby, or L0s (required)
- L1 ASPM (optional)

Both of these states are managed autonomously by hardware and completely invisible to software. A critical element associated with ASPM is returning to the L0 state with very short latencies. Additional configuration registers permit software to calculate the worst case latencies to determine if ASPM will violate latency requirements of the transactions.

D1 & D2 — When software places a device into either the D1 or D2 state the link is required to transition to the L1 state. The downstream component signals the port in the upstream device (root or switch) to which it attaches, to enter the

L1 state. During L1 the reference clock and power remain active.

D3$_{hot}$ — When software places a device into the D3 state, the device signals a transition to L1 just as done in the D1 and D2 states. However, because the device is in the D3$_{hot}$ state software may choose to remove the reference clock and power from the device called D3$_{cold}$. Prior to removing the clock and power, software initiates a handshake process that places a device into the L2/L3 Ready state (i.e., power and clock still on, but ready for power to be removed)

D3$_{cold}$ — This state indicates that the clock and power have been removed. However, auxiliary (AUX) Power may remain available after the main power rails are powered down. In this case, the link state is referred to as L2. When main power is removed and no AUX power is available it is referred to as L3.

Table 16-16: Relationship Between Device and Link Power States

Downstream Component D- State	Permissible Upstream Component D- State	Permissible Interconnect State
D0	D0	L0, L0s, & L1 (optional)
D1	D0-D1	L1
D2	D0-D2	L1
D3 hot	D0-D3 hot	L1, L2/L3 Ready
D3 cold	D0-D3 cold	L2 (AUX Pwr),L3

Table 16-17 on page 608 provides additional information regarding the Link power states.

Table 16-17: Link Power State Characteristics

State	Description	PM SW Directed	Active State Link PM	Reference Clocks	Main Power	PLL	Vaux
L0	Fully Active	Yes (D0)	On	On	On	On	On/Off
L0s	Standby	No	Yes (D0)	On	On	On	On/Off
L1	Low Power Standby	Yes* (D1-D3hot)	Yes (option) (D0)	On	On	On/Off	On/Off
L2/L3 Ready	Staging for power removal	Yes (PME_Turn_Off handshake seq.)	No	On	On	On/Off	On/Off
L2	Low Power Sleep	Yes**	No	Off	Off	Off	On
L3	Off (Zero Power)	N/A	N/A	Off	Off	Off	Off

* The L1 state is entered due to PM software placing a device into the D1, D2, or D3 states or optionally L1 is entered autonomously under hardware control when Active State Power Management is supported for L1.

** The specification describes the L2 state as being software directed. The other L-states in the table are listed as software directed because software initiates the transition into these states. For example, when software initiating a device power state change to D1, D2, or D3 devices must respond by entering the L1 state. Software also causes the transition to the L2/L3 Ready state by initiating a PME_Turn_Off message. Finally, software also initiates the removal of power from a device after the device has transitioned to the L2/L3 Ready state. This results in a transition to either the L2 or L3 pseudo-states (so called because power is removed from the devices and actual link state transitions do not apply). Because Vaux power is available in L2, a wakeup event can be signaled causing software to be notified.

Link Active State Power Management

PCI Express includes a feature that requires link power conservation even though the device has not been placed in a low-power state by software. Consequently this feature is call "Active State" power management and functions only when the device is in the DO state. Transitions into and out of Active State Power Management (ASPM) are handled solely by Hardware.

Two low power states are defined for ASPM:

1. L0 standby (L0s) — this state is required by all PCI Express devices and applies to a single direction on the link. The latency to return to the L0 state is specified to be very short.
2. L1 ASPM — this state is optional and can be entered to achieve a greater degree of power conservation than L0s. This state also results in both directions of the link being placed into the L1 state.

Figure 16-11 illustrates the link state transitions and highlights the transitions between L0, L0s, and L1. Note that transitions between L0s and L1 require the link to be returned to the L0 state.

Figure 16-11: ASPM Link State Transitions

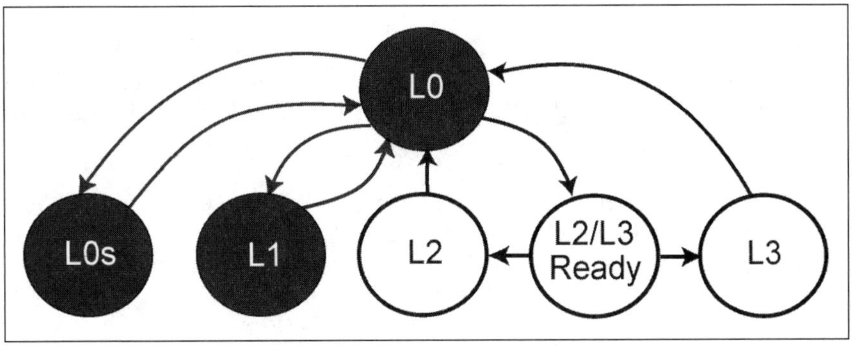

The Link Capability register specifies a device's support for Active State Power Management. Figure 16-12 on page 610 illustrates the *ASPM Support* field within this register. Notice that the only two combinations are supported via this register:

- L0s only and
- L0s and L1.

Figure 16-12: ASPM Support

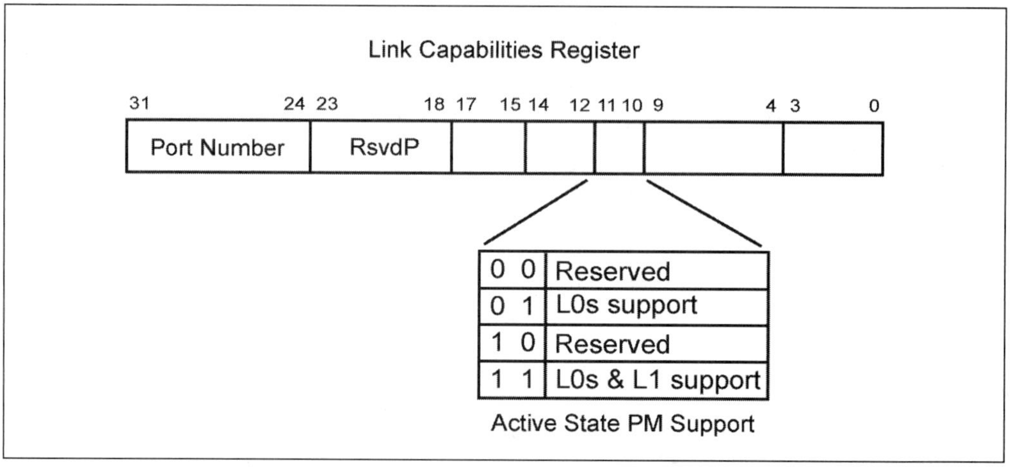

Software can enable and disable ASPM via the *Active State PM Control* field of the Link Control Register as illustrated in Figure 16-13 on page 611. The possible settings are listed in Table 16-18 on page 610. The following discussion of ASPM presume that the related features are enabled.

Note: The specification recommends that ASPM be disabled for all components in the path associated with Isochronous transactions, if the additional latencies associated with ASPM exceeds the limits of the isochronous transactions.

Table 16-18: Active State Power Management Control Field Definition

Setting	Description
00b	L0s and L1 ASPM disabled
01b	L0s enabled and L1 disabled
10b	L1 enabled and L0s disabled
11b	L0s and L1 enabled

Figure 16-13: Active State PM Control Field

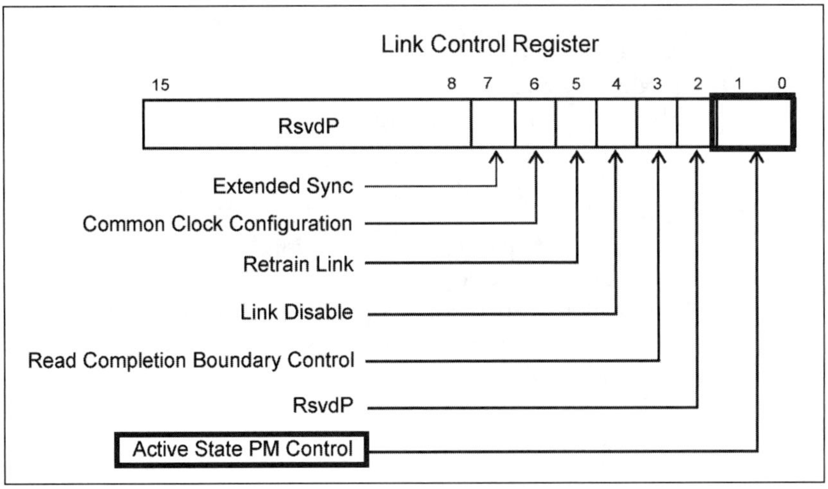

L0s State

L0s is a link power state that can be entered by any port and applied to a single direction of the link. For example, a large volume of traffic in conventional PC-based systems results from PCI and PCI Express devices sending data to main system memory. This means that the upstream lanes will have heavy traffic, while the downstream lanes will carry occasional ACK TLPs. These downstream lanes can enter the L0s state to conserve power during the stretches of idle bus time.

Entry into L0s

A transmitting port initiates the transition from L0 to L0s after detecting a period of idle time on the transmit link. Details regarding the meaning of idle, how L0s is entered, and the resulting transmitter and receiver states after L0s has been entered is discussed in this section.

Entry into L0s Triggered by Link Idle Time. Entry into L0s is managed for a single direction of the link based on detecting a period of link idle time. Ports are required to enter L0s after detecting idle time of no greater than 7µs. Idle is defined by the specification differently for each category of device. Each category must satisfy the bulleted items listed to be considered in the idle state:

- **Endpoint Port or Root Port**:
  - o No TLPs are pending transmission or Flow Control credits for a pending TLP are temporarily unavailable.
  - o No DLLPs are pending transmission.
- **Upstream Switch Port**:
  - o The receive lane of all downstream ports are already in the L0s state.
  - o No TLPs are pending transmission, or no FC credits are available for pending TLPs.
  - o No DLLPs are pending transmission.
- **Downstream Switch Port**:
  - o The Switch's Upstream Port's Receive Lanes are in the L0s state
  - o No TLPs are pending transmission, or no FC credits are available for pending TLPs.
  - o No DLLPs are pending for transmission

The Transaction and Data Link Layers have no knowledge of whether the transmitting side of the Physical Layer has entered L0s; however, the conditions that trigger a transition to L0s must be continuously reported from the Transaction and Link layers to the Physical Layer.

Note that the receiving side of a port must always support entering L0s even if software has disabled ASPM for this port. This allows a device at the other end of the link (that is enabled for ASPM) to still transition one side of the link to the L0s state.

Flow Control Credits Must be Delivered. A pending TLP that cannot be sent due to insufficient FC credits satisfies one of the requirements for an idle condition for all device categories listed above. Consequently, if flow control credits are received during L0s that permits delivery of the pending TLP, the transmitting port must initiate the return to L0. Also, if the receive buffer (associated with the transmit side that is in L0s) makes additional flow control credits available, a transmitter must initiate the return to L0 and deliver the related FC_Update DLLP to the port at the opposite end of the link.

Transmitter Initiates Entry to L0s. When sufficient idle time has been observed on the transmit side of the link, the transmitter forces the transition from L0 to L0s by taking the following steps. Following the sequence of events, both the transmitter and receiver will have transitioned to L0s:

1. Transmitter delivers an "electrical idle" ordered set to the receiver and places its transmitter into the Hi-Z state.

2. When the receiver detects the "electrical idle" ordered set, it places its receiver into the Lo-Z state.

The transmitter and receiver are now in their electrical idle states and have reduced power consumption. Synchronization between the transmitter and receiver has been lost and retraining is required. The specification requires that the PLL in the receiver must remain active to allow quick re-synchronization and recovery from L0s back to L0.

Exit from L0s State

If the transmitter detects that the idle condition has disappeared, it must initiate the sequence necessary to exit L0s and a return to L0. The specification encourages designers to monitor events that give an early indication that L0s exit is imminent and to start the recovery process to speed up the transition back to L0. For example, if the receiving side of the link receives a non-posted TLP, the transmitter side knows that it will shortly receive a request to send a completion transaction. Consequently, the transmitter can start the transition back to L0 prior to receiving the completion request.

Transmitter Initiates L0s Exit. When the transmitter whether in the upstream or downstream component recognizes that it must transition the link from L0s to L0, it initiates a sequence that re-establishes the connection with the receiver:

1. Transmitter exits Hi-Z state and issues one or more Fast Training Sequence (FTS) Ordered Sets needed by the receiver. The number of FTS Ordered Sets required by the receiver to re-synchronize (N_FTS) was previously communicated during link training following fundamental reset.
2. Following N_FTS one Skip ordered set is delivered.
3. The receiver receives the number of FTS (N_FTS) Ordered Sets it needs to establish bit lock (PLL), symbol lock (alignment of 10-bit symbols), and lane-to-lane deskew. After receiving the Skip ordered set the receiver is ready to resume normal operation.

Actions Taken by Switches that Receive L0s Exit. A switch's receiving port in the L0s state that receives the L0s to L0 transition sequence must also transmit an L0s exit to other switch ports currently in the L0s state. Two specific cases must be considered:

- **Switch Port Receives L0s to L0 transition from Downstream.** The switch must signal an L0s to L0 on the upstream port if it is currently in the L0s state. This prepares the link facing the Root Complex for transmission of a transaction that will likely be coming from the endpoint or downstream switch that signaled the transition.
- **Switch Port Receives L0s to L0 transition from Upstream.** The switch must signal an L0s to L0 transition on all downstream ports currently in the L0s state.

Any switch port in the L1 state (not L1 ASPM) has been placed into L1 due to software having previously transitioned the device to a D1 or higher power savings state. These ports remains unaffected by L0s to L0 transitions. However, once the upstream link has completed the transition to L0, a subsequent transaction may target this port, causing a transition from L1 to L0.

L1 ASPM State

The optional L1 ASPM state provides power savings greater than L0s, but with the cost of much greater recovery latency. This state also results in both directions of the link being placed into the L1 state and results in Link and Transaction layer deactivation within each device.

Entry into this state is initiated only by the downstream component (an endpoint or the upstream port of a switch). Note that a switch may support L1 ASPM on any combination of its ports. The port at the opposite end of the link can be a root port or the downstream port of a switch. In either case, the upstream component must agree to enter the L1 state through a negotiation process with the downstream component. (See Figure 16-14 on page 615) Note that exiting the L1 ASPM state can be initiated by either the downstream or upstream port.

Figure 16-14: Ports that Initiate L1 ASPM Transitions

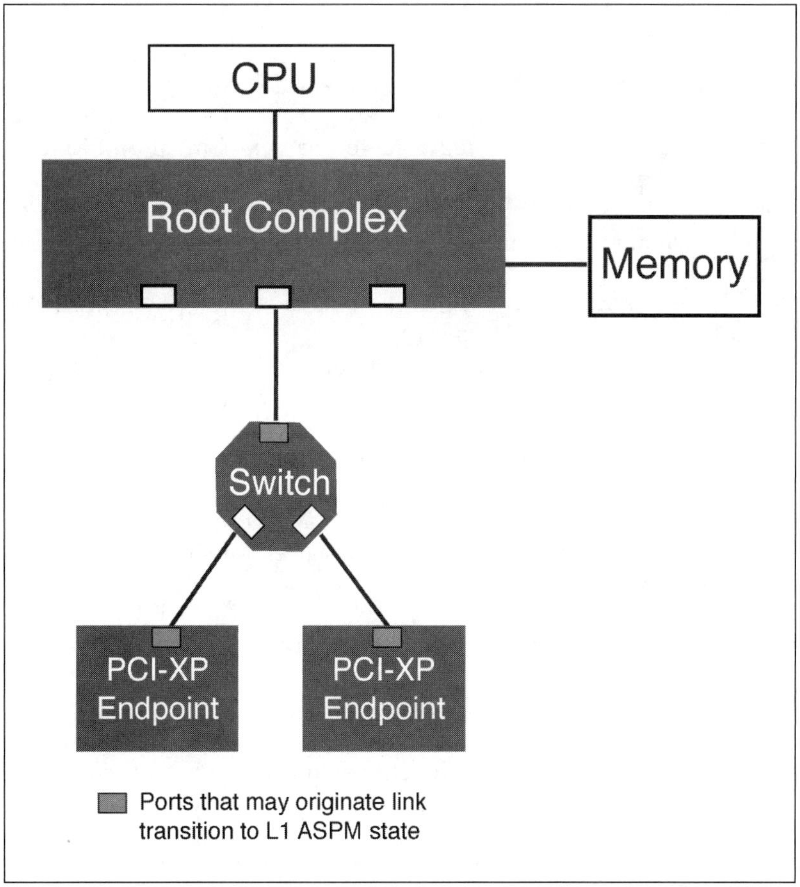

Downstream Component Decides to Enter L1 ASPM

The specification does not precisely define all conditions under which an endpoint or upstream port of a switch decides to attempt entry into the L1 ASPM state. The specification does suggest that one requirement might be that both directions of the link have entered L0s and have been in this state for a preset amount of time. The requirements specified include:

- ASPM L1 entry is supported and enabled
- Device-specific requirements for entering L1 have been satisfied
- No TLPs are pending transmission
- No DLLPs are pending transmission

- If the downstream component is a switch, then all of the switch's downstream ports must be in the L1 or higher power conservation state, before the upstream port can initiate L1 entry.

Negotiation Required to Enter L1 ASPM

Because of the long latency required to recover from L1 ASPM, a negotiation process is employed to ensure that the port at the other end of the link is enabled for L1 ASPM entry and is prepared to enter it. The negotiation involves sending several transactions:

- PM_ Active_State_Request_L1 — this DLLP is issued by the downstream port to start the negotiation process.
- PM_ Request_Ack — this DLLP is returned by the upstream port when all of its requirements to enter L1 ASPM have been satisfied.
- PM_Active_State_Nak — this TLP is returned by the upstream port when it is unable to enter the L1 ASPM state.

The upstream component may or may not accept the transition to the L1 ASPM state. The following scenarios describe a variety of circumstances that result in both conditions.

Scenario 1: Both Ports Ready to Enter L1 ASPM State

Figure 16-15 on page 618 summarizes the sequence of events that must occur to enable transition to the L1 ASPM state. This scenario assumes that all transactions have completed in both directions and no new transaction requirements emerge during the negotiation.

Downstream Component Issues Request to Enter L1 State. Once the downstream component has fulfilled all the requirements to transition to the L1 state, it can issue the request to enter L1 once the following steps have completed:

1. TLP scheduling is blocked at the Transaction Layer.
2. The Link Layer has received acknowledgement for the last TLP it had previously sent (i.e., the replay buffer is empty).
3. Sufficient flow control credits are available to allow transmission of the largest possible packet for any FC type. This ensures that the component can issue a TLP immediately upon exiting the L1 state.

The downstream component delivers the PM_ Active_State_Request_L1 DLLP to notify the upstream component of the request to enter the L1 state. This transaction is sent repeatedly until the upstream component returns a response — either a PM_Request_ACK DLLP or a PM_Active_State_NAK TLP.

Upstream Component Requirements to Enter L1 ASPM. As illustrated in Figure 16-14 on page 615 the upstream component may be either a Root Complex Port, or a Switch Downstream Port. These ports must accept a request to enter a low power L1 state if all of the following conditions are true:

- The Port supports ASPM L1 entry and is enabled to do so
- No TLP is scheduled for transmission
- No Ack or Nak DLLP is scheduled for transmission

Upstream Component Acknowledges Request to Enter L1. The upstream component sends a PM_Request_ACK DLLP to notify the downstream component of its agreement to enter the L1 ASPM state. Prior to sending this acknowledgement, it must complete the following:

1. Block scheduling of any TLPs.
2. The Upstream component must have received acknowledgement for the last TLP previously sent (i.e., its replay buffer is empty).
3. Sufficient flow control credits are available to allow transmission of the largest possible packet for any FC type. This ensures that the component can issue a TLP immediately upon exiting the L1 state.

The Upstream component then sends a PM_Request_Ack DLLP and continues sending the transaction continuously until it receives the Electrical Idle ordered set on its receive lanes.

Downstream Component Detects Acknowledgement. When the Downstream component detects a PM_Request_Ack DLLP, it knows that the upstream device has accepted the request. In response, the downstream component stops sending the PM_Active_State_Request_L1 DLLP, disables DLLP and TLP transmission, and places its transmit (upstream) lanes into the Electrical Idle state.

Upstream Component Receives Electrical Idle. When the Upstream component receives an Electrical Idle ordered set on its Receive Lanes (signaling that the Downstream component has entered the L1 state), it then stops sending the PM_Request_Ack DLLP, disables DLLP and TLP transmission, and places its transmit (downstream) lanes into the Electrical Idle state.

Figure 16-15: Negotiation Sequence Required to Enter L1 Active State PM

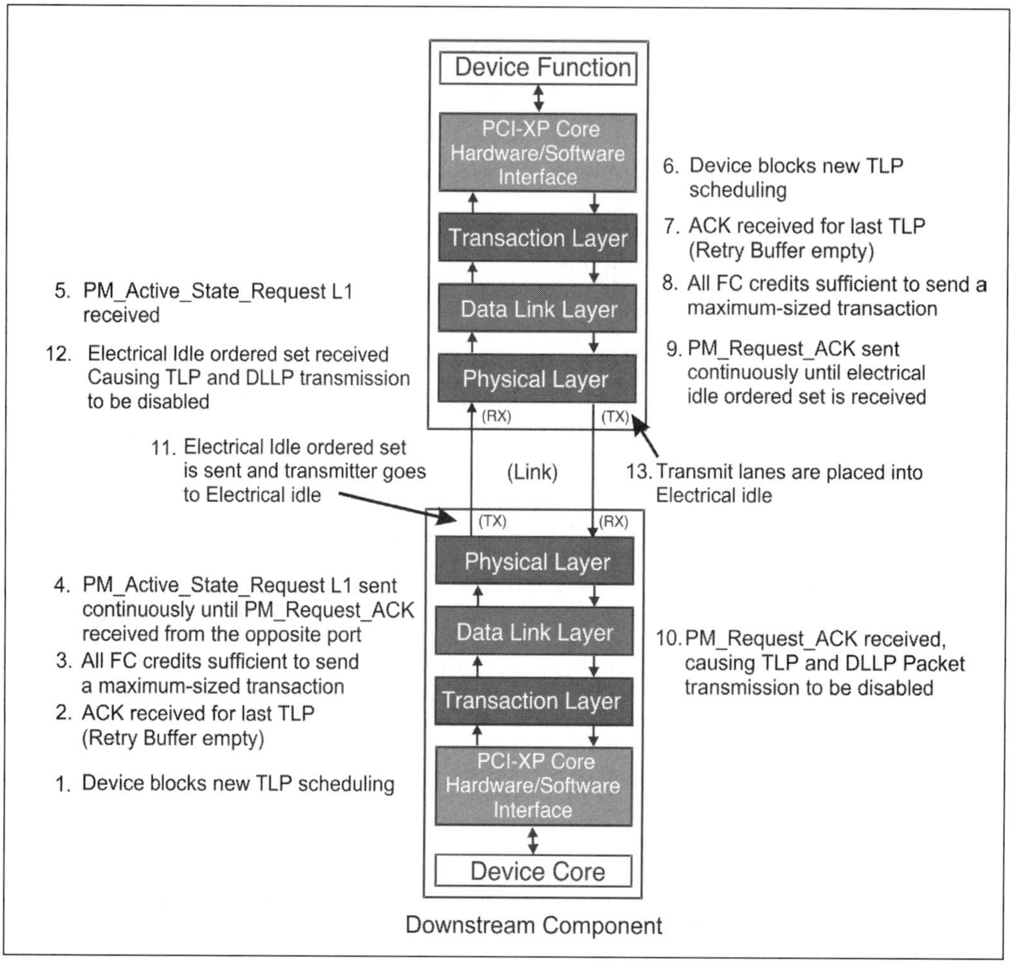

Scenario 2: Upstream Component Transmits TLP Just Prior to Receiving L1 Request

This scenario presumes that the upstream component has just received a request to send a TLP to the downstream component as it prepares to request entry in to the L1 state. Currently, the downstream device is unaware of the TLP being sent and the upstream device is unaware of the request to entry L1. Several negotiation rules define the actions that ensure that this situation is managed correctly.

TLP Must Be Accepted by Downstream Component. Note that after the downstream device sends the PM_Active_State_L1 DLLP it must wait for a response from the upstream component. While waiting, the receive side of the downstream component must be able to accept TLPs and DLLPs from the upstream device. Furthermore, it must also be able to send a DLLP as required. In this example the downstream component must respond to the TLP. Two possibilities exist:

- an ACK DLLP is returned to verify successful receipt of the TLP.
- a NAK DLLP is returned if a TLP transmission error is detected. This results in a transaction retry of the TLP from the upstream component. Retries are permitted during negotiation.

In summary, the specification requires that all TLPs be acknowledged prior to entering the L1 state.

Upstream Component Receives Request to Enter L1. The specification requires that the upstream component immediately accept or reject the request to enter the L1 state. However, it further states that prior to sending a PM_Request_ACK DLLP it must:

1. Block scheduling of new TLPs
2. Wait for acknowledgement of the last TLP previously sent, if necessary. The specification further states that the upstream component may issue retries in the event that a NAK DLLP is received from the downstream component, or a Link Acknowledgement timeout condition occurs.

Once all outstanding TLPs have been acknowledged, and all other conditions are satisfied, the upstream device must return a PM_Request_ACK DLLP.

Scenario 3: Downstream Component Receives TLP During Negotiation

During the negotiation sequence the downstream device may receive a new TLP targeting the upstream device. Recall that when a device begins the L1 ASPM negotiation process, it must block new TLP scheduling. This prevents a race condition between completing the transition to L1 and sending a new TLP that would otherwise prevent entry into L1 ASPM. Consequently, once all requirements to enter L1 have been satisfied and the downstream device has scheduled delivery of the PM_Request_L1 DLLP it must complete the transition to the L1 state (if a PM_Request_ACK is received). Then it can initiate the transition from L1 ASPM to L0 and send the TLP.

Scenario 4: Upstream Component Receives TLP During Negotiation

Note that in the event that the upstream component needs to transfer a TLP or DLLP after sending the PM_Request_Ack DLLP, it is required to complete the transition to L1. It must then initiate a transition from L1 to L0, after which the TLP or DLLP can be sent.

Scenario 5: Upstream Component Rejects L1 Request

Figure 16-16 on page 621 summarizes the negotiation sequence when the upstream component rejects the request to enter the L1 ASPM state.

The negotiation begins normally with the downstream component sending the request DLLP to enter L1. However, the upstream device returns a PM_Active_State_Nak TLP to indicate rejection of the request. The reasons for the upstream component rejecting the request to enter L1 include:

- does not support L1 ASPM
- supports L1 ASPM, but software has not enabled this feature within the Link Control register
- One or more TLPs are scheduled for transfer across the link
- ACK or NAK DLLPs are scheduled for transfer

Once the upstream component sends the rejection message, it can send TLPs and DLLPs as required.

If the downstream component receives a rejection it must transition to L0s if possible.

Figure 16-16. Negotiation Sequence Resulting in Rejection to Enter L1 ASPM State

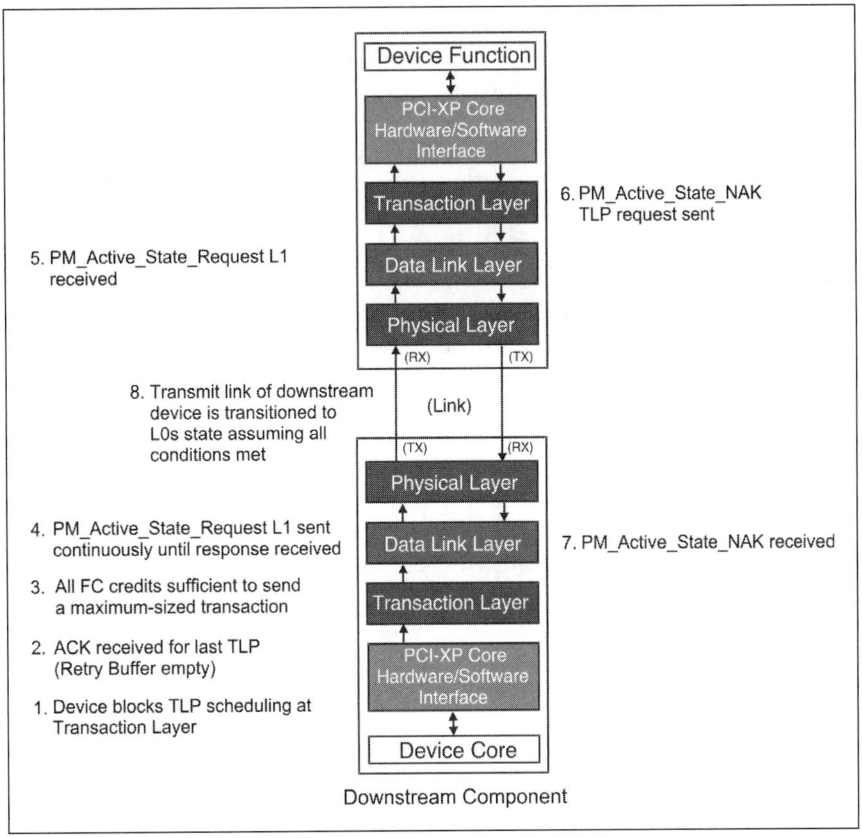

Exit from L1 ASPM State

Either component can initiate the transition from L1 to L0 when it needs to communicate via the link. Whether the upstream or downstream component initiates the exit from L1, the procedure is the same and does not involve any negotiation as does L1 entry. When switches are involved in exiting from L1 the specification requires that other switch ports in the ASPM low power states must also transition to the L0 state if they are possibly in the path of the transaction causing the exit. These issues are discussed in subsequent sections.

L1 ASPM Exit Signaling. The specification states that exit from L1 is invoked by exiting electrical idle, which could consist of a variety of signaled states. However, because re-training (recovery) is required to transition the link back to the L0 state, it seems reasonable that exit signaling would begin by transmitting the TS1 ordered set to the opposite port. The receiving port, in turn initiates recovery by signaling the TS1 ordered set back to the originating devices's receive port. The Physical Layer's Link Training State Machine completes the Recovery state after which the link will be returned to L0. Refer to"Recovery State" on page 532 for details.

Switch Receives L1 Exit from Downstream Component. This sections describes the switch behavior when a downstream component initiates exit from L1 (TS1 ordered set) to the switch. As pictured in Figure 16-17 on page 623, the Switch must respond to L1 exit signaling by returning the TS1 ordered set to the downstream component, and within 1µs (from signal L1 Exit downstream) it must also transmit the TS1 ordered set on its upstream link (but only when the upstream port is also in the L1 ASPM state).

The expectation is that the downstream component, having initiated L1 exit, is preparing to send a TLP traveling in the upstream direction. Because L1 exit latencies are relatively long, the specification states that a switch "must not wait until its Downstream Port Link has fully exited to L0 before initiating an L1 exit transition on its Upstream Port Link." This prevents accumulated latencies that would otherwise result if all L1 to L0 transitions occurred in a linear fashion.

Figure 16-17: Switch Behavior When Downstream Component Signals L1 Exit

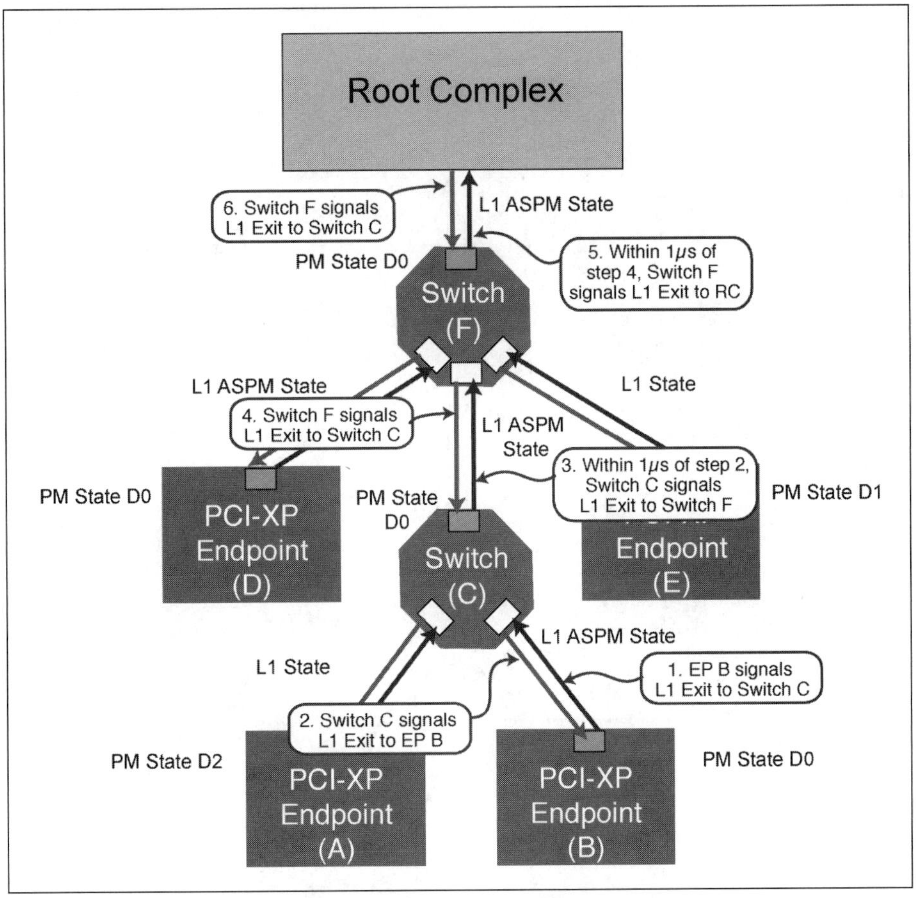

Switch Receives L1 Exit from Upstream Component. This section describes the switch behavior when an upstream component signals L1 Exit (TS1 ordered set) to a switch. In this case, the switch must send the TS1 ordered set back upstream, and within 1µs it must also signal the TS1 ordered set to force all downstream ports that are in the L1 ASPM state to also return to L0. The goal as in the previous example is to shorten the overall latency in returning to the L0 state. Figure 16-18 on page 624 summarizes these requirements. Note that the link attaching Switch F and EndPoint (EP) E is in the L1 state due to software having previously placed EP E into the D1 state, which caused the link to transition to L1. Only links in the L1 ASPM state are transitioned to L0 as a result of the Root Complex (RC) initiating the exit from L1 ASPM.

Figure 16-18: Switch Behavior When Upstream Component Signals L1 Exit

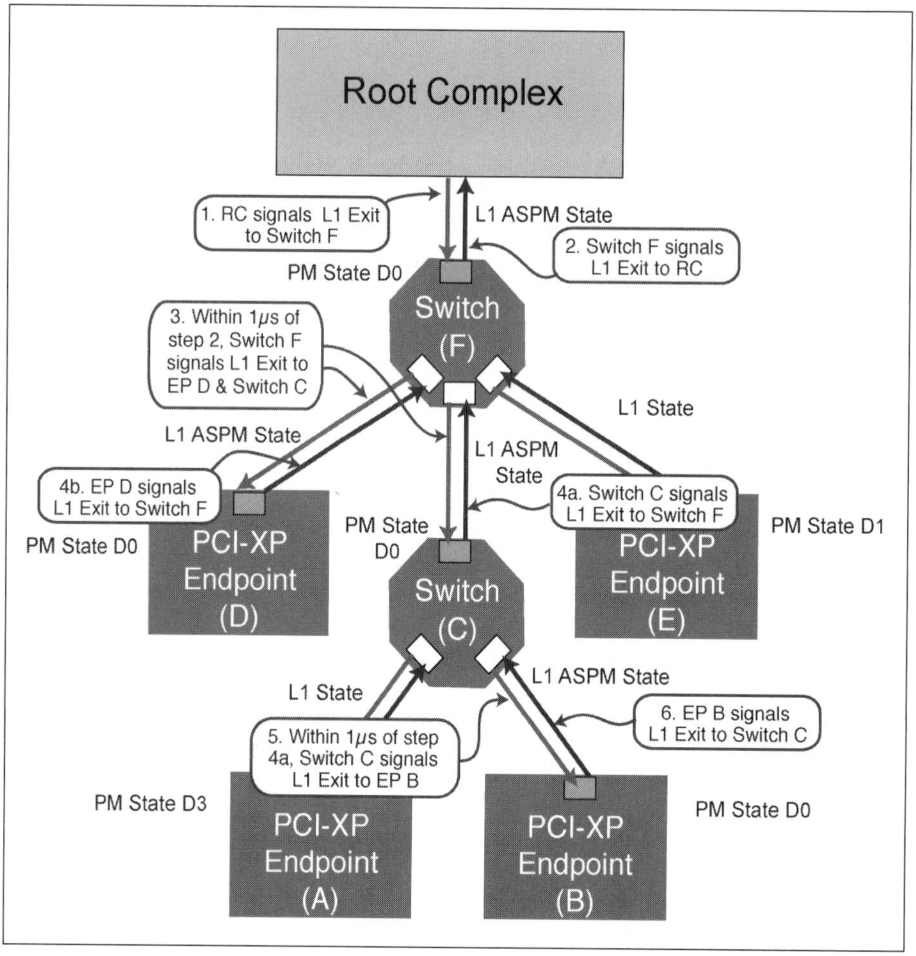

ASPM Exit Latency

PCI Express provides the mechanisms to ensure that the ASPM exit latencies for L0s and L1 do not exceed the latency requirements of the endpoint devices. Each device must report its L0s and L1 exit latencies from the moment ASPM exit is signaled. Endpoints also report the total acceptable latency that they can tolerate when performing accesses (typically to and from main memory). This latency is a function of the data buffer size within the device. If the chain of devices that reside between the endpoint and target device have a total latency that exceeds the acceptable latency reported by the endpoint, software can disable ASPM to avoid unacceptable latency for a given endpoint.

The exit latencies reported by a device will change depending on whether the devices on each end of a link share a common reference clock or not. Consequently, the Link Status register includes a bit called *Slot Clock* that specifies whether the component uses an external reference clock provided by the platform, or an independent reference clock (perhaps generated internally). Software checks these bits within devices at both ends of each link to determine whether they use a common clock. If so, software sets the *Common Clock* bit to report the common clock implementation to both devices. Figure 16-20 on page 628 illustrates the registers and related bit fields involved in managing the ASPM exit latency.

Reporting a Valid ASPM Exit Latency

Because the clock configuration affects the exit latency that a device will experience, devices must report the source of their reference clock via the *Slot Clock* status bit within the Link Status register. This bit is initialized by the component to report the source of its reference clock. If this bit is set (1), the clock uses the platform generated reference clock and cleared (0) if it uses an independent clock.

If system firmware or software determines that the components at each end of the link use the platform clock then the reference clocks within both devices will be in phase. This results in shorter exit latencies from L0s and L1, and is reported in the *Common Clock* field of the Link Control register. Components must then update their reported exit latencies to reflect the correct value. Note that if the clocks are not common then the default values will be correct and no further action is required.

L0s Exit Latency Update. Exit latency for L0s is reported in the Link Capability register based on the default assumption that a common clock implementation does not exist. L0s exit latency is also reported during link training (via the TS1 Ordered Sets) by specifying the number of FTS Ordered Sets (N_FTS) required to exit L0s. Consequently, if software detects a common clock implementation, the Common Clock field is set and System firmware or software must write to the *Retrain Link* bit in the Link Control register, to force retraining. During retraining new N_FTS values are reported to the transmitter at the opposite end of the link and new values are also reported in *L0s Latency* field of the Link Capability register.

L1 Exit Latency Update. Following link retraining, new values will also be reported in the *L1 Latency* field.

Calculating Latency Between Endpoint to Root Complex

Figure 16-19 on page 627 illustrates an endpoint whose transactions must transverse 2 switches in the path between the endpoints and Root Complex. This example presumes that all links in the path are in the L1 state.

1. Endpoint B needs to send a packet to main memory and begins the wake sequence by initiating a TS1 ordered set on link B/C at time "T." The L1 exit latency for EP B is a maximum of 8, but Switch C has a maximum exit latency of 16µs. Therefore, the exit latency for this link is 16µs.
2. Within 1µs of detecting the L1 exit on link B/C, Switch C signals L1 exit on link C/F at T+1µs.
3. Link C/F completes exit from L1 in 16µs, completing at T+17µs.
4. Switch F signals exit from L1 to the Root Complex within 1µs of detecting L1 exit from Switch C (T+2µs).
5. Link F/RC completes exit from L1 in 8µs, completing at T+10µs.
6. Total latency to transition path to target back to L0 = T+17µs.

Figure 16-19: Example of Total L1 Latency

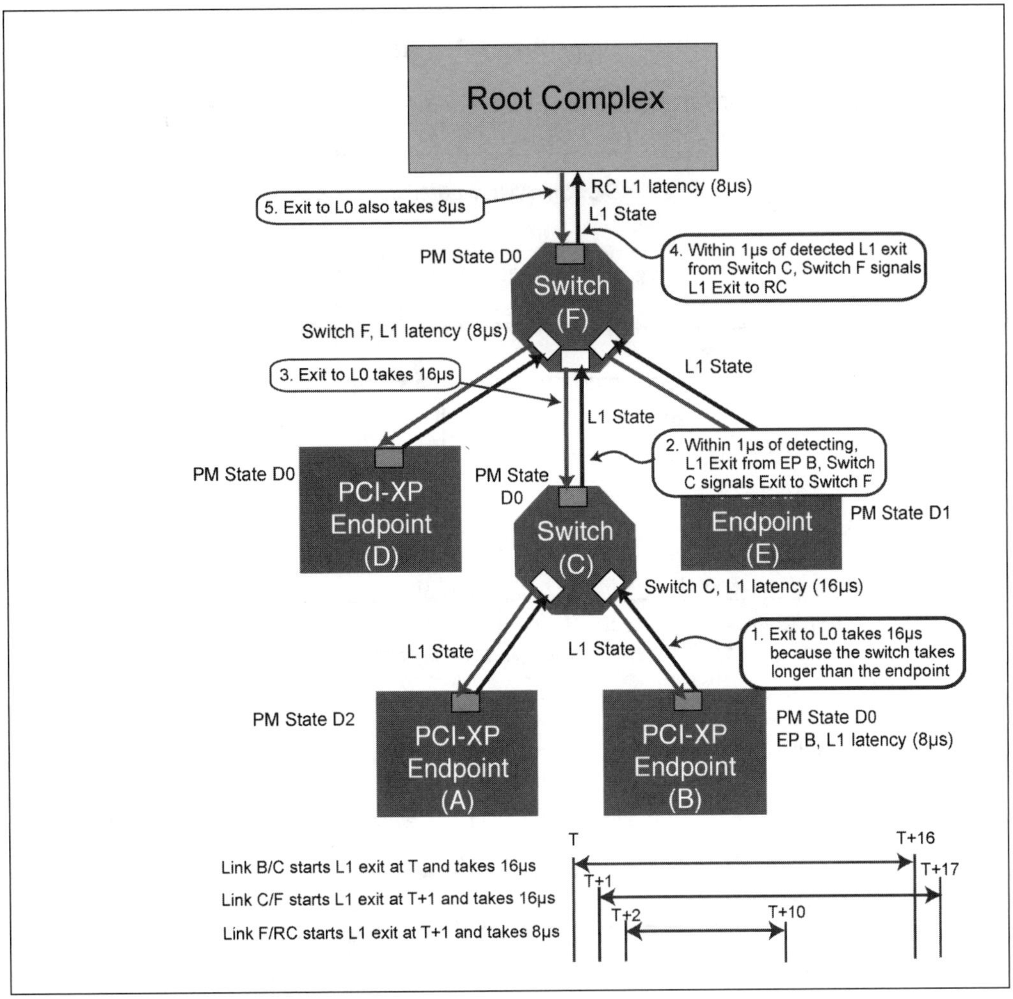

Figure 16-20: Config. Registers Used for ASPM Exit Latency Management and Reporting

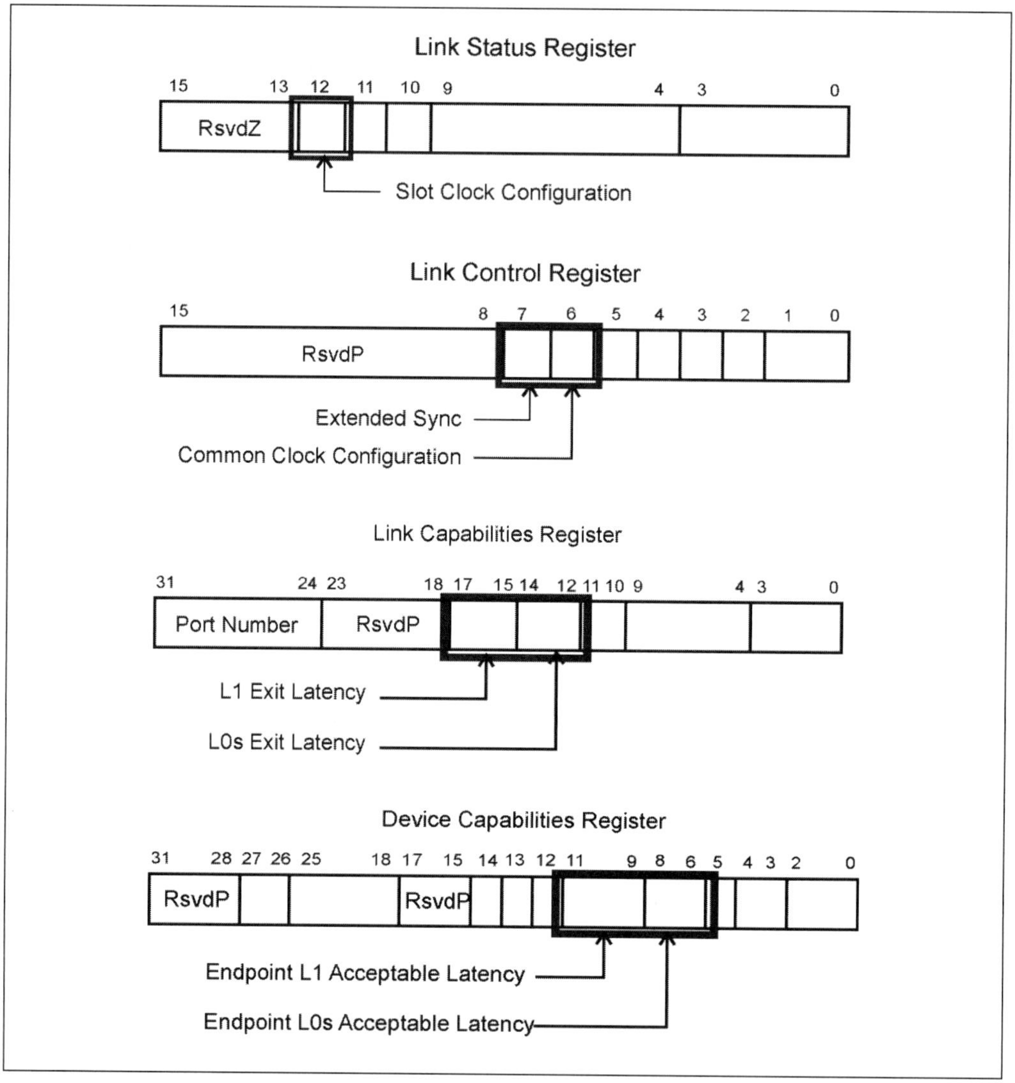

Software Initiated Link Power Management

When software initiates configuration write transactions to transition the power state of a device to conserve power, devices must respond by transitioning their link to the corresponding low power state.

D1/D2/D3$_{Hot}$ and the L1 State

The specification requires that when all functions within a device have been placed into any of the low power states (D1, D2, or D3$_{hot}$) by software, the device must initiate a transition to the L1 state. A device returns to L0 as a result of software intitiating a configuration access to the device or due to a device initiated Power Management Event (PME). See Figure 16-21.

Figure 16-21: Devices Transition to L1 When Software Changes their Power Level from D0

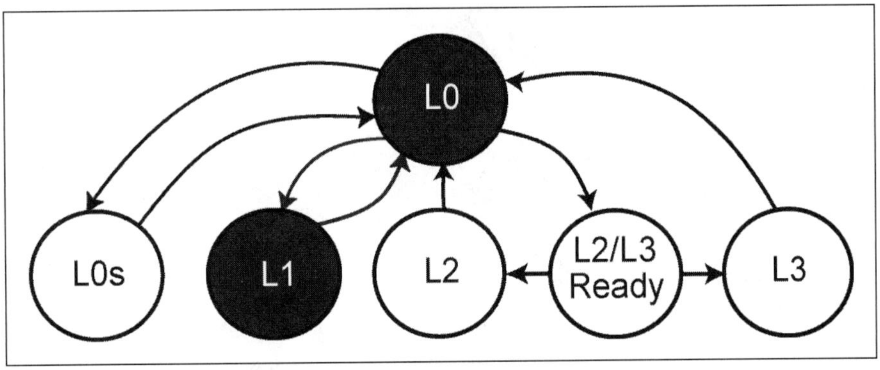

Upon receiving a configuration write transaction to the *Power State* field of the PMCSR register a device initiates the transition from L0 to L1 by sending a PM_Enter_L1 DLLP to the upstream component. Figure 16-22 on page 630 illustrates the sequence of events. In the example, software places the EndPoint (EP) device into the D2 state.

Figure 16-22: Software Placing a Device into a D2 State and Subsequent Transition to L1

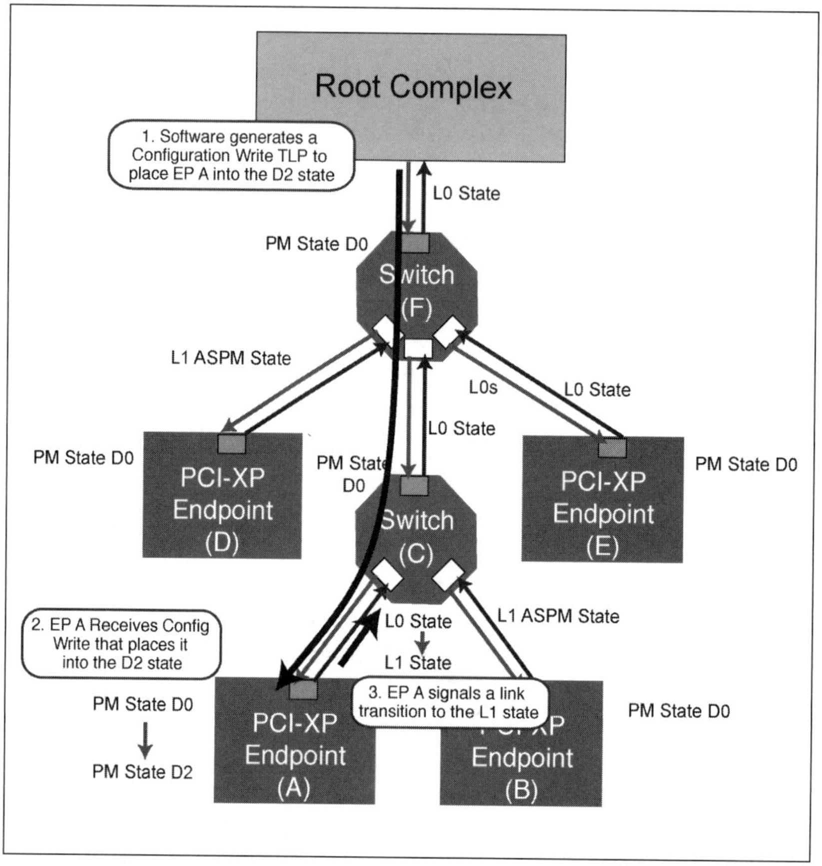

Entering the L1 State

The procedure required to place the link into an L1 state is illustrated in Figure 16-23 on page 632. Each step referenced in the figure is described in greater detail below:

1. Once the device recognizes that all its functions are in the D2 state, the device must prepare to transition the link into its L1 state. This process begins with blocking new TLPs from being scheduled.
2. A TLP may have been sent by endpoint A prior to receiving the request to enter D2 that has not yet received a TLP acknowledgement. The device must not attempt to signal a link transition request until all outstanding TLPs have been acknowledged. This means that the Replay Buffer must be empty before proceeding to the L1 state.

3. Because of the long latencies required to return the device and link to their active states, a device must be prepared to send a maximum-sized TLP immediately upon return to the active state. Recall that insufficient Flow Control credits result in TLP transmission being blocked; therefore, before entering L1 the endpoint must have sufficient credits to permit transmission of the maximum-sized packet supported for each Flow Control type.
4. When the above items have been completed the device sends a PM_Enter_L1 DLLP to the upstream device. This DLLP acts as a command to instruct the upstream component to place its transmit link into the L1 state. The PM_Enter_L1 DLLP is sent continuously on the link until a PM_Request_ACK DLLP is received from the upstream device.
5. The upstream component upon receipt of the PM_Enter_L1 DLLP, begins its preparation for entering L1 by performing steps 6, 7, and 8. This is the same preparation as performed by the downstream component prior to signaling the L1 transition.
6. All new TLP scheduling is blocked.
7. In the event that a previous TLP has not yet been acknowledged, the upstream device will wait until all transactions in the Replay Buffer have been acknowledged before proceeding.
8. Flow Control credits must be accumulated to ensure that the largest TLP can be transmitted for each Flow Control type before entering L1.
9. The upstream component sends a PM_Request_ACK DLLP to confirm that it's ready to enter the L1 state. This DLLP is sent continuously until an Electrical Idle ordered set is received, indicating that the acknowledgement has been accepted.
10. The downstream component upon receiving the acknowledgement DLLP knows that the upstream component is prepared to enter the L1 state.
11. The downstream device sends an Electrical Idle ordered set after which it places its transmit lanes into electrical idle (transmitter is in Hi-Z state).
12. The upstream component recognizes the Electrical Idle ordered set and places its transmit lanes into electrical idle. The link has now entered the L1 state.

Figure 16-23: Procedure Used to Transition a Link from the L0 to L1 State

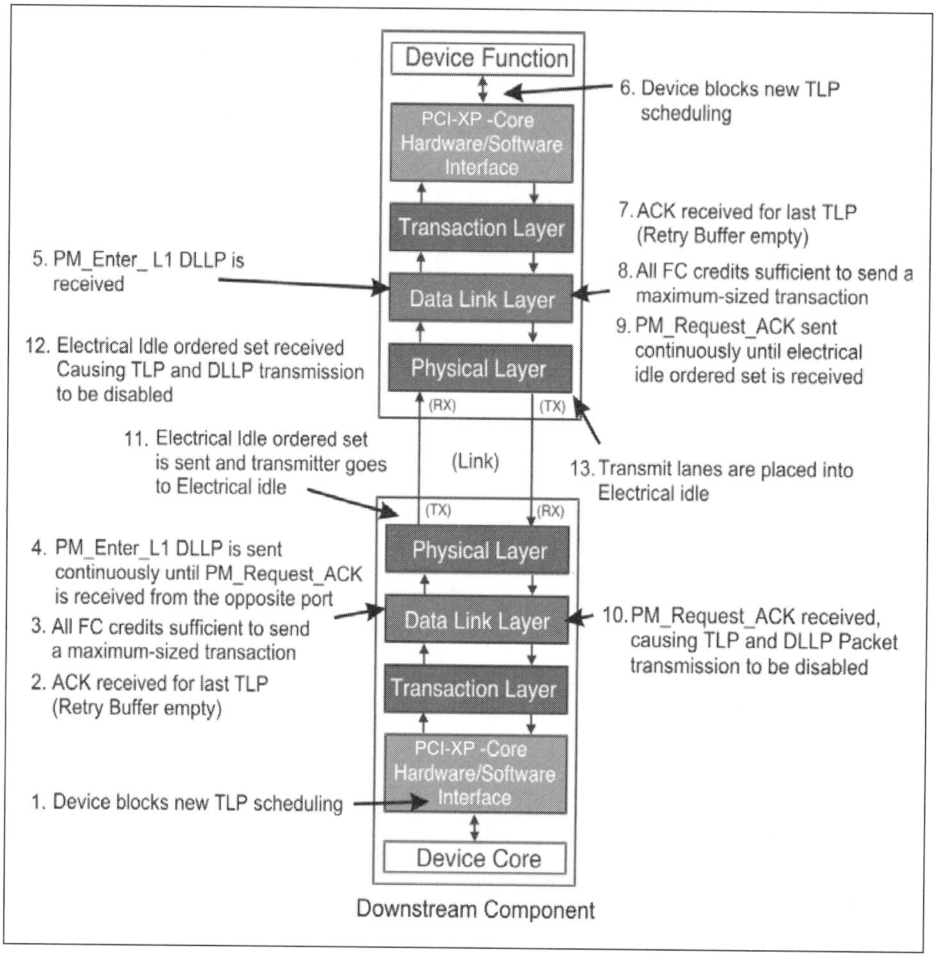

Exiting the L1 State

The exit from the L1 state can be initiated by either the upstream or downstream component. The trigger that causes an exit from L1 back to L0 is different for upstream and downstream devices as discussed below. This section also summarizes the signaling protocol used to exit L1.

Upstream Component Initiates L1 to L0 Transition. Software having placed a device into a power saving state (D1, D2, or D3) may need to transition the device back to D0 to permit device access. Power Management software must issue a configuration write transaction to change the power state back to D0. When the configuration transaction arrives at the upstream component (a Root Port or downstream Switch Port) the port will exit the electrical idle state which initiates re-training and return of the link to the L0 state.

Once the link is active, the configuration write transaction can be delivered to the device causing the transition back to D0. The device is now ready for normal operation again.

Downstream Component Initiates L1 to L0 Transition. When a link is in the L1 state the reference clock is still active and power is still applied to devices attached to the link. A downstream device may be designed to monitor external events that would trigger a Power Management Event (PME). In conventional PCI, a PME is reported via a signal of the same name — PME#. This signal is routed to system board logic that is responsible for notifying software (typically via an interrupt) of the need to exit L1. PCI Express uses the same concept but eliminates the sideband signal with a virtual wire message that reports the PME. (See "The PME Message" on page 639 for details.)

The L1 Exit Protocol. When in the L1 state both directions of the link are in the electrical idle state. A device signals an exit from L1 by transmitting the TS1 Ordered Sets, thereby causing the exit from electrical idle. When the device at the other end of the link detects the exit from electrical idle it sends the TS1 Ordered Sets back to the originating device. This sequence triggers both devices to enter re-training (recovery). Following recovery both devices will have returned to the L0 state.

L2/L3 Ready — Removing Power from the Link

Once software has placed all functions within a device into the $D3_{hot}$ state power can be removed from the device. A typical application for this would be to place all devices in the fabric into D3 and put all devices to sleep by removing power to all devices. Depending on the system design power can also be removed from devices selectively based on the implementation of separate power planes that permits power to be removed selectively. The specification does not specify the actual mechanism that would be used to remove clock and power (main power rails).

The state transitions required to prepare devices for removing power involve the preliminary steps of entering L1 and then via a handshake protocol returning to L0 and then to the L2/L3 Ready state as illustrated in Figure 16-24.

Figure 16-24: Link States Transitions Associated with Preparing Devices for Removal of the Reference Clock and Power

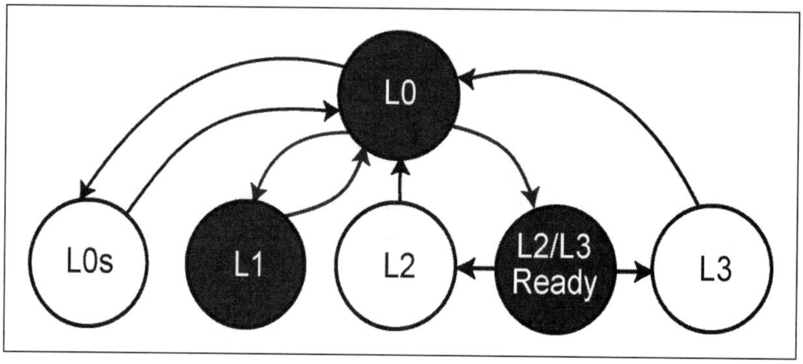

L2/L3 Ready Handshake Sequence

The specification however requires a handshake sequence when transitioning to the L2/L3 Ready state. This handshake has two purposes:

- to ensure that all devices are ready for reference clock and power removal.
- ensure that inband PME messages being sent to the Root Complex are not lost when power is removed.

Below is an example of the handshake sequence that is required before removing the reference clock and power from all PCI Express devices in the fabric. This example assumes a system-wide power down is being initiated. However the sequence can also apply to smaller segments of the PCI Express fabric or individual devices. The required steps are summarized below and in Figure 16-25 on page 636 (which illustrates a single Root Port). The overall sequence is represented in two parts labeled A and B. The Link transitions involved in the complete sequence include:

- L0 --> L1 (caused by software placing a device into D3)
- L1 --> L0 (caused by software initiating a PME_Turn_Off message)
- L0 --> L2/L3 Ready (caused by completion of PME_Turn_Off message handshake sequence, which culminates in a PM_Enter_L23 DLLP being sent by the device and the link going to electrical idle)

The following steps detail the sequence illustrated in Figure 16-25.

1. Power Management software must first place all functions within PCI Express fabric into their D3 state.
2. All devices initiate transitions of their links to the L1 state upon entering D3.
3. Power Management initiates a PME_Turn_Off TLP message that is broadcast from all Root Complex ports to all devices. (This prevents PME Messages from being sent upstream when power is removed. Otherwise a message would be lost if it is being sent when power is cut.) Note that delivery of this TLP requires each link to transition from L1 to L0 as it is forwarded downstream.
4. All devices must receive and acknowledge the PME_Turn_Off message by returning a PME_TO_ACK TLP message while in the D3 state.
5. Switches must collect the PME_TO_ACK messages from all of their enabled downstream ports and forward an aggregate PME_TO_ACK message upstream toward the Root Complex.
6. Subsequently, each device sends a PM_Enter_L23 DLLP when it is ready to have the reference clock and power removed. This causes each link to enter the L2/L3 Ready state. The specification states that the PM_Enter_L23 DLLP must be sent repeatedly until a PM_Request_ACK DLLP is returned. The links that enter the L2/L3 Ready state last are those attached to the device originating the PME_Turn_Off message (the Root Complex in this example).
7. The reference clock and power can finally be removed when all links have transitioned to the L2/L3 state. The specification further requires that clock and power cannot be removed sooner than 100ns after all links attached directly to the Root Port (i.e., point of origin) have transitioned to the L2/L3 Ready state. If auxiliary (AUX) power is supplied to the devices, the link transitions to L2 and if no AUX power is available the devices are referred to as being in the L3 state.

Figure 16-25: Negotiation for Entering L2/L3 Ready State

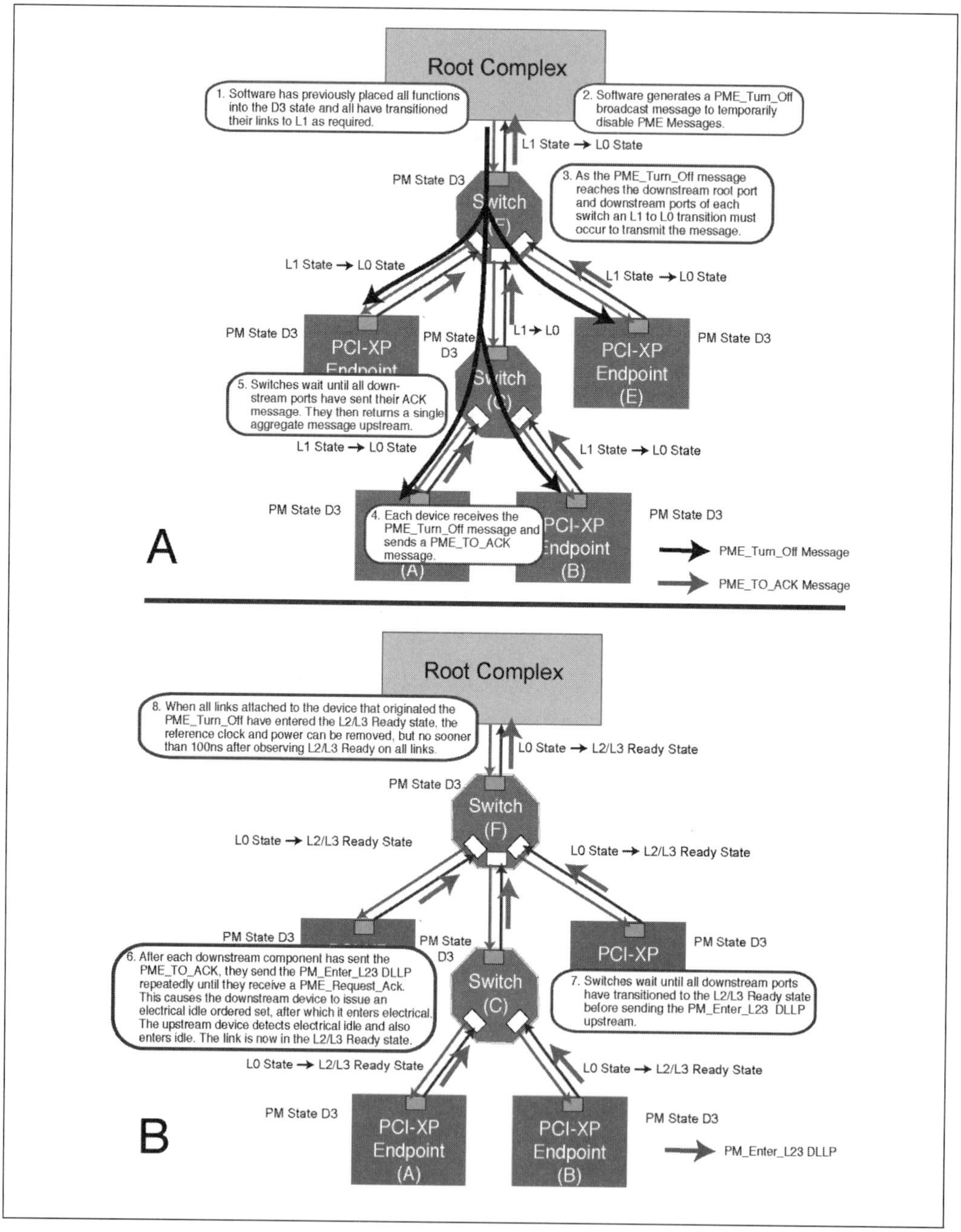

Exiting the L2/L3 Ready State — Clock and Power Removed

As illustrated in the state diagram in Figure 16-26, a device may only exit the L2/L3 Ready state when power is removed. Note that when Vaux is available the transition is to L2 and when all power is removed the transition is to L3.

Link state transitions are normally under control of the Link Training Sequence State Machine (LTSSM) within the Physical Layer. However, transitions to the L2 and L3 states result from main power being removed. Because the LTSSM operates typically on main power only, the specification refers to the L2 and L3 states as pseudo-states. These states are defined for explaining the resulting condition of a device when power is removed under Power Management software control, and are not associated with LTSSM actions.

Figure 16-26: State Transitions from L2/L3 Ready When Power is Removed

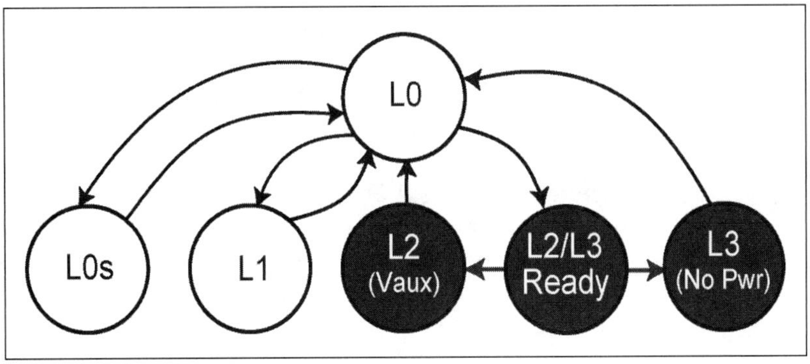

The L2 State

Some devices are designed to monitor external events and initiate a wakeup sequence so that an external event can be handled normally. Because main power is removed from the device, these device may need AUX power to monitor the events and to signal wakeup to notify software that the device needs to be revived.

The L3 State

When in this state the device has no power and therefore no means of communication. Recovery from this state requires the system to re-establish power and reference clock and receive fundamental reset.

Link Wake Protocol and PME Generation

The wake protocol provides a method for devices to reactivate the upstream link and request that Power Management software return the devices to D0 so they can perform required operations. The procedures and signaling methods used in PCI Express are different from the PCI-PM specified methods. However, PCI Express PM is designed to be compatible with PCI-PM software.

Rather than using the PCI-defined PME# sideband signal, PCI Express devices employ an inband PME message to notify PM software of a request to return the device to the full power state (D0). The ability to generate PME messages may be supported optionally within any of the low power states. Recall that devices report the PM states they support and from which of these states they can send a PME message. See Figure 16-8 on page 597.

PME messages can only be delivered once the link power state transitions to L0. The level of difficulty and latency required to reactivate the link so that a PME message can be sent is a function of a device's PM and Link state. Consequently, the steps required to complete a wakeup can include the following depending on the current link state:

1. Link is in non-communicating (L2) state — when a link is in the L2 state it cannot communicate because the reference clock and main power have been removed. Thus, a PME message cannot be sent until clock and power are restored, Fundamental Reset is asserted, and the link is re-trained. These events are triggered when a device signals a wakeup. This may result in all links being re-awakened that are in the path between the device needing to communicate and the Root Complex.
2. Link is in communicating (L1) state — when a link is in the L1 state clock and main power are still active; thus, a device simply exits the L1 state, re-trains the link (via the Recovery state) and returns the link to L0. This is the procedure discussed earlier in this chapter (See "Exiting the L1 State" on page 632.) Once the link is in L0 the PME message is delivered. Note that the devices never send a PME message while in the L2/L3 Ready state because entry into that state only occurs after PME notification has been turned off, in preparation for clock and power to be removed. (See "L2/L3 Ready Handshake Sequence" on page 634.)
3. PME is delivered (L0) — Once the link is in the L0 state, the device transfers the PME message to the Root Complex; thereby, notifying Power Management software that the device has observed an event that requires the device be placed back into its D0 state. Note that the message contains the

ID (Bus#, Device#, and Function#) of the device that originated the message. This permits software to immediately target the device's Power State to permit quicker return to the active state.

The PME Message

The PME message is delivered by devices that support PME notification. The message format is illustrated in Table 16-27 on page 639. The message may be initiated by a device in a low power state (D1, D2, $D3_{hot}$, and $D3_{cold}$) and is sent immediately upon return of the link to L0.

Figure 16-27: PME Message Format

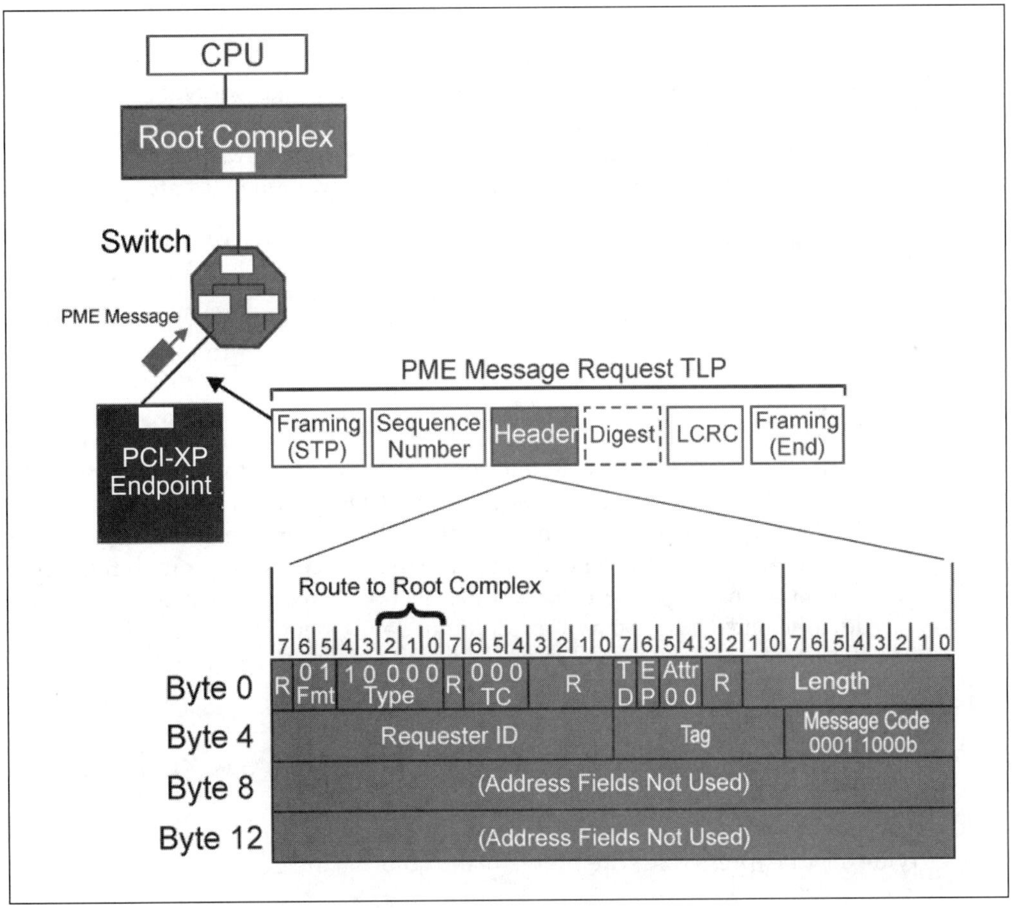

The PME message is a Transaction Layer Packet that has the following characteristics:

- TC and VC values are zero (000b)
- Routed implicitly to the Root Complex
- Handled as Posted Transaction
- Relaxed Ordering is not permitted, forcing all transactions in the fabric between the signaling device and the Root Complex to be delivered to the Root Complex ahead of the PME message

The PME Sequence

Devices may support PME in any of the low power states as specified in the PM Capabilities register. This register also specifies the amount of AUX current required by the device if it supports wakeup in the $D3_{cold}$ state. The basic sequence of events associated with signaling a PME to software is specified below and presumes that the device and system are enabled to generate PME (See "Scenario—Setup a Function-Specific System WakeUp Event" on page 583.) and the link has already been transitioned to the L0 state:

1. The device issues the PME message on its upstream port.
2. PME messages are implicitly routed to the Root Complex. Any switches in the path transition their upstream ports to L0 (if necessary) and send the packet upstream.
3. A root port receives the PME and forwards it to the Power Management Controller.
4. The controller calls power management software (typically via an interrupt). Software uses the Requester ID contained within the message to read and clear the PME_Status bit in the PMCSR and return the device to the D0 state. Depending on the degree of power conservation, the PCI Express driver may also need to restore the devices configuration registers.
5. PM Software may also call the device's software driver in the event that device context was lost as a result of the device being placed in a low power state. In this case, device software restores information within the device.

PME Message Back Pressure Deadlock Avoidance

The specification describes a potential deadlock scenario that is solved by specifying a PCI Express rule. The problem and solution are described below:

Background

The Root Complex typically stores the PME messages it receives in a queue, and calls PM software to handle each PME. A PME is held in this queue until PM software reads the PME_Status bit from the requesting device's PMCSR register. Once the configuration read transaction completes, this PME message can be removed from the internal queue.

The Problem

Deadlock can occur if the following scenario develops:

1. Incoming PME Messages have filled the PME message queue. Additional PME messages have been issued by other devices that are in the same hierarchy (downstream from the same root port) as the oldest message in the queue.
2. PM software, initiates a configuration read request from the Root Complex to read PME_Status from the oldest PME requester's PMCSR.
3. The corresponding split completion must push all previously posted PM_PME messages ahead of it (based on ordering rules).
4. The Root Complex cannot accept the incoming PME messages because the queue is full, and the read completion being behind the PME messages cannot reach the Root Complex to clear an entry from the queue.
5. No progress can be made, thus deadlock occurs.

The Solution

The deadlock is avoided if the Root Complex accepts any arriving PME messages, even when these message would overflow the queue. However, the Root Complex in this case simply discards the incoming PME message, because there is no place to store it. Consequently, the PME message is lost. Note that acceptance of a PME message still requires sufficient flow control credits.

To prevent a discarded PME message from being lost permanently, the device that sends a PME message is required to re-send it following a time-out interval, called the PME Service Time-out. If after sending a PME message, the device's PME_Status bit is not cleared with 100 ms (+ 50%/- 5%), it must re-issue the message.

The PME Context

Devices that generate PME must continue to power portions of the device that are used for detecting, signaling, and handling PME events. These items are called the PME context. Devices that support PME in the $D3_{cold}$ state use AUX power to maintain the PME context when the main power is removed. Following is a list of items that are typically part of the PME context.

- the function's PME_Status bit (required) — this bit is set when a device sends a PME message and is cleared by PM software. Devices that support PME in the $D3_{cold}$ state must implement the PME_Status bit as "sticky," meaning that the value is maintained across a fundamental reset.
- the functions's PME_Enable bit (required) — this bit must remain set to continue enabling a function's ability to generate PME messages and signal wakeup (if required). Devices that support PME in the $D3_{cold}$ state must implement PME_Enable as "sticky," meaning that the value is maintained across a fundamental reset.
- device-specific status information — for example, a device might preserve event status information in cases where several different types of events can trigger a PME.
- application-specific information — for example, modems that initiate wakeup would preserve Caller ID information if supported.

Waking Non-Communicating Links

When a device that supports PME in the D3cold state needs to send a PME message, it must first initiate the sequence of events needed to transition the link to the L0 state so that the message can be sent. This is typically referred to as wakeup. PCI Express defines two methods of triggering the wakeup of non-communicating links:

- Beacon — a signaling technique that is driven by AUX power
- WAKE# Signal — a sideband signal that is driven by AUX power

In both cases, PM software must be notified so that it can re-apply main power and restart the reference clock. This also causes generation of fundamental reset that forces a device into the $D0_{uninitialized}$ state. Once the link transitions to the L0 state, the device sends the PME message. Because reset is required to re-activate the link so that PME can be signaled, devices must maintain PME context across the reset sequence described above.

Beacon

PCI Express includes a signaling mechanism designed to operate on AUX power that does not require the differential drivers and receivers to be used. The beacon is simply a way of notifying the upstream component that software should be notified of the wakeup request. Switches upon receiving beacon on one of their downstream ports signal beacon on the upstream port. Ultimately, the beacon signal reaches the root complex, causing an interrupt that calls PM software.

Some form-factor types require support for the beacon signalling for waking the system, while others do not. The specification requires compliance with the specific form-factor specifications, and does not require beacon support for devices used in form-factors not requiring this support. However, for "universal" PCI Express components (those designed for use in a variety of form-factors) beacon support is required.

See "Beacon Signaling" on page 469 for details.

WAKE# (AUX Power)

PCI Express also provides a sideband signal called WAKE#, as a alternative to beacon signaling. This signal may be routed directly to the Root Complex or other motherboard logic, thereby causing an interrupt that will call PM software. It's also possible that a hybrid implementation can be used. In this case, WAKE# is sent to a switch, which in turn signal beacon on its upstream port. The options are illustrated in Figure 16-28 on page 644 A and B. Note that when asserted, the WAKE# signal remains low until the PME_Status bit is cleared by software.

This signal must be implemented by ATX or ATX-based form factor and by the minis. motherboard connectors and cards as well as for the mini-card form factor. No requirement is specified for embedded devices to use the WAKE# signal.

Figure 16-28: WAKE# Signal Implementations

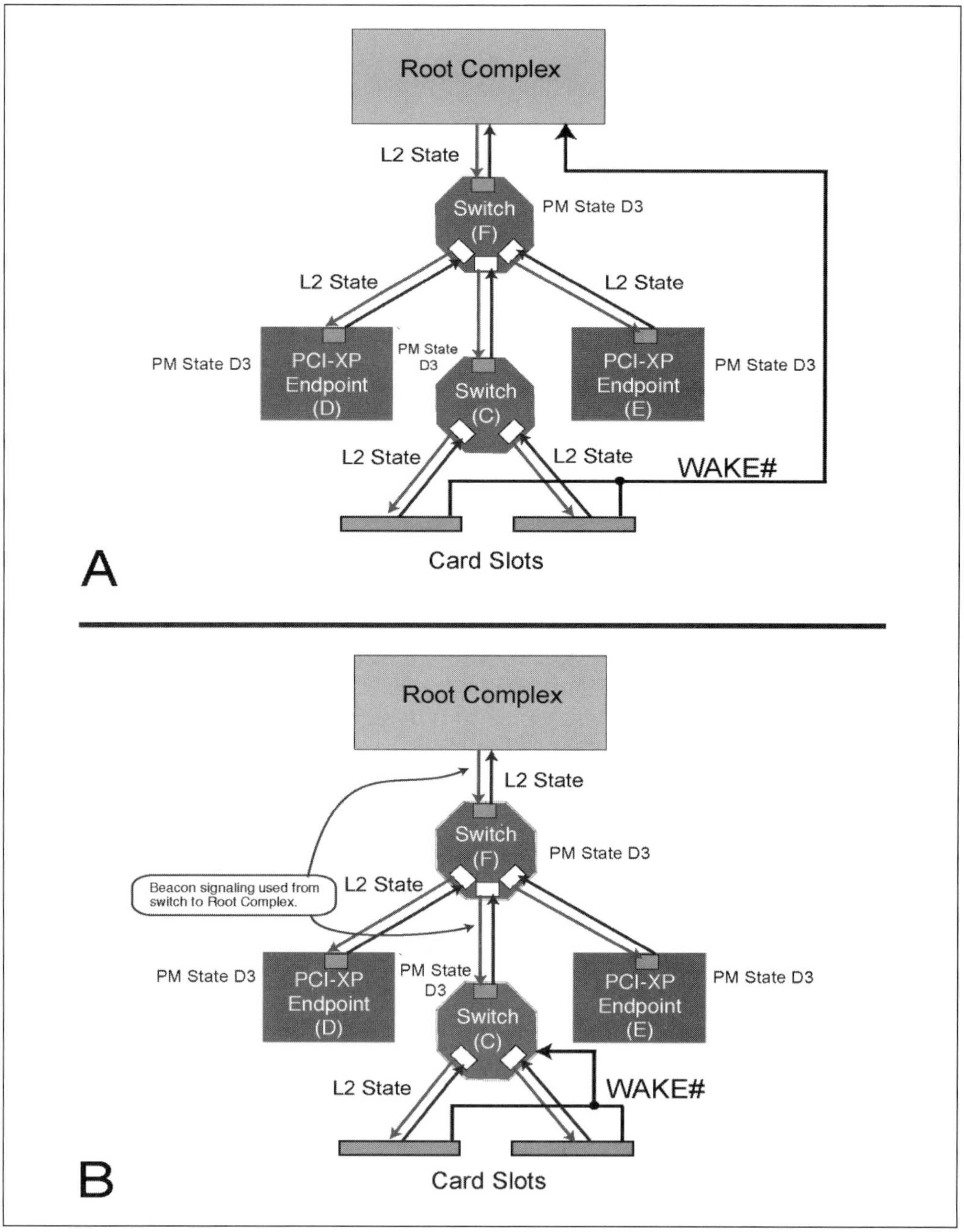

Auxiliary Power

Devices that support PME in the $D3_{cold}$ state must support the wakeup sequence (via beacon signaling or the sideband Wake# pin) and are allowed to consume the maximum auxiliary current of 375 mA (20mA maximum otherwise). The amount of current that they need is reported via the *Aux_Current* field within the PM Capability registers. Auxiliary power is enabled when the *PME_Enable* bit is set within the PMCSR register. PCI-PM limits the use of Auxiliary Current as specified above.

PCI Express extends the use of auxiliary power beyond the limitations specified by PCI-PM. Now devices that have PME disabled or that do not support PME can also consume the maximum amount of auxiliary current allowed. This new capability is enabled via software by setting the *Aux Power PM Enable* bit in the Device Control register, illustrated in Figure 16-29 on page 645. This capability permits devices the opportunity to support other functions such as SM Bus functionality while in a low power state. As in PCI-PM the amount of current consumed by a device is reported in the *Aux_Current* field in the PMC register.

Figure 16-29: Auxiliary Current Enable for Devices Not Supporting PMEs

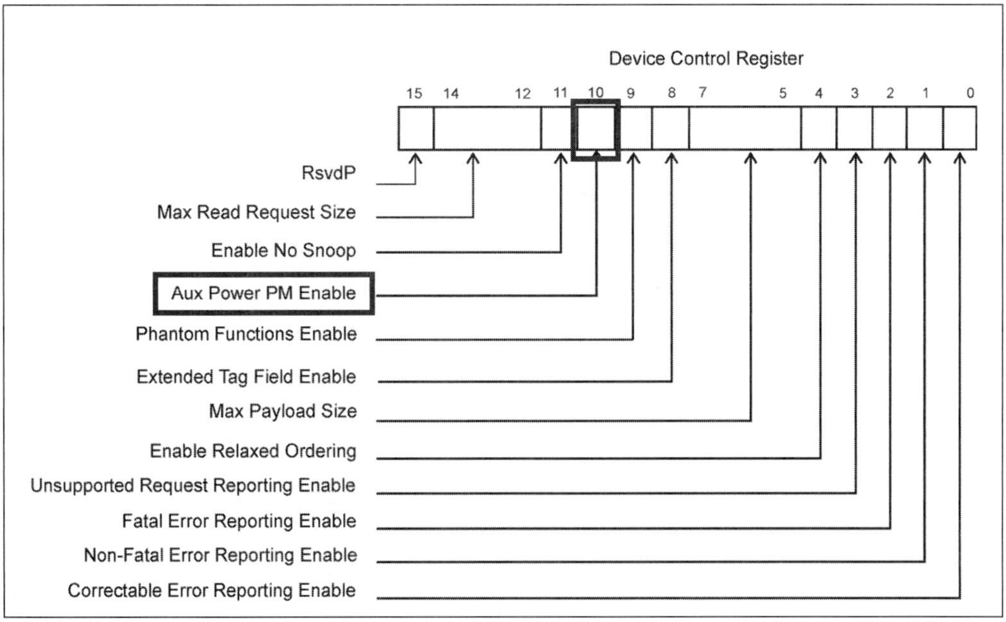

Part Five

Optional Topics

17 Hot Plug

The Previous Chapter

The previous chapter provided a detailed description of PCI Express power management, which is compatible with revision 1.1 of the *PCI Bus PM Interface Specification* and the *Advanced Configuration and Power Interface,* revision 2.0 (ACPI). In addition PCI Express defines extensions that are orthogonal to the PCI-PM specification. These extensions focus primarily on Link Power and PM event management. This chapter also provides an overall context for the discussion of power management, by including a description of the OnNow Initiative, ACPI, and the involvement of the Windows OS is also provided.

This Chapter

PCI Express includes native support for hot plug implementations. This chapter discusses hot plug and hot removal of PCI Express devices. The specification defines a standard usage model for all device and platform form factors that support hot plug capability. The usage model defines, as an example, how push buttons and indicators (LED's) behave, if implemented on the chassis, add-in card or module. The definitions assigned to the indicators and push buttons, described in this chapter, apply to all models of hot plug implementations.

The Next Chapter

The next chapter provides an introduction to the PCI Express add-in card electromechanical specifications. It describes the card form factor, the connector details, and the auxiliary signals with a description of their function. Other card form factors are also briefly described.

Background

Some systems that employ the use of PCI and PCI-X require high availability or non-stop operation. For example, many customers require computer systems that experience downtimes of just a few minutes a year, or less. Clearly, manufacturers must focus on equipment reliability, and also provide a method of identifying and repairing equipment failures quickly. An important feature in supporting these goals is the Hot Plug/Hot Swap solutions that provide three important capabilities:

1. a method of replacing failed expansion cards without turning the system off
2. keeping the O/S and other services running during the repair
3. shutting down and restarting software associated with the failed device

Prior to the widespread acceptance of PCI many proprietary Hot Plug solutions were available to support this type of removal and replacement of expansion cards. However the original PCI implementation was not designed to support hot removal and insertion of cards, but a standardized solution for supporting this capability in PCI was needed. Consequently, two major approaches to hot replacement of PCI expansion devices have been developed. These approaches are:

- Hot Plug PCI Card — used in PC Server motherboard and expansion chassis implementations
- Hot Swap — used in CompactPCI systems based on a passive PCI backplane implementation.

In both solutions, control logic is implemented to isolate the card logic from the PCI bus via electronic switches. In conjunction with isolation logic, power, reset, and clock are controlled to ensure an orderly power down and power up of cards when they are removed and replaced. Also, status and power LEDs provide indications to the user that it is safe to remove or install the card.

The need to extend hot plug support to PCI Express cards is clear. Designers of PCI Express have incorporated Hot removal and replacement of cards as a "native" feature. The specification defines configuration registers, Hot Plug Messages, and procedures to support Hot Plug solutions.

Hot Plug in the PCI Express Environment

PCI Express Hot Plug is derived from the 1.0 revision of the Standard Hot Plug Controller specification (SHPC 1.0) for PCI. The goals of PCI Express Hot Plug are to:

- support the same "Standardized Usage Model" as defined by the Standard Hot Plug Controller specification. This ensures that the PCI Express hot plug is identical from the user perspective to existing implementations based on the SHPC 1.0 specification
- support the same software model implemented by existing operating systems. However, if the OS includes a SHPC 1.0 compliant driver, it will not work with PCI Express Hot Plug controllers, which have a different programming interface.

PCI Express defines the registers necessary to support the integration of a Hot Plug Controller within individual root and switch ports. Under Hot Plug software control, these Hot Plug controllers and the associated port interface within the root or switch port must control the card interface signals to ensure orderly power down and power up as cards are removed and replaced. Hot Plug controllers must:

- assert and deassert the PERST# signal to the PCI Express card connector
- remove or apply power to the card connector.
- Selectively turn on or turn off the Power and Attention Indicators associated with a specific card connector to draw the user's attention to the connector and advertise whether power is applied to the slot.
- Monitor slot events (e.g. card removal) and report these events to software via interrupts.

PCI Express Hot-Plug (like PCI) is designed as a "no surprises" Hot-Plug methodology. In other words, the user is not permitted to install or remove a PCI Express card without first notifying software. System software then prepares both the card and slot for the card's removal and replacement, and finally indicates to the end user (via visual indicators) status of the hot plug process and notification that installation or removal may be performed.

Surprise Removal Notification

PCI Express cards (unlike PCI) must implement the edge contacts with card presence detect pins (PRSNT1# and PRSNT2#) that break contact first (when the card is removed from the slot). This gives advanced notice to software of a "surprise" removal and enough time to remove power prior to the signals breaking contact.

Differences between PCI and PCI Express Hot Plug

The elements needed to support hot plug are essentially the same between PCI and PCI Express hot plug solutions. Figure 17-1 on page 653 depicts the PCI hardware and software elements required to support hot plug. PCI solutions implement a single standardized hot plug controller on the system board that permits all hot plug slots on the bus to be controlled by a single controller. Also, isolation logic is needed in the PCI environment to electrically disconnect a single card slot from the bus prior to card removal.

PCI Express Hot Plug differs from the PCI implementation due to point-to-point connections. (See Figure 17-2 on page 654) Point-to-point connections eliminate the need for isolation logic and permit the hot plug controller to be distributed to each port interface to which a connector is attached. A standardized software interface defined for each root and switch port permits a standardized software interface to control hot plug operations. Note that the programming interface for the PCI Express and PCI Hot Plug Controllers vary and require different software drivers.

Figure 17-1: PCI Hot Plug Elements

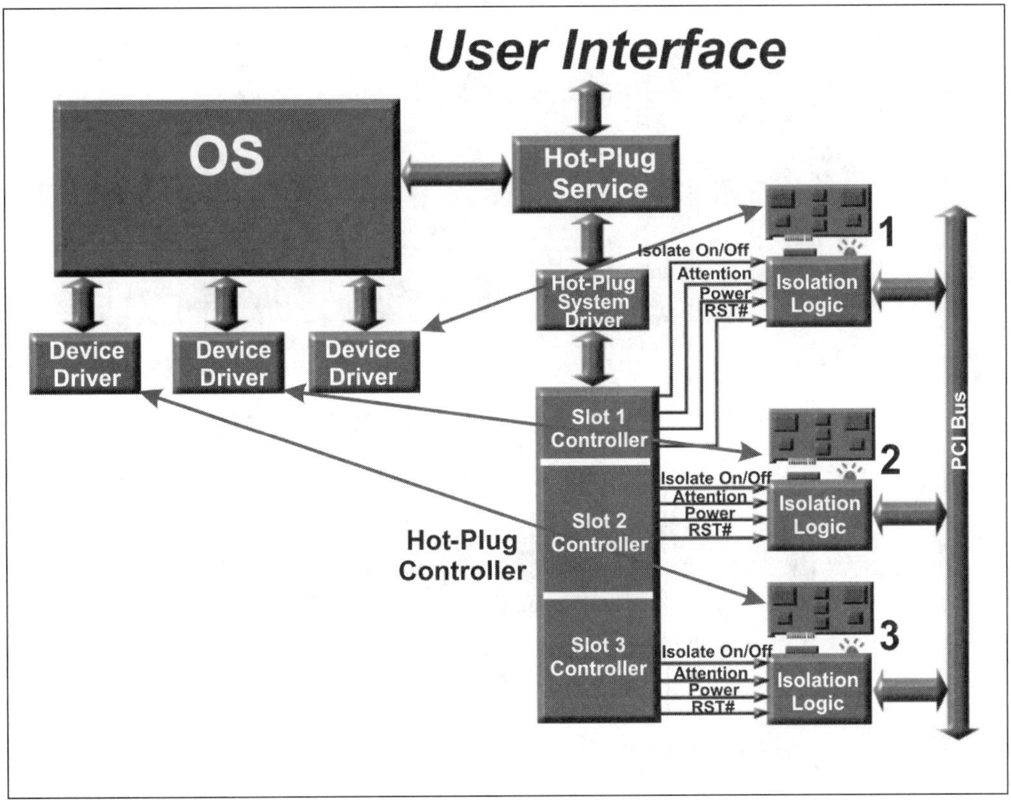

Figure 17-2: PCI Express Hot-Plug Hardware/Software Elements

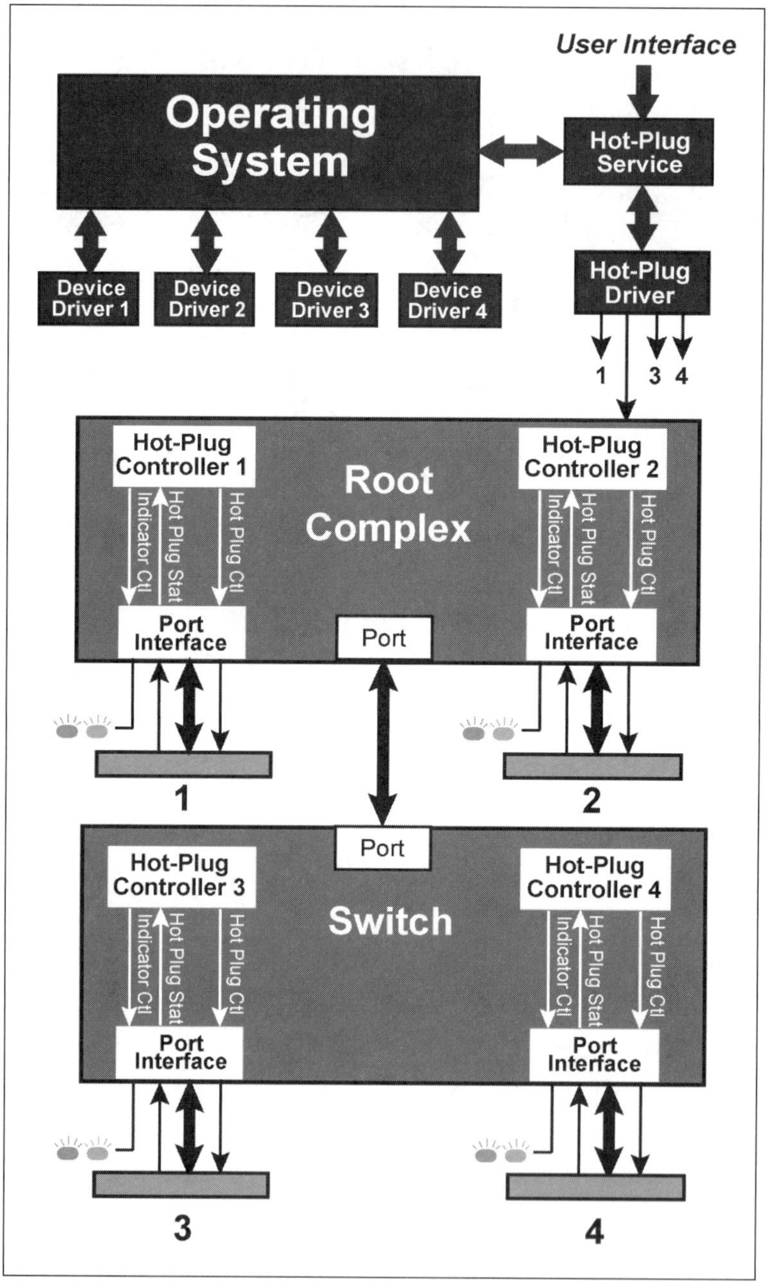

Elements Required to Support Hot Plug

This section describes the hardware and software elements required to support the Hot Plug environment. Refer to Figure 17-2 on page 654 during this discussion.

Software Elements

Table 17-1 on page 655 describes the major software elements that must be modified to support Hot-Plug capability. Also refer to Figure 17-2 on page 654.

Table 17-1: Introduction to Major Hot-Plug Software Elements

Software Element	Supplied by	Description
User Interface	OS vendor	An OS-supplied utility that permits the end-user to request that a card connector be turned off in order to remove a card or turned on to use a card that has just been installed.
Hot-Plug Service	OS vendor	A service that processes requests (referred to as Hot-Plug Primitives) issued by the OS. This includes requests to: • provide slot identifiers • turn card On or Off • turn Attention Indicator On or Off • return current state of slot (On or Off) The Hot-Plug Service interacts with the Hot-Plug System Driver to satisfy the requests. The interface (i.e., API) with the Hot-Plug System Driver is defined by the OS vendor.
Standardized Hot-Plug System Driver	System Board vendor or OS	Receives requests (aka Hot-Plug Primitives) from the Hot-Plug Service within the OS. Interacts with the hardware Hot-Plug Controllers to accomplish requests.

Table 17-1: Introduction to Major Hot-Plug Software Elements (Continued)

Software Element	Supplied by	Description
Device Driver	Adapter card vendor	Some special, Hot-Plug-specific capabilities must be incorporated in a Hot-Plug capable device driver. This includes: • support for the **Quiesce** command. • optional implementation of the **Pause** command. • Support for **Start** command or optional **Resume** command.

A Hot-Plug-capable system may be loaded with an OS that doesn't support Hot-Plug capability. In this case, although the system BIOS would contain Hot-Plug-related software, the Hot-Plug Service would not be present. Assuming that the user doesn't attempt hot insertion or removal of a card, the system will operate as a standard, non-Hot-Plug system.

- The system startup firmware must ensure that all Attention Indicators are Off.
- The spec also states: "the Hot-Plug slots must be in a state that would be appropriate for loading non-Hot-Plug system software."

Hardware Elements

Table 17-2 on page 656 and Figure 17-2 on page 654 illustrate the major hardware elements necessary to support PCI Express Hot-Plug operation.

Table 17-2: Major Hot-Plug Hardware Elements

Hardware Element	Description
Hot-Plug Controller	Receives and processes commands issued by the Hot-Plug System Driver. One Controller is associated with each root or switch port that supports hot plug operation. The PCI Express Specification defines a standard software interface for the Hot-Plug Controller.

Table 17 2: Major Hot Plug Hardware Elements (Continued)

Hardware Element	Description
Card Slot Power Switching Logic	Permits the power supply voltages to a slot to be turned on or off under program control. Controlled by the Hot Plug controller under the direction of the Hot-Plug System Driver.
Card Reset Logic	Permits the selective assertion or deassertion of the PERST# signal to a specific slot under program control. Controlled by the Hot Plug Controller under the direction of the Hot-Plug System Driver.
Power Indicator	One per slot. Indicates whether power is currently applied to the card slot or not. Controlled by the Hot Plug logic associated with each port, at the direction of the Hot Plug System Driver.
Attention Indicator	One per slot. The Attention Indicator is used to draw the attention of the operator to indicate a Hot Plug problem or failure. Controlled by the Hot Plug logic associated with this port, at the direction of the Hot-Plug System Driver.
Attention Button	One per slot. This button is pressed by the operator to notify Hot Plug software of a Hot Plug request.
Card Present Detect Pins	Two Card Present signals are defined by the PCI Express specification: PRSNT1# and PRSNT2#. PRSNT1# is located at one end of the card slot and PRSNT2# at the opposite end. These two pins are shorter that the other slot pins, allowing break-first capability upon card removal. The system board must tie PRSNT1# to ground and connect PRSNT2# to a pull-up resistor on the system board. Additional PRSNT2# pins are defined for wider connectors to support the insertion and recognition of shorter cards installed into longer connectors. The card must connect PRSNT1# to PRSNT2# to complete the current path between ground and Vcc. "Auxiliary Signals" on page 693.

Card Removal and Insertion Procedures

The descriptions of typical card removal and insertion that follow are intended to be introductory in nature. Additional detail can be found later in this chapter.

It should be noted that the procedures described in the following sections assume that the OS, rather than the Hot-Plug System Driver, is responsible for configuring a newly-installed device. If the Hot-Plug System Driver has this responsibility, the Hot-Plug Service will call the Hot-Plug System Driver and instruct it to configure the newly-installed device.

On and Off States

Definition of On and Off

A slot in the On state has the following characteristics:

- Power is applied to the slot.
- REFCLK is on.
- The link is active or in the standby (L0s or L1) low power state due to Active State Power Management.
- The PERST# signal is deasserted.

A slot in the Off state has the following characteristics:

- Power to the slot is turned off.
- REFCLK is off.
- The link is inactive. (Driver at the root of switch port is in Hi Z state)
- The PERST# signal is asserted.

Turning Slot Off

Steps required to turn off a slot that is currently in the On state:

1. Deactivate the link. This may involve issuing a Electrical Idle ordered set (a sequence initiated at the Physical Layer that forces the Card's driver to enter the Hi Z state.
2. Assert the PERST# signal to the slot.
3. Turn off REFCLK to the slot.
4. Remove power from the slot.

Turning Slot On

Steps to turn on a slot that is currently in the off state:

1. Apply power to the slot.
2. Turn on REFCLK to the slot
3. Deassert the PERST# signal to the slot. The system must meet the setup and hold timing requirements (specified in the PCI Express spec) relative to the rising edge of PERST#.

Once power and clock have been restored and PERST# removed, the physical layers at both ports will perform link training and initialization. When the link is active, the devices will initialize VC0 (including flow control), making the link ready to transfer TLPs.

Card Removal Procedure

When a card must be removed, a number of steps must occur to not only prepare software and hardware for safe removal of the card, but also to control indicators that provide visual evidence of the request to remove the card being processed. The condition of the indicators during normal operation are:

- Attention Indicator (Amber or Yellow) — "Off" during normal operation.
- Power Indicator (Green) — "On" during normal operation

Software issues "Requests" to the Hot Plug Controller via configuration write transactions that target the "Slot Control Registers implemented by Hot-Plug capable ports." These requests control power to the slot and the state of the indicators.

The exact sequence of events that occur when performing a Hot Plug card removal vary slightly depending on whether the Hot Plug operation is initiated by pressing the Attention Button or via the User Interface software utility. Each sequence is described below.

Attention Button Used to Initiate Hot Plug Removal

The sequence of events is as follows:

1. The operator initiates the card removal request by depressing the slot's "attention button." The Hot-Plug Controller detects this event and delivers an interrupt to the root complex. As a result of the interrupt the Hot Plug

service calls the Hot Plug System Driver, which reads slot status information and detects the Attention Button request.

2. Next, the Hot-Plug Service issues a request to the Hot-Plug System Driver commanding the Hot Plug Controller to blink the slot's Power Indicator. The operator is granted a 5 second abort interval, from the time that the indicators starts to blink, during which the operator may press the button a second time to abort the request.
3. The Power Indicator continues to blink while the Hot Plug software validates the request. Note that software may fail to validate the request (e.g., the card may currently be used for some critical system operation).*
4. If the request is validated, the Hot-Plug Service utility commands the card's device driver to quiesce. That is, the driver must stop issuing requests to the card and complete or terminate all outstanding requests as well as disable its ability to generate transactions (including interrupt messages).
5. Software then issues a command to disable the card's link via the Link Control register within the root or switch port to which the slot is attached. This causes ports at both ends of the link to be disabled.
6. Next, software commands the Hot Plug Controller to turn the slot off.
7. Following successful power down software issues the Power Indicator Off Request. The operator knows that the card may be removed safely from the slot when the Power Indicator is Off.
8. The operator releases the Mechanical Retention Latch, causing the Hot Plug Controller to remove all switched signals from the slot (e.g., SMBus and JTAG signals). The card can now be removed.
9. The OS deallocates the memory space, IO space, interrupt line, etc. that had been assigned to the device and makes these resources available for assignment to other devices in the future.

* If the request is not validated, software will deny the request and issue a command to the Hot Plug controller to turn the Power Indicator back ON. The specification also recommends that software notify the operator via a message or by logging an entry indicating the cause of the request denial.

Hot Plug Removal Request Issued via User Interface

The sequence of events is as follows:

1. The operator initiates the card removal request by selecting the Physical Slot number associated with the card to be removed. Software opens a window or presents a message requesting the operator confirm the request. Note that the Power Indicator remains on during this process.
2. When the operator confirms the request, the Hot-Plug Service issues a request to the Hot-Plug System Driver commanding the Hot Plug Controller to blink the slot's Power Indicator. During this time, software validates

the Hot Plug request. Note that software may fail to validate the request (e.g., the card may currently being used for some critical system operation)*.

3. If the request is validated, the Hot-Plug Service utility commands the card's device driver to quiesce. That is, the driver must stop issuing requests to the card and complete or terminate all outstanding requests as well as disable its ability to generate transactions (including interrupt messages).
4. Software then issues a command to disable the card's link via the Link Control register located in the root or switch port to which the slot connects. This causes ports at both ends of the link to be disabled.
5. Next, software commands the Hot Plug Controller to disable the slot.
6. Following successful power down software issues the Power Indicator Off Request. The operator knows that the card may be removed safely from the slot when the Power Indicator is Off.
7. The operator releases the Manual Retention Latch (MRL), causing the Hot Plug Controller to remove all switched signals from the slot (e.g., SMBus and V_{aux} signals). The card can now be removed.
8. The OS deallocates the memory space, IO space, interrupt line, etc. that had been assigned to the device and makes these resources available for assignment to other devices in the future.

* If the request is not validated, software will deny the request and issue a command to the Hot Plug controller to turn the Power Indicator back ON. The specification also recommends that software notify the operator via a message or by logging an entry indicating the cause of the request denial.

Card Insertion Procedure

The procedure for installing a new card basically reverses the steps listed for card removal. The following steps assume that the card slot was left in the same state that it was in immediately after a card was removed from the connector (in other words, the Power Indicator is in the Off state, indicating the slot is ready for card insertion). Variations between the two methods of initiation are described below.

Card Insertion Initiated by Pressing Attention Button

The steps taken to Insert and enable a card are as follows:

1. The operator installs the card and secures the MRL. If implemented, the MRL sensor will signal the Hot-Plug Controller that the latch is closed, causing switched auxillary signals and V_{aux} to be connected to the slot.

2. Next, the operator notifies the Hot-Plug Service that the card has been installed by pressing the Attention Button. This signals the Hot Plug controller of the event, resulting in status register bits being set and causing a system interrupt to be sent to the Root Complex. Subsequently, Hot Plug software reads slot status from the port and recognizes the request.
3. The Hot-Plug Service issues a request to the Hot-Plug System Driver commanding the Hot Plug Controller to blink the slot's Power Indicator to inform the operator that the card must not be removed. The operator is granted a 5 second abort interval, from the time that the indicators starts to blink, to abort the request by pressing the button a second time.
4. The Power Indicator continues to blink while Hot Plug software validates the request. Note that software may fail to validate the request (e.g., the security policy settings may prohibit the slot being enabled).*
5. The Hot-Plug Service issues a request to the Hot-Plug System Driver commanding the Hot Plug Controller to turn the slot on.
6. Once power is applied, software issues a command to turn the Power Indicator ON.
7. Once link training is complete, the OS commands the Platform Configuration Routine to configure the card function(s) by assigning the necessary resources.
8. The OS locates the appropriate driver(s) (using the Vendor ID and Device ID, or the Class Code, or the Subsystem Vendor ID and Subsystem ID configuration register values as search criteria) for the function(s) within the PCI Express device and loads it (or them) into memory.
9. The OS then calls the driver's initialization code entry point, causing the processor to execute the driver's initialization code. This code finishes the setup of the device and then sets the appropriate bits in the device's PCI configuration Command register to enable the device.

* If the request is not validated, software will deny the request and issue a command to the Hot Plug controller to turn the Power Indicator back OFF. The specification also recommends that software notify the operator via a message or by logging an entry indicating the cause of the request denial.

Card Insertion Initiated by User Interface

The steps taken to Re-enable the card are as follows:

1. The operator installs the card and secures the MRL. The MRL sensor signals the Hot Plug Controller to connect the switched signals to the slot.
2. Next, the operator informs the Hot-Plug Service (via the Hot Plug Utility program) that the card has been installed and is ready to be re-enabled. Software then prompts the user to verify that it is safe to re-enable the slot.

3. After the operator requests card insertion, the Hot-Plug Service issues a request to the Hot-Plug System Driver commanding the Hot Plug Controller to blink the slot's Power Indicator to inform the operator that the card must not be removed.
4. The Power Indicator continues to blink while Hot Plug software validates the request. Note that software may fail to validate the request (e.g., the security policy settings may be prohibit the slot being enabled).*
5. The Hot-Plug Service issues a request to the Hot-Plug System Driver commanding the Hot Plug Controller to reapply power to the slot.
6. Once power is applied, software issues a command to turn the Power Indicator ON.
7. Once link training is complete, the OS commands the Platform Configuration Routine to configure the card function(s) by assigning the necessary resources.
8. The OS locates the appropriate driver(s) (using the Vendor ID and Device ID, or the Class Code, or the Subsystem Vendor ID and Subsystem ID configuration register values as search criteria) for the function(s) within the PCI Express device and loads it (or them) into memory.
9. The OS then calls the driver's initialization code entry point, causing the processor to execute the driver's initialization code. This code finishes the setup of the device and then sets the appropriate bits in the device's PCI configuration Command register to enable the device.

* If the request is not validated, software will deny the request and issue a command to the Hot Plug controller to turn the Power Indicator back OFF. The specification also recommends that software notify the operator via a message or by logging an entry indicating the cause of the request denial.

Standardized Usage Model

Background

Systems based on the original 1.0 version of the PCI Hot Plug specification implemented hardware and software designs that varied widely because the specification did not define standardized registers or user interfaces. Consequently, customers who purchased Hot Plug capable systems from different vendors were confronted with a wide variation in user interfaces that required retraining operators when new systems were purchased. Furthermore, every board designer was required to write software to manage their implementation-specific hot plug controller. The 1.0 revision of the PCI Hot-Plug Controller (HPC) specification defines:

- a standard user interface that eliminates retraining of operators
- a standard programming interface for the hot plug controller, which permits a standardized hot plug driver to be incorporated into the operating system. PCI Express implements registers not defined by the HPC specification, hence the standard Hot Plug Controller driver implementations for PCI and PCI Express are slightly different.

The following sections discuss the standard user interface.

Standard User Interface

The user interface includes the following features:

- Attention Indicator — shows the attention state of the slot. The indicators are specified to be on, off, or blinking. The specification defines the blinking frequency as 1 to 2 Hz and 50% (+/- 5%) duty cycle. The state of this indicator is strictly under software control.
- Power Indicator (called Slot State Indicator in PCI HP 1.1) — shows the power status of the slot. Power indicator states are on, off, or blinking. The specification defines the blinking frequency as 1 to 2 Hz and 50% (+/- 5%) duty cycle. This indicator is controlled by software; however, the specification permits an exception in the event of a power fault condition.
- Manually Operated Retention Latch and Optional Sensor — secures card within slot and notifies the system when the latch is released
- Electromechanical Interlock (optional) — prevents card being removed from a slot while power is applied.
- Software User Interface — allows operator to request hot plug operation
- Attention Button (optional) — allows operator to manually request hot plug operation.
- Slot Numbering Identification — provides visual identification of slot on the board.

Attention Indicator

As mentioned in the previous section, the specification requires the system vendor to include an Attention Indicator associated with each Hot-Plug slot. This indicator must be located in close proximity to the corresponding slot and is yellow or amber in color. This Indicator draws the attention of the end user to the slot due to the hot plug request having failed due to an operational problem. The specification makes a clear distinction between operational and validation error and does not permit the attention indicator to report validation errors. Validation errors are problems detected and reported by software prior to beginning the hot plug operation. The behavior of the Attention Indicator is listed in Table 17-3 on page 665.

Table 17-3: Behavior and Meaning of the Slot Attention Indicator

Indicator Behavior	Attention State
Off	Normal — Normal Operation
On	Attention — Hot Plug Operation Failed due to an operational problem (e.g., problems with external cabling, add-in cards, software drivers, and power faults)
Blinking	Locate — Slot is being identified at operator's request

Power Indicator

The power indicator simply reflects the state of main power at the slot, and is controlled by Hot Plug software. The color of this indicator is green and is illuminated when power to the slot is "on."

The specification specifically prohibits Root or switch port hardware to change the power indicator state autonomously as a result of power fault or other events. A single exception to this rule allows a platform implementation that is capable of detecting stuck-on power faults. A stuck-on fault is simply a condition in which commands issued to remove slot power are ineffective. If the system is designed to detect this condition the system may override the root or switch port's command to turn the power indicator off and force it to the "on" state. This notifies the operator that the card should not be removed from the slot even though the operator has requested the slot to be powered down. The specification further states that supporting stuck-on faults is optional and if handled via system software "the platform vendor must ensure that this optional feature of the Standard Usage Model is addressed via other software, platform documentation, or by other means."

The behavior of the power indicator and the related power states are listed in Table 17-4 on page 666. Note that V_{aux} remains on and switch signals are still connected until the retention latch is released or when the card is removed as detected by the Prsnt1# and Prsnt2# signals.

Table 17-4: Behavior and Meaning of the Power Indicator

Indicator Behavior	Power State
Off	Power Off — it is safe to remove or insert a card. All power has been removed as required for hot plug operation. Vaux is only removed when the Manual Retention Latch is released.
On	Power On — removal or insertion of a card is not allowed. Power is currently applied to the slot.
Blinking	Power Transition — card removal or insertion is not allowed. This state notifies the operator that software is currently removing or applying slot power in response to a hot plug request.

Manually Operated Retention Latch and Sensor

The Manual Retention Latch (MRL) is required and it holds PCI Express cards rigidly in the slot. Each MRL can implement an optional sensor that notifies the Hot-Plug Controller that the latch has been closed or opened. The specification also allows a single latch that can hold down multiple cards. Such implementations do not support the MRL sensor.

An MRL Sensor is a Switch, optical device, or other type of sensor. The sensor reports only two conditions: fully closed and open. If an unexpected latch release is detected, the port automatically disables the slot and notifies system software. Note however, that the specification prohibits ports from changing the state of the Power or Attention indicators autonomously.

The switched signals and auxillary power (Vaux) must be automatically removed from the slot when the MRL Sensor indicates that the MRL is open and must be restored to the slot when the MRL Sensor indicates that the latch is re-established. The switched signals are:

- V_{aux}
- SMBCLK
- SMBDAT

The specification also describes an alternate method for removing V_{aux} and SMBus power when an MRL sensor is not present. In this case, the PRSNT#1 and PRSNT#2 pins, which indicate whether a card is installed into the slot, can be used to trigger the port to remove the switched signals.

Electromechanical Interlock (optional)

The optional electromechanical card interlock mechanism provides a more sophisticated method of ensuring that a card is not removed when power is still applied to the slot. The specification does not define the specific nature of the interlock, but states that it can physically lock the add-in card or lock the MRL in place.

The lock mechanism is controlled via software; however, there is no specific programming interface defined to control the electromechanical interlock. Instead an interlock is controlled by the same port output signal that enables main power to the slot.

Software User Interface

An operator may use a software interface to request card removal or insertion. This interface is provided by system software, which also monitors slots and reports status information to the operator. The specification states that the user interface is implemented by the Operating System and consequently is beyond the scope of the specification.

The operator must be able to initiate operations at each slot independent of all other slots. Consequently, the operator may initiate a hot-plug operation on one slot using the software user interface or attention button while a hot-plug operation on another slot is in process. This can be done regardless of which interface the operator used to start the first Hot-Plug operation.

Attention Button

The Attention Button is a momentary-contact push-button switch, located near the corresponding Hot-Plug slot or on a module. The operator presses this button to initiate a hot-plug operation for this slot (e.g., card removal or insertion). Once the Attention Button is depressed, the Power Indicator starts to blink. From the time the blinking begins the operator has 5 seconds to abort the Hot Plug operation by depressing the button a second time.

The specification recommends that if an operation initiated by an Attention Button fails, the system software should notify the operator of the failure. For example, a message explaining the nature of the failure can be reported or logged.

Slot Numbering Identification

Software and operators must be able to identify a physical slot based on its slot number. Each hot-plug capable port must implement registers that software uses to identify the physical slot number. The registers include a Physical Slot number and a chassis number. The main chassis is always labeled chassis 0. The chassis number for other chassis' must be a non-zero value and are assigned via the PCI-to-PCI bridge's Chassis Number register ("Introduction To Chassis/ Slot Numbering Registers" on page 859).

Standard Hot Plug Controller Signaling Interface

Figure 17-3 on page 669 represents a more detailed view of the logic within root and switch ports, along with the signals routed between the slot and port. The importance of the standardized Hot Plug Controller is the common software interface that allows the device driver to be integrated into operating systems.

The PCI Express specification in conjunction with the Card ElectroMechanical (CEM) specification define the slot signals and the support required for Hot Plug PCI Express. Following is a list of required and optional port interface signals needed to support the Standard Usage Model:

- PWRLED# (required) — port output that controls state of Power Indicator
- ATNLED# (required) — port output controls state of Attention Indicator
- PWREN (required, if reference clock is implemented) — port output that controls main power to slot
- REFCLKEN# (required) — port output that controls delivery of reference clock to the slot
- PERST# (required) — port output that controls PERST# at slot
- PRSNT1# (required) — Grounded at the connector
- and PRSNT2# (required) — port input indicates presence of card in slot. Also pulled up on system board
- PWRFLT# (required) — port input that notifies the Hot-Plug controller of a power fault condition detected by external logic
- AUXEN#(required, if AUX power is implemented) — port output that controls switched AUX signals and AUX power to slot when MRL is opened and closed. The MRL# signal is required with AUX power is present.
- MRL# (required if MRL Sensor is implemented, otherwise it's optional) — port input from the MRL sensor
- BUTTON# (required if Attention Button is implemented, otherwise it's optional) — port input indicating operator wishes to perform a Hot-Plug operation

Figure 17-3: Hot Plug Control Functions within a Switch

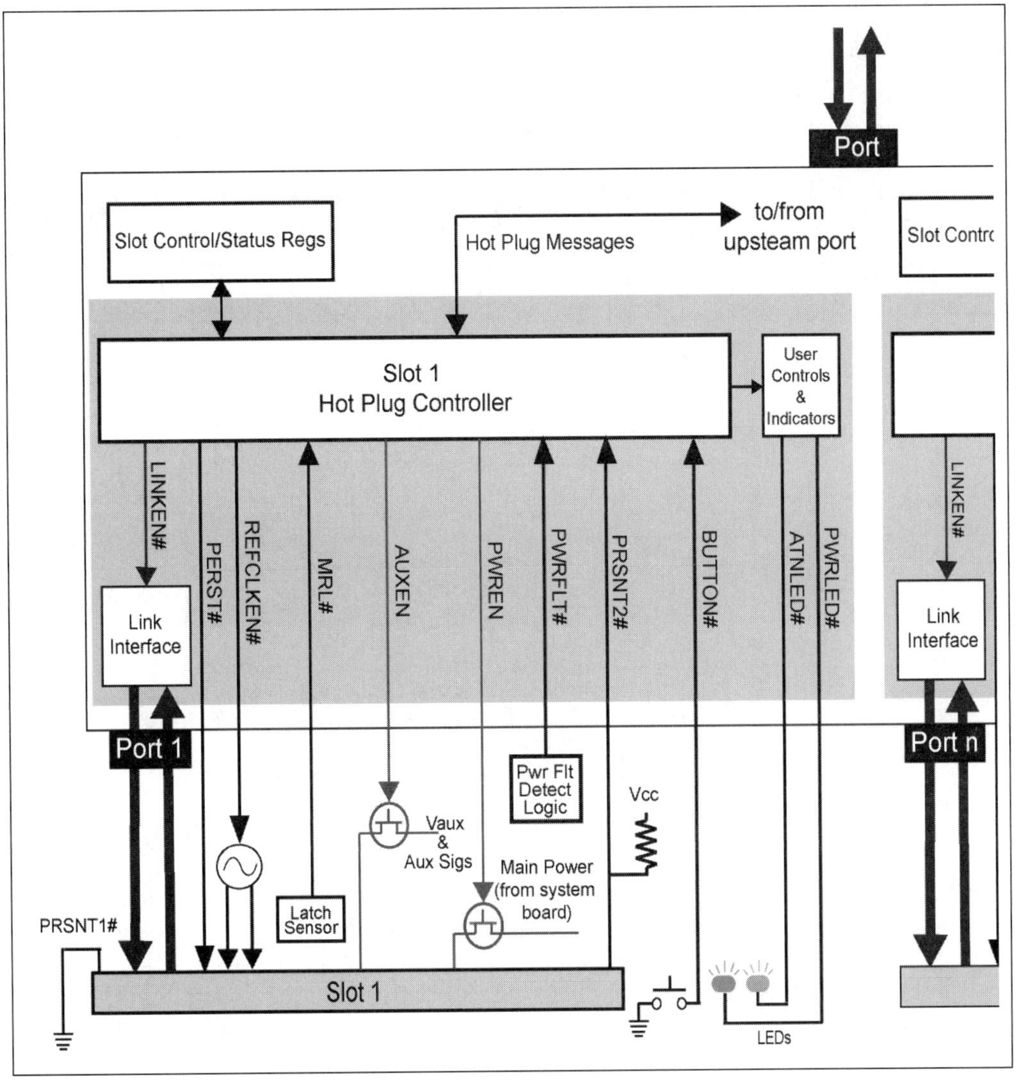

The Hot-Plug Controller Programming Interface

The standard programming interface to the Hot-Plug Controller is provided via the PCI Express Capability register block. Figure 17-4 on page 670 illustrates these registers and highlights the registers that are implemented by the different types of devices. Hot Plug features are primarily provided via Slot Registers that are defined for root and switch ports. The Device Capability register is also used in some implementations as described later in this chapter.

Figure 17-4: PCI Express Configuration Registers Used for Hot-Plug

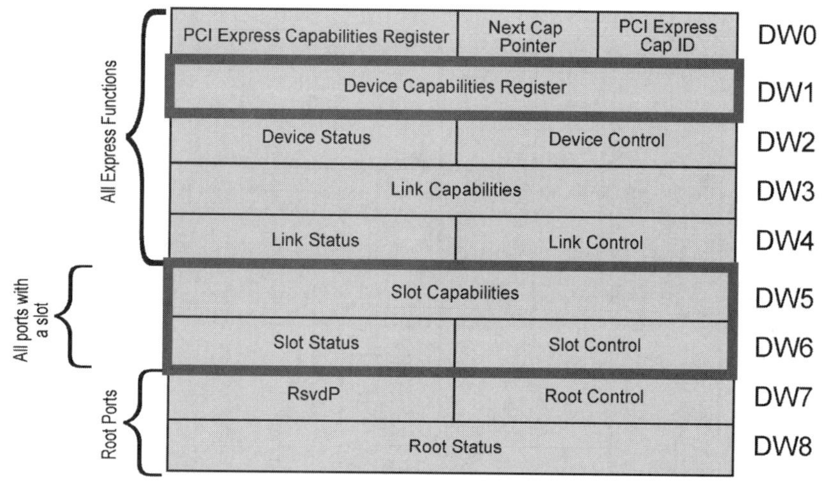

Slot Capabilities

Figure 17-5 on page 671 illustrates the slot capability register and bit fields. Hardware must initialize the capability register fields to reflect the features implemented by this port. This register applies to both card slots and rack mount implementations, except for the indicators and attention button. Software must read from the device capability register within the module to determine if indicators and attention buttons are implemented. Table 17-5 on page 671 lists and defines the slot capability fields.

Figure 17-5: Attention Button and Hot Plug Indicators Present Bits

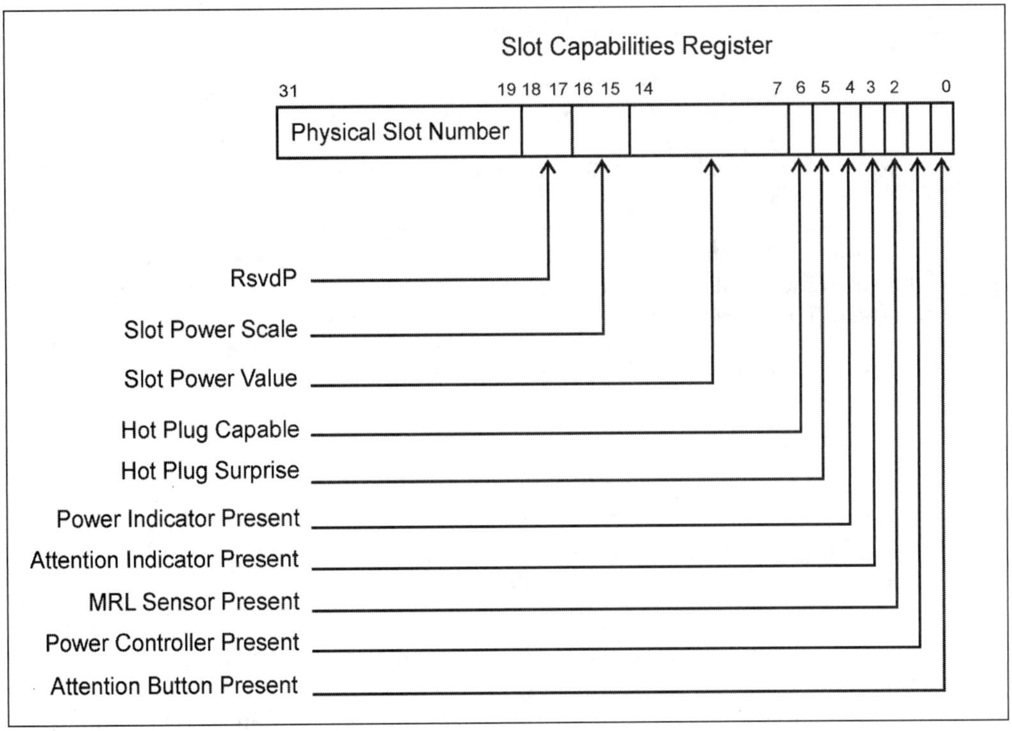

Table 17-5: Slot Capability Register Fields and Descriptions

Bit(s)	Register Name and Description
0	**Attention Button Present** — when set, indicates that an attention button is located on the chassis adjacent to the slot.
1	**Power Controller Present** — when set, indicates that a power controller is implemented for this slot.
2	**MRL Sensor Present** — when set, indicates that a MRL Sensor is located on the slot.
3	**Attention Indicator Present** — when set, indicates that an attention indicator is located on the chassis adjacent to the slot.
4	**Power Indicator Present** — when set, indicates that a power indicator is located on the chassis adjacent to the slot.

Table 17-5: Slot Capability Register Fields and Descriptions (Continued)

Bit(s)	Register Name and Description
5	**Hot-Plug Surprise** — when set, indicates that it is possible that the user can remove the card from the system without notification.
6	**Hot-Plug Capable** — when set, indicates that this slot supports hot plug operation.
14:7	**Slot Power Limit Value** — specifies the maximum power that can be supplied by this slot. This limit value is multiplied by the scale specified in the next field.
16:15	**Slot Power Limit Scale** — specifies the scaling factor for the Slot Power Limit Value.
31:19	**Physical Slot Number** — Indicates the physical slot number associated with this port.

Slot Power Limit Control

The specification provides a method for software to limit the amount of power consumed by a card installed into an expansion slot or backplane implementation. The registers needed to support this feature are included in the hot plug capable port within the Slot Capability register and within the expansion card or module within the device capability register.

Slot Control

Software controls the Hot Plug events via the Slot Control register. This register permits software to enable various Hot Plug features and to control hot plug operations. Figure 17-6 on page 673 depicts the slot control register and bit fields. Table 17-6 on page 673 lists and describes each field. This register acts as the programming interface to control various Hot-Plug features and to enable interrupt generation as well as enabling the sources of Hot-Plug events that can result in interrupt generation.

Figure 17-6: Slot Control Register Fields

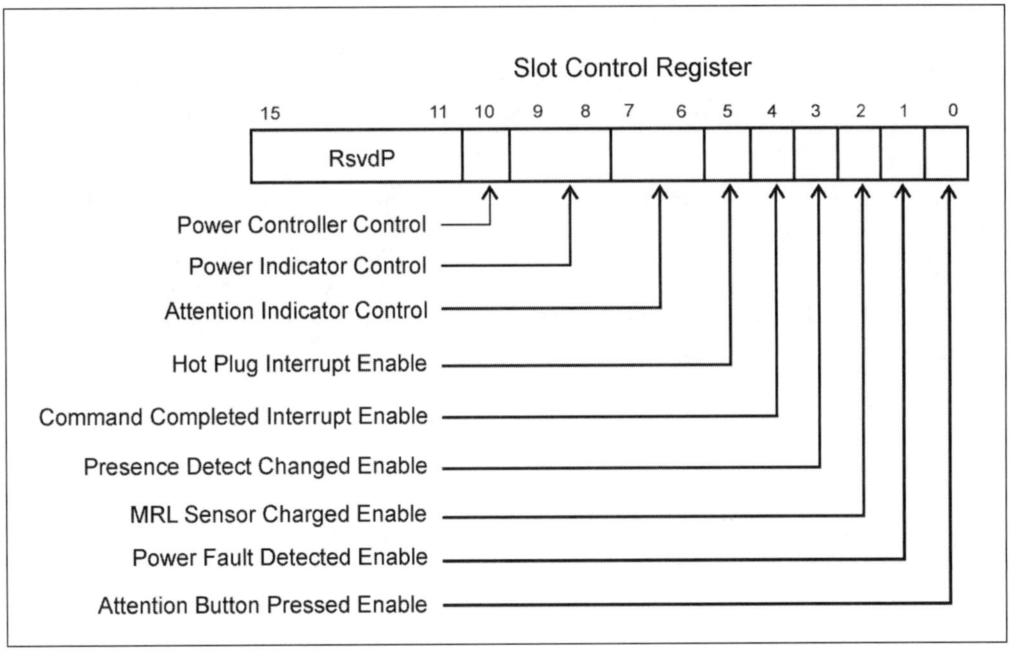

Table 17-6: Slot Control Register Fields and Descriptions

Bit(s)	Register Name and Description
0	**Attention Button Pressed Enable.** When set, this bit enables the generation of a hot-plug interrupt (if enabled) or assertion of the Wake# message, when the attention button is pressed.
1	**Power Fault Detected Enable.** When set, enables generation of a hot-plug interrupt (if enabled) or Wake# message upon detection of a power fault.
2	**MRL Sensor Changed Enable.** When set, enables generation of a hot-plug interrupt or Wake# (if enabled) message upon detection of a MRL sensor changed event.
3	**Presence Detect Changed Enable.** When set this bit enables the generation of the hot-plug interrupt or a Wake message when the presence detect changed bit in the Slot Status register is set.

Table 17-6: Slot Control Register Fields and Descriptions (Continued)

Bit(s)	Register Name and Description
4	**Command Completed Interrupt Enable.** When set, enables a Hot- Plug interrupt to be generated that informs software that the hot-plug controller is ready to receive the next command.
5	**Hot-Plug Interrupt Enable.** When set, enables the generation of Hot-Plug interrupts.
6	**Attention Indicator Control.** Writes to the field control the state of the attention indicator and reads return the current state, as follows: • 00b = Reserved • 01b = On • 10b = Blink • 11b = Off
7	**Power Indicator Control.** Writes to the field control the state of the power indicator and reads return the current state, as follows: • 00b = Reserved • 01b = On • 10b = Blink • 11b = Off
8	**Power Controller Control.** Writes to the field switch main power to the slot and reads return the current state, as follows: • 0b = Power On • 1b = Power Off

Slot Status and Events Management

The Hot Plug Controller monitors a variety of events and reports these events to the Hot Plug System Driver. Software can use the "detected" bits to determine which event has occurred, while the status bit identifies that nature of the change. The changed bits must be cleared by software in order to detect a subsequent change. Note that whether these events get reported to the system (via a system interrupt) is determined by the related enable bits in the Slot Control Register.

Figure 17-7: Slot Status Register Fields

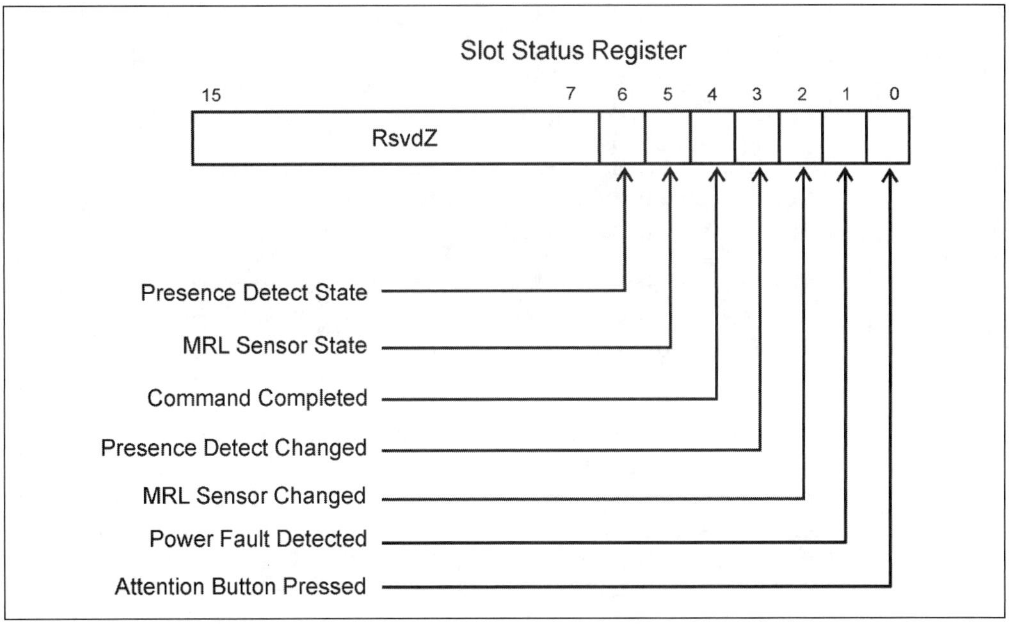

Table 17-7: Slot Status Register Fields and Descriptions

Bit Location	Register Name and Description
0	**Attention Button Pressed** — set when the Attention Button is pressed. Notification of the attention button being pushed depends on the form-factor implemented: • standard card slots use a signal trace to report the event • rack and backplane implementations may rely on the Attention_Button_Pressed message. • refer to other form-factor specs for details regarding those implementations.
1	**Power Fault Detected** — set when the Power Controller detects a power fault at this port.
2	**MRL Sensor Changed** — set when a MRL Sensor state change is detected.

Table 17-7: Slot Status Register Fields and Descriptions

Bit Location	Register Name and Description
3	**Presence Detect Changed** — set when a change has been detected in the state of the Prsnt1# or Prsnt2# signals.
4	**Command Completed** — set when the Hot Plug Controller completes a software command.
5	**MRL Sensor State** — when set, indicates the current state of the MRL sensor, if implemented. 0b = MRL Closed 1b = MRL Open
6	**Presence Detect State** — this bit reflects whether a card is installed into a slot or not (set if card present, clear if card not present). It is required for all root and switch ports that have a slot attached to the link. The specification also states that if a slot is not attached to the link, then this bit "should be hardwired to 1."

Card Slot vs Server IO Module Implementations

PCI Express supports two form factors that determine the location of the Hot-Plug indicators and attention button (See Figure 17-8 on page 677):

- Standard Cards that reside in PCI-like slots — motherboard or expansion chassis implementations place Hot Plug indicators, the attention button, and MRL sensor adjacent to each slot on the board.
- Server IO Modules (SIOMs) that install into racks — when modules are installed into a rack-mounted system the hot-plug indicators and attention button may be located more conveniently on the PCI Express modules as opposed to a Rack. However the specification does not preclude the possibility of indicators and buttons being located on module bays.

Figure 17-8. Location of Attention Button and Indicators

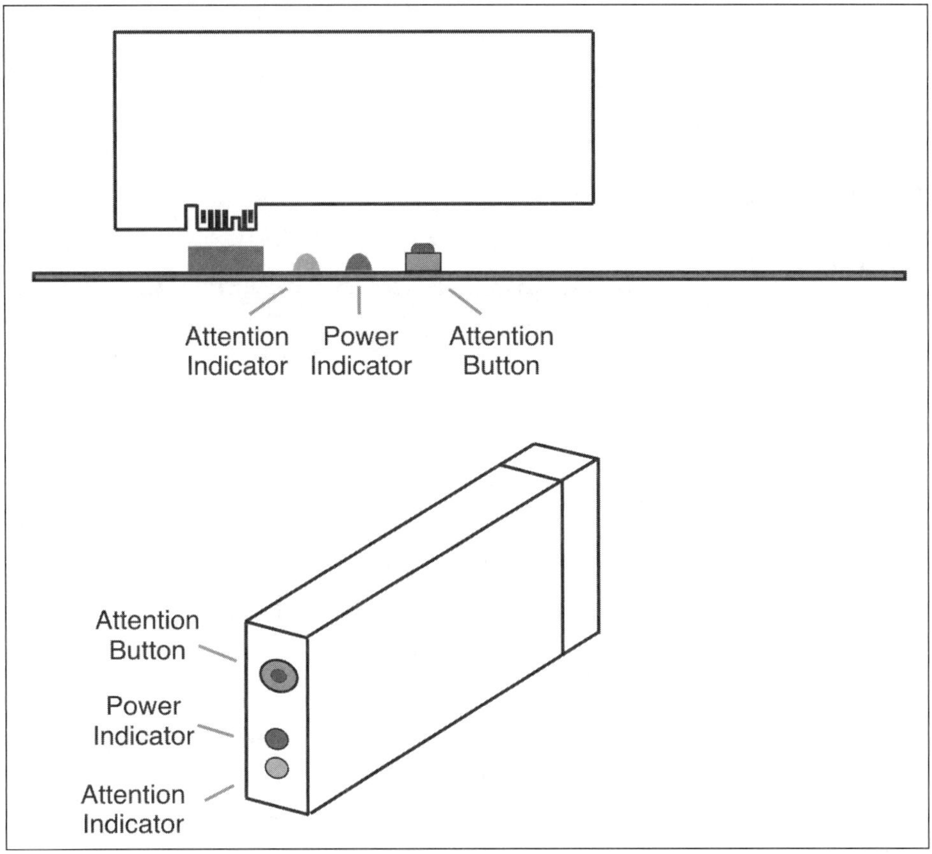

In addition to Server IO Modules, cards (or blades) that install into backplanes may also have indicators and the attention button located on the card. These implementations were not defined at the time of this writing. However, proposted SIOM implementations route the attention button and attention indicator signals through the connector.

The specification also defines messages that act as virtual wires for controlling the attention indicators and for reporting when the attention button has been pressed. The approach eliminates the need to route signals between the port and connector for the attention indicators and attention button, as done with card slots as illustrated in Figure 17-3 on page 669. See "Hot Plug Messages" on page 678.

Detecting Module and Blade Capabilities

Hot-Plug ports that attach to rack and backplane connectors may not know whether a given module or blade includes indicators or an attention button. Consequently, the specification includes this information within the Device Capabilities register. See Figure 17-9 on page 678.

Figure 17-9: Hot-Plug Capability Bits for Server IO Modules

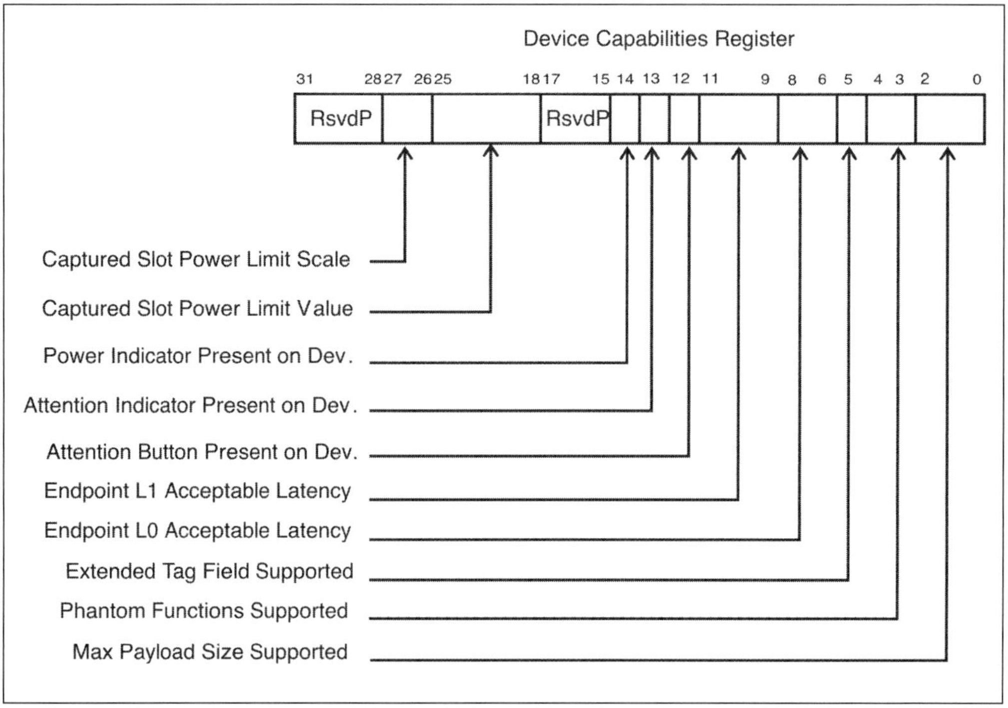

Hot Plug Messages

When the Hot-Plug indicators and attention button are located on a module or blade, messages can be used as virtual wires to control the indicators and to report that the button has been pressed.

Attention and Power Indicator Control Messages. As discussed in Table 17-6 on page 673, the attention and power indicators each have three states: on, off, and blinking. The message transactions act as virtual wires to signal the attention indicator state. Figure 17-10 on page 680 illustrates the Hot Plug Message format and lists the values associated with each of the messages.

- **Attention_Indicator_On.** This message is issued by the Hot Plug Controller when software writes a value of 01b into the Attention Indicator Control field of the Slot Control Register indicating that the Attention Indicator is to be turned on. The endpoint device that receives the message terminates it and causes the card's attention indicator to turn on.
- **Attention_Indicator_Blink.** This message is issued by the Hot Plug Controller when software writes a value of 10b into the Attention Indicator Control field of the Slot Control Register indicating that the Attention Indicator is to blink on and off. The endpoint device that receives the message terminates it and causes the card's attention indicator to start blinking.
- **Attention_Indicator_Off**. This message is issued by the Hot Plug Controller when software writes a value of 11b into the Attention Indicator Control field of the Slot Control Register indicating that the Attention Indicator is to be turned off. The endpoint device that receives the message terminates it and causes the card's indicator to turn off.
- **Power_Indicator_On**. This message is issued by the Hot Plug Controller when software writes a value of 01b into the Power Indicator Control field of the Slot Control Register indicating that the Power Indicator is to be turned on. The endpoint device that receives the message terminates it and causes the card's power indicator to turn on.
- **Power_Indicator_Blink.** This message is issued by the Hot Plug Controller when software writes a value of 10b into the Power Indicator Control field of the Slot Control Register indicating that the Power Indicator is to blink on and off. The endpoint device that receives the message terminates it and causes the power indicator to blink.
- **Power_Indicator_Off**. This message is issued by the Hot Plug Controller when software writes a value of 11b into the Power Indicator Control field of the Slot Control Register indicating that the Power Indicator is to be turned off. The endpoint device that receives the message terminates it and causes the card's power indicator to turn off.

Attention Button Pressed Message. A module or blade that employs an attention button must signal the Hot Plug Controller that the button has been pressed. The module generates an Attention_Button_Pressed message (Figure 17-10 on page 680) that targets the upstream device (root or switch port). The message results in an Attention Button Pressed Event that causes the *Attention Button Pressed* status bit in the Slot Status register bit to be set, and may also result in an interrupt if enabled.

Limitations of the Hot Plug Messages. Note that these features function only when the card is installed and operational. Thus, indicators can be controlled prior to card removal and similarly the card can report that the attention button has been pressed (e.g., to signal a request for card removal). However, when a new card is installed, the attention button message cannot be sent from the card and attention indicator messages cannot be received until the card is re-powered, reconfigured, and enabled. This means that software will have to be notified that a card is ready to be reinstalled.

Figure 17-10: Hot Plug Message Format

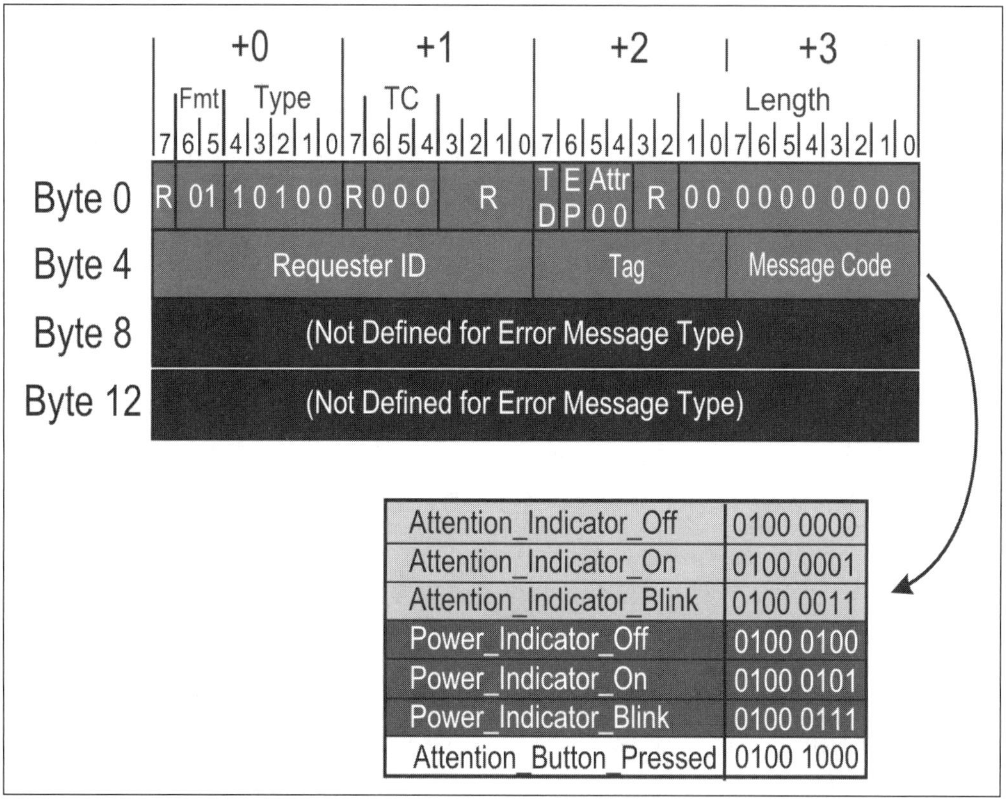

Slot Numbering

Physical Slot ID

An operator who wishes to prepare a slot for card removal or insertion must specify the Physical Slot ID. The physical slot number is designated by the system designer and this assignment must be communicated to the Root or Switch port. This is required because hardware must initialize the Physical Slot ID status bit within the Slot Status Register. When configuration accesses are made to read the physical slot ID software makes an association between the Logical Slot ID (Bus# and Device #) and physical Slot ID.

Quiescing Card and Driver

General

Prior to removing a card from the system, two things must occur:

1. The device's driver must cease accessing the card.
2. The card must cease generation transaction and interrupts.

How this is accomplished is OS-specific, but the following must take place:

- The OS must stop issuing new requests to the device's driver or must instruct the driver to stop accepting new requests.
- The driver must terminate or complete all outstanding requests.
- The card must be disabled from generating interrupts or transactions.

When the OS commands the driver to quiesce itself and its device, the OS must not expect the device to remain in the system (in other words, it could be removed and not replaced with a similar card).

Pausing a Driver (Optional)

Optionally, an OS could implement a "Pause" capability to temporarily stop driver activity in the expectation that the same card or a similar card will be reinserted. If the card is not reinstalled within a reasonable amount of time, however, the driver must be quiesced and then removed from memory.

A card may be removed and an identical card installed in its place. As an example, this could be because the currently-installed card is bad or is being replaced with a later revision as an upgrade. If it is intended that the operation appear seamless from a software and operational perspective, the driver would have to quiesce, save the current device's context (i.e., the contents of all of its registers, etc.). The new card would then be installed, the context restored, and normal operation would resume. It should be noted that if the old card had failed, it may or may not be possible to have the operation appear seamless.

Quiescing a Driver That Controls Multiple Devices

If a driver controls multiple cards and it receives a command from the OS to quiesce its activity with respect to a specific card, it must only quiesce its activity with that card as well as quiescing the card itself.

Quiescing a Failed Card

If a card has failed, it may not be possible for the driver to complete requests previously issued to the card. In this case, the driver must detect the error and must terminate the requests without completion and attempt to reset the card.

The Primitives

This section discusses the hot-plug software elements and the information passed between them. For a review of the software elements and their relationships to each other, refer to Table 17-1 on page 655. Communications between the Hot-Plug Service within the OS and the Hot-Plug System Driver is in the form of requests. The spec doesn't define the exact format of these requests, but does define the basic request types and their content. Each request type issued to the Hot-Plug System Driver by the Hot-Plug Service is referred to as a *primitive*. They are listed and described in Table 17-8 on page 682.

Table 17-8: The Primitives

Primitive	Parameters	Description
Query Hot-Plug System Driver	**Input**: None **Return**: Set of Logical Slot IDs for slots controlled by this driver.	Requests that the Hot-Plug System Driver return a set of Logical Slot IDs for the slots it controls.

Table 17-8: The Primitives (Continued)

Primitive	Parameters	Description
Set Slot Status	**Inputs**: • Logical Slot ID • New slot state (on or off). • New Attention Indicator state. • New Power Indicator state. **Return**: Request completion status: • status change successful • fault—wrong frequency • fault—insufficient power • fault—insufficient configuration resources • fault—power fail • fault—general failure	This request is used to control the slots and the Attention Indicator associated with each slot. Good completion of a request is indicated by returning the Status Change Successful parameter. If a fault is incurred during an attempted status change, the Hot-Plug System Driver should return the appropriate fault message (see middle column). Unless otherwise specified, the card should be left in the off state.
Query Slot Status	**Input**: Logical Slot ID **Return**: • Slot state (on or off) • Card power requirements.	This request returns the state of the indicated slot (if a card is present). The Hot-Plug System Driver must return the Slot Power status information.
Async Notice of Slot Status Change	**Input**: Logical Slot ID **Return**: none	This is the only primitive (defined by the spec) that is issued to the Hot-Plug Service by the Hot-Plug System Driver. It is sent when the Driver detects an unsolicited change in the state of a slot. Examples would be a run-time power fault or card installed in a previously-empty slot with no warning.

18 Add-in Cards and Connectors

The Previous Chapter

PCI Express includes native support for hot plug implementations. The previous chapter discussed hot plug and hot removal of PCI Express devices. The specification defines a standard usage model for all device and platform form factors that support hot plug capability. The usage model defines, as an example, how push buttons and indicators (LED's) behave, if implemented on the chassis, add-in card or module. The definitions assigned to the indicators and push buttons, described in this chapter, apply to all models of hot plug implementations.

This Chapter

This chapter provides an introduction to the PCI Express add-in card electromechanical specifications. It describes the card form factor, the connector details, and the auxiliary signals with a description of their function. Other card form factors are also briefly described, but it should be stressed that some of them have not yet been approved by the SIG as of this writing.

The Next Chapter

The next chapter provides an introduction to configuration in the PCI Express envionment. It introduces the configuration space in which a function's configuration registers are implemented, how a function is discovered, how configuration transactions are routed, PCI-compatible space, PCI Express extended configuration space, and how to differentiate between a normal function and a bridge.

Introduction

One goal of the PCI Express add-in card electromechanical spec was to encourage migration from the PCI architecture found in many desktop and mobile devices today by making the migration path straightforward and minimizing the required hardware changes. Towards this end, PCI Express add-in cards are defined to be very similar to the current PCI add-in card form factor, allowing them to readily coexist with PCI slots in system boards designed to the ATX or micro-ATX standard. PCI Express features like automatic polarity inversion and lane reversal also help reduce layout issues on system boards, so they can still be designed using the four-layer FR4 board construction commonly used today. As a result, much of an existing system board design can remain the same when it is modified to use the new architecture, and no changes are required for existing chassis designs.

Add-in Connector

The PCI Express add-in card connector (see Figure 18-1 on page 687 and Figure 18-2 on page 688) is physically very similar to the legacy PCI connector, but uses a different pinout and does not supply -12V or 5V power. The physical dimensions of a card are the same as the PCI add-in cards and the same IO bracket is used. Table 18-1 on page 689 shows the pinout for a connector that supports PCI Express cards up to x16 (16 lanes wide). Several signals are referred to as auxiliary signals in the spec, and these are highlighted and described in more detail in the section that follows the table.

Note that cards with fewer lanes can be plugged into larger connectors that will accommodate more lanes. This is referred to as **Up-plugging**. The opposite case, installing a larger card into a smaller slot is called **Down-plugging** and, unlike PCI, is physically prevented in PCI Express by the connector keying.) Consequently, the connector described by the table will accommodate a card that is x1, x4, x8, or x16. This flexibility in the connector is highlighted by notes in the table that indicate each group of signals. For example, a x4 card plugged into this slot would only make use of pins 1 through 32, and so the note indicating the end of the x4 group of signals appears after pin 32. These segment indicators do not represent physical spaces or keys, however, because there is only one mechanical key on the connector, located between pins 11 and 12.

Figure 18-1. PCI Express x1 connector

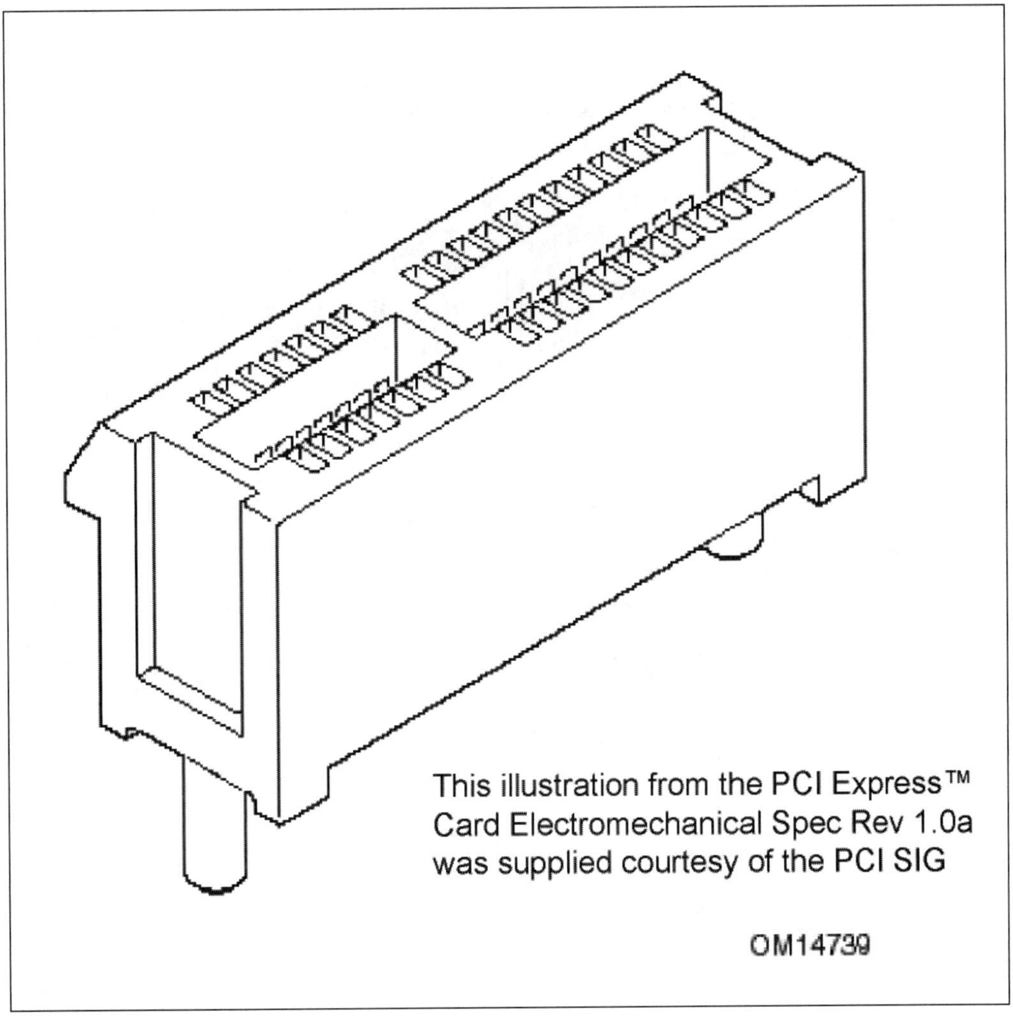

Figure 18-2: PCI Express Connectors on System Board

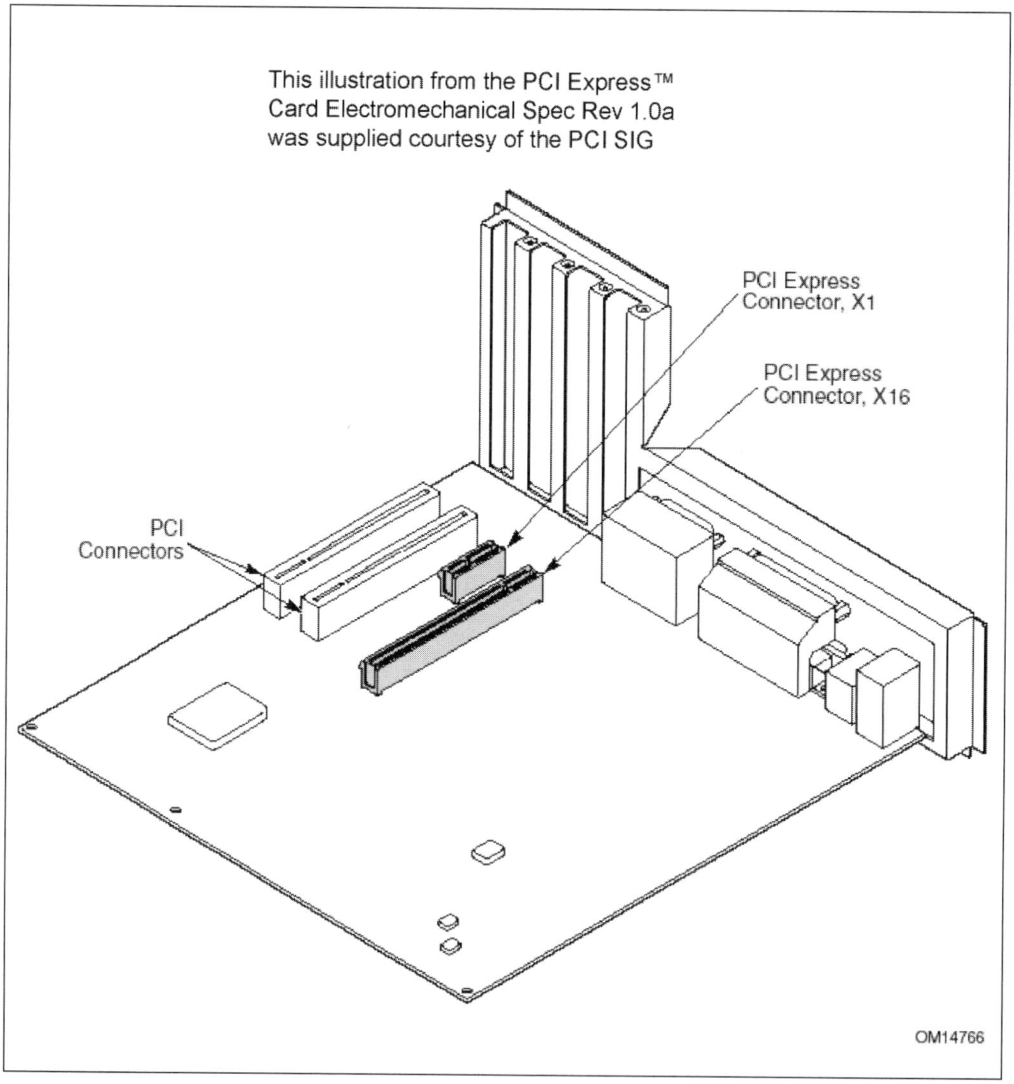

Table 18-1: PCI Express Connector Pinout

Pin #	Side B		Side A	
	Name	Description	Name	Description
1	+12V	12V Power	PRSNT1#	Hot-Plug presence detect
2	+12V	12V Power	+12V	12V Power
3	RSVD	Reserved	+12V	12V Power
4	GND	Ground	GND	Ground
5	SMCLK	SMBus (System Management Bus) Clock	JTAG2	TCK (Test Clock), clock input for JTAG interface
6	SMDAT	SMBus (System Management Bus) data	JTAG3	TDI (Test Data Input)
7	GND	Ground	JTAG4	TDO (Test Data output)
8	+3.3V	3.3 V Power	JTAG5	TMS (Test Mode Select)
9	JTAG1	TRST# (Test Reset) resets the JTAG interface	+3.3V	3.3 V Power
10	$3.3V_{AUX}$	3.3 V Auxiliary Power	+3.3V	3.3 V Power
11	WAKE#	Signal for link reactivation	PERST#	Fundamental reset
Mechanical Key				
12	RSVD	Reserved	GND	Ground
13	GND	Ground	REFCLK+	Reference Clock (differential pair)
14	PETp0	Transmitter differential pair, Lane 0	REFCLK-	
15	PETn0		GND	Ground

Table 18-1: PCI Express Connector Pinout (Continued)

Pin #	Side B		Side A	
	Name	Description	Name	Description
16	GND	Ground	PERp0	Receiver differential pair, Lane 0
17	PRSNT2#	Hot-Plug presence detect	PERn0	
18	GND	Ground	GND	Ground
End of the x1 connector				
19	PETp1	Transmitter differential pair, Lane 1	RSVD	Reserved
20	PETn1		GND	Ground
21	GND	Ground	PERp1	Receiver differential pair, Lane 1
22	GND	Ground	PERn1	
23	PETp2	Transmitter differential pair, Lane 2	GND	Ground
24	PETn2		GND	Ground
25	GND	Ground	PERp2	Receiver differential pair, Lane 2
26	GND	Ground	PERn2	
27	PETp3	Transmitter differential pair, Lane 3	GND	Ground
28	PETn3		GND	Ground
29	GND	Ground	PERp3	Receiver differential pair, Lane 3
30	RSVD	Reserved	PERn3	
31	PRSNT2#	Hot-Plug presence detect	GND	Ground
32	GND	Ground	RSVD	Reserved
End of the x4 connector				
33	PETp4	Transmitter differential pair, Lane 4	RSVD	Reserved
34	PETn4		GND	Ground

Table 18-1: PCI Express Connector Pinout (Continued)

Pin #	Side B		Side A	
	Name	Description	Name	Description
35	GND	Ground	PERp4	Receiver differential pair, Lane 4
36	GND	Ground	PERn4	
37	PETp5	Transmitter differential pair, Lane 5	GND	Ground
38	PETn5		GND	Ground
39	GND	Ground	PERp5	Receiver differential pair, Lane 5
40	GND	Ground	PERn5	
41	PETp6	Transmitter differential pair, Lane 6	GND	Ground
42	PETn6		GND	Ground
43	GND	Ground	PERp6	Receiver differential pair, Lane 6
44	GND	Ground	PERn6	
45	PETp7	Transmitter differential pair, Lane 7	GND	Ground
46	PETn7		GND	Ground
47	GND	Ground	PERp7	Receiver differential pair, Lane 7
48	PRSNT2#	Hot-Plug presence detect	PERn7	
49	GND	Ground	GND	Ground
End of the x8 connector				
50	PETp8	Transmitter differential pair, Lane 8	RSVD	Reserved
51	PETn8		GND	Ground
52	GND	Ground	PERp8	Receiver differential pair, Lane 8
53	GND	Ground	PERn8	
54	PETp9	Transmitter differential pair, Lane 9	GND	Ground
55	PETn9		GND	Ground

Table 18-1: PCI Express Connector Pinout (Continued)

Pin #	Side B		Side A	
	Name	Description	Name	Description
56	GND	Ground	PERp9	Receiver differential pair, Lane 9
57	GND	Ground	PERn9	
58	PETp10	Transmitter differential pair, Lane 10	GND	Ground
59	PETn10		GND	Ground
60	GND	Ground	PERp10	Receiver differential pair, Lane 10
61	GND	Ground	PERn10	
62	PETp11	Transmitter differential pair, Lane 11	GND	Ground
63	PETn11		GND	Ground
64	GND	Ground	PERp11	Receiver differential pair, Lane 11
65	GND	Ground	PERn11	
66	PETp12	Transmitter differential pair, Lane 12	GND	Ground
67	PETn12		GND	Ground
68	GND	Ground	PERp12	Receiver differential pair, Lane 12
69	GND	Ground	PERn12	
70	PETp13	Transmitter differential pair, Lane 13	GND	Ground
71	PETn13		GND	Ground
72	GND	Ground	PERp13	Receiver differential pair, Lane 13
73	GND	Ground	PERn13	
74	PETp14	Transmitter differential pair, Lane 14	GND	Ground
75	PETn14		GND	Ground
76	GND	Ground	PERp14	Receiver differential pair, Lane 14
77	GND	Ground	PERn14	

Table 18-1: PCI Express Connector Pinout (Continued)

Pin #	Side B		Side A	
	Name	Description	Name	Description
78	PETp15	Transmitter differential pair, Lane 15	GND	Ground
79	PETn15		GND	Ground
80	GND	Ground	PERp15	Receiver differential pair, Lane 15
81	PRSNT2#	Hot-Plug presence detect	PERn15	
82	RSVD	Reserved	GND	Ground

Auxiliary Signals

General

Several signals highlighted in Table 18-1 as auxiliary signals are described here in more detail. These signals are provided to assist with certain system level functions and are not required by the general PCI Express architecture, although some are required for add-in cards. For reference, these signals are summarized in Table 18-2.

Table 18-2: PCI Express Connector Auxiliary Signals

Signal Name	Required or Optional	Signal Type	Definition
REFCLK+	Required	Low-voltage differential clock	100MHz (+/- 300ppm) Reference clock used to synchronize devices on both ends of a link.
REFCLK-			
PERST#	Required	Low speed	Indicates when main power is within tolerance and stable. PERST# goes inactive after a delay of T_{PVPERL} once power is stable.

Table 18-2: PCI Express Connector Auxiliary Signals (Continued)

Signal Name	Required or Optional	Signal Type	Definition
WAKE#	Required if wakeup functionality is supported.	Open-drain	Driven low by a function to request that the main power and reference clock be reactivated.
SMBCLK	Optional	Open-drain	SMBus clock signal.
SMBDAT	Optional	Open-drain	SMBus address/data signal.
JTAG Group	Optional	Low speed	This group of signals (TCLK, TDI, TDO, TMS, and TRST#) can optionally be used to support the IEEE 1149.1 boundary scan spec.
PRSNT1#	Required		These signals are used to indicate that a card is installed into the connector.
PRSNT2#			

Reference Clock

This differential clock must be provided by the system board (although its use is optional for add-in cards). Its purpose is to allow both the transmitter and the receiver on a link to derive their internal clocks from the same source clock. While using the reference clock is not required, it does simplify the task of keeping the internal clocks between devices on either end of a link within the specified 600ppm of each other, since any two reference clocks are required to be within +/- 300ppm of their nominal 100MHz frequency. In addition, the base spec states that minimizing the L0s exit latency (i.e., the time required for the link to transition from the lower power L0s state back to L0) requires using a common reference clock. Finally, if Spread Spectrum Clocking (SSC) is to be used, it generally requires that both transmitters and receivers on a link must use the same reference clock. SSC allows the clock to be "down-modulated", or reduced in frequency, by as much as 0.5% and then brought back up to its nominal frequency at a rate not higher than 33KHz. Trying to modulate the clock frequency among devices that were not using the same reference clock would clearly be very difficult.

PERST#

This signal, similar in function to an inverted version of the POWERGOOD signal in a typical PC, is deasserted 100ms after the power supply is stable and within tolerance (see Figure 18-3 on page 695). PERST# is also aware of power management activity and so can also be used to give PCI Express devices some advance notice that power is about to be removed as a result of a power management operation (see Figure 18-4 on page 696). As long as PERST# remains asserted, all PCI Express functions are held in reset.

Figure 18-3: PERST Timing During Power Up

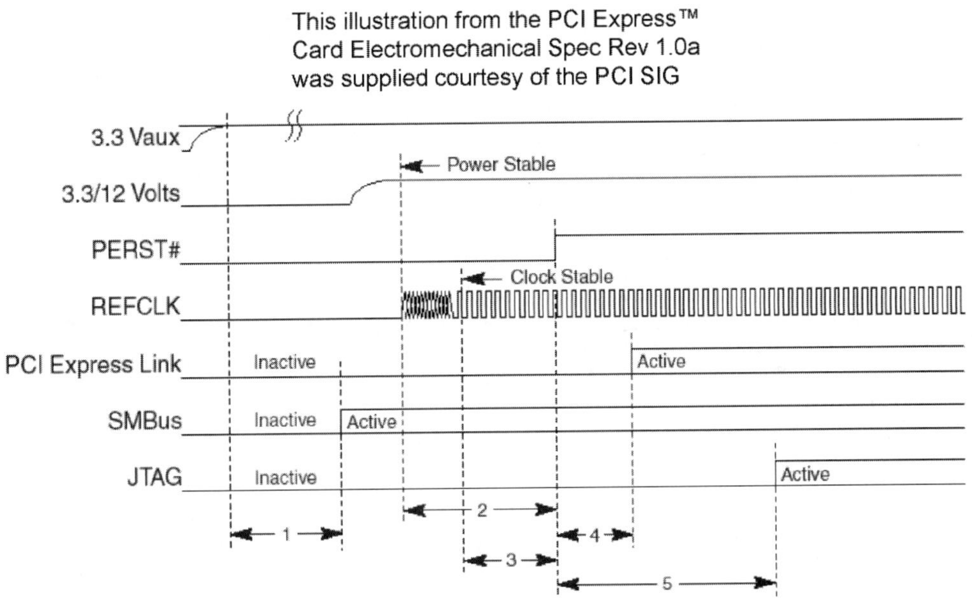

1. 3.3Vaux stable to SMBus driven (optional). If no 3.3Vaux on platform, the delay is from +3.3V stable
2. Minimum time from power rails within specified tolerance to PERST# inactive (T_{PVPERL})
3. Minimum clock valid to PERST# inactive ($T_{PERST\text{-}CLK}$)
4. Minimum PERST# inactive to PCI Express link out of electrical idle
5. Minimum PERST# inactive to JTAG driven (optional)

OM14742A

Figure 18-4: PERST# Timing During Power Management States

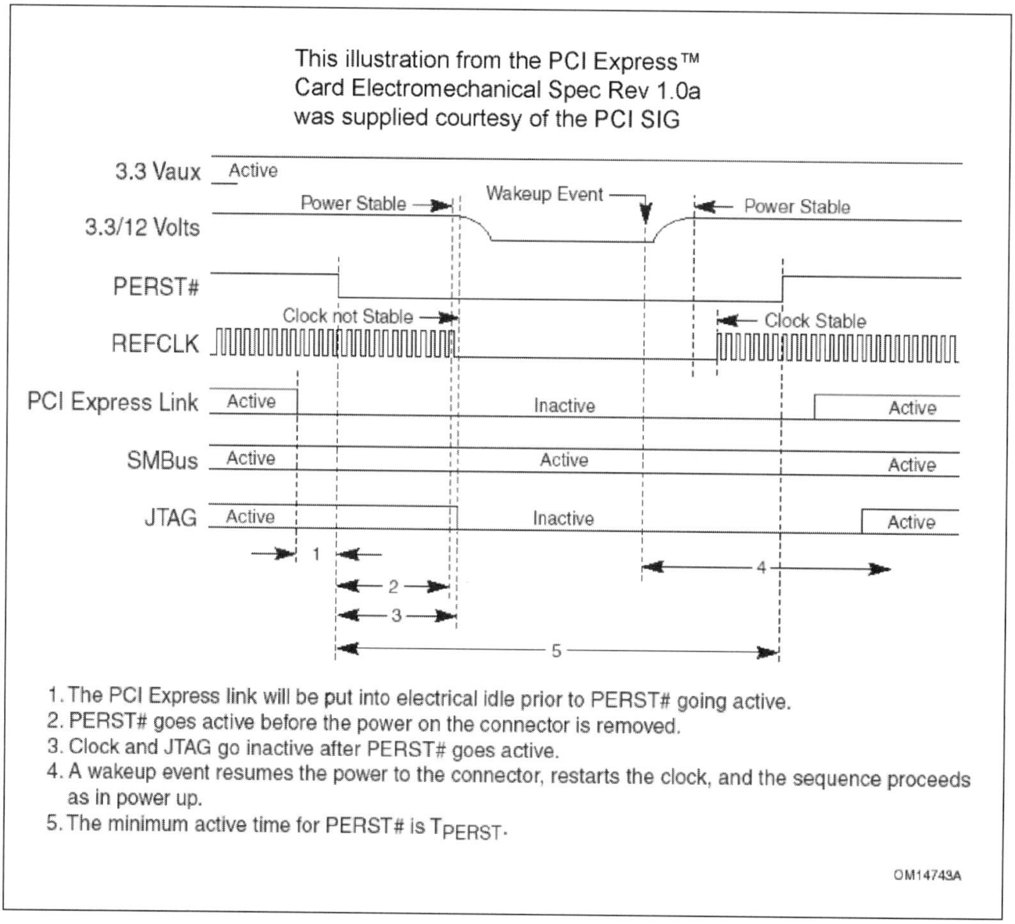

WAKE#

This open-drain signal is driven by a PCI Express device that supports the wakeup function to request reactivation of the main power and reference clock. If an add-in card supports the wakeup process, it must implement this pin, and a system board must support the function if it connects to the WAKE# pin on the slot. There are actually two defined wakeup mechanisms, the side-band WAKE# signal and an in-band indicator called the Beacon. The Beacon is required for all components with the exception of certain form factors, of which the PCI Express add-in card is one example. Systems that support wakeup for these form factors are required to support the WAKE# signal for them although they are also encouraged to support the Beacon. Add in cards that can generate a wakeup event are also required to support the Beacon operation. It is not clear why two mechanisms have been defined. One emphasis in PCI Express has been to reduce side-band signals, which would argue against adding a side-band wakeup signal. On the other hand, the use of the WAKE# signal may serve to reduce the latency involved in waking up the system enough to justify its use for add-in cards.

If a slot supports WAKE#, the signal is routed to the platform power management controller, which might reside, for example, inside the Root Complex. The WAKE# signals from all the slots can be bussed together into a single input or they can each be used as separate inputs to the controller. WAKE# must have a system board pullup to a reference voltage that will be present when the main power rails are turned off, and the pullup must be a value that will allow it to pull WAKE# high in no more than 100ns. Note that Hot plug requires WAKE# to be isolated (between connectors) and driven inactive during hot-add or hot-remove operations.

WAKE# functions in a way that is similar to PME# in a conventional PCI system, but it is not the same and must not be connected directly to the PME# signal. The spec also makes it clear that WAKE# must not directly cause an interrupt. As was true of the PME# signal in PCI, care must be taken to ensure that the generation of WAKE# in one device does not damage the WAKE# generation circuitry in another device. This could present a problem if one device has $3.3V_{AUX}$ supplied while another does not, permitting the output buffers of the device without power to be reverse-biased by the assertion of WAKE# and possibly damaged. One solution to this problem is to add a circuit like the one shown in Figure 18-5. As would be expected, a card can only initiate a wakeup event if $3.3V_{AUX}$ is supplied to it, since the other power rails may be turned off when the link is put into a sleep state.

Figure 18-5: Example of WAKE# Circuit Protection

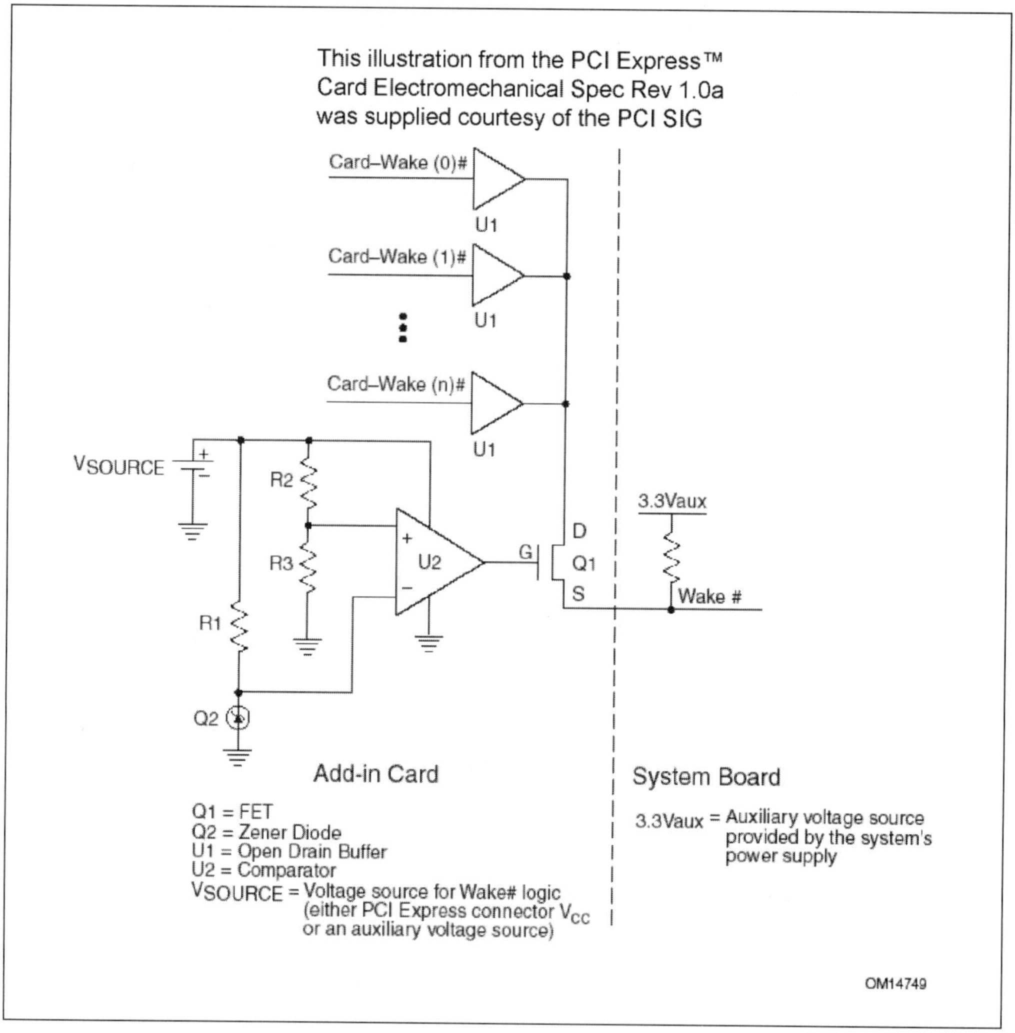

SMBus

This optional 2-wire bus provides a simple, inexpensive bus for system control and power management, reducing pin count and improving flexibility. One purpose for this bus is to reduce the number of control lines needed for the PCI Express bus, since it can be used to send SMBus messages between system devices. These messages can report manufacturer information, save state for a suspended event, report errors, accept control parameters, or supply status. The operation and requirements of the SMBus are described in detail in the *System Management Bus Specification, Version 2.0.*

JTAG

This optional interface provides a Test Access Port (TAP) to facilitate testing of a card that implements it. The TAP pins operate at 3.3V, as do the other single-ended IO signals of the PCI Express connector. JTAG stands for Joint Test Action Group and is commonly used to refer to the *IEEE Standard 1149.1, Test Access Port and Boundary Scan Architecture.*

PRSNT Pins

Refer to Figure 18-6 on page 700. These pins are used by the system to indicate whether a card has been plugged into a connector. On the add-in card, the PRSNT1# pin is wired to the farthest available PRSNT2# pin on the connector. For example, a x4 card would wire pins 1A (PRSNT1#) and 31B (PRSNT2#) together on the card. On the system board the PRSNT1# pin on the slot is grounded, while all the PRSNT2# pins of the slot are bussed together and pulled high, so the system is able to detect that a card has been installed in the slot by observing that the PRSNT2# signal has been pulled low.

Detecting that a card has been added is useful in a system that implements either hot-plug or hot-swap mechanisms, since a slot could be left powered off when no card is detected. Upon insertion of a new card, the hardware could detect the change and begin the process of preparing the system to bring the new card online. When the new card goes active, the link will automatically detect that a device is present and begin the process of training the link.

As an aside, the fact that an add-in card is required to connect PRSNT1# to the farthest possible PRSNT2# pin may mean that the spec designers considered using the presence detect pins to indicate information such as the link width on an add-in card. However, if the system board simply connects all the PRSNT2# pins together, this indication is not available. Visibility of the link width may have presented no real advantage anyway, since the link will automatically establish the usable link width during training.

Figure 18-6: Presence Detect

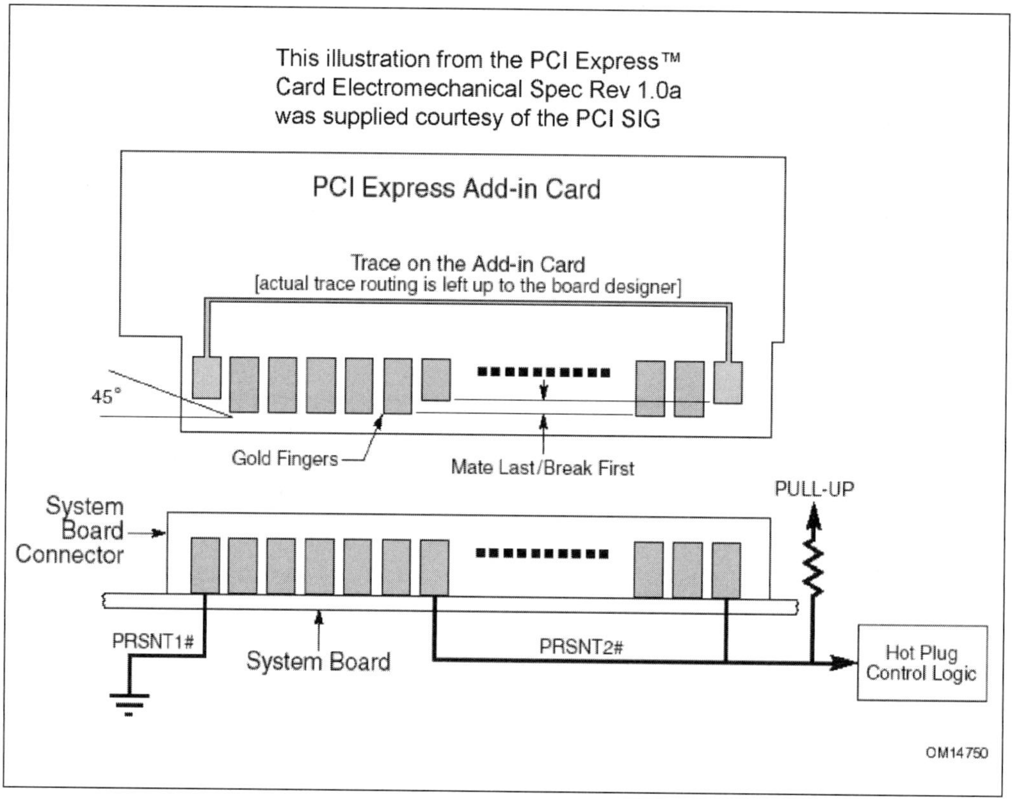

Electrical Requirements

Power Supply Requirements

Table 18-3 describes the power supplied to an add-in card. Note that the current provided by the +3.3V and +3.3V_{AUX} supplies does not change as a function of the link width, while it does for the +12V supply, indicating that the +12V supply provides the power needed for add-in cards that have higher wattage requirements. Both the +3.3V and +12V power supplies are required for an add-in connector, while +3.3V_{AUX} is optional. The current limits shown in the table for +3.3V_{AUX} indicate that the higher allowance is only for devices that support wakeup. This resembles the power limits in PCI assigned for 3.3V_{AUX}, in which the limit is based on whether a card is PME enabled, but there is an exception to the rule implied by this table in PCI Express. The configuration bit called Auxiliary Power PM Enable found in the Device Control Register (see "Device Control Register" on page 905), when set, indicates that a device has permission to use the full 375mA of auxiliary power regardless of whether it supports the wakeup function.

Table 18-3: Power Supply Requirements

Power Rail	x1 Connector	x4/x8 Connector	x16 Connector
+3.3V Voltage Tolerance Supply Current Capacitive Load	+/- 9% (max) 3.0A (max) 1000 uF (max)		
+12V Voltage Tolerance Supply Current Capacitive Load	+/- 8% 0.5A 300 uF (max)	+/- 8% 2.1A 300 uF (max)	+/- 8% 4.4A 300 uF (max)
+3.3V$_{AUX}$ Voltage Tolerance Supply Current Wakeup enabled Non-Wakeup enabled Capacitive Load	+/- 9% (max) 375 mA (max) 20 mA (max) 150 uF (max)		

Power Dissipation Limits

The power consumption limits for different link widths and card types are listed in Table 18-4. The table indicates, for example, that a x1 card cannot exceed 10W unless it is a high power device intended for server applications, in which case the maximum is 25W. At the high end, a x16 graphics card is allowed to consume up to 60W (increasing this value to 75W is under currently under consideration).

Table 18-4: Add-in Card Power Dissipation

Card Type	x1		x4/x8	x16	
Standard Height	10W (max) Desktop application	25W (max) Server application	25W (max)	25W (max) Server application	60W (max) Graphics application
Low Profile card	10W (max)		10W (max)	25W (max)	

The difference between the types of cards is described in more detail in the electromechanical spec, but basically, the standard height cards intended for desktop applications are limited to half-length add-in cards with lower wattages, while cards intended for server applications must be from at least 7.0 inches long up to a full-length card and are allowed to use higher wattages. Low-profile cards are limited to half-length and lower wattages.

Note that devices designated as high power are constrained to start up using the low power limits until they have been configured as high power devices. As a result, all x1 cards are initially limited to 10W, and cards intended for graphics applications are limited to 25W at initial power up until configured as a high power device, at which time they can use up to 60W (this may be increased to 75W in the future). See section "Slot Power Limit Control" on page 562 for more information on power configuration.

Add-in Card Interoperability

As mentioned earlier, it is possible for a PCI Express add-in card to be plugged into a slot that was intended for a wider card. This is illustrated in Table 18-5, which also points out that all the slot widths must support the basic x1 card. There are basically three size-mismatch scenarios to consider:

1. **Up-plugging**. Inserting a smaller link card into a larger link slot is fully allowed.
2. **Down-plugging**. Inserting a larger link card into a smaller link slot is not allowed and is physically prevented.
3. **Down-shifting**. Installing a card into a slot that is not fully routed for all of the lanes. This is not allowed except for the case of a x8 connector for which the system designer may choose to route only the first four lanes. A x8 card functions as a x4 card in this situation.

Table 18-5: Card Interoperability

Card \ Slot	x1	x4	x8	x16
x1	Required	Required	Required	Required
x4	No	Required	Allowed	Allowed
x8	No	No	Required	Allowed
x16	No	No	No	Required

Form Factors Under Development

General

In addition to the cards and slots that are defined with the PCI Express Card Electromechanical spec, there are other form factors currently under development by various groups. These form factors are usually designed for a particular class of applications and thus have different constraints. A card designed for a server application for example, will typically have a bigger power budget and more space available than one designed for a mobile application. The specs for these form factors were still under development at the time of this publication and are therefore subject to change.

Server IO Module (SIOM)

The PCI SIG is currently developing a module for the server environment called the Server IO Module (SIOM). It has four form factors: a base version and a full version, both of which can use a single- or double-width card. The built in hot swap capability of PCI Express helps make this module attractive to the server market because it allows changes to be readily made to the system on the fly.

Riser Card

Figure 18-7 on page 704 illustrates an example of a PCI Express riser card.

Figure 18-7: PCI Express Riser Card

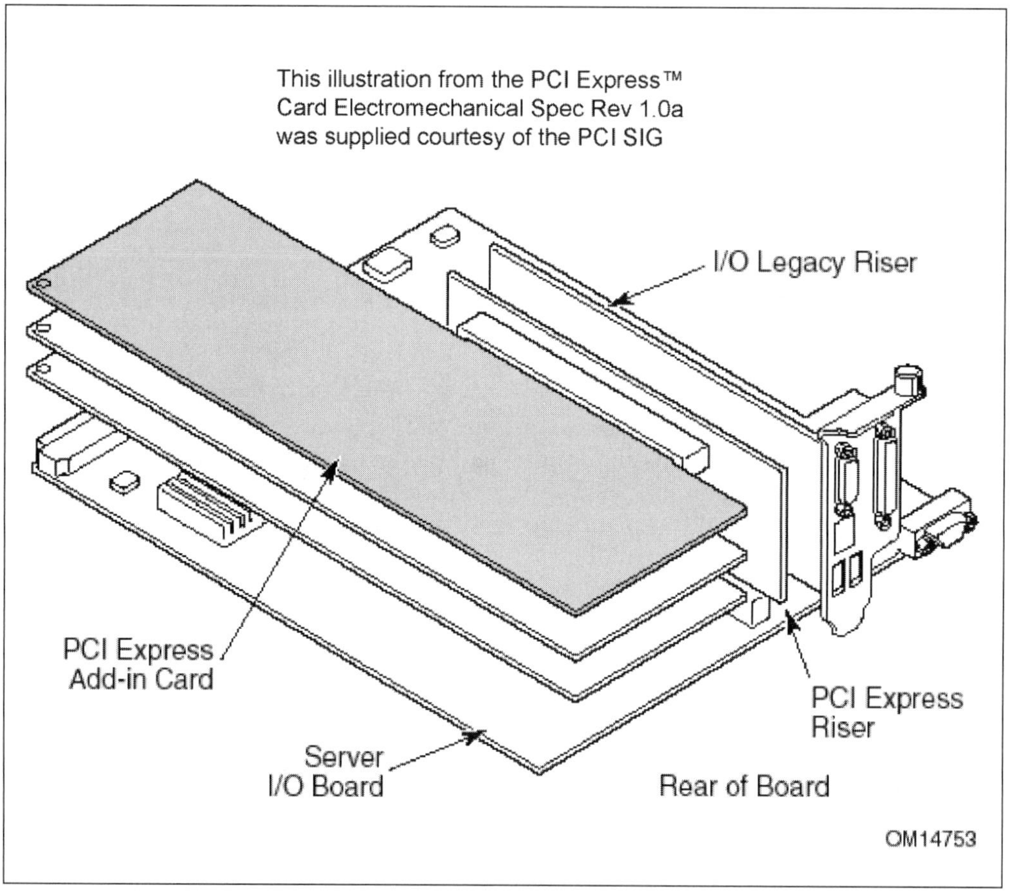

Mini PCI Express Card

Refer to Figure 18-8 on page 705, Figure 18-9 on page 706 and Figure 18-10 on page 706. The Mini PCI Express add-in card is similar to the conventional Mini PCI card, but is about half the size, uses smaller connectors and is optimized for mobile computing platforms and communications applications. It is designed with an interface that includes a x1 PCI Express connector, a USB 2.0 connector, and several LED indicators. While this form factor is designed for adding functionality internal to the system and therefore does not allow the user to readily make changes to the system, it does facilitate build-to-order or configure-to-order manufacture by making it easy to customize the functionality of a machine simply by choosing which cards to add or leave out of a product during assembly. This spec is being developed by the PCI SIG.

Figure 18-8: Mini PCI Express Add-in Card Installed in a Mobile Platform

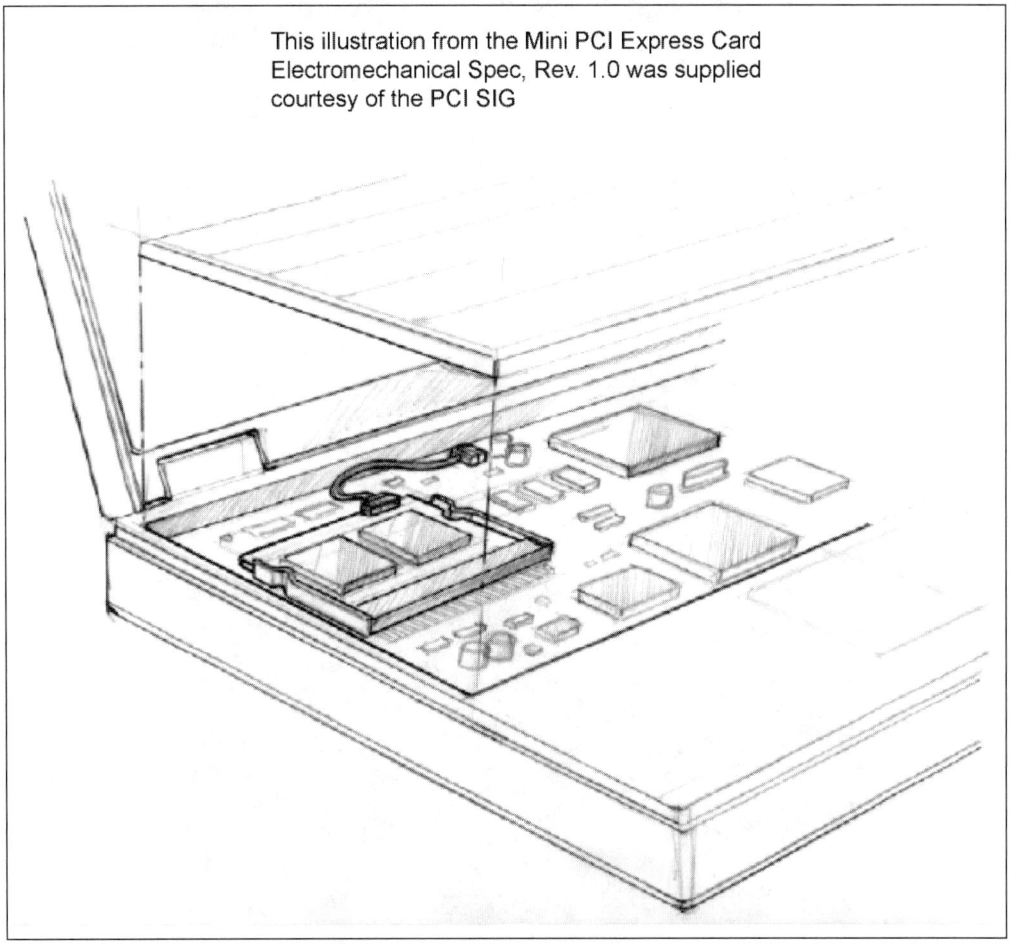

Figure 18-9: Mini PCI Express Add-in Card Photo 1

This illustration from a presentation slide
at the PCI Developer's Conference was
supplied courtesy of the PCI SIG

Figure 18-10: Mini PCI Express Add-in Card Photo 2

This illustration from a presentation slide
at the PCI Developer's Conference was
supplied courtesy of the PCI SIG

NEWCARD form factor

NEWCARD is a standard that is similar to the Mini PCI Express in functionality but is designed for the user to readily install or remove. This spec is being developed by the PCMCIA group (Personal Computer Memory Card International Association) for use in desktop and mobile devices, and is expected to ultimately replace the existing CardBus PC card solution for these computers. Like the Mini PCI Express standard, the NEWCARD interface is defined to contain a x1 PCI Express connector, a USB 2.0 connector, and several LED indicators.

For desktop machines, NEWCARD will offer the hot plug and hot swap capabilities of PCI Express and USB, and allow a user to upgrade or expand the machine without having to open it. Since the card will be able to fit into mobile computers, it will also be possible for the user to share a NEWCARD device between desktop and mobile computers.

For a communications-specific card, the IO interface side of the card might include wired connections such as a modem or Ethernet interface, or a wireless port such as a cellular or Bluetooth connection.

Part Six

PCI Express Configuration

19 Configuration Overview

The Previous Chapter

The previous chapter provided an introduction to the PCI Express add-in card electromechanical specifications. It described the card form factor, the connector details, and the auxiliary signals with a description of their function. Other card form factors were also briefly described, but it should be stressed that some of them have not yet been approved by the SIG as of this writing.

This Chapter

This chapter provides an introduction to configuration in the PCI Express environment. It introduces the configuration space in which a function's configuration registers are implemented, how a function is discovered, how configuration transactions are routed, PCI-compatible space, PCI Express extended configuration space, how a function is discovered, and how to differentiate between a normal function and a bridge.

The Next Chapter

The next chapter provides a detailed description of the two configuration mechanisms used in a PCI Express platform: the PCI-compatible configuration mechanism, and the PCI Express enhanced configuration mechanism. It provides a detailed description of the initialization period immediately following power-up, as well as error handling during this period.

Definition of Device and Function

Just as in the PCI environment, a device resides on a bus and contains one or more functions (a device containing multiple functions is referred to as a multifunction device). Each of the functions within a multifunction device provides a stand-alone functionality. As an example, one function could be a graphics controller while another might be a network interface.

Just as in PCI, a device may contain up to a maximum of eight functions numbered 0-through-7:

- The one-and-only function implemented in a single-function device must be function 0.
- In a multifunction device, the first function must be function 0, while the remaining functions do not have to be implemented in a sequential manner. In other words, a device could implement functions 0, 2, and 7.

In Figure 19-1 on page 713, Device 0 on Bus 3 is a multifunction device containing two functions, each of which implements its own set of configuration registers.

Figure 19-1: Example System

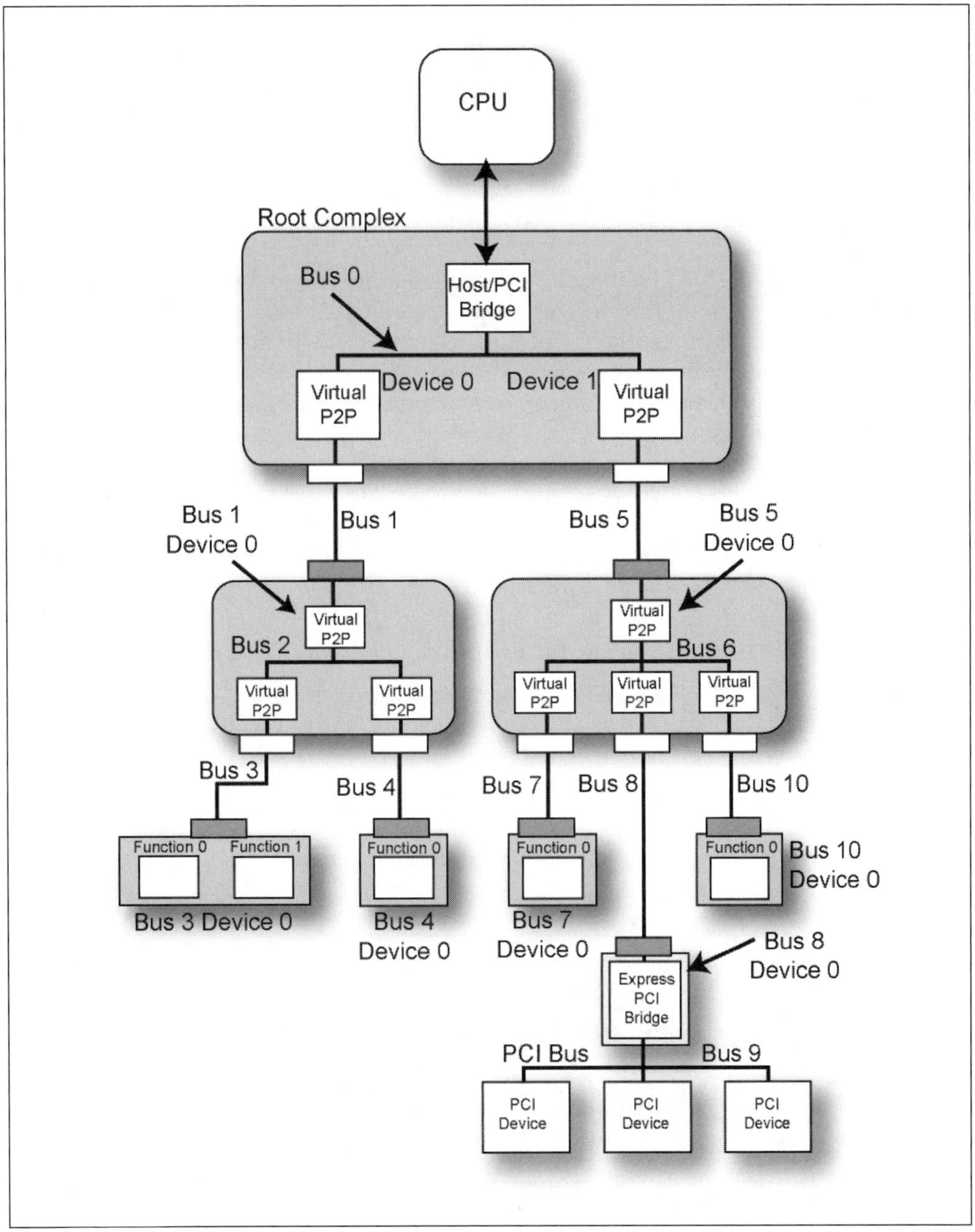

Definition of Primary and Secondary Bus

The bus connected to the upstream side of a bridge is referred to as its primary bus, while the bus connected to its downstream side is referred to as its secondary bus.

Topology Is Unknown At Startup

Refer to Figure 19-2 on page 714. When the system is first powered up, the configuration software has not yet scanned the PCI Express fabric to discover the machine topology and how the fabric is populated. The configuration software is only aware of the existence of the Host/PCI bridge within the Root Complex and that bus number 0 is directly connected to the downstream (i.e., secondary) side of the bridge.

It has not yet scanned bus 0 and therefore does not yet know how many PCI Express ports are implemented on the Root Complex. The process of scanning the PCI Express fabric to discover its topology is referred to as the *enumeration* process.

Figure 19-2: Topology View At Startup

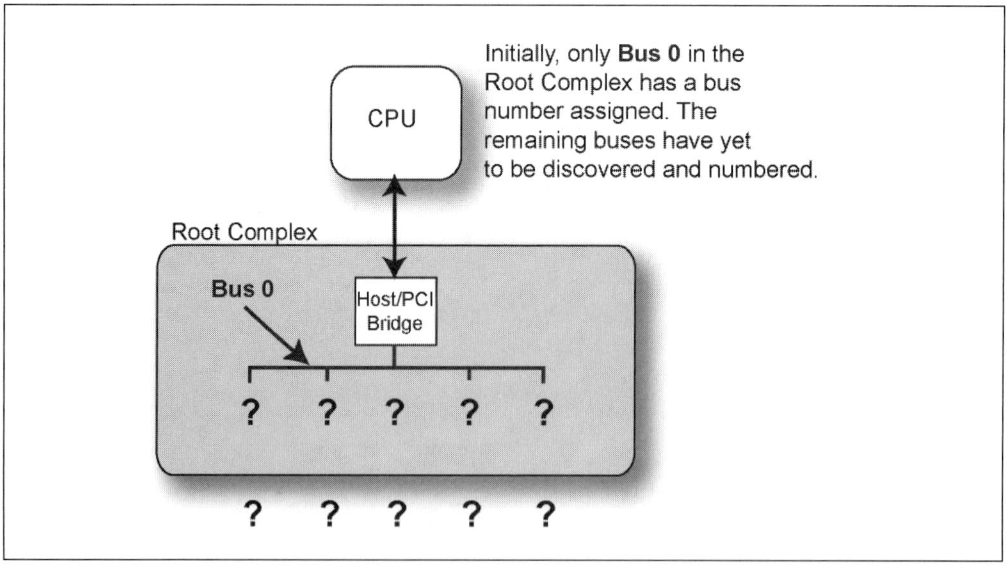

Each Function Implements a Set of Configuration Registers

Introduction

At the behest of software executing on the processor, the Root Complex initiates configuration transactions to read from or write to a function's configuration registers. These registers are accessed to discover the existence of a function as well as to configure it for normal operation. In addition to memory, IO, and message space, PCI Express also defines a dedicated block of configuration space allocated to each function within which its configuration registers are implemented.

Function Configuration Space

Refer to Figure 19-3 on page 717. Each function's configuration space is 4KB in size and is populated as described in the following two subsections.

PCI-Compatible Space

The 256 byte (64 dword) PCI-compatible space occupies the first 256 bytes of this 4KB space. It contains the function's PCI-compatible configuration registers. This area can be accessed using either of two mechanisms (both of which are described later):

- The PCI configuration access mechanism (see "PCI-Compatible Configuration Mechanism" on page 723).
- The PCI Express Enhanced Configuration mechanism (see "PCI Express Enhanced Configuration Mechanism" on page 731).

The first 16 dwords comprises the PCI configuration header area, while the remaining 48 dword area is reserved for the implementation of function-specific configuration registers as well as PCI New Capability register sets. It is mandatory that each PCI Express function must implement the PCI Express Capability Structure (defined later) within this area. A full description of the PCI-compatible registers may be found in "PCI Compatible Configuration Registers" on page 769.

PCI Express Extended Configuration Space

The remaining 3840 byte (960 dword) area is referred to as the PCI Express Extended Configuration Space. It is utilized to implement the optional PCI Express Extended Capability registers:

- Advanced Error Reporting Capability register set.
- Virtual Channel Capability register set.
- Device Serial Number Capability register set.
- Power Budgeting Capability register set.

A full description of the these optional register sets may be found in "Express-Specific Configuration Registers" on page 893.

Host/PCI Bridge's Configuration Registers

The Host/PCI bridge's configuration register set does not have to be accessed using either of the spec-defined configuration mechanisms mentioned in the previous section. Rather, it is mapped into a Root Complex design-specific address space (almost certainly memory space) that is known to the platform-specific BIOS firmware. However, its configuration register layout and usage must adhere to the standard Type 0 template defined by the PCI 2.3 spec (see "Header Type 0" on page 770 for details on the Type 0 register template).

Figure 19-3: 4KB Configuration Space per PCI Express Function

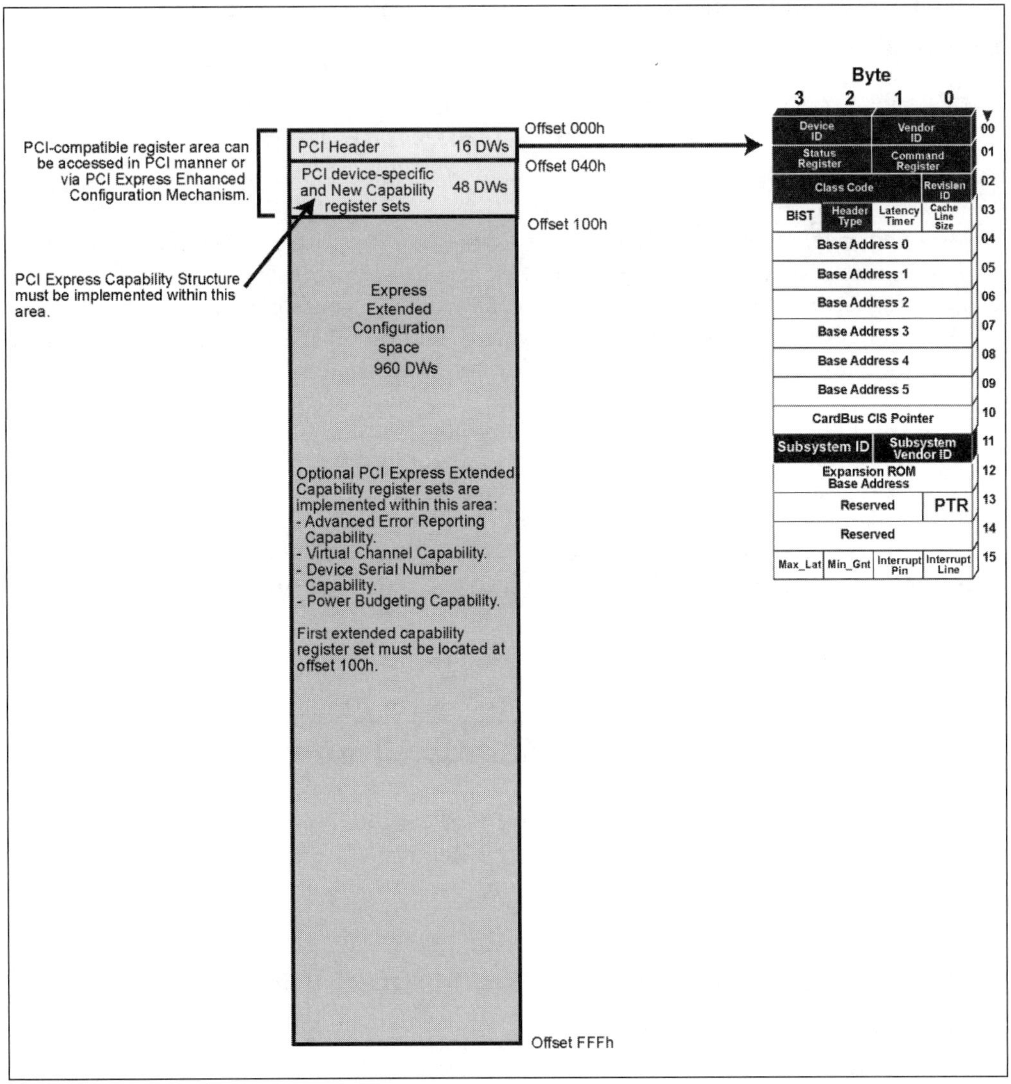

Configuration Transactions Are Originated by the Processor

Only the Root Complex Can Originate Configuration Transactions

The spec states that only the Root Complex is permitted to originate configuration transactions. The Root Complex acts as the processor's surrogate to inject transaction requests into the fabric, as well as to pass completions back to the processor. The configuration software executing on the processor is responsible for detecting and configuring all devices in the system.

The ability to originate configuration transactions is restricted to the processor/Root Complex to avoid the anarchy that would result if any device had the ability to change the configuration of other devices.

Configuration Transactions Only Move DownStream

This restriction exists for the same reason stated in the previous section.

No Peer-to-Peer Configuration Transactions

The following rule applies to Root Ports, Switches, and PCI Express-to-PCI Bridges: Propagation of Configuration Requests from peer-to-peer are not supported.

Configuration Transactions Are Routed Via Bus, Device, and Function Number

The transaction types that are routed via a bus, device, and function number (i.e., they use ID routing rather than address-based routing) are:

- Configuration transactions.
- Vendor-defined Messages may optionally be routed in this manner.
- Completion transactions.

This chapter focuses on configuration-related issues.

How a Function Is Discovered

The configuration software executing on the processor typically discovers the existence of a function by performing a read from its PCI-compatible Vendor ID register. A unique 16-bit value is assigned to each vendor by the PCI-SIG and is hardwired into the Vendor ID register of each function designed by that vendor. The Vendor ID of FFFFh is reserved and will never be assigned to any vendor.

A function is considered present if the value read from its Vendor ID register is a value other than FFFFh. In a system that depends on a return of all ones for a configuration read from a non-existent register, the Root Complex must be designed to return all ones for a configuration read request that results in a UR (Unsupported Request) completion status.

How To Differentiate a PCI-to-PCI Bridge From a Non-Bridge Function

Refer to Figure 19-3 on page 717 and Figure 19-4 on page 719. The lower 7 bits of the Header Type register identifies the basic category of the function:

- 0 = the function is not a bridge.
- 1 = the function is a PCI-to-PCI bridge (aka P2P) interconnecting two buses.
- 2 = the function is a CardBus bridge.

In Figure 19-1 on page 713, the Header Type field in each of the Virtual P2Ps would return a value of 1, as would the PCI Express-to-PCI bridge (Bus 8, Device 0), while those in the following Endpoint functions would return 0:

- Bus 3, Device 0.
- Bus 4, Device 0.
- Bus 7, Device 0.
- Bus 10, Device 0.

Figure 19-4: Header Type Register

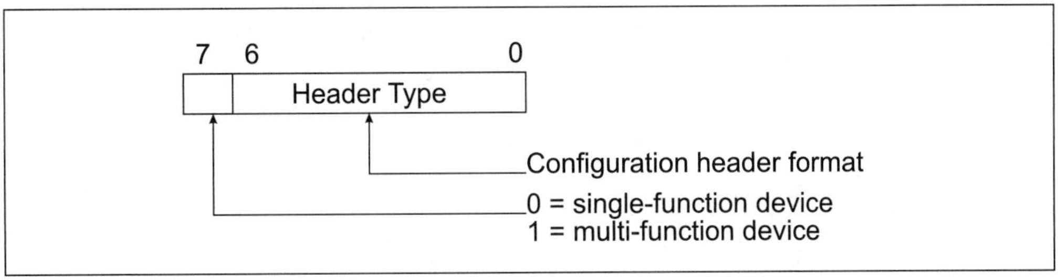

20 Configuration Mechanisms

The Previous Chapter

The previous chapter provided an introduction to configuration in the PCI Express environment. It introduced the configuration space in which a function's configuration registers are implemented, how a function is discovered, how configuration transactions are routed, PCI-compatible space, PCI Express extended configuration space, and how to differentiate between a normal function and a bridge.

This Chapter

This chapter provides a detailed description of the two configuration mechanisms used in a PCI Express platform: the PCI-compatible configuration mechanism, and the PCI Express enhanced configuration mechanism. It provides a detailed description of the initialization period immediately following power-up, as well as error handling during this period.

The Next Chapter

The next chapter provides a detailed description of the discovery process and bus numbering. It describes:

- Enumerating a system with a single Root Complex
- Enumerating a system with multiple Root Complexes
- A multifunction device within a Root Complex or a Switch
- An Endpoint embedded in a Switch or Root Complex
- Automatic Requester ID assignment.
- Root Complex Register Blocks (RCRBs)

Introduction

Refer to Figure 20-1 on page 723. Each function implements a 4KB configuration space. The lower 256 bytes (64 dwords) is the PCI-compatible configuration space, while the upper 960 dwords is the PCI Express extended configuration space.

There are two mechanisms available that allow configuration software running on the processor to stimulate the Root Complex to generate configuration transactions:

- The PCI 2.3-compatible configuration access mechanism.
- The PCI express enhanced configuration mechanism.

These two mechanisms are described in this chapter.

Intel x86 and PowerPC processors (as two example processor families) do not possess the ability to perform configuration read and write transactions. They use memory and IO (IO is only in the x86 case) read and write transactions to communicate with external devices. This means that the Root Complex must be designed to recognize certain IO or memory accesses initiated by the processor as requests to perform configuration accesses.

Figure 20-1: A Function's Configuration Space

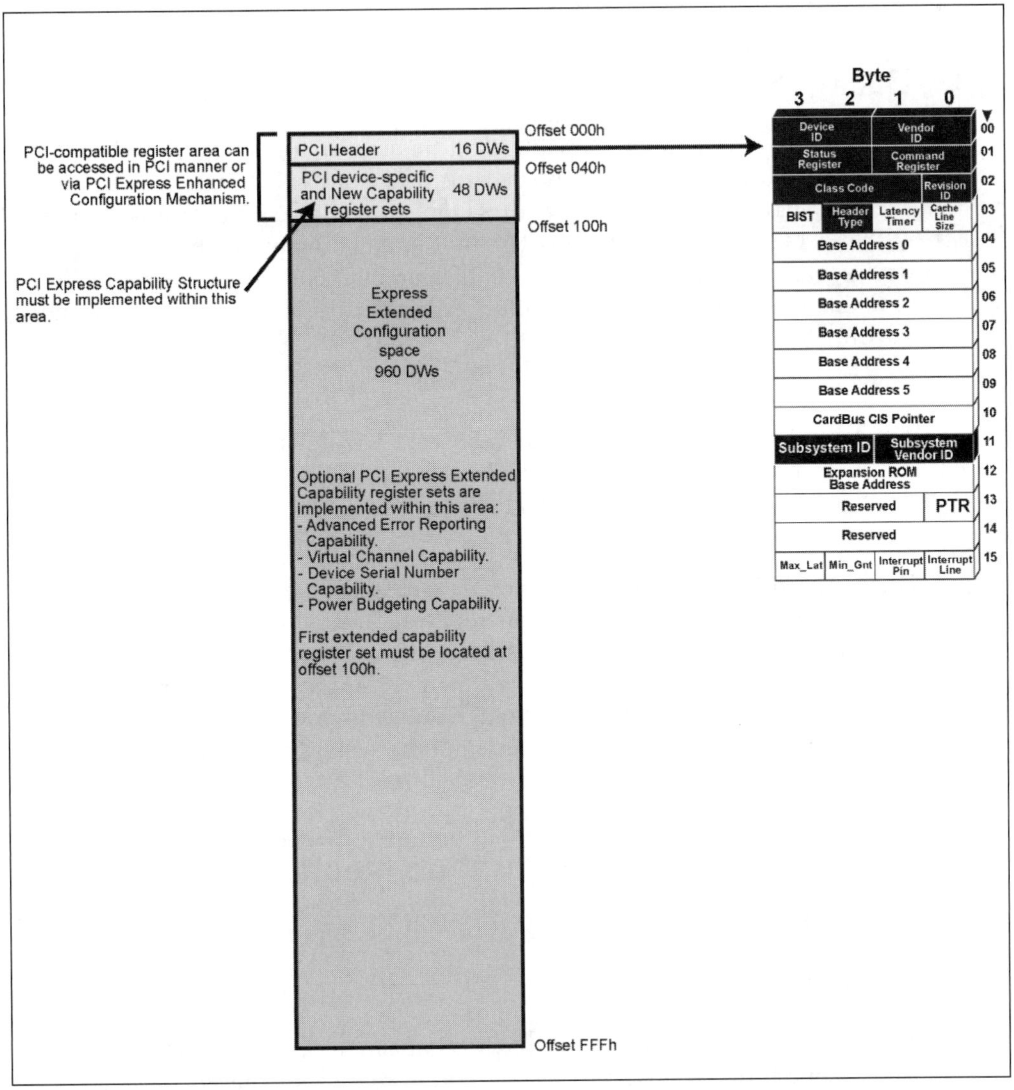

PCI-Compatible Configuration Mechanism

For x86-based PC-AT compatible systems, the 2.3 PCI spec defines a method that utilizes processor-initiated IO accesses to instruct the host/PCI bridge (in this case, within the Root Complex) to perform PCI configuration accesses.The spec does not define a configuration mechanism to be used in systems other than PC-AT compatible systems.

Background

The x86 processor family is capable of addressing up to, but no more than, 64KB of IO address space. In the EISA spec, the usage of this IO space was defined in such a manner that the only IO address ranges available for the implementation of the PCI Configuration Mechanism (without conflicting with an ISA or EISA device) were 0400h - 04FFh, 0800h - 08FFh, and 0C00h - 0CFFh. Many EISA system board controllers already resided within the 0400h - 04FFh address range, making it unavailable.

Consider the following:

- As with any other PCI function, a host/PCI bridge may implement up to 64 dwords of configuration registers.
- Each PCI function on each PCI bus requires 64 dwords of dedicated configuration space.

Due to the lack of available IO real estate within the 64KB of IO space, it wasn't feasible to map each configuration register directly into the processor's IO address space. Alternatively, the system designer could implement the configuration registers within the processor's memory space. The amount of memory space consumed aside, the address range utilized would be unavailable for allocation to regular memory. This would limit the system's flexibility regarding the mapping of actual memory.

PCI-Compatible Configuration Mechanism Description

General

The PCI-Compatible Configuration Mechanism utilizes two 32-bit IO ports implemented in the Host/PCI bridge within the Root Complex, located at IO addresses 0CF8h and 0CFCh. These two ports are:

- The 32-bit **Configuration Address Port**, occupying IO addresses 0CF8h through 0CFBh.
- The 32-bit **Configuration Data Port**, occupying IO addresses 0CFCh through 0CFFh.

Accessing one of a function's PCI compatible configuration registers is a two step process:

1. Write the target bus number, device number, function number and dword number to the Configuration Address Port and set the Enable bit in it to one.
2. Perform a one-byte, two-byte, or four-byte IO read from or a write to the Configuration Data Port.

In response, the host/PCI bridge within the Root Complex compares the specified target bus to the range of buses that exist on the other side of the bridge and, if the target bus resides beyond the bridge, it initiates a configuration read or write transaction (based on whether the processor is performing an IO read or write with the Configuration Data Port).

Configuration Address Port

Refer to Figure 20-2 on page 726. The Configuration Address Port only latches information when the processor performs a full 32-bit write to the port. A 32-bit read from the port returns its contents. The assertion of reset clears the port to all zeros. Any 8- or 16-bit access within this IO dword is treated as an 8- or 16-bit IO access. The 32-bits of information written to the Configuration Address Port must conform to the following template (illustrated in Figure 20-2 on page 726):

- bits **[1:0]** are hard-wired, read-only and must return **zeros** when read.
- bits **[7:2]** identify the **target dword** (1-of-64) within the target function's PCI-compatible configuration space. When the Root Complex subsequently generates the resultant configuration request packet, this bit field supplies the content of the packet's Register Number field and the packet's Extended Register Number field is set to all zeros. This configuration access mechanism is therefore limited to addressing the first 64 dwords of the targeted function's configuration space (i.e., the function's PCI-compatible address space).
- bits **[10:8]** identify the **target function** number (1-of-8) within the target device.
- bits **[15:11]** identify the target device number (1-of-32).
- bits **[23:16]** identifies the **target bus** number (1-of-256).
- bits **[30:24]** are **reserved** and must be zero.
- bit **31 must be** set to a **one**, enabling the translation of a subsequent processor IO access to the Configuration Data Port into a configuration access. If bit 31 is zero and the processor initiates an IO read from or IO write to the Configuration Data Port, the transaction is treated as an IO transaction request.

Figure 20-2: Configuration Address Port at 0CF8h

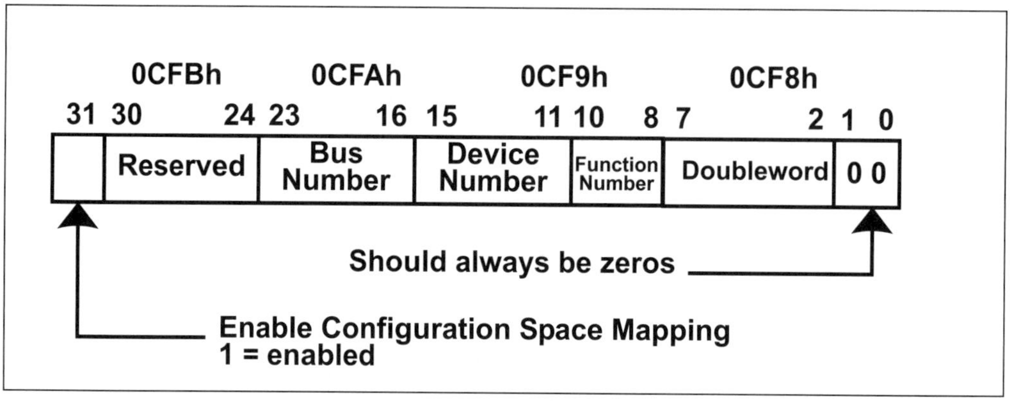

Bus Compare and Data Port Usage

Refer to Figure 20-3 on page 728. The Host/PCI bridge within the Root Complex implements a Bus Number register and a Subordinate Bus Number register. In a chipset that only supports one Root Complex, the bridge may have a bus number register that is hardwired to 0, a read/write register that reset forces to 0, or it just implicitly knows that it is the bridge to bus 0. If bit 31 in the Configuration Address Port (see Figure 20-2 on page 726) is enabled (i.e., set to one), the bridge compares the target bus number to the range of buses that exists beyond the bridge.

Target Bus = 0. If the target bus is the same as the value in the Bus Number register, this is a request to perform a configuration transaction on bus 0. A subsequent IO read from or write to the bridge's Configuration Data Port at 0CFCh causes the bridge to generate a Type 0 configuration read or write transaction. When devices that reside on a PCI bus detect a Type 0 configuration transaction in progress, this informs them that one of them is the target device (rather than a device on one of the subordinate buses beneath the bus the Type 0 transaction is being performed on).

Bus Number < Target Bus ≤ Subordinate Bus Number. If the target bus specified in the Configuration Address Port is > than the value in the bridge's Bus Number register, but is ≤ the value in the bridge's Subordinate Bus Number register, the bridge converts the subsequent processor IO access to its Configuration Data Port into a Type 1 configuration transaction on bus 0. When devices (other than PCI-to-PCI bridges) that reside on a bus detect a Type 1 configuration access in progress, they ignore the transaction.

The only devices on a bus that pay attention to the Type 1 configuration transaction are PCI-to-PCI bridges. Each of them must determine if the target bus number (delivered in the packet's header) is within the range of buses that reside behind them:

- If the target bus is not within range, then a PCI-to-PCI bridge ignores the Type 1 access.
- If it's in range, the access is passed through the PCI-to-PCI bridge as either a Type 0 configuration transaction (if the target bus = the bus number in the bridge's Secondary Bus Number register), or as
- a Type 1 transaction (if the target bus number ≤ the value in the bridge's Subordinate Bus Number register and > than the value in the bridge's Bus Number register).

The subject of Type 0 configuration accesses is covered in detail in "Type 0 Configuration Request" on page 732. The subject of Type 1 configuration accesses is covered in detail in "Type 1 Configuration Request" on page 733.

Single Host/PCI Bridge

Refer to Figure 20-3 on page 728. The information written to the Configuration Address Port is latched by the Host/PCI bridge within the Root Complex. If bit 31 is set to one and the target bus number = the value in the bridge's Bus Number register (or is ≤ the value in the bridge's Subordinate Bus Number register), the bridge is enabled to convert a subsequent processor access targeting its Configuration Data Port into a configuration access on bus 0 within the Root Complex. The processor then initiates a one-byte, two-byte, or four-byte (for an x86 processor indicated by the processor's byte enable signals; or, if a PowerPC 60x processor, by A[29:31] and TSIZ[0:2]) IO read or write transaction to the Configuration Data Port at 0CFCh. This stimulates the bridge to perform a configuration read (if the processor is reading from the Configuration Data Port) or a configuration write (if the processor is writing to the Configuration Data Port). It will be a Type 0 configuration transaction if the target bus is bus 0, or a Type 1 configuration transaction if the target bus is further out in the bus hierarchy beyond bus 0.

Figure 20-3: Example System

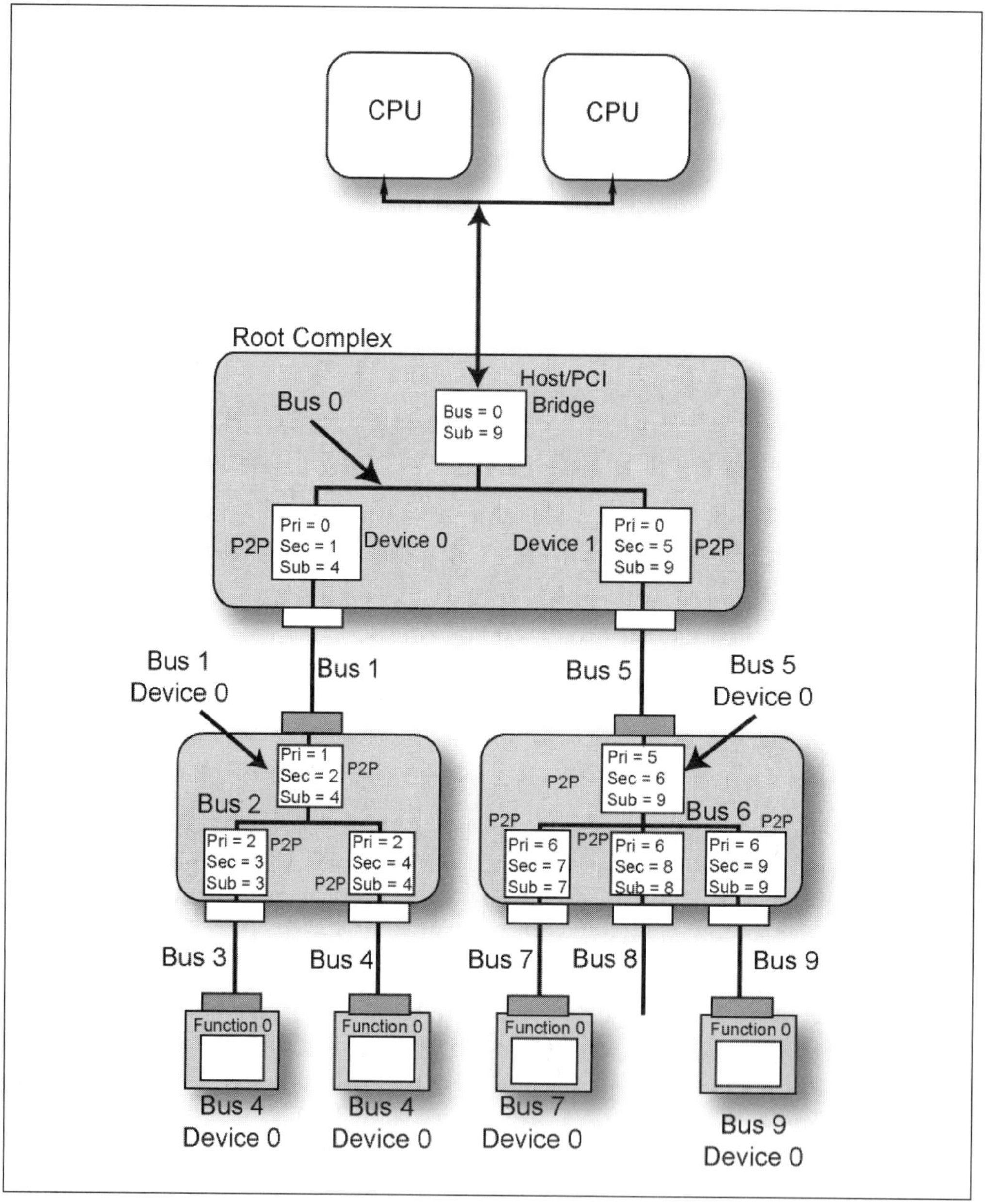

Multiple Host/PCI Bridges

If there are multiple Root Complexes present on the processor's FSB (refer to Figure 20-4 on page 730), the Configuration Address and Data ports are duplicated at the same IO addresses in each of their respective host/PCI bridges. In order to prevent contention on the processor's FSB signals, only one of the bridges responds to the processor's accesses to the configuration ports.

1. When the processor initiates the IO write to the Configuration Address Port, only one of the host/PCI bridges actively participates in the transaction. The other bridge quietly snarfs the data as it's written to the active participant.
2. Both bridges then compare the target bus number to their respective Bus Number and Subordinate Bus Number registers. If the target bus doesn't reside behind a particular host/PCI bridge, that bridge doesn't convert the subsequent access to its Configuration Data Port into a configuration access on its bus (in other words, it ignores the transaction).
3. A subsequent read or write access to the Configuration Data Port is only accepted by the host/PCI bridge that is the gateway to the target bus. This bridge responds to the processor's transaction and the other ignores it.
4. When the access is made to the Configuration Data Port, the bridge with a bus compare tests the state of the Enable bit in its Configuration Address Port. If the Enabled bit = 1, the bridge converts the processor's IO access into a configuration access:
   - o If the target bus is the bus immediately on the other side of the Host/PCI bridge, the bridge converts the access to a Type 0 configuration access on its secondary bus.
   - o Otherwise, it converts it into a Type 1 configuration access.

Figure 20-4: Peer Root Complexes

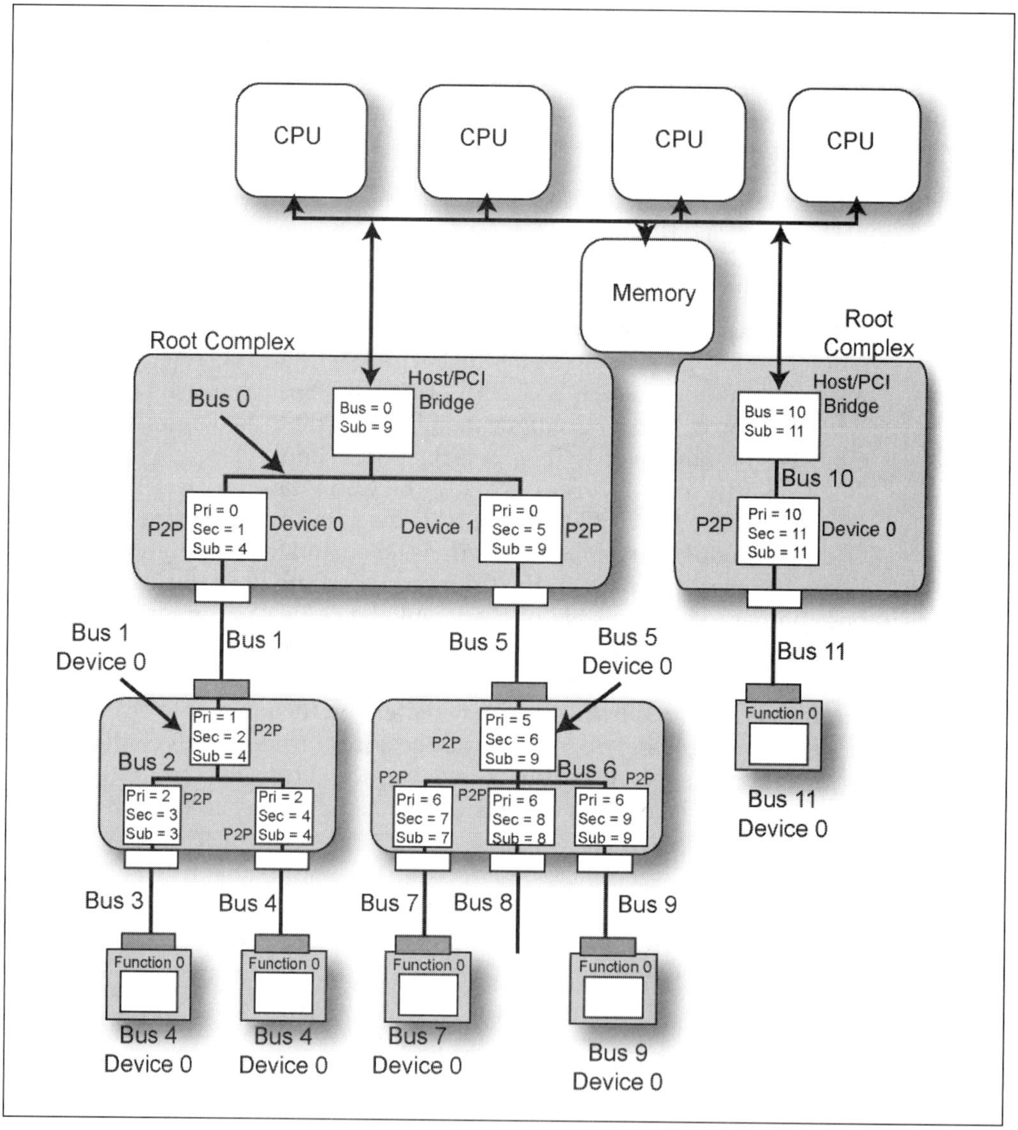

PCI Express Enhanced Configuration Mechanism

Description

Refer to Table 20 - 1 on page 732. Each function's 4KB configuration space starts at a 4KB-aligned address within the 256MB memory space set aside as configuration space:

- Address bits 63:28 indicates the 256MB-aligned base address of the overall Enhanced Configuration address range.
- Address bits 27:20 select the target bus (1-of-256).
- Address bits 19:15 select the target device (1-of-32) on the bus.
- Address bits 14:12 select the target function (1-of-8) within the device.
- Address bits 11:2 selects the target dword (1-of-1024) within the selected function's configuration space.
- Address bits 1:0 define the start byte location within the selected dword.

Some Rules

A Root Complex design is not required to support an access to the enhanced configuration memory space that crosses a dword address boundary (i.e., the access straddles two adjacent memory dwords.

In addition, some processor types can perform a series of memory accesses as an atomic, locked, transaction series. A Root Complex design is not required to support an access to the enhanced configuration memory space using this locking mechanism.

This being the case, software should avoid both of the scenarios just described unless it is known that the Root Complex implementation being used supports the translation.

Table 20 - 1: Enhanced Configuration Mechanism Memory-Mapped IO Address Range

Memory Address Bit Field	Description
A[63:28]	Upper bits of the 256MB-aligned base address of the 256MB memory-mapped IO address range allocated for the Enhanced Configuration Mechanism. The manner in which the base address is allocated is implementation-specific. It is supplied to the OS by system firmware.
A[27:20]	Target Bus Number (1-of-256).
A[19:15]	Target Device Number (1-of-32).
A[14:12]	Target Function Number (1-of-8).
A[11:2]	A[11:8] is the upper four bits of the target Dword Number (1-of-1024).
	A[7:2] is the lower six bits of the target Dword Number.
A[1:0]	Along with the access size, defines the Byte Enable setting.

Type 0 Configuration Request

A configuration read or write takes the form of a Type 0 configuration read or write when it arrives on the destination bus. On discerning that it is a Type 0 configuration operation:

1. The devices on the bus decode the header's Device Number field to determine which of them is the target device.
2. The selected device decodes the header's Function Number field to determine the selected function within the device.
3. The selected function uses the concatenated Extended Register Number and Register Number fields to select the target dword in the function's configuration space.
4. Finally, the function uses the First Dword Byte Enable field to select the byte(s) to be read or written within the selected dword.

Figure 20-5 and Figure 20-6 illustrate the Type 0 configuration read and write request header formats. In both cases, the Type field = 00100, while the state of the Fmt field's msb indicates whether it's a read or a write.

Figure 20-5: Type 0 Configuration Read Request Packet Header

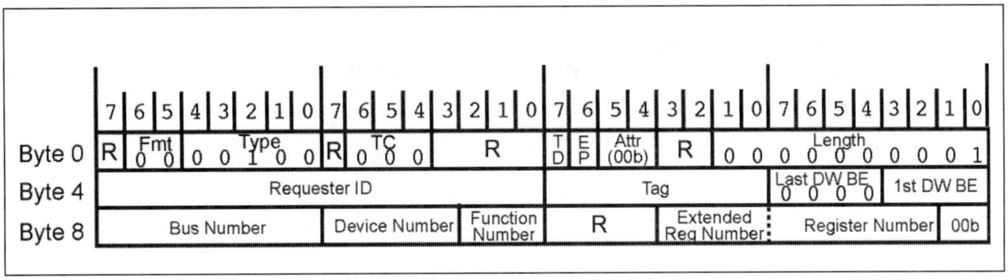

Figure 20-6: Type 0 Configuration Write Request Packet Header

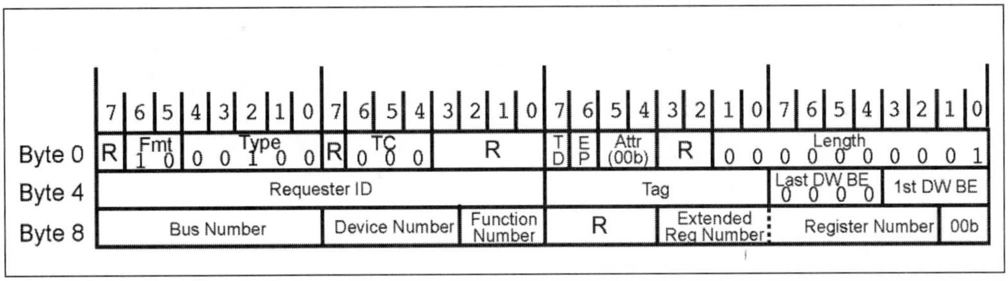

Type 1 Configuration Request

While in transit to the destination bus, a configuration read or write takes the form of a Type 1 configuration read or write when it is performed on each bus on the way to the destination bus. The only devices that pay attention to a Type 1 configuration read or write are PCI-to-PCI bridges. Upon receipt of a Type 1 configuration read or write request packet, a PCI-to-PCI bridge compares the target bus number in the packet header to the range of buses that reside behind the bridge (as defined by the contents of the bridge's Secondary Bus Number and Subordinate Bus Number configuration registers; see Figure 20-3 on page 728 and Figure 20-4 on page 730).

- If the target bus is the bridge's secondary bus, the packet is converted from a Type 1 to a Type 0 configuration request when it is passed to the secondary bus. The devices on that bus then decode the packet header as previously described in "Type 0 Configuration Request" on page 732.
- If the target bus is not the bridge's secondary bus but is a bus that resides beneath its secondary bus, the Type 1 request is passed through to the bridge's secondary bus as is.

Figure 20-7 and Figure 20-8 illustrate the Type 1 configuration read and write request header formats. In both cases, the Type field = 00101, while the state of the Fmt field's msb indicates whether it's a read or a write.

Figure 20-7: Type 1 Configuration Read Request Packet Header

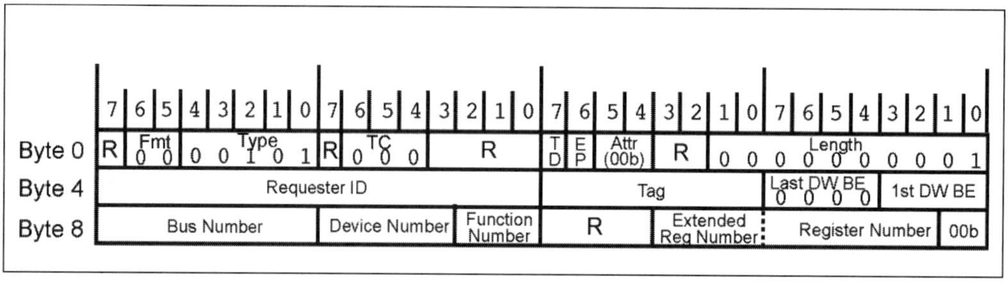

Figure 20-8: Type 1 Configuration Write Request Packet Header

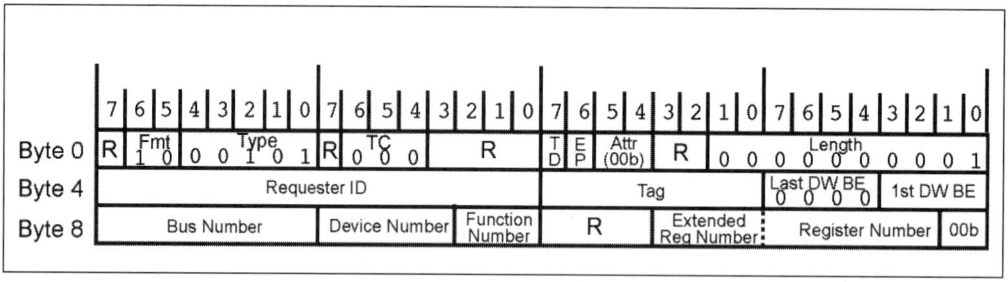

Example PCI-Compatible Configuration Access

Refer to Figure 20-9 on page 737. The following x86 code sample will cause the Root Complex to perform a read from Bus 4, Device 0, Function 0's Vendor ID configuration register:

```
mov    dx,0CF8      ;set dx = config address port address
mov    eax,80040000;enable=1, bus 4, dev 0, Func 0, DW 0
out    dx,eax       ;set up address port
mov    dx,0CFC      ; set dx = config data port address
in     ax,dx        ;2 byte read from config data port
```

1. On execution of the `out` (IO Write) instruction, the processor generates an IO write transaction on its FSB targeting the Configuration Address Port in the Root Complex Host/PCI bridge. The data sourced from the eax register is latched into the Configuration Address Port (see Figure 20-2 on page 726).
2. The Host/PCI bridge compares the target bus number (4) specified in the Configuration Address Port to the range of buses (0-through-10) that reside downstream of the bridge. The target bus falls within the range, so the bridge is primed.
3. On execution of the `in` (IO Read) instruction, the processor generates an IO read transaction on its FSB targeting the Configuration Data Port in the Root Complex Host/PCI bridge. It's a 2-byte read from the first two locations in the Configuration Data Port.
4. Since the target bus is not bus 0, the Host/PCI bridge initiates a Type 1 Configuration read on bus 0.
5. All of the devices on bus 0 latch the transaction request and determine that it is a type 1 Configuration Read request. As a result, both of the virtual PCI-to-PCI bridges in the Root Complex compare the target bus number in the Type 1 request to the range of buses that reside downstream of each of them.
6. The destination bus (4) is within the range of buses downstream of the left-hand bridge, so it passes the packet through to its secondary bus (bus 1). It is passed through as a Type 1 request because this is not the destination bus.
7. The upstream port on the left-hand switch receives the packet and delivers it to the upstream PCI-to-PCI bridge.
8. The bridge determines that the destination bus resides beneath it, so it passes the packet through to bus 2 as a Type 1 request.
9. Both of the bridge's within the switch receive the Type 1 request packet and the right-hand bridge determines that the destination bus is directly beneath it.

10. The bridge passes the Type 1 request packet through to bus 4, but converts into a Type 0 Configuration Read request (because the packet has arrived at the destination bus.
11. Device 0 on bus 4 receives the packet and decodes the target device number.
12. Device 0 decodes the target function number.
13. Function 0 in Device 0 uses the concatenated Extended Register Number and Register Number fields to select the target dword (dword 0; see Figure 20-1 on page 723) in the function's configuration space.
14. The first two Byte Enables in the First Dword Byte Enable field are asserted, so the function returns its Vendor ID in the resulting Completion packet. The Completion packet is routed back to the Host/PCI bridge using the Requester ID field obtained from the Type 0 request packet.
15. The two bytes of read data are delivered to the processor over its FSB, thereby completing the execution of the `in` instruction. The Vendor ID is placed in the processor's ax register.

Example Enhanced Configuration Access

Refer to Figure 20-9 on page 737. The following x86 code sample will cause the Root Complex to perform a read from Bus 4, Device 0, Function 0's Vendor ID configuration register. The example assumes that the 256MB-aligned base address of the Enhanced Configuration memory-mapped IO range is 50000000h:

```
mov   ax,[50400000];memory-mapped IO read
```

- Address bits 63:28 indicates the upper 36 bits of the 256MB-aligned base address of the overall Enhanced Configuration address range (in this case, 000000005h).
- Address bits 27:20 select the target bus (in this case, 4).
- Address bits 19:15 select the target device (in this case, 0) on the bus.
- Address bits 14:12 select the target function (in this case, 0) within the device.
- Address bits 11:2 selects the target dword (in this case, 0) within the selected function's configuration space.
- Address bits 1:0 define the start byte location within the selected dword (in this case, 0).

The processor initiates a 2-byte memory read from memory locations 50400000h and 50400001h on its FSB. The request is latched by the Host/PCI bridge in the Root Complex. It decodes the address and determines that it is a configuration read request for the first two bytes in dword 0, function 0, device 0, bus 4. The remainder of the operation is the same as that described in the previous section.

Figure 20-9: Example Configuration Access

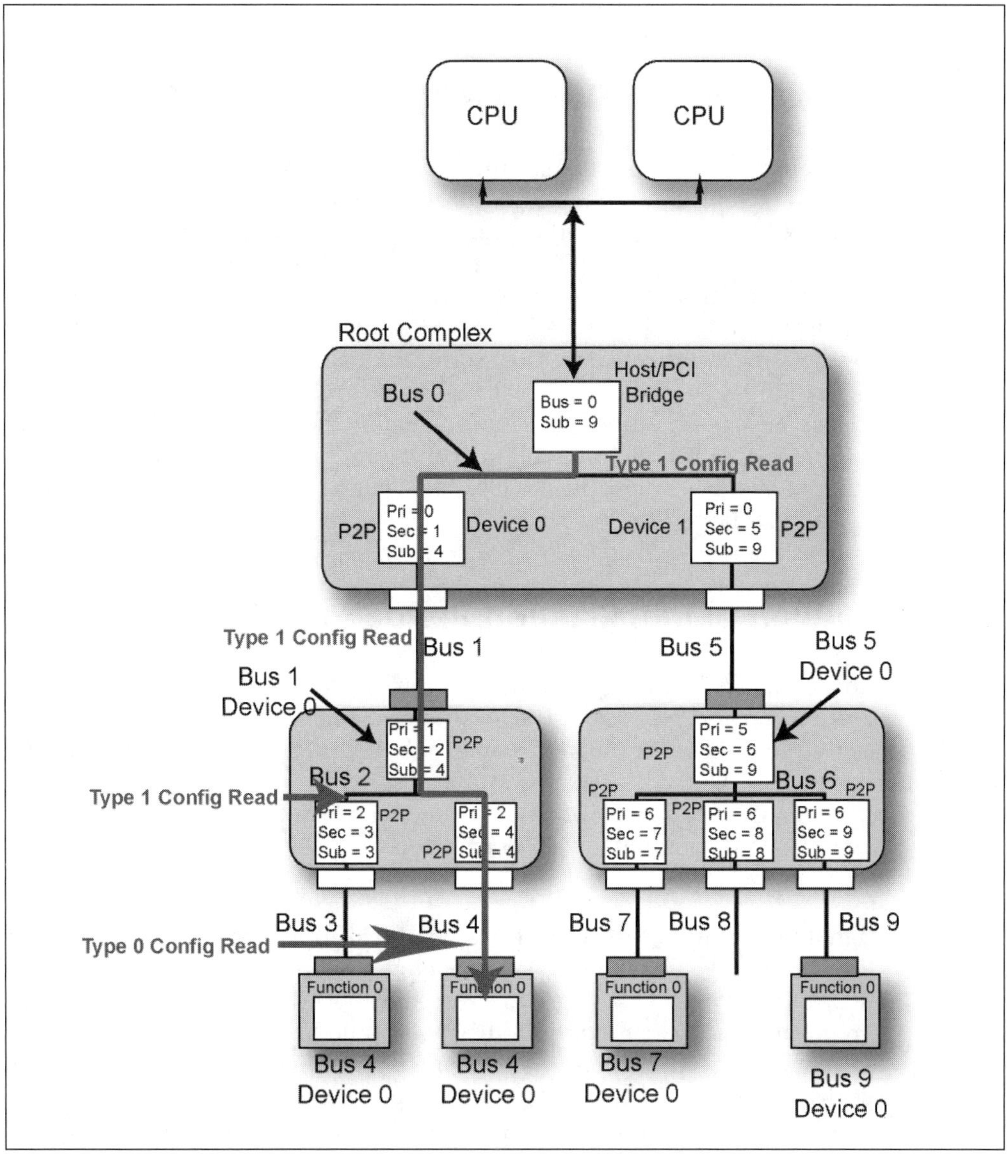

Initial Configuration Accesses

What's Going On During Initialization Time?

During initialization time, the startup configuration software is accessing the configuration registers within each function to determine the presence of a function as well as its resource requirements. Immediately after RST# is removed from a PCI or a PCI-X function, it may not be prepared to service configuration accesses on a timely basis. As an example, a function's configuration registers might not contain valid default values immediately after RST# is removed. Perhaps the function must start backloading this information into its configuration registers from a serial EEPROM. In this case, it could be a substantial amount of time after RST# removal before the function can provide read data from or accept write data into its configuration registers. For this reason, functions do not have obey the 16 clock first Data Phase completion rule during initialization time.

Definition of Initialization Period In PCI

As defined in the PCI 2.3 spec, Initialization Time (Trhfa) begins when RST# is deasserted and completes 2^{25} PCI clocks later (32 mega-cycles). This parameter is referred to in the spec as Trhfa (Time from Reset High-to-First-Access). At a bus speed of 33MHz, this equates to 1.0066 seconds, while it equates to 0.5033 seconds at a bus speed of 66MHz. Run-time follows initialization-time. If a target is accessed during initialization-time, it is allowed to do any of the following:

- Ignore the request (except if it is a boot device). A boot device is one that must respond as a target in order to allow the processor to access the boot ROM. In a typical PC design, this would be ICH (IO Control Hub). Devices in the processor's path to the boot ROM should be prepared to be the target of a transaction immediately after Trhff expires (five clock cycles after RST# is deasserted).
- Claim the access and hold in Wait States until it can complete the request, not to exceed the end of Initialization Time.
- Claim the access and terminate with Retry.

Definition of Initialization Period In PCI-X

In PCI-X, Trhfa is 2^{26} clocks (64 mega-cycles) in duration rather than 2^{25} as it is in PCI. This is because the PCI-X clock speed can be substantially faster than (up to 133MHz) the PCI clock speed and if this parameter remained the same as the PCI Trhfa spec, Initialization Time would be reduced to 0.25 seconds (at a clock speed of 133MHz).

During Initialization Time, a PCI-X target has the same options available as a PCI target does (see previous section).

PCI Express and Initialization Time

Just as in PCI or PCI-X, some devices in a PCI Express environment may go through a rather long self-initialization sequence to before they are able to service configuration access requests.

When a PCI Express device receives a configuration request it may respond with a Configuration Request Retry Completion Status (CRS). Requester receipt of a Completion with Configuration Request Retry Status terminates the configuration access request on PCI Express.

Initial Configuration Access Failure Timeout

After a PCI Express device is reset, the Root Complex and/or system software must allow 1.0s (+50%/-0%) for the device to return a Successful Completion status before deciding that the device has malfunctioned. This is analogous to the PCI/PCI-X Trhfa parameter.

When attempting a configuration access to a device on a PCI or PCI-X bus downstream of a PCI Express-to-PCI or -PCI-X bridge, Trhfa must be taken into account.

Delay Prior To Initial Configuration Access to Device

After system hardware or software causes one or more devices to be reset, software must wait at least 100ms from the end of reset before issuing any configuration requests to those devices. This time period is allocated to allow the device(s) to complete internal initialization.

The system design must guarantee (in a design-specific manner) that all components that must be software visible at boot time are ready to receive configuration requests within 100ms of the deassertion of Fundamental Reset at the Root Complex.

A Device With a Lengthy Self-Initialization Period

If a PCI Express device requires additional time to finish its self initialization, the system design must provide a design-specific mechanism for re-issuing configuration requests terminated with CRS status after the initial 1s timeout has elapsed.

To ensure proper enumeration of the system in a system running legacy PCI/PCI-X based software, the Root Complex hardware must re-issue the configuration request.

RC Response To CRS Receipt During Run-Time

After initialization time has elapsed, the action(s) taken by the Root Complex upon receipt of a Configuration Request Retry Completion Status is implementation-specific. It may re-issue the configuration request as a new request or may indicate failed completion to the processor.

If the Root Complex is designed to automatically retry the request, the number of retries attempted before indicating a failure to the processor is design-specific.

During Run-Time, support for a Completion Timeout (and the duration of the timeout) for configuration requests are implementation-specific.

The default setting in a PCI Express-to-PCI or -PCI-X bridge prevents it from returning a Configuration Request Retry Status (CRS) for a configuration request that targets a PCI or PCI-X device downstream of the bridge. This can result in a lengthy completion delay that must be taken into account by the Completion Timeout value used by the Root Complex. Configuration software can enable such a bridge to return Configuration Request Retry Status by setting the Bridge Configuration Retry Enable bit in the bridge's Device Control register.

21 PCI Express Enumeration

The Previous Chapter

The previous chapter provided a detailed description of the two configuration mechanisms used in a PCI Express platform: the PCI-compatible configuration mechanism, and the PCI Express enhanced configuration mechanism. It provided a detailed description of the initialization period immediately following power-up, as well as error handling during this period.

This Chapter

This chapter provides a detailed description of the discovery process and bus numbering. It describes:

- Enumerating a system with a single Root Complex
- Enumerating a system with multiple Root Complexes
- A multifunction device within a Root Complex or a Switch
- An Endpoint embedded in a Switch or Root Complex
- Automatic Requester ID assignment.
- Root Complex Register Blocks (RCRBs)

The Next Chapter

The next chapter provides a detailed description of the configuration registers residing a function's PCI-compatible configuration space. This includes the registers for both non-bridge and bridge functions.

Introduction

The discussions associated with Figure 19-1 on page 713 and Figure 20-4 on page 730 assumed that, each of the buses had been discovered and numbered earlier in time.

In reality, at power up time, the configuration software only knows of the existence of bus 0 (the bus that resides on the downstream side of the Host/PCI bridge) and does not even know what devices reside on bus 0 (see Figure 21-1 on page 742).

This chapter describes the enumeration process: the process of discovering the various buses that exist and the devices and functions which reside on each of them.

Figure 21-1: Topology View At Startup

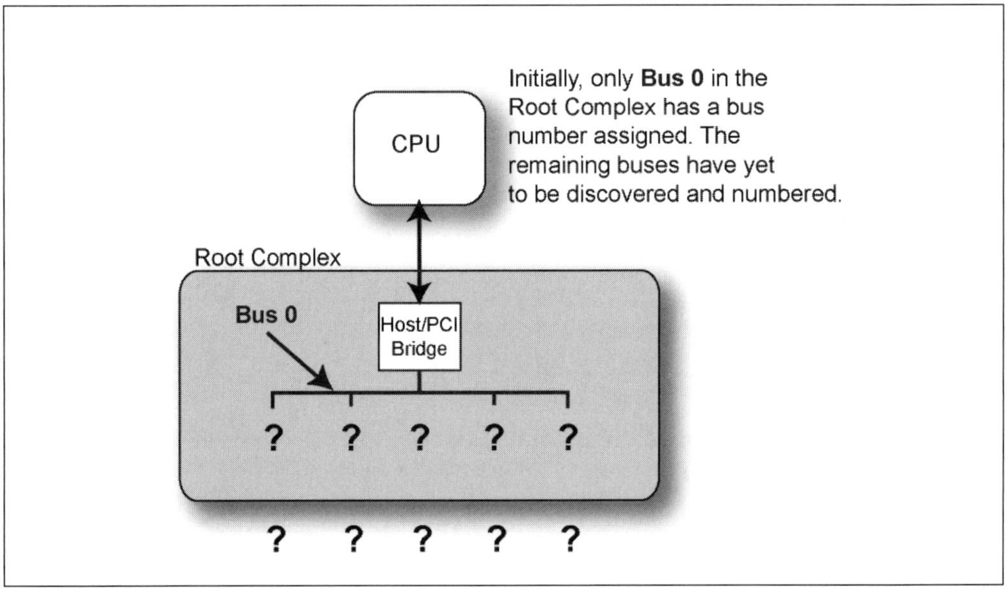

Enumerating a System With a Single Root Complex

Figure 21-2 on page 748 illustrates an example system before the buses and devices have been enumerated, while Figure 21-3 on page 749 shows the same system after the buses and devices have been enumerated. The discussion that follows assumes that the configuration software uses either of the two configuration mechanisms defined in the previous chapter. At startup time, the configuration software executing on the processor performs bus/device/function enumeration in the following manner:

1. Starting with device 0 (bridge A), the enumeration software attempts to read the Vendor ID from function 0 in each of the 32 possible devices on bus 0.
   - If a valid (not FFFFh) Vendor ID is returned from bus 0, device 0, function 0, this indicates that the device is implemented and contains at least one function. Proceed to the next step.
   - If a value of FFFFh were returned as the Vendor ID, this would indicate that function 0 is not implemented in device 0. Since it is a rule that the first function implemented in any device must be function 0, this would mean that device was not implemented and the enumeration software would proceed to probe bus 0, device 1, function 0.
2. The Header Type field (see Figure 21-6 and Figure 21-7) in the Header register (see Figure 21-4) contains the value one (0000001b) indicating that this is a PCI-to-PCI bridge with the PCI-compatible register layout shown in Figure 21-7 on page 752. This discussion assumes that the Multifunction bit (bit 7) in the Header Type register is 0, indicating that function 0 is the only function in this bridge. *It should be noted that the spec does not preclude implementing multiple functions within this bridge and each of these functions, in turn, could represent virtual PCI-to-PCI bridges.*
3. Software now performs a series of configuration writes to set the bridge's bus number registers as follows:
   - Primary Bus Number Register = 0.
   - Secondary Bus Number Register = 1.
   - Subordinate Bus Number Register = 1.

   The bridge is now aware that the number of the bus directly attached to its downstream side is 1 (Secondary Bus Number = 1) and the number of the bus farthest downstream of it is 1 (Subordinate Bus Number = 1).
4. Software updates the Host/PCI bridge's Subordinate Bus Number register to 1.
5. The enumeration software reads bridge A's Capability Register (Figure 21-5 on page 750 and Table 21 - 1 on page 753; a detailed description of this register can be found in "PCI Express Capabilities Register" on page 898). The value 0100b in the register's Device/Port Type field indicates that this a Root Port on the Root Complex.
6. The specification states that the enumeration software must perform a depth-first search, so before proceeding to discover additional functions/devices on bus 0, it must proceed to search bus 1.
7. Software reads the Vendor ID of bus 1, device 0, function 0. A valid Vendor ID is returned, indicating that bus 1, device 0, function 0 exists.
8. The Header Type field in the Header register contains the value one (0000001b) indicating that this is a PCI-to-PCI bridge. In addition, bit 7 is a 0, indicating that bridge C is a single-function device.

9. Bridge C's Capability Register contains the value 0101b in the Device/Port Type field indicating that this is the upstream Port on a switch.
10. Software now performs a series of configuration writes to set bridge C's bus number registers as follows:
    - Primary Bus Number Register = 1.
    - Secondary Bus Number Register = 2.
    - Subordinate Bus Number Register = 2.

    Bridge C is now aware that the number of the bus directly attached to its downstream side is 2 (Secondary Bus Number = 2) and the number of the bus farthest downstream of it is 2 (Subordinate Bus Number = 2).
11. Software updates the Subordinate Bus Number registers in the Host/PCI bridge and in bridge A to 2.
12. Continuing with its depth-first search, a read is performed from bus 2, device 0, function 0's Vendor ID register. The example assumes that bridge D is device 0, function 0 on bus 2.
13. A valid Vendor ID is returned, indicating that bus 2, device 0, function 0 exists.
14. The Header Type field in the Header register contains the value one (0000001b) indicating that this is a PCI-to-PCI bridge. In addition, bit 7 is a 0, indicating that bridge D is a single-function device.
15. Bridge D's Capability Register contains the value 0110b in the Device/Port Type field indicating that this is the downstream Port on a switch.
16. Software now performs a series of configuration writes to set bridge D's bus number registers as follows:
    - Primary Bus Number Register = 2.
    - Secondary Bus Number Register = 3.
    - Subordinate Bus Number Register = 3.

    Bridge D is now aware that the number of the bus directly attached to its downstream side is 3 (Secondary Bus Number = 3) and the number of the bus farthest downstream of it is 3 (Subordinate Bus Number = 3).
17. Software updates the Subordinate Bus Number registers in the Host/PCI bridge, bridge A, and bridge C to 3.
18. Continuing with its depth-first search, a read is performed from bus 3, device 0, function 0's Vendor ID register.
19. A valid Vendor ID is returned, indicating that bus 3, device 0, function 0 exists.
20. The Header Type field in the Header register contains the value zero (0000000b) indicating that this is an Endpoint device. In addition, bit 7 is a 1, indicating that this is a multifunction device.
21. The device's Capability Register contains the value 0000b in the Device/Port Type field indicating that this is an Endpoint device.
22. The enumeration software performs accesses to the Vendor ID of functions

1-through-7 in bus 3, device 0 and determines that only function 1 exists in addition to function 0.

23. Having exhausted the current leg of the depth first search, the enumeration software backs up one level (to bus 2) and moves on to read the Vendor ID of the next device (device 1). The example assumes that bridge E is device 1, function 0 on bus 2.
24. A valid Vendor ID is returned, indicating that bus 2, device 1, function 0 exists.
25. The Header Type field in bridge E's Header register contains the value one (0000001b) indicating that this is a PCI-to-PCI bridge. In addition, bit 7 is a 0, indicating that bridge E is a single-function device.
26. Bridge E's Capability Register contains the value 0110b in the Device/Port Type field indicating that this is the downstream Port on a switch.
27. Software now performs a series of configuration writes to set bridge E's bus number registers as follows:
    - Primary Bus Number Register = 2.
    - Secondary Bus Number Register = 4.
    - Subordinate Bus Number Register = 4.

    Bridge E is now aware that the number of the bus directly attached to its downstream side is 4 (Secondary Bus Number = 4) and the number of the bus farthest downstream of it is 4 (Subordinate Bus Number = 4).
28. Software updates the Subordinate Bus Number registers in the Host/PCI bridge, bridge A, and bridge C to 4.
29. Continuing with its depth-first search, a read is performed from bus 4, device 0, function 0's Vendor ID register.
30. A valid Vendor ID is returned, indicating that bus 4, device 0, function 0 exists.
31. The Header Type field in the Header register contains the value zero (0000000b) indicating that this is an Endpoint device. In addition, bit 7 is a 0, indicating that this is a single-function device.
32. The device's Capability Register contains the value 0000b in the Device/Port Type field indicating that this is an Endpoint device.
33. Having exhausted the current leg of the depth first search, the enumeration software backs up one level (to bus 2) and moves on to read the Vendor ID of the next device (device 2). The example assumes that devices 2-through-31 are not implemented on bus 2, so no additional devices are discovered on bus 2.
34. The enumeration software backs up to the bus within the Root Complex (bus 0) and moves on to read the Vendor ID of the next device (device 1). The example assumes that bridge B is device 1, function 0 on bus 0.
35. In the same manner as previously described, the enumeration software discovers bridge B and performs a series of configuration writes to set bridge

B's bus number registers as follows:
- Primary Bus Number Register = 0.
- Secondary Bus Number Register = 5.
- Subordinate Bus Number Register = 5.

Bridge B is now aware that the number of the bus directly attached to its downstream side is 5 (Secondary Bus Number = 5) and the number of the bus farthest downstream of it is 5 (Subordinate Bus Number = 5).

36. The Host/PCI's Subordinate Bus Number is updated to 5.
37. Bridge F is then discovered and a series of configuration writes are performed to set its bus number registers as follows:
    - Primary Bus Number Register = 5.
    - Secondary Bus Number Register = 6.
    - Subordinate Bus Number Register = 6.

    Bridge F is now aware that the number of the bus directly attached to its downstream side is 6 (Secondary Bus Number = 6) and the number of the bus farthest downstream of it is 6 (Subordinate Bus Number = 6).
38. The Host/PCI bridge's and bridge B' Subordinate Bus Number registers are updated to 6.
39. Bridge G is then discovered and a series of configuration writes are performed to set its bus number registers as follows:
    - Primary Bus Number Register = 6.
    - Secondary Bus Number Register = 7.
    - Subordinate Bus Number Register = 7.

    Bridge F is now aware that the number of the bus directly attached to its downstream side is 7 (Secondary Bus Number = 7) and the number of the bus farthest downstream of it is 7 (Subordinate Bus Number = 7).
40. The Host/PCI bridge's Subordinate Bus Number register is updated to 7. Bridge B's and F's Subordinate Bus Number registers are also updated to 7.
41. A single-function Endpoint device is discovered at bus 7, device 0, function 0.
42. Bridge H is then discovered and a series of configuration writes are performed to set its bus number registers as follows:
    - Primary Bus Number Register = 6.
    - Secondary Bus Number Register = 8.
    - Subordinate Bus Number Register = 8.

    Bridge F is now aware that the number of the bus directly attached to its downstream side is 8 (Secondary Bus Number = 8) and the number of the bus farthest downstream of it is 8 (Subordinate Bus Number = 8).
43. The Host/PCI bridge's Subordinate Bus Number register is updated to 8. Bridge B's and F's Subordinate Bus Number registers are also updated to 8.
44. Bridge J is discovered and its Capability register's Device/Port Type fields identifies it as a PCI Express-to-PCI bridge.
45. A series of configuration writes are performed to set bridge J's bus number registers as follows:

- Primary Bus Number Register = 8
- Secondary Bus Number Register = 9.
- Subordinate Bus Number Register = 9.

Bridge F is now aware that the number of the bus directly attached to its downstream side is 9 (Secondary Bus Number = 9) and the number of the bus farthest downstream of it is 9 (Subordinate Bus Number = 9).

46. The Host/PCI bridge's Subordinate Bus Number register is updated to 9. Bridge B's, bridge F's, and bridge H's Subordinate Bus Number registers are also updated to 9.
47. All devices and their respective functions on bus 9 are discovered and none of them are bridges.
48. Bridge I is then discovered and a series of configuration writes are performed to set its bus number registers as follows:
    - Primary Bus Number Register = 6.
    - Secondary Bus Number Register = 10.
    - Subordinate Bus Number Register = 10.

    Bridge I is now aware that the number of the bus directly attached to its downstream side is 10 (Secondary Bus Number = 10) and the number of the bus farthest downstream of it is 10 (Subordinate Bus Number = 10).
49. The Host/PCI bridge's Subordinate Bus Number register is updated to 10. Bridge B's and bridge F's Subordinate Bus Number registers are also updated to 10.
50. A single-function Endpoint device is discovered at bus 10, device 0, function 0.

Figure 21-2: Example System Before Bus Enumeration

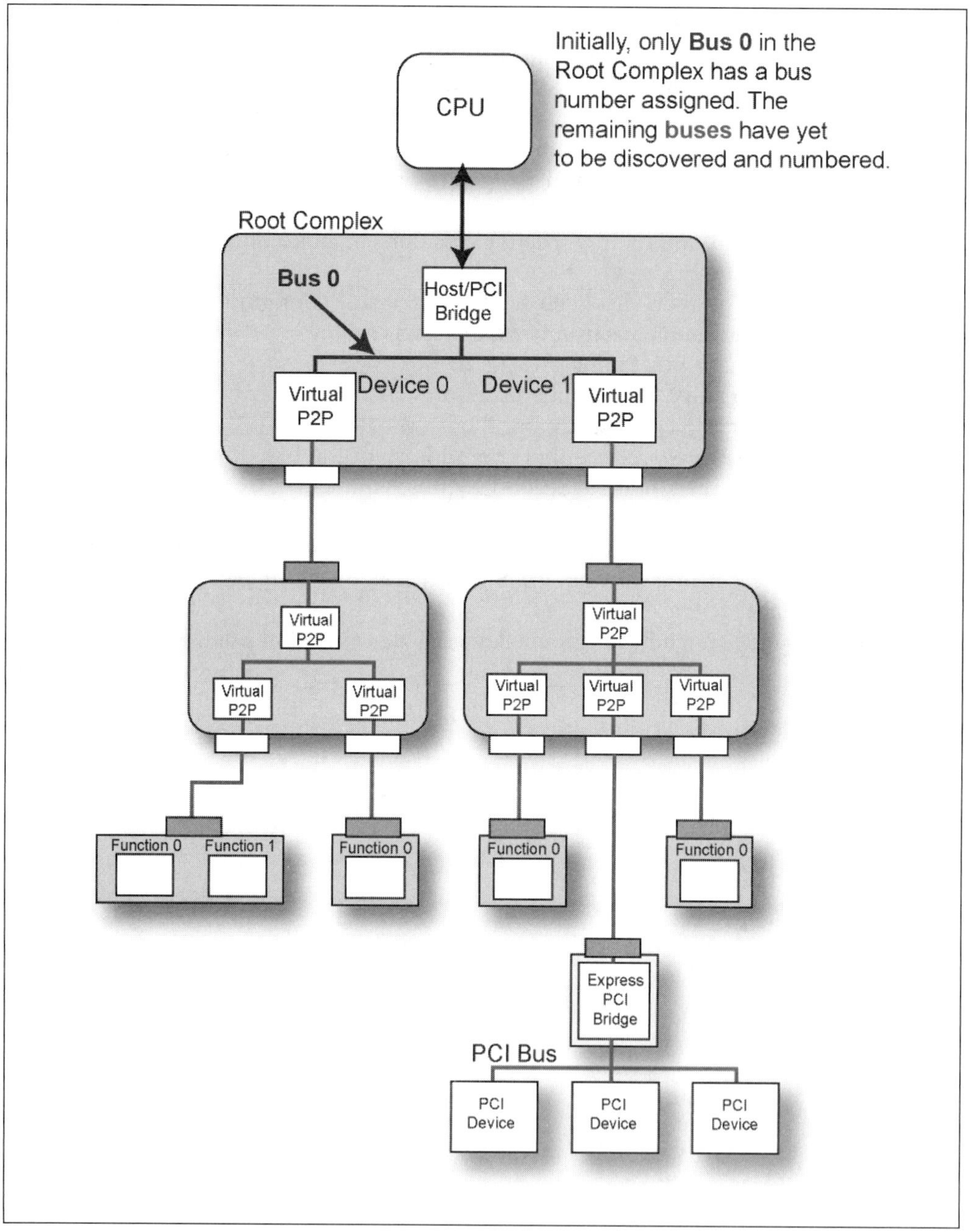

Figure 21-3: Example System After Bus Enumeration

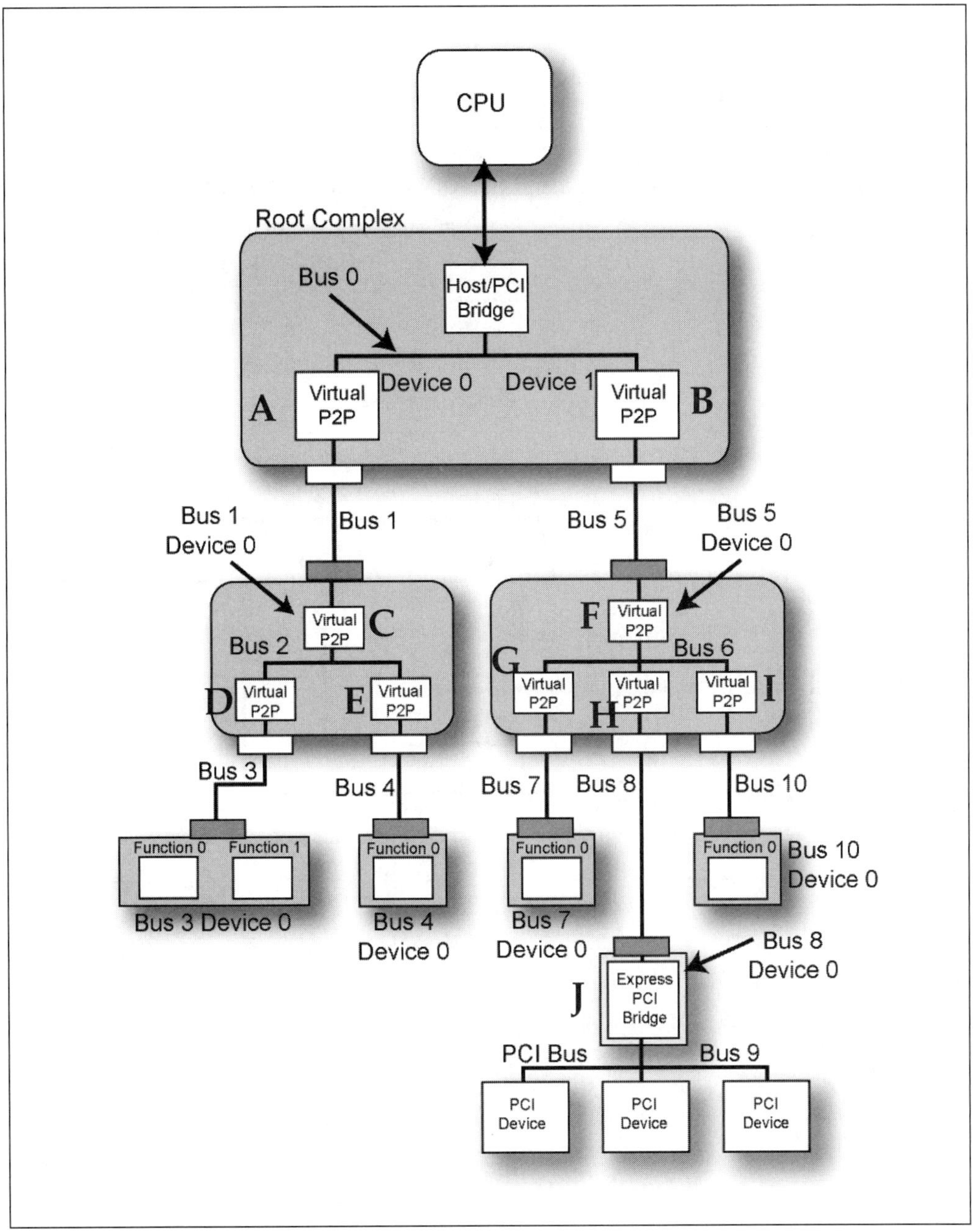

Figure 21-4: Header Type Register

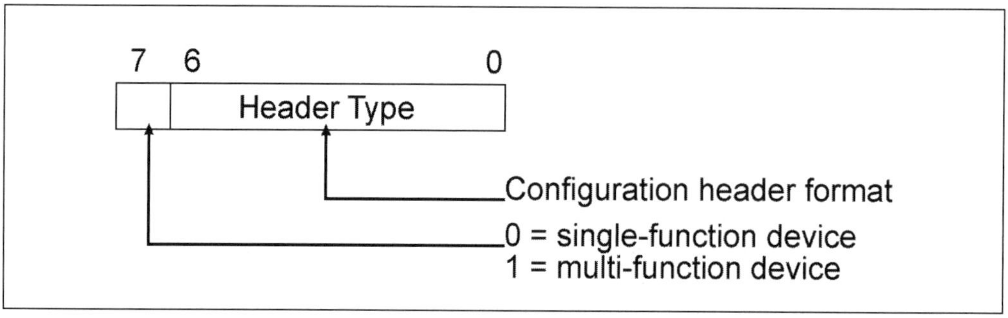

Figure 21-5: Capability Register

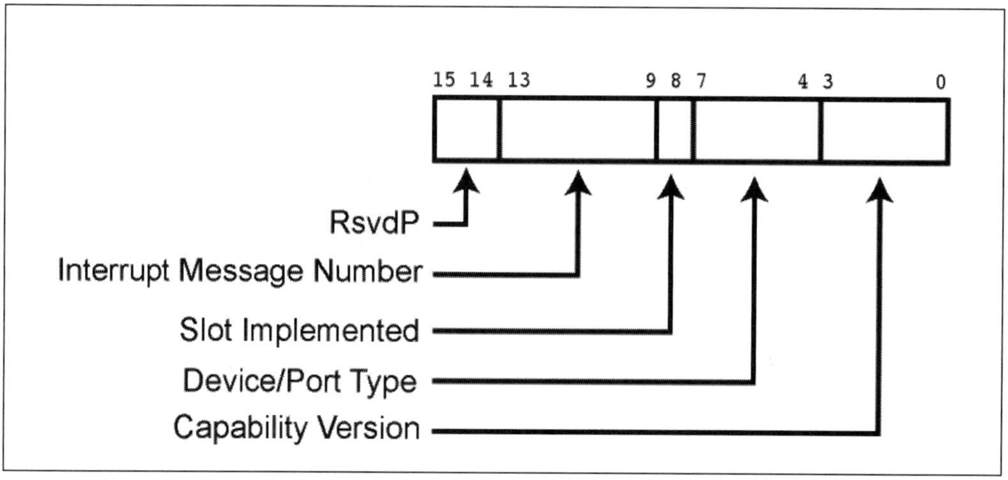

Figure 21-6: Header Type 0

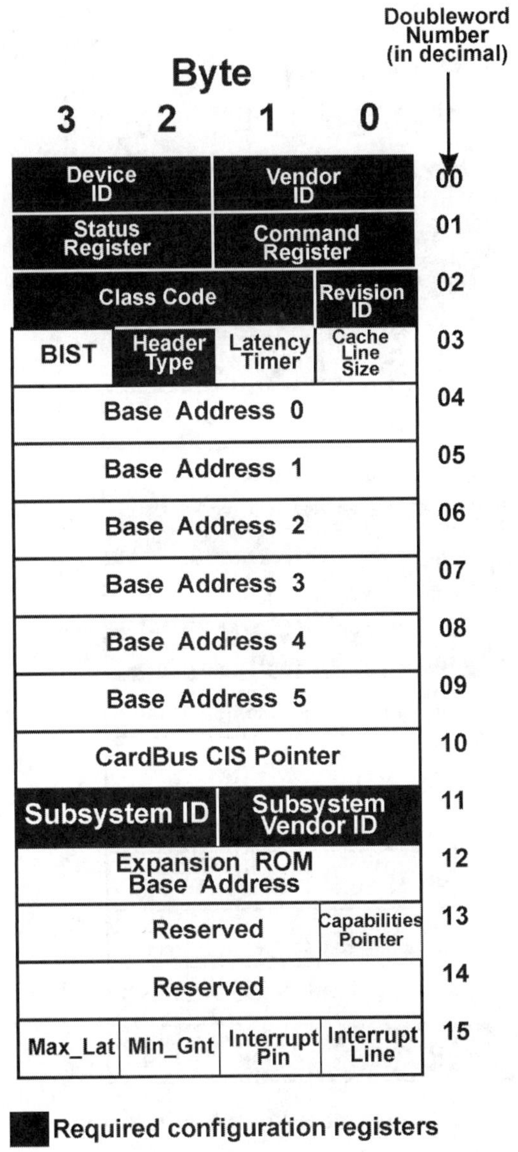

Figure 21-7: Header Type 1

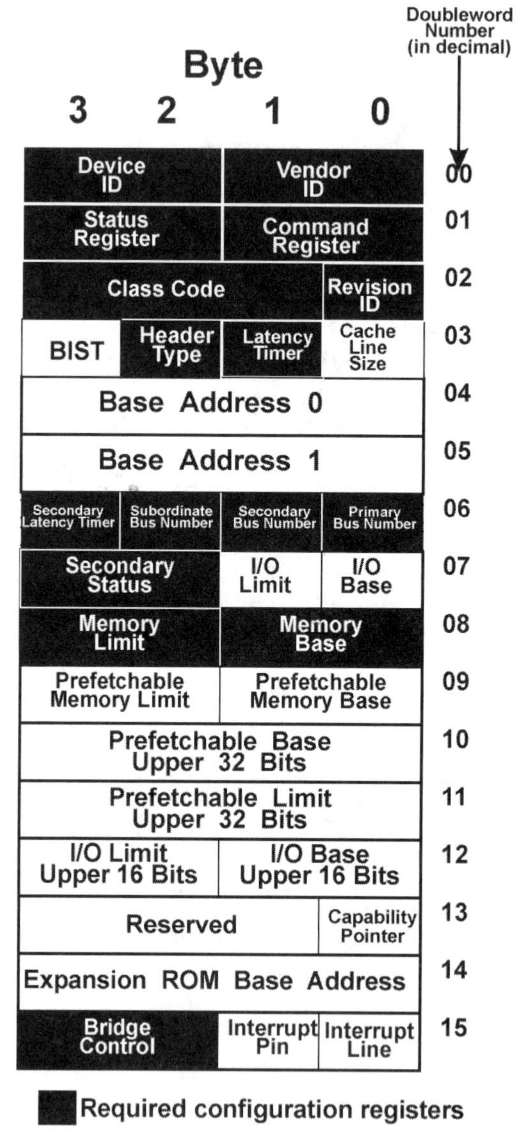

Table 21 - 1: Capability Register's Device/Port Type Field Encoding

Value	Description
0000b	PCI Express Endpoint device.
0001b	Legacy PCI Express Endpoint device.
0100b	Root Port of PCI Express Root Complex. This value is only valid for devices/functions that implement a Type 01h PCI Configuration Space header.
0101b	Upstream Port of PCI Express Switch. This value is only valid for devices/functions that implement a Type 01h PCI Configuration Space header.
0110b	Downstream Port of PCI Express Switch. This value is only valid for devices/functions that implement a Type 01h PCI Configuration Space header.
0111b	PCI Express-to-PCI/PCI-X Bridge. This value is only valid for devices/functions that implement a Type 01h PCI Configuration Space header.
1000b	PCI/PCI-X to PCI Express Bridge. This value is only valid for devices/functions that implement a Type 01h PCI Configuration Space header.
All other encodings are reserved.	

Enumerating a System With Multiple Root Complexes

Refer to Figure 21-8 on page 757. In a system with multiple Root Complexes, each Root Complex:

- Implements the Configuration Address Port and the Configuration Data Port at the same IO addresses (if it's an x86-based system).
- Implements the Enhanced Configuration Mechanism.
- Contains a Host/PCI bridge.
- Implements the Bus Number and Subordinate Bus Number registers at separate addresses known to the configuration software.

In the example illustration, each Root Complex is a member of the chipset and one of them is designated as the bridge to bus 0 (let's call this the primary Root Complex) while the other one is designated as the bridge to bus 255 (bus FFh; let's call it the secondary Root Complex). The default Bus Number and Subordinate Bus Number register values at startup time are:

- In the primary Root Complex, both the Bus Number and Subordinate Bus Number registers are set to 0.
- In the secondary Root Complex, both the Bus Number and Subordinate Bus Number registers are set to FFh (255d).

Operational Characteristics of the PCI-Compatible Mechanism

In order to prevent contention on the processor's FSB signals, only one of the bridges responds to the processor's accesses to the configuration ports:

1. When the processor initiates the IO write to the Configuration Address Port, only one of the Host/PCI bridges (typically the one in the primary Root Complex) actively participates in the transaction. The other bridge quietly snarfs the data as it's written to the active participant.
2. Both bridges then compare the target bus number to their respective Bus Number and Subordinate Bus Number registers. If the target bus doesn't reside behind a particular Host/PCI bridge, that bridge doesn't convert the subsequent access to its Configuration Data Port into a configuration access on its bus (in other words, it ignores the transaction).
3. A subsequent read or write access to the Configuration Data Port is only accepted by the Host/PCI bridge that is the gateway to the target bus. This bridge responds to the processor's transaction and the other ignores it.
4. When the access is made to the Configuration Data Port, the selected bridge tests the state of the Enable bit in its Configuration Address Port. If the Enabled bit = 1, the bridge converts the processor's IO access into a configuration access:
   - o If the target bus is the bus immediately on the other side of the Host/PCI bridge, the bridge converts the access to a Type 0 configuration access on its secondary bus.
   - o Otherwise, it converts it into a Type 1 configuration access.

Operational Characteristics of the Enhanced Configuration Mechanism

In order to prevent contention on the processor's FSB signals, only one of the bridges responds to the processor's accesses to the enhanced configuration memory-mapped IO space:

1. When the processor initiates a memory-mapped IO access to a memory location within the enhanced configuration memory-mapped IO address range, the Host/PCI bridges in each Root Complex examines address bits A[27:20] to determine the target bus number.
2. The bridge wherein the target bus falls within the range of buses downstream of that bridge (as defined by the contents of its Bus Number and Subordinate Bus Number registers) acts as the target of the processor's FSB transaction while the other bridge does not actively participate in the transaction.
3. The bridge with a bus compare converts the processor's memory access into a configuration access:
   - o If the target bus is the bus immediately on the other side of the Host/PCI bridge, the bridge converts the access to a Type 0 configuration access on its secondary bus.
   - o Otherwise, it converts it into a Type 1 configuration access.

The Enumeration Process

Refer to Figure 21-8 on page 757. The process of enumerating the buses downstream of the primary Root Complex is identical to that described in "Enumerating a System With a Single Root Complex" on page 742. During the enumeration of the left-hand tree structure, the Host/PCI bridge in the secondary Root Complex ignored all of the memory-mapped IO configuration accesses because, in each case, the target bus number that was specified was less than bus 255. It should be noted that, although detected and numbered, bus 8 has no device attached.

Once that enumeration process has been completed, the enumeration software takes the following steps to enumerate the buses and devices downstream of the secondary Root Complex:

1. The enumeration software changes both the Bus Number and Subordinate Bus Number register values in the secondary Root Complex's Host/PCI

bridge to bus 11 (one greater than the highest-numbered bus beneath the primary Root Complex).

2. The enumeration software then starts searching on bus 11 and discovers the PCI-to-PCI bridge attached to the downstream Root Port.
3. A series of configuration writes are performed to set its bus number registers as follows:
   - Primary Bus Number Register = 11.
   - Secondary Bus Number Register = 12.
   - Subordinate Bus Number Register = 12.

   The bridge is now aware that the number of the bus directly attached to its downstream side is 12 (Secondary Bus Number = 12) and the number of the bus farthest downstream of it is 12 (Subordinate Bus Number = 12).
4. The Host/PCI's Subordinate Bus Number is updated to 12.
5. A single-function Endpoint device is discovered at bus 12, device 0, function 0.
6. Enumeration continues on bus 11 and no additional devices are discovered. This completes the bus/device enumeration process.

Figure 21-8: Peer Root Complexes

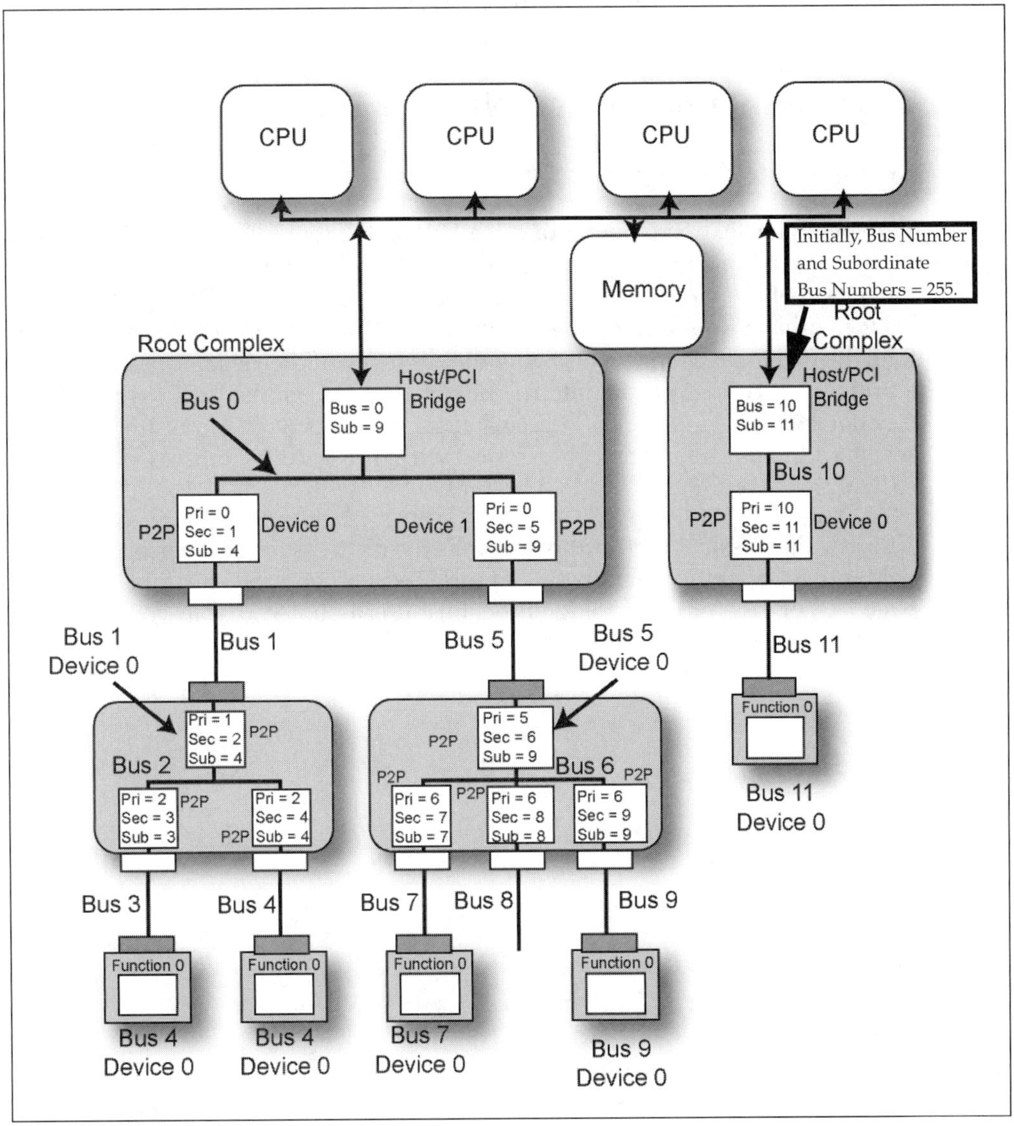

A Multifunction Device Within a Root Complex or a Switch

A Multifunction Device Within a Root Complex

Refer to Figure 21-9 on page 759.

The spec is unclear on whether or not a P2P on the root bus within a Root Complex can be a multifunction device. It states that the rules regarding the implementation of the Header Register (see Figure 21-7 on page 752) in a PCI-to-PCI bridge within a Root Complex or a Switch are defined by the PCI 2.3 spec rather than the PCI Express spec. This being the case, it would be legal for function 0 in a bridge that resides on the internal bus of a Root Complex to have the Multifunction bit (bit 7) in the Header Register set to 1. This would indicate that up to seven additional functions could reside within this Root Complex device and each of them could be PCI-to-PCI bridges.

The only open issue in the authors' eyes is the contents of the Device/Port Type field in the Capability register (see Figure 21-5 on page 750 and Table 21 - 1 on page 753) of each of these bridge functions. It is assumed that it would have to be 0100b (i.e., Root Port of PCI Express Root Complex).

Figure 21-9: Multifunction Bridges in Root Complex

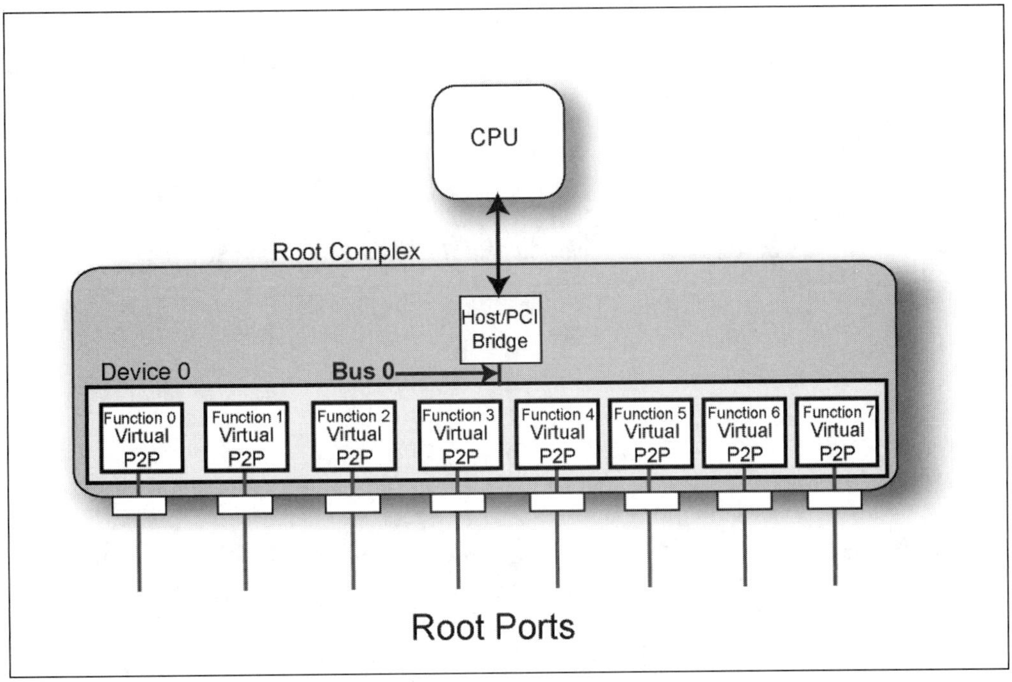

A Multifunction Device Within a Switch

Refer to Figure 21-10 on page 760 and Figure 21-11 on page 761. The spec doesn't preclude the inclusion of a multifunction device within a switch wherein each of the functions represents a PCI-to-PCI bridge to a downstream link.

In the first example the switch's internal bus implements two multifunction devices each of which contains four functions, and each function is the bridge to one of the switch's downstream ports. In the switch's upstream port bridge, the contents of the Device/Port Type field in the Capability register (see Figure 21-5 on page 750 and Table 21 - 1 on page 753) is 0101b (i.e., Upstream Port of PCI Express Switch).

In the second example, the bridge representing the switch's upstream port is device 0 on the link (i.e. bus) entering the switch and it is a multifunction device containing two functions each of which is a bridge to a separate internal switch bus. The contents of the Device/Port Type field in the Capability register (see

Figure 21-5 on page 750 and Table 21 - 1 on page 753) of each of these functions is 0101b (i.e., Upstream Port of PCI Express Switch). Each of the internal buses has two multifunction devices attached, and each function is the bridge to one of the switch's downstream ports. The contents of the Device/Port Type field in the Capability register (see Figure 21-5 on page 750 and Table 21 - 1 on page 753) of each of these functions is 0110b (i.e., Downstream Port of PCI Express Switch).

Figure 21-10: First Example of a Multifunction Bridge In a Switch

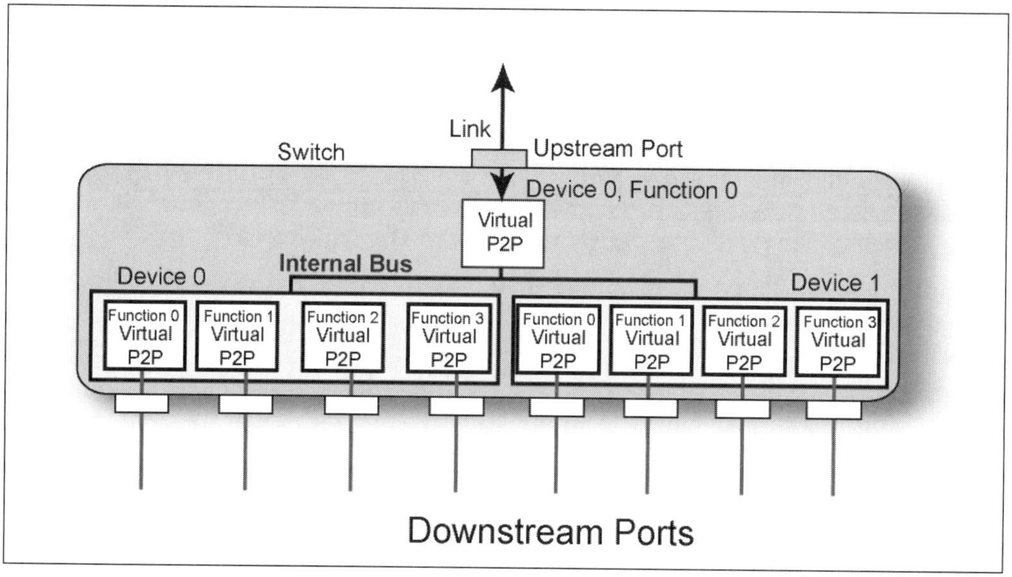

Figure 21-11: Second Example of a Multifunction Bridge In a Switch

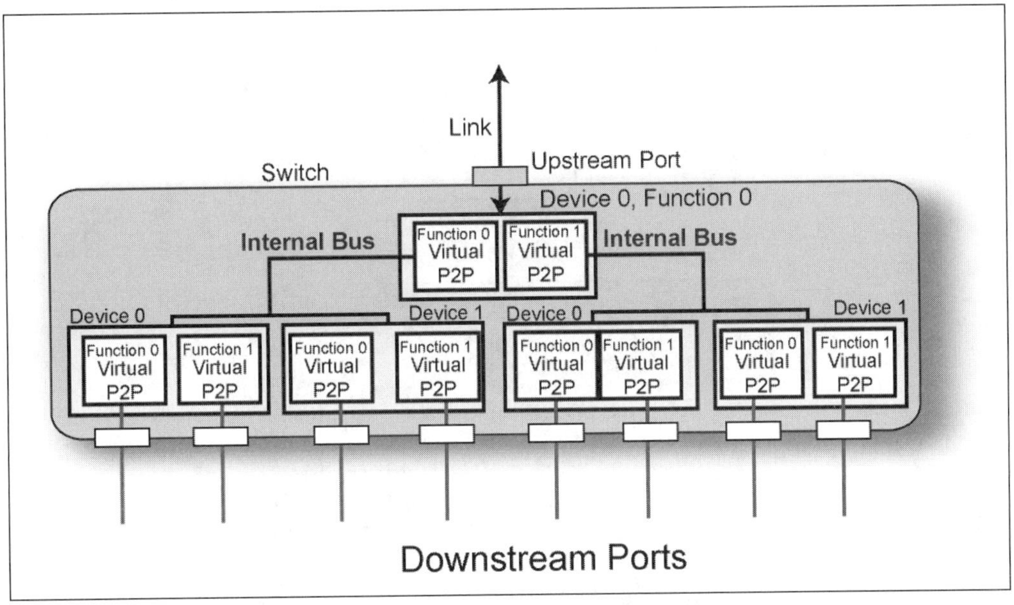

An Endpoint Embedded in a Switch or Root Complex

The spec contains the following two statements:

- "Endpoint devices (represented by Type 00h Configuration Space headers) may not appear to configuration software on the switch's internal bus as peers of the virtual PCI-to-PCI Bridges representing the Switch Downstream Ports."
- "Switch Downstream Ports are PCI-PCI Bridges bridging from the internal bus to buses representing the Downstream PCI Express Links from a PCI Express Switch. Only the PCI-PCI Bridges representing the Switch Downstream Ports may appear on the internal bus. Endpoints, represented by Type 0 configuration space headers, may not appear on the internal bus."

Nothing in this text forbids the implementation of an Endpoint device within a switch. In addition, nothing in the spec forbids the implementation of an Endpoint device within a Root Complex. Figure 21-12 on page 762 and Figure 21-13 on page 763 illustrate examples of these design cases.

Figure 21-12: Embedded Root Endpoint

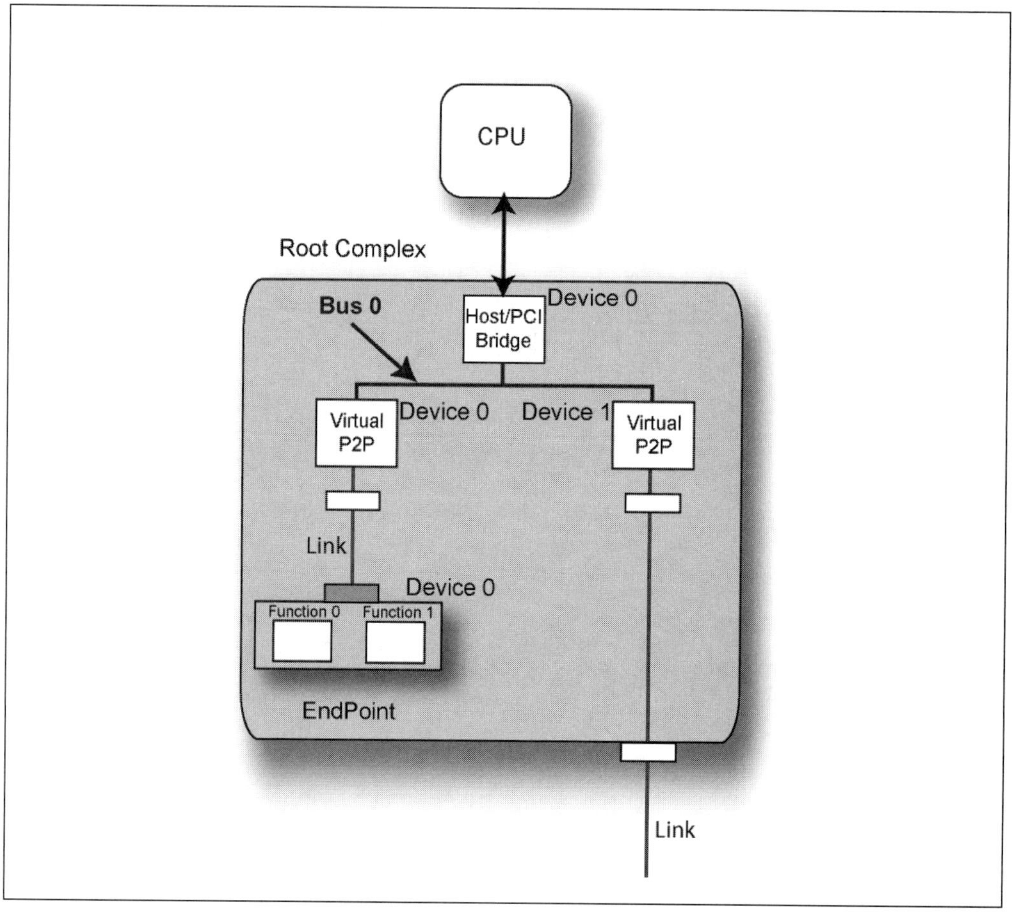

Figure 21-13: Embedded Switch Endpoint

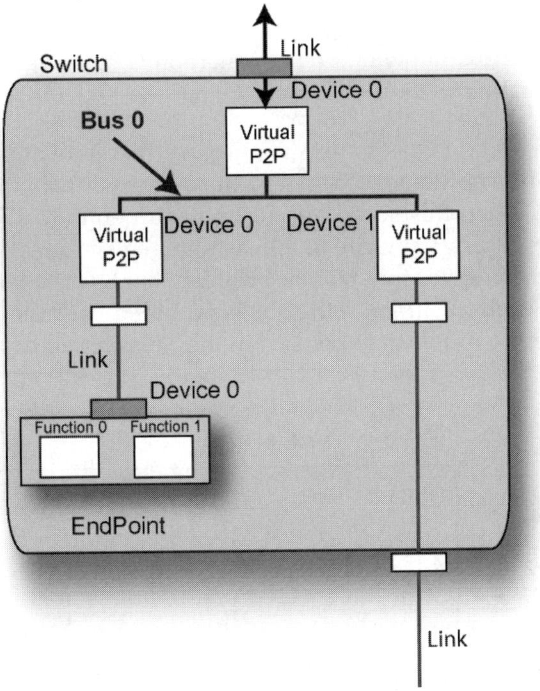

Memorize Your Identity

General

Whenever a function initiates a transaction as a requester, it must supply its Requester ID in the packet's header. Likewise, when a function initiates a transaction as a Completer, it must supply its Completer ID in the packet header. Both of these IDs are comprised of the Bus Number, Device Number and Function Number.

The function "knows" which function number it is within its device, but how does it know the device it resides within and what bus it resides on?

Each time that the source bridge for a bus initiates a type 0 configuration write transaction (see Figure 21-14 on page 764), it supplies the targeted function with the bus number from its Secondary Bus Number register and the number of the device that the function resides within. The function is required to save this information for use in forming its IDs when it initiates a transaction as either a Requester or as a Completer. The information is not saved in program readable registers but rather in a function-specific manner.

A hot-plug event such as the installation or the removal of a device can cause the enumeration software to re-assign bus numbers in a portion of the bus hierarchy. If and when this should occur, the enumeration software is required to perform a configuration write to at least one register (any register) within each function in each device that resides on a bus that has received a new number. In this manner, each function on the bus is provided with the new bus number (as well as its device number) to be used in their respective IDs.

Figure 21-14: Type 0 Configuration Write Request Packet Header

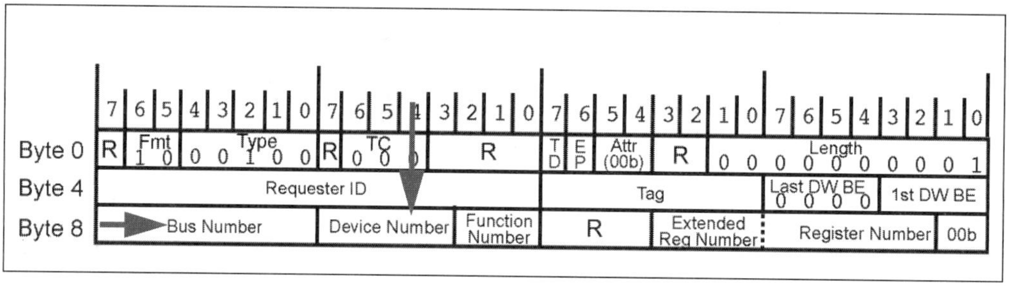

Root Complex Bus Number/Device Number Assignment

The manner in which the bus number and device number are assigned to functions residing on the internal bus of a Root Complex is design-specific.

Initiating Requests Prior To ID Assignment

Before the first type 0 configuration write is performed to a function, it does not know the bus number and device number portion of its ID. While it remains in this state, a function is not permitted to initiate non-posted requests (memory write requests and message requests). There is one exception:

- Functions within a Root Complex are permitted to initiate requests for accesses to system boot device(s).

Initiating Completions Prior to ID Assignment

If a function must generate a Completion before the first type 0 configuration write is performed to it, the Bus Number and Device Number fields in its Completer ID must be set to zeros. The Request issuer (the Requester) must ignore the value returned in the Completer ID field.

Root Complex Register Blocks (RCRBs)

What Problem Does an RCRB Address?

Refer to Figure 21-15 on page 766. Main memory is an extremely popular target. In addition to the processor, it is accessed by the graphics controller and is frequently accessed by PCI, PCI-X and PCI Express devices. This being the case, at a given moment in time, the Root Complex may simultaneously receive memory access requests through multiple ingress ports:

- The FSB interface.
- The graphics link.
- One or more Root Ports.

It should be obvious that a traffic director (labeled "Port/VC Arbitration") must be implemented within the Root Complex. In its simplest form, the Root Complex may implement a hardwired traffic director.

In addition to simply handling multiple simultaneous requests, the traffic director may also have to deal with QoS issues. Some of the memory access requesters may require faster access than others. The Root Complex Register Block would be used to program the memory controller's egress port logic regarding TC-to-VC mapping and the VC arbitration algorithm.

Additional Information on RCRBs

Additional information on RCRBs may be found in "RCRB" on page 957.

Figure 21-15: RCRB Example

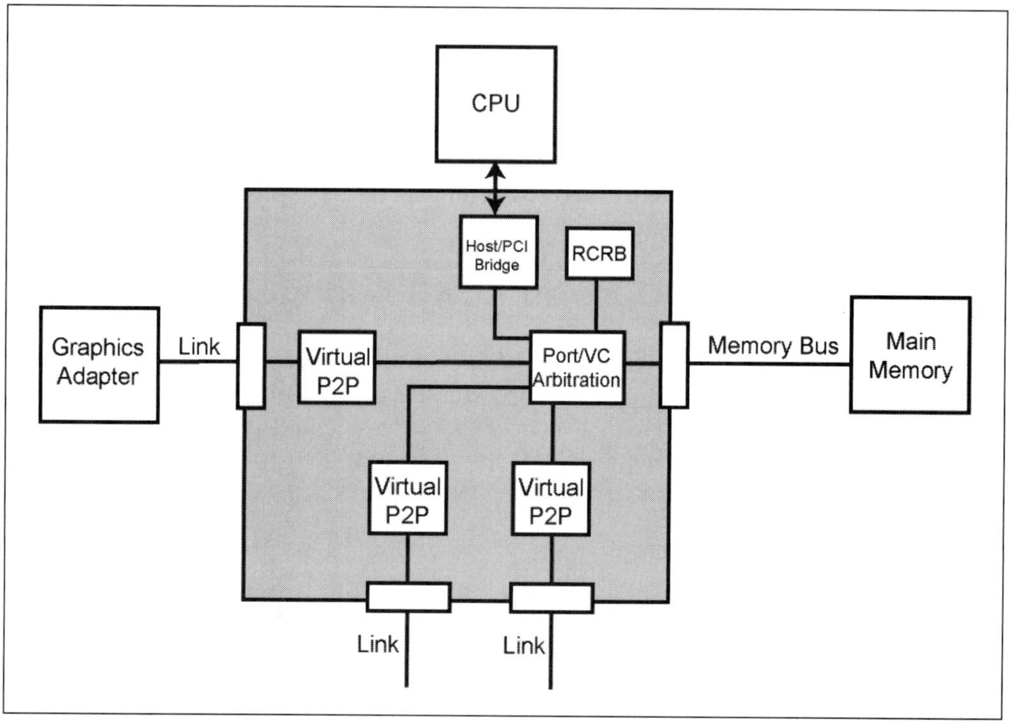

Miscellaneous Rules

A Split Configuration Transaction Requires a Single Completion

If a configuration transaction is split, the Requester expects to receive one and only one Completion transaction containing the dword or less of requested read data.

An Issue For PCI Express-to-PCI or -PCI-X Bridges

If such a bridge receives a configuration request targeting a PCI or PCI-X function and the Extended Register Address field is non-zero, the bridge must return a UR (Unsupported Request) status to the Requester.

PCI Special Cycle Transactions

If software must cause a PCI Special Cycle transaction to be generated on a PCI or PCI-X bus, it takes the following actions.

To prime the Host/PCI bridge to generate a PCI Special Cycle transaction, software must write a 32-bit value with the following content to the Configuration Address Port at IO address 0CF8h:

- Bus Number = the target PCI Bus that the Special Cycle transaction is to be performed on.
- Device Number = all ones (31d, or 1Fh).
- Function Number = all ones (7d).
- Dword Number = all zeros.

After this has been accomplished, the next write to the Configuration Data Port at IO port 0CFCh causes the Host/PCI bridge to pass the transaction through as a Type 1 configuration write (so that it can be submitted to PCI-to-PCI bridges farther out in the hierarchy). The type 1 configuration write request will flow unchanged through all of the bridges in the path to the target PCI/PCI-X bus until it finally arrives at the destination PCI Express-to-PCI/PCI-X bridge. This bridge converts the request in to a PCI Special Cycle transaction and the data written to the Host/PCI bridge's Configuration Data Port is supplied as the message in the Data Phase of the resultant PCI or PCI-X transaction.

22 PCI Compatible Configuration Registers

The Previous Chapter

The previous chapter provides a detailed description of the discovery process and bus numbering. It described:

- Enumerating a system with a single Root Complex
- Enumerating a system with multiple Root Complexes
- A multifunction device within a Root Complex or a Switch
- An Endpoint embedded in a Switch or Root Complex
- Automatic Requester ID assignment.
- Root Complex Register Blocks (RCRBs)

This Chapter

This chapter provides a detailed description of the configuration registers residing a function's PCI-compatible configuration space. This includes the registers for both non-bridge and bridge functions.

The Next Chapter

The next chapter provides a detailed description of device ROMs associated with PCI, PCI Express, and PCI-X functions. This includes the following topics:

- device ROM detection.
- internal code/data format.
- shadowing.

- initialization code execution.
- interrupt hooking.

Header Type 0

General

Figure 22-1 on page 771 illustrates the format of a function's Header region (for functions other than PCI-to-PCI bridges and CardBus bridges). The registers marked in black are always mandatory. Note that although many of the configuration registers in the figure are not marked mandatory, a register may be mandatory for a particular type of device. The subsequent sections define each register and any circumstances wherein it may be mandatory.

As noted earlier, this format is defined as Header Type 0. The registers within the Header are used to identify the device, to control its functionality and to sense its status in a generic manner. The usage of the device's remaining 48 dwords of PCI-compatible configuration space is intended for device-specific registers, but, with the advent of the 2.2 PCI spec, is also used as an overflow area for some new registers defined in the PCI spec (for more information, refer to "Capabilities Pointer Register" on page 779).

Figure 22-1: Header Type 0

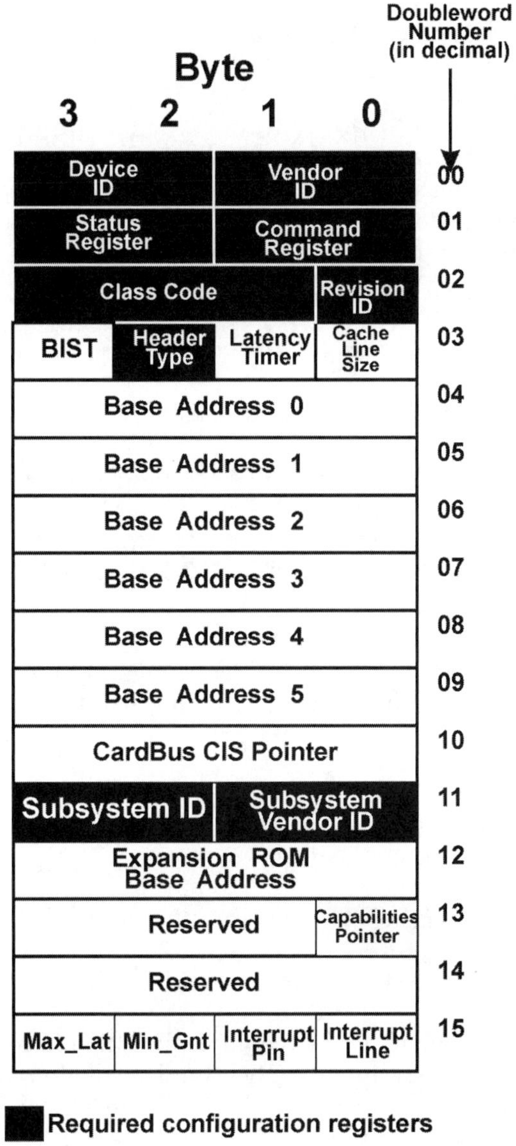

Header Type 0 Registers Compatible With PCI

The Header Type 0 PCI configuration registers that are implemented and used identically in PCI and PCI Express are:

- Vendor ID register.
- Device ID register.
- Revision ID register.
- Class Code register.
- Subsystem Vendor ID register.
- Subsystem ID register.
- Header Type register.
- BIST register.
- Capabilities Pointer register.
- CardBus CIS Pointer register.
- Expansion ROM Base Address register.

The sections that follow provide a description of each of these registers.

Header Type 0 Registers Incompatible With PCI

In a non-bridge PCI Express function, the definitions of the following configuration registers in the function's PCI-compatible configuration space differ from the PCI spec's definition of the respective register definitions:

- Command Register
- Status Register
- Cache Line Size Register
- Master Latency Timer Register
- Interrupt Line Register
- Interrupt Pin Register
- Base Address Registers
- Min_Gnt/Max_Lat Registers

The sections that follow define the implementation/usage differences of these registers. For a full description of their implementation in a PCI function, refer to the MindShare book entitled *PCI System Architecture, Fourth Edition* (published by Addison-Wesley). For a full description of their implementation in a PCI-X function, refer to the MindShare book entitled *PCI-X System Architecture,* First Edition (published by Addison-Wesley).

Registers Used to Identify Device's Driver

The OS uses some combination of the following mandatory registers to determine which driver to load for a device:

- Vendor ID.
- Device ID.
- Revision ID.
- Class Code.
- SubSystem Vendor ID.
- SubSystem ID.

Vendor ID Register

PCI-Compatible register. Always mandatory. This 16-bit register identifies the manufacturer of the function. The value hardwired in this read-only register is assigned by a central authority (the PCI SIG) that controls issuance of the numbers. The value FFFFh is reserved and must be returned by the Host/PCI bridge when an attempt is made to perform a configuration read from a configuration register in a non-existent function. In PCI or PCI-X, the read attempt results in a Master Abort, while in PCI Express it results in the return of UR (Unsupported Request) completion status. In either case, the bridge must return a Vendor ID of FFFFh. The error status returned is not considered to be an error, but the specification says that the bridge must nonetheless set its Received Master Abort bit in its configuration Status register.

Device ID Register

PCI-Compatible register. Always mandatory. This 16-bit value is assigned by the function manufacturer and identifies the type of function. In conjunction with the Vendor ID and possibly the Revision ID, the Device ID can be used to locate a function-specific (and perhaps revision-specific) driver for the function.

Revision ID Register

PCI-Compatible register. Always mandatory. This 8-bit value is assigned by the function manufacturer and identifies the revision number of the function. If the vendor has supplied a revision-specific driver, this is handy in ensuring that the correct driver is loaded by the OS.

Class Code Register

General. *PCI-Compatible register. Always mandatory.* The Class Code register is pictured in Figure 22-2 on page 775. It is a 24-bit, read-only register divided into three fields: base Class, Sub Class, and Programming Interface. It identifies the basic function of the function (e.g., a mass storage controller), a more specific function sub-class (e.g., IDE mass storage controller), and, in some cases, a register-specific programming interface (such as a specific flavor of the IDE register set).

- The upper byte defines the base Class of the function,
- the middle byte defines a sub-class within the base Class,
- and the lower byte defines the Programming Interface.

The currently-defined base Class codes are listed in Table 22-1 on page 775. Table 2 on page 1020 through Table 19 on page 1031 define the Subclasses within each base Class. For many Class/SubClass categories, the Programming Interface byte is hardwired to return zeros (in other words, it has no meaning). For some, such as VGA-compatible functions and IDE controllers, it does have meaning.

This register is useful when the OS is attempting to locate a function that a Class driver can work with. As an example, assume that a particular device driver has been written to work with any display adapter that is 100% XGA register set-compatible. If the OS can locate a function with a Class of 03h (see Table 22-1 on page 775) and a Sub Class of 01h (see Table 5 on page 1022), the driver will work with that function. A Class driver is more flexible than a driver that has been written to work only with a specific function from a specific vendor.

The Programming Interface Byte. For some functions (such as the XGA display adapter used as an example in the previous section) the combination of the Class Code and Sub Class Code is sufficient to fully-define its level of register set compatibility. The register set layout for some function types, however, can vary from one implementation to another. As an example, from a programming interface perspective there are a number of flavors of IDE mass storage controllers, so it's not sufficient to identify yourself as an IDE mass storage controller. The Programming Interface byte value (see Table 20 on page 1031) provides the final level of granularity that identifies the exact register set layout of the function.

Detailed Class Code Description. A detailed description of the currently-defined Classes, SubClasses, and Programming Interface Byte values can be found in Appendix D.

Figure 22-2: Class Code Register

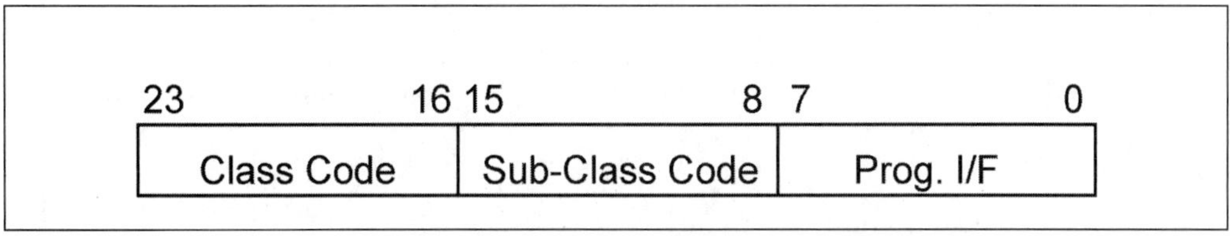

Table 22-1: Defined Class Codes

Class	Description
00h	Function built before class codes were defined (in other words: before rev 2.0 of the PCI spec).
01h	Mass storage controller.
02h	Network controller.
03h	Display controller.
04h	Multimedia device.
05h	Memory controller.
06h	Bridge device.
07h	Simple communications controllers.
08h	Base system peripherals.
09h	Input devices.
0Ah	Docking stations.
0Bh	Processors.
0Ch	Serial bus controllers.
0Dh	Wireless controllers.
0Eh	Intelligent IO controllers.

Table 22-1: Defined Class Codes (Continued)

Class	Description
0Fh	Satellite communications controllers.
10h	Encryption/Decryption controllers.
11h	Data acquisition and signal processing controllers.
12h-FEh	Reserved.
FFh	Device does not fit any of the defined class codes.

Subsystem Vendor ID and Subsystem ID Registers

General. *PCI-Compatible register. Mandatory.* This register pair was added in revision 2.1 of the PCI spec and was optional. The 2.2 PCI spec and the PCI-X spec state that they are mandatory except for those functions that have a base Class of 06h (a Bridge) with a Sub Class of 00h-04h (refer to Table 8 on page 1023), or a base Class of 08h (Base System Peripherals) with a Sub Class of 00h-03h (see Table 10 on page 1026). This excludes bridges of the following types:

- Host/PCI
- PCI-to-EISA
- PCI-to-ISA
- PCI-to-Micro Channel
- PCI-to-PCI

It also excludes the following generic system peripherals:

- Interrupt Controller
- DMA Controller
- Programmable Timers
- RTC Controller

The Subsystem Vendor ID is obtained from the SIG, while the vendor supplies its own Subsystem ID (the full name of this register is really "Subsystem Device ID", but the "device" is silent). A value of zero in these registers indicates there isn't a Subsystem Vendor and Subsystem ID associated with the function.

The Problem Solved by This Register Pair. A function may reside on a card or within an embedded device. Functions designed around the same

PCI/PCI-X, or PCI Express core logic (produced by a third-party) may have the same Vendor and Device IDs (if the core logic vendor hardwired their own IDs into these registers). If this is the case, the OS would have a problem identifying the correct driver to load into memory for the function.

These two mandatory registers (Subsystem Vendor ID and Subsystem ID) are used to uniquely identify the add-in card or subsystem that the function resides within. Using these two registers, the OS can distinguish the difference between cards or subsystems manufactured by different vendors but designed around the same third-party core logic. This permits the Plug-and-Play OS to locate the correct driver to load into memory.

Must Contain Valid Data When First Accessed. These two registers must contain their assigned values before the system first accesses them. If software attempts to access them before they have been initialized, the device must issue:

- a Retry to the master (in PCI).
- a Completion with CRS (Configuration Request Retry Completion Status) in PCI Express.

The values in these registers could be hardwired, loaded from a serial EEPROM, determined from hardware strapping pins, etc.

Header Type Register

PCI-Compatible register. Always mandatory. Figure 22-3 on page 778 illustrates the format of the Header Type register. Bits [6:0] of this one byte register define the format of dwords 4-through-15 of the function's configuration Header (see Figure 22-1 on page 771 and Figure 22-13 on page 803). In addition, bit seven defines the device as a single- (bit 7 = 0) or multifunction (bit 7 = 1) device. During configuration, the programmer determines if there are any other functions in this device that require configuration by testing the state of bit seven.

Currently, the only Header formats defined other than that pictured in Figure 22-1 on page 771 (**Header Type Zero**) are:

- **Header Type One** (PCI-to-PCI bridge Header format; description can be found in "Header Type 1" on page 802).
- and **Header Type Two** (CardBus bridge; detail can be found in the PC Card specification and in the MindShare book entitled *CardBus System Architecture* (published by Addison-Wesley).

Future versions of the specification may define other formats.

Figure 22-3: Header Type Register Bit Assignment

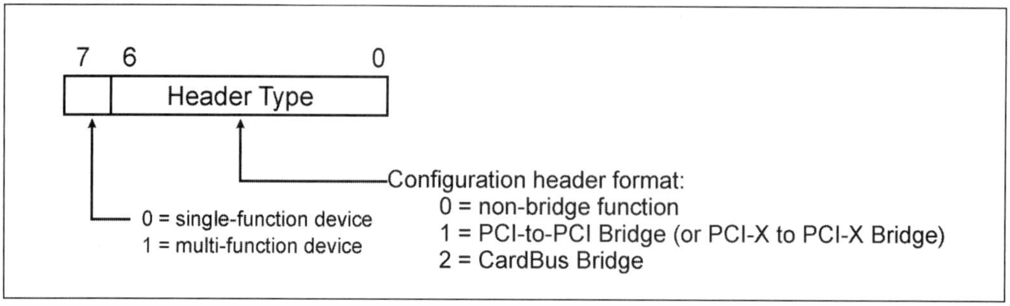

BIST Register

PCI-Compatible register. Optional. This register may be implemented by both Requester and Completer functions. If a function implements a Built-In Self-Test (BIST), it must implement this register as illustrated in Figure 22-4 on page 778. Table 22-2 on page 779 describes each bit's function. If the function doesn't support a BIST, this register must return zeros when read. The function's BIST is invoked by setting bit six to one. The function resets bit six upon completion of the BIST. Configuration software must fail the function if it doesn't reset bit six within two seconds. At the conclusion of the BIST, the test result is indicated in the lower four bits of the register. A completion code of zero indicates successful completion. A non-zero value represents a function-specific error code.

The time limit of two seconds may not be sufficient time to test a very complex function or one with an extremely large buffer that needs to be tested. In that case, the remainder of the test could be completed in the initialization portion of the function's device driver when the OS loads it into memory and calls it.

Figure 22-4: BIST Register Bit Assignment

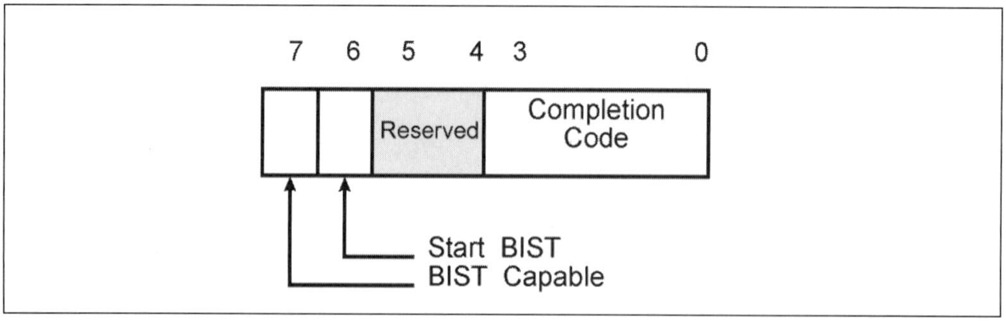

Table 22-2. BIST Register Bit Assignment

Bit	Function
3:0	**Completion Code**. A value of zero indicates successful completion, while a non-zero result indicates a function-specific error.
5:4	Reserved.
6	**Start BIST**. Writing a one into this bit starts the function's BIST. The function resets this bit automatically upon completion. Software should fail the function if the BIST does not complete within two seconds.
7	**BIST Capable**. Should return a one if the function implements a BIST, a zero if it doesn't.

Capabilities Pointer Register

PCI-Compatible register. Optional for a PCI function. Mandatory for a PCI-X or PCI Express function.

Configuration Header Space Not Large Enough

The 2.1 PCI spec defined the first 16 dwords of a function's PCI-compatible configuration space as its configuration Header space. It was originally intended that all of the function's PCI spec-defined configuration registers would reside within this region and that all of its function-specific configuration registers would reside within the lower 48 dwords of its PCI-compatible configuration space. Unfortunately, they ran out of space when defining new configuration registers in the 2.2 PCI spec. For this reason, the 2.2 and 2.3 PCI specs permit some spec-defined registers to be implemented in the lower 48 dwords of a function's PCI-compatible configuration space.

Discovering That Capabilities Exist

If the Capabilities List bit in the Status register (see Figure 22-5 on page 780) is set to one, the function implements the Capabilities Pointer register in byte zero of dword 13 in its PCI-compatible configuration space (see Figure 22-1 on page 771). This implies that the pointer contains the dword-aligned start address of the Capabilities List within the function's lower 48 dwords of PCI-compatible configuration space. It is a rule that the two least-significant bits must be hardwired to zero and must be ignored (i.e., masked) by software when reading the register. The upper six bits represents the upper six bits of the 8-bit, dword-aligned start address of the new registers implemented in the lower 48 dwords of the function's PCI-compatible space. The two least-significant bits are assumed to be zero.

Figure 22-5: Status Register

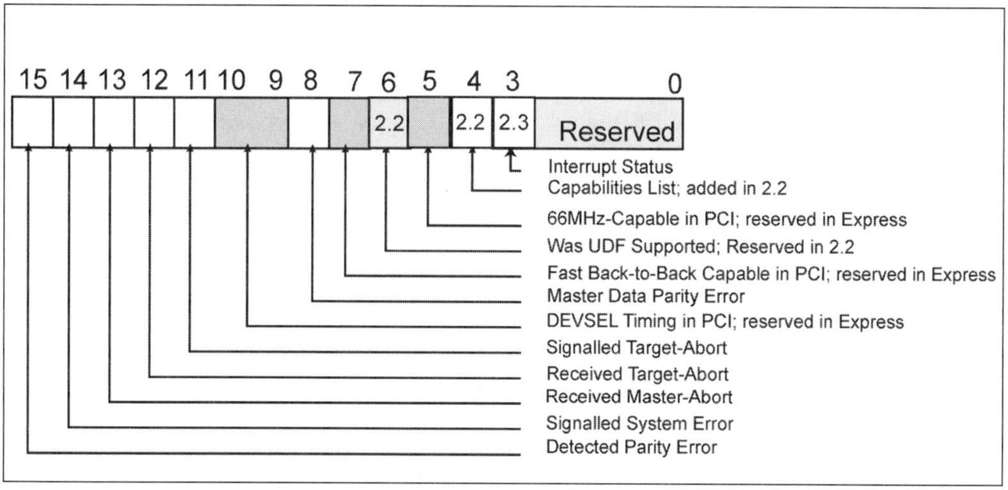

What the Capabilities List Looks Like

The configuration location pointed to by the Capabilities Pointer register is the first entry in a linked series of one or more configuration register sets, each of which supports a feature. Each entry has the general format illustrated in Figure 22-6 on page 782. The first byte is referred to as the Capability ID (assigned by the PCI SIG) and identifies the feature associated with this register set (e.g., 2 = AGP), while the second byte either points to another feature's register set, or indicates that there are no additional register sets (with a pointer value of zero) associated with this function. In either case, the least-significant two bits must return zero. If a pointer to the next feature's register set is present in the second byte, it points to a dword within the function's lower 48 dwords of PCI-compatible configuration space (it can point either forward or backward in the function's configuration space). The respective feature's register set always immediately follows the first two bytes of the entry, and its length and format are defined by what type of feature it is. The Capabilities currently defined in the 2.3 PCI spec are those listed in Table 22-3 on page 781.

Table 22-3: Currently-Assigned Capability IDs

ID	Description
00h	Reserved.
01h	**PCI Power Management Interface**. Refer to "The PM Capability Register Set" on page 585.
02h	**AGP**. Refer to "AGP Capability" on page 845. Also refer to the MindShare book entitled *AGP System Architecture, Second Edition* (published by Addison-Wesley).
03h	**VPD**. Refer to "Vital Product Data (VPD) Capability" on page 848.
04h	**Slot Identification**. This capability identifies a bridge that provides external expansion capabilities (i.e., an expansion chassis containing add-in card slots). Full documentation of this feature can be found in the revision 1.1 *PCI-to-PCI Bridge Architecture Specification*. For a detailed, Express-oriented description, refer to "Introduction To Chassis/Slot Numbering Registers" on page 859 and "Chassis and Slot Number Assignment" on page 861.
05h	**Message Signaled Interrupts**. Refer to "The MSI Capability Register Set" on page 332.
06h	**CompactPCI Hot Swap**. Refer to the chapter entitled *Compact PCI and PMC* in the MindShare book entitled *PCI System Architecture, Fourth Edition* (published by Addison-Wesley).
07h	**PCI-X device**. For a detailed description, refer to the MindShare book entitled *PCI-X System Architecture* (published by Addison-Wesley).
08h	**Reserved for AMD**.
09h	**Vendor Specific capability register set**. The layout of the register set is vendor specific, except that the byte immediately following the "Next" pointer indicates the number of bytes in the capability structure (including the ID and Next pointer bytes). An example vendor specific usage is a function that is configured in the final manufacturing steps as either a 32-bit or 64-bit PCI agent and the Vendor Specific capability structure tells the device driver which features the device supports.
0Ah	**Debug port**.
0Bh	**CompactPCI central resource control**. A full definition of this capability can be found in the PICMG 2.13 Specification (http://www.picmg.com).

Table 22-3: Currently-Assigned Capability IDs (Continued)

ID	Description
0Ch	**PCI Hot-Plug**. This ID indicates that the associated device conforms to the Standard Hot-Plug Controller model.
0Dh-0Fh	Reserved.
10h	**PCI Express Capability register set** (aka PCI Express Capability Structure). For a detailed explanation, refer to "PCI Express Capability Register Set" on page 896.
11h-FFh	Reserved.

Figure 22-6: General Format of a New Capabilities List Entry

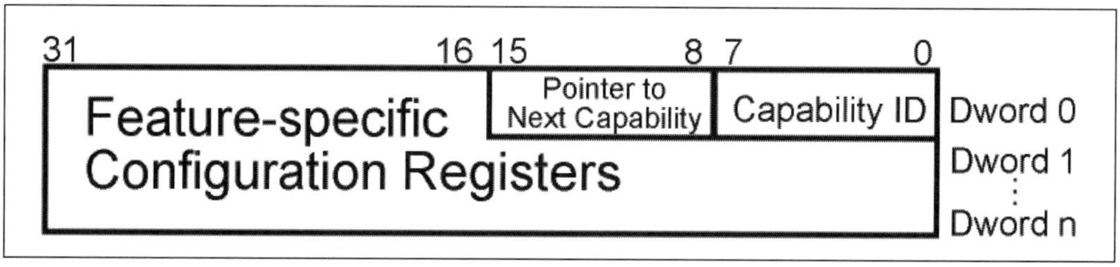

CardBus CIS Pointer Register

PCI-Compatible register. Optional. This optional register is implemented by functions that share silicon between a Cardbus device and a PCI or PCI Express function. This field points to the Card Information Structure (CIS) on the CardBus card. The register is read-only and indicates that the CIS can be accessed from the indicated offset within one of the following address spaces:

- Offset within the function's function-specific PCI-compatible configuration space (after dword 15d in the function's PCI-compatible configuration space).
- Offset from the start address indicated in one of the function's Memory Base Address Registers (see Figure 22-10 on page 796 and Figure 22-11 on page 797).
- Offset within a code image in the function's expansion ROM (see "Expansion ROM Base Address Register" on page 783 and "Expansion ROMs" on page 871).

The format of the CardBus CIS Pointer register is defined in the revision 3.0 PC Card specification. A detailed description of the CIS can be found in the MindShare architecture series book entitled *CardBus System Architecture* (published by Addison-Wesley).

Expansion ROM Base Address Register

PCI-Compatible register. Required if a function incorporates a device ROM. Many PCI functions incorporate a device ROM (the spec refers to it as an expansion ROM) that contains a device driver for the function. The expansion ROM start memory address and size is specified in the Expansion ROM Base Address Register at configuration dword 12d in the configuration Header region. As described in the section entitled "Base Address Registers" on page 792, on power-up the system must be automatically configured so that each function's IO and memory decoders recognize mutually-exclusive address ranges. The configuration software must be able to detect how much memory space an expansion ROM requires. In addition, the system must have the capability of programming a ROM's address decoder in order to locate its ROM in a non-conflicting address range.

When the start-up configuration program detects that a function has an Expansion ROM Base Address Register implemented (by writing all ones to it and reading it back), it must then check the first two locations in the ROM for an Expansion ROM signature to determine if a ROM is actually installed (i.e., there may be an empty ROM socket). If installed, the configuration program must shadow the ROM and execute its initialization code. This process is described in "Expansion ROMs" on page 871.

The format of the expansion ROM Base Address Register is illustrated in Figure 22-7 on page 785:

- A one in bit zero enables the function's ROM address decoder (assuming that the Memory Space bit in the Command register is also set to one).
- Bits [10:1] are reserved.
- Bits [31:11] are used to specify the ROM's start address (starting on an address divisible by the ROM's size).

As an example, assume that the programmer writes FFFFFFFEh to the ROM's Base Address Register (bit 0, the Expansion ROM Enable bit, is cleared so as not to enable the ROM address decoder until a start memory address has been assigned). A subsequent read from the register in the example yields FFFE0000h. This indicates the following:

- Bit 0 is a zero, indicating that the ROM address decoder is currently disabled.
- Bits [10:1] are reserved.
- In the Base Address field (bits [31:11]), bit 17 is the least-significant bit that the programmer was able to set to one. It has a binary-weighted value of 128K, indicating that the ROM decoder requires 128KB of memory space be assigned to the ROM. The programmer then writes a 32-bit start address into the register to assign the ROM start address on a 128K address boundary.

The PCI 2.3 spec recommends that the designer of the Expansion ROM Base Address Register should request a memory block slightly larger than that required by the current revision ROM to be installed. This permits the installation of subsequent ROM revisions that occupy more space without requiring a redesign of the logic associated with the function's Expansion ROM Base Address Register. The spec sets a limit of 16MB as the maximum expansion ROM size.

The Memory Space bit in the Command register has precedence over the Expansion ROM Enable bit. The function's expansion ROM should respond to memory accesses only if both its Memory Space bit (in its Command register) and the Expansion ROM Enable bit (in its expansion ROM Base Address register) are both set to one.

In order to minimize the number of address decoders that a function must implement, one address decoder can be shared between the Expansion ROM Base Address Register and one of the function's Memory Base Address Registers. The two Base Address Registers must be able to hold different values at the same time, but the address decoder will not decode ROM accesses unless the Expansion ROM Enable bit is set in the Expansion ROM Base Address Register.

A more detailed description of expansion ROM detection, shadowing and usage can be found in "Expansion ROMs" on page 871.

Figure 22-7: Expansion ROM Base Address Register Bit Assignment

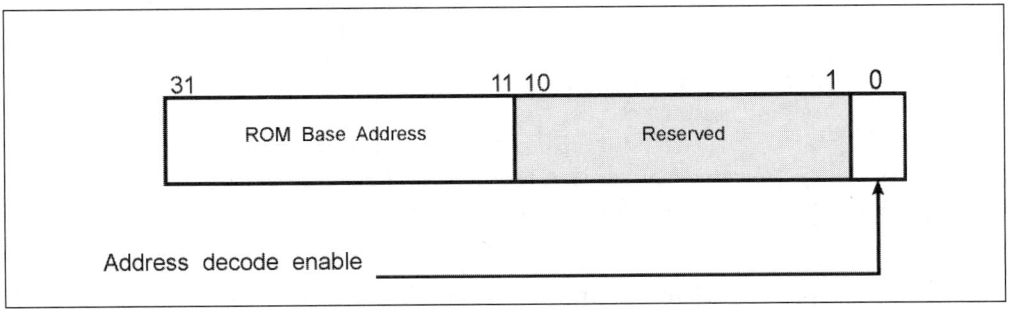

Command Register

Differs from the PCI spec. Mandatory. Refer to Figure 22-8 on page 785. Table 22 - 4 on page 786 provides a description of each bit in the Command register of a non-bridge function (i.e., one with a Type 0 Header format).

Figure 22-8: Command Register

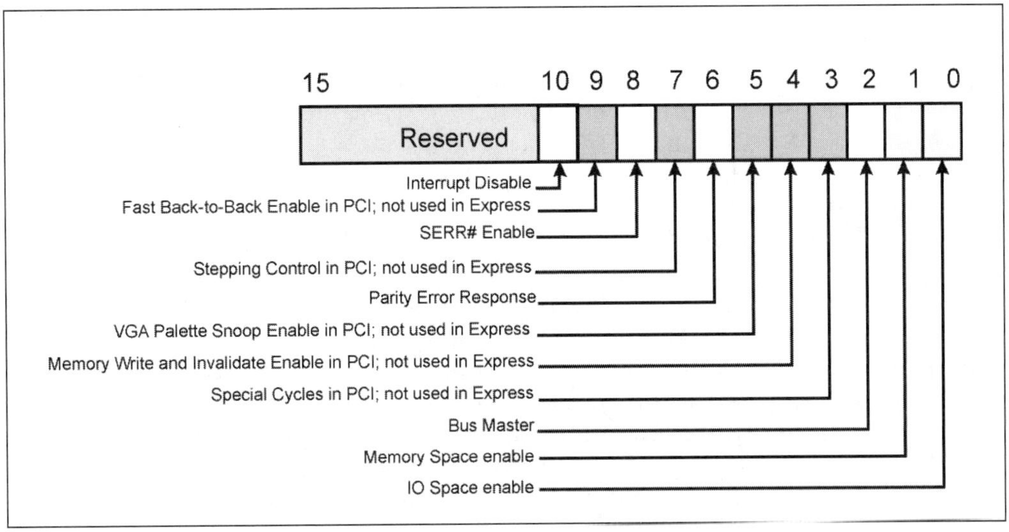

Table 22 - 4: Command Register

Bit	Type	Description
0	RW	**IO Address Space Decoder Enable.** • **Endpoints:** – **0.** IO decoder is disabled and IO transactions targeting this device return completion with 'Unsupported Request' status. – **1.** IO decoder is enabled andIO transactions targeting this device are accepted.
1	RW	**Memory Address Space Decoder Enable.** • **Endpoints and Memory-mapped devices within Switch**: – **0.** Memory decoder is disabled and Memory transactions targeting this device return completion with 'Unsupported Request' completion status. – **1.** Memory decoder is enabled and Memory transactions targeting this device are accepted.
2	RW	**Bus Master Enable.** • **Endpoints**: – **0.** Disables an Endpoint function from issuing memory or IO requests. Also disables the ability to generate MSI messages. – **1.** Enables the Endpoint to issue memory or IO requests, including MSI messages. – Requests other than memory or IO requests are not controlled by this bit. – Default =0. – Hardwired to 0 if an Endpoint function does not generate memory or IO requests. • **Root and Switch Port**: – Controls the forwarding of memory or IO requests by a Switch or Root Port in the upstream direction. – **0.** Memory and IO requests received at a Root Port or the downstream side of a Switch port must return an Unsupported Requests (UR) Completion. – Does not affect the forwarding of Completions in either the upstream or downstream direction. – Does not control the forwarding of requests other than memory or IO requests. – Default value of this bit is 0b.
3	RO	**Special Cycle Enable.** Does not apply to PCI Express and must be 0.

Table 22 - 4: Command Register (Continued)

Bit	Type	Description
4	RO	**Memory Write and Invalidate**. Does not apply to PCI Express and must be 0.
5	RO	**VGA Palette Snoop**. Does not apply to PCI Express and must be 0.
6	RW	**Parity Error Response**. In the Status register (see Figure 22-5 on page 780), the Master Data Parity Error bit is set by a Requester if its Parity Error Response bit is set and either of the following two conditions occurs: • If the Requester receives a poisoned Completion. • If the Requester poisons a write request. If the Parity Error Response bit is cleared, the Master Data Parity Error status bit is never set. The default value of this bit is 0.
7	RO	**IDSEL Stepping/Wait Cycle Control**. Does not apply to PCI Express and must be 0.
8	RW	**SERR Enable**. When set, this bit enables the non-fatal and fatal errors detected by the function to be reported to the Root Complex. The function reports such errors to the Root Complex if it is enabled to do so either through this bit or through the PCI Express specific bits in the Device Control register (see "Device Control Register" on page 905). The default value of this bit is 0.
9	RO	**Fast Back-to-Back Enable**. Does not apply to PCI Express and must be 0.

Table 22 - 4: Command Register (Continued)

Bit	Type	Description
10	RW	**Interrupt Disable.** Controls the ability of a PCI Express function to generate INTx interrupt messages. • 0 = Function enabled to generate INTx interrupt messages. • 1 = Function's ability to generate INTx interrupt messages is disabled. If the function had already transmitted any Assert_INTx emulation interrupt messages and this bit is then set, it must transmit a corresponding Deassert_INTx message for each assert message transmitted earlier. Note that INTx emulation interrupt messages forwarded by Root and Switch Ports from devices downstream of the Root or Switch Port are not affected by this bit. The default value of this bit is 0.

Status Register

Differs from the PCI spec. Mandatory. Table 22 - 5 on page 789 provides a description of each bit in the Status register (also refer to Figure 22-9 on page 788). The bit fields with the RW1C attribute have the following characteristics:

- Register bits return status when read, and a status bit may be cleared by writing a one to it. Writing a 0 to RW1C bits has no effect.

Figure 22-9: PCI Configuration Status Register

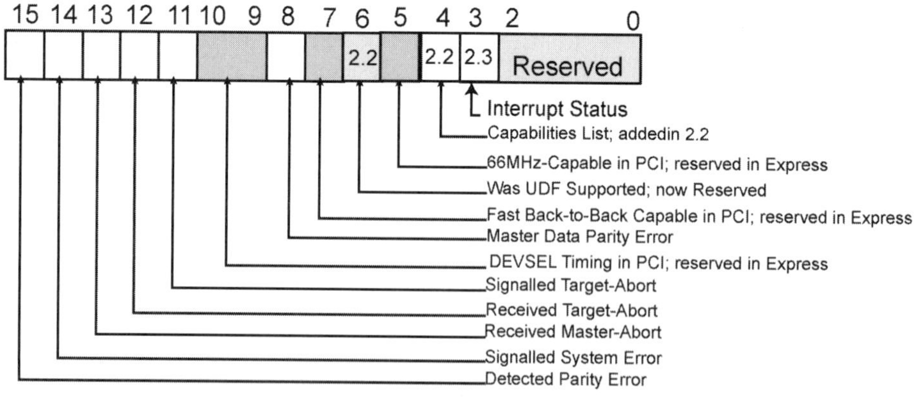

Table 22 - 5: Status Register

Bit	Attributes	Description
3	RO	**Interrupt Status**. Indicates that the function has an interrupt request outstanding (that is, the function transmitted an interrupt message earlier in time and is awaiting servicing). Note that INTx emulation interrupts forwarded by Root and Switch Ports from devices downstream of the Root or Switch Port are not reflected in this bit. The default state of this bit is 0. *Note* : this bit is only associated with INTx messages, and has no meaning if the device is using Message Signaled Interrupts.
4	RO	**Capabilities List**. Indicates the presence of one or more extended capability register sets in the lower 48 dwords of the function's PCI-compatible configuration space. Since, at a minimum, all PCI Express functions are required to implement the PCI Express capability structure, this bit must be set to 1.
5	RO	**66MHz-Capable**. Does not apply to PCI Express and must be 0.
7	RO	**Fast Back-to-Back Capable**. Does not apply to PCI Express and must be 0.
8	RW1C	**Master Data Parity Error**. The Master Data Parity Error bit is set by a Requester if the Parity Error Enable bit is set in its Command register and either of the following two conditions occurs: • If the Requester receives a poisoned Completion. • If the Requester poisons a write request. If the Parity Error Enable bit is cleared, the Master Data Parity Error status bit is never set. The default value of this bit is 0.
10:9	RO	**DEVSEL Timing**. Does not apply to PCI Express and must be 0.

Table 22 - 5: Status Register (Continued)

Bit	Attributes	Description
11	RW1C	**Signaled Target Abort**. This bit is set when a function acting as a Completer terminates a request by issuing Completer Abort Completion Status to the Requester. The default value of this bit is 0.
12	RW1C	**Received Target Abort**. This bit is set when a Requester receives a Completion with Completer Abort Completion Status. The default value of this bit is 0.
13	RW1C	**Received Master Abort**. This bit is set when a Requester receives a Completion with Unsupported Request Completion Status. The default value of this bit is 0.
14	RW1C	**Signaled System Error**. This bit is set when a function sends an ERR_FATAL or ERR_NONFATAL message, and the SERR Enable bit in the Command register is set to one. The default value of this bit is 0.
15	RW1C	**Detected Parity Error**. Regardless of the state the Parity Error Enable bit in the function's Command register, this bit is set if the function receives a Poisoned TLP. The default value of this bit is 0.

Cache Line Size Register

Differs from the PCI spec. Optional.

This field is implemented by PCI Express devices as a read-write field for legacy compatibility purposes but has no impact on any PCI Express device functionality.

Master Latency Timer Register

Differs from the PCI spec. Optional.

This register does not apply to PCI Express and must be hardwired to 0.

Interrupt Line Register

Differs from the PCI spec. Optional.

Usage In a PCI Function

Required if a PCI function is capable of generating interrupt requests via an INTx# pin (i.e., INTA#, INTB#, INTC#, or INTD#). The PCI spec allows a function to generate interrupts either using an interrupt pin, or using MSI-capability (for more information, see "Message Signaled Interrupts" on page 331).

The read/writable Interrupt Line register is used to identify which input on the interrupt controller the function's PCI interrupt request pin (as specified in its Interrupt Pin register; see "Interrupt Pin Register" on page 792) is routed to. For example, in a PC environment the values 00h-through-0Fh in this register correspond to the IRQ0-through-IRQ15 inputs on the interrupt controller. The value 255d (FFh) indicates "unknown" or "no connection." The values from 10h-through-FEh, inclusive, are reserved. Although it doesn't state this in the PCI spec, it is the author's opinion that RST# should initialize the Interrupt Line register to a value of FFh, thereby indicating that interrupt routing has not yet been assigned to the function.

The OS or device driver can examine a device's Interrupt Line register to determine which system interrupt request line the device uses to issue requests for service (and, therefore, which entry in the interrupt table to "hook").

In a non-PC environment, the value written to this register is architecture-specific and therefore outside the scope of the specification.

Usage In a PCI Express Function

A PCI Express function may generate interrupts in the legacy PCI/PCI-X manner. As an example, when a PCI Express-to-PCI or PCI-X bridge detects the assertion or deassertion of one of its INTA#, INTB#, INTC#, or INTD# inputs on the legacy side of the bridge, it sends an INTx Assert or Deassert message upstream towards the Root Complex (specifically, to the interrupt controller within the Root Complex).

As in PCI, the Interrupt Line register communicates interrupt line routing information. The register is read/write and must be implemented by any function that contains a valid non-zero value in its Interrupt Pin configuration register (described in the next section). The OS or device driver can examine a device's

Interrupt Line register to determine which system interrupt request line the device uses to issue requests for service (and, therefore, which entry in the interrupt table to "hook").

In a non-PC environment, the value written to this register is architecture-specific and therefore outside the scope of the specification.

Interrupt Pin Register

Differs from the PCI spec. Optional.

Usage In a PCI Function

Required if a PCI function is capable of generating interrupt requests via an INTx# pin. The PCI spec allows a function to generate interrupts either using an interrupt pin, or using MSI-capability (for more information, see "Two Methods of Interrupt Delivery" on page 330).

The read-only Interrupt Pin register defines which of the four PCI interrupt request pins, INTA#-through-INTD#, a PCI function is connected (i.e., bonded) to. The values 01h-through-04h correspond to PCI interrupt request pins INTA#-through-INTD#. A return value of zero indicates that the device doesn't generate interrupts. All other values (05h-FFh) are reserved.

Usage In a PCI Express Function

This read-only register identifies the legacy INTx interrupt Message (INTA, INTB, INTC, or INTD) the function transmits upstream to generate an interrupt. The values 01h-through-04h correspond to legacy INTx interrupt Messages INTA-through-INTD. A return value of zero indicates that the device doesn't generate interrupts using the legacy method. All other values (05h-FFh) are reserved. Note that, although the function may not generate interrupts via the legacy method, it may generate them via the MSI method (see "Determining if a Function Uses INTx# Pins" on page 343 for more information).

Base Address Registers

Differ from the PCI spec. Required if a function implements memory and/or IO decoders.

Chapter 22: PCI Compatible Configuration Registers

Introduction

Virtually all functions implement some memory, and/or a function-specific register set to control the function and sense its status. Some examples are:

- A parallel port's Status, Command and Data registers could reside in IO or memory-mapped IO space.
- A network interface's control registers (Command/Status, etc.) could reside in IO or memory-mapped IO space.
- The network interface may also incorporate a RAM memory buffer that must be mapped into the system's memory space.
- In addition, a ROM containing the function's BIOS and interrupt service routine may be present in a function.

On power-up, the system must be automatically configured so that each function's IO and memory functions occupy mutually-exclusive address ranges. In order to accomplish this, the system must be able to detect how many memory and IO address ranges a function requires and the size of each. Obviously, the system must then be able to program the function's address decoders in order to assign non-conflicting address ranges to them.

The Base Address Registers (BARs), located in dwords 4-through-9 of the function's configuration Header space (see Figure 22-1 on page 771), are used to implement a function's programmable memory and/or IO decoders. Each register is 32-bits wide (or 64-bits wide if it's a memory decoder and its associated memory block can be located above the 4GB address boundary). Figure 22-10 on page 796, Figure 22-11 on page 797, and Figure 22-12 on page 798 illustrate the three possible formats of a Base Address Register. Bit 0 is a read-only bit and indicates whether it's a memory or an IO decoder:

- If bit 0 = 0, the register is a memory address decoder.
- If bit 0 = 1, the register is an IO address decoder.

Decoders may be implemented in any of the Base Address Register positions. If more than one decoder is implemented, there may be holes. During configuration, the configuration software must therefore look at all six of the possible Base Address Register positions in a function's Header to determine which registers are actually implemented.

IO Space Usage

In a PC environment, IO space is densely populated and will only become more so in the future. For this reason and because some processors are only capable of performing memory transactions, the following rules related to IO space usage are defined in the PCI Express spec:

- **Native PCI Express Endpoint Function** (as indicated by a value of 0000b in the Device/Port Type field in the function's PCI Express Capabilities Register; see Figure 22-31 on page 865). Some operating systems and/or processors may not support IO accesses (i.e., accesses using IO rather than memory addresses). This being the case, the designer of a native PCI Express function should avoid the use of IO BARs.
  However, the target system that a function is designed for may use the function as one of the boot devices (i.e., the boot input device, output display device, or boot mass storage device) and may utilize a legacy device driver for the function at startup time. The legacy driver may assume that the function's device-specific register set resides in IO space. In this case, the function designer would supply an IO BAR to which the configuration software will assign an IO address range. When the OS boot has completed and the OS has loaded a native PCI Express driver for the function, however, the OS may deallocate all legacy IO address ranges previously assigned to the selected boot devices. From that point forward and for the duration of the power-up session, the native driver will utilize memory accesses to communicate with its associated function through the function's memory BARs.
- **Legacy PCI Express Endpoint Function** (as indicated by a value of 0001b in the Device/Port Type field in the function's PCI Express Capabilities Register; see Figure 22-31 on page 865). A legacy PCI Express Endpoint function consists of a legacy PCI or PCI-X function supplied with a PCI Express front end to interface it to the PCI Express fabric. As many legacy functions implemented IO BARs, IO BARs are tolerated in this type of function.

Memory Base Address Register

This section provides a detailed description of the bit fields within a Memory BAR. The section entitled "Finding Block Size and Assigning Address Range" on page 799 describes how the register is probed to determine its existence, the size of the memory associated with the decoder, and the assignment of the base address to the decoder.

Decoder Width Field. In a Memory Base Address Register, bits [2:1] define whether the decoder is 32- or 64-bits wide:

- If 00b = it's a **32-bit register** (see Figure 22-10 on page 796). The configuration software therefore will write a 32-bit start memory address into it specifying any address in the first 4GB of memory address space.
- If 10b = it's a **64-bit register** (see Figure 22-11 on page 797). The configu-

ration software therefore writes a 64-bit start memory address into it that specifies a start address in a 2^{64} memory address space. This means that this **Base Address Register consumes two consecutive dwords** of the configuration Header space. The first dword is used to set the lower 32-bits of the start address and the second dword is used to specify the upper 32-bits of the start address.

Prefetchable Attribute Bit. Bit three defines the block of memory as Prefetchable or not. A block of memory space may be marked as Prefetchable only if it can guarantee that:

- there are **no side effects from reads** (e.g., the read doesn't alter the contents of the location or alter the state of the function in some manner). It's permissible for a bridge that resides between a Requester and a memory target to prefetch read data from memory that has this characteristic. If the Requester doesn't end up asking for all of the data that the bridge read into a read-ahead buffer, the bridge must discard the data (see "Bridge Must Discard Unconsumed Prefetched Data" on page 801). The data remains unchanged in the target's memory locations.
- on a read, it **always returns all bytes** irrespective of the byte enable settings.
- the memory device **continues to function correctly if** a bridge that resides between the Requester and the memory target performs **byte merging** (for more information, refer to "Byte Merging" on page 801) in its posted memory write buffer when memory writes are **performed** within the memory target's range.

In a nutshell, regular memory is prefetchable while memory-mapped IO (or any other badly-behaved memory region) is not. The configuration software can determine that a memory target is prefetchable or not by checking the Prefetchable bit in the memory target's Base Address Register (BAR).

All memory BAR registers in PCI Express Endpoint functions with the Prefetchable bit set to one must be implemented as 64-bit memory BARs. Memory BARs that do not have the prefetchable bit set to one may be implemented as 32-bit BARs.

As an example, the address decoder for a block of memory-mapped IO ports may hardwire the Prefetchable bit to zero, while the address decoder for well-behaved memory would hardwire it to one. For performance reasons, the spec urges that, wherever possible, memory-mapped IO ranges be marked as prefetchable memory.

The configuration software checks this bit to determine a memory target's operational characteristics, assigns a memory range to its decoder (i.e., its Memory BAR), and then backtracks to all upstream bridges between the memory target and the processor and configures the bridges to treat the assigned memory range in the appropriate manner:

- If it's Prefetchable memory, it's permissible for a bridge to perform read prefetching to yield better performance, and it's also permissible for the bridge to perform byte merging in its posted memory write buffer for writes performed to the memory.
- If it's non-Prefetchable memory, bridge read prefetching and byte merging are not allowed within the assigned region of memory space. This will not allow bridges to optimize accesses to the function, but you're assured the function will work correctly (and that's pretty important!).

Base Address Field. This field consists of bits [31:7] for a 32-bit memory decoder and bits [63:7] for a 64-bit memory decoder. It is used:

- to determine the size of the memory associated with this decoder, and
- to assign a start (i.e., base) address to the decoder.

Programming of an example Memory Base Address Register is provided in "Finding Block Size and Assigning Address Range" on page 799.

The minimum memory range requested by a BAR is 128 bytes.

Figure 22-10: 32-Bit Memory Base Address Register Bit Assignment

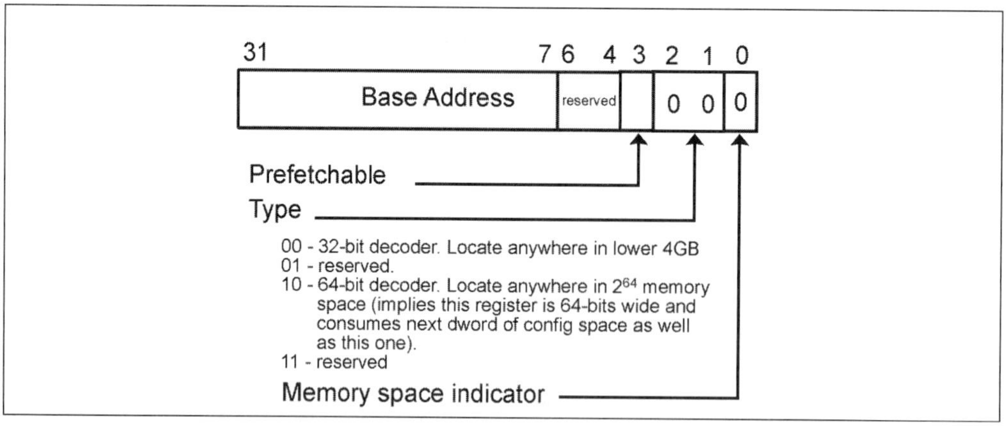

Figure 22-11: 64-Bit Memory Base Address Register Bit Assignment

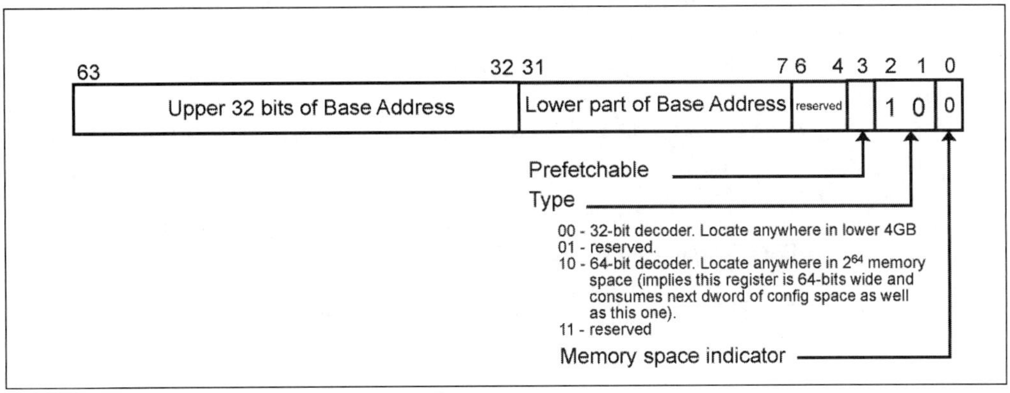

IO Base Address Register

Introduction. This section provides a detailed description of the bit fields within an IO Base Address Register. The section entitled "Finding Block Size and Assigning Address Range" on page 799 describes:

- how the register is probed to determine its existence,
- how to determine the size of the IO register set associated with the decoder and therefore the amount of IO space that must be assigned to it, and
- how to assign the base address to the decoder.

IO BAR Description. Refer to Figure 22-12 on page 798. Bit zero returns a one, indicating that this is an IO, rather than a memory, decoder. Bit one is reserved and must always return zero. Bits [31:2] comprises the Base Address field and is used to:

- determine the size of the IO block required and
- to set its start address.

The PCI spec requires that a device that maps its control register set into IO space must not request more than 256 locations per IO Base Address Register.

PC-Compatible IO Decoder. The upper 16-bits of the IO BAR may be hardwired to zero when a function is designed specifically for a PC-compatible, x86-based machine (because Intel x86 processors are incapable of generating IO addresses over 64KB). The function must still perform a full 32-bit decode of the IO address, however.

Legacy IO Decoders. Legacy PC-compatible devices such as VGA and IDE controllers frequently expect to be located within fixed legacy IO ranges. Such functions do not implement Base Address Registers. Instead, the configuration software identifies them as legacy functions via their respective Class Code and then enables their IO decoder(s) by setting the IO Space bit in its Command register to one.

A legacy IO function may or may not own all of the byte locations within a dword of IO space:

- A legacy IO function that does own all of the bytes within the currently-addressed dword can perform its decode using the dword-aligned address supplied by A[31:2].
- A legacy IO function that does not own all of the byte locations within a dword must decode the byte enables to determine if it owns the byte-specific location being addressed. It must examine the byte enables to determine if the Requester is addressing additional, higher byte locations within the target IO dword (identified via A[31:2]). If it owns all of the addressed IO ports, the function can honor the request. However, if it doesn't own them all it must issue a Completer Abort to the Requester.

Figure 22-12: IO Base Address Register Bit Assignment

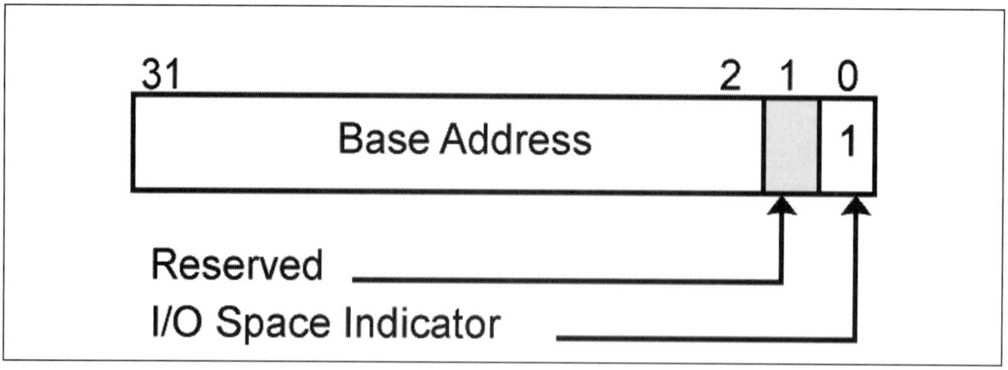

Finding Block Size and Assigning Address Range

How It Works. The configuration program must probe each of a function's possible Base Address Registers to determine:

- Is the Base Address Register implemented?
- Is it a memory or an IO address decoder?
- If it's a memory decoder, is it a 32- or 64-bit Base Address Register?
- If it's a memory decoder, is the memory associated with the register Prefetchable or non-Prefetchable?
- How much memory or address space does it require and with what alignment?

All of this information can be ascertained simply by writing all ones to the Base Address Register and then reading it back. A return value of zero indicates that the Base Address Register isn't implemented. Assuming that the value read is non-zero, scanning the returned value (assuming its non-zero) upwards starting at the least-significant bit of the Base Address field, the programmer determines the size of the required memory or the IO space by finding the least-significant bit that was successfully set to one. Bit zero of the register has a binary-weighted value of one, bit one a value of two, bit two a value of four, etc. The binary-weighted value of the least-significant bit set to one in the Base Address field indicates the required amount of space. This is also the first read/writable bit in the register and all of the bits above it are by definition read/writable. After discovering this information, the program then writes a base 32- or 64-bit memory address, or the base 32-bit IO address into the Base Address Register.

A Memory Example. As an example, assume that FFFFFFFFh is written to the Base Address Register at configuration dword 04d and the value read back is FFF00000h. The fact that any bits could be changed to one indicates that the Base Address Register is implemented.

- Bit 0 = 0, indicating that this is a memory address decoder.
- Bits [2:1] = 00b, indicating that it's a 32-bit memory decoder.
- Bit 3 = 0, indicating that it's not Prefetchable memory.
- Bit 20 is the first one bit found in the Base Address field. The binary-weighted value of this bit is 1,048,576, indicating that this is an address decoder for 1MB of memory.

The programmer then writes a 32-bit base address into the register. However, only bits [31:20] are writable. The decoder accepts bits [31:20] and assumes that bits [19:0] of the assigned base address are zero. This means that the base address is divisible by 1MB, the size of the requested memory range. It is a characteristic of PCI, PCI-X, and PCI Express decoders that the assigned start address is always divisible by the size of requested range.

As an example, it is possible to program the example memory address decoder for a 1MB block of memory to start on the one, two, or three meg boundary, but it is not possible to set its start address at the 1.5, 2.3, or 3.7 meg boundary.

An IO Example. As a second example, assume that FFFFFFFFh is written to a function's Base Address Register at configuration dword address 05d and the value read back is FFFFFF01h. Bit 0 is a one, indicating that this is an IO address decoder. Scanning upwards starting at bit 2 (the least-significant bit of the Base Address field), bit 8 is the first bit that was successfully changed to one. The binary-weighted value of this bit is 256, indicating that this is an IO address decoder requesting 256 bytes of IO space.

The programmer then writes a 32-bit base IO address into the register. However, only bits [31:8] are writable. The decoder accepts bits [31:8] and assumes that bits [7:0] of the assigned base address are zero. This means that the base address is divisible by 256, the size of the requested IO range.

Smallest/Largest Decoder Sizes

Smallest/Largest Memory Decoders. The smallest memory address decoder is implemented as a Base Address Register that permits bits [31:7] to be written. Since the binary-weighted value of bit seven is 128, 128 bytes is the smallest memory block a memory decoder can be designed for.

If a 32-bit memory BAR only permits bit 31 to be written, it is requesting 2GB of memory space.

A 64-bit memory BAR could request more than 2GB of memory address space, resulting in none of the lower 32 bits in the BAR being writable. If this is the case, the programmer must also write all ones in the high dword of the BAR to determine how big a memory space the decoder requires.

Smallest/Largest IO Decoders. The smallest IO decoder would be implemented as a Base Address Register that permitted bits [31:2] to be programmed. Since the binary-weighted value of bit two is 4, 4 bytes (a dword) is the smallest IO block an IO decoder can be designed for.

The largest IO decoder would permit bits [31:8] to be written. The binary-weighted value of bit 8 is 256 and this is therefore the largest range that an IO decoder can request.

Byte Merging

A bridge may combine writes to a single dword within one entry in the posted-write buffer. This feature is recommended to improve performance and is only permitted in memory address ranges that are designated as prefetchable.

As an example, assume that a Requester performs two memory writes:

- the first writes to locations 00000100h and 00000101h and
- the second writes to locations 00000102h and 00000103h.

These four locations reside within the same dword. The bridge could absorb the first two-byte write into a dword buffer entry and then absorb the second two byte write into the same dword buffer entry. When the bridge performs the memory write, it can complete it as a single access. It is a violation of the spec, however, for a bridge to combine separate byte writes to the same location into a single write. As an example, assume that a Requester performs four separate memory writes to the same dword: the first writes to location zero in the dword, the second to location zero again, the third to location one and the fourth to location two. When the bridge performs the posted writes, it has to perform a single memory write transaction to write the first byte to location zero. It then performs a second memory write transaction to write to locations zero (the second byte written to it by the Requester), one and two.

Bridge Must Discard Unconsumed Prefetched Data

A bridge that has prefetched memory read data for a Requester must discard any prefetched read data that the Requester doesn't actually end up reading. The following is an example scenario that demonstrates a problem that will result if a bridge doesn't discard prefetched data that wasn't consumed:

1. The processor has two buffers in main memory that occupy adjacent memory regions. The memory is designated as prefetchable memory.
2. The processor writes data into the first memory buffer and then instructs a PCI Express Requester to read and process the data.
3. The Requester starts its memory read and the bridge between the Requester and the target memory performs read aheads from the memory because it is prefetchable, well-behaved memory. The bridge ends up prefetching past the end of the first memory buffer into the second one, but the Requester

only actually reads the data from the first buffer area.

4. The bridge does not discard the unused data that was prefetched from the second buffer.
5. The processor writes data into the second memory buffer and then instructs a Requester (the same Requester or a different one) beyond the same bridge to read and process the data.
6. The Requester starts its memory read at the start address of the second buffer. The bridge delivers the data that it prefetched from the beginning of the second buffer earlier. *This is stale data and doesn't reflect the latest data written into the second memory buffer.*

Min_Gnt/Max_Lat Registers

Differs from the PCI spec. Optional.

These registers do not apply to PCI Express. They must be read-only and hardwired to 0.

Header Type 1

General

Figure 22-13 on page 803 illustrates the layout of a PCI-to-PCI bridge's configuration header space.

Figure 22-13: Header Type 1

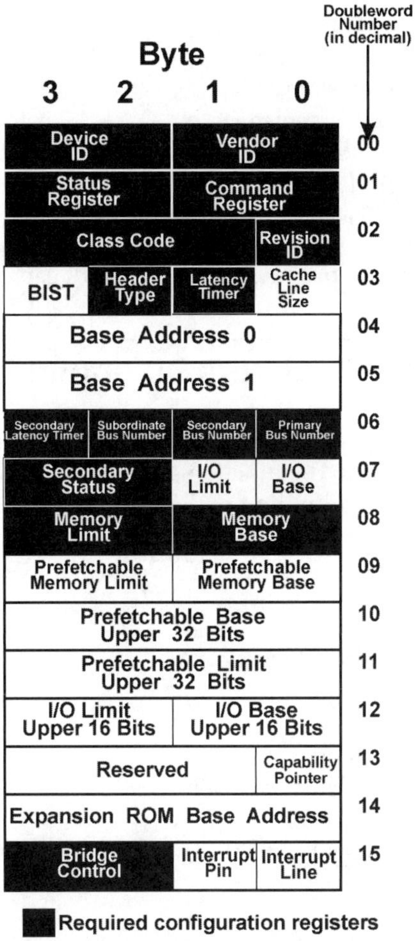

Header Type 1 Registers Compatible With PCI

The Header Type 1 PCI configuration registers that are implemented and used identically in both PCI and PCI Express are:

- Vendor ID register.
- Device ID register.

- Revision ID register.
- Class Code register.
- Header Type register.
- BIST register.
- Capabilities Pointer register.
- Subordinate Bus Number register.
- Secondary Bus Number register.
- Primary Bus Number register.
- IO Base, Limit and Upper registers.
- Memory Base and Limit registers.
- Expansion ROM Base Address register.

The sections that follow provide a description of each of these registers.

Header Type 1 Registers Incompatible With PCI

In a Header Type 1 bridge PCI Express function, the definitions of the following configuration registers in the function's PCI-compatible configuration space differ from the PCI spec's definition of the respective register definitions:

- Command Register
- Status Register
- Cache Line Size Register
- Master Latency Timer Register
- Interrupt Line Register
- Interrupt Pin Register
- Base Address Registers
- Secondary Latency Timer register.
- Secondary Status register.
- Prefetchable Memory Base, Limit, and Upper registers.
- Bridge Control register.

The sections that follow define the implementation/usage differences of these registers. For a full description of their implementation in a PCI-to-PCI bridge function, refer to the MindShare book entitled *PCI System Architecture*, Fourth Edition (published by Addison-Wesley). For a full description their implementation in a PCI-X to PCI-X bridge function, refer to the MindShare book entitled *PCI-X System Architecture*, First Edition (published by Addison-Wesley).

Chapter 22: PCI Compatible Configuration Registers

Terminology

Before proceeding, it's important to define some basic terms associated with an actual or a virtual PCI-to-PCI bridge. Each PCI-to-PCI bridge is connected to two buses, referred to as its primary and secondary buses:

- **Downstream**. When a transaction is initiated and is passed through one or more PCI-to-PCI bridges flowing away from the host processor, it is said to be moving downstream.
- **Upstream**. When a transaction is initiated and is passed through one or more PCI-to-PCI bridges flowing towards the host processor, it is said to be moving upstream.
- **Primary bus**. PCI bus that is directly connected to the upstream side of a bridge.
- **Secondary bus**. PCI bus that is directly connected to the downstream interface of a PCI-to-PCI bridge.
- **Subordinate bus**. Highest-numbered PCI bus on the downstream side of the bridge.

Bus Number Registers

PCI-Compatible registers. Mandatory.

Introduction

Each PCI-to-PCI bridge must implement three mandatory bus number registers. All of them are read/writable and are cleared to zero by reset. During configuration, the configuration software initializes these three registers to assign bus numbers. These registers are:

- the Primary Bus Number register.
- the Secondary Bus Number register.
- the Subordinate Bus Number register.

The combination of the Secondary and the Subordinate Bus Number register values defines the range of buses that exists on the downstream side of the bridge. The information supplied by these three registers is used by the bridge to determine whether or not to pass a packet through to the opposite interface.

Primary Bus Number Register

PCI-Compatible register. Mandatory. Located in Header byte zero of dword six. The Primary Bus Number register is initialized by software with the number of the bus that is directly connected to the bridge's primary interface. This register exists for three reasons:

- **To route Completion packets**.
- **To route a Vendor-defined message that uses ID-based routing**.
- **To route a PCI Special Cycle Request that is moving upstream**. A bridge that connects a PCI Express link to a PCI or PCI-X bus receives a Special Cycle Request (as defined in the PCI spec) on its secondary interface. A Special Cycle Request is a request to perform a Special Cycle transaction on the destination PCI or PCI-X bus. The request takes the form of a Type 1 Configuration write request packet (see Figure 20-8 on page 734) wherein the destination ID has the following characteristics:
  — All ones in the Device Number and Function Number fields, and
  — All zeros in the Register Number and Extended Register Number fields.
  If the destination bus number in the request packet matches the value in the Primary Bus Number register and the other fields are as stated above, the request is converted into a Special Cycle transaction on the primary bus and the write data is delivered as the message in the transaction's Data Phase.
  If it doesn't match the bridge's Primary Bus Number register and it's outside the range of buses defined by the bridge's Secondary Bus Number and Subordinate Bus Number registers, the bridge accepts the packet (the target bus is not on the downstream side of the bridge and therefore it must be passed upstream). The bridge accepts the packet and passes it to its opposite interface.

Secondary Bus Number Register

PCI-Compatible register. Mandatory. Located in Header byte one of dword six. The Secondary Bus Number register is initialized by software with the number of the bus that is directly connected to the bridge's secondary interface. This register exists for three reasons:

- When a Special Cycle Request is latched on the primary side, the bridge uses this register (and, possibly, the Subordinate Bus Number register) to determine if it should be passed to the bridge's secondary interface as either a PCI Special Cycle transaction (if the bus connected to the secondary interface is the destination PCI or PCI-X bus) or as is (i.e., as a Type 1 configuration write request packet).

- When a Type 1 Configuration transaction (read or write and not a PCI Special Cycle Request) is latched on the primary side, the bridge uses this register (and, possibly, the Subordinate Bus Number register) to determine if it should be passed to the bridge's secondary interface as either a Type 0 configuration transaction (if the bus connected to the secondary interface is the destination PCI or PCI-X bus) or as is (i.e., as a Type 1 configuration write request packet).
- When a Completion packet is latched on the primary side, the bridge uses this register (and, possibly, the Subordinate Bus Number register) to determine if it should be passed to the bridge's secondary interface.

Subordinate Bus Number Register

PCI-Compatible register. Mandatory. Located in Header byte two of dword six. The Subordinate Bus Number register is initialized by software with the number of the highest-numbered bus that exists on the downstream side of the bridge. If there are no PCI-to-PCI bridges on the secondary bus, the Subordinate Bus Number register is initialized with the same value as the Secondary Bus Number register.

Bridge Routes ID Addressed Packets Using Bus Number Registers

When one of the bridge's interfaces latches a Completion packet, an ID-routed Vendor-defined message, or a PCI Special Cycle request, it uses its internal bus number registers to decide whether or not to accept the packet and pass it to the opposite bridge interface:

- The routing of PCI Special Cycle requests was described in the previous sections.
- When the bridge latches a Completion packet or an ID-routed Vendor-defined message on its primary interface, it compares the Bus Number portion of destination ID to its Secondary Bus Number and Subordinate Bus Number register values. If the target bus number falls within the range of buses defined by the bridge's Secondary Bus Number and Subordinate Bus Number registers, the bridge accepts the packet and passes it to its opposite interface.
- When the bridge latches a Completion packet or an ID-routed Vendor-defined message on its secondary interface, it compares the Bus Number portion of the destination ID to its Primary Bus Number register.
  - — If it matches, the bridge accepts the packet and passes it to the primary interface.
  - — If it doesn't match the bridge's Primary Bus Number register and it's outside the range of buses defined by the bridge's Secondary Bus Num-

ber and Subordinate Bus Number registers, the bridge accepts the packet (the target bus is not on the downstream side of the bridge and therefore it must be passed upstream) and passes it to its primary interface.
   — If the destination bus falls within the range of buses defined by the bridge's Secondary Bus Number and Subordinate Bus Number registers, then the target bus is on the downstream side of the bridge. The bridge therefore does not accept the packet.
- These registers are also used to route Type 1 configuration packets.

Vendor ID Register

PCI-Compatible register. Mandatory. See "Vendor ID Register" on page 773.

Device ID Register

PCI-Compatible register. Mandatory. See "Device ID Register" on page 773.

Revision ID Register

PCI-Compatible register. Mandatory. See "Revision ID Register" on page 773.

Class Code Register

PCI-Compatible register. Mandatory. Refer to Figure 22-2 on page 775. The Class field in the Class Code register of a Virtual PCI-to-PCI bridge, or a PCI Express bridge to a PCI or PCI-X bus will contain the value 06h (see Table 22-1 on page 775), the SubClass field will contain the value 04h (see Table 8 on page 1023), and the Programming Interface Byte will contain 00h.

Header Type Register

PCI-Compatible register. Mandatory. Refer to "Header Type Register" on page 777. The Header Type field in the Header Type register of a Virtual PCI-to-PCI bridge, or a PCI Express bridge to a PCI or PCI-X bus will be 01h, thereby indicating the register layout shown in Figure 22-13 on page 803.

BIST Register

*PCI-Compatible register. Optional.*Refer to "BIST Register" on page 778.

Capabilities Pointer Register

PCI-Compatible register. Mandatory. Refer to "Capabilities Pointer Register" on page 779.

Basic Transaction Filtering Mechanism

PCI devices that reside on the downstream side of a PCI-to-PCI bridge may incorporate internal memory (mapped into memory space) and/or an internal, device-specific register set mapped into either IO or memory-mapped IO space. The configuration program automatically detects the presence, type and address space requirements of these devices and allocates space to them by programming their address decoders to recognize the address ranges it assigns to them.

The configuration program assigns all IO devices that reside behind a PCI-to-PCI bridge mutually-exclusive address ranges that are blocked together within a common overall range of IO locations. The PCI-to-PCI bridge is then programmed to pass any IO transactions detected on the primary side of the bridge to the secondary side if the target address is within the range associated with the community of IO devices that reside behind the bridge. Conversely, any IO transactions detected on the secondary side of the bridge are passed to the primary side if the target address is outside the range associated with the community of IO devices that reside on the secondary side (because the target device doesn't reside on the secondary side, but may reside on the primary side).

All memory-mapped IO devices (i.e., non-prefetchable memory) that reside behind a PCI-to-PCI bridge are assigned mutually-exclusive memory address ranges within a common block of memory locations. The PCI-to-PCI bridge is then programmed to pass any memory-mapped IO transactions detected on the primary side of the bridge to the secondary side if the target address is within the range associated with the community of memory-mapped IO devices that reside behind the bridge. Conversely, any memory-mapped IO transactions detected on the secondary side of the bridge are passed to the primary side if the target address is outside the range associated with the community of memory-mapped IO devices that reside on the secondary side (because the target device doesn't reside on the secondary side, but may reside on the primary side).

All memory devices (i.e., regular memory, not memory-mapped IO) that reside behind a PCI-to-PCI bridge are assigned mutually-exclusive memory address ranges within a common overall range of memory locations. The PCI-to-PCI bridge is then programmed to pass any memory transactions detected on the primary side of the bridge to the secondary side if the target address is within the range associated with the community of memory devices that reside behind the bridge. Conversely, any memory transactions detected on the secondary side of the bridge are passed to the primary side if the target address is outside the range associated with the community of memory devices that reside on the secondary side (because the target device doesn't reside on the secondary side, but may reside on the primary side).

The bridge itself may incorporate:

- a memory buffer.
- an IO register set that is used to control the bridge
- a device ROM that contains a device driver for the bridge.

The bridge must incorporate programmable address decoders for these devices.

Bridge's Memory, Register Set and Device ROM

Introduction

A PCI-to-PCI bridge designer may choose to incorporate the following entities within the bridge:

- A set of internal, device-specific registers that are used to control the bridge's operational characteristics or check its status. These registers are outside the scope of the PCI specification.
- A memory buffer within the bridge.
- A device ROM that contains a device driver for the bridge.

The register set must be mapped into memory or IO address space (or both). The designer implements one or two Base Address Registers (programmable address decoders) for this purpose.

If there is a device ROM within the bridge, the designer must implement an Expansion ROM base address register used by configuration software to map the ROM into memory space.

Likewise, if the bridge incorporates a memory buffer, the design must include a Base Address Register used to assign a base address to the memory.

Base Address Registers

Differs from PCI. Optional. Only necessary if the bridge implements a device-specific register set and/or a memory buffer.

Located in Header dwords four and five. If the designer doesn't implement any internal, device-specific register set or memory, then these address decoders aren't necessary. These Base Address Registers are used in the same manner as those described for a non-bridge PCI function (see "Base Address Registers" on page 792). If implemented, both may be implemented as memory decoders, both as IO decoders, one as memory and one as IO, or only one may be implemented as either IO or memory.

If a BAR is implemented as a memory BAR with the prefetchable bit set to one, it must be implemented as a 64-bit memory BAR and would therefore consume both dwords four and five.

Expansion ROM Base Address Register

PCI-Compatible register. Optional. Only necessary if the bridge implements a bridge-specific device ROM. Located in Header dword 14. This register is optional (because there may not be a device ROM incorporated within the bridge). The format and usage of this register is precisely the same as that described for a non-bridge PCI function (see "Expansion ROM Base Address Register" on page 783).

Bridge's IO Filter

PCI-Compatible registers. Optional.

Introduction

There is no requirement for a bridge to support devices that reside in IO space within or behind the bridge. For this reason, implementation of the IO decode-related configuration registers is optional.

When the bridge detects an IO transaction initiated on either of its bus interfaces, it must determine which of the following actions to take:

1. **Ignore the transaction** because the target IO address isn't located on the other side of the bridge, nor is it targeting an IO location embedded within the bridge itself.
2. When the **target IO address is one of the bridge's internal IO registers**, the Requester is permitted to access the targeted internal register and the **transaction is not passed through the bridge**.
3. **When** the target IO location is located on the other side of the bridge, the **transaction is passed through the bridge** and is initiated on the opposite bus.

The optional configuration registers within the bridge that support this "filtering" capability are:

- **Base Address Registers**. If present, the Base Address Register or registers can be designed as IO or memory decoders for an internal register set or memory.
- **IO Base and IO Limit registers**. If the bridge supports IO space on the downstream side of the bridge, the IO Base register defines the start address and the IO Limit register defines the end address of the range to recognize and pass through to the secondary bus.
- **IO Extension registers** (IO Base Upper 16-Bits and IO Limit Upper 16-Bits registers). If the bridge supports a 4GB (rather than a 64KB) IO address space on the downstream side of the bridge (as indicated in the IO Base and IO Limit registers), the combination of the IO Base and the IO Base Upper 16 Bits registers define the start address, and the combination of the IO Limit and the IO Limit Upper 16-Bits registers define the end address of the range to recognize and pass to the secondary side.

The sections that follow describe each of these scenarios.

Bridge Doesn't Support Any IO Space Behind Bridge

Assume that a bridge doesn't support any devices that reside in IO space on the downstream side of the bridge. In other words, it doesn't recognize any IO addresses as being implemented behind the bridge and therefore ignores all IO transactions detected on its primary bus. In this case, the bridge designer does not implement the optional IO Base, IO Limit, or IO Extension registers (i.e., IO Base Upper 16-bits and IO Limit Upper 16-Bits registers).

The bridge ignores all IO request packets detected on the primary bus (other than transactions that may target an optional set of bridge-specific registers contained within the bridge itself).

Any IO transactions detected on the bridge's secondary bus would be claimed and passed through to the primary bus in case the target IO device is implemented somewhere upstream of the bridge.

Bridge Supports 64KB IO Space Behind Bridge

Assume that a bridge is designed to support IO transactions initiated on the primary bus that may target locations within the first 64KB of IO space (IO locations 00000000h through 0000FFFFh) on the secondary side of the bridge. It ignores any primary side IO accesses over the 64KB address boundary. In other words, the bridge supports a 64KB IO space, but not a 4GB IO space on the secondary side of the bridge.

In this case, the bridge designer must implement the IO Base and the IO Limit registers, but does not implement the IO Extension registers (i.e., the IO Base Upper 16-Bits and the IO Limit Upper 16-Bits registers).

The IO Base and IO Limit register pair comprise the global IO address decoder for all IO targets that reside on the secondary side of the bridge:

1. Before the registers are initialized by the configuration software, they are first read from to determine whether they support 64KB or a 4GB of IO space on the secondary side of the bridge. In this scenario, assume that the registers are hardwired to indicate that the bridge only supports a 64KB IO space.
2. The configuration software then walks the secondary bus (and any subordinate buses it discovers) and assigns to each IO decoder it discovers an exclusive IO address range within the first 64KB of IO space. The subranges assigned to the devices are assigned in sequential blocks to make efficient use of IO space.
3. The IO Base and Limit register pair are then initialized by the startup configuration software with the start and end address of the IO range that all IO devices that were discovered behind the bridge (on the secondary and on any subordinate buses) have been programmed to reside within. In this case, since the bridge only supports the first 64KB of IO space, the defined range will be a subset of the first 64KB of IO space.
4. After they have been initialized, these two registers provide the bridge with the start and the end address of the IO address range to recognize. After they have been initialized, these two registers provide the bridge with the start and the end address of the IO address range to recognize for passing IO transactions through the bridge.

The bridge only supports the lower 64KB of IO space, but the IO address decoder comprised of the IO Base and Limit registers must perform a full IO address decode of address bits [31:2] to determine whether or not to accept an IO access on the primary bus and pass it to the secondary bus.

The format of the IO Base and IO Limit registers are illustrated in Figure 22-14 on page 815 and Figure 22-15 on page 815. Both registers have the same format:

- the upper hex digit, bits [7:4], defines the most-significant hex digit of a 16-bit IO address;
- the lower hex digit, bits [3:0], defines whether the bridge performs a 16-bit or 32-bit IO address decode.

In the scenario under discussion, the lower hex digit of both registers is hard-wired with the value 0h, indicating that it performs a 16-bit IO address decode and therefore only supports addresses within the first 64KB of IO space.

Assume that the configuration software programs the upper digit of the IO Base register with the value 2h and the upper digit of the IO Limit register with the value 3h. This indicates that the start of the IO range to recognize is 2000h and the end address is 3FFFh—an 8KB block. As another example, assume that the upper digit in the base and limit registers are both set to 3h. The IO address range to recognize is then 3000h through 3FFFh—a 4KB block. In other words, this register pair defines the start address aligned on a 4KB address boundary, and the size, also referred to as the granularity, of the defined block is in increments of 4KB.

It should be noted that, if there aren't any IO devices on the bridge's secondary side, the IO Limit register can be programmed with a numerically lower IO address than the IO Base register. The bridge will not pass any IO transactions latched on the primary side through to the secondary side, but will pass any IO transactions latched on the secondary side through to the primary side.

Figure 22-14: IO Base Register

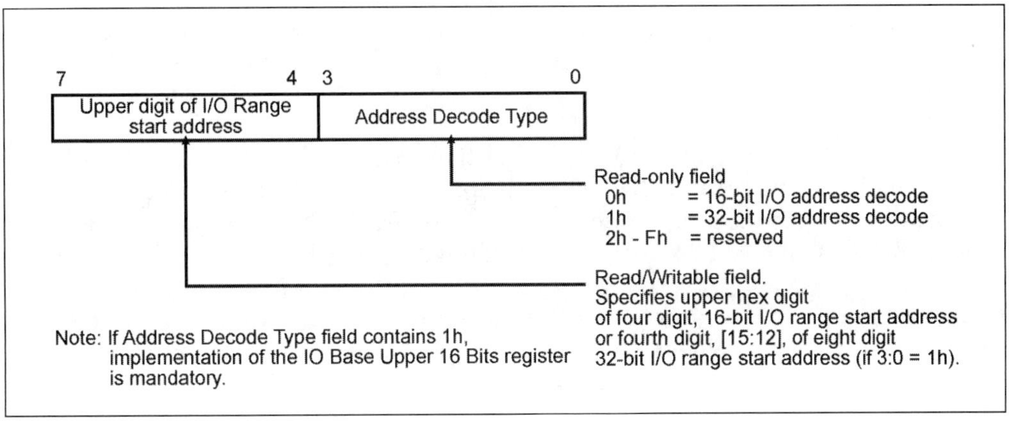

Figure 22-15: IO Limit Register

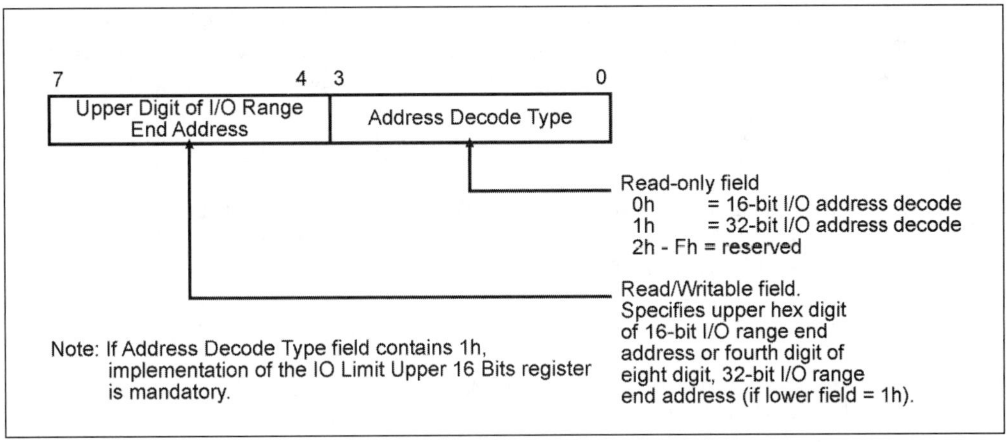

Example. Assume that the IO base is set to 2h and the IO Limit is set to 3h. The bridge is now primed to recognize any IO transaction on the primary bus that targets an IO address within the range consisting of 2000h through 3FFFh. Refer to Figure 22-16 on page 817.

Anytime that the bridge detects an IO transaction on the primary bus with an address inside the 2000h through 3FFFh range, it accepts the transaction and passes it through (because it's within the range defined by the IO Base and Limit registers and may therefore be for an IO device that resides behind the bridge).

Anytime that the bridge detects an IO transaction on the primary bus with an address outside the 2000h through 3FFFh range, it ignores the transaction (because the target IO address is outside the range of addresses assigned to IO devices that reside behind the bridge).

Anytime that the bridge detects an IO transaction on the secondary bus with an address inside the 2000h through 3FFFh range, it ignores the transaction (because the target address falls within the range assigned to IO devices that reside on the secondary side of the bridge).

Anytime that the bridge detects an IO transaction on the secondary bus with an address outside the 2000h through 3FFFh range, it accepts the transaction and passes it through to the primary side (because the target address falls outside the range assigned to IO devices that reside on the secondary side of the bridge, but it may be for an IO device on the primary side).

Figure 22-16: Example of IO Filtering Actions

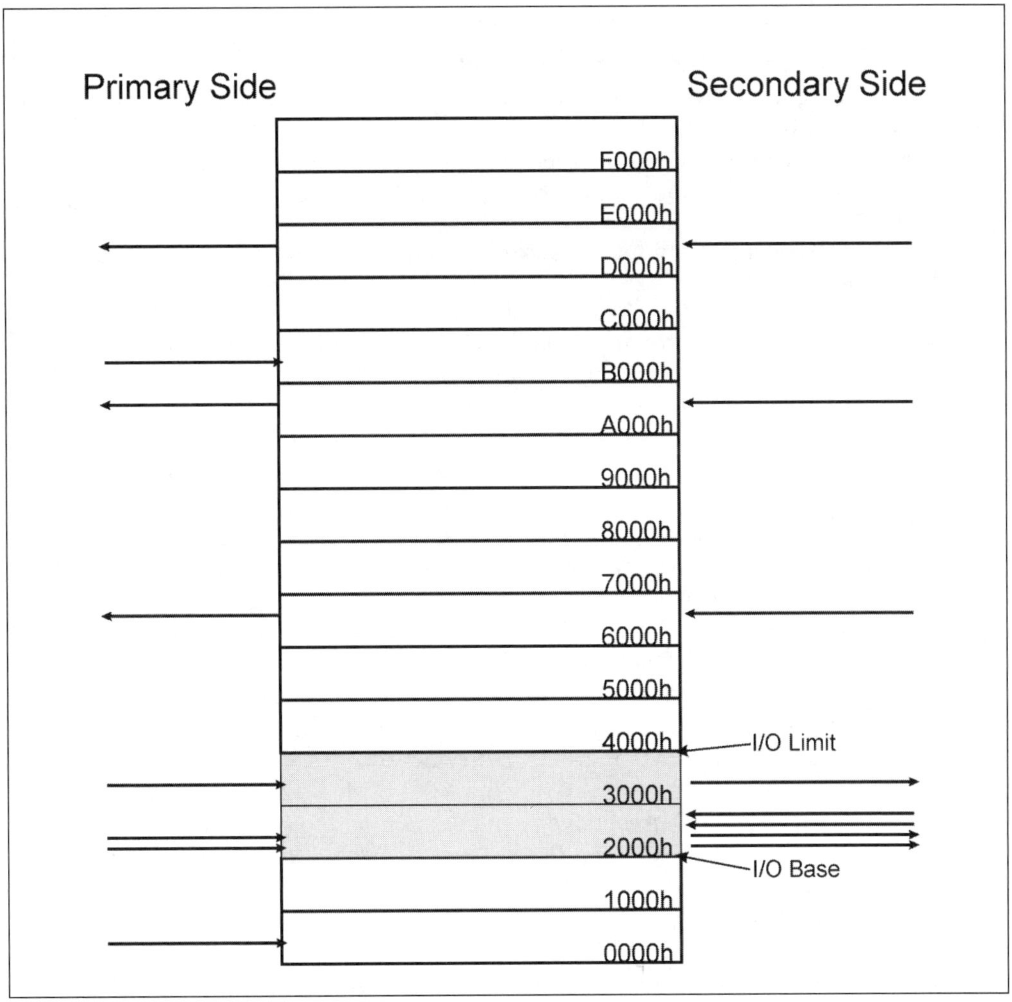

Bridge Supports 4GB IO Space Behind Bridge

Assume a bridge is designed to recognize IO transactions initiated on the primary bus that target locations anywhere within 4GB of IO space (IO locations 00000000h through FFFFFFFFh) on the downstream side of the bridge.

In this case, in addition to the IO Base and the IO Limit registers, the bridge designer must also implement the IO Extension registers—IO Base Upper 16-bits and the IO Limit Upper 16-bits registers:

- The IO Base register is initialized with the fourth digit of the 32-bit start IO address.
- The IO Base Upper 16 bits register is initialized with the fifth through the eight digits of the 32-bit start address of the range.
- The IO Limit register is initialized with the fourth digit of the 32-bit end IO address.
- The IO Limit Upper 16 bits register is initialized with the fifth through eighth digits of the 32-bit end address of the range.

The IO Base and IO Limit register pair comprise an IO address decoder. They are used as follows:

1. Before the registers are initialized by the configuration software, they are read from to determine if they are capable of supporting a 64KB or a 4GB IO address space behind the bridge. In this scenario, the Address Decode Type field (see Figure 22-14 on page 815) within each of the registers is hardwired (with a value of 1h) to indicate that a 4GB IO space is supported on the secondary side.
2. The configuration software than walks the secondary bus (and any subordinate buses it discovers beneath the secondary bus) and assigns each IO device that it discovers an exclusive IO address range within the 4GB IO space. The sub-ranges assigned to the devices are assigned in sequential blocks to make efficient use of IO space.
3. The IO Base and IO Base Extension (i.e., the IO Base Upper 16-bits) register pair is then initialized by the startup configuration software with the upper five digits of the 4KB-aligned, 32-bit start address of the IO range that all IO devices that were discovered behind the bridge (on the secondary and on any subordinate buses) have been programmed to reside within.
4. The IO Limit and IO Limit Extension (i.e., the IO Limit Upper 16 bits) register pair is initialized with the 4KB-aligned end address of the range that the devices occupy.

In the scenario under discussion, since the bridge supports the entire 4GB IO space, the defined range is a subset of the overall 4GB IO space. After they have been initialized, these four registers provide the bridge with the start and the end address of the IO address range to recognize.

Since the bridge supports the entire 4GB IO space, the IO address decoder comprised of the four registers (Base and Limit registers plus their Extension registers) performs an IO address decode within address bits [31:12] to determine whether or not to pass an IO access detected on the primary bus through to the secondary bus and vice versa.

The format of the IO Base and IO Limit registers was illustrated earlier in Figure 22-14 on page 815 and Figure 22-15 on page 815. In the scenario under discussion, the lower hex digit of the Base and Limit registers is hardwired with the value 1h, indicating a 32-bit IO address decode, supporting address recognition within the entire 4GB IO space. Simply put, the IO Base and IO Limit Upper 16-bits registers are used to hold the upper four digits of the start and end IO address boundaries, respectively.

Assume that the configuration software programs the registers as follows:

- Upper digit of the IO Base = 2h.
- IO Base Upper 16-bits register = 1234h.
- Upper digit of the IO Limit register = 3h.
- IO Limit Upper 16-bits register = 1235h.

This indicates a 72KB range consisting of:

- start of IO range = 12342000h
- end address = 12353FFFh.

As another example, assume the following:

- Upper digit of the IO Base = 3h.
- IO Base Upper 16-bits register = 1234h.
- Upper digit of the IO Limit register = 3h.
- IO Limit Upper 16-bits register = 1234h.

This indicates a 4KB range consisting of:

- start of IO range = 12343000h
- end address = 12343FFFh.

In other words, the four registers define the start address aligned on a 4KB address boundary, and the size of the defined block is an increment of 4KB.

Bridge's Prefetchable Memory Filter

Differs from PCI. Optional.

An Important Note From the Authors

Although the Express spec appears to support the concept of a bridge within a Root Complex or a Switch reading more data than is actually requested from areas of memory defined as prefetchable (see the spec statements included below), it is the opinion of the authors that a bridge within a Root Complex or a Switch will not do so. Our rationale is provided below.

In PCI. When a PCI bus master initiates a memory read transaction, it issues the start memory address but does not indicate how much data is to be read. The only exception is a single Data Phase memory read. In that case, the total amount of data to be read is represented by the Byte Enables that are presented in that Data Phase.

When the device acting as the target on the initiating bus receives the transaction request, the manner in which the request is handled depends on the device type (bridge or ultimate memory target), as well as the transaction type used by the bus master:

- **If device acting as the target is the ultimate target of the read**:
  - **and the memory is well-behaved, prefetchable memory**, then the target may perform internal prefetches (i.e., read-aheads) and queue up data to be supplied to the requester if the transaction ends up asking for the data. This is to enhance performance. If the transaction ends without all of the prefetched data being asked for, the remaining data in the target's read-ahead buffer should be discarded (unless the target can guarantee the continued freshness of the data).
  - **and the memory is not prefetchable memory** (e.g., it's a memory-mapped IO register set), then the memory target must wait until the Byte Enables are presented in each Data Phase and only read and supply the requested bytes. No prefetching is permitted.
- **If the device acting as the target is a bridge in the path to the target**, the bridge latches the request and issues a Retry to the initiating master:
  - **and the transaction type is Memory Read**, there are two possibilities:
    - If the memory address is **within a range defined as prefetchable memory**, the bridge may turn the read into a burst read when it initiates the request on the other side of the bridge and prefetch data into a bridge buffer. When the original master then retries the transaction, the bridge sources data from the fast read-ahead buffer yielding better performance. If the master ultimately doesn't consume all of the data, it is discarded by the bridge.
    - **and the memory is not prefetchable memory** (e.g., it's a memory-mapped IO register set), then no prefetching by the bridge is permitted when it re-initiates the read on the opposite side of the bridge.

— **and the transaction type is Memory Read Line (MRL),** this tells the bridge that the master has specific knowledge that the memory range from the transaction's start address up to the end of the addressed line of memory space is prefetchable memory. Even if the bridge's prefetchable memory range registers indicate this is not prefetchable memory, the bridge may turn the read into a burst read when it initiates the request on the other side of the bridge and prefetch data up to the end of the current line into a bridge buffer. When the original master then retries the transaction, the bridge sources data from the fast read-ahead buffer yielding better performance. If the master ultimately doesn't consume all of the data, it is discarded by the bridge.

— **and the transaction type is Memory Read Multiple (MRM),** this tells the bridge that the master has specific knowledge that the memory range from the transaction's start address and up to the end of the line immediately following the addressed line of memory space is prefetchable memory. Even if the bridge's prefetchable memory range registers indicate this is not prefetchable memory, the bridge may turn the read into a burst read when it initiates the request on the other side of the bridge and prefetch data across cache line boundaries into a bridge buffer. When the original master then retries the transaction, the bridge sources data from the fast read-ahead buffer yielding better performance. If the master ultimately doesn't consume all of the data, it is discarded by the bridge.

In PCI Express. When a PCI Express Requester issues a memory read request, it indicates the exact amount of data it wishes to read:

- The First DW Byte Enable field in the request packet header indicates the byte(s) to be read from the first dword.
- The Length field in the request packet header indicates the overall number of dwords in the transfer.
- The Last DW Byte Enable field in the request packet header indicates the byte(s) to be read from the last dword.

Since the exact amount of requested data is known at the onset of a memory read request, there is no reason for prefetching to achieve better performance (as there is in PCI).

Spec References To Prefetchable Memory. The following Express spec 1.0a references represent all of its references to prefetching:

- Page 33, line 5: "A PCI Express Endpoint requesting memory resources through a BAR must set the BAR's Prefetchable bit unless the range contains locations with read side-effects or locations in which the device does not tolerate write merging".
- Page 33, line 8: "For a PCI Express Endpoint, 64-bit addressing must be supported for all BARs that have the prefetchable bit set. 32-bit addressing is permitted for all BARs that do not have the prefetchable bit set."
- Page 52, line 13: "For each bit of the Byte Enables fields: a value of 0b indicates that the corresponding byte of data must not be written or, if non prefetchable, must not be read at the Completer."
- Page 54, line 9: "This is really just a specific case of the rule that in a non-prefetchable space, non-enabled bytes must not be read at the Completer."
- Page 265, line 26: "For example, if a Read is issued to prefetchable memory space and the Completion returns with a Unsupported Request Completion Status, perhaps due to a temporary condition, the initiator may choose to reissue the Read Request without side effects."
- Page 326, line 5: "A PCI Express Endpoint requesting memory resources through a BAR must set the BAR's Prefetchable bit unless the range contains locations with read side-effects or locations in which the device does not tolerate write merging. It is strongly encouraged that memory-mapped resources be designed as prefetchable whenever possible. PCI Express devices other than legacy Endpoints must support 64-bit addressing for any Base Address register that requests prefetchable memory resources".
- Page 328, line 1: "A PCI Express Endpoint requesting memory resources through a BAR must set the BAR's Prefetchable bit unless the range contains locations with read side-effects or locations in which the device does not tolerate write merging. It is strongly encouraged that memory-mapped resources be designed as prefetchable whenever possible. PCI Express devices other than legacy Endpoints must support 64-bit addressing for any Base Address register that requests prefetchable memory resources."
- Page 329: "The Prefetchable Memory Base and Prefetchable Memory Limit registers must indicate that 64-bit addresses are supported, as defined in PCI Bridge 1.1." *Please note that this not so. Section 3.2.5.10 in the 1.1 bridge spec states "The Prefetchable Base Upper 32 Bits and Prefetchable Limit Upper 32 Bits registers are optional extensions to the Prefetchable Memory Base and Prefetchable Memory Limit registers."*

Characteristics of Prefetchable Memory Devices

While the Memory Base and Limit registers are mandatory (to support memory-mapped IO behind the bridge). The Prefetchable Memory Base and Limit registers (and their extensions) are optional (there is no requirement for a bridge to support prefetchable memory on its downstream side). The PCI-to-PCI bridge specification recognizes the fact that while both groups are mapped into memory address space, memory devices and memory-mapped IO devices can have distinctly different operational characteristics.

An optional set of registers are provided in the bridge's configuration space that permit the configuration software to define the start and end address of the prefetchable memory space that is occupied by well-behaved memory devices behind the bridge. A mandatory register pair permits the configuration software to define the start and end address of the memory-mapped IO space that is occupied by well-behaved memory devices behind the bridge.

Multiple Reads Yield the Same Data. A well-behaved memory device always returns the same data from a location no matter how many times the location is read from. In other words, reading from a memory device doesn't in any way alter the contents of memory. This is one of the characteristics of a prefetchable memory target.

Byte Merging Permitted In the Posted Write Buffer. A bridge incorporates a posted-write buffer that quickly absorbs data to be written to a memory device on the other side of the bridge. Since the initiating Requester is able to immediately complete a memory write and doesn't have to delay until the write to the memory device has actually been completed, posting yields better performance during memory write operations. The bridge would ensure that, before any subsequent memory read is permitted to propagate through the bridge, the bridge would flush its posted-write buffer to the memory device. Byte merging is permitted in a bridge's posted memory write buffer when handling writes to prefetchable memory (for more information, refer to "Byte Merging" on page 801).

Characteristics of Memory-Mapped IO Devices

Memory-mapped IO devices exhibit a different set of operational characteristics.

Read Characteristics. Performing a memory read from a memory-mapped IO location often has the effect of altering the contents of the location. As examples, one of the following may be true:

- The location may be occupied by a memory-mapped IO status port. Reading from the location causes the IO device to deassert any status bits that were set in the register (on the assumption that they've been read and will therefore be dealt with by the device driver). If the read was caused by a prefetch and the prefetched data is never actually read by the device driver, then status information has just been discarded.
- The location may be the front-end of a FIFO data buffer. Performing a read from the location causes the delivery of its current contents and the next data item is then automatically placed in the location by the IO device. The device assumes that the first data item has just been read by the device driver and sets up the next data item in the FIFO location. If the read was caused by a prefetch and the prefetched data is never actually read by the device driver, then the data has just been discarded.

Reads within an area of memory space occupied by memory-mapped IO devices must never result in prefetching by a bridge. A mandatory set of registers are provided that permit the configuration software to define the start and end address of the memory space that is occupied by memory-mapped IO devices that reside on the bridge's secondary side.

Write Characteristics. See "Byte Merging" on page 801.

Determining If Memory Is Prefetchable or Not

The configuration software determines that a memory target supports prefetching by testing the state of the *Prefetchable* attribute bit in the memory target's Base Address Register (see "Base Address Registers" on page 792 and "Prefetchable Attribute Bit" on page 795).

- Prefetchable = 1 indicates that the memory is prefetchable. The memory target must be mapped into Prefetchable memory space using the bridge's Prefetchable Base and Limit configuration registers (if they are implemented).
- Prefetchable = 0 indicates that it's not. In this case, the memory target must be mapped into memory-mapped IO space using the Memory Base and Limit registers.

Bridge Support For Downstream Prefetchable Memory Is Optional

If the bridge does not support Prefetchable memory on its secondary side, the Prefetchable Memory Base and Limit registers must be implemented as read-only registers that return zero when read, and the Prefetchable Memory Base and Prefetchable Memory Limit registers are not implemented.

Must Support > 4GB Prefetchable Memory On Secondary Side

Whether or not a bridge supports prefetchable memory on the bridge's downstream side is optional. If the designer chooses to support this capability, then the following registers must be implemented to define the start and end address of the memory range occupied by prefetchable memory devices on the downstream side of the bridge:

- Prefetchable Memory Base register.
- Prefetchable Memory Limit register.

These two registers are used to define the start (base) and end (limit) address of the memory range and are illustrated in Figure 22-17 on page 827 and Figure 22-18 on page 828. Any address within the lower 4GB can be specified. The start address is 1MB-aligned and the size of the range is specified in 1MB increments. The Express spec states that all memory BARs for prefetchable memory must be implemented as 64-bit registers (see Figure 22-11 on page 797). To support this, the extensions to Base and Limit registers must also be implemented:

- Prefetchable Memory Base Upper 32-bits register.
- Prefetchable Memory Limit Upper 32-bits register.

The 4-bit Address Decode Type field in the Base and Limit registers is hardwired to indicate that the extension registers are present.

The configuration software walks the secondary bus and any buses subordinate to the bridge and assigns each Prefetchable memory target a sub-range in a global overall range within the 2^{64} memory space. After completing the address assignment process, the software then writes the upper eight hex digits of the range's 64-bit start address into the Prefetchable Memory Base Upper register and the next three hex digits into the upper three digits of the Base register. The upper eight hex digits of the range's 64-bit end address is written into the Prefetchable Memory Limit Upper register and the next three hex digits into the upper three digits of the Limit register.

As an example, assume that these four registers are set as follows:

- FF00000h is written into the Prefetchable Memory Base Upper 32-bits register.
- 123h is written into the upper three digits of the Base register.
- FF000000h is written into Prefetchable Memory Limit Upper 32-bits register.
- 124h is written into the upper three digits of the Limit register.

This defines the Prefetchable memory address range as the 2MB range from FF00000012300000h through FF000000124FFFFFh. As another example, assume they are programmed as follows:

- 00000230h is written into the Prefetchable Memory Base Upper 32-bits register.
- 222h written into the upper three digits of the Base register.
- 00000230h is written into Prefetchable Memory Limit Upper 32-bits register.
- 222h written into the upper three digits of the Limit register.

This defines the Prefetchable memory address range as the 1MB range from 0000023022200000h through 00000230222FFFFFh.

Figure 22-17: Prefetchable Memory Base Register

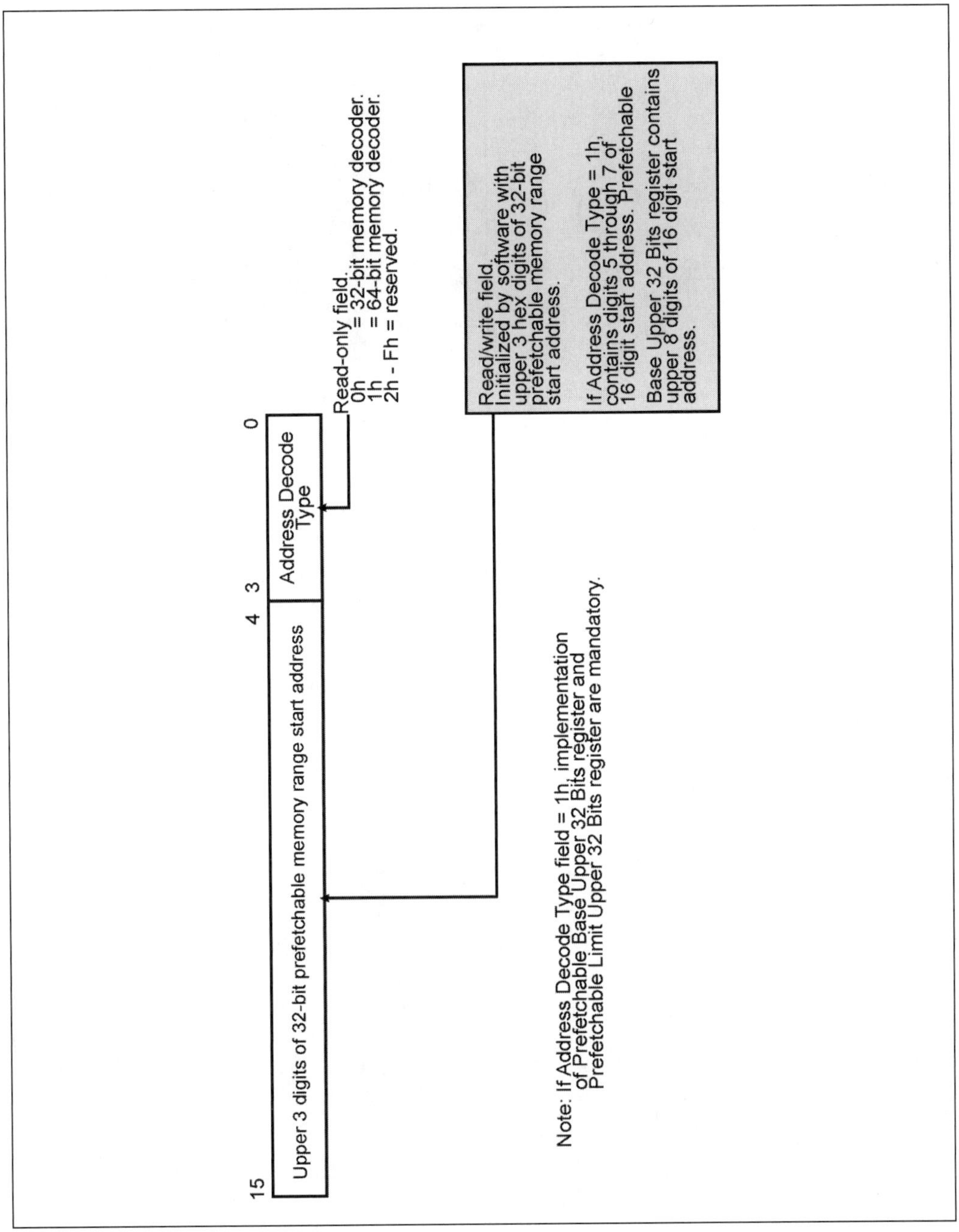

Figure 22-18: Prefetchable Memory Limit Register

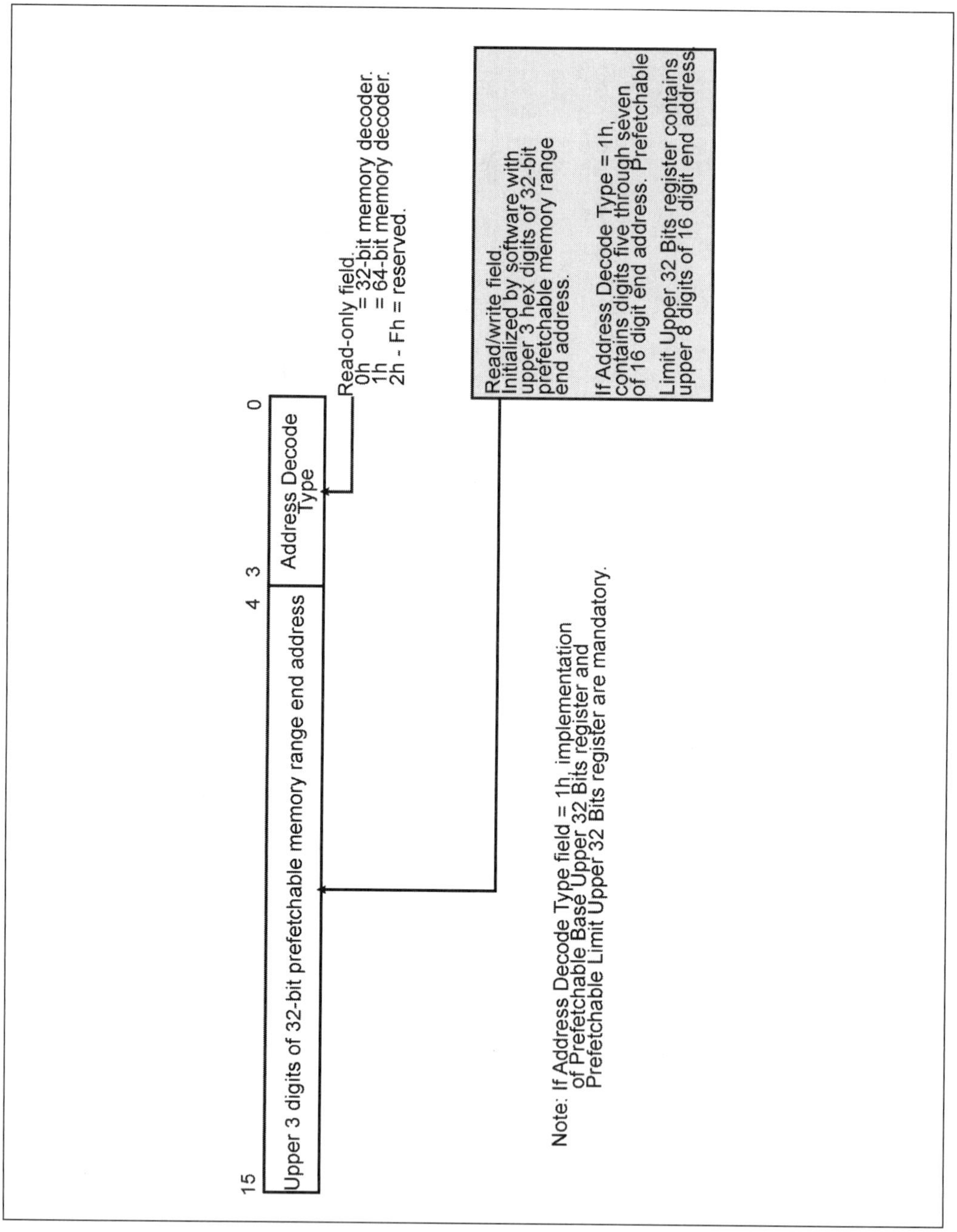

Rules for Bridge Prefetchable Memory Accesses

The following rules apply to Prefetchable memory:

1. Bridge support for Prefetchable memory on its secondary side is optional.
2. If the bridge does not support Prefetchable memory on its secondary side, the Prefetchable Memory Base and Limit registers must be implemented as read-only registers that return zero when read.
3. If the bridge does support prefetchable memory on its downstream side, it must implement the Prefetchable Memory Base and Limit registers, as well as the Prefetchable Memory Base and Limit Upper 32-bits registers (as indicated by hardwiring the first digit in the Base and Limit registers to a value of 1h).
4. Memory transactions are forwarded from the primary to the secondary bus if the address is within the range defined by the Prefetchable Memory Base and Limit registers or that defined by the Memory Base and Limit registers (for memory-mapped IO).
5. Memory transactions are forwarded from the secondary to the primary bus when the address is outside the ranges defined by the extended Prefetchable Memory Base and Limit registers and the Memory Base and Limit registers (for memory-mapped IO).
6. When 2^{64} memory is supported on the downstream side of the bridge, transactions targeting addresses within the address range specified by the Prefetchable Memory Base and Limit registers (and their extensions) are permitted to cross the 4GB boundary.
7. The bridge designer must support memory access requests above the 4GB address boundary received by its downstream interface. Prior to the 1.1 PCI-to-PCI bridge spec, it was optional on both sides. This was changed to ensure that Requesters on the secondary side can access main memory above the 4GB address boundary.
8. Assume that the bridge supports Prefetchable memory anywhere in 2^{64} memory space on the downstream side, but the configuration software maps all Prefetchable memory behind the bridge below the 4GB boundary. In this case, the upper extensions of the Prefetchable Base and Limit registers must be set to zero and the bridge does not respond to memory access requests above the 4GB address boundary received on the upstream interface. Those received by the bridge's downstream interface would be passed to the upstream interface (in case the Requester is addressing main memory above the 4GB boundary).
9. Assume that the bridge supports Prefetchable memory anywhere in 2^{64} memory space on the downstream side and that the configuration software maps all Prefetchable memory on the downstream side above the 4GB

boundary. In this case, the upper extensions of the Prefetchable Base and Limit registers contain non-zero values and the bridge responds only to prefetchable memory access requests received on its upstream interface that are above the 4GB address boundary and within the defined prefetchable memory address range.

10. Assume that the bridge supports Prefetchable memory anywhere in 2^{64} memory space behind the bridge and that the configuration software maps the Prefetchable memory on the bridge's downstream side into a space that straddles the 4GB boundary. In this case, the extension to the Prefetchable Base register is set to zero and the extension to the Limit register contains a non-zero value. When a memory request with an address below the 4GB boundary is detected on either interface, the bridge compares the address only to the Prefetchable Memory Base register. If the address is $\geq$ the start address specified in the register, the address is in range. When a memory request with an address above the 4GB boundary is detected on either interface, the bridge compares the lower 32-bits of the address to the Limit register and the Upper 32-bits of the address to the Limit Upper 32-bits register. If the address is $\leq$ the end address specified in the two registers, the address is in range.
11. The bridge may be designed to assume that all memory accesses received by its downstream interface that are passed to the primary bus are prefetchable. This assumes that the destination of all memory reads traveling upstream is system memory (which is prefetchable). If a bridge makes this assumption, it must implement a device-specific bit in its configuration space that allows this ability to be disabled.
12. Memory writes received by either of the bridge's interfaces are accepted into the bridge's downstream or upstream posted memory write buffer. As described in "Byte Merging" on page 801, the bridge is permitted to perform byte merging in the buffer for writes to prefetchable memory, but not to memory-mapped IO.

Bridge's Memory-Mapped IO Filter

PCI-Compatible registers. Mandatory. The bridge designer is required to implement the Memory Base and Limit registers used to define a memory-mapped IO range. These two registers are used to define a range of memory occupied by memory-mapped IO devices that reside on the downstream side of the bridge. Figure 22-19 on page 831 and Figure 22-20 on page 831 illustrate the Memory Base and Limit registers. The lower digit of each register is hardwired to zero and the upper three digits are used to define the upper three hex digits of the eight-digit start and end addresses, respectively. Unlike the Prefetchable Base and Limit and IO Base and Limit register pairs, there are no Extension registers associated with the Memory Base and Limit register pair. This means that all memory-mapped IO devices in the system must reside in the lower 4GB of memory address space.

As an example, assume that the configuration software has written the following values to the Memory Base and Limit registers:

- The upper three digits of the Memory Base register contain 555h.
- The upper three digits of the Memory Limit register contain 678h.

This defines a 292MB memory-mapped IO region on the downstream side of the bridge starting at 55500000h and ending at 678FFFFFh.

Figure 22-19: Memory-Mapped IO Base Register

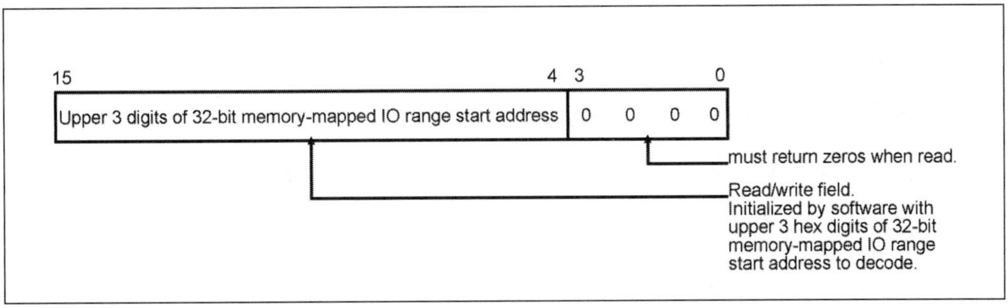

Figure 22-20: Memory-Mapped IO Limit Register

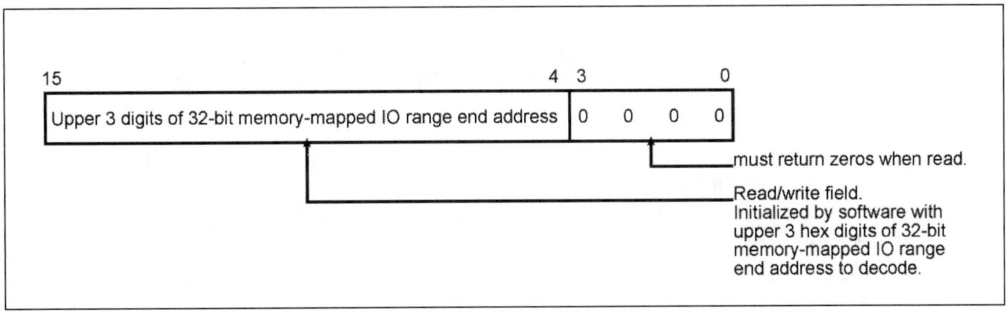

Bridge Command Registers

Differs from PCI. Mandatory.

Introduction

The bridge designer must implement two required command registers in the bridge's configuration Header region:

- The Command register is the standard configuration Command register defined by the spec for any function. It is associated with the bridge's primary bus interface.
- The Bridge Control register is an extension to the standard Command register and is associated with the operation of both of the bridge's bus interfaces.

These two registers are described in the next two sections.

Bridge Command Register

Differs from PCI. Mandatory. The Command register format, pictured in Figure 22-21 on page 832, is the same as that for a non-bridge function. Some of the bits, however, have different effects. Each of the bits is described in Table 22-6 on page 833.

Figure 22-21: Command Register

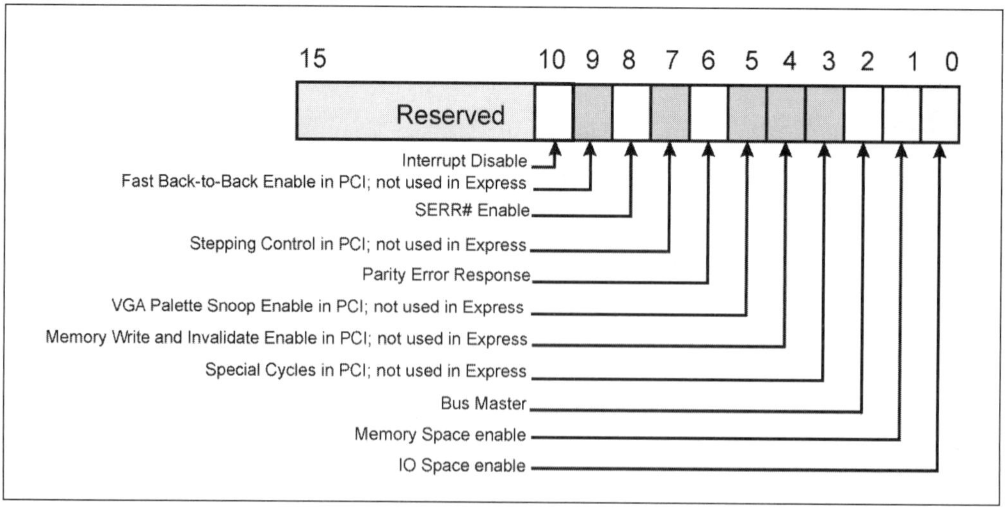

Table 22-6: Bridge Command Register Bit Assignment

Bit	Attributes	Description
0	RW	**IO Address Space Decoder Enable.** – **0**. IO transactions received at the downstream side of a bridge that are moving in the upstream direction are not forwarded and bridge returns completion with 'Unsupported Request' completion status. – **1**. IO transactions received at the downstream side of a bridge that are moving in the upstream direction are forwarded from the secondary to primary side of the bridge.
1	RW	**Memory Address Space Decoder Enable.** • **Memory-mapped devices within Bridge**: – **0**. Memory decoder is disabled and Memory transactions targeting this device results in bridge returning completion with 'Unsupported Request' completion status. – **1**. Memory decoder is enabled and Memory transactions targeting this device are accepted. • **Memory transactions targeting device on the upstream side of a bridge**: – **0**. Memory transactions received at the downstream side of a bridge are not forwarded to the upstream side and bridge returns 'Unsupported Request' completion status. – **1**. Memory transactions received at the dowstream side of a bridge that target a device residing on the upstream side of a bridge are forwarded from the secondary to the primary side of the bridge.
2	RW	**Bus Master.** – Controls the ability of a Root Port or a downstream Switch Port to forward memory or IO requests in the upstream direction. – **If this bit is 0,** when a Root Port or a downstream Switch Port receives an upstream-bound memory request or IO request, it returns Unsupported Requests (UR) status to the requester. – This bit does not affect forwarding of Completions in either the upstream or downstream direction. – The forwarding of requests other than those mentioned above are not controlled by this bit. – Default value of this bit is 0.

Table 22-6: Bridge Command Register Bit Assignment (Continued)

Bit	Attributes	Description
3	RO	**Special Cycles**. Does not apply to PCI Express and must be hardwired to 0.
4	RO	**Memory Write and Invalidate Enable**. Does not apply to PCI Express and must be hardwired to 0.
5	RO	**VGA Palette Snoop**. Does not apply to PCI Express and must be hardwired to 0.
6	RW	**Parity Error Response**. When forwarding a Poisoned TLP from Primary to Secondary: • The primary side must set the Detected Parity Error bit in the bridge Status register. • If the Parity Error Response bit in the Bridge Control register is set, the secondary side must set the Master Data Parity Error bit in the Secondary Status register. When forwarding a Poisoned TLP from Secondary to Primary: • The secondary side must set the Detected Parity Error bit in the Secondary Status register. • If the Parity Error Response bit in the Bridge Control register is set, the primary side must set the Master Data Parity Error bit in the bridge Status register. If the Parity Error Response bit is cleared, the Master Data Parity Error status bit in the bridge Status register is never set. The default value of this bit is 0.
7	RO	**Stepping Control**. Does not apply to PCI Express. Must be hardwired to 0.
8	RW	**SERR# Enable**. When set, this bit enables the non-fatal and fatal errors detected by the bridge's primary interface to be reported to the Root Complex. The function reports such errors to the Root Complex if it is enabled to do so either through this bit or through the PCI Express specific bits in the Device Control register (see "Device Control Register" on page 905). The default value of this bit is 0.
9	RO	**Fast Back-to-Back Enable.** Does not apply to PCI Express and must be hardwired to 0.

Table 22-6: Bridge Command Register Bit Assignment (Continued)

Bit	Attributes	Description
10	RW	**Interrupt Disable.** Controls the ability of a bridge to generate INTx interrupt messages: • 0 = The bridge is enabled to generate INTx interrupt messages. • 1 = The bridge's ability to generate INTx interrupt messages is disabled. If the bridge had already transmitted any Assert_INTx emulation interrupt messages and this bit is then set, it must transmit a corresponding Deassert_INTx message for each assert message transmitted earlier. Note that INTx emulation interrupt messages forwarded by Root and Switch Ports from devices downstream of the Root or Switch Port are not affected by this bit. The default value of this bit is 0.
15:11		**Reserved**. Read-only and must return zero when read.

Bridge Control Register

Differs from PCI. Mandatory. The Bridge Control register is a required extension to the bridge's Command register and is associated with the operation of both the primary and the secondary bridge interfaces. Figure 22-22 on page 835 illustrates this register and Table 22-7 on page 836 defines its bit assignment. Bits 8 - through - 11 were first defined in the 2.2 PCI spec.

Figure 22-22: Bridge Control Register

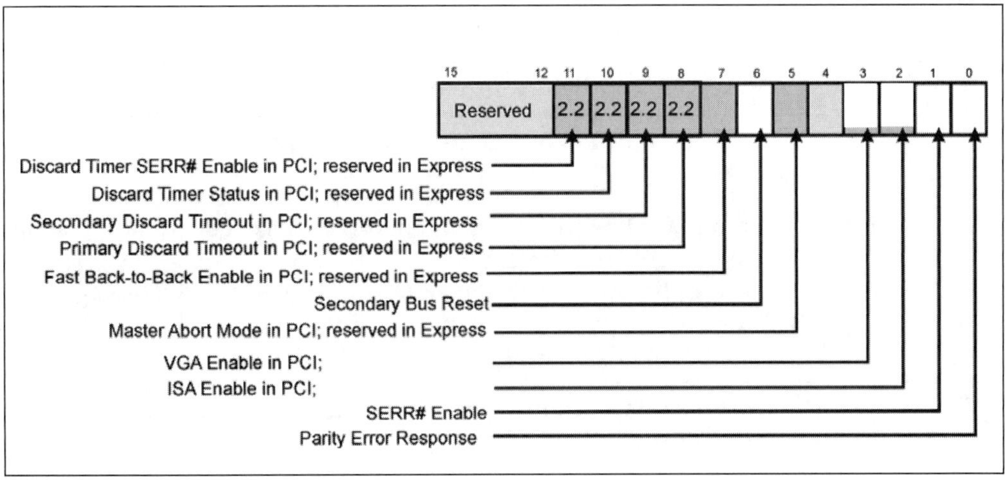

Table 22-7: Bridge Control Register Bit Assignment

Bit	Attributes	Description
0	RW	**Parity Error Response.** When forwarding a Poisoned TLP from Primary to Secondary: • The primary side must set the Detected Parity Error bit in the bridge Status register. • If the Parity Error Response bit in the Bridge Control register is set, the secondary side must set the Master Data Parity Error bit in the Secondary Status register. When forwarding a Poisoned TLP from Secondary to Primary: • The secondary side must set the Detected Parity Error bit in the Secondary Status register. • If the Parity Error Response bit in the Bridge Control register is set, the primary side must set the Master Data Parity Error bit in the bridge Status register. If the Parity Error Response bit is cleared, the Master Data Parity Error status bit in the Secondary Status register is never set. The default value of this bit is 0.
1	RW	**SERR# Enable.** This bit controls the forwarding of ERR_COR (correctable errors), ERR_NONFATAL (non-fatal errors), and ERR_FATAL (fatal errors) received on the secondary side to the primary side. Default value of this field is 0.
2	RW	**ISA Enable.** See page 582 of the MindShare PCI book.
3	RW	**VGA Enable.** See page 608 of the MindShare PCI book.
4	RO	**Reserved.** Hardwired to zero.
5	RO	**Master Abort Mode.** Not used in Express and must be hardwired to zero.
6	RW	**Secondary Bus Reset.** Setting this bit to one triggers a hot reset on the Express downstream port. Port configuration registers must not be affected, except as required to update port status. Default value of this field is 0.
7	RO	**Fast Back-to-Back Enable.** Not used in Express and must be hardwired to zero.

Table 22-7: Bridge Control Register Bit Assignment (Continued)

Bit	Attributes	Description
8	RO	**Primary Discard Timeout**. Not used in Express and must be hard-wired to zero.
9	RO	**Secondary Discard Timeout**. Not used in Express and must be hardwired to zero.
10	RO	**Discard Timer Status**. Not used in Express and must be hard-wired to zero.
11	RO	**Discard Timer SERR# Enable**. Not used in Express and must be hardwired to zero.

Bridge Status Registers

Introduction

The bridge contains two required status registers, each of which is associated with one of the two interfaces.

Bridge Status Register (Primary Bus)

Differs from PCI. Mandatory. Refer to Figure 22-23 on page 838 and Table 22 - 8 on page 838. This required register is completely compatible with the Status register definition for a non-bridge function (see "Status Register" on page 788) and only reflects the status of the bridge's primary interface.

If the Capabilities List bit (bit 4) is set to one, this indicates that the bridge implements the Capability Pointer register in byte 0 of dword 13 in its configuration Header (see Figure 22-13 on page 803). For a general description of the New Capabilities, refer to "Capabilities Pointer Register" on page 779. In subsequently traversing the New Capabilities list, software may discover that the bridge implements the Slot Numbering registers. For a description of this feature, refer to "Introduction To Chassis/Slot Numbering Registers" on page 859 and "Chassis and Slot Number Assignment" on page 861.

Figure 22-23: Primary Interface Status Register

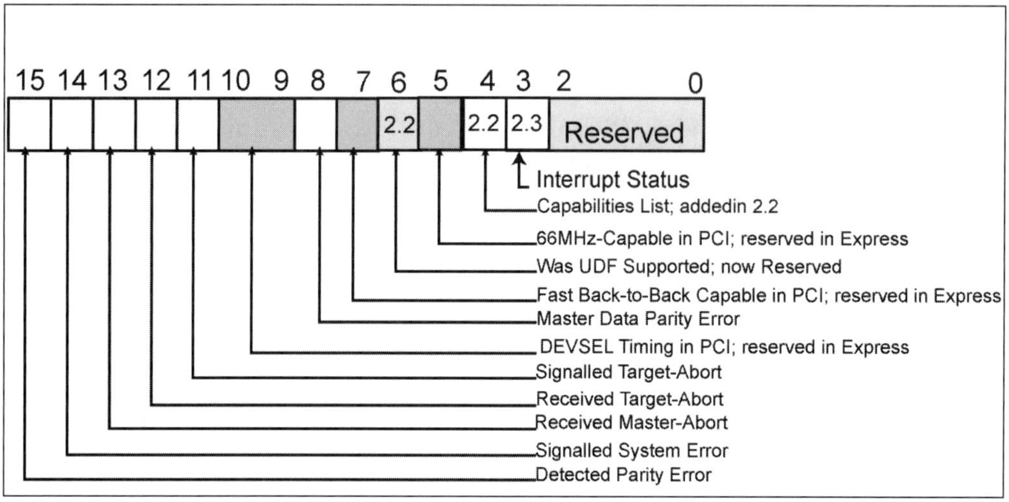

Table 22 - 8: Bridge Primary Side Status Register

Bit	Attributes	Description
3	RO	**Interrupt Status**. Indicates that the bridge itself had previously transmitted an interrupt request to its driver (that is, the function transmitted an interrupt message earlier in time and is awaiting servicing). Note that INTx emulation interrupts forwarded by Root and Switch Ports from devices downstream of the Root or Switch Port are not reflected in this bit. The default state of this bit is 0.
4	RO	**Capabilities List**. Indicates the presence of one or more extended capability register sets in the lower 48 dwords of the function's PCI-compatible configuration space. Since, at a minimum, all PCI Express functions are required to implement the PCI Express capability structure, this bit must be set to 1.
5	RO	**66MHz-Capable**. Does not apply to PCI Express and must be 0.

Table 22 - 8: Bridge Primary Side Status Register (Continued)

Bit	Attributes	Description
7	RO	**Fast Back-to-Back Capable**. Does not apply to PCI Express and must be 0.
8	RW1C	**Master Data Parity Error**. When forwarding a Poisoned TLP from Primary to Secondary: • The primary side must set the Detected Parity Error bit in the bridge Status register. • If the Parity Error Response bit in the Bridge Control register is set, the secondary side must set the Master Data Parity Error bit in the Secondary Status register. When forwarding a Poisoned TLP from Secondary to Primary: • The secondary side must set the Detected Parity Error bit in the Secondary Status register. • If the Parity Error Response bit in the Bridge Control register is set, the primary side must set the Master Data Parity Error bit in the bridge Status register. If the Parity Error Response bit in the Bridge Command register is cleared, the Master Data Parity Error status bit in the Secondary Status register is never set. The default value of this bit is 0.
10:9	RO	**DEVSEL Timing**. Does not apply to PCI Express and must be 0.
11	RW1C	**Signaled Target Abort**. This bit is set when the bridge's primary interface completes a received request by issuing a Completer Abort Completion Status. Default value of this field is 0.
12	RW1C	**Received Target Abort**. This bit is set when the bridge's primary interface receives a Completion with Completer Abort Completion Status. Default value of this field is 0.
13	RW1C	**Received Master Abort**. This bit is set when the bridge's primary interface receives a Completion with Unsupported Request Completion Status. Default value of this field is 0.

Table 22 - 8: Bridge Primary Side Status Register (Continued)

Bit	Attributes	Description
14	RW1C	**Signaled System Error**. This bit is set when the bridge's primary interface sends an ERR_FATAL (fatal error) or ERR_NONFATAL (non-fatal error) message (if the SERR Enable bit in the bridge Command register is set to one). The default value of this bit is 0.
15	RW1C	**Detected Parity Error**. This bit is set by the bridge's primary interface whenever it receives a Poisoned TLP, regardless of the state the Parity Error Enable bit in the bridge Command register. Default value of this bit is 0.

Bridge Secondary Status Register

Differs from PCI. Mandatory. Refer to Figure 22-24 on page 841. With the exception of the Received System Error bit, this required register is completely compatible with the Status register definition for a non-bridge function (see "Status Register" on page 788) and only reflects the status of the secondary side. It should be noted that the Capabilities List bit (bit 4) is never implemented in this register.

While bit 14 is the Signaled System Error bit in the primary side Status register, it is the Received System Error bit in the Secondary Status register. When set, this bit indicates that SERR# was detected asserted on the secondary side. Writing a one to it clears the bit, while a zero doesn't affect it. Reset clears this bit.

Figure 22-24: Secondary Status Register

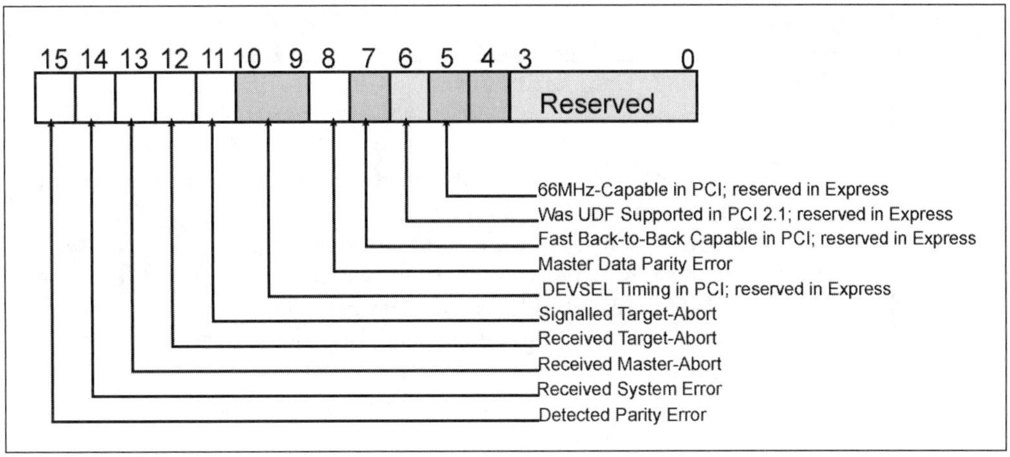

Table 22 - 9: Bridge Secondary Side Status Register

Bit	Attributes	Description
5	RO	**66MHz-Capable**. Does not apply to Express and must be 0.
7	RO	**Fast Back-to-Back Capable**. Does not apply to PCI Express and must be 0.

Table 22 - 9: Bridge Secondary Side Status Register (Continued)

Bit	Attributes	Description
8	RW1C	**Master Data Parity Error.** When forwarding a Poisoned TLP from Primary to Secondary: • The primary side must set the Detected Parity Error bit in the bridge Status register. • If the Parity Error Response bit in the Bridge Control register is set, the secondary side must set the Master Data Parity Error bit in the Secondary Status register. When forwarding a Poisoned TLP from Secondary to Primary: • The secondary side must set the Detected Parity Error bit in the Secondary Status register. • If the Parity Error Response bit in the Bridge Control register is set, the primary side must set the Master Data Parity Error bit in the bridge Status register. If the Parity Error Response bit in the Bridge Control register is cleared, the Master Data Parity Error status bit in the Secondary Status register is never set. The default value of this bit is 0.
10:9	RO	**DEVSEL Timing**. Does not apply to Express and must be 0.
11	RW1C	**Signaled Target Abort**. This bit is set when the bridge's secondary interface completes a received request by issuing a Completer Abort Completion Status. Default value of this field is 0.
12	RW1C	**Received Target Abort**. This bit is set when the bridge's secondary interface receives a Completion with Completer Abort Completion Status. Default value of this field is 0.
13	RW1C	**Received Master Abort**. This bit is set when the bridge's secondary interface receives a Completion with Unsupported Request Completion Status. Default value of this field is 0.
14	RW1C	**Signaled System Error**. This bit is set when the bridge's secondary interface sends an ERR_FATAL (fatal error) or ERR_NONFATAL (non-fatal error) message (if the SERR Enable bit in the Bridge Control register is set to one. The default value of this bit is 0.

Table 22 - 9: Bridge Secondary Side Status Register (Continued)

Bit	Attributes	Description
15	RW1C	**Detected Parity Error.** This bit is set by the bridge's secondary interface whenever it receives a Poisoned TLP, regardless of the state the Parity Error Enable bit in the Bridge Control register. Default value of this bit is 0.

Bridge Cache Line Size Register

Differs from PCI. Mandatory.

This field is implemented by PCI Express devices as a read-write field for legacy compatibility purposes but has no impact on any PCI Express device functionality.

Bridge Latency Timer Registers

Differs from PCI. Mandatory.

Bridge Latency Timer Register (Primary Bus)

Differs from PCI. Mandatory. This register does not apply to PCI Express and must be read-only and hardwired to 0.

Bridge Secondary Latency Timer Register

Differs from PCI. Mandatory. This register does not apply to PCI Express and must be read-only and hardwired to 0.

Bridge Interrupt-Related Registers

Differs from PCI. Optional. Only required if the bridge itself generates interrupts.

Interrupt Line Register

A bridge may generate interrupts in the legacy PCI/PCI-X manner due to an internal, bridge-specific event. The interrupt handler is within the bridge's device driver. When the bridge detects such an internal event, it sends an INTx Assert message upstream towards the Root Complex (specifically, to the interrupt controller within the Root Complex).

As in PCI, the Interrupt Line register communicates interrupt line routing information. The register is read/write and must be implemented if the bridge contains a valid non-zero value in its Interrupt Pin configuration register (described in the next section). The OS or device driver can examine the bridge's Interrupt Line register to determine which system interrupt request line the bridge uses to issue requests for service (and, therefore, which entry in the interrupt table to "hook").

In a non-PC environment, the value written to this register is architecture-specific and therefore outside the scope of the specification.

Interrupt Pin Register

This read-only register identifies the legacy INTx interrupt Message (INTA, INTB, INTC, or INTD) the bridge transmits upstream to generate an interrupt. The values 01h-through-04h correspond to legacy INTx interrupt Messages INTA-through-INTD. A return value of zero indicates that the bridge doesn't generate interrupts using the legacy method. All other values (05h-FFh) are reserved. Note that, although the bridge may not generate interrupts via the legacy method, it may generate them via the MSI method (see "Determining if a Function Uses INTx# Pins" on page 343 for more information).

PCI-Compatible Capabilities

AGP Capability

The 2.2 spec assigns the Capability ID of 02h to AGP. The remainder of this section is only included as an example of a New Capability.

Refer to Figure 22-25 on page 845.

- The AGP's Capability ID is 02h.
- The second byte is the register that points to the register set associated with the next New Capability (if there is one).
- Following the pointer register are two, 4-bit read-only fields designating the major and minor rev of the AGP spec that the AGP device is built to (at the time of this writing, the major rev is 2h and the minor is 0h).
- The last byte of the first dword is reserved and must return zero when read.
- The next two dwords contain the AGP device's AGP Status and AGP Command registers.

The sections that follow define these registers and the bits within them.

For a detailed description of AGP, refer to the MindShare book entitled *AGP System Architecture* (published by Addison-Wesley).

Figure 22-25: Format of the AGP Capability Register Set

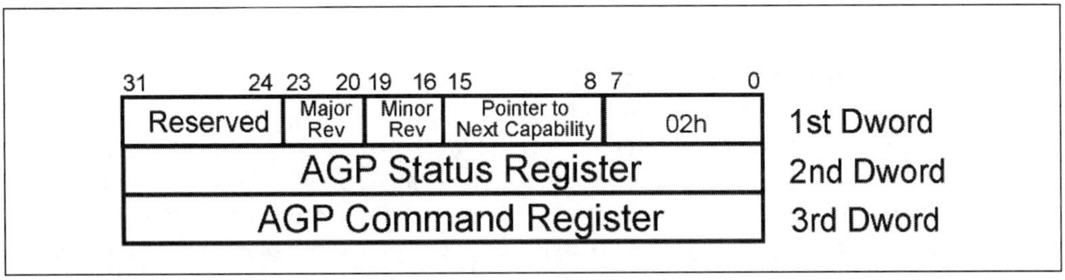

AGP Status Register

The AGP Status register is defined in Table 22-10 on page 846. This is a read-only register. Writes have no effect. Reserved or unimplemented fields or bits always return zeros when read.

Table 22-10: AGP Status Register (Offset CAP_PTR + 4)

Bits	Field	Description
31:24	RQ	The RQ field contains the maximum depth of the AGP request queue. Therefore, this number is the maximum number of transaction requests this device can manage. A "0" is interpreted as a depth of one, while FFh is interpreted as a depth of 256.
23:10	Reserved	Writes have no effect. Reads return zeros.
9	SBA	If set, this device supports Sideband Addressing.
8:6	Reserved	Writes have no effect. Reads return zeros.
5	4G	If set, this device supports addresses greater than 4GB.
4	FW	If set, this device supports Fast Write transactions.
3	Reserved	Writes have no effect. Reads return a zero
2:0	RATE	The RATE field is a bit map that indicates the data transfer rates supported by this device. AGP devices must report all that apply. The RATE field applies to AD, C/BE#, and SBA buses. **Bit Set** **Transfer Rate** 0 1X 1 2X 2 4X

AGP Command Register

The AGP Command register is defined in Table 22-11 on page 847. This is a read/writable register, with reserved fields hard-wired to zeros. All bits in the AGP Command register are cleared to zero after reset. This register is programmed during configuration. With one exception, the behavior of a device if this register is modified during runtime is not specified. If the AGP_Enable bit is cleared, the AGP master is not allowed to initiate a new request.

Table 22-11: AGP Command Register (Offset CAP_PTR + 8)

Bits	Field	Description
31:24	RQ_Depth	**Master**: The RQ_DEPTH field must be programmed with the maximum number of transaction requests the master is allowed to enqueue into the target. The value programmed into this field must be equal to or less than the value reported by the target in the RQ field of its AGP Status Register. A "0" value indicates a request queue depth of one entry, while a value of FFh indicates a request queue depth of 256. **Target**: The RQ_DEPTH field is reserved.
23:10	Reserved	Writes have no effect. Reads return zeros.
9	SBA_Enable	When set, the Sideband Address mechanism is enabled in this device.
8	AGP_Enable	**Master**: Setting the AGP_Enable bit allows the master to initiate AGP operations. When cleared, the master cannot initiate AGP operations. Also when cleared, the master is allowed to stop driving the SBA port. If bits 1 or 2 are set, the master must perform a re-synch cycle before initiating a new request. **Target**: Setting the AGP_Enable bit allows the target to accept AGP operations. When cleared, the target ignores incoming AGP operations. The target must be completely configured and enabled before the master is enabled. The AGP_Enable bit is the last to be set. Reset clears this bit.
7:6	Reserved	Writes have no effect. Reads return zeros.

Table 22-11: AGP Command Register (Offset CAP_PTR + 8) (Continued)

Bits	Field	Description
5	4G	**Master**: Setting the 4G bit allows the master to initiate AGP requests to addresses at or above the 4GB address boundary. When cleared, the master is only allowed to access addresses in the lower 4 GB of addressable space. **Target**: Setting the 4G bit enables the target to accept AGP DAC (Dual-Address Commands) commands, when bit 9 is cleared. When bits 5 and 9 are set, the target can accept a Type 4 SBA command and utilize A[35:32] of the Type 3 SBA command.
4	FW_Enable	When this bit is set, memory write transactions initiated by the core logic will follow the fast write protocol. When this bit is cleared, memory write transactions initiated by the core logic will follow the PCI protocol.
3	Reserved	Writes have no effect. Reads return zeros.
2:0	Data_Rate	No more than one bit in the Data_Rate field must be set to indicate the maximum data transfer rate supported. The same bit must be set in both the master and the target. **Bit Set** **Transfer Rate** 0 1X 1 2X 2 4X

Vital Product Data (VPD) Capability

Introduction

The 2.1 spec defined the optional Vital Product Data as residing in a PCI function's expansion ROM.

The 2.2 spec has deleted this information from the ROM and instead places the VPD (if present) in a function's PCI configuration register space (see "Capabilities Pointer Register" on page 779). This section describes the 2.2 implementation of the VPD and provides an example from the 2.2 spec.

It's Not Really Vital

It's always brought a smile to my face that despite its name, the VPD has never been vital. It's always been named "Vital" in the spec, but its *content* was *not initially defined*. Then in the 2.1 spec, although *vital*, it was defined as residing in a function's ROM, but its inclusion was *optional*. The 2.2 spec has now moved it from the ROM to the configuration space, but it's still *optional*.

What Is VPD?

The configuration registers present in a PCI function's configuration Header region (the first 16 dwords of its configuration space) provide the configuration software with quite a bit of information about the function. However, additional useful information such as

- a board's part number
- the EC (Engineering Change) level of a function
- the device's serial number
- an asset tag identifier

could be quite useful in a repair, tech support or asset management environments. If present, the VPD list provides this type of information.

Where Is the VPD Really Stored?

It is intended that the VPD would reside in a device such as a serial EEPROM associated with the PCI function. The configuration access mechanism described in the next section defines how this information would be accessed via the PCI function's VPD feature registers.

VPD On Cards vs. Embedded PCI Devices

Each add-in card may optionally contain VPD. If it's a multifunction card, only one function may contain VPD or each function may implement it. Embedded functions may or may not contain VPD.

How Is VPD Accessed?

Figure 22-26 on page 851 illustrates the configuration registers that indicate the presence of VPD information and permit the programmer to access it. The Capability ID of the VPD registers is 03h, while the registers used to access to the VPD data consists of the VPD Address and Data registers in conjunction with the one-bit Flag register. The programmer accesses the VPD information using the procedures described in the following two sections.

Reading VPD Data. Use the following procedure to read VPD data:

1. Using a PCI configuration write, write the dword-aligned VPD address into the Address register and simultaneously set the Flag bit to zero.
2. Hardware then reads the indicated dword from VPD storage and places the four bytes into the Data register. Upon completion of the operation, the hardware sets the Flag bit to one.
3. When software sees the Flag bit set to one by the hardware, it can then perform a PCI configuration read to read the four VPD bytes from the Data register.

If either the Address or Data registers are written to prior to hardware setting the Flag bit to one, the results of the read are unpredictable.

Writing VPD Data. Use the following procedure to write VPD data. Please note that only Read/Write VPD Data items may be written to.

1. Write four bytes of data into the Data register.
2. Write the dword-aligned VPD address into the Address register and simultaneously set the Flag bit to one.
3. When software detects that the Flag bit has been cleared to zero by hardware, the VPD write has been completed.

If either the Address or Data registers are written to prior to hardware clearing the Flag bit to zero, the results of the VPD write are unpredictable.

Rules That Apply To Both Read and Writes. The following rules apply to both VPD data reads and writes:

1. Once a VPD read or write has been initiated, writing to either the Address or Data registers prior to the point at which the hardware changes the state of the Flag bit yields unpredictable results.
2. Each VPD data read or write always encompasses all four bytes within the VPD dword indicated in the Address register.
3. The least-significant byte in the Data register corresponds to the least-significant byte in the indicated VPD dword.
4. The initial values in the Address and Data registers after reset are indeterminate.
5. Reading or writing data outside the scope of the overall VPD data structure is not allowed. The spec doesn't say what the result will be if you do it, so it is hardware design-specific.
6. The values contained in the VPD are only stored information and have no effect upon the device.

7. The two least-significant bits in the Address register must always be zero (i.e., it is illegal to specify an address that is not aligned on a dword address boundary).

Figure 22-26: VPD Capability Registers

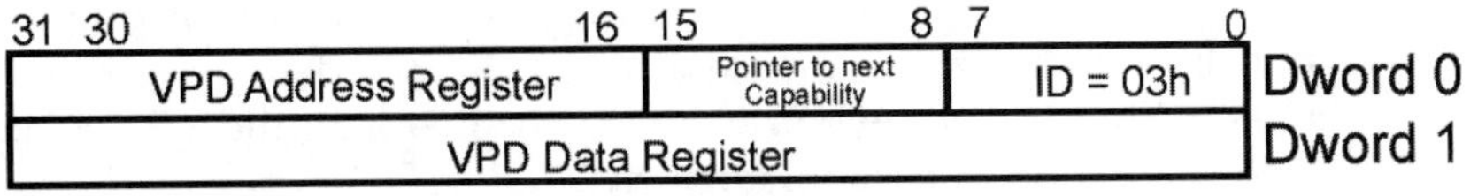

VPD Data Structure Made Up of Descriptors and Keywords

As mentioned earlier, the VPD actually consists of a data structure accessed using the VPD Address and Data registers. The individual data items that comprise the VPD data structure are themselves small data structures known as descriptors. The basic format of two of the descriptors used in the VPD was first defined in the version 1.0a *ISA Plug and Play* spec. For more information about this spec, refer to the MindShare book entitled *Plug and Play System Architecture* (published by Addison-Wesley). The two ISA-like descriptor types are:

- **Identifier String descriptor**. This descriptor contains the alphanumeric name of the card or embedded device. If the VPD is implemented, this descriptor is mandatory and is always the first one in the VPD. It is illustrated in Table 22-13 on page 853.
- **End Tag descriptor**. If the VPD is implemented, this descriptor is mandatory and is used to identify the end of VPD data structure. Its value is always 78h.

In addition to these two descriptors, the 2.2 spec has defined two new descriptor types referred to as:

- **VPD-R descriptor**. This descriptor type identifies the **start and** overall **length of** a **series of** one or more **read-only keywords** within the VPD data structure. The last keyword in the list of read-only keywords must be the Checksum keyword. This checksum encompasses the VPD from its first location to the end of the read-only area. A detailed description of this descriptor can be found in "VPD Read-Only Descriptor (VPD-R) and Keywords" on page 853.

- **VPD-W descriptor**. If used, this optional descriptor type is used to identify the **start and** overall **length of** the **read/write** descriptors within the VPD data structure. A detailed description of this descriptor can be found in "VPD Read/Write Descriptor (VPD-W) and Keywords" on page 856.

The basic format of the overall VPD data structure is illustrated in Table 22-12 on page 852. It has the following characteristics:

1. The VPD always **starts with** an **Identifier String descriptor**, followed by an optional list of one or more read-only VPD keywords.
2. The **list of read-only keywords** always begins with the VPD-R descriptor and ends with the Checksum keyword.
3. Immediately following the list of read-only keywords is an **optional list of read/write keywords**. If present, the read-write keyword list is prefaced with the VPD-W descriptor. Because the VPD read-write keywords can be altered, there is no checksum at the end of the read/write keywords.
4. The overall **VPD** data structure is **always terminated by** a special descriptor known as the **End Tag**. Its value is always 78h.

Table 22-12: Basic Format of VPD Data Structure

<table>
<tr><th>Typical Descriptor List</th><th>Comments</th></tr>
<tr><td>String Identifier Descriptor</td><td>Always the first entry.</td></tr>
<tr><td>Read-Only Descriptor</td><td>Heads the list of read-only keywords.</td></tr>
<tr><td>Read-Only Keyword</td><td rowspan="4">List of Read-Only keywords.</td></tr>
<tr><td>Read-Only Keyword</td></tr>
<tr><td>Read-Only Keyword</td></tr>
<tr><td>Checksum Keyword</td></tr>
<tr><td>Read/Write Descriptor</td><td>Heads the list of read-write keywords.</td></tr>
<tr><td>Read/Write Keyword</td><td rowspan="2">List of Read/Write keywords.</td></tr>
<tr><td>Read/Write Keyword</td></tr>
<tr><td>End Tag descriptor</td><td>Always used to indicate the end of the VPD. Its value is always 78h.</td></tr>
</table>

Table 22-13: Format of the Identifier String Tag

Byte	Description
0	Must be 82h.
1	Least-significant byte of identifier string length (the length encompasses bytes 3-through-n).
2	Most-significant byte of identifier string length (the length encompasses bytes 3-through-n).
3-through-n	ASCII name of function.

VPD Read-Only Descriptor (VPD-R) and Keywords

Table 22-14 on page 853 illustrates the format of the VPD-R descriptor. As mentioned earlier, this descriptor begins the list of one or more read-only keywords and indicates the length of the list. Each keyword is a minimum of four bytes in length and has the format illustrated in Table 22-15 on page 854. The read-only keywords currently-defined are listed in Table 22-16 on page 854.

Table 22-14: Format of the VPD-R Descriptor

Byte	Description
0	Must be 90h.
1	Least-significant byte of read-only keyword list length (the length encompasses bytes 3-through-n).
2	Most-significant byte of read-only keyword list length (the length encompasses bytes 3-through-n).
3-through-n	List of Read-Only keywords.

Table 22-15: General Format of a Read or a Read/Write Keyword Entry

Byte(s)	Description
0 and 1	ASCII Keyword (see Table 22-16 on page 854 and Table 22-20 on page 856).
2	Length of Keyword field (encompassing bytes 3-through-n).
3-through-n	Keyword data field.

Table 22-16: List of Read-Only VPD Keywords

ASCII Read-Only Keyword	Description of Keyword Data Field
PN	Device Part Number in ASCII.
EC	Engineering Change level (alphanumeric) of device in ASCII.
MN	Manufacturer ID in ASCII.
SN	Serial Number (alphanumeric) in ASCII.
Vx	Vendor-Specific field (alphanumeric) in ASCII. "x" can be any value 0-through-Z.
CP	Extended Capability. If present, this keyword indicates that the function implements an additional New Capability within its IO or memory space. See Table 22-17 on page 855 for a complete description.
RV	Checksum. See Table 22-18 on page 855 for complete description.

Table 22-17. Extended Capability (CP) Keyword Format

Byte	Description
0	New Capability ID.
1	Index of Base Address Register (value between 0 and 5) that points to space containing this capability.
2	Least-significant byte of offset within BAR's range where this New Capability's register set begins.
3	Most-significant byte of offset within BAR's range where this New Capability's register set begins.

Table 22-18: Format of Checksum Keyword

Byte	Description
0	Checksum from start of VPD up to and including this byte. Checksum is correct if sum of all bytes equals zero.
1	Reserved.
2	Reserved.
3-through-n	Reserved read-only space (as much as desired).

Is Read-Only Checksum Keyword Mandatory?

The spec doesn't say if the Checksum is mandatory, but it is the author's opinion that it is. In other words, even if the VPD contained no other read-only keywords, it must contain the VPD-R descriptor followed by the Checksum keyword. This provides the programmer with the checksum for the portion of the VPD that encompasses the String Identifier descriptor, the VPD-R descriptor and the Checksum keyword itself. In other words, it provides the checksum for everything other than the read-write portion of the VPD. It stands to reason the portion of the VPD that can be written to should not be included within the checksummed area.

VPD Read/Write Descriptor (VPD-W) and Keywords

The VPD may optionally contain a list of one or more read/write keyword fields. If present, this list begins with the VPD-W descriptor which indicates the start and length of the read/write keyword list. There is no checksum stored at the end of the read-write keyword list.

Table 22-19 on page 856 illustrates the format of the VPD-W descriptor and Table 22-20 on page 856 provides a list of the currently-defined read/write keyword fields.

Table 22-19: Format of the VPD-W Descriptor

Byte(s)	Description
0	Must be 91h
1	Least-significant byte of read/write keyword list length (the length encompasses bytes 3-through-n).
2	Most-significant byte of read/write keyword list length (the length encompasses bytes 3-through-n).
3-through-n	List of Read/Write keywords.

Table 22-20: List of Read/Write VPD Keywords

ASCII Read/Write Keyword	Description of Keyword Data Field
Vx	Vendor-Specific (alphanumeric in ASCII). "x" may be any character from 0-through-Z.
YA	Asset Tag Identifier. ASCII alphanumeric code supplied by system owner.
Yx	System-specific alphanumeric ASCII item. "x" may be any character from 0-through-9 and B-through-Z.
RW	Remaining read/write area. Identifies the unused portion of the r/w space. The description in the spec is very confusing and defies interpretation by the author (maybe I'm just being thick-headed).

Example VPD List

Table 22-21 on page 857 contains the sample VPD data structure provided in the spec. The author has made a few minor corrections, so it doesn't match the one in the spec exactly. In the draft version of the spec, the 3rd row, last column contained "ABC Super..." etc. and the offset in VPD-R Tag row was wrong. I fixed it by adjusting the offsets in the 1st column. It was fixed in the final version of the 2.2 spec by changing the Product Name to "ABCD Super...".

Table 22-21: Example VPD List

Offset (decimal)	Item	Value
0	String ID Tag	82h
1-2	String length (32d)	0020h (32d)
3-34	Product name in ASCII	"ABC Super-Fast Widget Controller"
Start of VPD Read-Only Keyword Area		
35	VPD-R Tag. Identifies start and length of read-only keyword area within VPD.	90h
36-37	Length of read-only keyword area.	5Ah (90d)
38-39	Read-only Part Number keyword.	"PN"
40	Length of Part Number data field.	08h (8d)
41-48	Part Number in ASCII.	"6181682A"
49-50	Read-Only Engineering Change (EC) level keyword.	"EC"
51	Length of EC data field.	0Ah (10d)
52-61	EC data field.	"4950262536"
62-63	Read-only Serial Number keyword.	"SN"
64	Serial Number length field.	08h (8d)
65-72	Serial Number data field.	"00000194"

Table 22-21: Example VPD List (Continued)

Offset (decimal)	Item	Value
73-74	Read-only Manufacturer ID keyword.	"MN"
75	Manufacturer ID length field.	04h (4d)
76-79	Manufacturer ID	"1037"
80-81	Read-only Checksum keyword.	"RV"
82	Length of reserved read-only VPD area.	2Ch (44d)
83	Checksum for bytes 0-through-83.	Checksum.
84-127	Reserved read-only area.	
Start of VPD Read/Write Keyword Area		
128	VPD-W Tag	91h
129-130	Length of read/write keyword area.	007Eh (126d)
131-132	Read/Write Vendor-Specific Keyword.	"V1"
133	Vendor-specific data field length.	05h (5d)
134-138	Vendor-specific data field.	"65A01"
139-140	System-specific keyword.	"Y1"
141	System-specific data field length.	0Dh (13d)
142-154	System-specific data field.	"Error Code 26"
155-156	Remaining Read/Write area keyword.	"RW"
157	Length of remaining read/write area.	61h (97d)
158-254	Remainder of read/write area.	reserved.
255	End Tag	78h

Introduction To Chassis/Slot Numbering Registers

Assuming that the Capabilities List bit is set in the bridge's primary Status register, the bridge implements the Capabilities Pointer register (see "Capabilities Pointer Register" on page 779). When software traverses the linked list of New Capability register sets for a bridge associated with a Root Port or a switch downstream port, it may encounter the Slot Numbering registers (if this is the bridge to an expansion chassis).

Figure 22-27 on page 859 pictures the Slot Numbering register set. It consists of the registers described in Table 22-22 on page 859. For additional information, refer to "Chassis and Slot Number Assignment" on page 861.

Figure 22-27: Chassis and Slot Number Registers

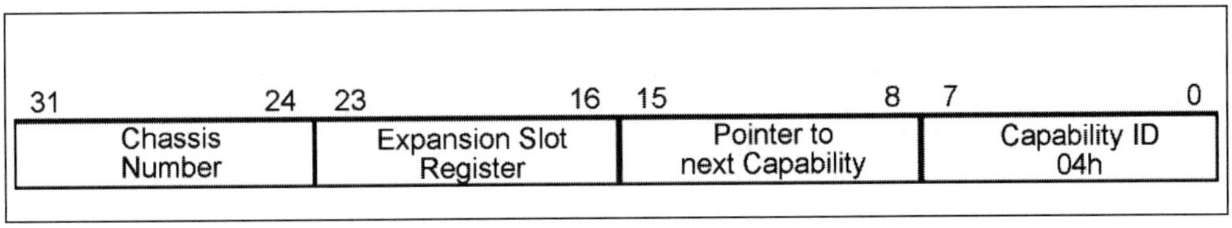

Table 22-22: Slot Numbering Register Set

Register	Description
Capability ID	**Read-Only**. **04h** identifies this as the Slot Numbering register set.
Next Capability Pointer	**Read-Only.** **00h** = Indicates that this is the last register set in the linked New Capabilities list. **Non-zero value** = dword-aligned pointer to the next register set in the linked list.

Table 22-22: Slot Numbering Register Set (Continued)

Register	Description
Expansion Slot	**Read-Only, automatically loaded by hardware after reset**. The configuration software uses the value in this register to determine the number of expansion card slots present in the chassis. The spec doesn't define where the hardware obtains this information. It could read a set of strapping pins on the trailing-edge of reset, or could obtain the information from a serial EEPROM.
Chassis Number	**Read/Write**. The value in this register identifies the chassis number assigned to this chassis. At reset time, this register may: • be pre-loaded with 00h, or • be implemented as a non-volatile register that "remembers" the chassis number assigned during a previous platform configuration. The configuration software will initialize all upstream bridges within the same chassis with the same Chassis Number and must guarantee that each chassis is assigned a mutually-exclusive Chassis Number. A bridge may implement the Chassis/Slot numbering registers and yet may not have any expansion card slots residing beneath it. The Chassis Number register may be cleared to zero by reset, or may be non-volatile (i.e., the current contents of the register will survive resets and power cycles). If it is non-volatile, its initial state after the first power up will be zero. When the configuration software detects zero in an expansion chassis' Chassis Number register, it must assign a number to it. Zero is not a valid Chassis Number for an expansion chassis because Chassis Zero is reserved for the card slots embedded on the system board.

Chassis and Slot Number Assignment

Problem: Adding/Removing Bridge Causes Buses to Be Renumbered

The best way to start this discussion is to illustrate the problem with an example. Assume the following set of conditions:

1. The system has several Express add-in card slots on the bus in the Root Complex.
2. There are one or more Root Ports and one or more of these Root Ports are connected to chasses, each of which has add-in card slots on the downstream side of the chassis' Switch upstream port (i.e., the Switch embedded in the chassis).
3. The system was shipped as described in items one and two and no cards have been added or removed.
4. Diagnostic software has detected a problem with an add-in card in one of the slots.

Now, the question: *When the software displays a message to identify the bad card to the end user, how will it identify the location of the card slot to the end user?* The software knows the following:

- The bus number that the device resides on.
- Which device number is assigned to the device.

So, let's say that the software identifies the bad boy to the end user by displaying its location using the bus and device numbers and let's say that someone at the factory was nice enough to physically label each card slot using that information (bus and device number). That would work just fine—as long as no one installs or removes a card that has a bridge on it. Remember that the configuration software discovers bridges each time that the machine is restarted and assigns a bus number to each bridge's secondary bus. In other words, if a bus is added or removed, that can change the bus numbers assigned to a number of the buses. *This would result in the labels on the card slots being wrong and the end user wouldn't know it.*

If Buses Added/Removed, Slot Labels Must Remain Correct

As stated in this section's heading, the addition or removal of a bus must not render the physical slot labels incorrect. This requirement highlights that the bus number cannot be used as part of the slot labeling (because it can change).

The only exception would be Bus 0 which cannot be removed and is always assigned bus number 0.

Definition of a Chassis

As defined in the 1.1 PCI-to-PCI bridge specification, there are two types of chasses:

- **Main Chassis**—Refer to Figure 22-28 on page 862. These add-in card **slots** are connected to Root Ports and are **not removable**. These card slots do not present a problem in that the physical labeling of the slots is always correct.
- **Expansion Chassis**—Refer to Figure 22-33 on page 869. An Expansion Chassis consists of a group of one or more buses each with card slots and the entire group can be installed in or removed from the system as a single entity. The slots within an expansion chassis are numbered sequentially and are identified by chassis number and slot number.

Figure 22-28: Main Chassis

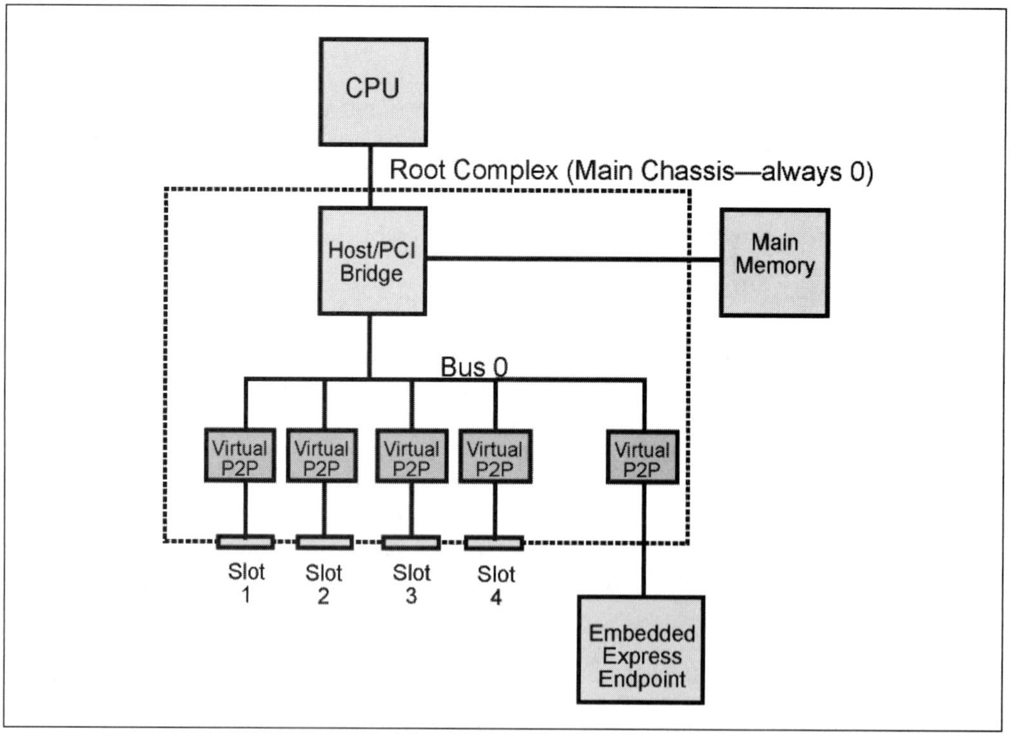

Chassis/Slot Numbering Registers

PCI-Compatible Chassis/Slot Numbering Register Set. "Introduction To Chassis/Slot Numbering Registers" on page 859 introduced the PCI-compatible configuration registers associated with chassis and slot numbering:

- The **Chassis Number register** (see Figure 22-27 on page 859 and Table 22-22 on page 859). The configuration software assigns a non-zero chassis number to each upstream bridge that implements the Slot Numbering capability register set and that has a non-zero value in its Expansion Slot register (indicating the number of slots implemented within the chassis).
- The **Expansion Slot register** (see Figure 22-29 on page 864 and Table 22-23 on page 864). The Expansion Slot register is preloaded with the indicated information by hardware before the configuration software is executed. As an example, the bridge could sample a set of strapping pins on the trailing-edge of reset to determine the contents of the Expansion Slot register. A bridge may implement the Chassis/Slot numbering registers and yet may not have any expansion slots on its secondary bus. 0 indicates that no slots are implemented on the downstream side of the bridge.

Express-Specific Slot-Related Registers. In addition to these PCI-compatible registers, the following PCI Express-specific configuration registers are also involved in the process:

- The **Slot Implemented bit in the PCI Express Capabilities register** (see Figure 22-31 on page 865). This bit is only implemented in the bridge to a Root Port or to a downstream switch port. If this bit is hardwired to one, this indicates that the downstream port is connected to an add-in slot rather than to an embedded device or to a disabled link.
- The **Physical Slot Number field in the PCI Express Slot Capability register** (see Figure 22-30 on page 865). This hardware initialized field indicates the physical slot number attached to this Port. The assigned slot number must be globally unique within this chassis. This field must be set to 0 for a port that is connected to a device that is either integrated on the system board or within the same silicon as the Switch device or the Root Port.

The Chassis and Expansion Slot registers must be implemented in each upstream bridge in an expansion chassis that has expansion slots on its secondary bus.

Figure 22-29: Expansion Slot Register

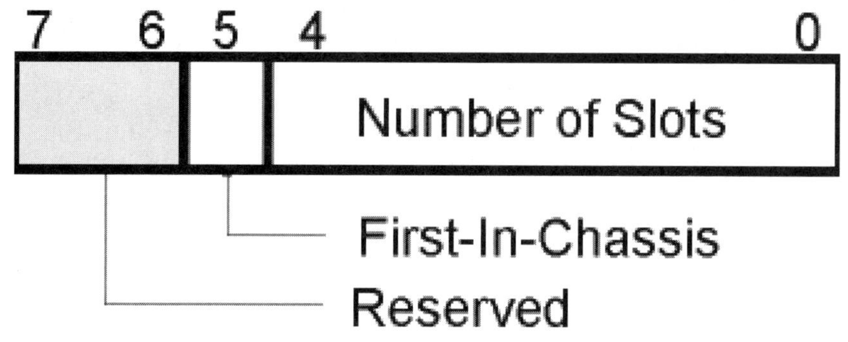

Table 22-23: Expansion Slot Register Bit Assignment

Bit Field	Description
7:6	**Reserved**. Read-only and must always return zero when read.
5	**First-In-Chassis bit**. This bit must be set to one in the first upstream bridge within each expansion chassis. This is defined as follows: • If there is only one expansion chassis and it contains only one upstream bridge with slots on its secondary side, that bridge is the First-In-Chassis. • If an expansion chassis contains a hierarchy of bridges springing from one parent upstream bridge (see Figure 22-33 on page 869), the parent upstream bridge is First-In-Chassis, while the other upstream bridges will have the First-In-Chassis bit cleared to zero.
4:0	**Number of Expansion Slots** on bridge's secondary bus. If there aren't any expansion slots on the bridge's secondary bus, this field must be hardwired to zero.

Figure 22-30: Slot Capability Register

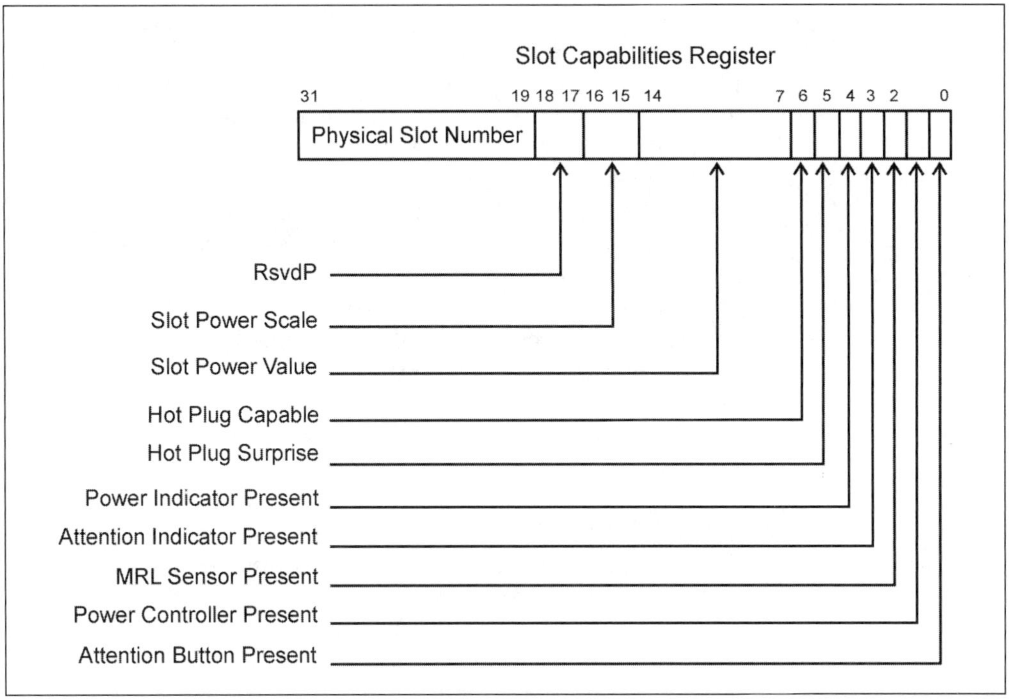

Figure 22-31: PCI Express Capabilities Register

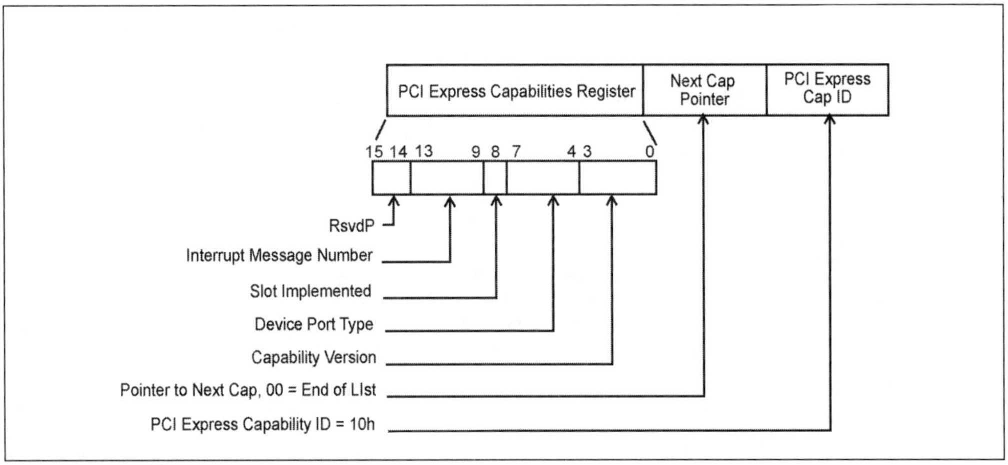

Two Examples

First Example. Figure 22-32 on page 867 illustrates a system wherein:

- The Root Complex has four Root Ports that are connected to add-in slot connectors, and one Root Port connected to an embedded device. With the exception of the Root Port that is connected to an embedded device, in each of the Root Port bridges:
  - — Slot Implemented bit = 1 (hardware in initialized).
  - — Physical Slot Number = the respective slot's hardware-assigned slot number (hardware in initialized).
  - — The Chassis register is not implemented.
  - — The Expansion Slot register is not implemented.
- The Root Port that is connected to the embedded device contains the following information:
  - — Slot Implemented bit = 0 (hardware in initialized).
  - — Physical Slot Number = not implemented.
  - — Chassis register not implemented.
  - — Expansion Slot register not implemented.
- A chassis is connected to add-in slot connector number one.
- In the upstream bridge of the chassis:
  - — The Chassis register in the chassis' upstream port is set to 01h by the configuration software.
  - — The First In Chassis bit is set to one (hardware in initialized).
  - — The upstream bridge's Expansion Slot register contains the value 2 (hardware in initialized) indicating that the chassis implements 2 add-in slot connectors on the downstream side of the bridge.
- In each of the chassis' downstream port bridges:
  - — Slot Implemented bit = 1 (hardware in initialized).
  - — Physical Slot Number = the respective slot's hardware-assigned slot number (hardware in initialized).
  - — The Chassis register is not implemented.
  - — The Expansion Slot register is not implemented.

Figure 22-32: Chassis Example One

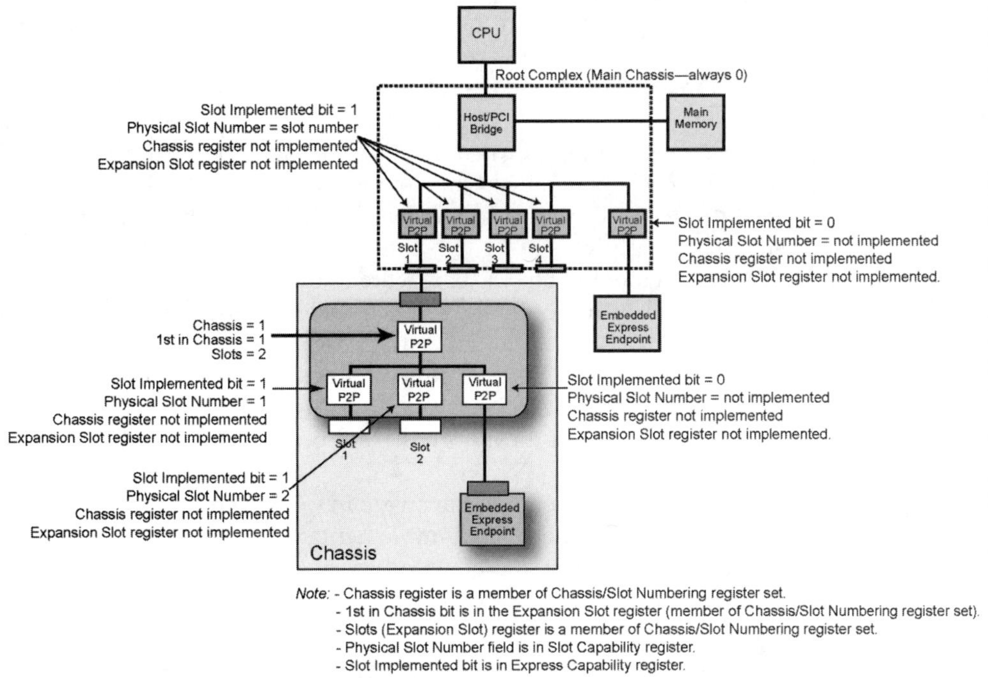

Second Example. Figure 22-33 on page 869 illustrates an example wherein:

- The Root Complex has four Root Ports that are connected to add-in slot connectors, and one Root Port connected to an embedded device. With the exception of the Root Port that is connected to an embedded device, in each of the Root Port bridges:
  — Slot Implemented bit = 1 (hardware in initialized).
  — Physical Slot Number = the respective slot's hardware-assigned slot number (hardware in initialized).
  — The Chassis register is not implemented.
  — The Expansion Slot register is not implemented.
- The Root Port that is connected to the embedded device contains the following information:
  — Slot Implemented bit = 0 (hardware in initialized).
  — Physical Slot Number = not implemented.
  — Chassis register not implemented.

  - Expansion Slot register not implemented.
- A chassis is connected to add-in slot connector number one.
- In the upstream bridge of the chassis:
  - The Chassis register in the chassis' upstream port is set to 01h by the configuration software.
  - The First In Chassis bit is set to one (hardware in initialized).
  - The upstream bridge's Expansion Slot register contains the value 7 (hardware in initialized) indicating that the chassis implements 7 add-in slot connectors on the downstream side of the bridge.
- In the bridge of each of the downstream switch ports that are connected to slots 1-through-5:
  - Slot Implemented bit = 1 (hardware in initialized).
  - Physical Slot Number = the respective slot's hardware-assigned slot number (hardware in initialized).
  - The Chassis register is not implemented.
  - The Expansion Slot register is not implemented.
- In the bridge of the left-most downstream port on the same bus as slots 1-through-5:
  - Slot Implemented bit = 0 (hardware in initialized).
  - Physical Slot Number = not implemented.
  - Chassis register not implemented.
  - Expansion Slot register not implemented.
- In the upstream bridge of the lower switch within the chassis:
  - The Chassis register in the chassis' upstream port is set to 01h by the configuration software.
  - The First In Chassis bit is cleared to zero (hardware in initialized).
  - The upstream bridge's Expansion Slot register contains the value 2 (hardware in initialized) indicating that the chassis implements 2 add-in slot connectors on the downstream side of this bridge.
- In the bridge of each of the downstream ports beneath the upstream bridge:
  - Slot Implemented bit = 1 (hardware in initialized).
  - Physical Slot Number = the respective slot's hardware-assigned slot number (hardware in initialized).
  - The Chassis register is not implemented.
  - The Expansion Slot register is not implemented.

Figure 22-33: Chassis Example Two

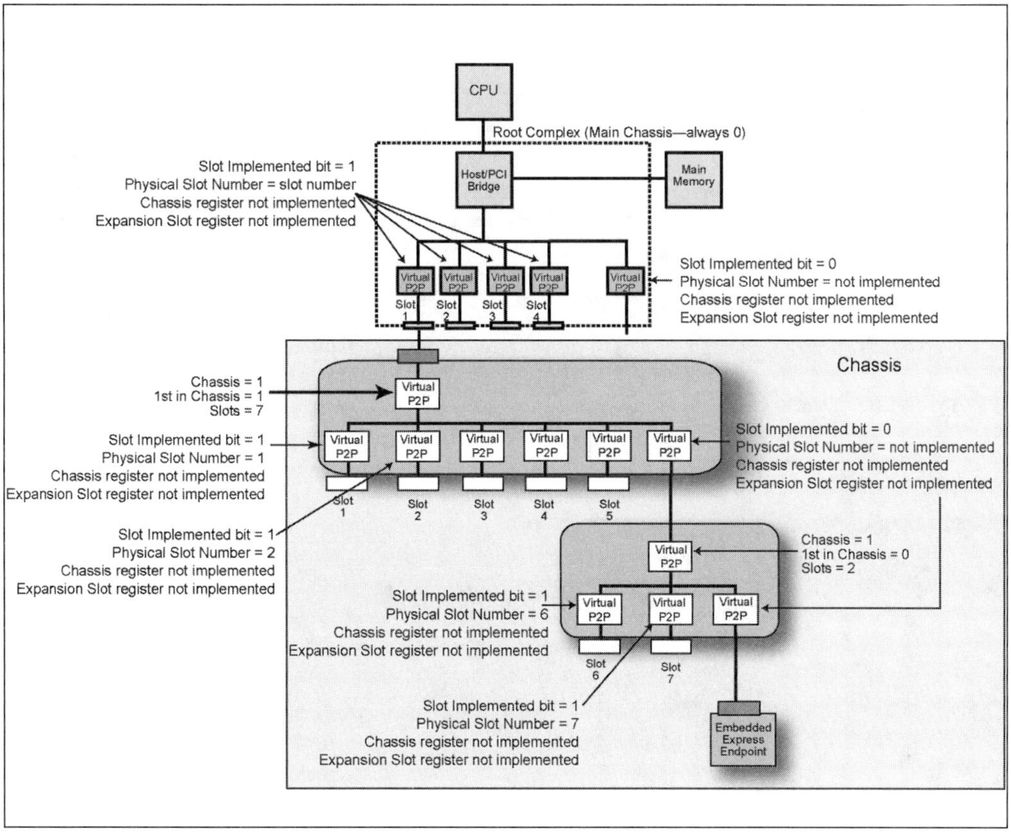

23 Expansion ROMs

The Previous Chapter

The previous chapter provided a detailed description of the configuration registers residing a function's PCI-compatible configuration space. This included the registers for both non-bridge and bridge functions.

This Chapter

This chapter provides a detailed description of device ROMs associated with PCI, PCI Express, and PCI-X functions. This includes the following topics:

- device ROM detection.
- internal code/data format.
- shadowing.
- initialization code execution.
- interrupt hooking.

The Next Chapter

The next chapter provides a description of:

- The PCI Express Capability register set in a function's PCI-compatible configuration space.
- The optional PCI Express Extended Capabilities register sets in a function's extended configuration space:
  - — The Advanced Error Reporting Capability register set.
  - — Virtual Channel Capability register set.
  - — Device Serial Number Capability register set.
  - — Power Budgeting Capability register set.
- RCRBs.

ROM Purpose—Device Can Be Used In Boot Process

In order to boot the OS into memory, the system needs three devices:

- A mass storage device to load the OS from. This is sometimes referred to as the **IPL** (Initial Program Load) **device** and is typically an IDE or a SCSI hard drive.
- A display adapter to enable progress messages to be displayed during the boot process. In this context, this is typically referred to as the **output device**.
- A keyboard to allow the user to interact with the machine during the boot process. In this context, this is typically referred to as the **input device**.

The OS must locate three devices that fall into these categories and **must also locate a device driver associated with each of the devices**. Remember that the OS hasn't been booted into memory yet and therefore hasn't loaded any loadable device drivers into memory from disk! This is the main reason that device ROMs exist. It contains a device driver that permits the device to be used during the boot process.

ROM Detection

When the configuration software is configuring a PCI, PCI-X, or PCI-Express function, it determines if a function-specific ROM exists by checking to see if the designer has implemented an Expansion ROM Base Address Register (refer to Figure 23-1 on page 873).

As described in "Expansion ROM Base Address Register" on page 783, the programmer writes all ones (with the exception of bit zero, to prevent the enabling of the ROM address decoder; see Figure 23-1 on page 873) to the Expansion ROM Base Address Register and then reads it back. If a value of zero is returned, then the register is not implemented and there isn't an expansion ROM associated with the device.

On the other hand, the ability to set any bits to ones indicates the presence of the Expansion ROM Base Address Register. This may or may not indicate the presence of a device ROM. Although the address decoder and a socket may exist for a device ROM, the socket may not be occupied at present. The programmer determines the presence of the device ROM by:

- assigning a base address to the register's Base Address field,
- enabling its decoder (by setting bit 0 in the register to one),
- and then attempting to read the first two locations from the ROM.

If the first two locations contain the ROM signature—AA55h—then the ROM is present.

Figure 23-1 on page 873 illustrates the format of the Expansion ROM Base Address Register. Assume that the register returns a value of FFFE0000h when read back after writing all ones to it. Bit 17 is the least-significant bit that was successfully changed to a one and has a binary-weighted value of 128K. This indicates that it is a 128KB ROM decoder and bits [24:17] within the Base Address field are writable. The programmer now writes a 32-bit start address into the register and sets bit zero to one to enable its ROM address decoder. The function's ROM address decoder is then enabled and the ROM (if present) can be accessed. The maximum ROM decoder size permitted by the PCI spec is 16MB, dictating that bits [31:25] must be read/write.

The programmer then performs a read from the first two locations of the ROM and checks for a return value of AA55h. If this pattern is not received, the ROM is not present. The programmer disables the ROM address decoder (by clearing bit zero of the Expansion ROM Base Address Register to zero). If AA55h is received, the ROM exists and a device driver code image must be copied into main memory and its initialization code must be executed. This topic is covered in the sections that follow.

Figure 23-1: Expansion ROM Base Address Register Bit Assignment

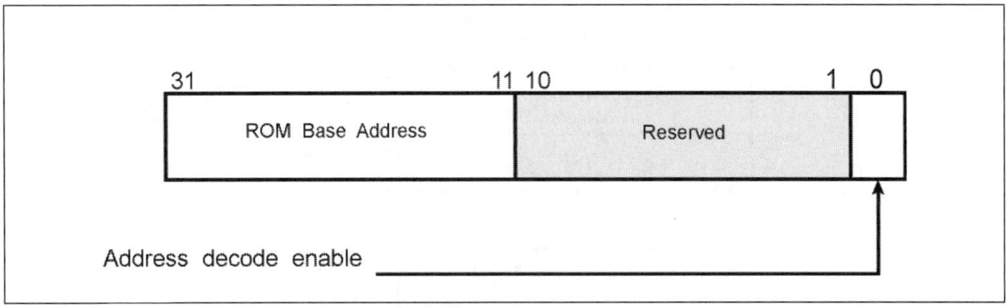

Figure 23-2: Header Type Zero Configuration Register Format

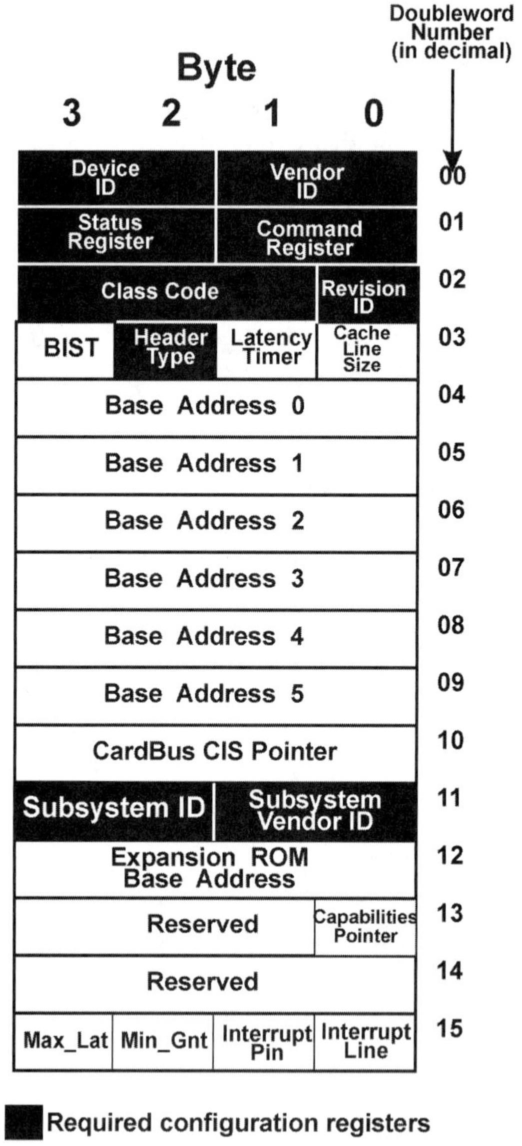

ROM Shadowing Required

The PCI spec requires that device ROM code is never executed in place (i.e., from the ROM). It must be copied to main memory. This is referred to as "shadowing" the ROM code. This requirement exists for two reasons:

- ROM access time is typically quite slow, resulting in poor performance whenever the ROM code is fetched for execution.
- Once the initialization portion of the device driver in the ROM has been executed, it can be discarded and the code image in main memory can be shortened to include only the code necessary for run-time operation. The portion of main memory allocated to hold the initialization portion of the code can be freed up, allowing more efficient use of main memory.

Once the presence of the device ROM has been established (see the previous section), the configuration software must copy a code image into main memory and then disable the ROM address decoder (by clearing bit zero of the Expansion ROM Base Address Register to zero). In a non-PC environment, the area of memory the code image is copied to could be anywhere in memory space. The specification for that environment may define a particular area.

In a PC environment, the ROM code image must be copied into main memory into the range of addresses historically associated with device ROMs: 000C0000h through 000DFFFFh. If the Class Code indicates that this is the VGA's device ROM, its code image must be copied into memory starting at location 000C0000h.

The next section defines the format of the information in the ROM and how the configuration software determines which code image (yes, there can be more than one device driver) to load into main memory.

ROM Content

Multiple Code Images

The PCI spec permits the inclusion of more than one code image in a PCI device ROM. Each code image would contain a copy of the device driver in a specific machine code, or in interpretive code (explained later). The configuration software can then scan through the images in the ROM and select the one best suited to the system processor type. The ROM might contain drivers for various types of devices made by this device's vendor. The code image copied into main memory should match up with the function's ID. To this end, each code image also contains:

- the Vendor ID and Device ID. This is useful for matching up the driver with a function that has a vendor/device match.
- the Class Code. This is useful if the driver is a Class driver that can work with any compatible device within a Class/SubClass. For more information, see "Class Code Register" on page 774.

Figure 23-3 on page 877 illustrates the concept of multiple code images embedded within a device ROM. Each image must start on an address evenly-divisible by 512. Each image consists of two data structures, as well as a run-time code image and an initialization code image. The configuration software interrogates the data structures in order to determine if this is the image it will copy to main memory and use. If it is, the configuration software:

1. Copies the image to main memory,
2. Disables the expansion ROM's address decoder,
3. Executes the initialization code,
4. If the initialization code shortens the length indicator in the data structure, the configuration software deallocates the area of main memory that held the initialization portion of the driver (in Figure 23-4 on page 879, notice that the initialization portion of the driver is always at the end of the image).
5. The area of main memory containing the image is then write-protected.

The sections that follow provide a detailed discussion of the code image format and the initialization process.

Figure 23-3: Multiple Code Images Contained In One Device ROM

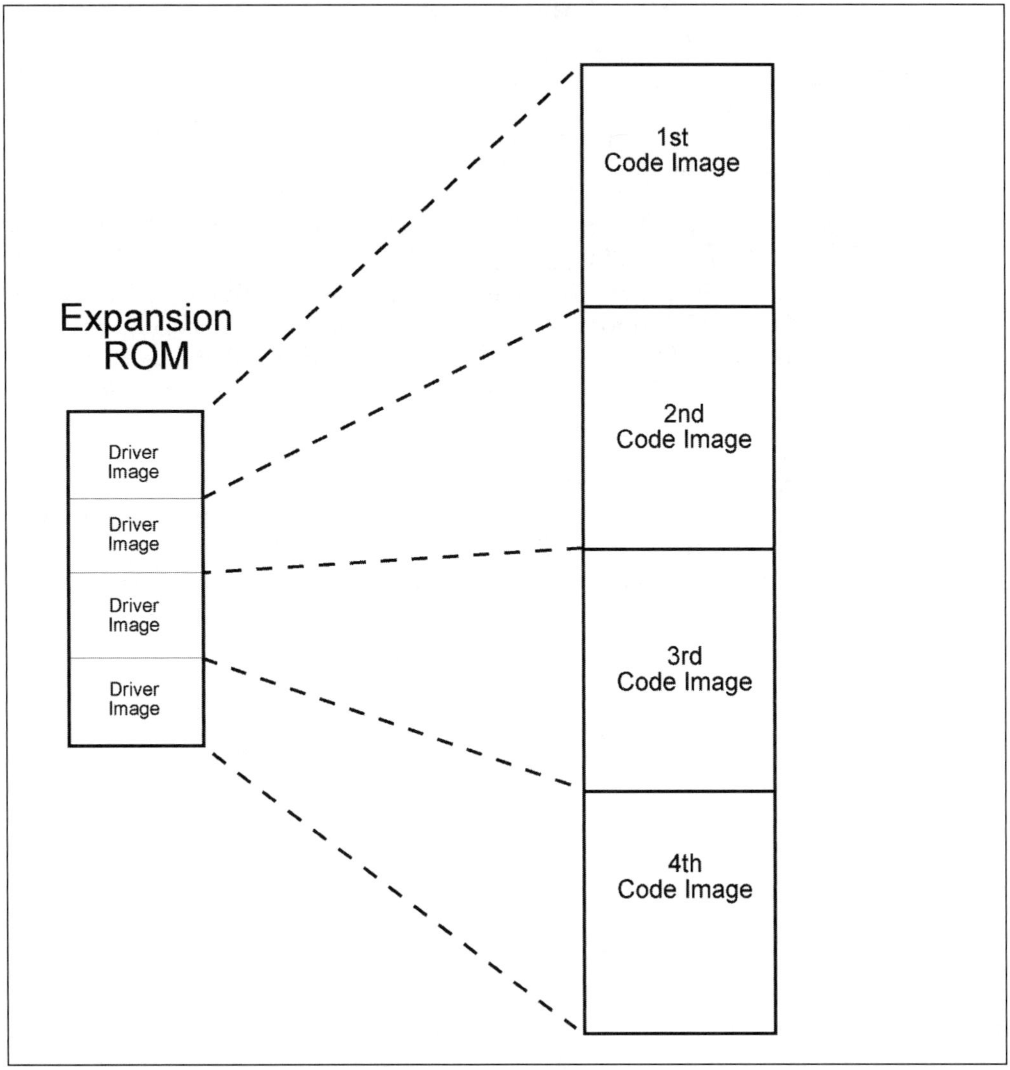

Format of a Code Image

General

Figure 23-4 on page 879 illustrates the format of a single code image. The image consists of the following components:

- **ROM Header**. Described in "ROM Header Format" on page 879. Also contains a 16-bit pointer to the ROM data structure.
- **ROM Data Structure.** Described in "ROM Data Structure Format" on page 881. Contains information about the device and the image.
- **Run-time code**. This is the portion of the device driver that remains in main memory after the OS loads and that remains available for execution on an on-going basis.
- **Initialization code**. This is the portion of the device driver that is called and executed immediately after loading the driver into main memory. It completes the setup of the device and enables it for normal operation. It must always reside at the end of the image so it can be abbreviated or discarded after its initial execution at system startup.

Figure 23-1: Code Image Format

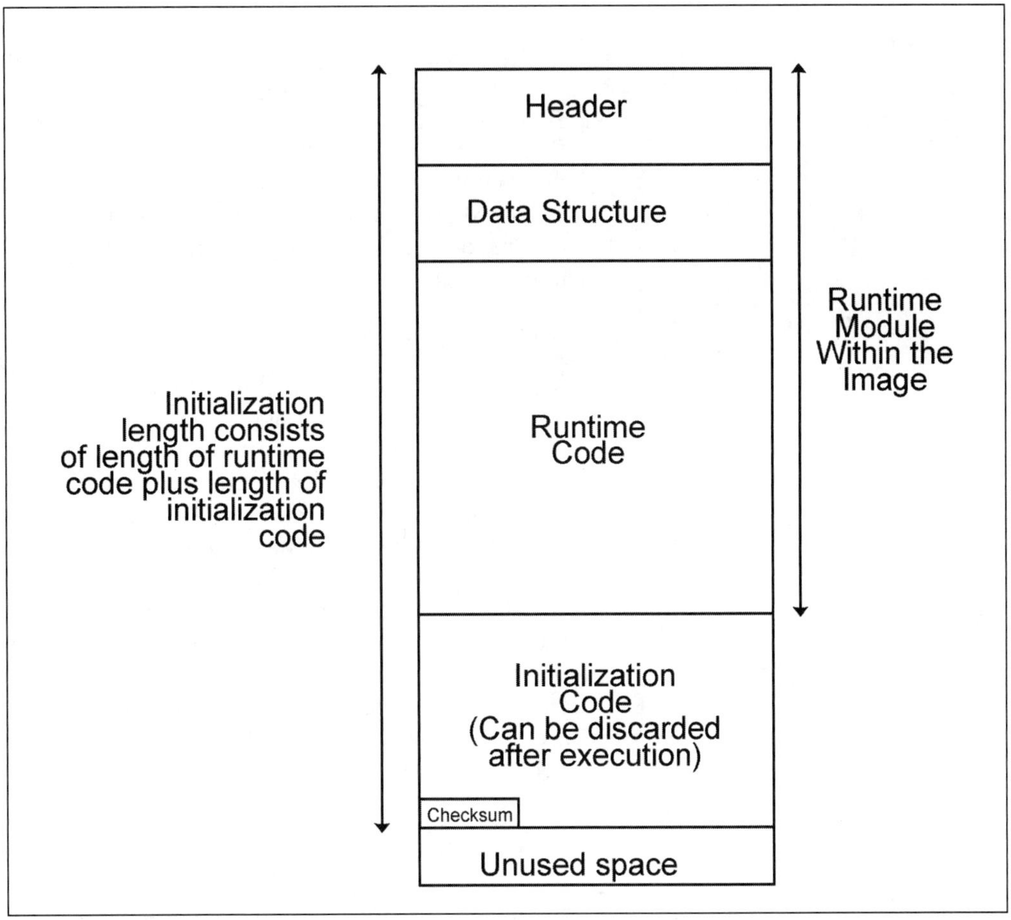

ROM Header Format

The ROM Header must be located at the very start of each image within the ROM (so a better name for it might be the Code Image Header). Table 23-1 on page 880 defines the format of the Header and the purpose of each field is further defined in the paragraphs that follow. The offset specified in the table is the offset from the first location in this ROM code image.

Table 23-1: PCI Expansion ROM Header Format

Offset	Length (bytes)	Value	Description
00h	1d	55h	ROM signature byte one. The first two bytes must contain AA55h, identifying this as a device ROM. This has always been the signature used for a device ROM in any PC-compatible machine.
01h	1d	AAh	ROM signature byte two.
02h - 17h	22d	n	Reserved for processor architecture unique data. See Table 23-2 on page 881. This block of 22d locations is reserved for processor/architecture unique data. For PC-compatible environments and images that identify the code as Intel x86-compatible in the Code Type field (see "Code Type" on page 885) of the ROM data structure, the PCI spec defines the structure of the processor/architecture unique data area in the image Header. For non-PC compatible environments, the content of this structure is architecture-specific. Table 23-2 on page 881 defines the fields that must be supplied for PC-compatibility. The offset specified in the table is the offset from the first location of this ROM code image.
18h - 19h	2d	n	Pointer to PCI Data Structure. Since this is a 16-bit pointer, the data structure can be anywhere within 64K forward of the first location in this code image. This is the 16-bit offset (in little-endian format) to the ROM data structure within this code image. It is an offset from the start address of this code image. Because this is only a 16-bit offset from the first location of this code image, the data structure must reside within 64KB forward of the first location of this code image.

Table 23-2: PC-Compatible Processor/Architecture Data Area In ROM Header

Offset	Length (in bytes)	Description
02h	1	Overall size of the image (in 512 byte increments). The total size of the runtime code plus the initialization code (runtime code + initialization code = initialization size). This sum is not necessarily the "overall size of the image." The overall size of the image (Image Length) could be greater than the initialization size. The Image Length or Image size is what specifies where the next image in the ROM starts, while the Initialization size (a better name for this field) is the actual code size that is copied into RAM.
03h-05h	3	Entry point for the initialization code. Contains a three-byte, x86 short jump to the initialization code entry point. The POST performs a far call to this location to initialize the device.
06h-17h	18d	Reserved (for application-unique data, such as the copyright notice).

ROM Data Structure Format

As stated earlier, the ROM Data Structure associated with each code image must reside within the first 64KB of each code image. The Data Structure must reside within the run-time code (assuming there is one). It's possible that a ROM may not contain a device driver for the device, but only an initialization module that tests the device and gets it ready for normal operation. If there isn't a run-time code module, the Data Structure must reside within the initialization code. The Data Structure's format is defined in Table 23-3 on page 882 and the purpose of each field is further defined in the sections that follow the table.

Table 23-3: PCI Expansion ROM Data Structure Format

Offset	Length	Description
00h	4	**Signature** consisting of the ASCII string "PCIR" (PCI ROM).
04h	2	**Vendor ID**. This is a duplication of the Vendor ID found in the function's configuration Vendor ID register (see "Vendor ID Register" on page 773). The ROM may contain multiple code images of the desired Code Type (e.g., x86 code), but they may be for different devices produced by the same (or a different) vendor. In order to ensure that it loads the correct one, the configuration software compares the Vendor ID, Device ID, and Class Code values contained in this Data Structure to those found in the function's Vendor ID, Device ID, and Class Code configuration registers.
06h	2	**Device ID**. This is a duplication of the Device ID found in the function's configuration Device ID register (see "Device ID Register" on page 773). See explanation of Vendor ID field in this table.
08h	2	**Reserved. Was the Pointer to the Vital Product Data**. The pointer to the optional VPD is provided as an offset from the start location of the code image. The 2.2 PCI spec redefined this as a Reserved bit field and the optional VPD (if present) was moved to the device's configuration registers. Refer to "Vital Product Data (VPD) Capability" on page 848.
0Ah	2	PCI **Data Structure Length** in bytes, little-endian format.
0Ch	1	PCI **Data Structure Revision**. The Data Structure format shown in this table is revision zero.
0Dh	3	**Class Code**. This is a duplication of the Class Code found in the function's configuration Class Code register (see "Class Code Register" on page 774). See explanation of Vendor ID field in this table.

Table 23-3: PCI Expansion ROM Data Structure Format (Continued)

Offset	Length	Description
10h	2	**Image length**. Code image length in increments of 512 bytes (little-endian format). The total size of the runtime code plus the initialization code (runtime code + initialization code = initialization size). This sum is not necessarily the "overall size of the image." The overall size of the image (Image Length) could be greater than the initialization size. The Image Length or Image size is what specifies where the next image in the ROM starts, while the Initialization size (a better name for this field) is the actual code size that is copied into RAM.
12h	2	**Revision level of code/data** in this code image.
14h	1	**Code type**. See "Code Type" on page 885.
15h	1	**Indicator byte**. Bit 7 indicates whether this is the last code image in the ROM (1 = last image). Bits [6:0] are reserved and must be zero.
16h	2	**Reserved**.

ROM Signature. This unique signature identifies the start of the PCI Data Structure. The "**P**" is stored at offset 00h, the "**C**" at offset 01h, etc. "**PCIR**" stands for PCI ROM.

Vendor ID field in ROM data structure. As stated in Table 23-3 on page 882, the configuration software does not select a code image to load into system memory unless it is the correct Code Type and the Vendor ID, Device ID, and Class Code in the image's Data Structure match the function's respective configuration registers. The ROM may contain code images for variations on the device, either from the same vendor or supplied by different vendors.

Device ID in ROM data structure. Refer to the description of the Vendor ID field in the previous section.

Pointer to Vital Product Data (VPD). The 2.2 PCI spec defined this as a Reserved field and the optional VPD (if present) was moved to the device's configuration registers. Refer to "Vital Product Data (VPD) Capability" on page 848. The following description is only provided as historical information.

The VPD pointer is the offset (from the start of the code image) to the Vital Product Data area. The offset was stored in little-endian format. Because the offset is only 16-bits in size, the Vital Product Data area had to reside within the first 64KB of the image. A value of zero indicates that the image contains no Vital Product Data. The revision 2.0 PCI spec said that the pointer was required, but the 2.1 PCI spec removed that requirement. If no device ROM was present on a device other than the one containing the VPD, there was only one image and it contained the VPD. If multiple code images were present, each image contained VPD for that device. The VPD data that described the device may be duplicated in each code image, but the VPD that pertains to software may be different for each code image.

PCI Data Structure Length. This 16-bit value is stored in the little-endian format. It defines the length (in bytes) of the PCI Data Structure for this image.

PCI Data Structure Revision. This 8-bit field reflects the revision of the image's Data Structure. The currently-defined data structure format (as of revision 2.2 PCI spec) is revision zero.

Class Code. The 24-bit class code field contains the same information as the Class Code configuration register within the function's configuration header. The configuration software examines this field to determine if this is a VGA-compatible interface. If it is, the ROM code image must be copied into system memory starting at location 000C0000h (for compatibility). Otherwise, it will typically be copied into the C0000h-through-DFFFFh region in a PC-compatible machine. Also refer to "Vendor ID field in ROM data structure" on page 883.

Image Length. This two-byte field indicates the length of the entire code image (refer to Figure 23-4 on page 879) in increments of 512 bytes. It is stored in little-endian format. The total size of the runtime code plus the initialization code (runtime code + initialization code = initialization size). This sum is not necessarily the "overall size of the image." The overall size of the image (Image Length) could be greater than the initialization size. The Image Length or Image size is what specifies where the next image in the ROM starts, while the Initialization size (a better name for this field) is the actual code size that is copied into RAM.

Revision Level of Code/Data. This two-byte field reflects the revision level of the code within the image.

Code Type. This one-byte field identifies the type of code contained in this image as either executable machine language for a particular processor/architecture, or as interpretive code.

- Code Type 00h = Intel **x86** (IBM PC-AT compatible) executable code.
- Code Type 01h = **OpenBoot interpretive code**. The Open Firmware standard (reference IEEE standard 1275-1994) defines the format and usage of the interpretive code. A basic description of the Open Firmware standard can be found in "Introduction to Open Firmware" on page 888.
- Code Type 02h = **HP PA/RISC** executable code (added in the 2.2 PCI spec).
- Code Type 03h = Extensible Firmware Interface (EFI).

The values from 04h-through-FFh are reserved.

Indicator Byte. Only bit seven is currently defined.

- 0 = not last code image in ROM.
- 1 = last code image in ROM.

Bits [6:0] are reserved.

Execution of Initialization Code

Prior to the discovery of the device's ROM, the configuration software has accomplished the following:

- Assigned one or more memory and/or IO ranges to the function by programming its Base Address Registers (see "Base Address Registers" on page 792).
- If the device is interrupt-driven, the interrupt routing information has been programmed into the device's Interrupt Line register (see "Interrupt Line Register" on page 791).
- In addition, if the UDF bit (this bit was in the 2.1 PCI spec and was deleted from the 2.2 PCI spec) was set in the device's configuration Status register, the user has been prompted to insert the diskette containing the PCI configuration file, or PCF, and the user selected any configuration options available from the file.

After the ROM is discovered, the configuration software copied a code image from the ROM into RAM memory. After the appropriate code image has been copied into system memory, the device ROM's address decoder is disabled. The configuration software must keep the area of RAM (the image resides in) read/writable. The sequence that follows assumes that the selected ROM image's Code Type field is 00h and that the device resides on a PC compatible platform. The configuration software then executes the following sequence:

1. Refer to Figure 23-5 on page 888. The software calls the initialization module within the image (through location 3h in the image), supplying it with three parameters in the AX register: the bus number, device number and function number of the function associated with the ROM:
   — The 8-bit bus number is supplied in AH,
   — the device number is supplied in the upper five bits of AL,
   — and the function number in the lower three bits of AL.
   It's necessary to supply the initialization code with this information so that it can determine how the function has been configured. For example, what IO and/or memory address range the configuration software has allocated to the function (via its base address registers), what input on the interrupt controller the function's interrupt pin has been routed to, etc.
2. The initialization code then issues a call to the PCI BIOS, supplying the bus number, device number, and function number as input parameters and requesting the contents of the function's Base Address Registers. Armed with this information, the initialization code can now communicate with the function's IO register set to initialize the device and prepare it for normal operation.
3. If the ROM image has a device-specific Interrupt Service Routine embedded within the run-time module, it reads from the device's Interrupt Line configuration register to determine which system interrupt request input on the interrupt controller the function's PCI interrupt pin has been routed to by the configuration software. Using this routing information, the initialization code knows which entry in the interrupt table in memory must be hooked. It first reads the pointer currently stored in that interrupt table entry and saves it within the body of the run-time portion of the image. It then stores the pointer to the interrupt service routine embedded within the run-time module of the code image into that interrupt table entry. In this way, it maintains the integrity of the interrupt chain. Since the area of system memory it has been copied into must be kept read/writable until the initialization code completes execution, the initialization code has no problem saving the pointer that it read from the interrupt table entry before hooking it to its own service routine.

4. The ROM image may also have a function-specific BIOS routine embedded within the run-time module of the code image. In this case, it needs to hook another interrupt table entry to this BIOS routine. Once again, it reads and saves the pointer currently stored in that interrupt table entry and then stores the pointer to the BIOS routine embedded within the run-time module of the code image. In this way, it maintains the integrity of the interrupt chain. *Note regarding steps 3 and 4: This procedure is different if the function will deliver interrupts via MSI instead of INTx messages. It would read the MSI capability structure of the function for the message address and message data fields and use that info to find the interrupt table entry. Then it would store the pointer to the interrupt service routine embedded within the run-time module of the code image into that interrupt table entry. No interrupt chaining would have to be supported.*
5. Since the area of system memory it resides in must be kept read/writable until the initialization code completes execution, the initialization code can adjust the code image length (in location 2h of the image). Very typically, at the completion of initialization code execution the programmer will adjust the image length field to encompass the area from the image's start through the end of the run-time code. The initialization code is typically only executed once and is then discarded. It must also recompute a new Checksum and store it at the end of the run-time code. If it sets the image length to zero, it doesn't need to recompute the image checksum and update it. When it returns control to the configuration software, a length of zero would indicate that the driver will not be used for some reason (perhaps a problem was detected during the setup of the device) and all of the memory it occupies can be deallocated and reused for something else.
6. Once the initialization code has completed execution, it executes a return to the system software that called it.

The configuration software then performs two final actions:

1. It interrogates the image size (at offset 2h in the image) to determine if it was altered. If it has, the configuration software adjusts the amount of memory allocated to the image to make more efficient use of memory. The image is typically shorter than it was.
2. It computes a new checksum for the image and stores it at the end of the image.
3. Write-protects the area of main memory the image resides in. This will keep the OS from using the area after it takes control of the machine.

The *ISA Plug-and-Play* spec refers to the PCI method of writing device ROM code and handling its detection, shadowing, and initialization, as the *DDIM (Device Driver Initialization Model)*. That spec stresses that this is the model that all device ROMs for other buses (i.e., other than PCI) should adhere to.

Figure 23-5: AX Contents On Entry To Initialization Code

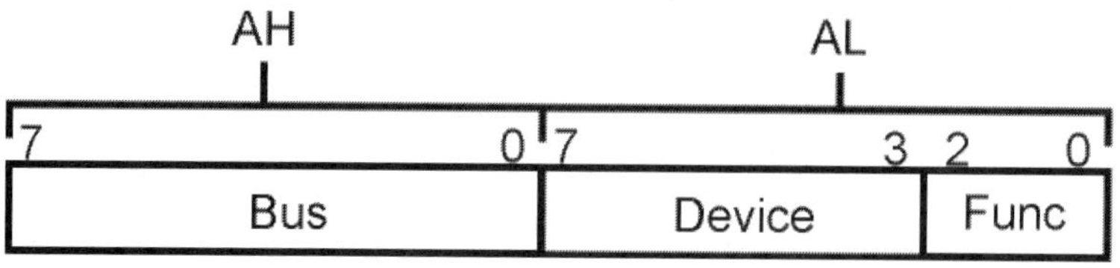

Introduction to Open Firmware

Introduction

The IEEE standard 1275-1994 entitled *Standard for Boot (Initialization, Configuration) Firmware Core Requirements and Practices* addresses two areas of concern regarding the boot process:

- The very first section in this chapter described the basic rationale for including a device ROM in the design of a device—it provides a **device driver** that allows the OS boot program **to use** the device **during** the **OS boot** process. That raises the question of what language to write the device driver in. This is one of the two major areas addressed by the OpenBoot standard. It is the one that the PCI spec is concerned with.
- After the OS is booted into memory, the BIOS passes control to it. If it's a Plug-and-Play capable OS, it would be nice if the BIOS **passed** a **pointer to** the OS that identified a **data structure** defining all of the devices that the OS has at its disposal. The OS could then traverse this data structure, determine the current state of all devices, and manage them for the remainder of the power-up session. In order for this to work, the exact format of this data structure must be standardized and understood by both the BIOS that builds it and the OS that subsequently takes ownership of it. This is the other major area addressed by the OpenBoot standard.

These two areas are discussed in more detail in the two sections that follow. It should be noted that this is only intended as an introduction to this standard. There's a lot more to it than is covered here: the standard is approximately 300 pages in length, 8.5″ x 11″ in size. A detailed discussion of Open Firmware is outside the scope of this book.

Universal Device Driver Format

Historically, most of the PC-compatible machines marketed in the past have been based on Intel x86 processors. When writing ROM code for an add-in subsystem on a card, it was a simple decision that the device driver image to be stored in the ROM would be an x86 machine language code image.

A number of system vendors have created systems incorporating PCI and based on processors other than the x86 processor family. These machines would take a substantial performance hit when executing expansion ROM code that isn't written in the processor's native machine language (i.e., x86 code is "foreign" to PowerPC and other types of non-Intel compatible processors). They would be forced to emulate the x86 code, an inherently inefficient solution.

Rather than writing an add-in device's ROM code in machine language native to a particular processor, the subsystem designer can write the ROM code in Fcode (tokenized Forth code) based on the Open Firmware specification, IEEE 1275-1994. In other words, the device driver is written in the high-order language Forth.

The Open Firmware components would consist of the following:

- The system BIOS contains the Fcode interpreter and possibly an individual Fcode device driver associated with each of the embedded subsystems that the system Open Firmware is already cognizant of.
- Each add-in subsystem would hopefully contain an Open Firmware Fcode image.

The Open Firmware language is based on the Forth programming language. The ROM code would be written in Forth source code. The source code is then supplied as input to a "tokenizer" program. The tokenizer processes the source code into a series of compressed commands, known as Fcode. As an example, an entire line of source code might be reduced to a single byte that represents the Forth command, only in a much more compact form.

The system BIOS that "discovered" the ROM (as described earlier in this chapter), incorporates an interpreter that converts the Fcode byte stream read from the ROM into machine language instructions specific to the system's processor.

The programmer only has to write this one universal version of the driver and any machine with an Fcode interpreter built into the system BIOS can then utilize this driver with the device during the boot process (allowing the device to be selected as the Input, Output, or IPL boot device). Obviously, executing a driver written in interpretive code would yield less than optimum performance. However, once the OS is booted into memory it then loads native code drivers for the three boot devices to replace the Fcode drivers. Performance of the devices is then optimized.

The PCI spec refers the reader to another document, *PCI Bus Binding to IEEE 1275-1994,* for implementation of Open Firmware in a PCI-based machine. This document is available using anonymous FTP to the machine playground.sun.com with the file name /pub/p1275/bindings/postscript/PCI.ps.

Passing Resource List To Plug-and-Play OS

BIOS Calls Bus Enumerators For Different Bus Environments

A machine architecture can contain many different device environments. Examples would be PCI, CardBus, Plug-and-Play ISA, etc. The methods that must be used to access the configuration registers associated with each of these different device types are very different from each other. In addition, the layout and format of their configuration registers are quite different as well.

The BIOS includes a separate, bus-specific program for each of these environments. This program is frequently referred to as a **Bus Enumerator**. The Bus Enumerator knows:

- how to access the configuration registers within devices of its specific type (e.g., PCI, PCI-X, PCI Express).
- how to "discover" devices within its environment. For example, in a PCI, PCI-X, or PCI Express environment, the programmer reads the Vendor ID from a function's Vendor ID register. Any value other than FFFFh represents a valid ID, while FFFFh indicates that no function resides at the currently-addressed location.
- how to probe the device's configuration registers to discover the device's resource requirements.
- how to allocate selected resources to the device.

The system BIOS must call the Bus Enumerators for each of the bus environments supported in the platform. When a specific Enumerator is called, it discovers all of the devices within its target environment, discovers the resources each requires, and allocates non-conflicting resources to each. It does not, however, enable the devices. The Enumerator builds a data structure in memory that lists all devices of its type that were found. It then passes a pointer to the start of that data structure back to the system BIOS.

When the system BIOS has called each of the Bus Enumerators for the different environments, it now has a list of pointers to the various, bus-specific data structures that list all of the devices that it has to work with.

BIOS Selects Boot Devices and Finds Drivers For Them

The system BIOS would then scan the data structures to locate an Input device, an Output device, and an IPL device to use in booting the OS into memory. In order to use each of these devices during the boot process, it would also require a device driver for each of them. The drivers would either be embedded within the BIOS itself or within device ROMs discovered with each of the devices.

For each of the three boot devices, the BIOS would then:

- call the initialization code within the device driver. The initialization code would then complete the preparation of the device for use.
- The BIOS would then set the appropriate bits in its configuration Command register (e.g., Bus Master Enable, etc.) to enable the device and bring it on-line.

BIOS Boots Plug-and-Play OS and Passes Pointer To It

The system BIOS then uses the three devices to boot the OS into memory and passes control to the OS. It also passes the OS a pointer that points to the head of the list of data structures that identify all of the devices that the OS has to work with.

OS Locates and Loads Drivers and Calls Init Code In Each

Note that *Init code* refers to the Initialization code portion of the driver. The OS then locates the disk-based drivers for each device and loads them into memory one-by-one. As it loads each driver, it then calls its initialization code entry point and the driver completes the device-specific setup of the device and brings the device on-line. The machine is now up and running and the OS manages the system devices from this point forward.

24 Express-Specific Configuration Registers

The Previous Chapter

The previous chapter provided a detailed description of device ROMs associated with PCI, PCI Express, and PCI-X functions. This included the following topics:

- device ROM detection.
- internal code/data format.
- shadowing.
- initialization code execution.
- interrupt hooking.

This Chapter

This chapter provides a description of:

- The PCI Express Capability register set in a function's PCI-compatible configuration space.
- The optional PCI Express Extended Capabilities register sets in a function's extended configuration space:
  - — The Advanced Error Reporting Capability register set.
  - — Virtual Channel Capability register set.
  - — Device Serial Number Capability register set.
  - — Power Budgeting Capability register set.
- RCRBs.

Introduction

Refer to Figure 24-1 on page 895. As described earlier in "Each Function Implements a Set of Configuration Registers" on page 715, each PCI Express function has a dedicated 4KB memory address range within which its configuration registers are implemented. Each Express function must implement the PCI Express Capability register set somewhere in the lower 48 dwords of the PCI-compatible register space (i.e., within the lower 48 dword region of the first 64 dwords of configuration space). In addition, the function may optionally implement any of the PCI Express Extended Capability register sets. The sections that follow provide a detailed description of each of these Express-specific register sets.

Figure 24-1: Function's Configuration Space Layout

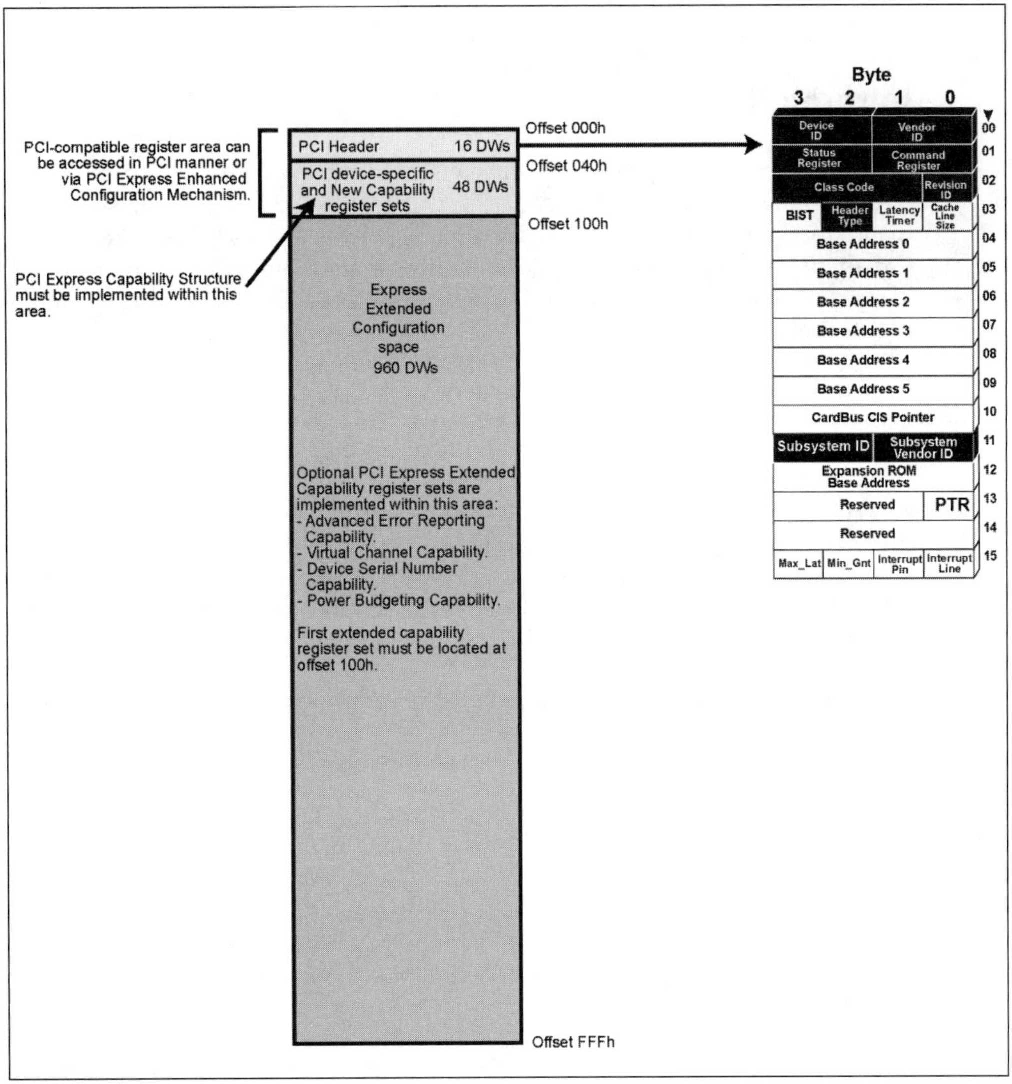

PCI Express Capability Register Set

Introduction

Refer to Figure 24-2 on page 897. Otherwise referred to as the PCI Express Capability Structure, implementation of the PCI Express Capability register set is mandatory for each function. It is implemented as part of the linked list of Capability register sets that reside in the lower 48 dwords of a function's PCI-compatible register area. It should be noted however, that some portions of this register set are optional.

Register implementation requirements:

- Every Express function must implement the registers that reside in dwords 0-through-4.
- The bridge associated with each Root Port must implement the registers that reside in dwords seven and eight.
- Each bridge associated with a Root Port or a downstream Switch Port that is connected to a slot (i.e., an add-in card slot) must implement the registers that reside in dwords five and six.

The sections that follow provide a detailed description of each of these registers.

Figure 24-2: PCI Express Capability Register Set

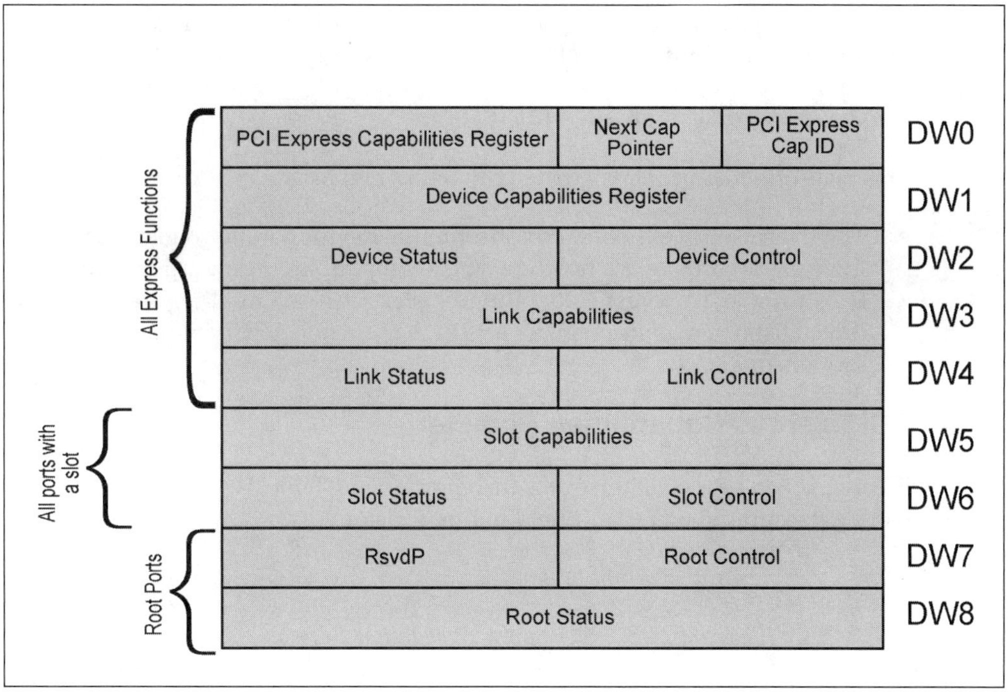

Required Registers

General

The sections that follow describe each of the required registers within the PCI Express Capability register set. The following registers must be implemented by all Express functions:

- PCI Express Capability ID Register
- Next Capability Pointer Register
- PCI Express Capabilities Register
- Device Capabilities Register
- Device Control Register
- Device Status Register
- Link Capabilities Register
- Link Control Register
- Link Status Register

PCI Express Capability ID Register

This read-only field must contain the value 10h, indicating this is the start of the PCI Express Capability register set.

Next Capability Pointer Register

This read-only field contains one of the following:

- The dword-aligned, non-zero offset to the next capability register set in the lower 48 dwords of the function's PCI-compatible configuration space.
- 00h, if the PCI Express Capability register set is the final register set in the linked list of capability register sets in the function's PCI-compatible configuration space.

PCI Express Capabilities Register

Figure 24-3 on page 898 illustrates this register and Table 24 - 1 on page 899 provides a description of each bit field in this register.

Figure 24-3: PCI Express Capabilities Register

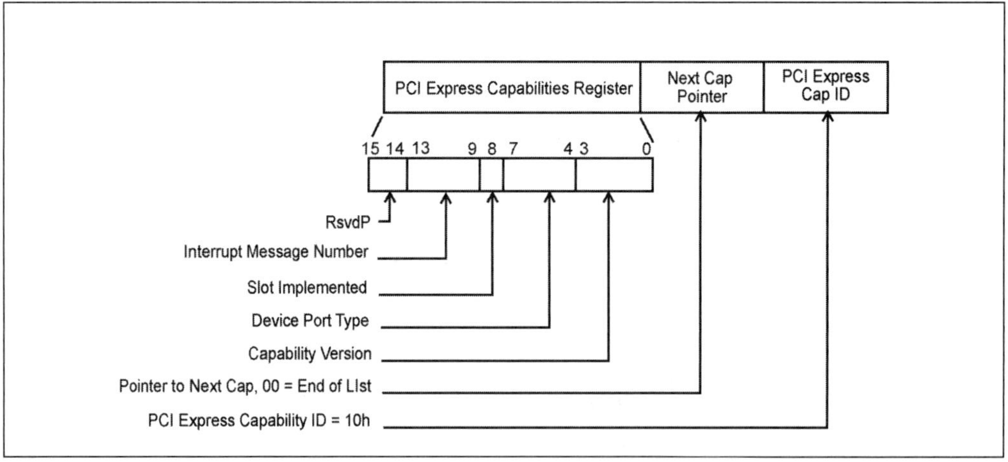

Table 24 - 1: PCI Express Capabilities Register

Bit(s)	Type	Description
3:0	RO	**Capability Version**. SIG-defined PCI Express capability structure version number (must be 1h).
7:4	RO	**Device/Port Type**. Express logical device type: • 0000b: **PCI Express Endpoint**. Some OSs and/or processors may not support IO accesses (i.e., accesses using IO rather than memory addresses). This being the case, the designer of a native PCI Express function should avoid the use of IO BARs. However, the target system that a function is designed for may use the function as one of the boot devices (i.e., the boot input device (e.g., keyboard), output display device, or boot mass storage device) and may utilize a legacy device driver for the function at startup time. The legacy driver may assume that the function's device-specific register set resides in IO space. In this case, the function designer would supply an IO BAR to which the configuration software will assign an IO address range. When the OS boot has completed and the OS has loaded a native PCI Express driver for the function, however, the OS may deallocate all legacy IO address ranges previously assigned to the selected boot devices. From that point forward and for the duration of the power-up session, the native driver will utilize memory accesses to communicate with its associated function through the function's memory BARs. • 0001b: **Legacy PCI Express Endpoint**. A function that requires IO space assignment through BARs for run-time operations. Extended configuration space capabilities, if implemented on legacy PCI Express Endpoint devices, may be ignored by software. • 0100b: **Root Port** of PCI Express Root Complex*. • 0101b: **Switch upstream port***. • 0110b: **Switch downstream port***. • 0111b: **Express-to-PCI/PCI-X bridge***. • 1000b: **PCI/PCI-X to Express bridge***. • All other encodings are reserved. * Only valid for functions with a Type 1 configuration register layout.

Table 24 - 1: PCI Express Capabilities Register (Continued)

Bit(s)	Type	Description
8	HWInit	**Slot Implemented**. When set, indicates that this Root Port or Switch downstream port is connected to an add-in card slot (rather than to an integrated component or being disabled). See "Chassis and Slot Number Assignment" on page 861 for more information.
13:9	RO	**Interrupt Message Number**. If this function is allocated more than one MSI interrupt message value (see "Message Data Register" on page 335), this register contains the MSI Data value that is written to the MSI destination address when any status bit in either the Slot Status register (see "Slot Status Register" on page 925) or the Root Status register (see "Root Status Register" on page 928) of this function are set. If system software should alter the number of message data values assigned to the function, the function's hardware must update this field to reflect the change.

Device Capabilities Register

Figure 24-4 on page 901 and Table 24 - 2 on page 901 provide a description of each bit field in this register. This register defines operational characteristics that are globally applicable to the device (and all functions that reside within it).

Figure 24-4: Device Capabilities Register

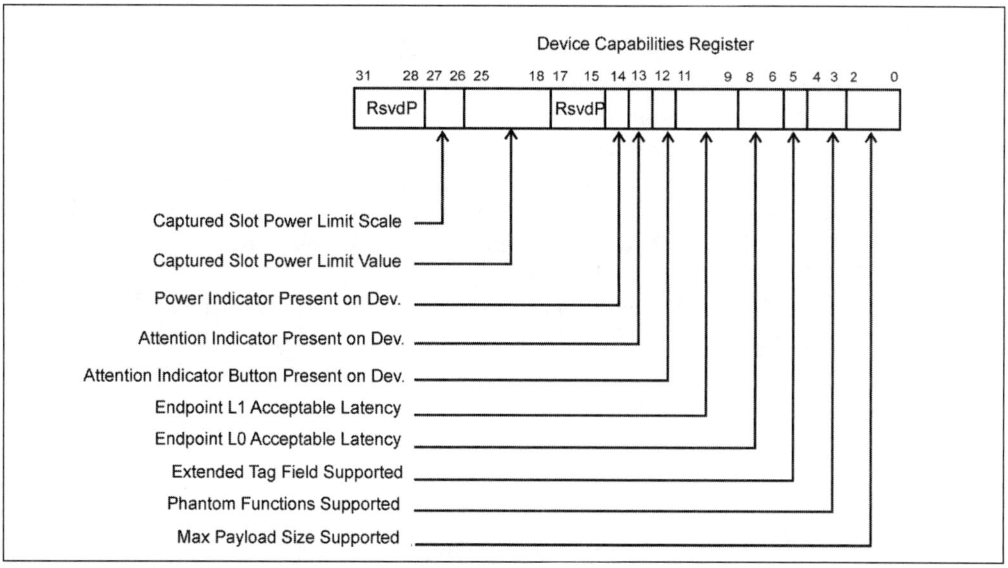

Table 24 - 2: Device Capabilities Register (read-only)

Bit(s)	Description
2:0	**Max Payload Size Supported**. Max data payload size that the function supports for TLPs: • 000b = 128 bytes max payload size • 001b = 256 bytes max payload size • 010b = 512 bytes max payload size • 011b = 1KB max payload size • 100b = 2KB max payload size • 101b = 4KB max payload size • 110b = Reserved • 111b = Reserved

Table 24 - 2: Device Capabilities Register (read-only) (Continued)

Bit(s)	Description
4:3	**Phantom Functions Supported.** **Background**: Normally, each Express function (when acting as a Requester) is limited to no more than 32 outstanding requests currently awaiting completion (as indicated by the lower five bits of the transaction Tag; the upper three bits of the Tag must be zero). However, a function may require more than this. If the Extended Tag Field is supported (see bit 5 in this table) and if the Extended Tag Field Enable bit in the Device Control register is set (see "Device Control Register" on page 905), the max is increased to 256 and all eight bits of the Requester ID Tag field are used when a function within the device issues a request packet. If a function requires a greater limit than 256, it may do this via Phantom Functions. **Description**: When the device within which a function resides does not implement all eight functions, a non-zero value in this field indicates that this is so. Assuming all functions are not implemented and that the programmer has set the Phantom Function Enable bit in the Device Control register (see "Device Control Register" on page 905), a function may issue request packets using its own function number as well as one or more additional function numbers. This field indicates the number of msbs of the function number portion of Requester ID that are logically combined with the Tag identifier. • 00b. The **Phantom Function feature is not available** within this device. • 01b. The msb of the function number in the Requestor ID is used for Phantom Functions. The device designer may implement functions 0-3. When issuing request packets, **Functions 0, 1, 2, and 3 may also use function numbers 4, 5, 6, and 7, respectively, in the packet's Requester ID**. • 10b. The two msbs of the function number in the Requestor ID are used for Phantom Functions. The device designer may implement functions 0 and 1. When issuing request packets, **Function 0 may also use function numbers 2, 4, and 6 in the packet's Requester ID. Function 1 may also use function numbers 3, 5, and 7 in the packet's Requester ID**. • 11b. All three bits of the function number in the Requestor ID are used for Phantom Functions. The device designer must only implement **Function 0** (and it **may use any function number in the packet's Requester ID**).

Table 24 - 2: Device Capabilities Register (read-only) (Continued)

Bit(s)	Description
5	**Extended Tag Field Supported**. Max supported size of the Tag field when this function acts as a Requester. • 0 = **5-bit Tag field supported** (max of 32 outstanding request per Requester). • 1 = **8-bit Tag field supported** (max of 256 outstanding request per Requester). If 8-bit Tags are supported and will be used, this feature is enabled by setting the Extended Tag Field Enable bit in the Device Control register (see "Device Control Register" on page 905) to one.
8:6	**Endpoint L0s Acceptable Latency**. Acceptable total latency that an Endpoint can withstand due to the transition from the L0s state to the L0 state (see "L0s Exit Latency Update" on page 625). This value is an indirect indication of the amount of the Endpoint's internal buffering. Power management software uses this value to compare against the L0s exit latencies reported by all components in the path between this Endpoint and its parent Root Port to determine whether ASPM L0s entry can be used with no loss of performance. • 000b = Less than 64ns • 001b = 64ns to less than 128ns • 010b = 128ns to less than 256ns • 011b = 256ns to less than 51 ns • 100b = 512ns to less than 1µs • 101b = 1µs to less than 2µs • 110b = 2µs-4µs • 111b = More than 4µs

Table 24 - 2: Device Capabilities Register (read-only) (Continued)

Bit(s)	Description
11:9	**Endpoint L1 Acceptable Latency**. Acceptable latency that an Endpoint can withstand due to the transition from L1 state to the L0 state (see "L1 Exit Latency Update" on page 626). This value is an indirect indication of the amount of the Endpoint's internal buffering. Power management software uses this value to compare against the L1 Exit Latencies reported by all components in the path between this Endpoint and its parent Root Port to determine whether ASPM L1 entry can be used with no loss of performance. • 000b = Less than 1µs • 001b = 1µs to less than 2µs • 010b = 2µs to less than 4µs • 011b = 4µs to less than 8µs • 100b = 8µs to less than 16µs • 101b = 16µs to less than 32µs • 110b = 32µs-64µs • 111b = More than 64µs
12	**Attention Button Present**. When set to one, indicates an Attention Button is implemented on the card or module. Valid for the following PCI Express device Types: • Express Endpoint device • Legacy Express Endpoint device • Switch upstream port • Express-to-PCI/PCI-X bridge
13	**Attention Indicator Present**. When set to one, indicates an Attention Indicator is implemented on the card or module. Valid for the following PCI Express device Types: • Express Endpoint device • Legacy Express Endpoint device • Switch upstream port • Express-to-PCI/PCI-X bridge

Table 24 - 2: Device Capabilities Register (read only) (Continued)

Bit(s)	Description
14	**Power Indicator Present**. When set to one, indicates a Power Indicator is implemented on the card or module. Valid for the following PCI Express device Types: • Express Endpoint device • Legacy Express Endpoint device • Switch upstream port • Express-to-PCI/PCI-X bridge
25:18	**Captured Slot Power Limit Value** (upstream ports only). In combination with the Slot Power Limit Scale value (see the next row in this table), specifies the upper limit on power supplied by slot: Power limit (in Watts) = Slot Power Limit value x Slot Power Limit Scale value This value is either automatically set by the receipt of a Set Slot Power Limit Message received from the port on the downstream end of the link, or is hardwired to zero. Refer to "Slot Power Limit Control" on page 562 for a detailed description.
27:26	**Captured Slot Power Limit Scale** (upstream ports only). Specifies the scale used for the calculation of the Power Limit (see the previous row in this table): • 00b = 1.0x • 01b = 0.1x • 10b = 0.01x • 11b = 0.001x This value is either automatically set by the receipt of a Set Slot Power Limit Message received from the port on the downstream end of the link, or is hardwired to zero.

Device Control Register

Figure 24-5 on page 906 and Table 24 - 3 on page 906 provide a description of each bit field in this register.

Figure 24-5: Device Control Register

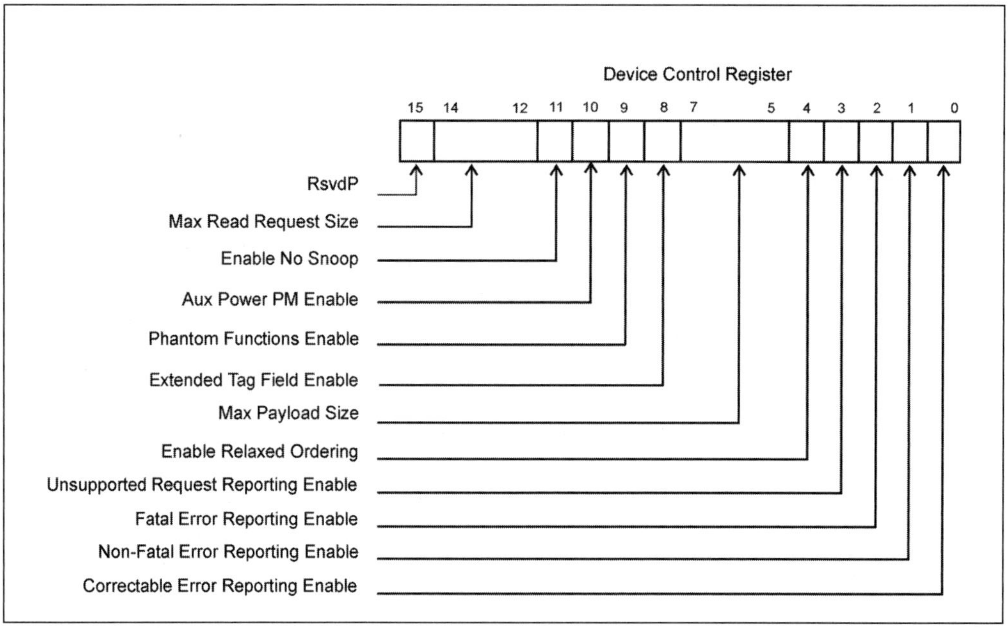

Table 24 - 3: Device Control Register (read/write)

Bit(s)	Description
0	**Correctable Error Reporting Enable**. For a multifunction device, this bit controls error reporting for all functions. For a Root Port, the reporting of correctable errors occurs internally within the Root Complex. No external ERR_COR Message is generated. Default value of this field is 0.
1	**Non-Fatal Error Reporting Enable.** This bit controls the reporting of non-fatal errors. For a multifunction device, it controls error reporting for all functions. For a Root Port, the reporting of non-fatal errors occurs internally within the Root Complex. No external ERR_NONFATAL Message is generated. Default value of this field is 0.

Table 24 - 3: Device Control Register (read/write) (Continued)

Bit(s)	Description
2	**Fatal Error Reporting Enable.** This bit controls the reporting of fatal errors. For a multifunction device, it controls error reporting for all functions within the device. For a Root Port, the reporting of fatal errors occurs internally within the Root Complex. No external ERR_FATAL Message is generated. Default value of this bit is 0.
3	**Unsupported Request (UR) Reporting Enable.** When set to one, this bit enables the reporting of Unsupported Requests. For a multifunction device, it controls UR reporting for all functions. The reporting of error messages (ERR_COR, ERR_NONFATAL, ERR_FATAL) received by a Root Port is controlled exclusively by the Root Control register (see "Root Control Register" on page 926). Default value of this bit is 0.
4	**Enable Relaxed Ordering.** When set to one, the device is permitted to set the Relaxed Ordering bit (refer to "Relaxed Ordering" on page 319) in the Attributes field of requests it initiates that do not require strong write ordering. Default value of this bit is 1, but it may be hardwired to 0 if a device never sets the Relaxed Ordering attribute in requests it initiates as a Requester.
7:5	**Max Payload Size.** Sets the max TLP data payload size for the device. As a Receiver, the device must handle TLPs as large as the set value; as a Transmitter, the device must not generate TLPs exceeding the set value. Permissible values that can be programmed are indicated by the Max Payload Size Supported in the Device Capabilities register (see "Device Capabilities Register" on page 900). • 000b = 128 byte max payload size • 001b = 256 byte max payload size • 010b = 512 byte max payload size • 011b = 1024 byte max payload size • 100b = 2048 byte max payload size • 101b = 4096 byte max payload size • 110b = Reserved • 111b = Reserved Default value of this field is 000b.

Table 24 - 3: Device Control Register (read/write) (Continued)

Bit(s)	Description
8	**Extended Tag Field Enable.** When set to one, enables a device to use an 8-bit Tag field as a requester. If cleared to zero, the device is restricted to a 5-bit Tag field. Also refer to the description of the Phantom Functions Supported field in Table 24 - 2 on page 901. The default value of this bit is 0. Devices that do not implement this capability hardwire this bit to 0.
9	**Phantom Functions Enable**. See the description of the Phantom Functions Supported field in Table 24 - 2 on page 901. Default value of this bit is 0. Devices that do not implement this capability hardwire this bit to 0.
10	**Auxiliary (AUX) Power PM Enable.** When set to one, this bit enables a device to draw Aux power independent of PME Aux power. In a legacy OS environment, devices that require Aux power should continue to indicate PME Aux power requirements. Aux power is allocated as requested in the Aux Current field of the Power Management Capabilities register (PMC; see "Auxiliary Power" on page 645), independent of the PME Enable bit in the Power Management Control/Status register (PMCSR; see "PM Control/Status (PMCSR) Register" on page 599). For multifunction devices, a component is allowed to draw Aux power if at least one of the functions has this bit set. • <u>Note</u>: Devices that consume Aux power must preserve the value in this field when Aux power is available. In such devices, this register value is not modified by hot, warm, or cold reset. • Devices that do not implement this capability hardwire this bit to 0.

Table 24 - 3: Device Control Register (read/write) (Continued)

Bit(s)	Description
11	**Enable No Snoop.** Software sets this bit to one if the area of memory this Requester will access is not cached by the processor(s). When a request packet that targets system memory is received by the Root Complex (i.e., the memory that the processors cache from), the Root Complex does not have to delay the access to memory to perform a snoop transaction on the processor bus if the No Snoop attribute bit is set. This speeds up the memory access. • Note that setting this bit to one should not cause a function to unequivocally set the No Snoop attribute on every memory requests that it initiates. The function may only set the bit when it knows that the processor(s) are not caching from the area of memory being accessed. • Default value of this bit is 1 and it may be hardwired to 0 if a device never sets the No Snoop attribute in Request transactions that it initiates.
14:12	**Max_Read_Request_Size.** Max read request size for the device when acting as the Requester. The device must not generate read requests with a size > this value. • 000b = 128 byte max read request size • 001b = 256 byte max read request size • 010b = 512 byte max read request size • 011b = 1KB max read request size • 100b = 2KB max read request size • 101b = 4KB max read request size • 110b = Reserved • 111b = Reserved Devices that do not generate read requests larger than 128 bytes are permitted to implement this field as Read Only (RO) with a value of 000b. Default value of this field is 010b.

Device Status Register

Figure 24-6 on page 910 and Table 24 - 4 on page 910 provide a description of each bit field in this register.

Figure 24-6: Device Status Register

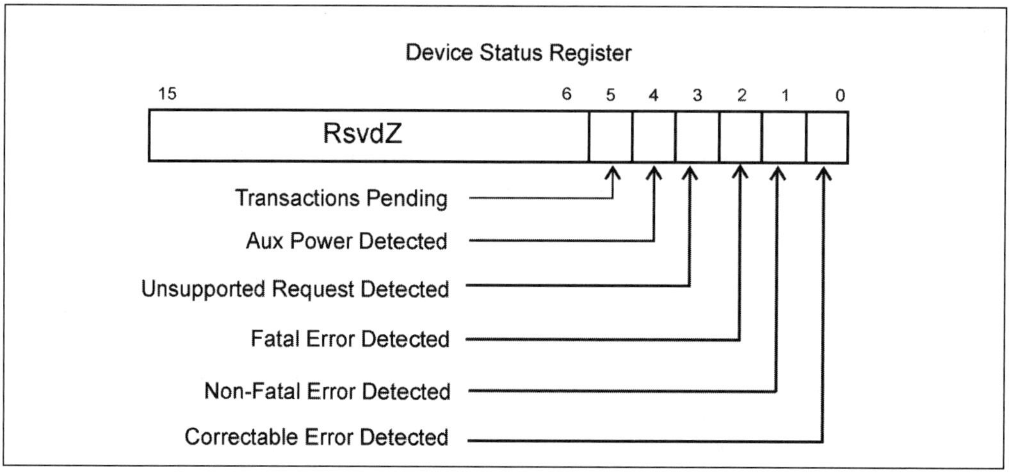

Table 24 - 4: Device Status Register

Bit(s)	Type	Description
0	RW1C	**Correctable Error Detected**. A one indicates that one or more correctable errors were detected since the last time this bit was cleared by software. Correctable errors are reflected by this bit regardless of whether error reporting is enabled or not in the Device Control register (see "Device Control Register" on page 905). In a multifunction device, each function indicates whether or not that function has detected any correctable errors using this bit. For devices supporting Advanced Error Handling (see "Advanced Error Reporting Mechanisms" on page 382), errors are logged in this register regardless of the settings of the Correctable Error Mask register. Default value of this bit is 0.

Table 24 - 4: Device Status Register (Continued)

Bit(s)	Type	Description
1	RW1C	**Non-Fatal Error Detected**. A one indicates that one or more non-fatal errors were detected since the last time this bit was cleared by software. Non-fatal errors are reflected in this bit regardless of whether error reporting is enabled or not in the Device Control register (see "Device Control Register" on page 905). In a multifunction device, each function indicates whether or not that function has detected any non-fatal errors using this bit. For devices supporting Advanced Error Handling, errors are logged in this register regardless of the settings of the Uncorrectable Error Mask register (*note that the 1.0a spec says "Correctable Error Mask register", but the authors think this is incorrect*). Default value of this bit is 0.
2	RW1C	**Fatal Error Detected**. A one indicates that one or more fatal errors were detected since the last time this bit was cleared by software. Fatal errors are reflected in this bit regardless of whether error reporting is enabled or not in the Device Control register (see "Device Control Register" on page 905). In a multifunction device, each function indicates whether or not that function has detected any fatal errors using this bit. For devices supporting Advanced Error Handling (see "Advanced Error Reporting Capability" on page 930), errors are logged in this register regardless of the settings of the Uncorrectable Error Mask register (*note that the 1.0a spec erroneously says "Correctable Error Mask register."*) Default value of this bit is 0.
3	RW1C	**Unsupported Request (UR) Detected**. When set to one, indicates that the function received an Unsupported Request. Errors are reflected in this bit regardless of whether error reporting is enabled or not in the Device Control register (see "Device Control Register" on page 905). In a multifunction device, each function indicates whether or not that function has detected any UR errors using this bit. Default value of this field is 0.
4	RO	**Aux Power Detected**. Devices that require Aux power set this bit to one if Aux power is detected by the device.

Table 24 - 4: Device Status Register (Continued)

Bit(s)	Type	Description
5	RO	**Transactions Pending**. When set to one, indicates that this function has issued non-posted request packets which have not yet been completed (either by the receipt of a corresponding Completion, or by the Completion Timeout mechanism). A function reports this bit cleared only when all outstanding non-posted requests have completed or have been terminated by the Completion Timeout mechanism. • **Root and Switch Ports**: Root and Switch Ports adhering solely to the 1.0a Express spec never issue non-posted requests on their own behalf. Such Root and Switch Ports hardwire this bit to 0b.

Link Registers (Required)

There are three link-related registers:

- The Link Capabilities Register.
- The Link Control Register.
- The Link Status Register.

Link Capabilities Register. Figure 24-7 on page 913 and Table 24 - 5 on page 913 provide a description of each bit field in this register.

Figure 24-7: Link Capabilities Register

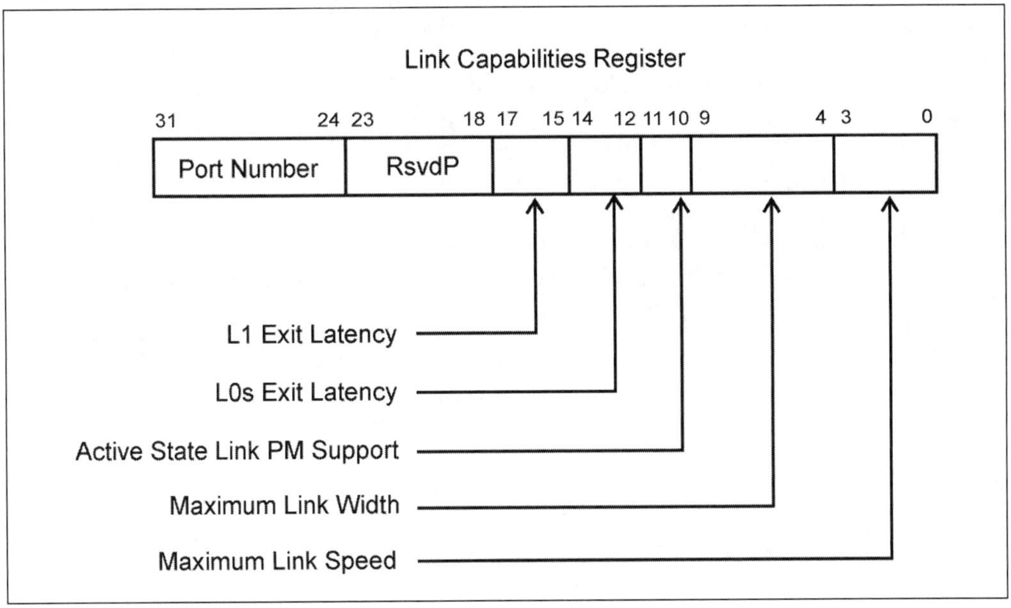

Table 24 - 5: Link Capabilities Register

Bit(s)	Type	Description
3:0	RO	**Maximum Link Speed**. • 0001b = 2.5 Gb/s • All other encodings are reserved.
9:4	RO	**Maximum Link Width**. • 000000b = Reserved • 000001b = x1 • 000010b = x2 • 000100b = x4 • 001000b = x8 • 001100b = x12 • 010000b = x16 • 100000b = x32 • All other values are reserved.

Table 24 - 5: Link Capabilities Register (Continued)

Bit(s)	Type	Description
11:10	RO	**Active State Power Management (ASPM) Support**. Indicates the level of ASPM supported on this Link. • 00b = Reserved • 01b = L0s Entry Supported • 10b = Reserved • 11b = L0s and L1 Supported Refer to "Link Active State Power Management" on page 608 for more information.
14:12	RO	**L0s Exit Latency**. Indicates the L0s exit latency for the Link (i.e., the length of time this Port requires to complete a transition from L0s to L0). • 000b = Less than 64ns • 001b = 64ns to less than 128ns • 010b = 128ns to less than 256ns • 011b = 256ns to less than 512ns • 100b = 512ns to less than 1µs • 101b = 1µs to less than 2µs • 110b = 2µs-4µs • 111b = More than 4µs *Note*: Exit latencies may be influenced by a port's reference clock configuration (i.e., whether the port uses the reference clock supplied by the port at the remote end of the link or it provides it own local reference clock). Refer to "ASPM Exit Latency" on page 624 for more information.

Table 24 - 5. Link Capabilities Register (Continued)

Bit(s)	Type	Description
17:15	RO	**L1 Exit Latency**. Indicates the L1 exit latency for the Link (i.e., the length of time this Port requires to complete a transition from L1 to L0). • 000b = Less than 1µs • 001b = 1µs to less than 2µs • 010b = 2µs to less than 4µs • 011b = 4µs to less than 8µs • 100b = 8µs to less than 16µs • 101b = 16µs to less than 32µs • 110b = 32µs-64µs • 111b = More than 64µs *Note*: Exit latencies may be influenced by a port's reference clock configuration (i.e., whether the port uses the reference clock supplied by the port at the remote end of the link or it provides it own local reference clock). Refer to "ASPM Exit Latency" on page 624 for more information.
31:24	HWInit	**Port Number**. Indicates the Port number associated with this Link. The port number is assigned by the hardware designer.

Link Control Register. Figure 24-8 on page 916 and Table 24 - 6 on page 916 provide a description of each bit field in this register.

Figure 24-8: Link Control Register

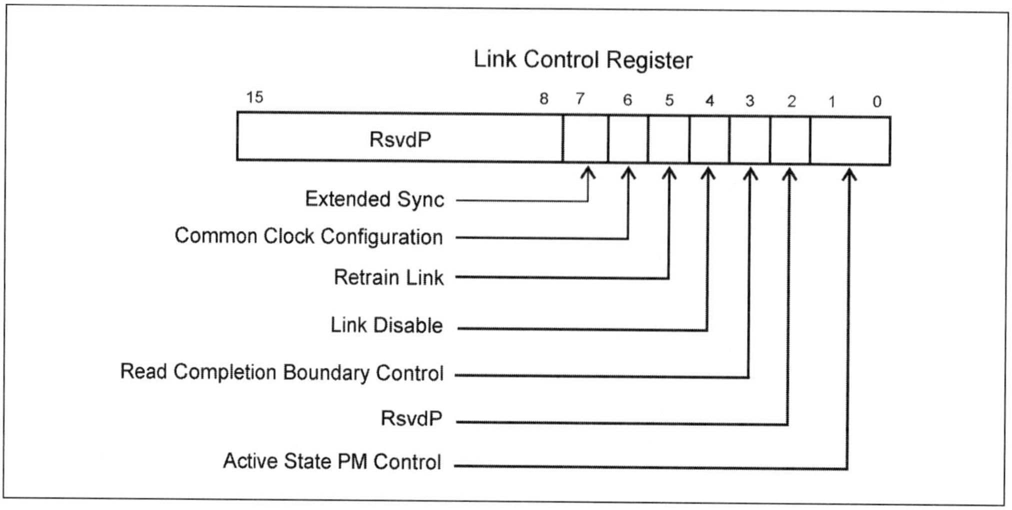

Table 24 - 6: Link Control Register

Bit(s)	Type	Description
1:0	RW	**Active State Power Management (ASPM) Control**. Controls the level of ASPM supported on the Link. • 00b = **Disabled.** • 01b = **L0s Entry Enabled**. Indicates the Transmitter entering L0s is supported. The Receiver must be capable of entering L0s even when this field is disabled (00b). • 10b = **L1 Entry Enabled.** • 11b = **L0s and L1 Entry Enabled.** Default value of this field is 00b or 01b depending on form factor. At the time of writing, only the Electromechanical specified had been released. This specification makes no mention of the default state of the ASPM bits.

Table 24 - 6. Link Control Register (Continued)

Bit(s)	Type	Description
3	**RO** for Root and Switch Ports **RW** for End-points	**Read Completion Boundary (RCB).** • **Root Ports**: Hardwired. Indicates the RCB value for the Root Port. It is a hardwired, read-only value indicating the RCB support capabilities: – 0b = 64 byte – 1b = 128 byte • **Endpoints**: Set by configuration software to indicate the RCB value of the Root Port upstream from the Endpoint. Devices that do not implement this feature must hardwire the field to 0b. – 0b = 64 byte – 1b = 128 byte • **Switch Ports**: Reserved and hardwired to 0b.
4	RW	**Link Disable**. 1 = disable the Link. Reserved on Endpoint devices and Switch upstream ports. The value written can be read back immediately, before the link has actually changed state. Default value of this bit is 0b.
5	RW	**Retrain Link**. • 1 = initiate Link retraining by changing the Physical Layer LTSSM to the Recovery state. • Reads of this bit always return 0b. • Reserved on Endpoint devices and Switch upstream ports. See "Link Errors" on page 379 for more information.
6	RW	**Common Clock Configuration**. • 1 indicates that this component and the component at the opposite end of this Link are using a common reference clock. • 0 indicates that this component and the component at the opposite end of this Link are using separate reference clocks. • A component factors this bit setting into its calculation of the L0s and L1 Exit Latencies (see Table 24 - 5 on page 913) that it reports in the Link Capabilities register. • After changing this bit in a component on either end of a Link, software must trigger the Link to retrain by setting the Retrain Link bit to one in this register. • Default value of this field is 0b. See "ASPM Exit Latency" on page 624 for more information.

Table 24 - 6: Link Control Register (Continued)

Bit(s)	Type	Description
7	RW	**Extended Sync**. When set to one, this bit forces the transmission of: • 4096 FTS Ordered Sets during the L0s state • followed by a single SKP ordered set prior to entering the L0 state, • as well as the transmission of 1024 TS1 Ordered Sets in the L1 state prior to entering the Recovery state. This mode gives external devices (e.g., logic analyzers) that may be monitoring Link activity time to achieve bit and symbol lock before the Link enters the L0 or Recovery state and resumes communication. Default value for this bit is 0b. See "L0s State" on page 611 for more information.

Link Status Register. Figure 24-9 on page 918 and Table 24 - 7 on page 919 provide a description of each bit field in this register.

Figure 24-9: Link Status Register

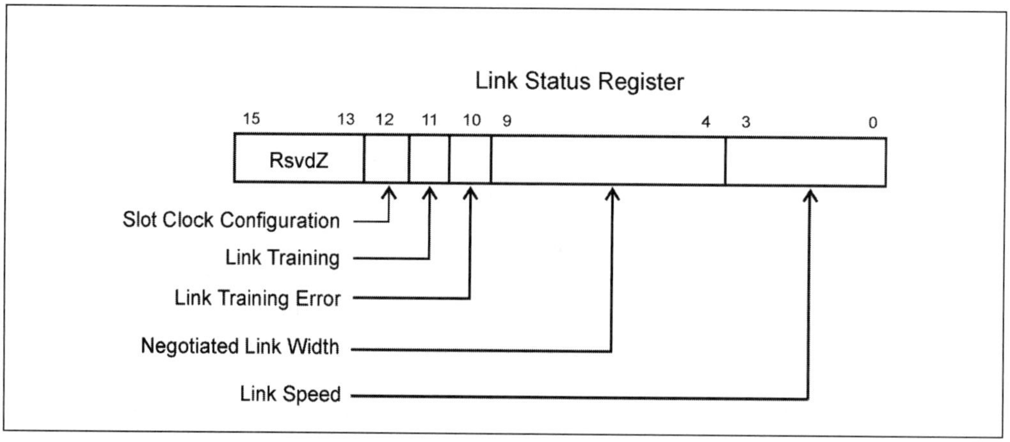

Table 24 - 7: Link Status Register

Bit(s)	Type	Description
3:0	RO	**Link Speed**. The negotiated Link speed. • 0001b = 2.5 Gb/s All other encodings are reserved.
9:4	RO	**Negotiated Link Width**. The negotiated Link width. • 000001b = x1 • 000010b = x2 • 000100b = x4 • 001000b = x8 • 001100b = x12 • 010000b = x16 • 100000b = x32 • All other encodings are reserved. See "Negotiate Link Width[9:4]" on page 551 for more information.
10	RO	**Training Error**. 1 = indicates that a Link training error occurred. Reserved on Endpoint devices and Switch upstream ports. Cleared by hardware upon successful training of the Link to the L0 Link state. See "Link Errors" on page 379 for more information.
11	RO	**Link Training**. When set to one, indicates that Link training is in progress (Physical Layer LTSSM is in the Configuration or Recovery state) or that the Retrain Link bit was set to one but Link training has not yet begun. • Hardware clears this bit once Link training is complete. • This bit is not applicable and reserved on Endpoint devices and the Upstream Ports of Switches. See "Link Errors" on page 379 for more information.
12	HWInit	**Slot Clock Configuration**. This bit indicates that the component uses the same physical reference clock that the platform provides on the connector. If the device uses an independent clock irrespective of the presence of a reference on the connector, this bit must be clear. See "Config. Registers Used for ASPM Exit Latency Management and Reporting" on page 628 for more information.

Slot Registers

Introduction

The slot-specific register set must be implemented for Root Port bridges and Switch downstream port bridges that are connected to add-in slot connectors. The registers are:

- Slot Capabilities Register
- Slot Control Register
- Slot Status Register

They are described in the sections that follow.

Slot Capabilities Register

Figure 24-10 on page 921 and Table 24 - 8 on page 921 provide a description of each bit field in this register.

Figure 24-10: Slot Capabilities Register

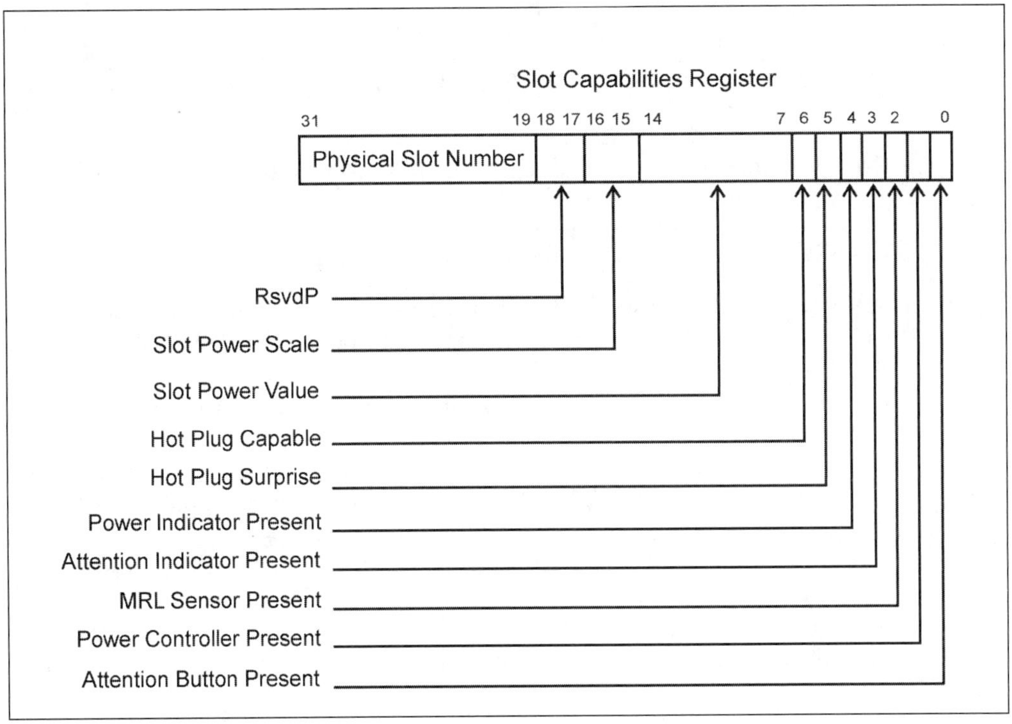

Table 24 - 8: Slot Capabilities Register (all fields are HWInit)

Bit(s)	Description
0	**Attention Button Present**. 1 = Attention Button is implemented on the chassis for this slot.
1	**Power Controller Present**. 1 = A Power Controller is implemented for this slot.
2	**MRL (Manually-operated Retention Latch) Sensor Present**. 1 = An MRL Sensor is implemented on the chassis for this slot.
3	**Attention Indicator Present**. 1 = An Attention Indicator is implemented on the chassis for this slot.

Table 24 - 8: Slot Capabilities Register (all fields are HWInit) (Continued)

Bit(s)	Description
4	**Power Indicator Present**. 1 = A Power Indicator is implemented on the chassis for this slot.
5	**Hot-Plug Surprise**. 1 = A device installed in this slot may be removed from the system without any prior notification.
6	**Hot-Plug Capable**. 1 = This slot supports Hot-Plug operations.
14:7	**Slot Power Limit Value**. In combination with the Slot Power Limit Scale value (see the next row in this table), specifies the max power (in Watts) available to the device installed in this slot. • **Max power limit = Slot Power Limit Value x Slot Power Limit Scale value**. • This field must be implemented if the Slot Implemented bit is set to one in the PCI Express Capabilities Register (see "PCI Express Capabilities Register" on page 898). • A write to this field causes the Port to send the Set Slot Power Limit Message upstream to the port at the other end of the Link. • The default value prior to hardware/firmware initialization is 0000 0000b. See "The Power Budget Capabilities Register Set" on page 564 for more information.
16:15	**Slot Power Limit Scale**. See the description in the previous row of this table. • Possible values: – 00b = 1.0x – 01b = 0.1x – 10b = 0.01x – 11b = 0.001x • This field must be implemented if the Slot Implemented bit is set to one in the PCI Express Capabilities Register (see "PCI Express Capabilities Register" on page 898). • A write to this field causes the Port to send the Set Slot Power Limit Message upstream to the port at the other end of the Link. • The default value prior to hardware/firmware initialization is 00b.

Table 24 - 8: Slot Capabilities Register (all fields are HWInit) (Continued)

Bit(s)	Description
31:19	**Physical Slot Number**. Indicates the physical slot number attached to this Port. Must be hardware initialized to a value that assigns a slot number that is globally unique within the chassis. Must be initialized to 0 for Ports connected to devices that are either integrated on the system board or integrated within the same silicon as the Switch downstream port or the Root Port. See "Chassis and Slot Number Assignment" on page 861 for more information.

Slot Control Register

Figure 24-11 on page 923 and Table 24 - 9 on page 924 provide a description of each bit field in this register.

Figure 24-11: Slot Control Register

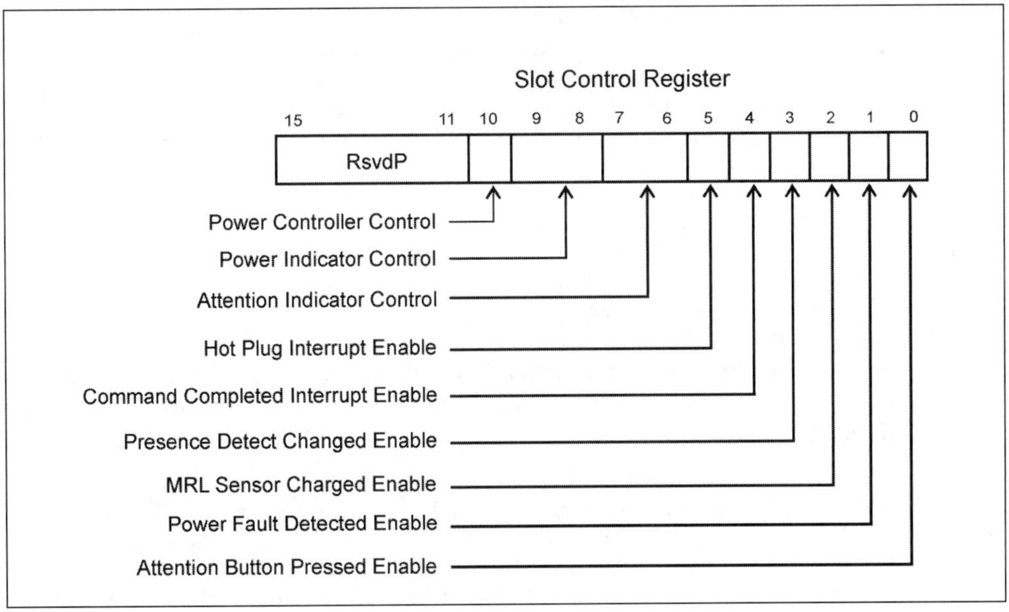

Table 24 - 9: Slot Control Register (all fields are RW)

Bit(s)	Description
0	**Attention Button Pressed Enable**. When set to one, enables the generation of a Hot-Plug interrupt or a wakeup event when the attention button is pressed. Default value of this field is 0. See "Attention Button" on page 667 for more information.
1	**Power Fault Detected Enable**. When set to one, enables the generation of a Hot-Plug interrupt or a wakeup event on a power fault event. Default value of this field is 0.
2	**MRL Sensor Changed Enable**. When set to one, enables the generation of a Hot-Plug interrupt or a wakeup event on an MRL sensor changed event. Default value of this field is 0. See "Electromechanical Interlock (optional)" on page 667 for more information.
3	**Presence Detect Changed Enable**. When set to one, enables the generation of a Hot-Plug interrupt or a wakeup event on a presence detect changed event. Default value of this field is 0. See "Slot Status and Events Management" on page 674 for more information.
4	**Command Completed Interrupt Enable**. When set to one, enables the generation of a Hot-Plug interrupt when a command is completed by the Hot-Plug Controller. Default value of this field is 0.
5	**Hot-Plug Interrupt Enable**. When set to one, enables the generation of a Hot-Plug interrupt on enabled Hot-Plug events. Default value of this field is 0.
7:6	**Attention Indicator Control**. A read from this field returns the current state of the Attention Indicator, while a write sets the Attention Indicator to the state indicated below: • 00b = Reserved • 01b = On • 10b = Blink • 11b = Off Writes to this field also cause the Port to send the respective Attention Indicator message.

Table 24 - 9: Slot Control Register (all fields are RW) (Continued)

Bit(s)	Description
9:8	**Power Indicator Control**. A read from this field returns the current state of the Power Indicator, while a write sets the Power Indicator to the state indicated below: • 00b = Reserved • 01b = On • 10b = Blink • 11b = Off Writes to this field also cause the Port to send the respective Power Indicator message.
10	**Power Controller Control**. A read from this field returns the current state of the power applied to the slot, while a write sets the power state of the slot to the state indicated below: • 0b = Power On • 1b = Power Off

Slot Status Register

Figure 24-12 on page 925 and Table 24 - 10 on page 926 provide a description of each bit field in this register.

Figure 24-12: Slot Status Register

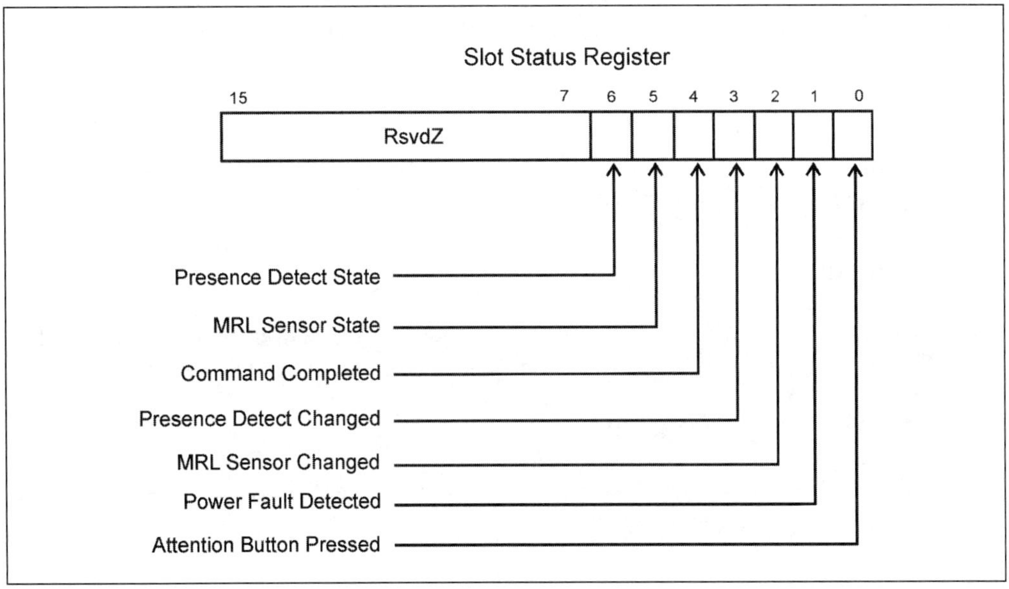

Table 24 - 10: Slot Status Register

Bit(s)	Type	Description
0	RW1C	**Attention Button Pressed**. 1 = attention button pressed.
1	RW1C	**Power Fault Detected**. 1 = Power Controller detected a power fault at this slot.
2	RW1C	**MRL Sensor Changed**. 1 = MRL Sensor state change detected.
3	RW1C	**Presence Detect Changed**. 1 = Presence Detect change detected.
4	RW1C	**Command Completed**. 1 = Hot-Plug Controller completed a command.
5	RO	**MRL Sensor State**. MRL sensor status (if MRL implemented). • 0b = MRL Closed • 1b = MRL Open
6	RO	**Presence Detect State**. When set to one, a card is present in the slot (as indicated either by an in-band mechanism or via the Presence Detect pins as defined in the PCI Express Card Electromechanical Specification). • 0b = Slot Empty • 1b = Card Present in slot This field must be implemented on all Switch downstream ports and on Root Ports that are attached to an add-in connector. It is hardwired to one if the port is not connected to an add-in slot connector.

Root Port Registers

Introduction

All Root Ports must implement the Root Control and Root Status registers. The following two sections provide a detailed description of these two registers.

Root Control Register

Figure 24-13 on page 927 and Table 24 - 11 on page 927 provide a description of each bit field in this register.

Figure 24-13: Root Control Register

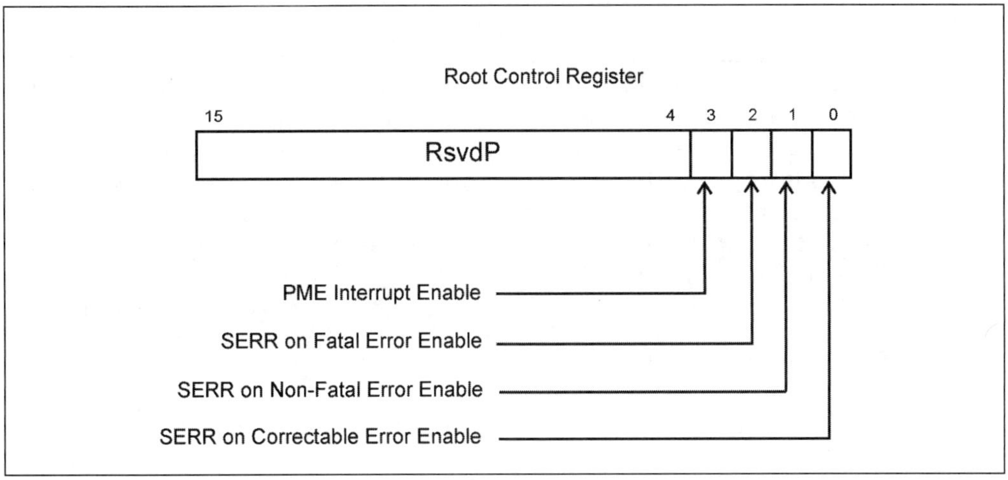

Table 24 - 11: Root Control Register (all fields are RW)

Bit(s)	Description
0	**System Error on Correctable Error Enable**. When set to one, a System Error is generated if a correctable error (ERR_COR) is reported by any of the child (i.e., downstream) devices associated with this Root Port, or by the Root Port itself. The mechanism for signaling a System Error to the system is system-specific (e.g., in an x86-based system, a Non-Maskable Interrupt—NMI—could be generated to the processor). Default value of this bit is 0. See "Reporting Errors to the Host System" on page 392 for more information.
1	**System Error on Non-Fatal Error Enable**. When set to one, a System Error is generated if a non-fatal error (ERR_NONFATAL) is reported by any of the child (i.e., downstream) devices associated with this Root Port, or by the Root Port itself. The mechanism for signaling a System Error to the system is system-specific (e.g., in an x86-based system, a Non-Maskable Interrupt—NMI—could be generated to the processor). Default value of this bit is 0. See "Reporting Errors to the Host System" on page 392 for more information.

Table 24 - 11: Root Control Register (all fields are RW) (Continued)

Bit(s)	Description
2	**System Error on Fatal Error Enable**. When set to one, a System Error is generated if a Fatal error (ERR_FATAL) is reported by any of the child (i.e., downstream) devices associated with this Root Port, or by the Root Port itself. The mechanism for signaling a System Error to the system is system-specific (e.g., in an x86-based system, a Non-Maskable Interrupt—NMI—could be generated to the processor). Default value of this field is 0. See "Reporting Errors to the Host System" on page 392 for more information.
3	**PME Interrupt Enable**. When set to one, enables interrupt generation on receipt of a PME Message from a child (i.e., downstream) device (which sets the PME Status bit in the Root Status register—see "Root Status Register" on page 928—to one). A PME interrupt is also generated when software sets this bit to one (assuming it was originally cleared to zero) when the PME Status bit in the Root Status register is set to one. Default value of this field is 0. See "The PME Sequence" on page 640 for more information.

Root Status Register

Figure 24-14 on page 928 and Table 24 - 12 on page 929 provide a description of each bit field in this register.

Figure 24-14: Root Status Register

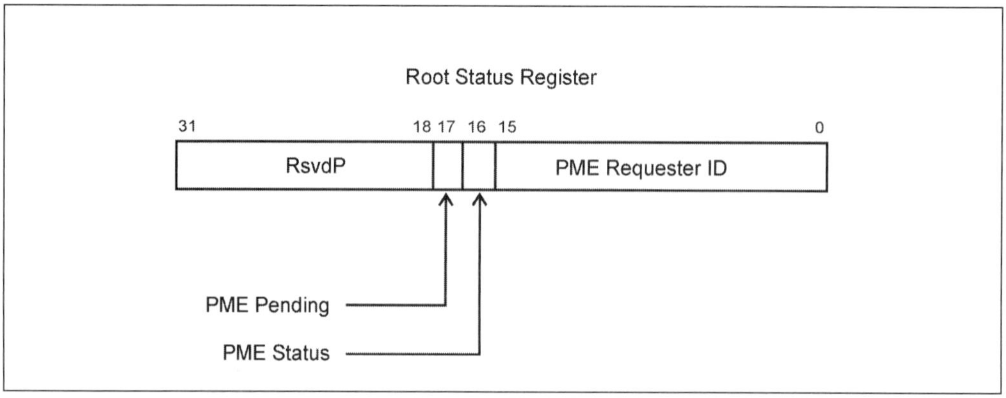

Table 24 - 12: Root Status Register

Bit(s)	Type	Description
15:0	RO	**PME Requestor ID**. Contains the Requester ID of the last child (i.e., downstream) device to issue a PME.
16	RW1C	**PME Status**. When set to one, indicates that PME was asserted by the Requester indicated in the PME Requestor ID field. Subsequent PMEs remain pending until this bit is cleared by software by writing a 1 to it.
17	RO	**PME Pending**. When set to one and the PME Status bit is set, indicates that another PME is pending. When the PME Status bit is cleared by software, the Root Port hardware indicates the delivery of the next PME by setting the PME Status bit again and updating the Requester ID field appropriately. The PME Pending bit is cleared by hardware when no more PMEs are pending.

PCI Express Extended Capabilities

General

A PCI Express function may optionally implement any, all, or none of the following Extended Capability register sets:

- Advanced Error Reporting Capability register set.
- Virtual Channel (VC) Capability register set.
- Device Serial Number Capability register set.
- Power Budgeting Capability register set.

Refer to Figure 24-1 on page 895. The first extended capability register set must be implemented at offset 100h in a function's 4KB configuration space and its Enhanced Capability Header register (see Figure 24-15 on page 930) contains a pointer (the Next Capability Offset field; this 12-bit field must contain either the dword-aligned start address of the next capability register set, or a value of zero if this is the last of the extended capability register sets) to the next extended capability register set in the list. The respective capability IDs of each register set are:

- Advanced Error Reporting Capability register set. ID = 0001h.
- Virtual Channel (VC) Capability register set. ID = 0002h.

- Device Serial Number Capability register set. ID = 0003h.
- Power Budgeting Capability register set. ID = 0004h.

The Capability Version field is assigned by the SIG and defines the layout of the register set. It must be 1h for all of the extended capabilities currently defined.

Figure 24-15: Enhanced Capability Header Register

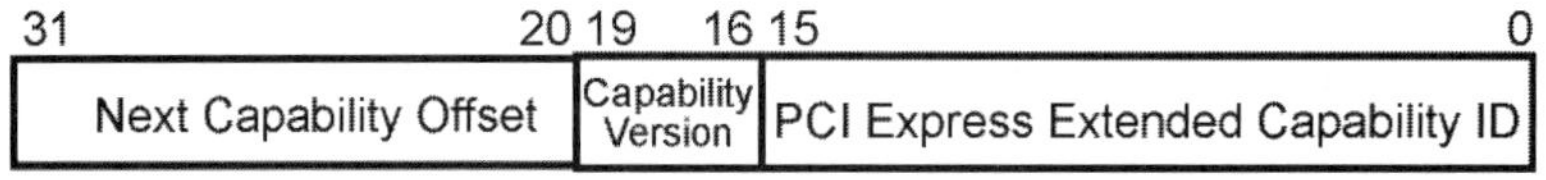

Advanced Error Reporting Capability

General

Figure 24-16 on page 931 illustrates the optional Advanced Error Reporting capability register set. Note that the registers in the last three dwords of this register set may only be implemented for a Root Port function (one that has a value of 0100b in the Device/Port Type field of the PCI Express Capabilities register in the function's PCI-compatible configuration space). This capability register set consists of the registers pictured in Figure 24-16 on page 931 and described in Table 24 - 13 on page 932.

Detailed Description

For a detailed description of the Advanced Error Reporting capability register set, refer to "Advanced Error Reporting Mechanisms" on page 382.

Figure 24-16: Advanced Error Reporting Capability Register Set

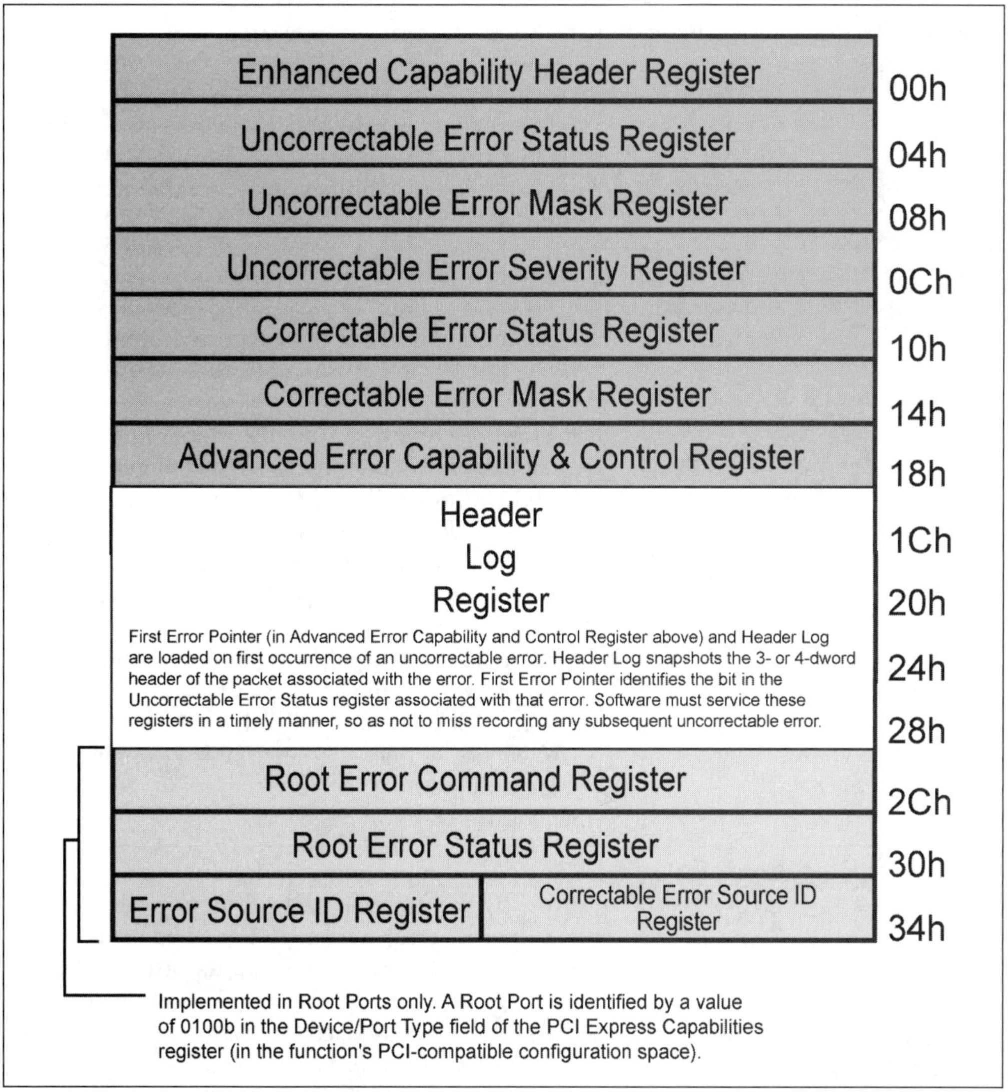

Table 24 - 13: Advanced Error Reporting Capability Register Set

Register Group	Register	Description
NA	Enhanced Capability Header	Capability ID = 0001h. The Capability Version field in this register is assigned by the SIG and defines the layout of the register set. It must be 1h for all of the extended capabilities currently defined. See Figure 24-17 on page 935.
NA	Capabilities and Control Register	Contains the following bits fields: • **First Error Pointer**. Read-only. Identifies the bit position of the first error reported in the Uncorrectable Error Status register (see Figure 24-23 on page 937). • **ECRC Generation Capable**. Read-only. 1 indicates that the function is capable of generating ECRC (End-to-End CRC; refer to "ECRC Generation and Checking" on page 361). • **ECRC Generation Enable**. Read/write sticky bit. When set to one, enables ECRC generation. Default = 0. • **ECRC Check Capable**. Read-only. 1 indicates that the function is capable of checking ECRC. • **ECRC Check Enable**. Read/write sticky bit. When set to one, enables ECRC checking. Default = 0. See Figure 24-18 on page 935.
Correctable Error Registers	Correctable Error Mask Register	Controls the reporting of individual correctable errors by the function to the Root Complex via a PCI Express error message. A masked error (respective bit set to one) is not reported to the Root Complex by the function. This register contains a mask bit for each corresponding error bit in the Correctable Error Status register (see the next row in this table and Figure 24-19 on page 935).
	Correctable Error Status Register	Reports the error status of the function's correctable error sources. Software clears a set bit by writing a 1 to the respective bit. See Figure 24-20 on page 936.

Table 24 - 13: Advanced Error Reporting Capability Register Set (Continued)

Register Group	Register	Description
Uncorrectable Error Registers	Uncorrectable Error Mask Register	Controls the function's reporting of errors to the Root Complex via a PCI Express error message. A masked error (respective bit set to 1b): • is not logged in the Header Log register (see Figure 24-16 on page 931), • does not update the First Error Pointer (see the description of the Capabilities and Control Register in this table), and • is not reported to the Root Complex. This register (see Figure 24-21 on page 936)contains a mask bit for each corresponding error bit in the Uncorrectable Error Status register.
	Uncorrectable Error Severity Register	Each respective bit controls whether an error is reported to the Root Complex via a non-fatal or fatal error message. An error is reported as fatal if the corresponding bit is set to one. See Figure 24-22 on page 937.
	Uncorrectable Error Status Register	Reports the error status of the function's uncorrectable error sources. See Figure 24-23 on page 937.

Table 24 - 13: Advanced Error Reporting Capability Register Set (Continued)

Register Group	Register	Description
Root Error Registers	Root Error Command Register	Controls the Root Complex's ability to generate an interrupt to the processor upon receipt of: • a correctable error message, • a non-fatal error message, or • a fatal error message from a child function downstream of the Root Port. See Figure 24-24 on page 938.
	Root Error Status Register	Tracks the Root Port's receipt of error messages received by the Root Complex from a child function downstream of the Root Port, and of errors detected by the Root Port itself. Non-fatal and fatal error messages are grouped together as uncorrectable. There is a first error bit and a next error bit associated with correctable and uncorrectable errors, respectively. When an error is received by a Root Port, the respective first error bit is set and the Requestor ID is logged in the Error Source Identification register. If software does not clear the first reported error before another error message is received of the same category (correctable or uncorrectable), the corresponding next error status bit will be set, but the Requestor ID of the subsequent error message is discarded. Updated regardless of the settings in the Root Control and the Root Error Command registers. See Figure 24-25 on page 938.
	Uncorrectable Error Source ID Register	Identifies the source (Requestor ID) of the first uncorrectable (non-fatal/fatal) error reported in the Root Error Status register. Updated regardless of the settings in the Root Control and the Root Error Command registers. See Figure 24-26 on page 938.
	Correctable Error Source ID Register	Identifies the source (Requestor ID) of the first correctable error reported in the Root Error Status register. Updated regardless of the settings in the Root Control and the Root Error Command registers. See Figure 24-26 on page 938.

Figure 24-17: Advanced Error Reporting Enhanced Capability Header

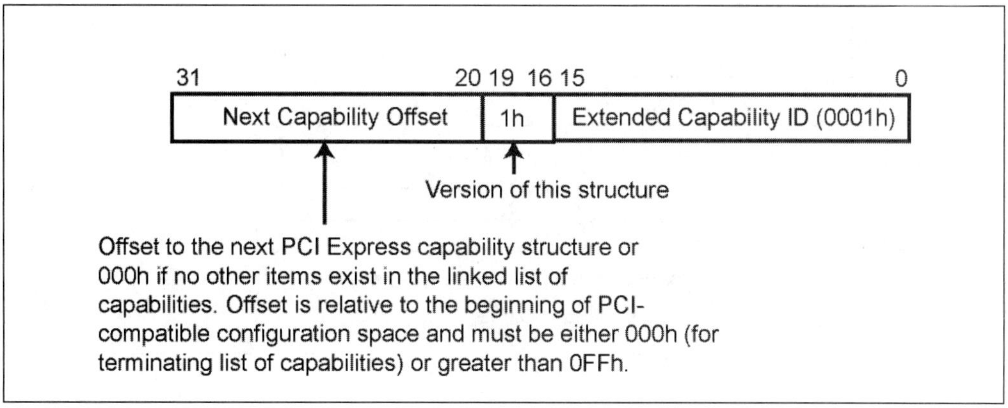

Figure 24-18: Advanced Error Capabilities and Control Register

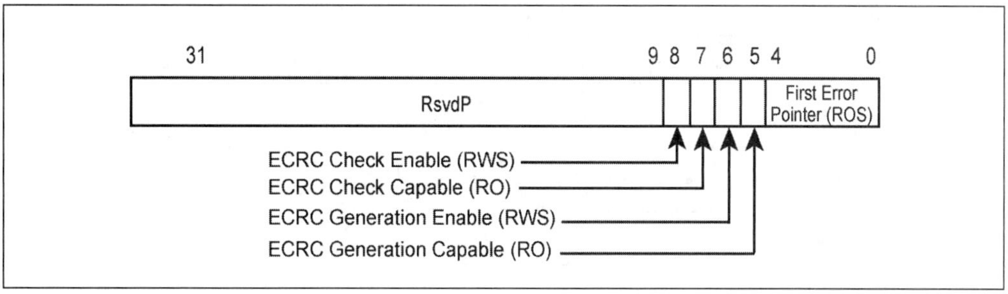

Figure 24-19: Advanced Error Correctable Error Mask Register

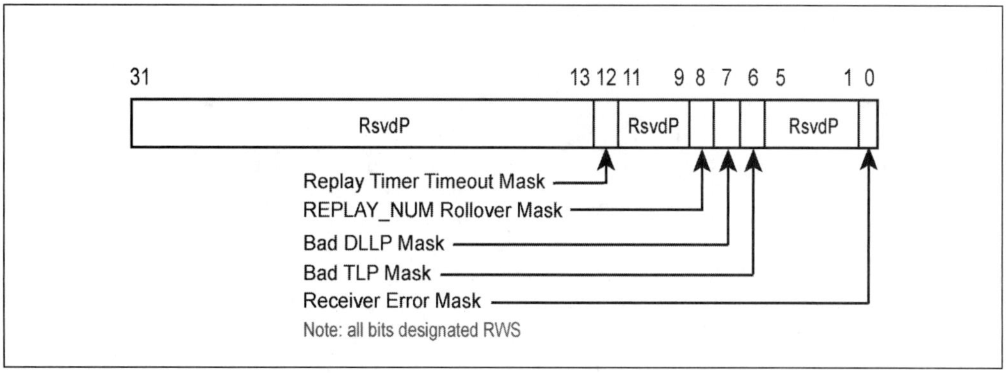

Figure 24-20: Advanced Error Correctable Error Status Register

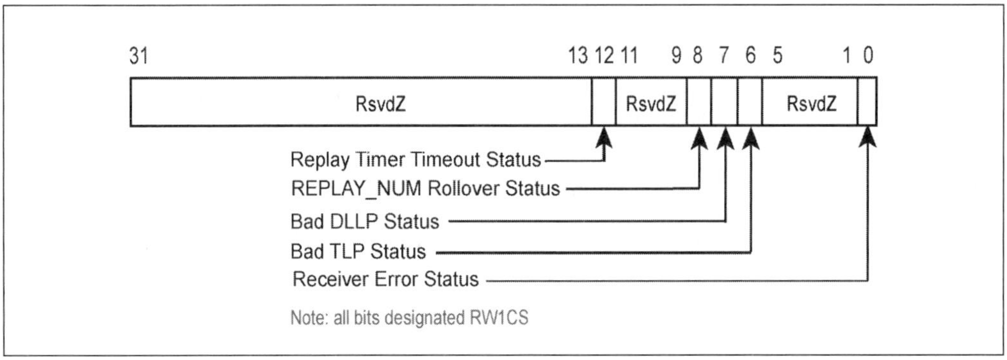

Figure 24-21: Advanced Error Uncorrectable Error Mask Register

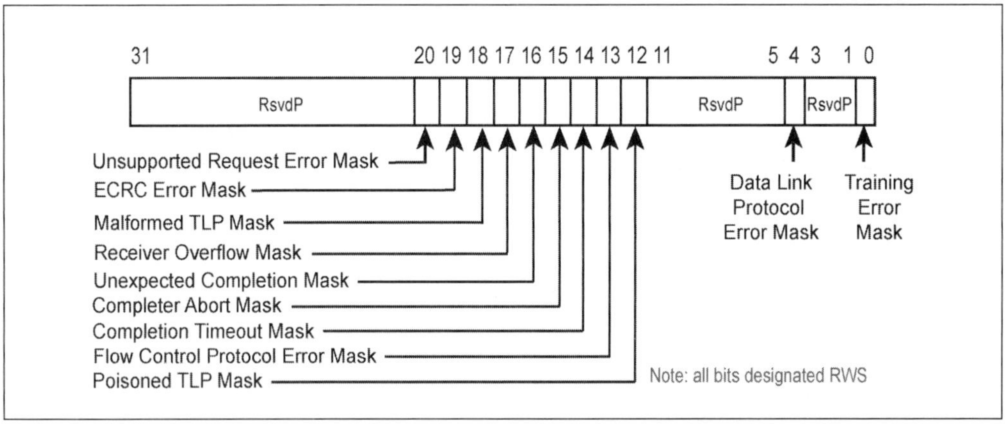

Figure 24-22: Advanced Error Uncorrectable Error Severity Register

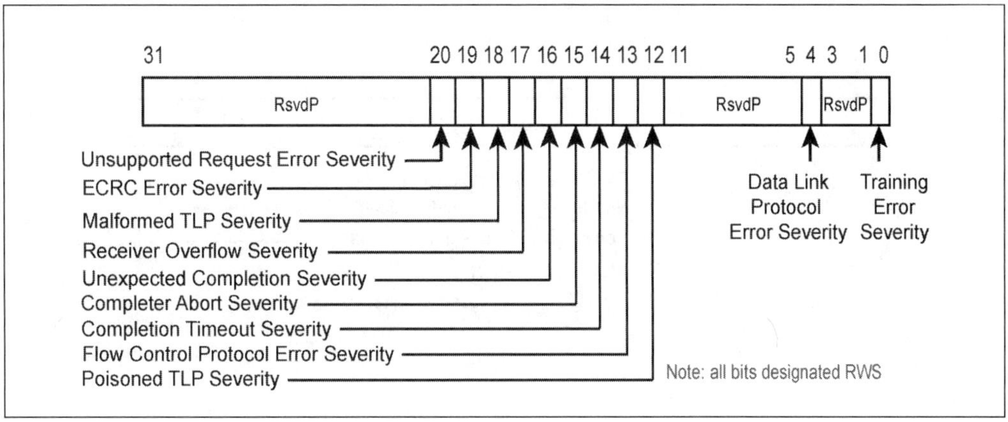

Figure 24-23: Advanced Error Uncorrectable Error Status Register

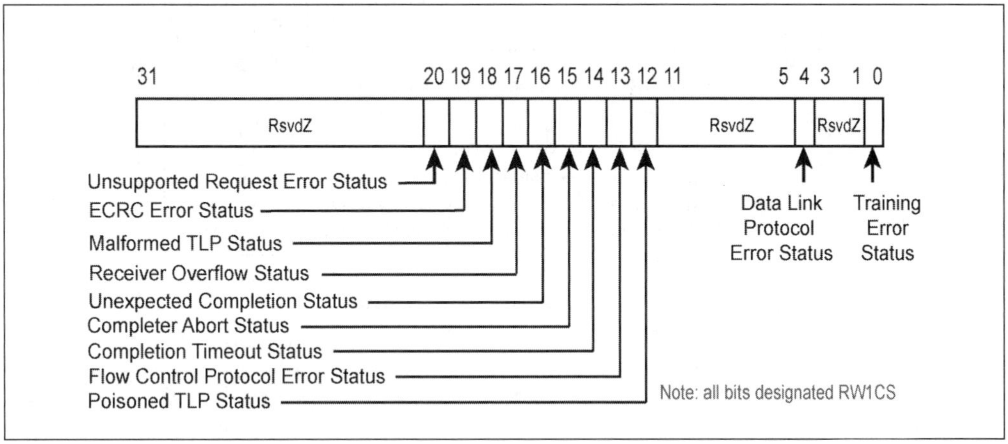

Figure 24-24: Advanced Error Root Error Command Register

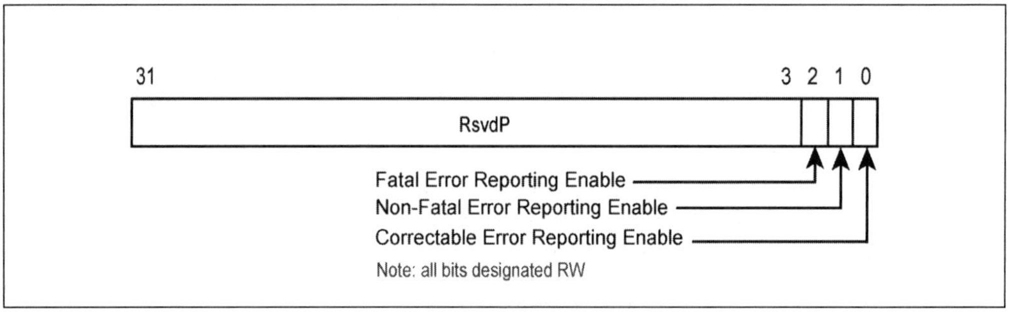

Figure 24-25: Advanced Error Root Error Status Register

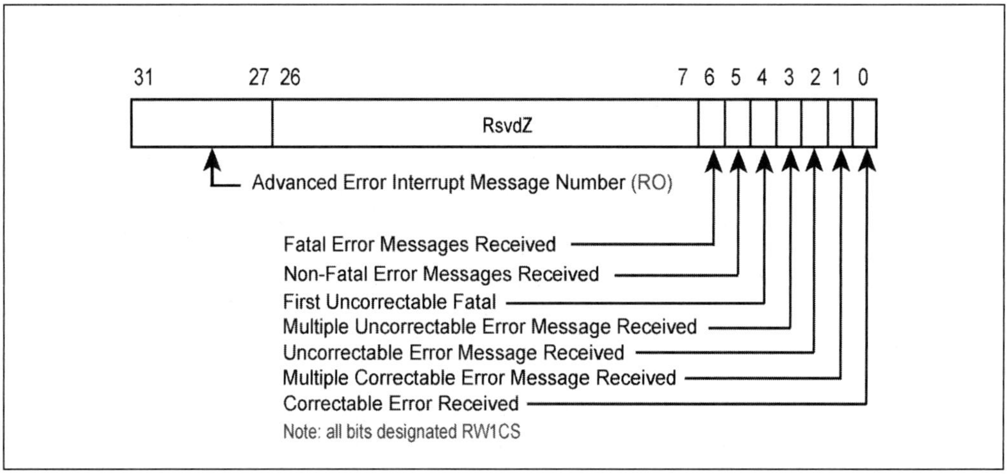

Figure 24-26: Advanced Error Uncorrectable and Uncorrectable Error Source ID Registers

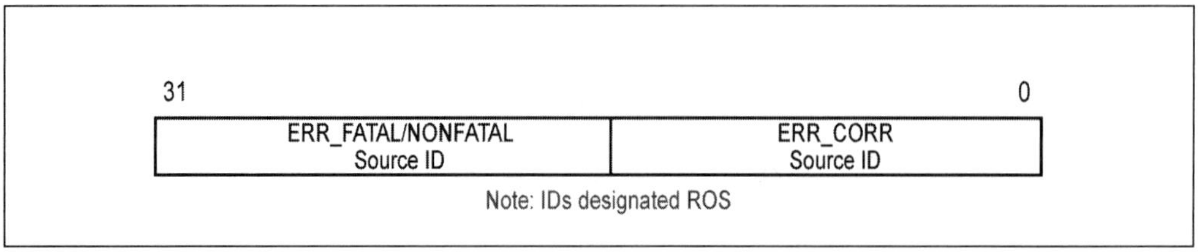

Virtual Channel Capability

The VC Register Set's Purpose

This register set serves several purposes:

- In a port that implements multiple VC buffers, it permits the configuration of the TC-to-VC mapping.
- See Figure 24-27 on page 939. In an egress port that implements multiple VC buffers, it permits the configuration of the arbitration scheme that defines the order in which each VC accepts packets from the various source ingress ports within the device. This is referred to as the VC's port arbitration scheme.
- See Figure 24-27 on page 939. In an egress port that implements multiple VC buffers, it permits the configuration of the arbitration scheme that defines the order in which the egress port accepts packets from its VC buffers for transmit onto the link. This is referred to as the port's VC arbitration scheme.
- In a port that only implements a single VC (VC0), the configuration software may specify that only packets with certain TCs be accepted into the VC0 buffer for transfer. This is referred to as TC filtering.

Figure 24-27: Port and VC Arbitration

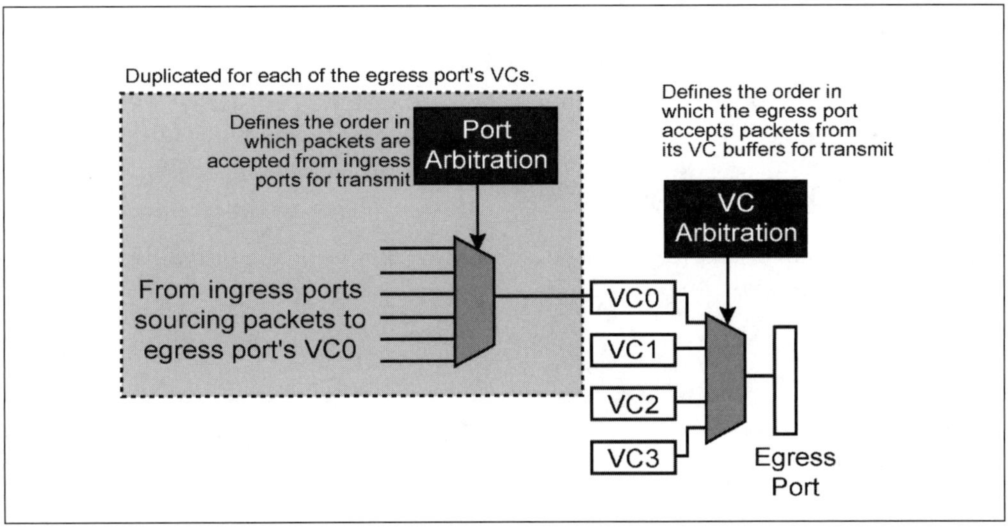

Who Must Implement This Register Set?

The following functions must implement this optional register set:

- A function (i.e., a port) that only implements VC0 but permits the configuration software to specify that only packets with certain TCs may be placed in the VC0 buffer for transfer.
- A function that implements VCs in addition to VC0.

This applies to Endpoint devices, upstream and downstream Switch ports, Root Ports, and RCRBs.

Multifunction Upstream Port Restriction

The spec contains the following statement:

"The PCI Express Virtual Channel Capability structure can be present in the Extended Configuration Space of all devices or in RCRB with the restriction that it is only present in the Extended Configuration Space of Function 0 for multifunction devices at their Upstream Ports."

The authors take this to mean that if the upstream port of a device is implemented as a multifunction device (see Figure 21-11 on page 761) and that port meets the criteria specified in "Who Must Implement This Register Set?" on page 940, this capability register set is only implemented in the Extended Configuration Space of function 0 of that device.

The Register Set

Figure 24-28 on page 941 illustrates the VC Capability register set and Figure 24-29 on page 941 illustrates the detail of its Enhanced Capability Header register.

Detailed Description of VCs

For a detailed description of VCs, refer to Chapter 6, entitled "QoS/TCs/VCs and Arbitration," on page 251.

Figure 24-28: Virtual Channel Capability Register Set

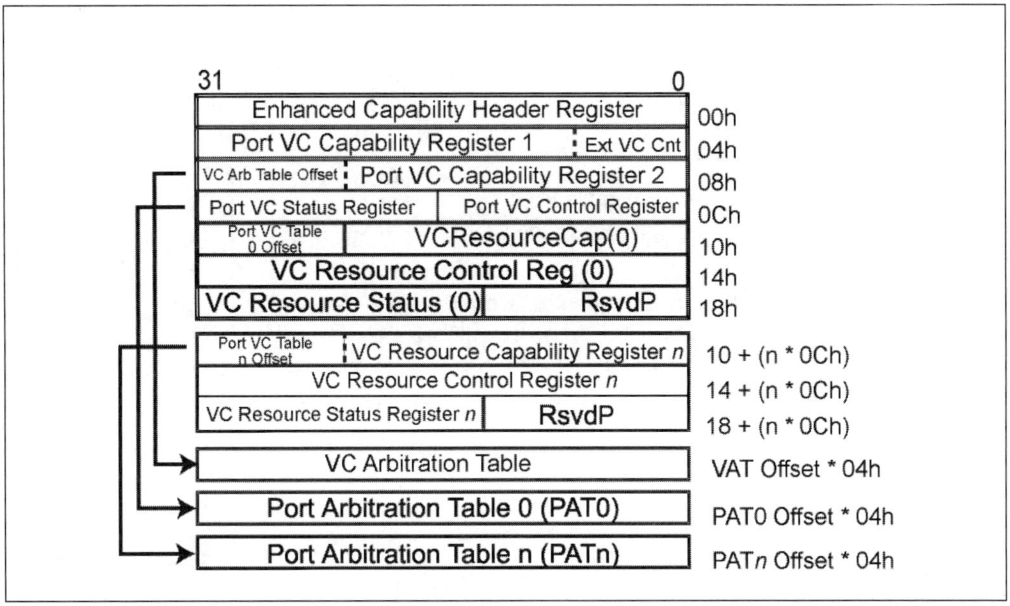

Figure 24-29: VC Enhanced Capability Header

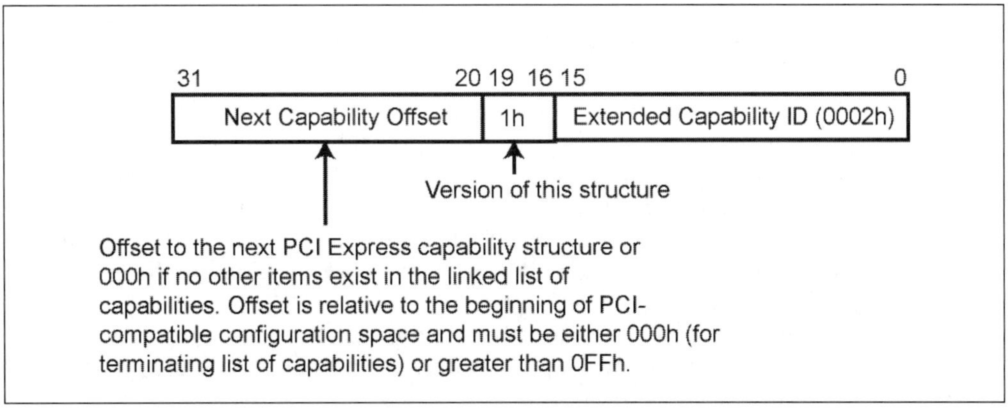

Port VC Capability Register 1

The register is illustrated in Figure 24-30 on page 942 and each bit field is described in Table 24 - 14 on page 942.

Figure 24-30: Port VC Capability Register 1 (Read-Only)

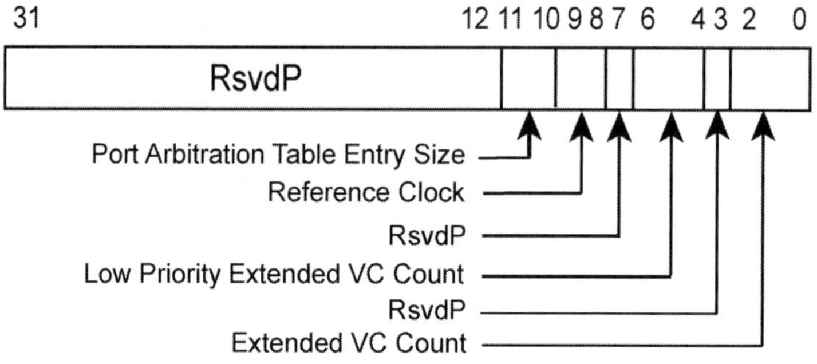

Table 24 - 14: Port VC Capability Register 1 (Read-Only)

Bit(s)	Description
2:0	**Extended VC Count**. The number of additional VCs supported by the device. • 0 = just VC0 is supported. • The maximum value is 7.
6:4	**Low Priority Extended VC Count**. Indicates the number of VCs (starting with VC0) that comprise the Low-Priority VC (LPVC) group. • **0**. There is **no LPVC group** and the sequence in which the port's VC buffers transfer is governed by the fixed-priority scheme wherein VC0 has the lowest priority and the highest-numbered VC that is implemented has the highest priority. • **Non-zero value (*n*).** VCs 0-through-*n* are members of the LPVC group. The value specified cannot be greater than that specified in the Extended VC Count field of this register. – The VCs above *n* are members of the high-priority group where VC*n*+1 has the lowest priority and the highest VC has the highest priority. – Control passes to the LPVC group only when the VCs in the upper group have no packets to transfer. The priority scheme used among the VCs that are members of the lower group is governed by the VC Arbitration Capability field in Port VC Capability Register 2 (see "Port VC Capability Register 2" on page 943).

Table 24 - 14: Port VC Capability Register 1 (Read-Only) (Continued)

Bit(s)	Description
9:8	**Reference Clock**. The reference clock for VCs that support time-based WRR Port Arbitration. This field is valid for RCRB and for Switch Ports and is not valid for Root Ports and Endpoint devices (must be hardwired to 0). • 00b = 100ns reference clock. • 01b – 11b are reserved.
11:10	**Port Arbitration Table Entry Size**. Indicates the size (in bits) of each entry in the device's Port Arbitration table. This field is valid only for an RCRB and for any Switch Port. It is hardwired to 0 for Endpoint devices and Root Ports. • 00b The size of each Port Arbitration table entry is 1 bit. • 01b The size of each Port Arbitration table entry is 2 bits. • 10b The size of each Port Arbitration table entry is 4 bits. • 11b The size of each Port Arbitration table entry is 8 bits.

Port VC Capability Register 2

The register is illustrated in Figure 24-31 on page 943 and each bit field is described in Table 24 - 15 on page 944.

Figure 24-31: Port VC Capability Register 2 (Read-Only)

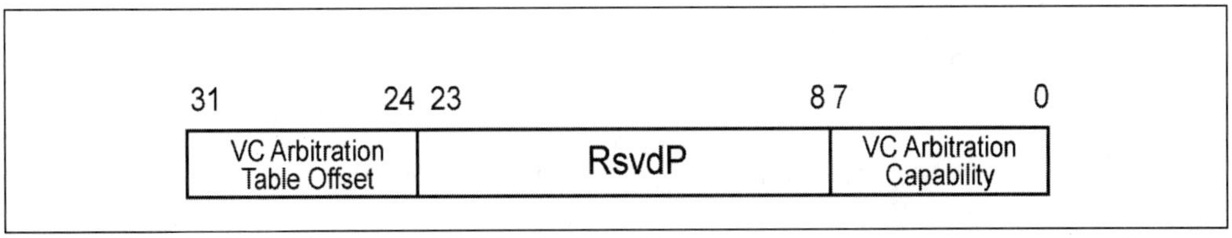

Table 24 - 15: Port VC Capability Register 2 (Read-Only)

Bit(s)	Description
7:0	**VC Arbitration Capability**. This bit mask indicates the arbitration scheme(s) supported by the device for the LPVC group. It is valid for all devices that report a Low Priority Extended VC Count greater than 0 (see the description in Table 24 - 14 on page 942). Each bit corresponds to an arbitration scheme defined below. When more than one bit is set, it indicates that the Port can be configured to provide different VC arbitration services. • Bit 0: Hardwired, fixed arbitration scheme (e.g., Round Robin). • Bit 1: Weighted Round Robin (WRR) arbitration with 32 phases. • Bit 2: WRR arbitration with 64 phases. • Bit 3: WRR arbitration with 128 phases. • Bits 4-7: Reserved. The desired arbitration scheme is selected via the VC Arbitration Select field in the Port VC Control Register (see Table 24 - 16 on page 945).
31:24	**VC Arbitration Table Offset**. Indicates the location of the VC Arbitration Table with reference to the start of the VC capability register set (specified in increments of dqwords—16 bytes). A value of 0 indicates that the table is not present.

Port VC Control Register

The register is illustrated in Figure 24-32 on page 944 and each bit field is described in Table 24 - 16 on page 945.

Figure 24-32: Port VC Control Register (Read-Write)

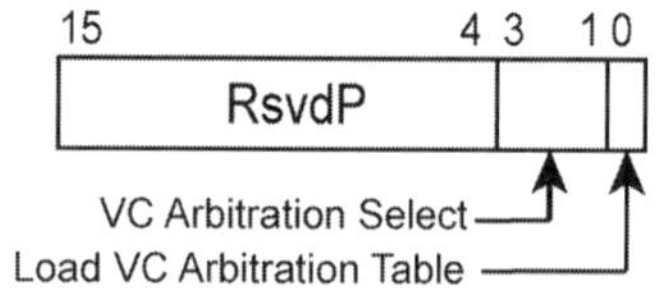

Table 24 - 16: Port VC Control Register (Read-Write)

Bit(s)	Description
0	**Load VC Arbitration Table**. In order to activate a port's VC Arbitration Table, the configuration software takes the following steps: 1. When software initially programs the VC Arbitration Table, or when any change is subsequently made to any entry in the table, the VC Arbitration Table Status bit in the Port VC Status register is automatically set to one by hardware. 2. Software then sets the Load VC Arbitration Table bit to one, causing the port to read the VC Arbitration Table from the capability register set and apply it. 3. When the port hardware has completed reading and applying the updated table, it automatically clears the VC Arbitration Table Status bit in the Port VC Status register. 4. Software can determine if the updated table has been applied by reading the state of the VC Arbitration Table Status bit in the Port VC Status register. – 0 indicates the updated table has been read and applied. – 1 indicates that the update is not yet complete. This bit is valid for a device when the selected VC Arbitration type (see the next row in this table) uses the VC Arbitration Table. Clearing this bit has no effect. This bit always returns 0 when read.
3:1	**VC Arbitration Select.** The configuration software selects one of the supported LPVC arbitration schemes by setting it to the BCD value of the bit corresponding to the desired scheme (see the description of bits 7:0 in Table 24 - 15 on page 944). The configuration software must select the arbitration scheme prior to enabling more than one VC in the LPVC group.

Port VC Status Register

The register is illustrated in Figure 24-33 on page 946 and each bit field is described in Table 24 - 17 on page 946.

Figure 24-33: Port VC Status Register (Read-Only)

Table 24 - 17: Port VC Status Register (Read-Only)

Bit(s)	Description
0	**VC Arbitration Table Status**. See the description of the Load VC Arbitration Table bit in Table 24 - 16 on page 945.

VC Resource Registers

General. At a minimum, each port implements a single VC, VC0, and it may optionally implement up to eight VCs, VC0-through-VC7. For each VC it supports, the port implements the following three registers:

— VC Resource Capability register.
— VC Resource Control register.
— VC Resource Status register.

The following three sections provide a description of each of these registers.

Each VC implements:

— A mandatory TC/VC bit map that defines the TCs that should be accepted into this VC.
— An optional Port Arbitration Table that defines the order in which the VC accepts packets from the device ingress ports that source packets to it for transmission.

VC Resource Capability Register. The register is illustrated in Figure 24-34 on page 947 and each bit field is described in Table 24 - 18 on page 947.

Figure 24-34: VC Resource Capability Register

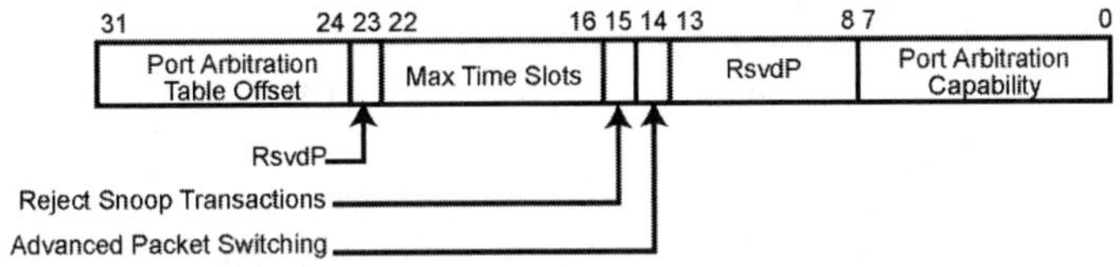

Table 24 - 18: VC Resource Capability Register

Bit(s)	Type	Description
7:0	RO	**Port Arbitration Capability**. This bit mask indicates the types of Port arbitration (one or more) supported by the VC. It is valid for all Switch Ports and an RCRB, but not for PCI Express Endpoint devices or Root Ports. Software selects one of these arbitration schemes by writing to the Port Arbitration Select field in the VC Resource Control register (see "VC Resource Control Register" on page 948). • Bit 0. Hardwired, fixed arbitration scheme (e.g., Round Robin). • Bit 1. Weighted Round Robin (WRR) arbitration with 32 phases. • Bit 2. WRR arbitration with 64 phases. • Bit 3. WRR arbitration with 128 phases. • Bit 4. Time-based WRR with 128 phases. • Bit 5. WRR arbitration with 256 phases. • Bits 6-7. Reserved.
14	RO	**Advanced Packet Switching**. • 1 = This VC only supports transactions optimized for Advanced Packet Switching (AS). This bit is valid for all PCI Express Ports and RCRB. • 0 = The VC is capable of supporting all transactions defined by the spec (including AS transport packets).

Table 24 - 18: VC Resource Capability Register (Continued)

Bit(s)	Type	Description
15	HwInit	**Reject Snoop Transactions.** • 0 = Transactions with or without the No Snoop bit set are allowed on this VC. • 1 = Transactions with No Snoop = 0 are rejected as an Unsupported Request. This bit is valid for Root Ports and RCRB, but not for Endpoint devices or Switch ports.
22:16	HwInit	**Maximum Time Slots**. Max time slots (minus one) that the VC supports when configured for time-based WRR port arbitration. This field is valid for all Switch ports, Root Ports and an RCRB, but not for Endpoint devices. Only valid when the Port Arbitration Capability field in this register indicates that the VC supports time-based WRR port arbitration.
31:24	RO	**Port Arbitration Table Offset**. Indicates the location of the Port Arbitration Table associated with this VC with reference to the start of the VC capability register set (specified in increments of dqwords—16 bytes). A value of 0 indicates that the table is not present. This field is valid for all Switch ports and an RCRB, but not for Endpoint devices or Root Ports.

VC Resource Control Register. The register is illustrated in Figure 24-35 on page 948 and each bit field is described in Table 24 - 19 on page 949.

Figure 24-35: VC Resource Control Register (Read-Write)

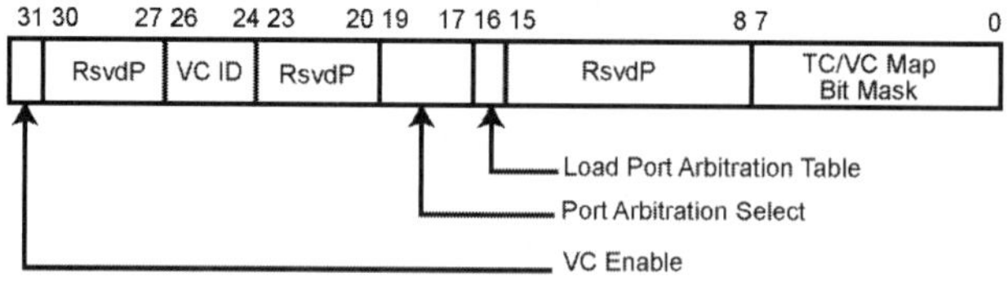

Table 24 - 19: VC Resource Control Register (Read-Write)

Bit(s)	Description
7:0	**TC/VC Map**. TC-to-VC mapping bit map. Each bit within this field corresponds to a TC that is mapped to this VC. Multiple bits may be set to one. **Bit** 7 1 = TC7 is mapped to this VC. 6 1 = TC6 is mapped to this VC. 5 1 = TC5 is mapped to this VC. 4 1 = TC4 is mapped to this VC. 3 1 = TC3 is mapped to this VC. 2 1 = TC2 is mapped to this VC. 1 1 = TC1 is mapped to this VC. 0 1 = TC0 is mapped to this VC. This bit is read-only. 1 for VC0 and 0 for all other enabled VCs. Before removing one or more TCs from the TC/VC Map of an enabled VC, software must ensure that no new or outstanding transactions with those TC labels are targeted at the given Link. The default value = FFh for VC0 and = 00h for other VCs.
16	**Load Port Arbitration Table**. In order to activate a VC's Port Arbitration Table, the configuration software takes the following steps: 1. When software initially programs the VC's Port Arbitration Table, or when any change is subsequently made to any entry in the table, the Port Arbitration Table Status bit in the VC's VC Resource Status register (see "VC Resource Status Register" on page 950) is automatically set to one. 2. Software then sets the Load Port Arbitration Table bit to one, causing the VC to read the updated Port Arbitration Table from the capability register set and apply it. 3. When the VC hardware has completed reading and applying the updated table, it automatically clears the Port Arbitration Table Status bit in its VC Resource Status register. 4. Software can determine if the updated table has been applied by reading the state of the Port Arbitration Table Status bit in the VC's VC Status register. – 0 indicates the updated table has been read and applied. – 1 indicates that the update is not yet complete. This bit is valid for a device when the selected Port Arbitration type (the next row in this table) uses the Port Arbitration Table. Clearing this bit has no effect. This bit always returns 0 when read. This bit is valid for all Switch Ports and an RCRB, but not for Endpoint devices or Root Ports. This bit always returns 0 when read and the default value of this bit is 0.

Table 24 - 19: VC Resource Control Register (Read-Write) (Continued)

Bit(s)	Description
19:17	**Port Arbitration Select**. The configuration software selects one of the supported port arbitration schemes by setting it to the BCD value of the bit corresponding to the desired scheme (see the description of bits 7:0 in Table 24 - 18 on page 947). The configuration software must select the arbitration scheme prior to enabling more than one VC in the LPVC group.
26:24	**VC ID**. This field assigns a VC ID (between 0 and 7) to the VC (for VC0, it is hardwired to zero). It cannot be modified if the VC has already been enabled.
31	**VC Enable**. • 1 = VC enabled. • 0 = VC disabled. The state of this bit is qualified by the state of the VC Negotiation Pending bit (in the VC's VC Resource Status register; see "VC Resource Status Register" on page 950). • 0 = negotiation has been completed (Flow Control initialization is completed for the PCI Express Port) and the VC Enable bit indicates the state of the VC. • 1 = the negotiation process has not yet completed and the state of the VC Enable bit therefore remains indeterminate. This bit is hardwired to 1 for VC0. It is read/write for the other VCs and its default is 0. To enable a VC, its VC Enable bit must be set to one in the ports at both ends of the link. To disable a VC, its VC Enable bit must be cleared to zero in the ports at both ends of the link. Before disabling a VC, software must ensure that no traffic is using the VC. Prior to re-enabling a VC, software must first fully disable the VC in both components on the Link.

VC Resource Status Register. The register is illustrated in Figure 24-36 on page 951 and each bit field is described in Table 24 - 20 on page 951.

Figure 24-36: VC Resource Status Register (Read-Only)

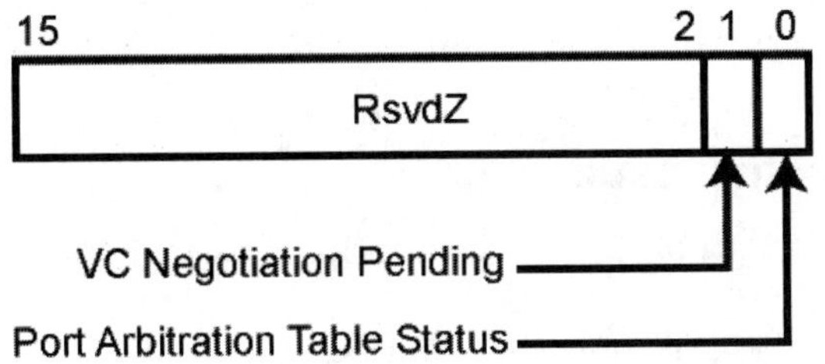

Table 24 - 20: VC Resource Status Register (Read-Only)

Bit(s)	Description
0	**Port Arbitration Table Status**. See the description of the Load Port Arbitration Table bit in Table 24 - 19 on page 949. The default value of this bit is 0.
1	**VC Negotiation Pending**. Indicates whether the VC negotiation process (initialization or disabling) is in the pending state. When this bit is set by hardware, it indicates that the VC is still in the process of negotiation. It is cleared by hardware after the VC negotiation completes. For VCs other than VC0, software uses this bit to enable or disable the VC. For VC0, this bit indicates the status of the Flow Control initialization process. Before using a VC, software must check whether the VC Negotiation Pending bit is cleared in the components at both ends of the Link.

VC Arbitration Table

A port implements a VC Arbitration Table if both of the following are true:

- The Port supports more than one VC.
- The Port implements a WRR arbitration scheme.

The table consists of a set of read/write registers and is only used if the configuration software selects (via the VC Arbitration Select field in Table 24 - 15 on page 944) one of the implemented WRR VC arbitration schemes (see VC Arbitration Capability in Table 24 - 15 on page 944).

The configuration software configures the table with the arbitration scheme that the egress port logic uses to service the VC transmit buffers associated with the port. See the description of the Load VC Arbitration Table bit in Table 24 - 16 on page 945 for a description of how the table is uploaded into the port's logic. For a detailed description of the VC Arbitration Table, refer to "Loading the Virtual Channel Arbitration Table" on page 270.

Port Arbitration Tables

A VC implements a Port Arbitration Table if both of the following are true:

- The Port supports more than one VC.
- The VC implements a WRR arbitration scheme.

The table consists of a set of read/write registers and is only used if the configuration software selects (via the Port Arbitration Select field in Table 24 - 19 on page 949) one of the implemented WRR Port arbitration schemes (see Port Arbitration Capability in Table 24 - 18 on page 947).

The configuration software configures the table with the arbitration scheme that defines in what order the VC accepts packets being sourced from the ingress ports that have packets to be passed to this VC buffer on the egress port. See the description of the Load VC Arbitration Table bit in Table 24 - 16 on page 945 for a description of how the table is uploaded into the port's logic.

This register array is valid for all Switch Ports and RCRBs, but not for Endpoint devices or Root Ports. For a detailed description of the Port Arbitration Tables, refer to "The Port Arbitration Mechanisms" on page 277.

Device Serial Number Capability

This optional register set can be implemented on any PCI Express device in accordance with the following rules:

- It consists of the Enhanced Capability Header pictured in Figure 24-37 on page 953 and the 64-bit Serial Number register pictured in Figure 24-38 on page 953.
- The device serial number is a unique, read-only 64-bit value assigned to the device when it is manufactured.
- A multifunction device with this feature only implements it on function 0 and other functions within the device must return the same serial number value as that reported by function 0.
- Any component (e.g., a Switch) that contains multiple devices must return

the same serial number for each device within the component.

Figure 24-37: Device Serial Number Enhanced Capability Header

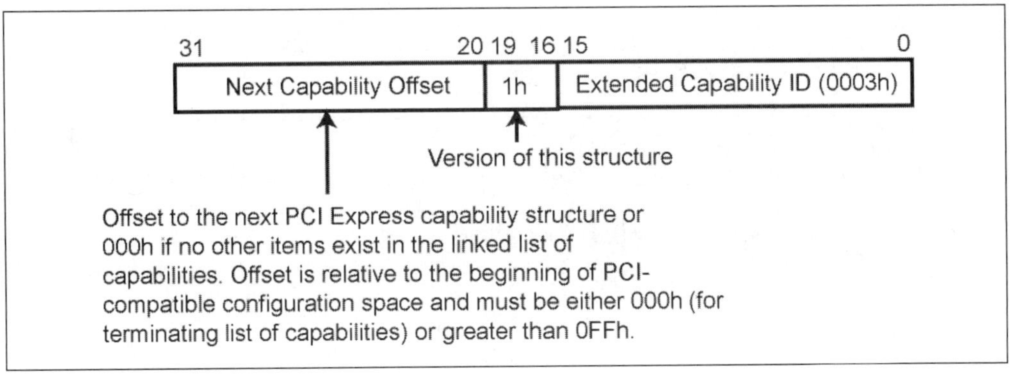

Figure 24-38: Device Serial Number Register

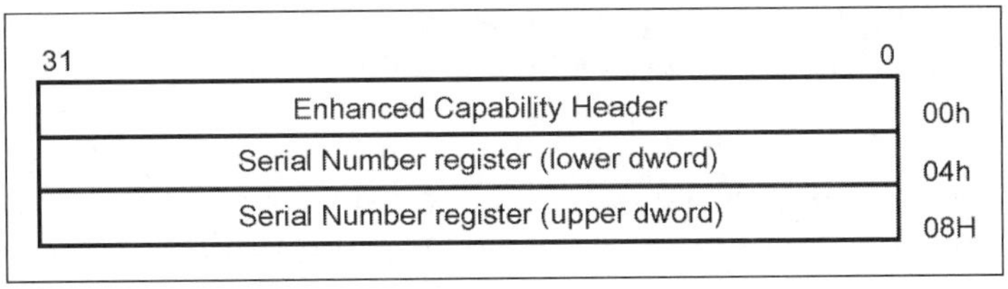

The serial number is also known as the EUI-64. Refer to Figure 24-39 on page 954. A portion of the Extended Unique Identifier (EUI)-64 is assigned by a registration authority operating under the auspices of the IEEE organization. The EUI-64 consists of:

- **24-bit company ID** value assigned by IEEE. Bit 6, the Universal/Local scope bit, is always set to one (Universal scope ID, not assigned to anything else in the universe) in the value assigned by the IEEE.
- **40-bit extension ID** assigned by the company that "owns" the assigned company ID. The interpretation of the company-assigned extension is outside the scope of the spec. As an example, it may represent the device ID and manufacturer-assigned serial number.

Figure 24-39: EUI-64 Format

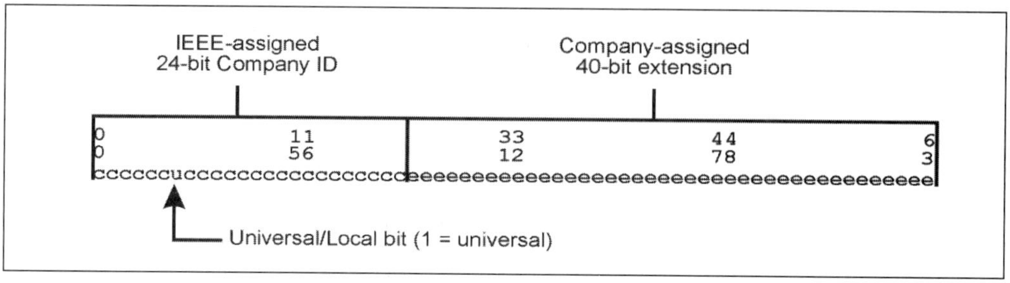

Power Budgeting Capability

General

Refer to Chapter 15, entitled "Power Budgeting," on page 557 for a detailed description of the Power Budgeting capability.

This optional capability permits the platform to properly allocate power to a device that is hot-plugged into the system during runtime. Using this register set, the device reports the following to the platform:

- The power it consumes on a variety of power rails.
- The power it consumes in different power management states.
- The power it consumes under different operating conditions.

The platform (i.e., the system and the OS) uses this information to ensure that the system can provide the proper power and cooling levels to the device.

Implementation of this capability register set (see Figure 24-40 on page 955) is optional for devices that are implemented either in a form factor which does not require hot-plug support, or that are integrated on the system board. Although the spec states that "PCI Express form factor specifications may require support for power budgeting," it does not indicate any specific cases where this is required.

Figure 24-40 on page 955 illustrates the register set and Figure 24-41 on page 955 illustrates its Enhanced Capability Header register.

How It Works

The power budgeting data for the function consists of a table of *n* entries starting with entry 0. Each entry is read by placing an index value in the Power Budgeting Data Select register (Figure 24-40 on page 955) and then reading the value returned in the Power Budgeting Data register (Figure 24-42 on page 956).The end of table is indicated by a return value of all 0's in the Data register.

In the Power Budgeting Capability register (see Figure 24-43 on page 956), the System Allocated bit is automatically set to one if the device is integrated onto the system board and its power requirements are therefore already taken into account in the system's power supply budget. In that case, the device's power requirements should be ignored by software in making power budgeting decisions.

Figure 24-40: Power Budget Register Set

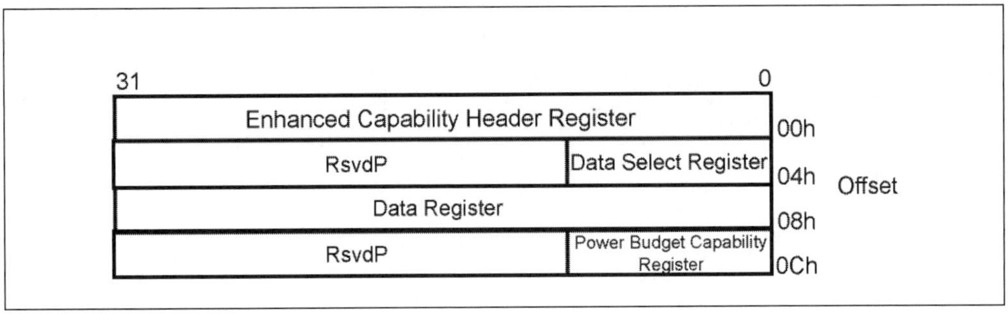

Figure 24-41: Power Budgeting Enhanced Capability Header

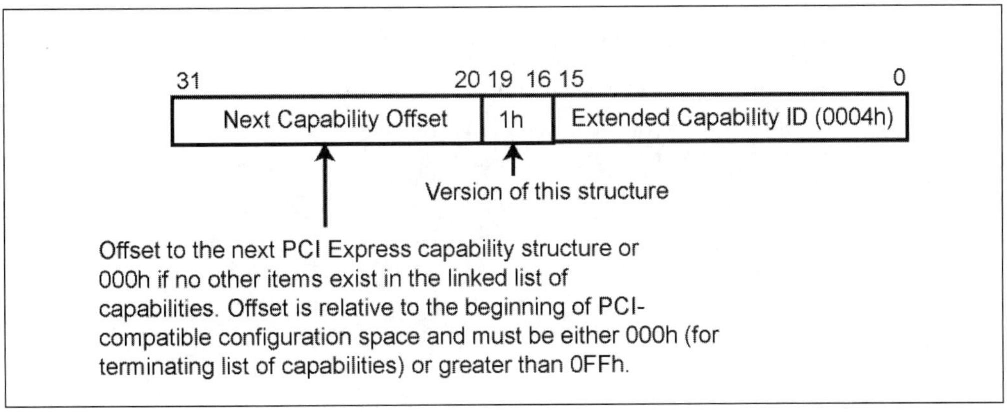

Figure 24-42: Power Budgeting Data Register

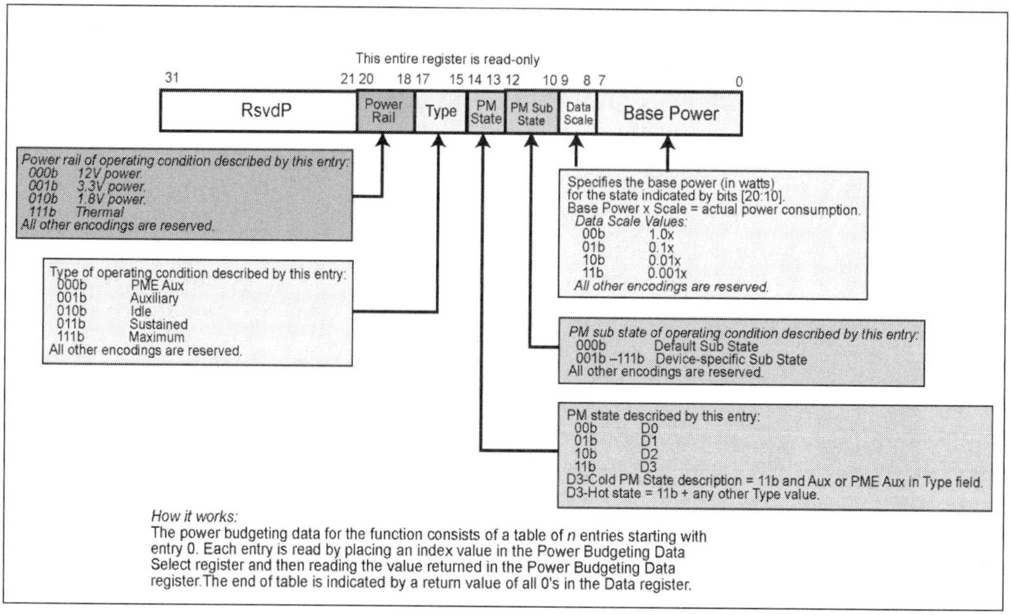

Figure 24-43: Power Budgeting Capability Register

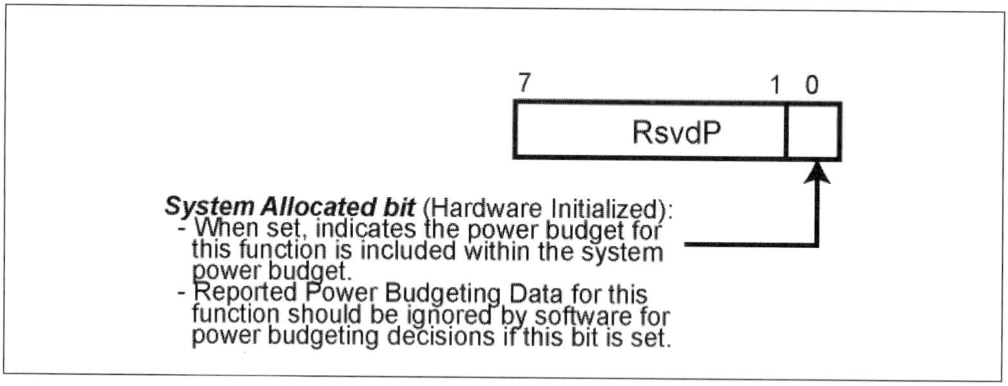

RCRB

General

As mentioned in "Root Complex Register Blocks (RCRBs)" on page 765, a Root Port may optionally implement a Root Complex Register Block (RCRB) as a 4KB block of memory-mapped IO registers that can include one or more of the optional PCI Express extended capabilities and other implementation specific registers that apply to the Root Complex. An RCRB must not reside in the same memory-mapped IO address space as that defined for normal PCI Express functions. Multiple Root Ports or internal devices may be associated with the same RCRB (see Figure 24-44 on page 958 for an example).

Firmware Gives OS Base Address of Each RCRB

The spec requires that the platform firmware must communicate the base address of the RCRB for each Root Port or internal device in the Root Complex to the OS. How this is accomplished is outside the scope of the spec.

Misaligned or Locked Accesses To an RCRB

A Root Complex is not required to support memory access requests to an RCRB that cross dword address boundaries or that are accomplished using a locked transaction series. Software should therefore not attempt an access of either type to an RCRB unless it is has device-specific knowledge that the Root Complex supports this access type.

Extended Capabilities in an RCRB

Any Extended Capability register sets in an RCRB must always begin at offset 0h within the RCRBs 4KB memory-mapped IO address space. If the RCRB does not implement any of the optional extended capability register sets, this is indicated by an Enhanced Capability header with a Capability ID of FFFFh and a Next Capability Offset of 0h.

The RCRB Missing Link

The 1.0a version of the spec does not identify any method for discovering the existence of RCRBs that may reside within a Root Complex, nor does it identify any method for associating an RCRB with one or more Root Ports. As of the time of this writing (6/6/03), there is a draft ECN (Engineering Change Notice) to the 1.0a spec that has not yet been approved that addresses this issue. As soon as it is approved, MindShare will immediately include this information in classes taught by MindShare and, of course, this information will be provided in the Second Edition of this book. It is not included in this edition because draft changes have a habit of mutating before they reach their finalized, approved form.

Figure 24-44: RCRB Example

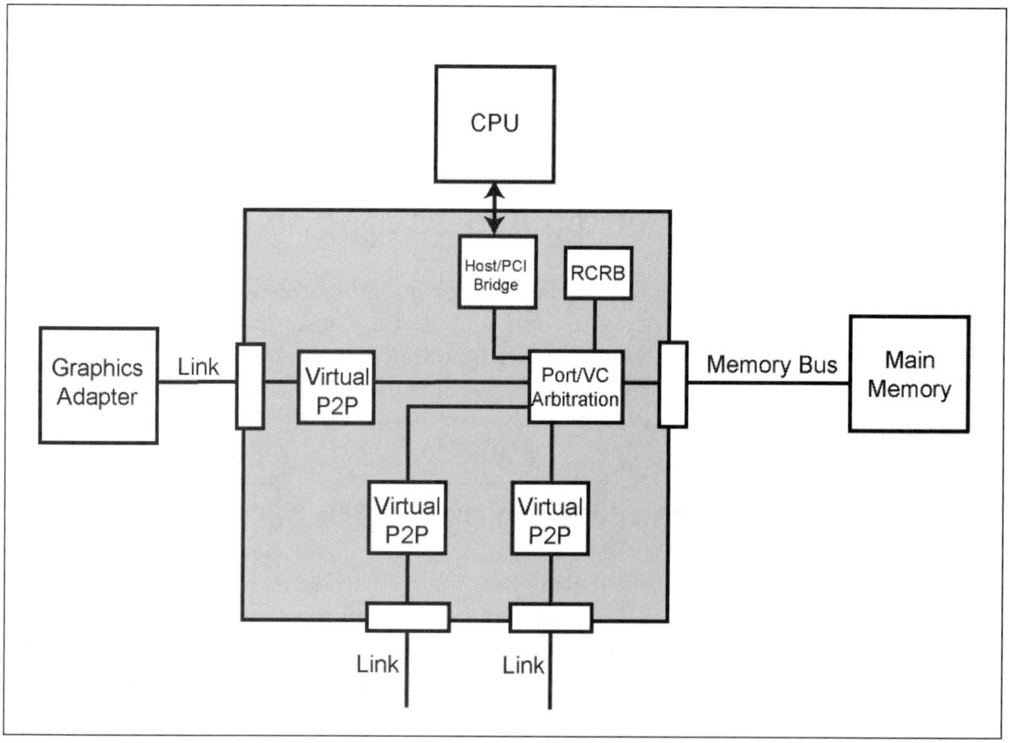

Appendices

Appendix A Test, Debug and Verification

Challenges, Issues and Hints

by Nader Saleh, Catalyst Enterprises, Inc.

Scope

IO interface bus technologies keep getting faster and more complex in order to provide more bandwidth.

The trend for PC bus technologies has been from a relatively slow asynchronous, parallel bus (ISA bus operating at 12 MHz and 16 bits) to synchronous and faster parallel busses (PCI operating at 66MHz and 64-bits and PCI-X at 133MHz and 64 bits).

Parallel bus technologies have experienced an exponentially increasing bandwidth, but this technology is reaching its practical limitation for offering more bandwidth. Therefore, the trend in PC bus technologies is a move towards new, high-speed serial buses.

PCI Express is an emerging serial bus technology that is expected to dominate the desktop and server market by 2005. There are several issues that make development for PCI Express radically different than development for parallel buses. These differences create a series of new challenges which designers and developers need to consider when entering into this new technology. Some of those are covered in this article.

Serial Bus Topology

PCI Express's serial bus topology represents a challenge for test and debug development tools.

In a parallel bus, as the name identifies, all of the protocol signals associated with data transfer are simultaneously presented and act in parallel. Developers can see bus signals and interpret bus conditions by just capturing and viewing raw bus signals with a relatively simple development tool.

An example of simultaneously active signals on a PCI bus (Captured by a Catalyst analyzer) is depicted in Figure A-1. In this example the user can see the individual signals which each have their own specific meaning. When FRAME# is asserted (low), it indicates that the initiator is requesting a data transfer. CBE = 0x0010, indicating that this transfer is an IO read and TRDY# = 0, indicating the data transfer of 0x99h completed.

Also, when all bus signals (except clock) are high it indicates that the bus is in the idle state.

Figure A-1: PCI Parallel Bus Start and End of a Transaction Easily Identified

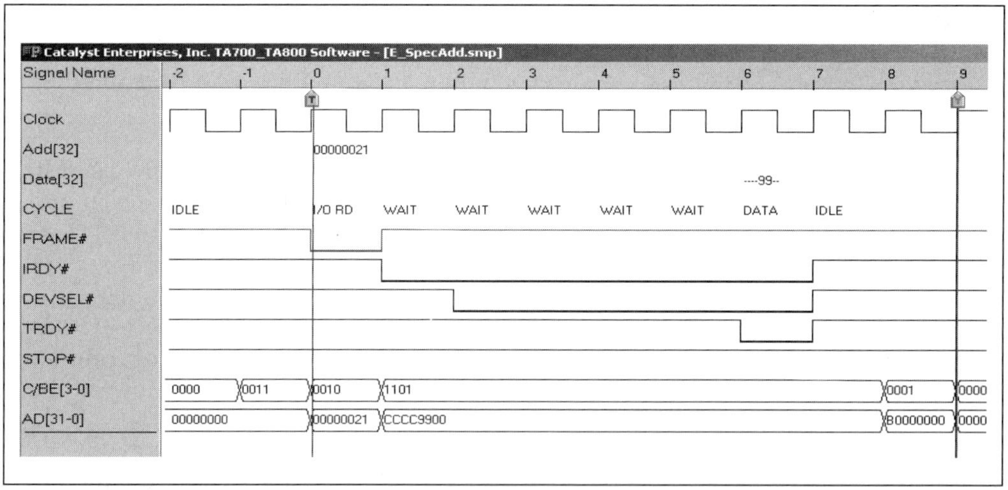

Start Request *Complete Transfer*

Unlike parallel buses, the status of serial buses cannot easily be identified by monitoring the individual bus signals. A more complex process is required for monitoring and interpretation of Serial buses such as PCI Express, for the following reasons:

1. The data is transferred serially in a differential pair and the request for data transfer, the type of transfer, address and clock are all embedded on the same signal line in a serialized sequence rather than having dedicated, independent signals.
2. The idle state of the bus cannot simply be quiet since activities are required to keep the clock recovery circuit active and enabled. These constant signal activities make it difficult to recognize the start and end points of transfers. These added activities are also scrambled to minimize the EMI effects.
3. Serial bus protocols require additional headers and footers, such as CRC, to make the data transfer more secure and error free. These additional bits are also added to the data packets and require interpretation.
4. PCI Express architecture has defined protocols that communicate in several different layers. Physical layer protocol is used for establishing and maintaining the links, the "Data Link Layer Packets" protocol is used for handshaking and "Transfer Layer" protocols used for transferring the data. To interpret bus conditions adequately, users must be able to convert raw bits into these layers.

Converting binary bits into a meaningful interpretation of all these layers requires an advanced and dedicated tool, beyond the capability of many low level monitoring development tools.

Figure A-2 indicates a data capture of a PCI Express bus transaction on a scope in its most primitive form. Comparing to the PCI bus, it would be impossible to interpret what is occurring on this serial bus.

Figure A-2: PCI Express Serial Bit Stream

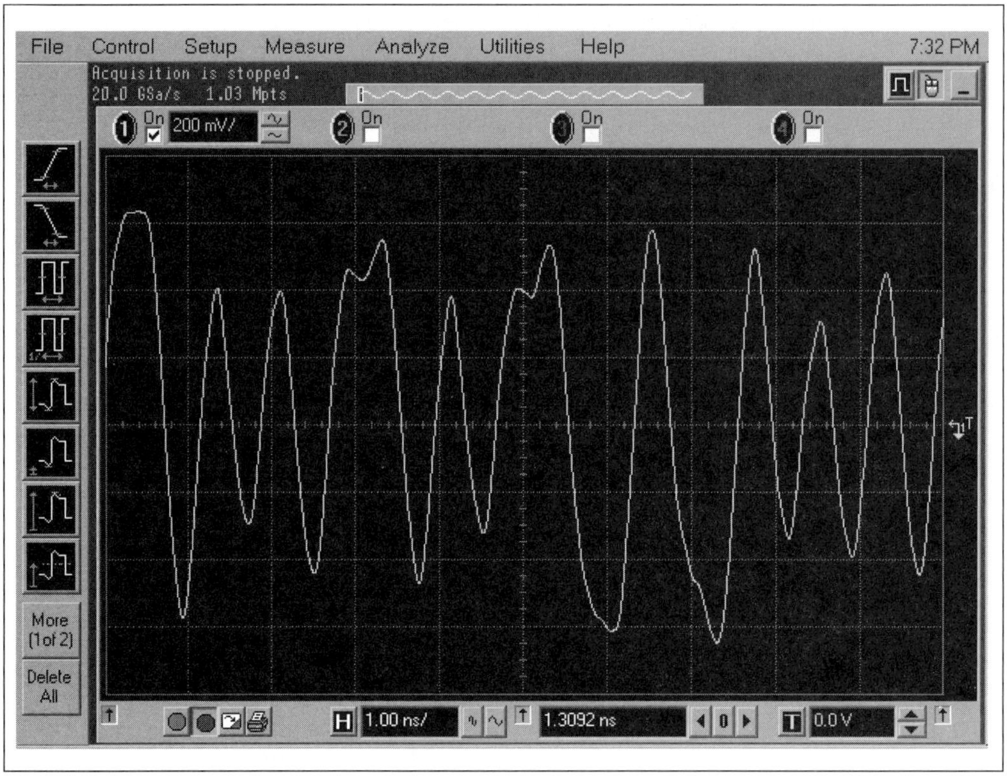

It should be noted that the PCI Express transmit/receive signals each consist of a differential signal pair and the sample shown here display the output of such a differential signal pair.

Dual-Simplex

The PCI Express serial bus is a dual-simplex bus (see Figure A-3 on page 965), unlike the parallel-based PCI bus where the start and end of a transfer can be seen on the same bus as shown in Figure A-1 on page 962.

This architecture requires the requester to transmit a "Request" for data transfer on one transmit pair, while it receives the "Completion" response on the receive signal pair. Considering that the response time can widely vary, developers need to be able to set the analyzer to filter the received and the transmitted data independent of each other.

Also the agents on the two ends of the PCI express link may be equally capable of being requesters and completers. This allows a transaction type to be generated in either direction on the link at different times. Therefore, being able to specify the trigger and data capture on both buses independently is very important, and users must specify the direction in order to trigger on the proper transfer they intend to view.

Figure A-3: PCI Express Dual-Simplex Bus

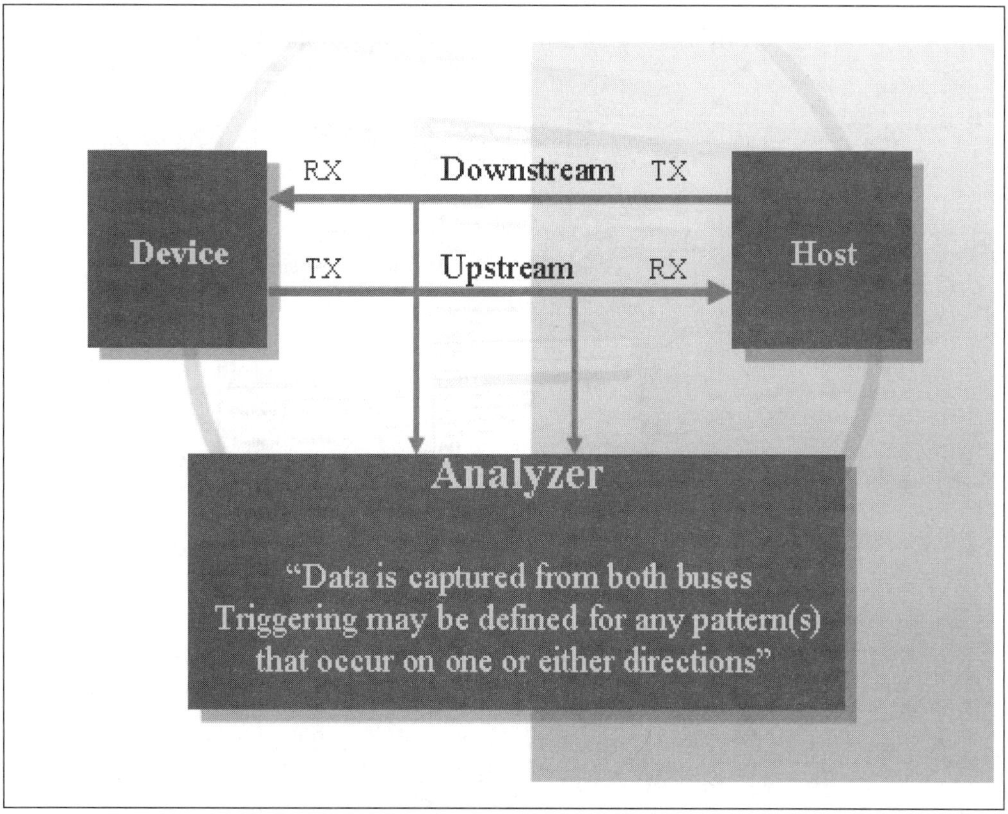

The two signal pairs from the host to the device are referred to as Upstream (towards the host processor) and Downstream (away from the host processor). The analyzer should be able to sample both signal pairs and trigger on occurrences of patterns on either pair or just one, per user defined settings.

Setting Up the Analyzer, Capturing and Triggering

Figure A-4 on page 966 and Figure A-5 on page 967 indicate various setups for capturing and triggering on possible PCI Express bus states.

To review the complete menus and features you may download and try the software from the Catalyst web site (www.getcatalyst.com).

Figure A-4: Capturing All Patterns on PCI Express

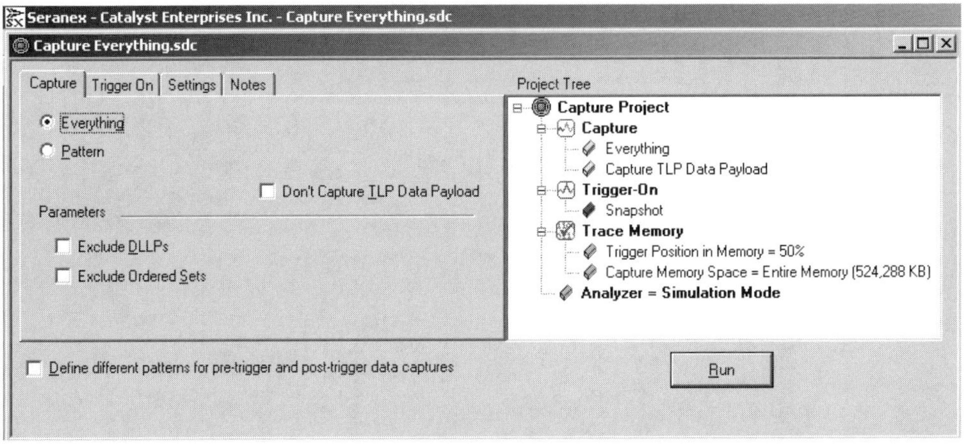

Figure A-4 provides a default setup for capturing anything on the bus and indicates whether or not there is any data transfer or the bus is in an idle state. Any transactions would be captured and displayed with all details included.

Further triggering selections will allow users to fully qualify the bus data and transaction type and to see exactly what sort of request and response is communicated between the agents on the bus.

Figure A-5 on page 967 shows a data capture setup for capturing all TLP packets on both buses and to trigger when a TLP memory read to address range 0x00FE8DXX....XX occurs, but only when it is initiated in the downstream bus.

Sequential triggering also allows the user to trigger on patterns only after a certain set of events has occurred (as defined by the user).

Figure A-5: Specific Trigger Definition for Upstream or Downstream Pair

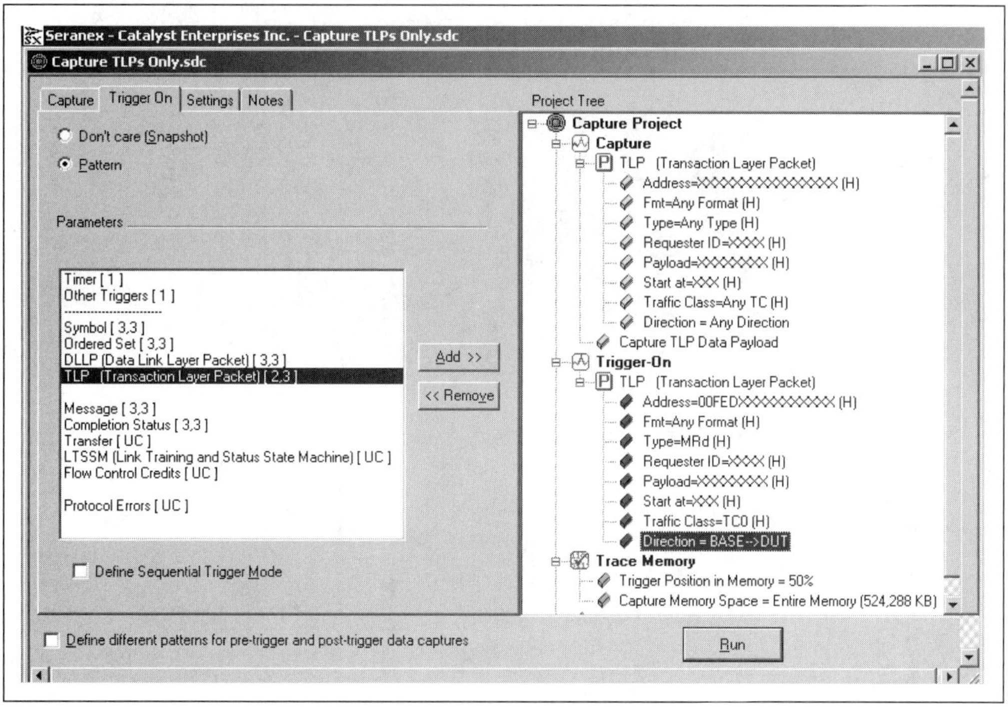

Link Training, the First Step in Communication

Link training is one of the first protocols that two agents perform to establish link configuration parameters such as link width, lane polarities, or maximum supported data rate. The following screenshots show the actual data captured for a X4 link training session between the Catalyst PX-4 Exerciser and a PCI Express system board. It should be noted that the link training exercise demonstrated here is based on the 1.0 specification. In the images that follow, several of the repeated packets (all of the idle state) are removed for clarity, but all of the sequences are shown. During the Link Training, the two agents start the communication by sending a low level "ordered set" TS1, and once they each recognize the expected packet from the other side they proceed with link width negotiation, confirmed by both agents with TS2. This is immediately followed by a sequence of three DLLPs (Data Link Layer Packets) to exchange flow control credit information.

Figure A-6: Start with TS1

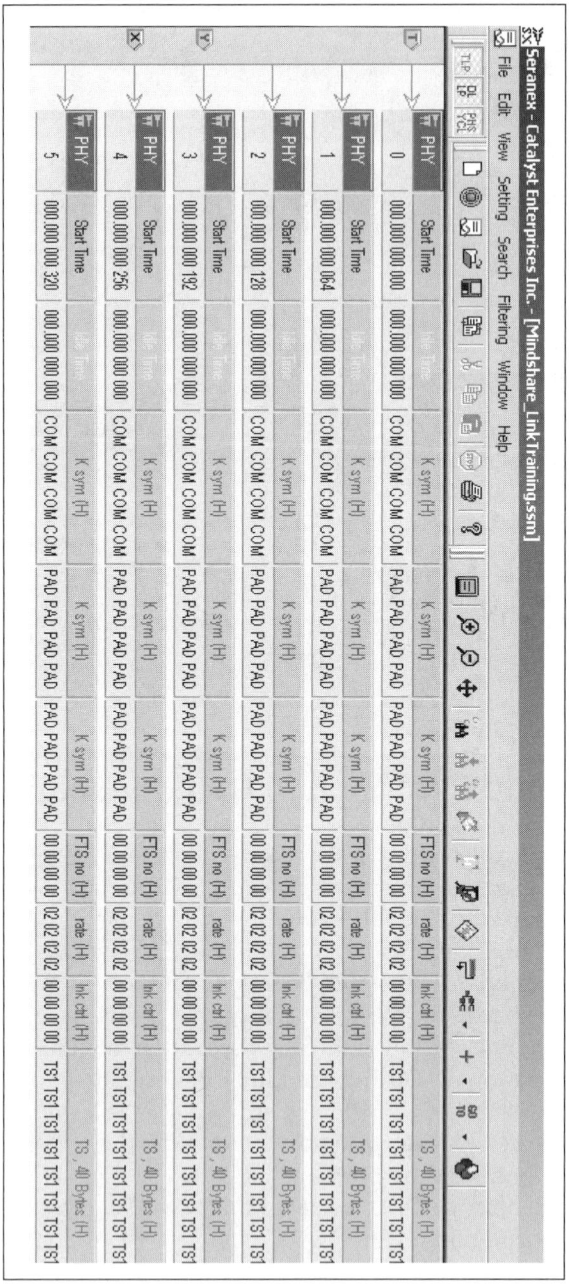

After detecting the receiver at opposite sides of the link, each device starts by sending at least 1024 TS1 packets to allow adequate time for starting communication, locking the clocks, and reversing lane polarity if necessary.

Figure A-7. SKIP

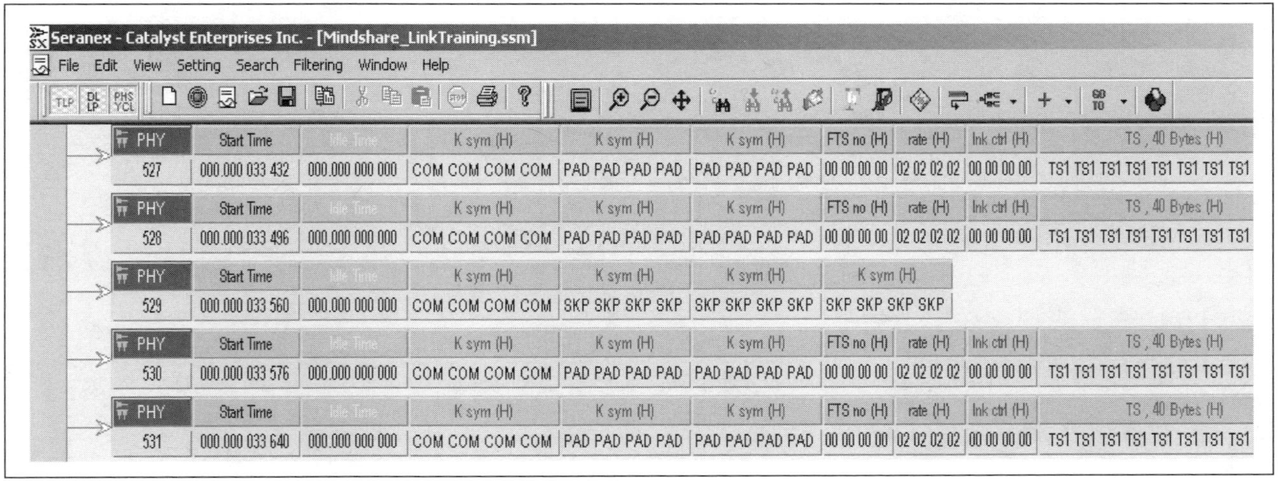

At all times, SKIP "Ordered Sets" are sent approximately every 5 microseconds to compensate for clock synchronization mismatch between the two agents.

Figure A-8: Completion of 1024 TS1

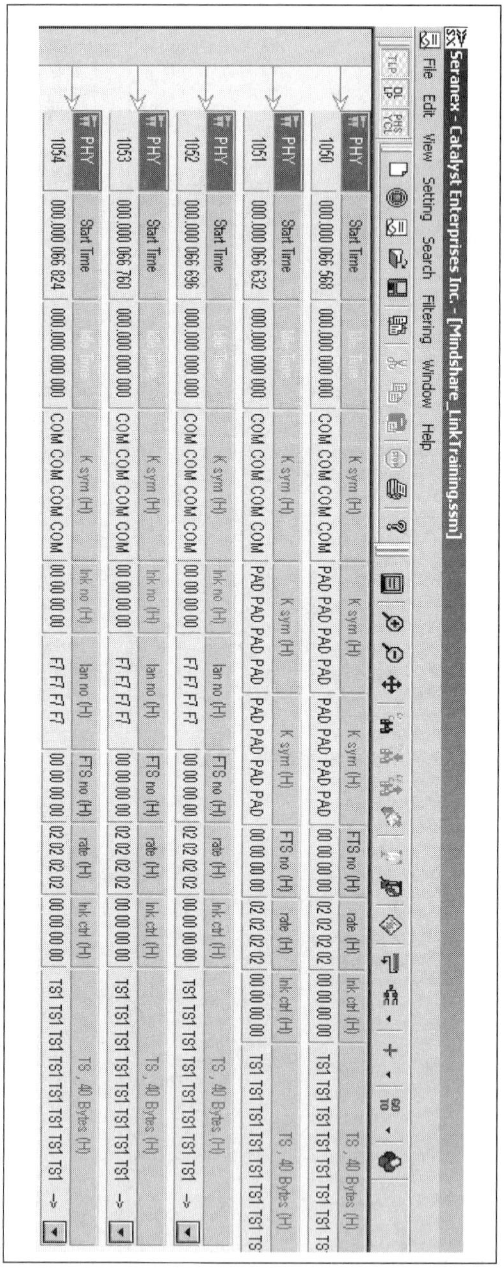

After 1024 TS1 PADs, TS1 packets with data are sent to announce the group of lanes that are eligible to become the active link lanes. As indicated in packet 1052, the link fields switch from being PAD to include a Link number.

Figure A-9: Lane Number Declaration

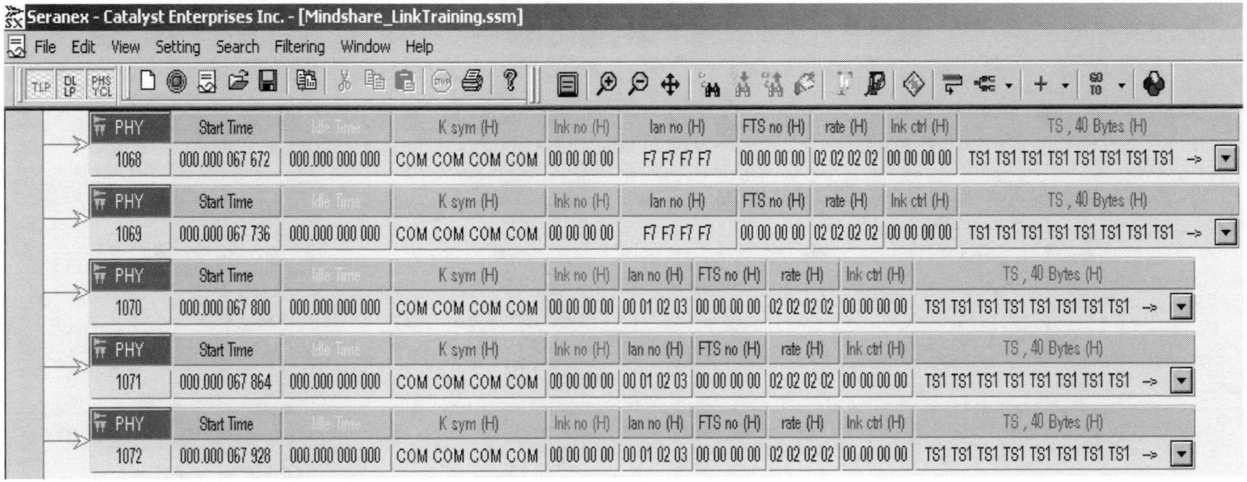

In this sequence, lane numbers are being declared after the communication has been established. As indicated in packet 1070, the lane fields switch from being PAD to include Lane numbers.

Figure A-10: Start of TS2

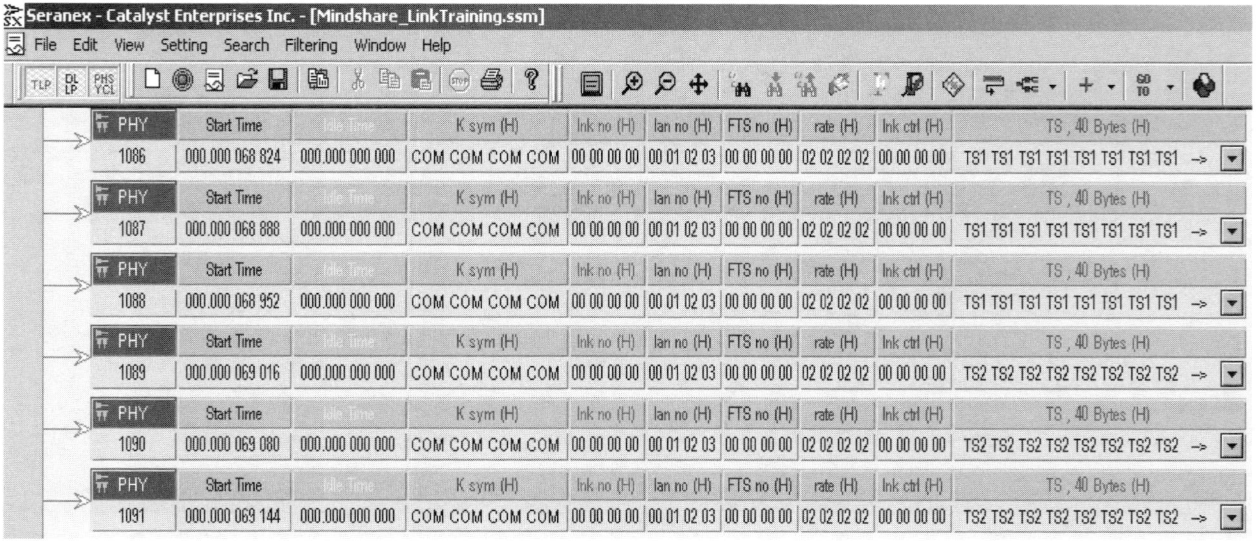

TS2 packets start after Link setup. TS2 packets are far fewer than TS1. These are sent as a confirmation of successful physical layer link negotiation.

Figure A-11: Initialization of Flow Control 1

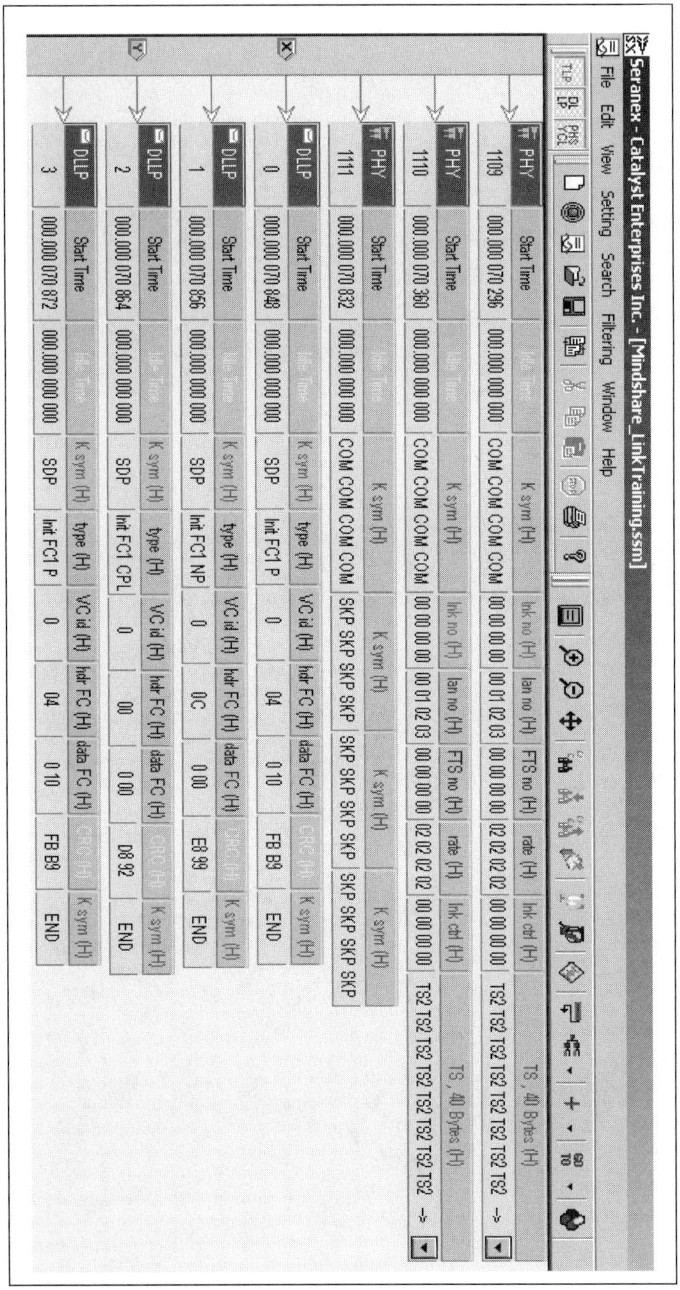

Initialization of Flow Control packets start after link training is completed by the physical layer. INIT FC1 sequences contain 3 packets to advertise available buffering for posted, non-posted and completion transaction types. These packets are repeated until both agents acknowledge it by starting the INIT FC2 transmissions.

Figure A-12: Initialization of Flow Control 2

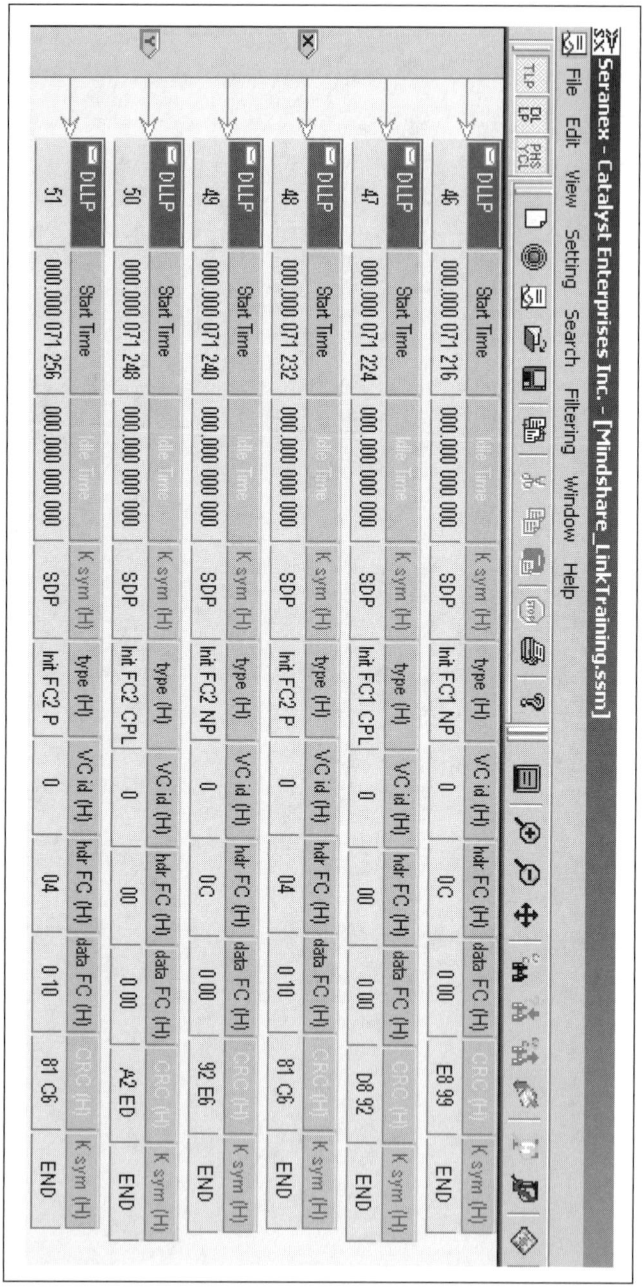

Packet	Start Time	Idle Time	K sym (H)	type (H)	VC id (H)	hdr FC (H)	data FC (H)	CRC (H)	K sym (H)
DLLP 46	000.000 071 216	000.000 000 000	SDP	Init FC1 NP	0	0C	0 00	E8 99	END
DLLP 47	000.000 071 224	000.000 000 000	SDP	Init FC1 CPL	0	00	0 00	D8 92	END
DLLP 48	000.000 071 232	000.000 000 000	SDP	Init FC2 P	0	04	0 10	81 C6	END
DLLP 49	000.000 071 240	000.000 000 000	SDP	Init FC2 NP	0	0C	0 00	92 E6	END
DLLP 50	000.000 071 248	000.000 000 000	SDP	Init FC2 CPL	0	00	0 00	A2 ED	END
DLLP 51	000.000 071 256	000.000 000 000	SDP	Init FC2 P	0	04	0 10	81 C6	END

There are three INIT FC2 packets which are repeated until both sides acknowledge by going into FC Updates. The Flow Control status of device is periodically updated using "Update FC" packets.

Figure A-13. Flow Control Updates

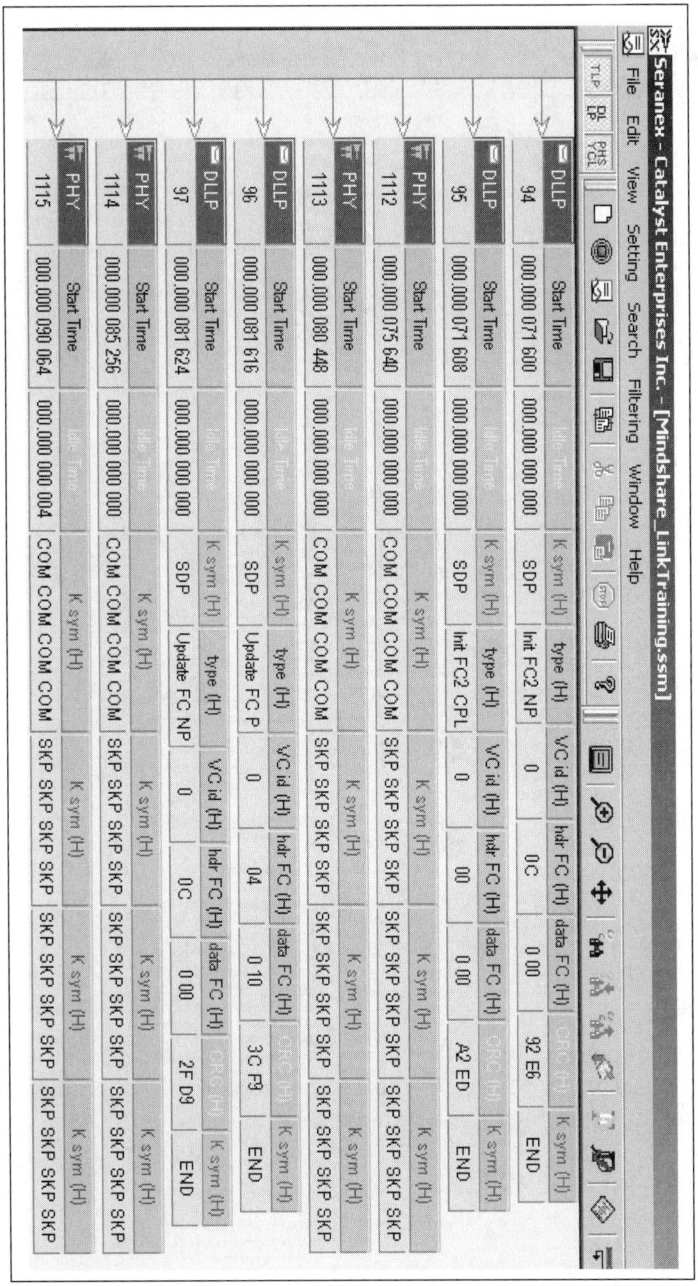

Packet	Start Time	Idle Time	K sym (H)	type (H)	VC id (H)	hdr FC (H)	data FC (H)	CRC (H)	K sym (H)
DLLP 94	000.000 071 600	000.000 000 000	SDP	Init FC2 NP	0	0C	0 00	92 E6	END
DLLP 95	000.000 071 608	000.000 000 000	SDP	Init FC2 CPL	0	00	0 00	A2 ED	END
PHY 1112	000.000 075 640	000.000 000 000	COM COM COM COM	SKP SKP SKP SKP	SKP SKP SKP SKP	SKP SKP SKP SKP	SKP SKP SKP SKP		
PHY 1113	000.000 080 448	000.000 000 000	COM COM COM COM	SKP SKP SKP SKP	SKP SKP SKP SKP	SKP SKP SKP SKP	SKP SKP SKP SKP		
DLLP 96	000.000 081 616	000.000 000 000	SDP	Update FC P	0	04	0 10	3C F9	END
DLLP 97	000.000 081 624	000.000 000 000	SDP	Update FC NP	0	0C	0 00	2F D9	END
PHY 1114	000.000 085 256	000.000 000 000	COM COM COM COM	SKP SKP SKP SKP	SKP SKP SKP SKP	SKP SKP SKP SKP	SKP SKP SKP SKP		
PHY 1115	000.000 090 064	000.000 000 004	COM COM COM COM	SKP SKP SKP SKP	SKP SKP SKP SKP	SKP SKP SKP SKP	SKP SKP SKP SKP		

Flow control updates and SKIPs are continuously repeated. At this time, TLP packets can be inserted anytime to perform data transfers.

Figure A-14: Alternate Display in Listing Format

Seranex - Catalyst Enterprises Inc. - [Mindshare_LinkTraining.ssm]

No.	TimeStamp	L0	L1	L2	L3	Status	Type	PE
	000.000 009 388	4A	4A	4A	4A			
	000.000 009 392	4A	4A	4A	4A			
	000.000 009 396	4A	4A	4A	4A			
	000.000 009 400	4A	4A	4A	4A			
	000.000 009 404	4A	4A	4A	4A			
	000.000 009 408	4A	4A	4A	4A			
	000.000 009 412	4A	4A	4A	4A			
148	000.000 009 416	BC	BC	BC	BC		PHY	
	000.000 009 420	F7	F7	F7	F7			
	000.000 009 424	F7	F7	F7	F7			
	000.000 009 428	0	0	0	0			
	000.000 009 432	2	2	2	2			
	000.000 009 436	0	0	0	0			
	000.000 009 440	4A	4A	4A	4A			
	000.000 009 444	4A	4A	4A	4A			
	000.000 009 448	4A	4A	4A	4A			
	000.000 009 452	4A	4A	4A	4A			
	000.000 009 456	4A	4A	4A	4A			
	000.000 009 460	4A	4A	4A	4A			
	000.000 009 464	4A	4A	4A	4A			
	000.000 009 468	4A	4A	4A	4A			
	000.000 009 472	4A	4A	4A	4A			
	000.000 009 476	4A	4A	4A	4A			
149	000.000 009 480	BC	BC	BC	BC		PHY	
	000.000 009 484	1C	1C	1C	1C			
	000.000 009 488	1C	1C	1C	1C			
	000.000 009 492	1C	1C	1C	1C			
150	000.000 009 496	BC	BC	BC	BC		PHY	
	000.000 009 500	F7	F7	F7	F7			
	000.000 009 504	F7	F7	F7	F7			
	000.000 009 508	0	0	0	0			
	000.000 009 512	2	2	2	2			
	000.000 009 516	0	0	0	0			
	000.000 009 520	4A	4A	4A	4A			
	000.000 009 524	4A	4A	4A	4A			

All bus activities may be viewed in the Symbol listing form which represents the bus data in raw form. In this listing, the SKP (1C) symbol after the COM (BC) identifies the SKIP type ordered set.

Slot Connector vs. Mid-Bus Pad

The PCI Express bus can also be used for chip-to-chip connections. In this case, there are no connectors for the analyzer to plug into. This requires a mid-bus probing technique.

The mid-bus probing does not allow for bus exercising since the bus stubs can create signal integrity issues. Developers wanting to characterize their products by fully exercising it should design a development card that includes their device and plug it into the Exerciser for characterization and verification.

Figure A-15 on page 978 illustrates one recommended interface to help developers and tool vendors to provide a common interface for analysis. However, this interface design is not part of the specifications and is intended only for prototype boards and does not include all required details at this time.

This interface is referred to as mid-bus probing and it defines a mechanical specification for the set of pads to probe the signals, mostly for chip-to-chip buses.

The figure indicates the mechanical pads that must be designed on the board if they are interested in using a mid-bus probe to analyze the bus.

Figure A-15: Mid-bus Pad Definition

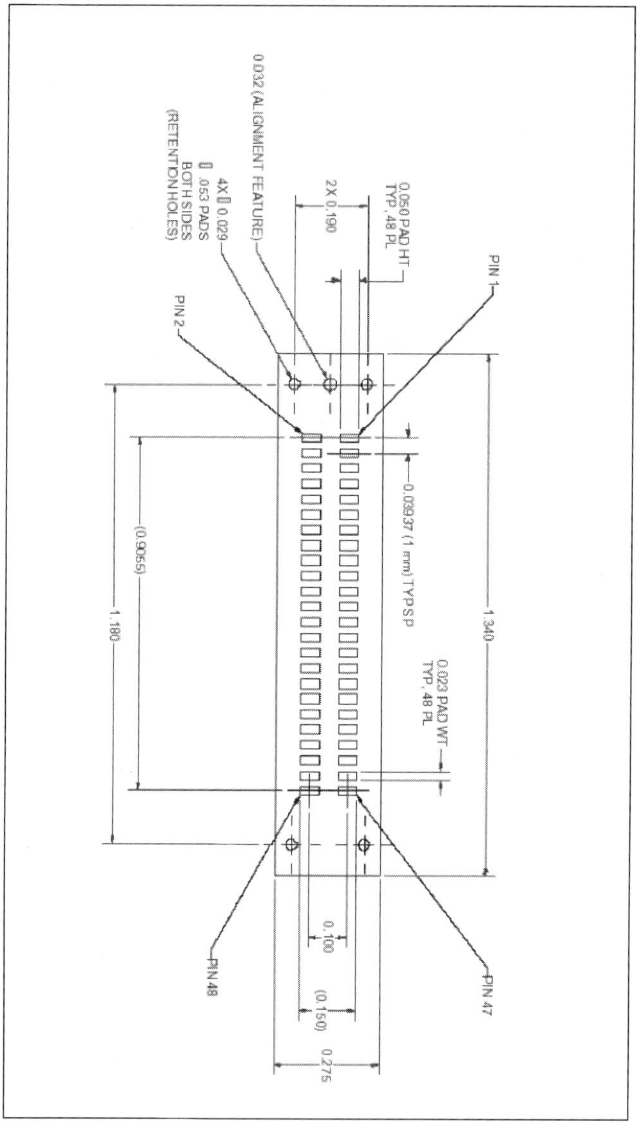

The exact implementation on how to mount the probe to the pads needs to be resolved or recommended by the development tool vendors. In this diagram only the position and sizes of mounting holes are defined

Suggested signal assignments for the probe are not defined in the specifications. Figure A-16 is a proposed suggestion that tool vendors are considering. Since there is an effect on the signals, the probe vendor must provide specifications of the probe loading effects and the developers must also consider these effects.

Figure A-16: Mid-Bus Suggested Signal Assignment

PAD#	Signal Description	PAD#	Signal Description
2	GND	1	IN+
4	IN+	3	IN-
6	IN-	5	GND
8	GND	7	IN+
10	IN+	9	IN-
12	IN-	11	GND
14	GND	13	IN+
16	IN+	15	IN-
18	IN-	17	GND
20	GND	19	IN+
22	IN+	21	IN-
24	IN-	23	GND
26	GND	25	IN+
28	IN+	27	IN-
30	IN-	29	GND
32	GND	31	IN+
34	IN+	33	IN-
36	IN-	35	GND
38	GND	37	IN+
40	IN+	39	IN-
42	IN-	41	GND
44	GND	43	IN+
46	IN+	45	IN-
48	IN-	47	GND

System developers must confirm with their analyzer/probe vendor to be sure that the probe vendor is also using the same signal assignment.

Exercising: In-Depth Verification

One of the most problematic issues developers have is to test, or characterize, their products in such a way that they can be sure they work in all expected conditions and with all other products. A common and easy way of testing is to have a few different other products available and test various combinations to verify the interoperability.

The problem with this common technique is that there is no assurance that all or even a small percentage of the possible expected conditions have been tested for. In most test cases, configurations cannot represent the conditions experienced when the system encounters high data traffic, errors or various termination responses.

The Bus Exerciser represents a premier tool that allows developers to test their new product beyond the typical limitations. Exercisers can generate errors, generate high throughput traffic, and even generate various different responses to transaction requests to verify that a new design can accommodate all expected conditions and that the system can properly recover.

A PCI Express bus Exerciser that can accommodate most of these requirements thta has an easy programming interface for all layers, and that allows users to fully manipulate the data would prove to be a useful tool for verifying and testing PCI Express products.

Samples taken from the PX-4, a Catalyst PCI Express bus Exerciser, are presented and explained here to indicate how this type of tool may be applied during test, debug and verification phases.

The Exerciser can also be used to verify various compliance requirements, as defined by the specifications.

To review the complete menus and features, you may download and try the software from catalyst web site www.getcatalyst.com

Figure A-17: Exerciser Covering All Possible Commands

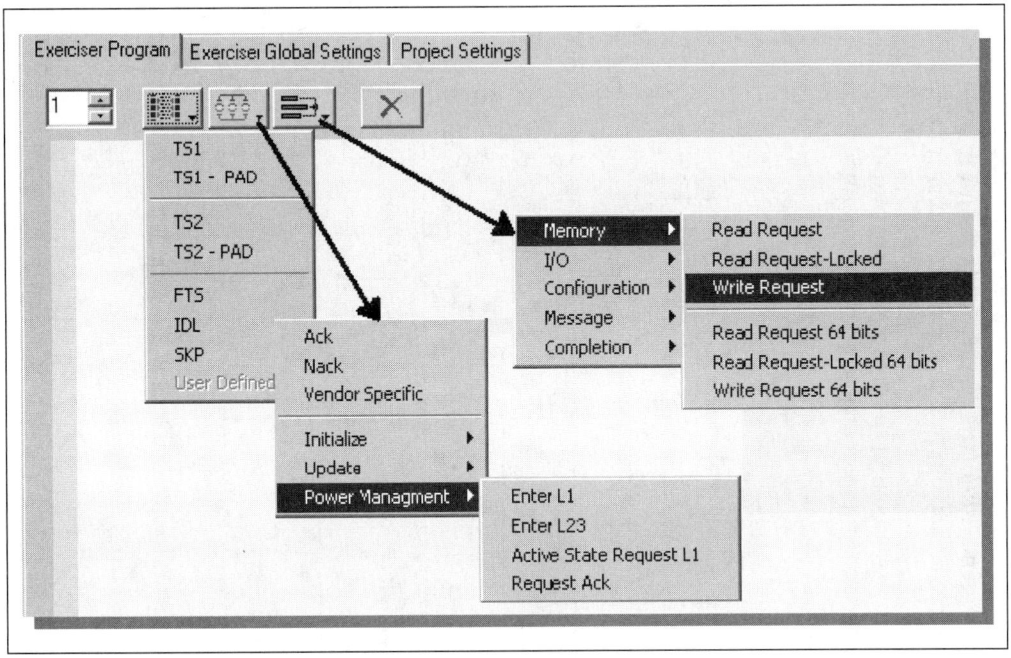

The PX-4 Exerciser interface indicates all possible commands and Ordered Sets in physical layer, data link layer and transactions layer packets.

Figure A-18: Exerciser Bit Level Manipulation Allowing Various Options

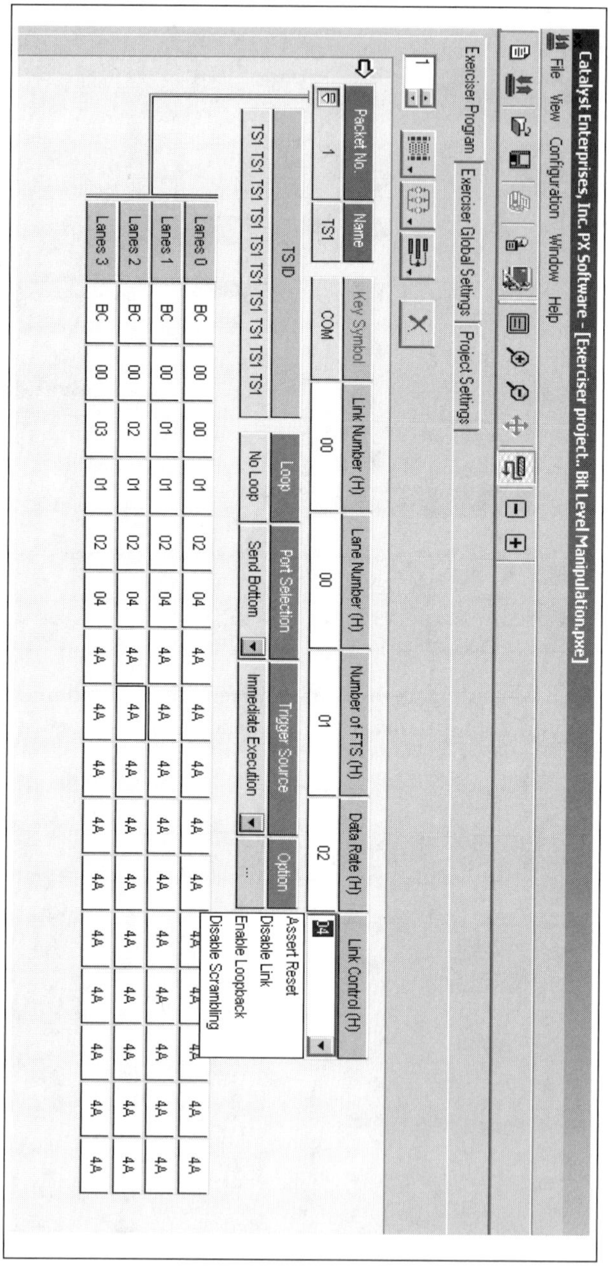

Setup for a TS1 packet, in a X4 link configuration, allowing the user various options to define the symbol values in the packet and change the bits within the symbols.

This packet can be sent to the device repeatedly in a predefined loop up to 4096 times or infinitely. By setting various available options users can test all possible responses.

Figure A-19: Supporting All Layers, Simultaneously

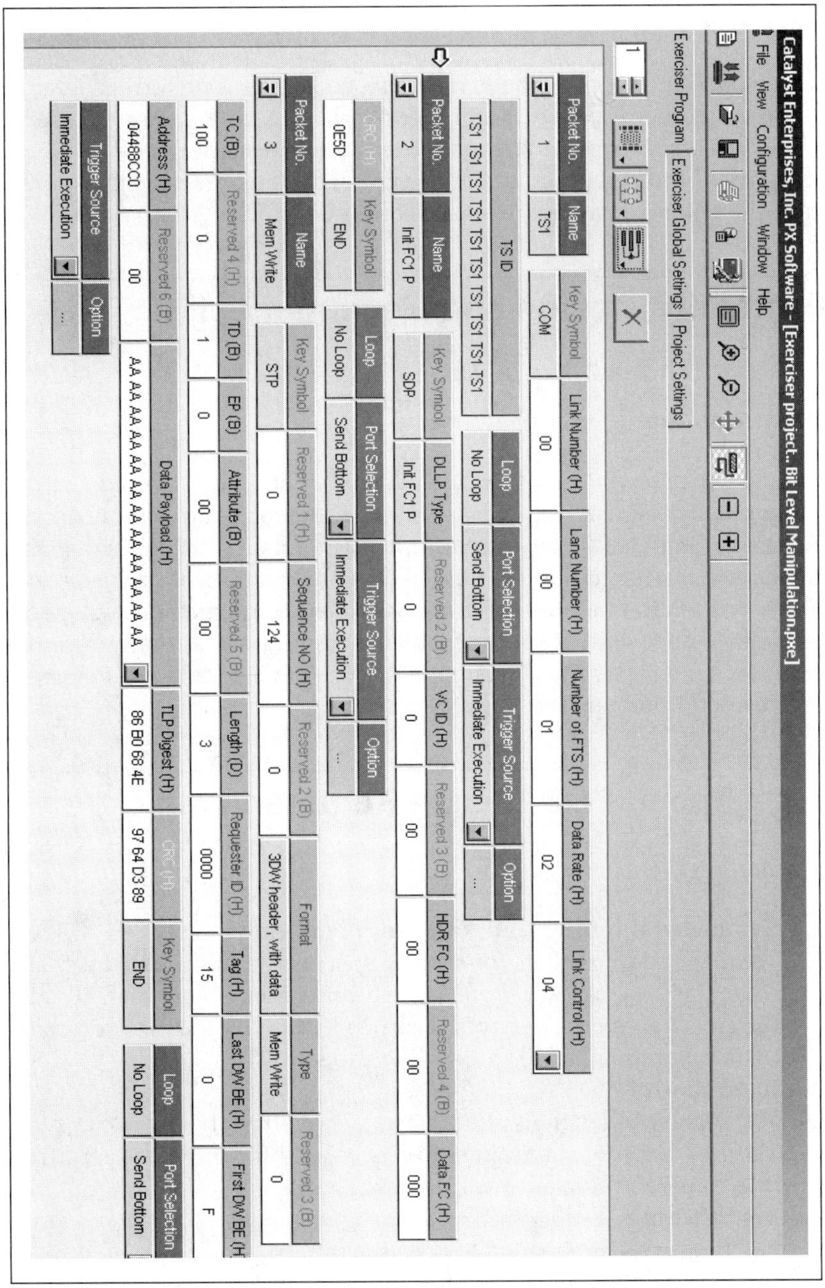

Several multi-layer commands may be defined to create a more in-depth program, such as Link training, Posted and Non-posted Transactions, or other various specific sequences.

Commands associated with different layers may be mixed, and each may be set with a different option and a number of loops. The commands may be issued immediately after each other or after a defined delay.

These packets and commands may also be sent as a pattern generator without considering the response and proper handshake. In this case the user may generate and repeat a pattern to measure the response of the device regardless of integrity of the response. In a more typical system, unless the response is accurate, the initiator may not repeat or continue.

Signal Integrity, Design and Measurement

General

The PCI Express bus runs at 2.5Gb/s and it should be noted that, without a proper PCB design, developers will not be able to produce a functional product. At these frequencies the losses impact the quality of the signal that passes through the transmission medium. Additional sources of problems may also be attributed to crosstalk. In short, more extensive research on high-speed design guidelines and simulation by system modeling are strongly recommended. Here are a few items that first time designers of Gigahertz technology should be aware of and pursue.

High Speed PCB Design Requirements

The designer must be aware of:

1. **Symmetrical routing and trace length matching**
   There are requirements for routing such as that high speed signals must be routed as a symmetrical pair with a difference of less than 20 mil between the two traces. These traces also need to be impedance controlled to 100 Ohm differential, or 50 Ohm single ended.
2. **Bend control**
   The high speed signals should also avoid sharp bends such as 90 degrees. The PCI Express signal integrity is based on controlling loss through the interconnect media as much as other factors.
3. **Via Stitching**
   Stitching is recommended to keep the number of vias for high speed signals to a minimum (such as two for add-in cards). It is sometimes a practice to

add a ground via next to the signal via to keep a uniform continuation for the return path (referred to as via stitching).

4. **Jitter control**
   One of the most common issues in signal integrity is controlling the jitter. A frequent source of jitter in a serial data stream is the reference clock. Jitter generally occurs due to excessive noise on the V_{CC} supply for clock distribution circuits and PCI Express transceivers. Proper filtering and decoupling for the power supply and around the clock oscillators and buffers must be implemented to keep the DC noise to a few millivolts in order to keep the jitter, and therefore the Eye pattern, of the output signals to an acceptable level. Also, clock sources (on board oscillators) must be of a high stability and low jitter.

   Figure A-20 on page 986 is a screenshot of a measurement made on a clock to show the acceptable jitter, and Figure A-21 on page 987 represents unacceptable jitter.

Figure A-20: Jitter Analysis of a Transceiver source clock—Acceptable (for a specific device)

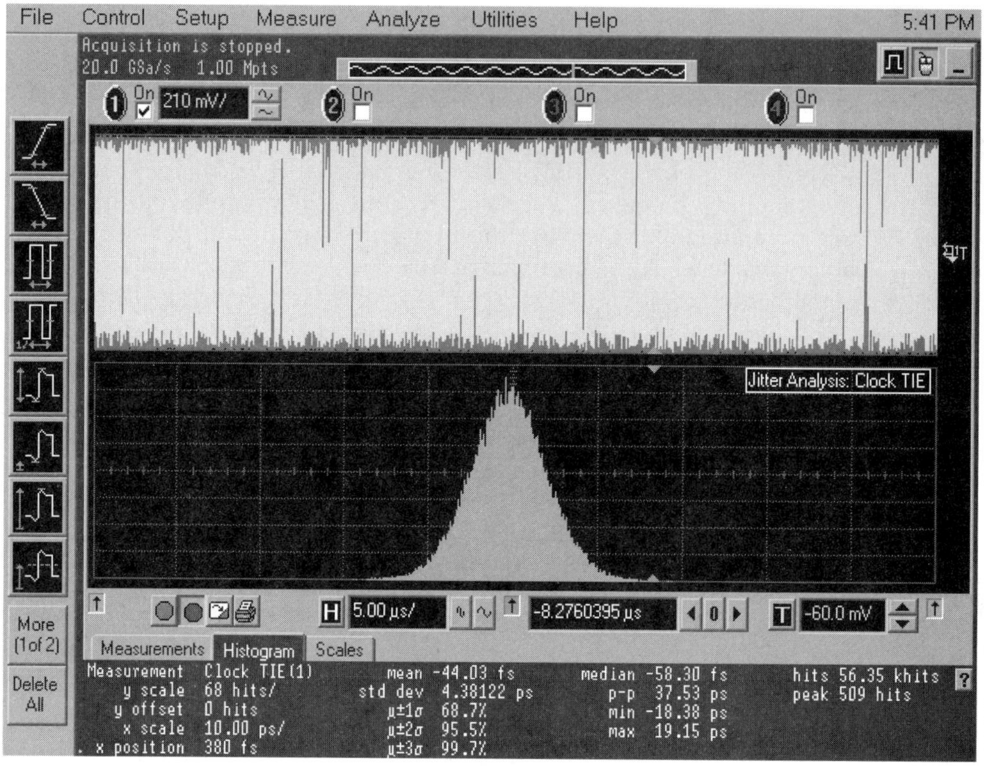

This measurement indicates a clock jitter of 39ps P-P and a stable clock at the desired frequency.

Figure A-21: Jitter analysis of a Transceiver source clock—Unacceptable (for a specific device)

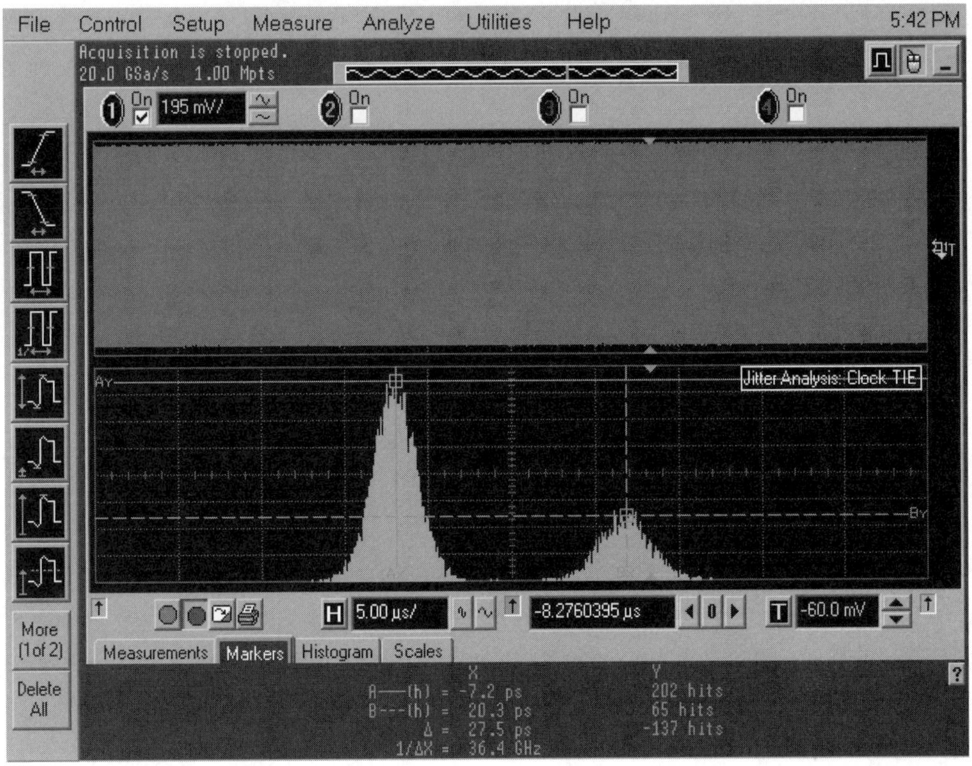

This measurement indicates a high clock jitter along with an unstable frequency.

The absolute jitter and stability is highly dependent on device specification requirements. Developers need to know the acceptable limits of their devices and use the measurement results accordingly.

Appendix B

Markets & Applications for the PCI Express™ Architecture

By Larry Chisvin, Akber Kazmi, and Danny Chi (PLX Technology, Inc.)

Introduction

Since its definition in the early 1990's, PCI has become one of the most successful interconnect technologies ever used in computers. Originally intended for personal computer systems, the PCI architecture has penetrated into virtually every computing platform category, including servers, storage, communications, and a wide range of embedded control applications. From its early incarnation as a 32-bit 33MHz interconnect, it has been expanded to offer higher speeds (currently in widespread use at 64-bit 133MHz, with faster versions on the way). Most importantly, each advancement in PCI bus speed and width provided backward software compatibility, allowing designers to leverage the broad code base.

As successful as the PCI architecture has become, there is a limit to what can be accomplished with a multi-drop, parallel shared bus interconnect technology. Issues such as clock skew, high pin count, trace routing restrictions in printed circuit boards (PCB), bandwidth and latency requirements, physical scalability, and the need to support Quality of Service (QoS) within a system for a wide variety of applications lead to the definition of the PCI Express™ architecture.

PCI Express is the natural successor to PCI, and was developed to provide the advantages of a state-of-the-art, high-speed serial interconnect technology and packet based layered architecture, but maintain backward compatibility with the large PCI software infrastructure. The key goal was to provide an optimized and universal interconnect solution for a great variety of future platforms, including desktop, server, workstation, storage, communications and embedded systems.

Figure B-1: Migration from PCI to PCI Express

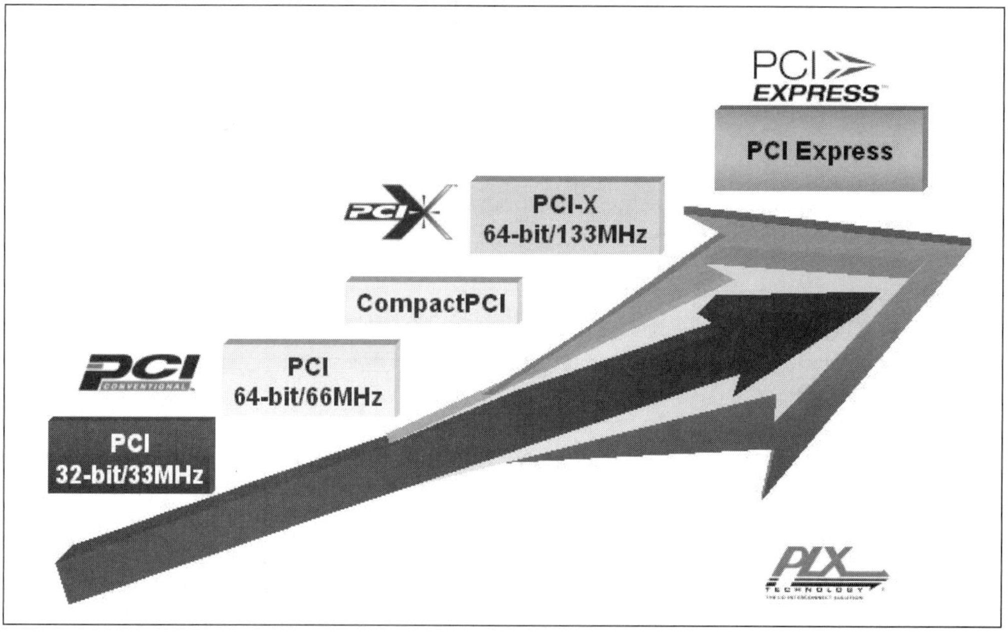

This chapter provides an overview of the markets and applications that PCI Express is expected to serve, with an explanation of how the technology will be integrated into each application, and some exploration of the advantages that PCI Express brings to each usage.

Let's review the key benefits of the PCI Express architecture before we discuss its application in different markets. Some of the key features of the architecture we reviewed in this book are:

- Packet-based layered architecture
- Serial interconnection at 2.5 GHz (5 GHz being considered)
- Link-to-link and end-to-end error detection (CRC check)
- Point-to-point data flow
- Differential low voltage signals for noise immunity

- Quality of Service (QoS)and Virtual Channels (VC)
- Scalable from 1x to 32x lanes
- Software (backward) compatibility with legacy PCI systems

Enterprise Computing Systems

PCI Express is expected to be deployed initially in desktop and server systems. These computers typically utilize a chipset solution that includes one or more microprocessors and two types of special interconnect devices, called northbridges and southbridges. Northbridges connect the CPU with memory, graphics and I/O. Southbridges connect to standardized I/O devices such as hard disk drives, networking modules or devices, and often PCI expansion slots.

Desktop Systems

Typical use of PCI Express in a desktop application is shown in Figure B-2 on page 992. The PCI Express ports come directly out of the northbridge, and are bridged to PCI slots that are used for legacy plug-in cards. In some implementations the PCI Express interconnections will be completely hidden from the user behind PCI bridges, and in other implementations there will be PCI Express slots in a new PCI Express connector form factor.

The major benefit for using PCI Express in this application is the low pin count associated with serial interface technology, which will translate into lower cost. This low pin count provides the ability to create northbridges and I/O bridges with smaller footprints, and a significantly fewer number of board traces between the components. This provides a major reduction in the area and complexity of the signal/trace routing in PCBs.

Server Systems

Figure B-3 on page 993 shows PCI Express used in an enterprise server system. This system has similarities to the desktop system, since there is a northbridge and southbridge providing functions that parallel their roles in the desktop system, and the form factor of the system is often similar. Servers, however, place a greater emphasis on performance than desktop systems do.

Figure B-2: PCI Express in a Desktop System

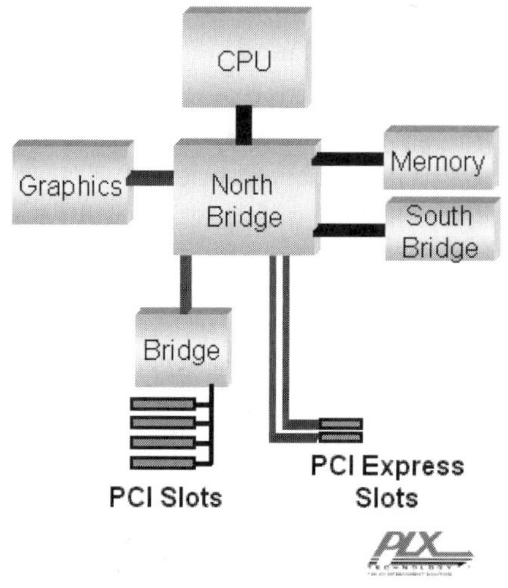

To achieve their performance and time to market objectives, server designers have adopted PCI-X. The primary attraction to PCI-X has been increased throughput, but with PCI code compatibility. PCI-X offers clear benefits compared to PCI, and will remain in server systems for a long while, but it suffers from the same shared bus limitations that have already been discussed. The high throughput of PCI Express serial interconnection provides a measurable benefit versus legacy interconnect technologies, especially as the speed of the I/O interconnect and the number of high speed I/O ports on each card increases.

Some systems will only provide PCI-X slots, but many newer systems will also offer several PCI Express slots. The number of PCI Express slots will grow over time compared to the PCI-X slots, and eventually will become dominant in the same way that PCI did with previous interconnect technologies. Since bandwidth is a primary motivator for a server, typical PCI Express slots will be either x4 or x8 lanes.

In most low to midrange server systems, the PCI-X bridging and PCI Express slots will be provided by using the ports right off of the northbridge. However, high-end systems will require more I/O slots of both kinds. Since PCI Express is a point-to-point technology, the only way to provide additional connection links is through a device called a fan out switch. Specifically, the purpose of a fan out switch is to multiply the number of PCI Express lanes from an upstream host port to a higher number of downstream PCI Express devices. Figure 3 below, shows a PCI Express switch used in the system for this purpose.

Figure B-3: PCI Express in a Server System

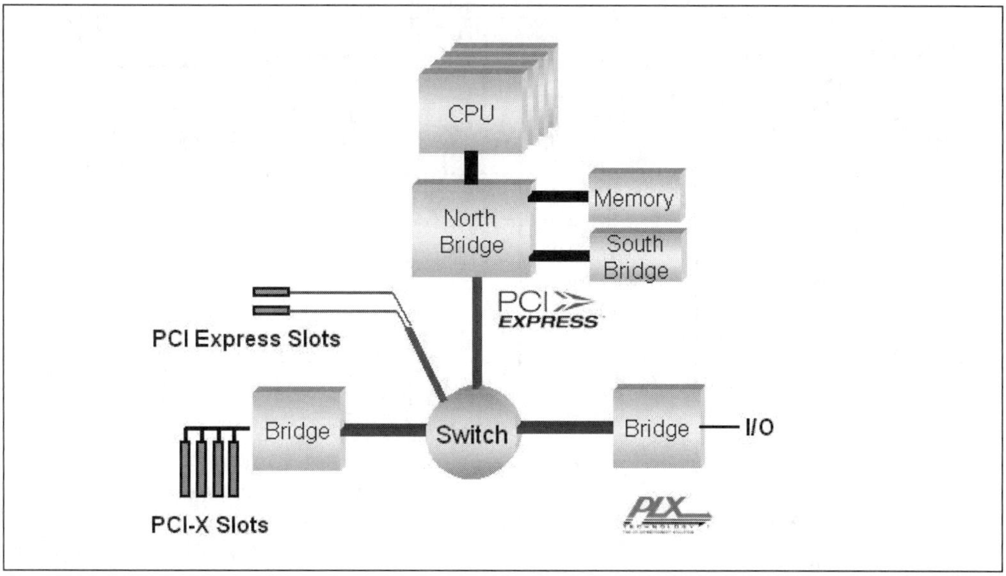

Embedded Control

One of the many areas that PCI has penetrated is embedded-control systems. This describes a wide range of applications that measure, test, monitor, or display data, and includes applications such as industrial control, office automation, test equipment, and imaging.

In these applications, system designers typically utilize embedded processors. In many instances, leading-edge companies will differentiate their products by utilizing some custom logic in the form of an ASIC or FPGA. A bridge is often used to translate the simple custom interface and connect it to the bus.

It is expected that the embedded-control market will quickly migrate to PCI Express, with a typical example shown in Figure B-4 on page 994. Applications such as imaging and video streaming are always hungry for bandwidth, and the additional throughput of x4 or x8 PCI Express links will translate into higher video resolution, or the handling of more video streams by the system. Others will implement PCI Express because of the noise resistance its LVDS traces provide, or because of its efficient routing and its ability to hook together subsystems through a standard cable. Still others will choose PCI Express simply because of its ubiquity.

Figure B-4: PCI Express in Embedded-Control Applications

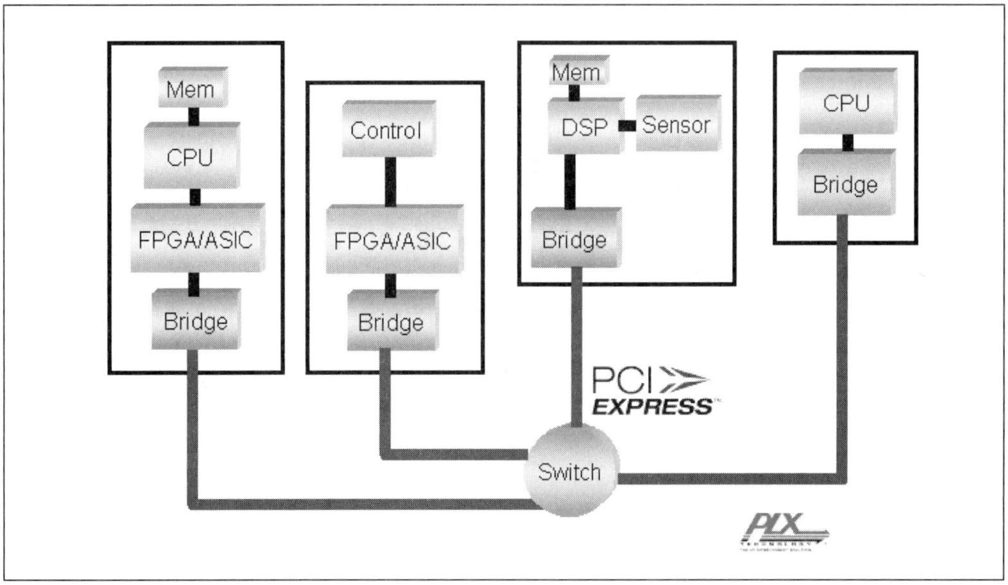

Storage Systems

PCI has become a common backplane technology for mainstream storage systems. Although it provides a good mix of features, low cost, and throughput, the "bus" has become a performance bottleneck. Figure B-5 on page 995 shows the use of PCI Express in a storage system. Systems similar to the one shown in Figure B-5 on page 995 can be built on a motherboard, or as part of a backplane. The discussion in this section applies to both form factors.

We have highlighted increased bandwidth as one of the advantages of moving to PCI Express, and nowhere is it more beneficial and obvious than in storage. The bandwidth demanded by I/O connections such as Ethernet, Fibre Channel, SCSI, and InfiniBand, is increasing rapidly. And the ability to move data between I/O modules and the host processor is critical to overall system performance.

Appendix B: Markets/Apps for PCI Express (by PLX)

In RAID based storage systems, for example, data to be archived is distributed across several disk drives to provide faster data retrieval and fault tolerance. As performance and complexity increase in these systems, the need for faster read and write operations from multiple I/O locations (disk drives) becomes extremely important. PCI Express, with its high performance, point-to-point architecture becomes very desirable for this application.

PCI Express provides a key reliability benefit in storage applications as well. The specification provides for two different types of error checking (CRC) schemes. There is CRC information between each link to ensure a reliable connection, and there is an optional end-to-end CRC that travels with the data from source to destination.

In High Availability (HA) applications, a separate host can reside in the system (as shown in Figure B-5 on page 995) for failover. If and when the primary host becomes unstable or non-operational, the secondary host will take over control of the system. This is an important feature for system level reliability when the designer is attempting to eliminate as many single points of failure as possible. This secondary host will be integrated into the system using non-transparent bridging (a detailed discussion of non-transparent bridging is provided in Appendix C).

Figure B-5: PCI Express in a Storage System

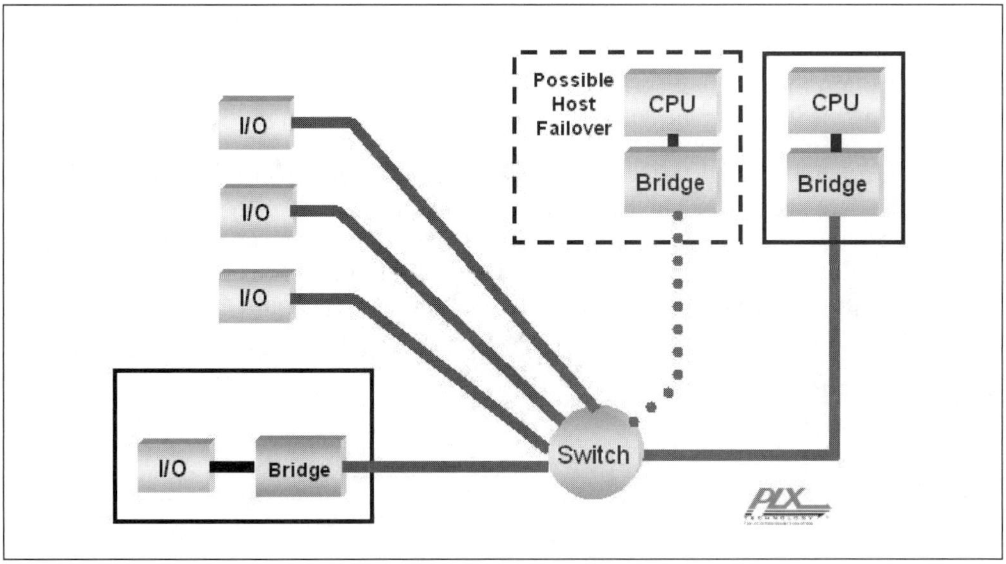

Communications Systems

The last application that we will explore is the use of PCI Express in communications systems. As with previous usage models, PCI technology has in the past made significant inroads into communication systems, but over time it has become less desirable due to the inherent limitations of a shared bus. In general, serial interconnects such as PCI Express have become attractive to backplane system designers by providing switch-based topologies that enable higher reliability, scalability, and robustness.

High end communications systems are based on one or more racks, with a midplane or backplane chassis used to interconnect each subsystem. Many systems use the CompactPCI architecture for their backplane implementations, and in some cases proprietary bus solutions are used to interconnect line cards, the switch fabric and the control modules. Some vendors are moving toward the AdvancedTCA™ (ATCA) architecture that supports a variety of different fabrics based upon a standard chassis for communication applications. ATCA has a range of benefits, but the PCI Express version of ATCA provides a smooth migration to higher speeds and a set of features that fit well with the communications paradigm.

One feature common to many communications systems is the ability to assign priorities to different data streams based on Quality of Service (QoS). PCI Express offers Traffic Classes (TC) that can be used to differentiate types of data. These TCs are then mapped onto Virtual Channels (VC) within the hardware. Each VC has its own set of queues in the subsystem, providing a separate path through the switch or bridge. This mechanism can be used to provide separate channels for different types of traffic (I/O, data, special messages).

Figure B-6 on page 997 shows a typical communication switch or router. Only 6 slots are shown for illustration purposes, but actual systems typically have 10+ slots. As shown in the figure, PCI Express technology can be used to support redundant switch fabrics and control modules, allowing communications equipment vendors to build high availability systems with a faster time to market.

Figure B-6: PCI Express in Communications Systems

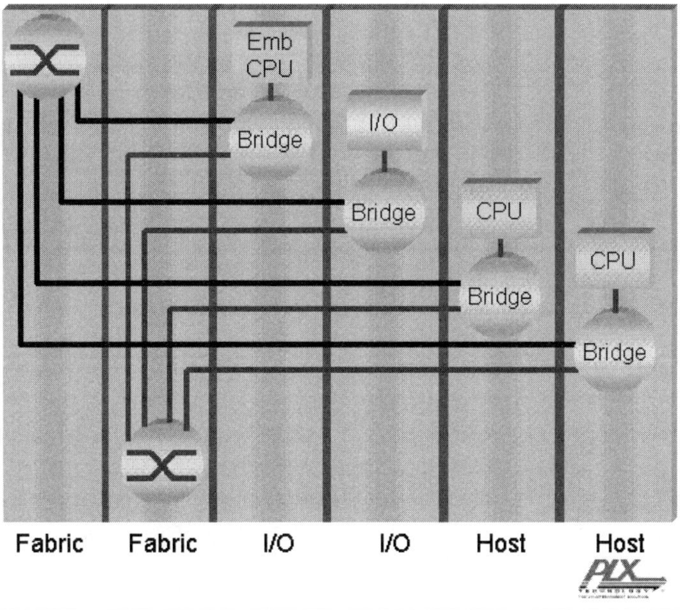

Summary

PCI Express technology offers an improvement in performance and the promise of features beyond PCI, but does so in a way that preserves investment made in PCI software over the last ten years. The combination of increased bandwidth, reduced cost, and extended capabilities with an easy migration path is likely to make the PCI Express architecture the next ubiquitous interconnection technology for a wide variety of applications.

Appendix C

Implementing Intelligent Adapters and Multi-Host Systems With PCI Express™ Technology

By Jack Regula, Danny Chi and Tim Canepa (PLX Technology, Inc.)

Introduction

Intelligent adapters, host failover mechanisms and multiprocessor systems are three usage models that are common today, and expected to become more prevalent as market requirements for next generation systems. Despite the fact that each of these was developed in response to completely different market demands, all share the common requirement that systems that utilize them require multiple processors to co-exist within the system. This appendix outlines how PCI Express can address these needs through non-transparent bridging.

Because of the widespread popularity of systems using intelligent adapters, host failover and multihost technologies, PCI Express silicon vendors must provide a means to support them. This is actually a relatively low risk endeavor; given that PCI Express is software compatible with PCI, and PCI systems have long implemented distributed processing. The most obvious approach, and the one that PLX espouses, is to emulate the most popular implementation used in the PCI space for PCI Express. This strategy allows system designers to use not only a familiar implementation but one that is a proven methodology, and one that can provide significant software reuse as they migrate from PCI to PCI Express.

This paper outlines how multiprocessor PCI Express systems will be implemented using industry standard practices established in the PCI paradigm. We first, however, will define the different usage models, and review the successful efforts in the PCI community to develop mechanisms to accommodate these requirements. Finally, we will cover how PCI Express systems will utilize non-transparent bridging to provide the functionality needed for these types of systems.

Usage Models

Intelligent Adapters

Intelligent adapters are typically peripheral devices that use a local processor to offload tasks from the host. Examples of intelligent adapters include RAID controllers, modem cards, and content processing blades that perform tasks such as security and flow processing. Generally, these tasks are either computationally onerous or require significant I/O bandwidth if performed by the host. By adding a local processor to the endpoint, system designers can enjoy significant incremental performance. In the RAID market, a significant number of products utilize local intelligence for their I/O processing.

Another example of intelligent adapters is an ecommerce blade. Because general purpose host processors are not optimized for the exponential mathematics necessary for SSL, utilizing a host processor to perform an SSL handshake typically reduces system performance by over 90%. Furthermore, one of the requirements for the SSL handshake operation is a true random number generator. Many general purpose processors do not have this feature, so it is actually difficult to perform SSL handshakes without dedicated hardware. Similar examples abound throughout the intelligent adapter marketplace; in fact, this usage model is so prevalent that for many applications it has become the de facto standard implementation.

Host Failover

Host failover capabilities are designed into systems that require high availability. High availability has become an increasingly important requirement, especially in storage and communication platforms. The only practical way to ensure that the overall system remains operational is to provide redundancy for all components. Host failover systems typically include a host based system attached to several endpoints. In addition, a backup host is attached to the system and is configured to monitor the system status. When the primary host fails, the backup host processor must not only recognize the failure, but then take steps to assume primary control, remove the failed host to prevent additional disruptions, reconstitute the system state, and continue the operation of the system without losing any data.

Appendix D: Intelligent Adapters & Multi-Host Systems

Multiprocessor Systems

Multiprocessor systems provide greater processing bandwidth by allowing multiple computational engines to simultaneously work on sections of a complex problem. Unlike systems utilizing host failover, where the backup processor is essentially idle, multiprocessor systems utilize all the engines to boost computational throughput. This enables a system to reach performance levels not possible by using only a single host processor. Multiprocessor systems typically consist of two or more complete sub-systems that can pass data between themselves via a special interconnect. A good example of a multihost system is a blade server chassis. Each blade is a complete subsystem, often replete with its own CPU, Direct Attached Storage, and I/O.

The History Multi-Processor Implementations Using PCI

To better understand the implementation proposed for PCI Express, one needs to first understand the PCI implementation.

PCI was originally defined in 1992 for personal computers. Because of the nature of PCs at that time, the protocol architects did not anticipate the need for multiprocessors. Therefore, they designed the system assuming that the host processor would enumerate the entire memory space. Obviously, if another processor is added, the system operation would fail as both processors would attempt to service the system requests.

1Several methodologies were subsequently invented to accommodate the requirement for multiprocessor capabilities using PCI. The most popular implementation, and the one discussed in this paper for PCI Express, is the use of non-transparent bridging between the processing subsystems to isolate their memory spaces.[1]

Because the host does not know the system topology when it is first powered up or reset, it must perform discovery to learn what devices are present and then map them into the memory space. To support standard discovery and configuration software, the PCI specification defines a standard format for Control and Status Registers (CSRs) of compliant devices. The standard PCI-to-PCI bridge CSR header, called a Type 1 header, includes primary, secondary and subordi-

1. Unless explicitly noted, the architecture for multiprocessor systems using PCI and PCI Express are similar and may be used interchangeably.

nate bus number registers that, when written by the host, define the CSR addresses of devices on the other side of the bridge. Bridges that employ a Type 1 CSR header are called transparent bridges.

A Type 0 header is used for endpoints. A Type 0 CSR header includes base address registers (BARs) used to request memory or I/O apertures from the host. Both Type 1 and Type 0 headers include a class code register that indicates what kind of bridge or endpoint is represented, with further information available in a subclass field and in device ID and vendor ID registers. The CSR header format and addressing rules allow the processor to search all the branches of a PCI hierarchy, from the host bridge down to each of its leaves, reading the class code registers of each device it finds as it proceeds, and assigning bus numbers as appropriate as it discovers PCI-to-PCI bridges along the way. At the completion of discovery, the host knows which devices are present and the memory and I/O space each device requires to function. These concepts are illustrated in Figure C - 1.

Figure C-1: Enumeration Using Transparent Bridges

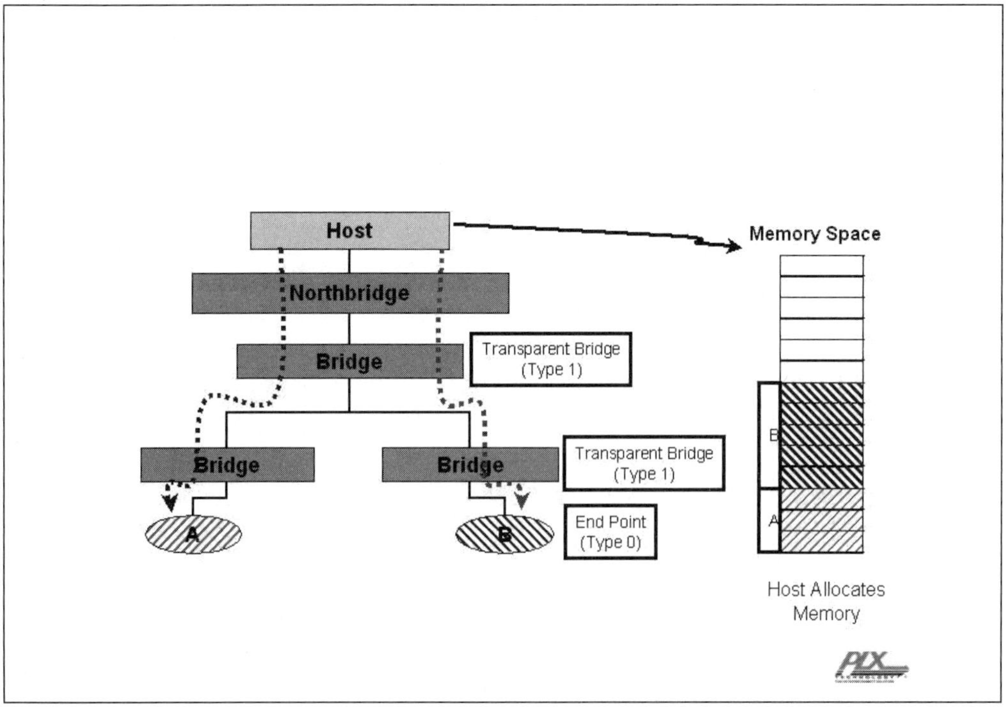

Appendix D: Intelligent Adapters & Multi-Host Systems

Implementing Multi-host/Intelligent Adapters in PCI Express Base Systems

Up to this point, our discussions have been limited to one processor with one memory space. As technology progressed, system designers began developing end points with their own native processors built in. The problem that this caused was that both the host processor and the intelligent adapter would, upon power up or reset, attempt to enumerate the entire system, causing system conflict and ultimately a non-functional system.[2]

To get around this, architects designed non-transparent bridges. A non-transparent PCI-to-PCI Bridge, or PCI Express-to-PCI Express Bridge, is a bridge that exposes a Type 0 CSR header on both sides and forwards transactions from one side to the other with address translation, through apertures created by the BARs of those CSR headers. Because it exposes a Type 0 CSR header, the bridge appears to be an endpoint to discovery and configuration software, eliminating potential discovery software conflicts. Each BAR on each side of the bridge creates a tunnel or window into the memory space on the other side of the bridge. To facilitate communication between the processing domains on each side, the non-transparent bridge also typically includes doorbell registers to send interrupts from each side of the bridge to the other, and scratchpad registers accessible from both sides.

A non-transparent bridge is functionally similar to a transparent bridge in that both provide a path between two independent PCI buses (or PCI Express links). The key difference is that when a non-transparent bridge is used, devices on the downstream side of the bridge (relative to the system host) are not visible from the upstream side. This allows an intelligent controller on the downstream side to manage the devices in its local domain, while at the same time making them appear as a single device to the upstream controller. The path between the two buses allows the devices on the downstream side to transfer data directly to the upstream side of the bus without directly involving the intelligent controller in the data movement. Thus transactions are forwarded across the bus unfettered just as in a PCI-to-PCI Bridge, but the resources responsible are hidden from the host, which sees a single device.

2. While we are using an intelligent endpoint as the examples, we should note that a similar problem exists for multi-host systems.

Because we now have two memory spaces, the PCI Express system needs to translate addresses of transactions that cross from one memory space to the other. This is accomplished via Translation and Limit Registers associated with the BAR. See "Address Translation" on page 1013 for a detailed description; Figure C-2 on page 1004 provides a conceptual rendering of Direct Address Translation. Address translation can be done by Direct Address Translation (essentially replacement of the data under a mask), table lookup, or by adding an offset to an address. Figure C-3 on page 1005 shows Table Lookup Translation used to create multiple windows spread across system memory space for packet originated in a local I/O processor's domain, as well as Direct Address Translation used to create a single window in the opposite direction.

Figure C-2: Direct Address Translation

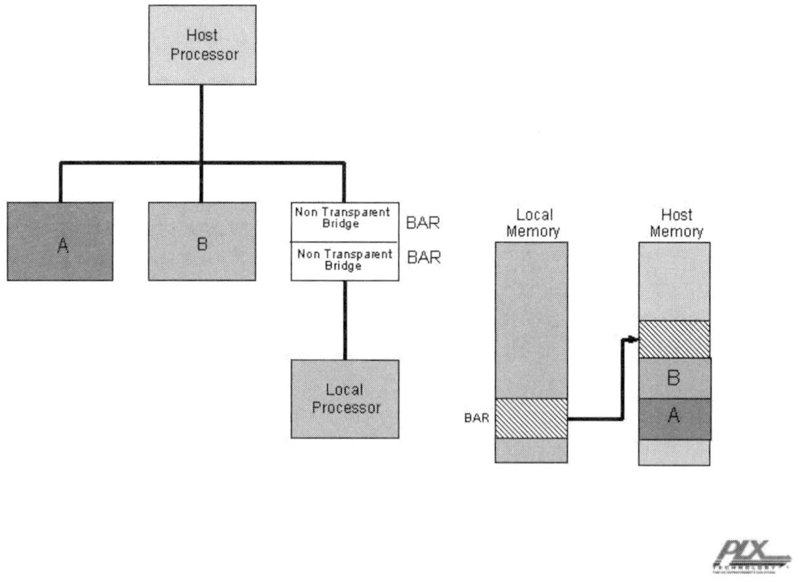

Figure C-3: Look Up Table Translation Creates Multiple Windows

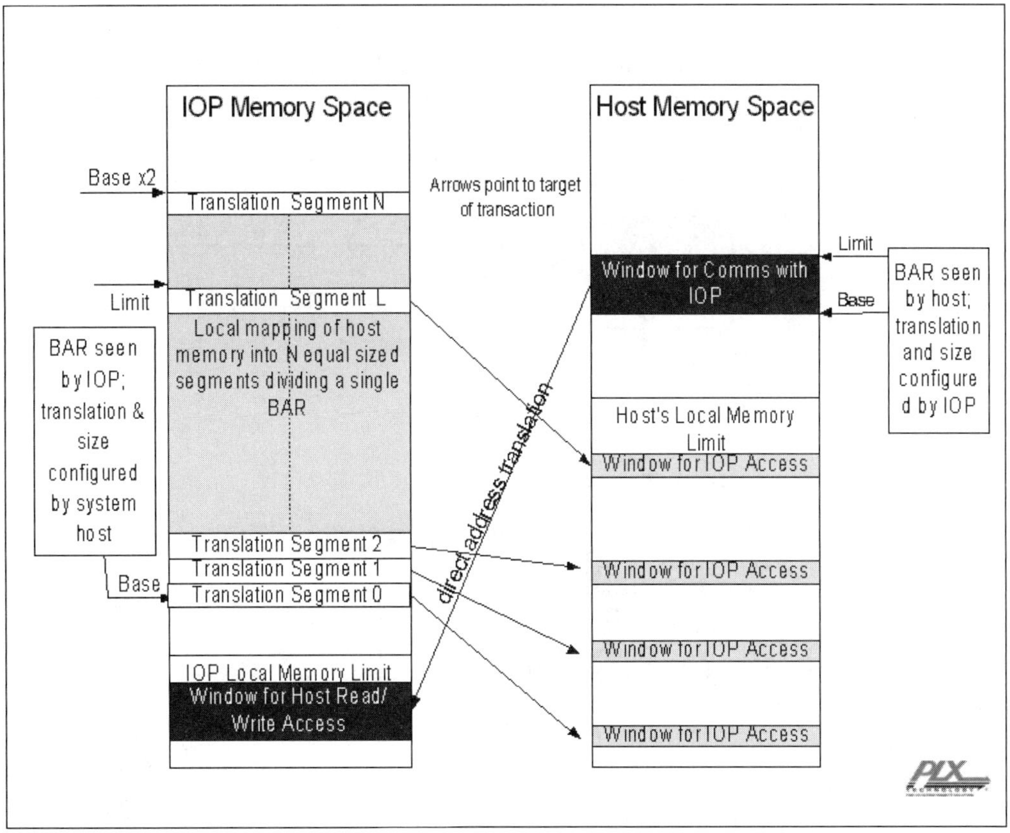

Example: Implementing Intelligent Adapters in a PCI Express Base System

Intelligent adapters will be pervasive in PCI Express systems, and will likely be the most widely used example of systems with "multiple processors".

Figure C-4 on page 1006 illustrates how PCI Express systems will implement intelligent adapters. The system diagram consists of a system host, a root complex (the PCI Express version of a Northbridge), a three port switch, an example endpoint, and an intelligent add-in card. Similar to the system architecture, the add-in card contains a local host, a root complex, a three port switch, and an example endpoint. However we should note two significant differences: the intelligent add-in card contains an EEPROM, and one port of the switch contains a back to back non-transparent bridge.

Figure C-4: Intelligent Adapters in PCI and PCI Express Systems

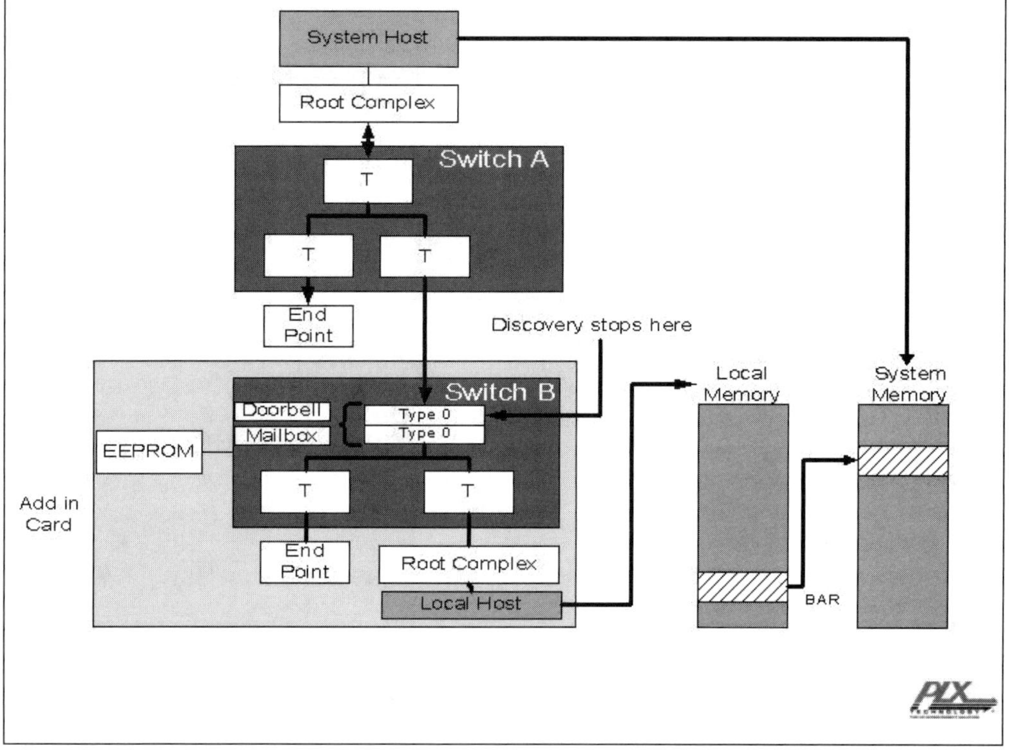

Upon power up, the system host will begin enumerating to determine the topology. It will pass through the Root Complex and enter the first switch (Switch A). Upon entering the topmost port, it will see a transparent bridge, so it will know to continue to enumerate. The host will then poll the leftmost port and, upon finding a Type 0 CSR header, will consider it an endpoint and explore no deeper along that branch of the PCI hierarchy. The host will then use the information in the endpoint's CSR header to configure base and limit registers in bridges and BARs in endpoints to complete the memory map for this branch of the system.

The host will then explore the rightmost port of Switch A and read the CSR header registers associated with the top port of Switch B. Because this port is a non-transparent bridge, the host finds a Type 0 CSR header. The host processor therefore believes that this is an endpoint and explores no deeper along that branch of the PCI hierarchy. The host reads the BARs of the top port of Switch B to determine the memory requirements for windows into the memory space on the other side of the bridge. The memory space requirements can be preloaded from an EEPROM into the BAR Setup Registers of Switch B's non-transparent port or can be configured by the processor that is local to Switch B prior to allowing the system host to complete discovery.

Similar to the host processor power up sequence, the local host will also begin enumerating its own system. Like the system host processor, it will allocate memory for end points and continue to enumerate when it encounters a transparent bridge. When the host reaches the topmost port of Switch B, it sees a non-transparent bridge with a Type 0 CSR header. Accordingly, it reads the BARs of the CSR header to determine the memory aperture requirements, then terminates discovery along this branch of its PCI tree. Again, the memory aperture information can be supplied by an EEPROM, or by the system host.

Communication between the two processor domains is achieved via a mailbox system and doorbell interrupts. The doorbell facility allows each processor to send interrupts to the other. The mailbox facility is a set of dual ported registers that are both readable and writable by both processors. Shared memory mapped mechanisms via the BARs may also be used for inter-processor communication.

Example: Implementing Host Failover in a PCI Express System

Figure C-5 on page 1008 illustrates how most PCI Express systems will implement host failover. The primary host processor in this illustration is on the left side of the diagram, with the backup host on the right side of the diagram. Like most systems with which we are familiar, the host processor connects to a root complex. In turn, the root complex routes its traffic to the switch. In this example, the switch has two ports to end points in addition to the upstream port for the primary host we have just described. Furthermore, this system also has another processor, which is connected to the switch via another root complex.

Figure C-5: Host Failover in PCI and PCI Express Systems

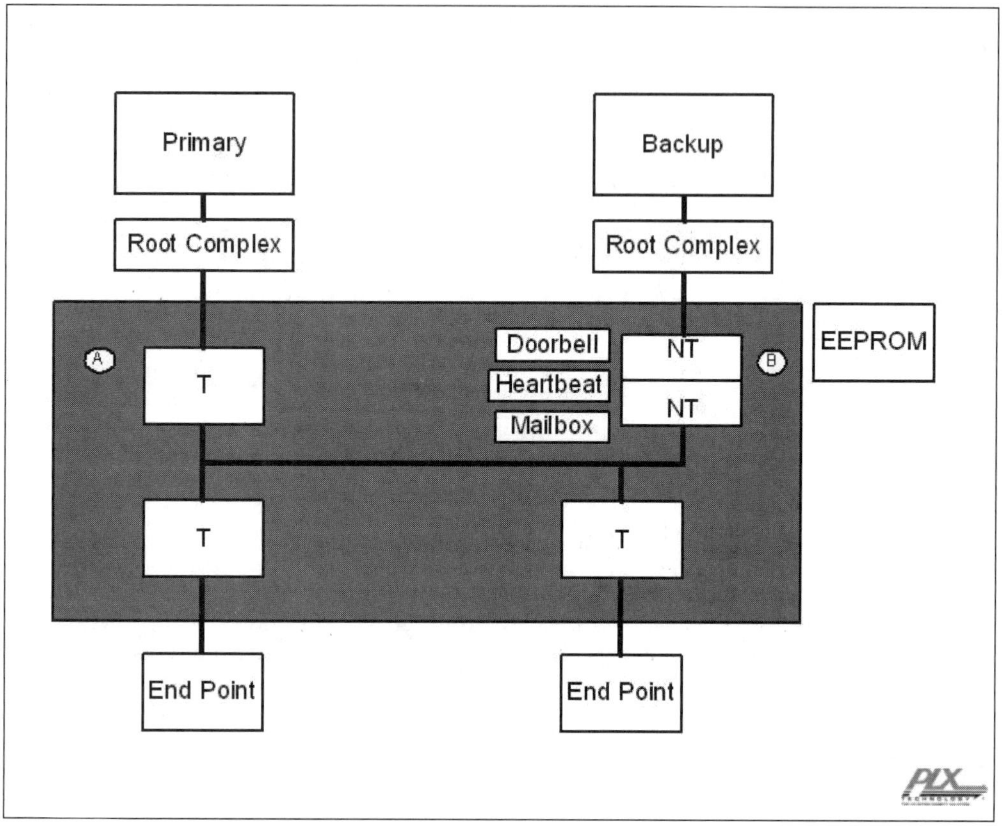

The switch ports to both processors need to be configurable to behave either as a transparent bridge or a non-transparent bridge. An EEPROM or strap pins on the switch can be used to initially bootstrap this configuration.

Under normal operation, upon power up, the primary host begins to enumerate the system. In our example, as the primary host processor begins its discovery protocol through the fabric, it discovers the two end points, and their memory requirements, by sizing their BARs. When it gets to the upper right port, it finds a Type 0 CSR header. This signifies to the primary host processor that it should not attempt discovery on the far side of the associated switch port. As in the previous example, the BARs associated with the non-transparent switch port may have been configured by EEPROM load prior to discovery or might be configured by software running on the local processor.

Again, similar to the previous example, the backup processor powers up and begins to enumerate. In this example, the backup processor chipset consists of the root complex and the backup processor only. It discovers the non-transparent switch port and terminates its discovery there. It is keyed by EEPROM loaded Device ID and Vendor ID registers to load an appropriate driver.

During the course of normal operation, the host processor performs all of its normal duties as it actively manages the system. In addition, it will send messages to the backup processor called heartbeat messages. Heartbeat messages are indications of the continued good health of the originating processor. A heartbeat message might be as simple as a doorbell interrupt assertion, but typically would include some data to reduce the possibility of a false positive. Checkpoint and journal messages are alternative approaches to providing the backup processor with a starting point, should it need to take over. In the journal methodology, the backup is provided with a list or journal of completed transactions (in the application specific sense, not in the sense of bus transactions). In the checkpoint methodology, the backup is periodically provided with a complete system state from which it can restart if necessary. The heartbeat's job is to provide the means by which the backup processor verifies that the host processor is still operational. Typically this data provides the latest activities and the state of all the peripherals.

If the backup processor fails to receive timely heartbeat messages, it will begin assuming control. One of its first tasks is to demote the primary port to prevent the failed processor from interacting with the rest of the system. This is accomplished by reprogramming the CSRs of the switch using a memory mapped view of the switch's CSRs provided via a BAR in the non-transparent port. To take over, the backup processor reverses the transparent/non-transparent modes at both its port and the primary processor's port and takes down the link to the primary processor. After cleaning up any transactions left in the queues or left in an incomplete state as a result of the host failure, the backup processor reconfigures the system so that it can serve as the host. Finally, it uses the data in the checkpoint or journal messages to restart the system.

Example: Implementing Dual Host in a PCI Express Base System

Figure C-6 on page 1010 illustrates how PCI Express systems might implement a dual host system[3]. In this example, the leftmost blocks are a typically complete system, with the rightmost blocks being a separate subsystem. As previously discussed, connecting the leftmost and rightmost diagram is a set of non-transparent bridges.

Figure C-6: Dual Host in a PCI and PCI Express System

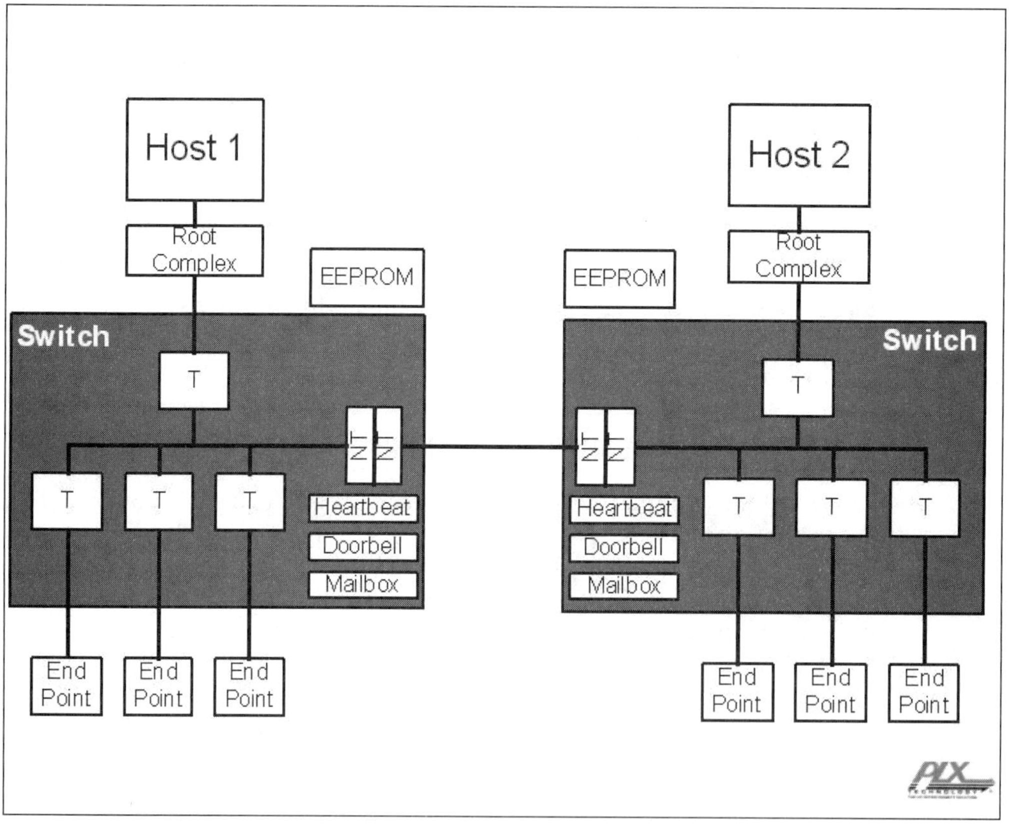

3. Back to back non-transparent (NT) ports are unnecessary but occur as a result of the use of identical single board computers for both hosts. A transparent backplane fabric would typically be interposed between the two NT ports.

Upon power up, both processors will begin enumerating. As before, the hosts will search out the endpoints by reading the CSR and then allocate memory appropriately. When the hosts encounter the non-transparent bridge port in each of their private switches, they will assume it is an endpoint and, using the data in the EEPROM, allocate resources. Both systems will use the doorbell and mailbox registers described above to communicate with each other.

[2]The dual-host system model may be extended to a fully redundant dual star system by using additional switches to dual-port the hosts and line cards into a redundant fabric as shown in Figure C-7 on page 1012. This is particularly attractive to vendors who employ chassis based systems for their flexibility, scalability and reliability.

Two host cards are shown. Host A is the primary host of Fabric A and the secondary host of Fabric B. Similarly, Host B is the primary host of Fabric B and the secondary host of Fabric A.

Each host is connected to the fabric it serves via a transparent bridge/switch port and to the fabric for which it provides only backup via a non-transparent bridge/switch port. These non-transparent ports are used for host-to-host communications and also support cross-domain peer-to-peer transfers where address maps do not allow a more direct connection.

Figure C-7: Dual-Star Fabric

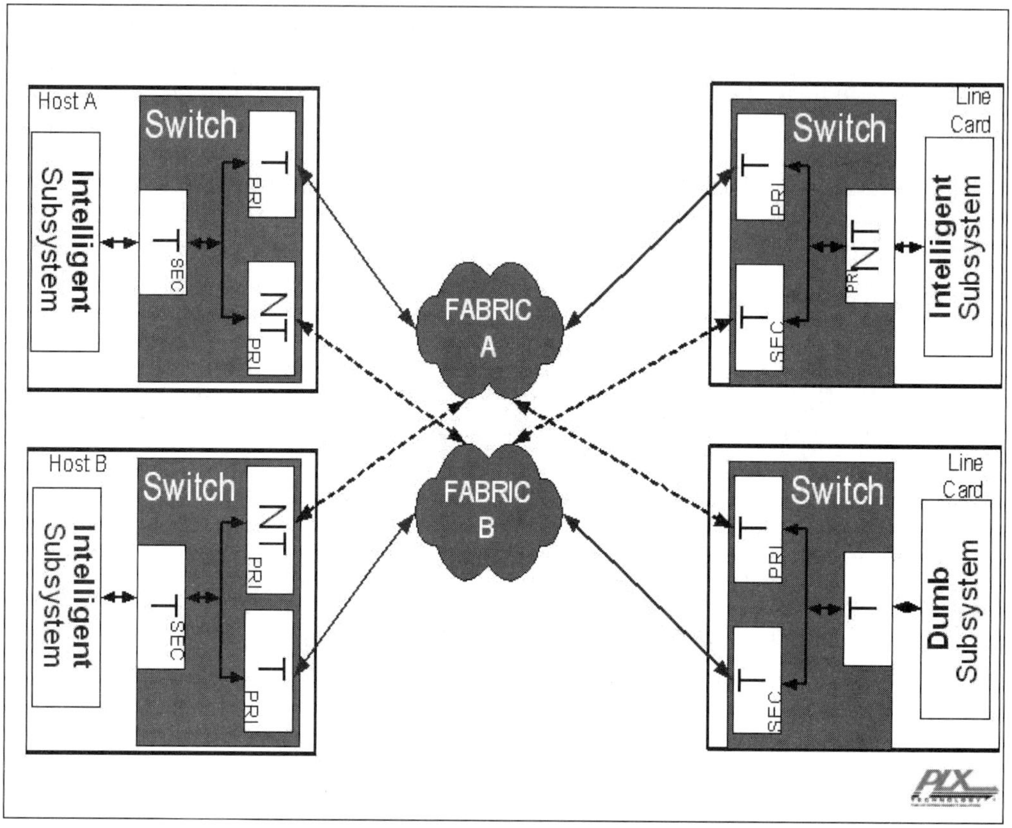

Summary

Through non-transparent bridging, PCI Express Base offers vendors the ability to integrate intelligent adapters and multi-host systems into their next generation designs. This appendix demonstrated how these features will be deployed using de-facto standard techniques adopted in the PCI environment and showed how they would be utilized for various applications. Because of this, we can expect this methodology to become the industry standard in the PCI Express paradigm.

Address Translation

This section provides an in-depth description of how systems that use non-transparent bridges communicate using address translation. We provide details about the mechanism by which systems determine not only the size of the memory allocated, but also about how memory pointers are employed. Implementations using both Direct Address Translation as well as Lookup Table Based Address Translation are discussed. By using the same standardized architectural implementation of non transparent bridging popularized in the PCI paradigm into the PCI Express environment, interconnect vendors can speed market adoption of PCI Express into markets requiring intelligent adapters, host failover and multihost capabilities.

The transparent bridge uses base and limit registers in I/O space, non-prefetchable memory space, and prefetchable memory space to map transactions in the downstream direction across the bridge. All downstream devices are required to be mapped in contiguous address regions such that a single aperture in each space is sufficient. Upstream mapping is done via inverse decoding relative to the same registers. A transparent bridge does not translate the addresses of forwarded transactions/packets.

The non-transparent bridges use the standard set of BARs in their Type 0 CSR header to define apertures into the memory space on the other side of the bridge. There are two sets of BARs: one on the Primary side and one on the Secondary. BARs define resource apertures that allow the forwarding of transactions to the opposite (other side) interface.

For each BAR bridge there exists a set of associated control and setup registers usually writable from the other side of the bridge. Each BAR has a "setup" register, which defines the size and type of its aperture, and an address translation register. Some bars also have a limit register that can be used to restrict its aperture's size. These registers need to be programmed prior to allowing access from outside the local subsystem. This is typically done by software running on a local processor or by loading the registers from EEPROM.

In PCI Express, the Transaction ID fields of packets passing through these apertures are also translated to support Device ID routing. These Device IDs are used to route completions to non-posted requests and ID routed messages.

The transparent bridge forwards CSR transactions in the downstream direction according to the secondary and subordinate bus number registers, converting Type 1 CSRs to Type 0 CSRs as required. The non-transparent bridge accepts only those CSR transactions addressed to it and returns an unsupported request response to all others.

Direct Address Translation

The addresses of all upstream and downstream transactions are translated (except BARs accessing CSRs). With the exception of the cases in the following two sections, addresses that are forwarded from one interface to the other are translated by adding a Base Address to their offset within the BAR that they landed in as seen in Figure C-8 on page 1014. The BAR Base Translation Registers are used to set up these base translations for the individual BARs.

Figure C-8: Direct Address Translation

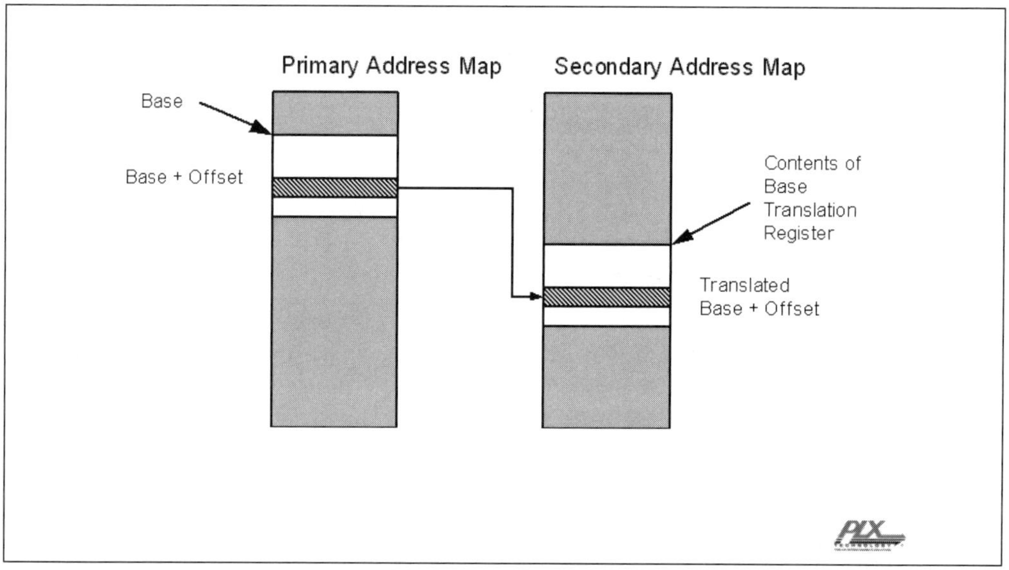

Lookup Table Based Address Translation

Following the de facto standard adopted by the PCI community, PCI Express should provide several BARs for the purposes of allocating resources. All BARs contain the memory allocation; however, in accordance with PCI industry conventions, BAR 0 contains the CSR information whereas BAR1 contains I/O information, BAR 2 and BAR 3 are utilized for Lookup Table Based Translation. BAR 4 and BAR 5 are utilized for Direct Address Translations.

On the secondary side, BAR3 uses a special lookup table based address translation for transactions that fall inside its window as seen in Figure C-9 on page 1015. The lookup table provides more flexibility in secondary bus local addresses to primary bus addresses. The location of the index field with the address bus is programmable to adjust aperture size.

Figure C-9: Lookup Table Based Translation

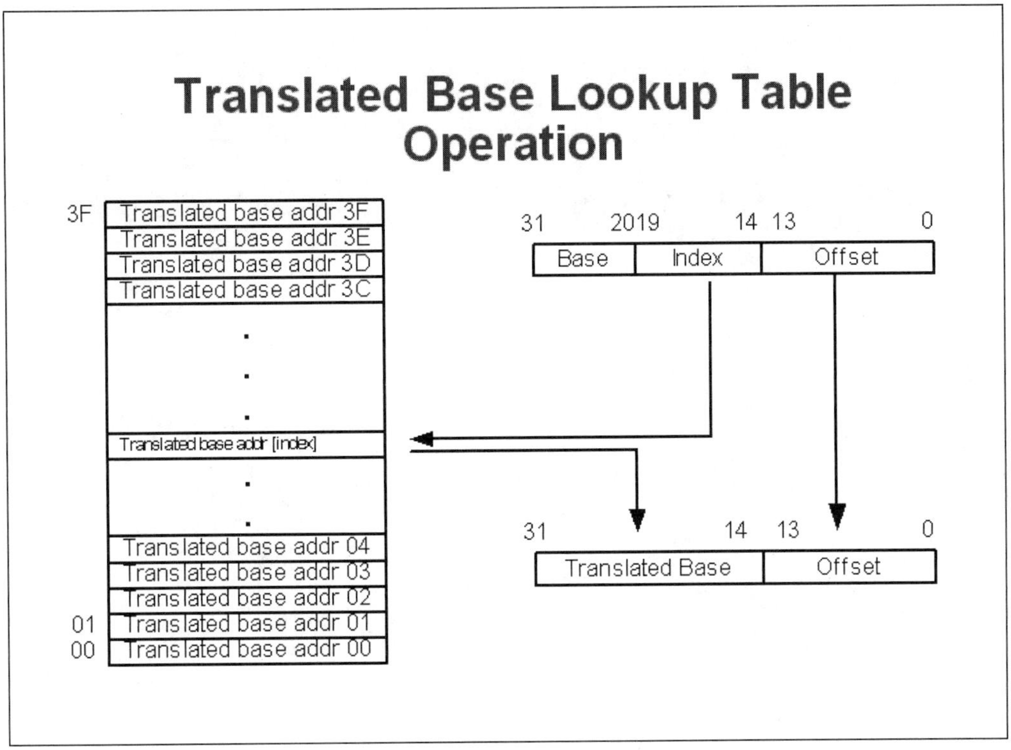

Downstream BAR Limit Registers

The two downstream BARs on the primary side (BAR2/3 and BAR4/5) also have Limit registers, programmable from the local side, to further restrict the size of the window they expose, as seen in Figure C-10 on page 1016. BARs can only be assigned memory resources in "power of two" granularity. The limit registers provide a means to obtain better granularity by "capping" the size of the BAR within the "power of two" granularity. Only transactions below the Limit registers are forwarded to the secondary bus. Transactions above the limit are discarded or return 0xFFFFFFFF, or a master abort equivalent packet, on reads.

Figure C-10: Use of Limit Register

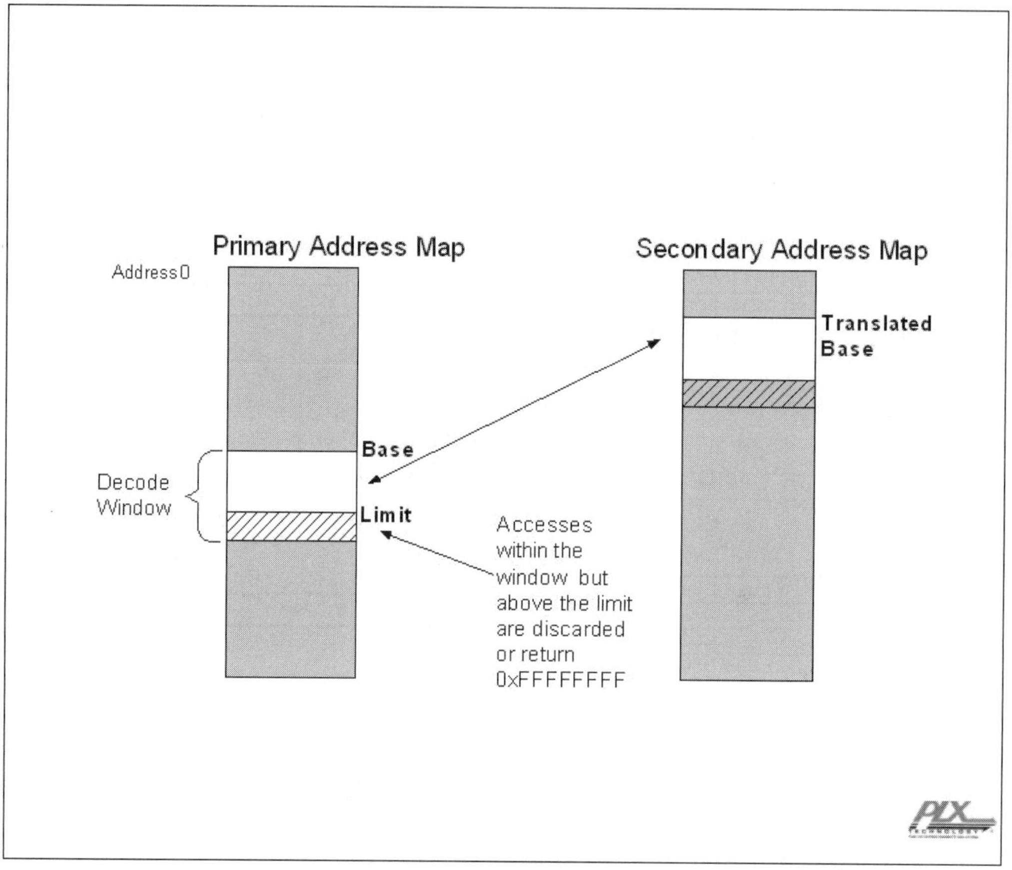

Forwarding 64bit Address Memory Transactions

Certain BARs can be configured to work in pairs to provide the base address and translation for transactions containing 64-bit addresses. Transactions that hit within these 64-bit BARs are forwarded using Direct Address Translation. As in the case of 32 bit transactions, when a memory transaction is forwarded from the primary to the secondary bus, the primary address can be mapped to another address in the secondary bus domain. The mapping is performed by substituting a new base address for the base of the original address.

A 64-bit BAR pair on the system side of the bridge is used to translate a window of 64-bit addresses in packets originated on the system side of the bridge down below 232 in local space.

Appendix D
Class Codes

This appendix lists the class codes, sub-class codes, and programming interface byte definitions currently provided in the 2.3 PCI specification.

Figure D-1: Class Code Register

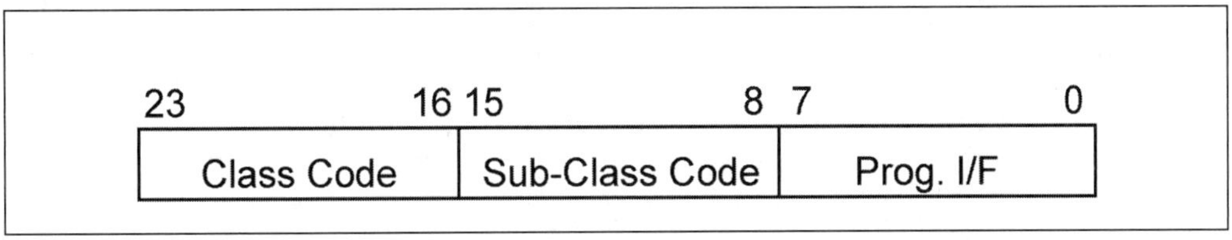

Table D-1: Defined Class Codes

Class	Description
00h	Function built before class codes were defined (in other words: before rev 2.0 of the PCI spec).
01h	Mass storage controller.
02h	Network controller.
03h	Display controller.
04h	Multimedia device.
05h	Memory controller.
06h	Bridge device.

Table D-1: Defined Class Codes (Continued)

Class	Description
07h	Simple communications controllers.
08h	Base system peripherals.
09h	Input devices.
0Ah	Docking stations.
0Bh	Processors.
0Ch	Serial bus controllers.
0Dh	Wireless controllers.
0Eh	Intelligent IO controllers.
0Fh	Satellite communications controllers.
10h	Encryption/Decryption controllers.
11h	Data acquisition and signal processing controllers.
12h-FEh	Reserved.
FFh	Device does not fit any of the defined class codes.

Table D-2: Class Code 0 (PCI rev 1.0)

Sub-Class	Prog. I/F	Description
00h	00h	All devices other than VGA.
01h	01h	VGA-compatible device.

Table D-3: Class Code 1: Mass Storage Controllers

Sub-Class	Prog. I/F	Description
00h	00h	SCSI controller.
01h	xxh	IDE controller. See Table D-20 on page 1031 for definition of Programming Interface byte.

Table D-3: Class Code 1: Mass Storage Controllers (Continued)

Sub-Class	Prog. I/F	Description
02h	00h	Floppy disk controller.
03h	00h	IPI controller.
04h	00h	RAID controller.
05h	20h	ATA controller with single DMA .
	30h	ATA controller with chained DMA.
80h	00h	Other mass storage controller.

Table D-4: Class Code 2: Network Controllers

Sub-Class	Prog. I/F	Description
00h	00h	Ethernet controller.
01h	00h	Token ring controller.
02h	00h	FDDI controller.
03h	00h	ATM controller.
04h	00h	ISDN Controller.
05h	00h	WorldFip controller.
06h		PICMG 2.14 Multi Computing. For information on the use of the Programming Interface Byte, see the PICMG 2.14 Multi Computing Specification (http://www.picmg.com).
80h	00h	Other network controller.

Table D-5: Class Code 3: Display Controllers

Sub-Class	Prog. I/F	Description
00h	00h	VGA-compatible controller, responding to memory addresses 000A0000h through 000BFFFFh (Video Frame Buffer), and IO addresses 03B0h through 3BBh, and 03C0h-through-03DFh and all aliases of these addresses.
	01h	8514-compatible controller, responding to IO address 02E8h and its aliases, 02EAh and 02EFh.
01h	00h	XGA controller.
02h	00h	3D Controller.
80h	00h	Other display controller.

Table D-6: Class Code 4: Multimedia Devices

Sub-Class	Prog. I/F	Description
00h	00h	Video device.
01h	00h	Audio device.
02h	00h	Computer Telephony device.
80h	00h	Other multimedia device.

Table D-7: Class Code 5: Memory Controllers

Sub-Class	Prog. I/F	Description
00h	00h	RAM memory controller.
01h	00h	Flash memory controller.
80h	00h	Other memory controller.

Table D-8: Class Code 6: Bridge Devices

Sub-Class	Prog. I/F	Description
00h	00h	Host/PCI bridge.
01h	00h	PCI/ISA bridge.
02h	00h	PCI/EISA bridge.
03h	00h	PCI/Micro Channel bridge.
04h	00h	PCI/PCI bridge.
	01h	Subtractive decode PCI-to-PCI bridge. Supports subtractive decode in addition to normal PCI-to-PCI functions. For a detailed discussion of this bridge type, refer to the MindShare *PCI System Architecture* book, Fourth Edition (published by Addison-Wesley).
05h	00h	PCI/PCMCIA bridge.
06h	00h	PCI/NuBus bridge.
07h	00h	PCI/CardBus bridge.
08h	xxh	RACEway bridge. RACEway is an ANSI standard (ANSI/VITA 5-1994) switching fabric. Bits 7:1 of the Interface bits are reserved, read-only and return zeros. Bit 0 is read-only and, if 0, indicates that the bridge is in Transparent mode, while 1 indicates that it's in End-Point mode.
09h	40h	Semi-transparent PCI-to-PCI bridge with the primary PCI bus side facing the system host processor.
	80h	Semi-transparent PCI-to-PCI bridge with the secondary PCI bus side facing the system host processor.
0Ah	00h	InfiniBand-to-PCI host bridge.
80h	00h	Other bridge type.

Table D-9: Class Code 7: Simple Communications Controllers

Sub-Class	Prog. I/F	Description
00h	00h	Generic XT-compatible serial controller.
	01h	16450-compatible serial controller.
	02h	16550-compatible serial controller.
	03h	16650-compatible serial controller.
	04h	16750-compatible serial controller.
	05h	16850-compatible serial controller.
	06h	16950-compatible serial controller.
01h	00h	Parallel port.
	01h	Bi-directional parallel port.
	02h	ECP 1.X-compliant parallel port.
	03h	IEEE 1284 controller.
	FEh	IEEE 1284 target device (not a controller).
02h	00h	Multiport serial controller.

Table D-9: Class Code 7: Simple Communications Controllers (Continued)

Sub-Class	Prog. I/F	Description
03h	00h	Generic modem.
	01h	Hayes-compatible modem, 16450-compatible interface. BAR 0 maps the modem's register set. The register set can be either memory- or IO-mapped (as indicated by the type of BAR).
	02h	Hayes-compatible modem, 16550-compatible interface. BAR 0 maps the modem's register set. The register set can be either memory- or IO-mapped (as indicated by the type of BAR).
	03h	Hayes-compatible modem, 16650-compatible interface. BAR 0 maps the modem's register set. The register set can be either memory- or IO-mapped (as indicated by the type of BAR).
	04h	Hayes-compatible modem, 16750-compatible interface. BAR 0 maps the modem's register set. The register set can be either memory- or IO-mapped (as indicated by the type of BAR).
04h	00h	GPIB (IEEE 488.1/2) controller.
05h	00h	Smart Card.
80h	00h	Other communications device.

Table D-10: Class Code 8: Base System Peripherals

Sub-Class	Prog. I/F	Description
00h	00h	Generic 8259 programmable interrupt controller (PIC).
	01h	ISA PIC.
	02h	EISA PIC.
	10h	IO APIC. Base Address Register 0 is used to request a minimum of 32 bytes of non-Prefetchable memory. Two registers within that space are located at Base + 00h (IO Select Register) and Base + 10h (IO Window Register). For a full description of the use of these registers, refer to the data sheet for the Intel 8237EB in the 82420/82430 PCIset EISA Bridge Databook #290483-003.
	20h	IO(x) APIC interrupt controller.
01h	00h	Generic 8237 DMA controller.
	01h	ISA DMA controller.
	02h	EISA DMA controller.
02h	00h	Generic 8254 timer.
	01h	ISA system timers.
	02h	EISA system timers.
03h	00h	Generic RTC controller.
	01h	ISA RTC controller.
04h	00h	Generic PCI Hot-Plug controller.
80h	00h	Other system peripheral.

Table D-11: Class Code 9: Input Devices

Sub-Class	Prog. I/F	Description
00h	00h	Keyboard controller.
01h	00h	Digitizer (pen).
02h	00h	Mouse controller.
03h	00h	Scanner controller.
04h	00h	Generic gameport controller.
	10h	Gameport controller. A gameport controller with a Programming Interface = 10h indicates that any Base Address registers in this function that request/assign IO address space, the registers in that IO space conform to the standard "legacy" game ports. The byte at offset 00h in an IO region behaves as a legacy gameport interface where reads to the byte return joystick/gamepad information and writes to the byte start the RC timer. The byte at offset 01h is an alias of the byte at offset 00h. All other bytes in an IO region are unspecified and can be used in vendor unique ways.
80h	00h	Other input controller.

Table D-12: Class Code A: Docking Stations

Sub-Class	Prog. I/F	Description
00h	00h	Generic docking station.
80h	00h	Other type of docking station.

Table D-13: Class Code B: Processors

Sub-Class	Prog. I/F	Description
00h	00h	386.
01h	00h	486.
02h	00h	Pentium.
10h	00h	Alpha.
20h	00h	PowerPC.
30h	00h	MIPS
40h	00h	Co-processor.

Table D-14: Class Code C: Serial Bus Controllers

Sub-Class	Prog. I/F	Description
00h	00h	Firewire (IEEE 1394).
	10h	IEEE 1394 using 1394 OpenHCI spec.
01h	00h	ACCESS.bus.
02h	00h	SSA (Serial Storage Architecture).
03h	00h	USB (Universal Serial Bus) controller using Universal Host Controller spec.
	10h	USB (Universal Serial Bus) controller using Open Host Controller spec.
	80h	USB (Universal Serial Bus) controller with no specific programming interface.
	FEh	USB device (not Host Controller).
04h	00h	Fibre Channel.
05h	00h	SMBus (System Management Bus).
06h	00h	InfiniBand.

Table D 14: Class Code C: Serial Bus Controllers (Continued)

Sub-Class	Prog. I/F	Description
07h	00h	IPMI SMIC Interface. The register interface definitions for the Intelligent Platform Management Interface Sub-Class 07h) are in the IPMI specification.
	01h	IPMI Kybd Controller Style Interface
	02h	IPMI Block Transfer Interface
08h	00h	SERCOS Interface Standard (IEC 61491). There is no register level definition for the SERCOS Interface standard. For more information see IEC 61491.
09h	00h	CANbus.
80h	00h	Other type of Serial Bus Controller.

Table D-15: Class Code D: Wireless Controllers

Sub-Class	Interface	Meaning
00	00h	iRDA compatible controller
01h	00h	Consumer IR controller
10h	00h	RF controller
11h	00h	Bluetooth.
12h	00h	Broadband.
80h	00h	Other type of wireless controller

Table D-16: Class Code E: Intelligent IO Controllers

Sub-Class	Interface	Meaning
00h	xxh	Intelligent IO controller adhering to the I2O Architecture spec. The spec can be downloaded from ftp.intel.com/pub/IAL/i2o/.
	00h	Message FIFO at offset 40h.
80h	00h	Other type of Intelligent IO Controller.

Table D-17: Class Code F: Satellite Communications Controllers

Sub-Class	Interface	Meaning
01h	00h	TV
02h	00h	Audio
03h	00h	Voice
04h	00h	Data
80h	00h	Other type of Satellite Communications Controller.

Table D-18: Class Code 10h: Encryption/Decryption Controllers

Sub-Class	Interface	Meaning
00h	00h	Network and computing Encrypt/Decrypt.
10h	00h	Entertainment Encrypt/Decrypt.
80h	00h	Other Encrypt/Decrypt.

Table D-19: Class Code 11h: Data Acquisition and Signal Processing Controllers

Sub-Class	Interface	Meaning
00h	00h	DPIO modules.
01h	00h	Performance counters.
10h	00h	Communications synchronization plus time and frequency test/measurement.
20h	00h	Management card.
80h	00h	Other Data Acquisition and Signal Processing Controllers.

Table D-20: Definition of IDE Programmer's Interface Byte Encoding

Bit(s)	Description
0	Operating mode (primary).
1	Programmable indicator (primary).
2	Operating mode (secondary).
3	Programmable indicator (secondary).
6:4	Reserved. Hardwired to zero.
7	Master IDE device.

Note: The SIG document *PCI IDE Controller Specification* completely describes the layout and meaning of bits 0 through 3 in the Programming Interface byte. The document *Bus Master Programming Interface for IDE ATA Controllers* describes the meaning of bit 7 in the Programming Interface byte. While the PCI 2.1 spec stated that this document could be obtained via FAX by calling (408)741-1600 and requesting document 8038, that reference was removed from the 2.3 spec.

Appendix E

Locked Transactions Series

Introduction

Native PCI Express implementations do not support lock. Support for Locked transaction sequences exist solely for supporting legacy device software executing on the host processor that performs a locked RMW (read-modify-write) operation on a memory semaphore that may reside within the memory of a legacy PCI device. This chapter defines the protocol defined by PCI Express for supporting locked access sequences that target legacy devices. Failure to support lock may result in deadlocks.

Background

PCI Express continues the PCI 2.3 tradition of supporting locked transaction sequences (RMW—ready-modify-write) to support legacy device software. PCI Express devices and their software drivers are never allowed to use instructions that cause the CPU to generate locked operations that target memory that resides beneath the Roor Complex level.

Locked operations consist of the basic RMW sequence, that is:

1. One or more memory reads from the target location to obtain the semaphore value.
2. The modification of the data within a processor register.
3. One or more writes to write the modified semaphore value back to the target memory location.

This transaction sequence must be performed such that no other accesses are permitted to the target locations (or device) during the locked sequence. This requires blocking other transactions during the operation. The result potentially can result in deadlocks and poor performance.

The devices required to support locked sequences are:

- The Root Complex.
- Any Switches in the path leading to a legacy devices that may be the target of a locked transaction series.
- A PCI Express - to - PCI Bridge.
- A PCI Express-to-PCI-X Bridge.
- Any legacy devices whose device drivers issue locked transactions to memory residing within the legacy device.

No other devices must support locked transactions and must ignore any locked transactions that they receive.

Lock in the PCI environment is achieved, in part, via the use of the PCI LOCK# signal. The equivalent functionality in PCI Express is accomplished via a transaction that emulates the LOCK signal functionality.

The PCI Express Lock Protocol

The only source of lock supported by PCI Express is the system processor, and, as a consequence, the source of all locked operations in PCI Express is the Root Complex (acting as the processor's surrogate). A locked operation is performed between a Root Complex downstream port and the PCI Express downstream port to which the targeted legacy device is attached. In most systems, the legacy device is typically a PCI Express-to-PCI or PCI Express-to-PCI-X bridge. Only one locked sequence at a time is supported for a given hierarchical path.

PCI Express limits locked transactions to Traffic Class 0 and Virtual Channel 0. All transactions with TC values other than zero that are mapped to a VC other than zero are permitted to traverse the fabric without regard to the locked operation. All transactions that are mapped to VC0 are subject to the lock rules described in this appendix. The discussion of the locked protocol in this appendix presumes that all transactions have been assigned to TC0 (unless otherwise indicated).

Lock Messages — The Virtual Lock Signal

PCI Express defines the following transactions that, together, act as a virtual wire that replaces the PCI LOCK# signal.

- **Memory Read Lock Request** (MRdLk) — Originates a locked sequence. The first MRdLk transaction blocks other requests from reaching the target device. One or more of these locked read requests may be issued during the sequence.
- **Memory Read Lock Completion with Data** (CplDLk) — Returns data and confirms that the path to the target is locked. A successful read Completion that returns data for the first Memory Read Lock request results in the path between the Root Complex and the target device being locked. That is, transactions traversing the same path from other ports are blocked from reaching either the root port or the target port. Transactions being routed in buffers for VC1-VC7 are unaffected by the lock.
- **Memory Read Lock Completion without Data** (CplLK) — A Completion without a data payload indicates that the lock sequence cannot complete currently and the path remains unlocked.
- **Unlock Message** — An unlock message is issued by the Root Complex from the locked root port. This message unlocks the path between the root port and the target port.

The Lock Protocol Sequence — an Example

This section explains the PCI Express lock protocol by example. The example includes the following devices:

- The Root Complex that initiates the Locked transaction series on behalf of the host processor.
- A Switch in the path between the root port and targeted legacy endpoint.
- A PCI Express-to-PCI Bridge in the path to the target.
- The target PCI device who's Device Driver initiated the locked RMW.
- A PCI Express endpoint is included to describe Switch behavior during lock.

In this example, the locked operation completes normally. The steps that occur during the operation are described in the two sections that follow.

The Memory Read Lock Operation

Figure E-1 on page 1037 illustrates the first step in the Locked transaction series (i.e., the initial memory read to obtain the semaphore):

1. The CPU initiates the locked sequence (a Locked Memory Read) as a result of a driver executing a locked RMW instruction that targets a PCI target.
2. The Root Port issues a Memory Read Lock Request from port 2. The Root Complex is always the source of a locked sequence.
3. The Switch receives the lock request on its upstream port and forwards the request to the target egress port (3). The switch, upon forwarding the request to the egress port, must block all requests from ports other than the ingress port (1) from being sent from the egress port.
4. A subsequent peer-to-peer transfer from the illustrated PCI Express endpoint to the PCI bus (switch port 2 to switch port 3) would be blocked until the lock is cleared. Note that the lock is not yet established in the other direction. Transactions from the PCI Express endpoint could be sent to the Root Complex.
5. The Memory Read Lock Request is sent from the Switch's egress port to the PCI Express-to-PCI Bridge. This bridge will implement PCI lock semantics (See the MindShare book entitled *PCI System Architecture, Fourth Edition*, for details regarding PCI lock).
6. The bridge performs the Memory Read transaction on the PCI bus with the PCI LOCK# signal asserted. The target memory device returns the requested semaphore data to the bridge.
7. Read data is returned to the Bridge and is delivered back to the Switch via a Memory Read Lock Completion with Data (CplDLk).
8. The switch uses ID routing to return the packet upstream towards the host processor. When the CplDLk packet is forwarded to the upstream port of the Switch, it establishes a lock in the upstream direction to prevent traffic from other ports from being routed upstream. The PCI Express endpoint is completely blocked from sending any transaction to the Switch ports via the path of the locked operation. Note that transfers between Switch ports not involved in the locked operation would be permitted (not shown in this example).
9. Upon detecting the CplDLk packet, the Root Complex knows that the lock has been established along the path between it and the target device, and the completion data is sent to the CPU.

Figure E-1: Lock Sequence Begins with Memory Read Lock Request

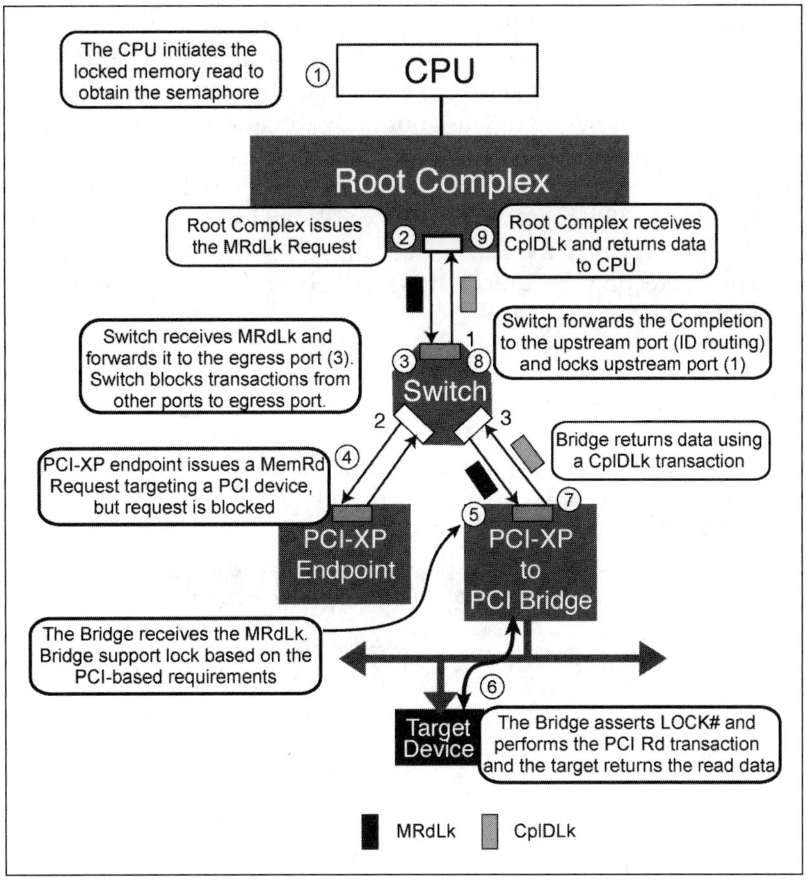

Read Data Modified and Written to Target and Lock Completes

The device driver receives the semaphore value, alters it, and then initiates a memory write to update the semaphore within the memory of the legacy PCI device. Figure E-2 on page 1038 illustrates the write sequence followed by the Root Complex's transmission of the Unlock message that releases the lock:

10. The Root Complex issues the Memory Write Request across the locked path to the target device.
11. The Switch forwards the transaction to the target egress port (3). The memory address of the Memory Write must be the same as the initial Memory Read request.

12. The bridge forwards the transaction to the PCI bus.
13. The target device receives the memory write data.
14. Once the Memory Write transaction is sent from the Root Complex, it sends an Unlock message to instruct the Switches and any PCI/PCI-X bridges in the locked path to release the lock. Note that the Root Complex presumes the operation has completed normally (because memory writes are posted and no Completion is returned to verify success).
15. The Switch receives the Unlock message, unlocks its ports and forwards the message to the egress port that was locked to notify any other Switches and/or bridges in the locked path that the lock must be cleared.
16. Upon detecting the Unlock message, the bridge must also release the lock on the PCI bus.

Figure E-2: Lock Completes with Memory Write Followed by Unlock Message

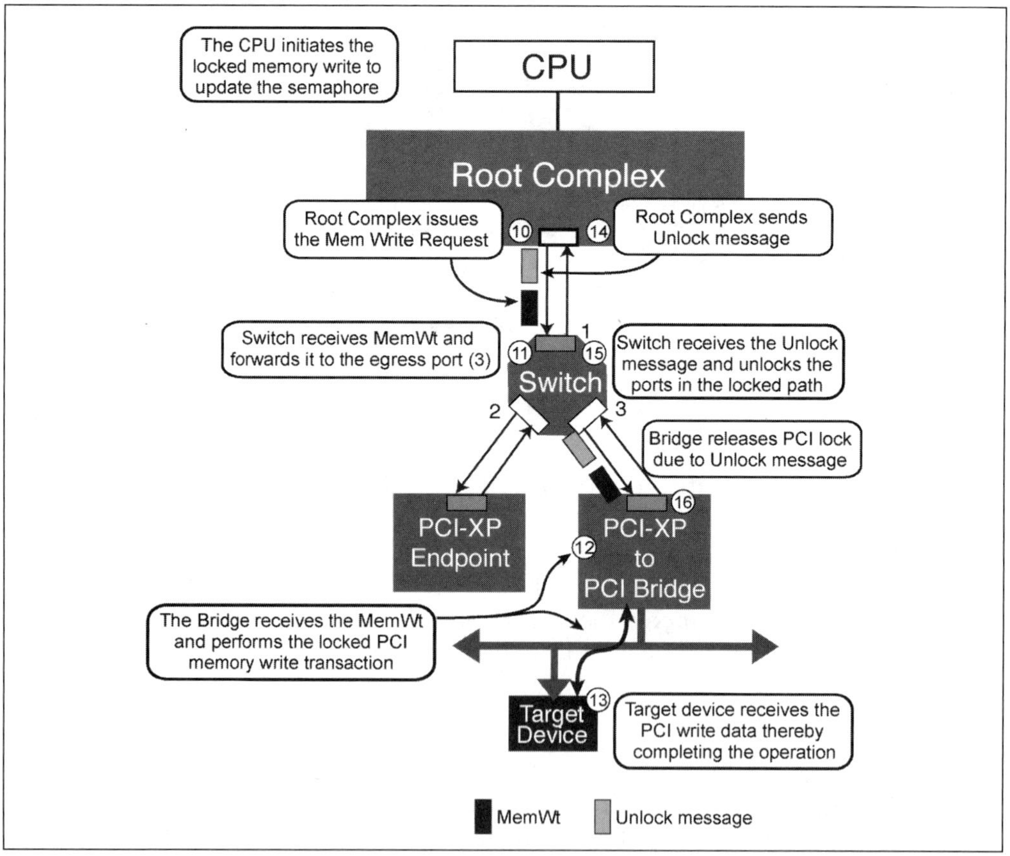

Notification of an Unsuccessful Lock

A locked transaction series is aborted when the initial Memory Read Lock Request receives a Completion packet with no data (CplLk). This means that the locked sequence must terminate because no data was returned. This could result from an error associated with the memory read transaction, or perhaps the target device is busy and cannot respond at this time.

Summary of Locking Rules

Following is a list of ordering rules that apply to the Root Complex, Switches, and Bridges.

Rules Related To the Initiation and Propagation of Locked Transactions

- Locked Requests which are completed with a status other than Successful Completion do not establish lock.
- Regardless of the status of any of the Completions associated with a locked sequence, all locked sequences and attempted locked sequences must be terminated by the transmission of an Unlock Message.
- MRdLk, CplDLk and Unlock semantics are allowed only for the default Traffic Class (TC0).
- Only one locked transaction sequence attempt may be in progress at a given time within a single hierarchy domain.
- Any device which is not involved in the locked sequence must ignore the Unlock Message.

The initiation and propagation of a locked transaction sequence through the PCI Express fabric is performed as follows:

- A locked transaction sequence is started with a MRdLk Request:
  - Any successive reads associated with the locked transaction sequence must also use MRdLk Requests.
  - The Completions for any successful MRdLk Request use the CplDLk Completion type, or the CPlLk Completion type for unsuccessful Requests.

- If any read associated with a locked sequence is completed unsuccessfully, the Requester must assume that the atomicity of the lock is no longer assured, and that the path between the Requester and Completer is no longer locked.
- All writes associated with a locked sequence must use MWr Requests.
- The Unlock Message is used to indicate the end of a locked sequence. A Switch propagates Unlock Messages through the locked Egress Port.
- Upon receiving an Unlock Message, a legacy Endpoint or Bridge must unlock itself if it is in a locked state. If it is not locked, or if the Receiver is a PCI Express Endpoint or Bridge which does not support lock, the Unlock Message is ignored and discarded.

Rules Related to Switches

Switches must detect transactions associated with locked sequences from other transactions to prevent other transactions from interfering with the lock and potentially causing deadlock. The following rules cover how this is done. Note that locked accesses are limited to TC0, which is always mapped to VC0.

- When a Switch propagates a MRdLk Request from an Ingress Port to the Egress Port, it must block all Requests which map to the default Virtual Channel (VC0) from being propagated to the Egress Port. If a subsequent MRdLk Request is received at this Ingress Port addressing a different Egress Port, the behavior of the Switch is undefined. Note that this sort of split-lock access is not supported by PCI Express and software must not cause such a locked access. System deadlock may result from such accesses.
- When the CplDLk for the first MRdLk Request is returned, if the Completion indicates a Successful Completion status, the Switch must block all Requests from all other Ports from being propagated to either of the Ports involved in the locked access, except for Requests which map to channels other than VC0 on the Egress Port.
- The two Ports involved in the locked sequence must remain blocked until the Switch receives the Unlock Message (at the Ingress Port which received the initial MRdLk Request)
  - The Unlock Message must be forwarded to the locked Egress Port.
  - The Unlock Message may be broadcast to all other Ports.
  - The Ingress Port is unblocked once the Unlock Message arrives, and the Egress Port(s) which were blocked are unblocked following the transmission of the Unlock Message out of the Egress Port(s). Ports that were not involved in the locked access are unaffected by the Unlock Message

Rules Related To PCI Express/PCI Bridges

The requirements for PCI Express/PCI Bridges are similar to those for Switches, except that, because these Bridges only use TC0 and VC0, all other traffic is blocked during the locked access. The requirements on the PCI bus side are described in the MindShare book entitled *PCI System Architecture, Fourth Edition* (published by Addison-Wesley).

Rules Related To the Root Complex

A Root Complex is permitted to support locked transactions as a Requester. If locked transactions are supported, a Root Complex must follow the rules already described to perform a locked access. The mechanism(s) used by the Root Complex to interface to the host processor's FSB (Front-Side Bus) are outside the scope of the spec.

Rules Related To Legacy Endpoints

Legacy Endpoints are permitted to support locked accesses, although their use is discouraged. If locked accesses are supported, legacy Endpoints must handle them as follows:

- The legacy Endpoint becomes locked when it transmits the first Completion for the first read request of the locked transaction series access with a Successful Completion status:
  - — If the completion status is not Successful Completion, the legacy Endpoint does not become locked.
  - — Once locked, the legacy Endpoint must remain locked until it receives the Unlock Message.
- While locked, a legacy Endpoint must not issue any Requests using Traffic Classes which map to the default Virtual Channel (VC0). Note that this requirement applies to all possible sources of Requests within the Endpoint, in the case where there is more than one possible source of Requests. Requests may be issued using Traffic Classes which map to VCs other than VC0.

Rules Related To PCI Express Endpoints

Native PCI Express Endpoints do not support lock. A PCI Express Endpoint must treat a MRdLk Request as an Unsupported Request.

Index

Index

Index

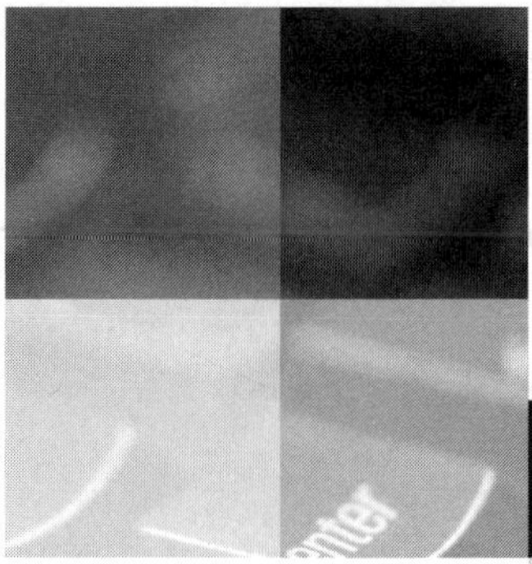